ike

“I work very hard to make sure that
the men I draw having sex are proud
men having happy sex!”

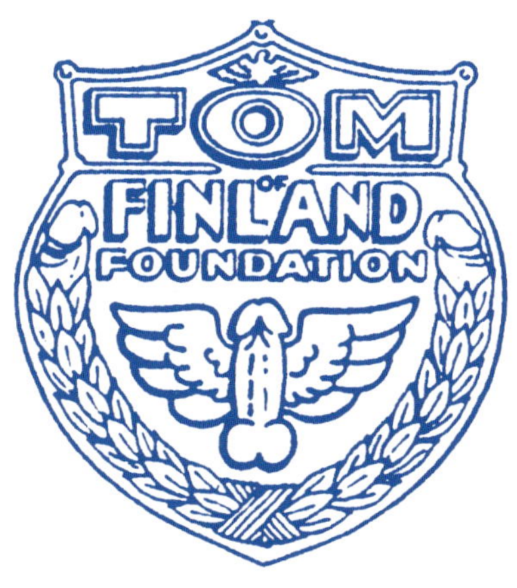

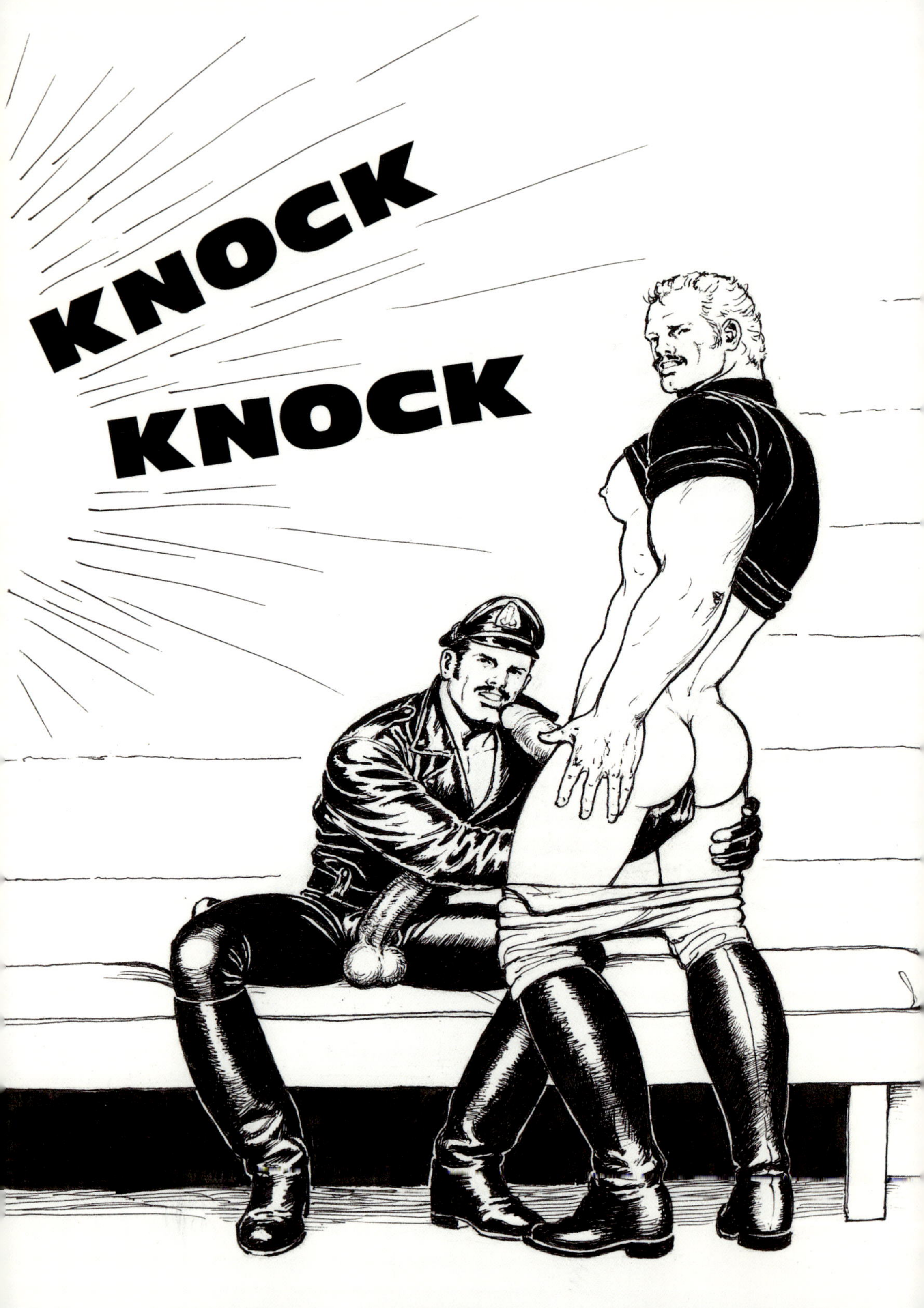

KNOCK
KNOCK

EDITED BY DIAN HANSON

THE COMPLETE kake COMICS 1968–1986

TASCHEN

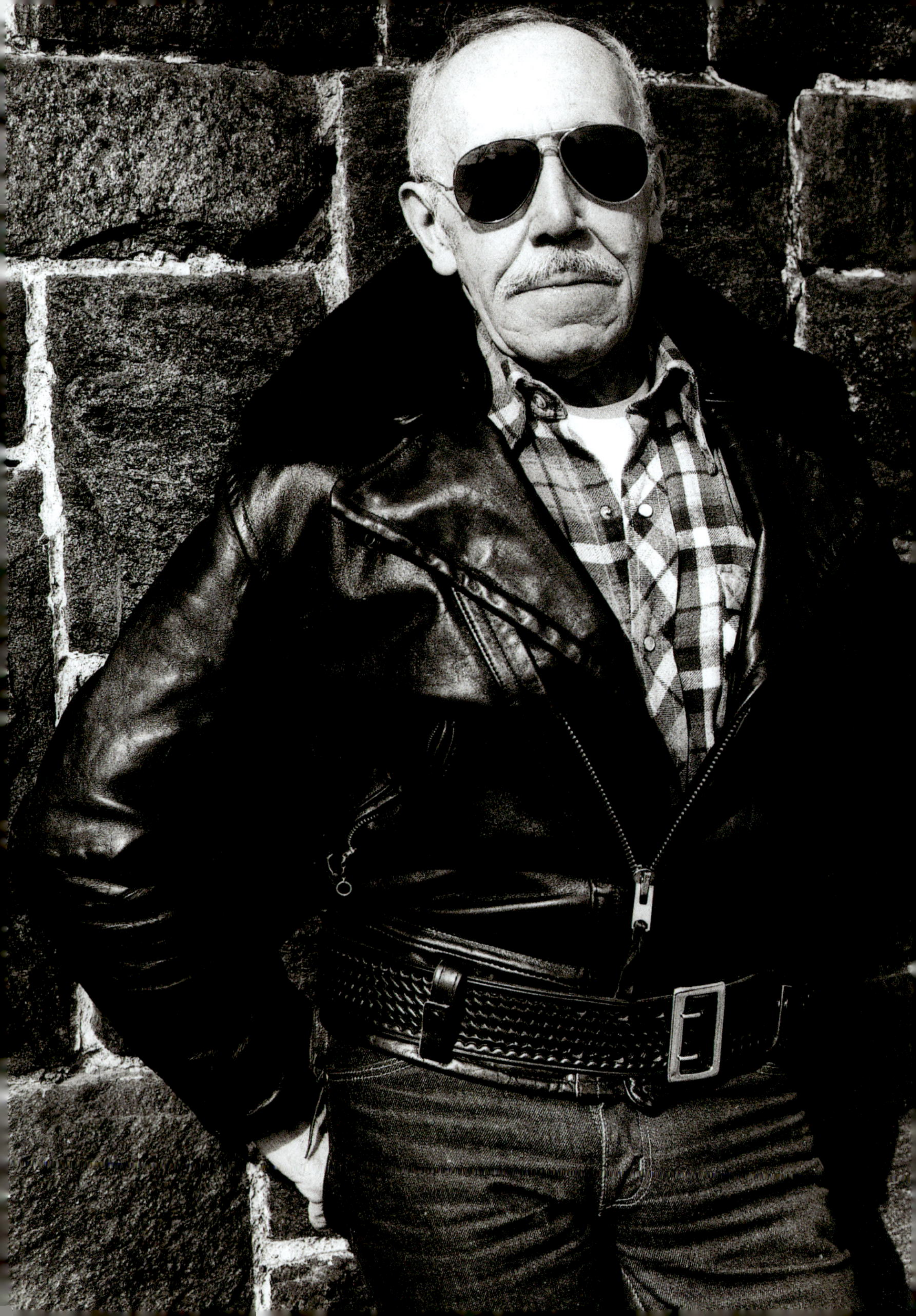

CONTENTS

Tom in his cop jacket, 1985.
Photo: Ralf Marsault and Heino Muller.

THE COMPLETE KAKE COMICS

Introduction by Dian Hanson

Touko Laaksonen was born in 1920 in the small Finnish village of Kaarina. The son of two teachers, he was kept indoors as a child, reading and practicing piano while other boys enjoyed the rugged rural life. Touko always admired these rough boys. He knew from an early age he was attracted to men, and accepted this as an inborn, if secret, part of his being. He had good reason to hide his desires; homosexuality was punishable by imprisonment in Finland. Drawing became an important escape at an early age, and he produced his first comic strips at age eight. At 10, with puberty approaching, Touko began drawing the loggers and manual laborers who stirred his secret fantasies. There was nothing explicitly sexual in the drawings, but since they aroused sexual feelings in him he kept them well hidden.

In 1939 Touko moved to Helsinki to attend art school. The port city introduced him to new masculine ideals, including policemen, construction workers and sailors. Uniforms and the power they conferred began to take a special place in his fantasies, one that increased exponentially when Russia invaded Finland later that year. To repel the Russians Finland formed a pact with Germany. Touko found the German soldiers, with their fine uniforms and shiny black boots, overwhelmingly attractive. Many found Lieutenant Laaksonen equally appealing. "All my early sexual experiences were with German soldiers," he said in the 1991 documentary *Daddy and the Muscle Academy*. "No one made a uniform like the Germans. And the boots!"

Touko's passion for high leather boots began in childhood. He prevailed upon his parents to buy him a pair when he was around 10 and secretly wore them to bed until caught by his mother. Through his teens he continued to find men in boots exciting, but nothing he'd seen of rustic Finnish footwear could compare to the glossy perfection of German jackboots. In the moral chaos of war Touko was able to indulge desires that might otherwise have remained suppressed for years. The boots, the uniforms, the genuinely masculine homoeroticism, all were firmly stamped on his psyche by the time the Germans withdrew in 1945.

After the war Touko was left sexually adrift. He found a good job in advertising, designing fashion campaigns and store displays, and was a popular piano player in Helsinki's bohemian bars at night, but sex was often just masturbating while drawing pictures based on his wartime experiences. "I always knew a drawing was good if I got an erection," he said years later. He tried for a while to fit into Helsinki's gay underground, but at that time society, even gay society, considered effeminacy a queer requirement. Touko tried to be one of the girls, but it wasn't in his nature. Rather than play fey he chose to live through his "deviant" fantasies of masculine man-to-man sex. One can see this cultural conflict in the first multi-panel story he created in 1946. The lead character is conspicuously feminine compared to the hearty Tom's Men to come.

By the '50s, encouraged by the work of George Quaintance, Touko was making art truer to his personal tastes. He now created panel stories as gifts for his friends in Finland as well as for his own sexual arousal. In 1956 one of these friends convinced him to send a few drawings to the prototypical American muscle mag *Physique Pictorial*. Publisher Bob Mizer immediately saw Touko's talent and used one of his smiling blonde loggers for the cover of *Physique*'s Spring 1957 issue. In the Winter 1957 issue Mizer bestowed the "Tom of Finland" name, playing up Touko's Finnish roots to make the artist seem as exotic as the men he drew.

These early *Physique* drawings featured Touko's first boyhood crushes—lumberjacks and rural roughnecks. Perhaps he was afraid to send the drawings revealing his fetish for the Wehrmacht high command uniform, an ensemble familiar to all Tom fans, featuring a tailored jacket with a "Sam Browne" style leather belt and shoulder strap over jodhpur pants with a wide decorative stripe down the outer leg. The uniform was customarily accessorized with knee-high glossy black riding boots, a black brimmed, peaked cap and gauntleted black leather gloves. For increased fetish panache Tom sometimes replaced the striped pants with the black leather jodhpurs favored by Luftwaffe pilots.

Some criticized Tom as glorifying Nazis, but it must be noted that his passion was entirely apolitical and that erotic fantasy frequently attaches to troubling stereotypes. Still, most were grateful when Tom shifted his obsession from the army officer to the leather-jacketed biker epitomized by Marlon Brando in *The Wild One*, released in 1953. It was a natural progression. Tom loved leather, and the biker jacket was cut much like a Wehrmacht

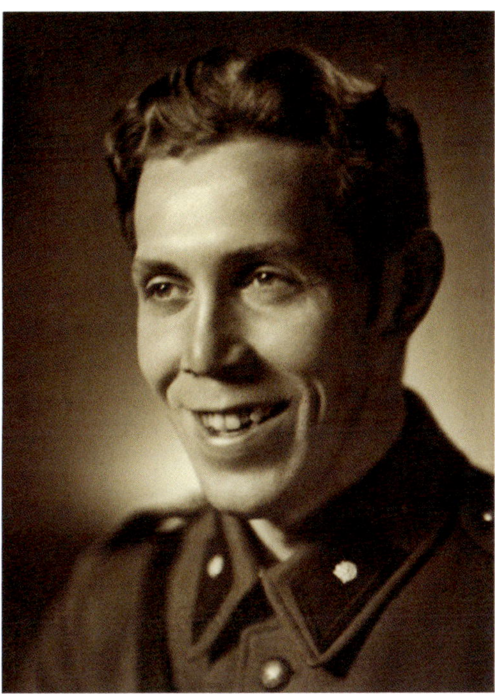

A formal portrait of Touko in his uniform, 1941.

jacket in black cowhide. Brando's cap, copied by many ex-military motorcyclists, was similar to a German officer's, and in the '50s bikers often wore their high boots outside tight pegged jeans. It was a uniform even more manly than a German officer's, with no moral baggage.

Tom's timing in submitting his work to *Physique* couldn't have been better. The magazine's most popular illustrator, George Quaintance, died in November 1957. Tom still had to compete with *Physique* mainstays Art-Bob and Etienne, and with the Quaintance archive, but Mizer was looking for a new main man. By 1960 Tom was that man, with work appearing in every issue. His first consecutive story panels (from *The Tattooed Sailor* series) appeared in the August 1961 issue. From then on it was common for a few panels of a story to appear accompanied by an ad offering readers the whole set of five to 15 panels at $1.50 per page. Durk Dehner of the Tom of Finland Foundation says Bob encouraged Tom to draw panel stories based on his own *Physique* model photos. Many of the bikers and sailors in the early '60s panels do bear a striking resemblance to popular models in the magazine.

In 1965 Tom began flirting with the idea of an ongoing character for his panel stories, the ultimate Tom's Man. He tried out a blonde named Vicky—a common male name in Finland—who was quickly renamed Mike. Then in 1968 Tom settled on Kake, a dark-haired, mustached leatherman who often wore a tight white t-shirt bearing the motto "Fucker." Kake was indeed a fucker, a sort of Johnny Appleseed traveling the world on his motorcycle spreading the seeds of liberated, mutually satisfying, ecstatically explicit gay sex. Tom once said, "I work very hard to make sure that the men I draw having sex are proud men having happy sex!" This was epitomized in the Kake stories, but no matter how physically imposing, all Tom's men were happy, their faces open, warm and welcoming. Sure, they were going to fuck you, and maybe hold you down or tie you up in the process, but it was all in the name of fun, and when they'd had theirs, they'd insist on turning the other cheek and letting you have yours. Tom's men were also the first to break the affection barrier, kissing and caressing as well as sucking, fucking and fisting. From the '50s onward Tom was a dedicated crusader against gay shame, first to please himself, and then to inspire men the world over to take pride in themselves and their preferences. Nowhere is this more apparent than in his panel stories, where we can follow

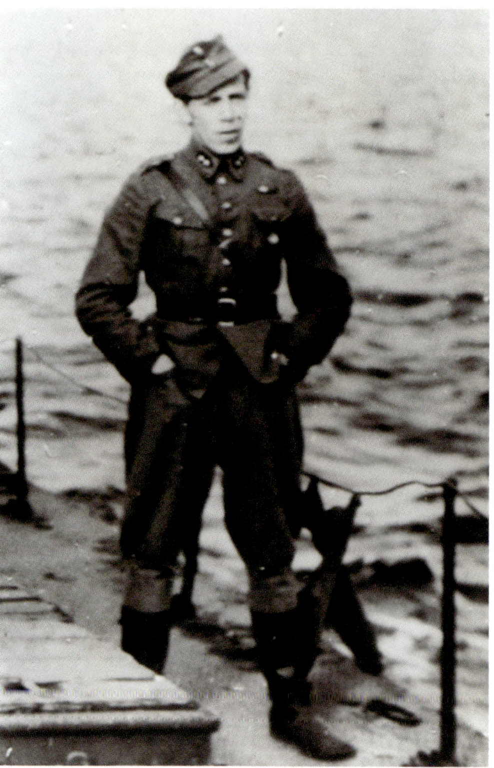

Touko in the Finnish army, 1941.

seduction (or abduction) through consumma-
tion on to affectionate aftermath.

In 1968 the first 20-page *Kake* storybook was
published by DFT of Denmark. The little books
came out regularly after that, first from DFT,
then from Coq of Denmark around 1971. Revolt
Press of Sweden started publishing Tom's
storybooks around the same time as Coq, and
through the '70s Tom worked for both compa-
nies, producing *Kake* episodes, as well as the
three volumes of *Jack*, two of *Beach Boys*, three
Pekkas (another common Finnish name), and
assorted one-offs. In 1979 Tom, in partnership
with Durk Dehner, set up the Tom of Finland
Company in Los Angeles, which became the
sole publisher of TOF storybooks. In 1984 Durk
persuaded Tom to create the Tom of Finland
Foundation to archive and preserve this great
body of work. Following Tom's death from
emphysema in 1991 the Foundation set about
rounding up all the lost art and restoring it.

Today, the Tom of Finland Foundation has
managed to find and preserve most of Tom's
panel stories as original art. This collection
represents all 26 of Tom's *Kake* adventures,
from the first 20-page episode, "The Intruder,"
created in 1968 to the final 30-page "Oversexed
Office," released in 1986.

Of course, Tom's art is nothing but Tom's
fantasies. Like every great erotic artist he drew
with one overriding purpose: to arouse himself.
That the personal fantasies of one shy Finn were
shared by millions of men around the world
was just fortuitous coincidence, because Touko
Laaksonen couldn't, and wouldn't, have done it
any other way.

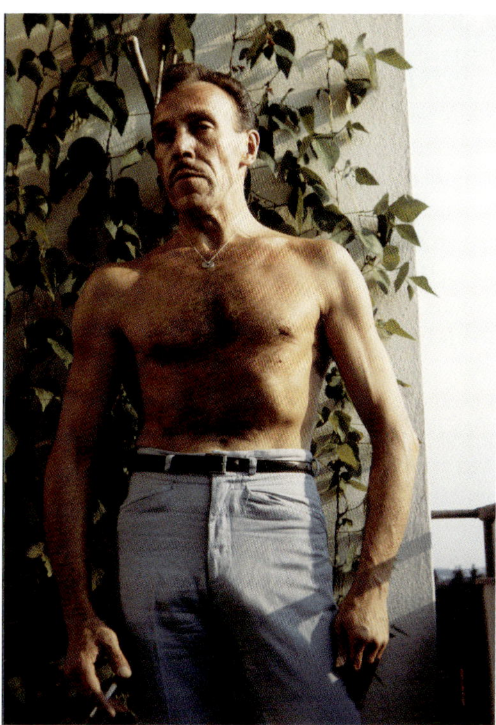

Tom as "Tom's Man," late 1960s.

DIE GESAMMELTEN KAKE COMICS

Einleitung von Dian Hanson

Touko Laaksonen wurde 1920 in der finnischen Kleinstadt Kaarina geboren. Der Sohn eines Lehrerehepaars musste als Kind viel Zeit im Haus verbringen, wo er Bücher las und Klavier übte, während andere Jungen seines Alters das Leben in der freien Natur genossen. Der kleine Touko beneidete diese rauen Jungs. Schon sehr früh fühlte er sich zu Männern hingezogen und akzeptierte dies als angeborene, wenn auch verborgene Seite seines Wesens. Und er hatte gute Gründe dafür, sein Verlangen geheim zu halten – zur damaligen Zeit galt Homosexualität in Finnland als Verbrechen und wurde mit Gefängnis bestraft. Das Zeichnen bot ihm die Möglichkeit zur Flucht aus der Wirklichkeit, und bereits im Alter von acht Jahren zeichnete er seine ersten Comics. Als Zehnjähriger, mit dem Einsetzen der Pubertät, zeichnete Touko erstmals die Holzfäller und Landarbeiter, die seine geheimen Fantasien bevölkerten. Diese Zeichnungen waren alles andere als freizügig, aber da sie ihn sexuell erregten, hielt er sie sorgfältig unter Verschluss.

1939 zog Touko nach Helsinki, um dort die Kunstakademie zu besuchen. In dieser Hafenstadt begegnete ihm eine ganze Reihe neuer maskuliner Wunschbilder, darunter Polizisten, Bauarbeiter und Matrosen. Uniformen und die Macht, die sie ausstrahlten, nahmen einen immer wichtigeren Platz in seinen Fantasien ein, und diese Entwicklung beschleunigte sich enorm, als Russland im selben Jahr in Finnland einfiel. Um die russische Armee zurückschlagen zu können, ging die finnische Regierung einen Pakt mit Deutschland ein. Touko fand die deutschen Soldaten mit ihren prächtigen Uniformen und den glänzenden schwarzen Stiefeln einfach unwiderstehlich – und der junge Leutnant Laaksonen erregte seinerseits unter den Deutschen großes Interesse. „Alle meine frühen sexuellen Erfahrungen hatte ich mit deutschen Soldaten“, erzählte er 1991 in dem Dokumentarfilm *Daddy and the Muscle Academy*. „Niemand machte solche Uniformen wie die Deutschen. Und erst die Stiefel!“

Schon in der Kindheit entwickelte Touko eine Leidenschaft für Lederstiefel. Mit zehn überredete er seine Eltern, ihm ein Paar zu kaufen, die er heimlich im Bett trug, bis seine Mutter ihn damit erwischte. Auch als Teenager fand er Männer in Stiefeln weiterhin aufregend – doch nichts, was er bisher an rustikalen finnischen Schuhen und Stiefeln gesehen hatte, ließ sich mit der glänzenden Perfektion der deutschen Schaftstiefel vergleichen. Das moralische Chaos der Kriegszeit bot Touko die Möglichkeit, Leidenschaften auszuleben, die andernfalls wahrscheinlich noch jahrelang unterdrückt worden wären. Die Stiefel, die Uniformen, die durch und durch maskuline Homoerotik – all dies hatte sich fest in seiner Psyche verankert, als sich die deutsche Wehrmacht 1945 aus Finnland zurückzog.

Nach dem Krieg war Touko sexuell heimatlos. Er fand eine gut bezahlte Stelle in der Werbebranche, wo er Modeanzeigen und Schaufensterauslagen entwarf, und war ein beliebter Pianist in den Nachtclubs und Bars von Helsinki – doch Sex bestand in dieser Zeit für ihn oft nur aus Masturbation, während er Bilder nach den Erfahrungen zeichnete, die er im Krieg gemacht hatte. „Ich wusste immer, dass eine Zeichnung gut war, wenn ich davon eine Erektion bekam", erzählte er Jahre später. Eine Zeit lang suchte er Anschluss in der Gay-Szene von Helsinki, doch zu dieser Zeit galt in der Gesellschaft, und selbst in der homosexuellen Gesellschaft, eine unmännliche Erscheinung als unbedingte Voraussetzung für Schwule. Touko versuchte sich anzupassen, doch das lag nicht in seiner Natur. Anstatt eine Tunte zu spielen, entschied er sich dafür, seine „abnormalen" Fantasien von maskulinem Männersex zu verarbeiten. Seine erste Bildergeschichte, die im Jahr 1946 entstand, spiegelt diesen kulturellen Konflikt wider: Verglichen mit den unverfälscht männlichen „Tom's Men" späterer Jahre, ist die Hauptfigur auffallend feminin.

Ermutigt durch die Arbeiten von George Quaintance, ging Touko in den 1950er-Jahren langsam dazu über, Werke zu schaffen, die eher seinem persönlichen Geschmack entsprachen. Inzwischen zeichnete er Bildergeschichten nicht nur zu seiner eigenen sexuellen Erregung, sondern auch als Geschenke für seinen Freundeskreis in Finnland. 1956 überredete ihn einer dieser Freunde, einige Zeichnungen an *Physique Pictorial* zu schicken, eines der ersten amerikanischen Muskelmagazine. Dessen Herausgeber Bob Mizer erkannte Toukos Talent sofort und verwendete einen seiner lächelnden blonden Holzfäller für das Cover der *Physique*-Frühjahrsausgabe 1957. In der Winterausgabe 1957 führte Mizer den Namen „Tom of Finland" ein – in Anspielung auf Toukos finnische Herkunft wie auch im Versuch, den Künstler so exotisch erscheinen zu lassen wie die Männer, die er zeichnete.

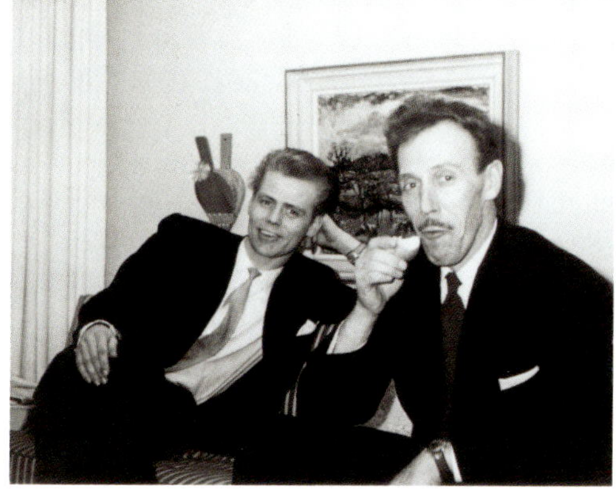

Tom with Veli, his partner of 21 years.

Die frühen *Physique*-Zeichnungen zeigen Toms heimliche Lieben der frühen Jugend – Holzfäller und raue Naturburschen. Wahrscheinlich scheute er noch davor zurück, die Zeichnungen einzusenden, die seinen Fetisch für die Uniform des Oberkommandos der Wehrmacht preisgaben. Dieses Ensemble – das mittlerweile jeder Tom-Fan kennt – besteht aus einer taillierten Jacke, einem Lederkoppel im „Sam Browne"-Stil mit Schulterriemen und einer Jodhpurhose mit breitem dekorativen Seitenstreifen. Diese Uniform wird gewöhnlich komplettiert durch kniehohe, blank polierte schwarze Reitstiefel, eine Schirmmütze mit schwarzem Rand und Stulpenhandschuhe aus schwarzem Leder. Um den Kick noch zu erhöhen, tauschte Tom manchmal die Reiterhosen mit Seitenstreifen gegen Jodhpurhosen aus schwarzem Leder aus, wie sie die Piloten der deutschen Luftwaffe trugen.

**Die Stiefel, die Uniformen, die durch
und durch maskuline Homoerotik – all dies
hatte sich fest in seiner Psyche verankert,
als sich die deutsche Wehrmacht 1945 aus
Finnland zurückzog.**

Zwar wurde Tom von manchen Kritikern beschuldigt, die Nazis zu verherrlichen, doch es sollte an dieser Stelle darauf hingewiesen werden, dass seine Leidenschaft völlig unpolitischer Natur war und dass sich erotische Fantasien häufig an verstörenden Stereotypen festmachen. Dennoch waren viele seiner Fans froh, als sich Toms Obsessionen vom Wehrmachtsoffizier auf den Biker mit der Lederjacke verschoben, den Marlon Brando im 1953 erschienenen Film *The Wild One* („Der Wilde") verkörperte. Es war ein logischer Schritt: Tom liebte Leder, und die Motorradjacken der damaligen Zeit sahen aus wie Wehrmachtsjacken, nur aus schwarzem Rindsleder. Brandos Schirmmütze, die von vielen Motorradfahrern und Ex-Soldaten kopiert wurde, ähnelte den deutschen Offiziersmützen, und in den 1950er Jahren steckten viele Biker ihre engen Jeans in hohe Lederstiefel. Es war eine Uniform, die noch männlicher wirkte als die der deutschen Offiziere, allerdings ohne deren moralischen Ballast.

Tom war mit seinen Arbeiten für *Physique* genau zur richtigen Zeit am richtigen Ort: Im November 1957 starb der bis dahin beliebteste Illustrator des Magazins, George Quaintance, und auch wenn Tom sich gegen solche Konkurrenz wie die *Physique*-Größen Art-Bob und Etienne – und gegen das große Quaintance-Archiv – behaupten musste, so suchte Mizer doch auf Dauer nach einem würdigen Nachfolger. Bis 1960 hatte Tom sich endgültig durchgesetzt, und seine Arbeiten erschienen in jeder Ausgabe des Magazins. Seine ersten zusammenhängenden Bildergeschichten (aus der Serie *The Tattooed Sailor*) erschienen in der August-Ausgabe 1961. Von da an veröffentlichte *Physique* in jeder Ausgabe einige Seiten einer Bildgeschichte, verbunden mit einer Anzeige, die den Lesern die vollständige Geschichte von 5–15 Seiten zum Preis von 1,50 Dollar pro Seite anbot. Wie Durk Dehner, Mitbegründer der Tom of Finland Foundation erzählt, hielt Bob Tom dazu an, seine Bildergeschichten auf Basis der Modellfotos aus *Physique* zu zeichnen – und so zeigen viele Biker und Matrosen in Toms Zeichnungen der frühen 1960er Jahre eine verblüffende Ähnlichkeit mit den beliebtesten Modellen des Magazins.

1965 dachte Tom erstmals darüber nach, seine Bildergeschichten rund um einen immer wiederkehrenden Helden zu zeichnen, sozusagen den ultimativen „Tom's Man". Zunächst versuchte er es mit einem blonden Charakter namens Vicky – ein in Finnland durchaus üblicher Männername –, der jedoch schon bald in Mike umbenannt wurde. Danach folgte der von Tarzan inspirierte Jack, und 1968 ersann Tom schließlich Kake, einen dunkelhaarigen Lederkerl mit Schnurrbart, der häufig ein weißes T-Shirt trug, auf dem sein Lebensmotto zu lesen war: „Fucker". Und Kake war genau das – eine Art Easy Rider mit einer Botschaft, der die Welt mit seinem Motorrad bereiste und überall freien, von beiden Seiten gewollten und unkompliziert genossenen schwulen Sex hatte. „Ich achte sorgfältig darauf, dass ich nur Männer zeichne, die ihren Sex mit Stolz und Freude ausleben!", sagte Tom einmal. Dies ist auch die Kernbotschaft der Kake-Storys: Egal wie physisch eindrucksvoll sie dargestellt sind, Toms Männer zeigen immer offene, freundliche und

einladende Gesichter. Natürlich wollen sie
jemanden ficken und denjenigen bei dieser
Gelegenheit auch festhalten oder fesseln – aber
all das geschieht aus purem sexuellen Vergnü-
gen, und wenn sie ihren Spaß gehabt haben,
sorgen sie immer dafür, dass der andere den
Spieß umdrehen kann und auch seinen Spaß
bekommt. Darüber hinaus waren Toms Männer
die Ersten, die die Zuneigungsgrenze durch-
brachen – hier ging es nicht nur ums Blasen,
Ficken und Faustficken, sondern auch ums
Küssen und Streicheln. Ab den 50er Jahren
widmete Tom sich dem Kampf gegen schwule
Scham – zum einen aus eigenem Interesse, zum
anderen, um Männer in aller Welt dazu zu inspi-
rieren, für sich selbst und ihre Neigungen ein-
zutreten. Nirgendwo kommt dies deutlicher
zum Ausdruck als in seinen Bildergeschichten,
die uns die Verführung (oder Entführung)
ebenso genussvoll miterleben lassen wie die
Erfüllung und das zärtliche Nachspiel.

1968 erschien unter dem Titel *Kake #1* der
erste, 21 Seiten starke Sammelband mit Tom-of-
Finland-Bildergeschichten bei dem dänischen
Verlag DFT. Danach kamen in regelmäßigen
Abständen weitere Bände auf den Markt,
zunächst bei DFT, dann ab 1971 bei Coq of
Denmark. Etwa zur gleichen Zeit wie Coq veröffentlichte auch Revolt Press in Schweden
den ersten Band mit Toms Bildergeschichten.
Während der 1970er-Jahre arbeitete er
regelmäßig für beide Verlage und produzierte
neben weiteren *Kake*-Episoden drei Bände mit
Jack-Geschichten, zwei Hefte unter dem Titel
Beach Boys, drei *Pekka*-Bände (ebenfalls ein
geläufiger finnischer Name) sowie eine ganze

Reihe von Einzelausgaben. Nach der Gründung
der Tom of Finland Foundation 1984 wurden
viele dieser frühen Arbeiten in Amerika wieder-
veröffentlicht; außerdem entstanden neue
Bücher, die die Foundation mit Hauptsitz in
Los Angeles herausgab. Nach Toms Tod an
einem Emphysem 1991 setzte die Stiftung sich
zum Ziel, sämtliche seiner Arbeiten aufzu-
spüren und zu sammeln, um so sein Lebens-
werk zu bewahren.

Inzwischen ist es der Tom of Finland Foundation gelungen, den größten Teil von Toms
Bildergeschichten zu finden und – in den meis-
ten Fällen im Original – zu archivieren. Die
Bandbreite der Arbeiten reicht von Toukos titel-
loser erster Geschichte aus dem Jahr 1946 bis
zu den 26 *Kake*-Abenteuern. Diese Sammlung
enthält alle 26 Kake-Abenteuer, von der ersten,
20 Seiten langen Episode „Der Eindringling“
von 1968 bis zu der 30 Seiten umfassenden
Geschichte „Bürohengste“ von 1986.

Natürlich ist Toms Kunst letztlich nichts
anderes als ein Ausdruck seiner Fantasien. Wie
jeder große erotische Künstler schuf er seine
Arbeiten in erster Linie nur aus einem einzigen
Grund: um sich selbst zu erregen. Dass die
persönlichen Fantasien eines schüchternen
Finnen von Millionen Männern in aller Welt
geteilt wurden, war nichts als ein glücklicher
Zufall, denn Touko Laaksonen hätte niemals
anders zeichnen können – oder wollen.

LES BANDES DESSINÉES KAKE COMPLÈTES

Préface de Dian Hanson

Touko Laaksonen est né en 1920 dans le petit village de Kaarina en Finlande. Fils de deux enseignants, il a passé son enfance à lire et à jouer du piano, sans guère sortir de chez lui, tandis que les autres garçons de son âge profitaient des plaisirs sauvages de la vie à la campagne. Touko a toujours admiré ces petits durs et il a très tôt pris conscience de son attirance pour les hommes, chose qu'il assumait comme un trait inné de sa personnalité, même s'il n'en parlait à personne. Il faut dire qu'il avait de bonnes raisons pour dissimuler cette inclination, l'homosexualité étant à l'époque passible d'emprisonnement en Finlande. Très vite, il trouva dans le dessin une échappatoire capitale et il réalisa ses premières bandes dessinées à l'âge de huit ans. À dix ans, à l'approche de la puberté, il se mit à représenter des bûcherons et des travailleurs manuels qui titillaient ses fantasmes secrets. Il n'y avait pourtant rien d'explicitement sexuel dans ces images, mais comme elles éveillaient en lui des pulsions sexuelles, il les tenait bien cachées.

En 1939, Touko déménagea à Helsinki pour poursuivre ses études aux Beaux-Arts. Là, dans cette ville portuaire, il fut amené à croiser de nouveaux idéaux masculins, parmi lesquels des policiers, des ouvriers du bâtiment et des marins. Les uniformes, et le pouvoir qu'ils conféraient à ceux qui en portaient, se mirent à occuper une place privilégiée dans ses fantasmes, et cette place décupla en importance au moment où la Russie envahit la Finlande un peu plus tard la meme année. Pour expulser les Russes, la Finlande signa alors un pacte avec l'Allemagne. Les soldats du nouveau pays allié,

équipés de splendides uniformes et de bottes noires lustrées, exerçaient sur Touko un attrait irrésistible ; en retour, ceux-ci étaient nombreux à ne pas rester insensibles aux charmes du lieutenant Laaksonen. « J'ai fait toutes mes premières expériences sexuelles avec des soldats allemands, déclara-t-il dans le documentaire *Daddy and the Muscle Academy* en 1991. Il n'y avait que les Allemands pour fabriquer des uniformes pareils. Sans parler de leurs bottes ! »

En réalité, la passion de Touko pour les hautes bottes de cuir remontait à son enfance. Vers l'âge de dix ans, il avait persuadé ses parents de lui en acheter une paire, qu'il portait en secret pour dormir jusqu'au jour où sa mère le surprit en flagrant délit. Les hommes bottés continuèrent à exciter son imagination pendant son adolescence, mais rien de ce qu'il connaissait des lourdes chaussures finlandaises ne soutenait la comparaison avec la perfection luisante des bottes militaires allemandes. C'est donc grâce à la confusion morale de la guerre qu'il eut l'occasion d'assouvir des désirs qui, sans cela, auraient pu rester longtemps refoulés. Au moment où les Allemands se retirèrent du pays en 1945, les bottes, uniformes et autres composantes de cet authentique homoérotisme avaient laissé une forte empreinte dans son esprit.

Après la guerre, Touko se retrouva perdu dans sa vie sexuelle. Il obtint un bon emploi dans la publicité, où il concevait des campagnes de mode et la décoration de vitrines de magasins, et il se tailla une belle réputation comme pianiste dans les bars de nuit d'Helsinki ; mais sa sexualité se bornait en général à des séances de masturbation auxquelles il s'adonnait en dessinant des images basées sur ses souvenirs d'expériences vécues en temps de guerre. « J'ai toujours su que j'avais réussi un dessin s'il me faisait bander », déclara-t-il des années plus tard. Pendant un certain temps, il tenta de s'intégrer au milieu clandestin homosexuel d'Helsinki, mais à cette époque, les gays étaient forcément efféminés aux yeux de la société (y compris aux yeux des homosexuels eux-mêmes). Touko essaya donc de jouer la femme, mais ce n'était pas dans sa nature. Au lieu de verser dans l'affectation, il choisit de prendre son mal en patience pour vivre ses fantasmes « déviants » d'une sexualité virile entre hommes. De ce conflit culturel témoigne la première série de dessins qu'il réalisa en 1946 : de toute évidence, le personnage principal possède des traits féminins, en comparaison des solides gaillards qui allaient caractériser sa production ultérieure.

Au début des années 1950, encouragé par le travail de George Quaintance, Touko créait déjà un art qui exprimait plus fidèlement ses goûts personnels. Il réalisait des bandes dessinées qu'il offrait à ses amis finlandais ou qu'il conservait pour assouvir ses propres pulsions. En 1956, l'un de ces amis le convainquit d'envoyer quelques images au principal magazine américain spécialisé dans la musculature, *Physique Pictorial*. Se rendant tout de suite compte du talent de Touko, l'éditeur, Bob Mizer, consacra la couverture du numéro du printemps 1957 à l'un de ses bûcherons blonds et souriants. Pendant l'hiver de la même année, il lui donna le pseudonyme Tom of Finland pour rehausser ses

origines finlandaises et harmoniser l'exotisme de l'artiste avec celui des hommes qu'il dessinait.

Les premiers dessins de Tom parus dans *Physique Pictorial* reprenaient des types masculins dont il s'était amouraché dans son enfance : des bûcherons et de robustes paysans. Peut-être avait-il peur d'envoyer les dessins où se manifestait son fétichisme pour les uniformes des hauts gradés de la Wehrmacht — collection bien connue de tous des adeptes —, avec leurs vestes ajustées, leurs ceintures en cuir et leurs épaulettes de style « Sam Browne », ainsi que les jodhpurs ornés d'une large rayure qui descendait le long de la jambe. S'y ajoutaient en général divers accessoires : bottes d'équitation noires qui montaient jusqu'aux genoux, casquette noire à visière, gants à crispin en cuir noir. Pour accroître la dimension fétichiste, Tom remplaçait parfois les pantalons rayés par les jodhpurs en cuir noir qu'affectionnaient particulièrement les pilotes de la Luftwaffe.

Quoique d'aucuns lui aient reproché d'avoir glorifié les nazis, il convient de souligner que la passion de Tom était totalement apolitique, les fantasmes érotiques étant souvent inspirés par des stéréotypes troublants. Cependant, la plupart des lecteurs lui surent gré de reporter son obsession pour l'officier militaire sur le motard en blouson de cuir, tel qu'il était parfaitement incarné par Marlon Brando dans *L'Équipée sauvage* (1953). Cette évolution était naturelle. Tom adorait le cuir, et le blouson de motard était coupé comme la veste des officiers de la Wehrmacht et taillé dans le même cuir noir de vachette. La casquette de Brando, reprise par de

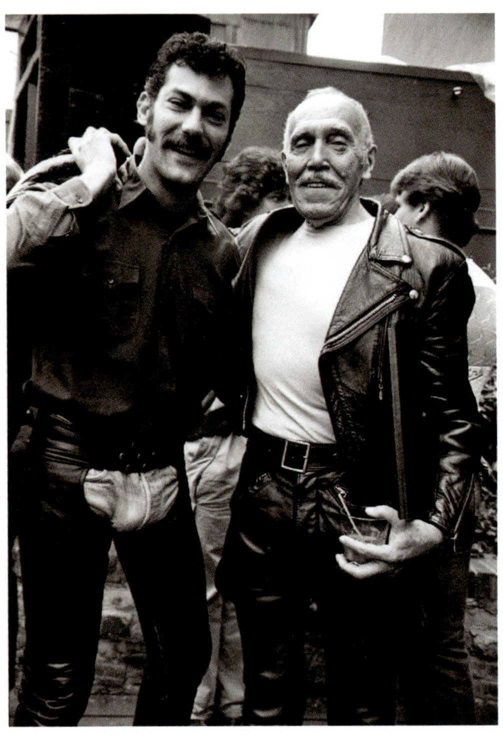

Tom with model Tony at a Foundation fundraiser,
Eagle Bar, San Francisco, 1985. Photo: Robert Pruzan.

nombreux motards qui avaient servi dans l'armée, ressemblait à celle des officiers allemands, et dans les années 1950, les motards rentraient leurs jeans très moulants dans leurs hautes bottes. C'était donc un uniforme encore plus viril que celui des officiers allemands, et il présentait en outre l'avantage de n'être pas chargé de connotations morales.

Le moment que choisit Tom pour soumettre son travail au magazine *Physique Pictorial*

n'aurait pu mieux tomber : l'illustrateur le plus populaire de la revue, George Quaintance, était décédé en novembre 1957. Certes, il restait encore deux piliers importants, Art-Bob et Etienne, et il fallait négocier avec les archives de Quaintance. Mais Mizer cherchait un nouvel homme de confiance et c'est en Tom qu'il le trouva avant la fin des années 1950. Par la suite, il fit paraître son travail dans chaque numéro de la revue. Les premières séries de dessins (tirées de l'album *The Tattooed Sailor* [« Le marin tatoué »]) furent publiées dans le numéro d'août 1961. À partir de là, il ne fut pas rare que paraissent plusieurs dessins d'une histoire, accompagnés d'une publicité proposant aux lecteurs la série complète, comprenant entre cinq et dix planches, pour 1 dollar 50 la page. D'après Durk Dehner, qui a participé à la création de la Fondation Tom of Finland, Bob encourageait Tom à dessiner en s'inspirant de ses propres photos de mannequins parues dans *Physique*. Nombreux sont au reste les motards et les marins qui, dans la production des années 1960, ressemblent beaucoup aux modèles populaires qui posaient pour la revue.

En 1965, Tom se prit à songer à un personnage qui reviendrait dans toutes ses histoires, et qui représenterait son image idéale de l'Homme. Il commença par un blond prénommé Vicky (prénom masculin courant en Finlande), lequel fut bientôt rebaptisé Mike. Suivit un Jack inspiré de Tarzan. Puis, en 1968, Tom se fixa sur Kake, un brun moustachu tout de cuir vêtu, à l'exception d'un tee-shirt blanc sur lequel était inscrit le mot « Fucker ». De fait, Kake était un baiseur, une sorte de Johnny

Au moment où les Allemands se retirèrent du pays en 1945, les bottes, uniformes et autres composantes de cet authentique homoérotisme avaient laissé une forte empreinte dans son esprit.

Appleseed qui sillonnait le monde à moto et propageait l'image explicite d'une sexualité gay sans tabous, jouissive et satisfaisante pour les deux partenaires. « Je fais tout mon possible, déclara Tom un jour, pour que les hommes que je représente en train de baiser soient des hommes fiers et heureux qui prennent leur pied ! » Les histoires de Kake illustraient ces propos à la perfection : les dessins montraient des hommes qui, malgré leur carrure, étaient heureux et avaient le visage ouvert, chaleureux, avenant. Certes, ils allaient vous baiser, et, le cas échéant, vous maintenir au sol ou vous attacher pendant l'acte, mais c'était au nom du plaisir ; et une fois qu'ils avaient joui, ils avaient tôt fait de se retourner pour vous faire jouir à votre tour. Les hommes de Tom furent aussi les premiers à franchir le cap de la sensualité, à s'embrasser et à se caresser autant qu'ils se suçaient, s'enculaient et se fistaient. À partir des années 1950, Tom lutta avec acharnement contre la honte des homos, d'abord pour se faire plaisir, ensuite pour inspirer à des hommes du monde entier la fierté d'être soi et de revendiquer ses préférences. Nulle part cette dimension n'apparaît plus clairement que dans ses séries de dessins où l'on passe de la séduction (ou de l'enlèvement) à la consommation de l'acte puis aux échanges de tendresse.

En 1968, la maison danoise DFT publia le premier recueil de bandes dessinées de Tom : c'était Kake n° 1 et il contenait 21 pages. Par la suite, d'autres petits livres semblables sortirent à intervalles réguliers, d'abord chez DFT, puis, aux alentours de 1971, chez Coq, toujours au

Danemark. À peu près à la même époque, la maison suédoise Revolt Press commença à publier les livres de Tom, lequel travailla pour ces deux éditeurs pendant les années 1970 : il créa les histoires de Kake en épisodes, trois volumes de Jack, deux de Beach Boys, trois Pekka (prénom également courant en Finlande), ainsi que d'autres albums de temps en temps.

Après la création de la Fondation Tom of Finland en 1984, nombreuses furent ces premières publications à être rééditées en Amérique, tandis que les nouvelles histoires furent en exclusivité publiées par les bureaux de la Fondation basée à Los Angeles. Après la disparition de Tom, mort d'un emphysème en 1991, la Fondation a entrepris de rassembler toutes les œuvres perdues et de les restaurer.

Aujourd'hui, la Fondation a réussi à retrouver la plupart des séries et à les préserver comme des œuvres d'art originales. Cette collection représente toutes les 26 aventures de Kake, du premier épisode de 20 pages, « L'Intrus », créé en 1968, au dernier volume de 30 pages, « Trop-plein sexuel au bureau », paru en 1986.

Certes, l'art de Tom ne consiste en rien d'autre qu'en ses propres fantasmes. Comme tout grand artiste érotique, il n'avait guère qu'un seul but lorsqu'il dessinait : s'exciter luimême. Mais que les fantasmes personnels d'un timide Finlandais soient partagés par des millions d'hommes aux quatre coins de la planète n'est que pure coïncidence, car jamais Touko Laaksonen n'aurait su ni voulu s'y prendre autrement.

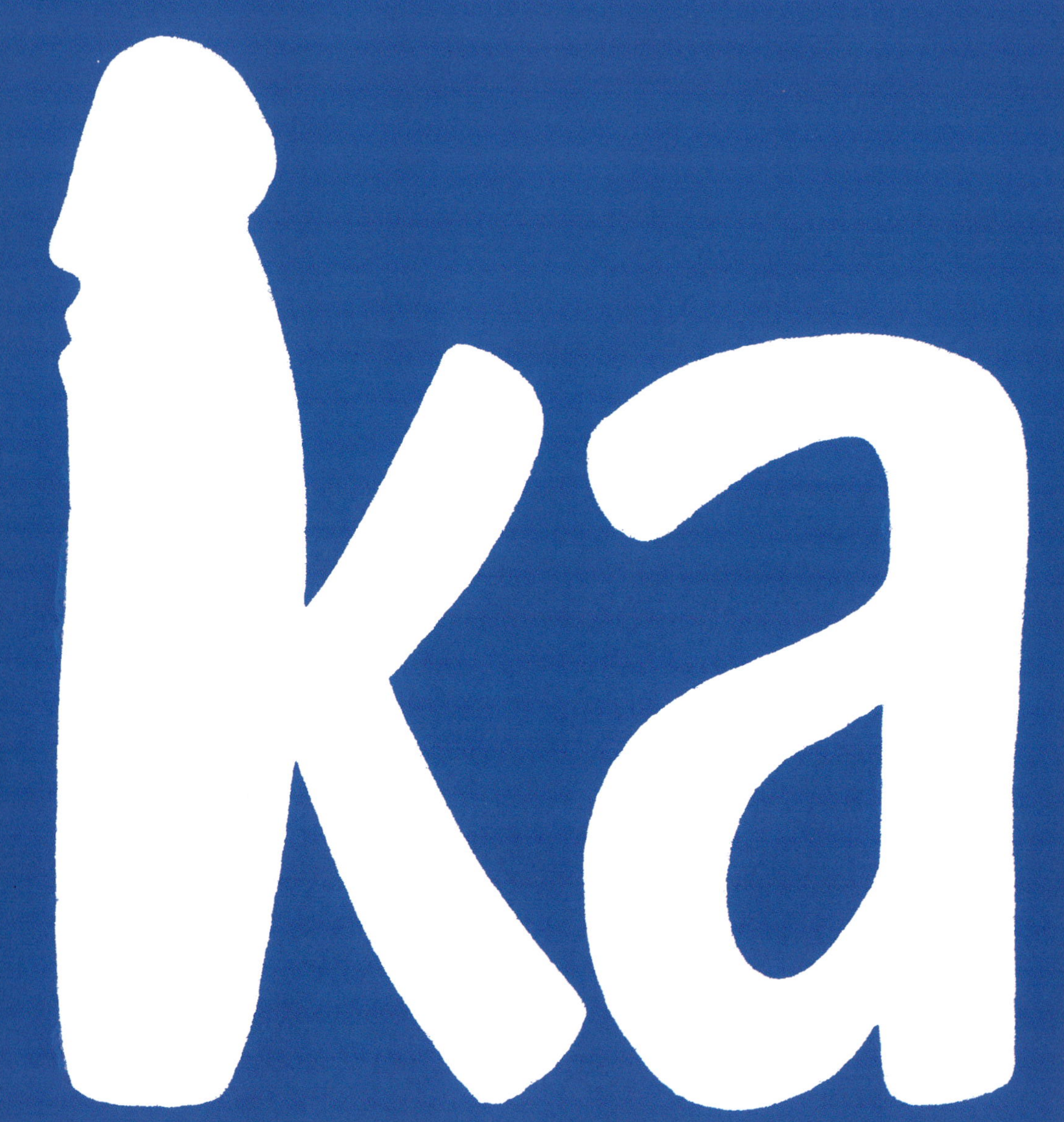

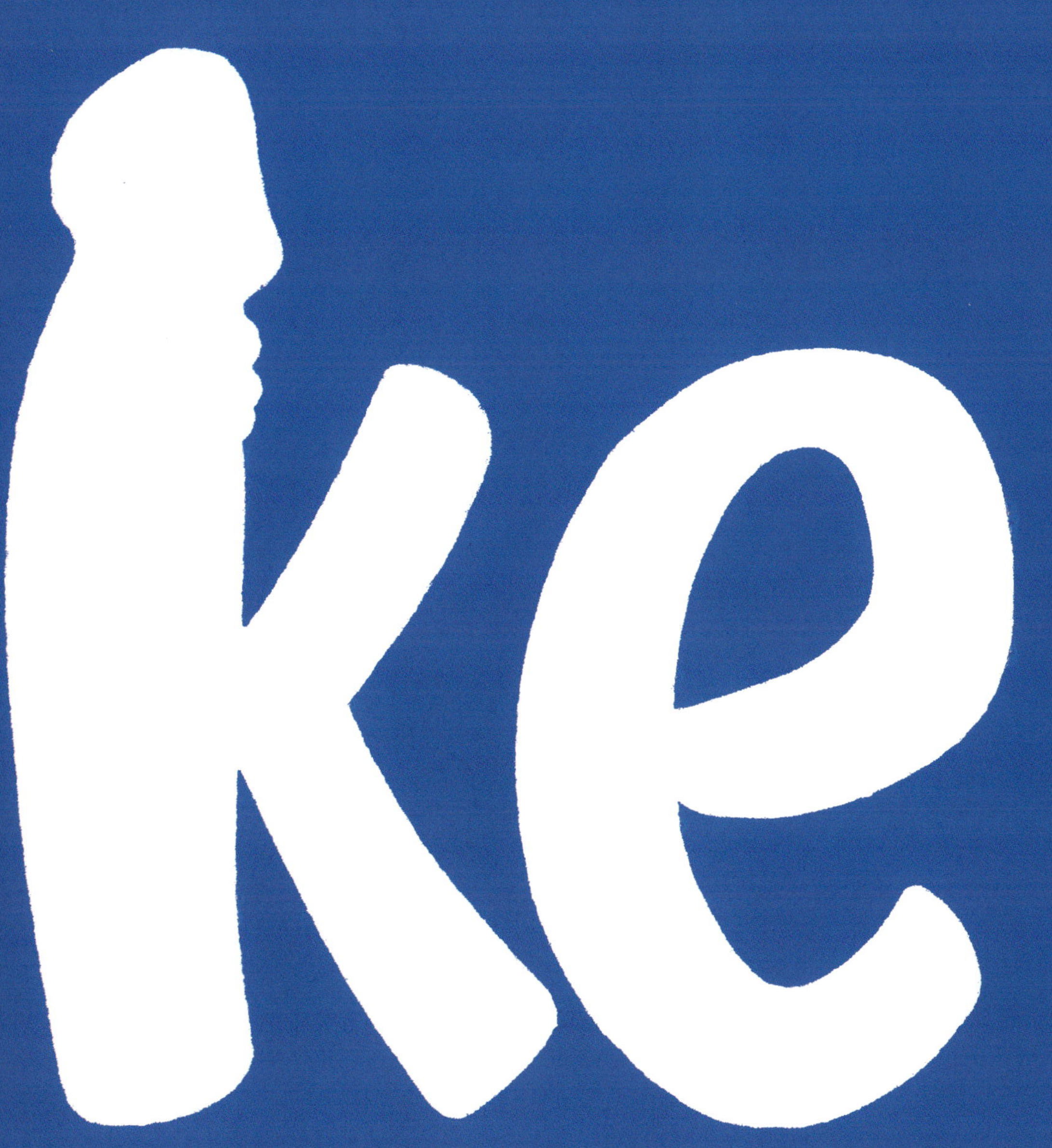

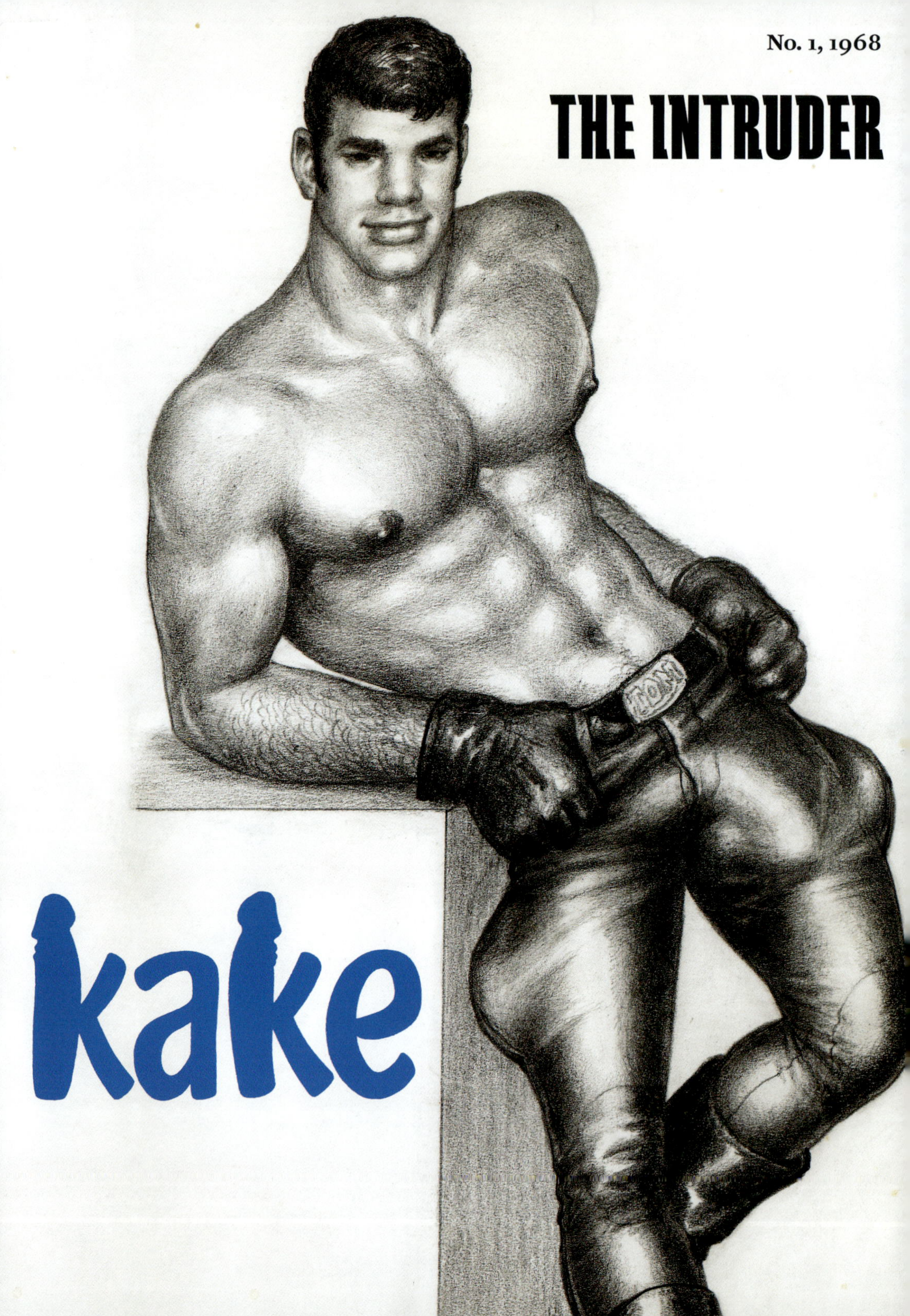

No. 1, 1968
THE INTRUDER
kake

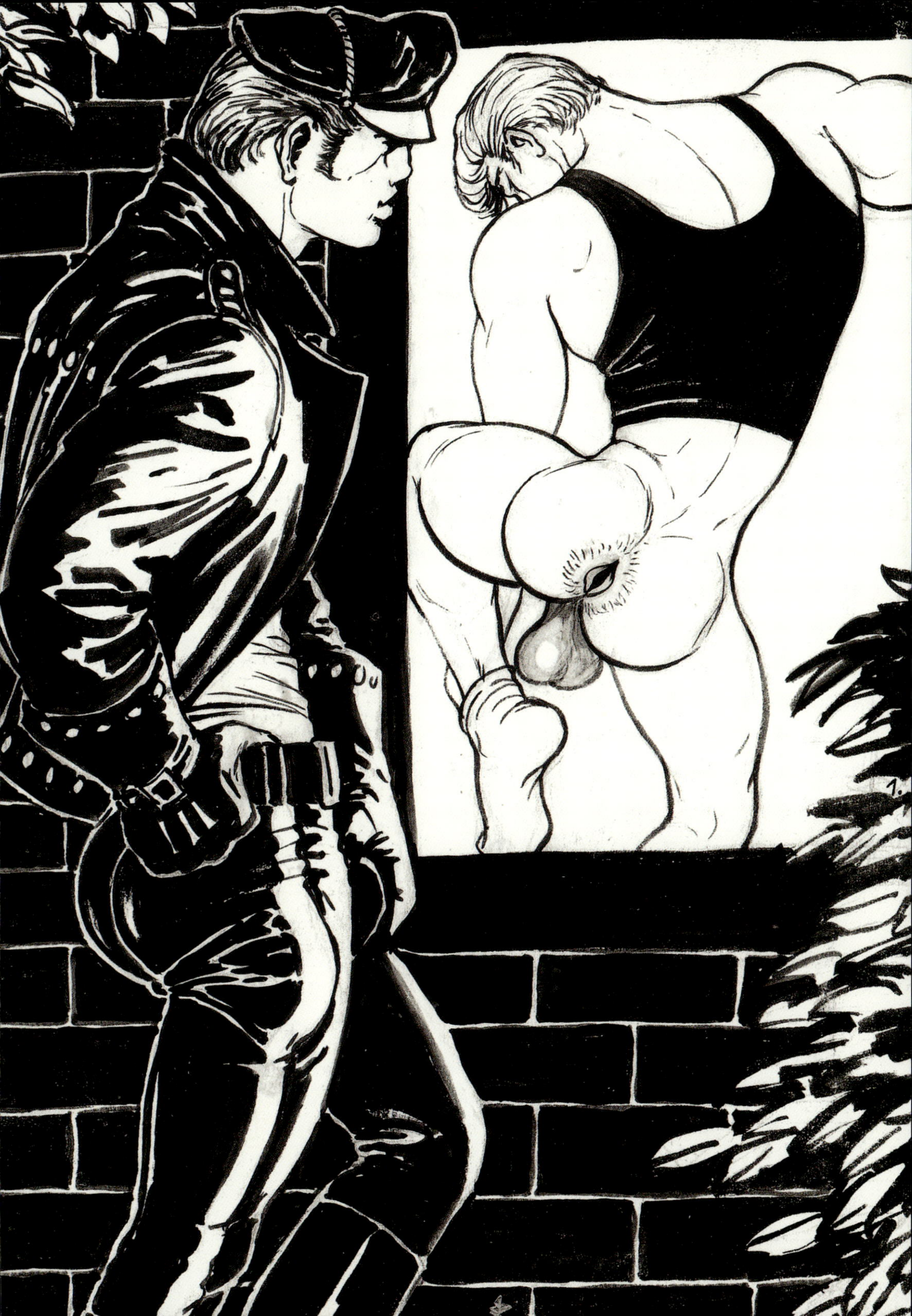

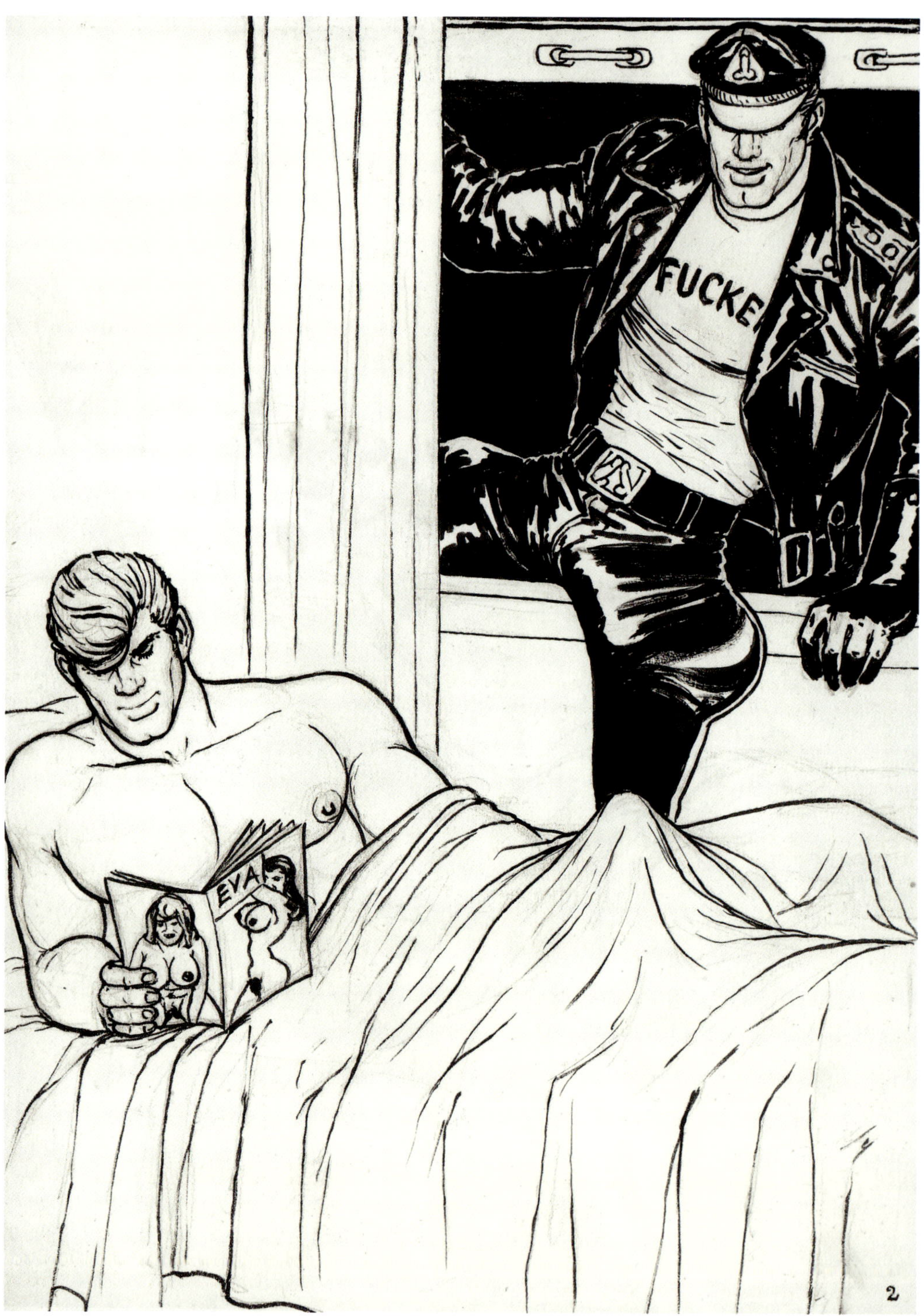

FUCKE
EYA

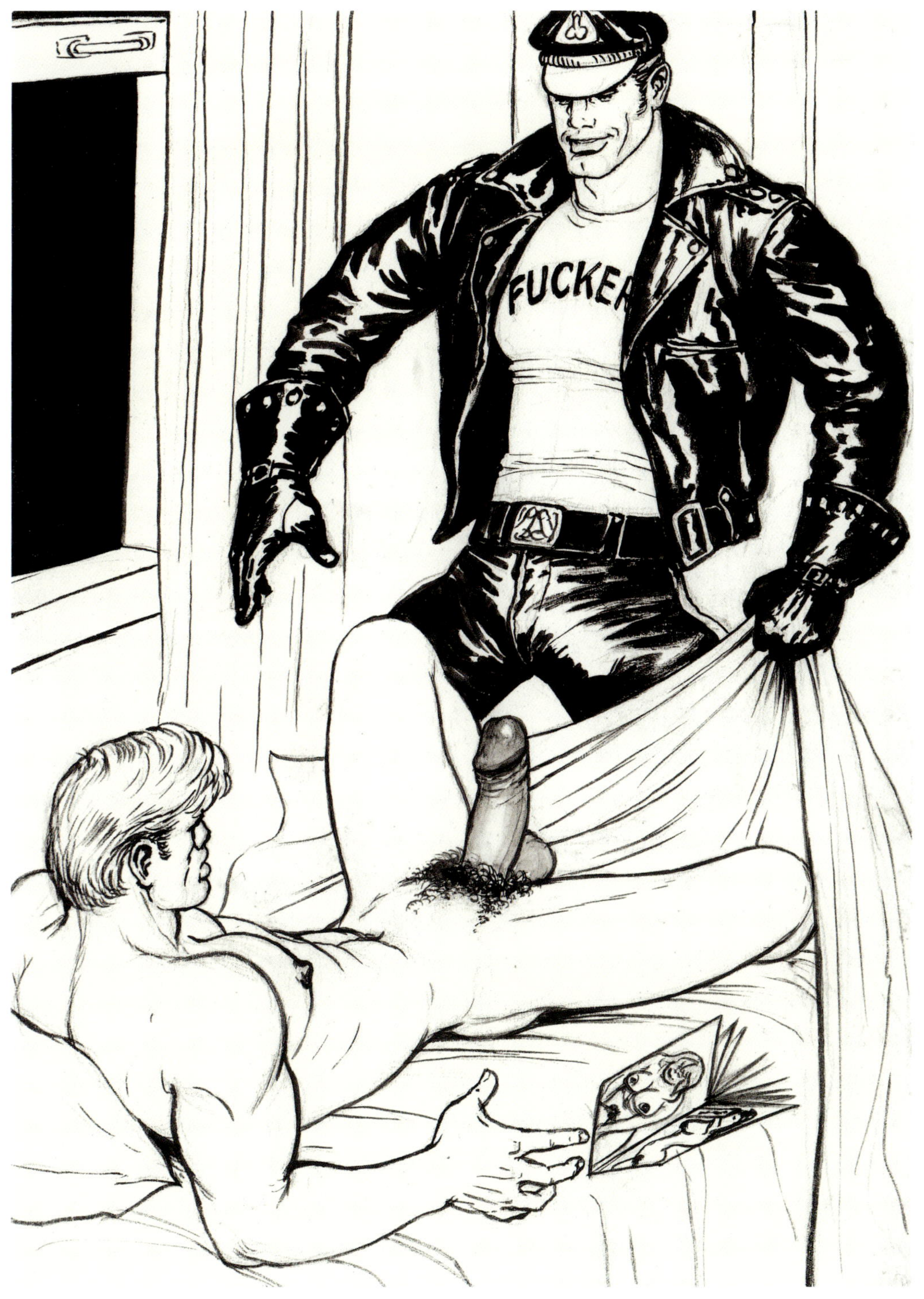

FUCKER

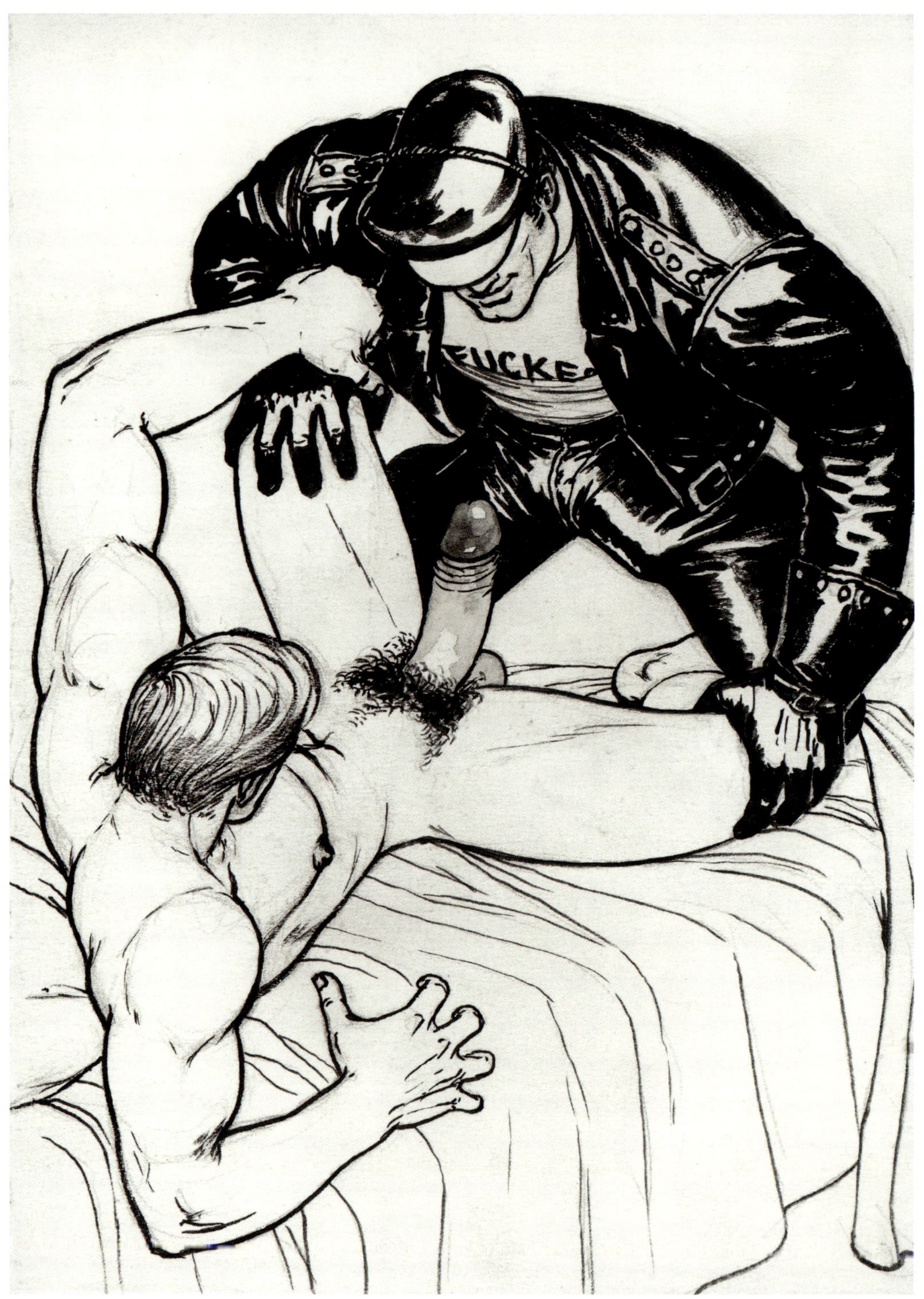
FUCKE

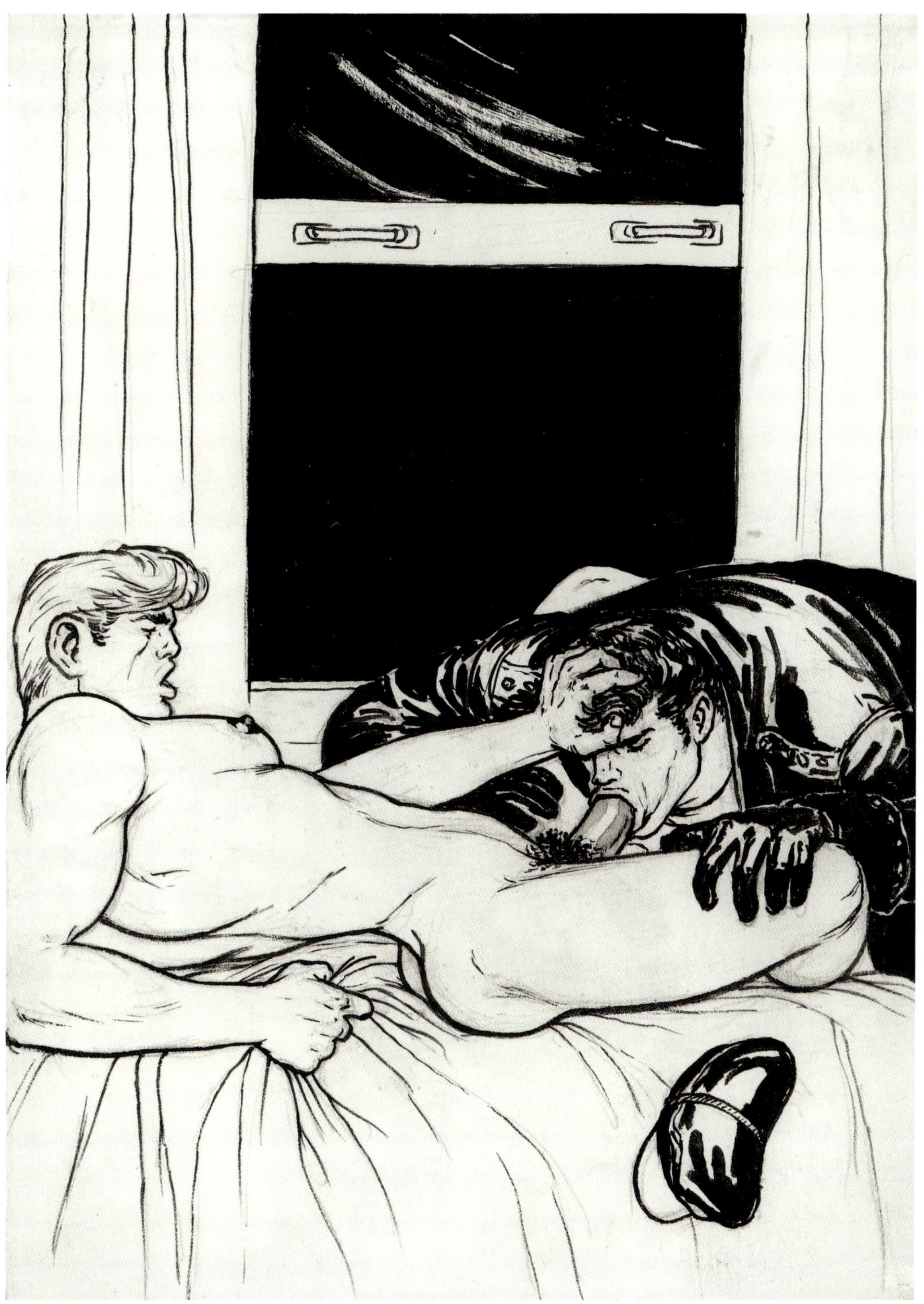

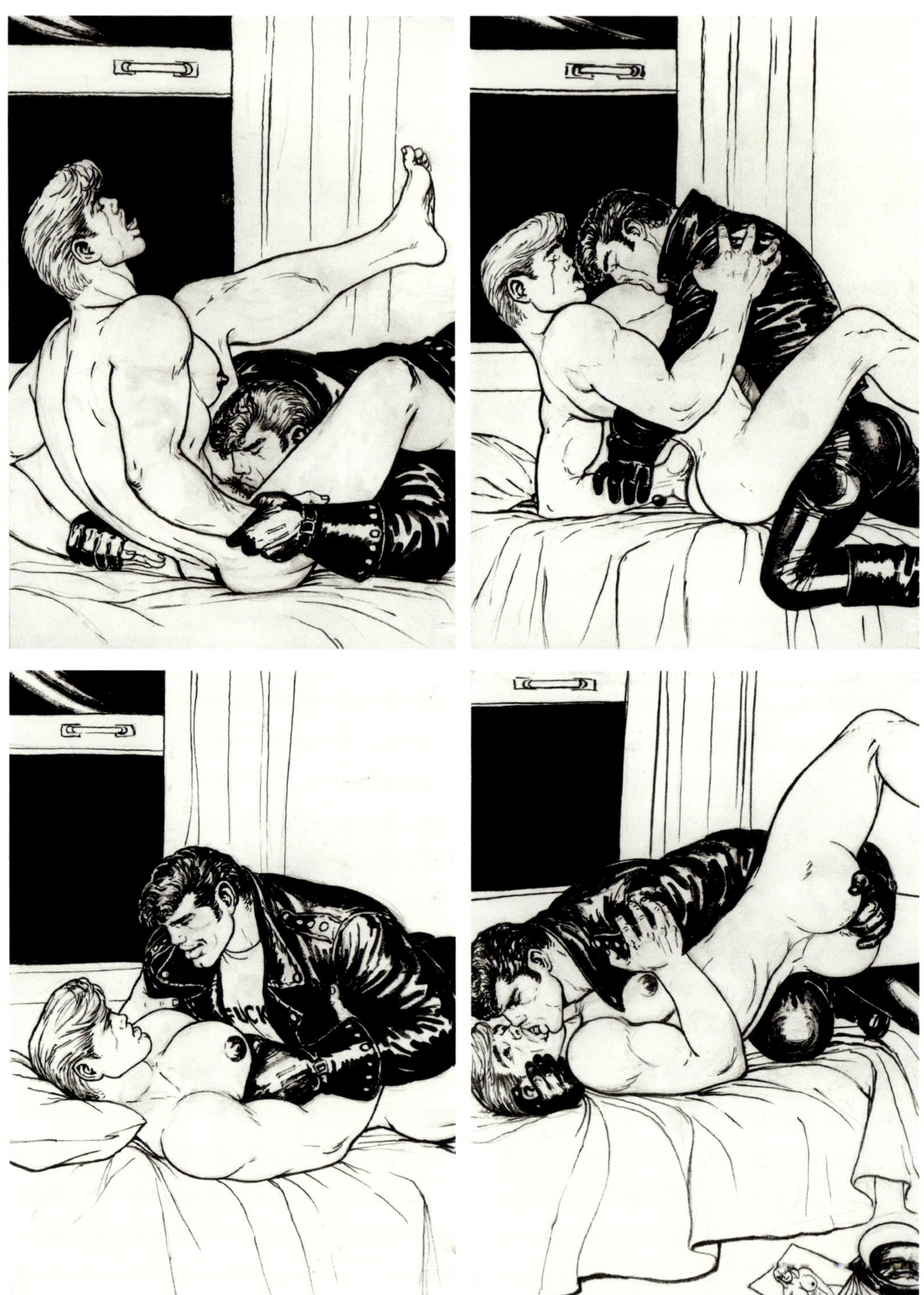

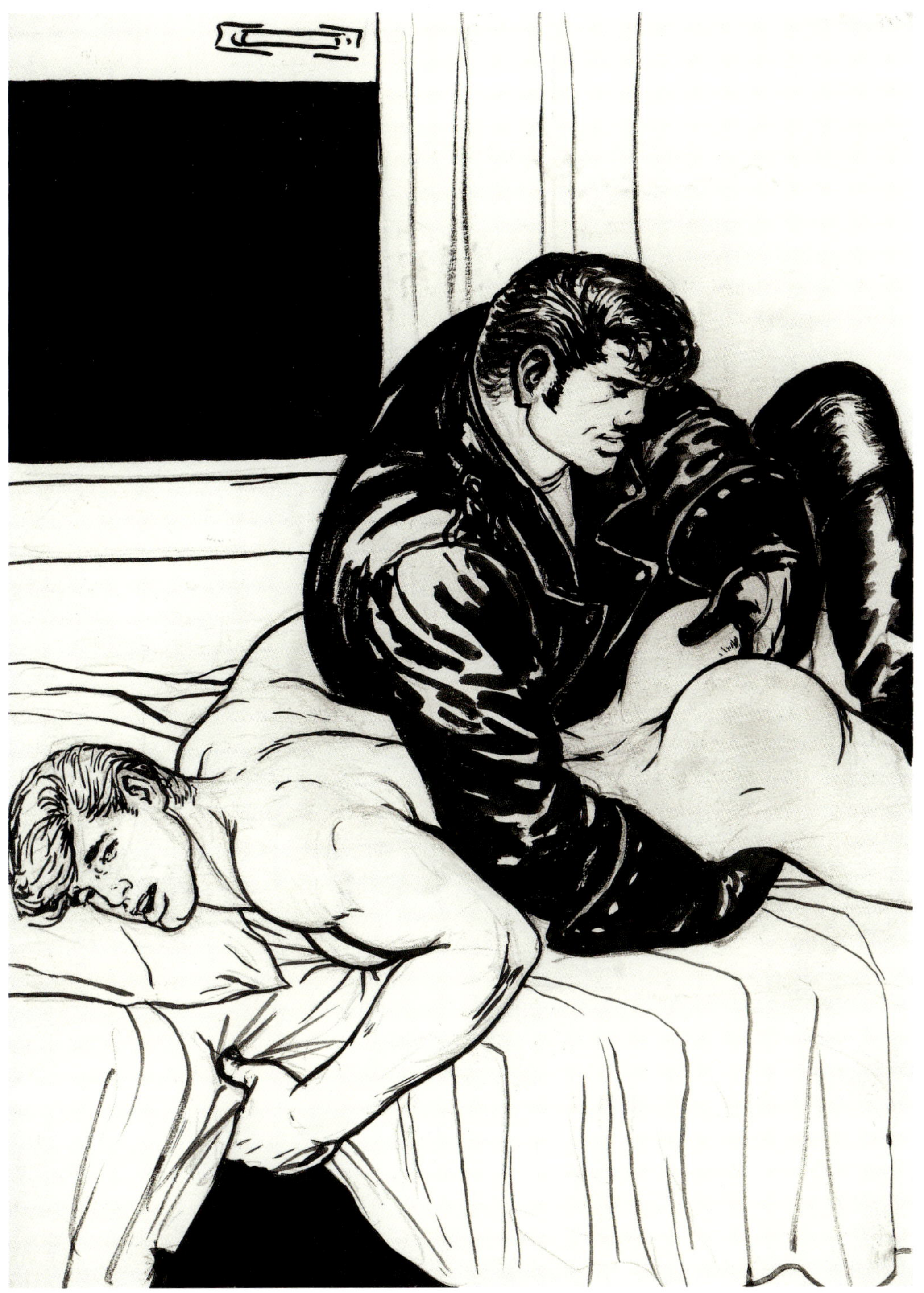

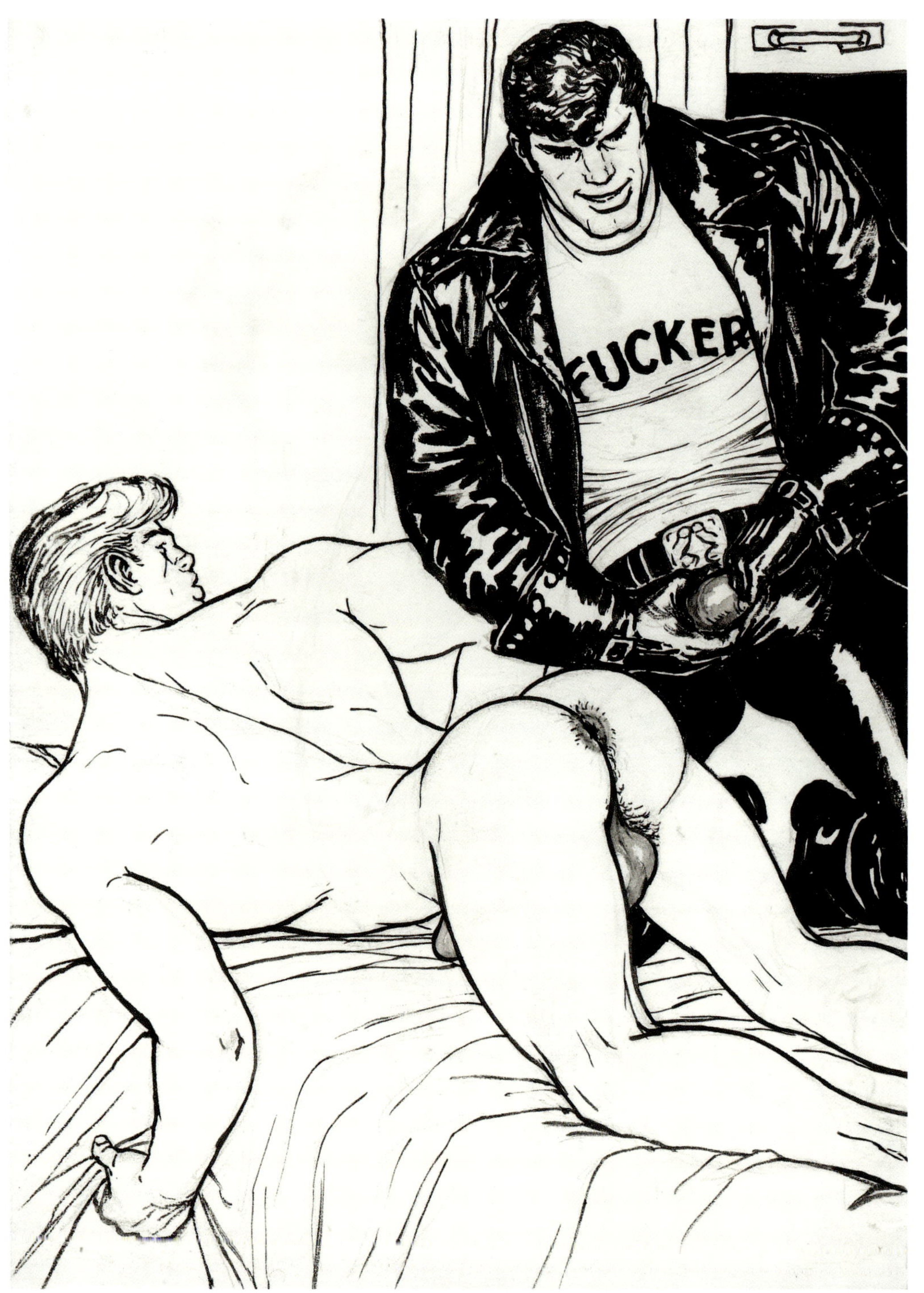
FUCKER

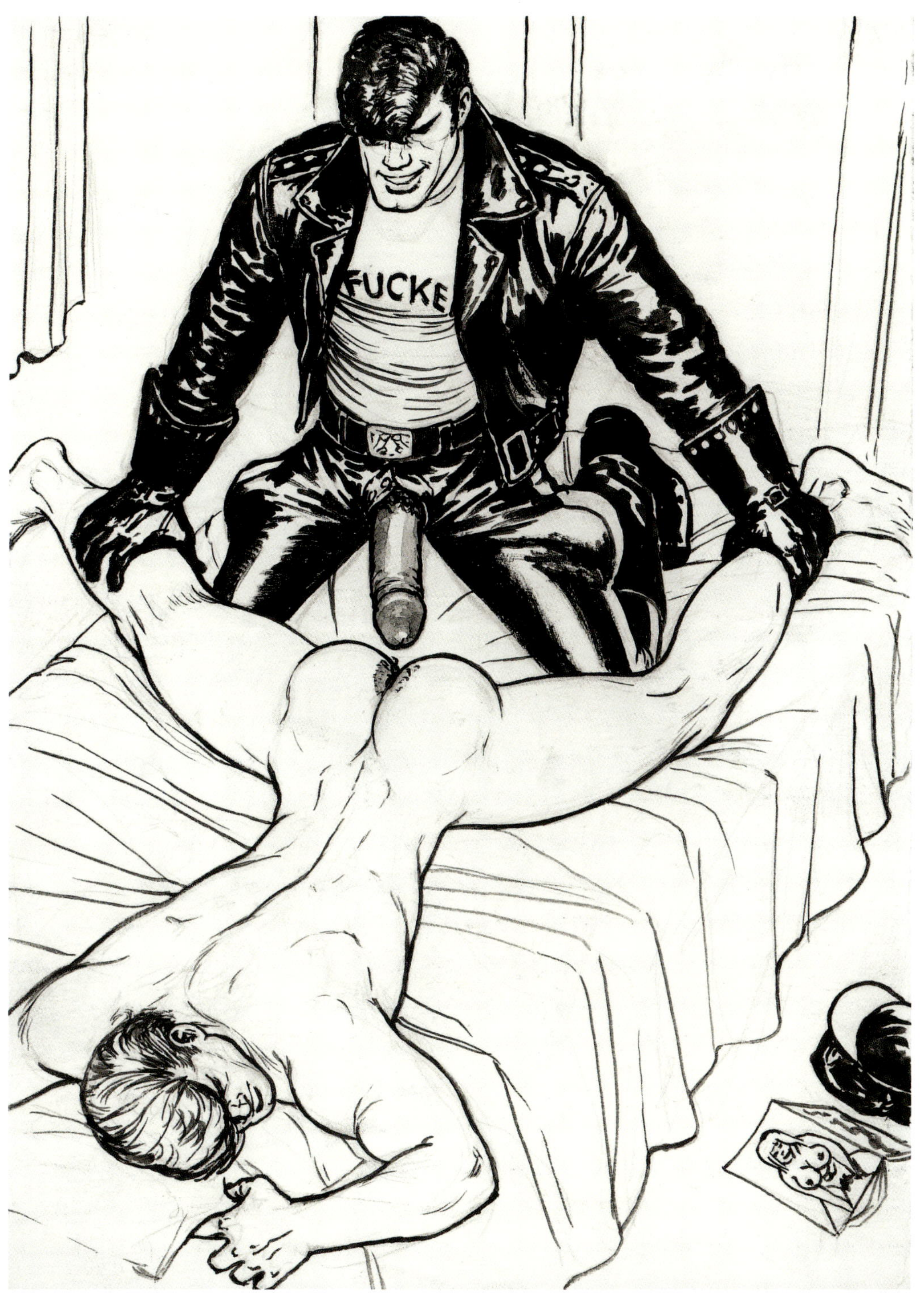
FUCKE

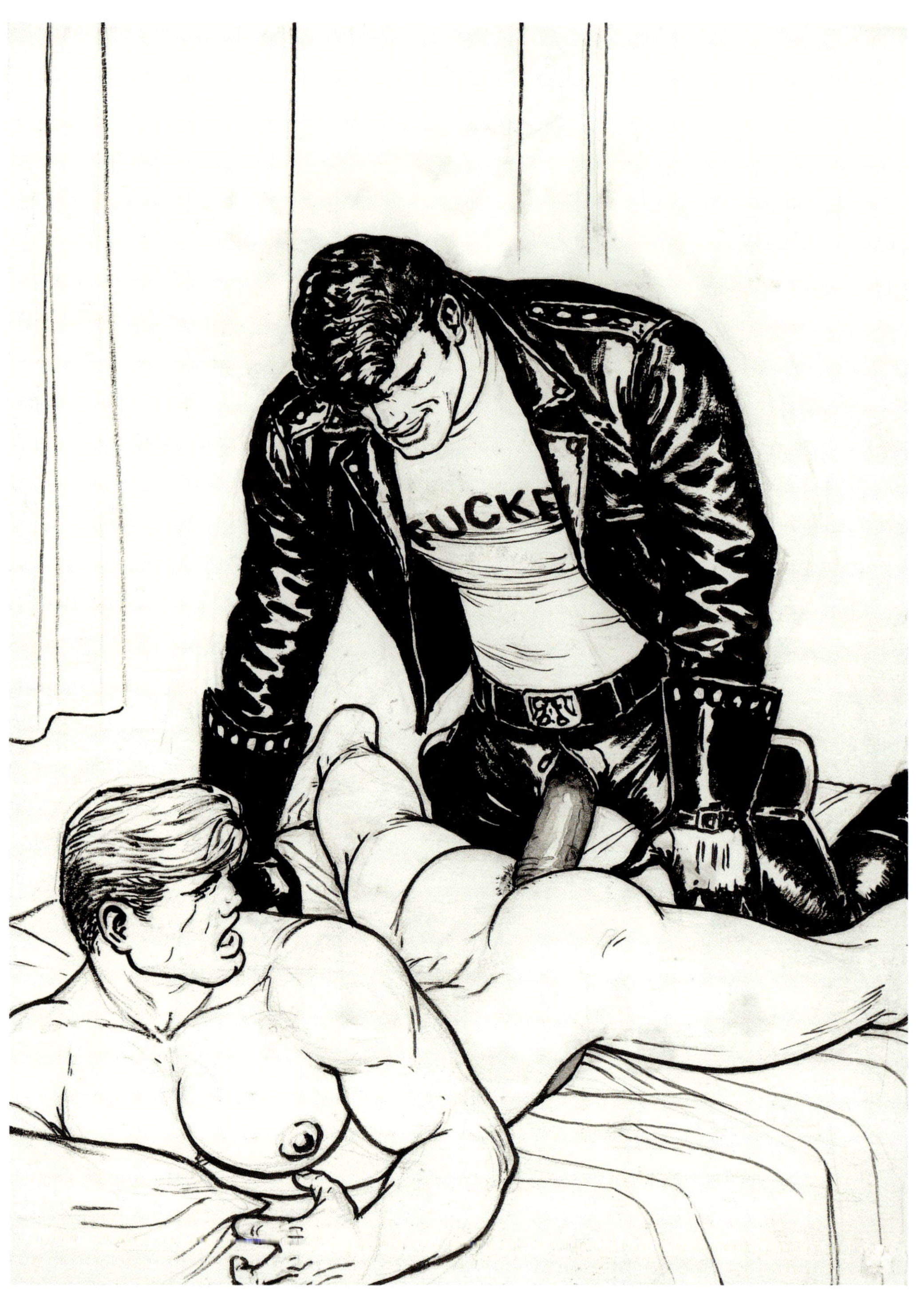
RUCKE

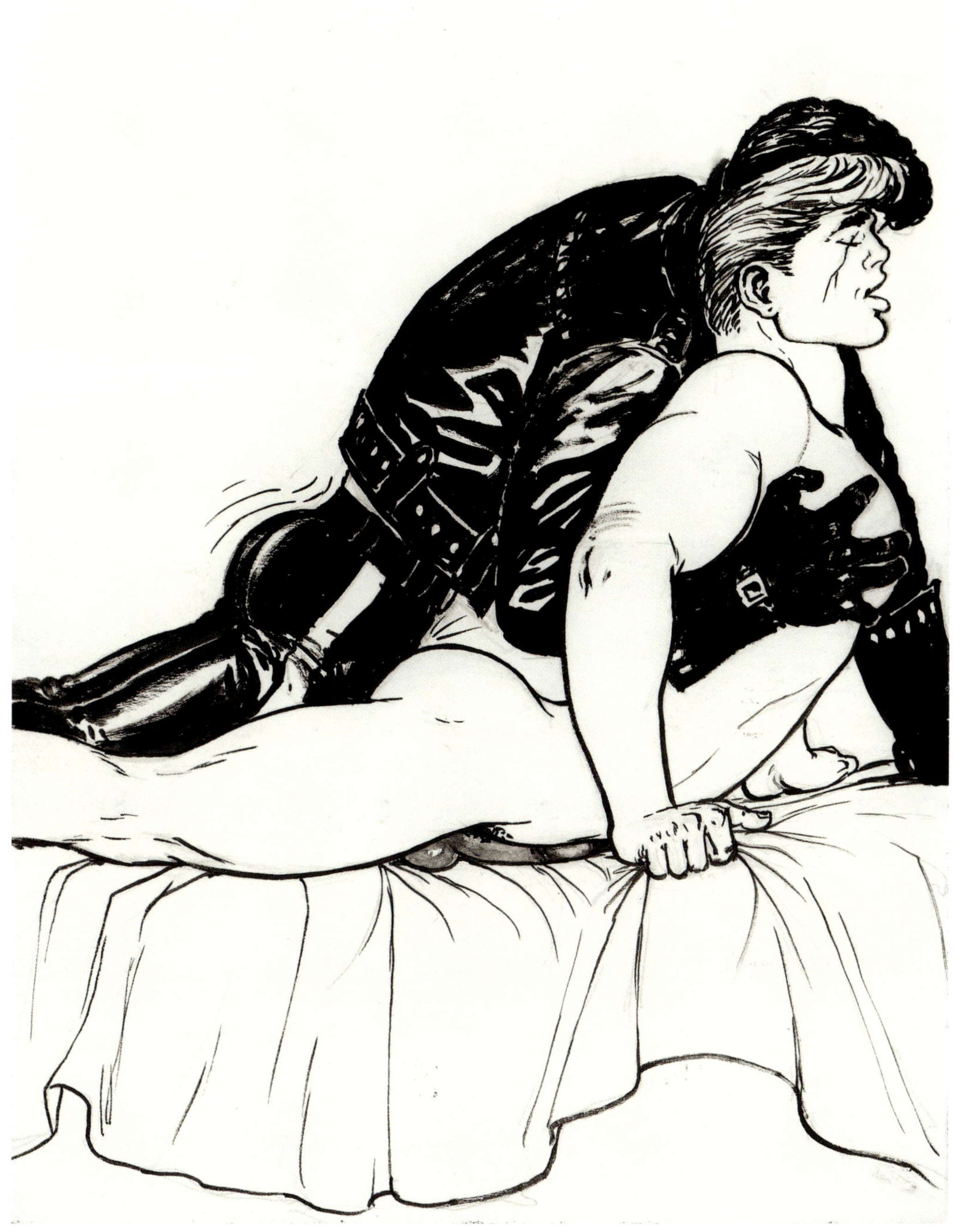

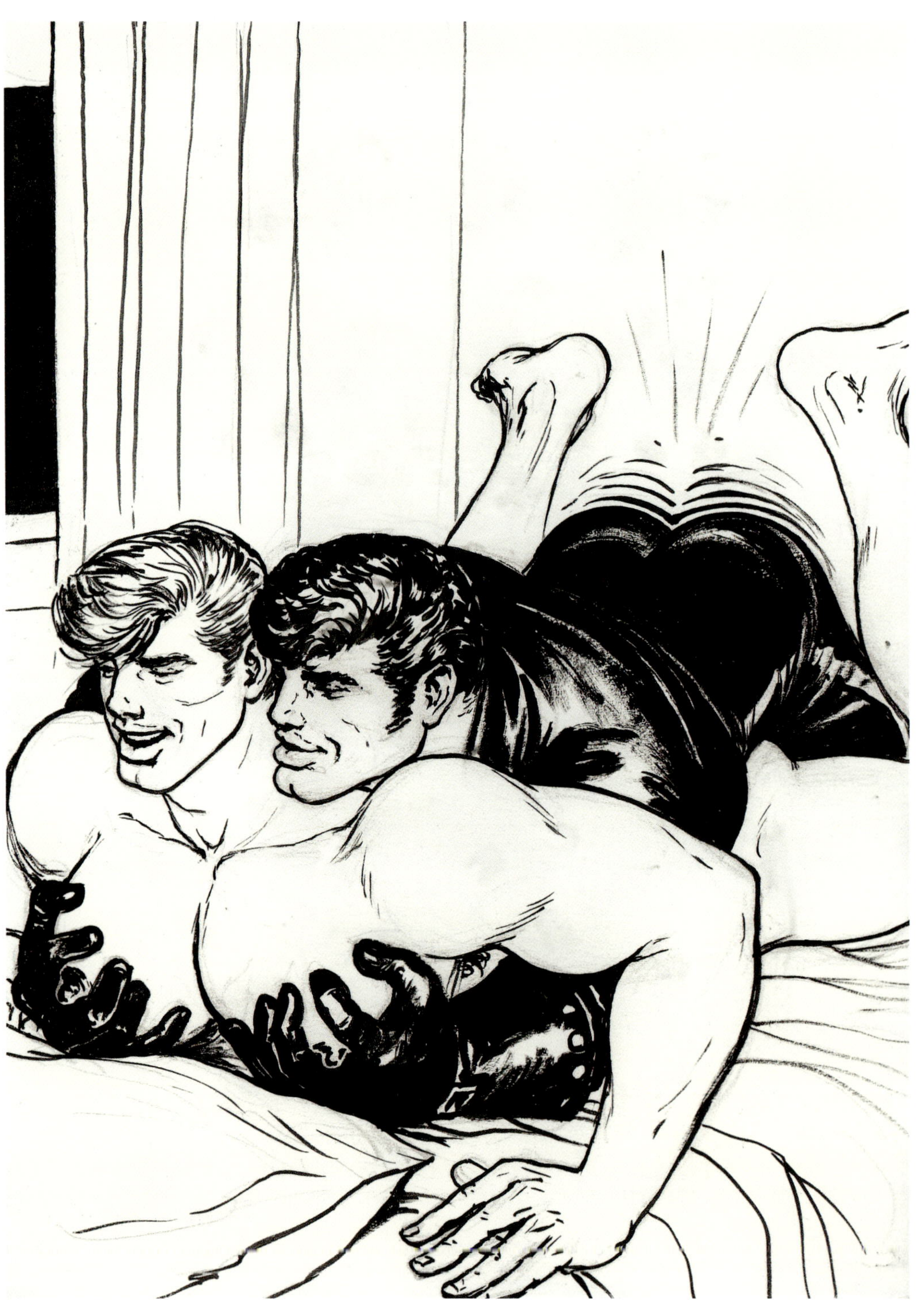

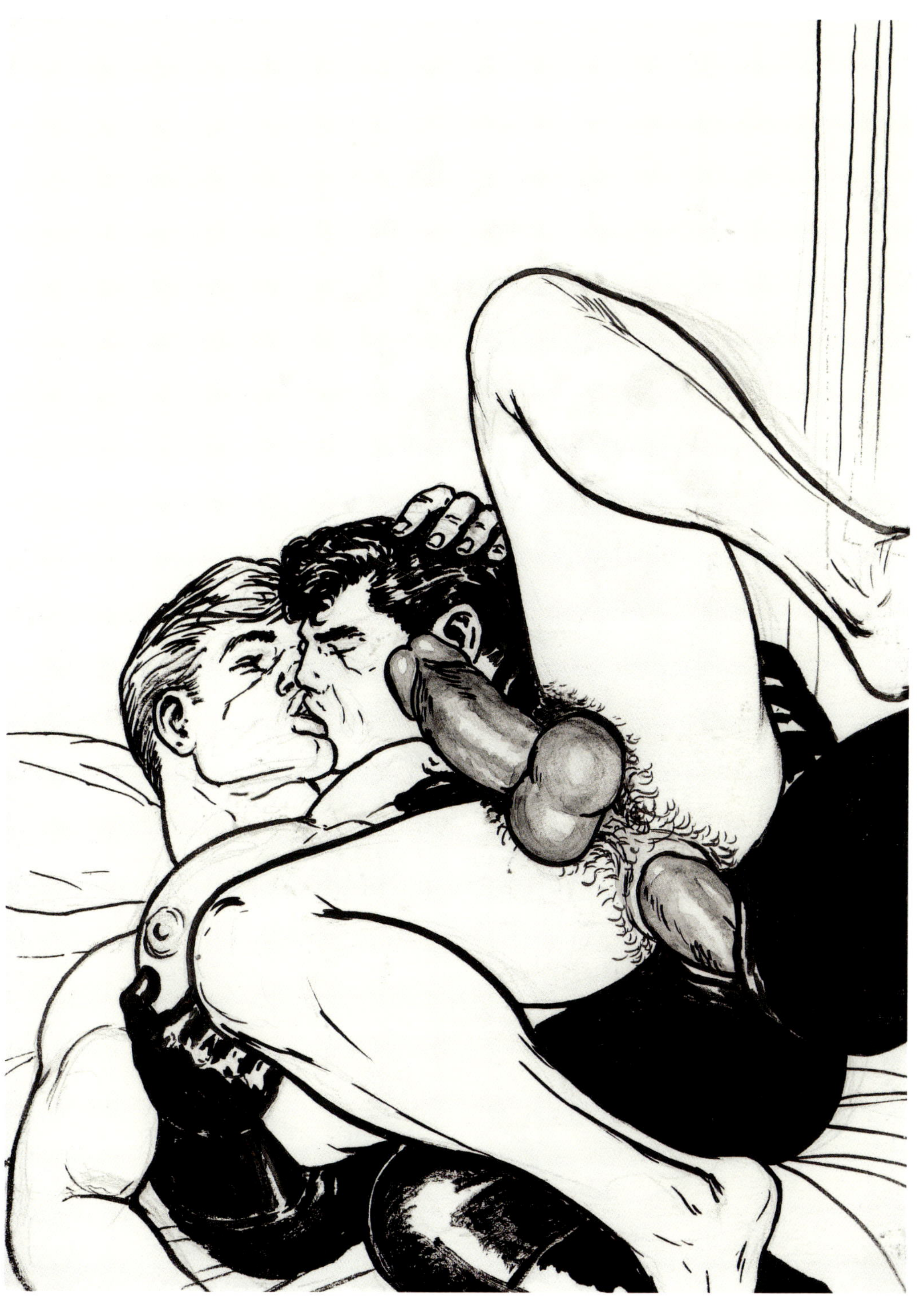

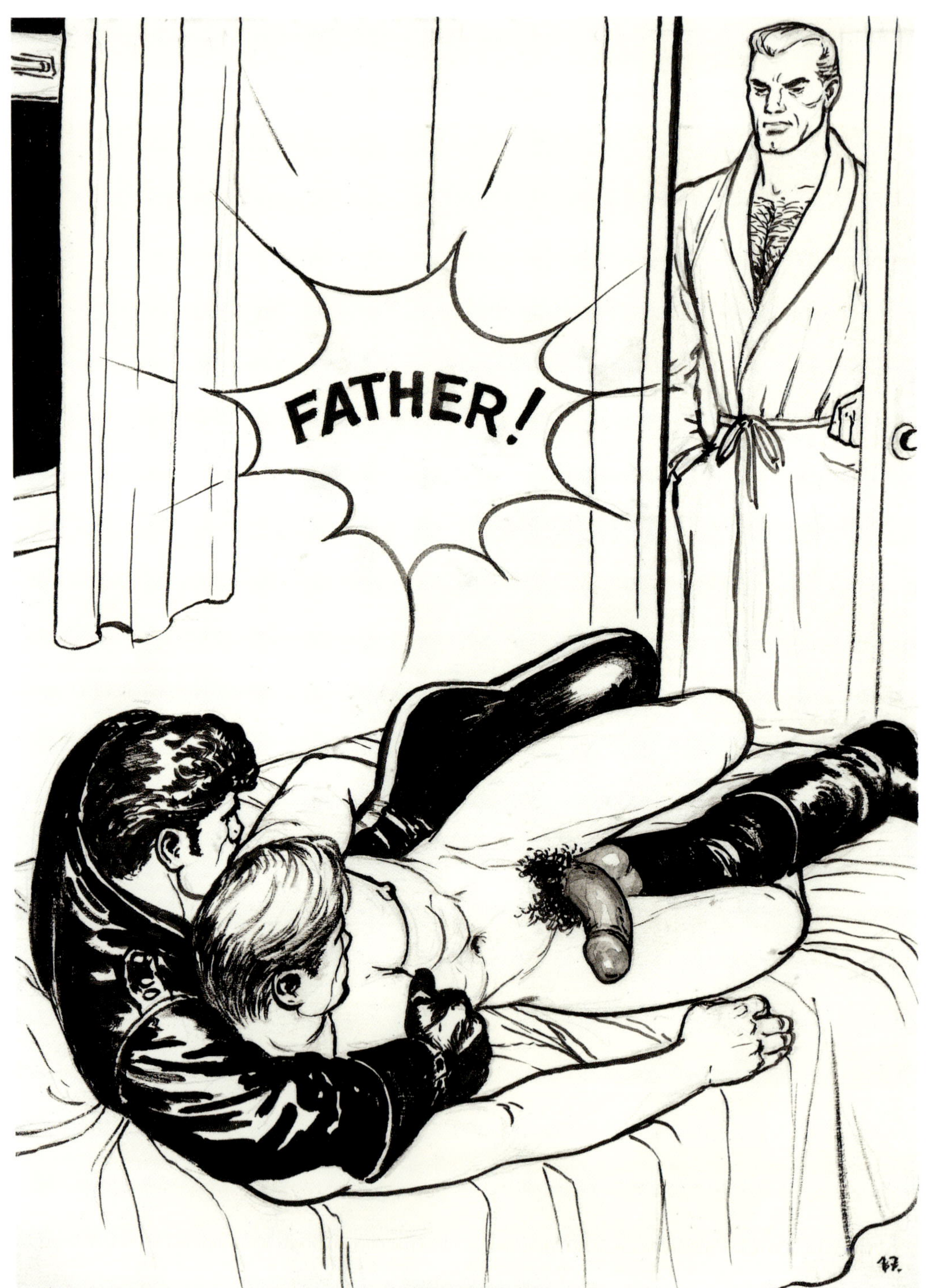
FATHER!

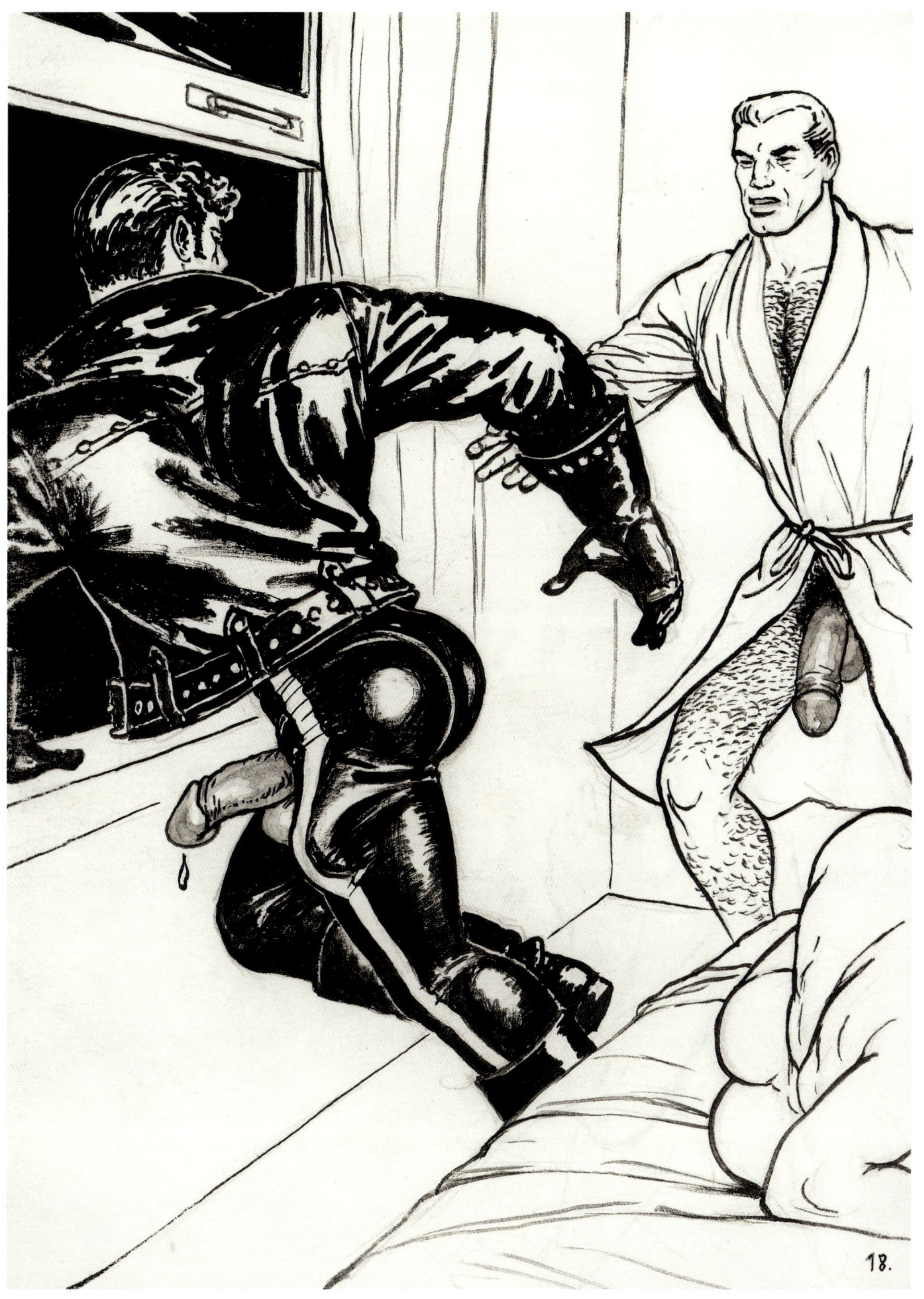

18.

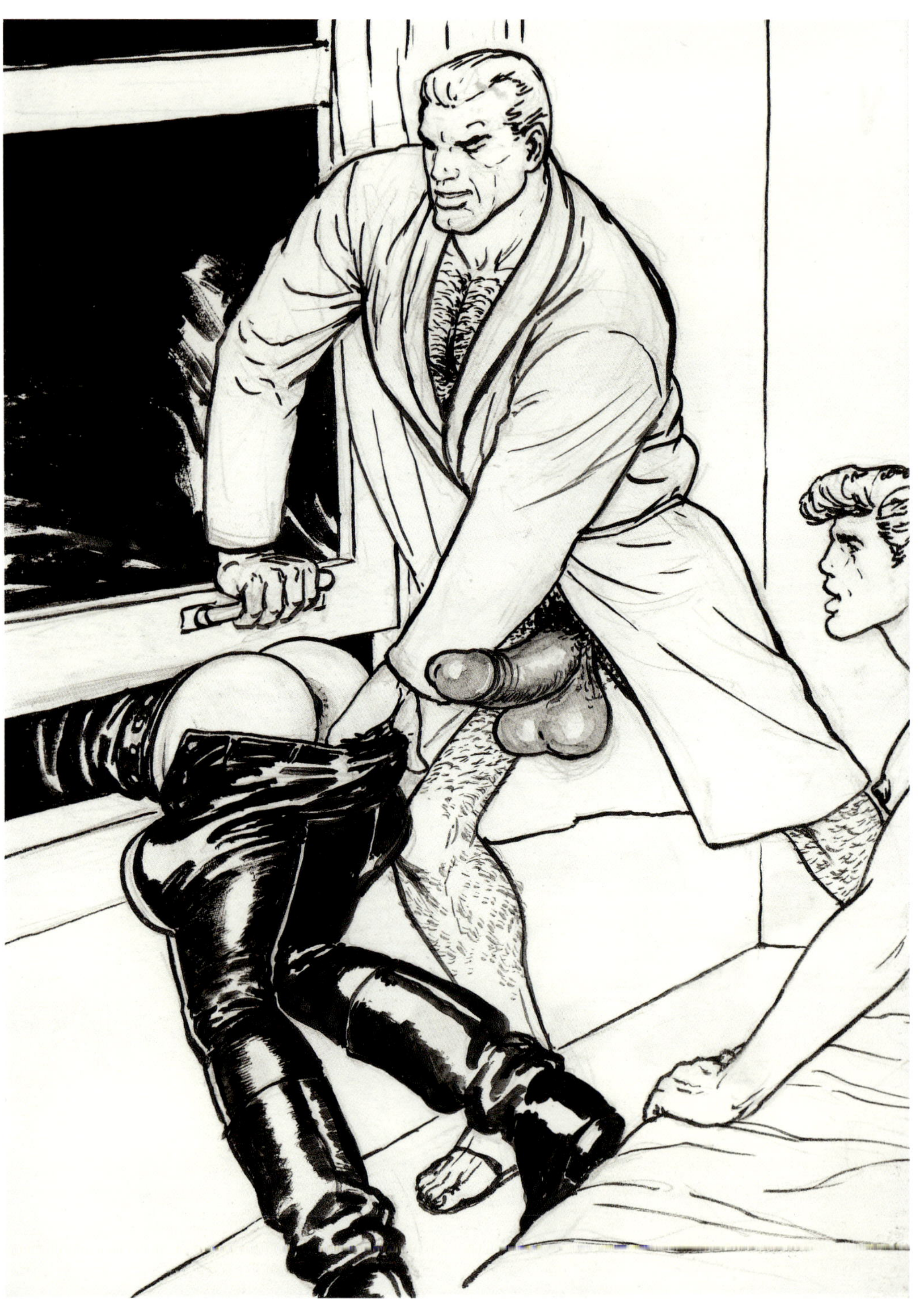

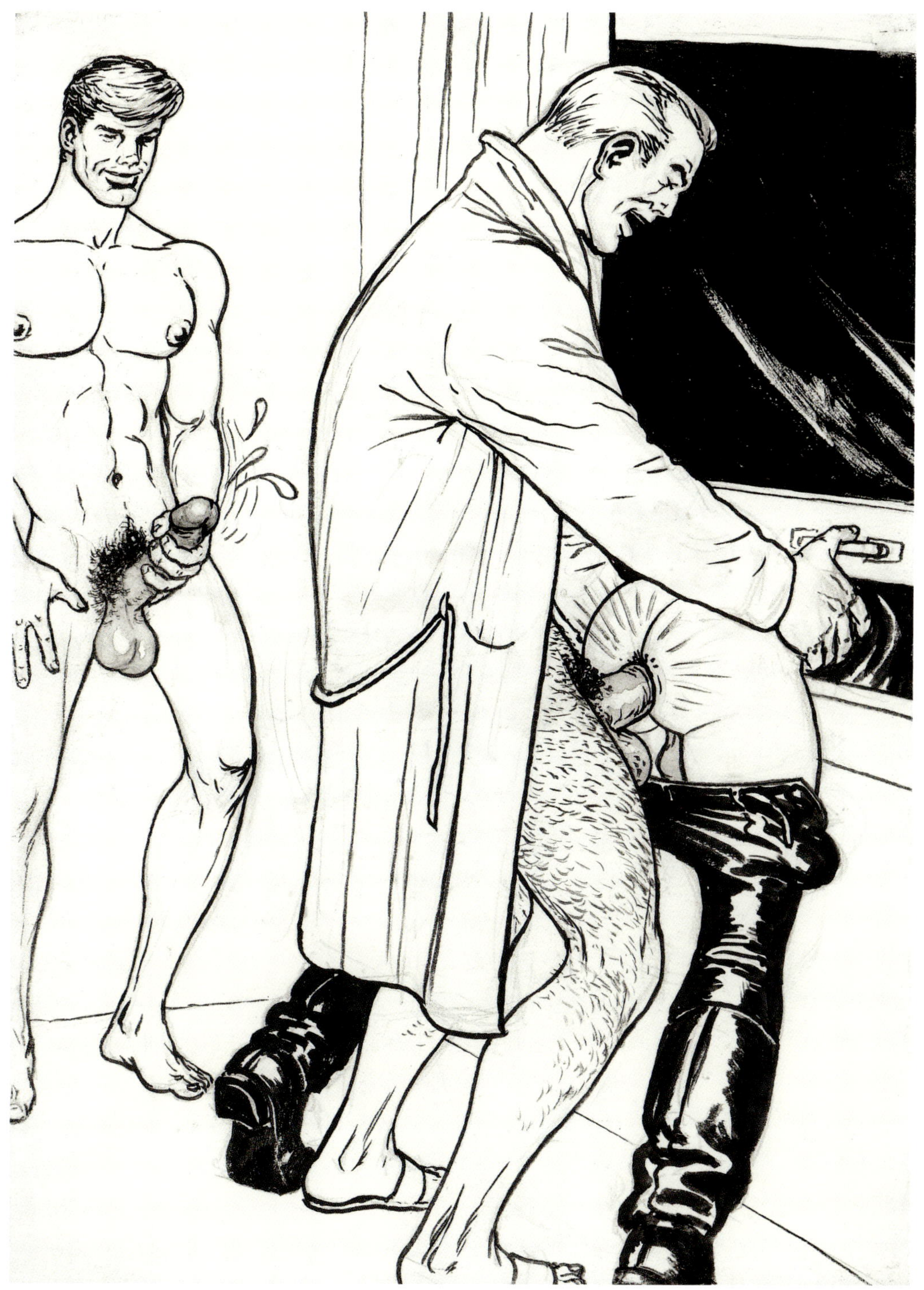

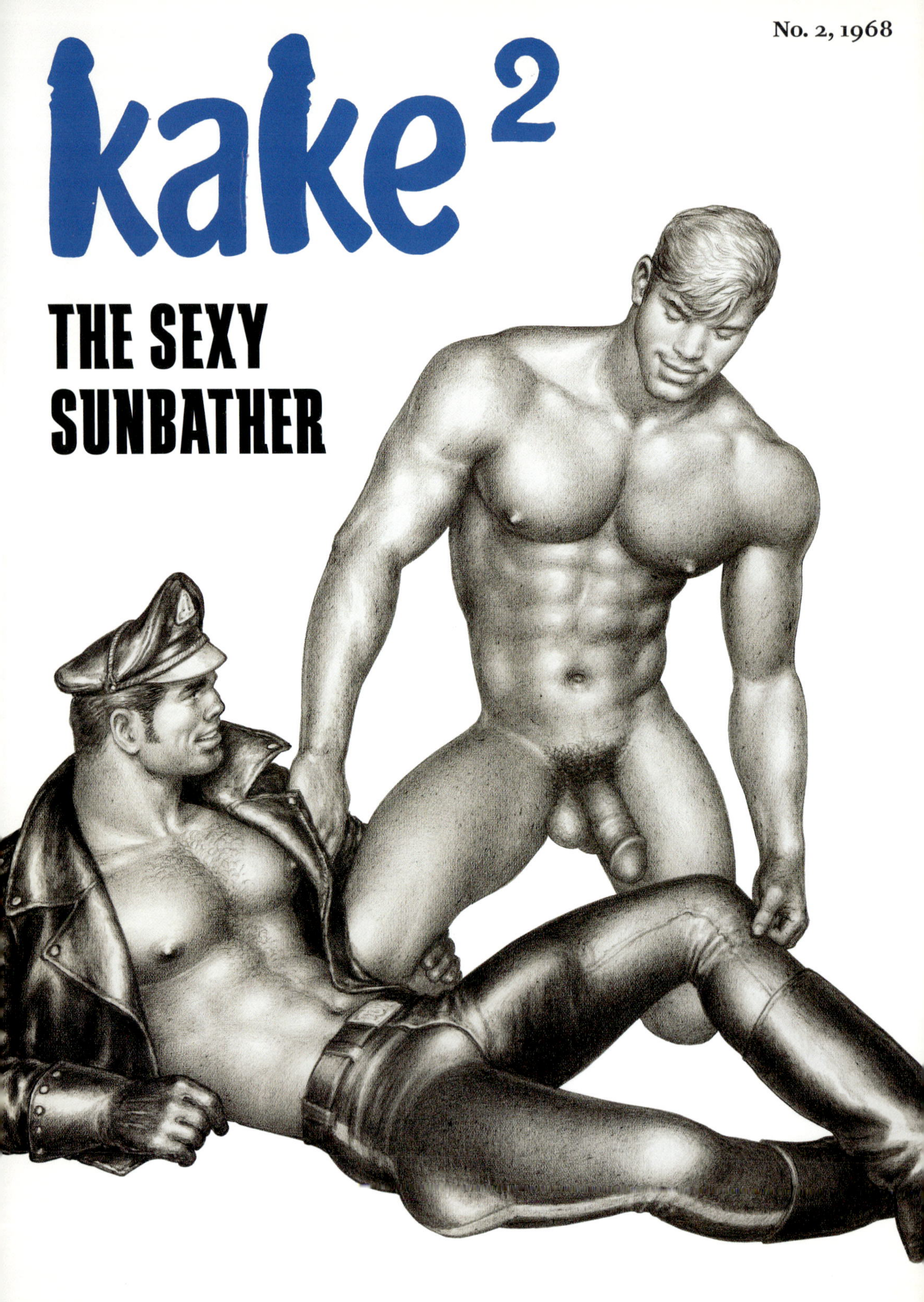
No. 2, 1968
kake²
THE SEXY
SUNBATHER

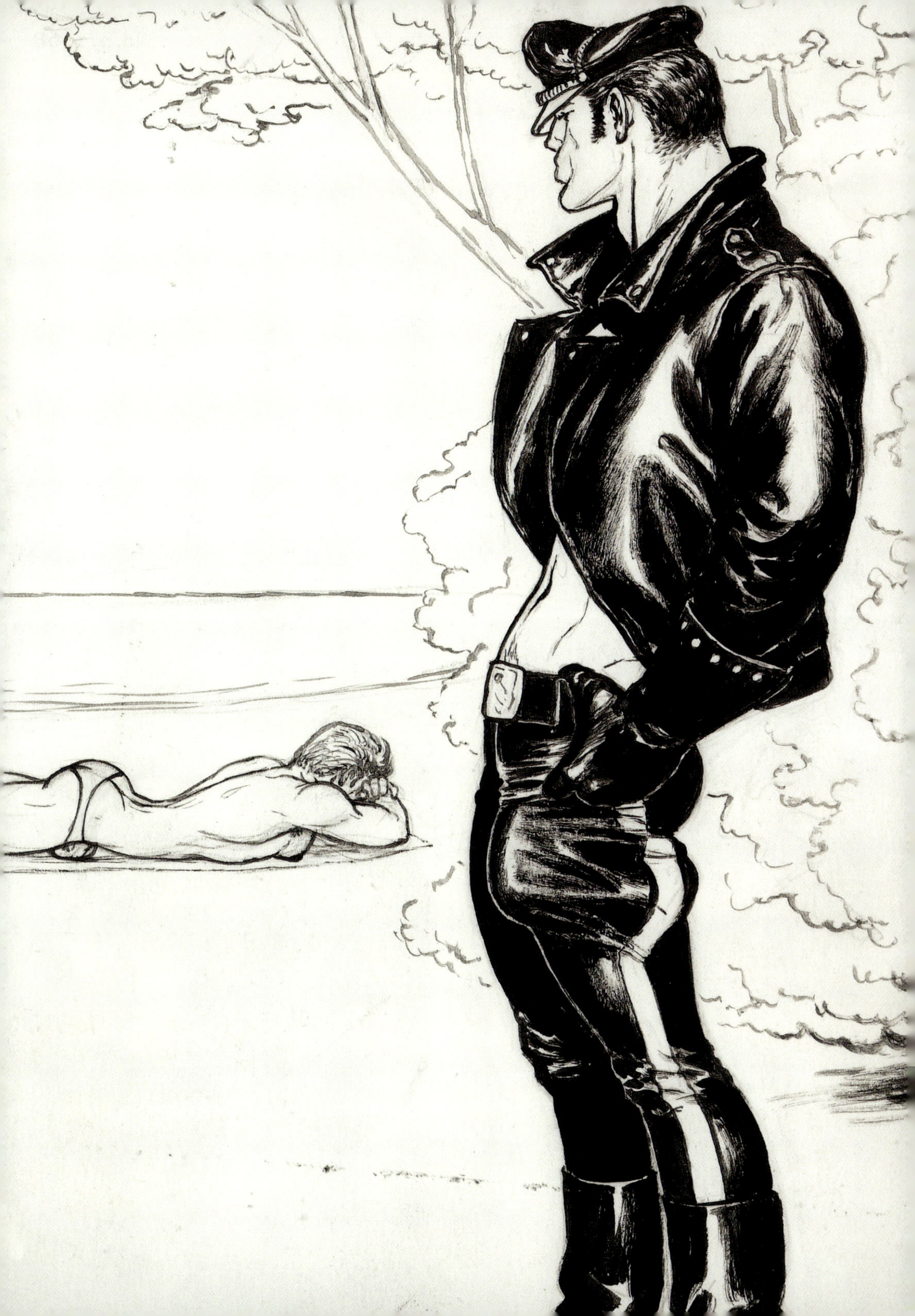

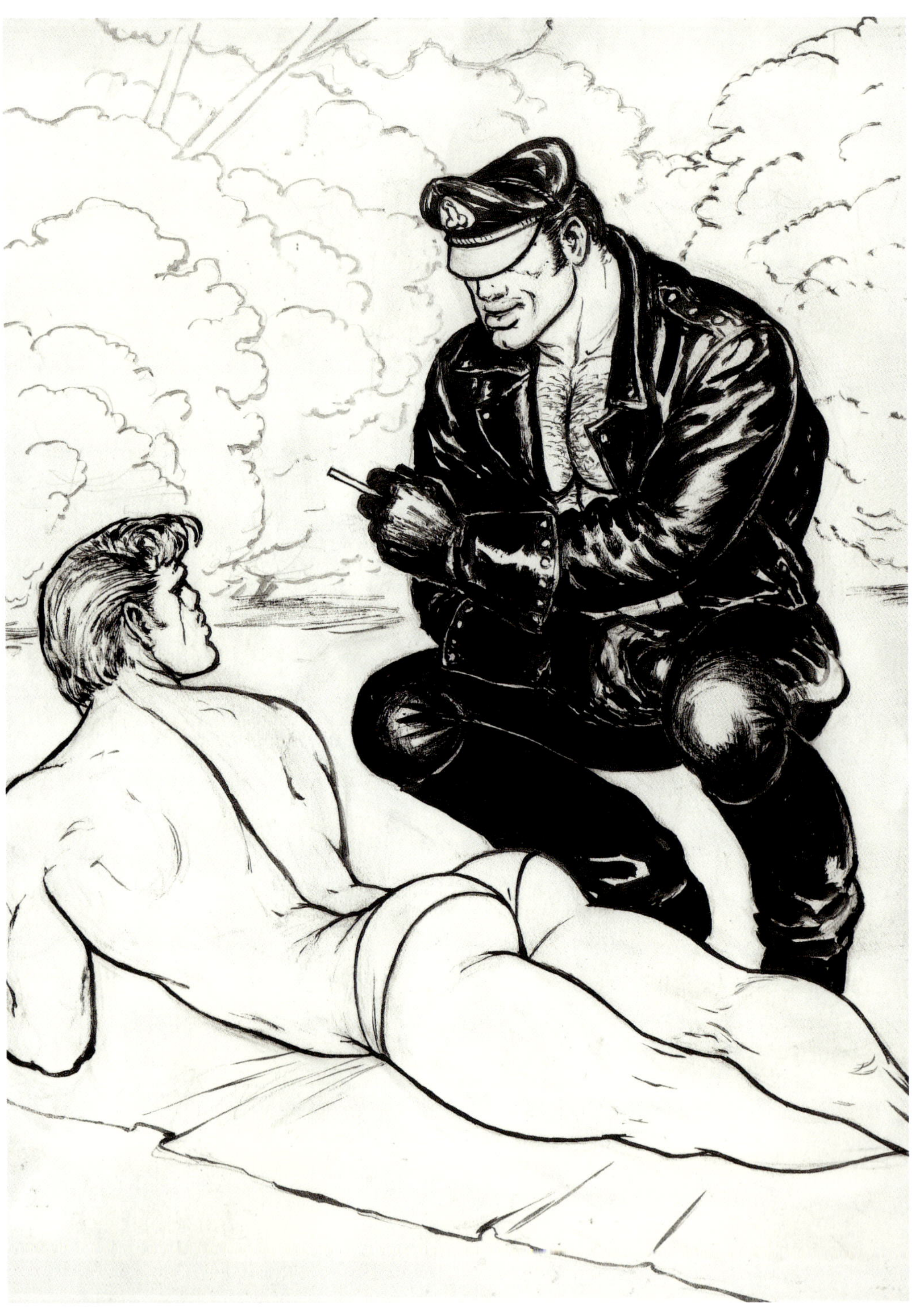

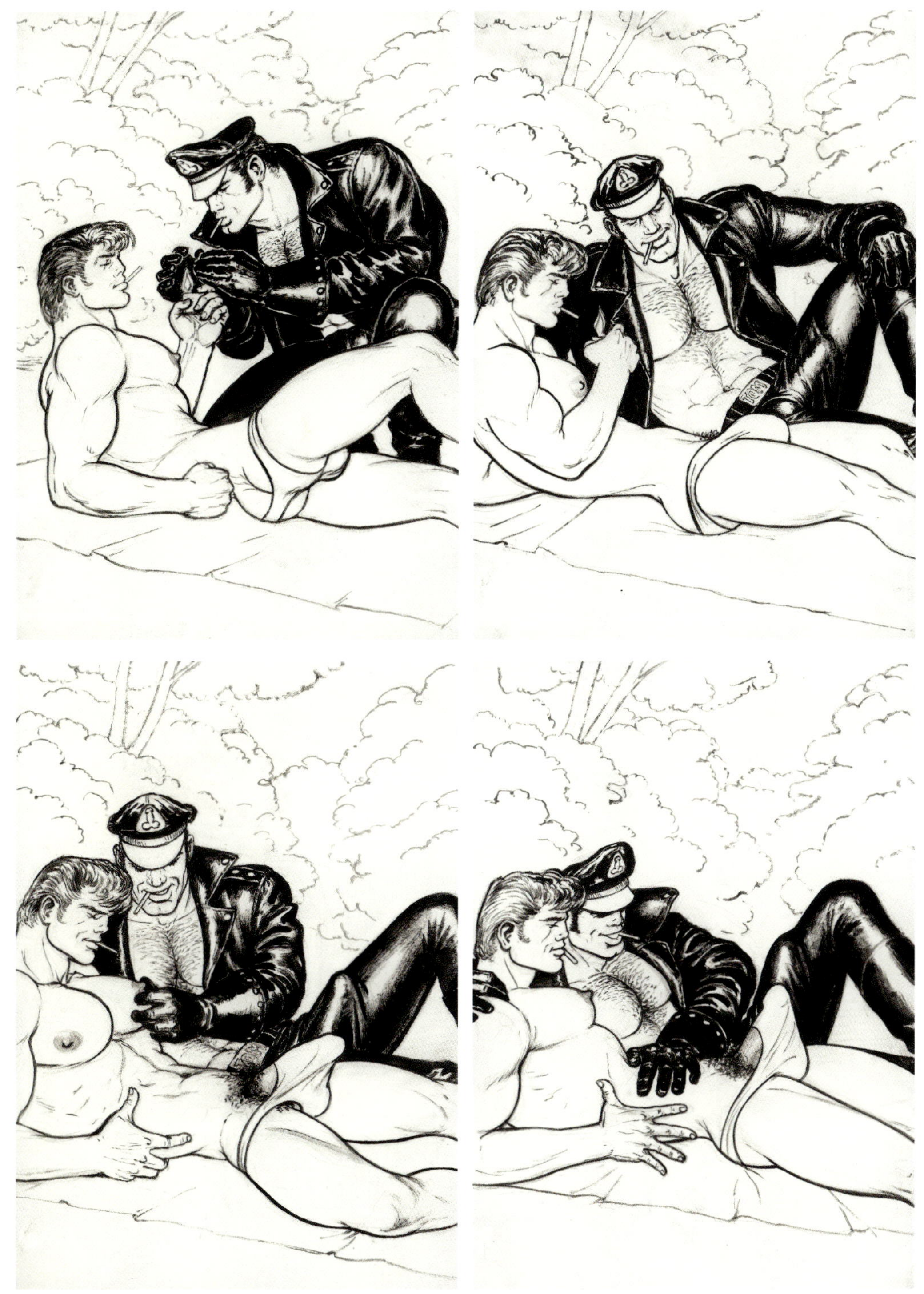

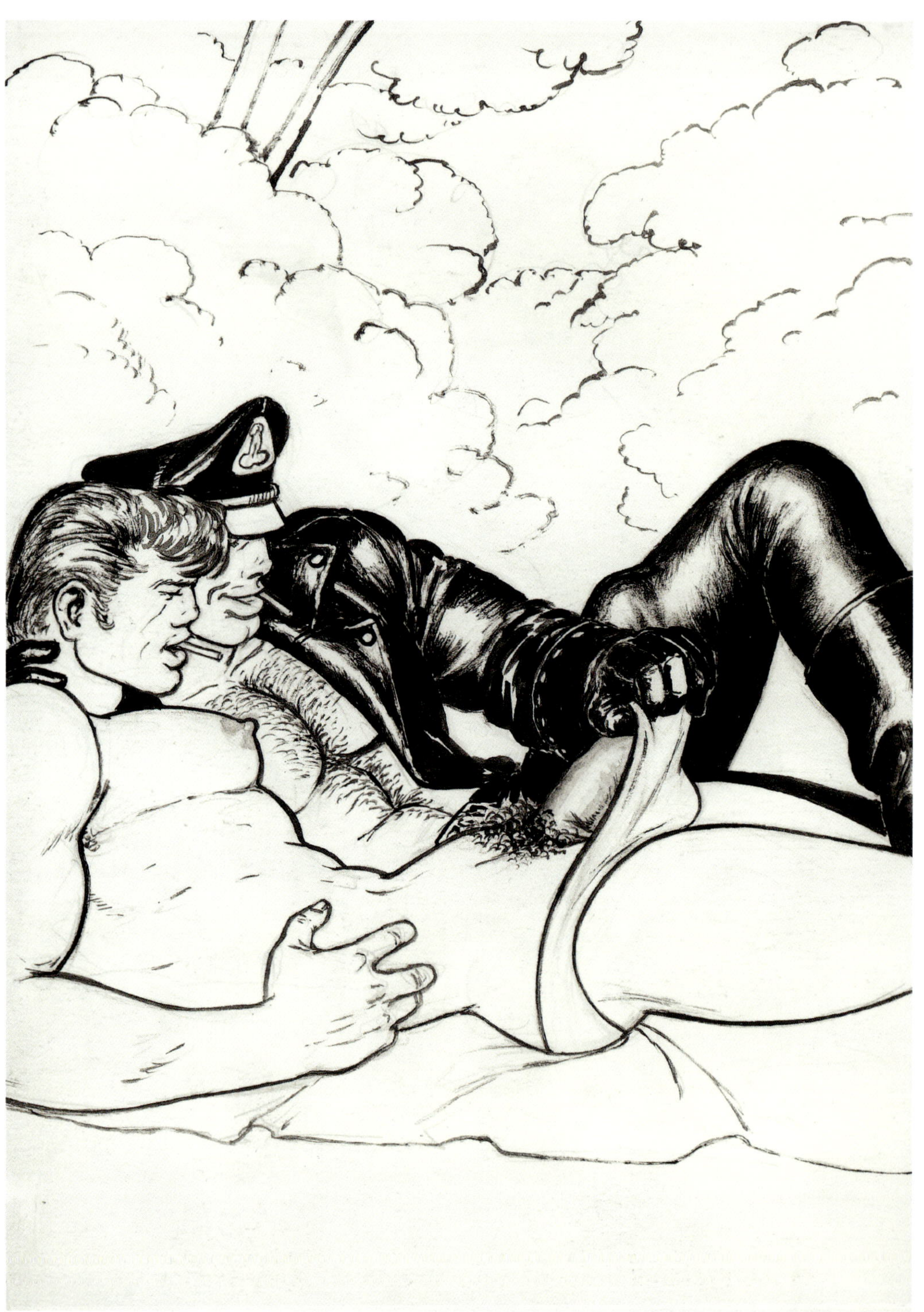

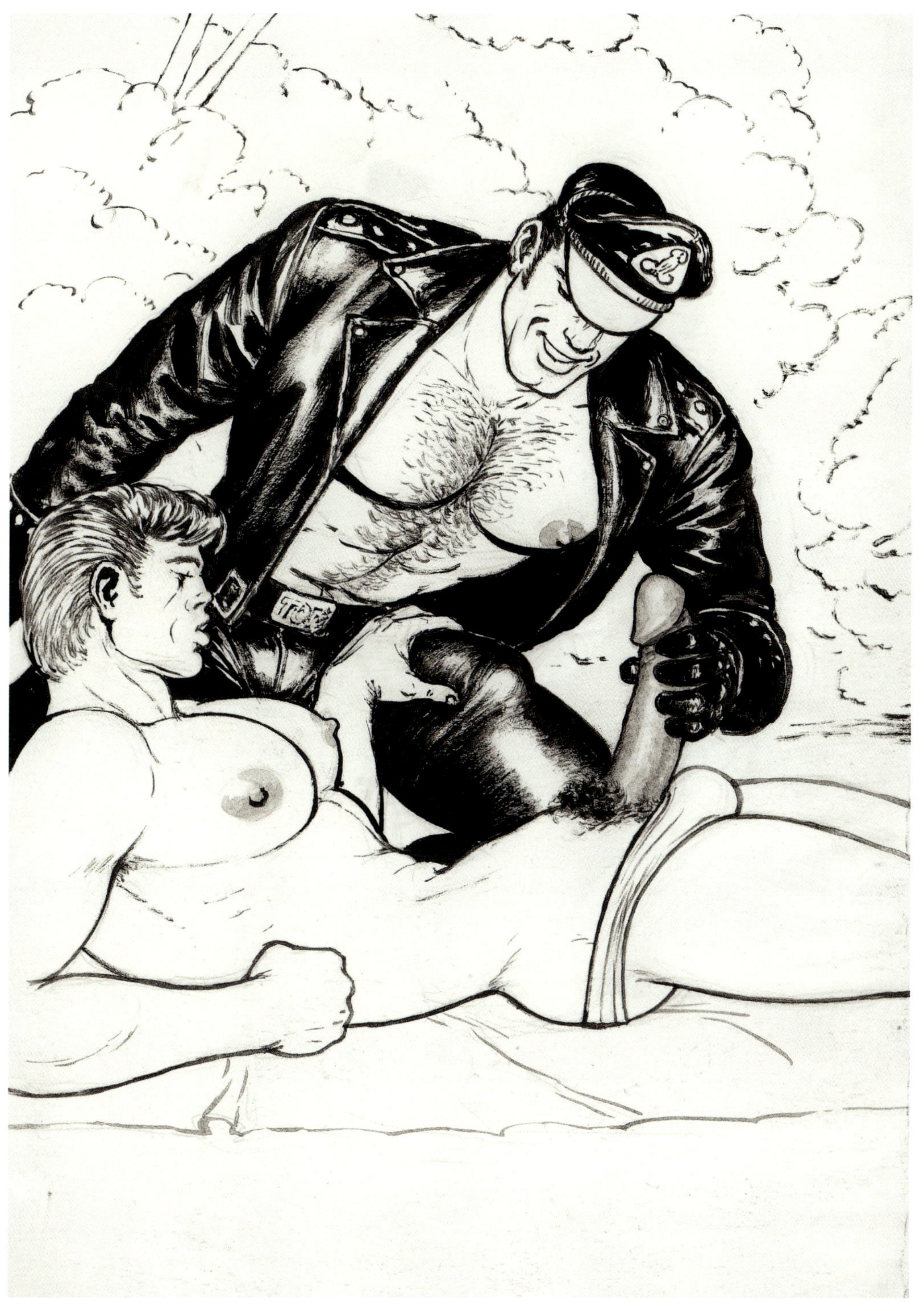

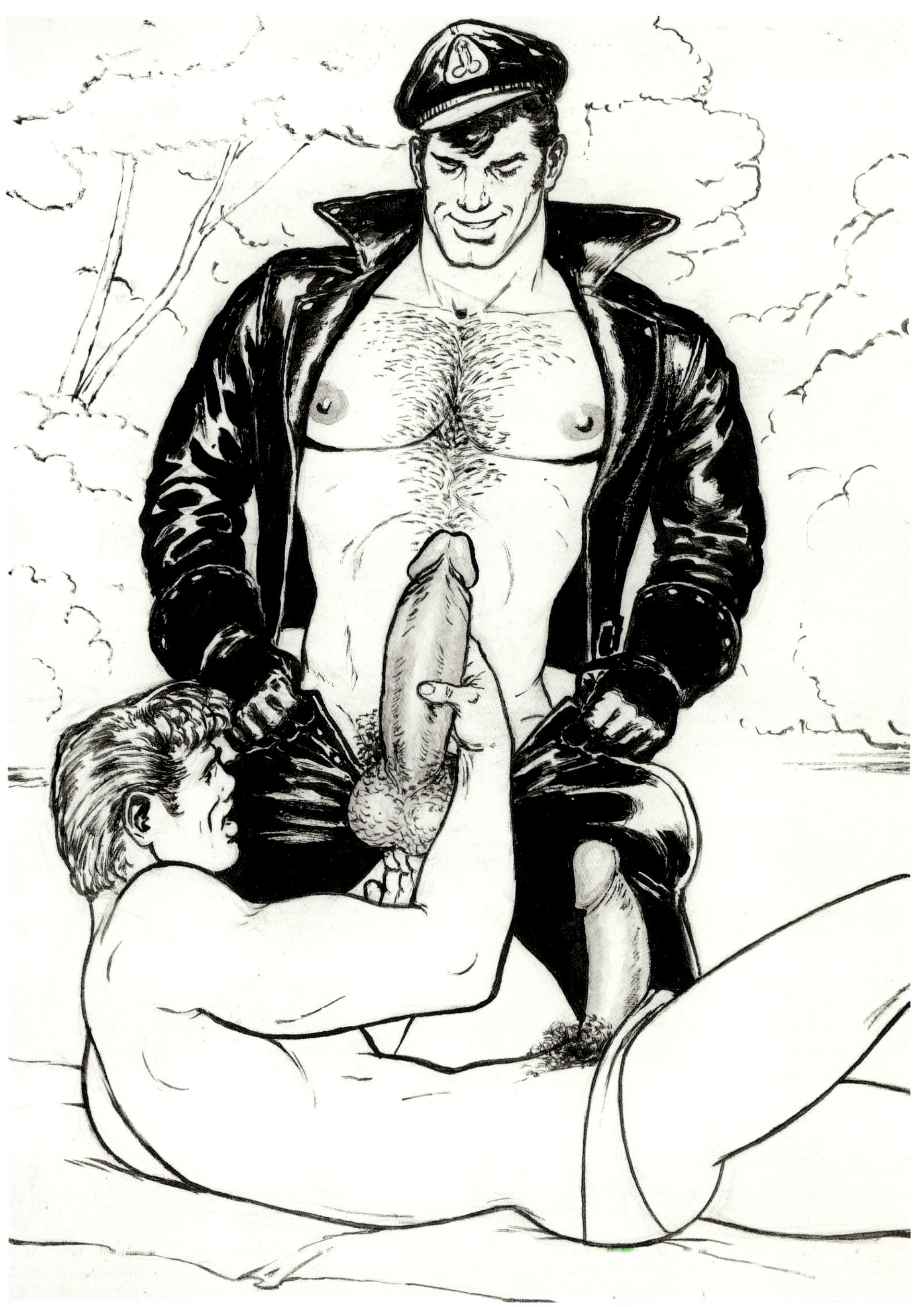

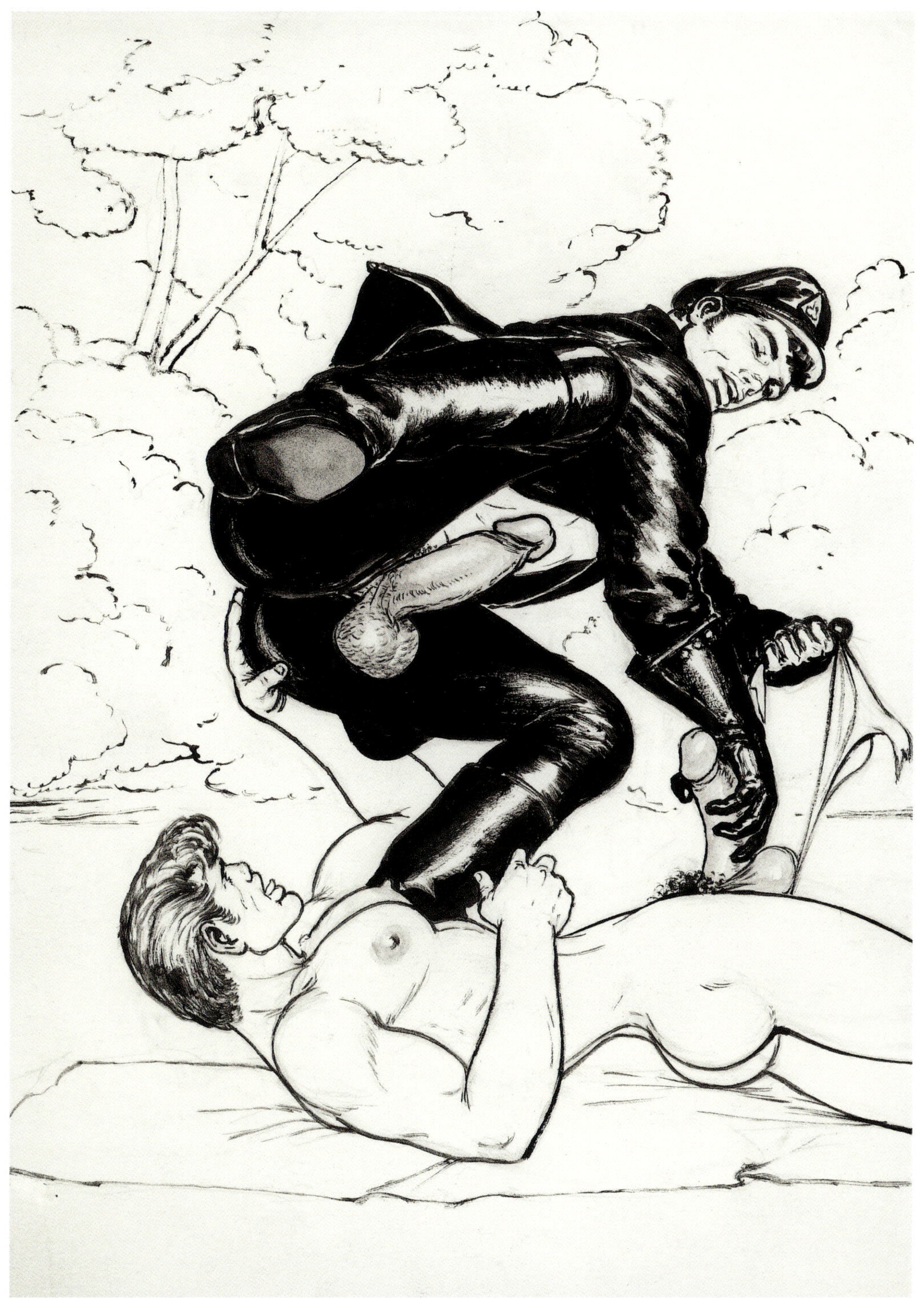

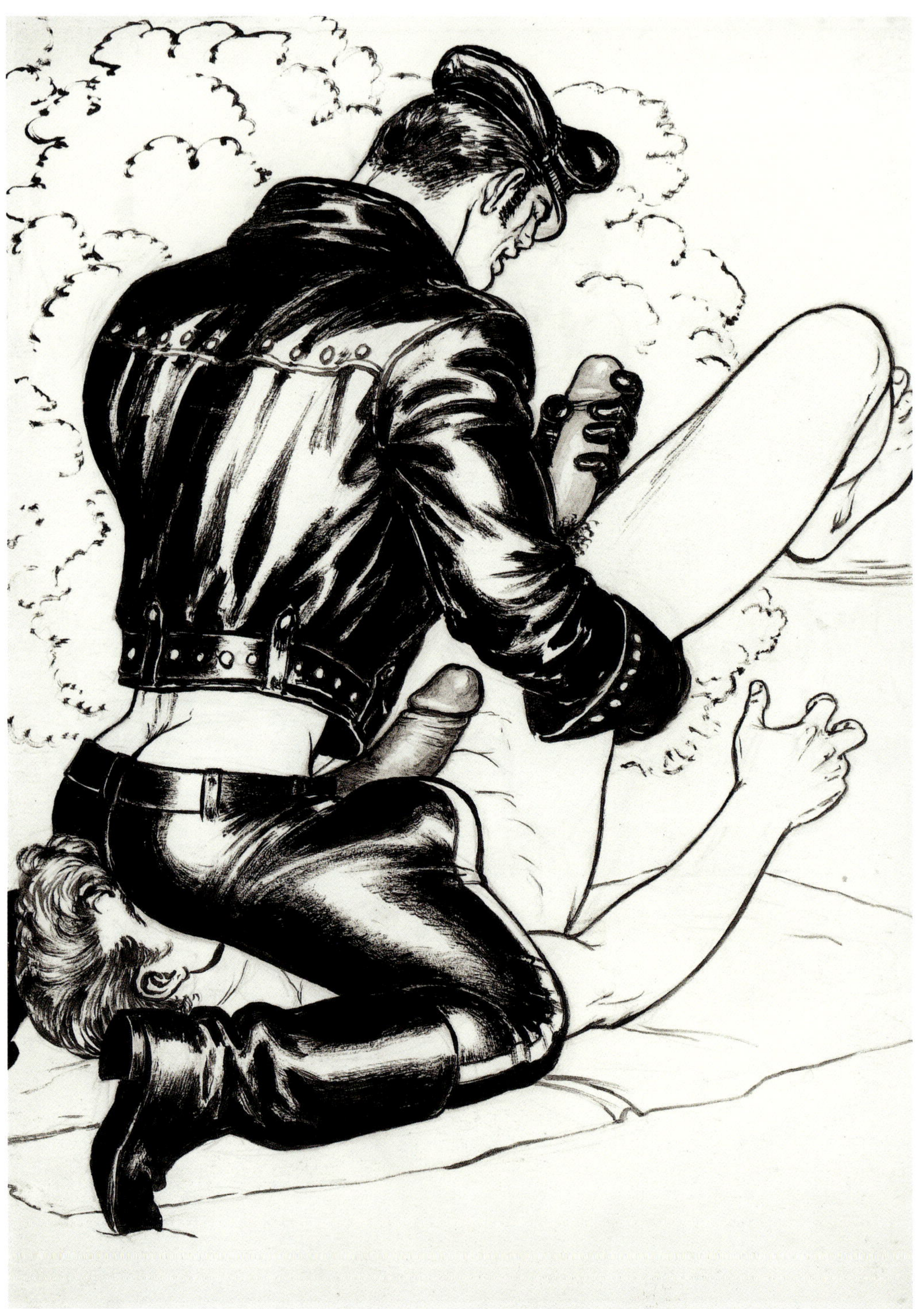

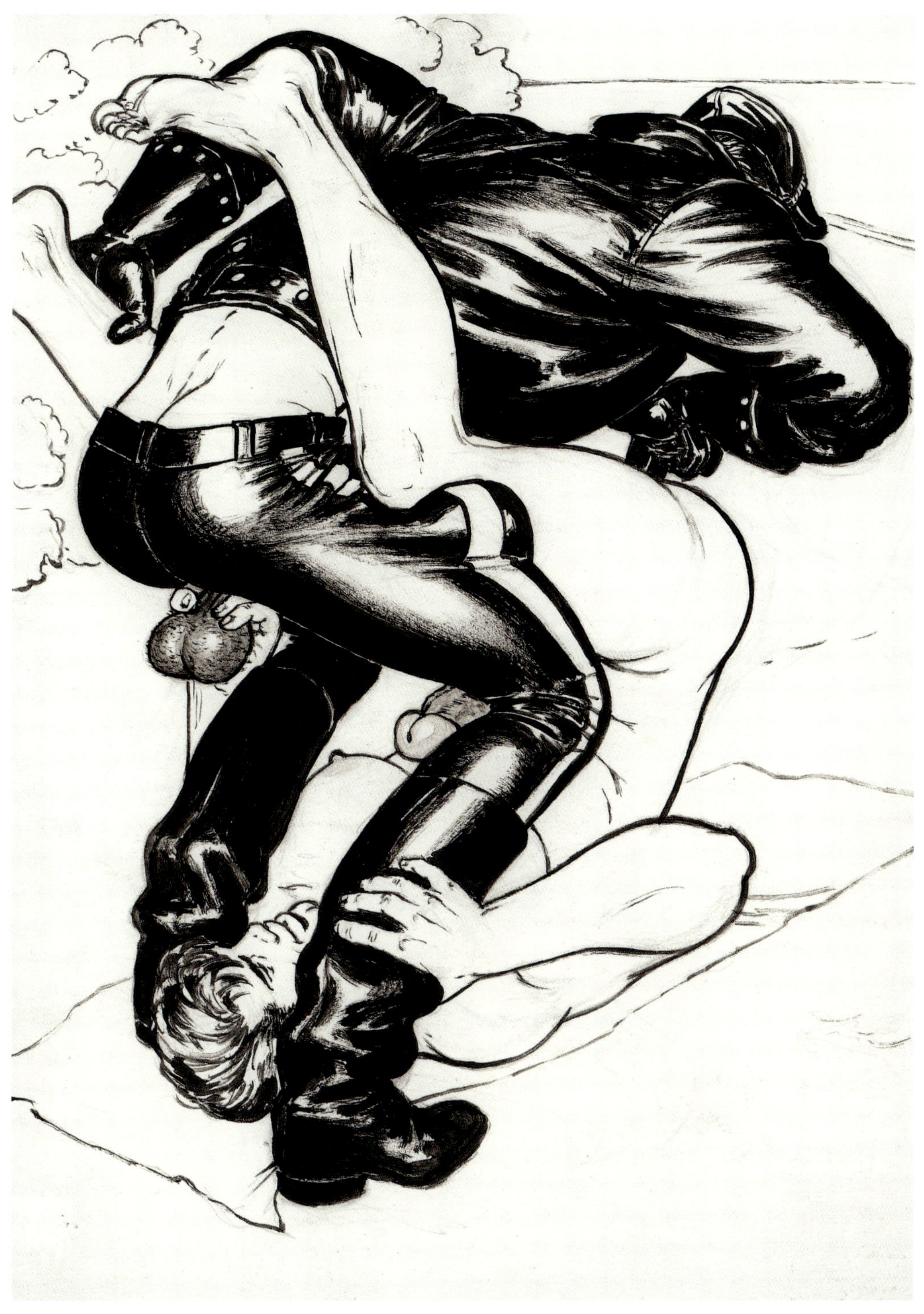

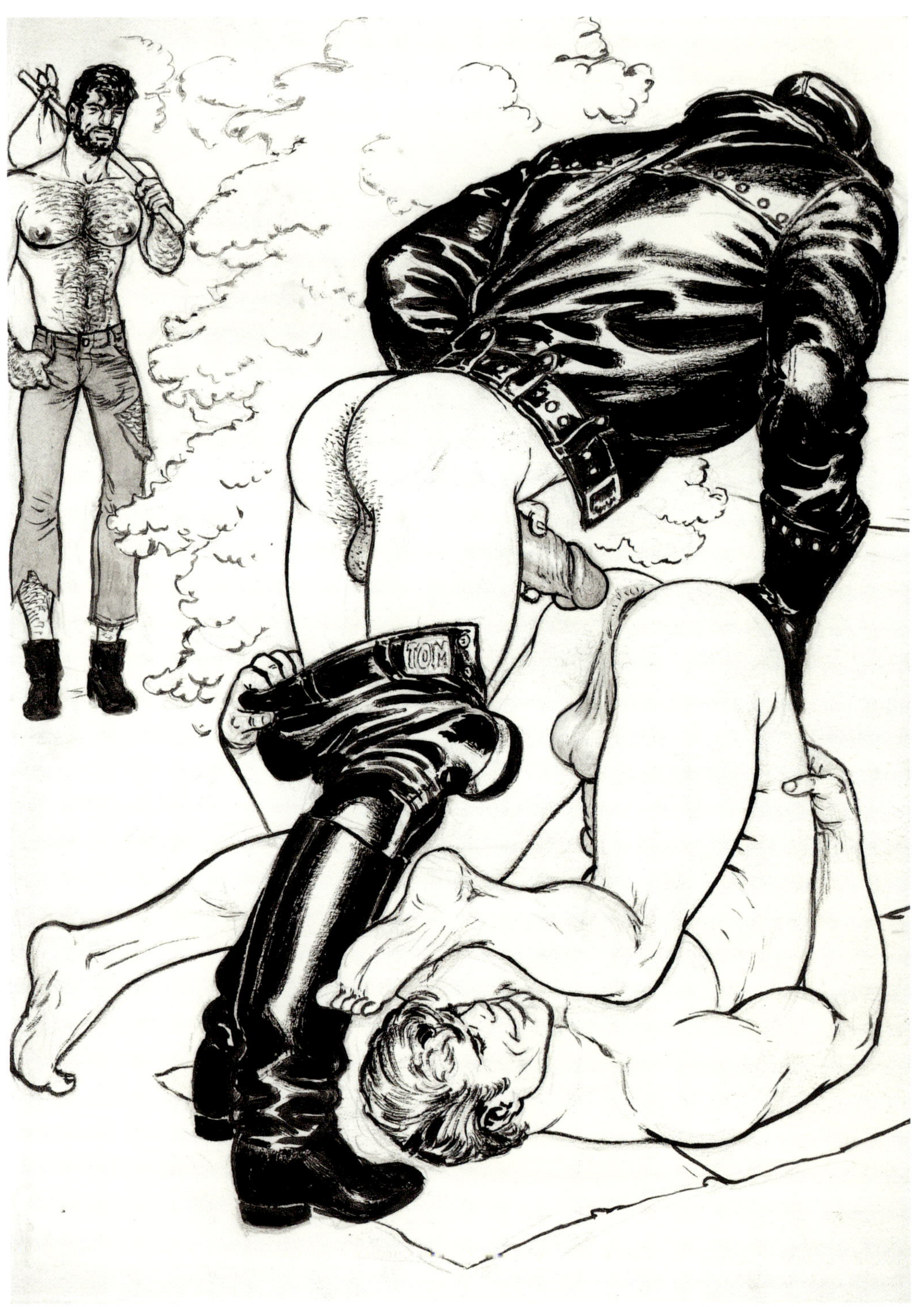

TOM

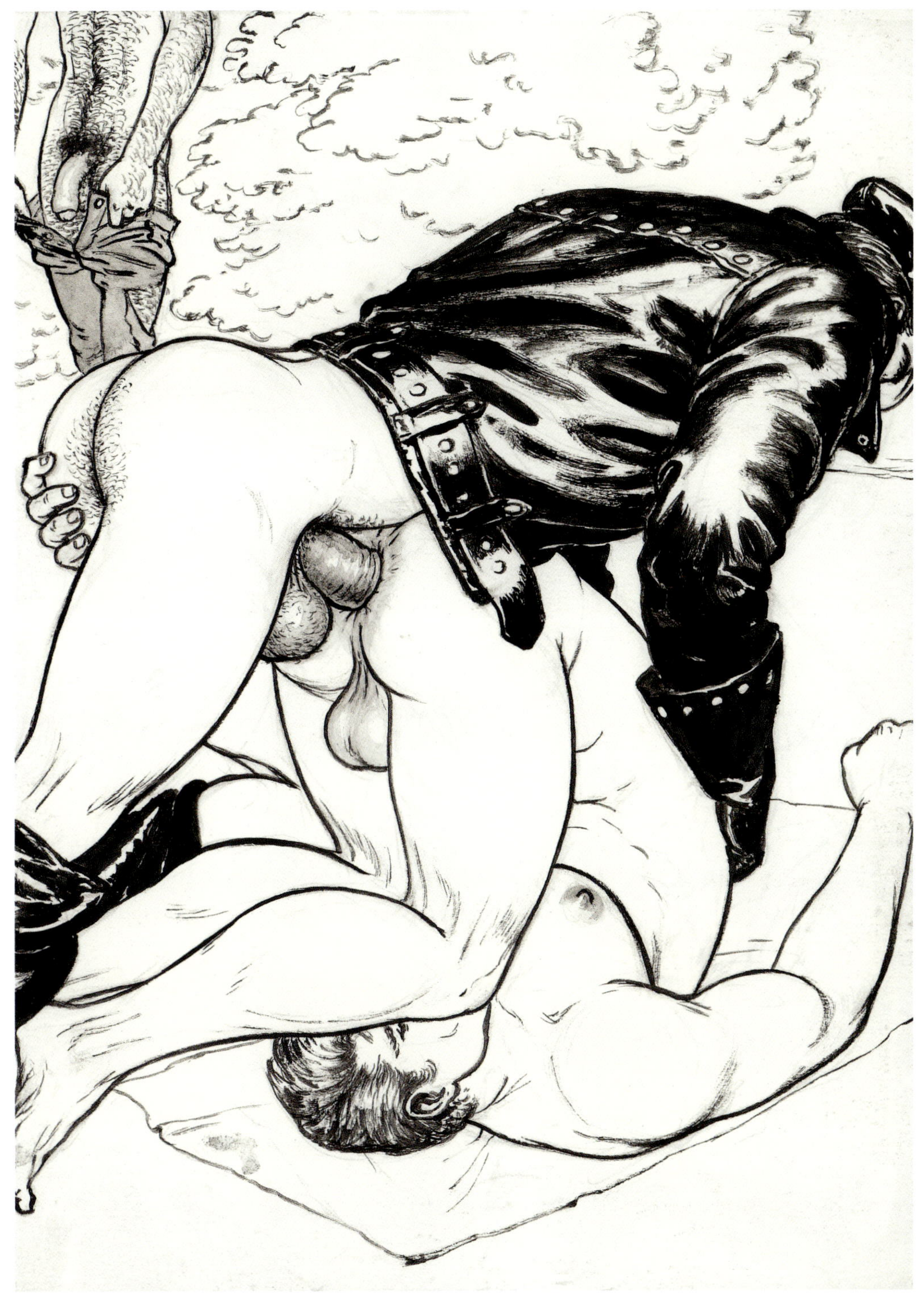

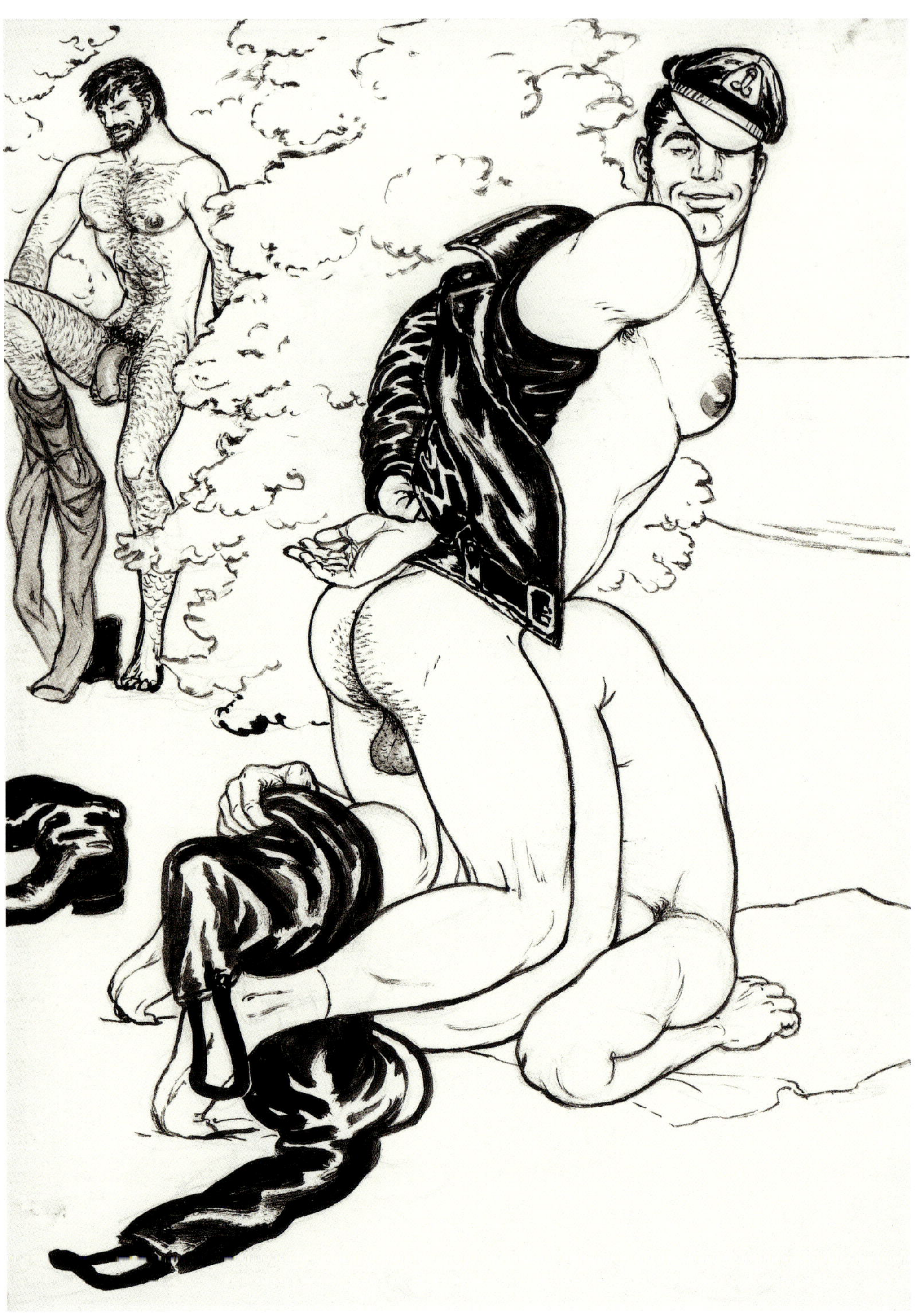

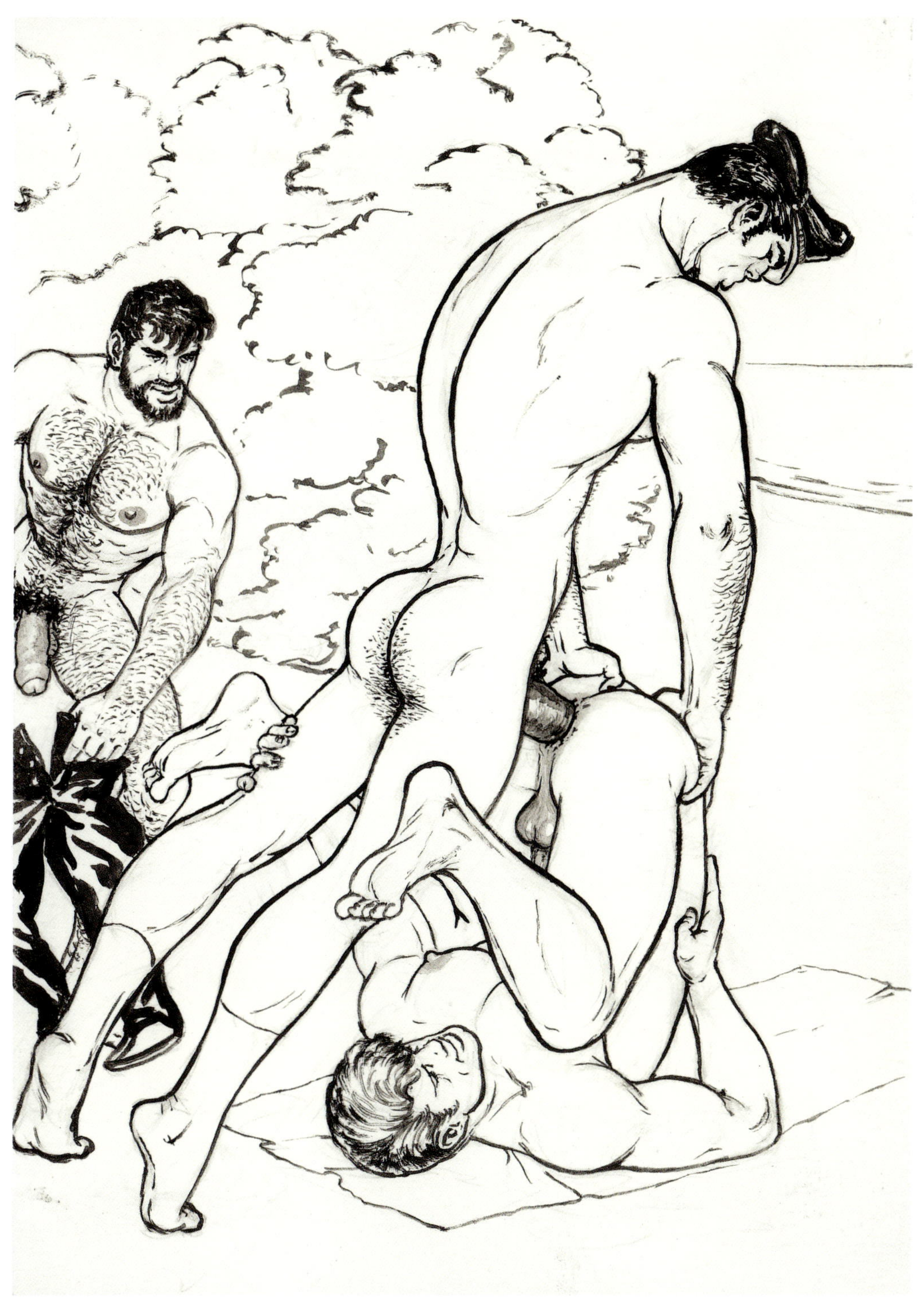

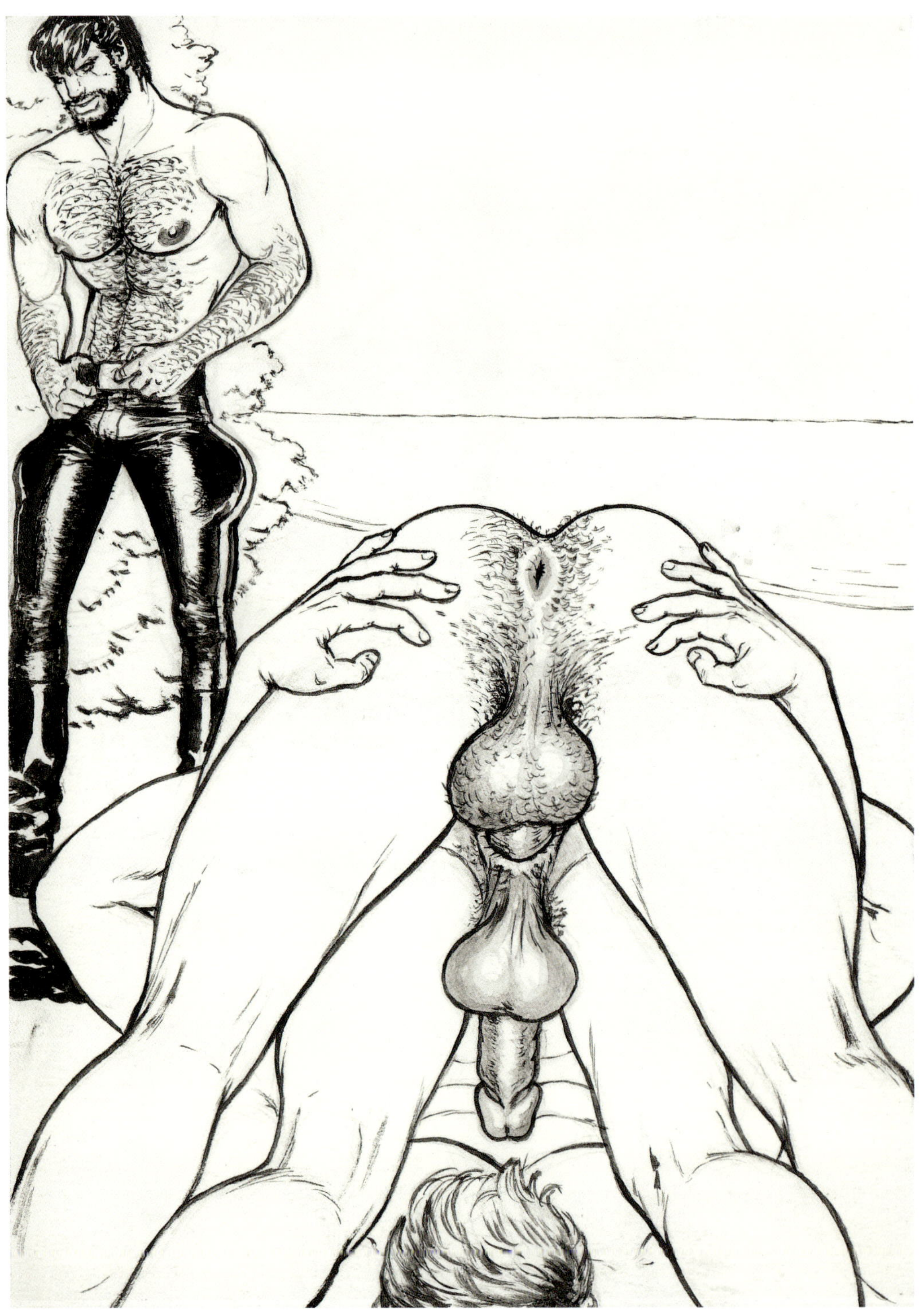

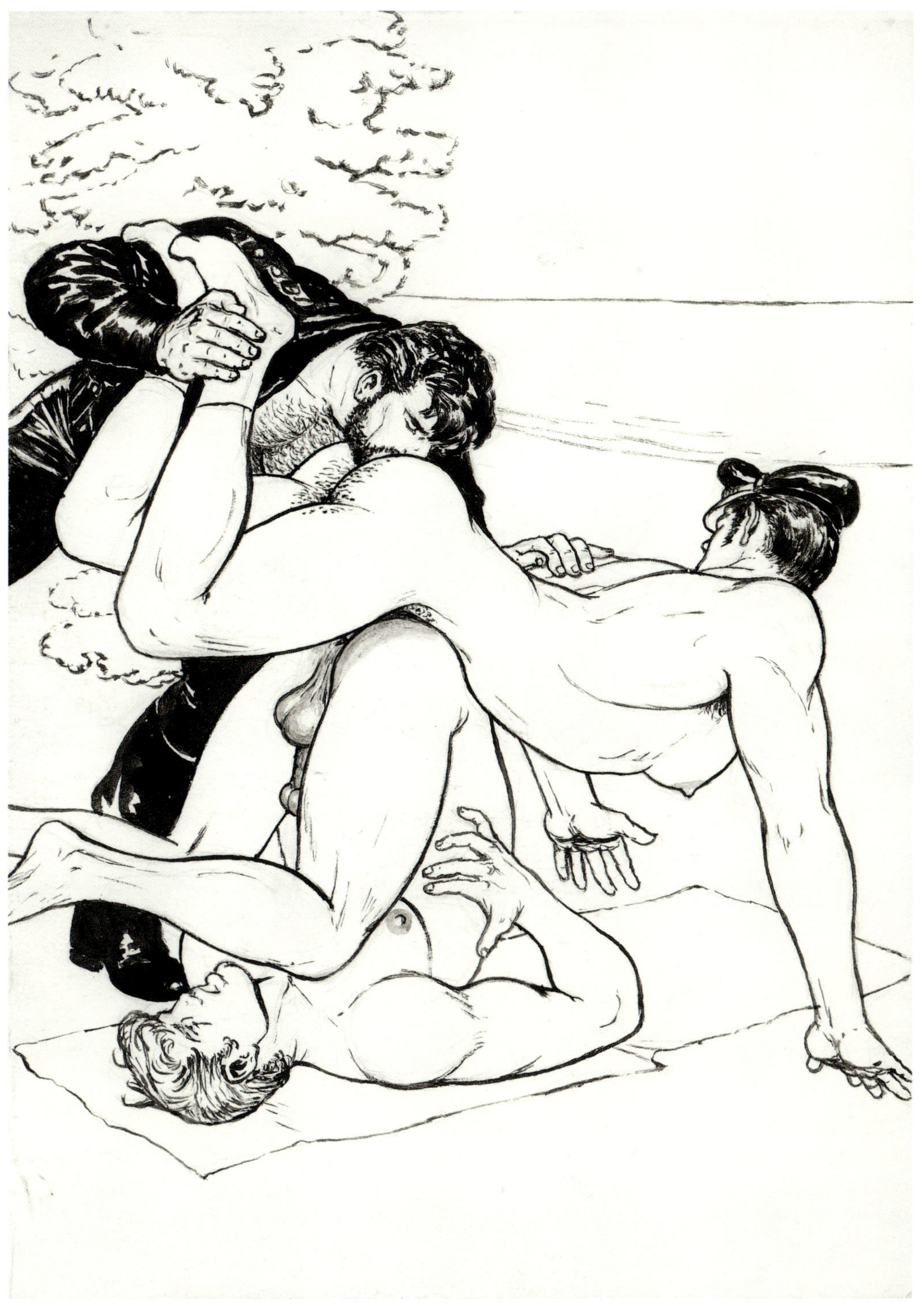

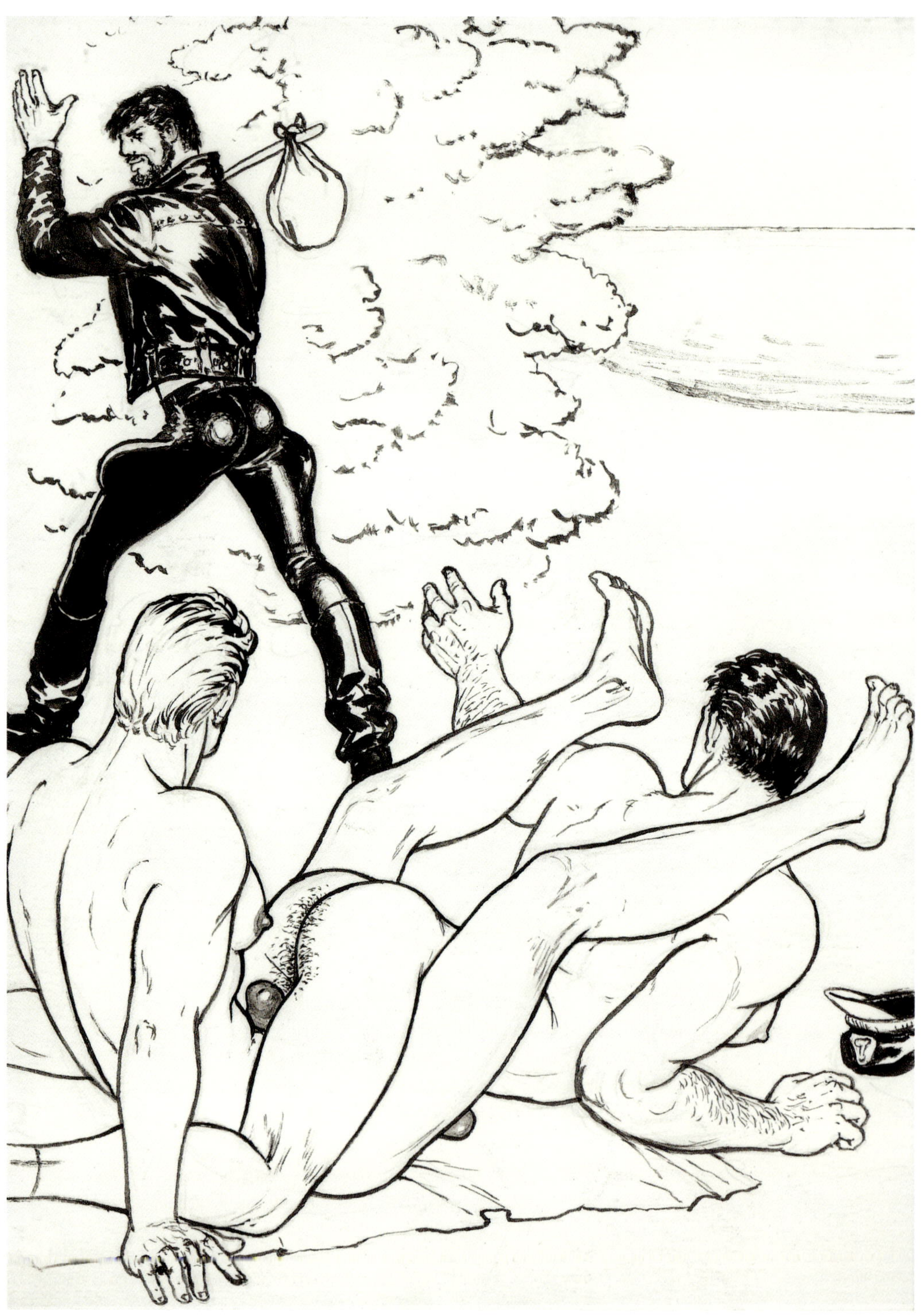

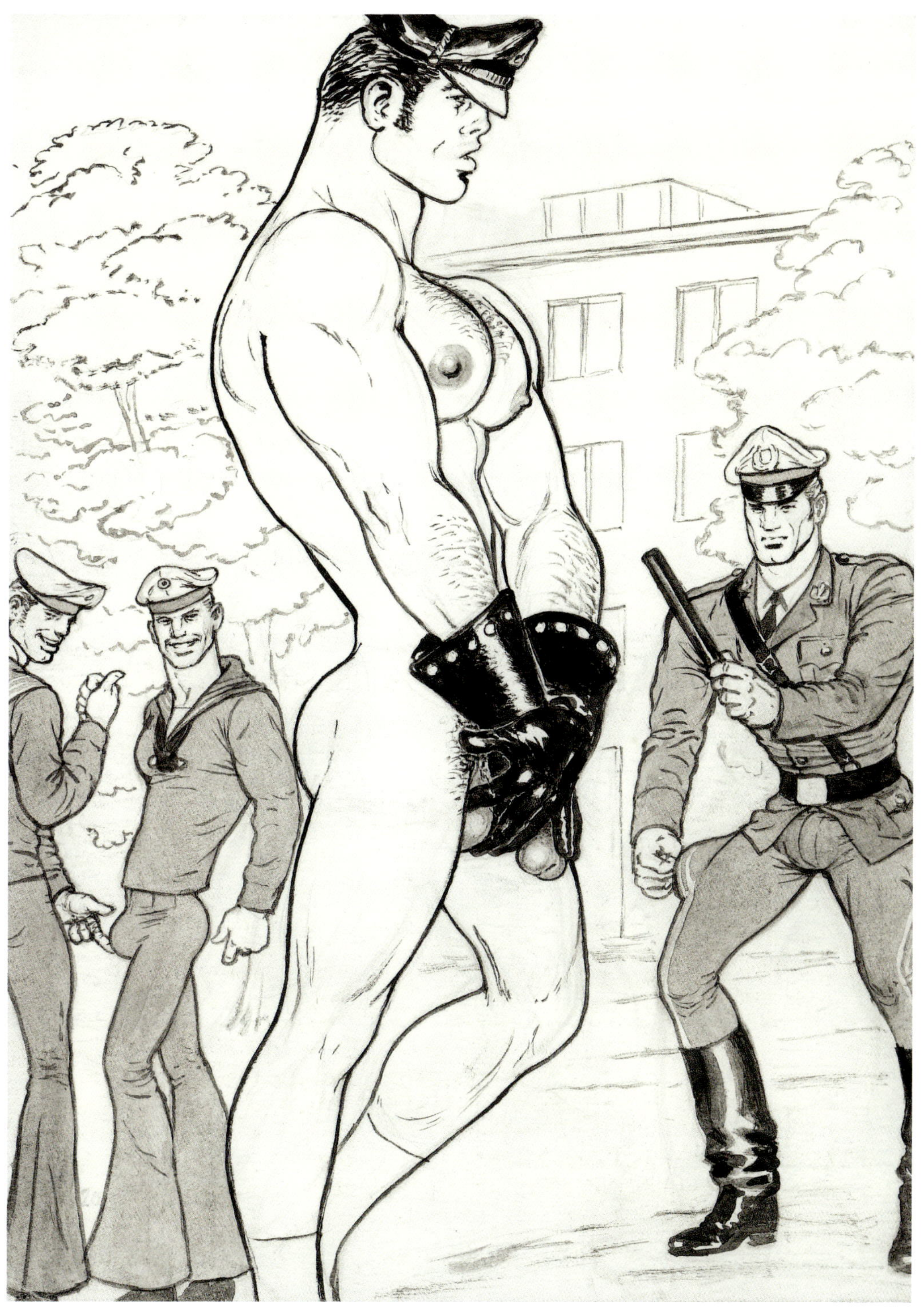

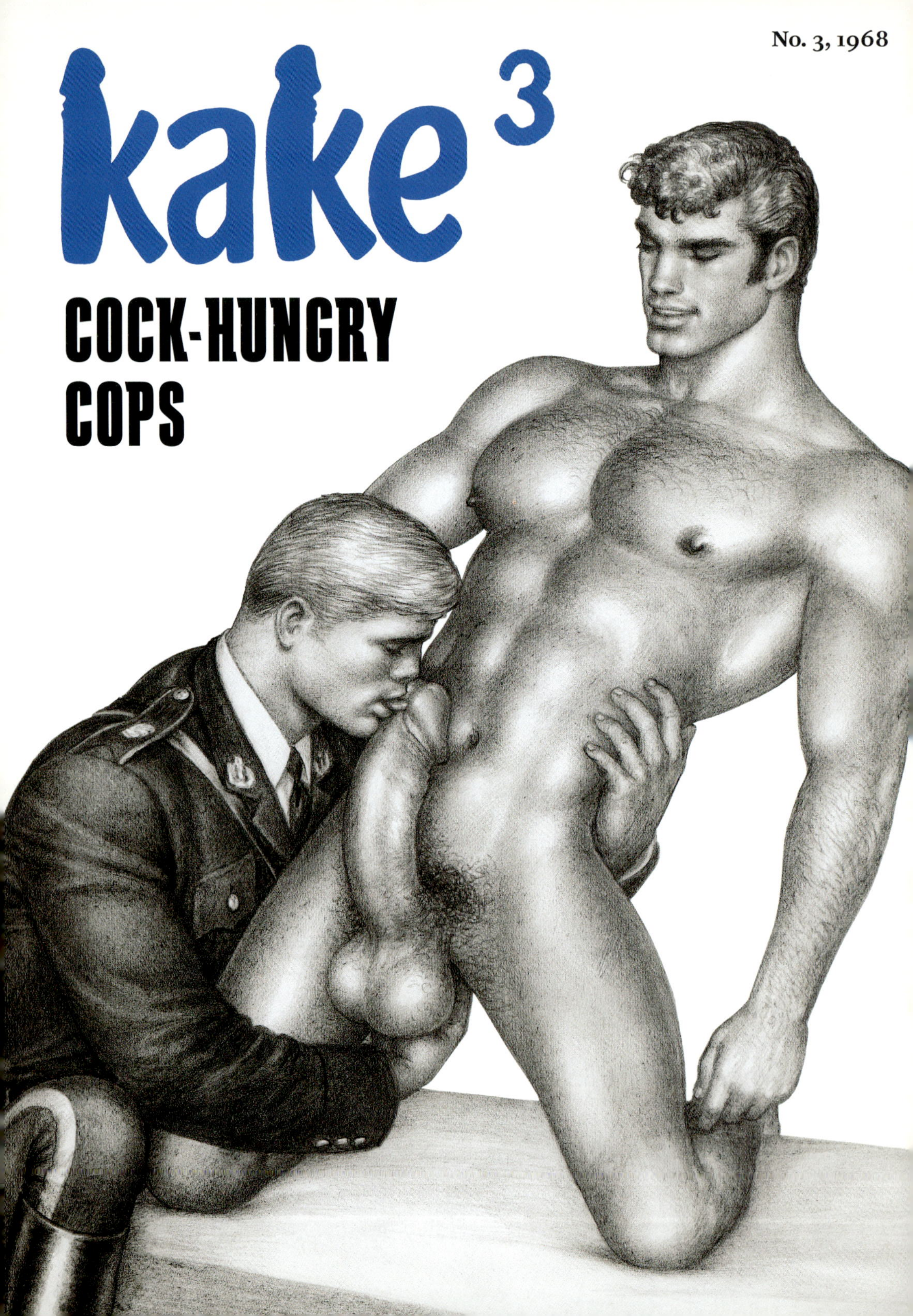

No. 3, 1968
kake³
COCK-HUNGRY COPS

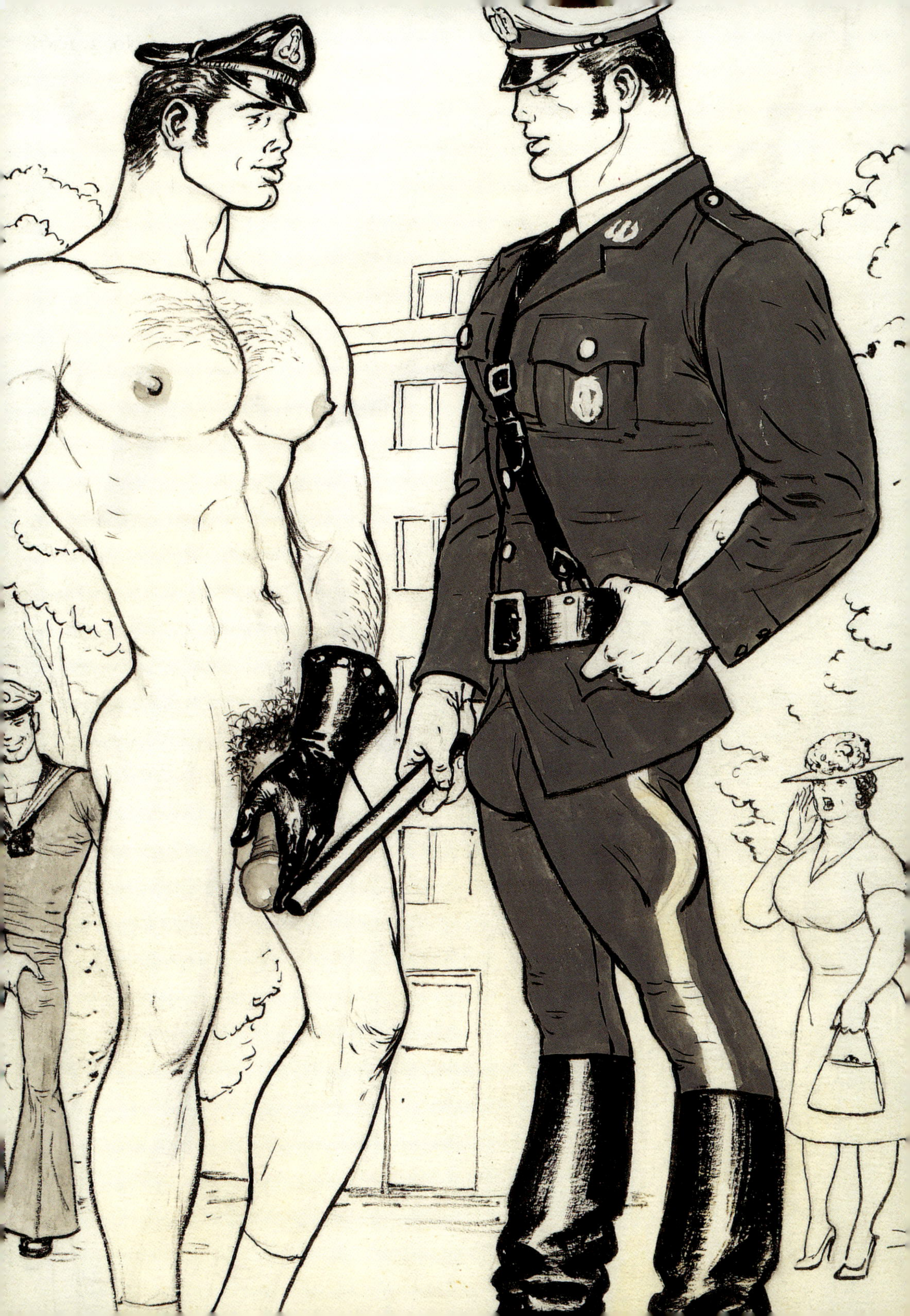

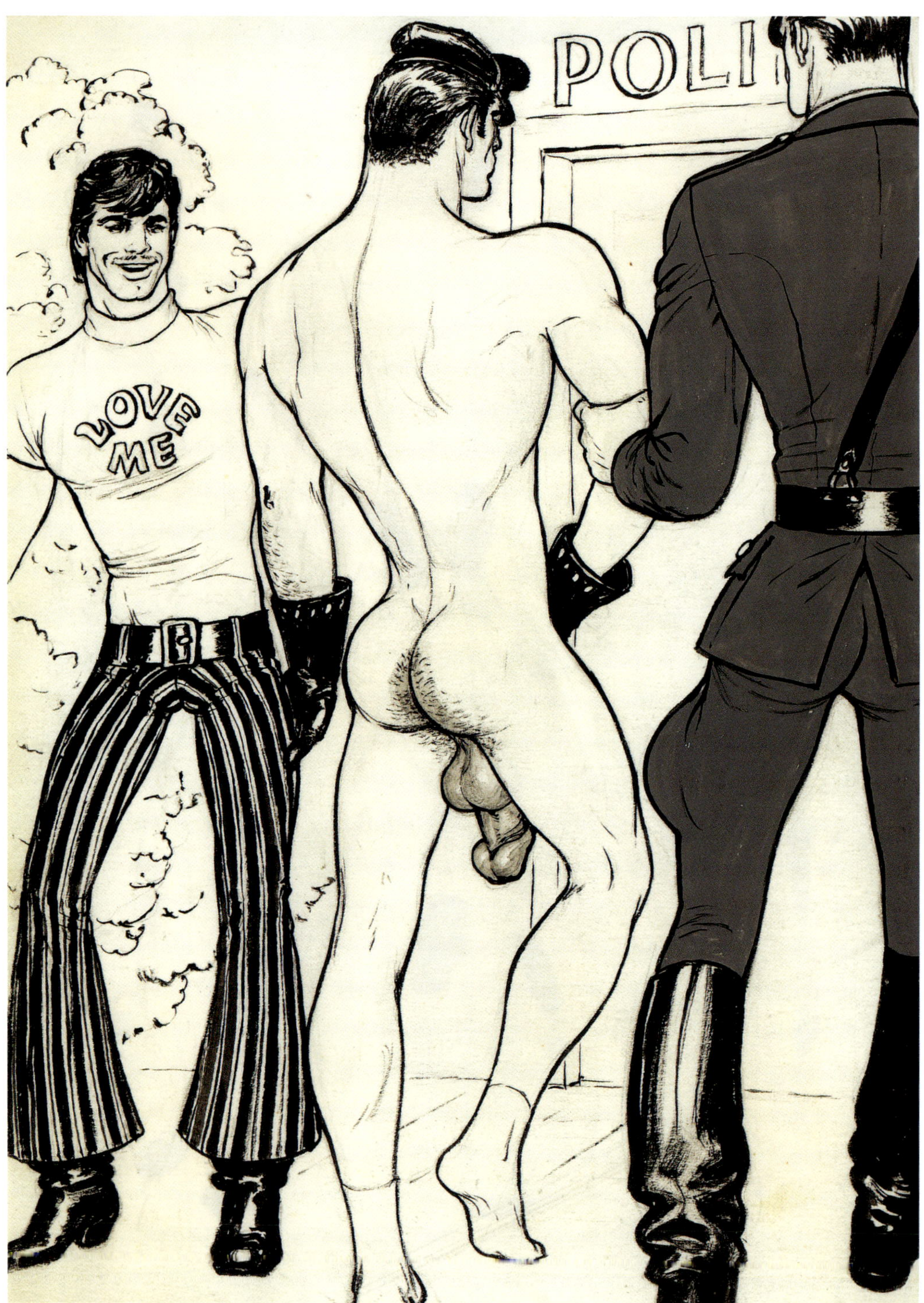

LOVE ME
POLI

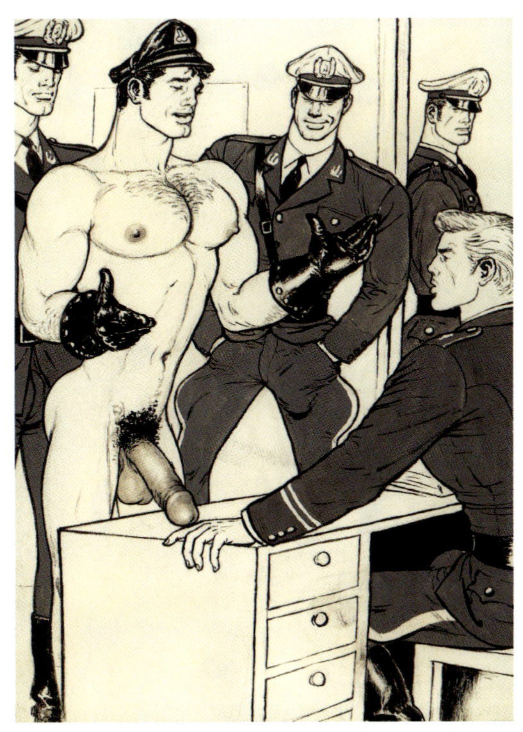
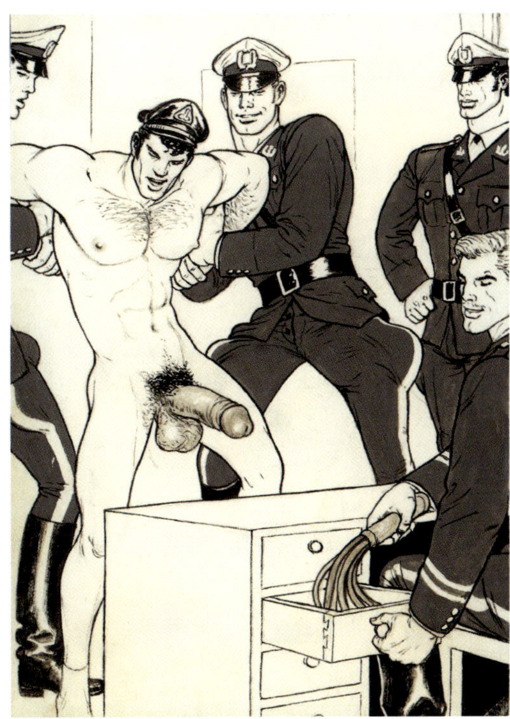
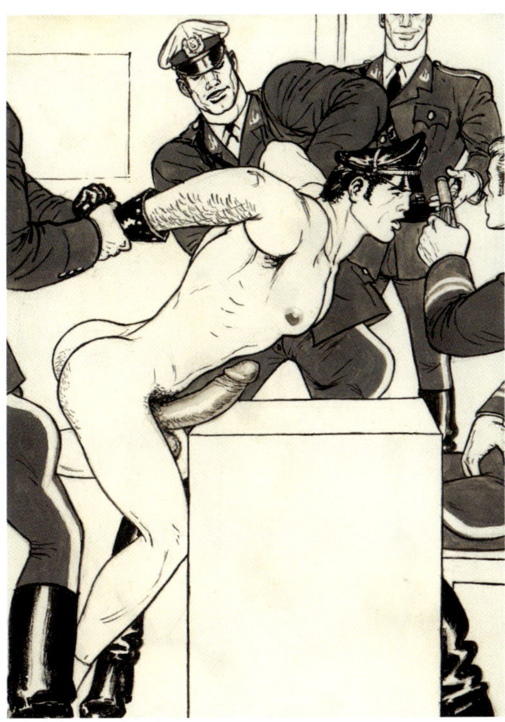
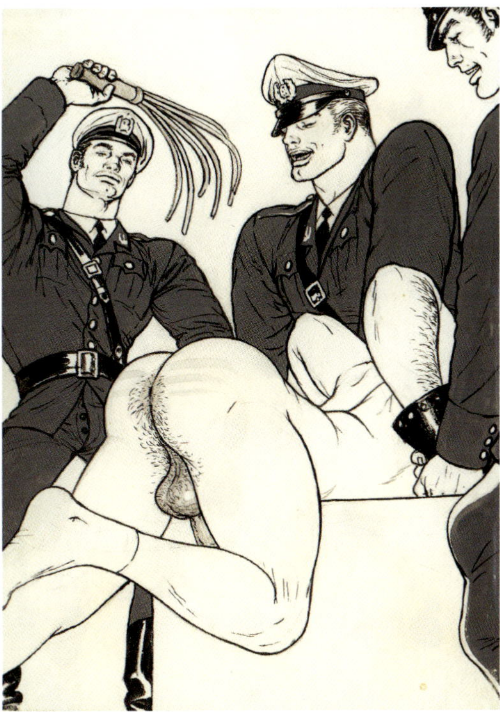

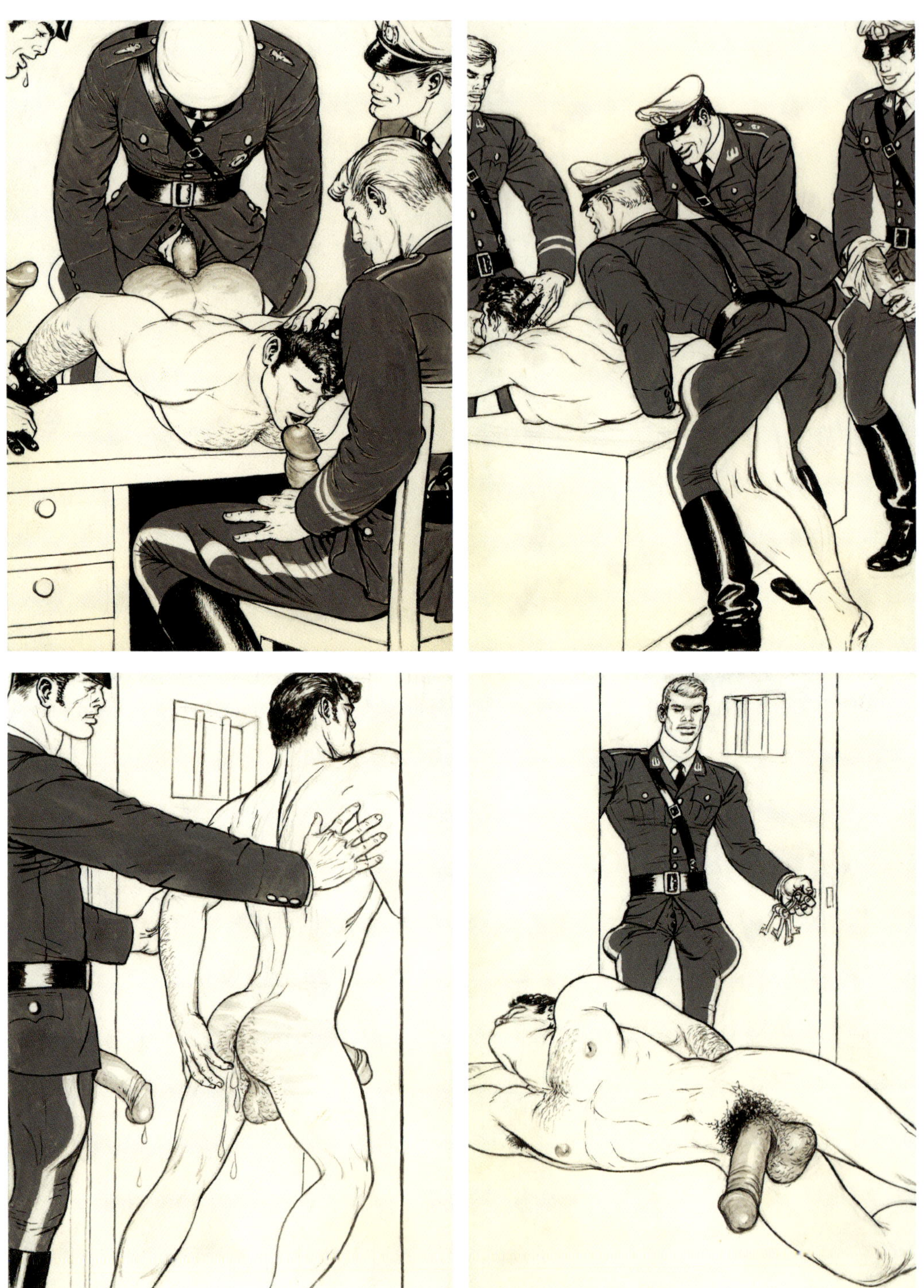

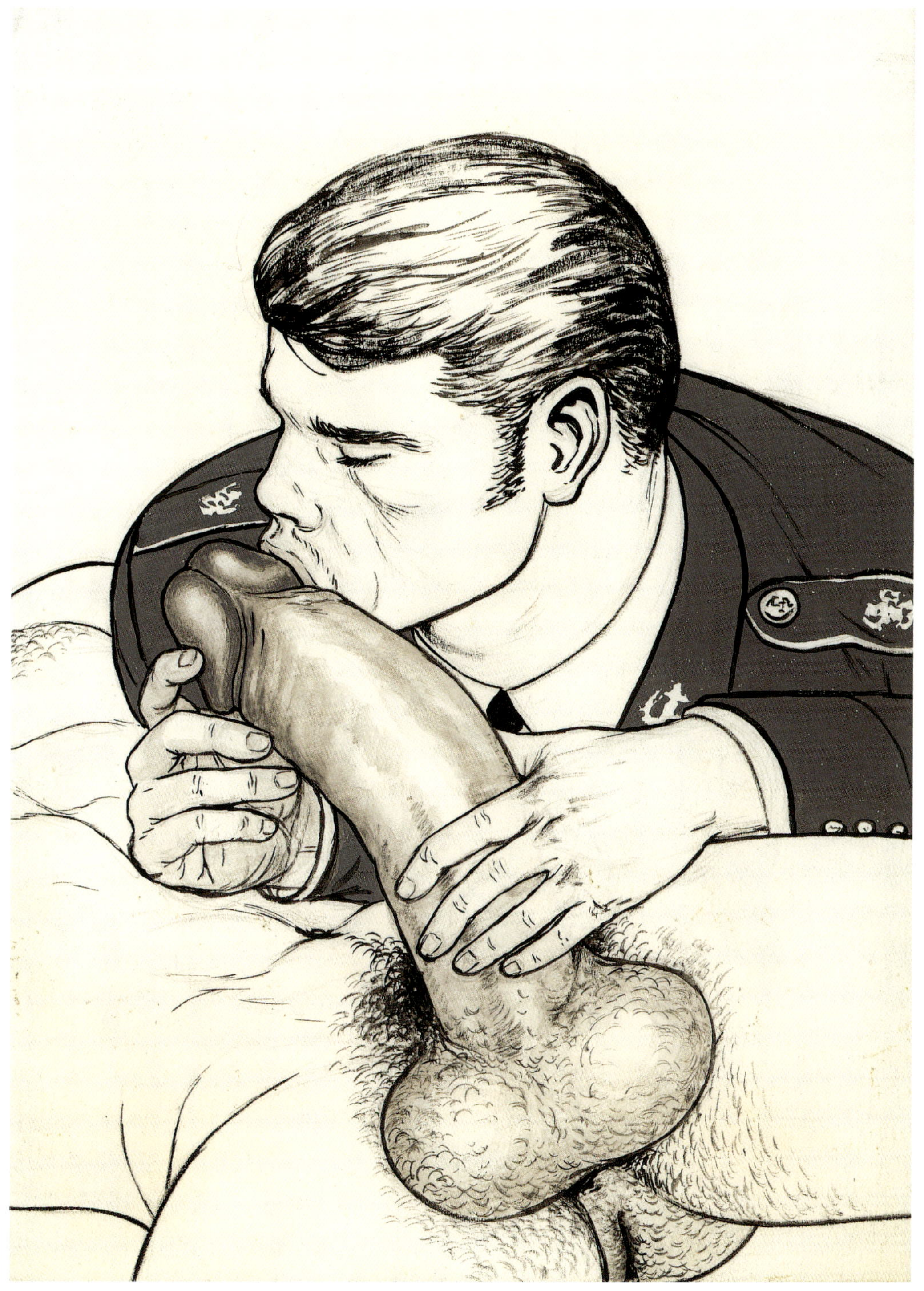

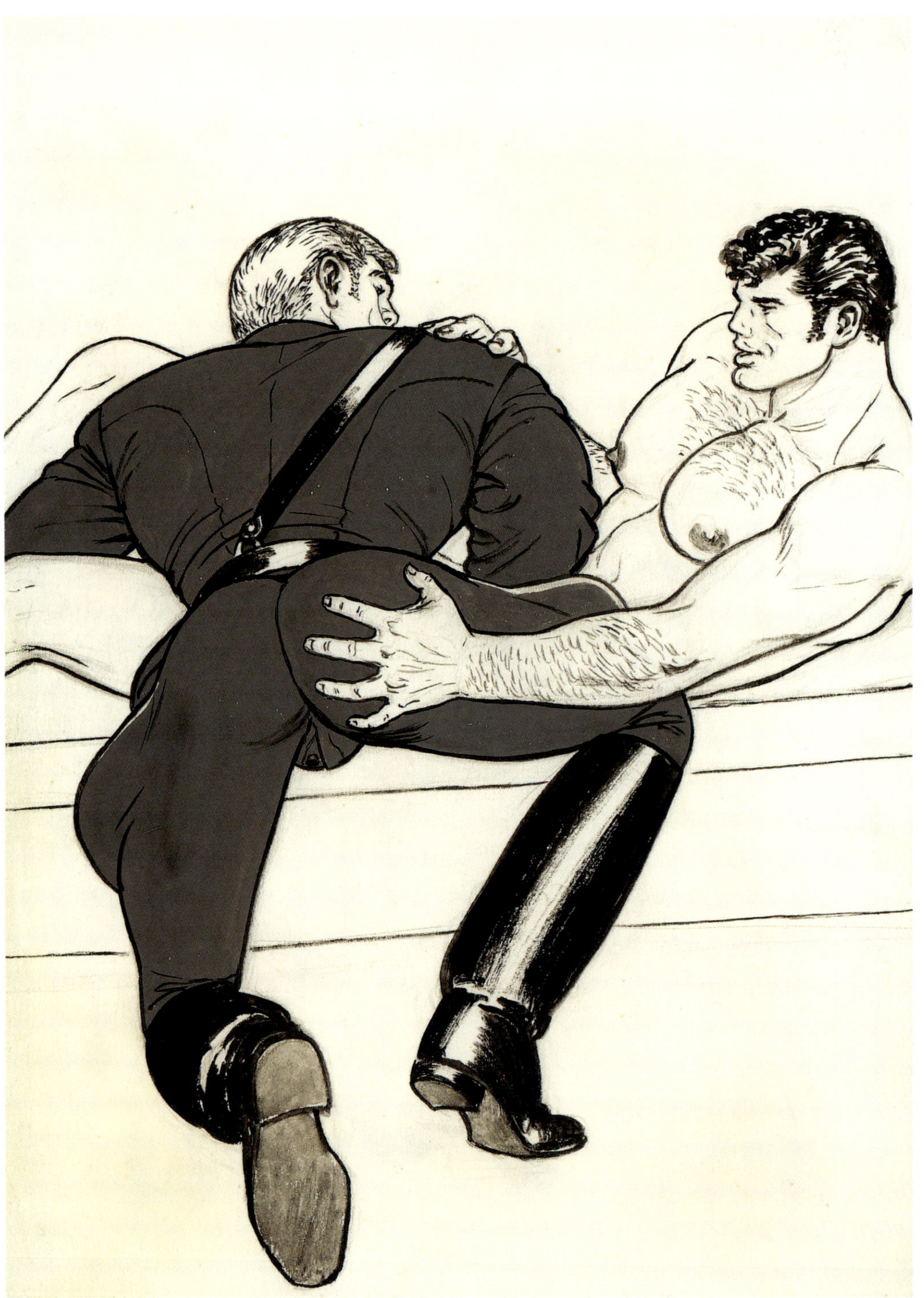

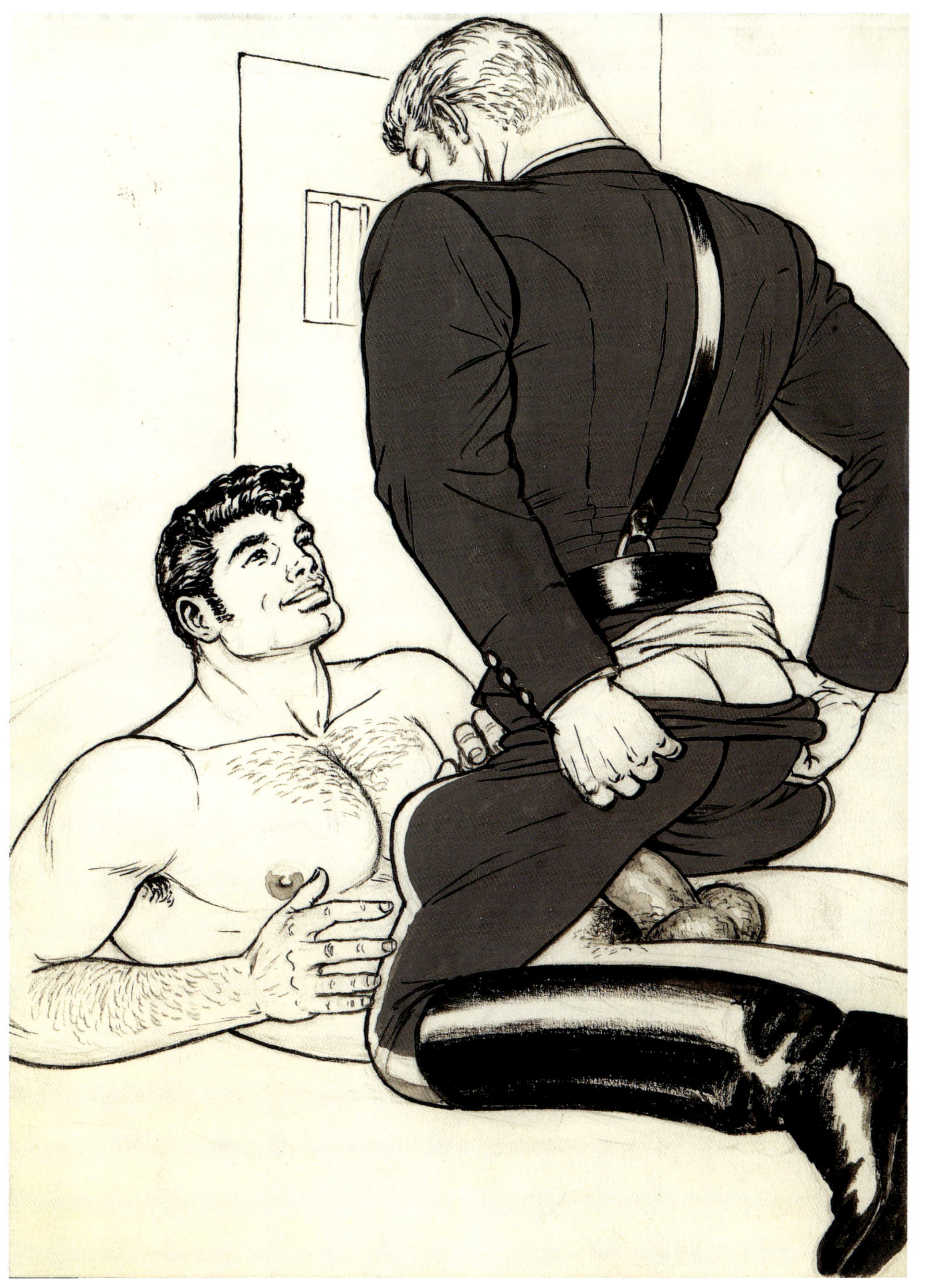

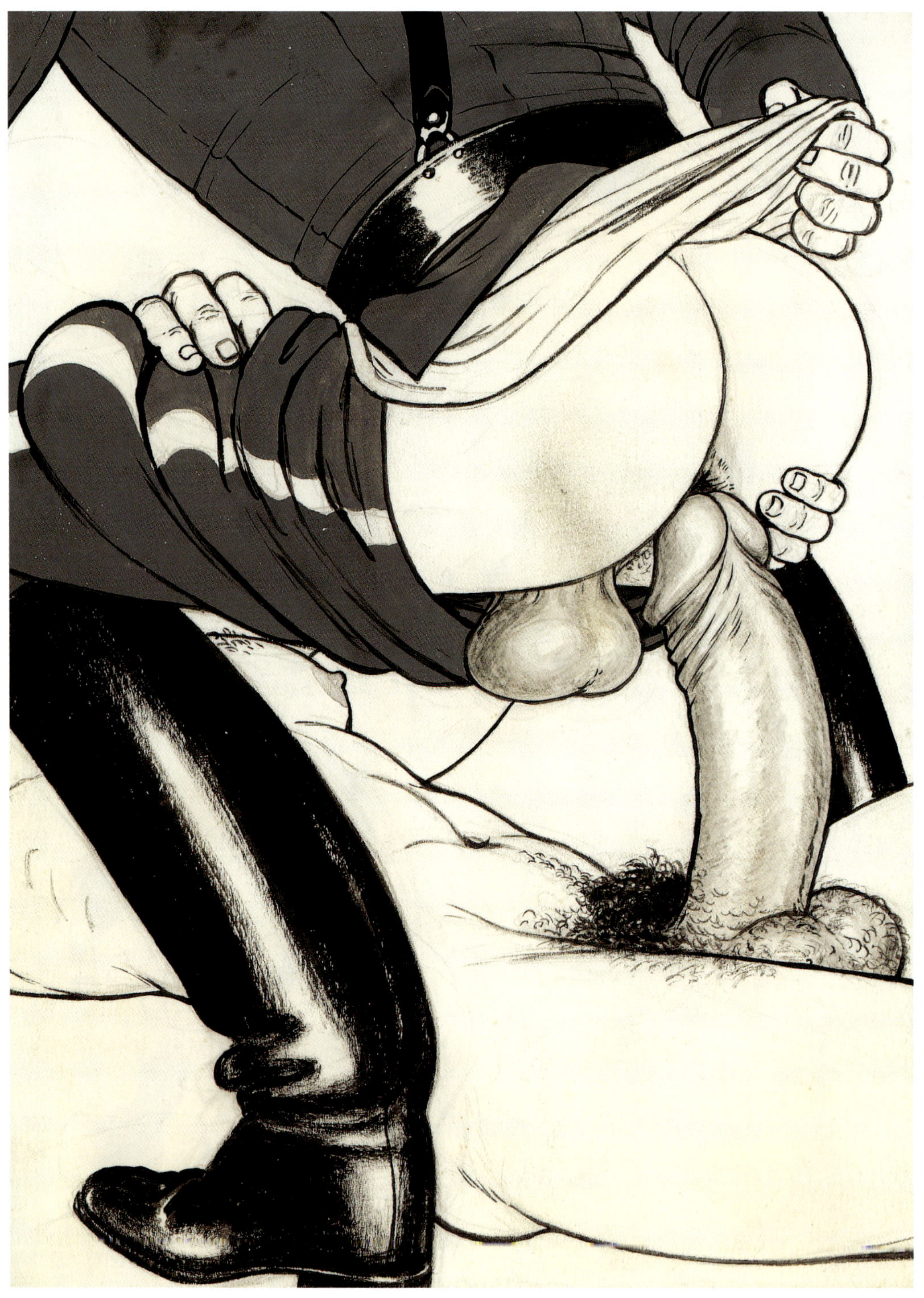

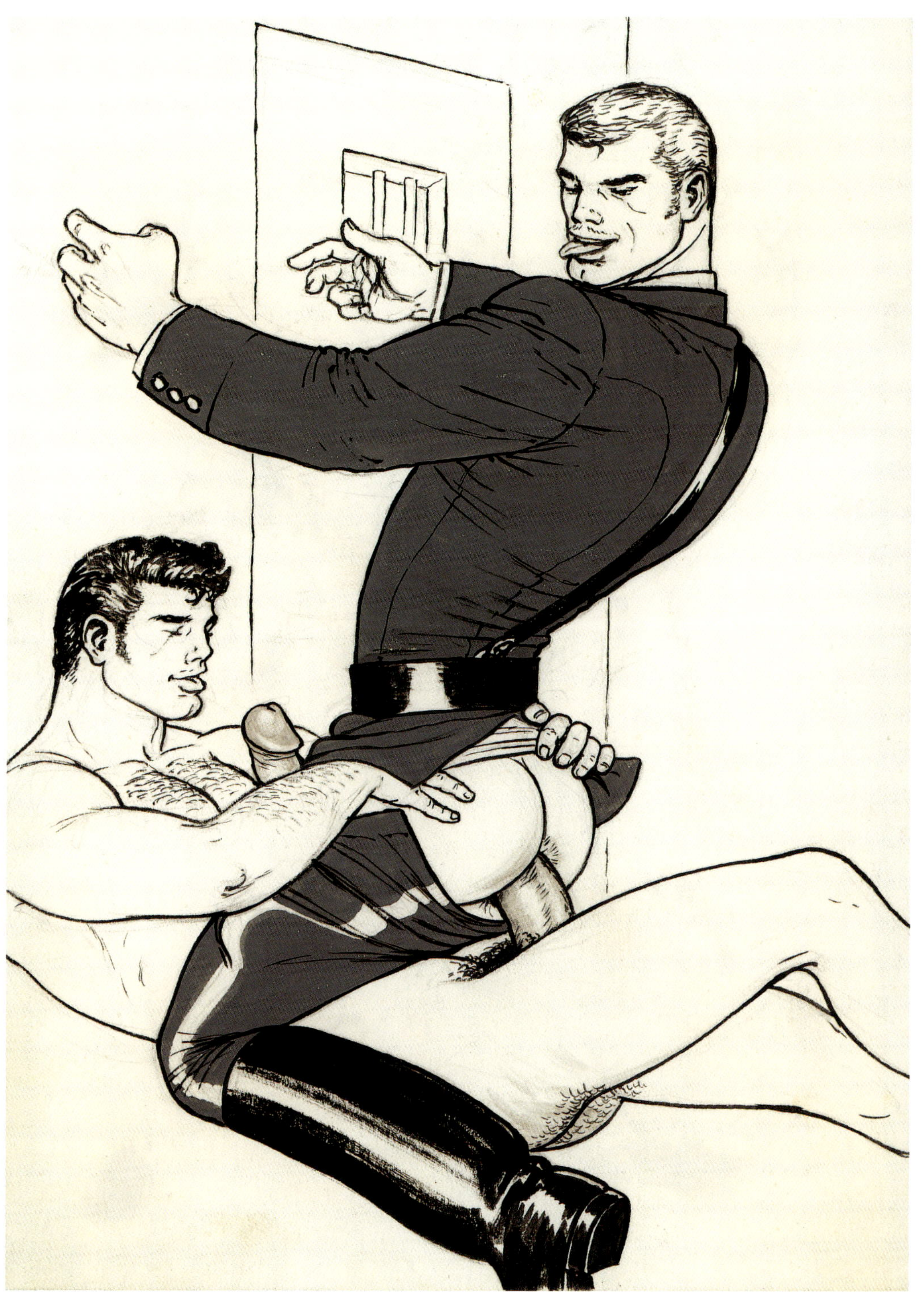

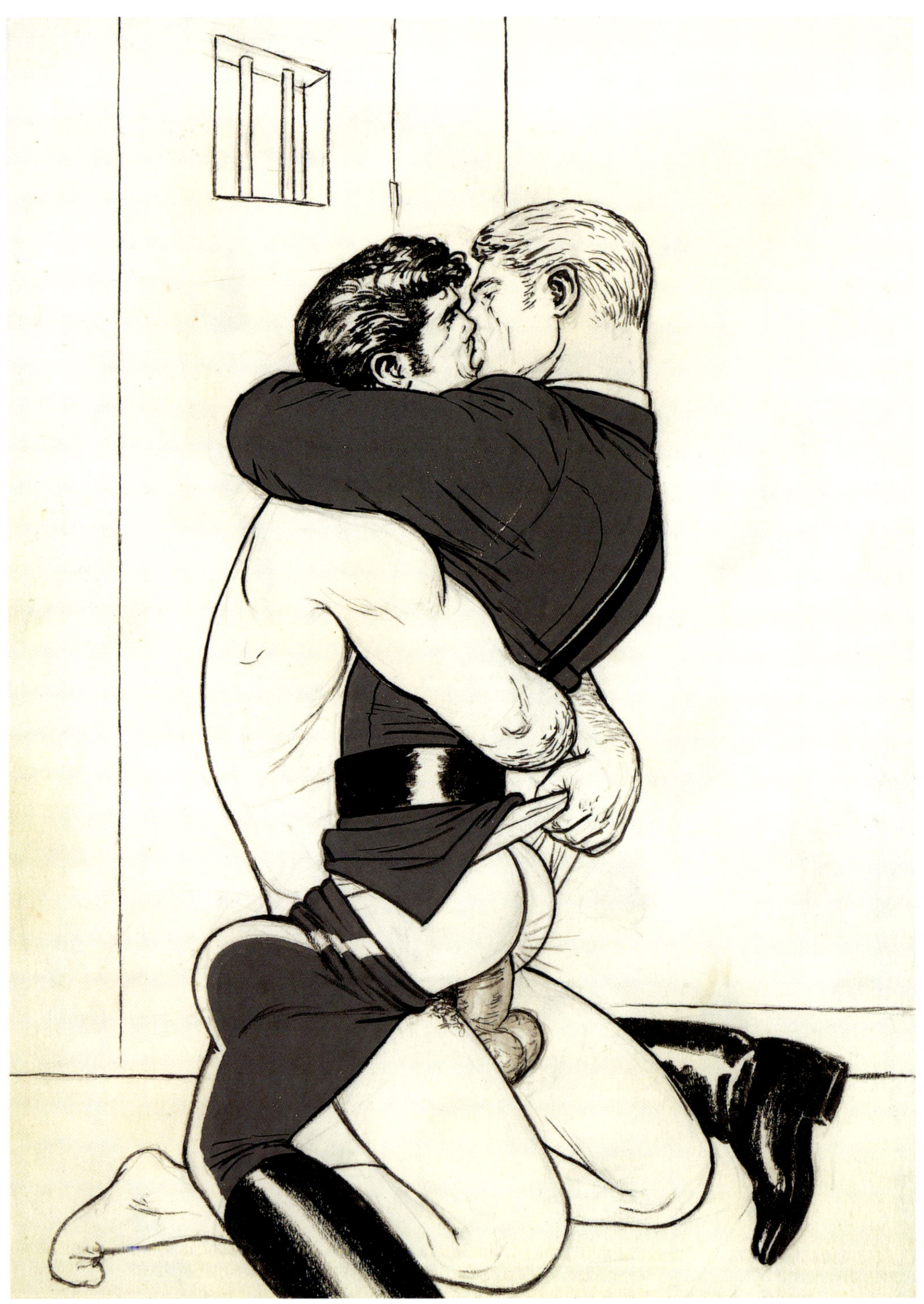

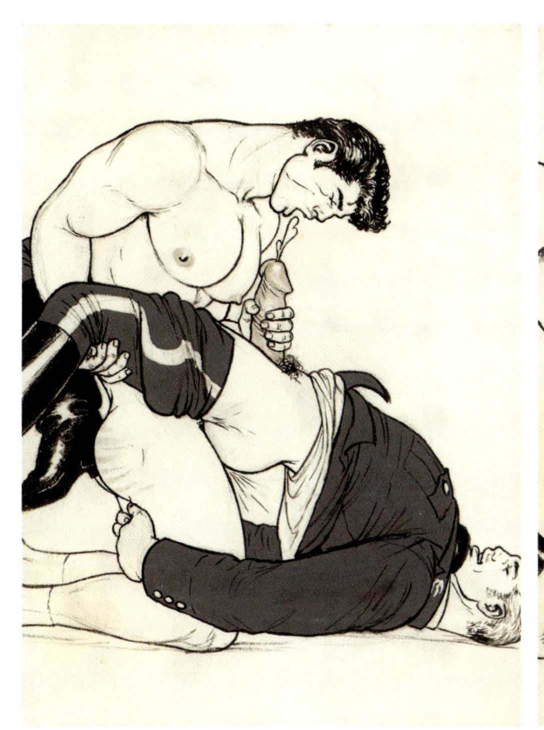

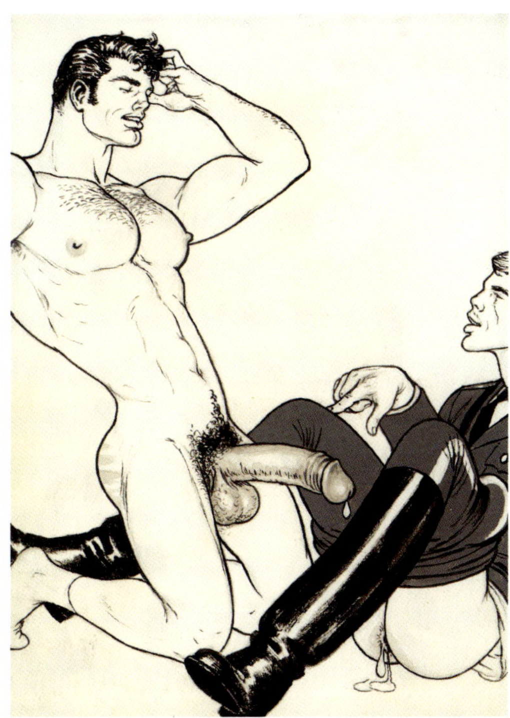

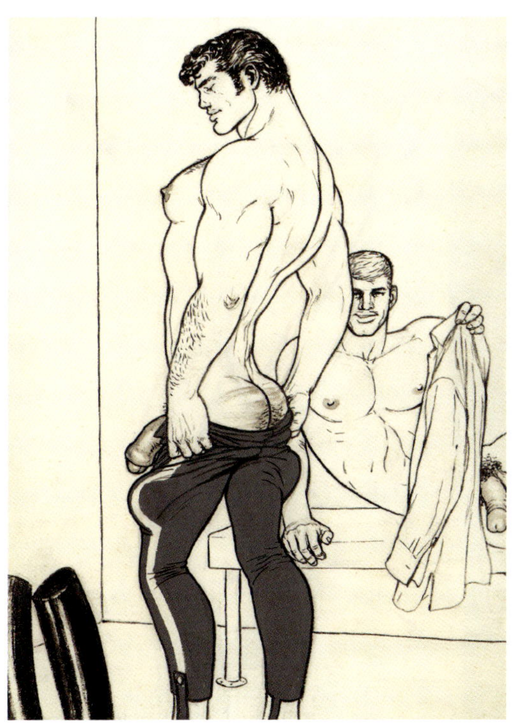

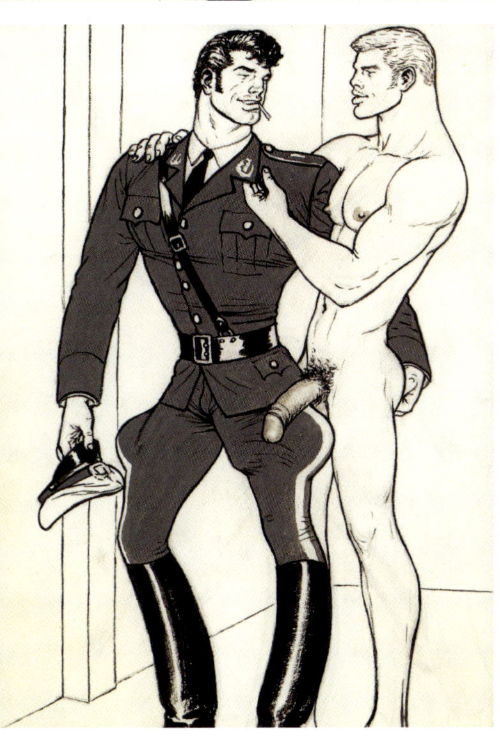

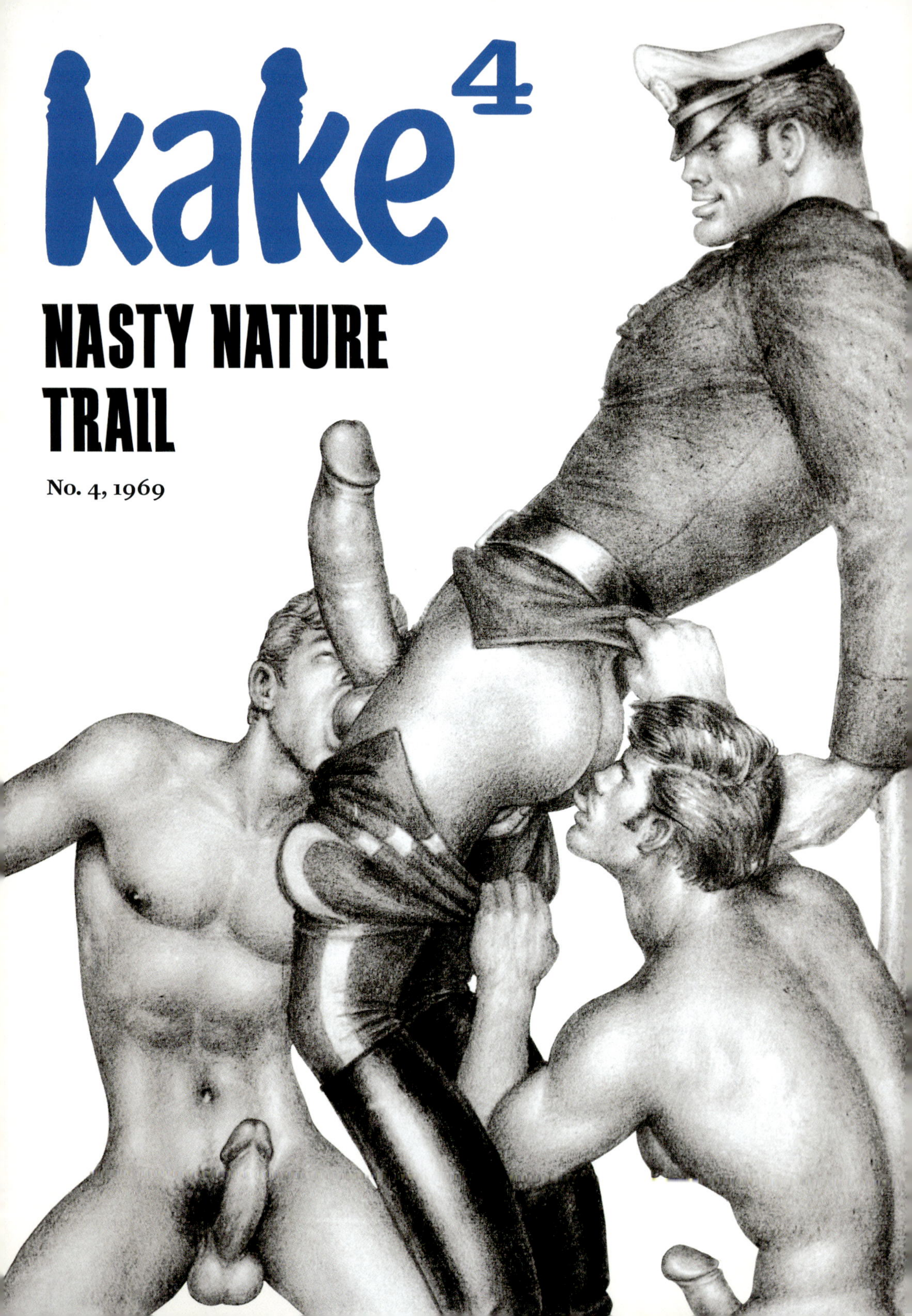

kake 4
NASTY NATURE
TRAIL
No. 4, 1969

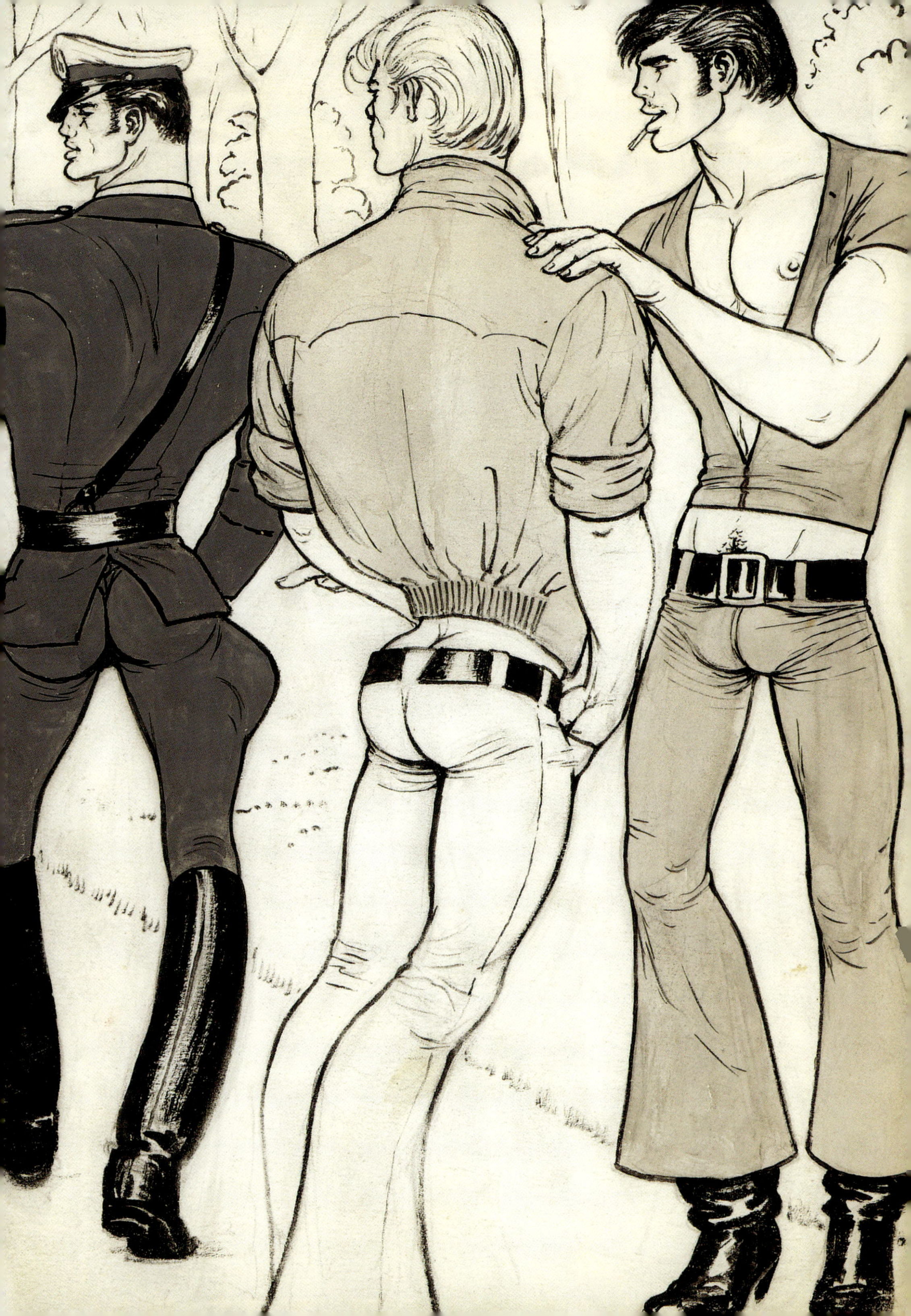

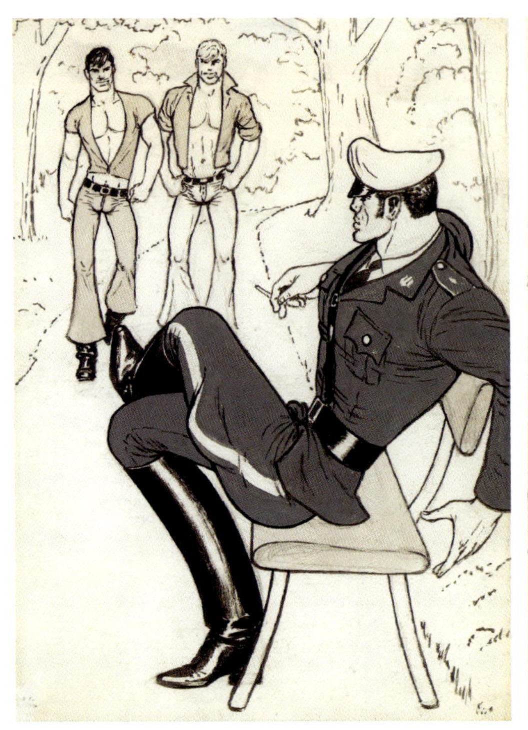
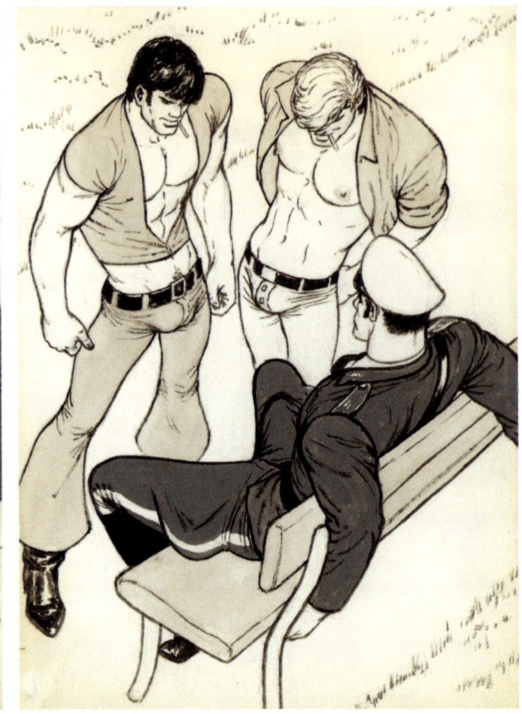
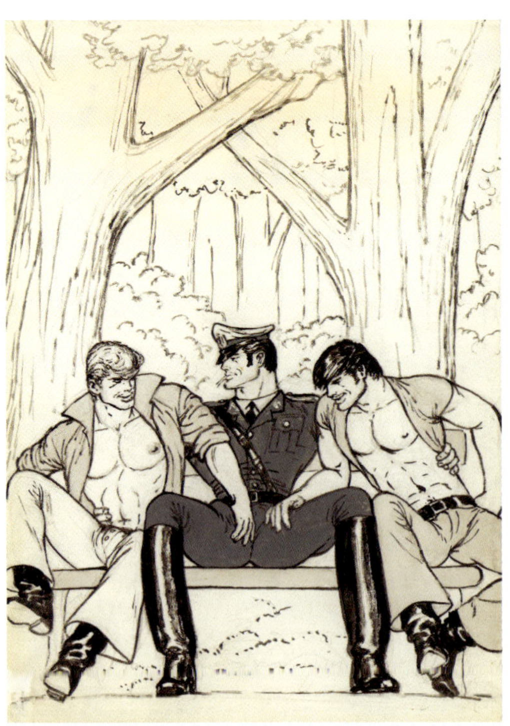
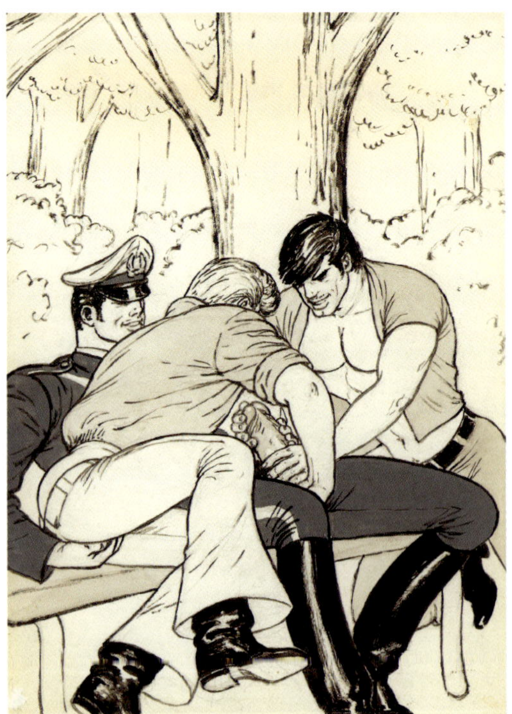

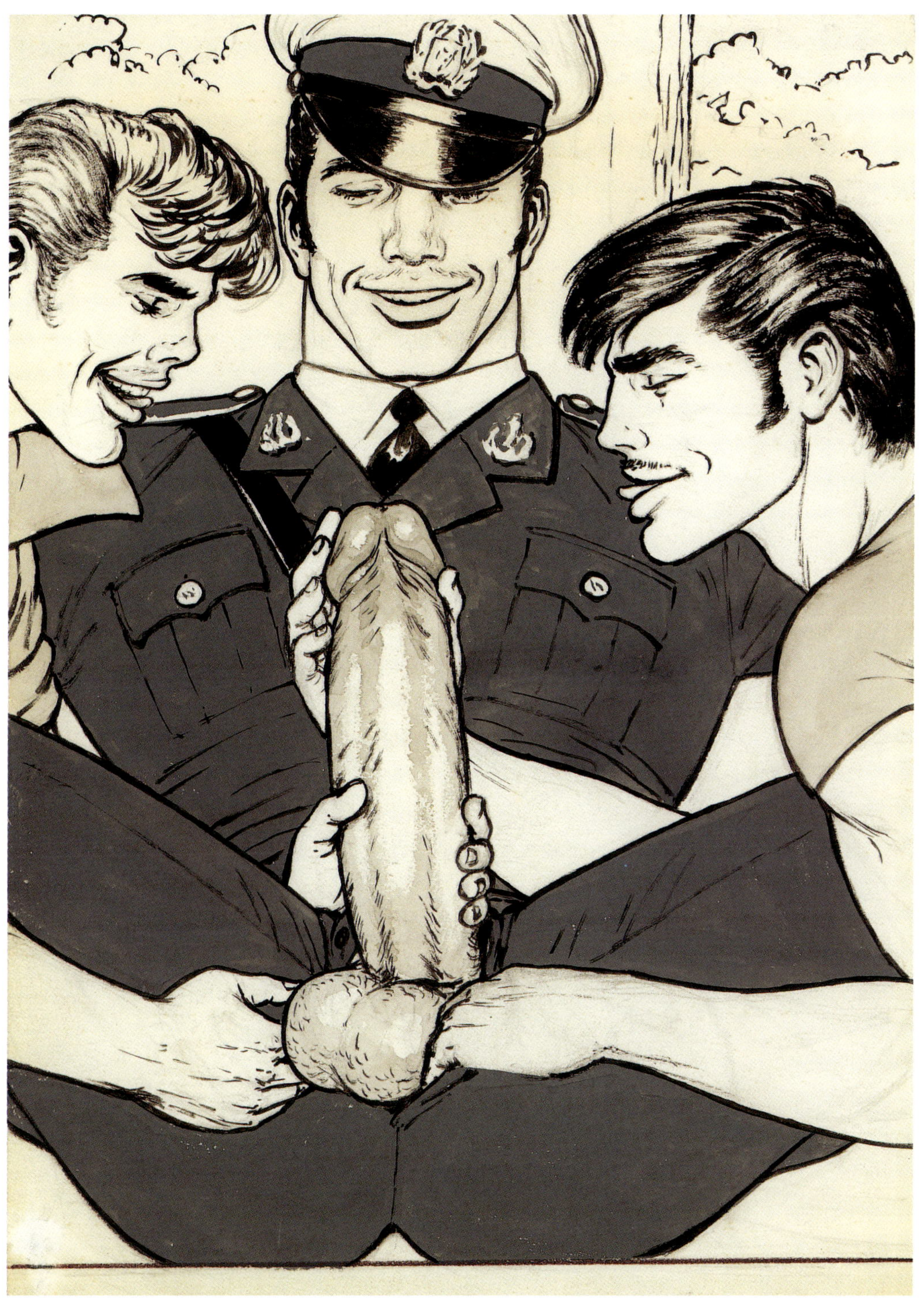

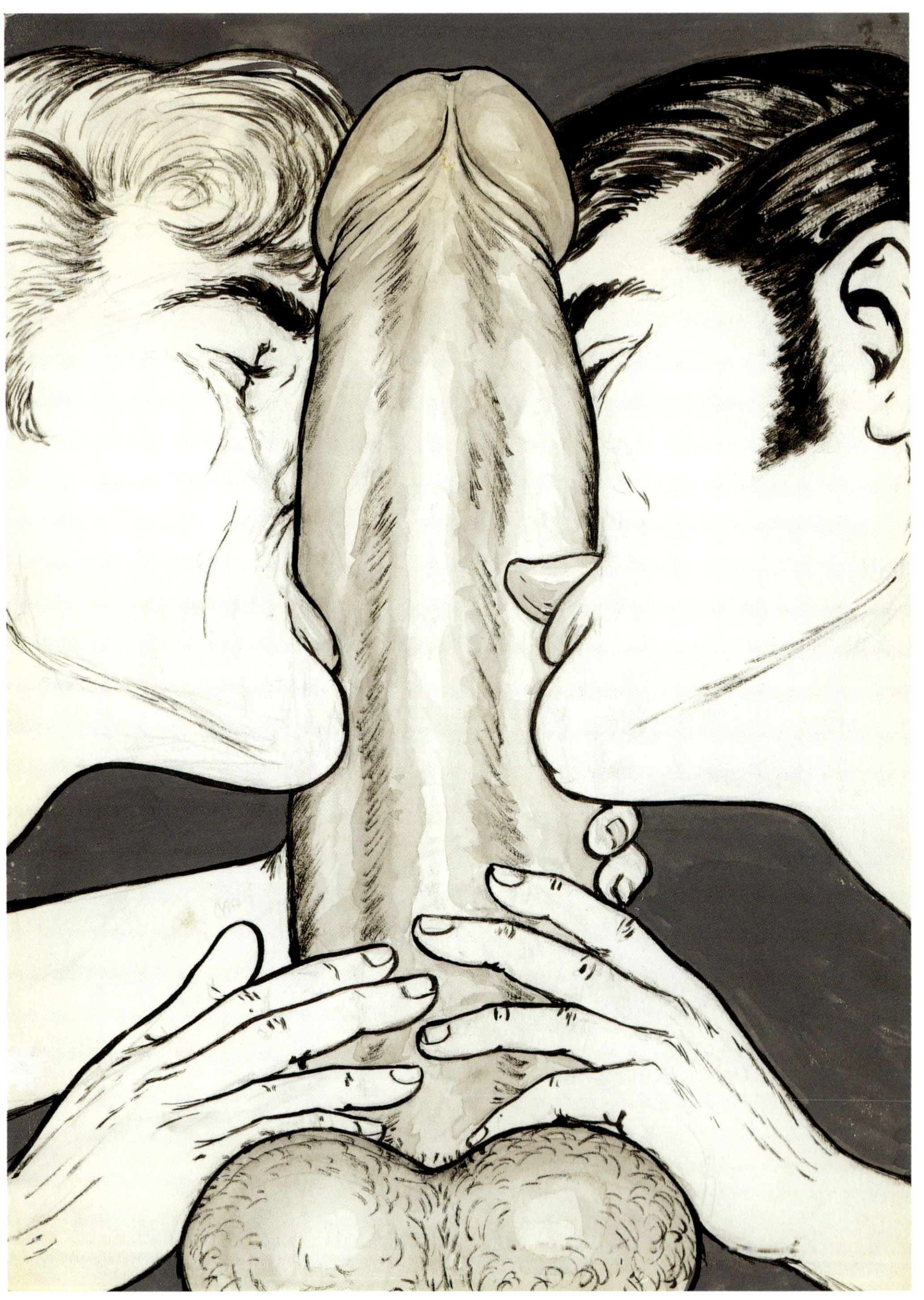

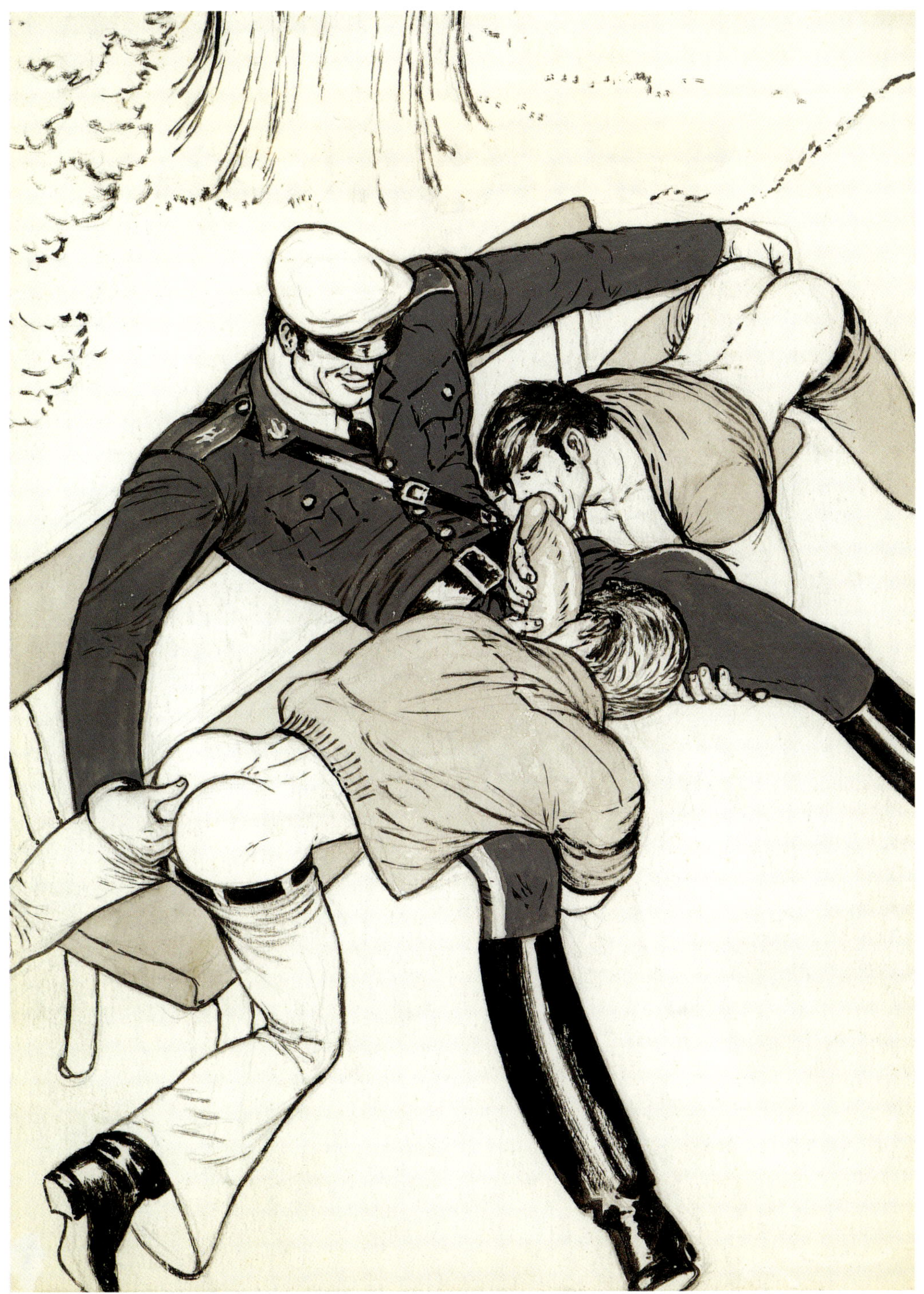

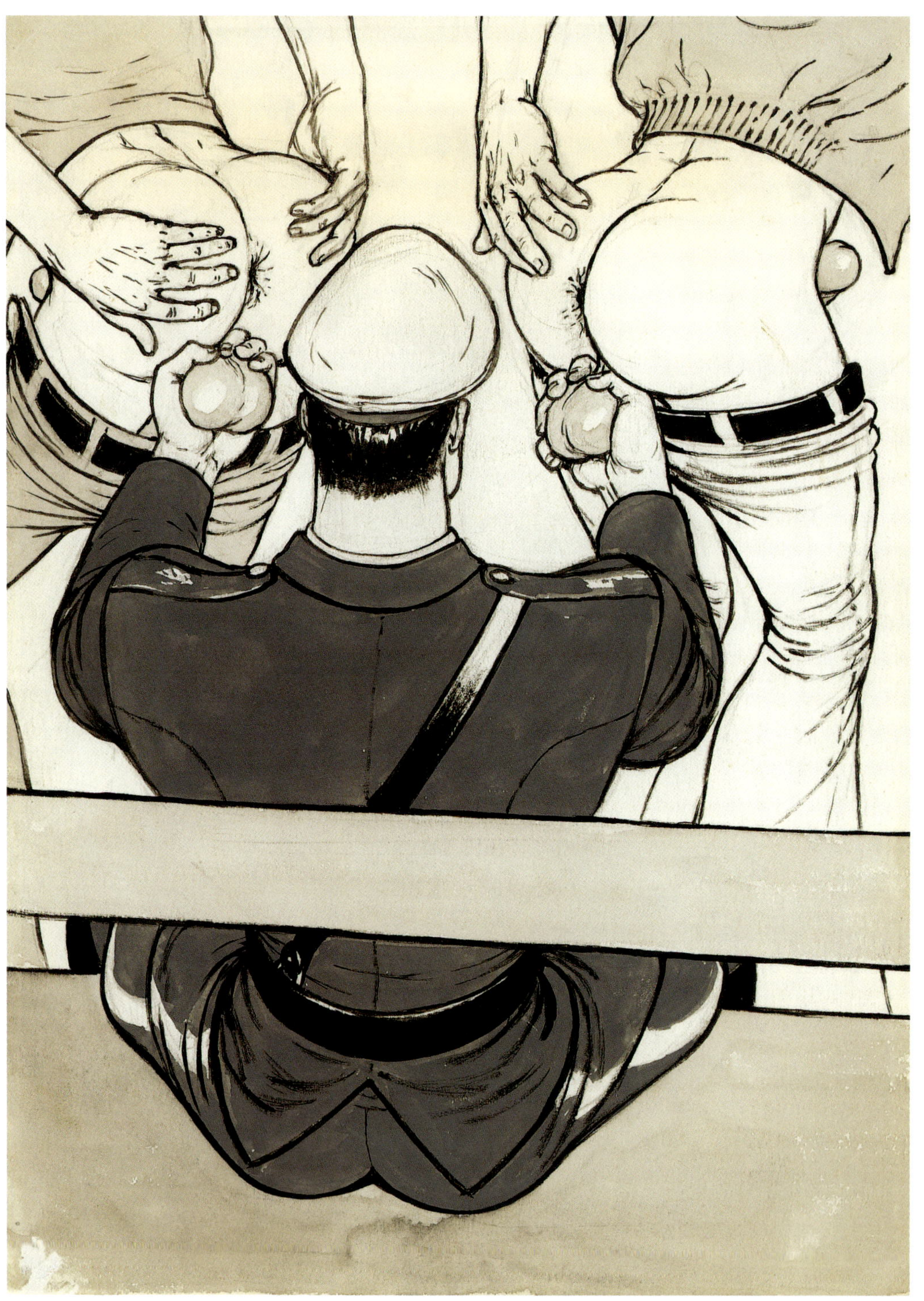

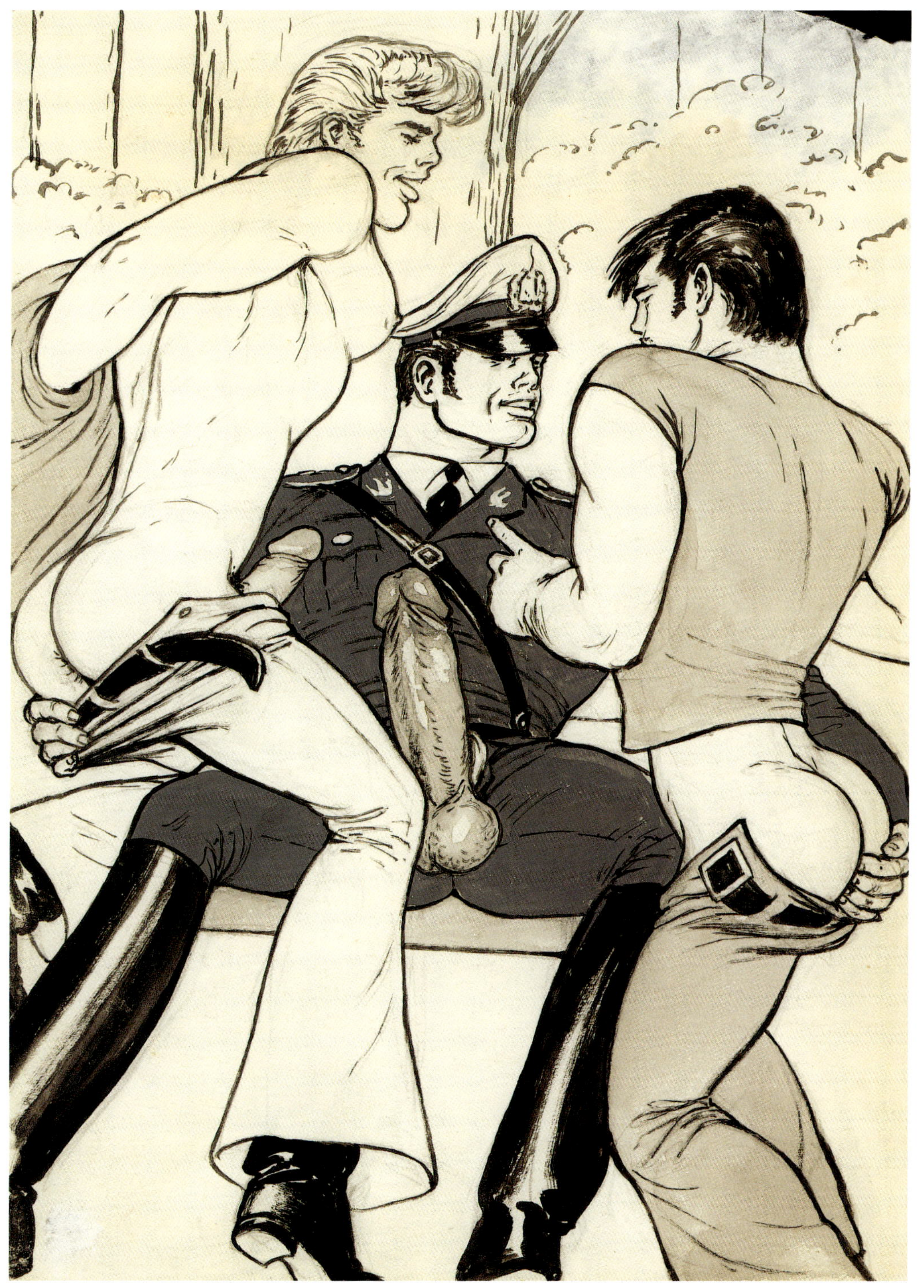

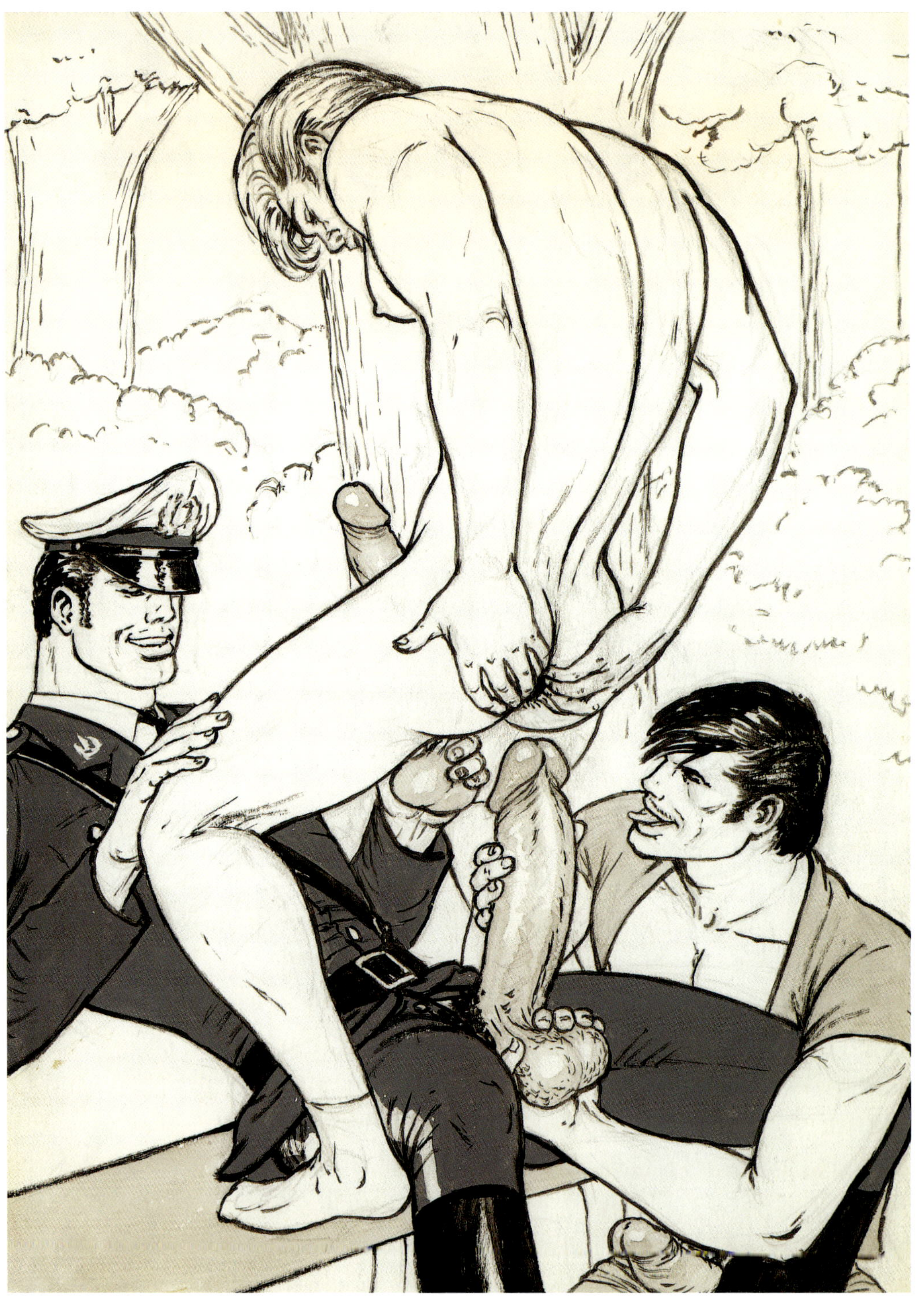

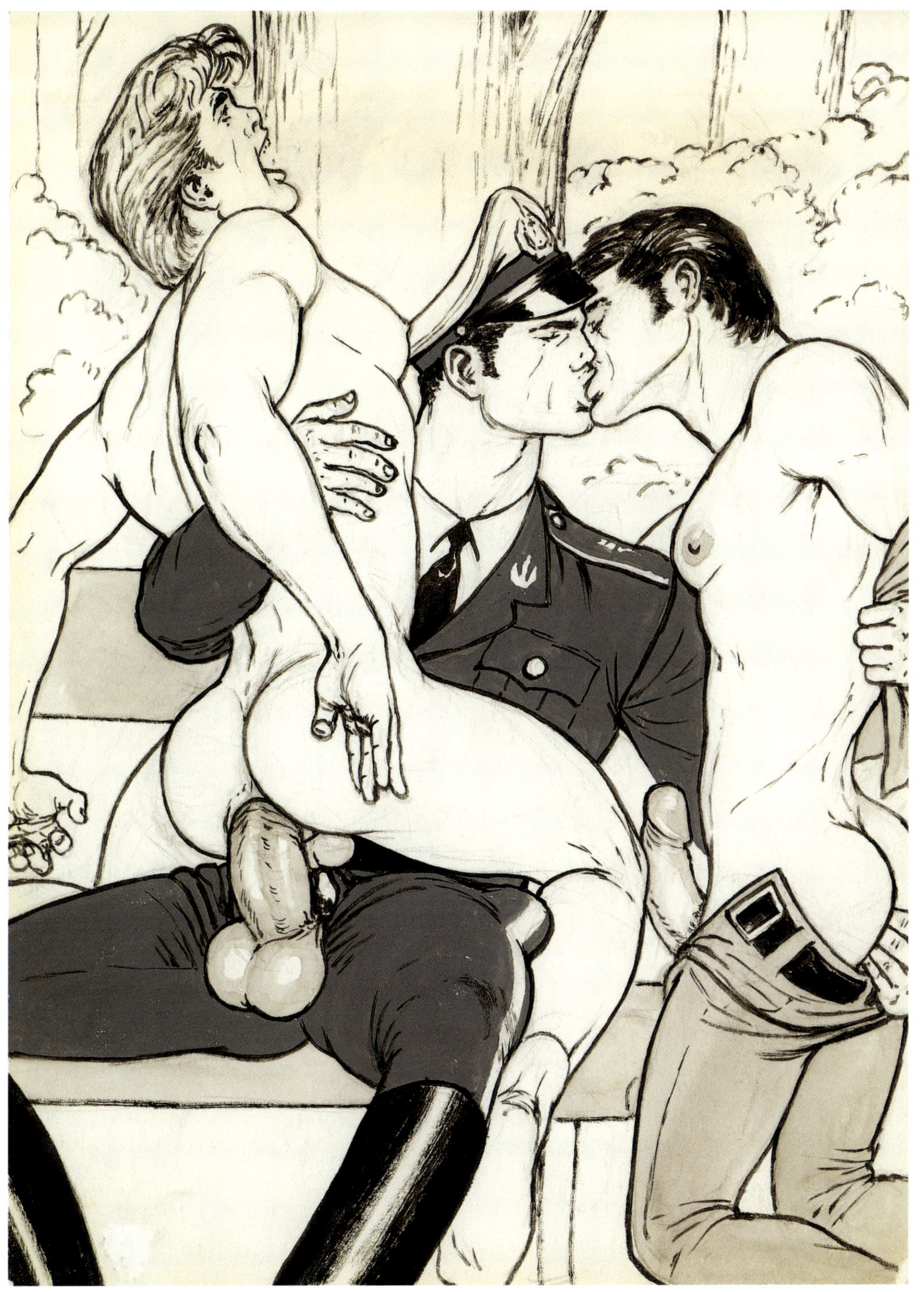

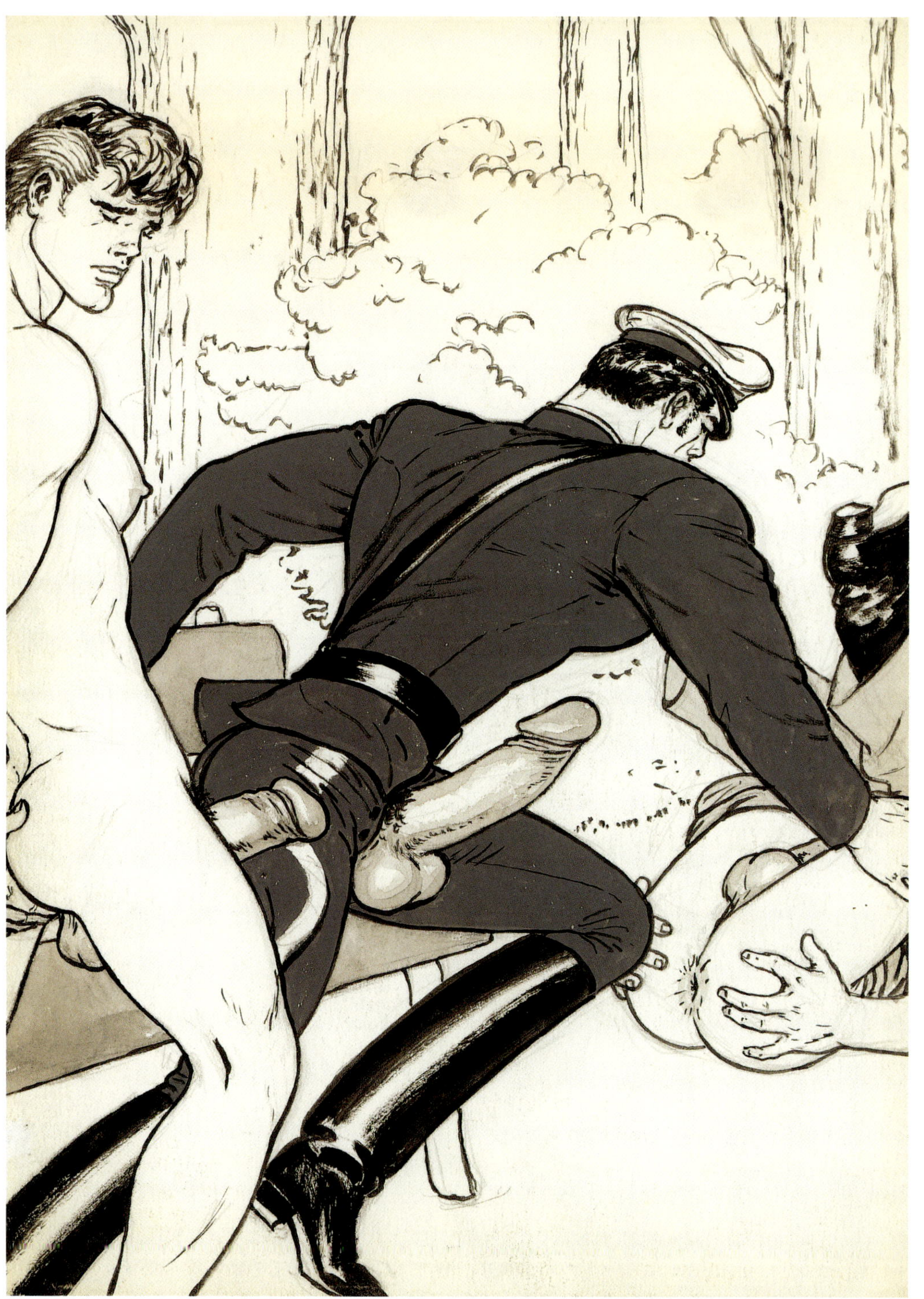

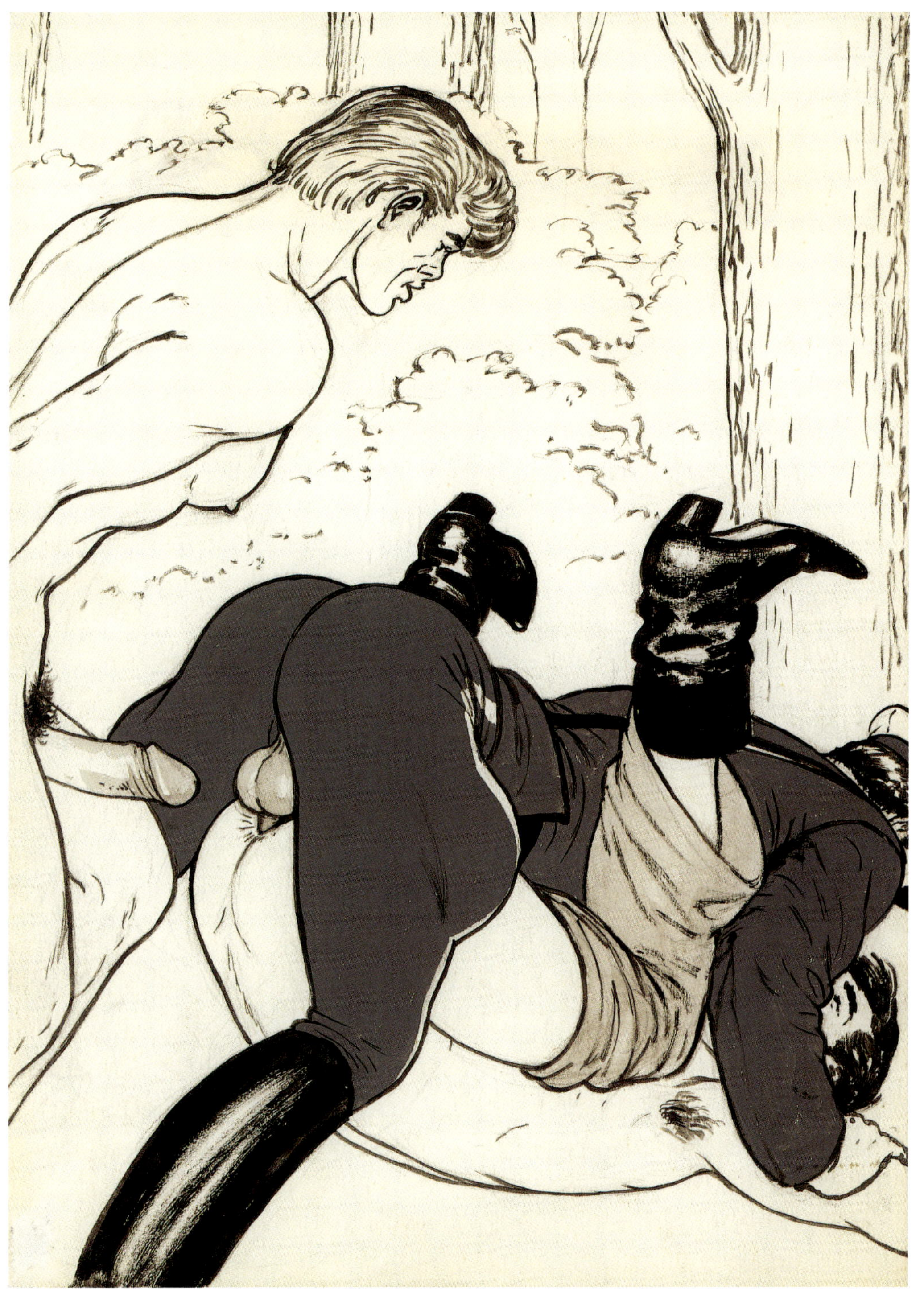

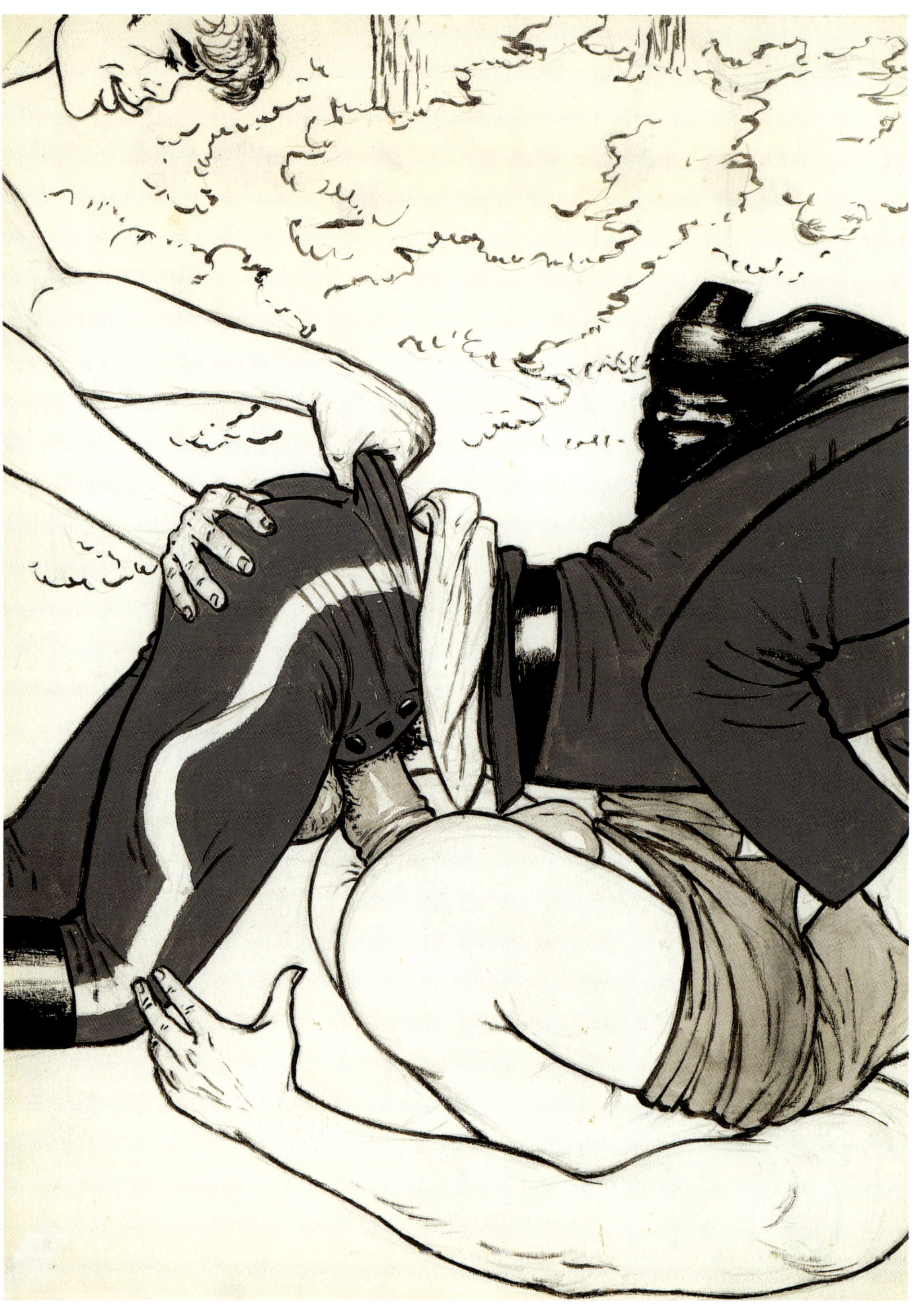

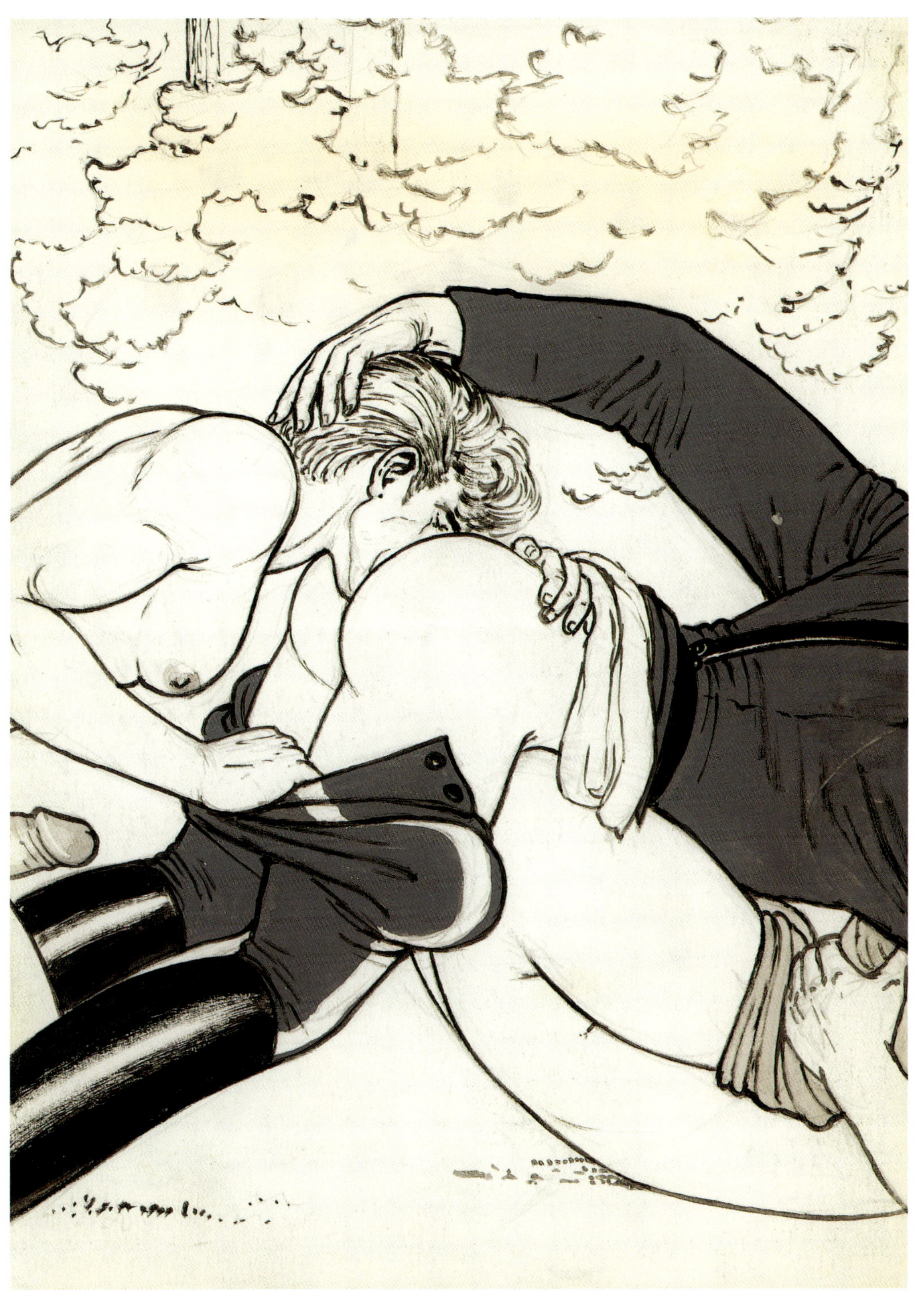

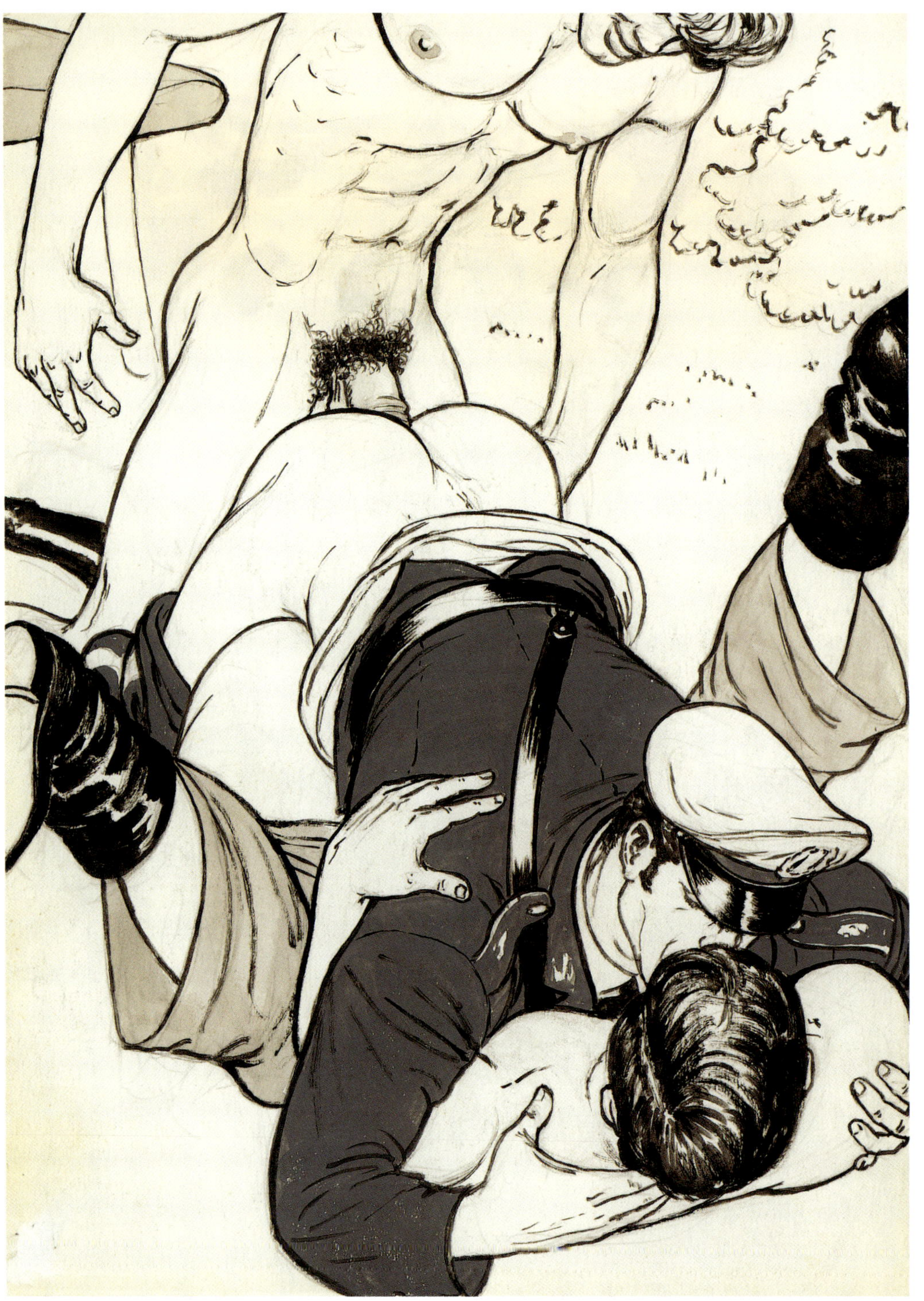

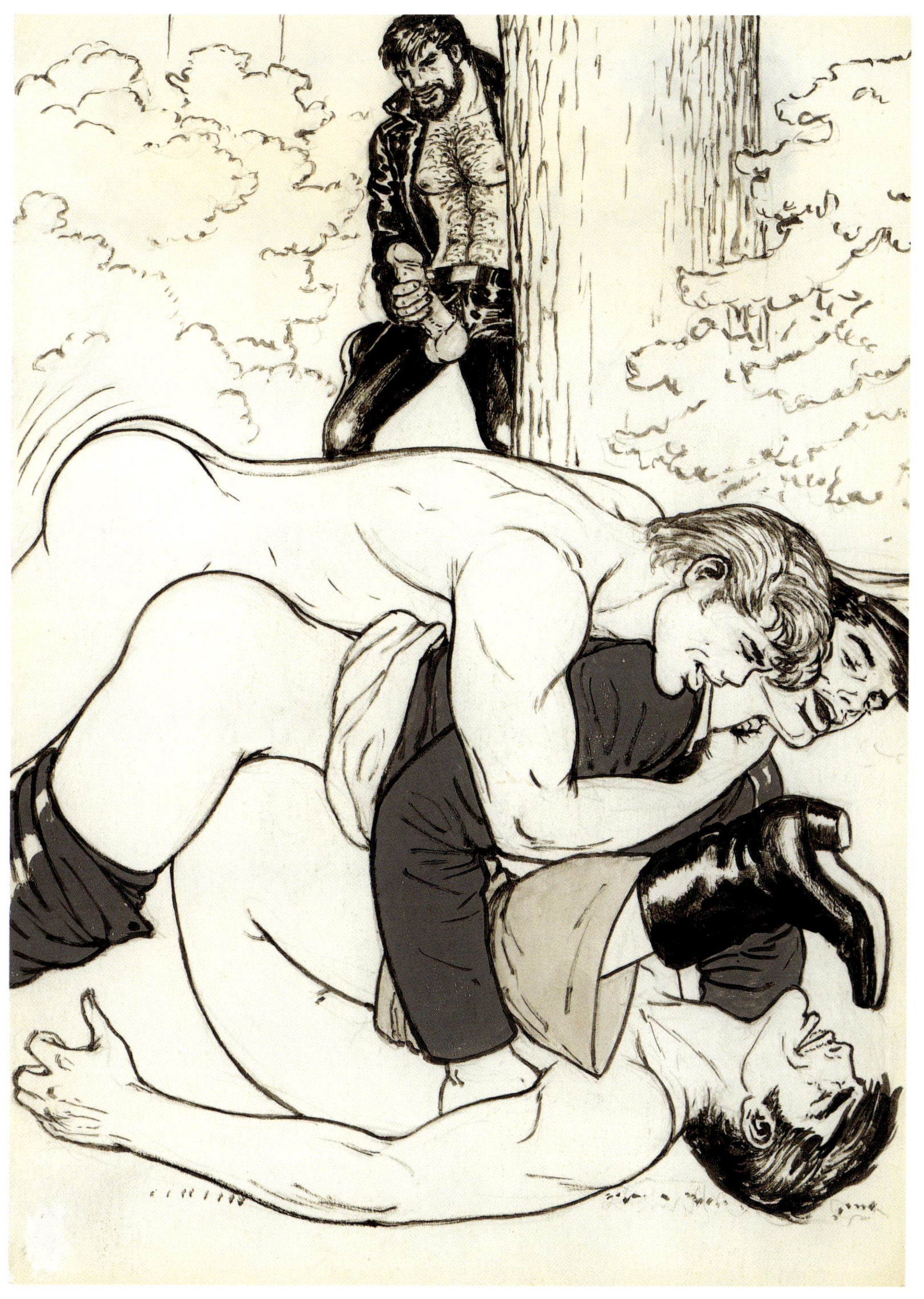

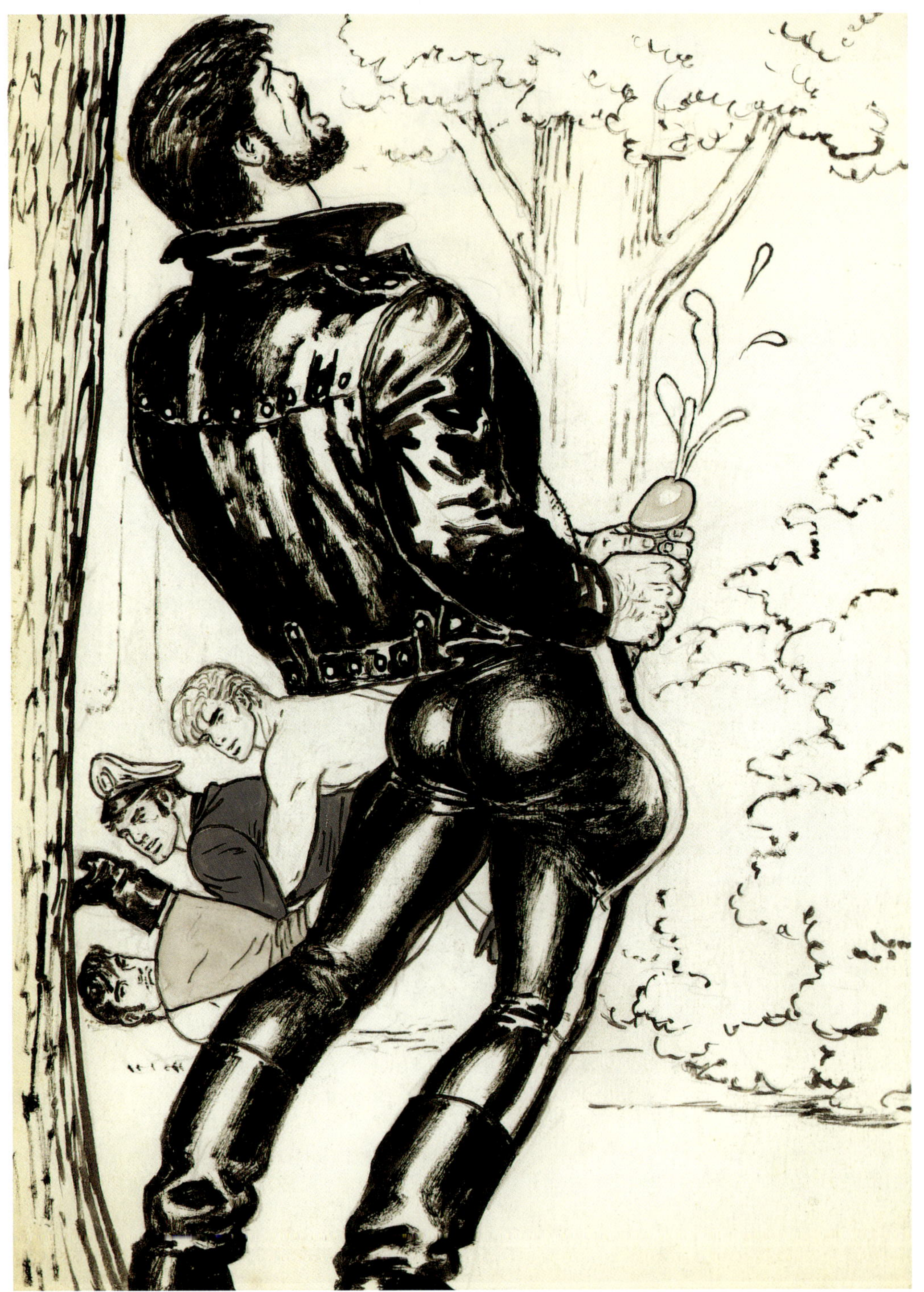

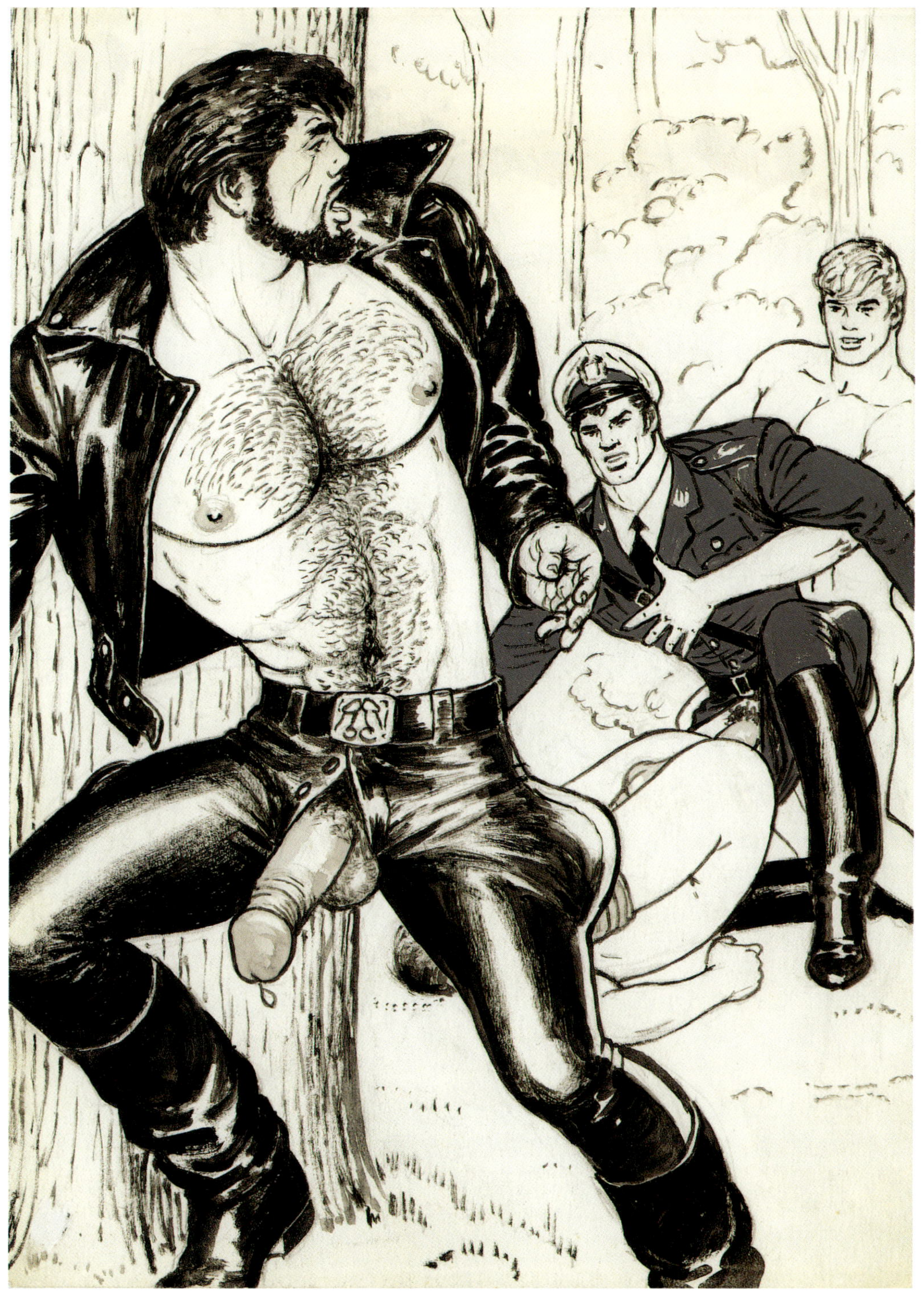

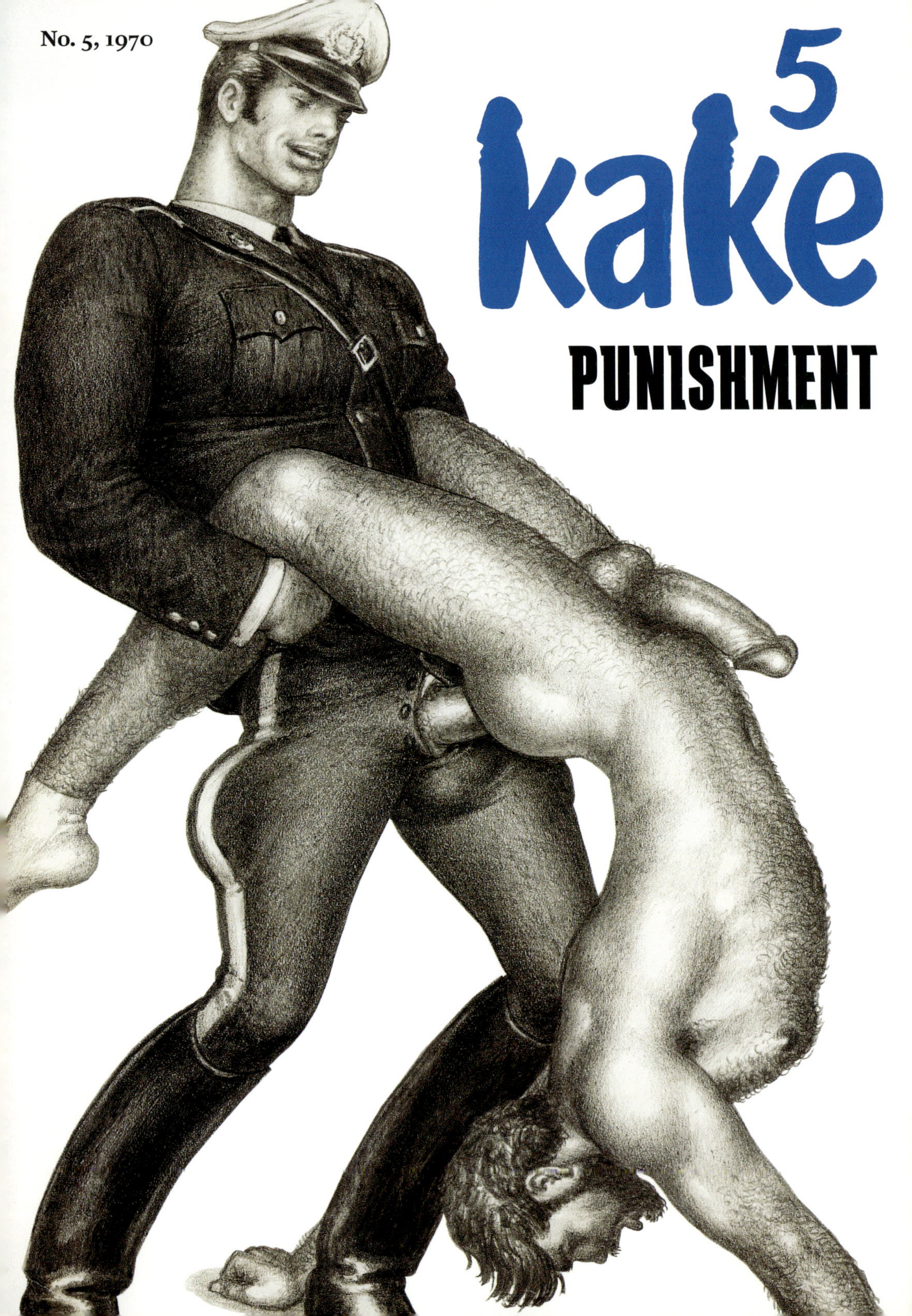
No. 5, 1970
5
kake
PUNISHMENT

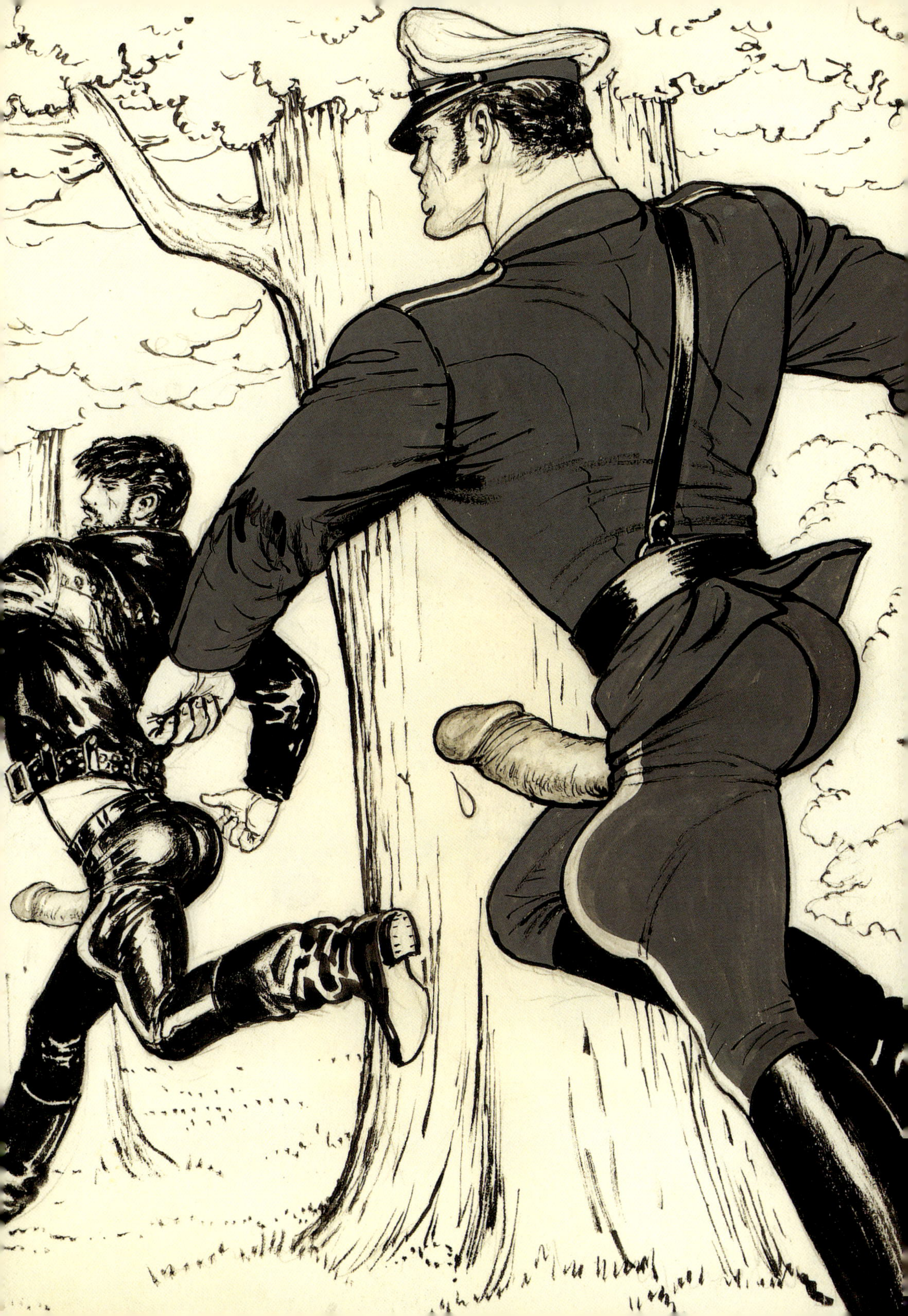

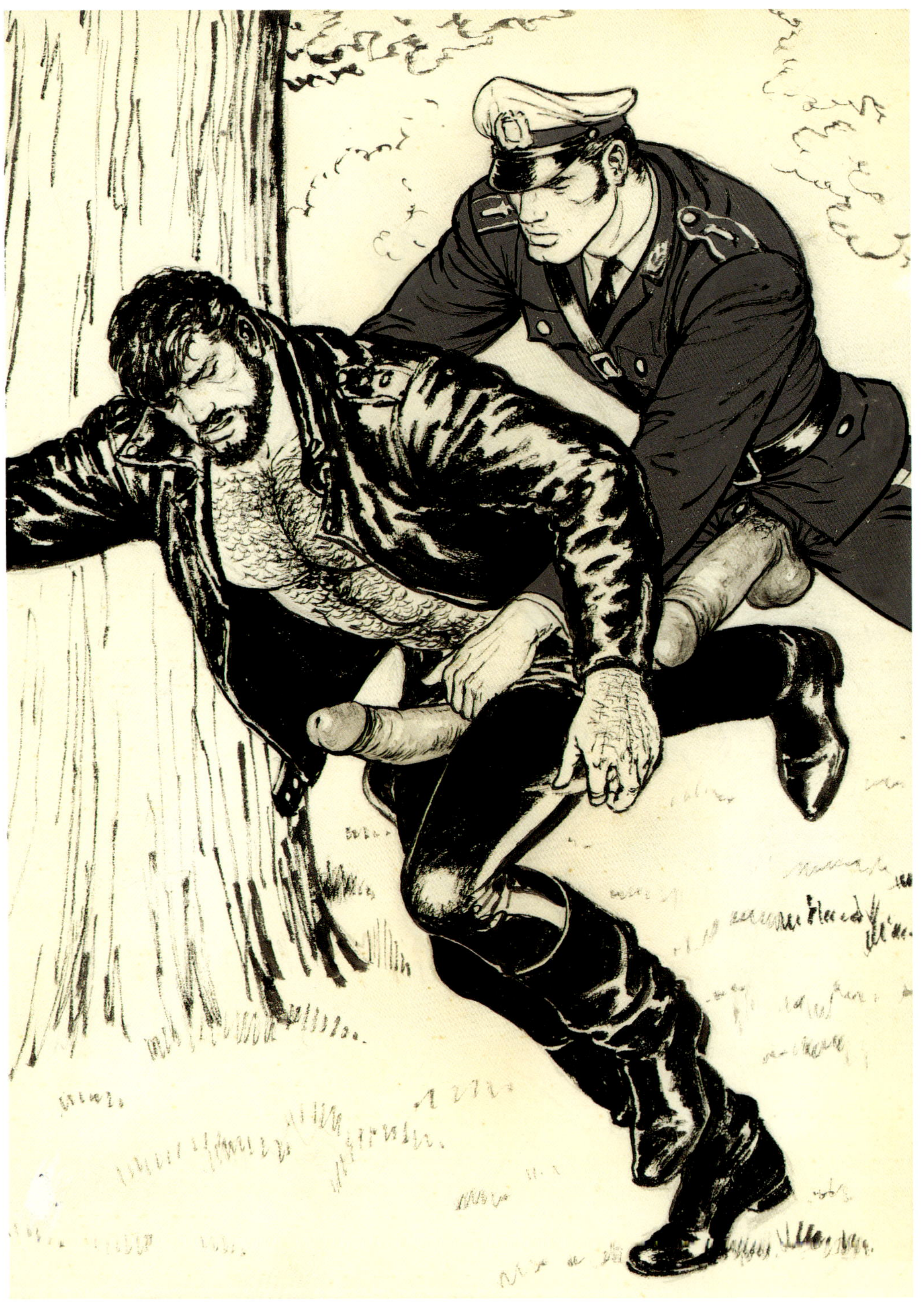

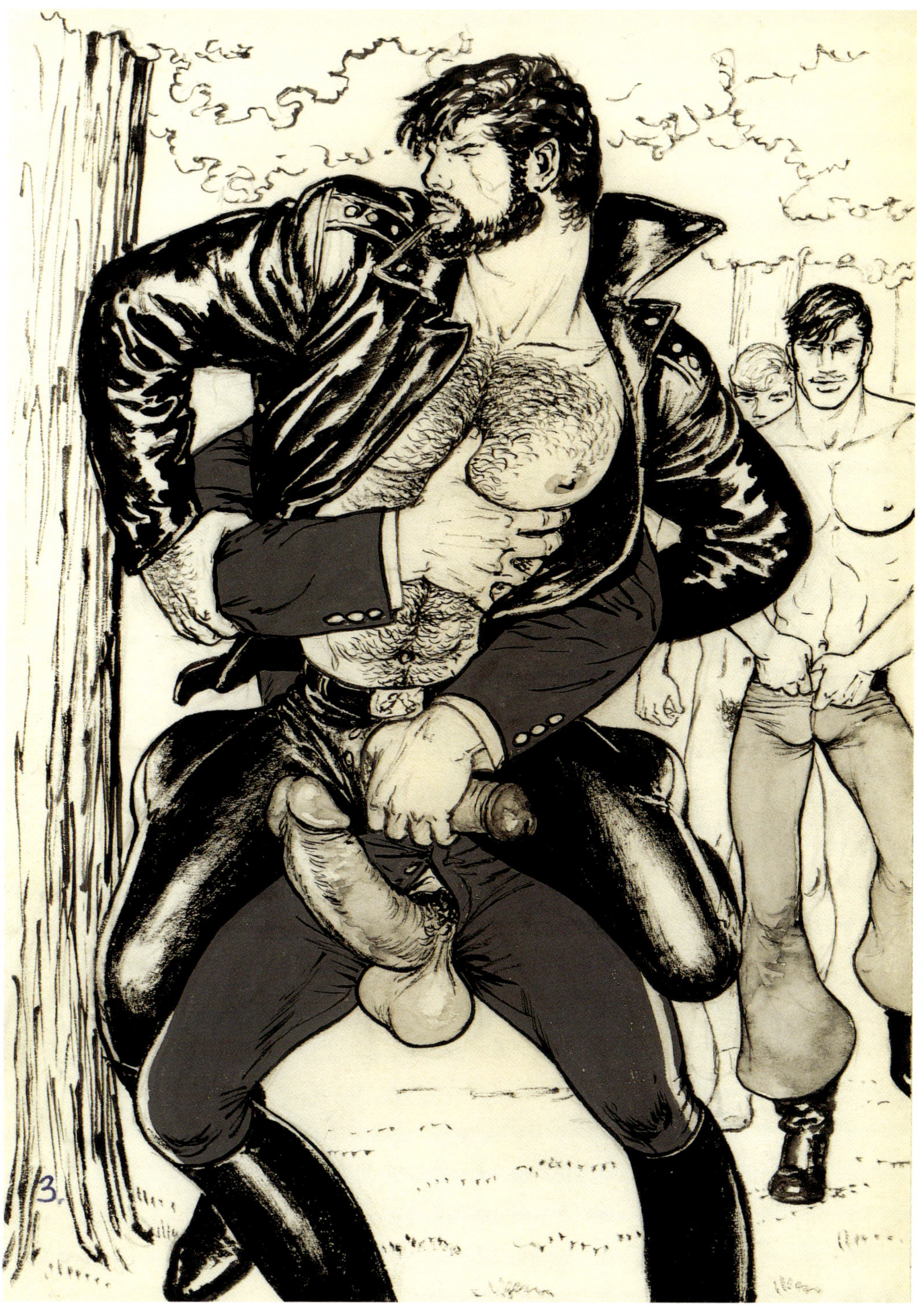

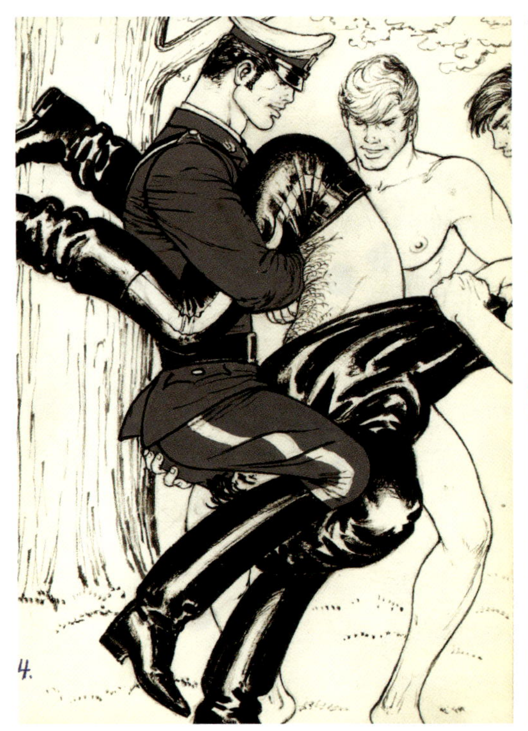
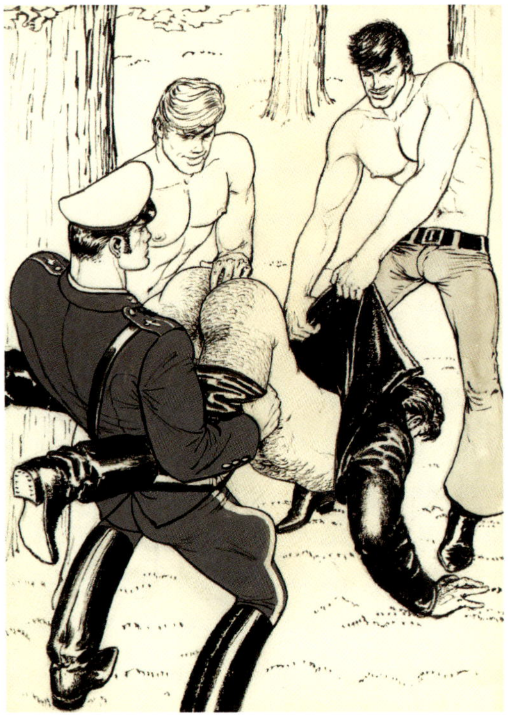
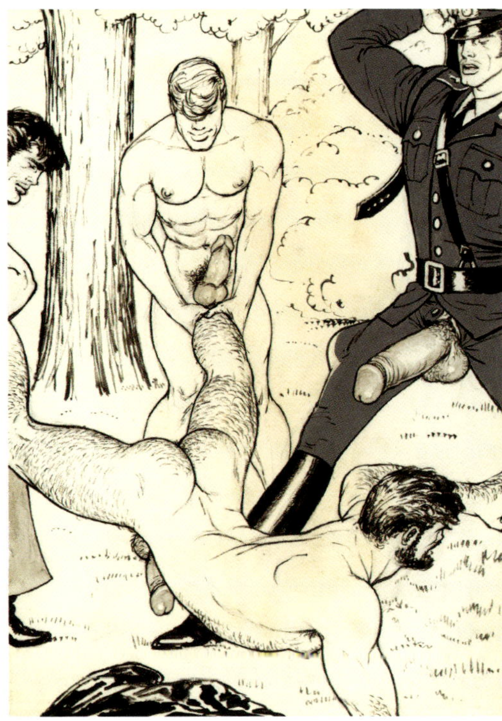
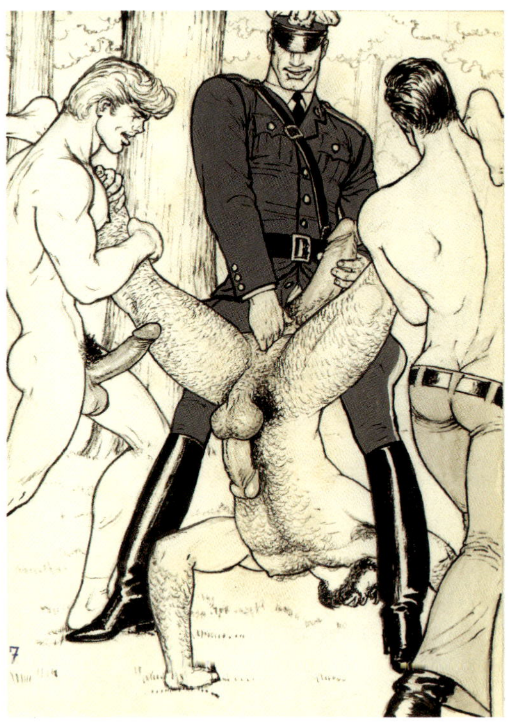

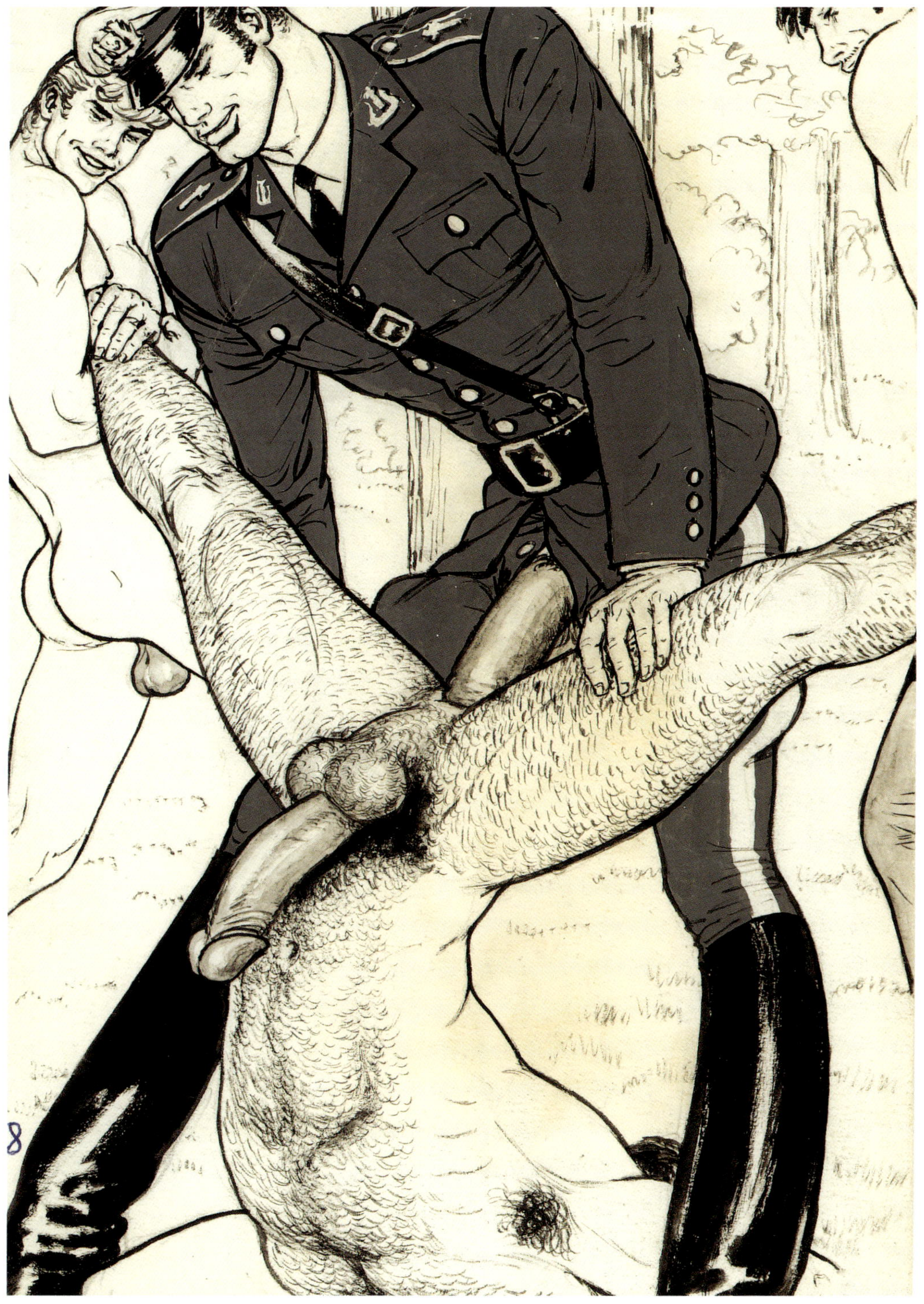

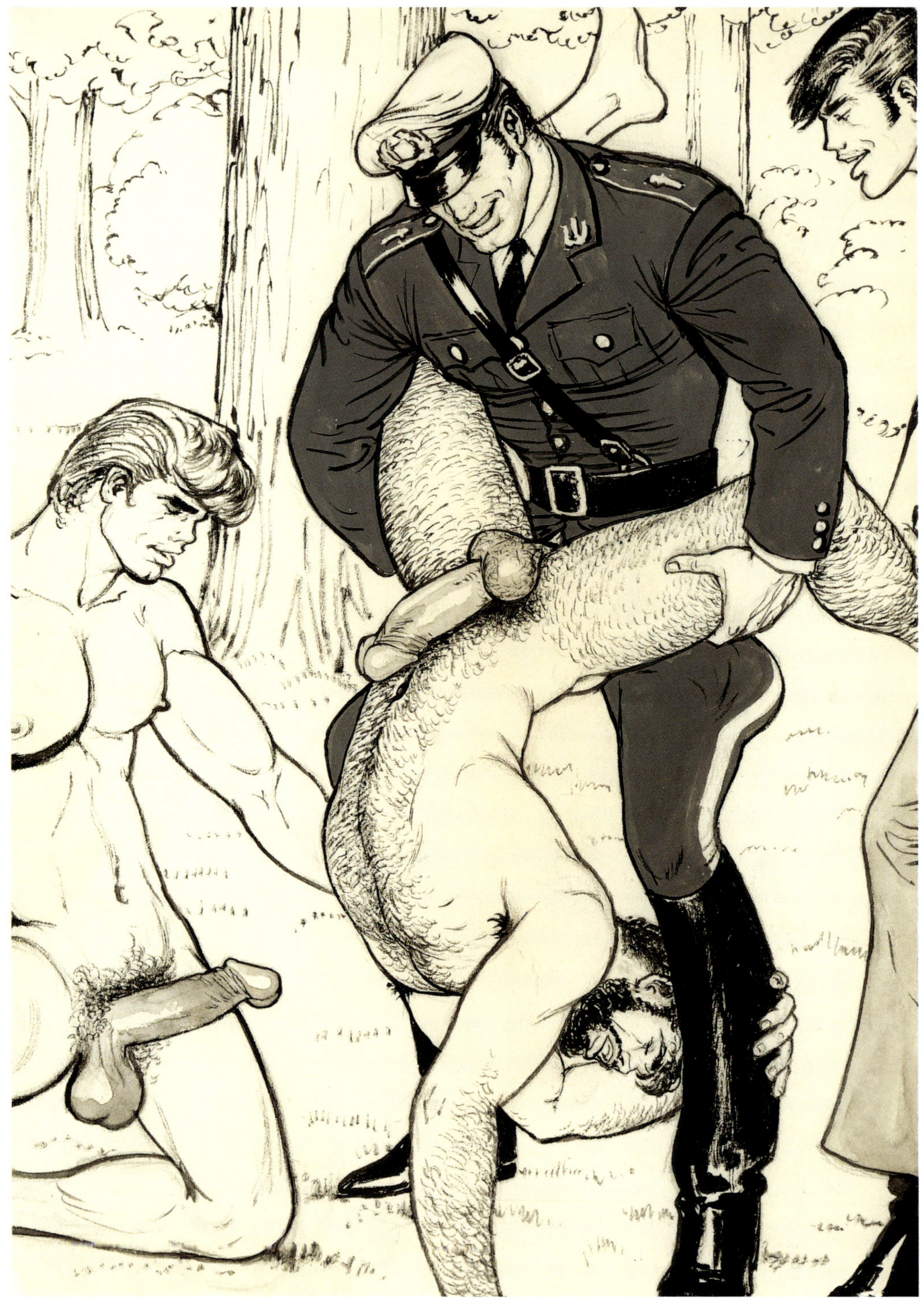

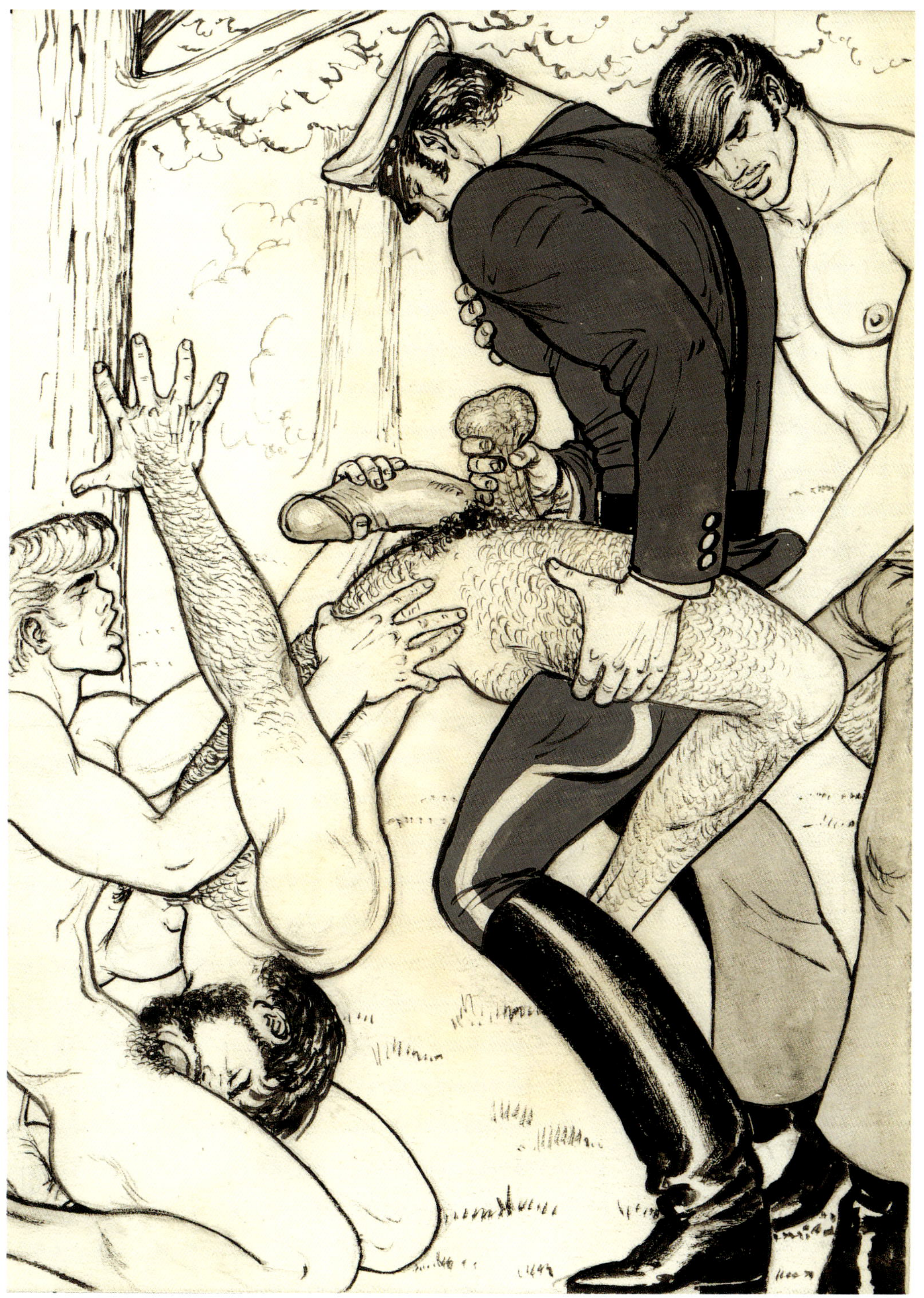

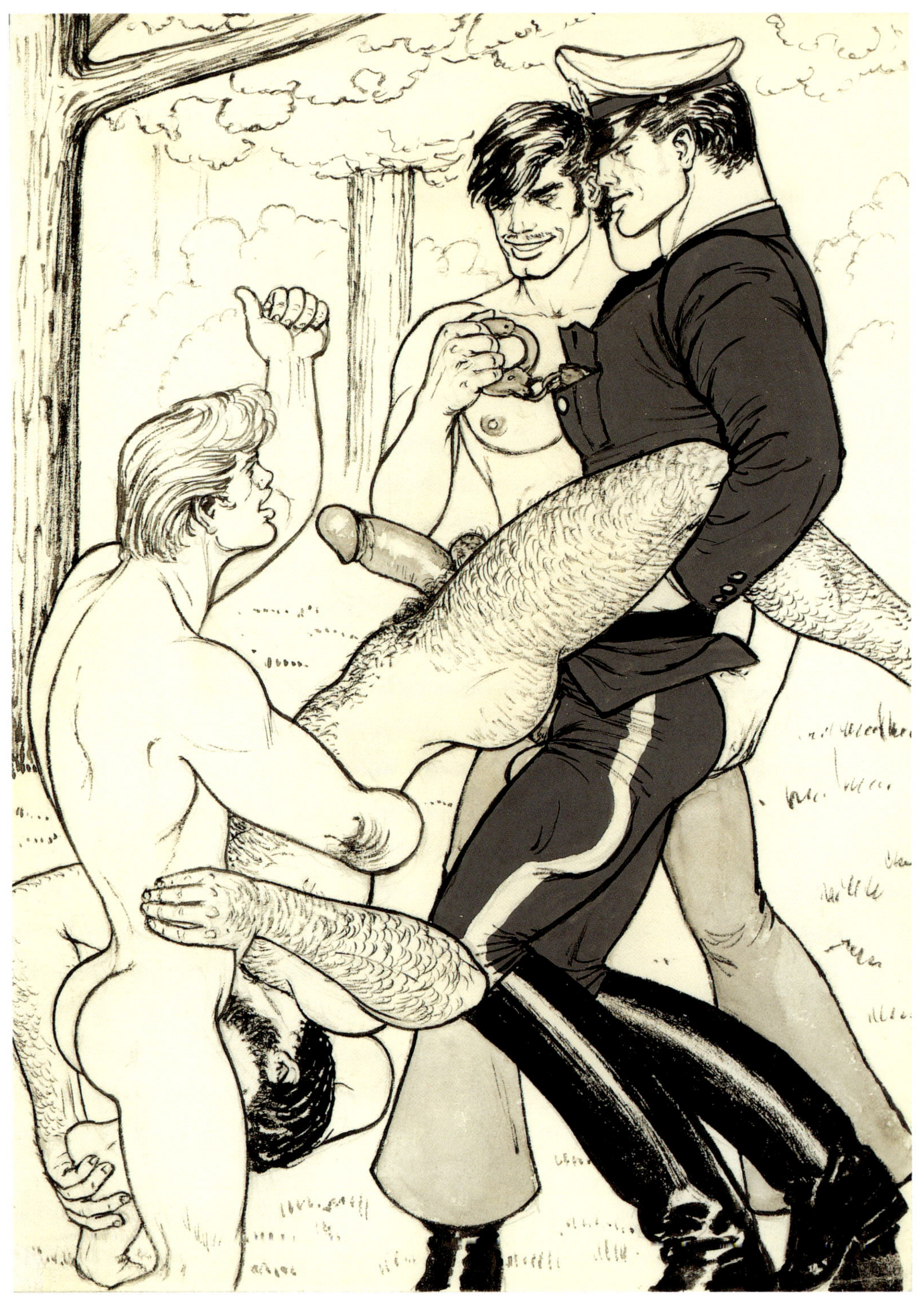

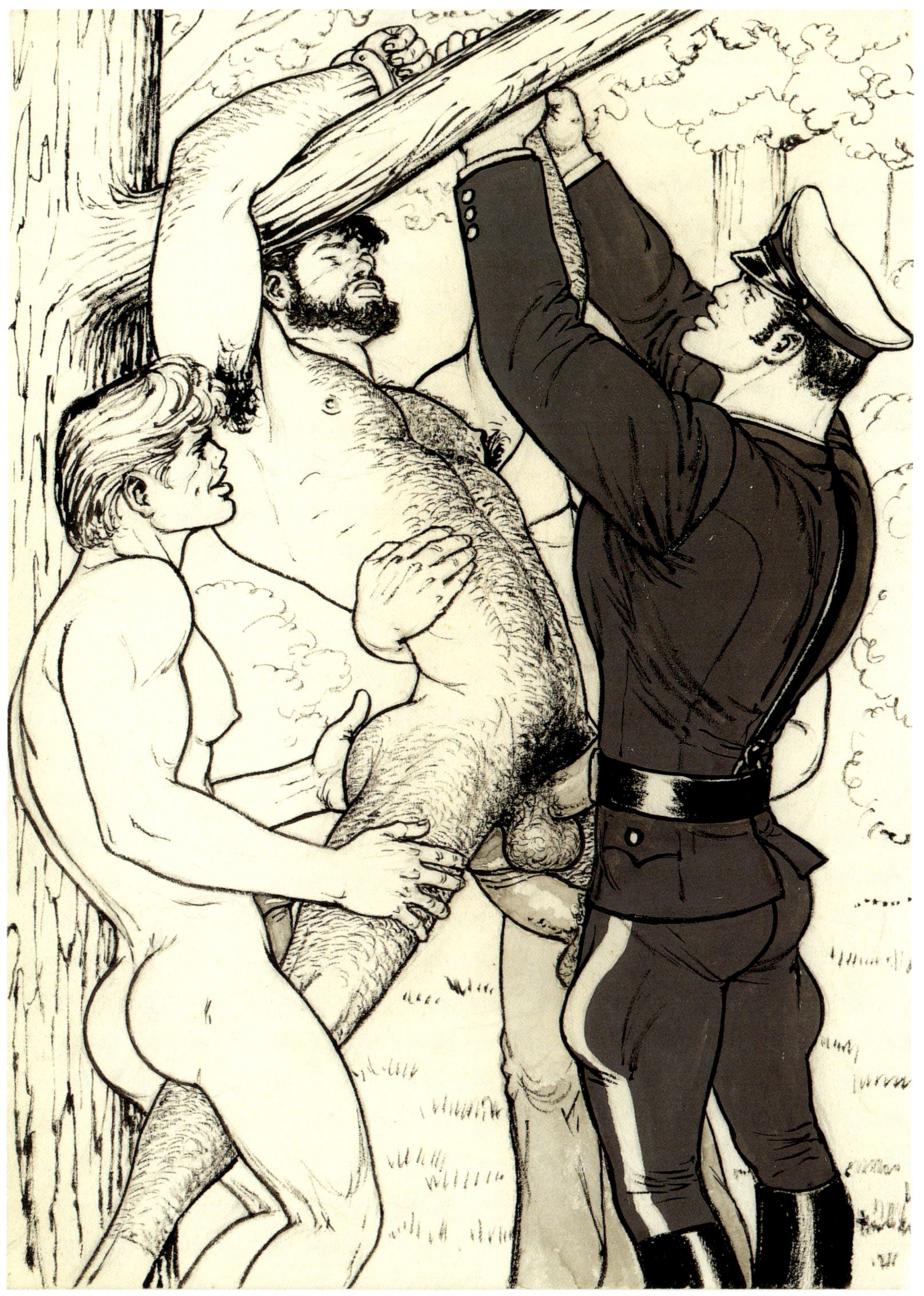

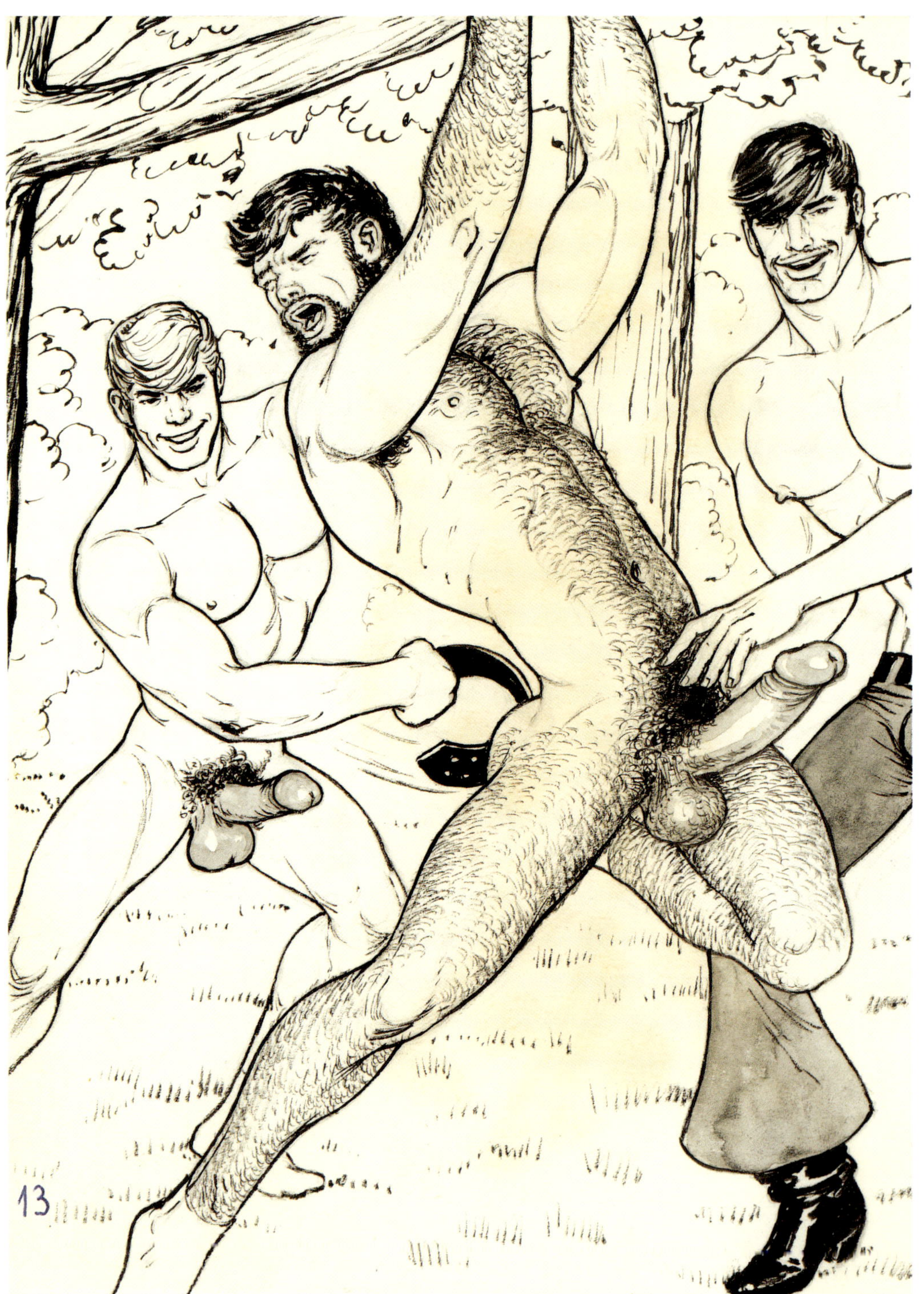

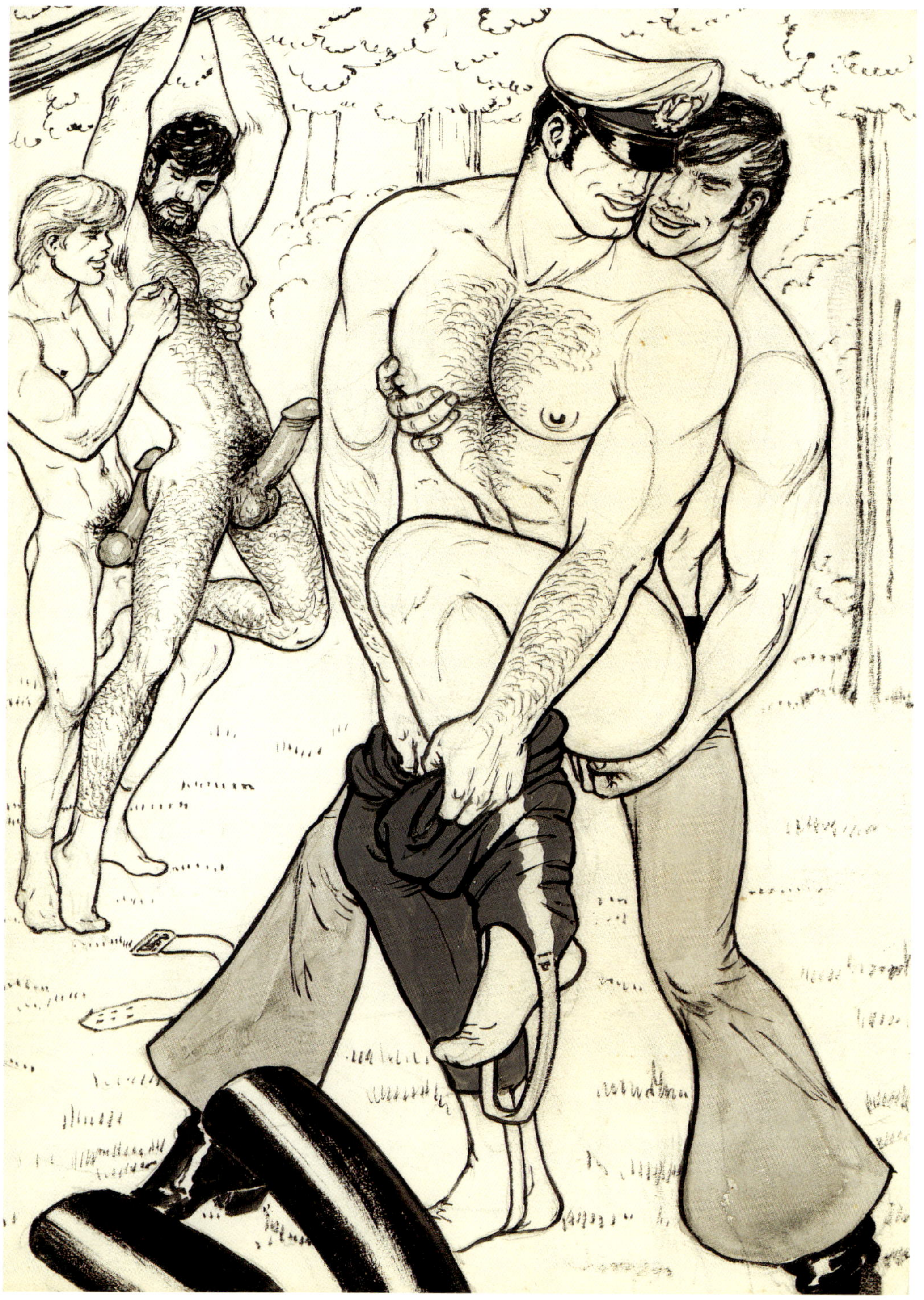

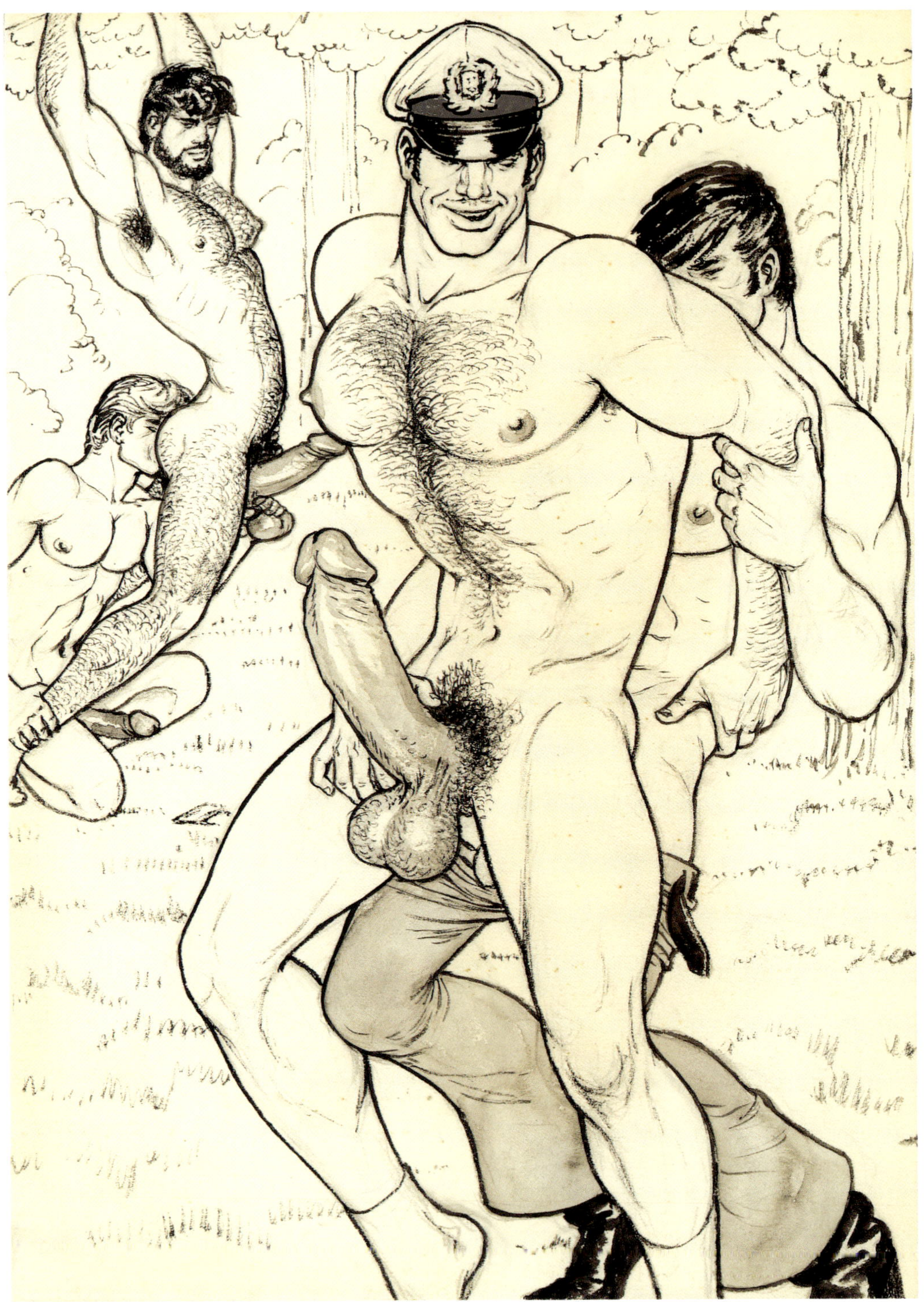

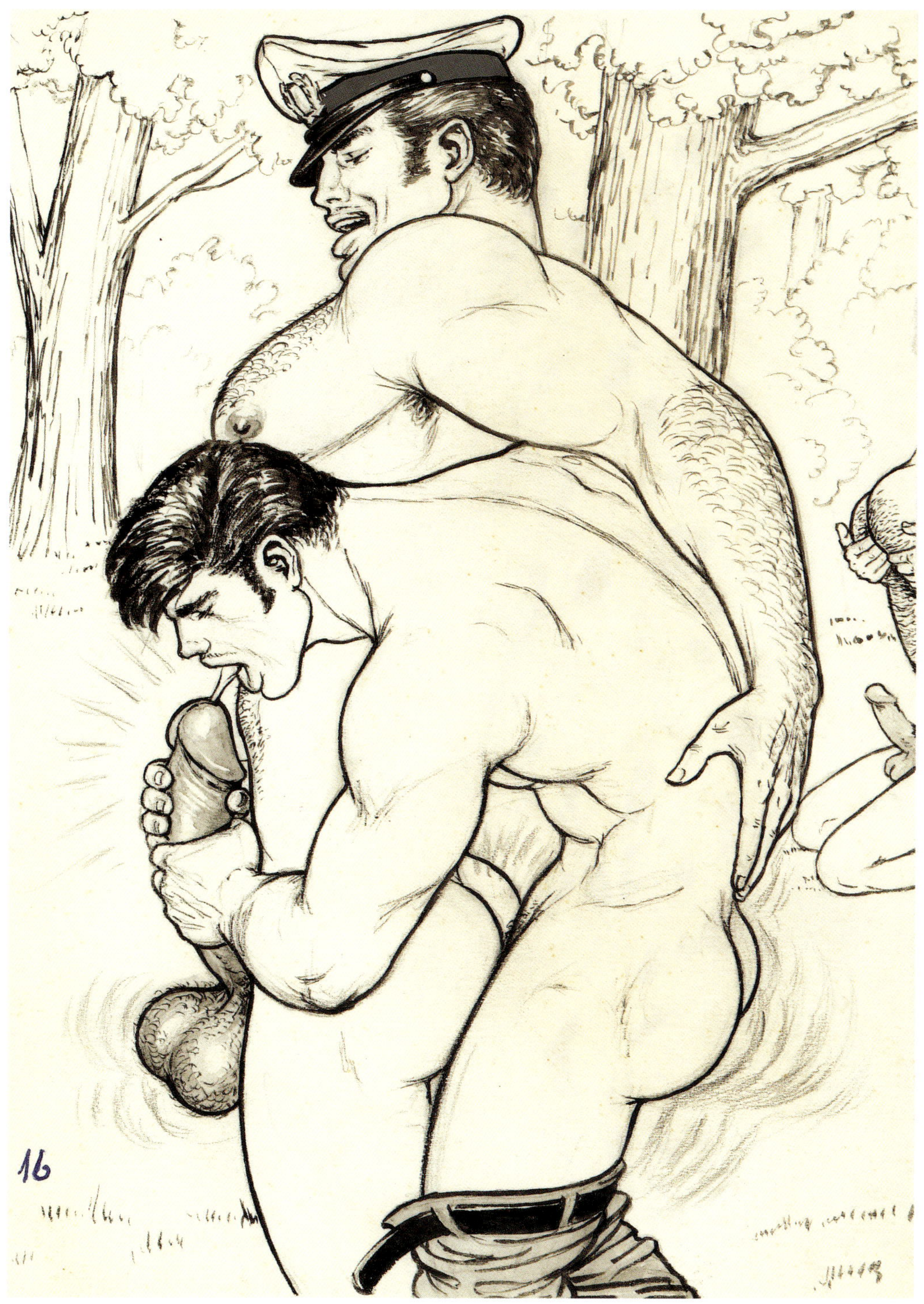

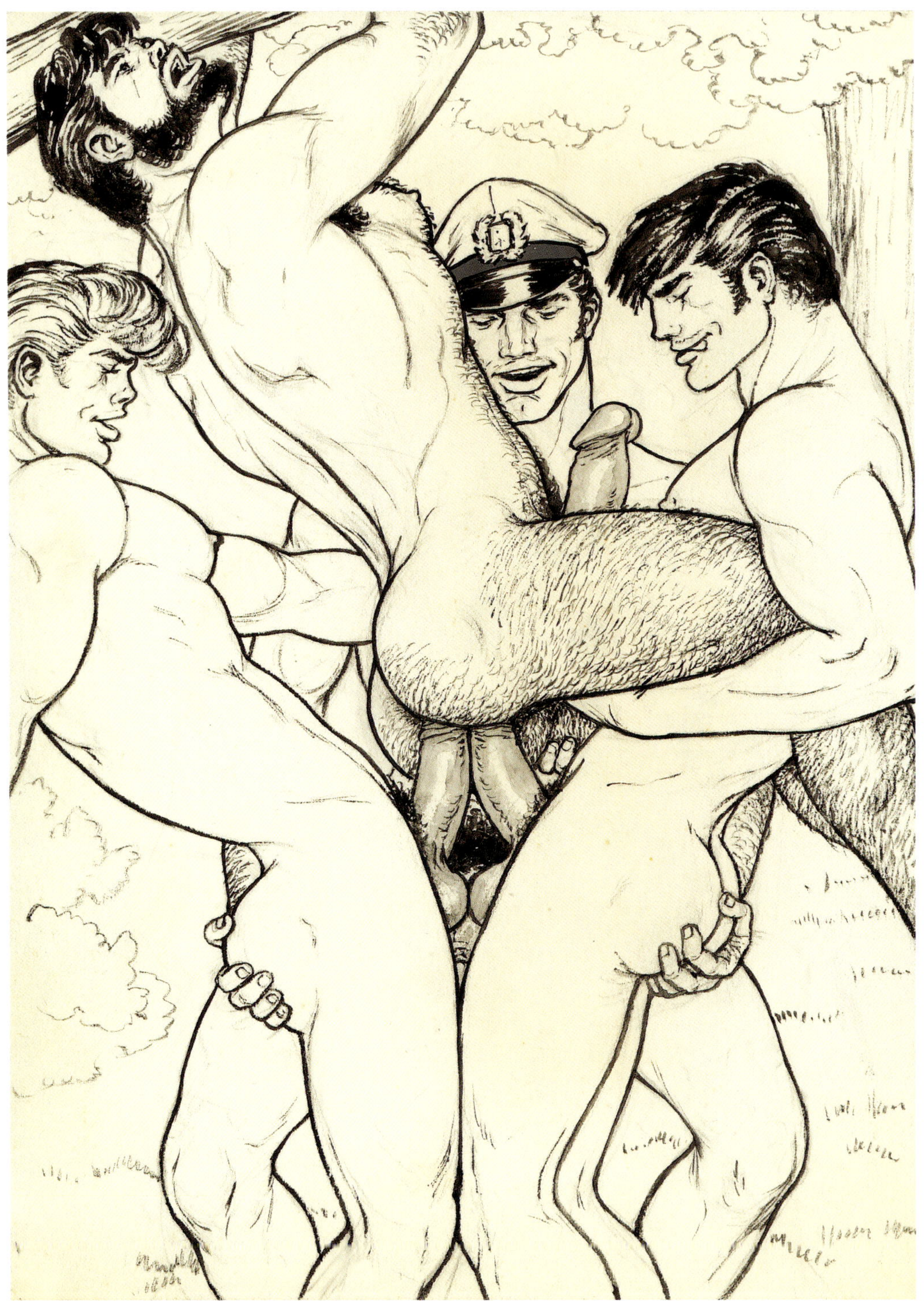

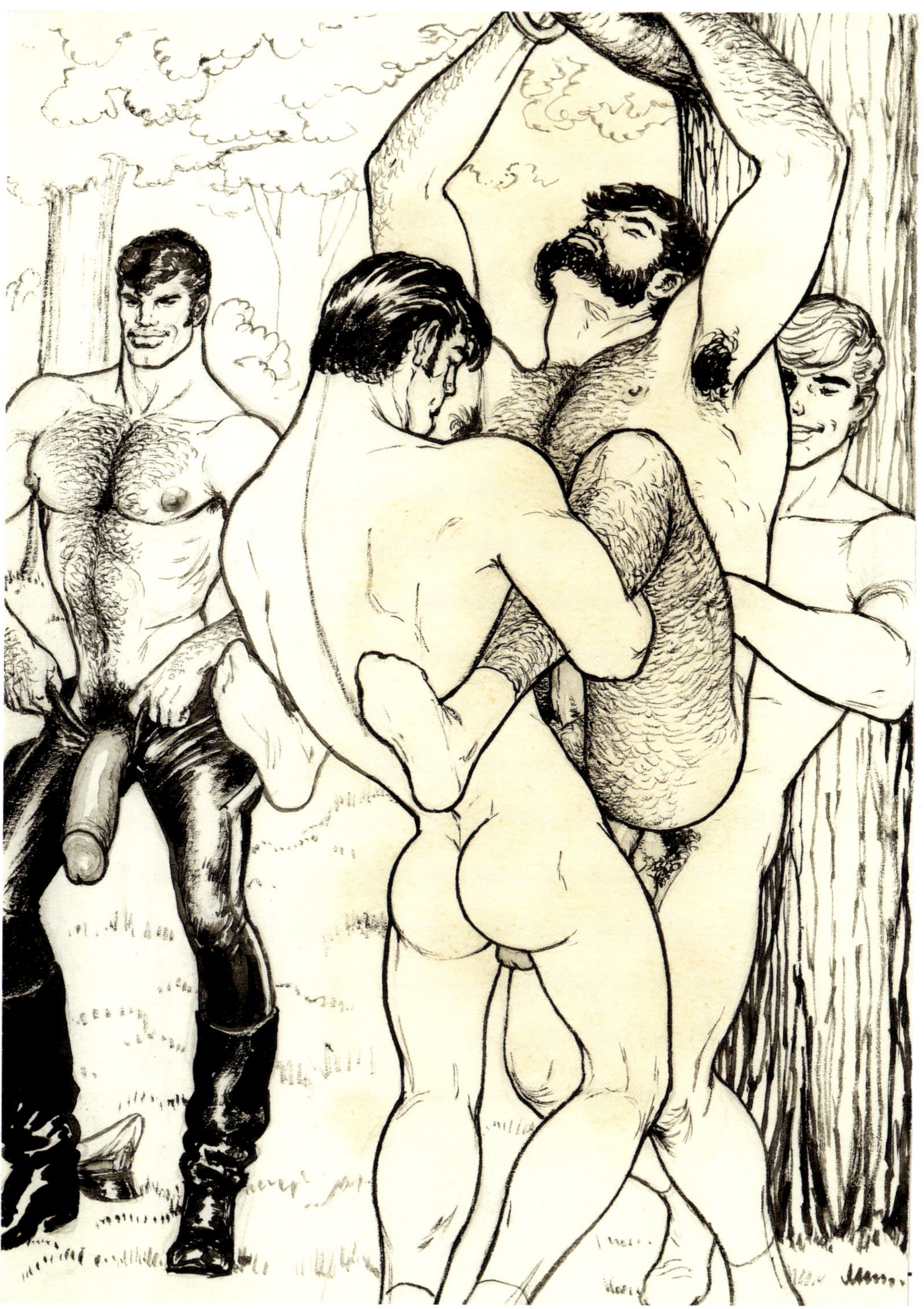

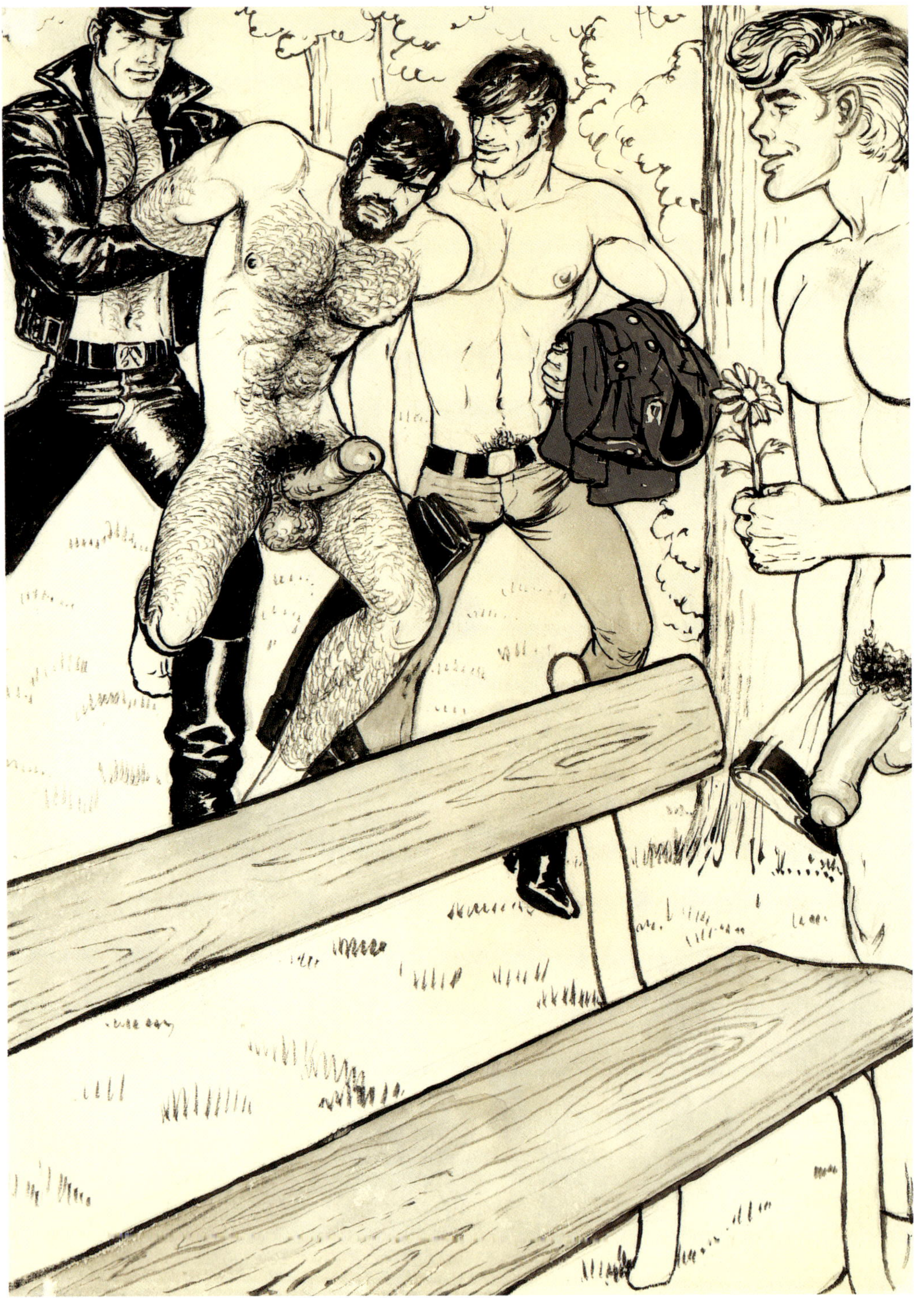

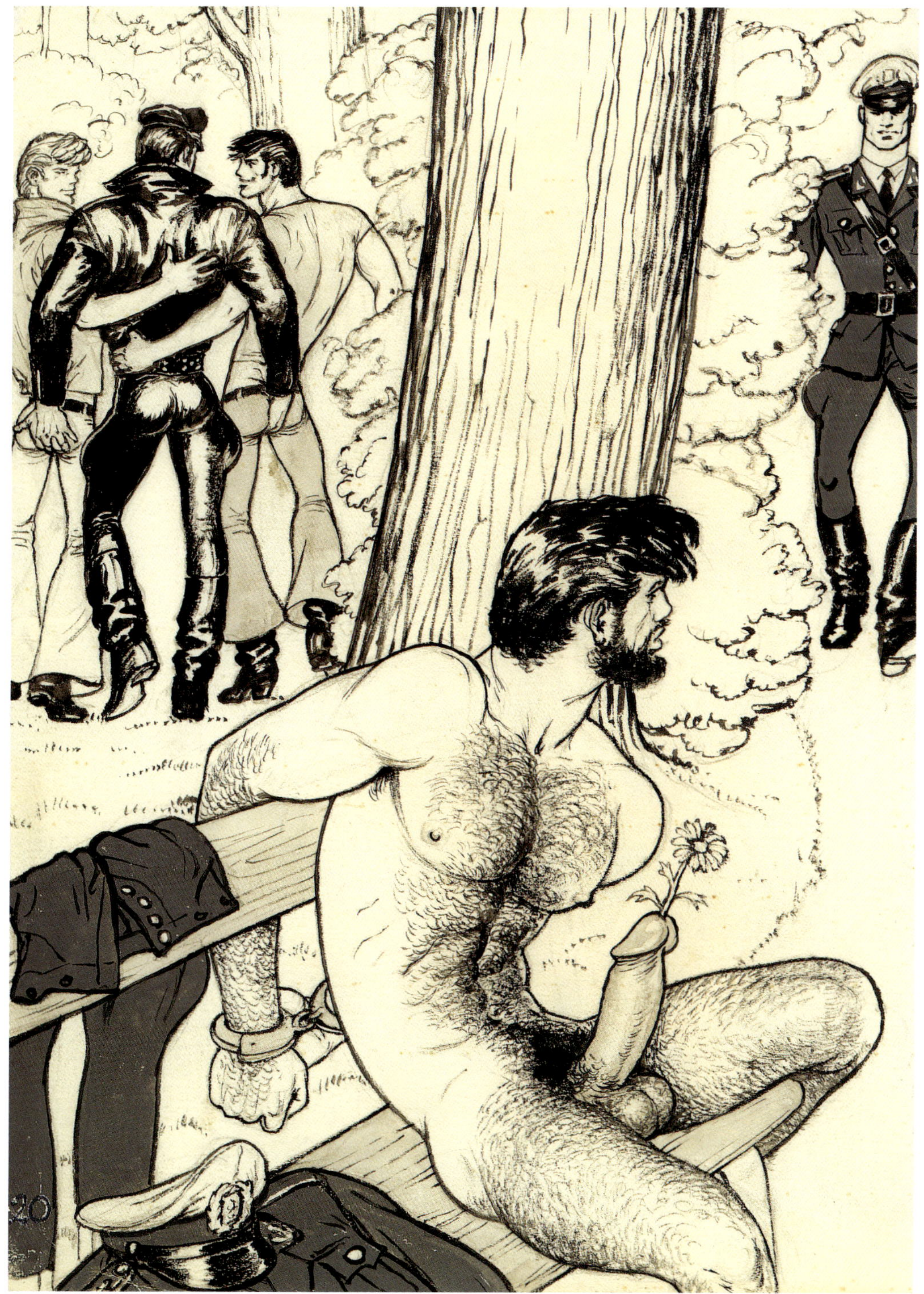

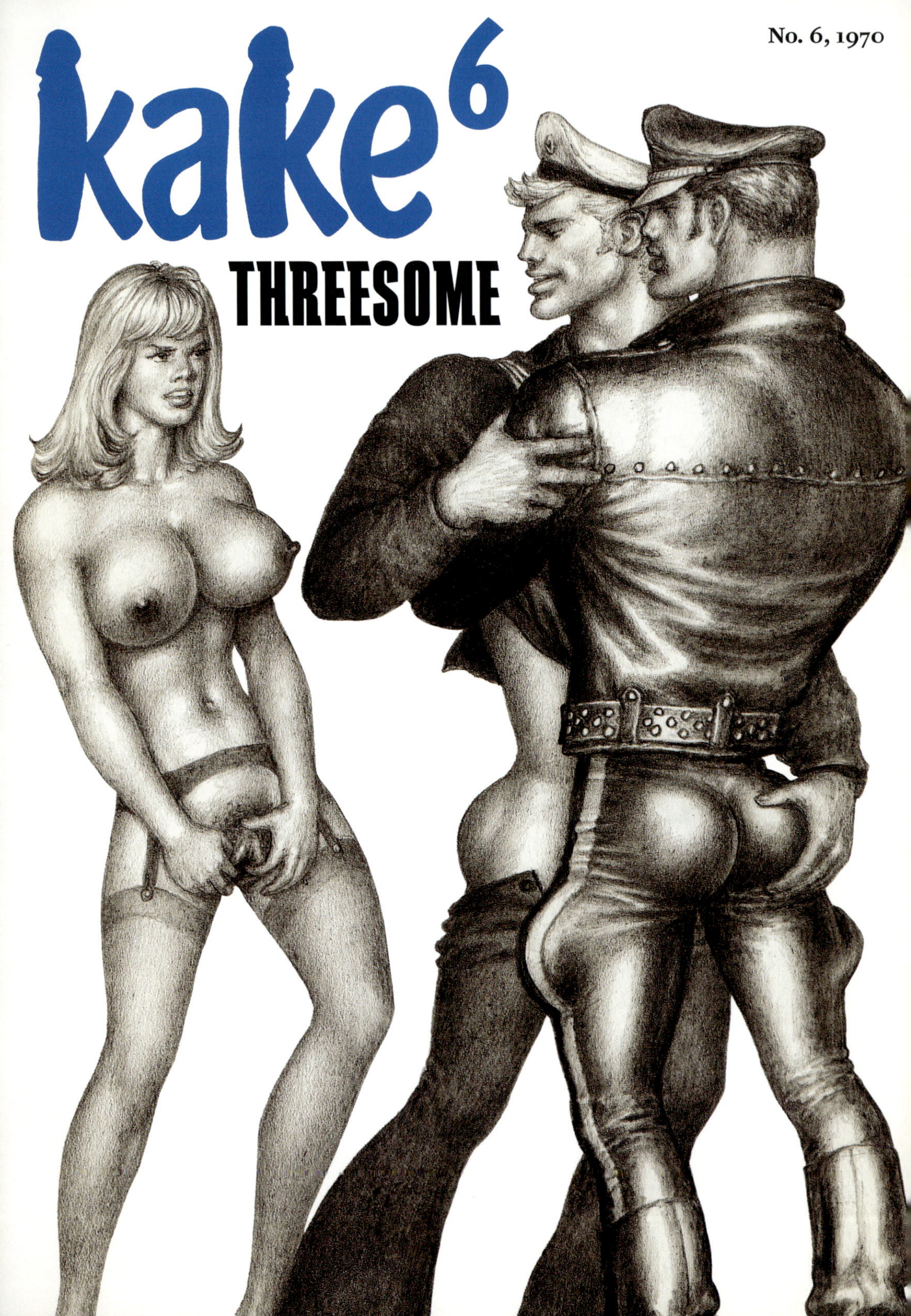

No. 6, 1970
kake 6
THREESOME

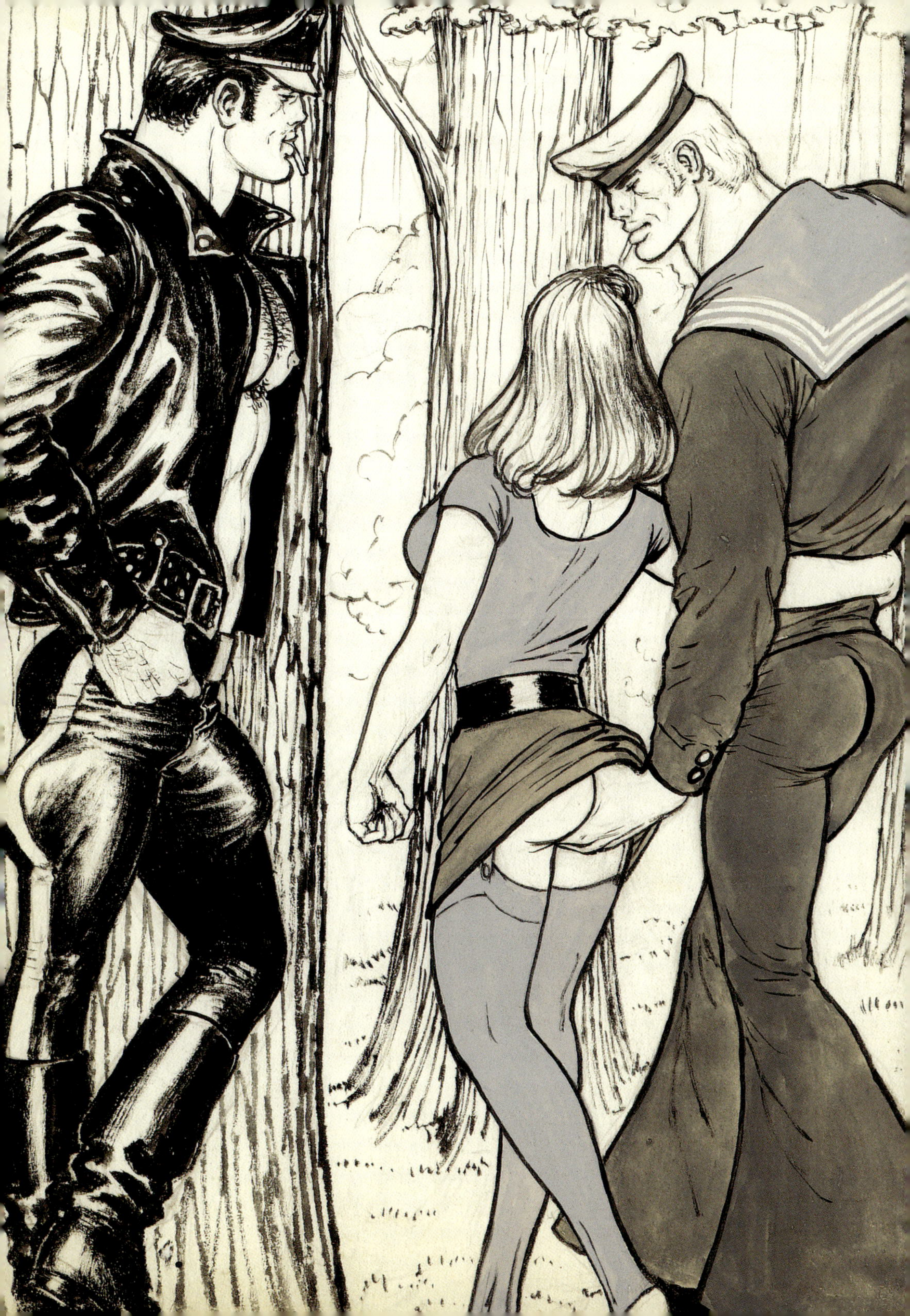

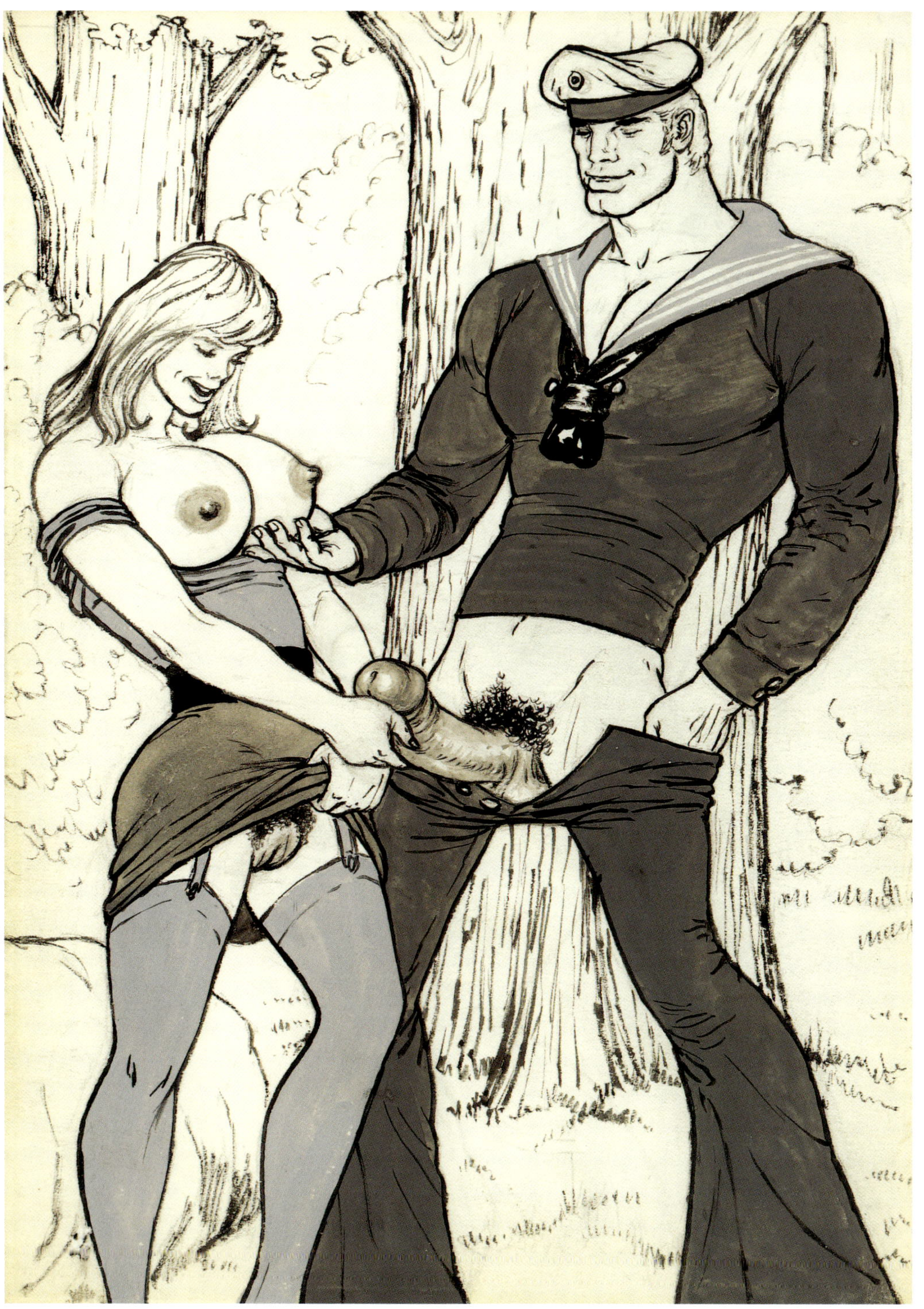

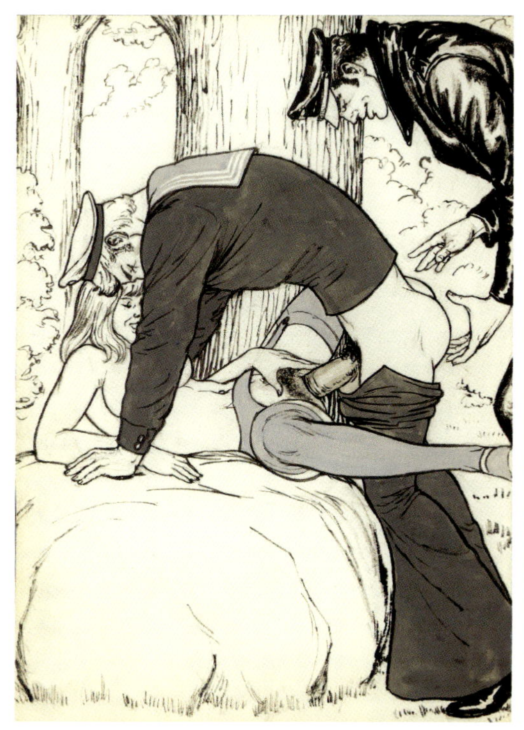

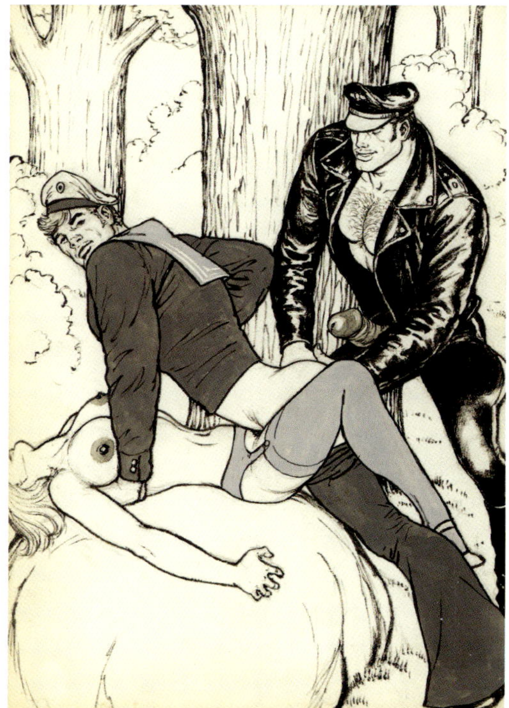

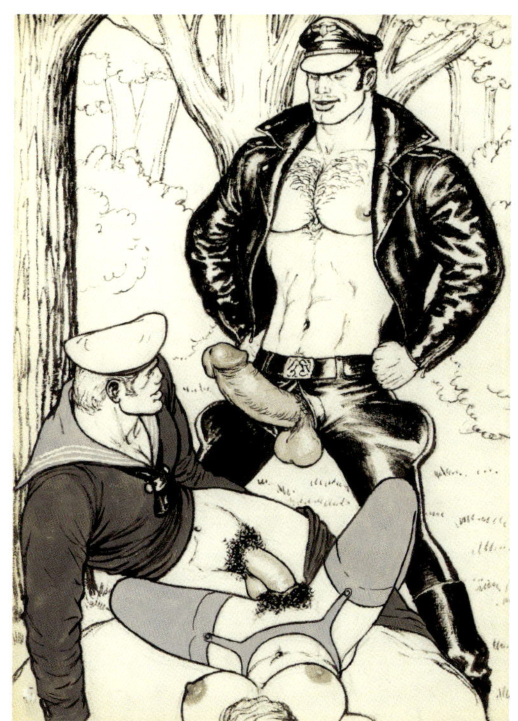

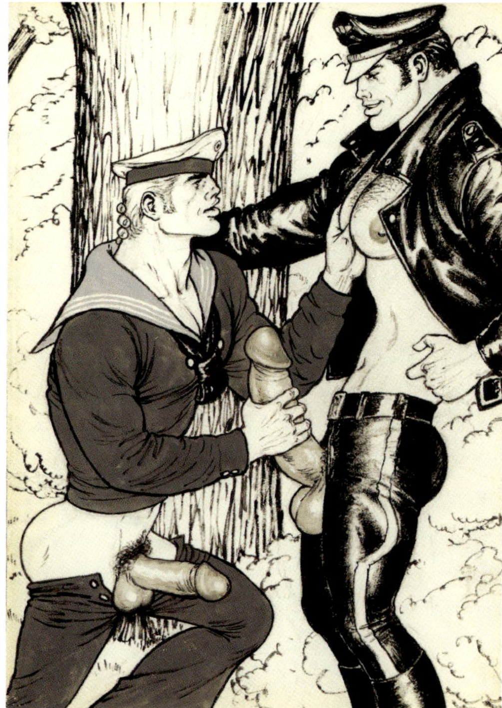

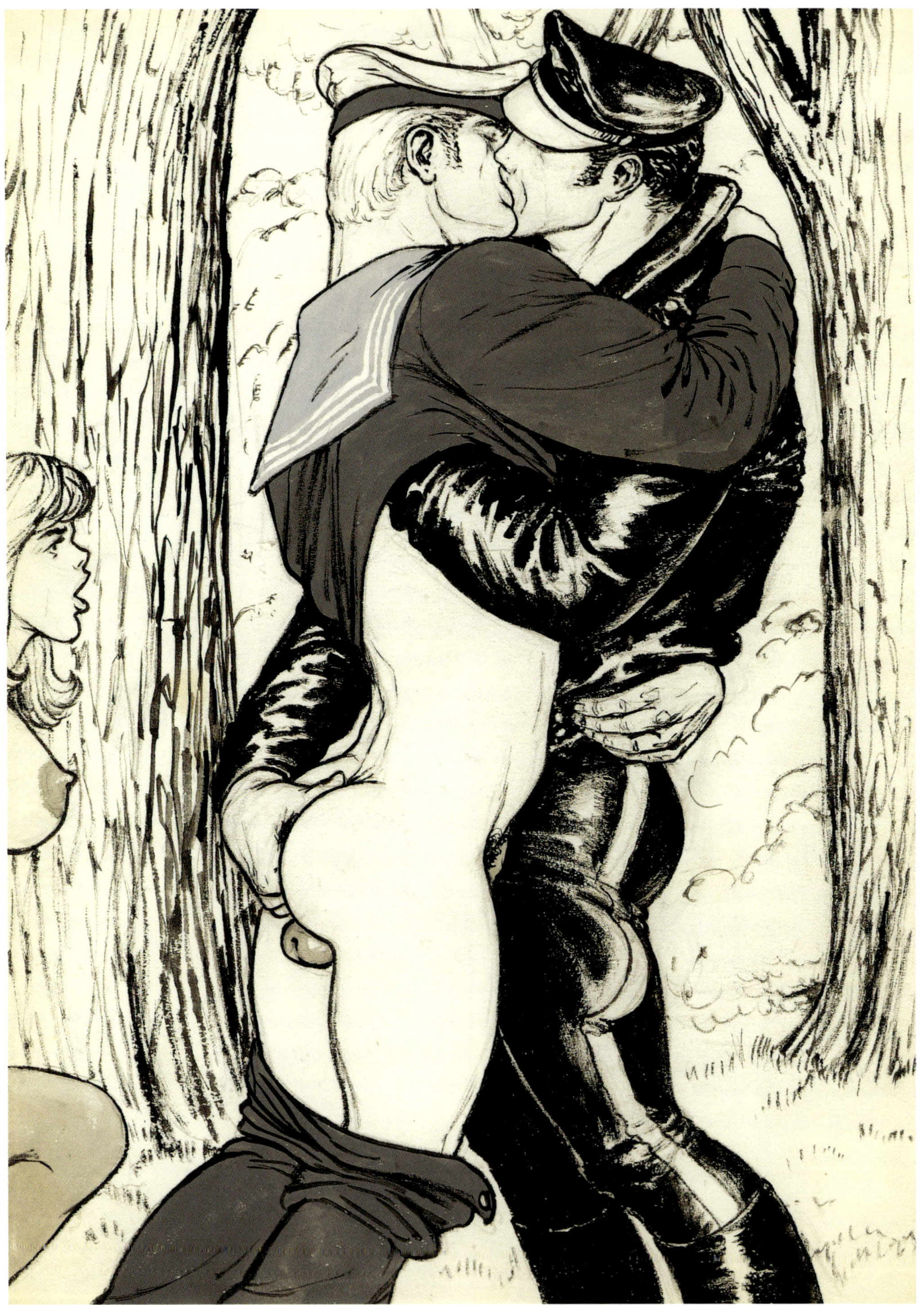

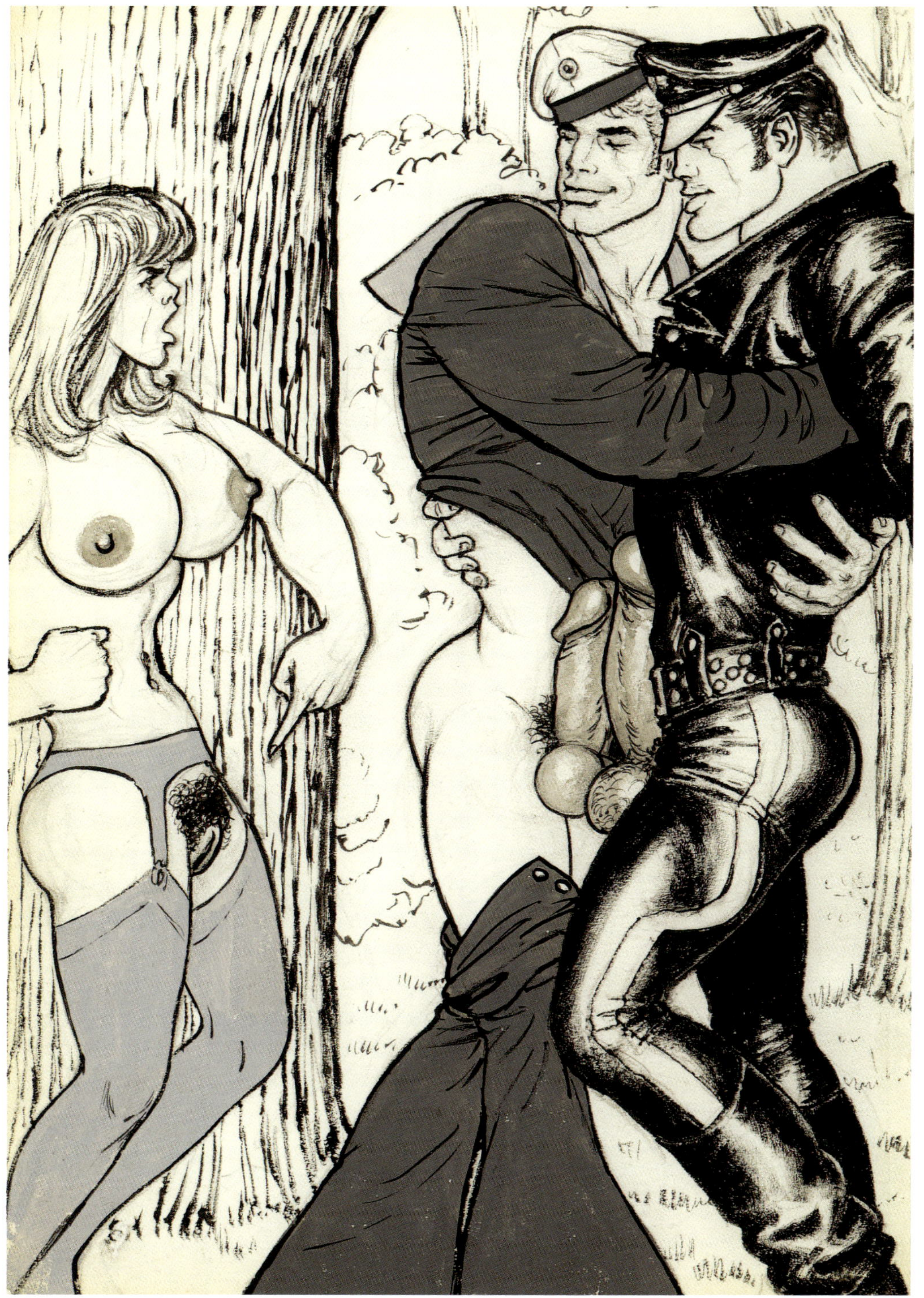

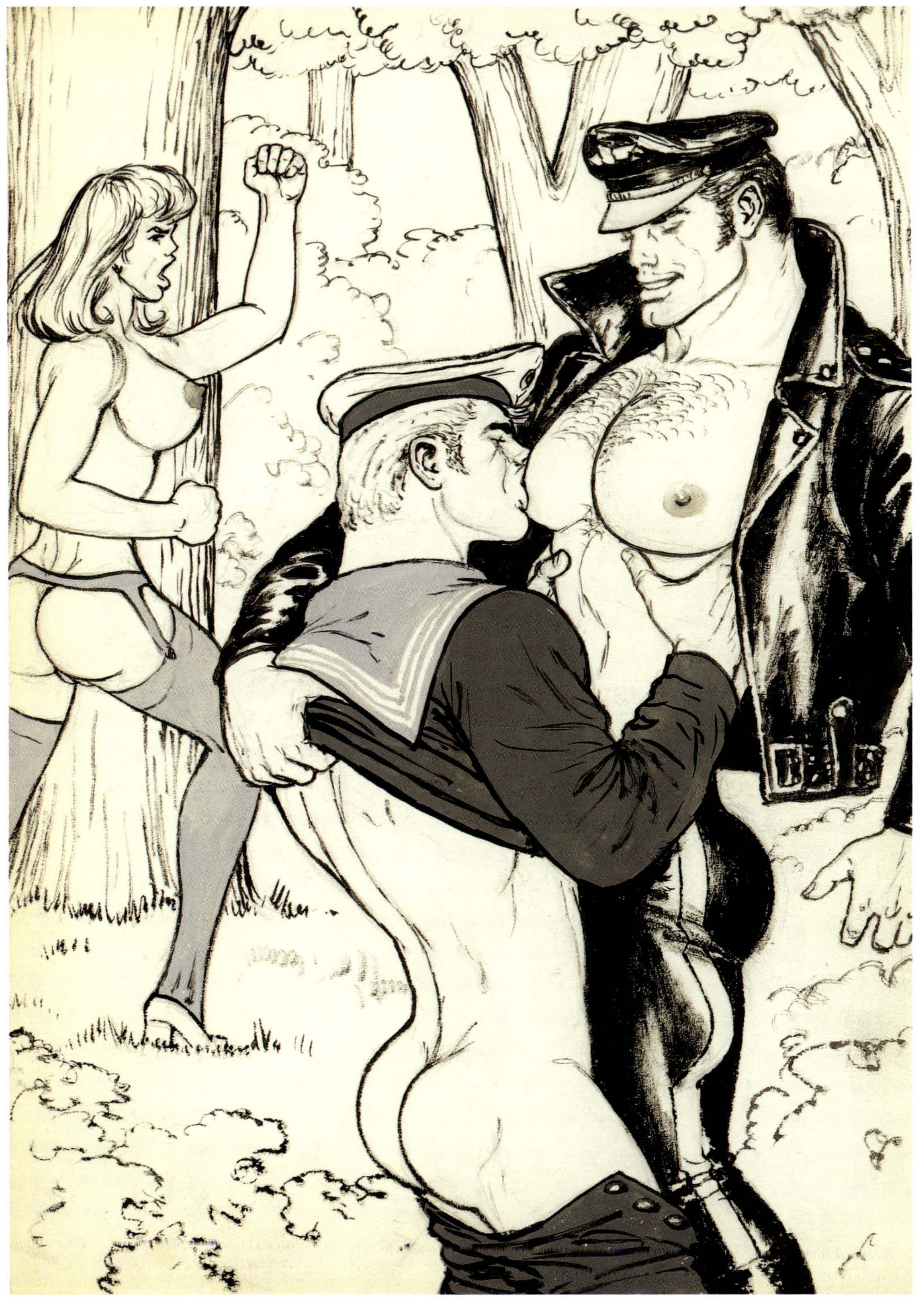

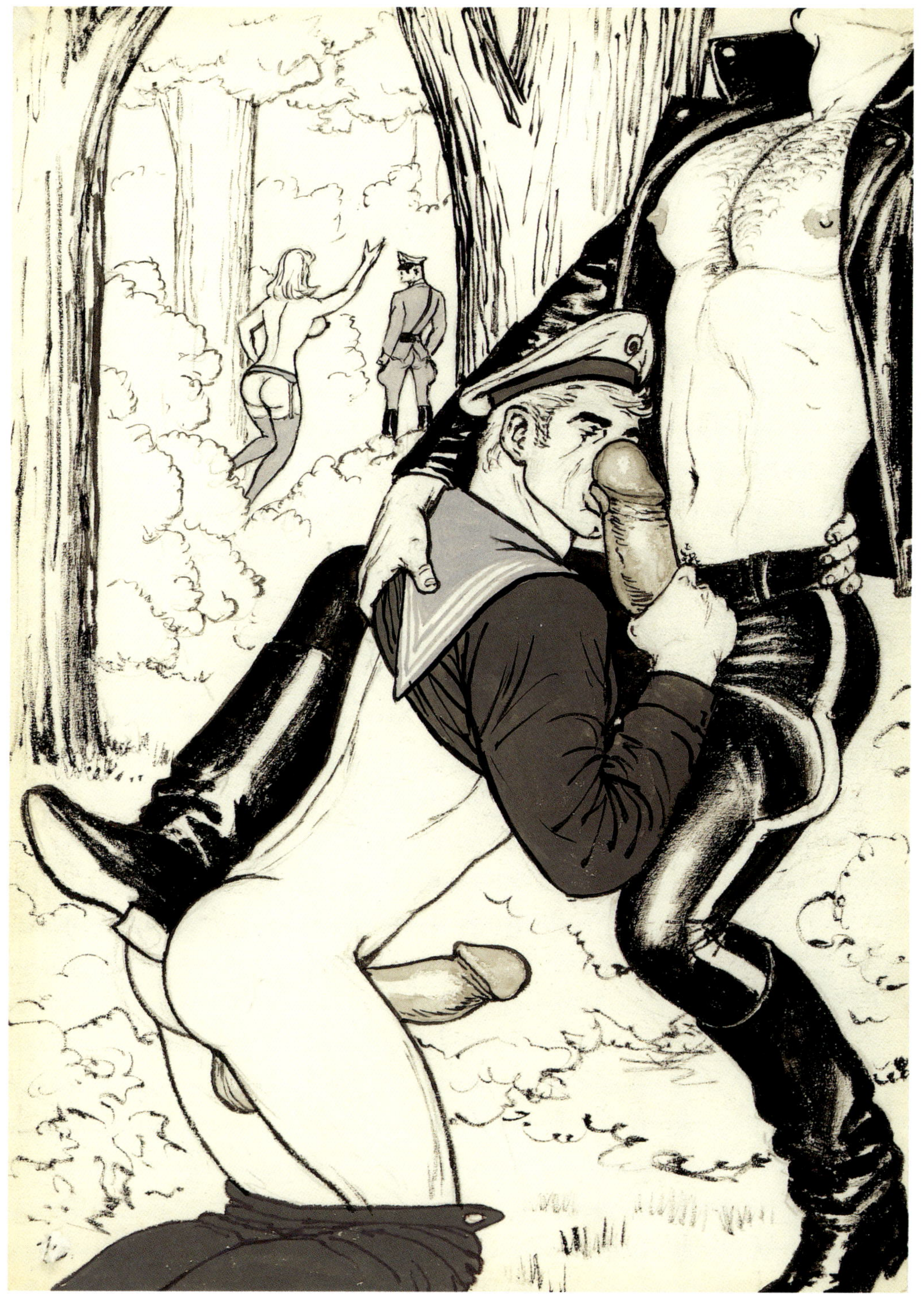

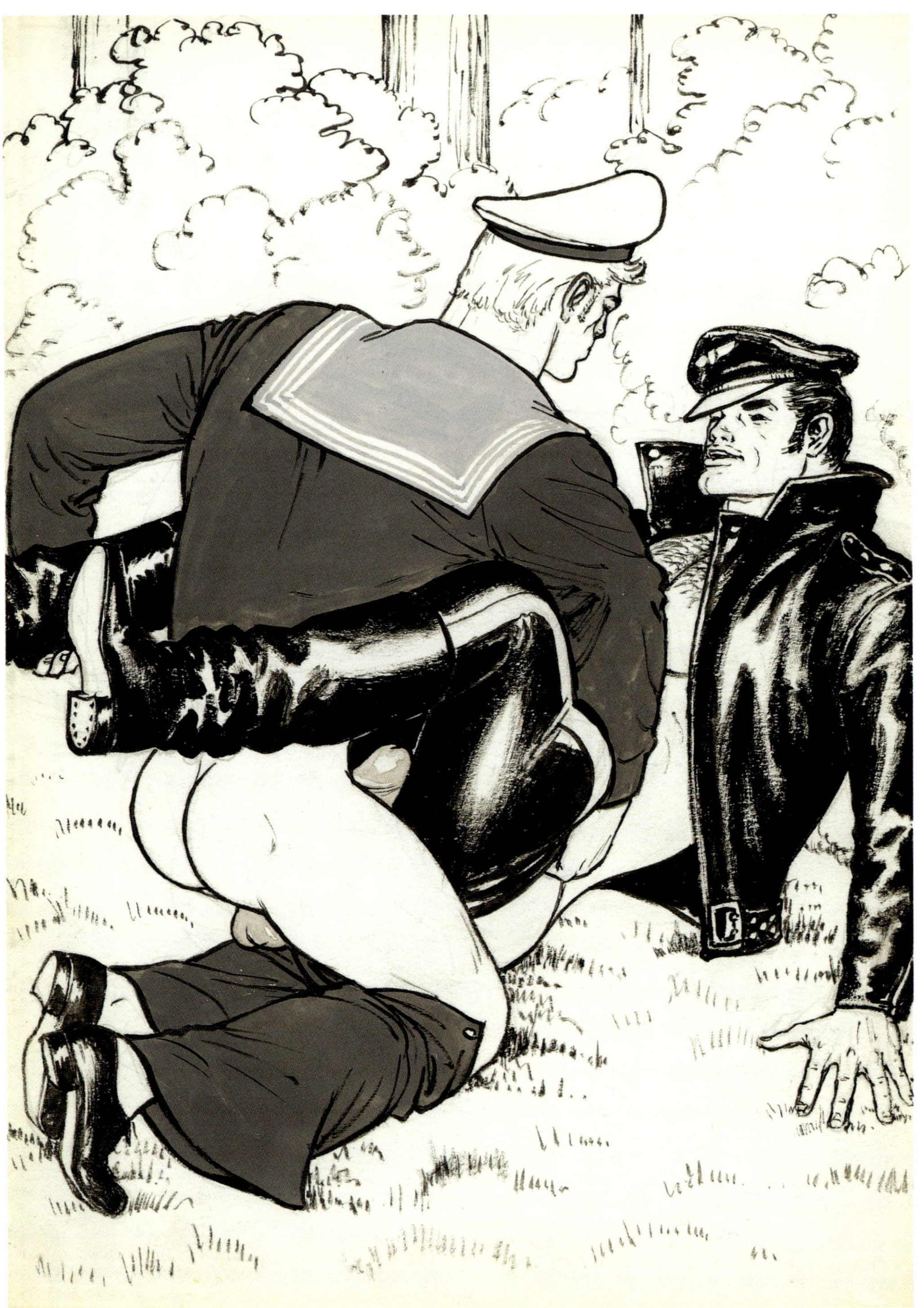

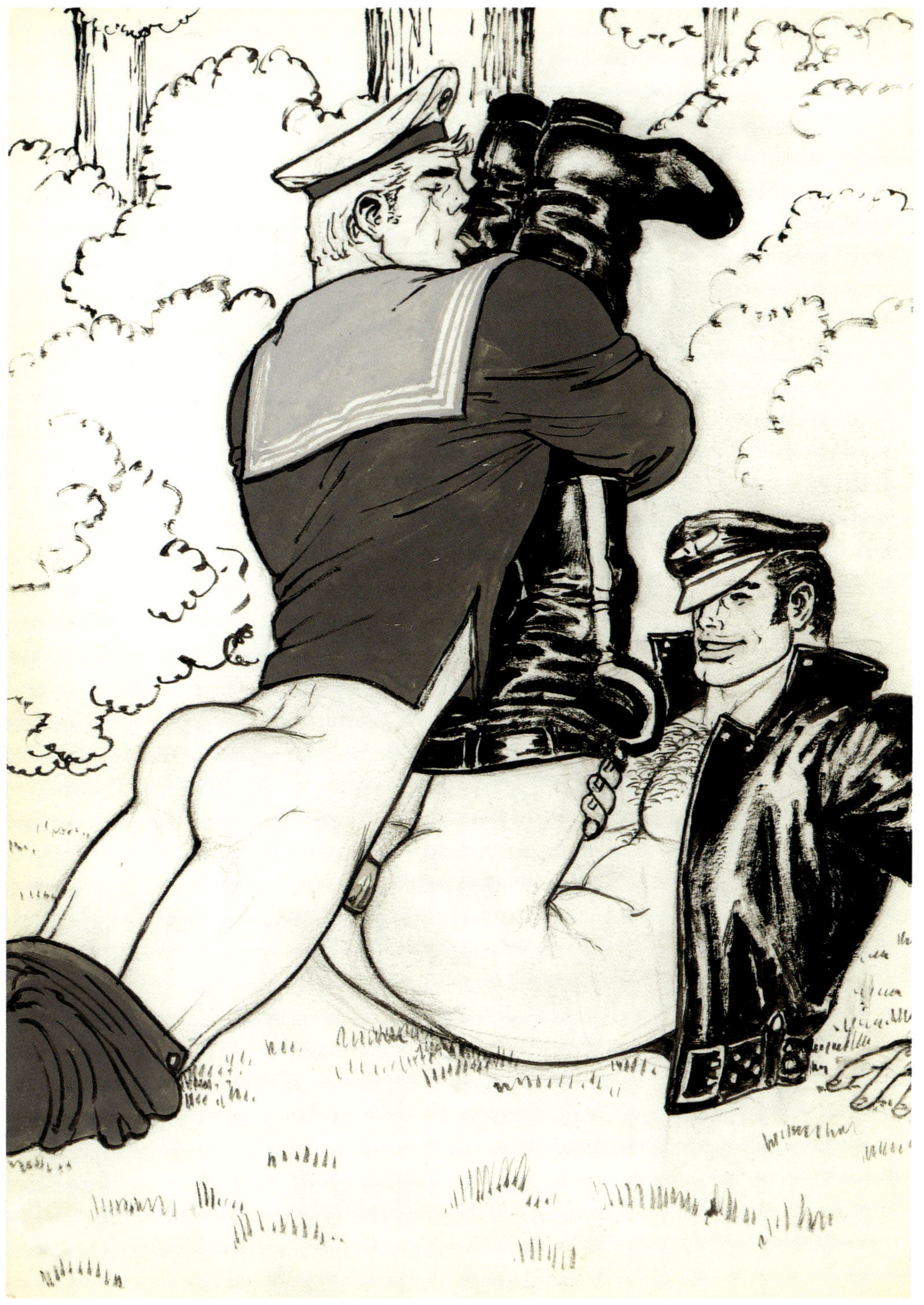

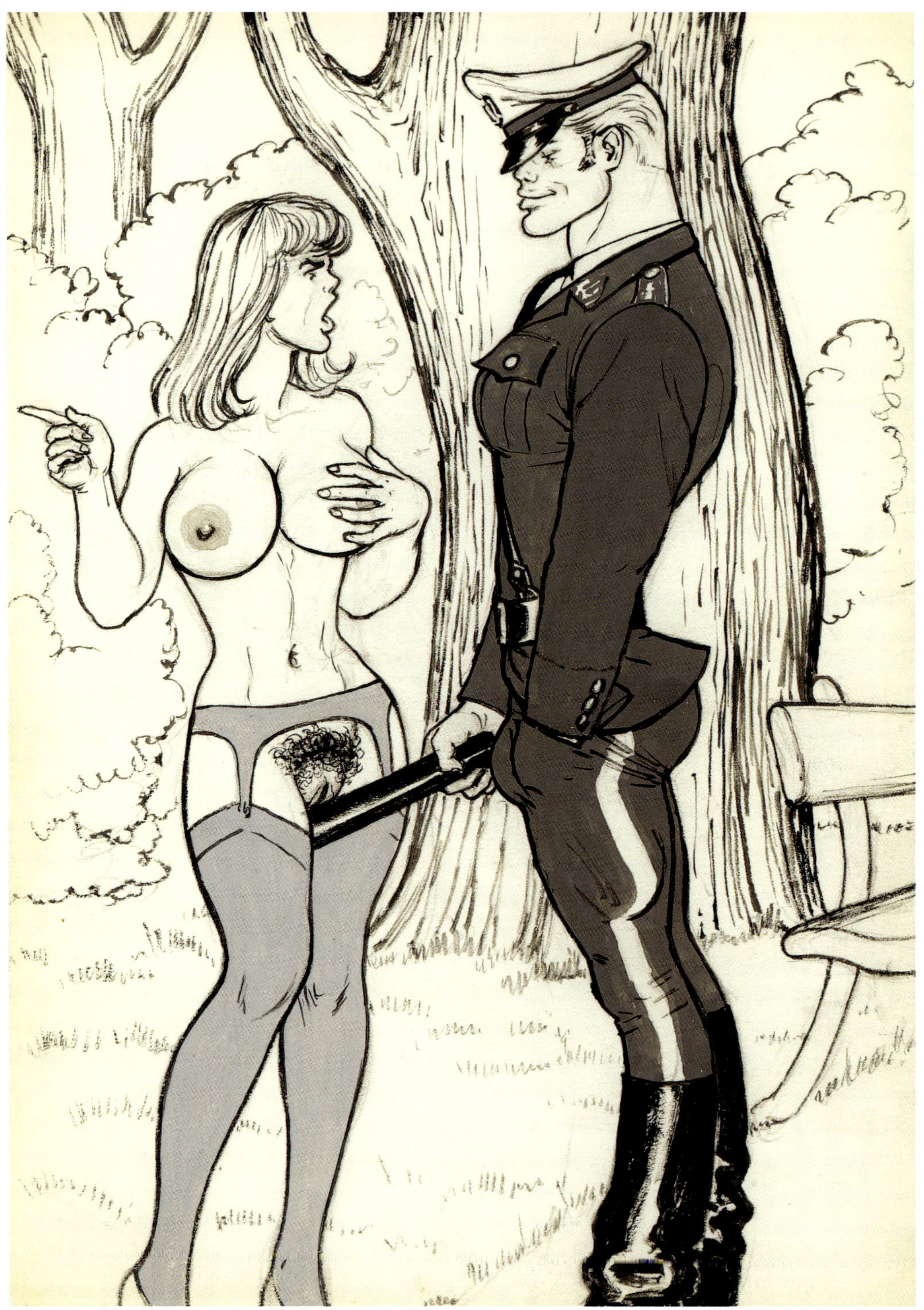

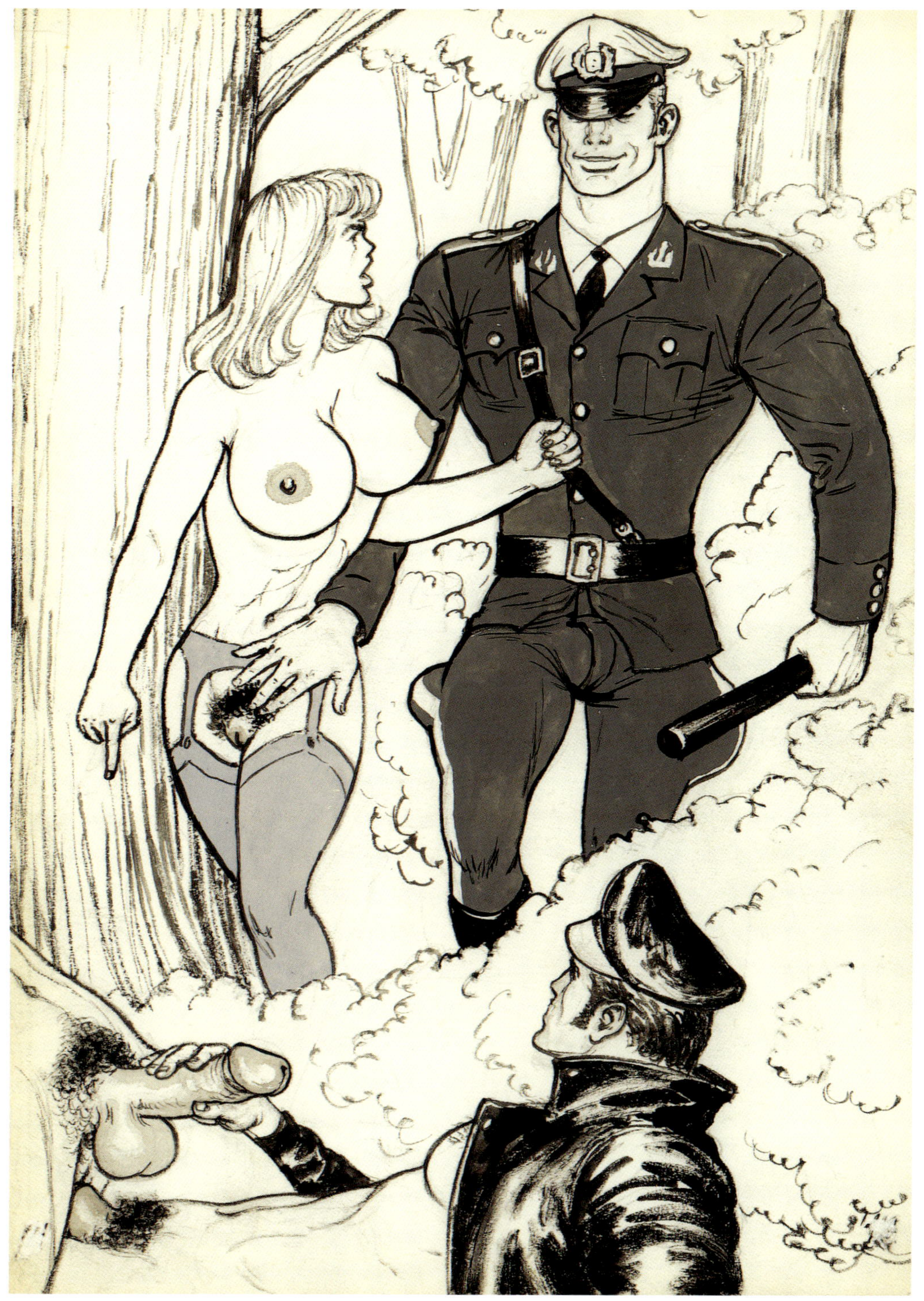

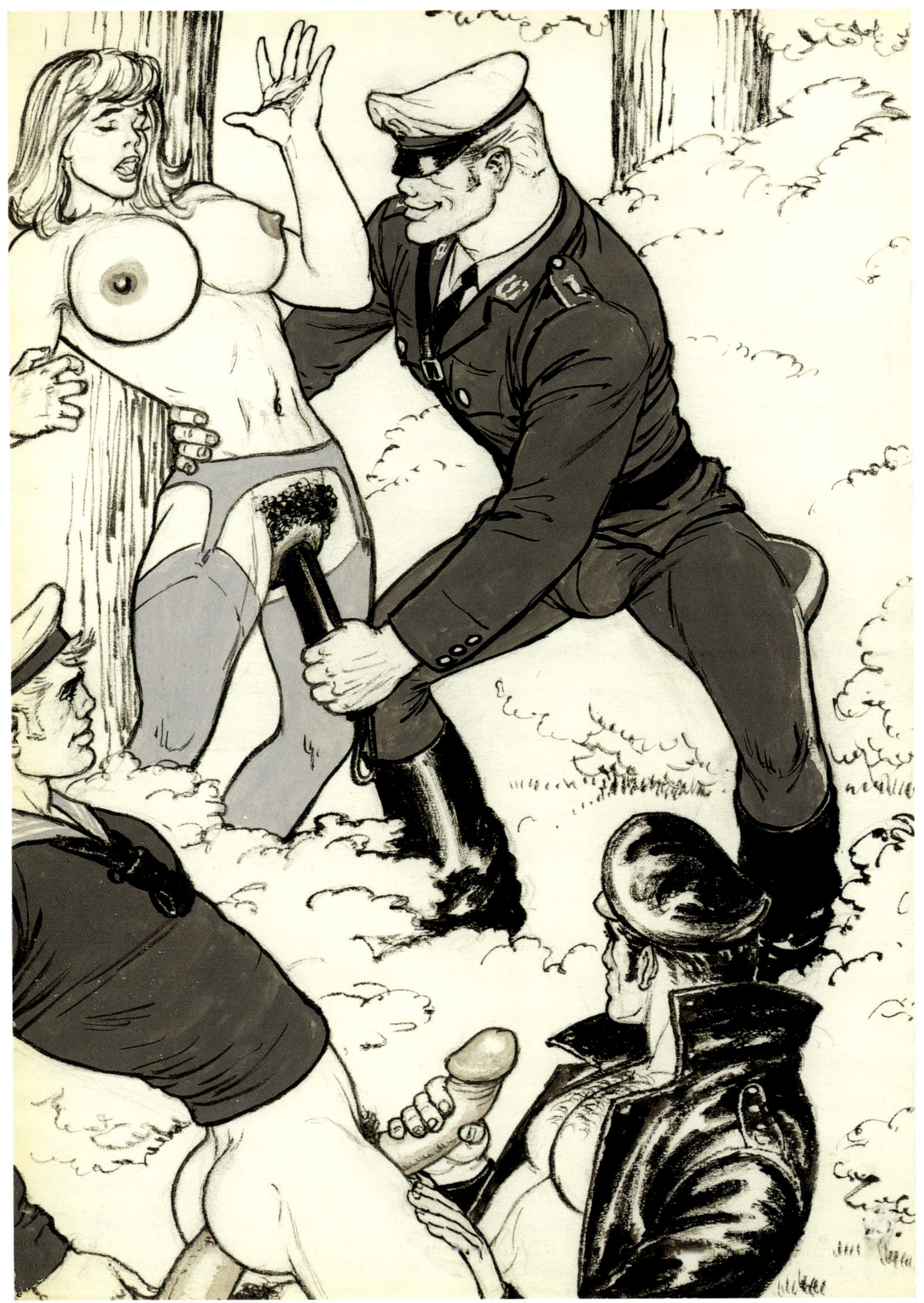

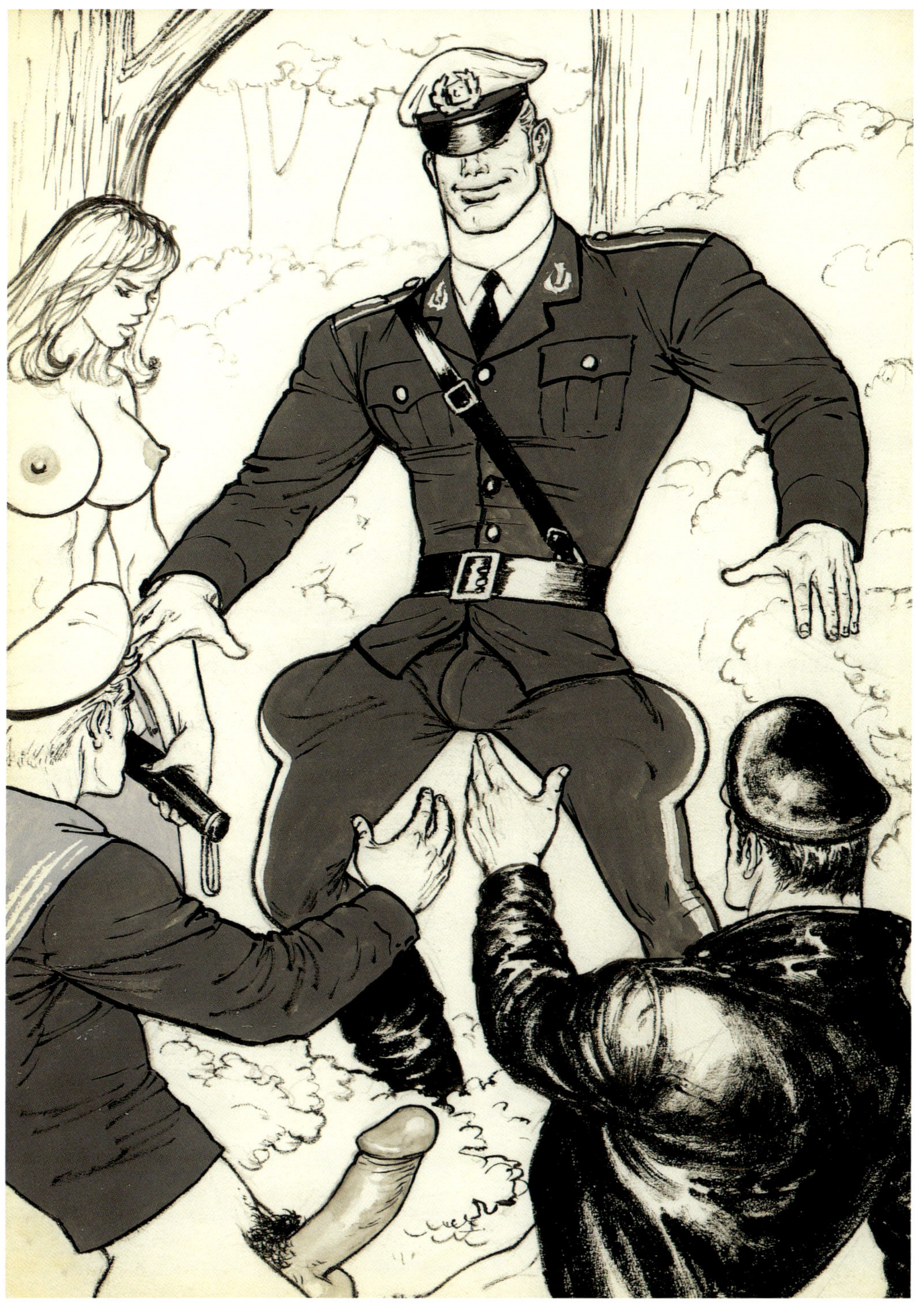

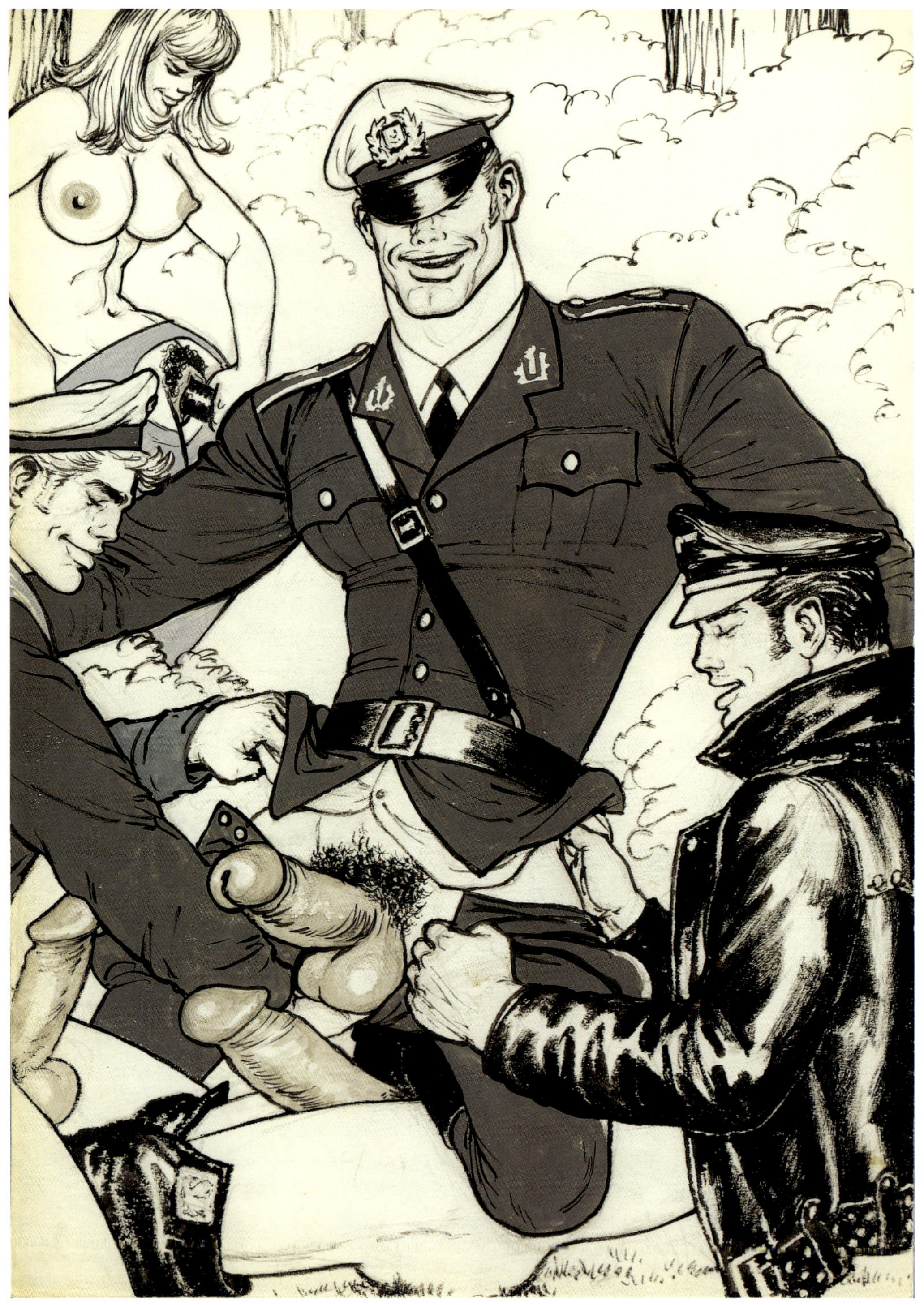

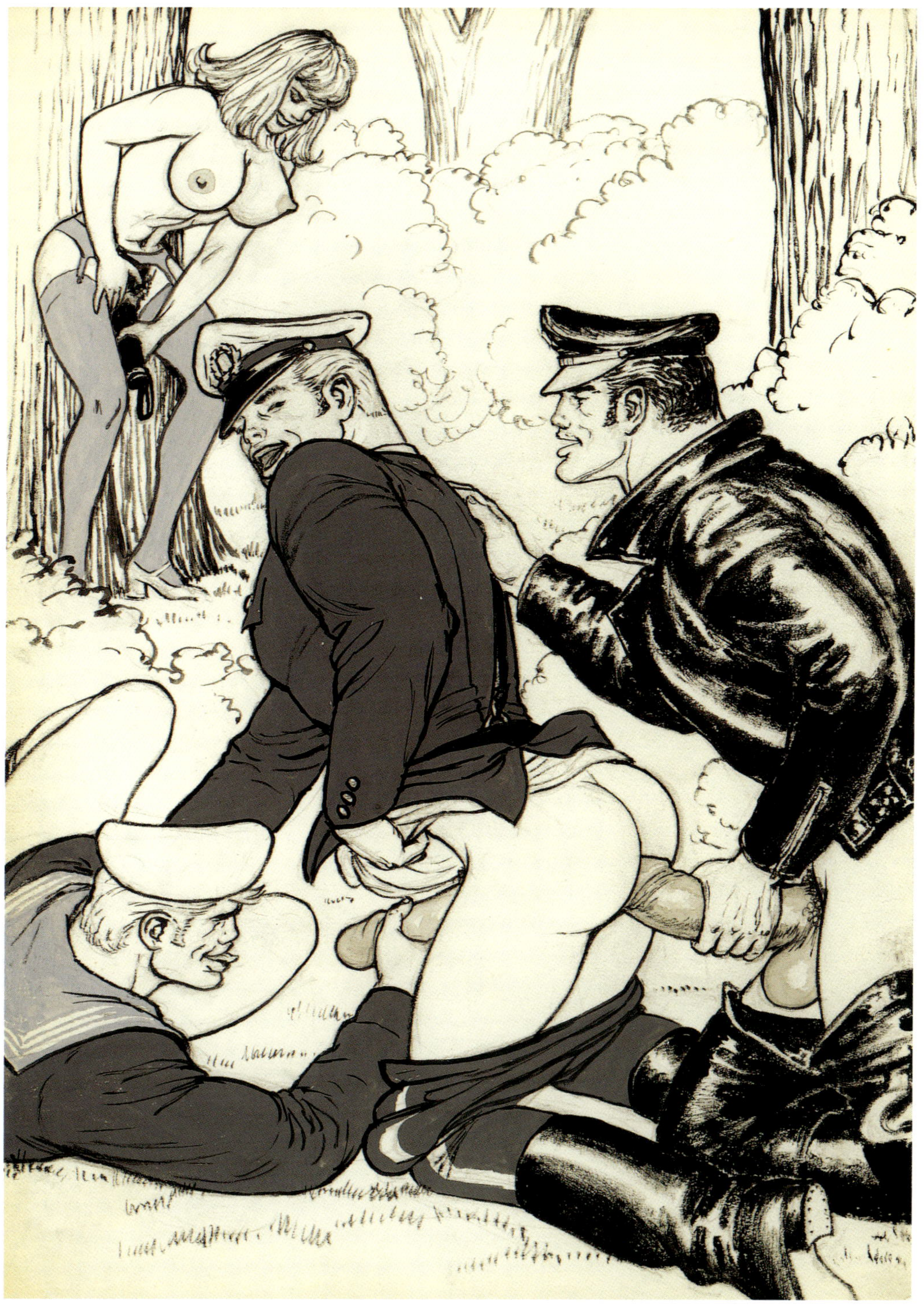

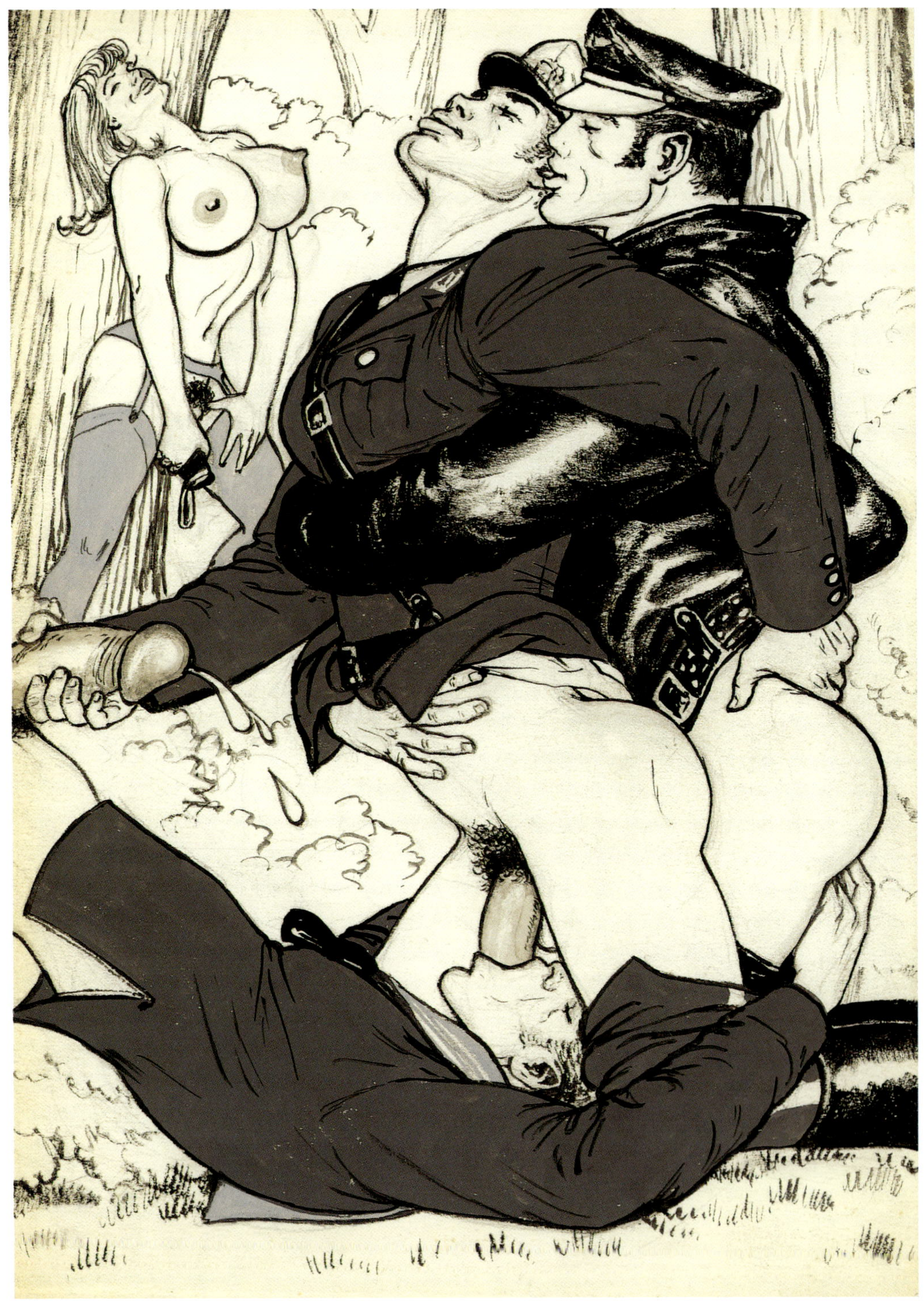

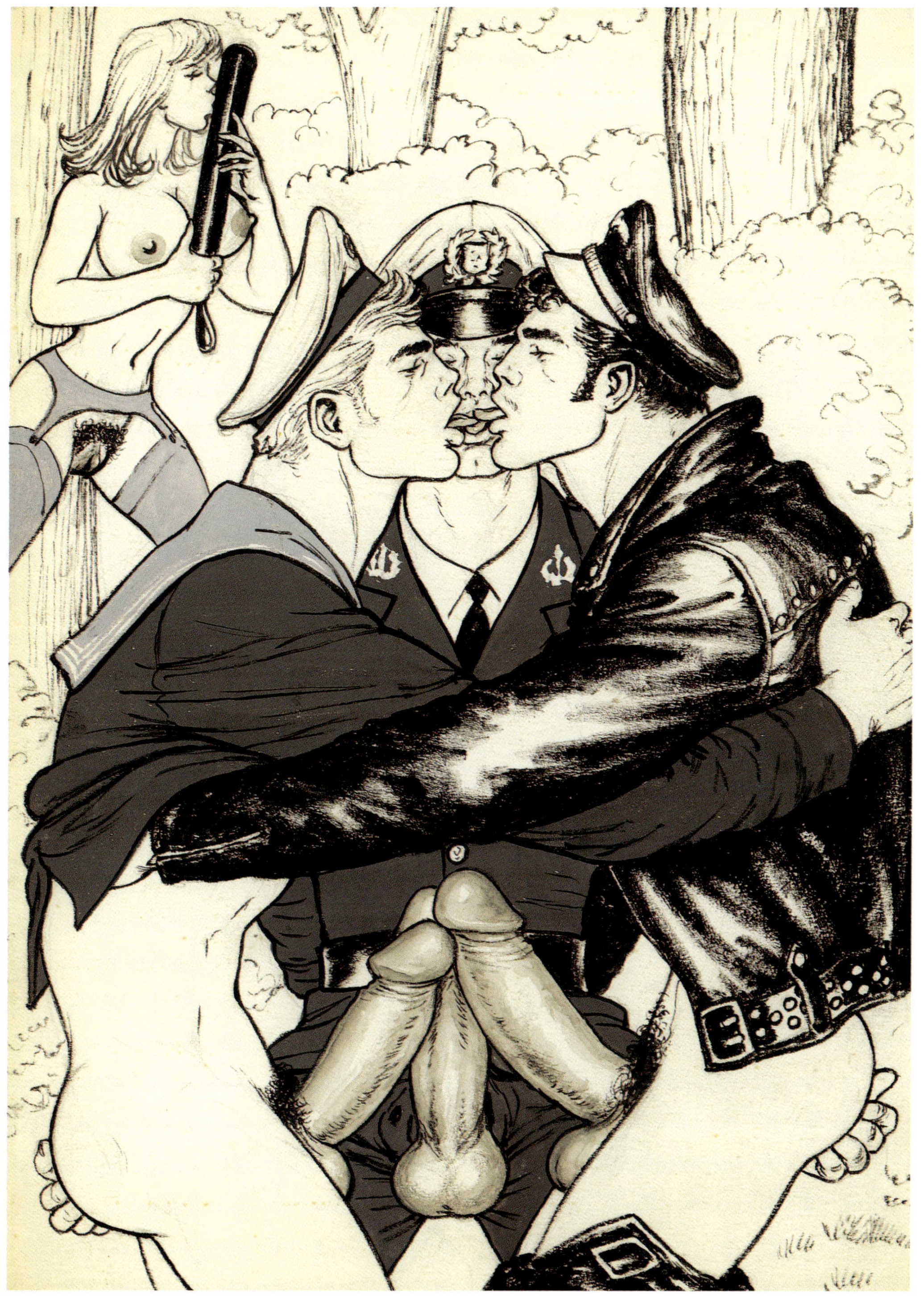

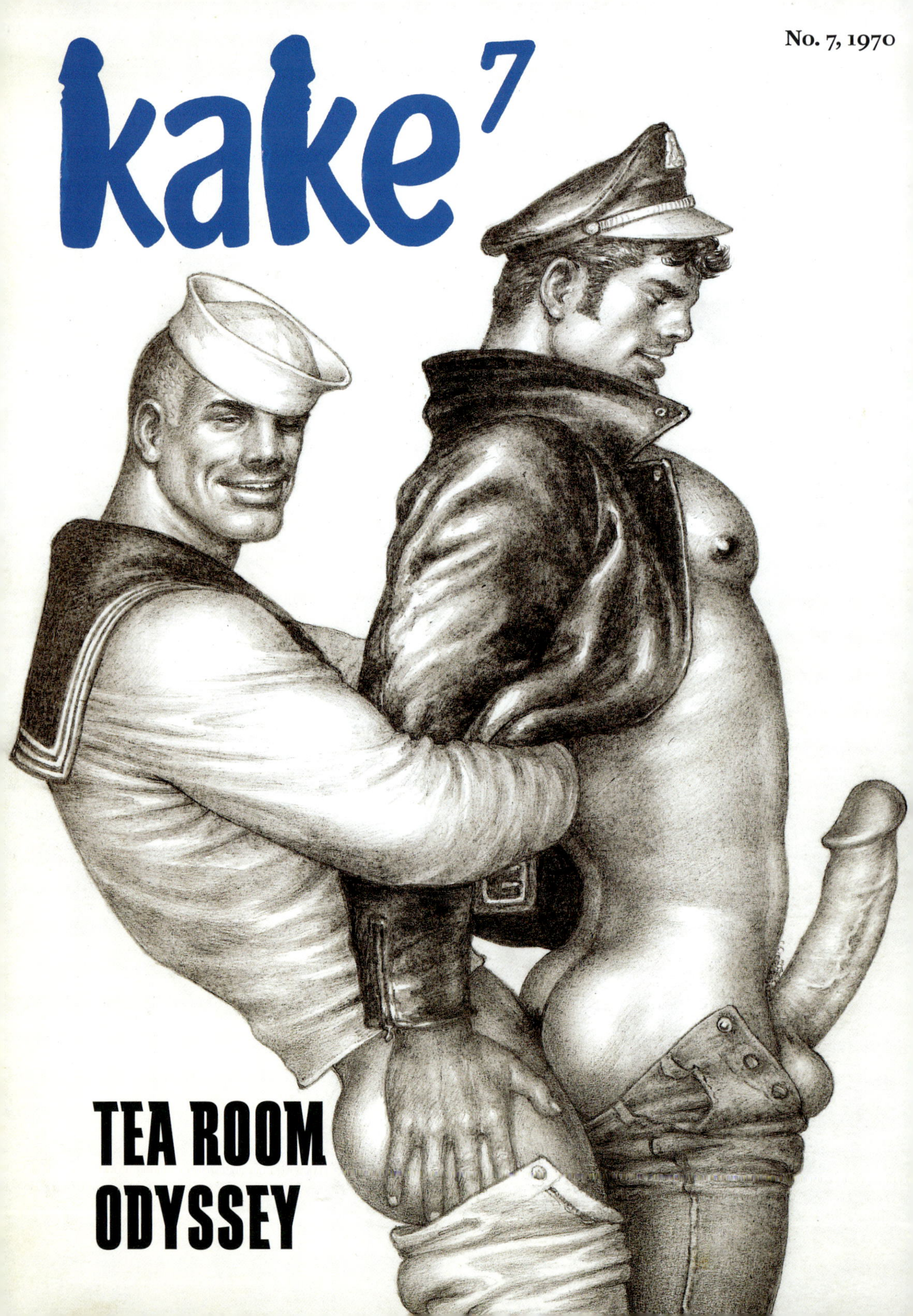
No. 7, 1970
kake 7
TEA ROOM
ODYSSEY

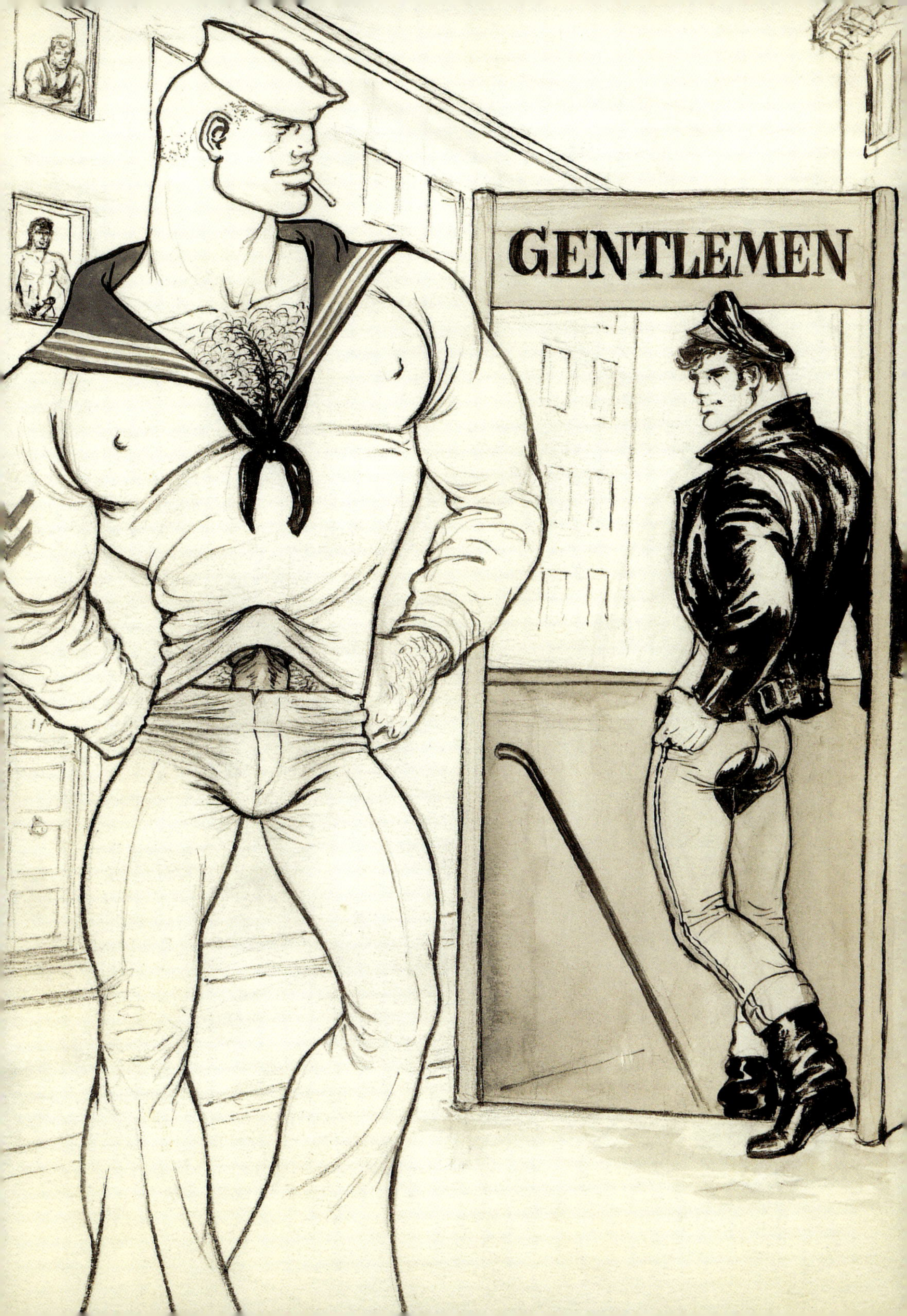

GENTLEMEN

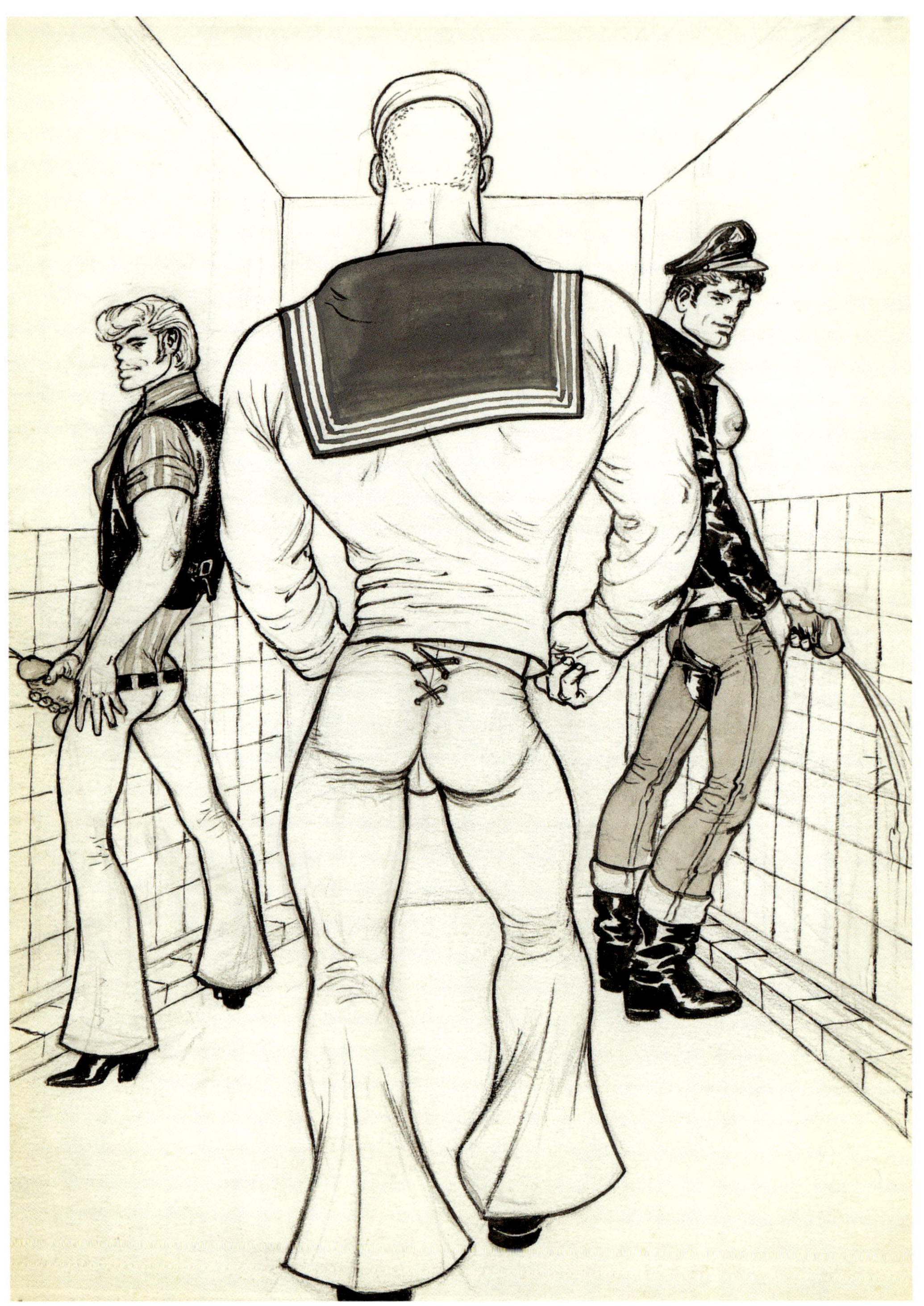

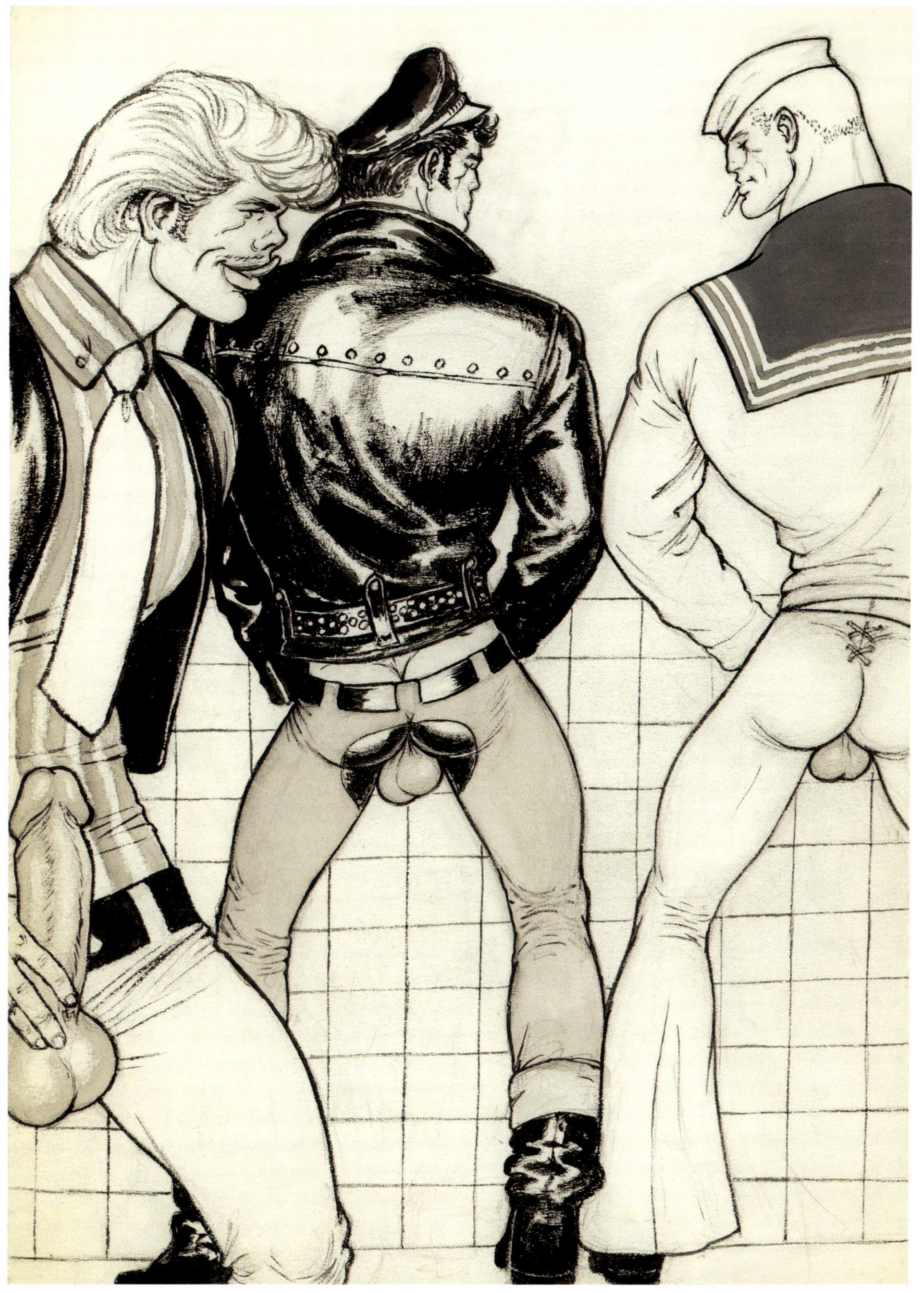

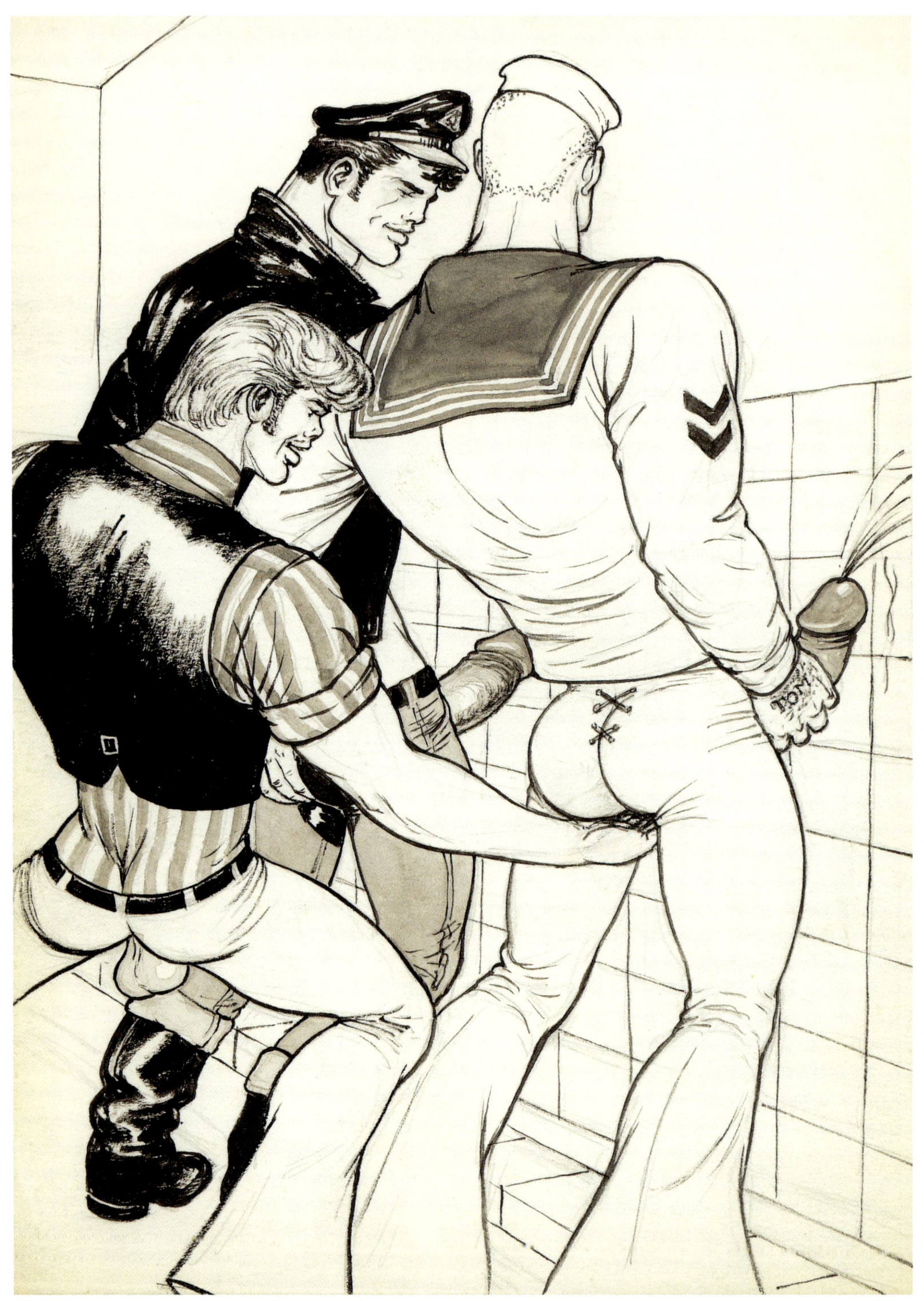

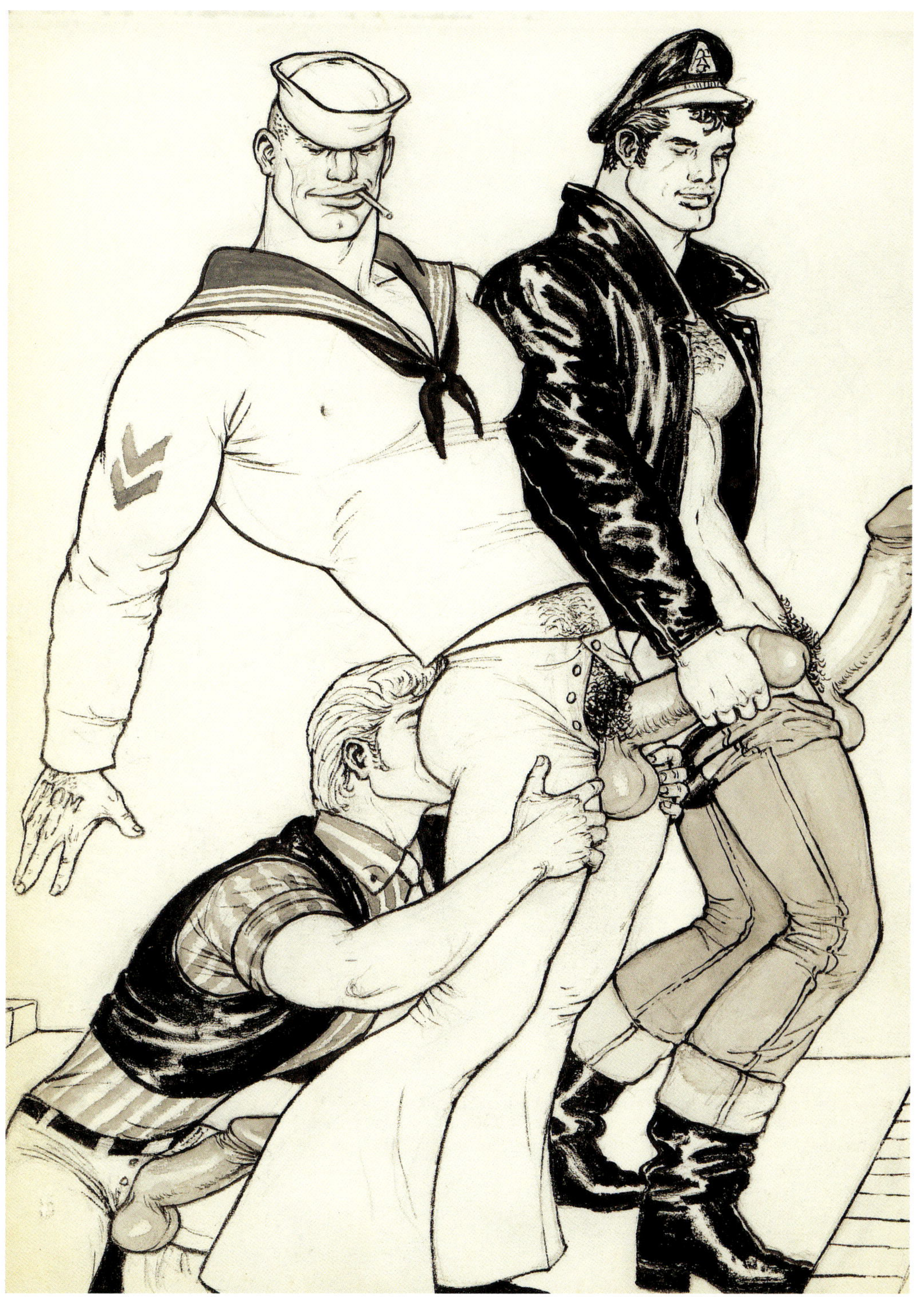

TOM

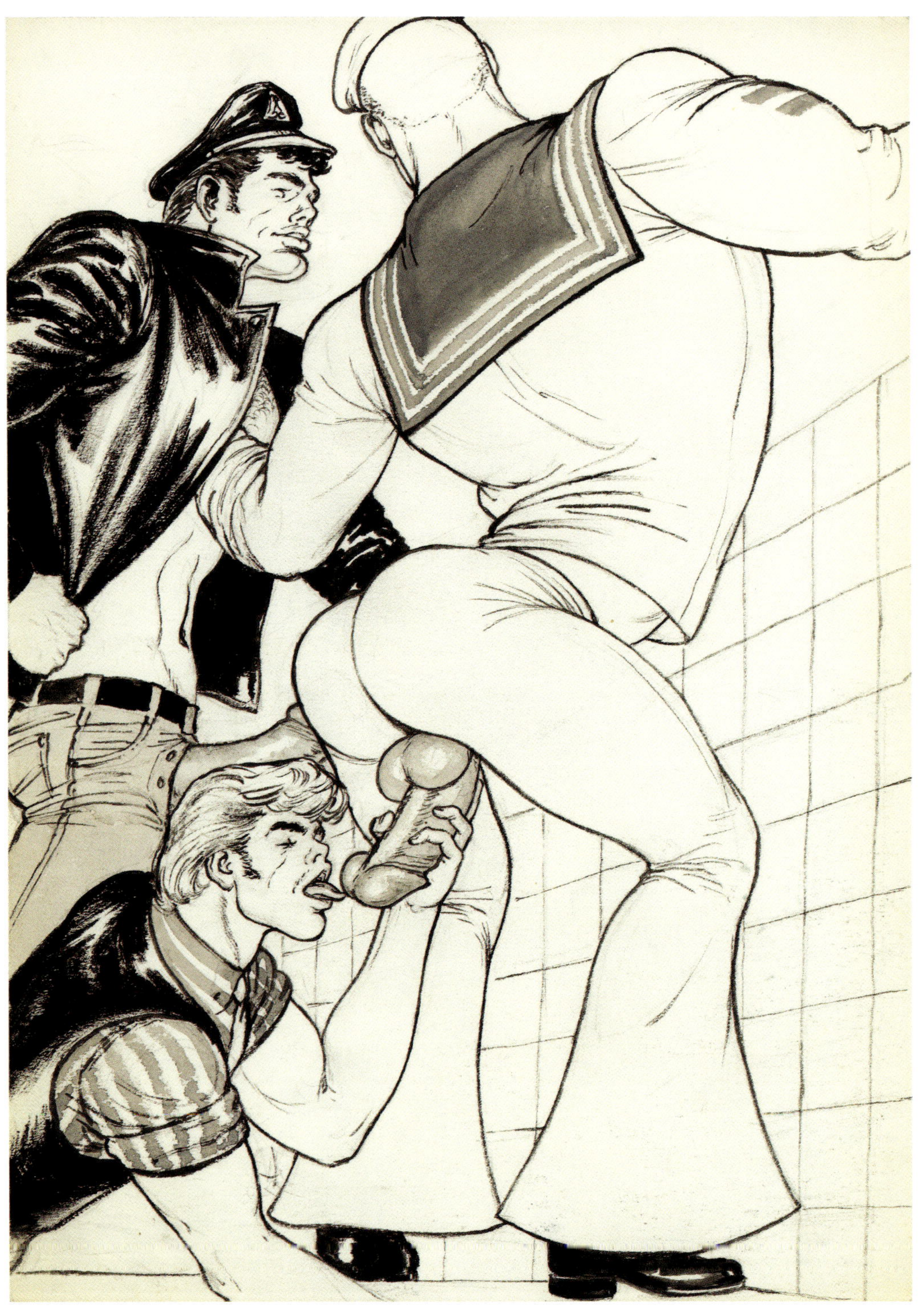

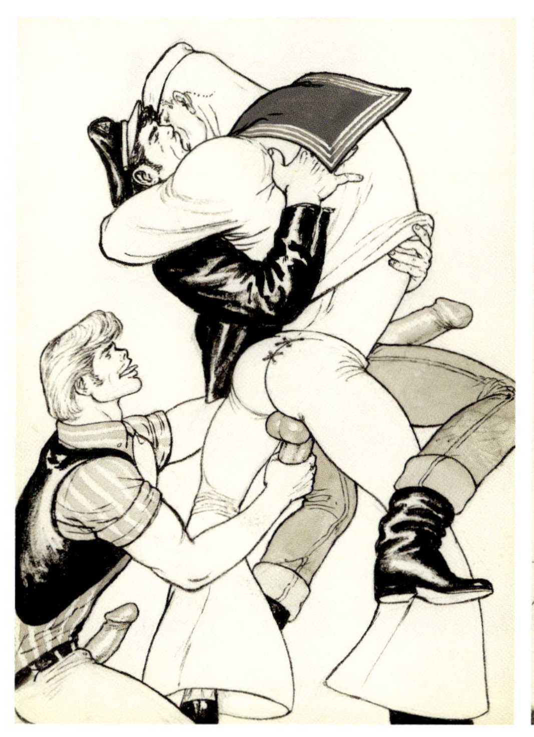
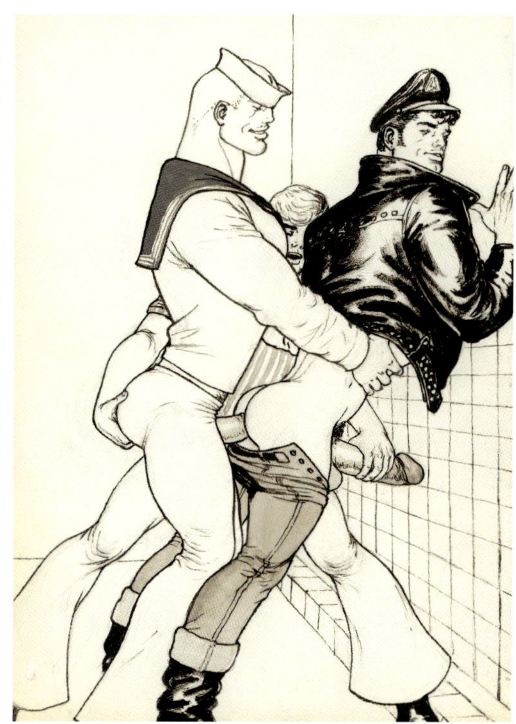
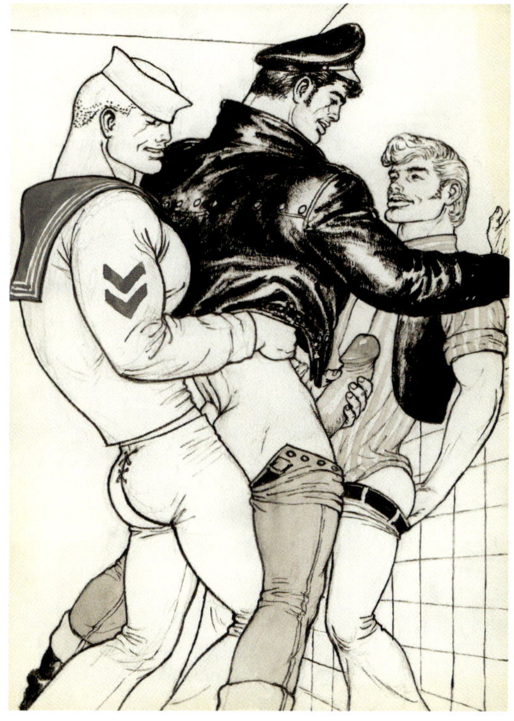
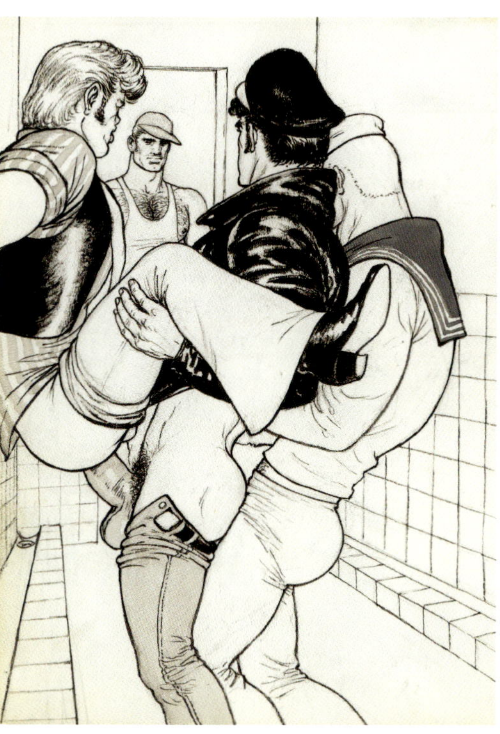

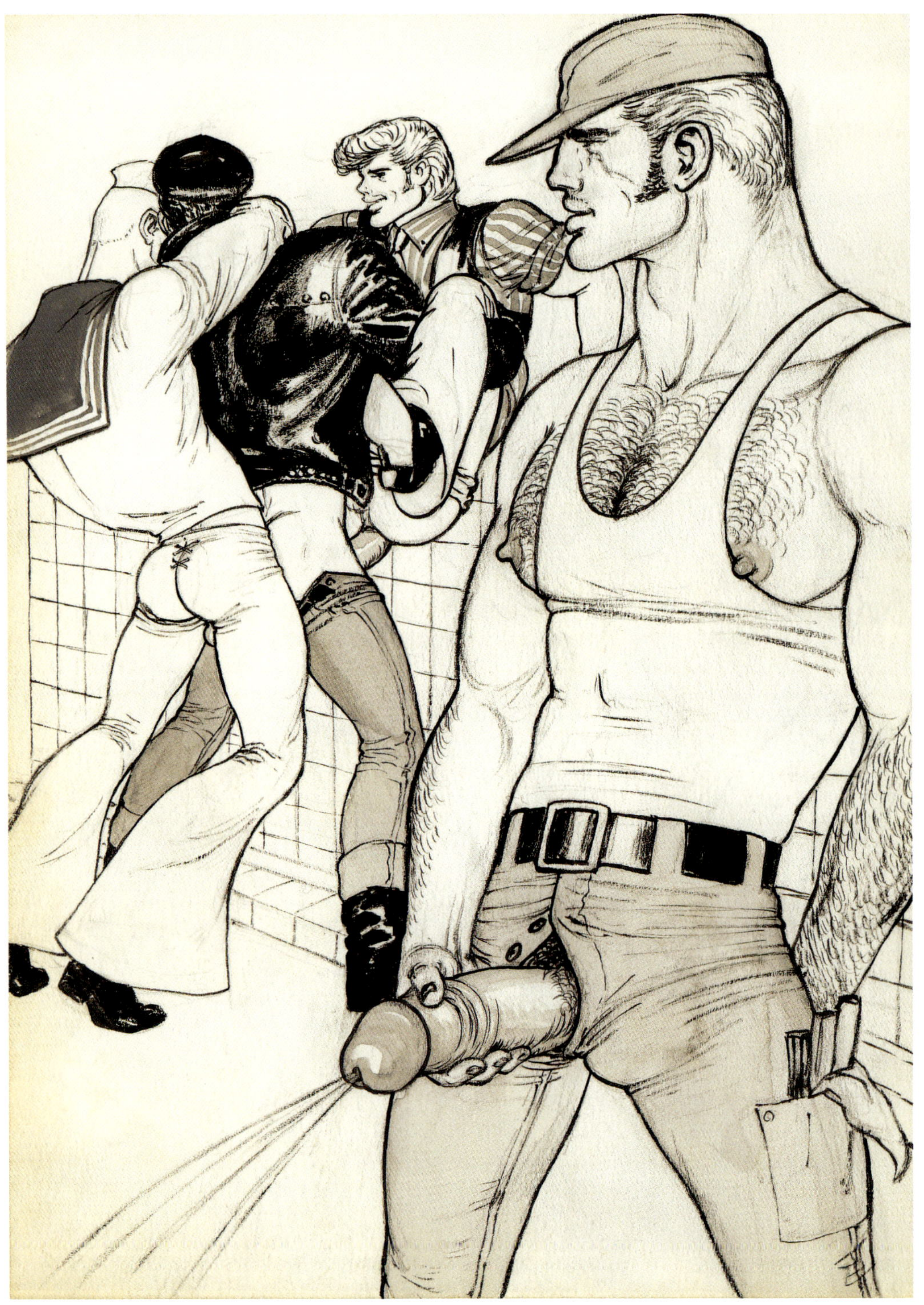

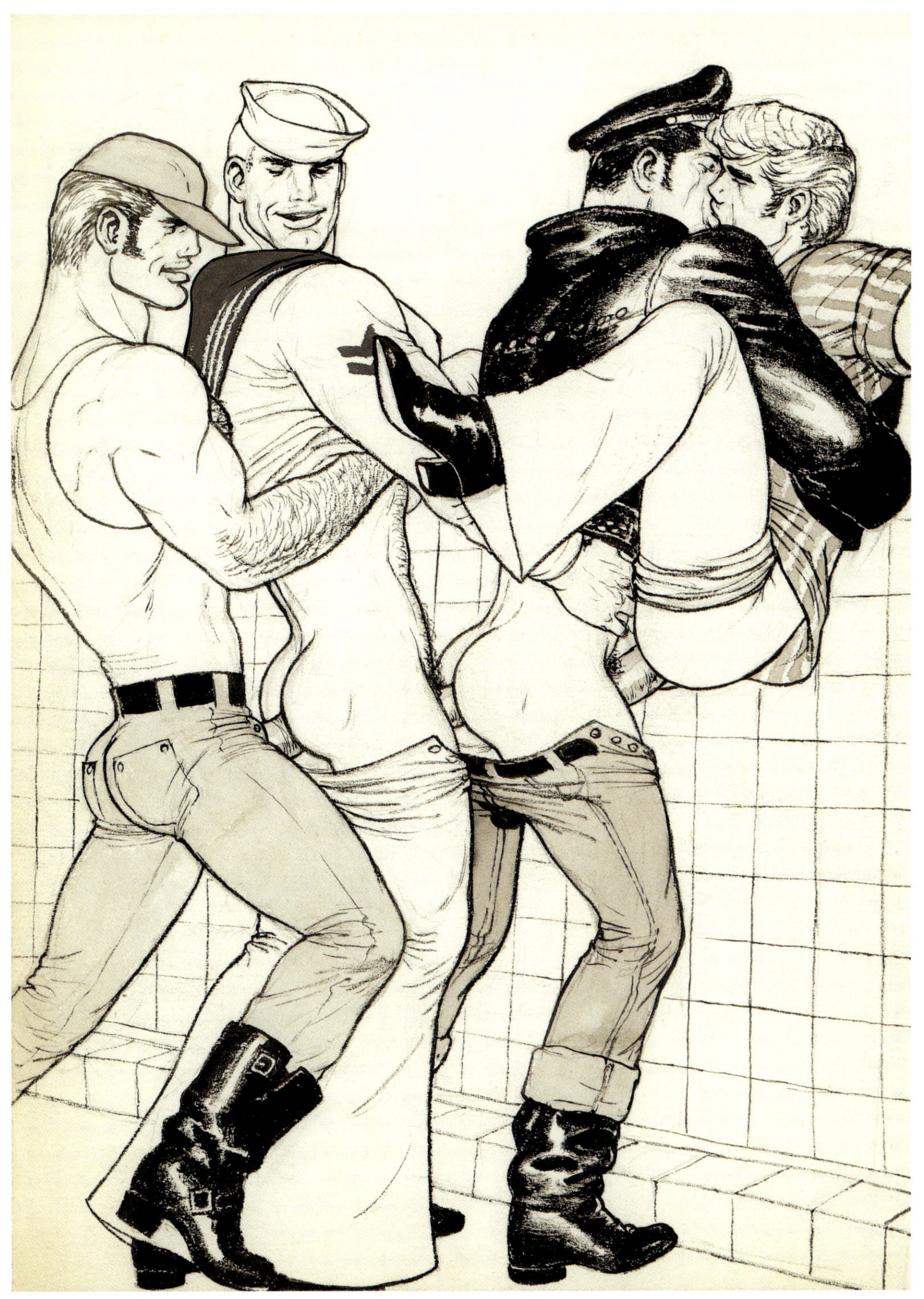

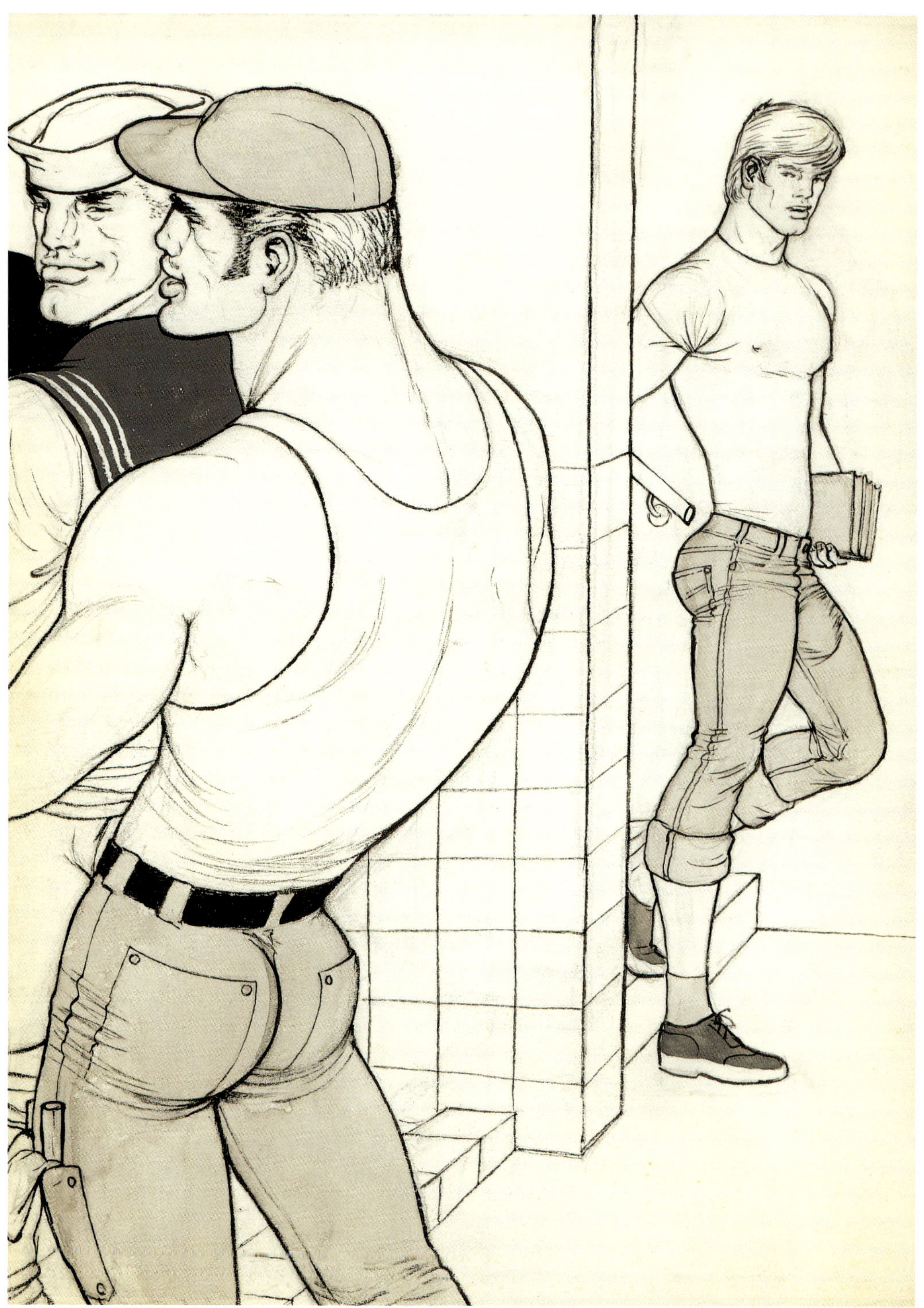

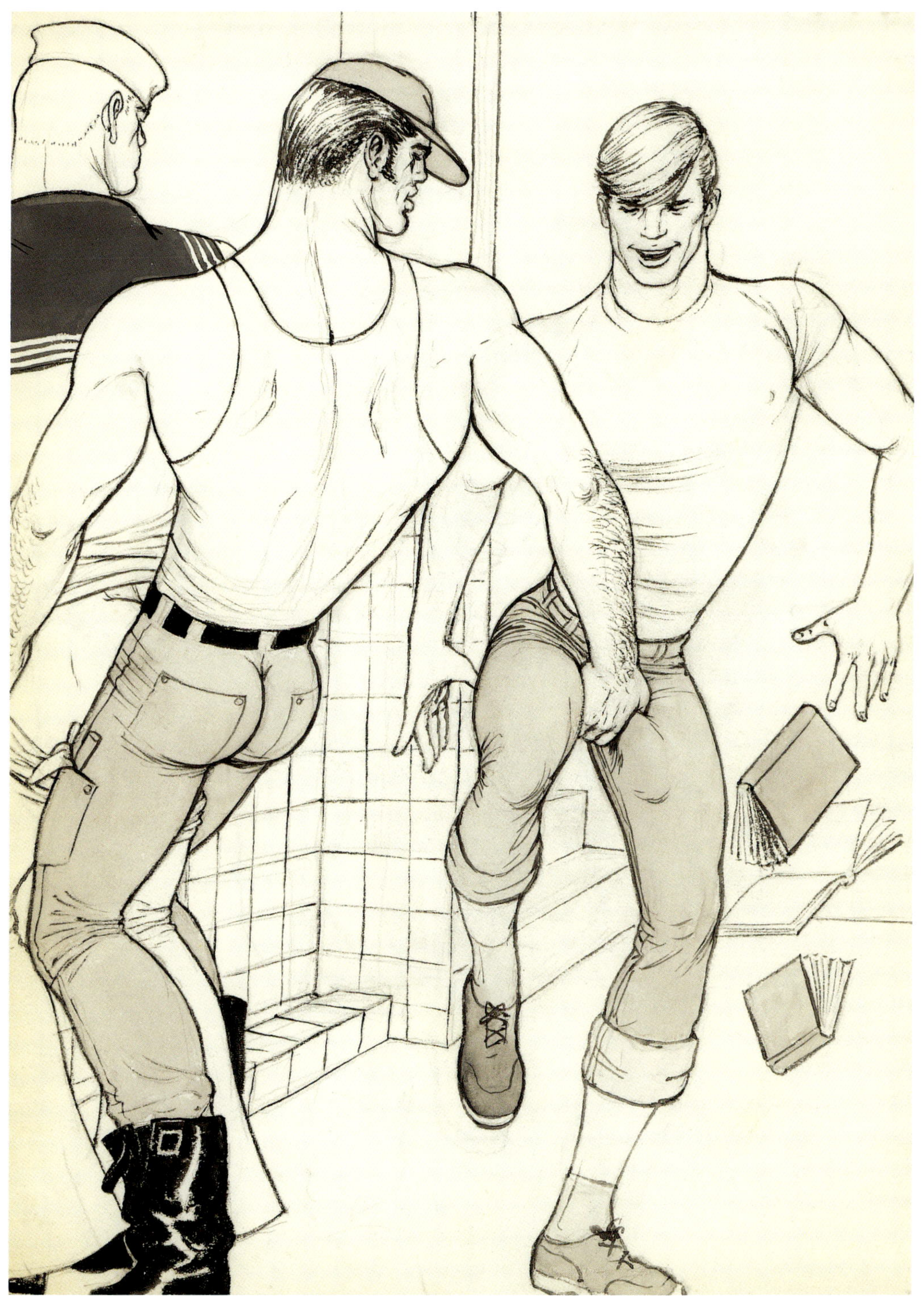

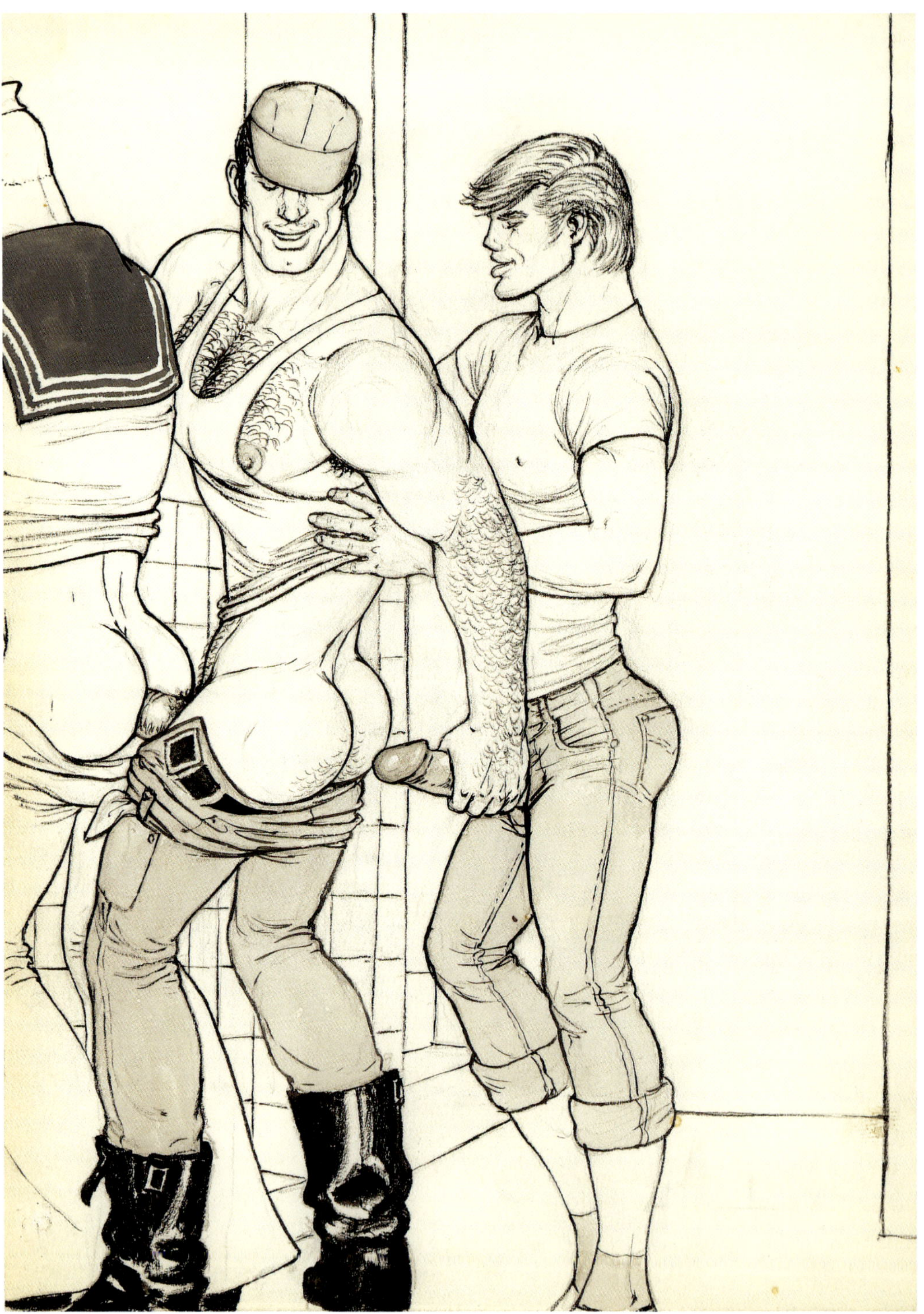

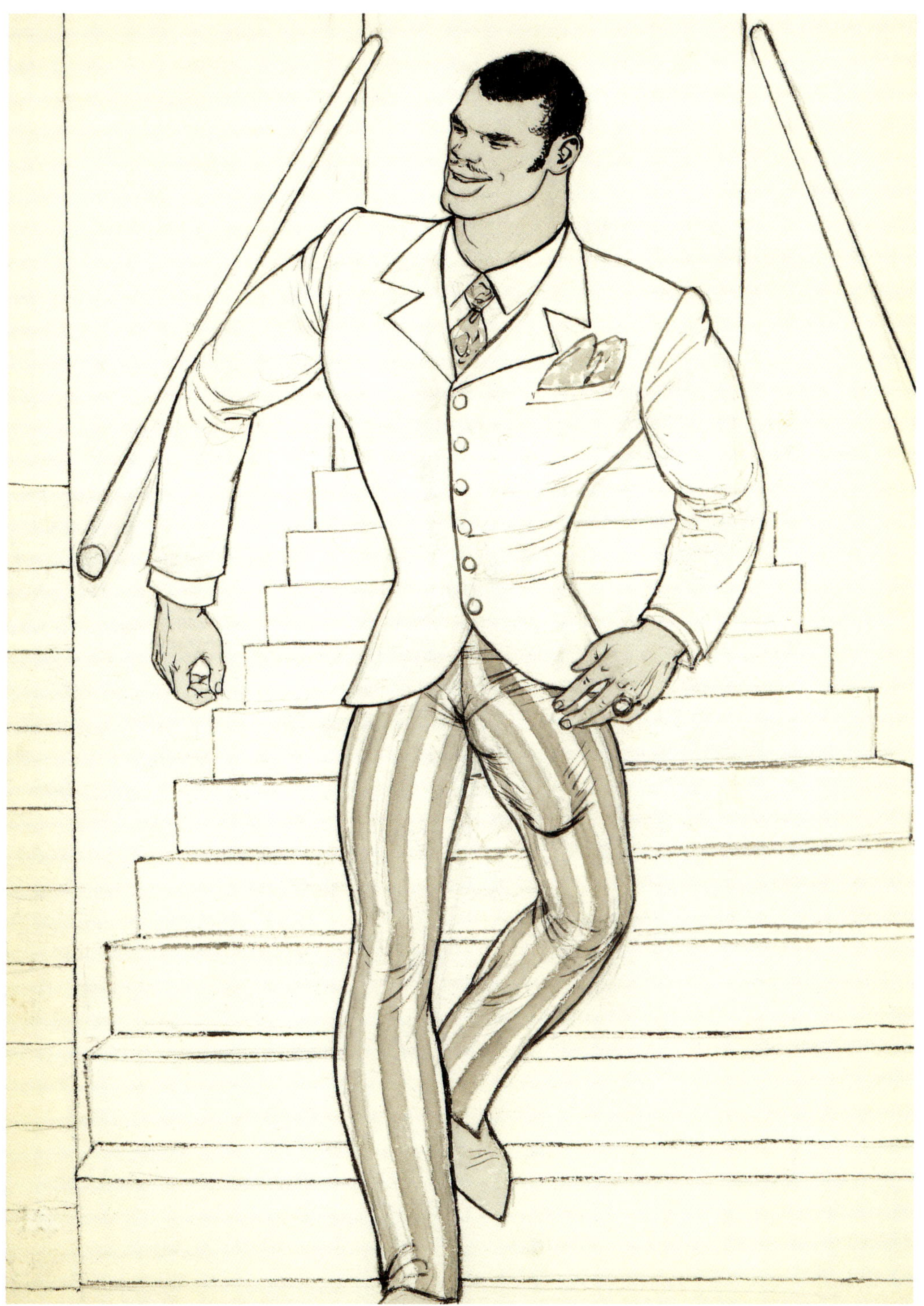

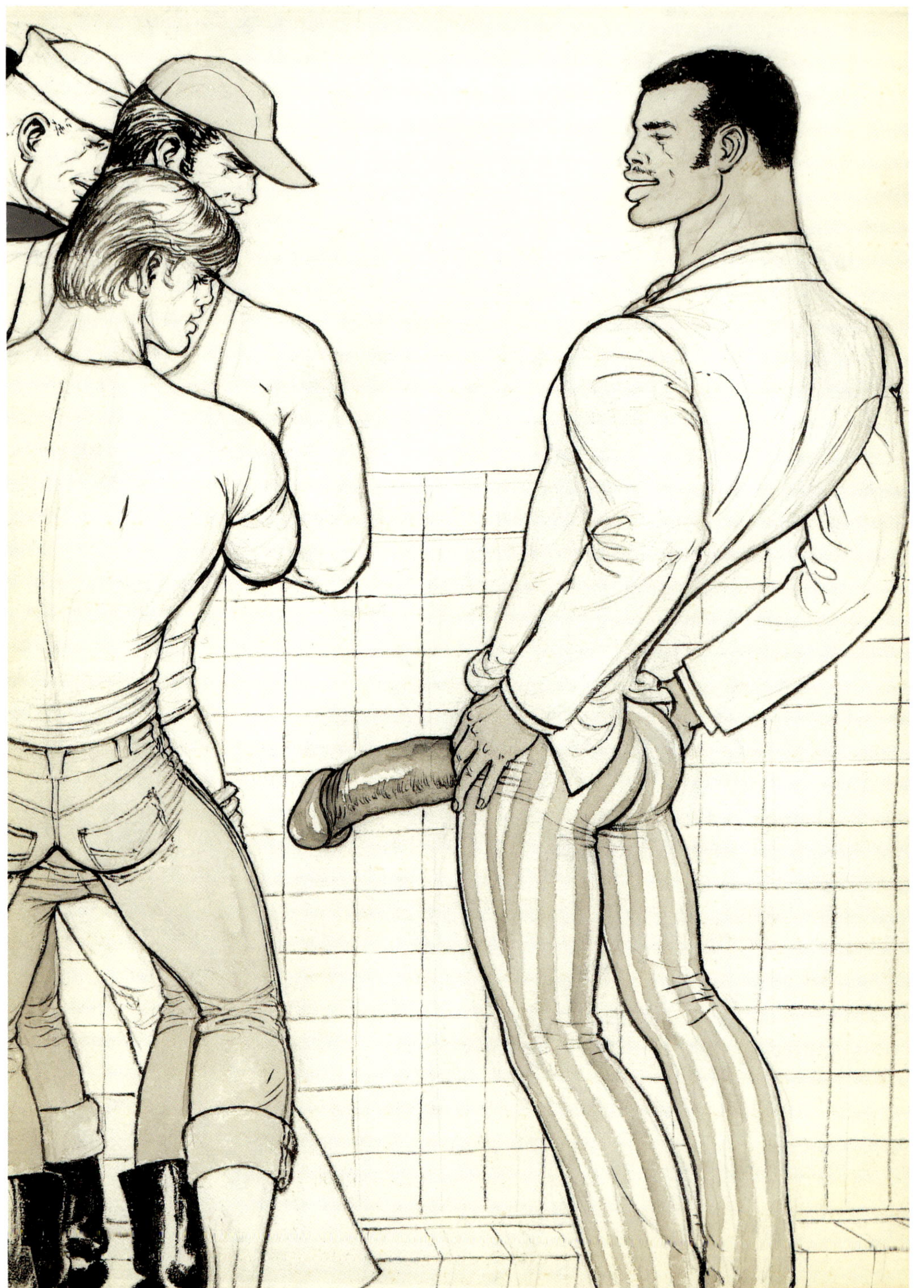

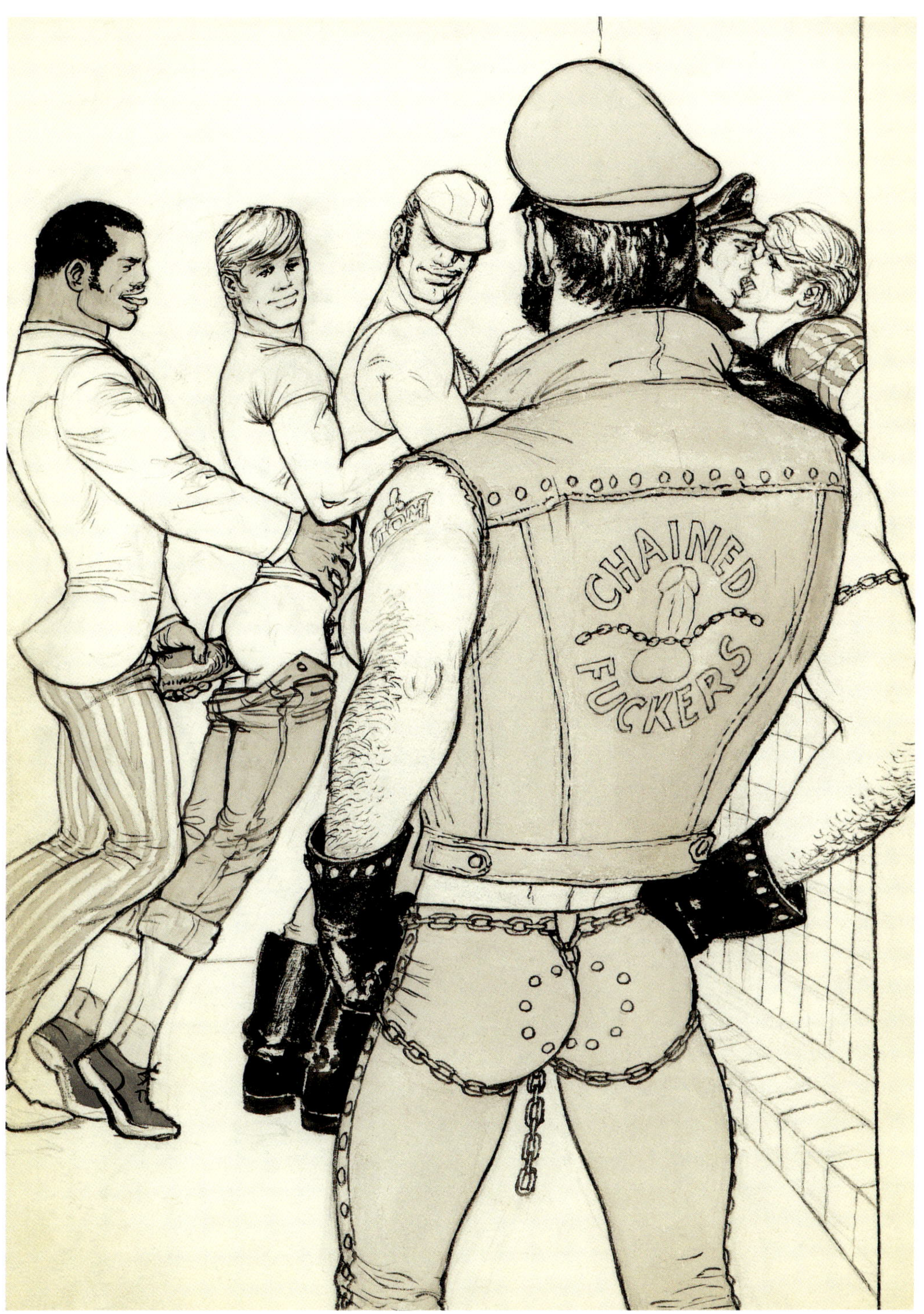
CHAINED
FUCKERS

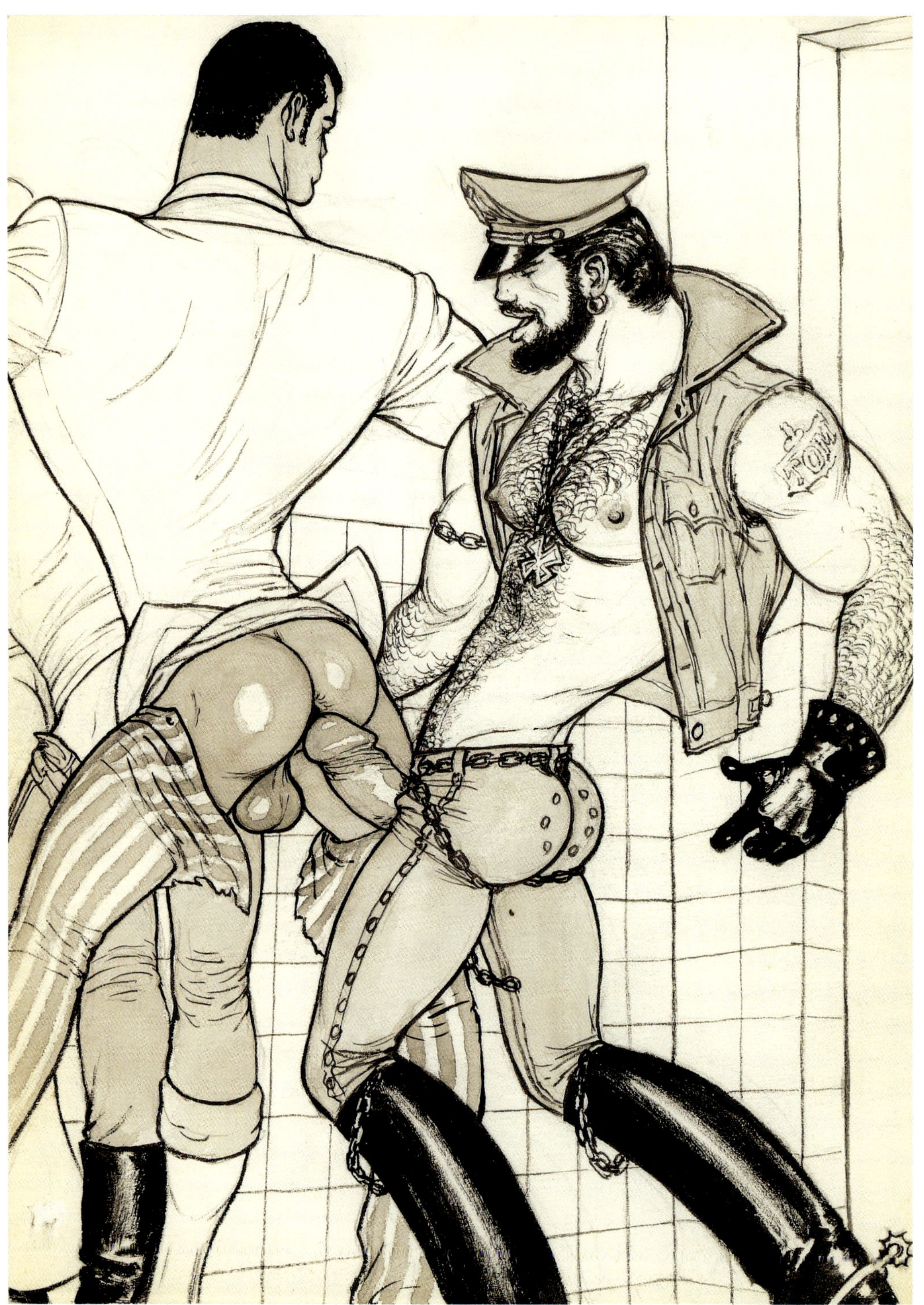

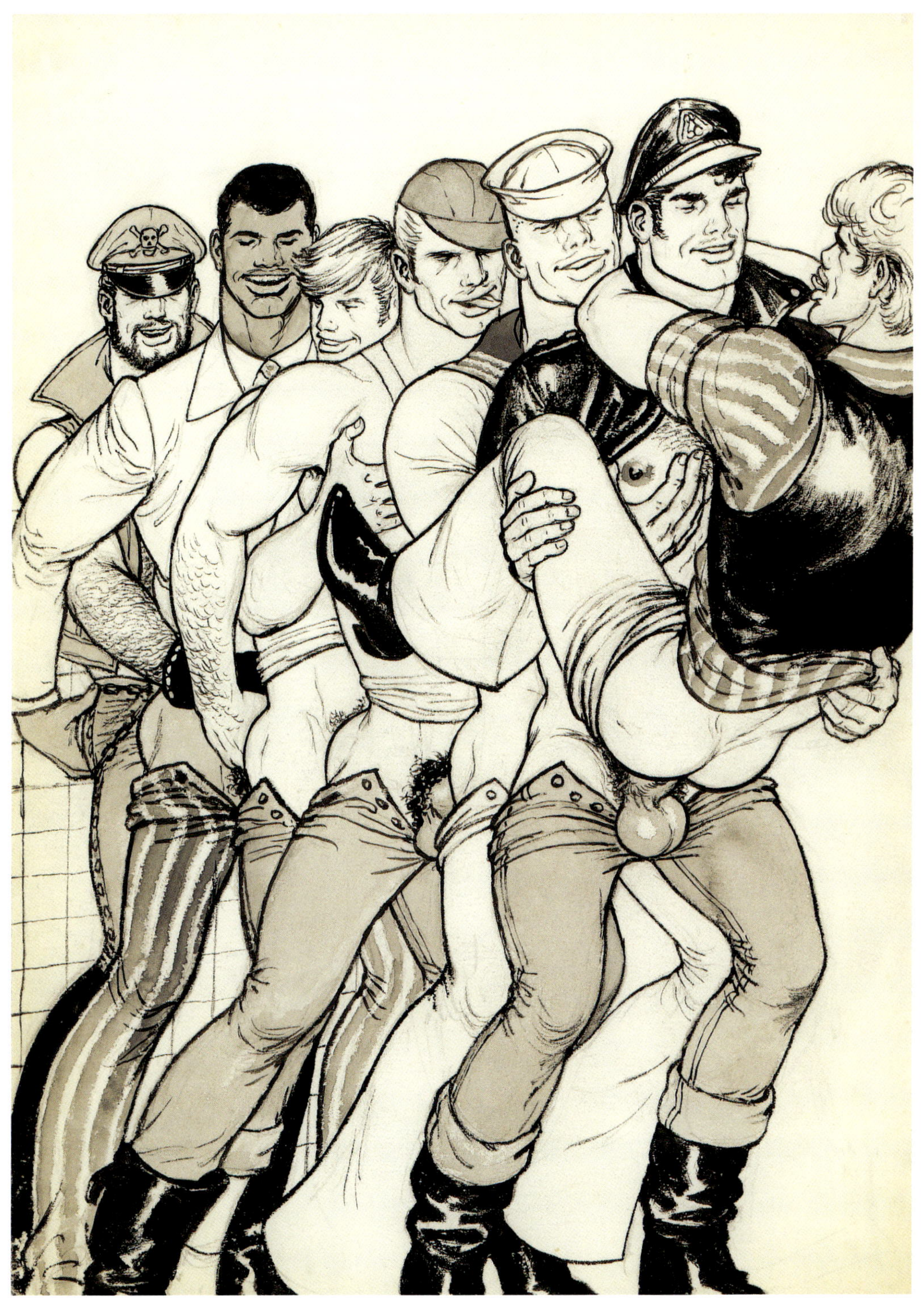

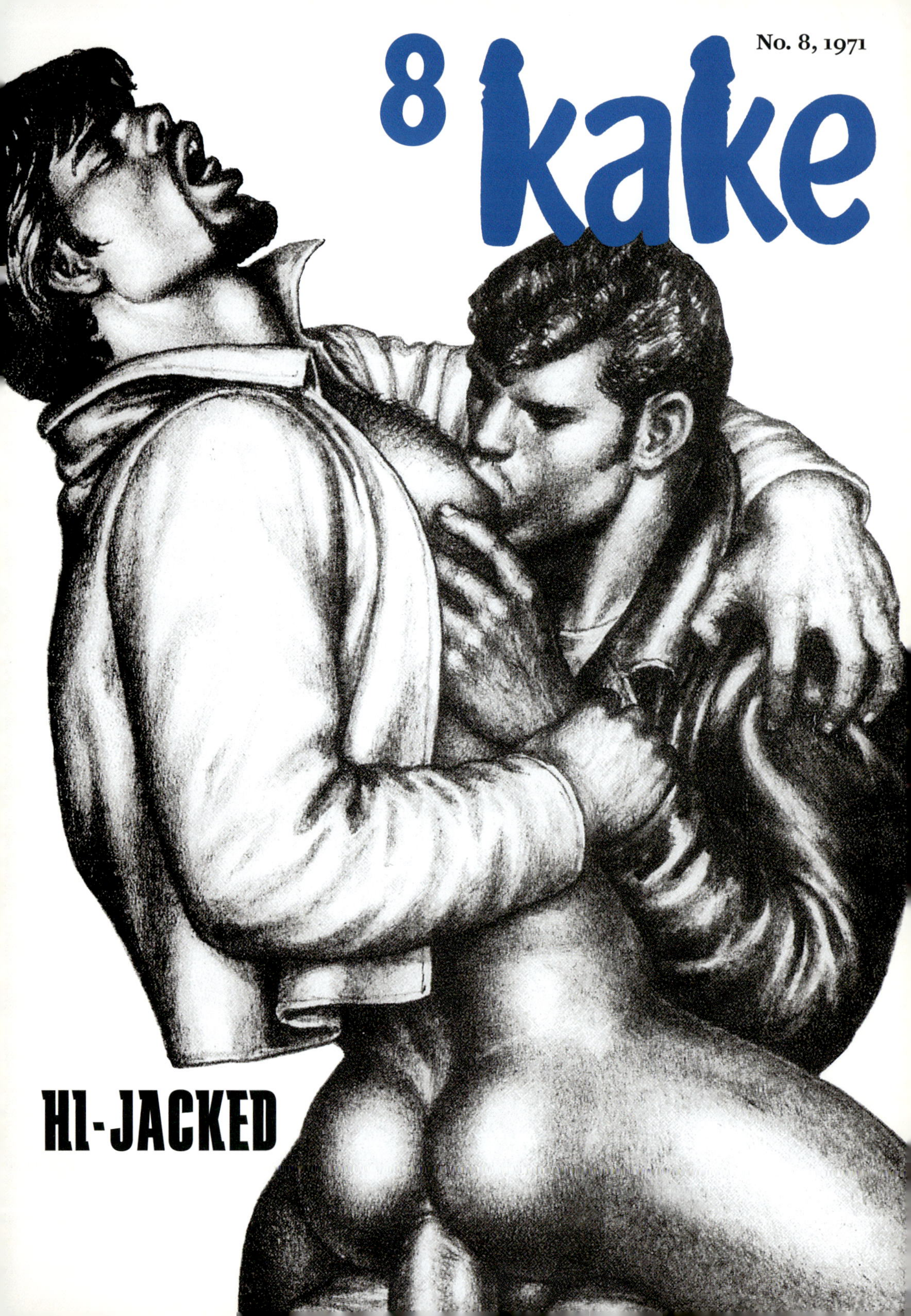
No. 8, 1971
8 kake
HI-JACKED

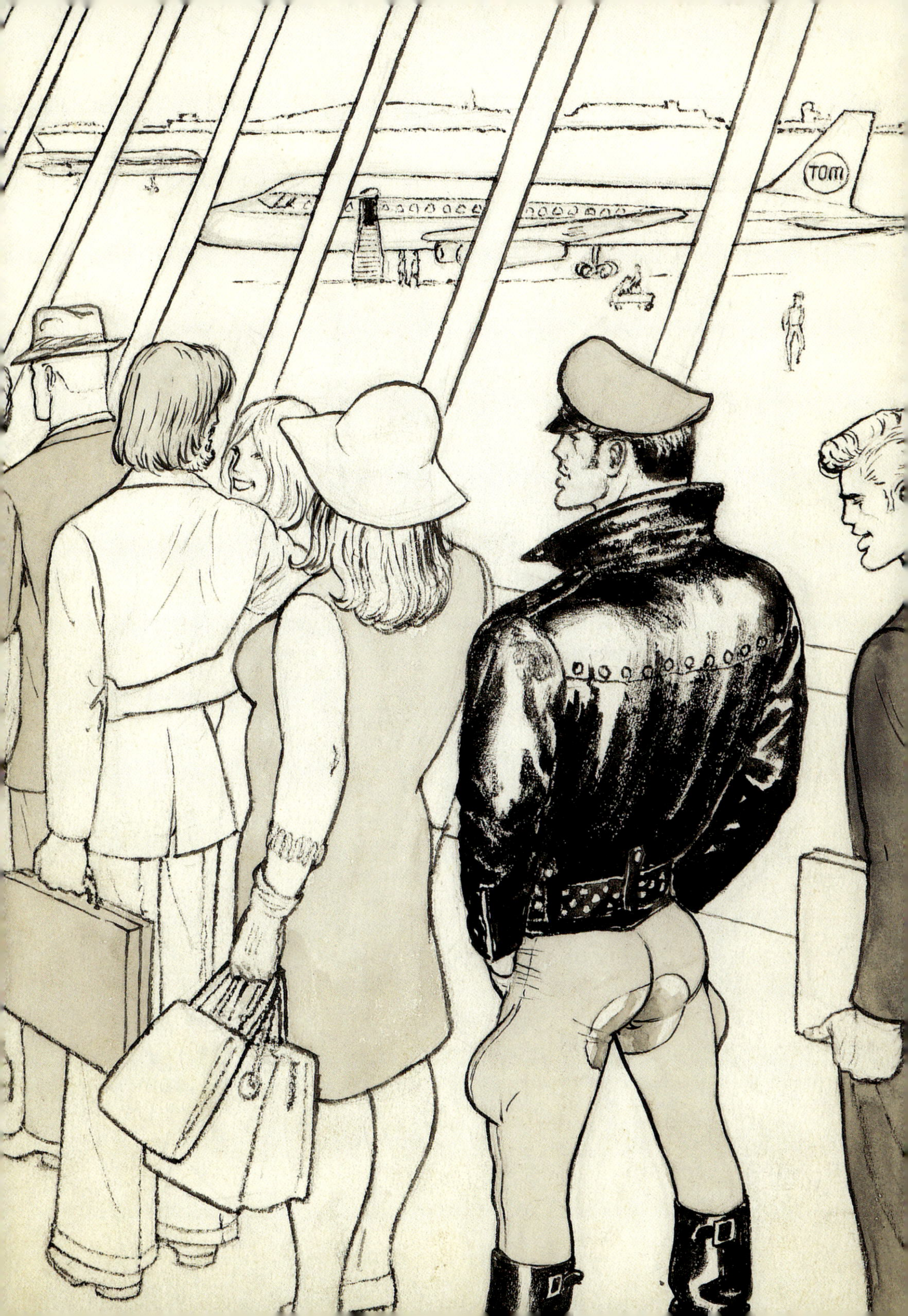

TOM

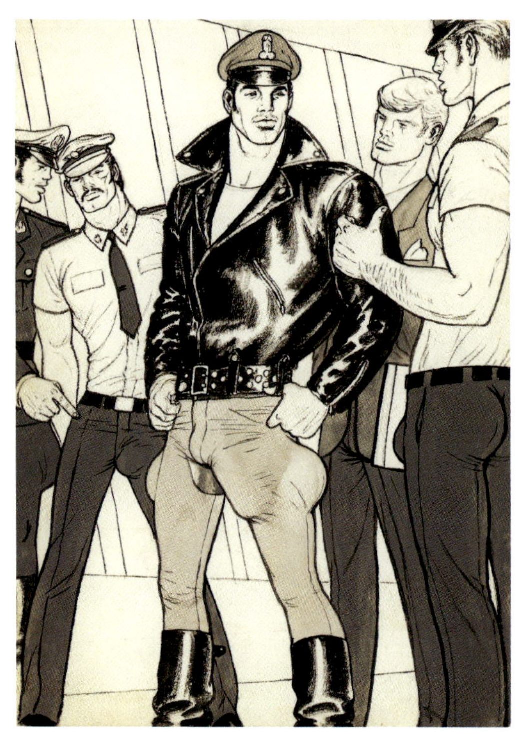
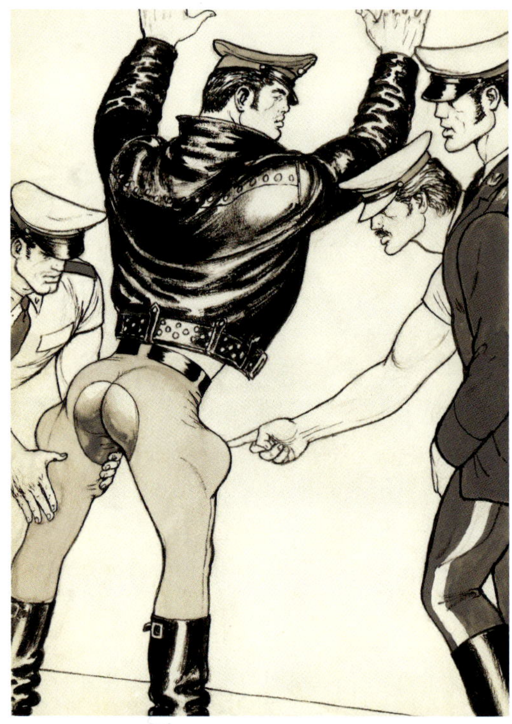
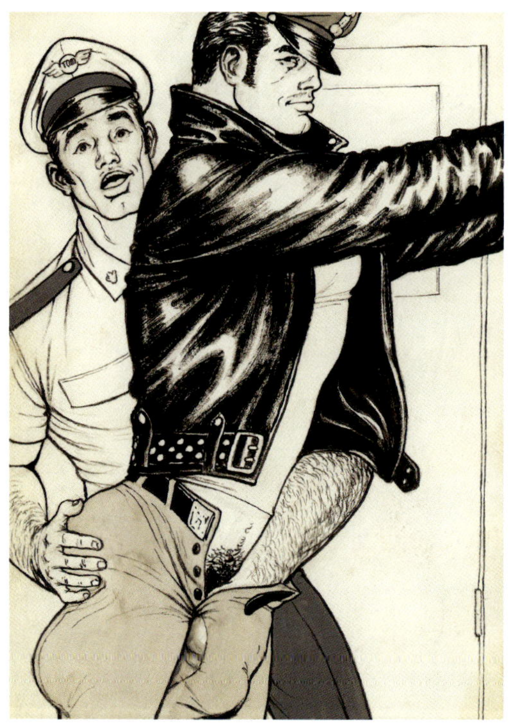
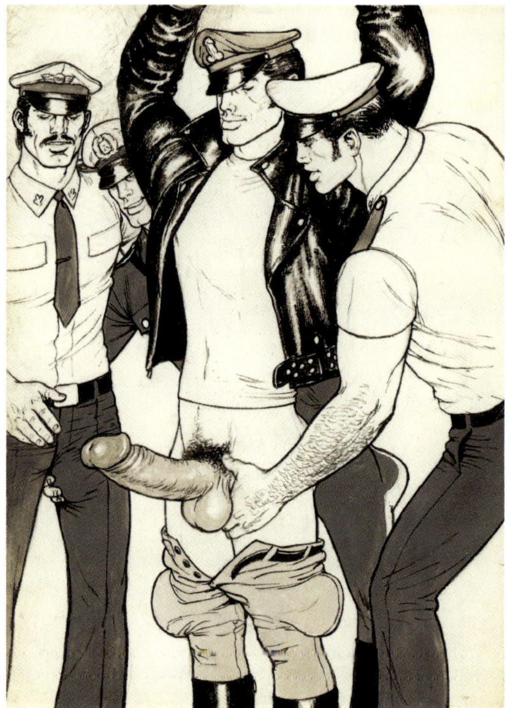

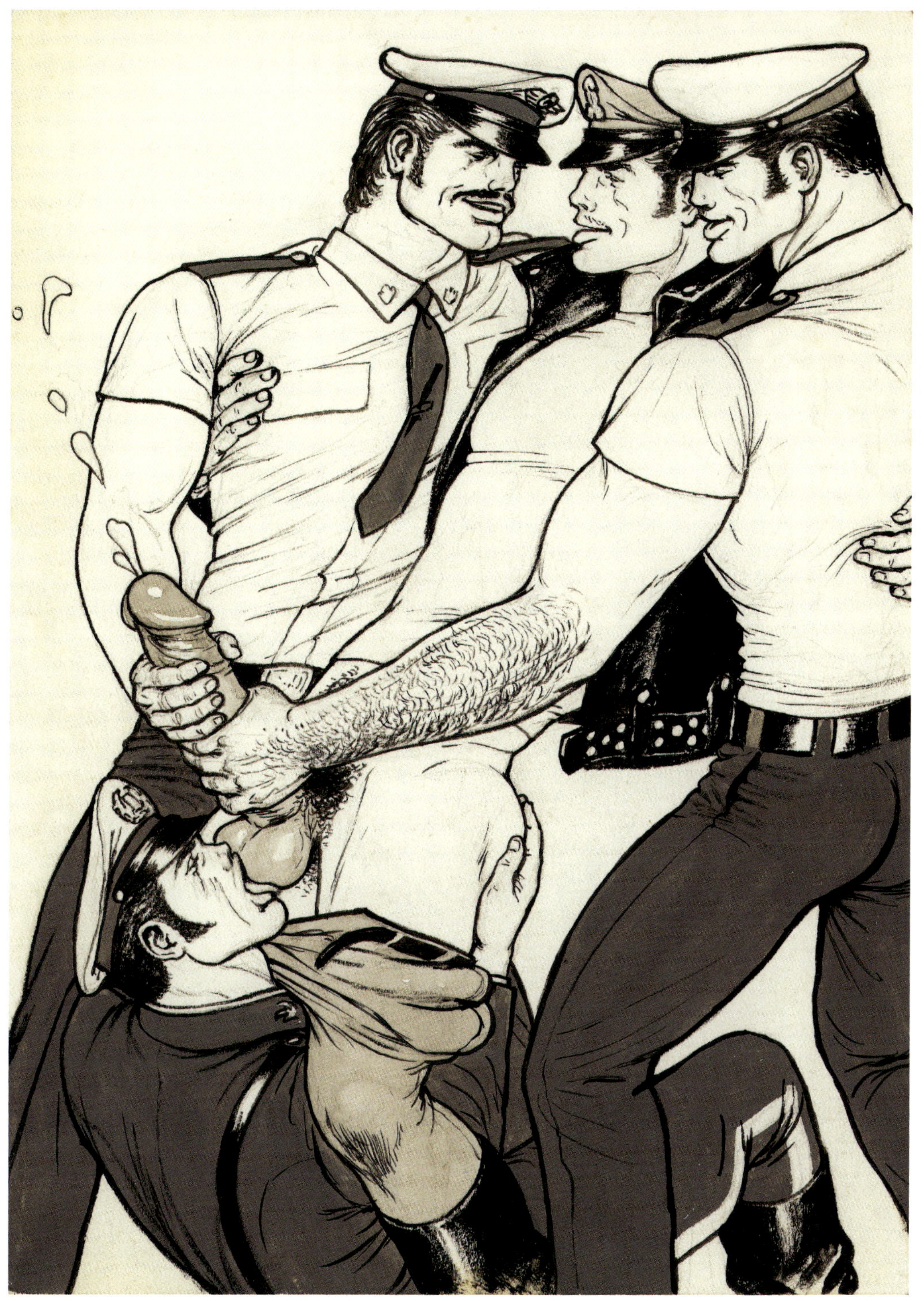

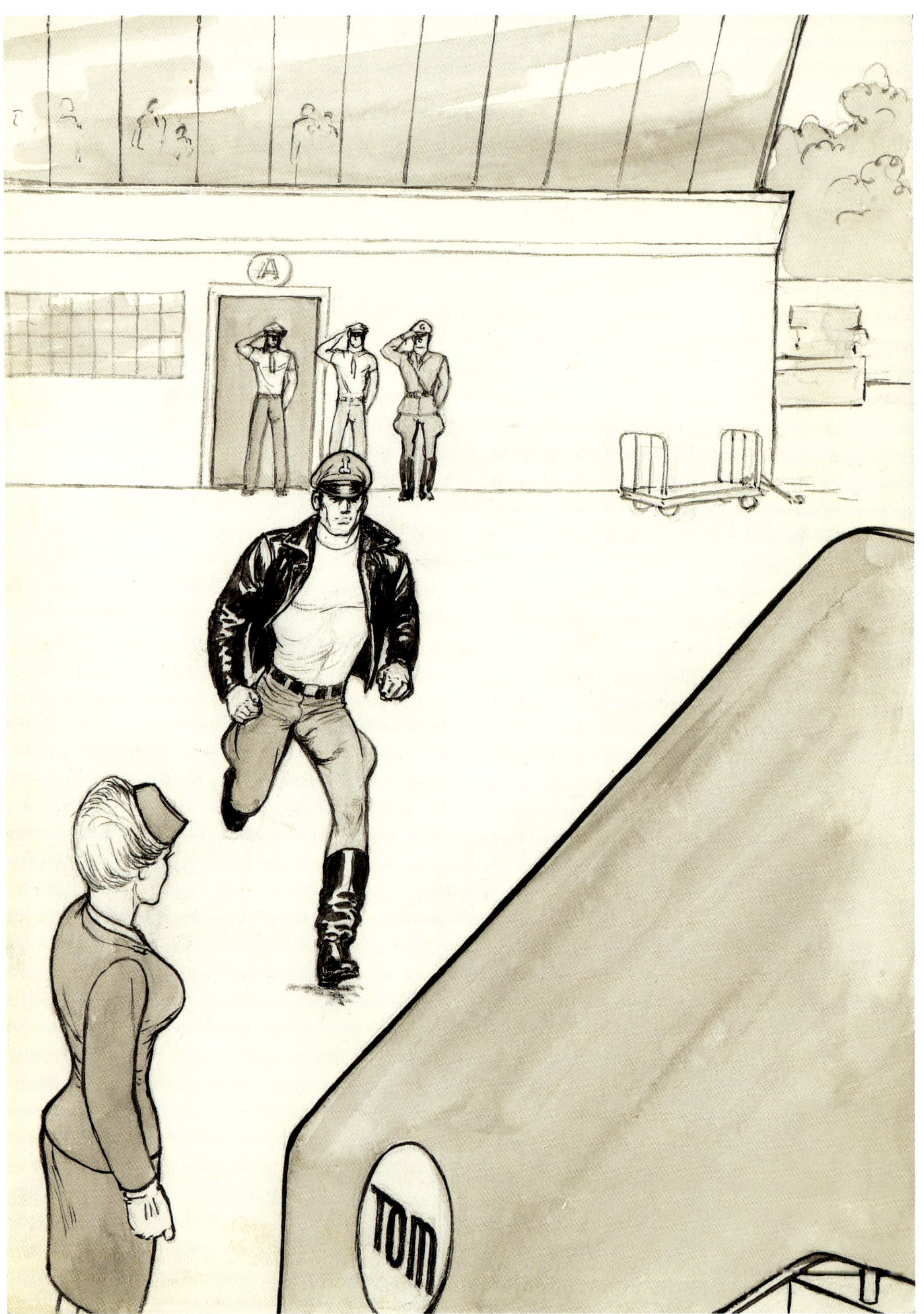
A
TOM

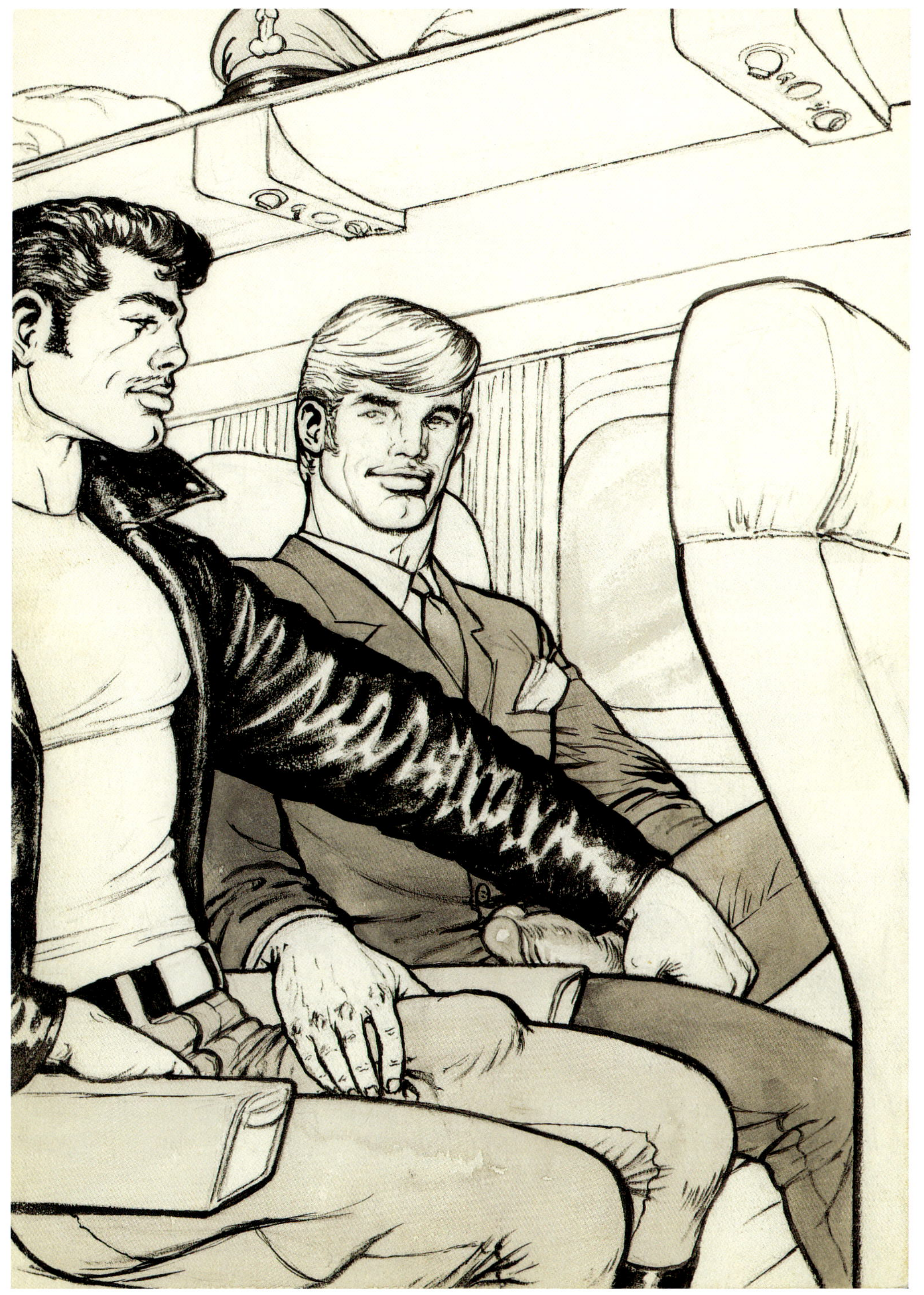

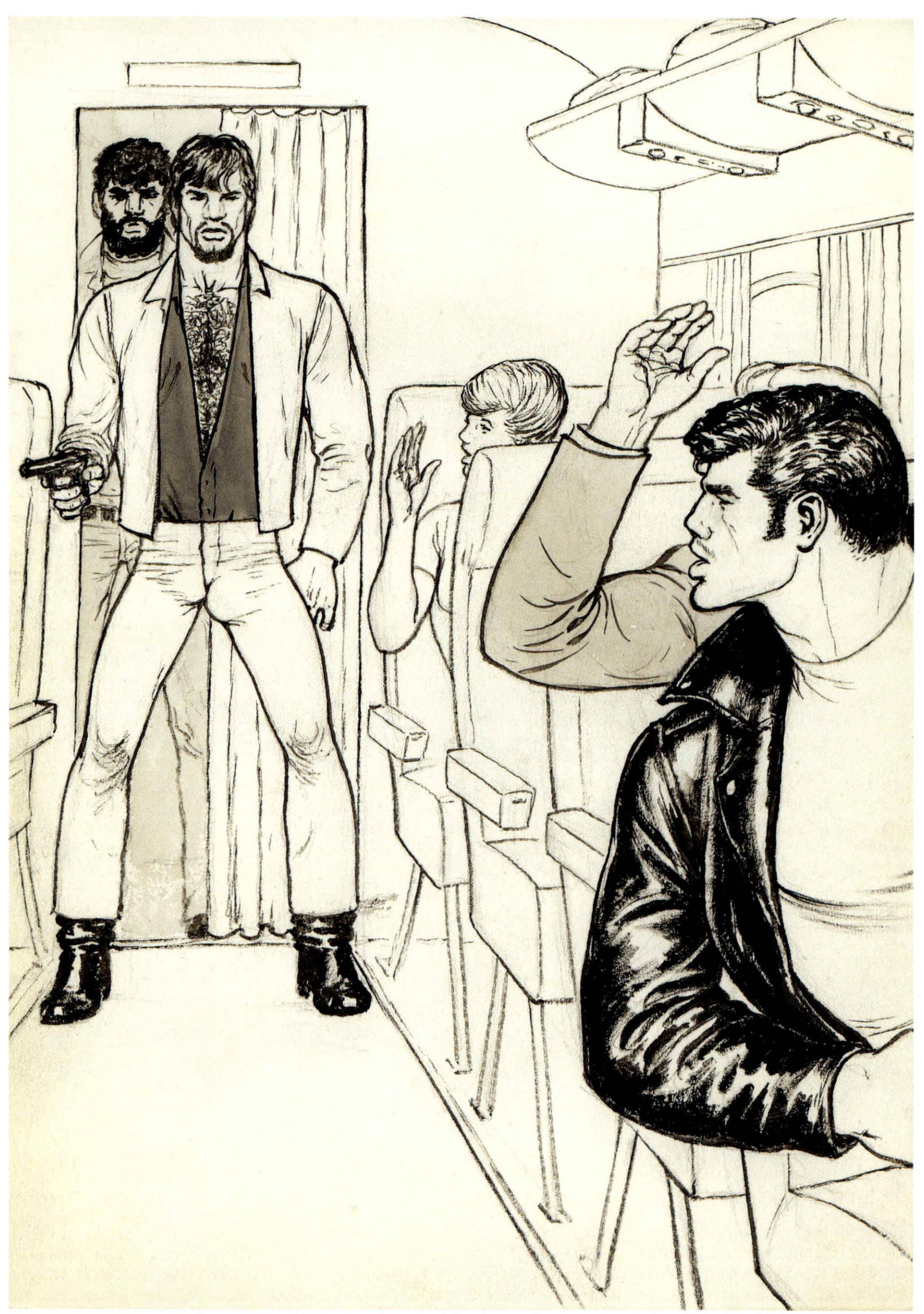

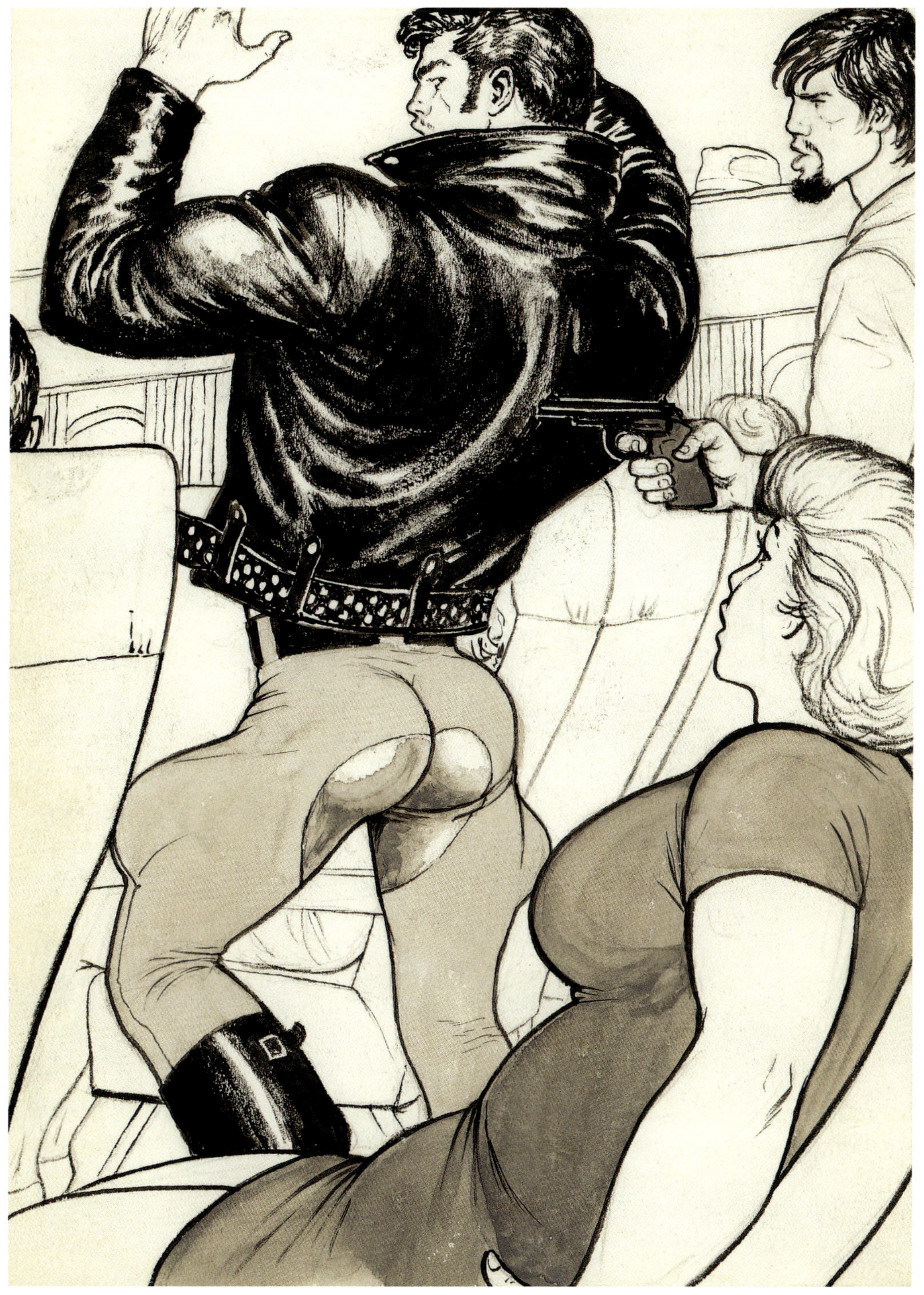

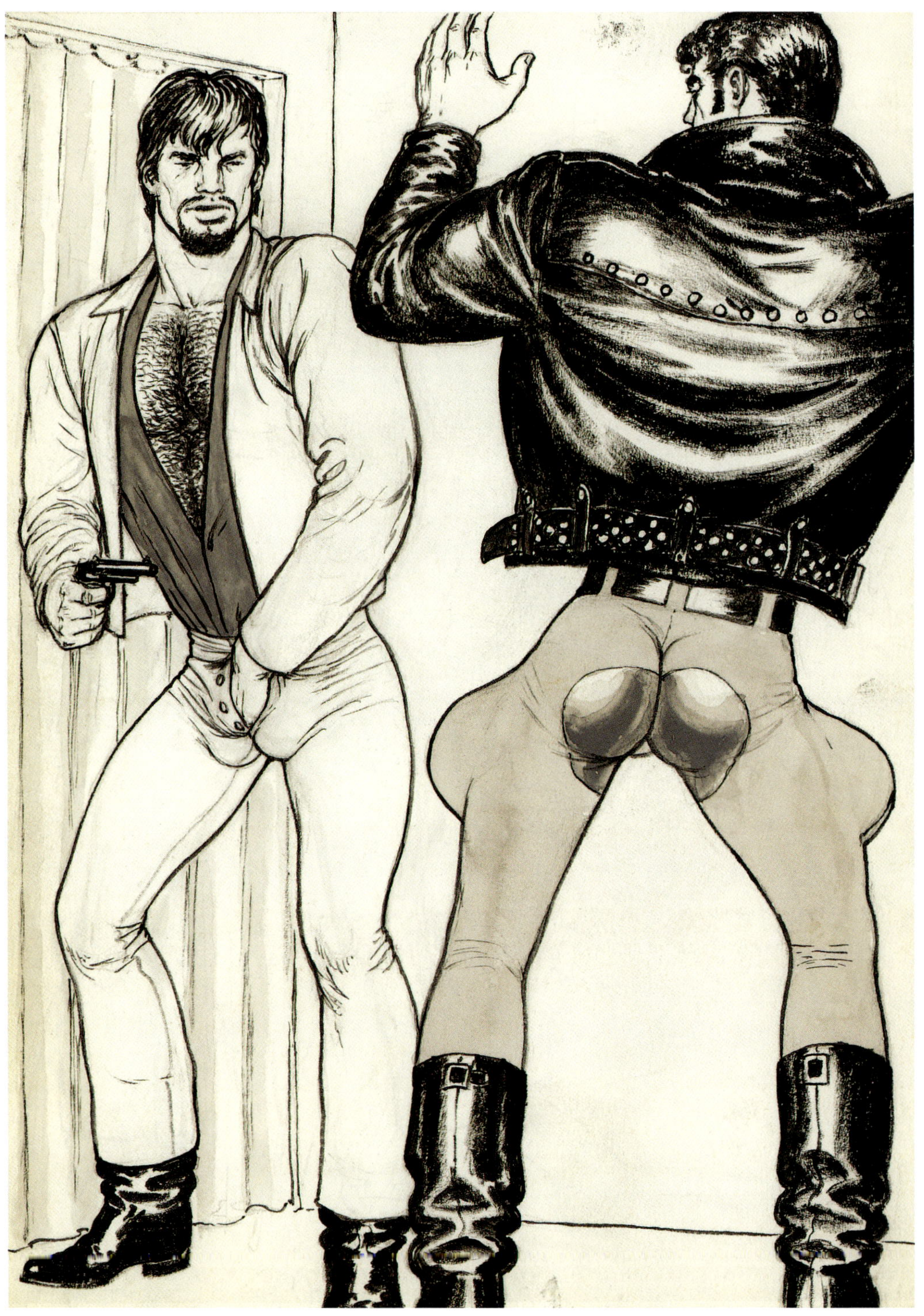

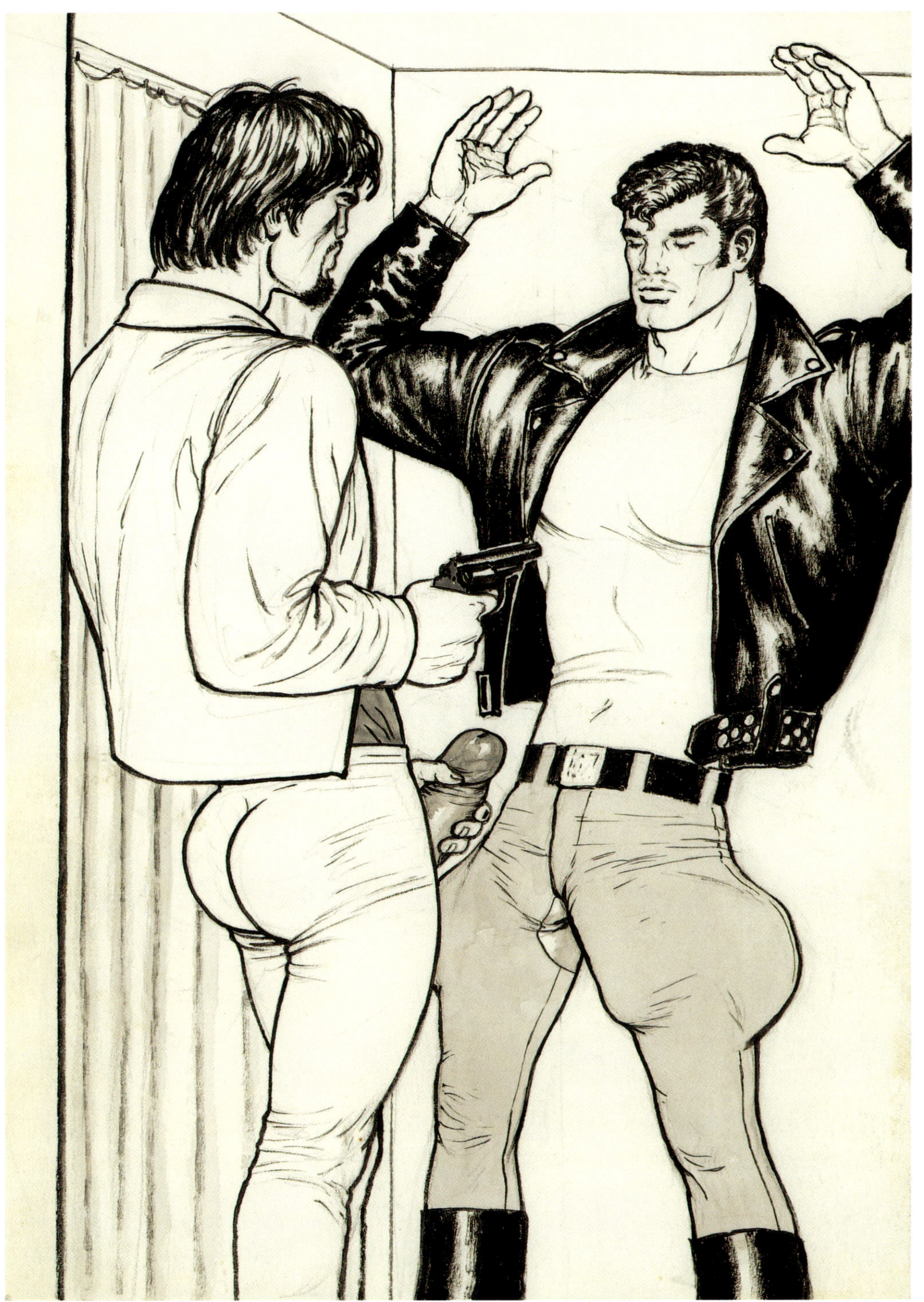

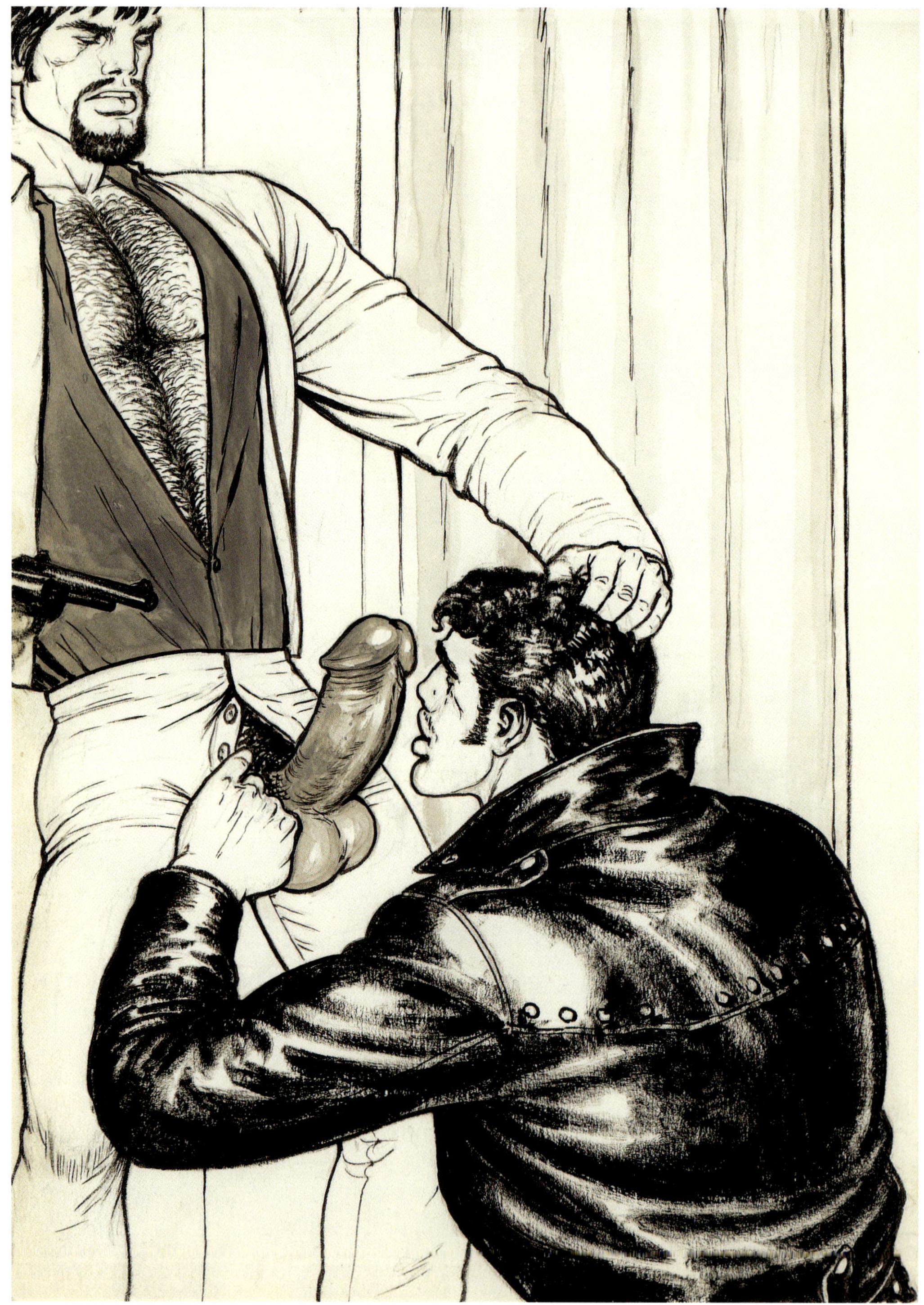

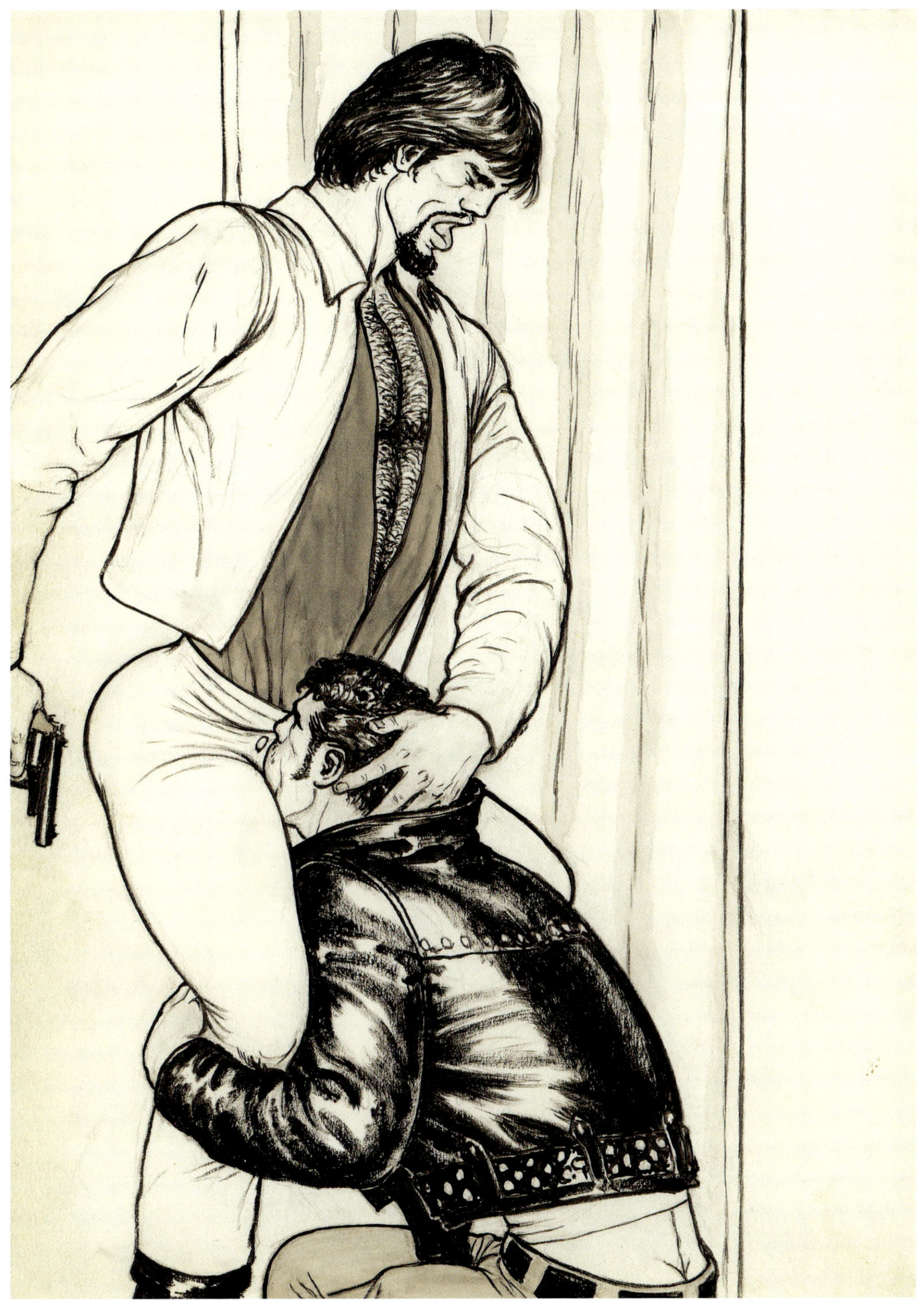

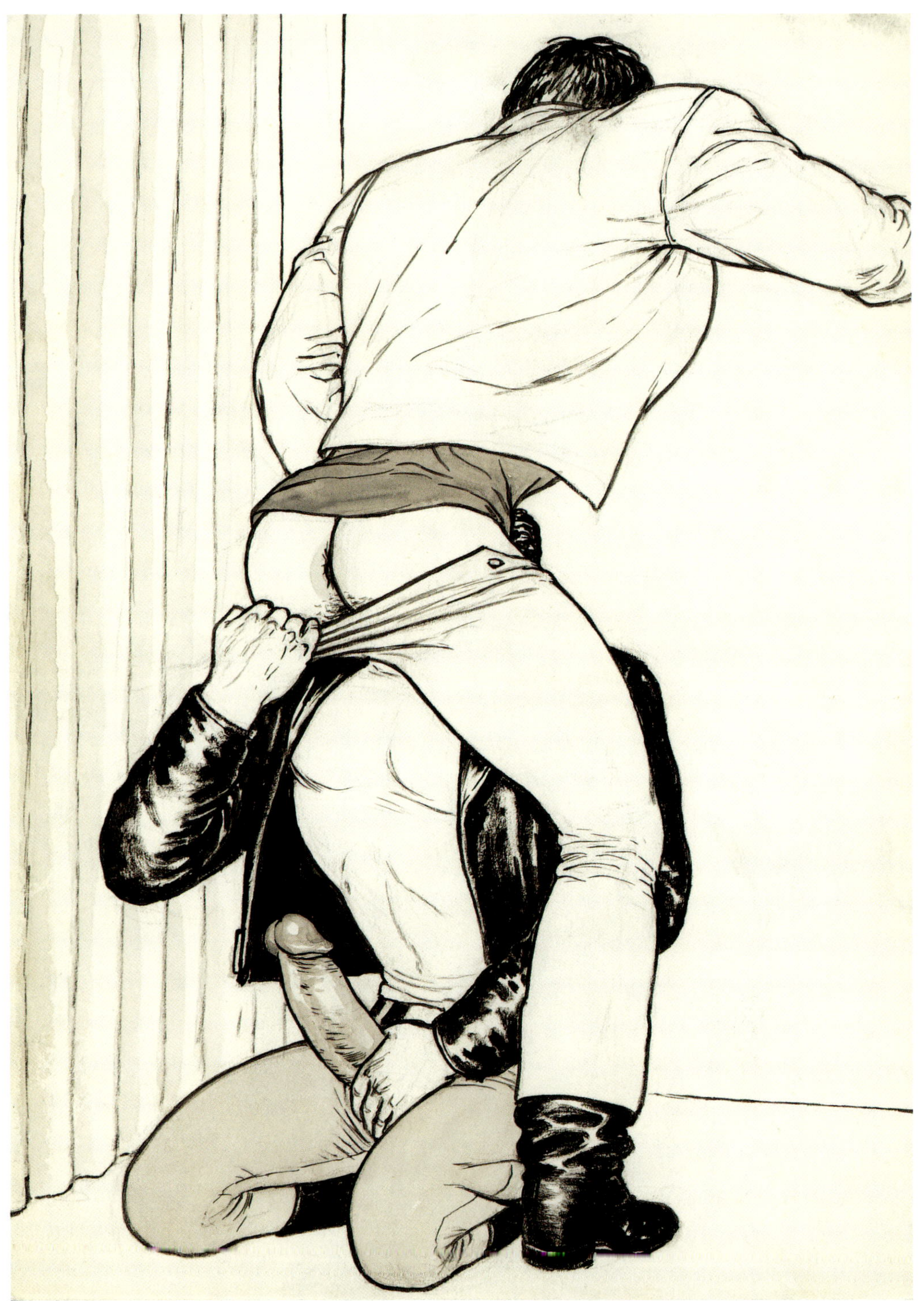

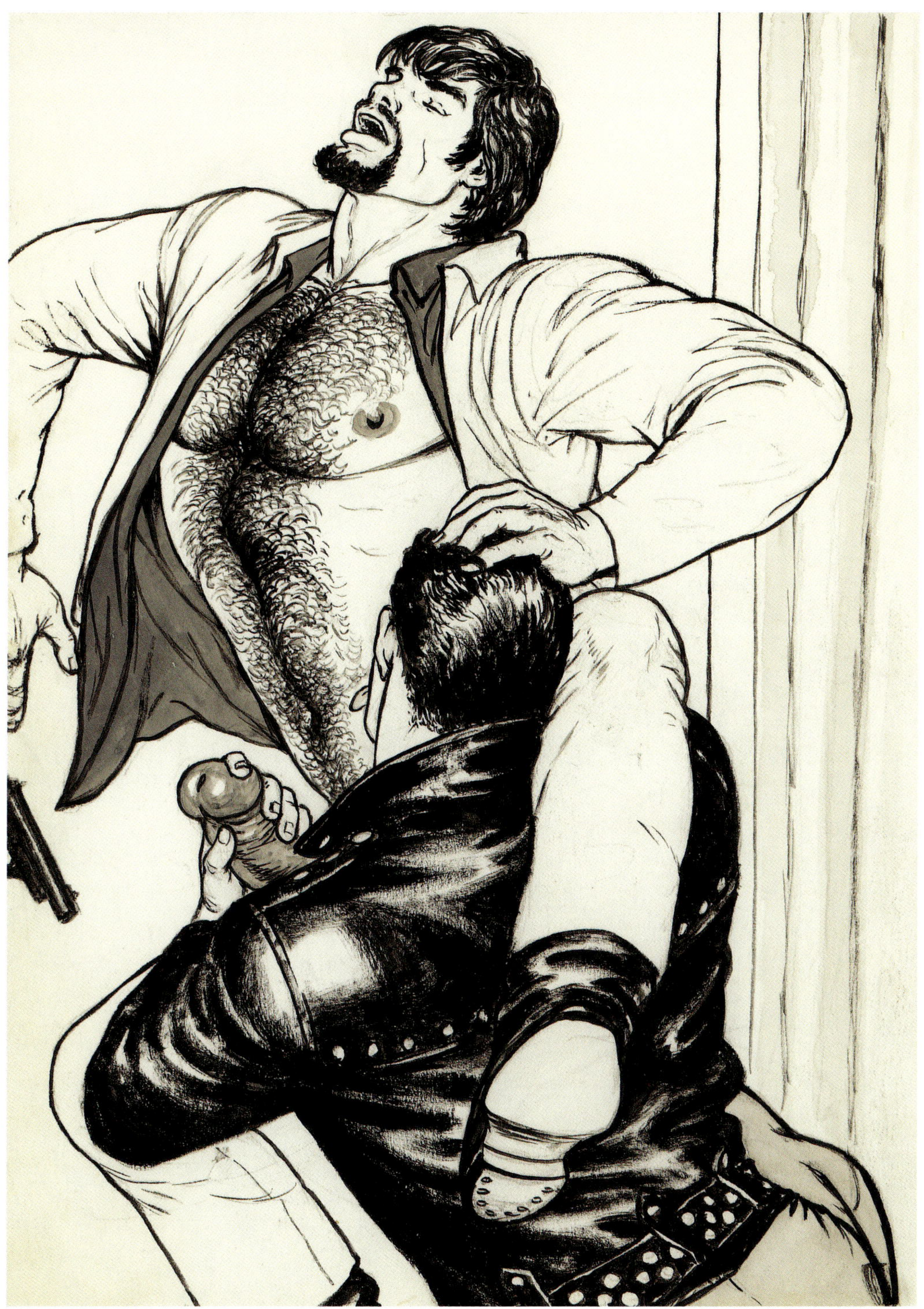

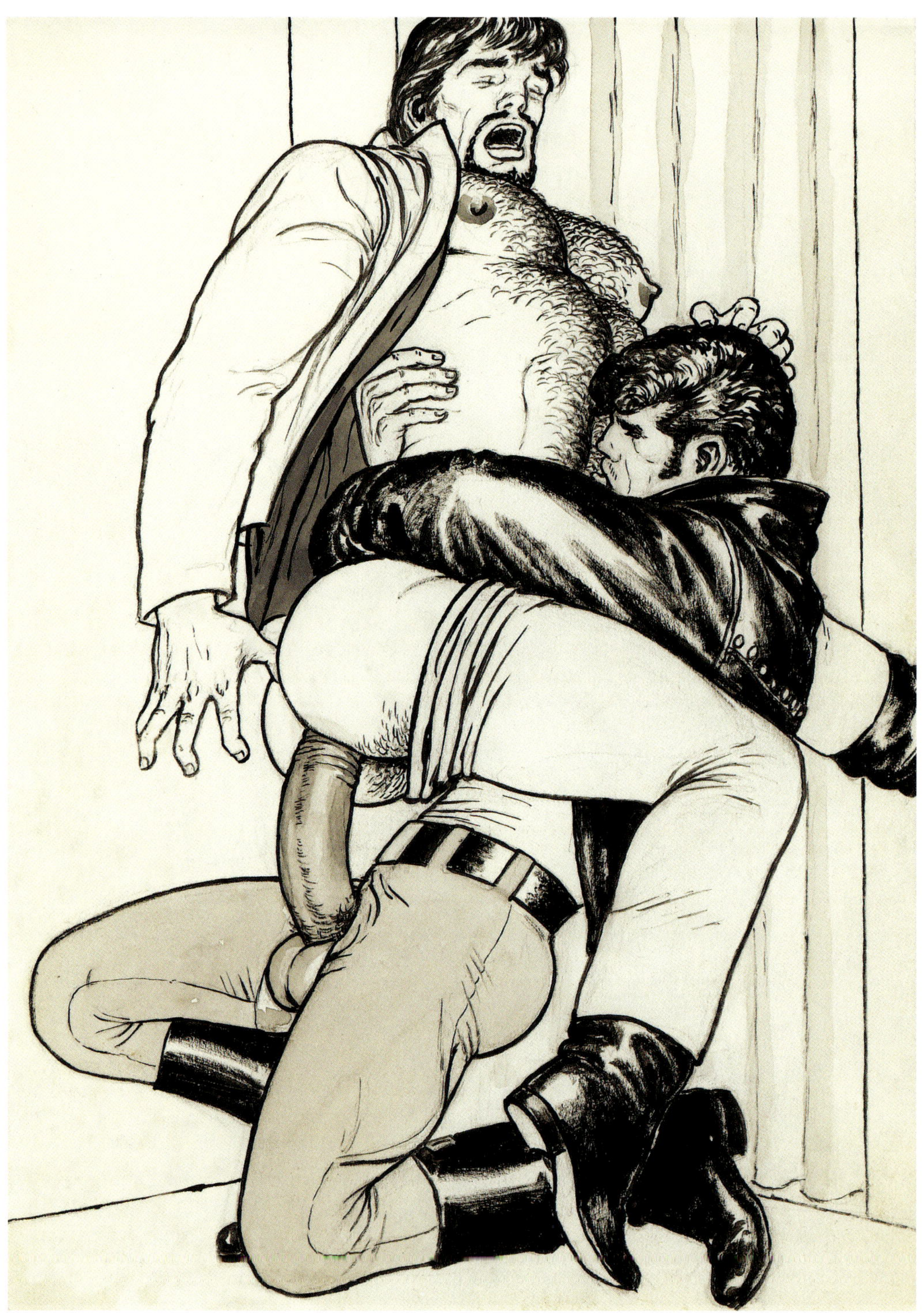

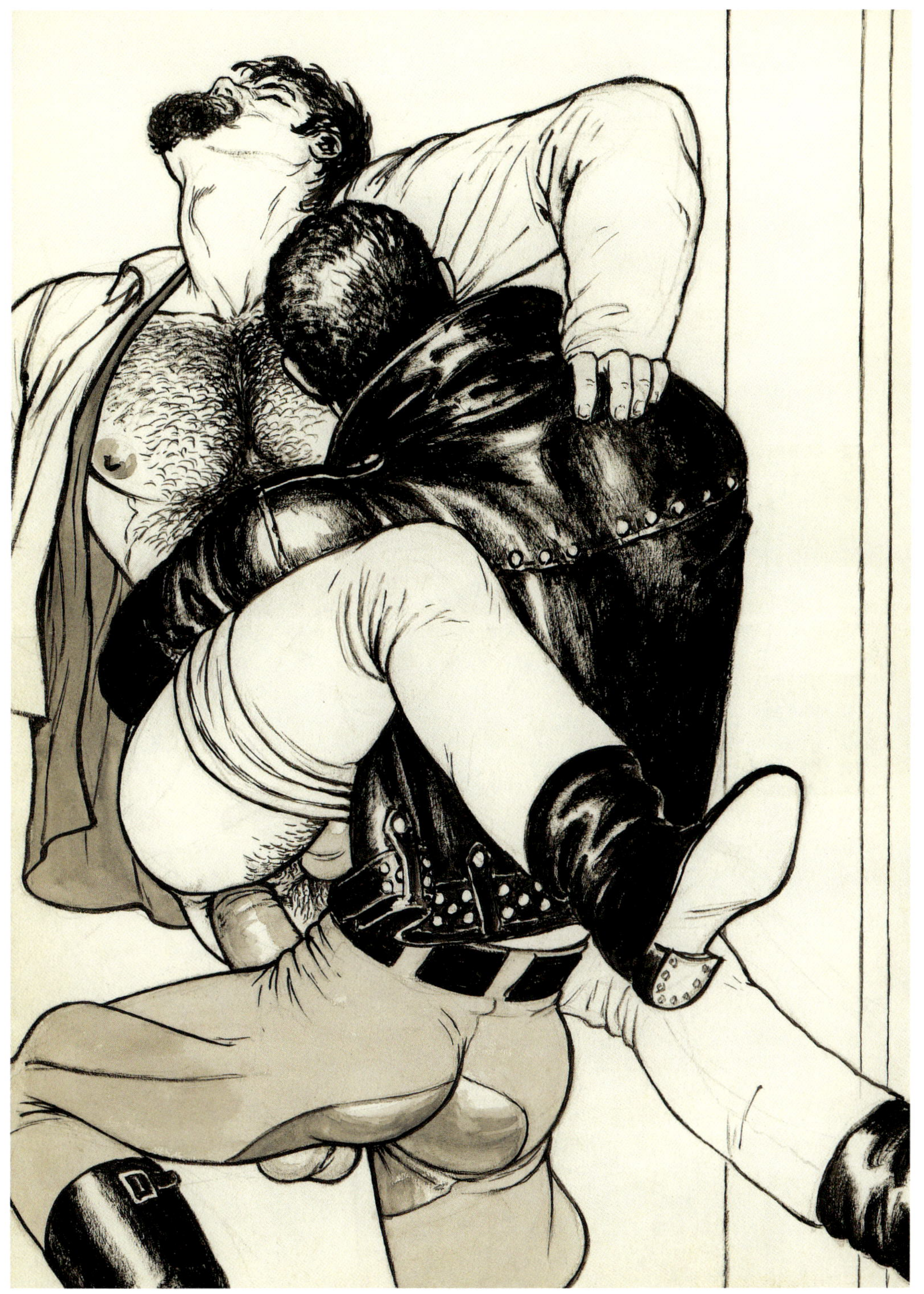

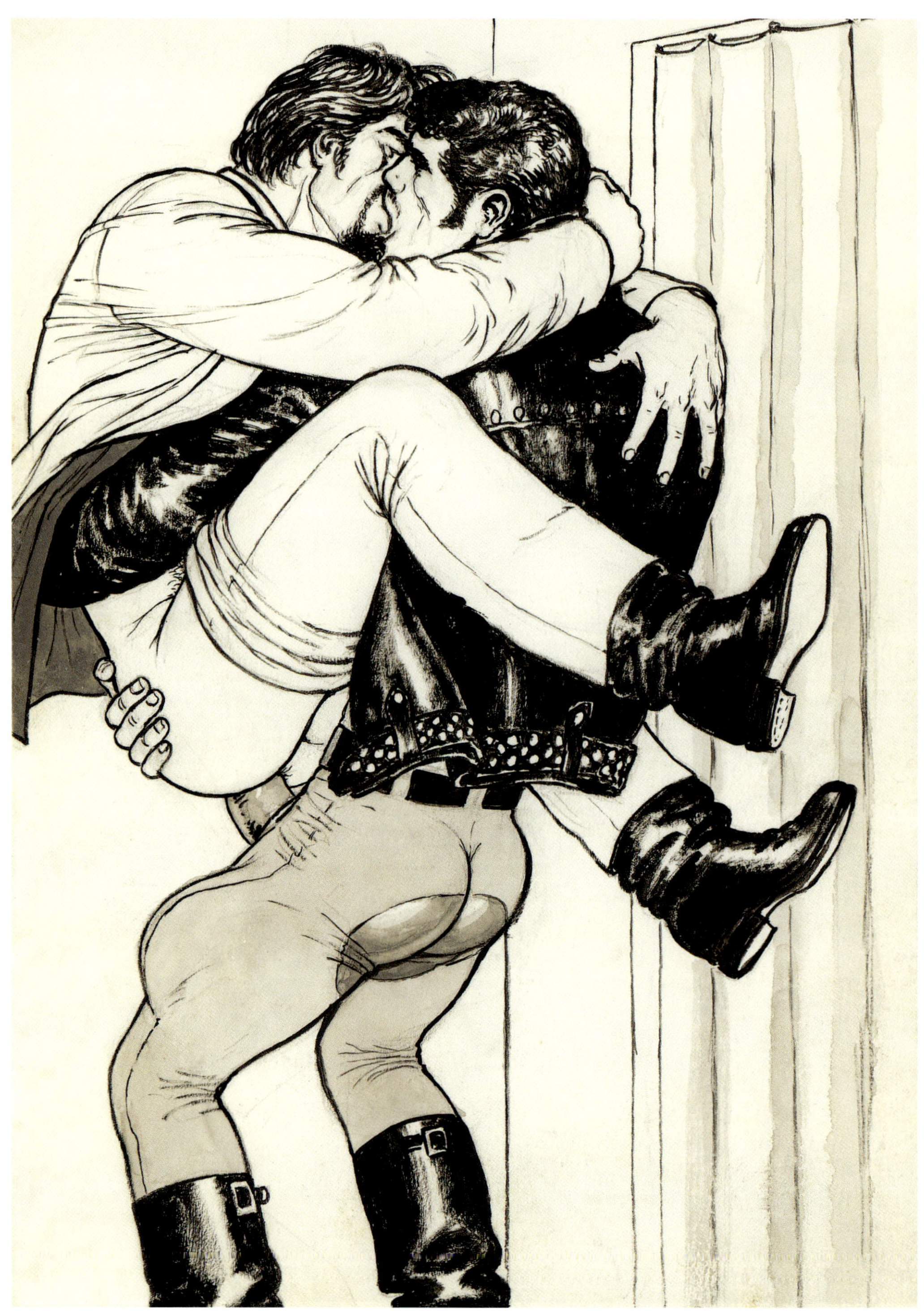

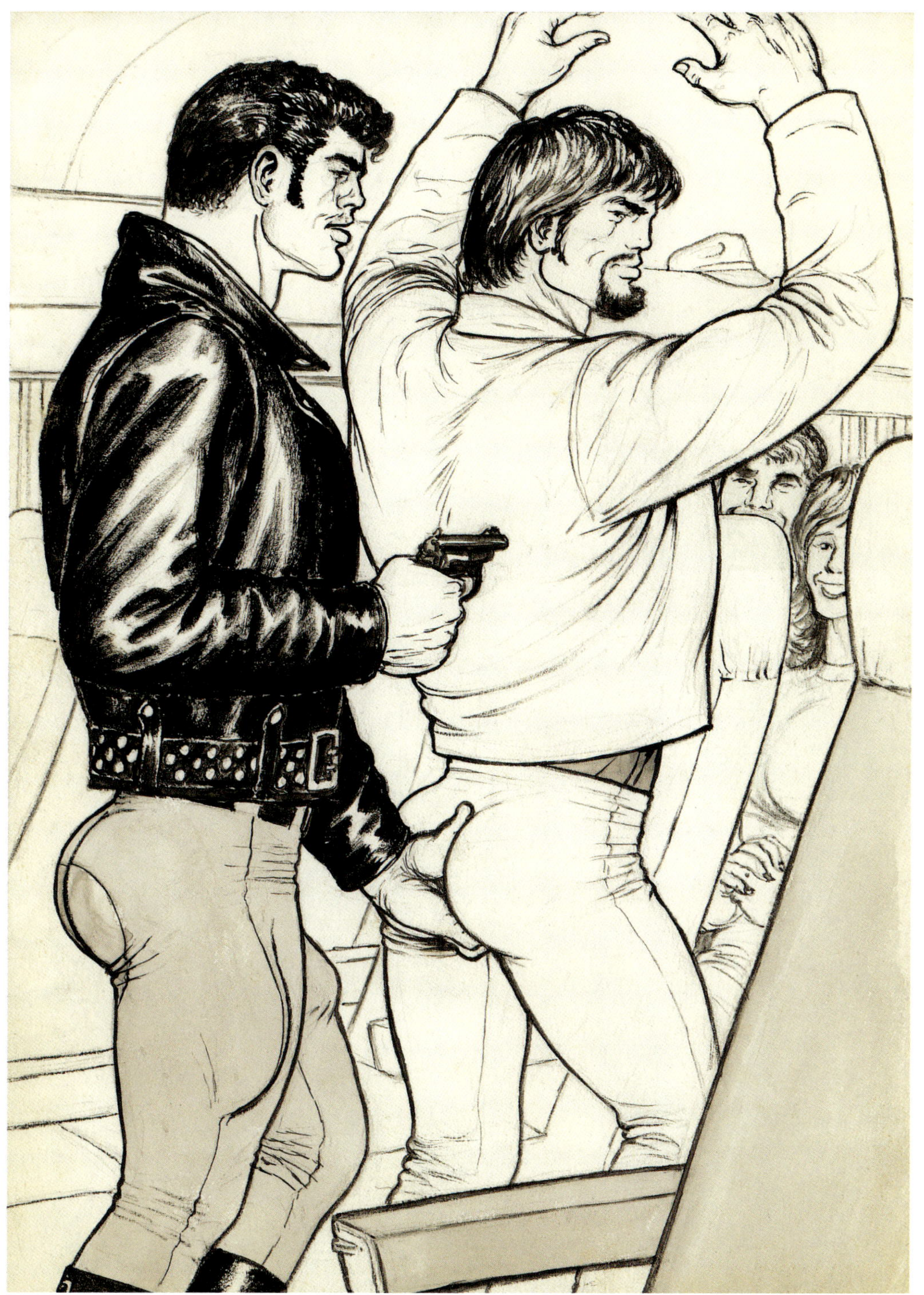

No. 9, 1971

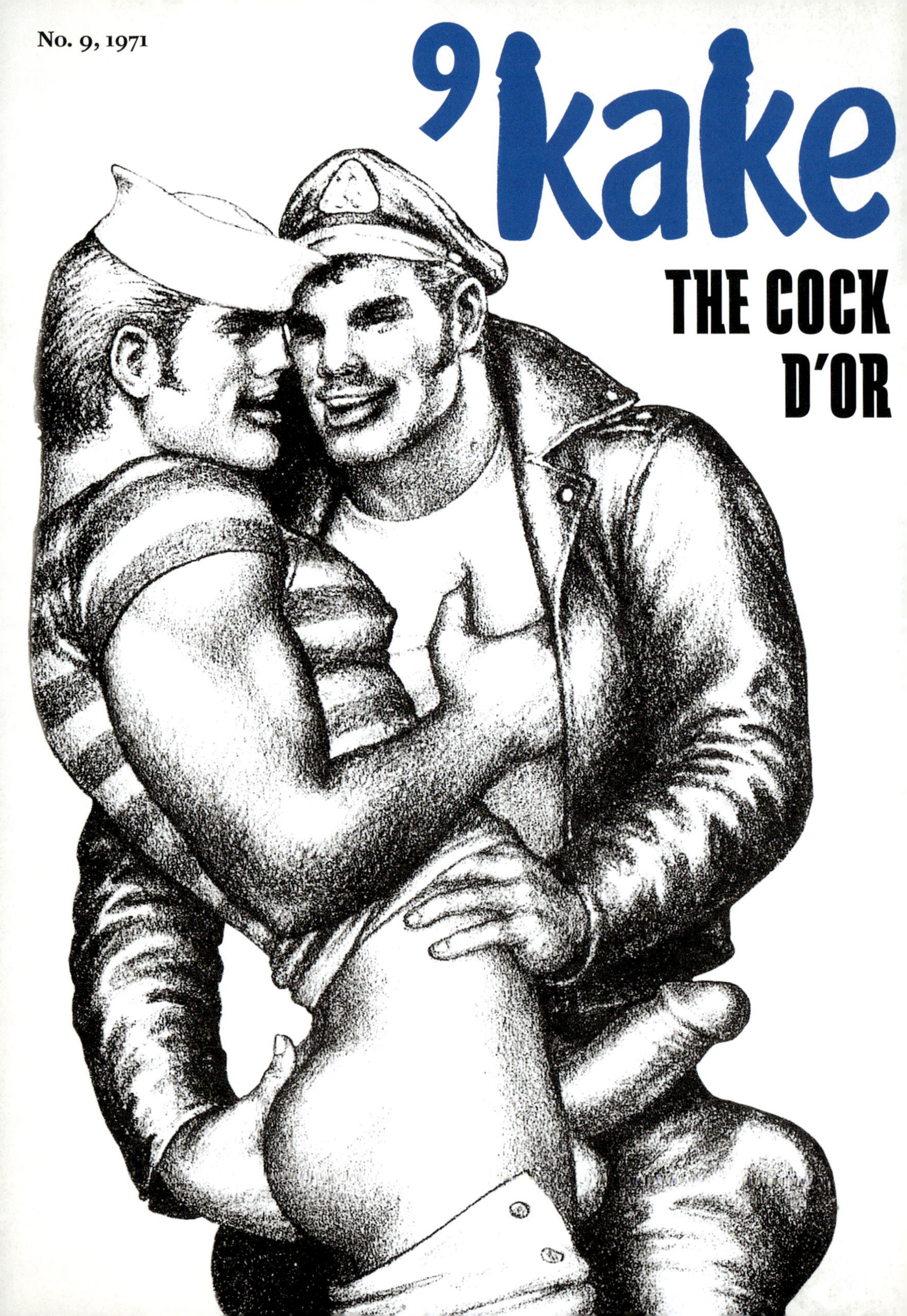

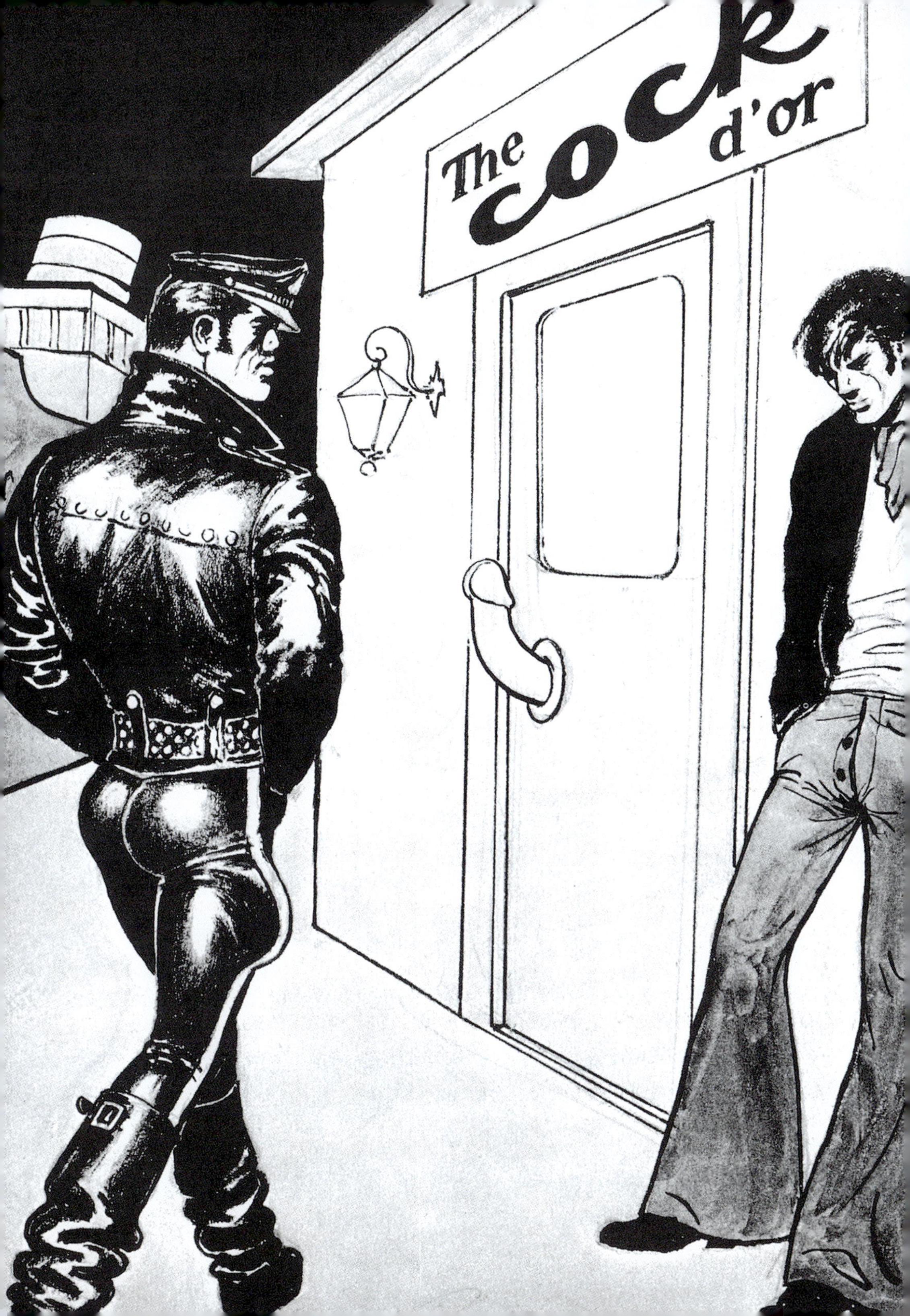

The CoCk d'or

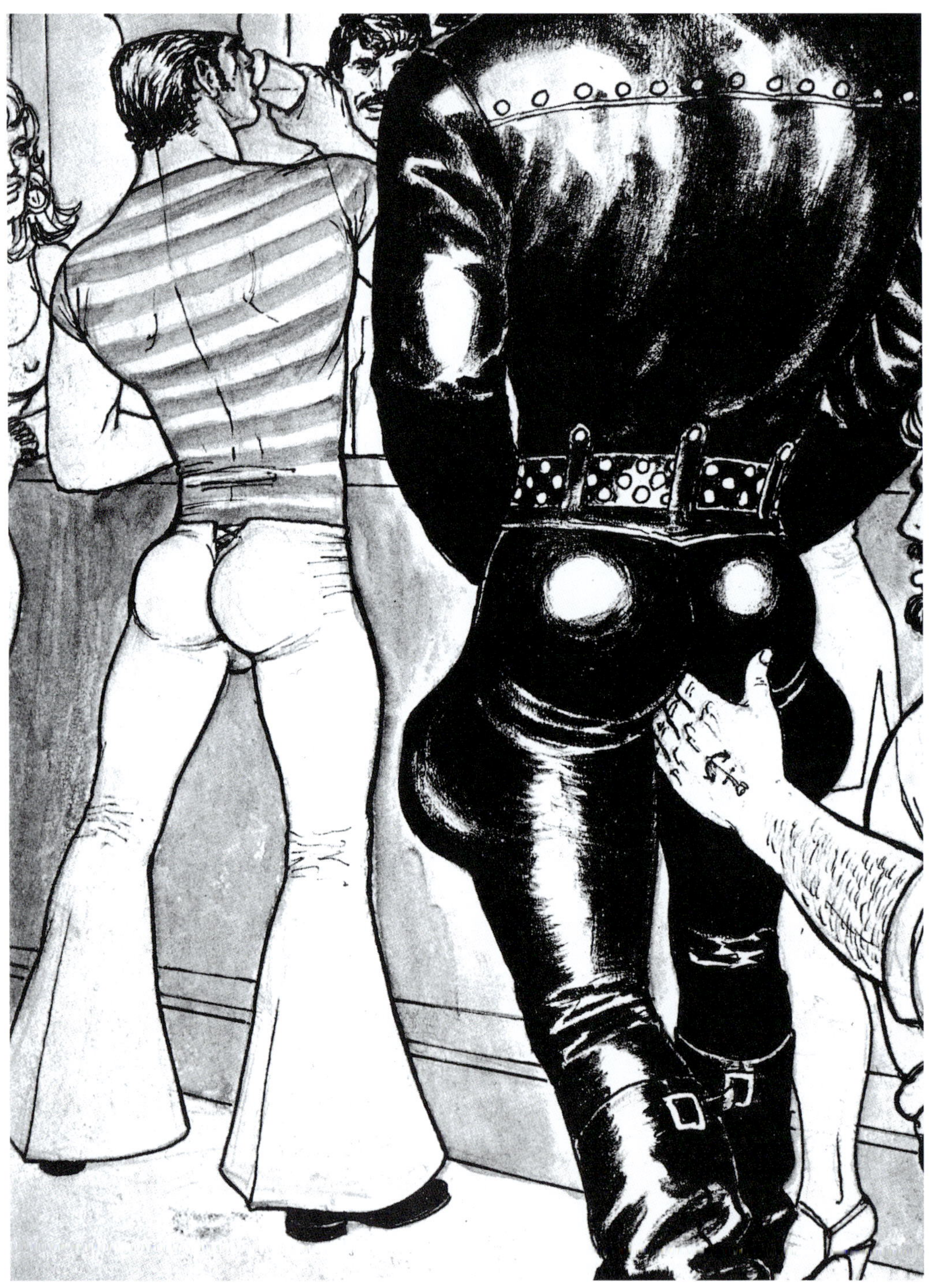

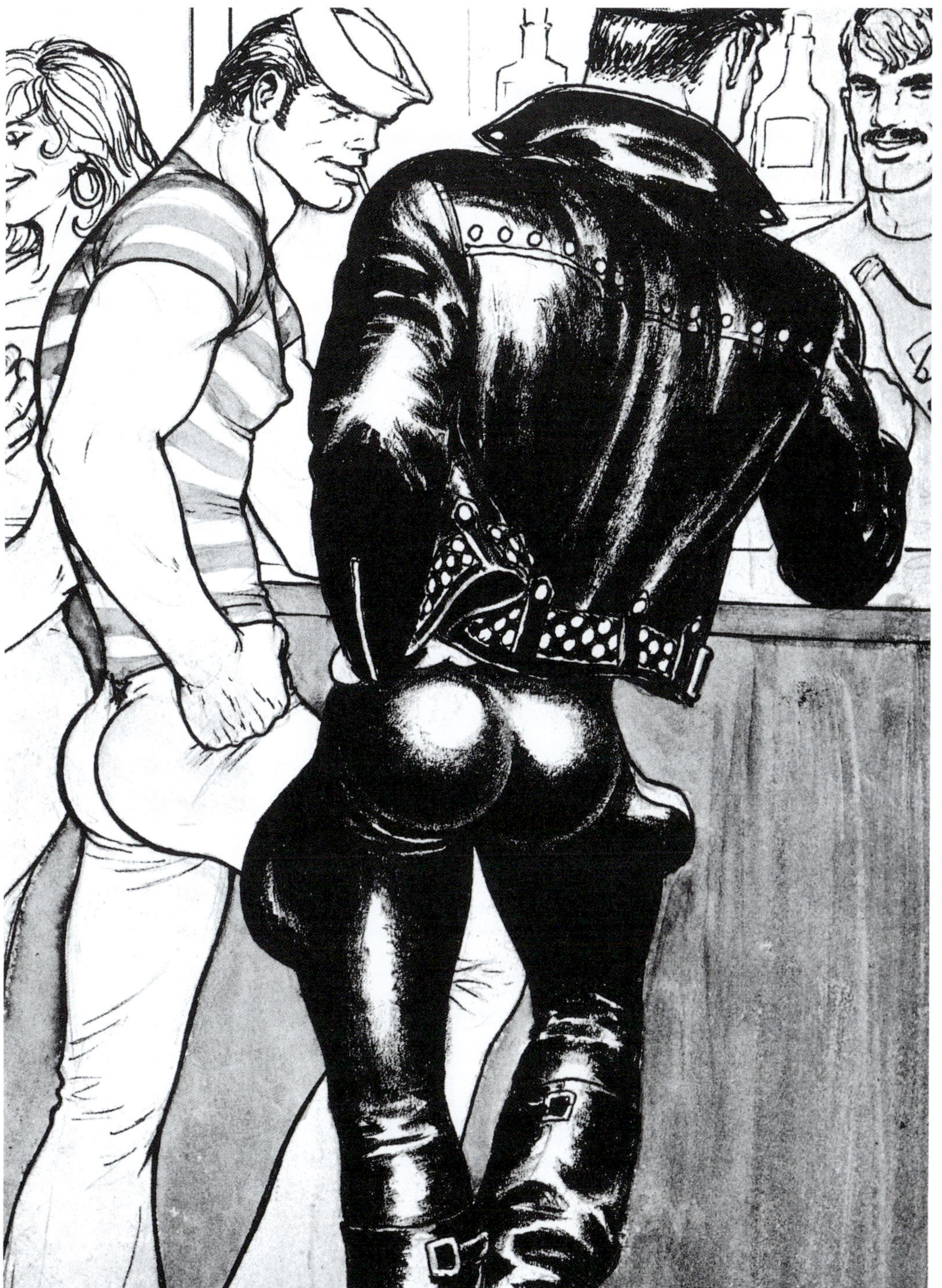

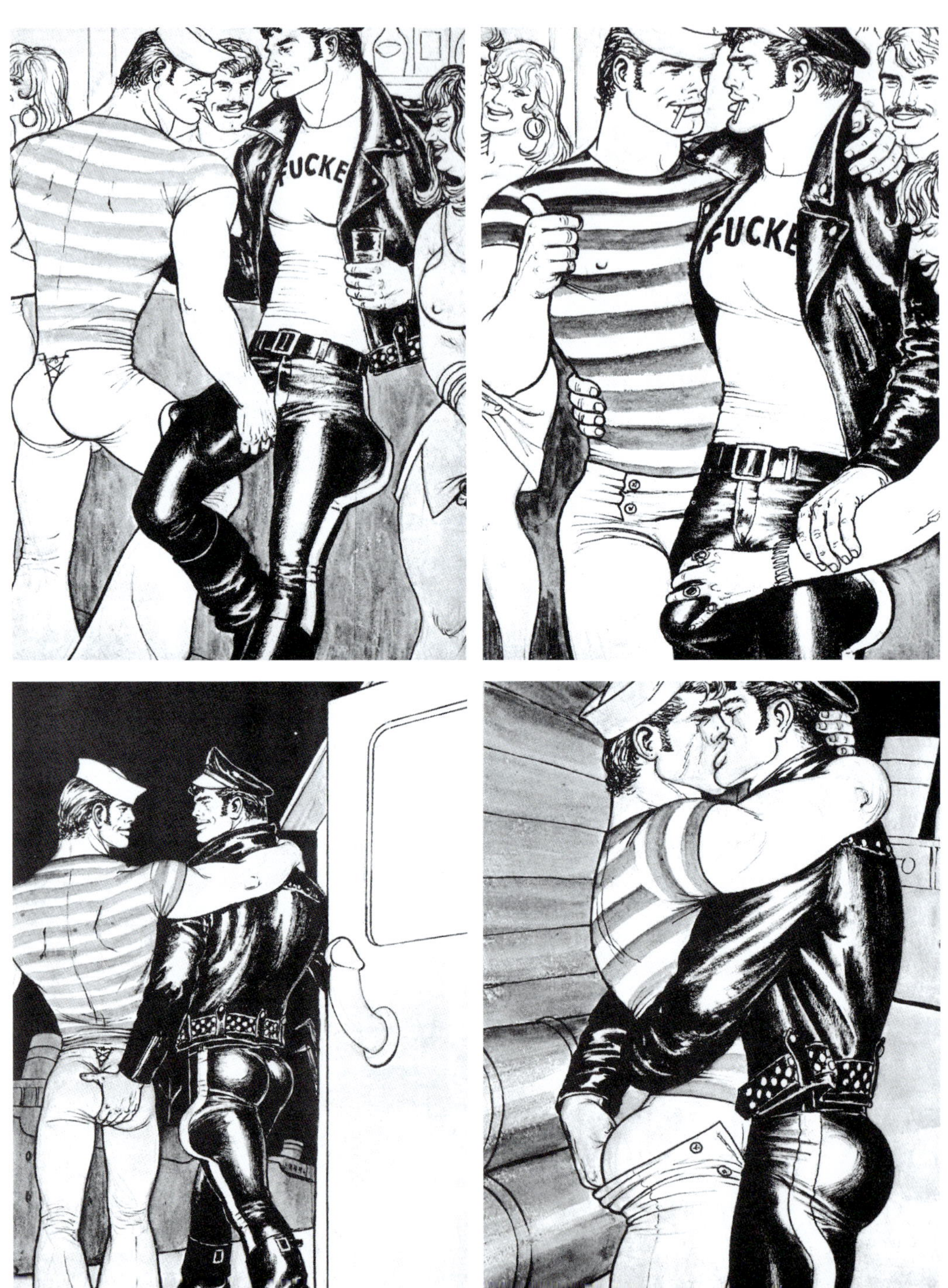

FUCKE
FUCKE

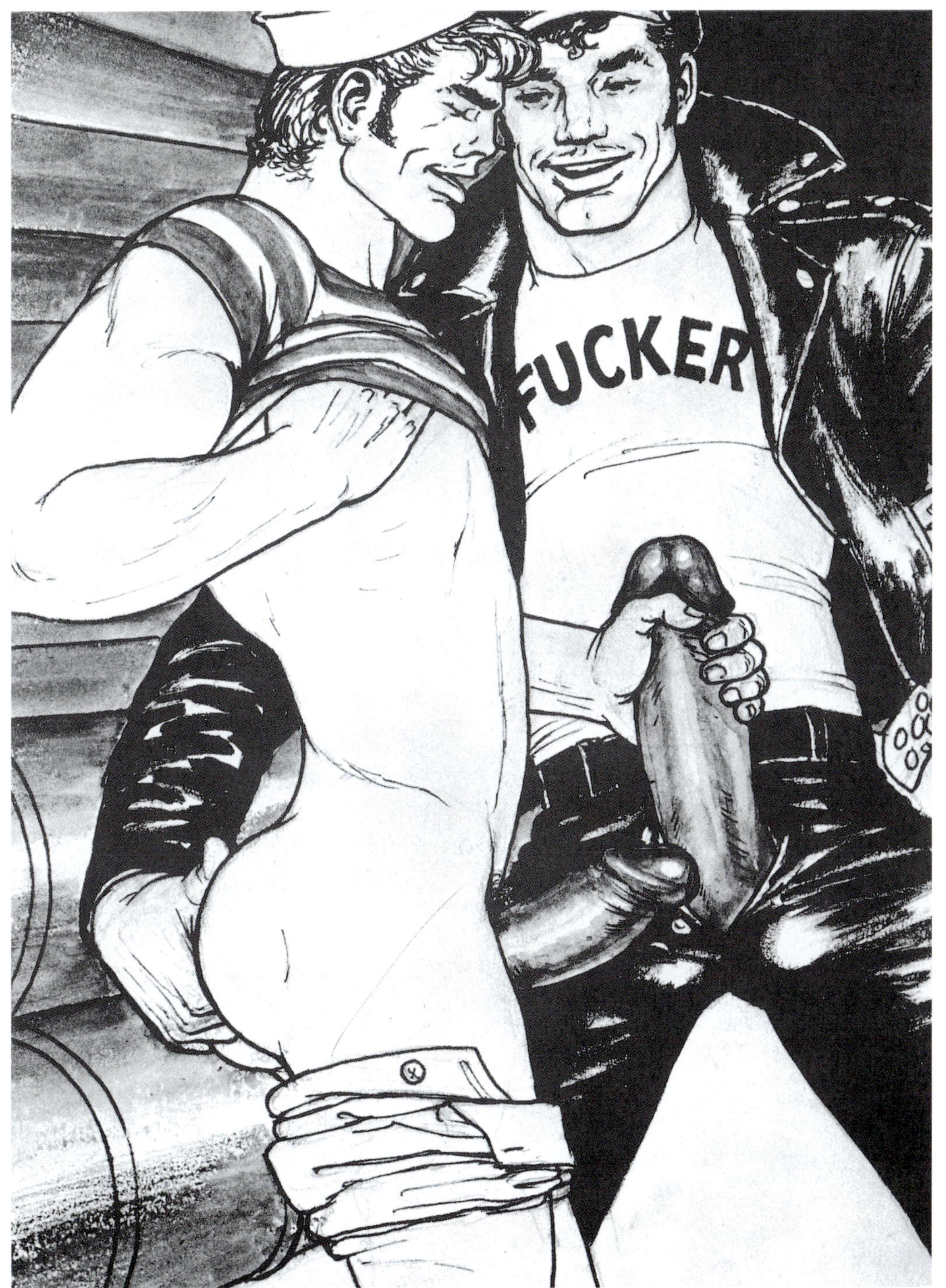
FUCKER

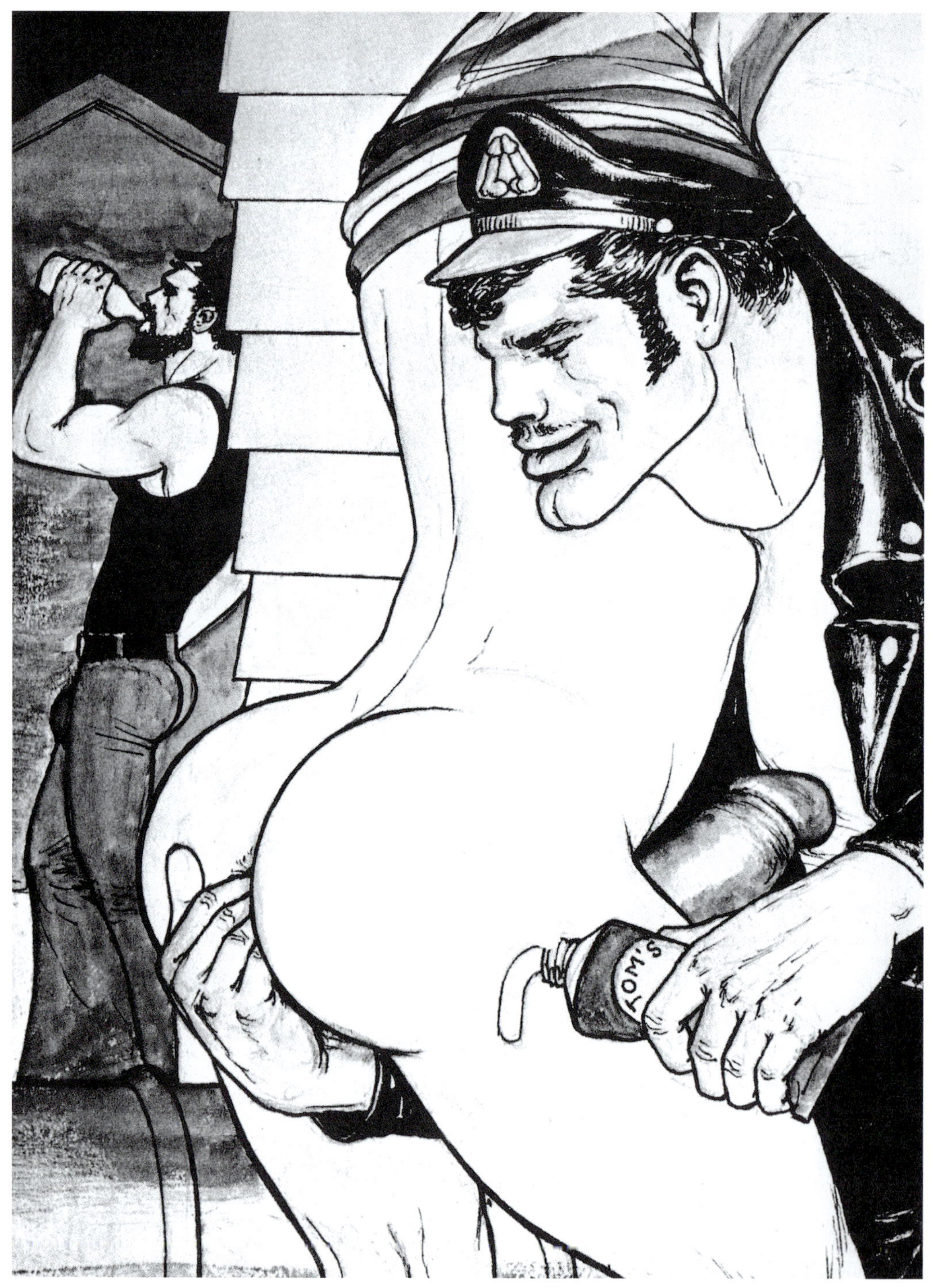
TOM'S

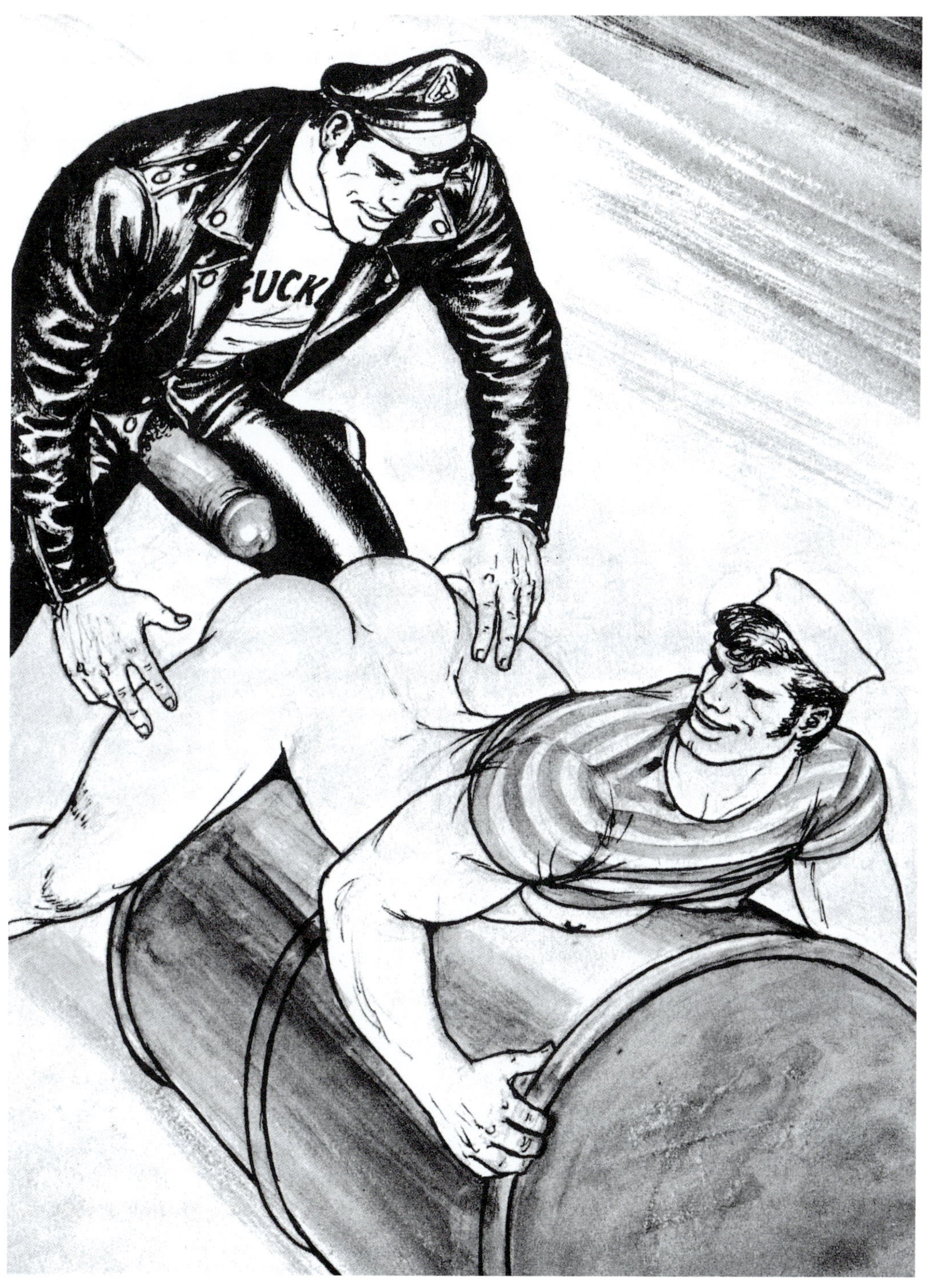
FUCK

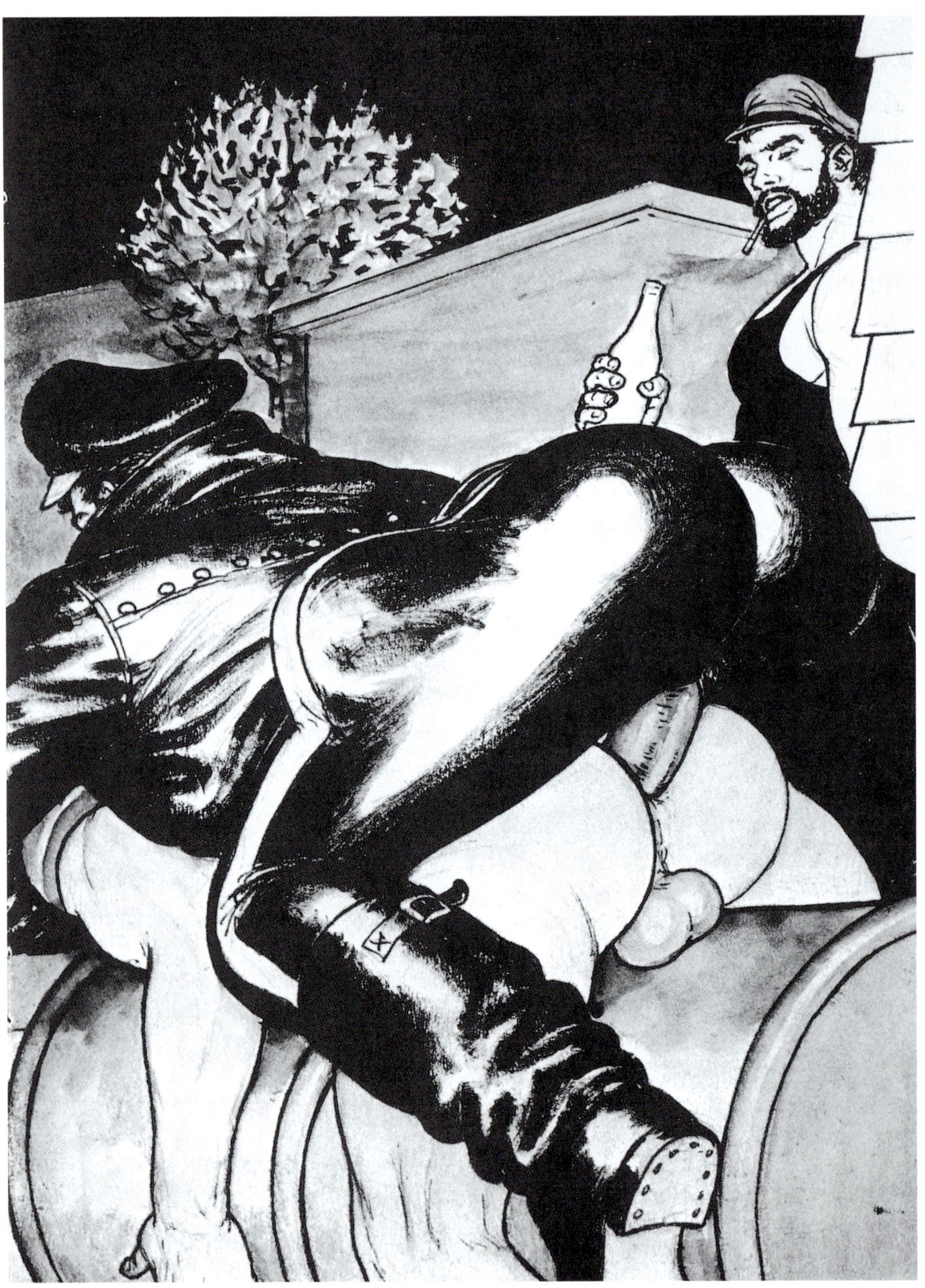

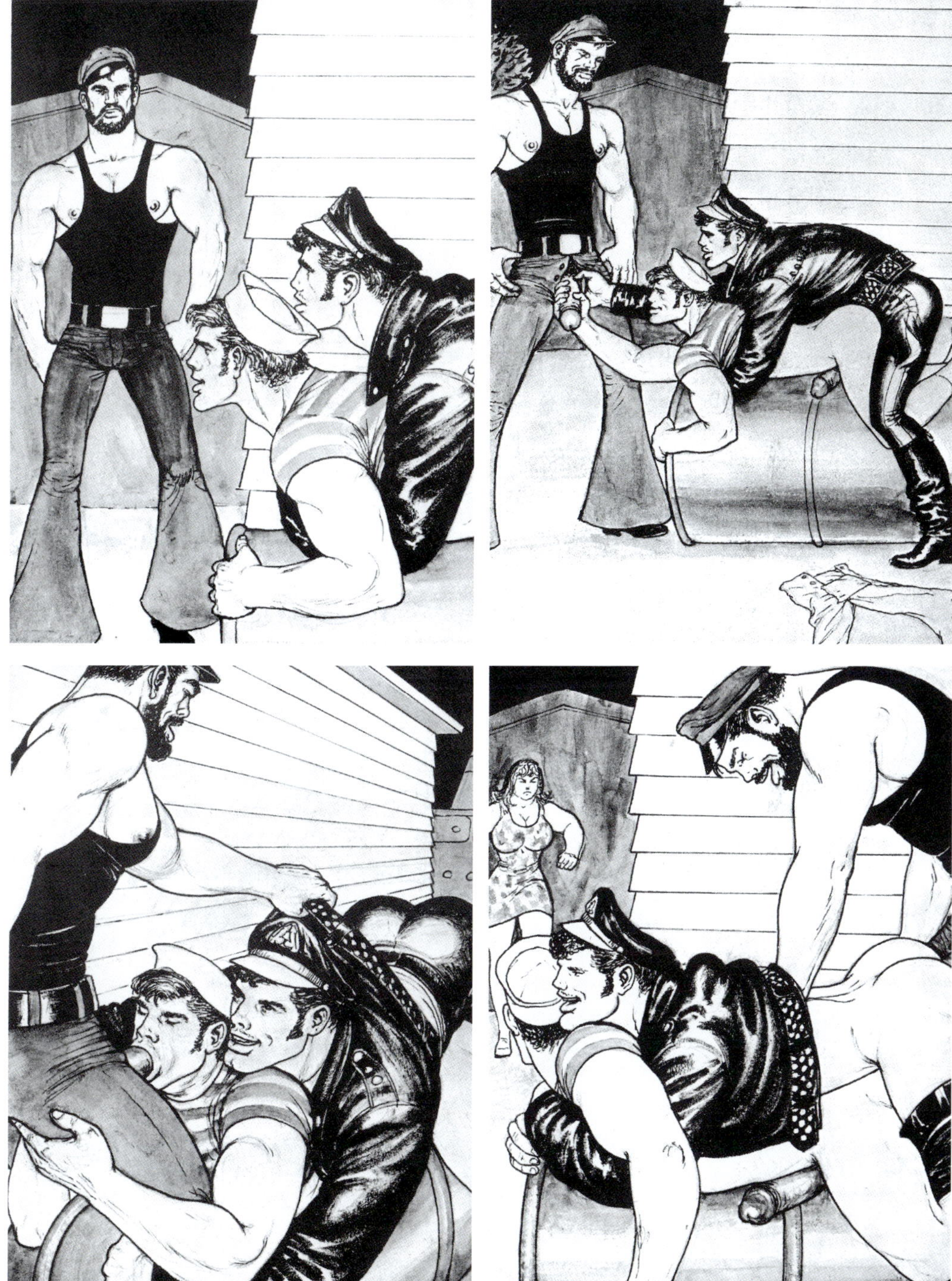

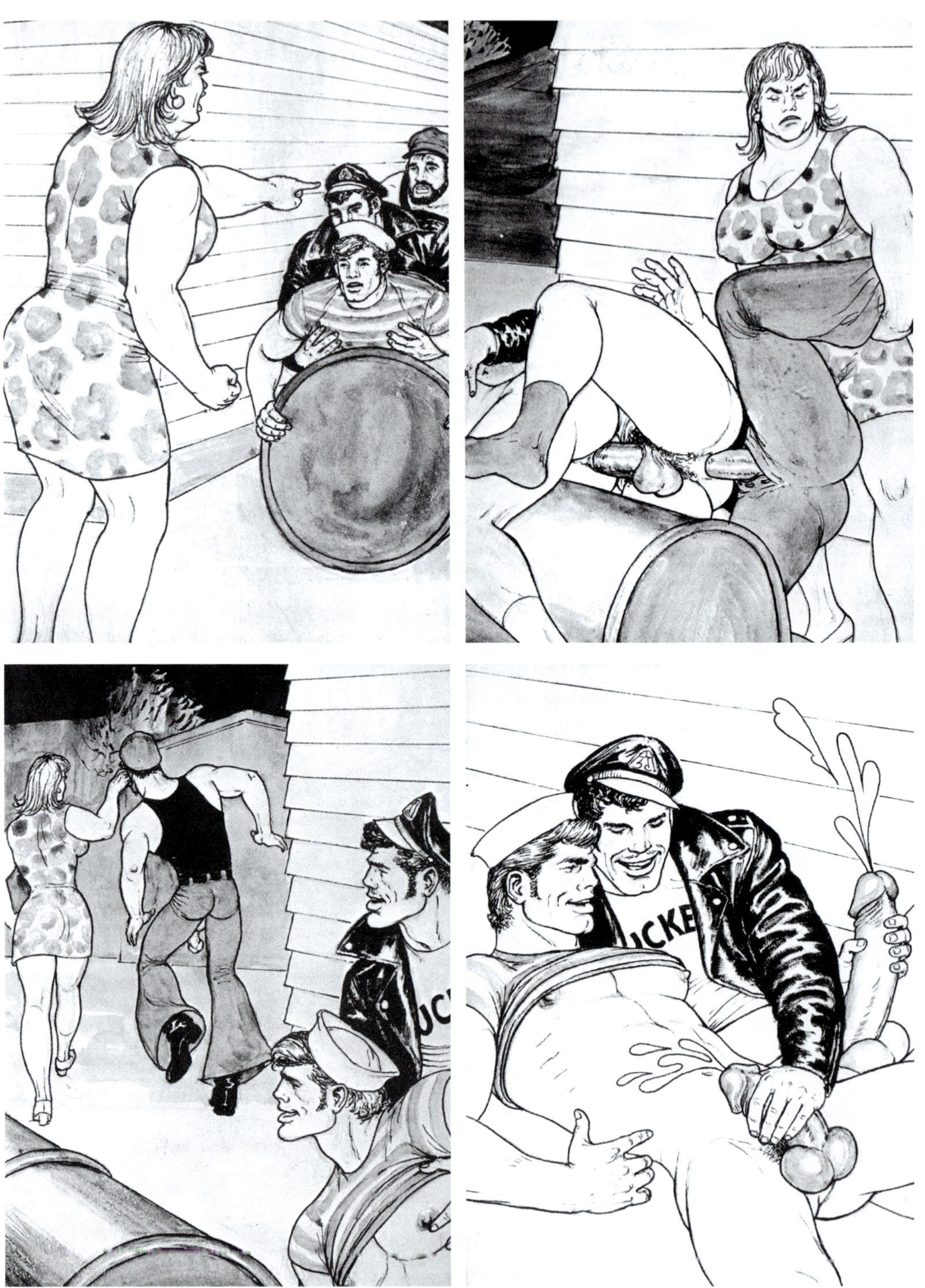
UCKE

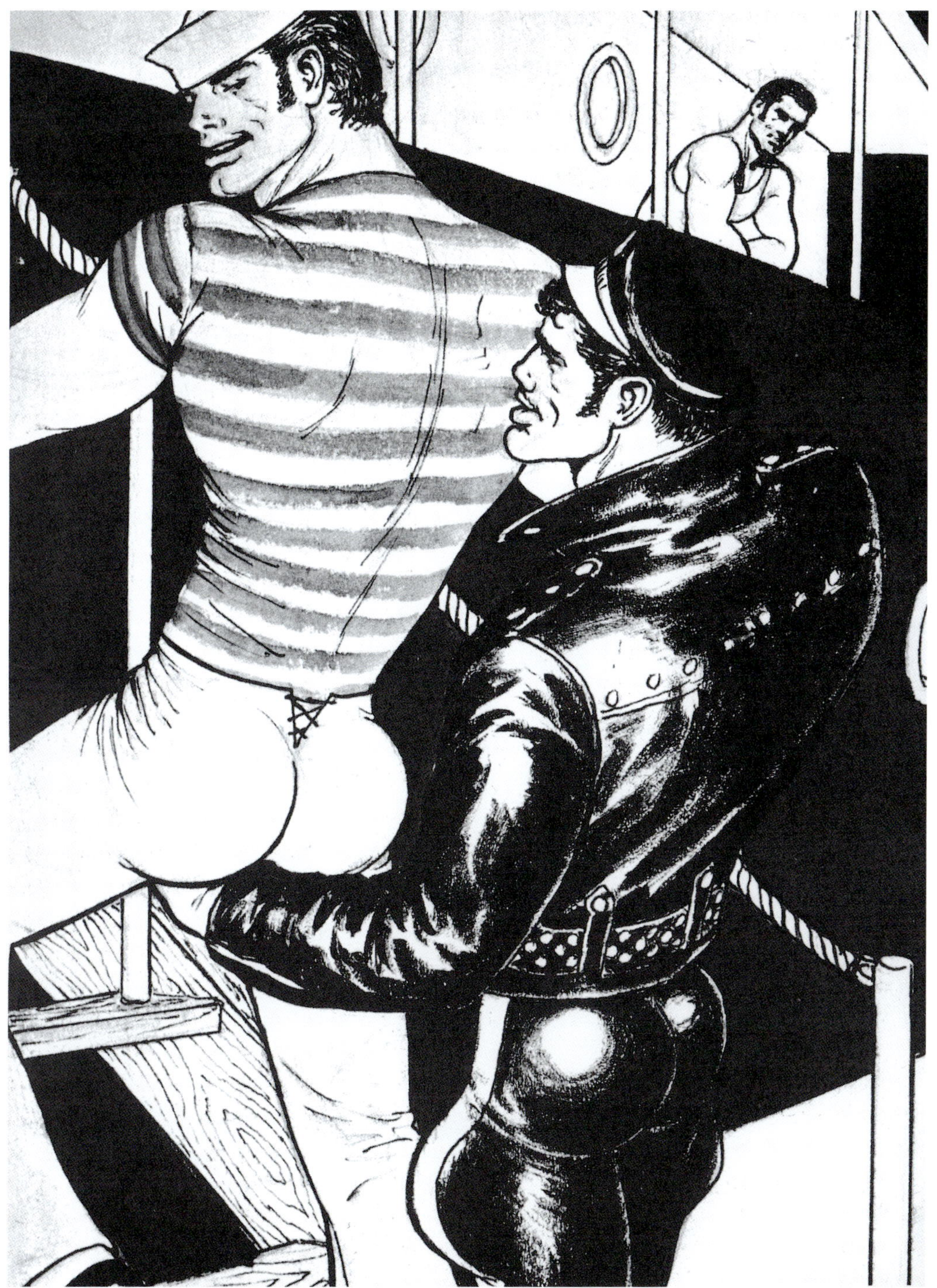

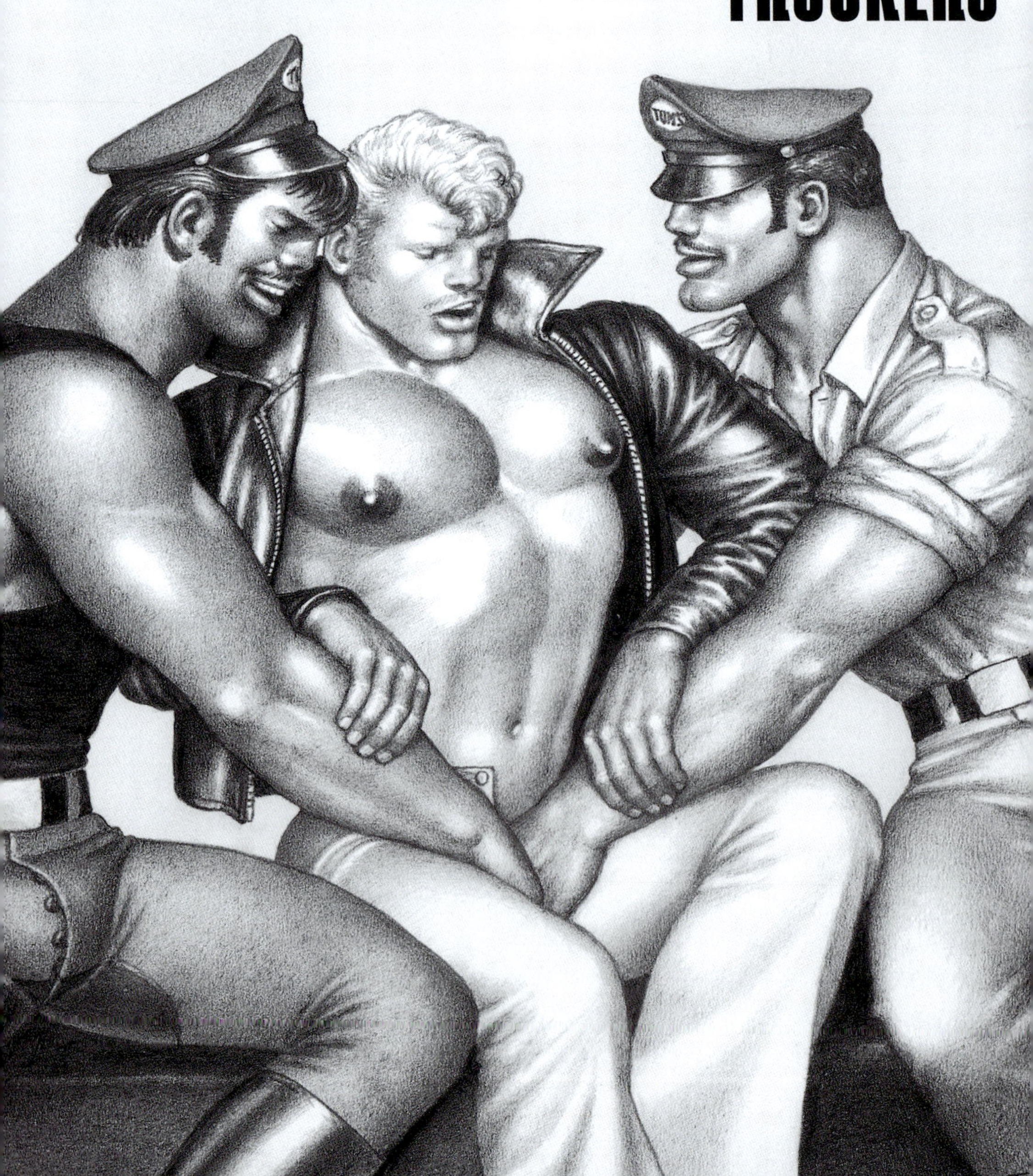

kake 10

RAUNCHY TRUCKERS

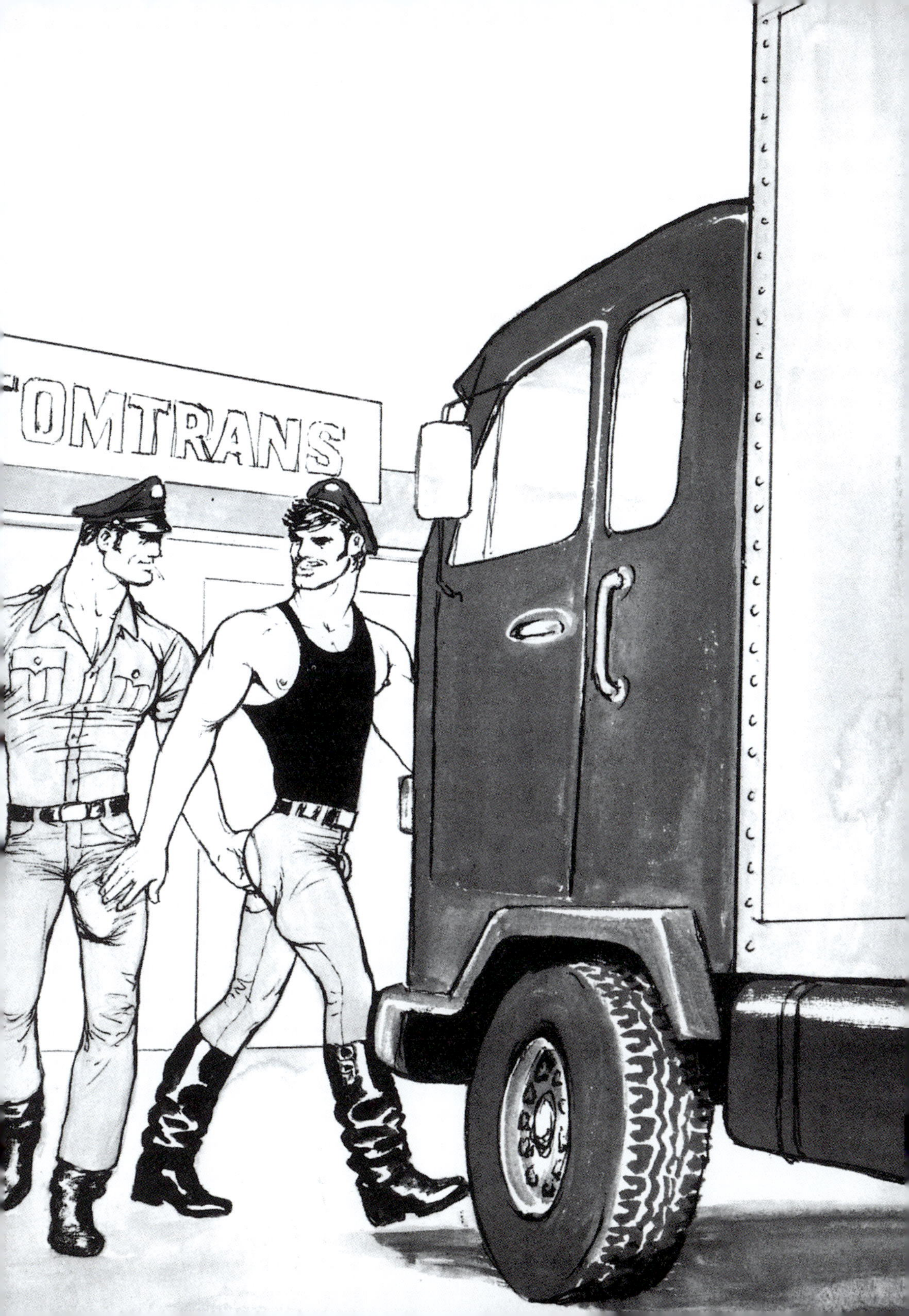

OMTRANS

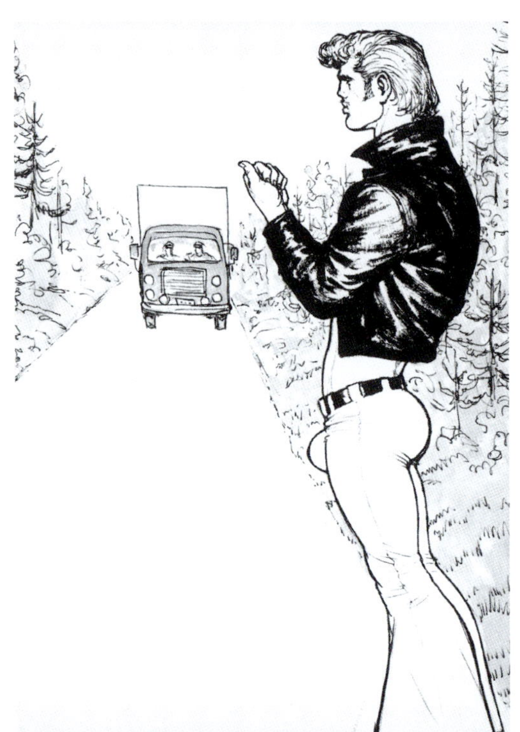
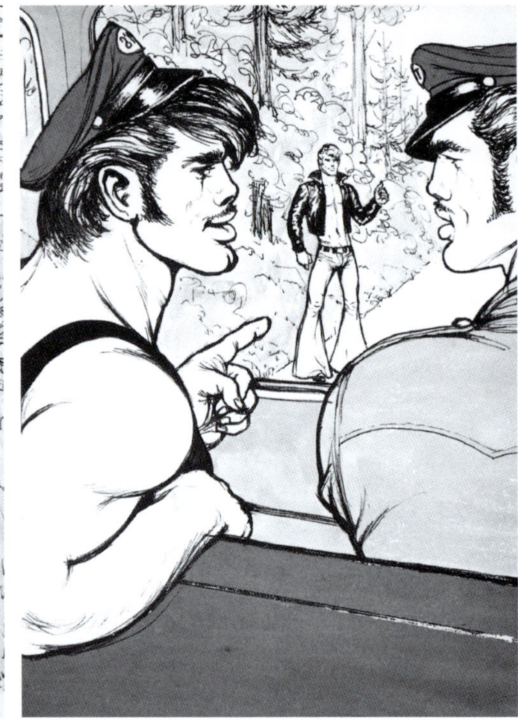
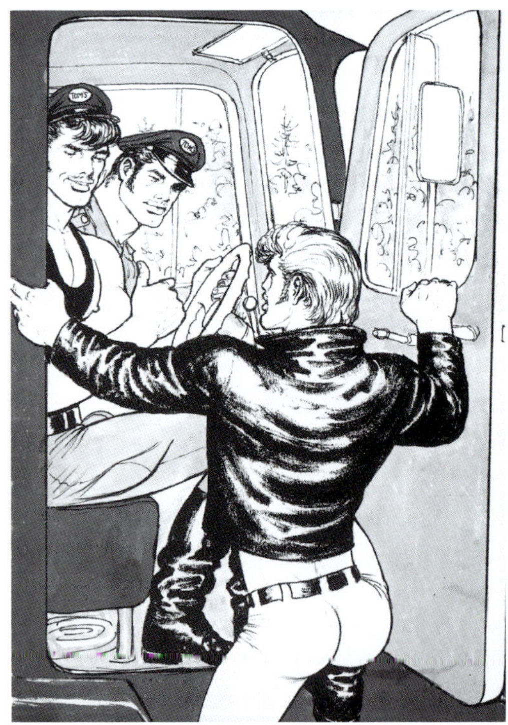
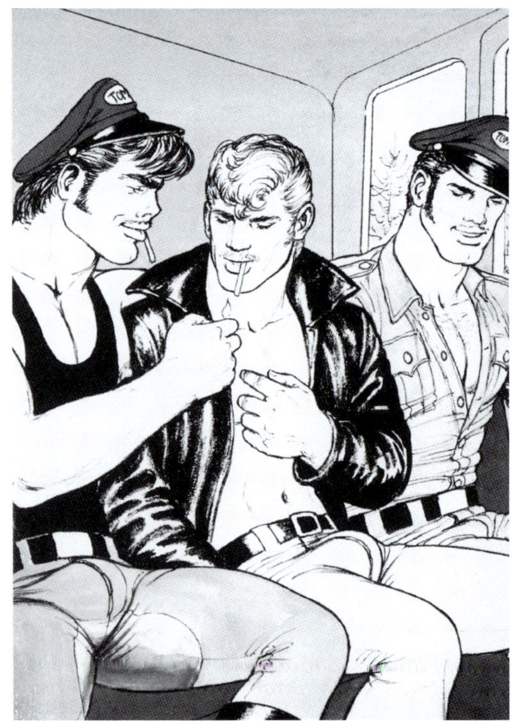

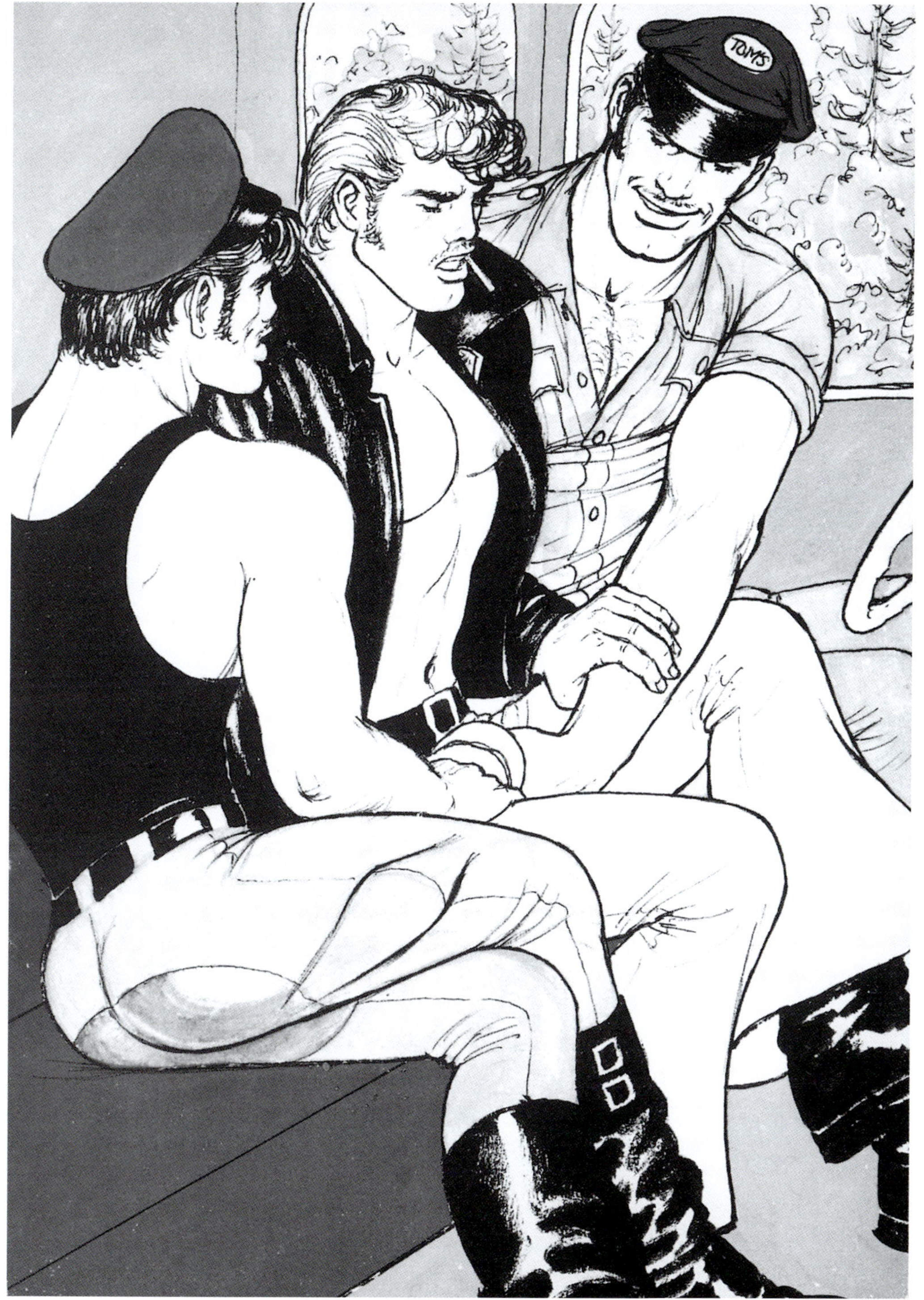
TOM'S

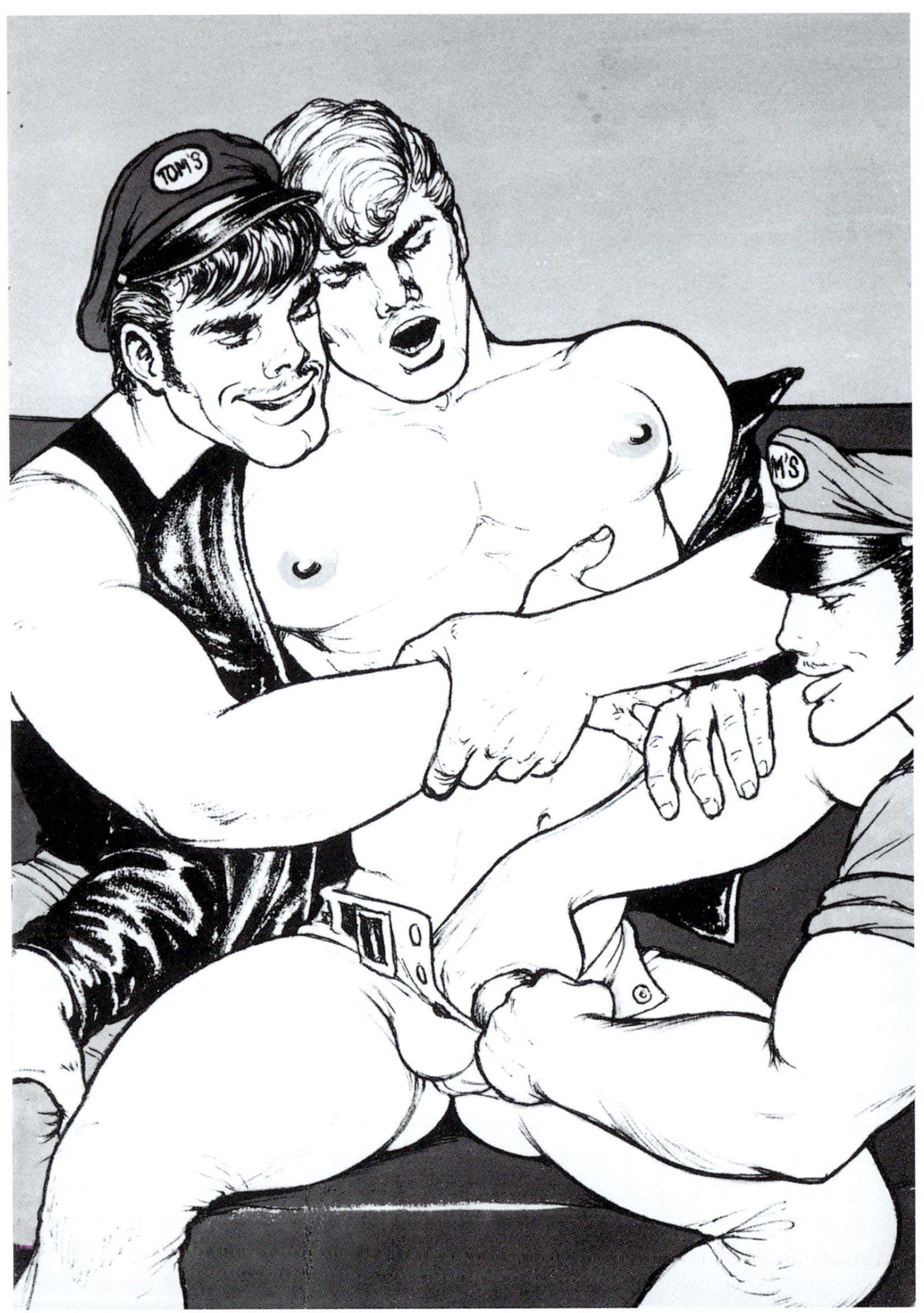

TOM'S
TOM'S

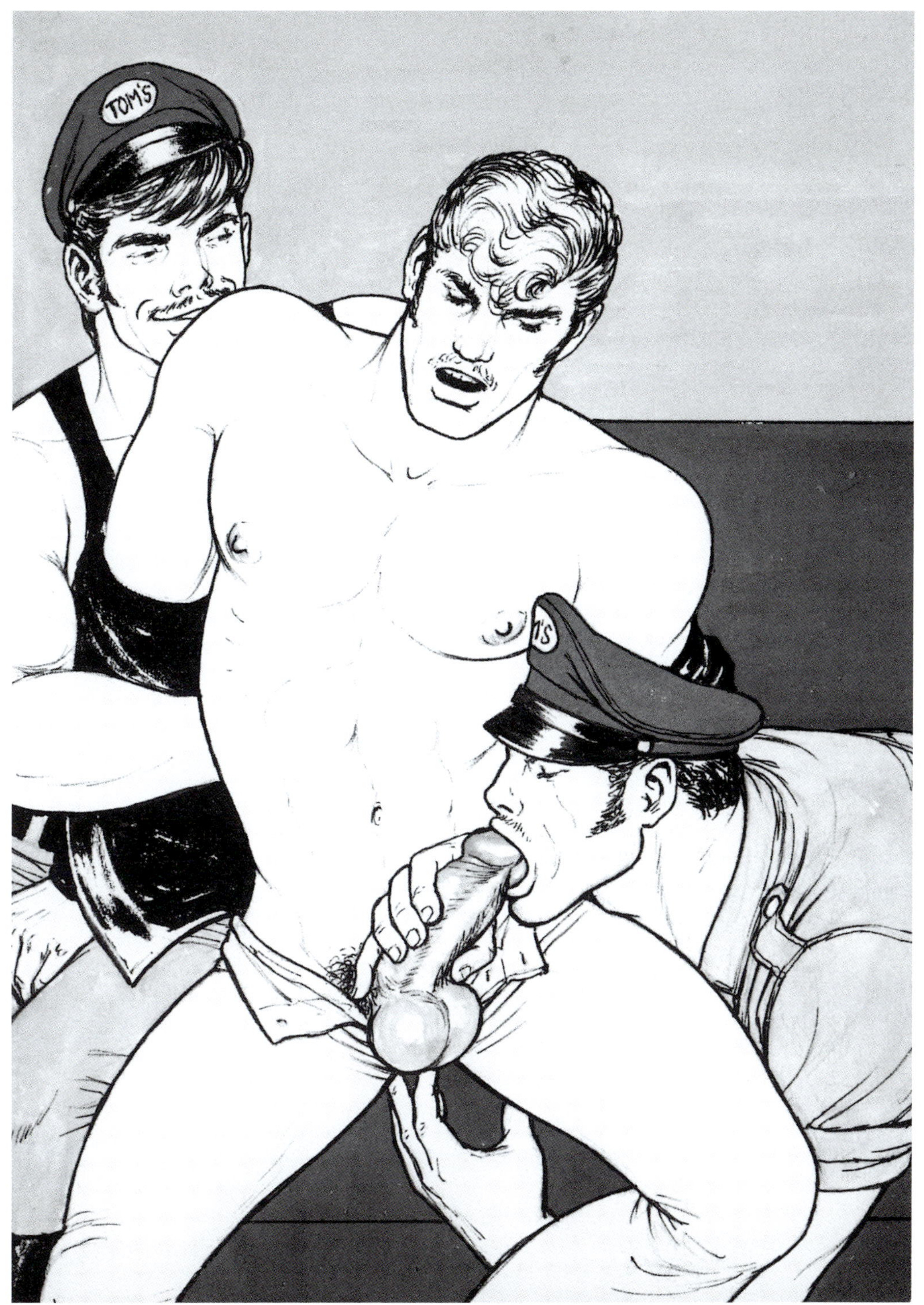

TOM'S
TOM'S

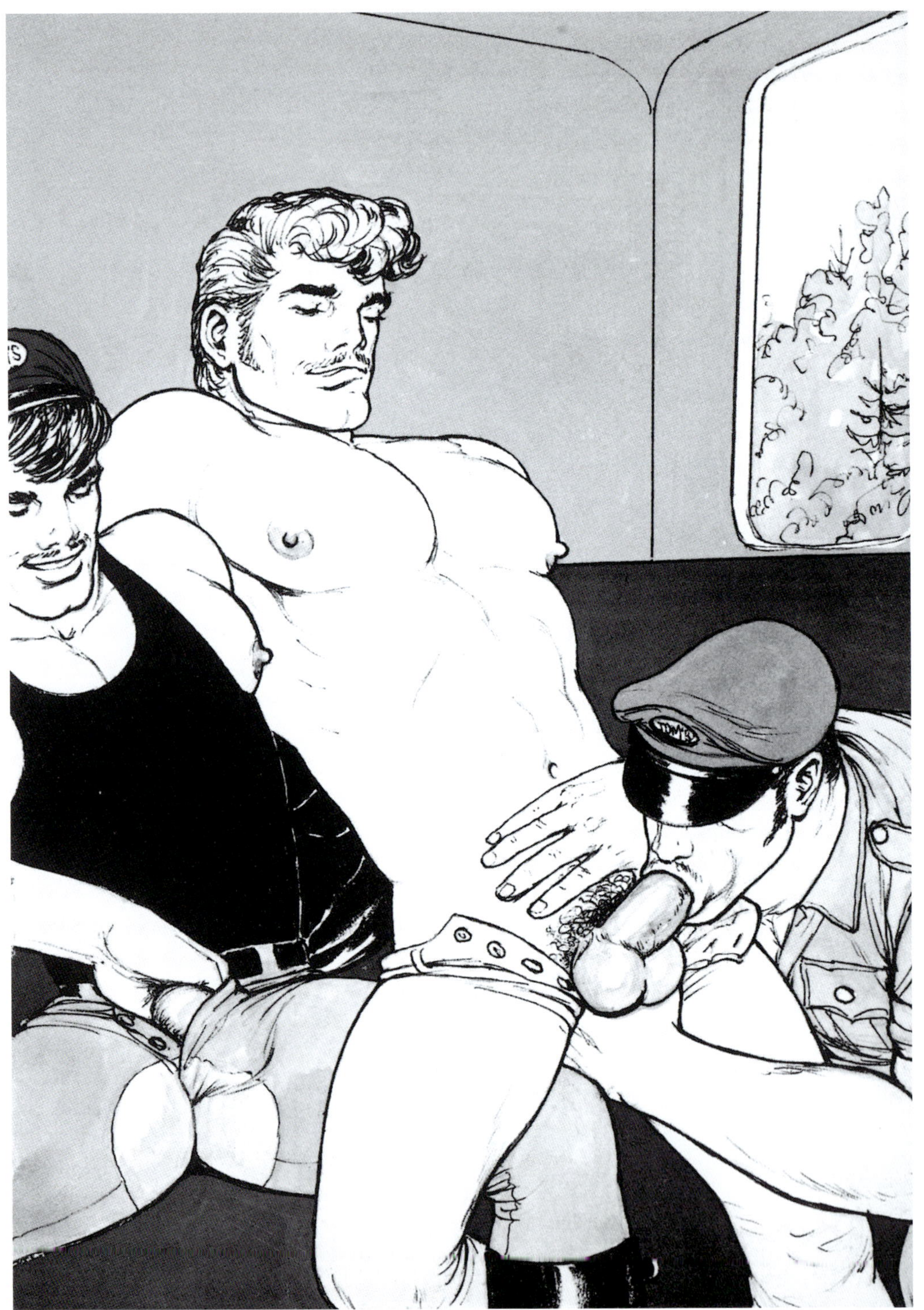

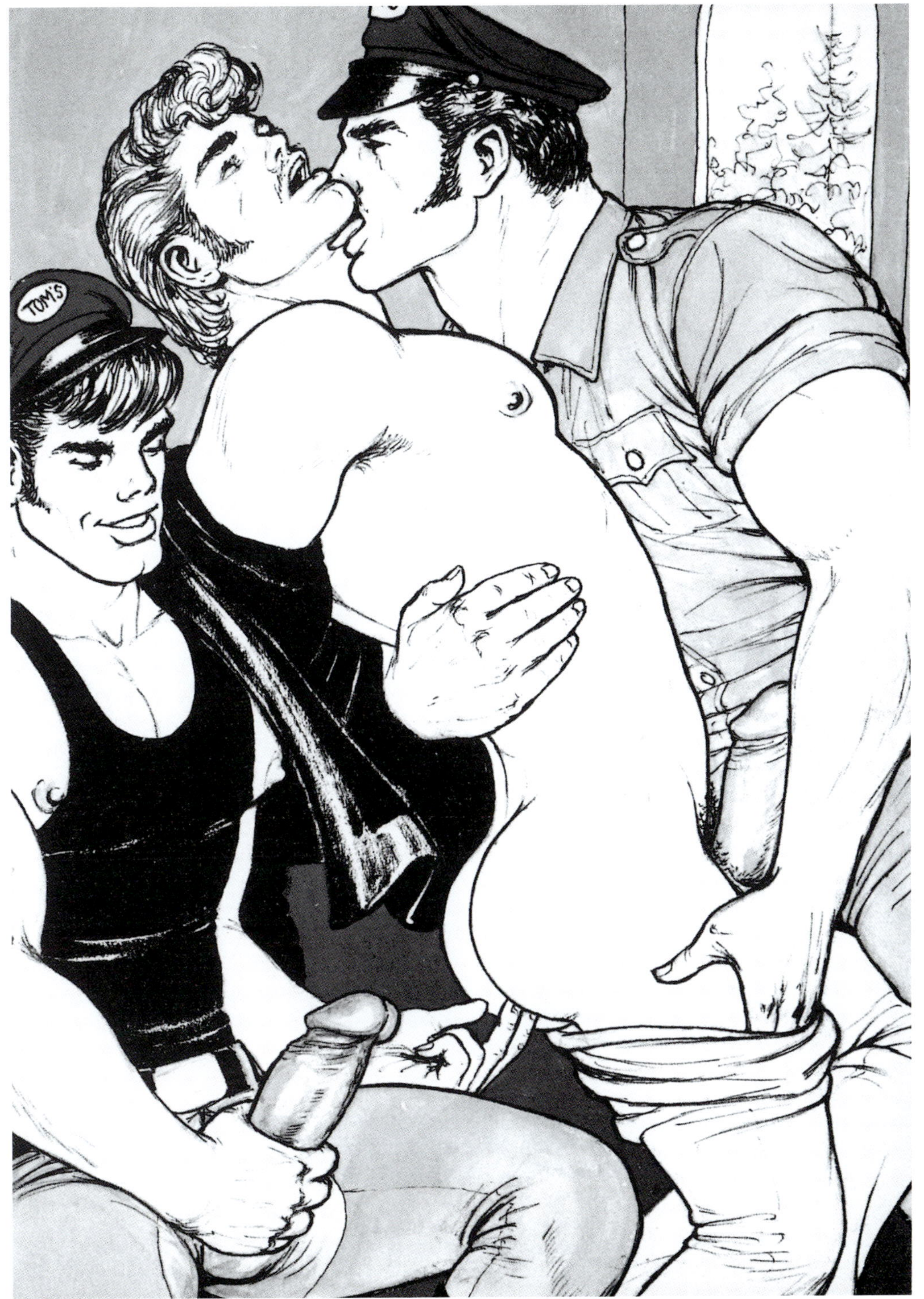
TOM'S

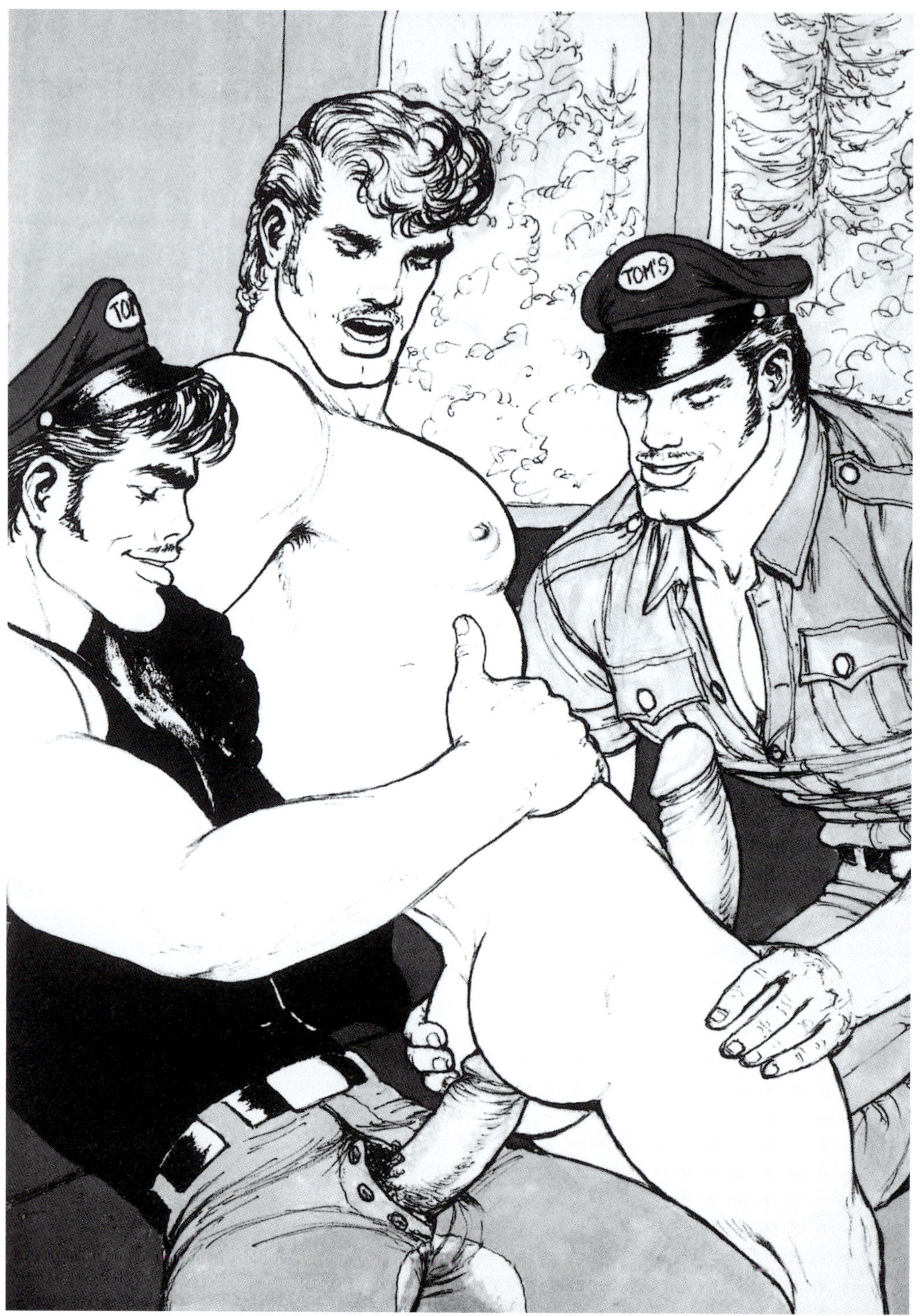

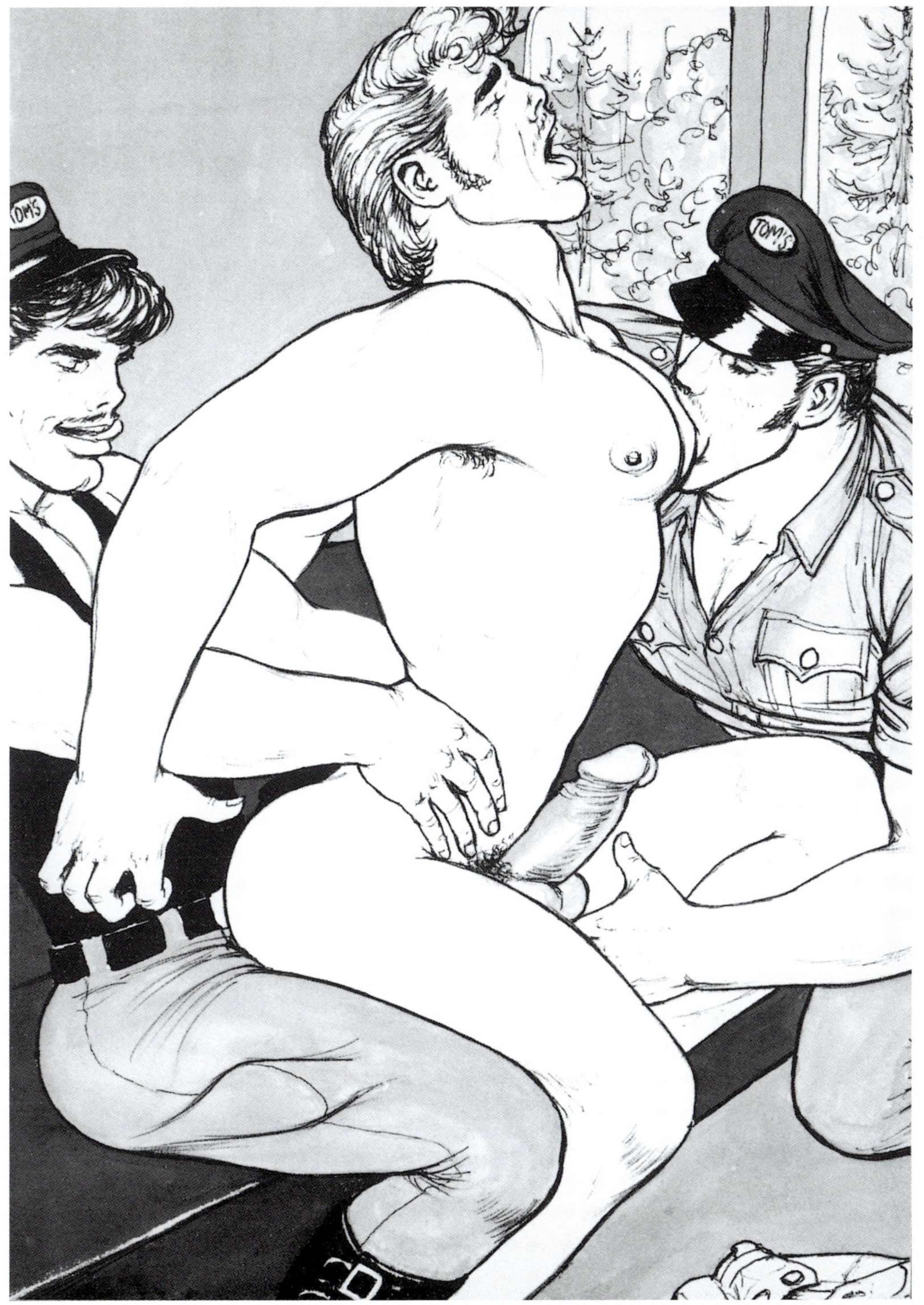
TOM'S
TOM'S

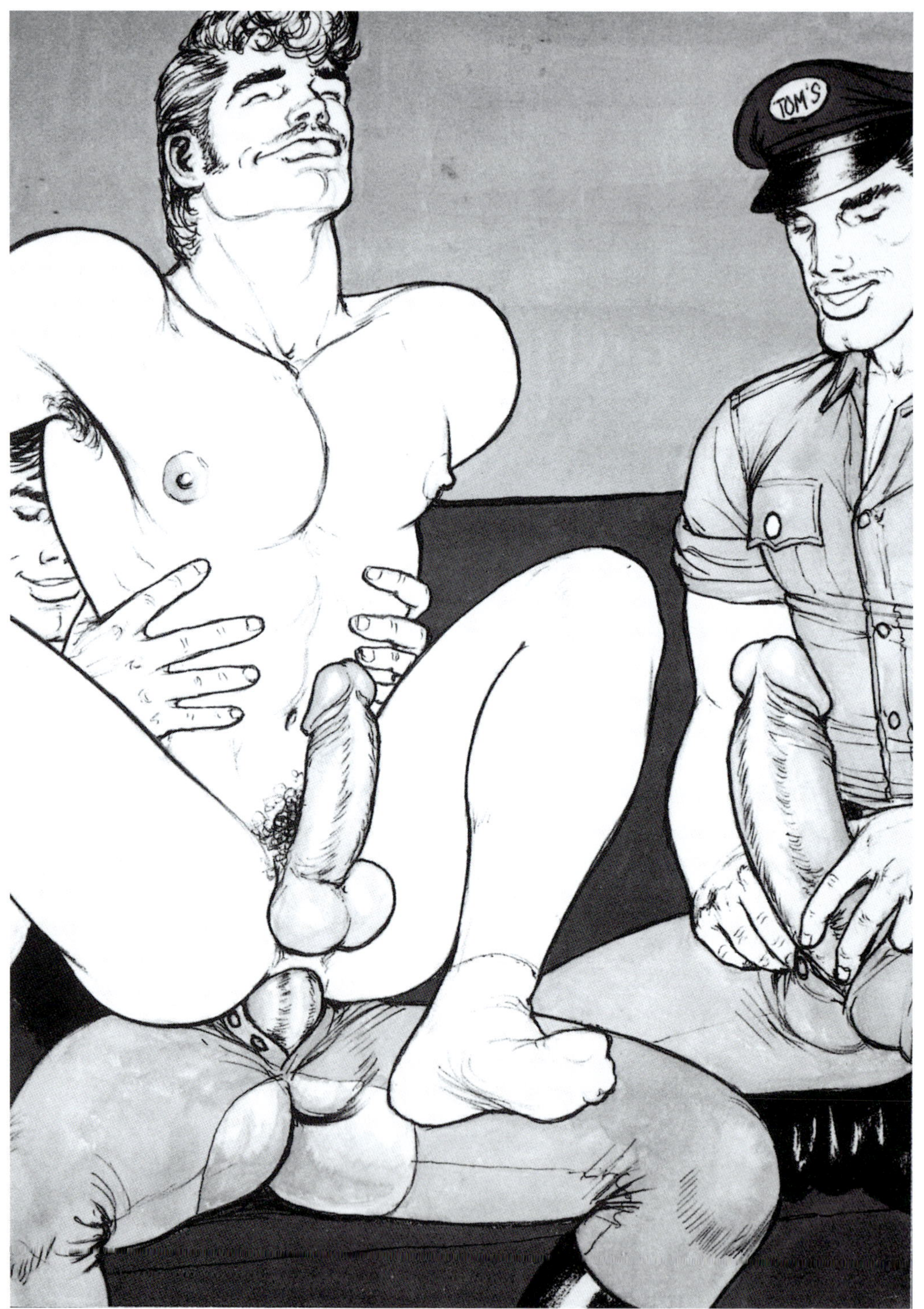
TOM'S

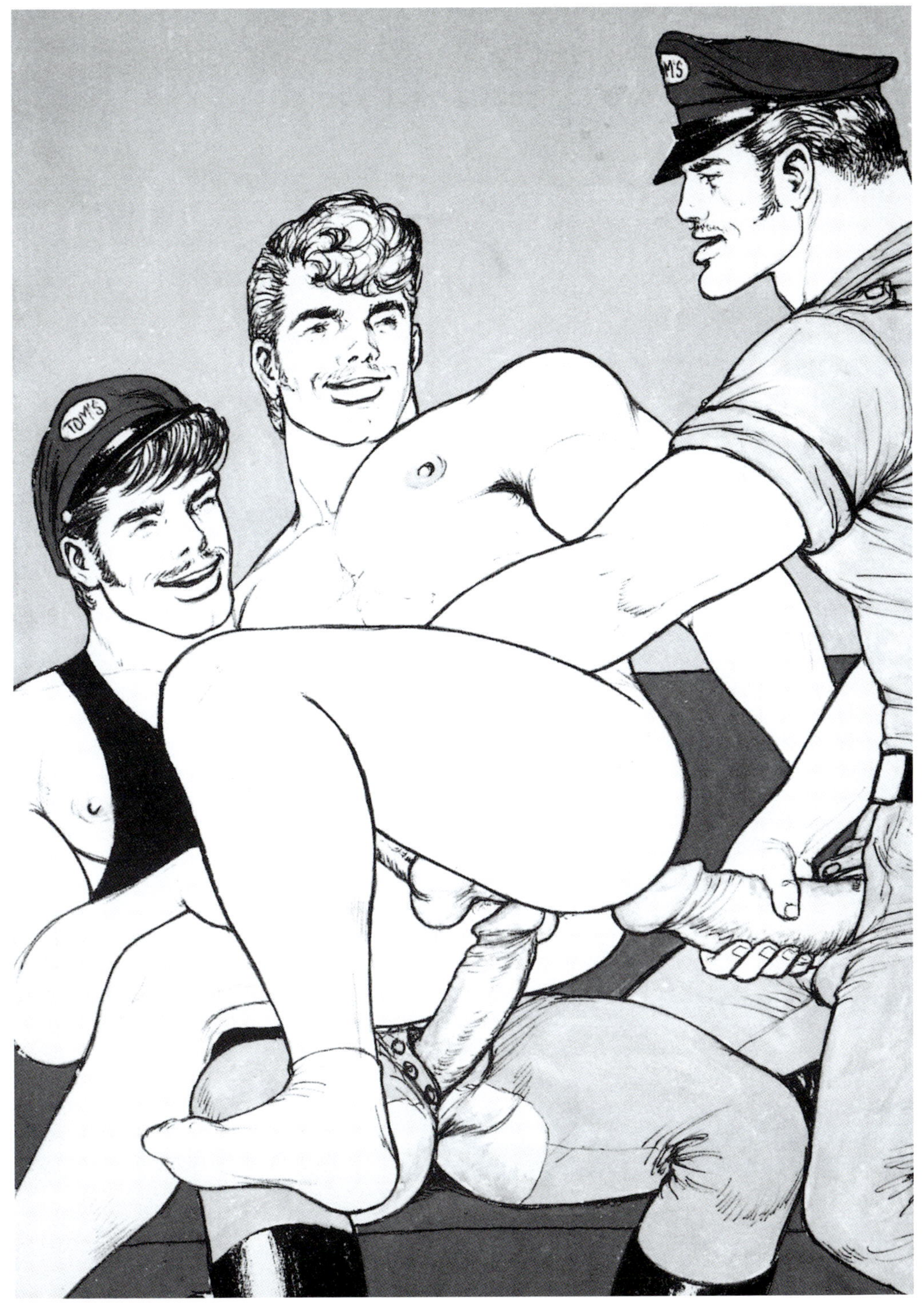

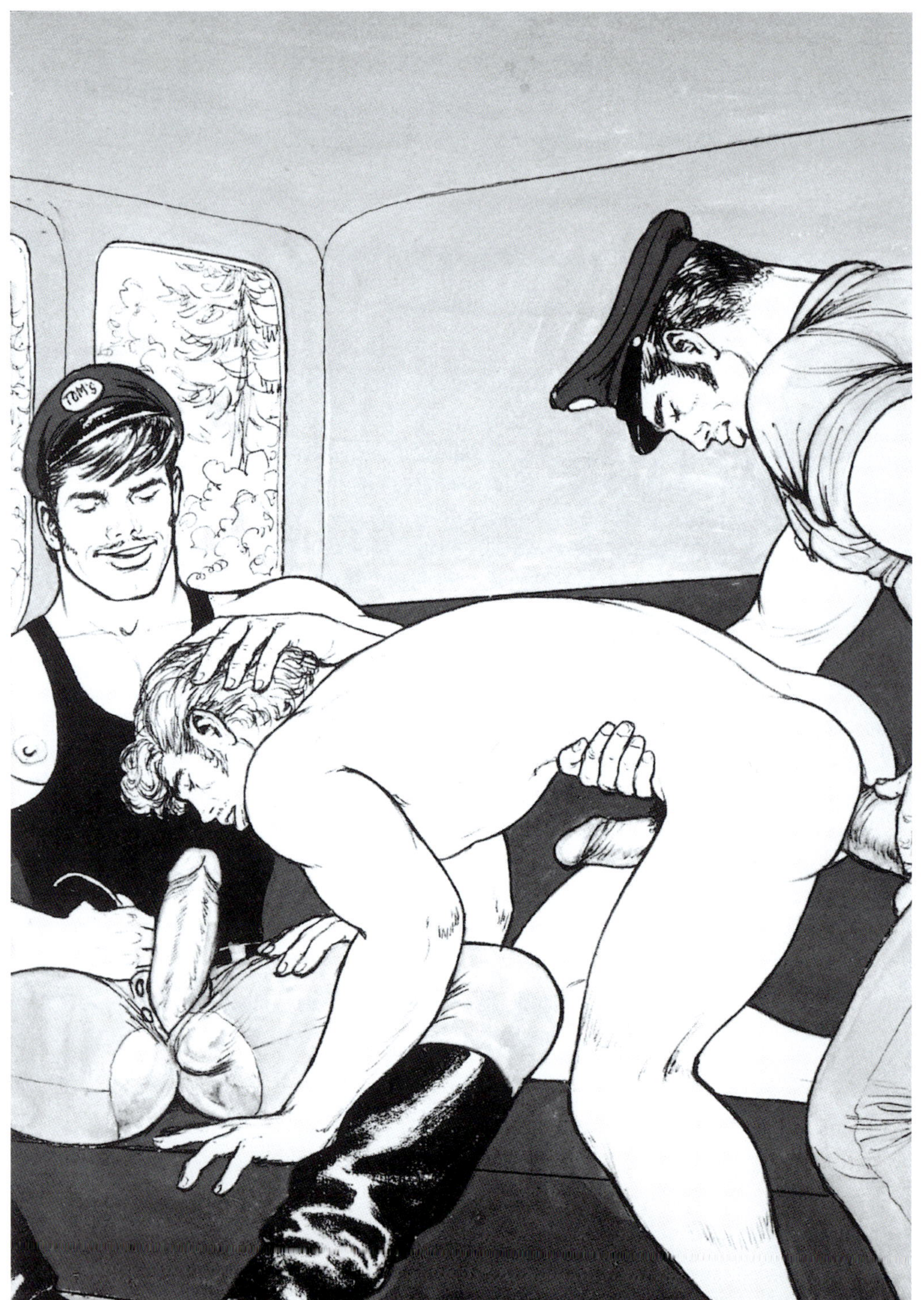
TOM'S

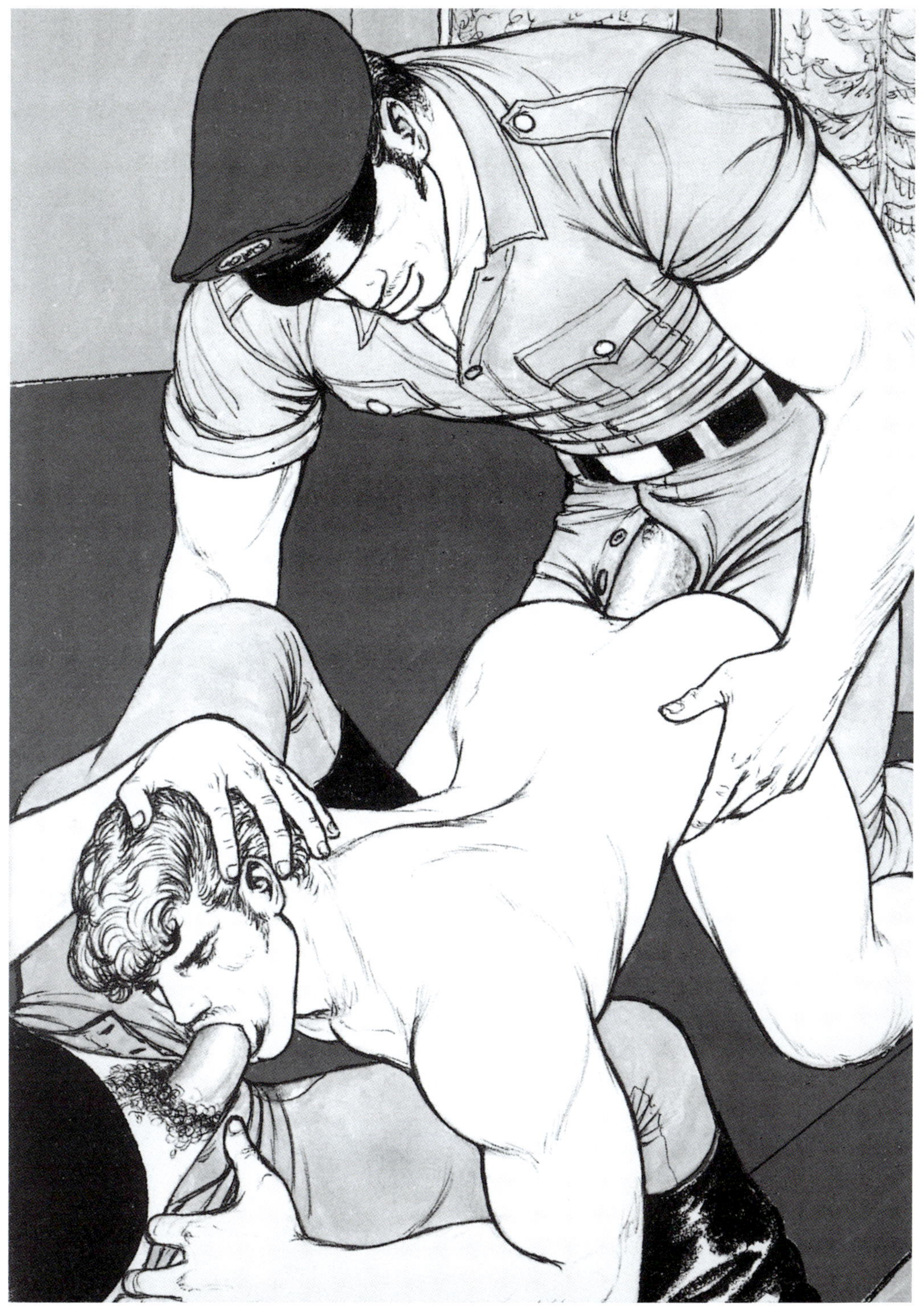

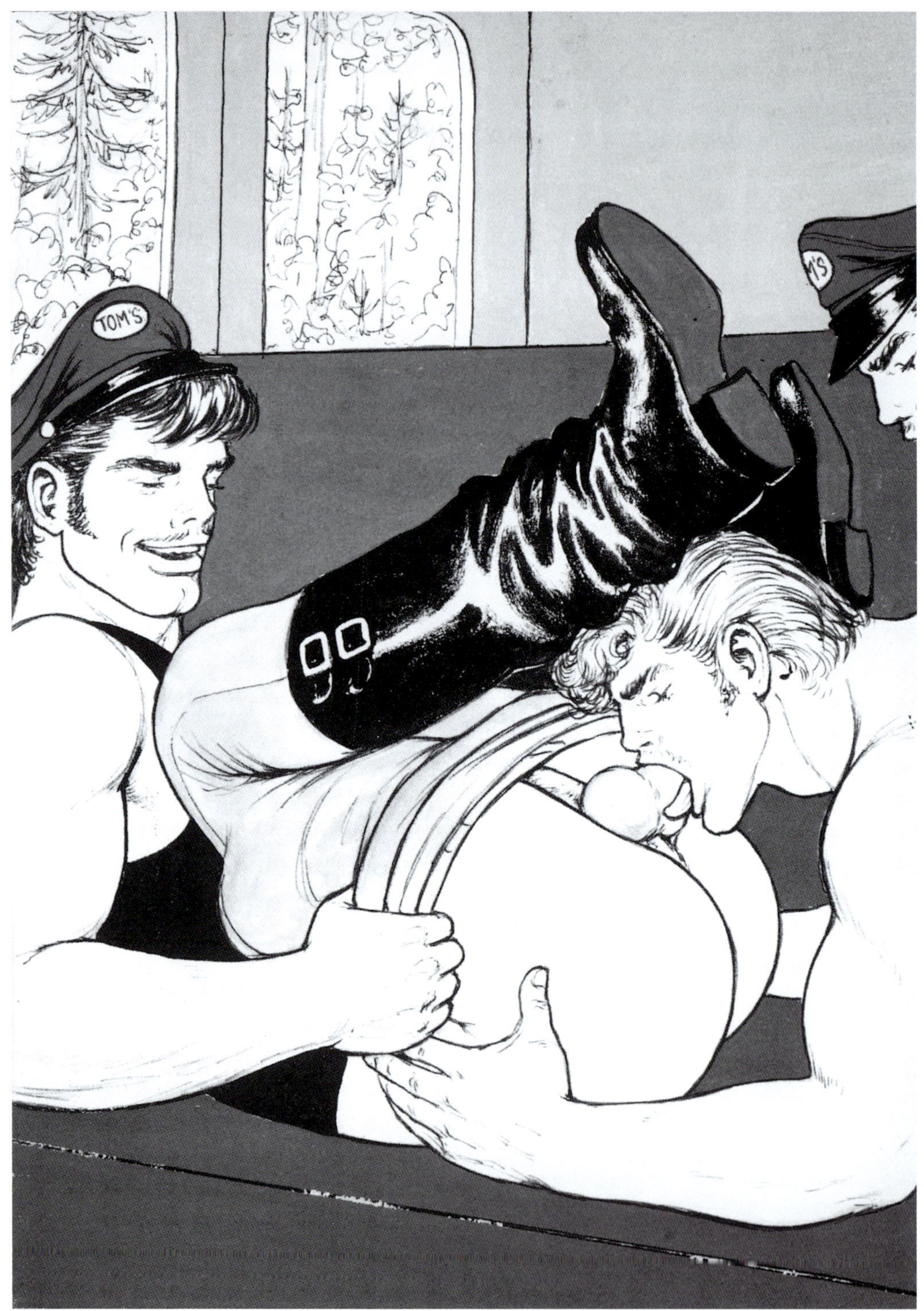

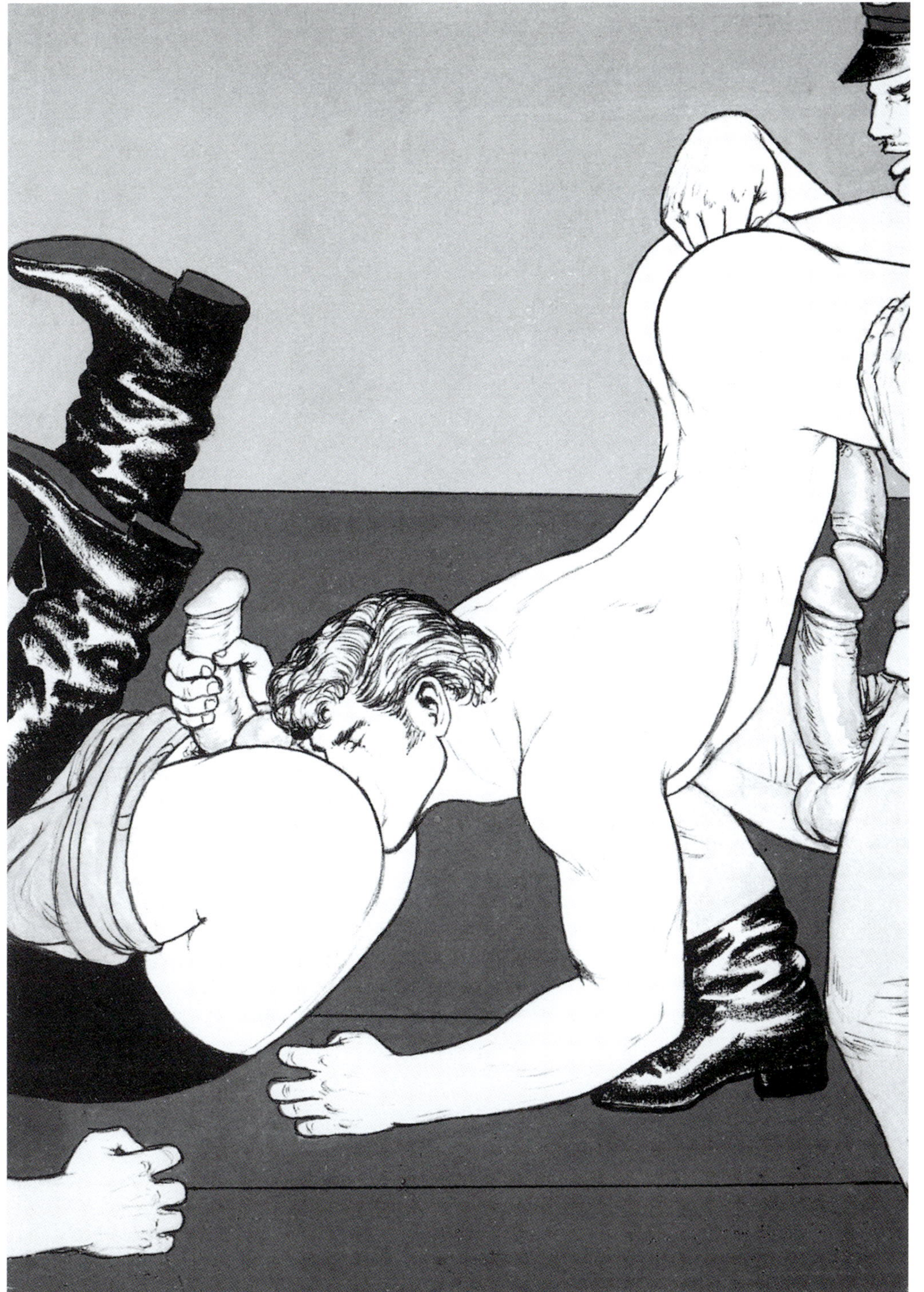

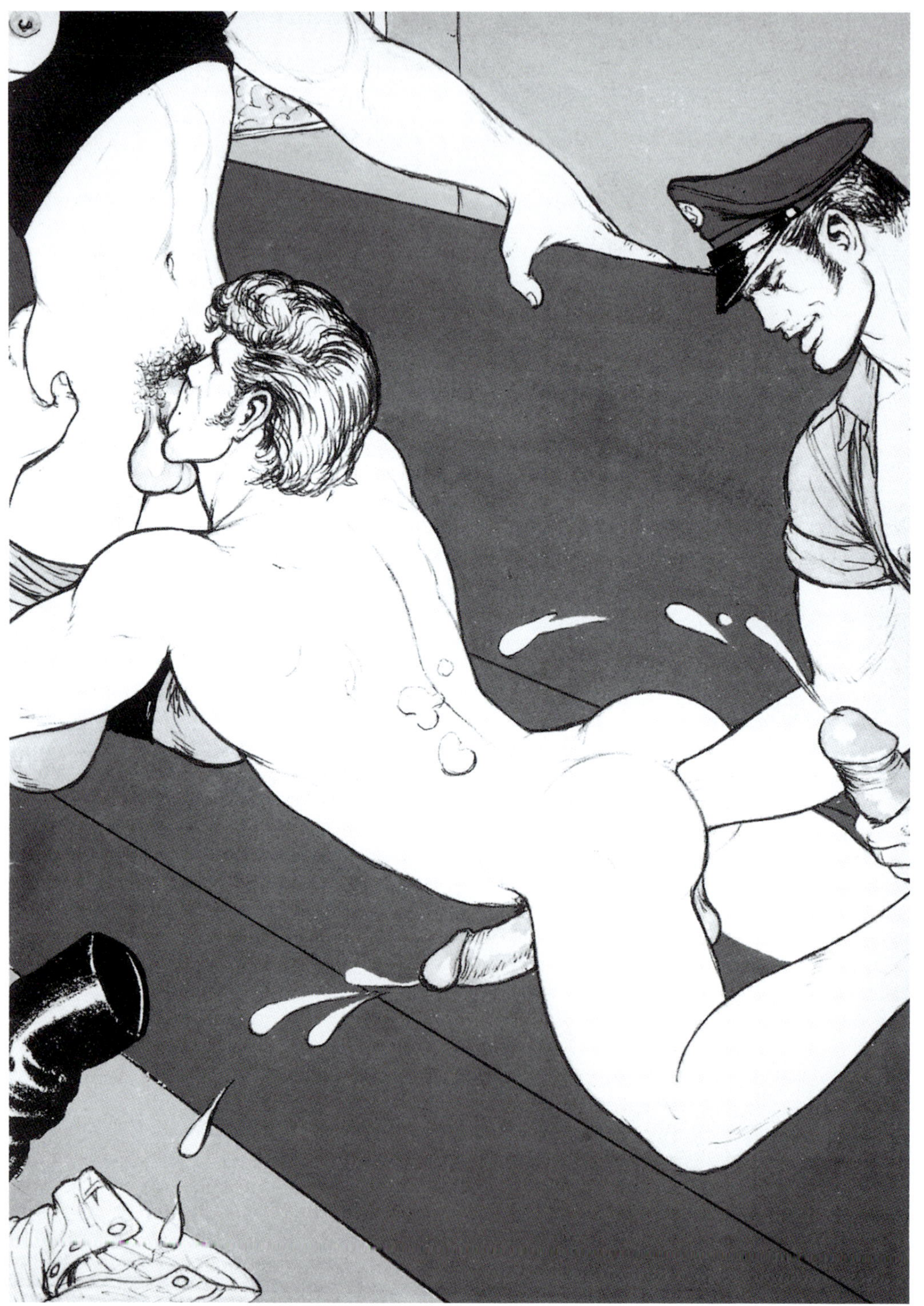

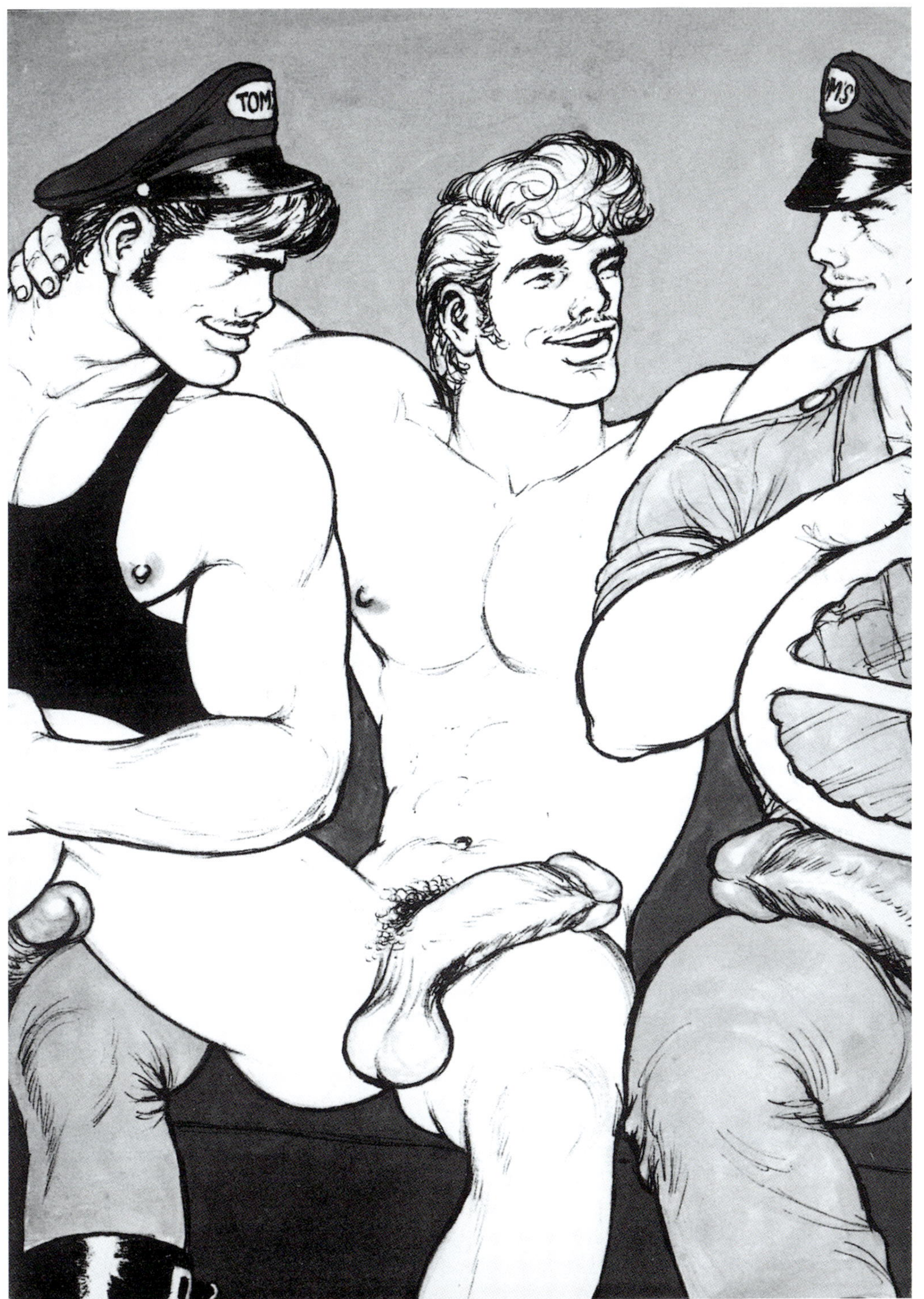

TOM'S
TOM'S

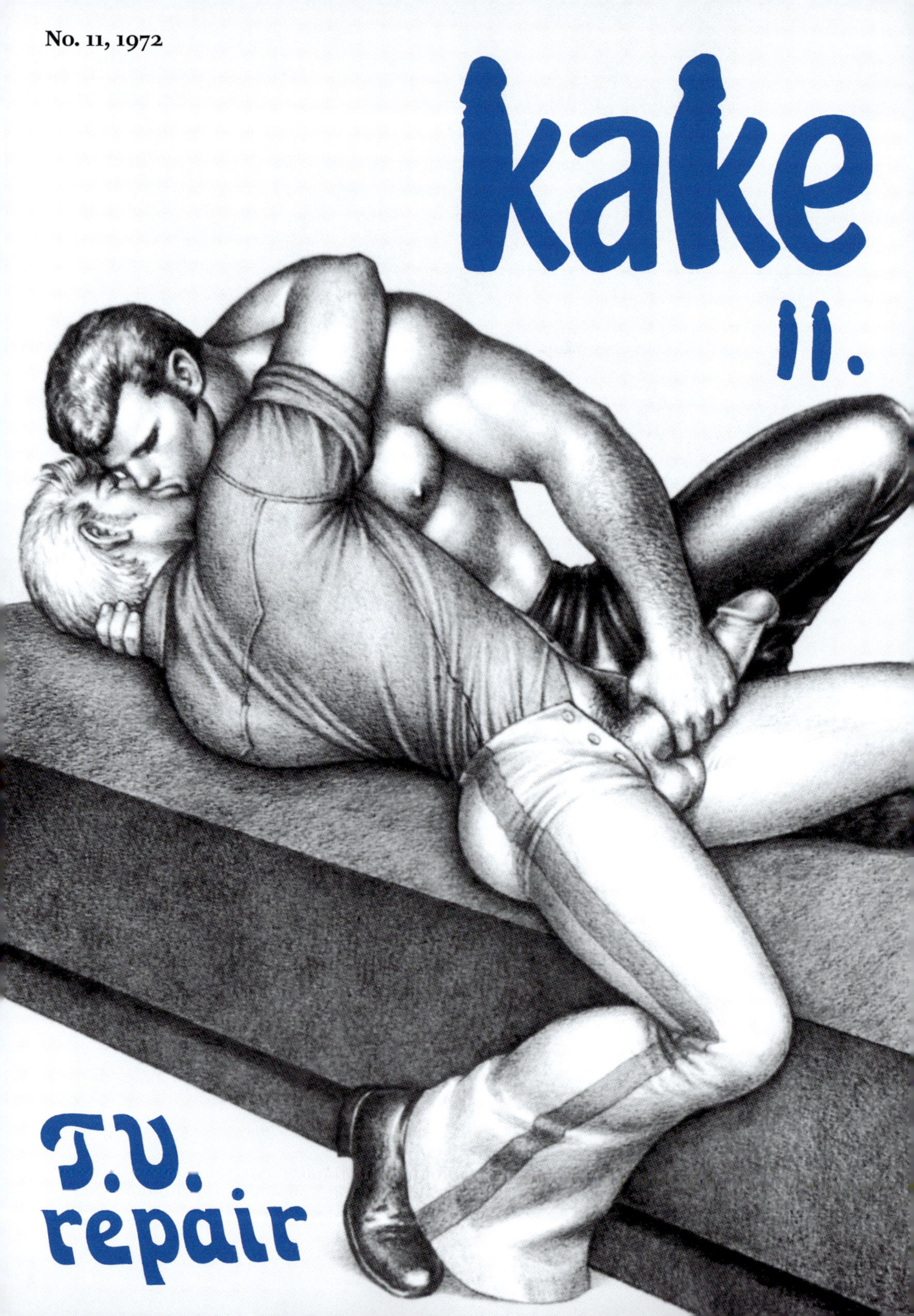

No. 11, 1972
kake
11.
T.V.
repair

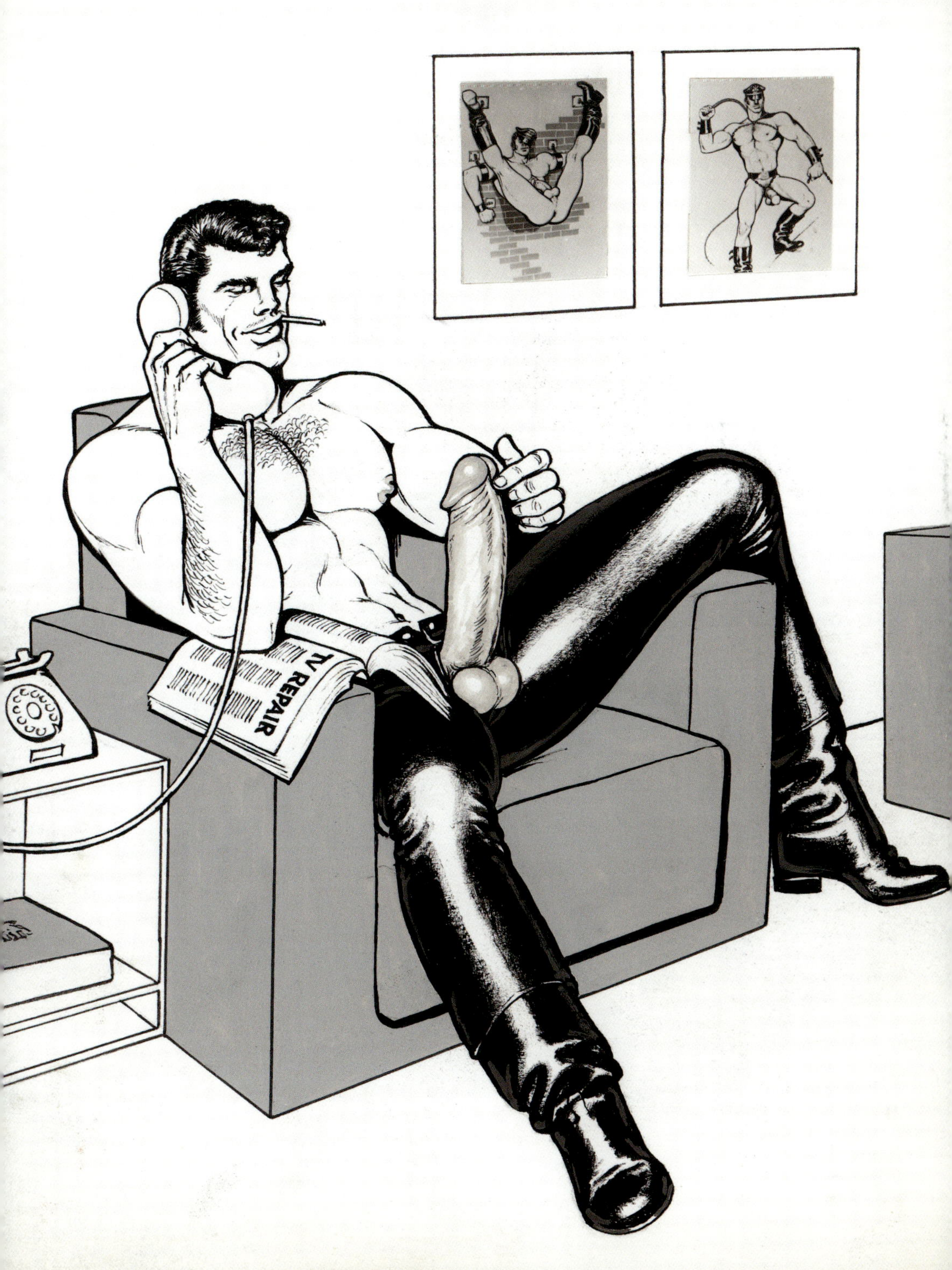

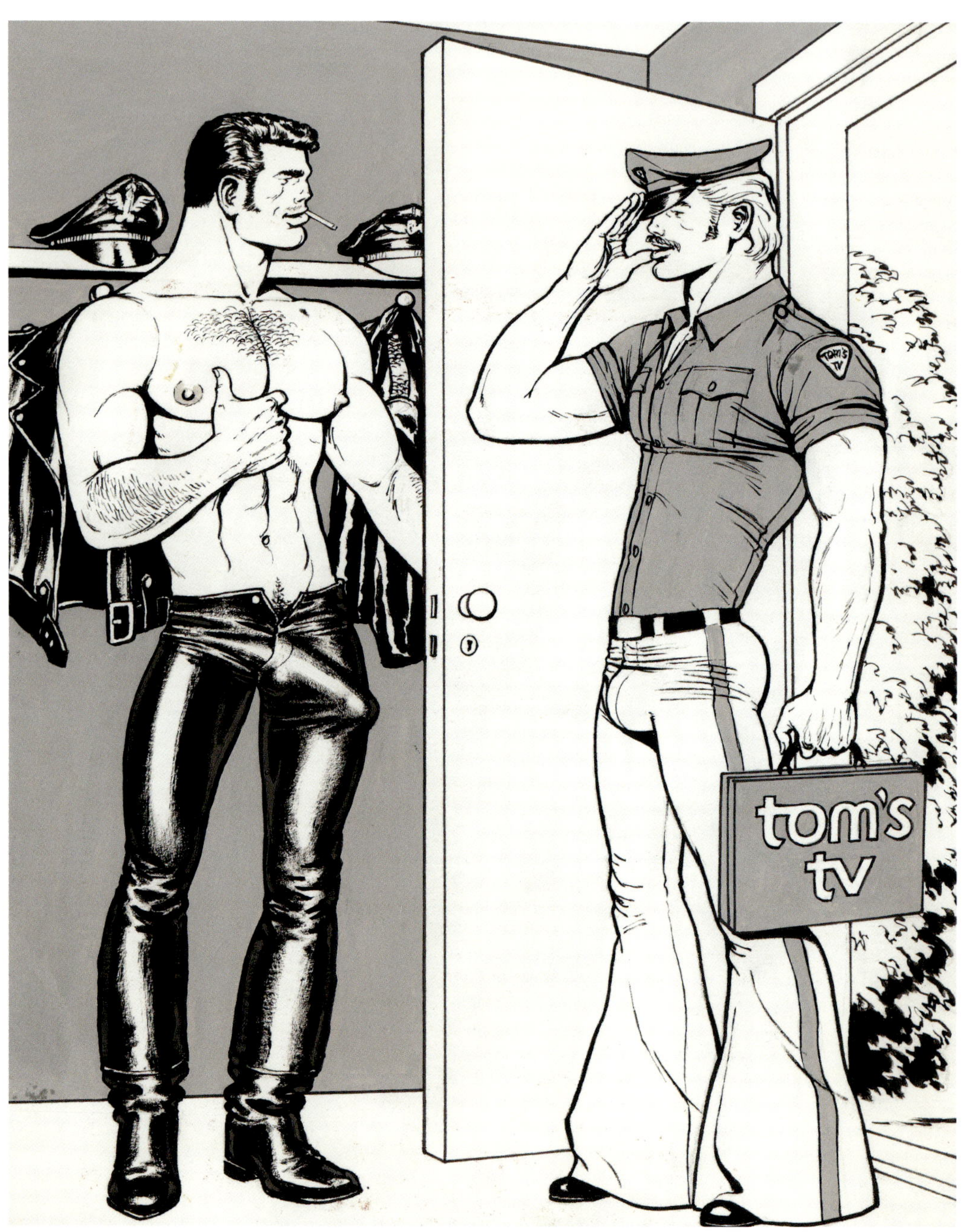

tom's tv

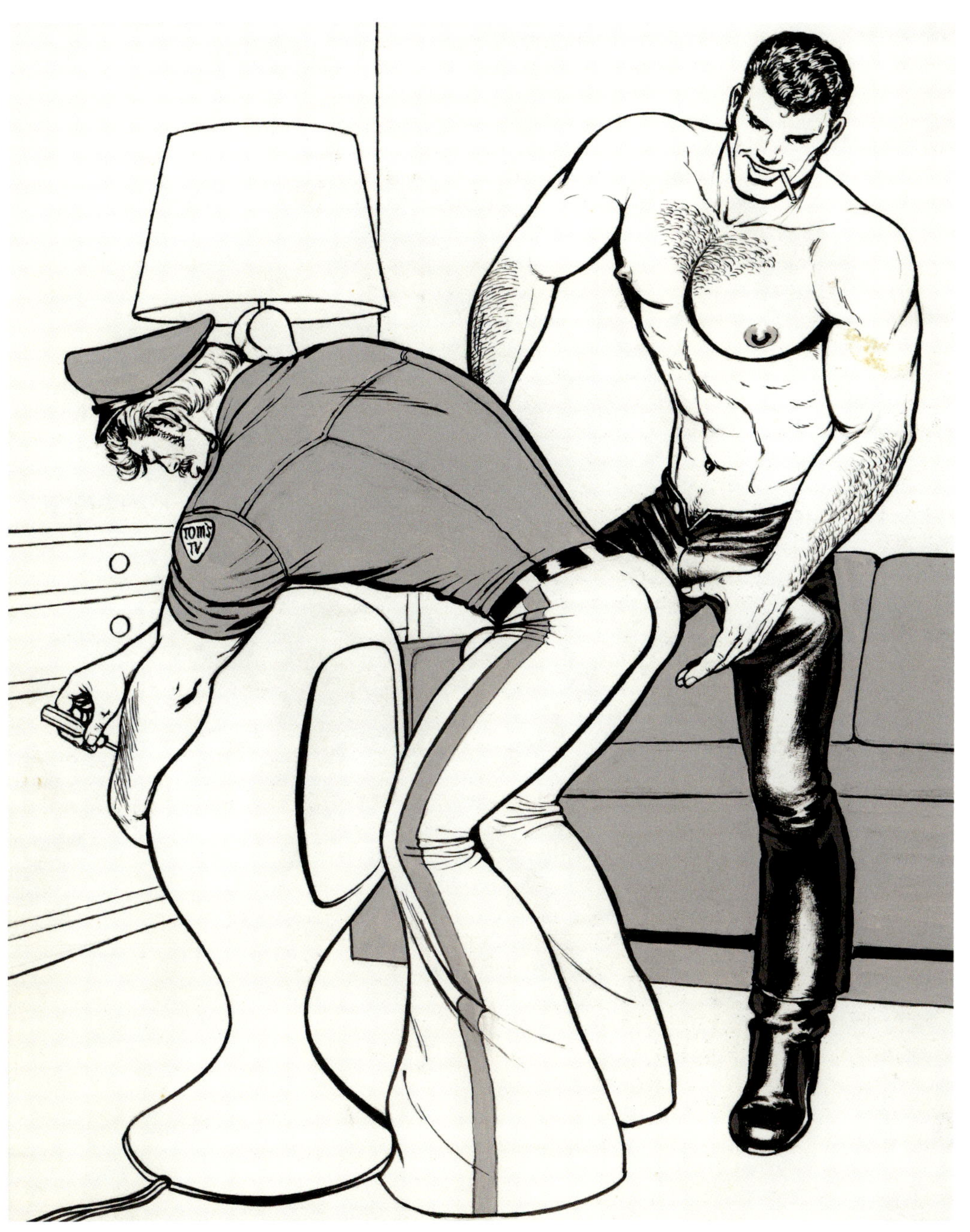

TOM'S
TV

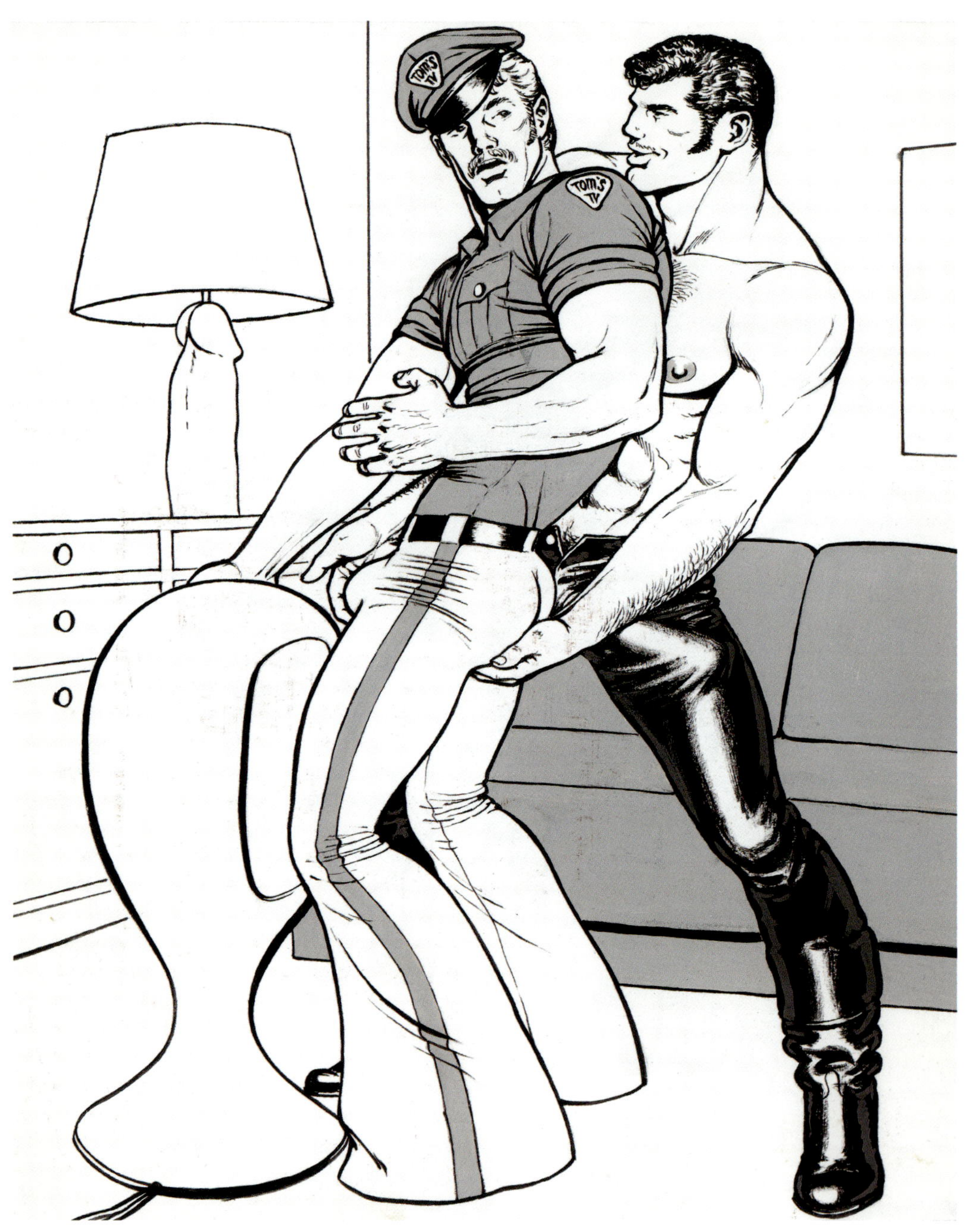

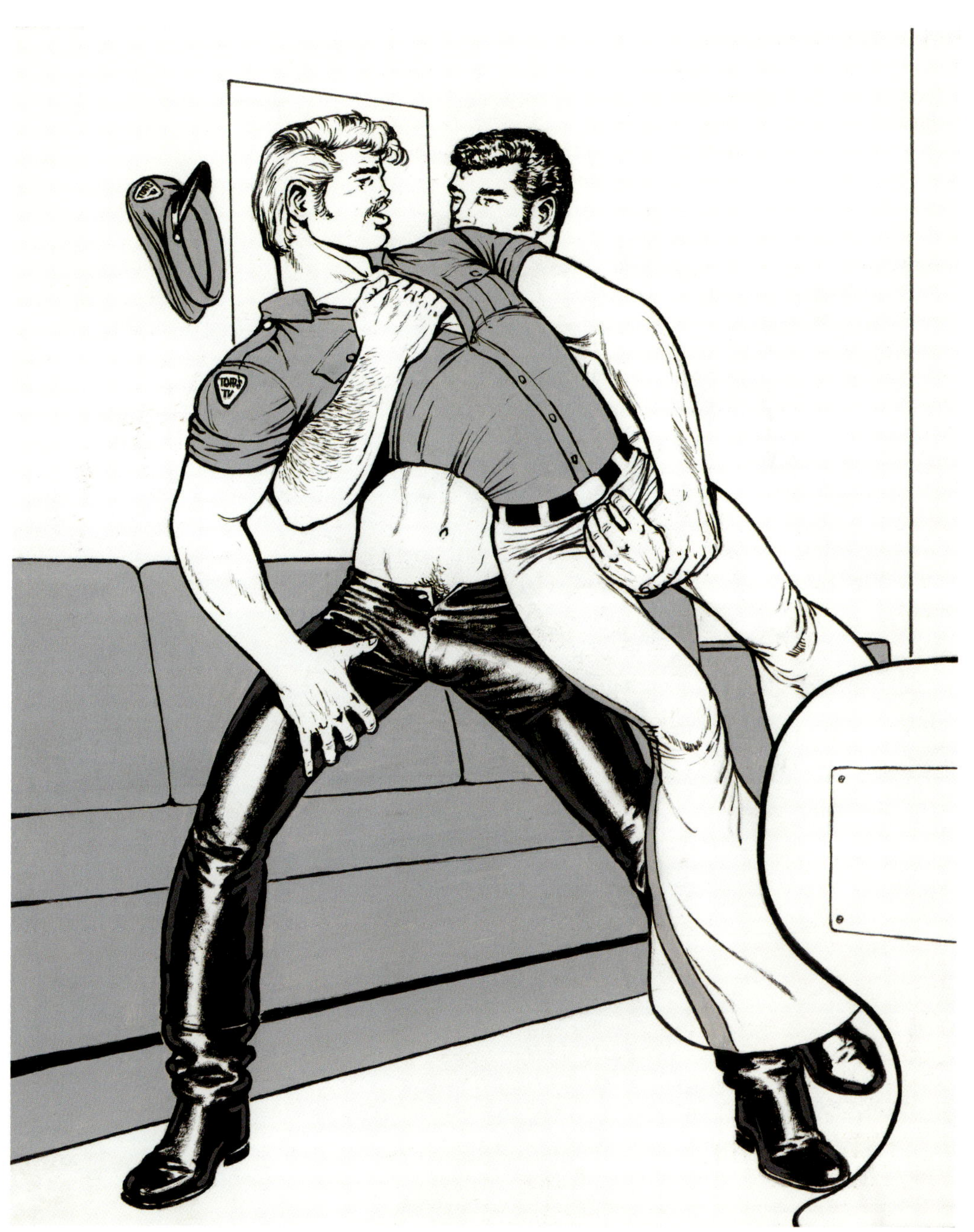

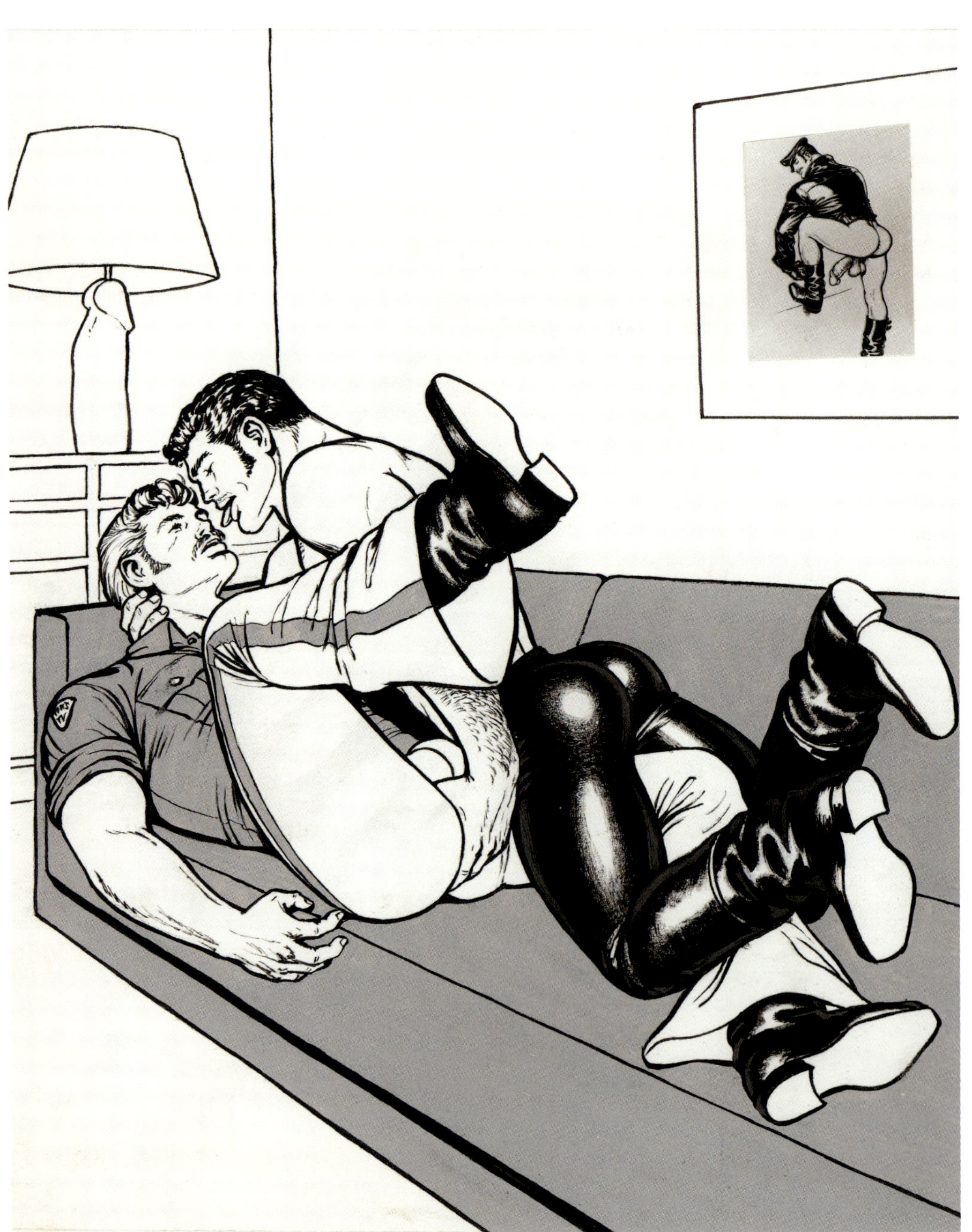

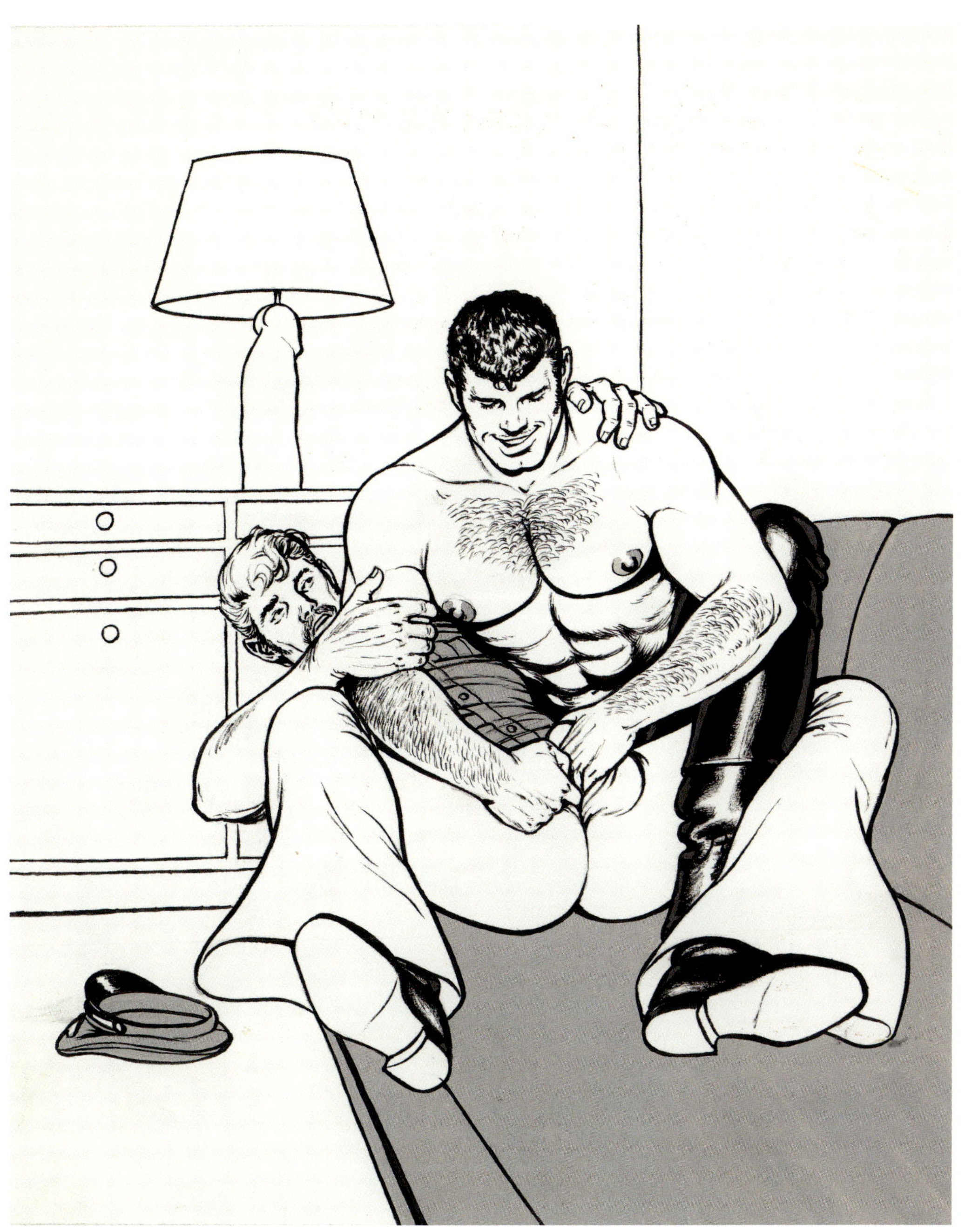

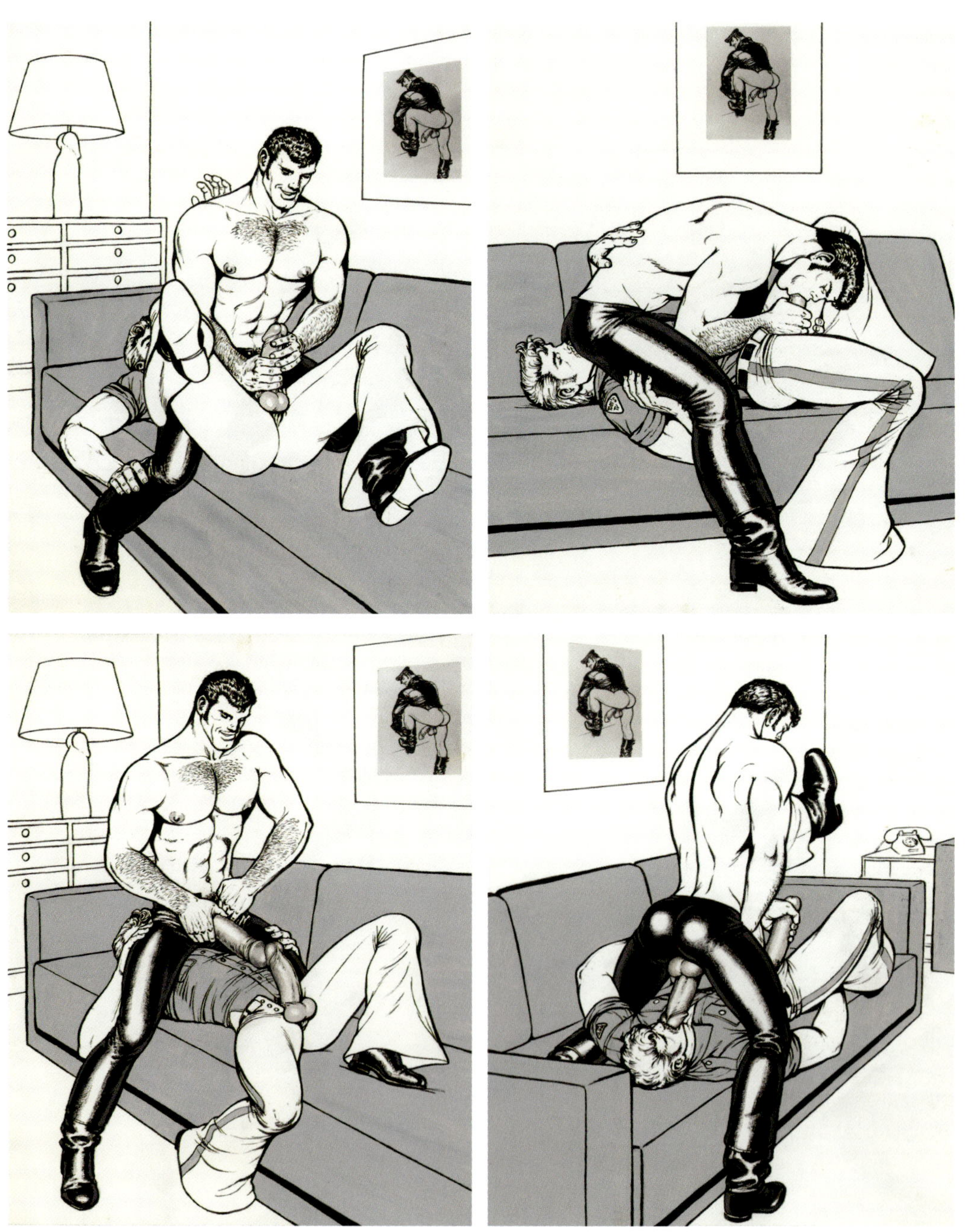

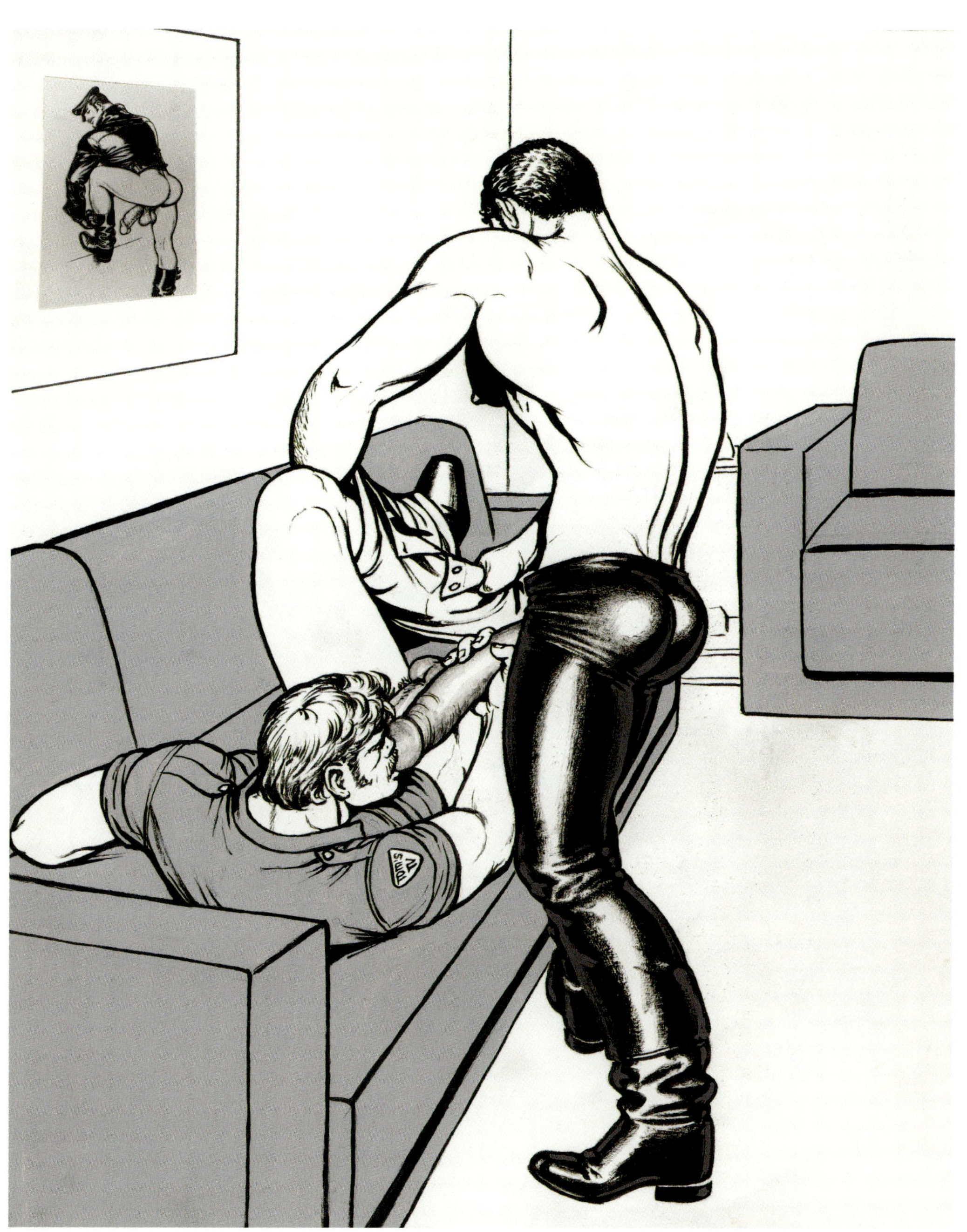

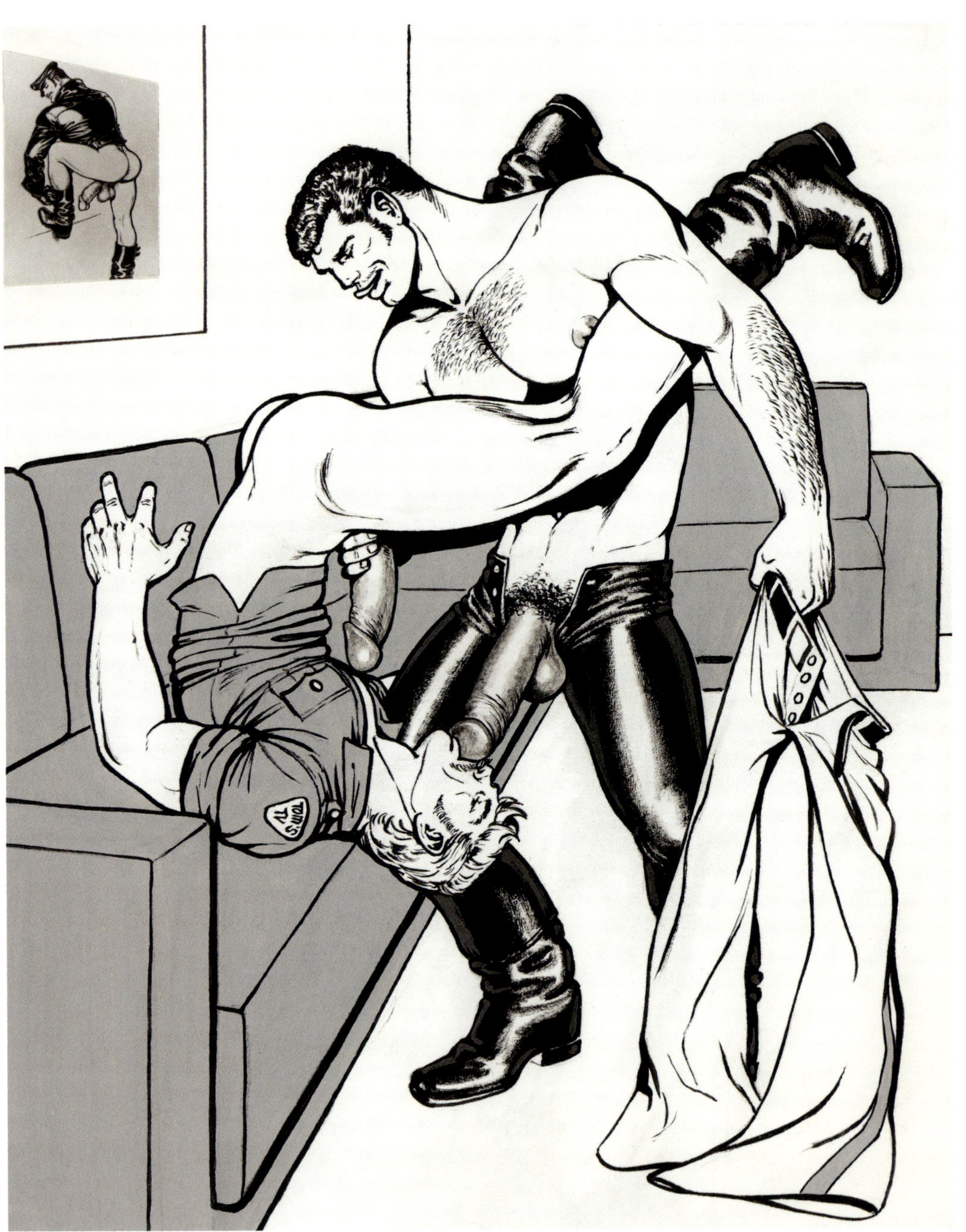

TOM'S 77

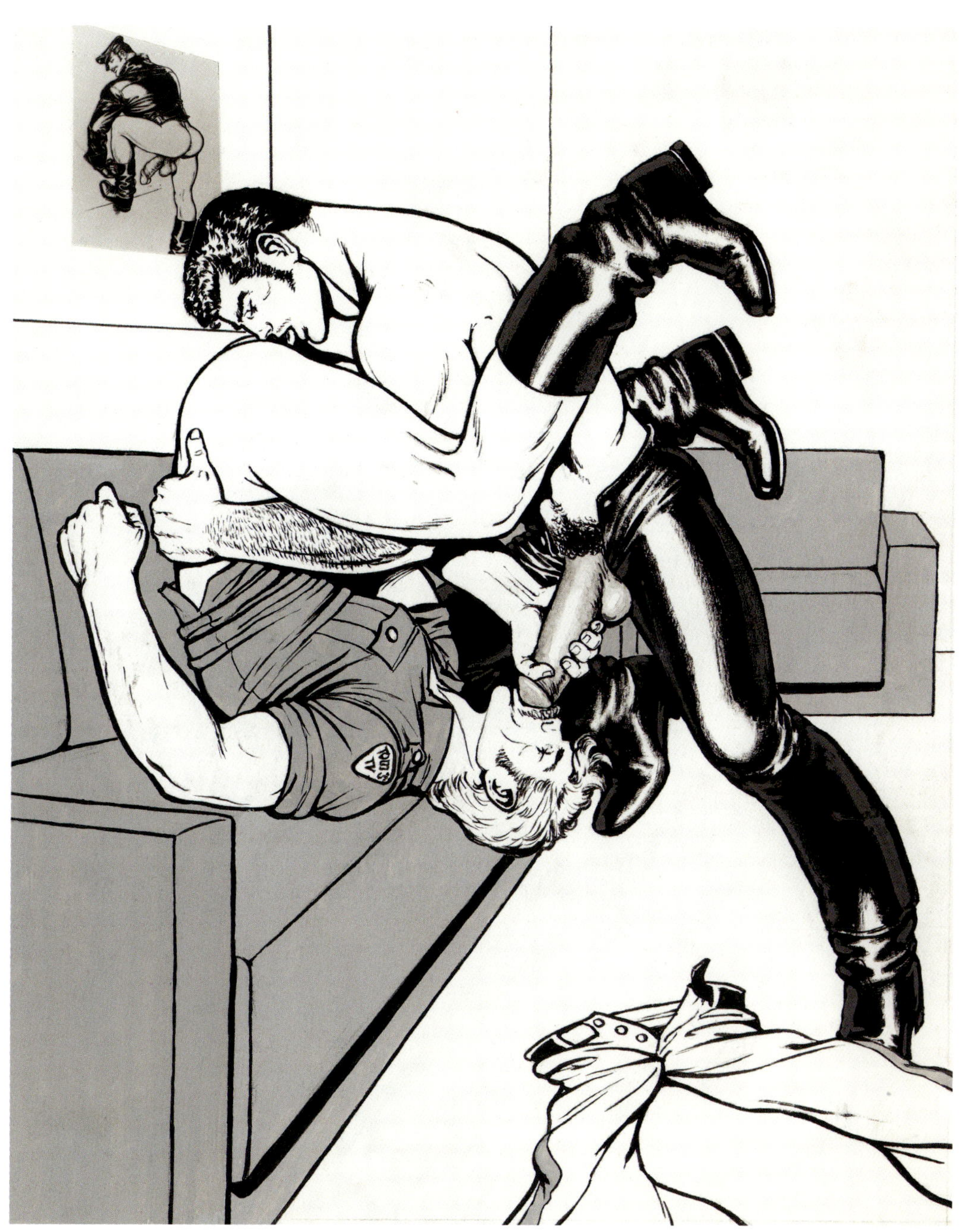

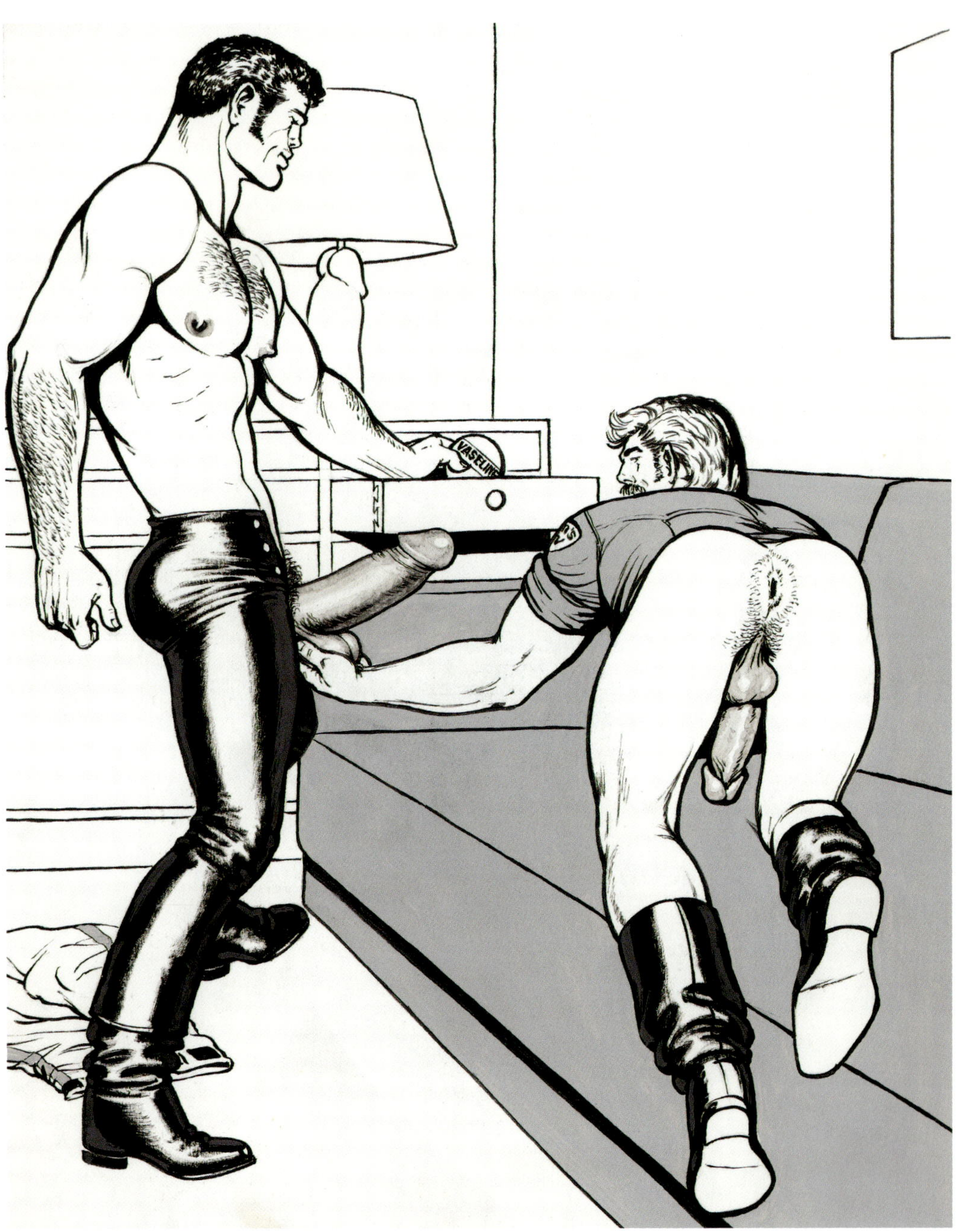
VASELINE

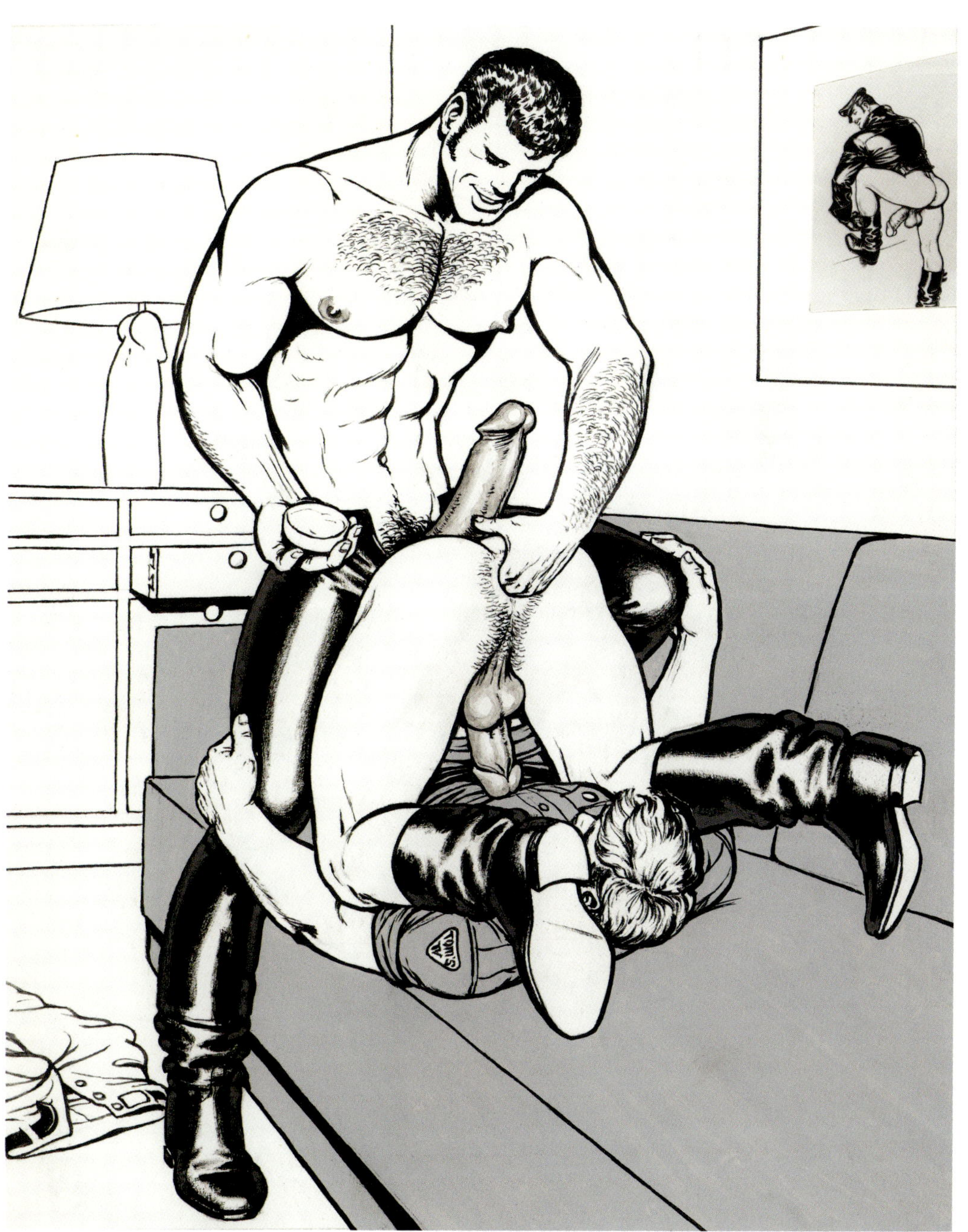

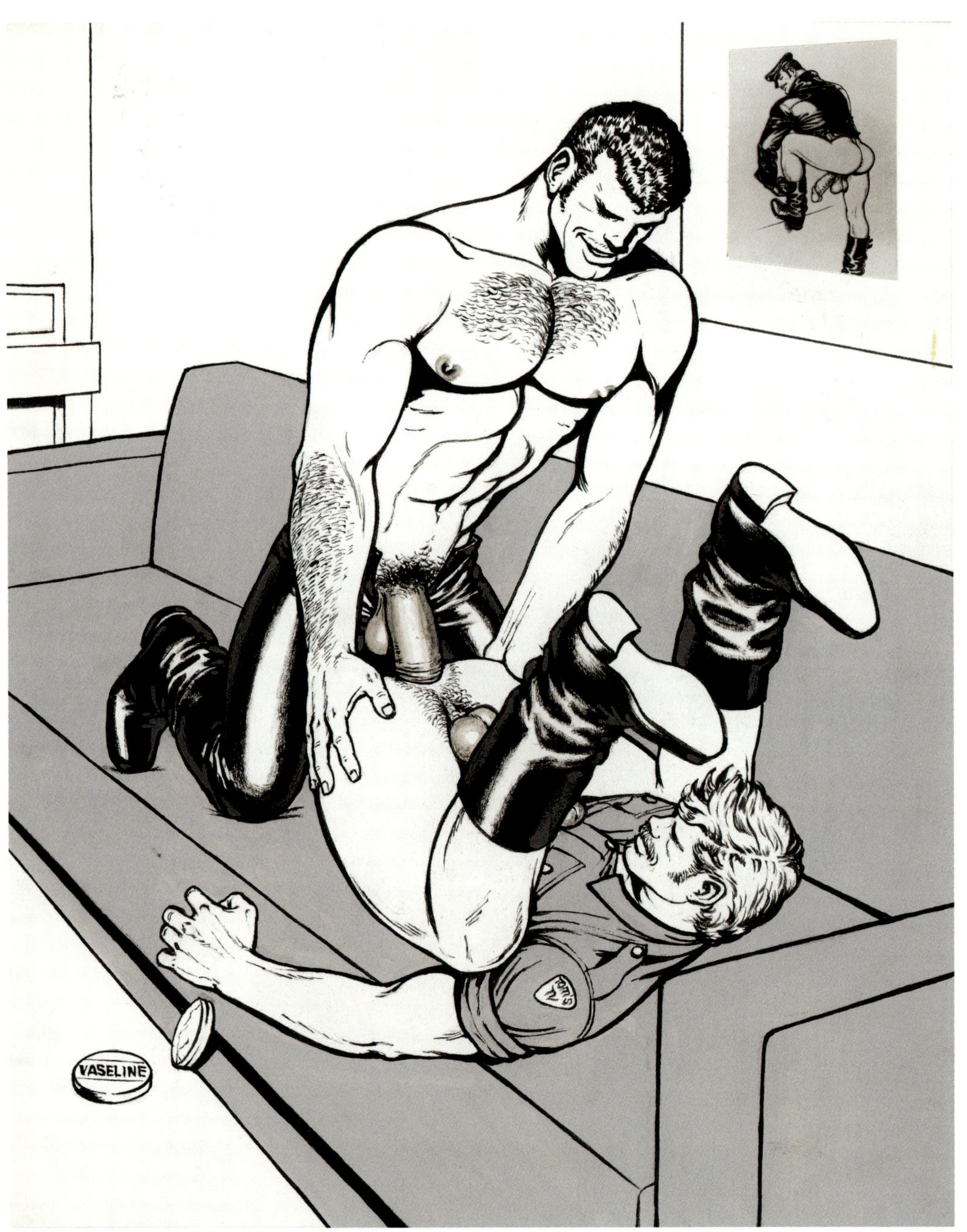
VASELINE

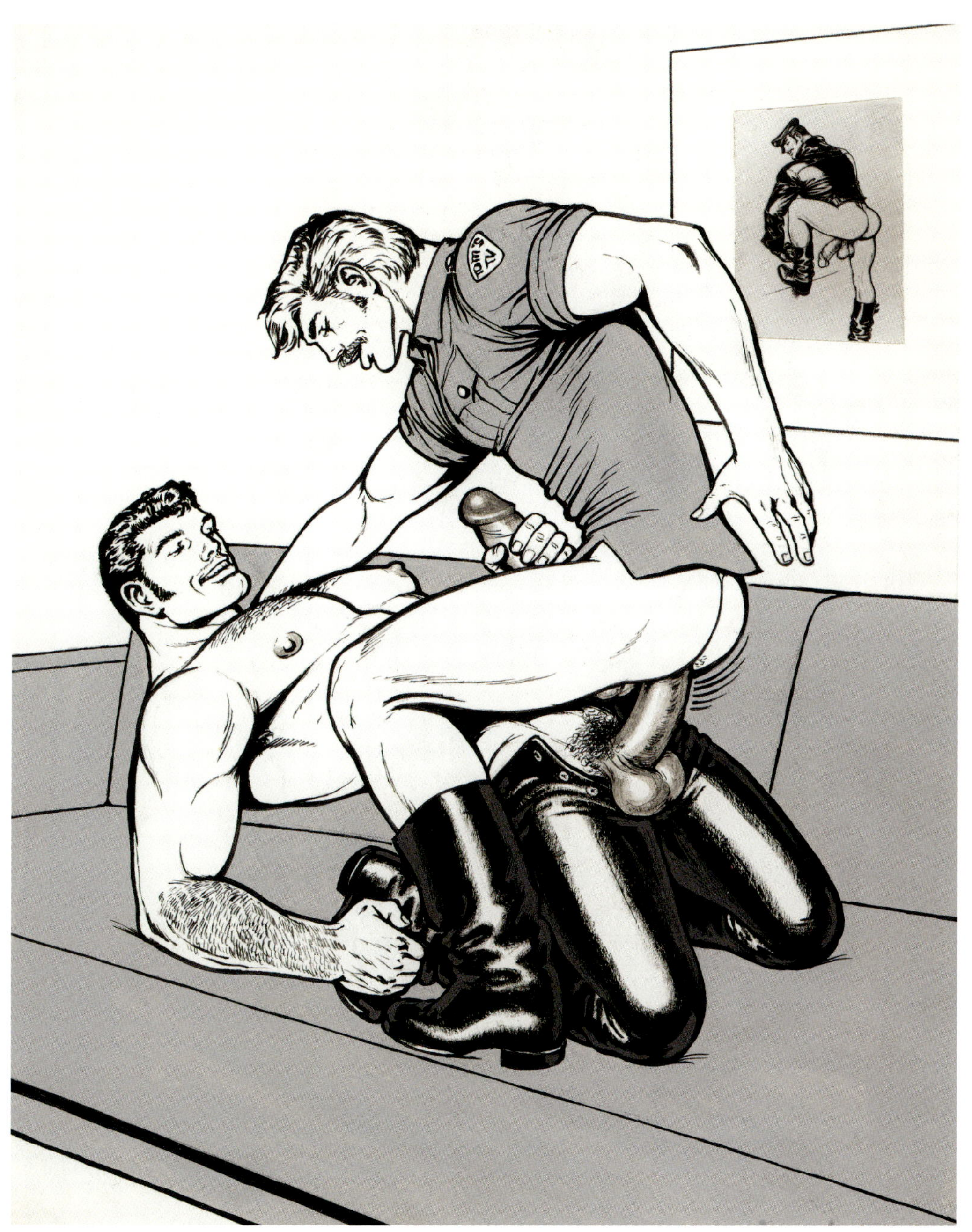

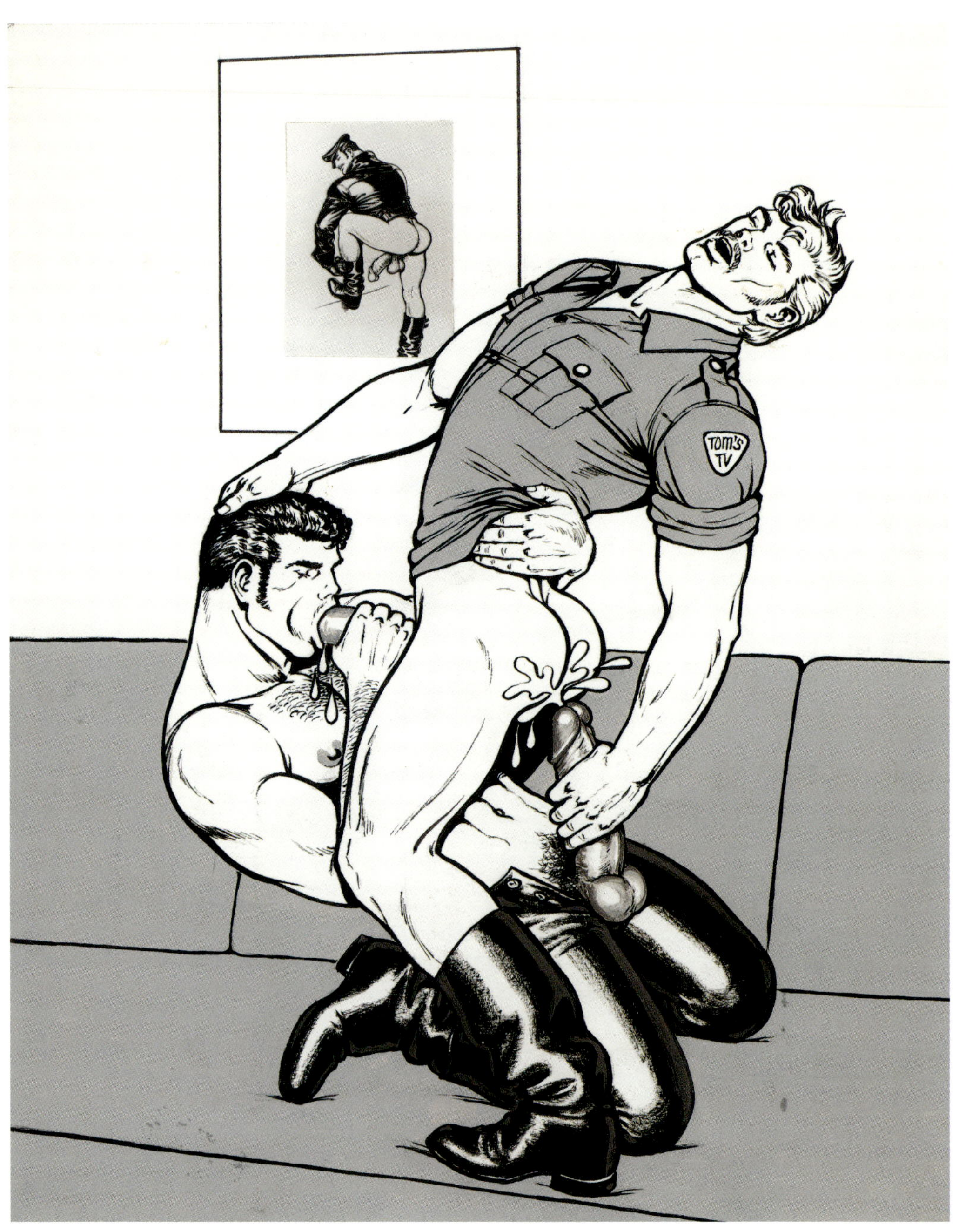

TOM'S
TV

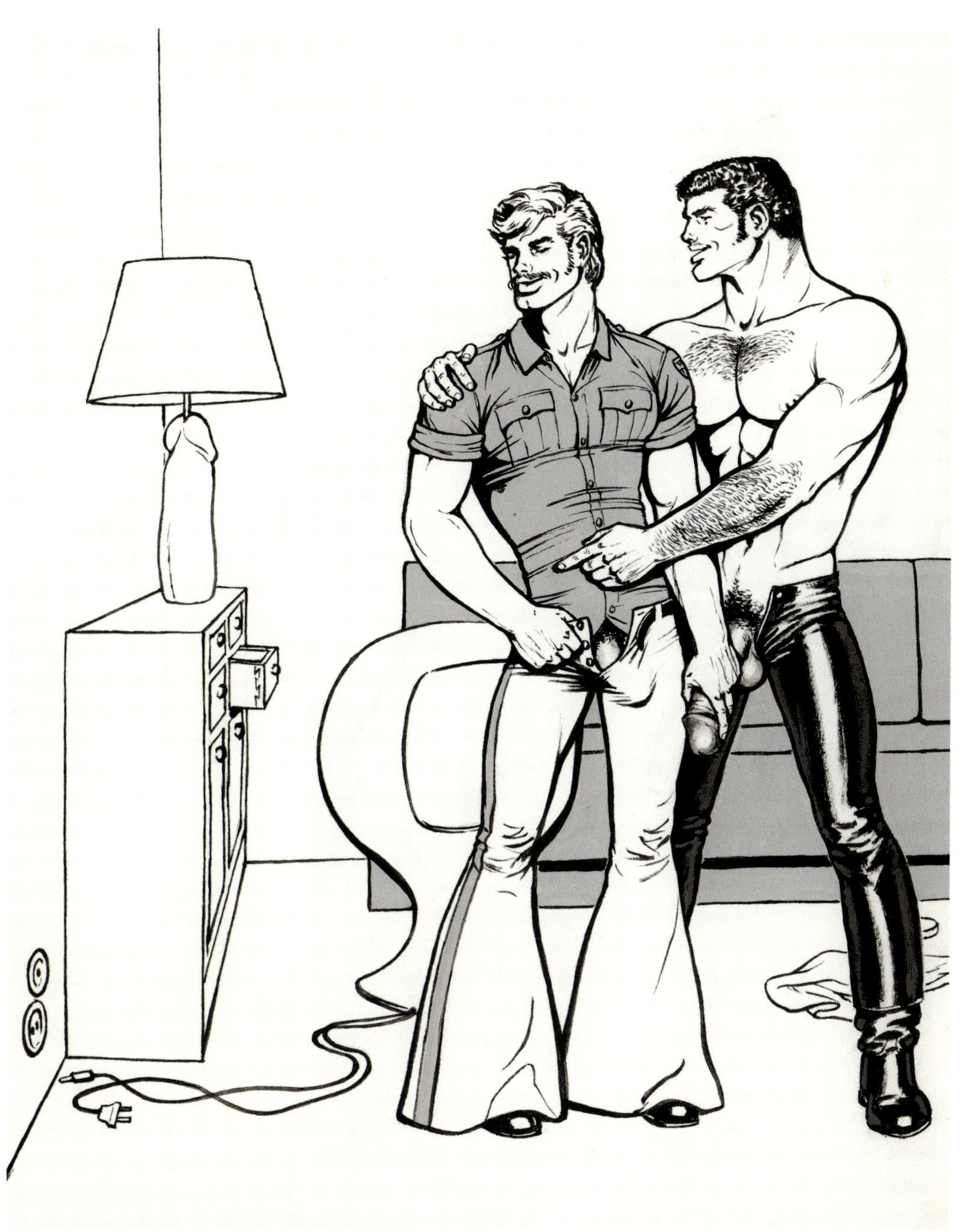

kake

12.

Service Station

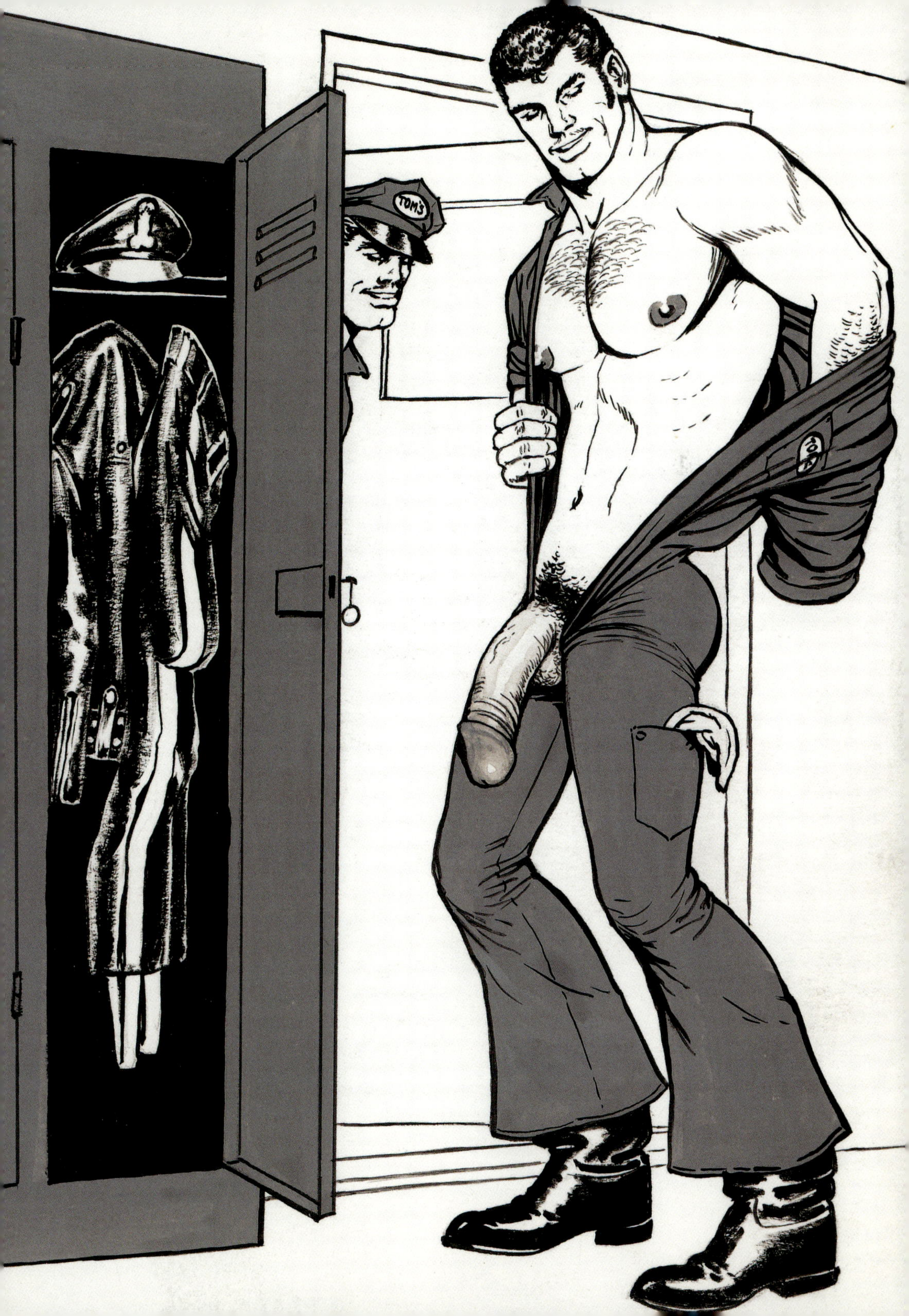

TOM'S

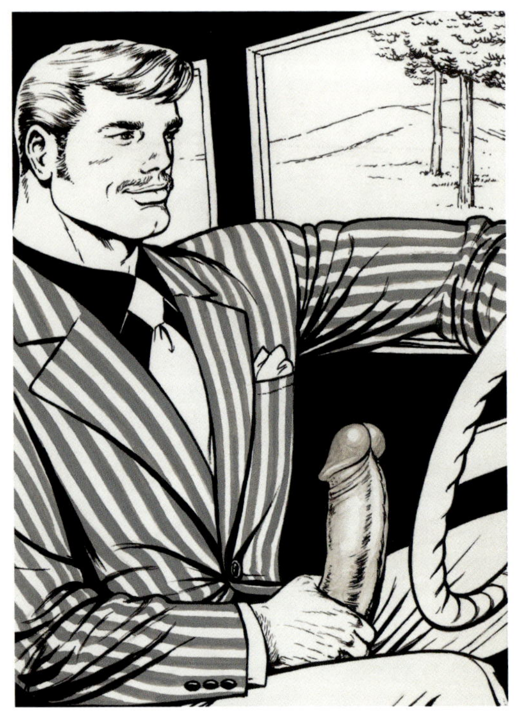

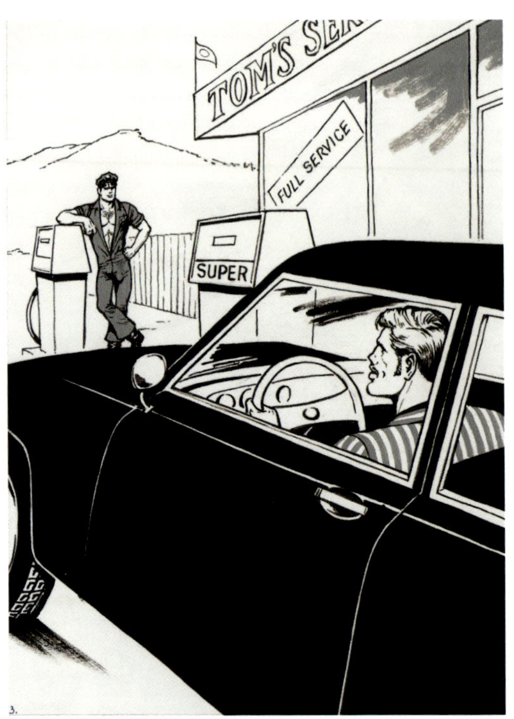
TOM'S SER
FULL SERVICE
SUPER
3.

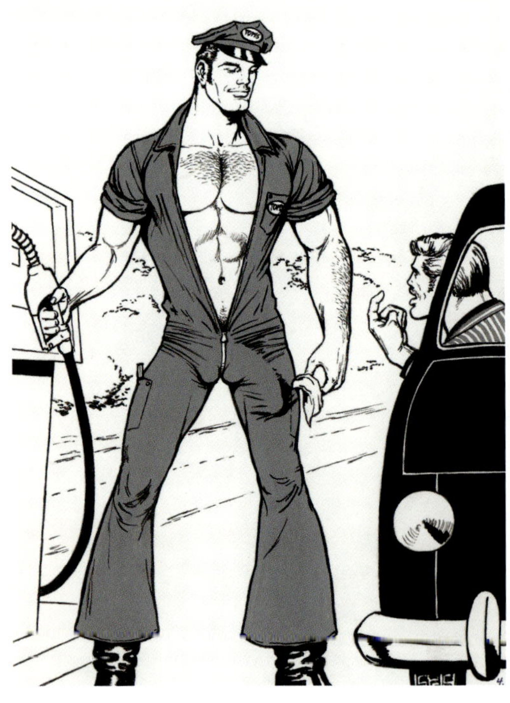
TOM'S

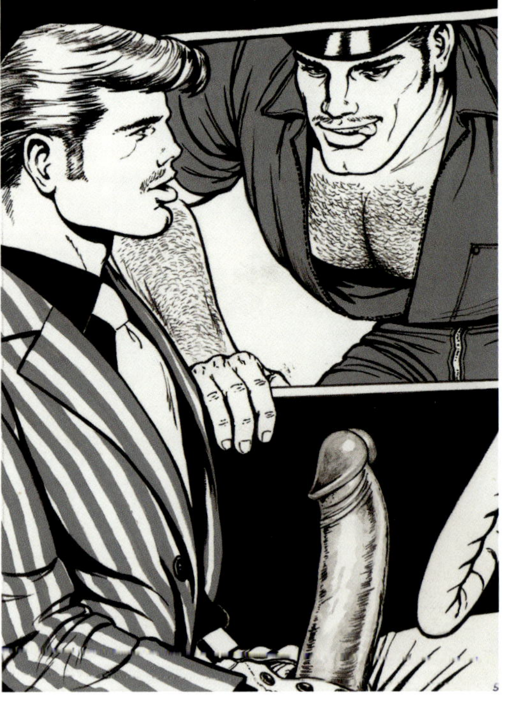

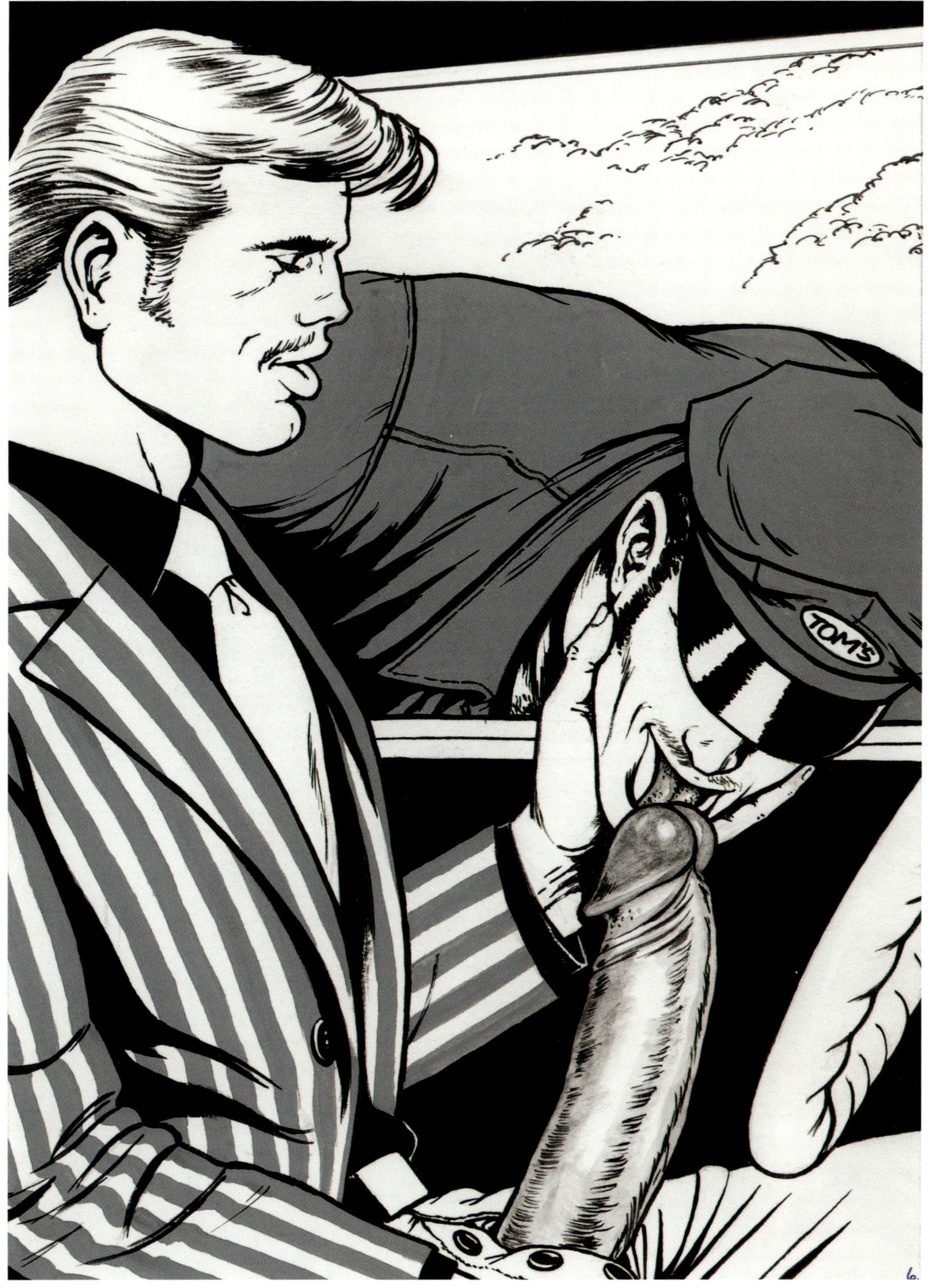

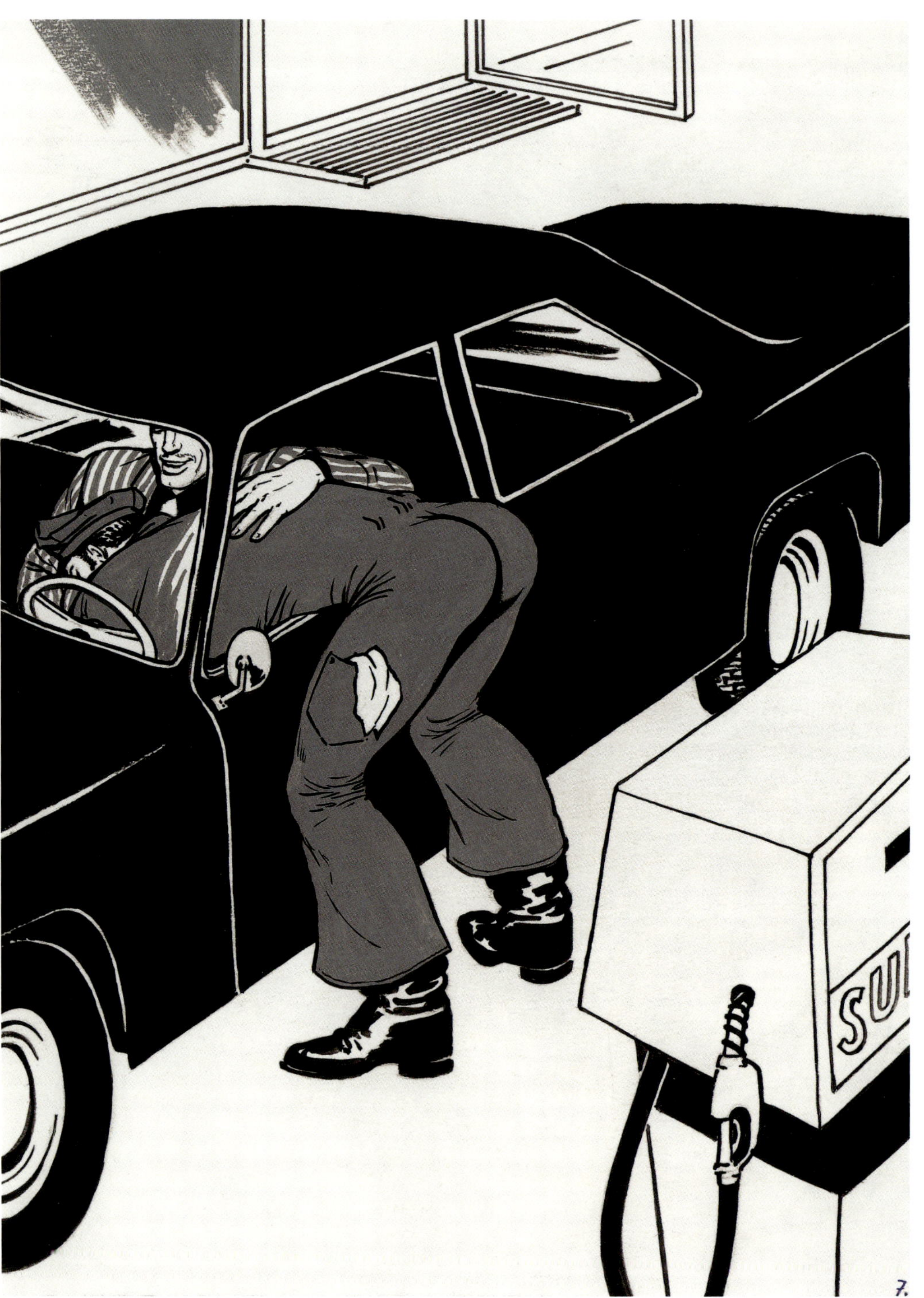
SU

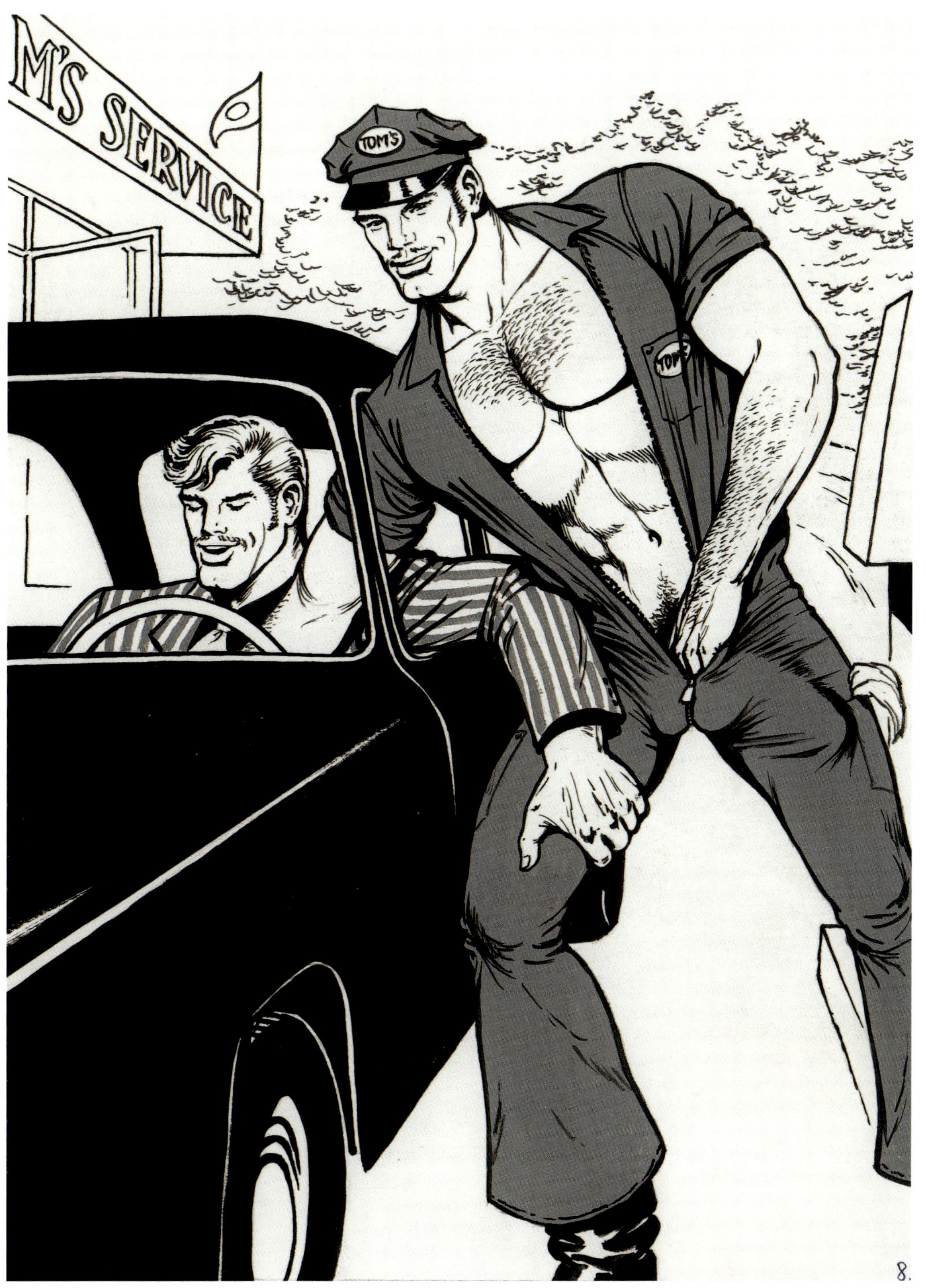

8.

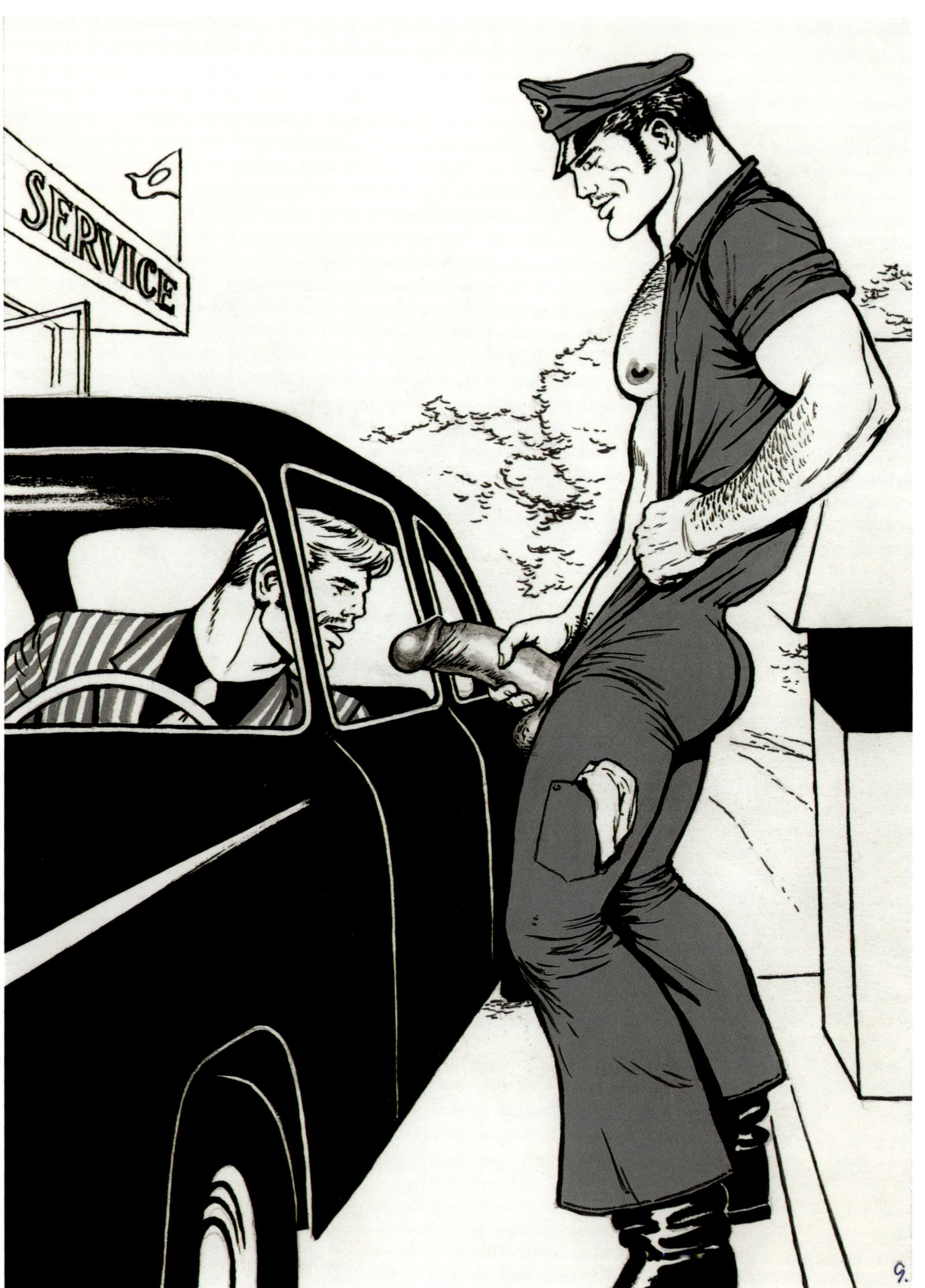
SERVICE

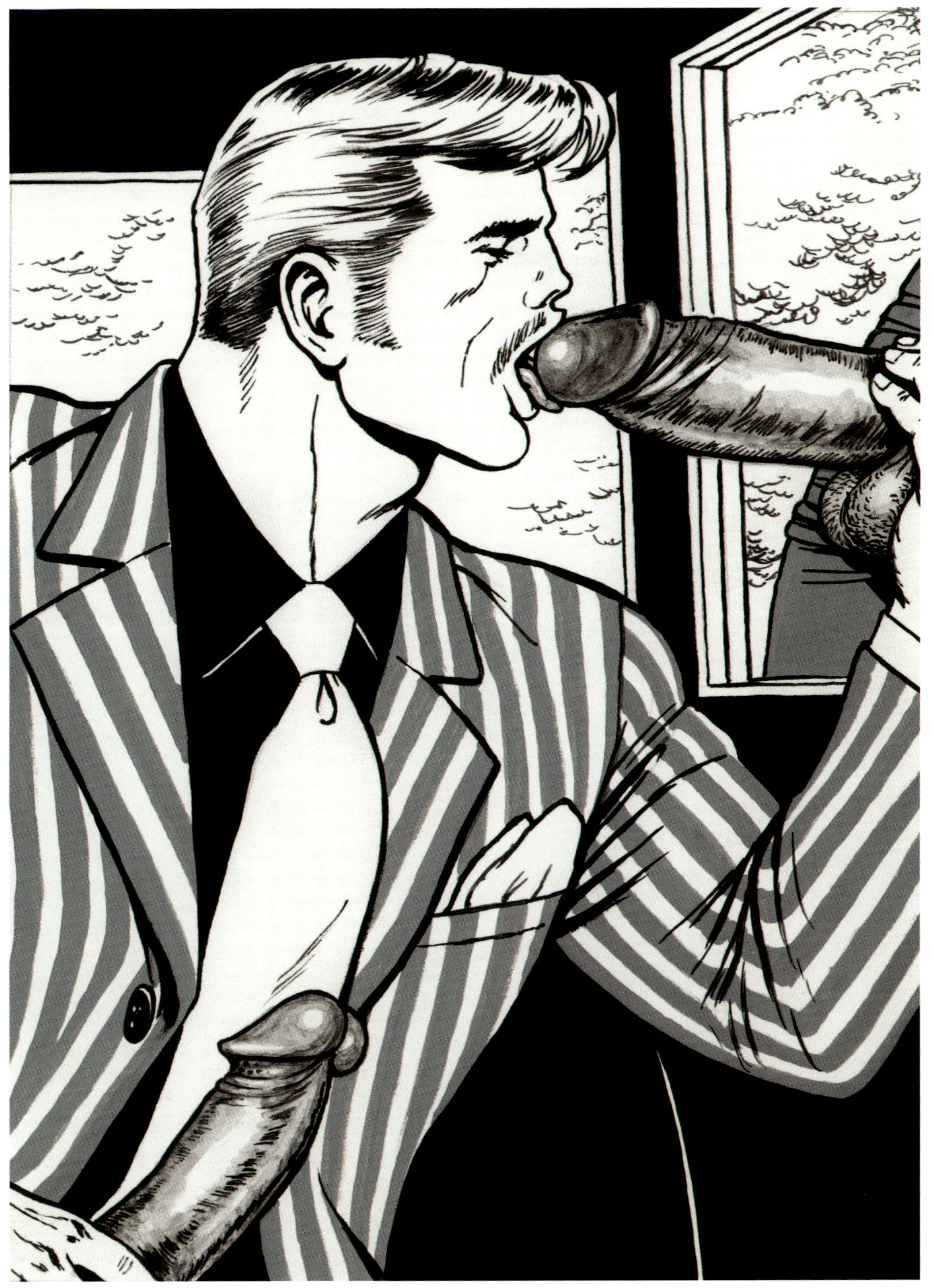

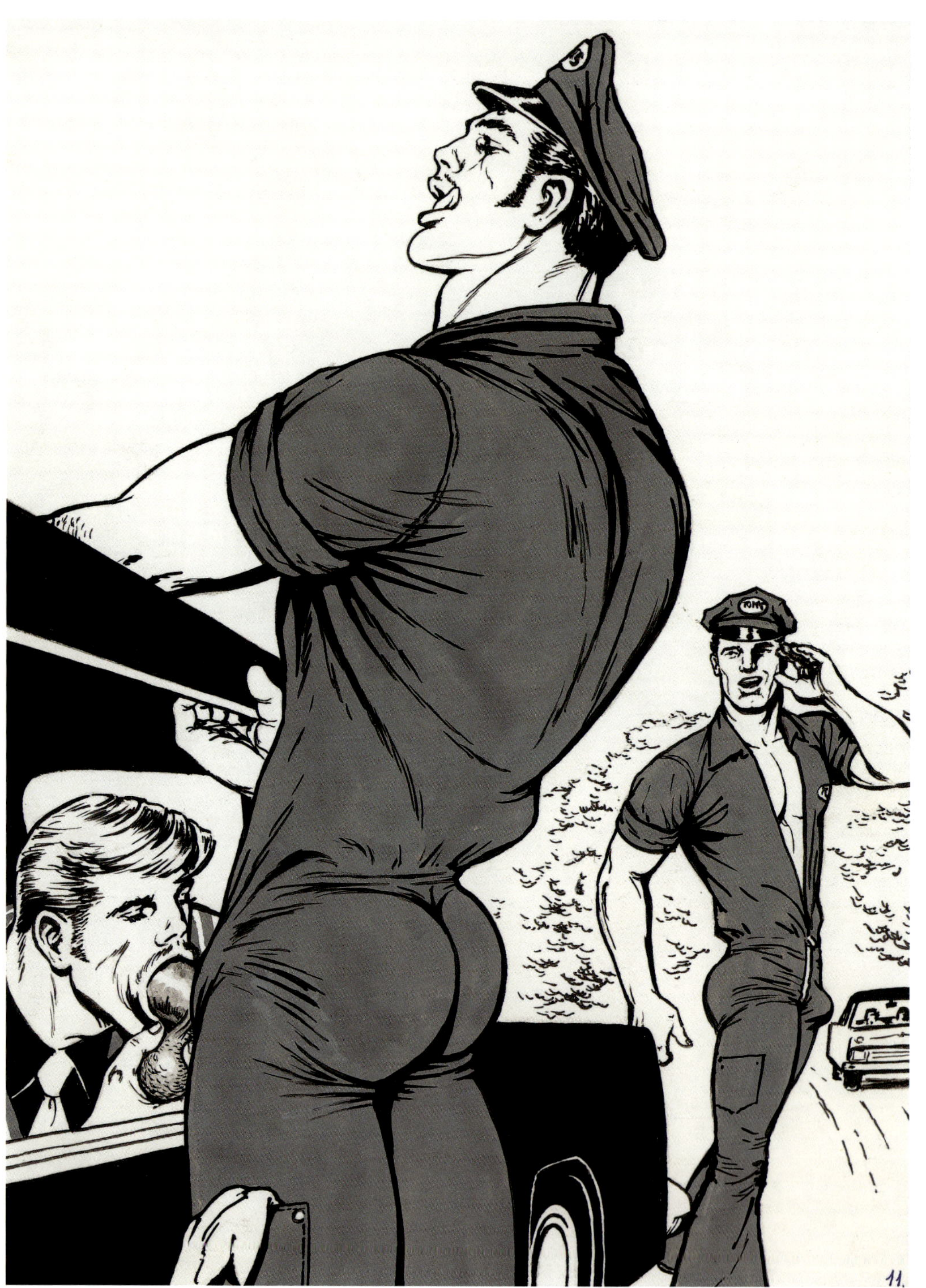

TOM

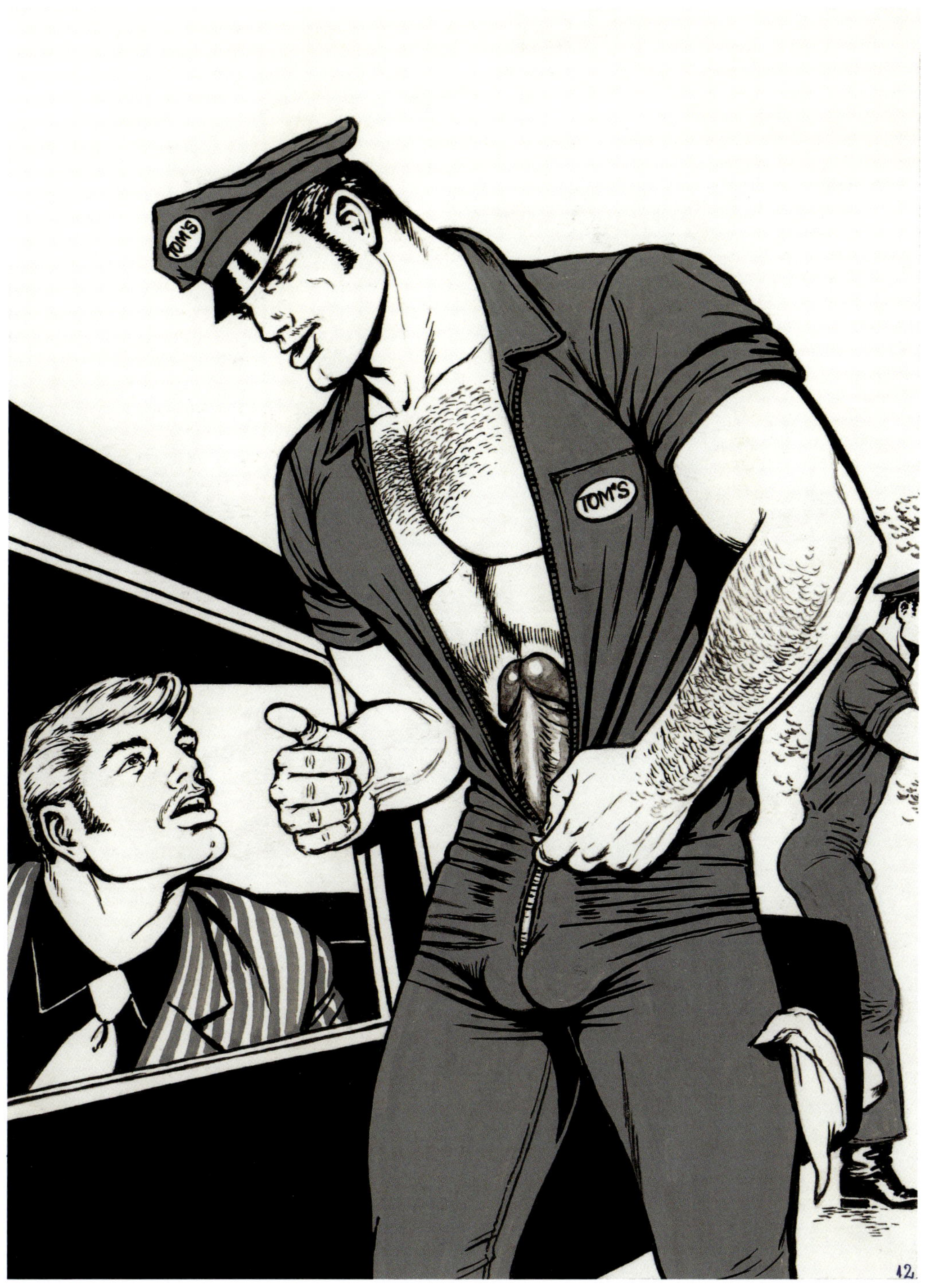
TOM'S
TOM'S

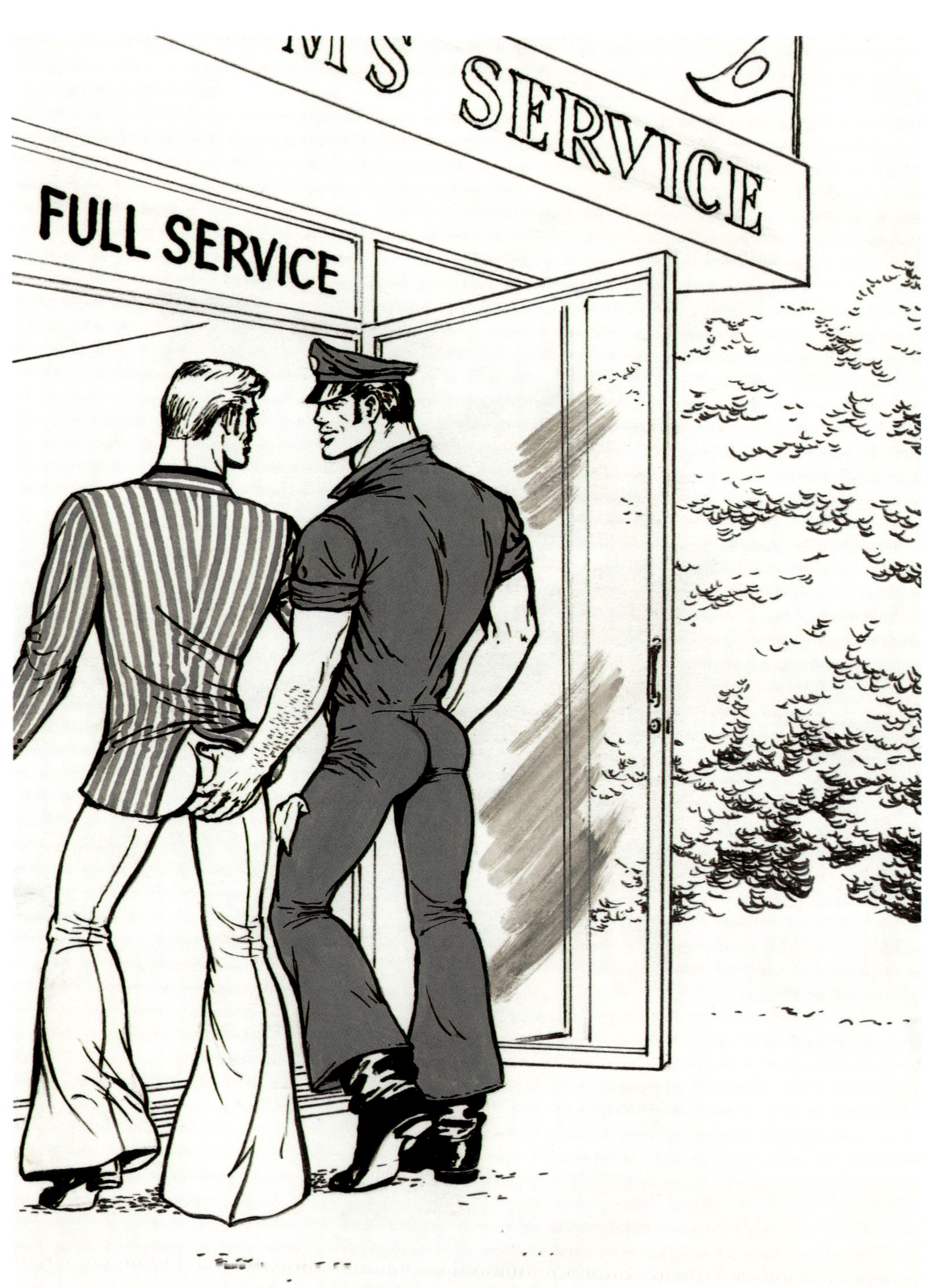

FULL SERVICE
M'S SERVICE

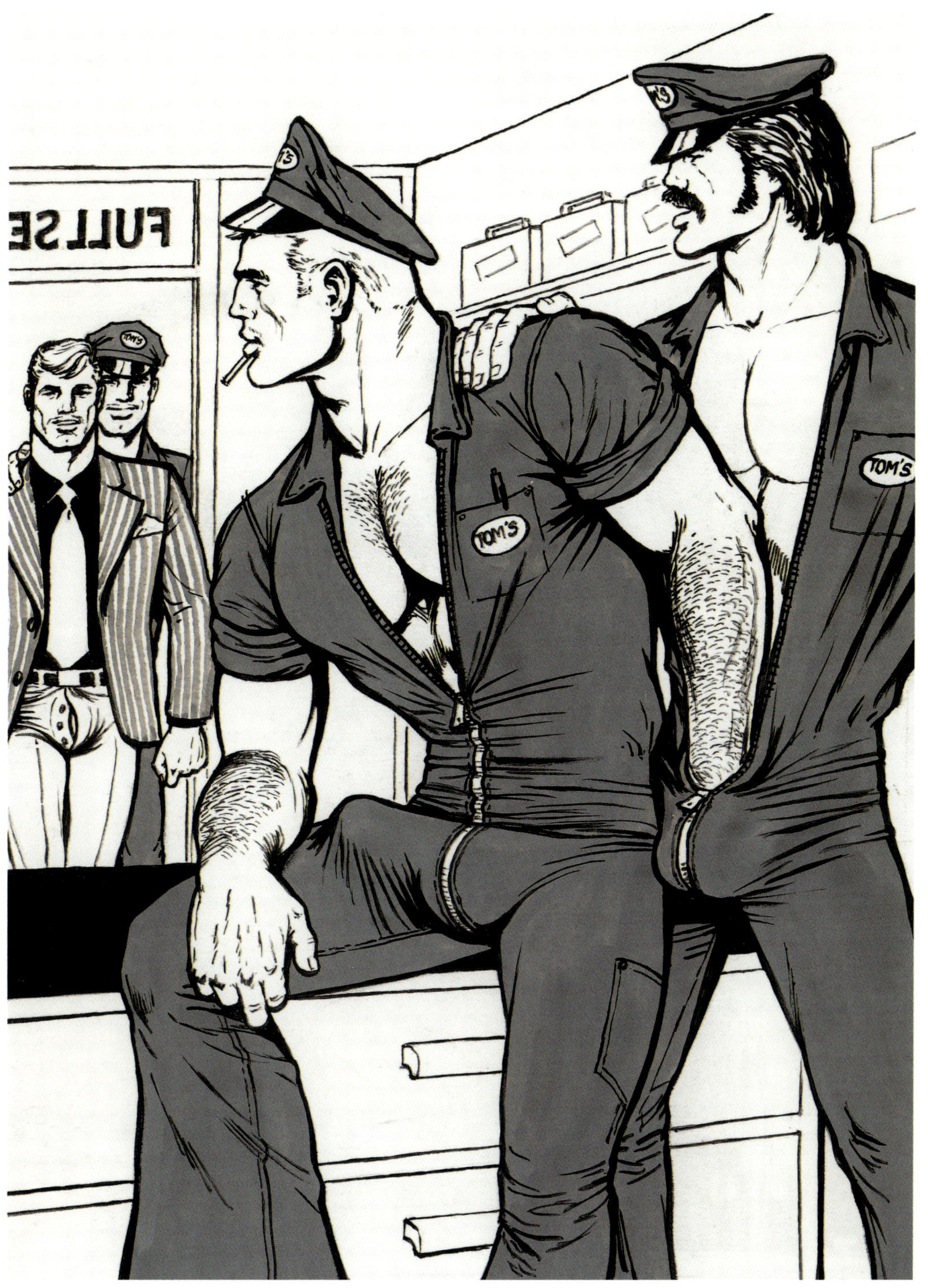

FULLSE
TOM'S
TOM'S
TOM'S

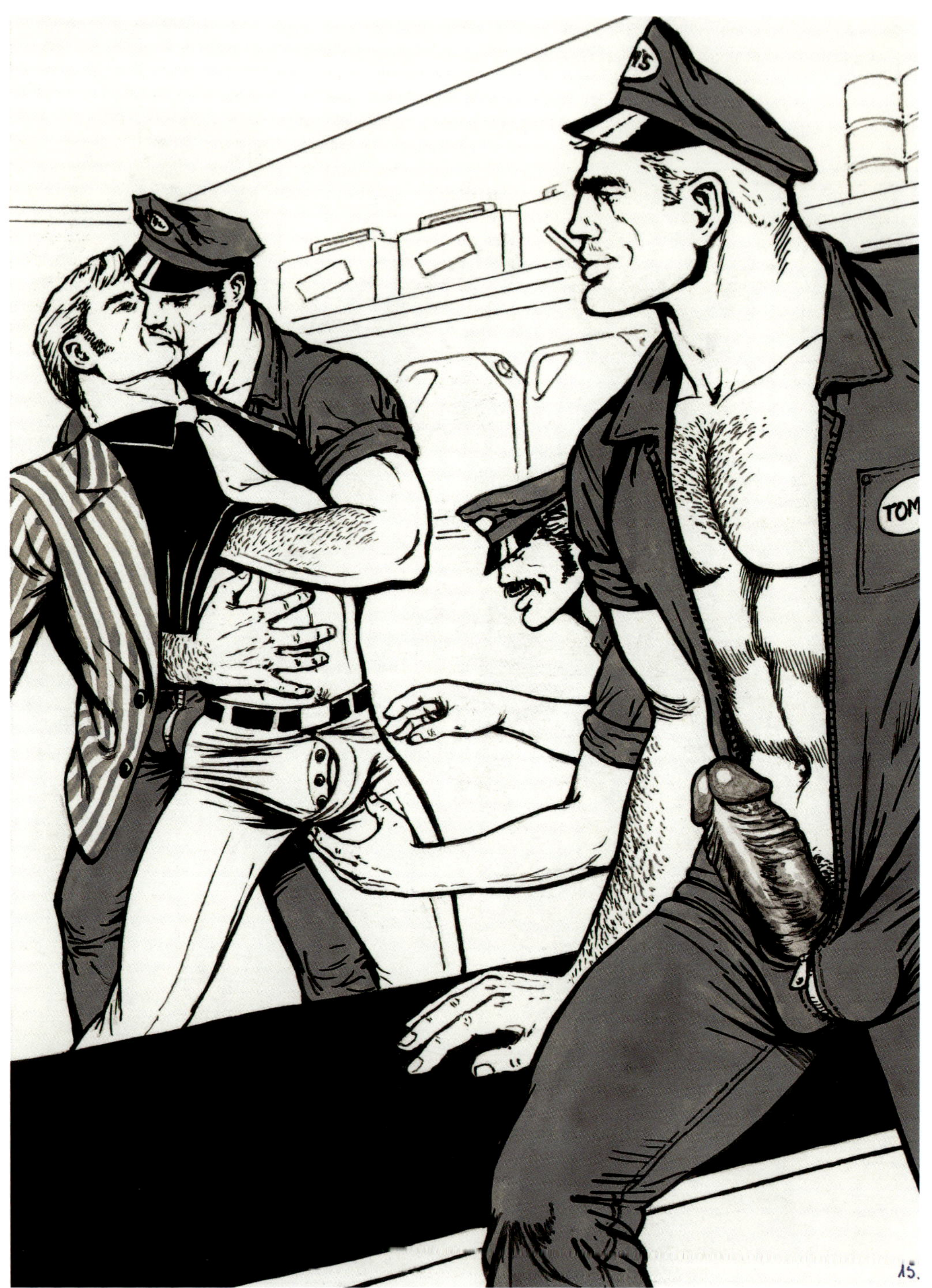
TOM

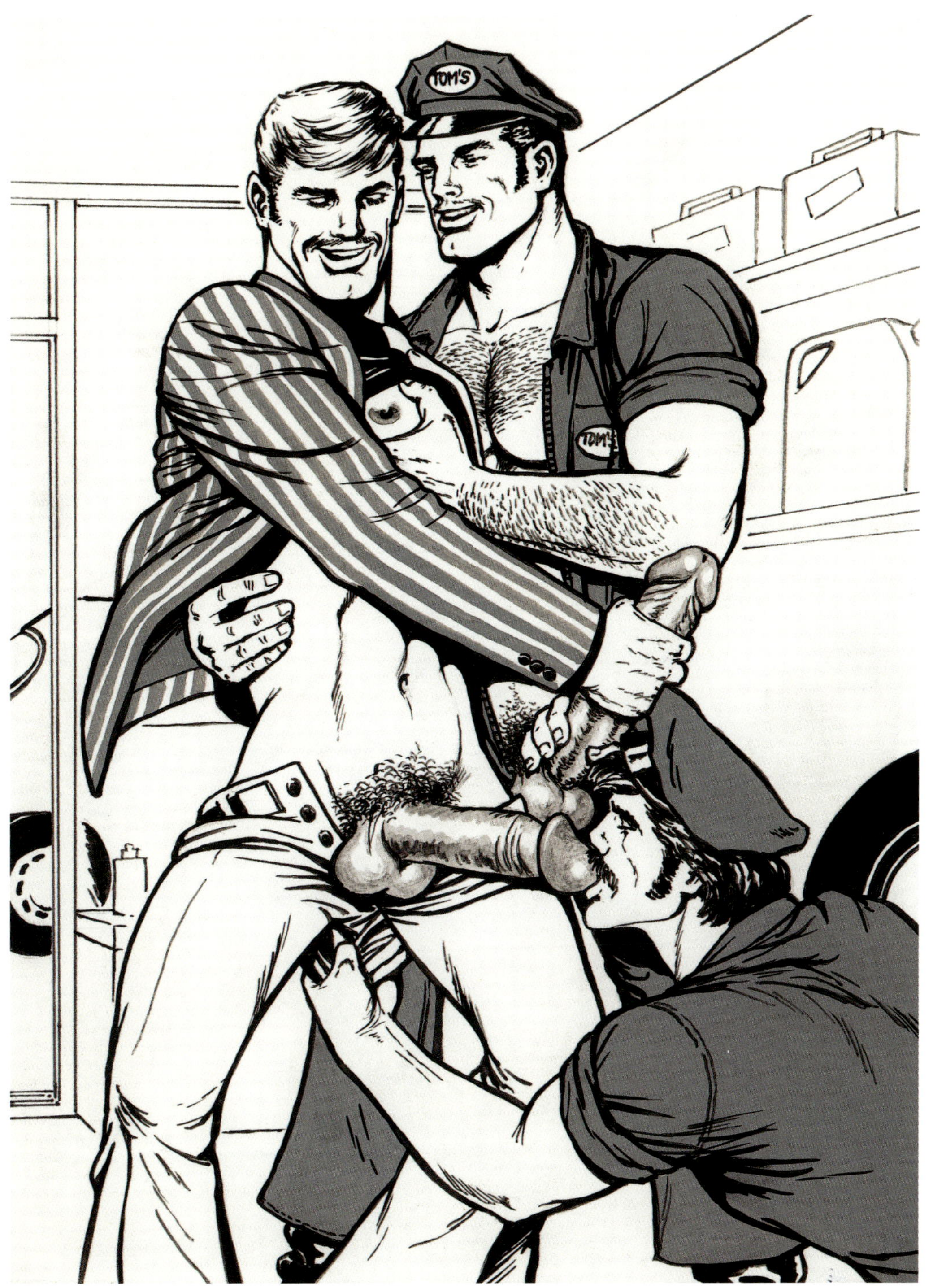

TOM'S
TOM'S

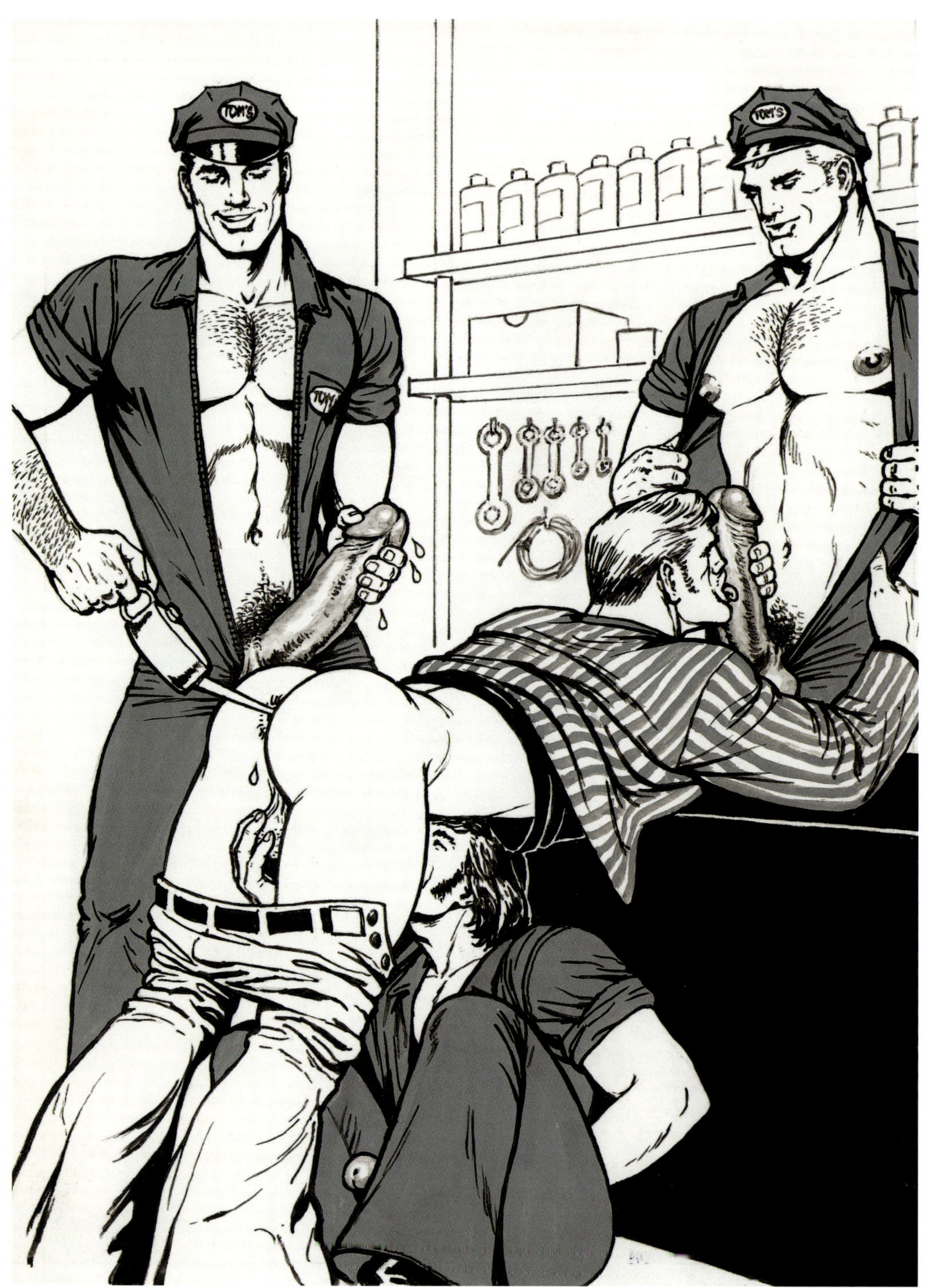

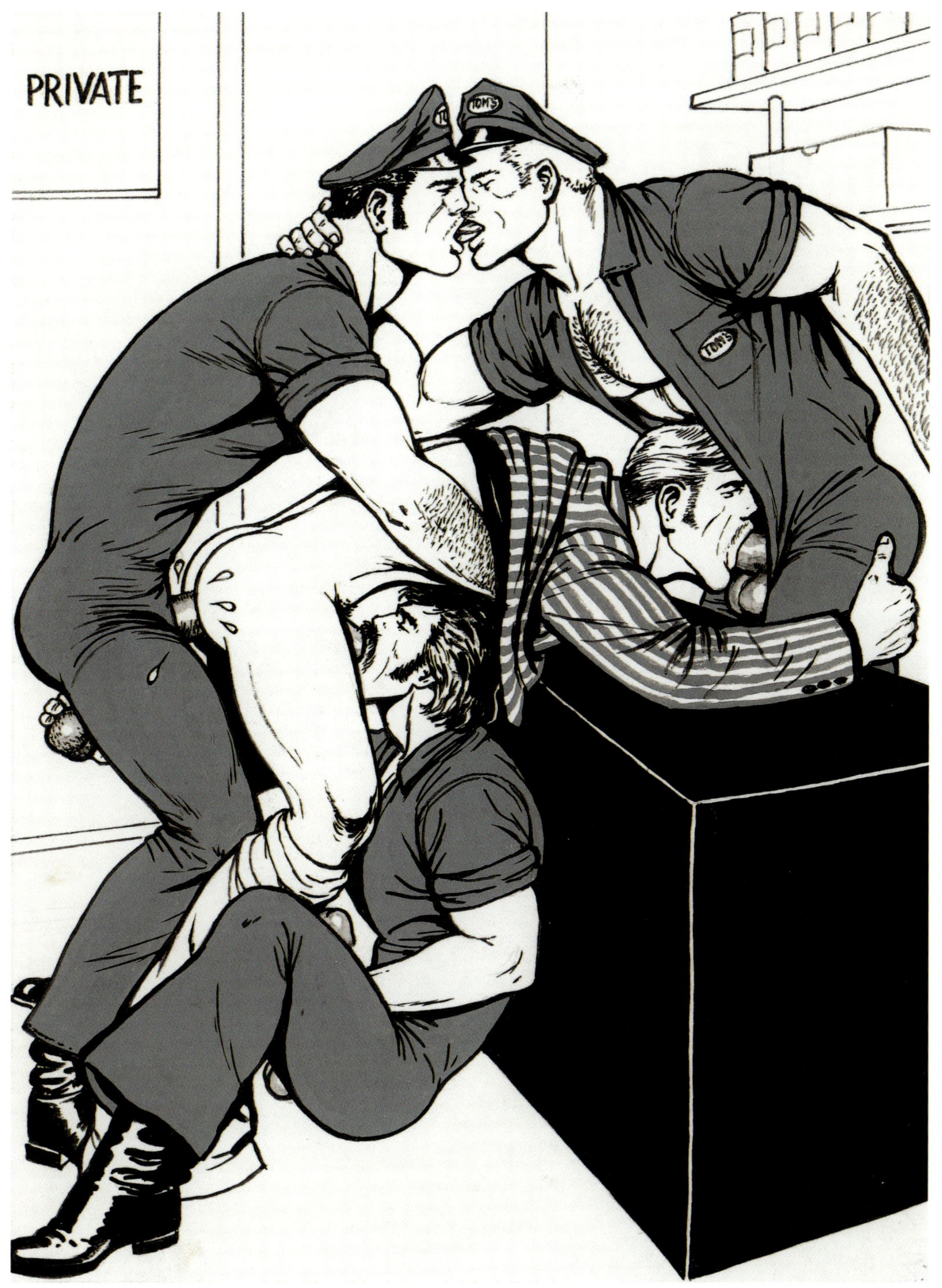
PRIVATE
TOM'S
TOM'S
TOM'S

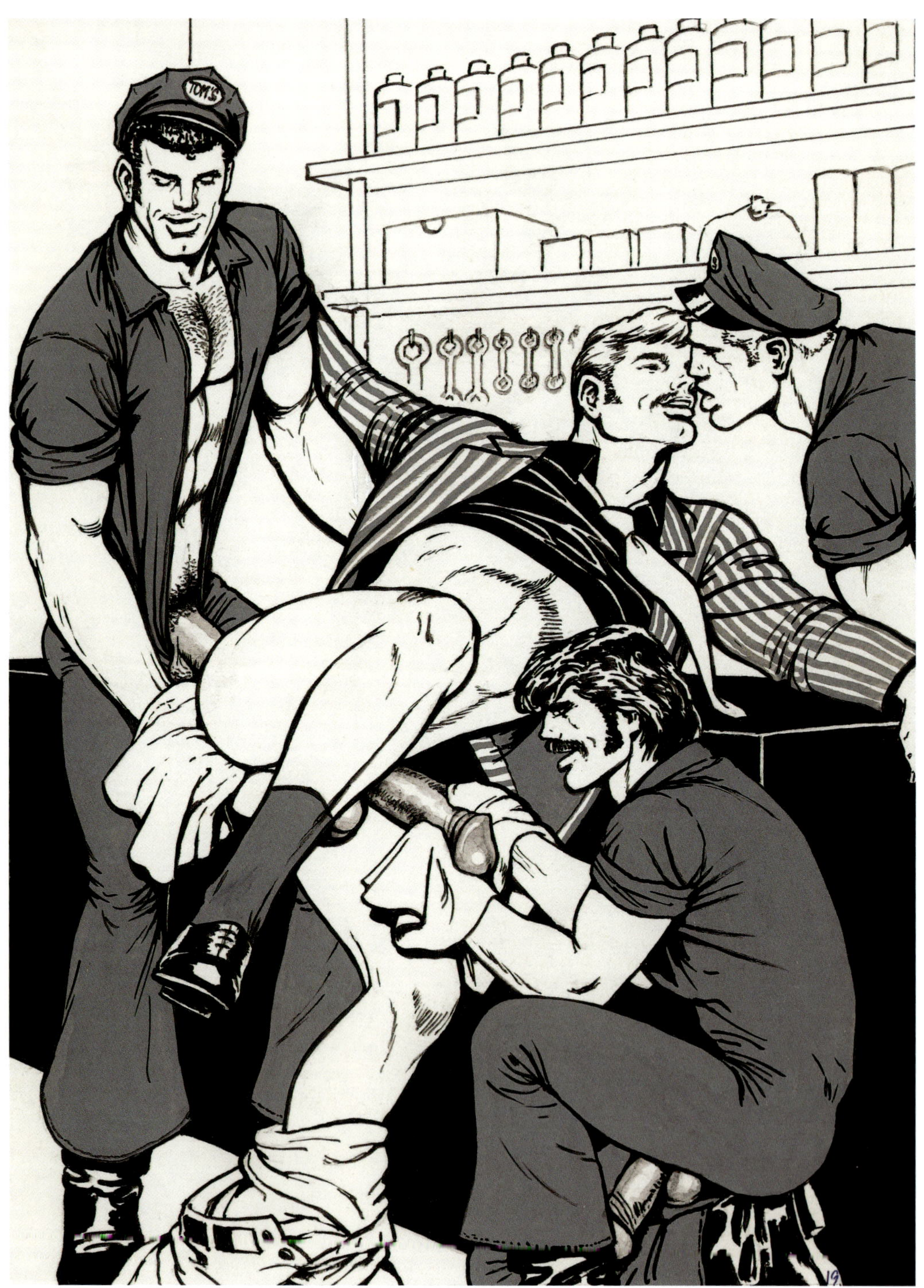

TOM'S

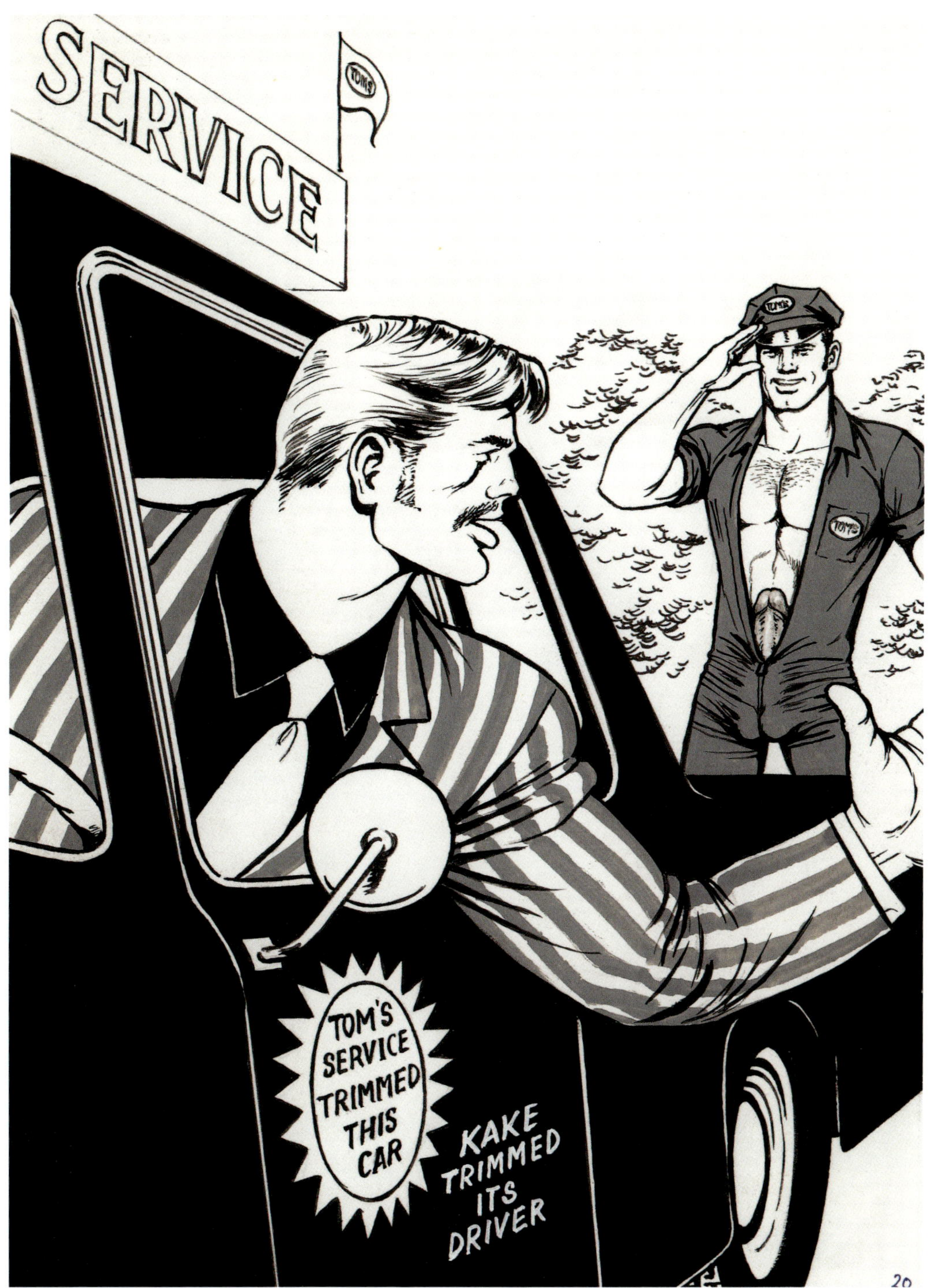

SERVICE
TOM'S
TOM'S
TOM'S
TOM'S SERVICE TRIMMED THIS CAR
KAKE TRIMMED ITS DRIVER

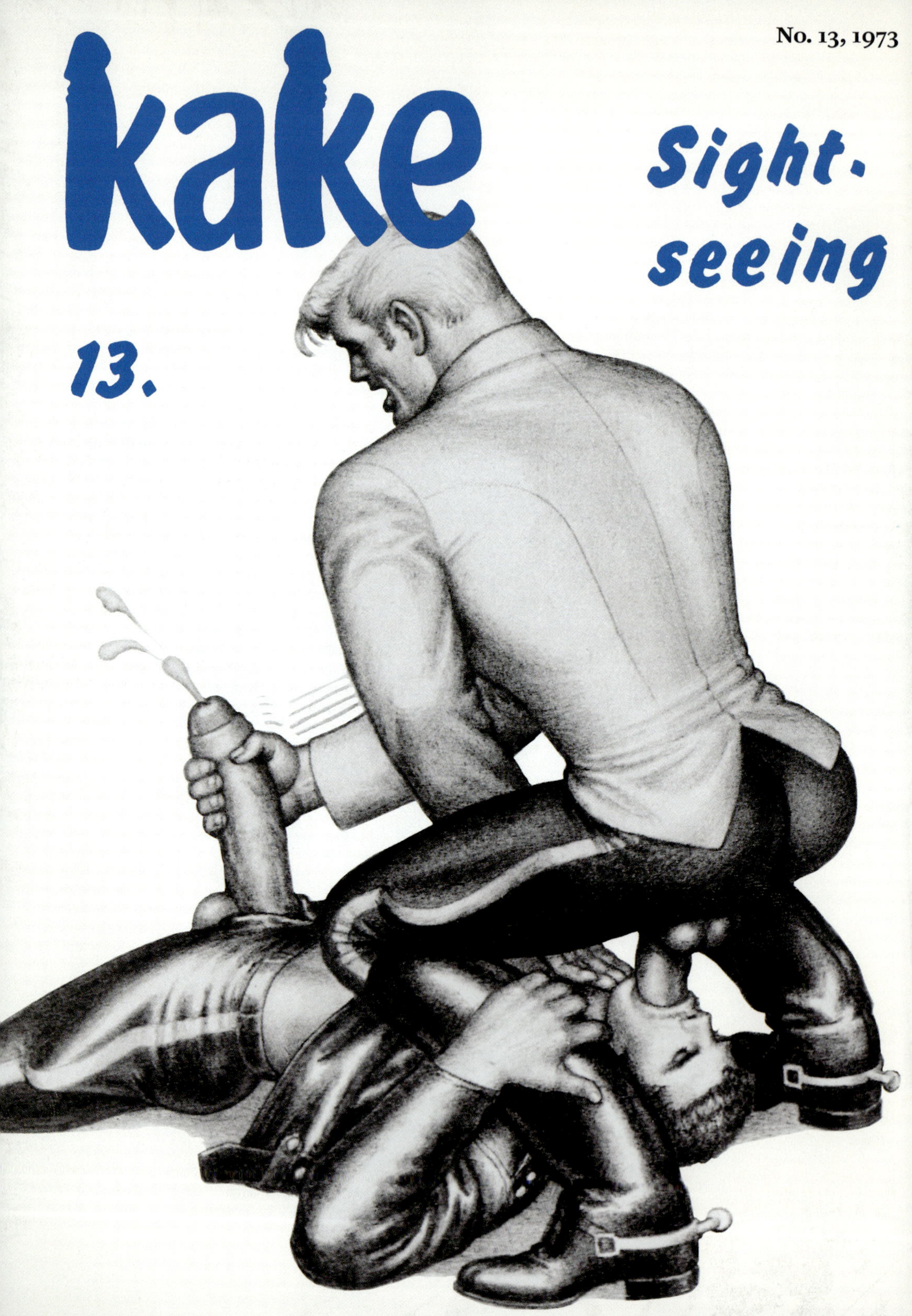
kake
13.
No. 13, 1973
Sight-
seeing

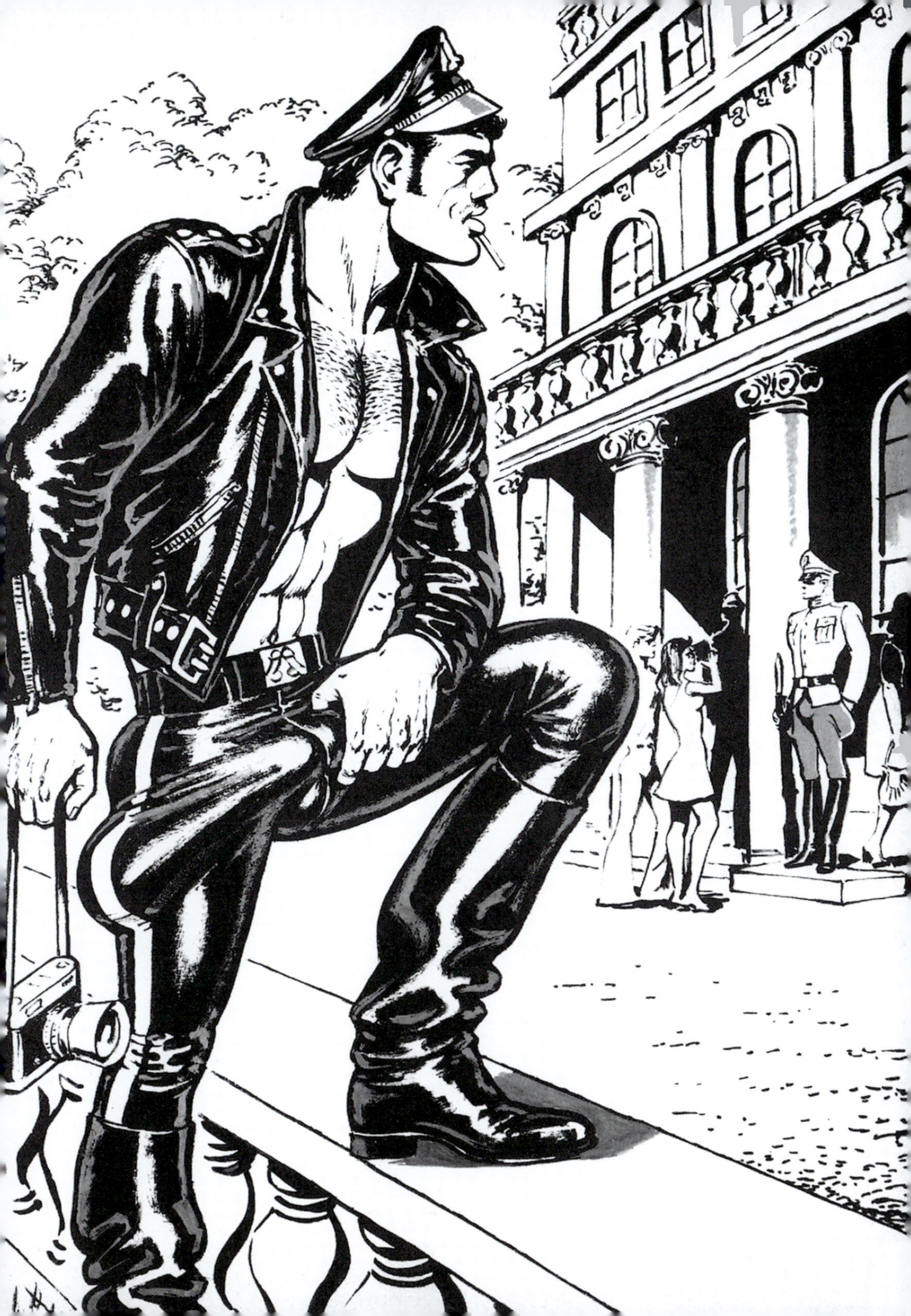

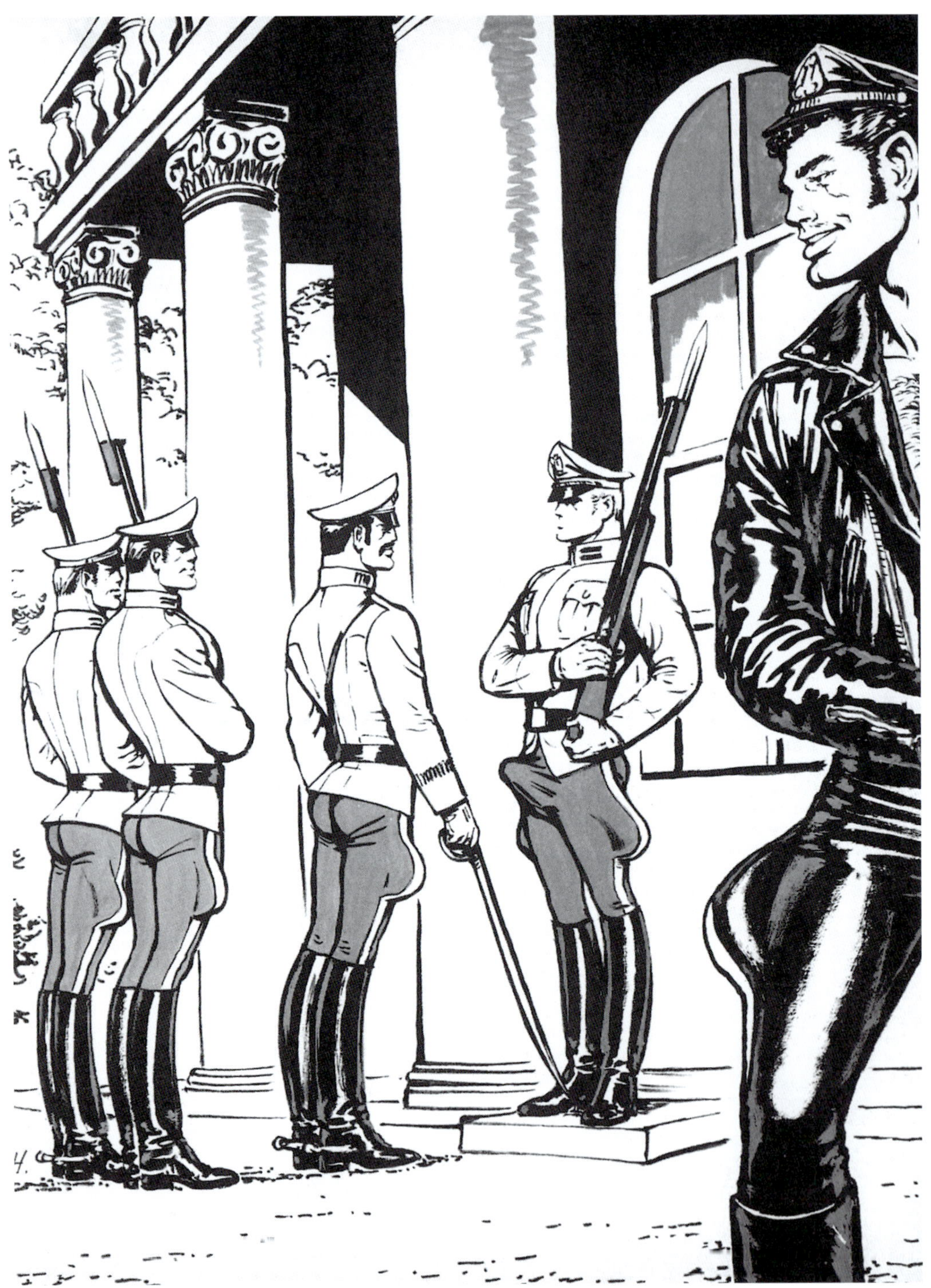

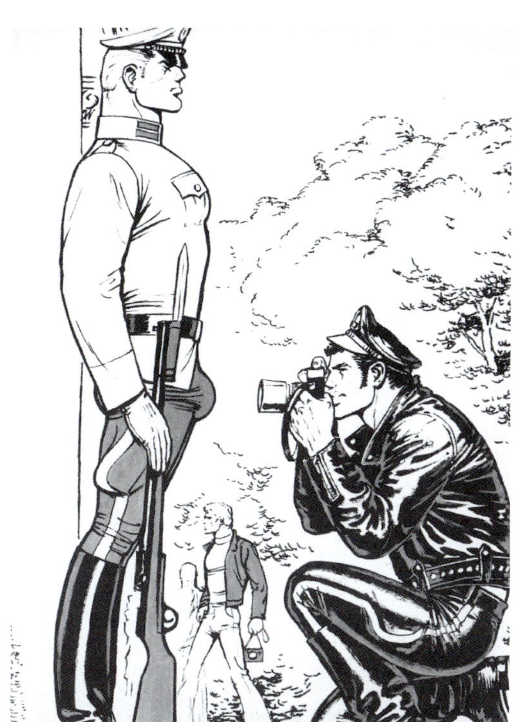
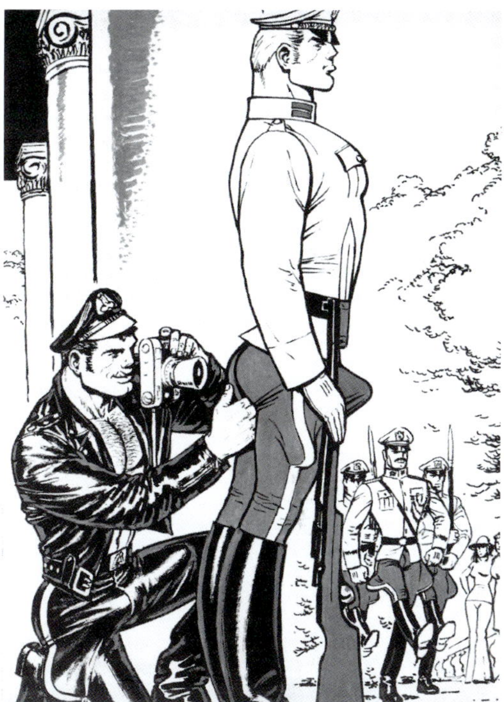
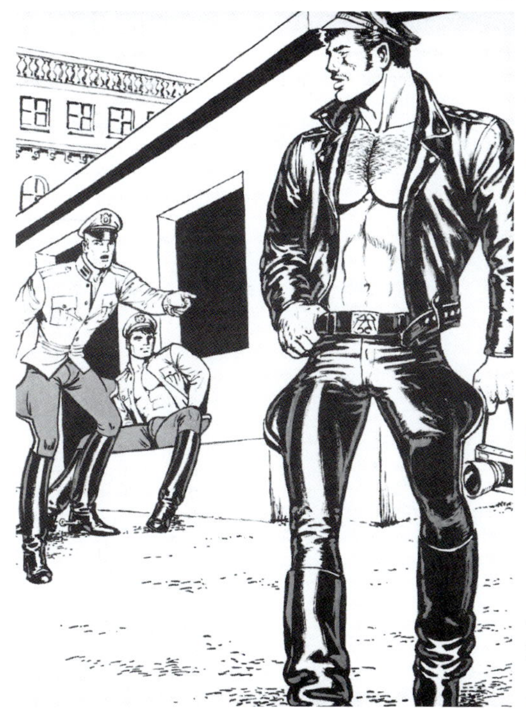
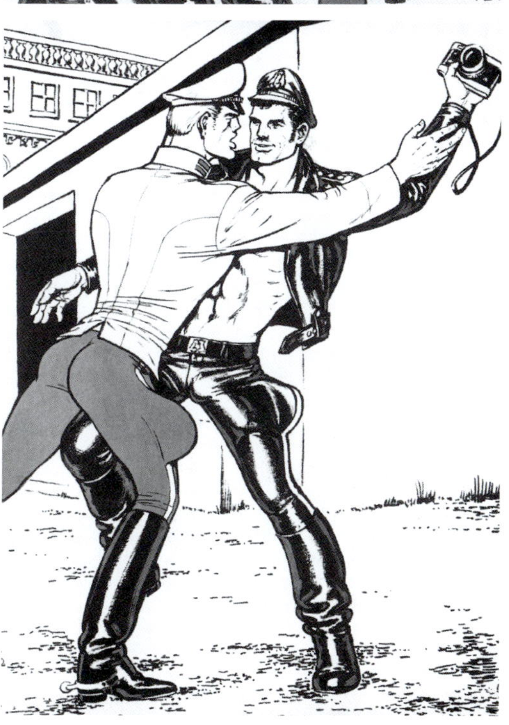

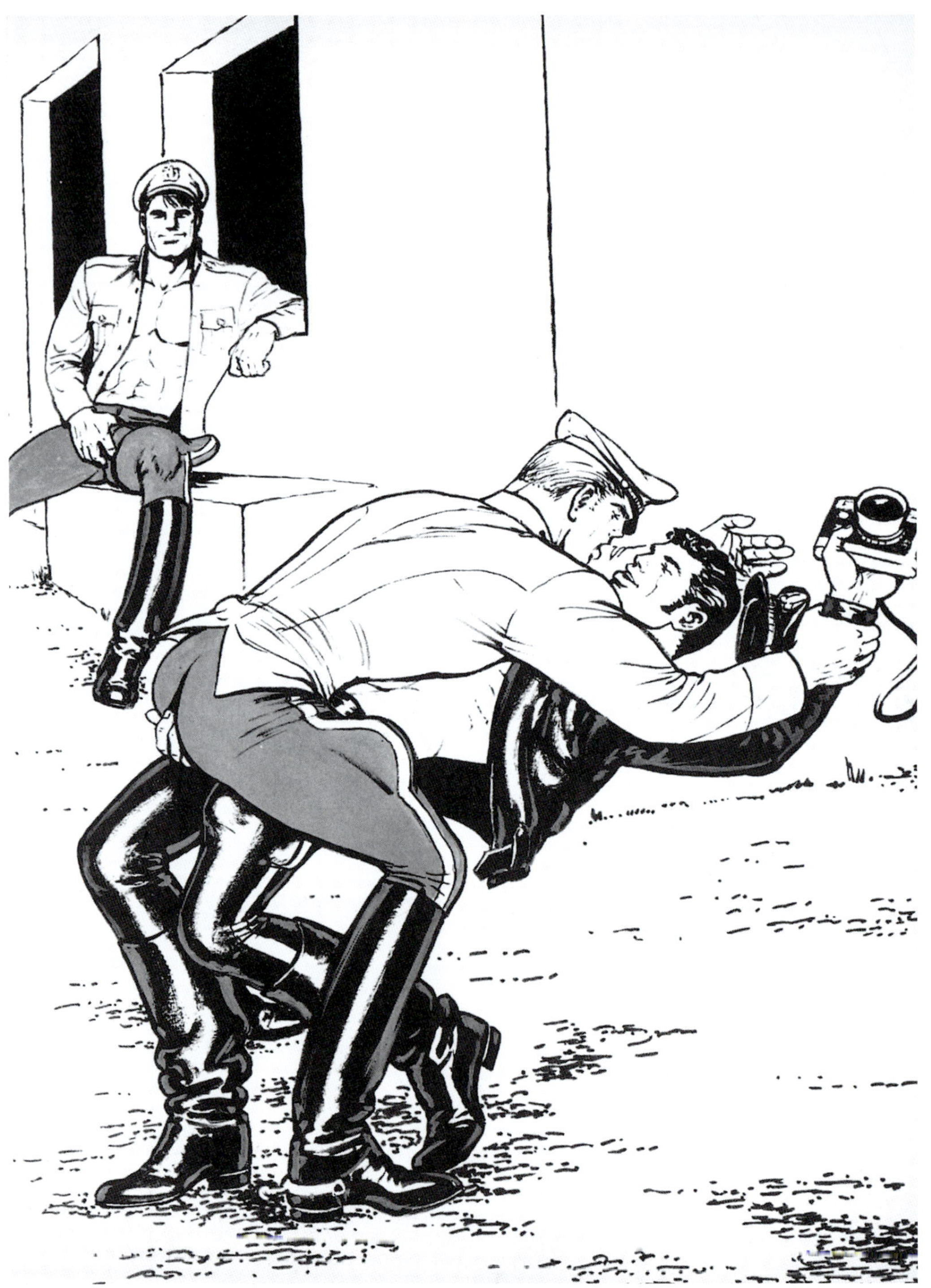

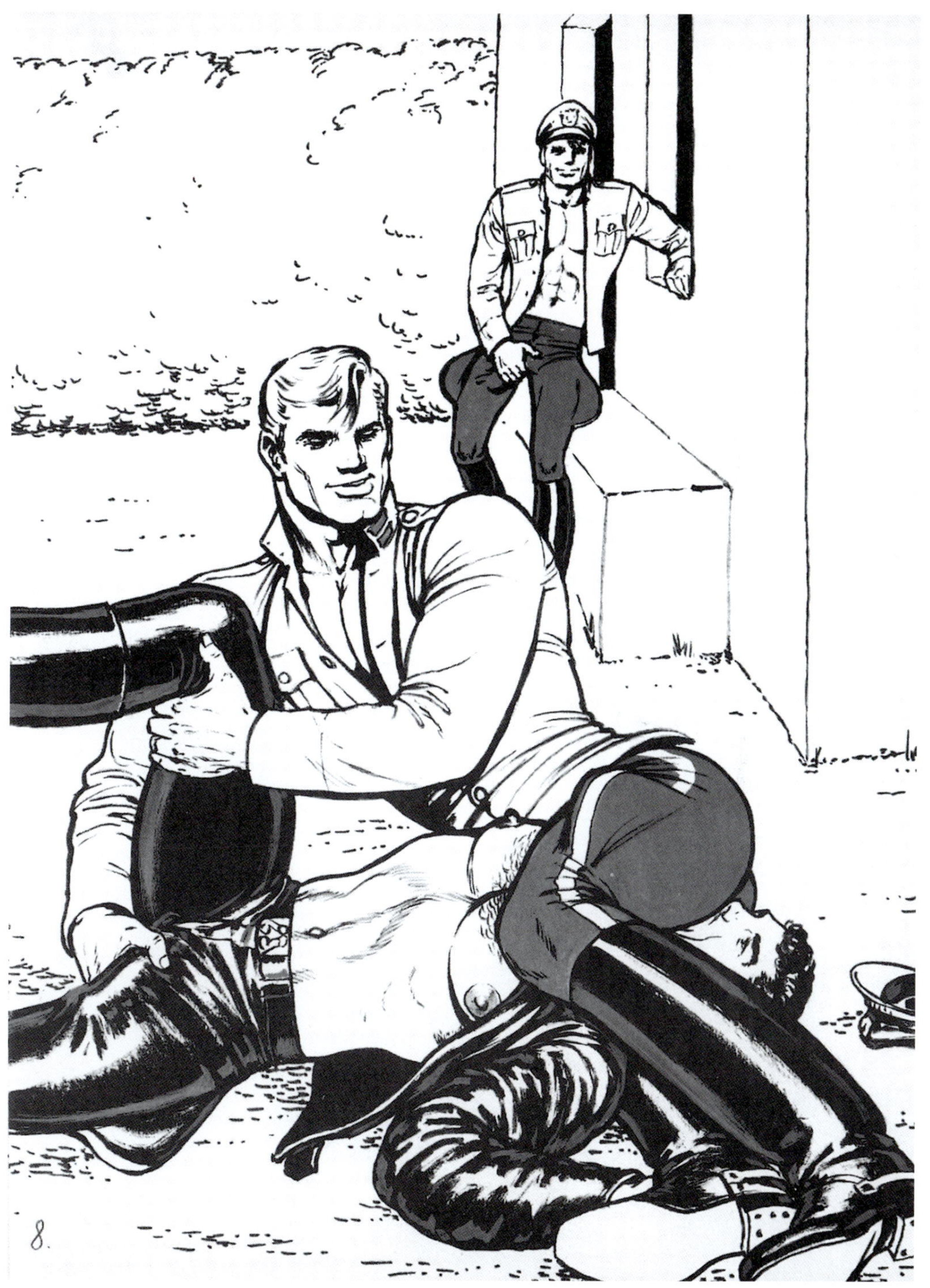

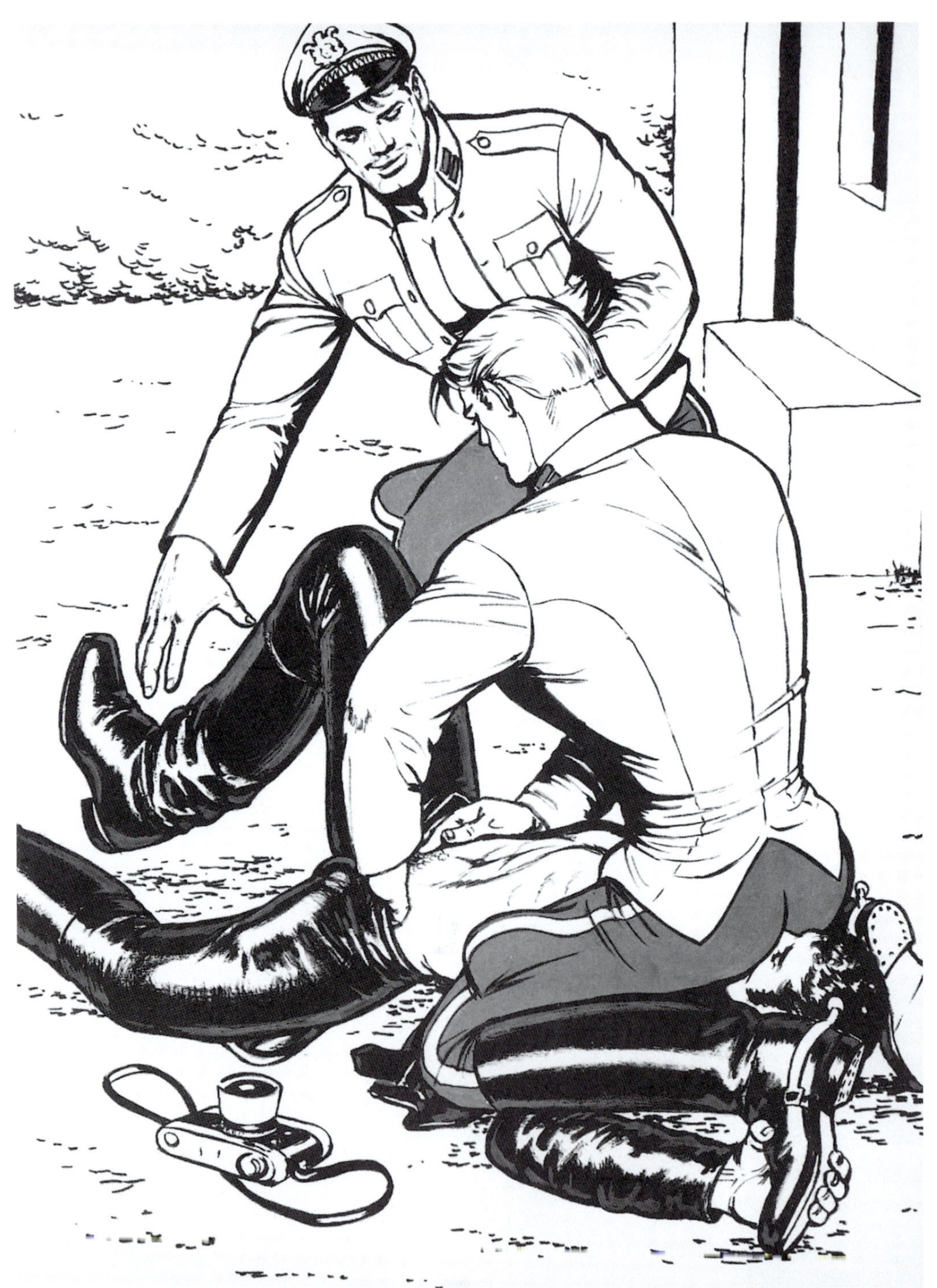

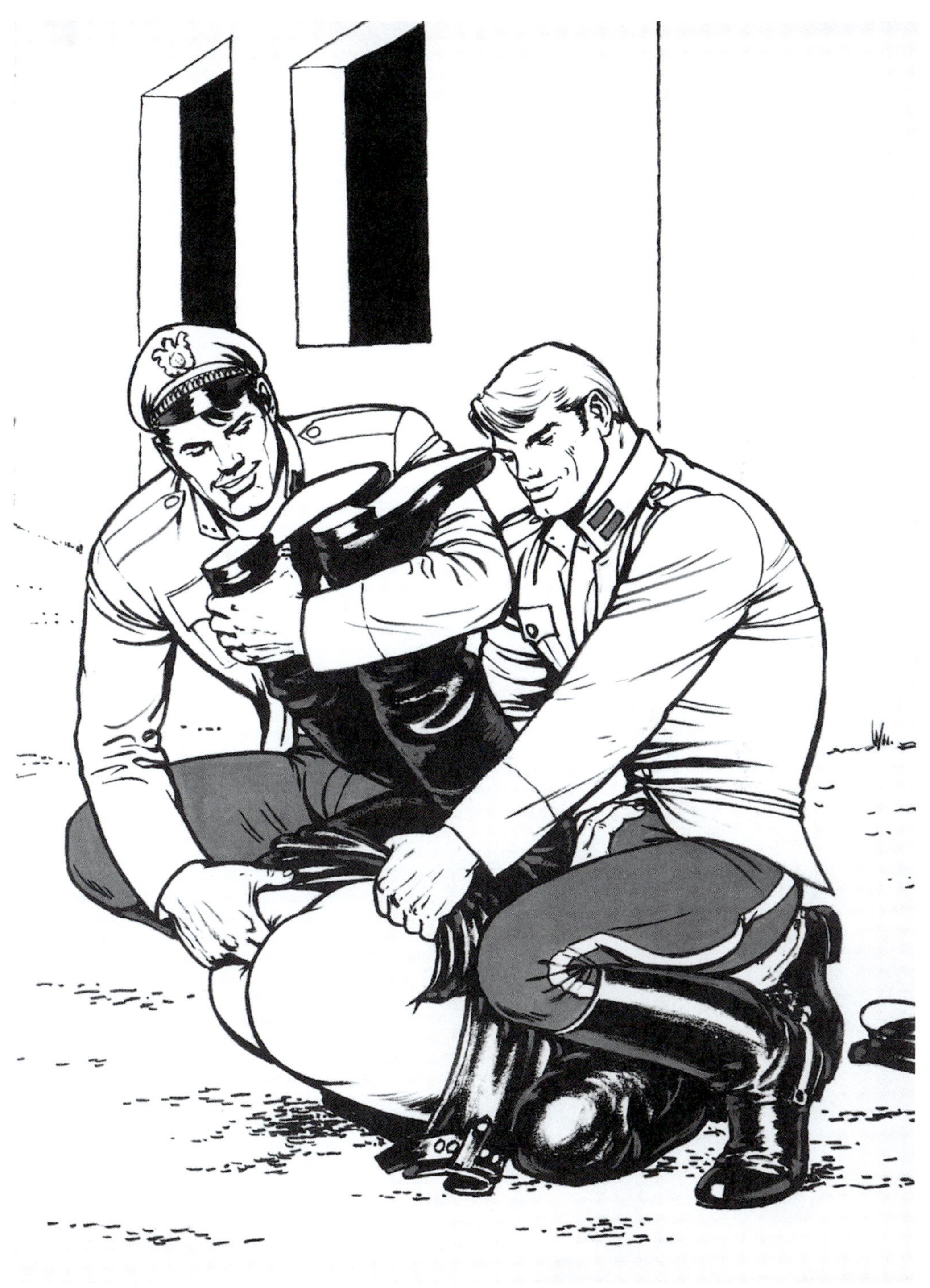

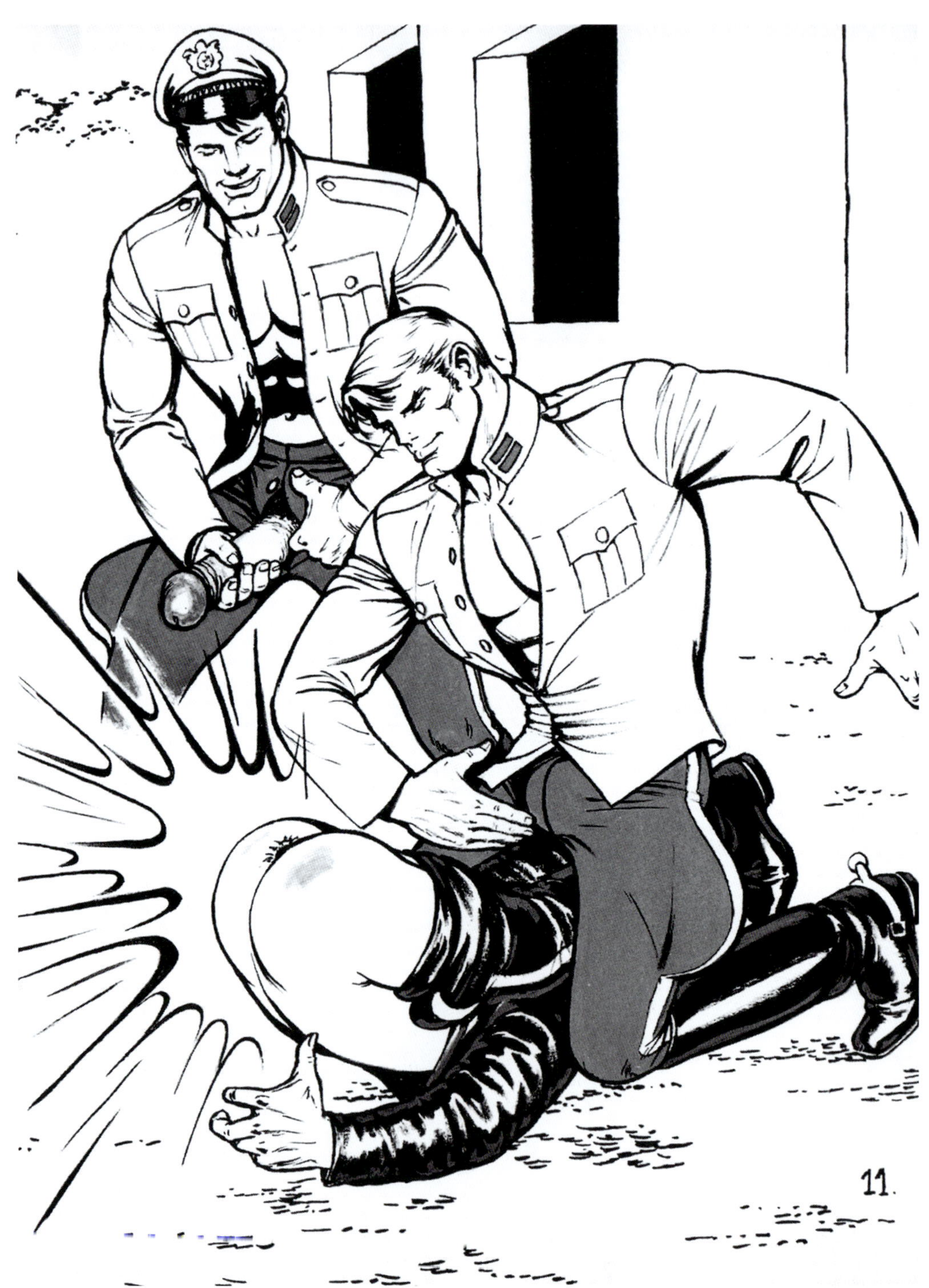

11.

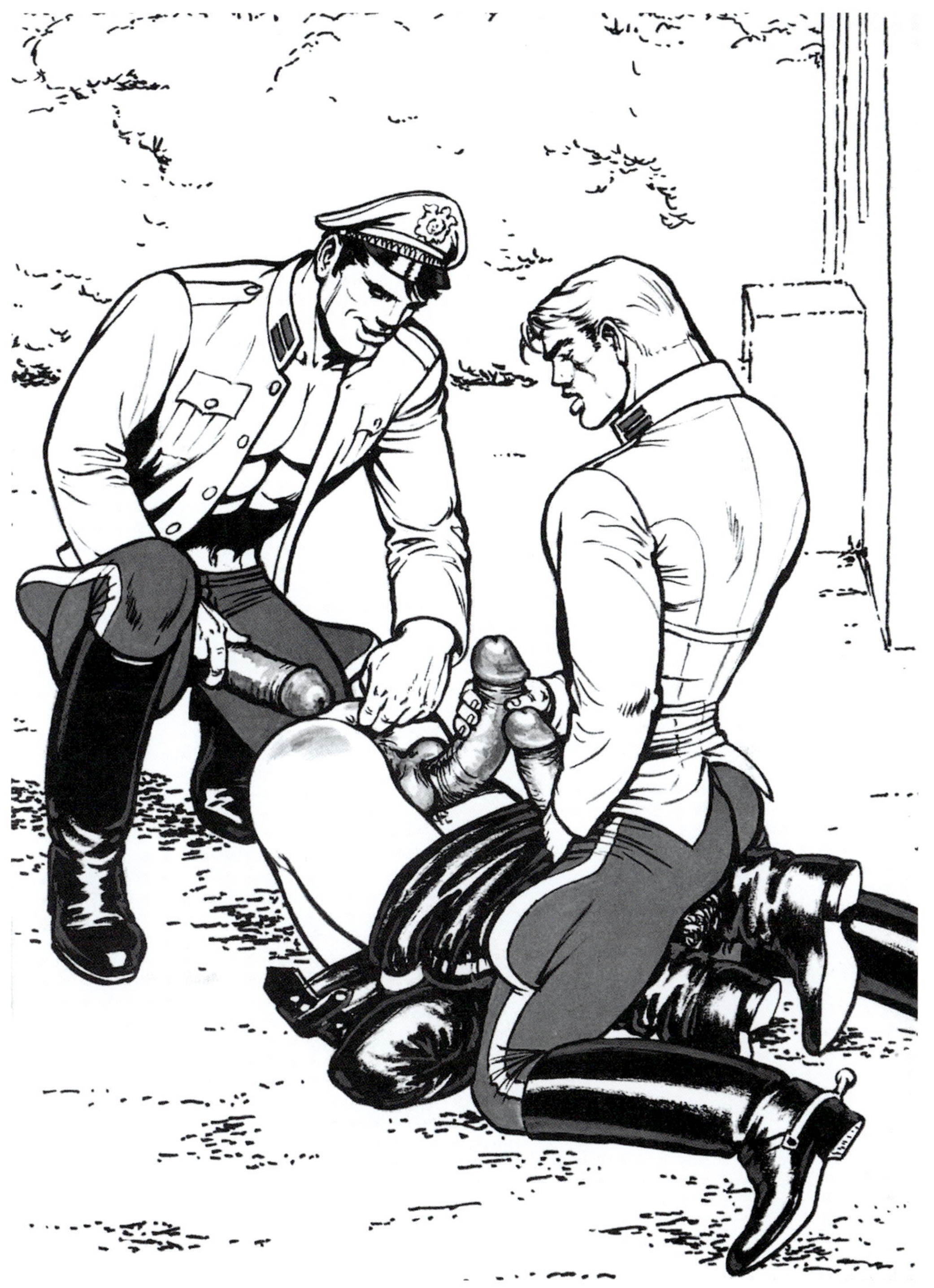

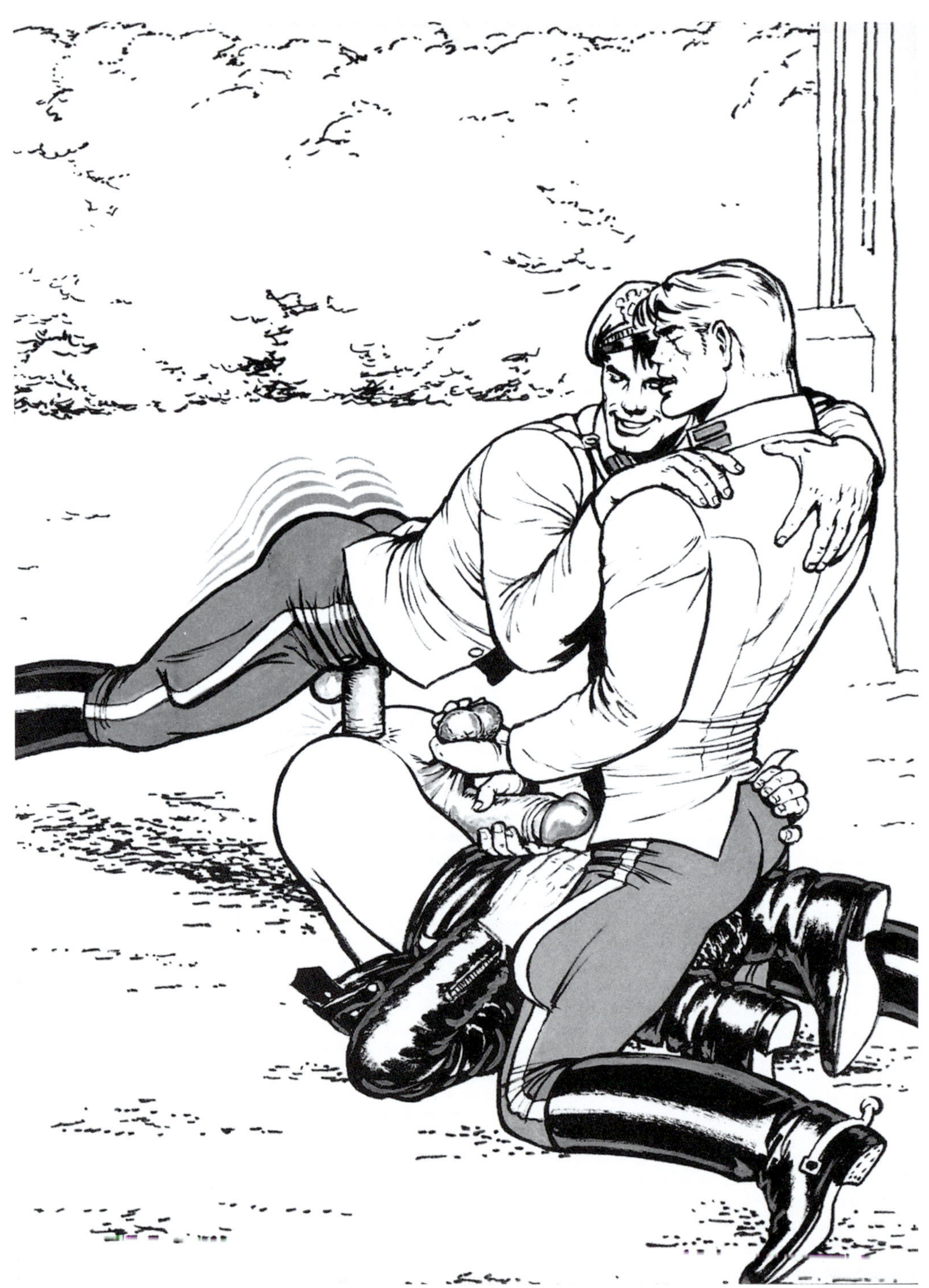

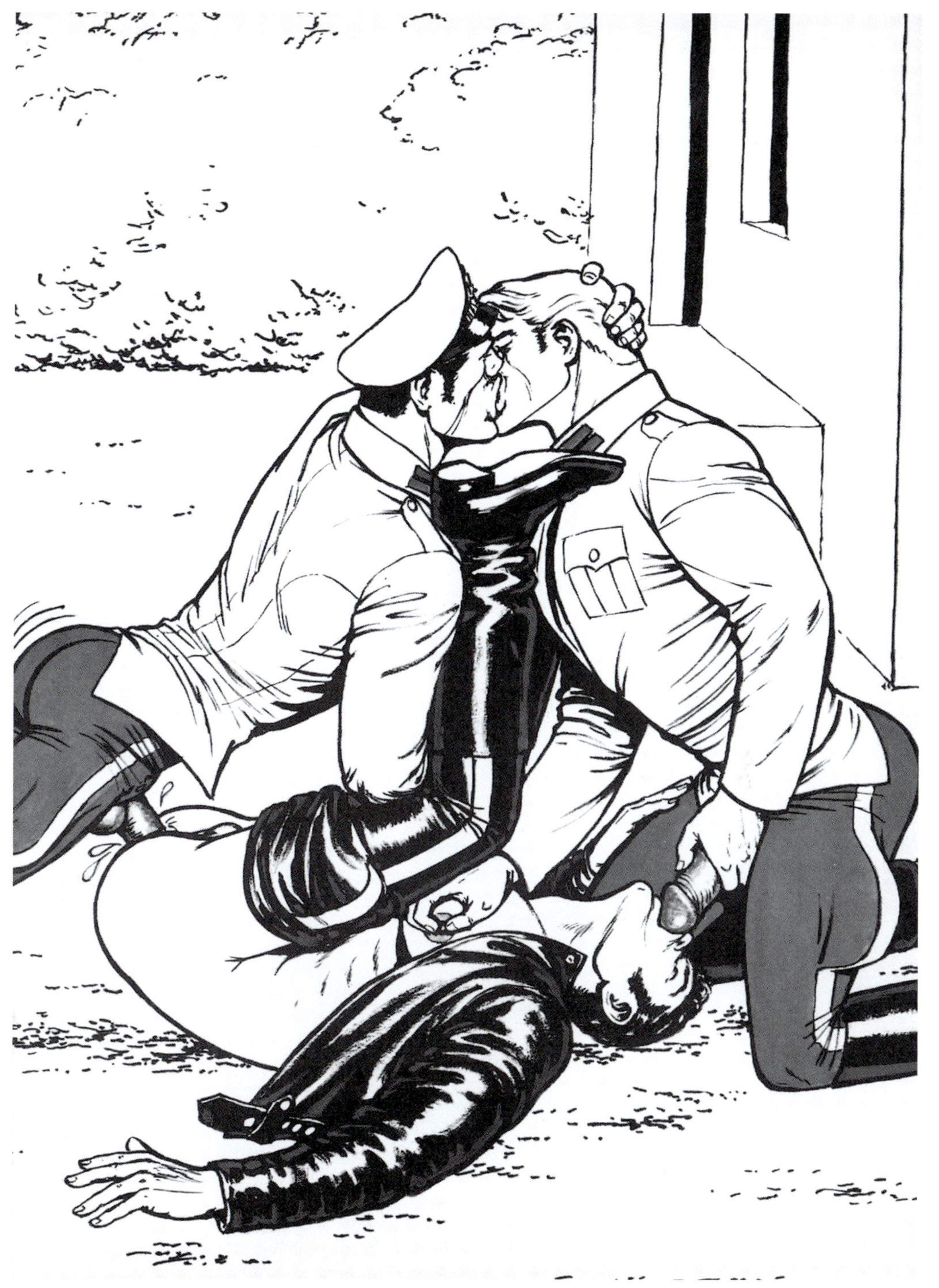

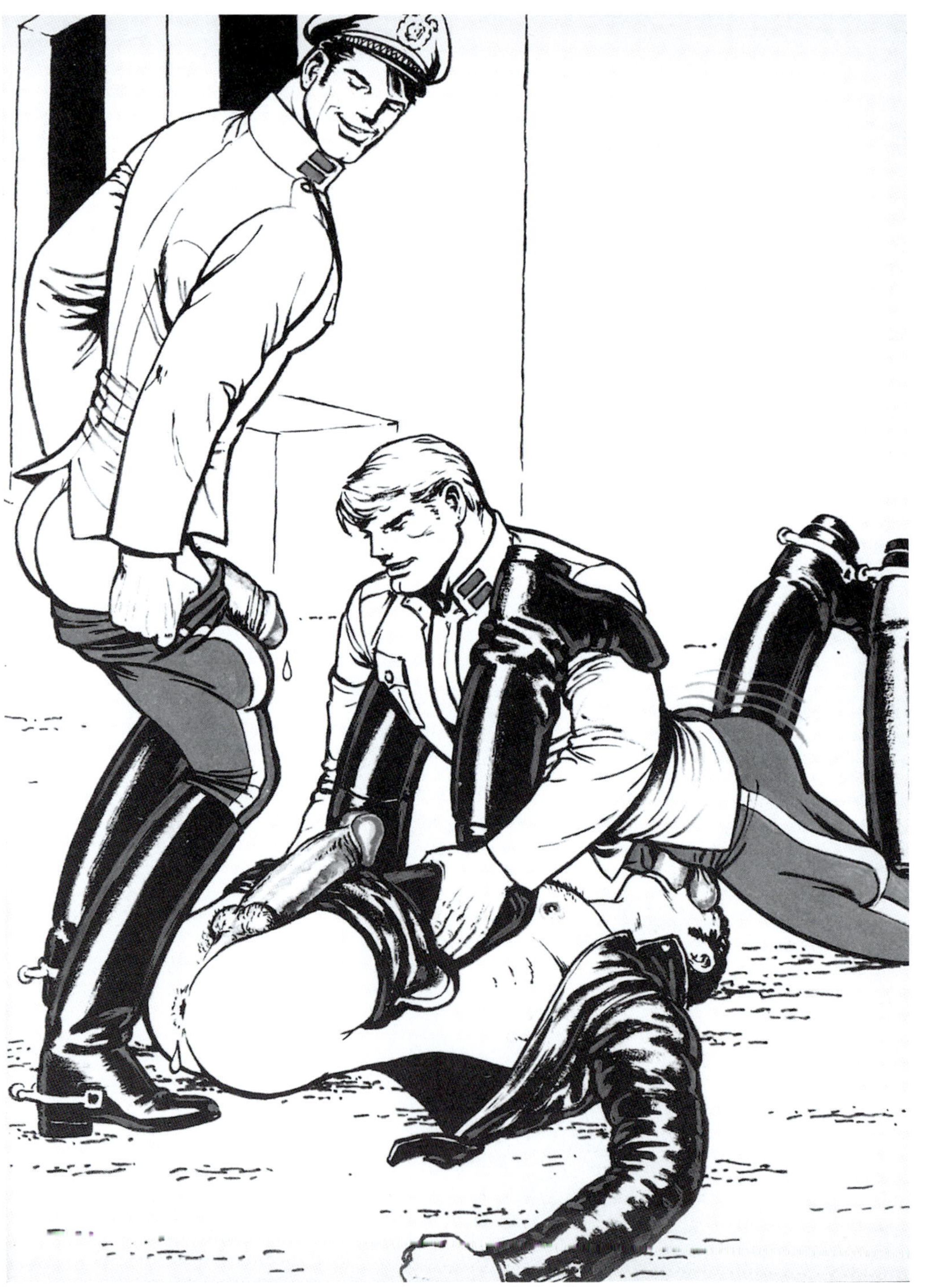

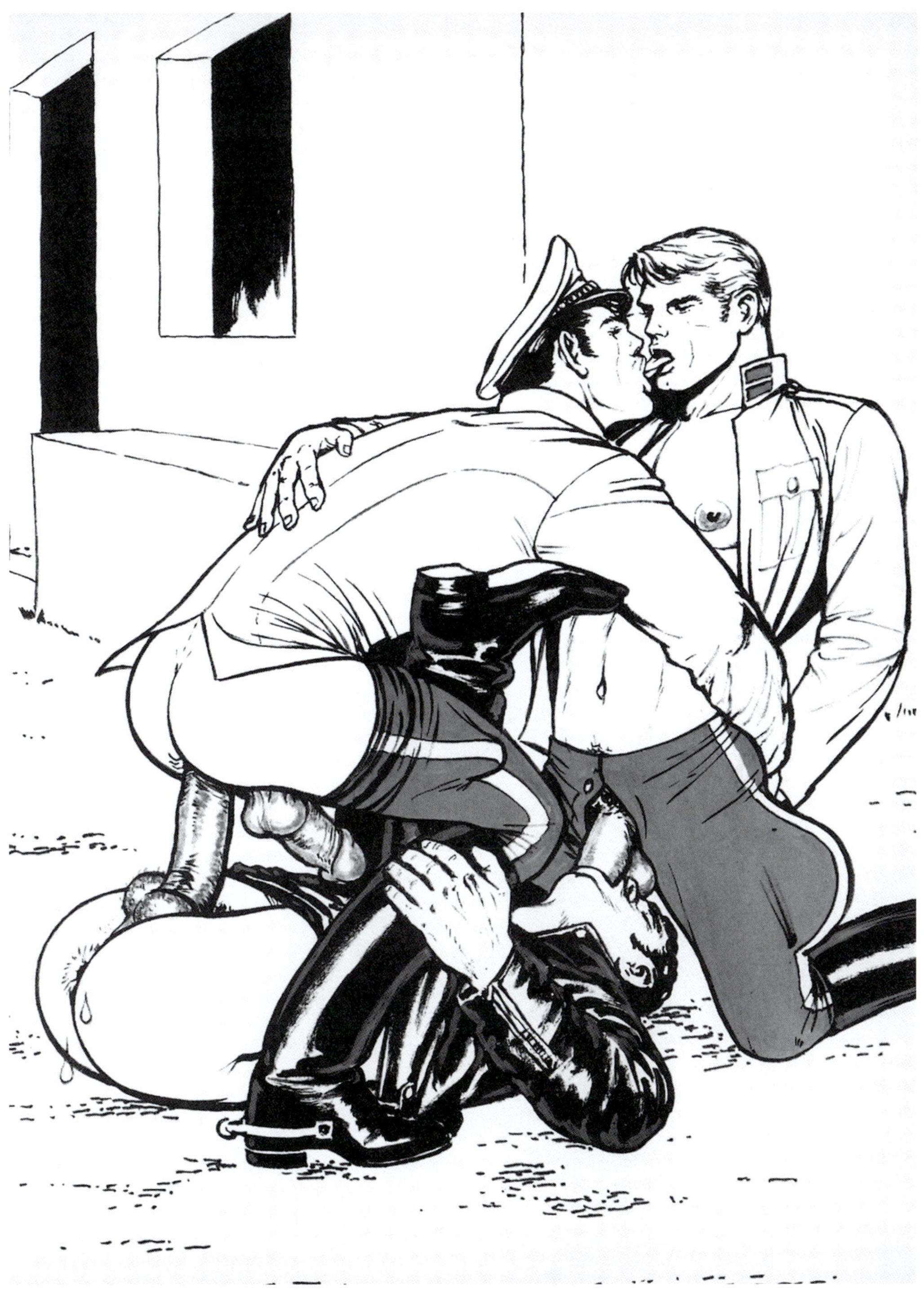

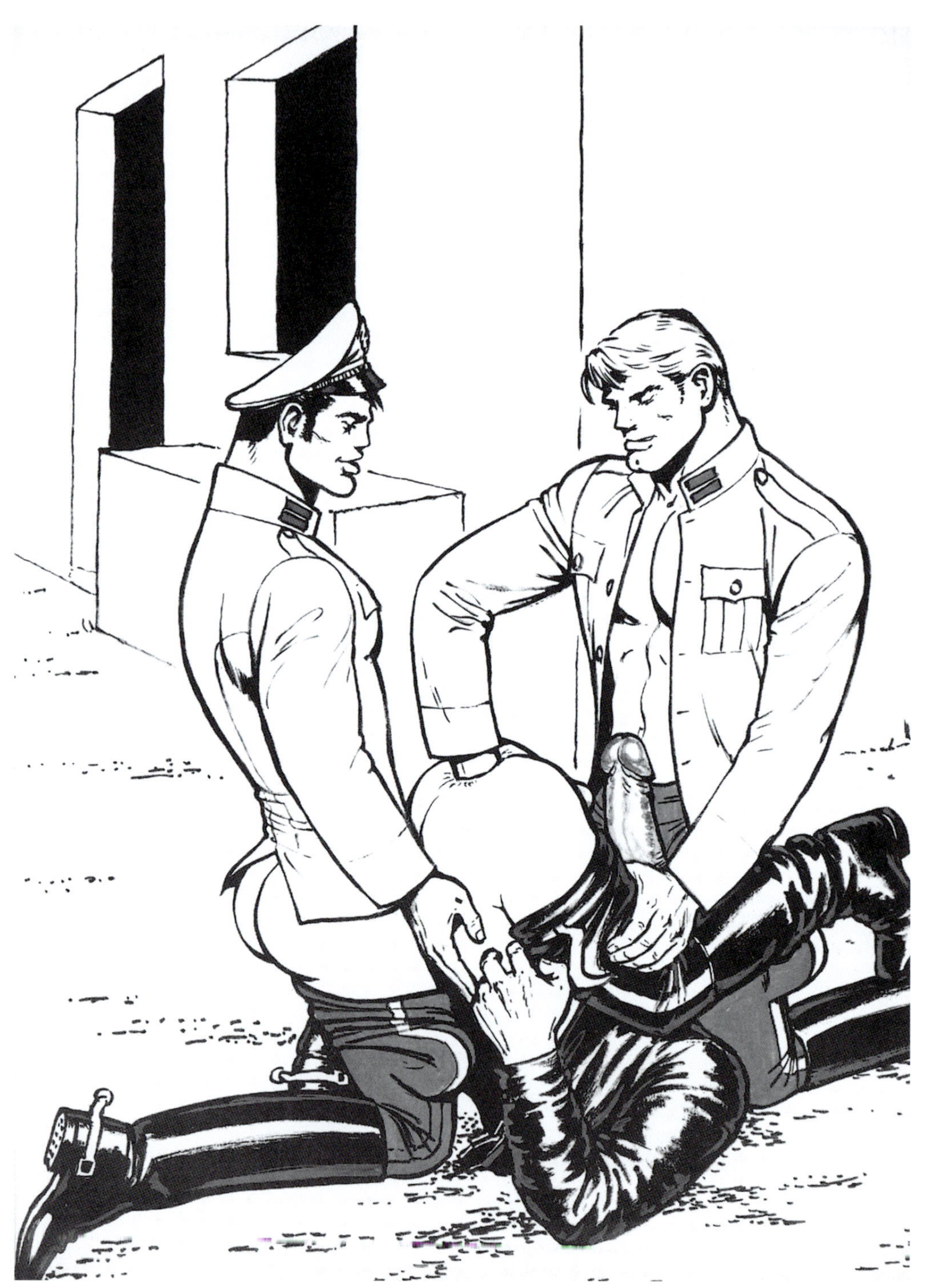

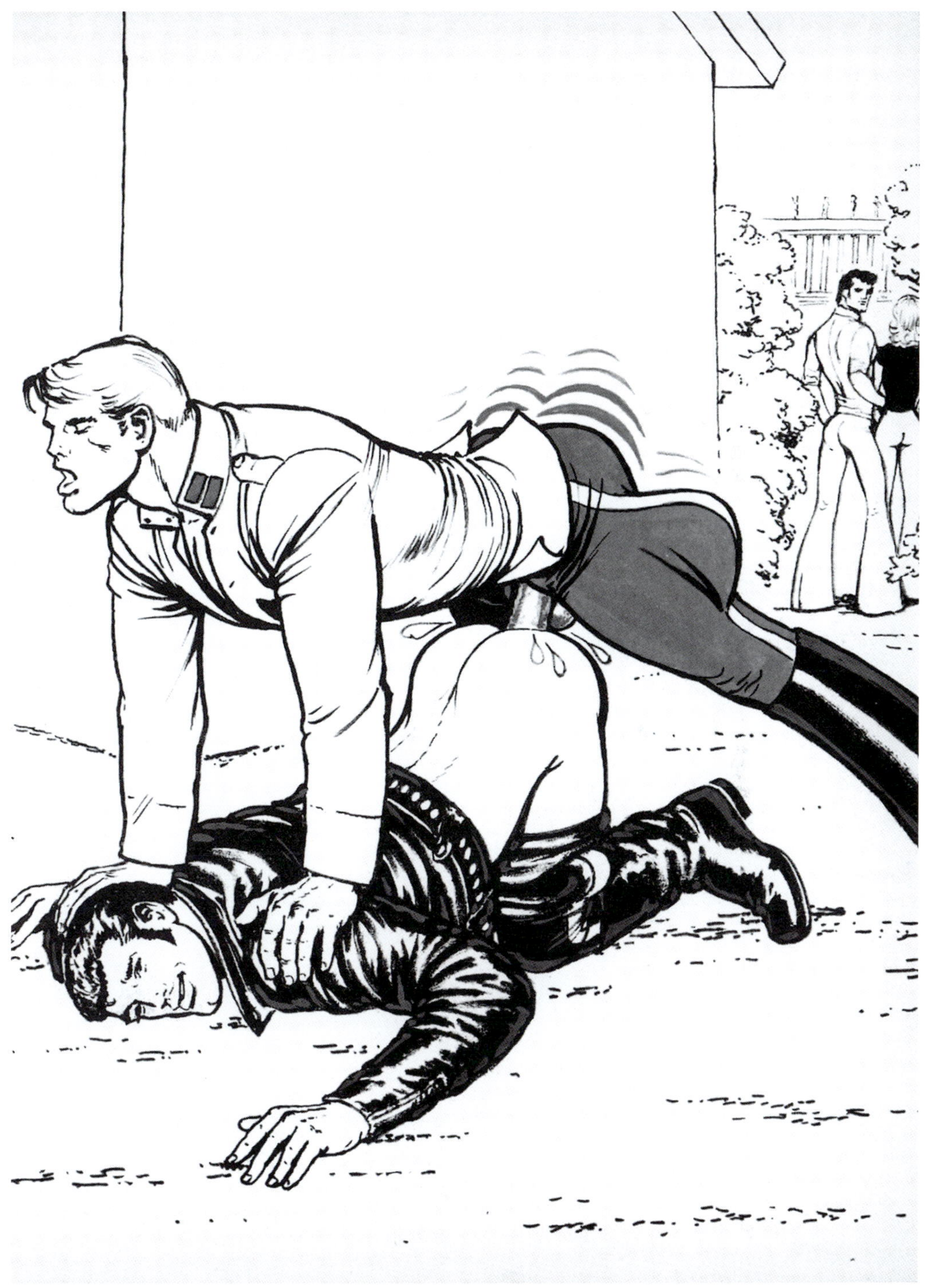

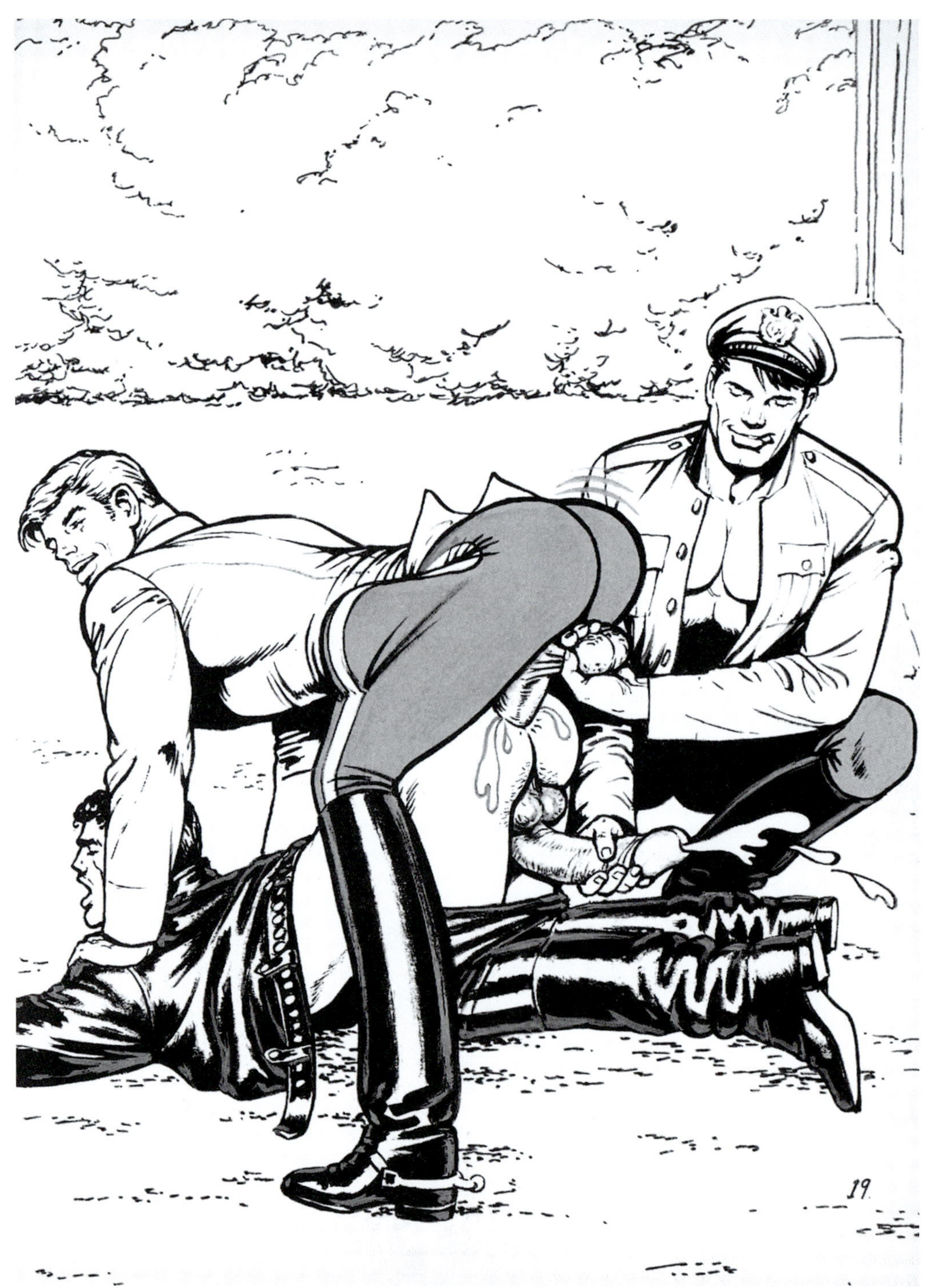

19

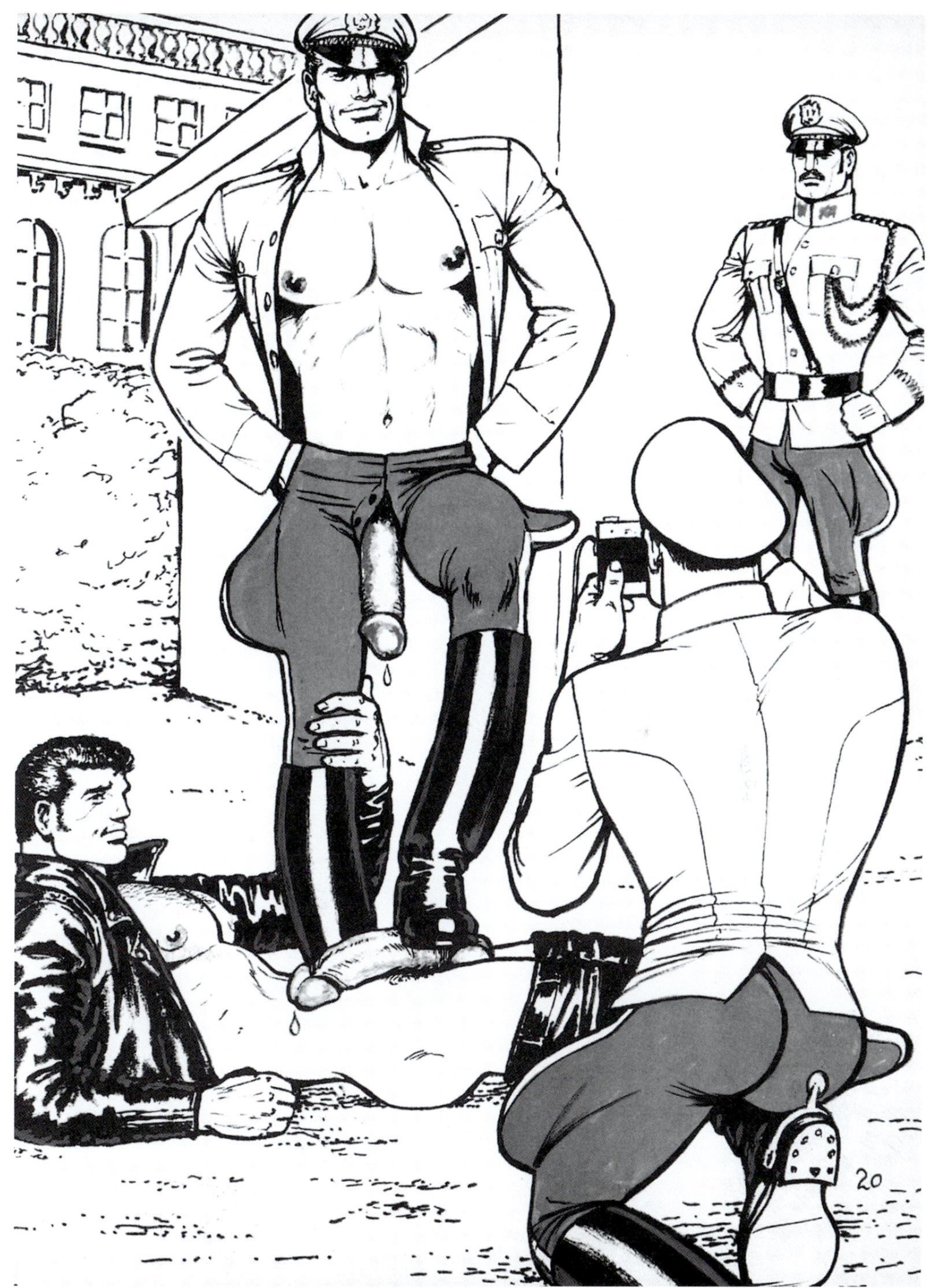

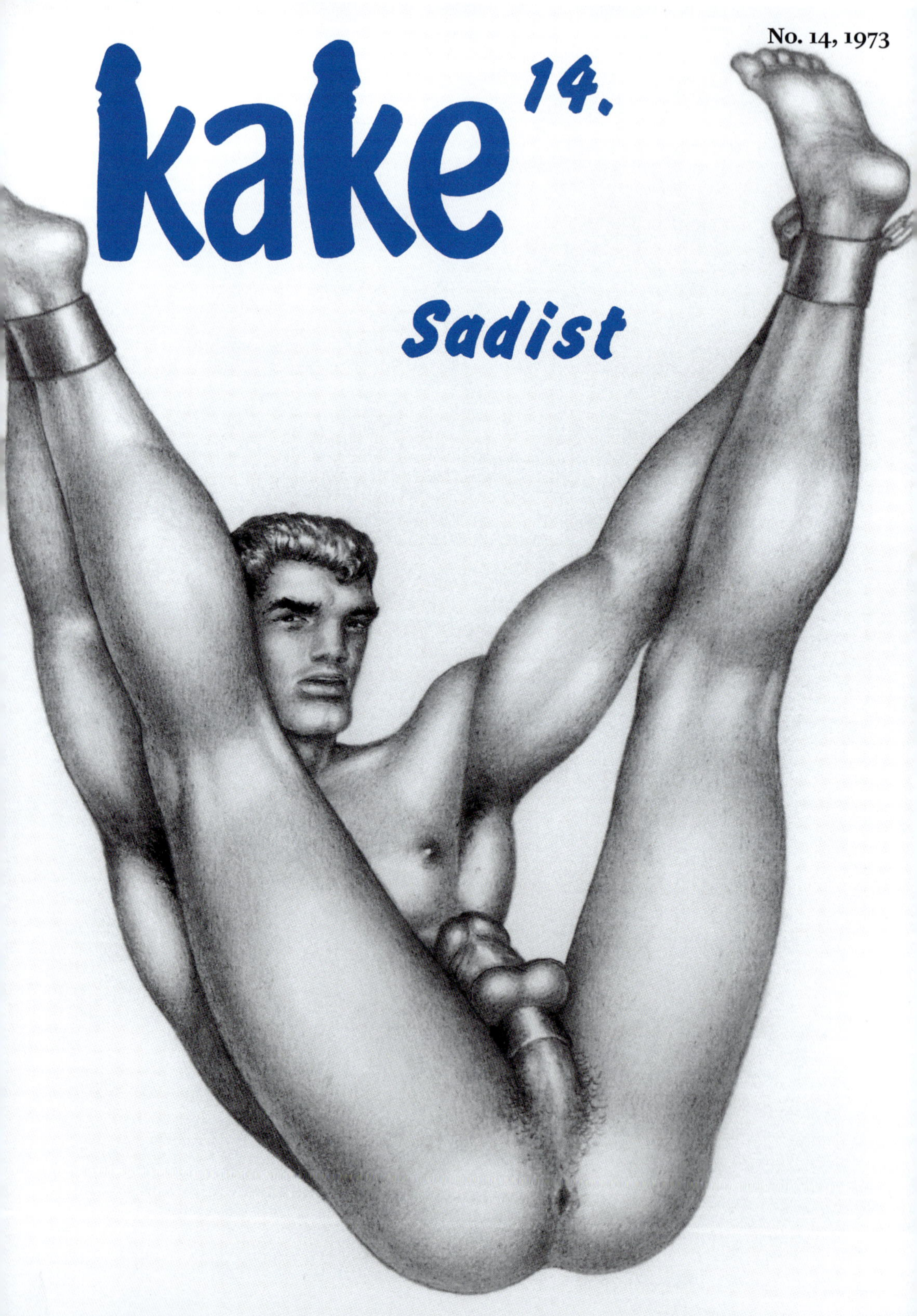
No. 14, 1973
kake 14.
Sadist

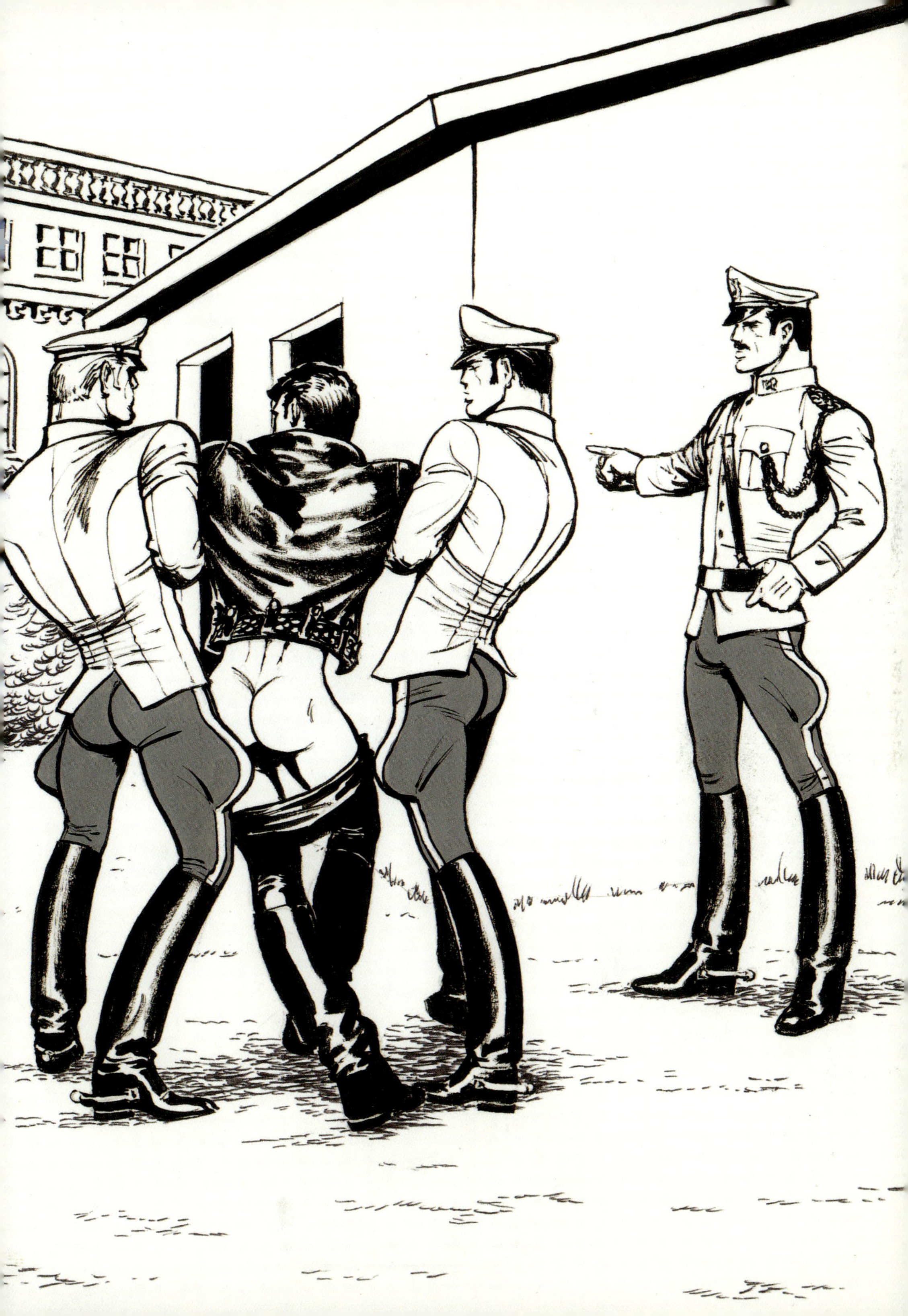

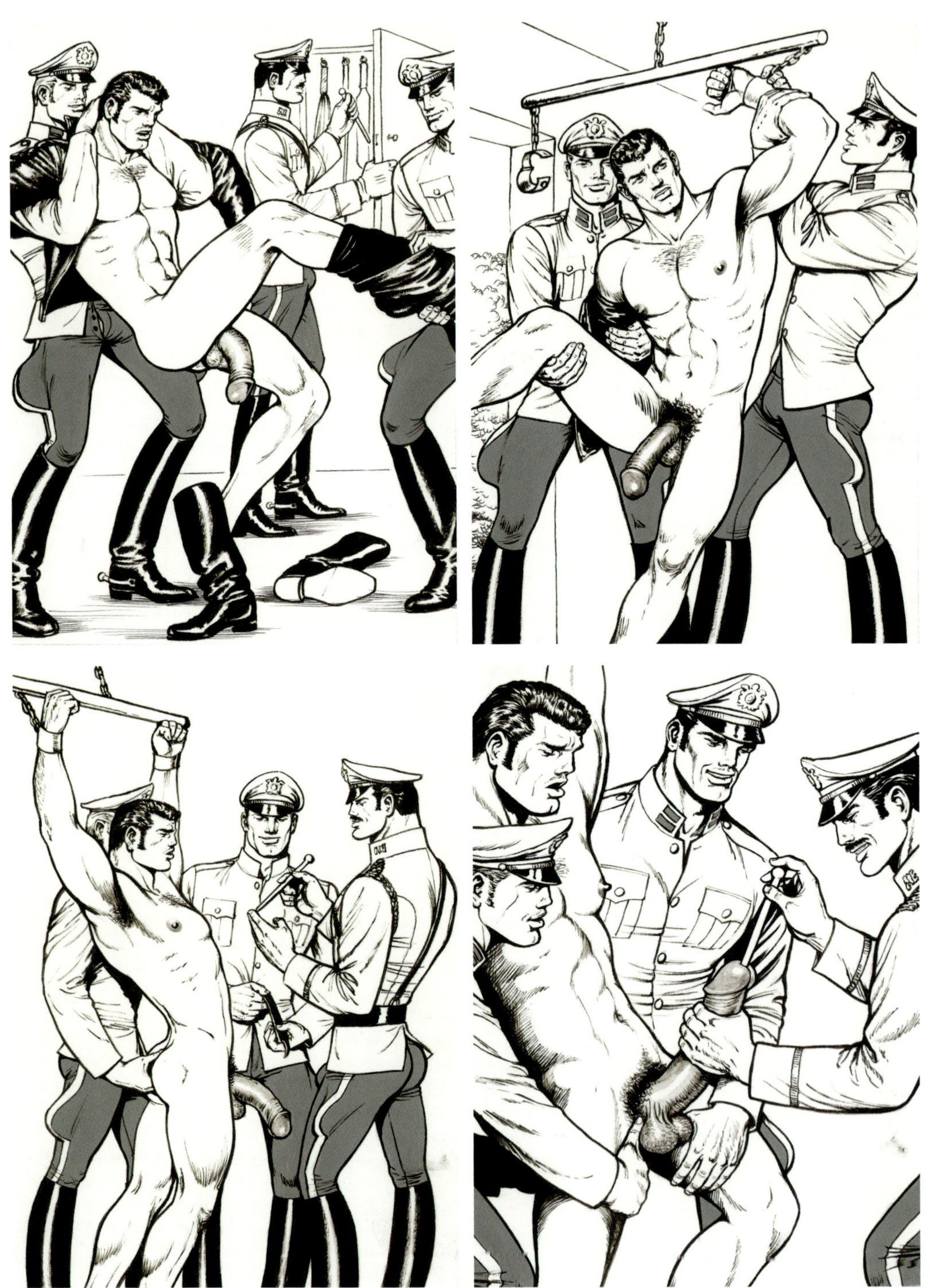

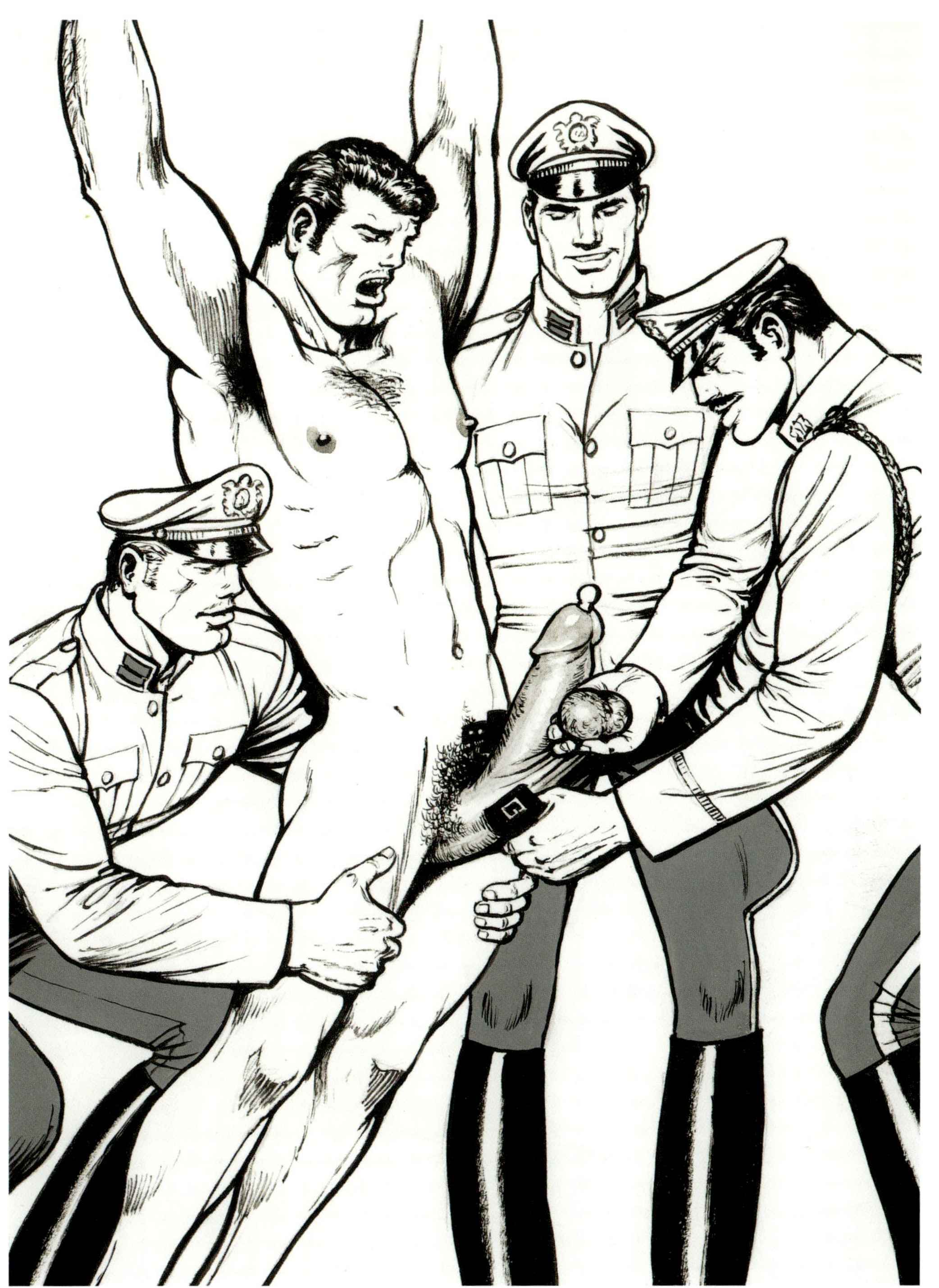

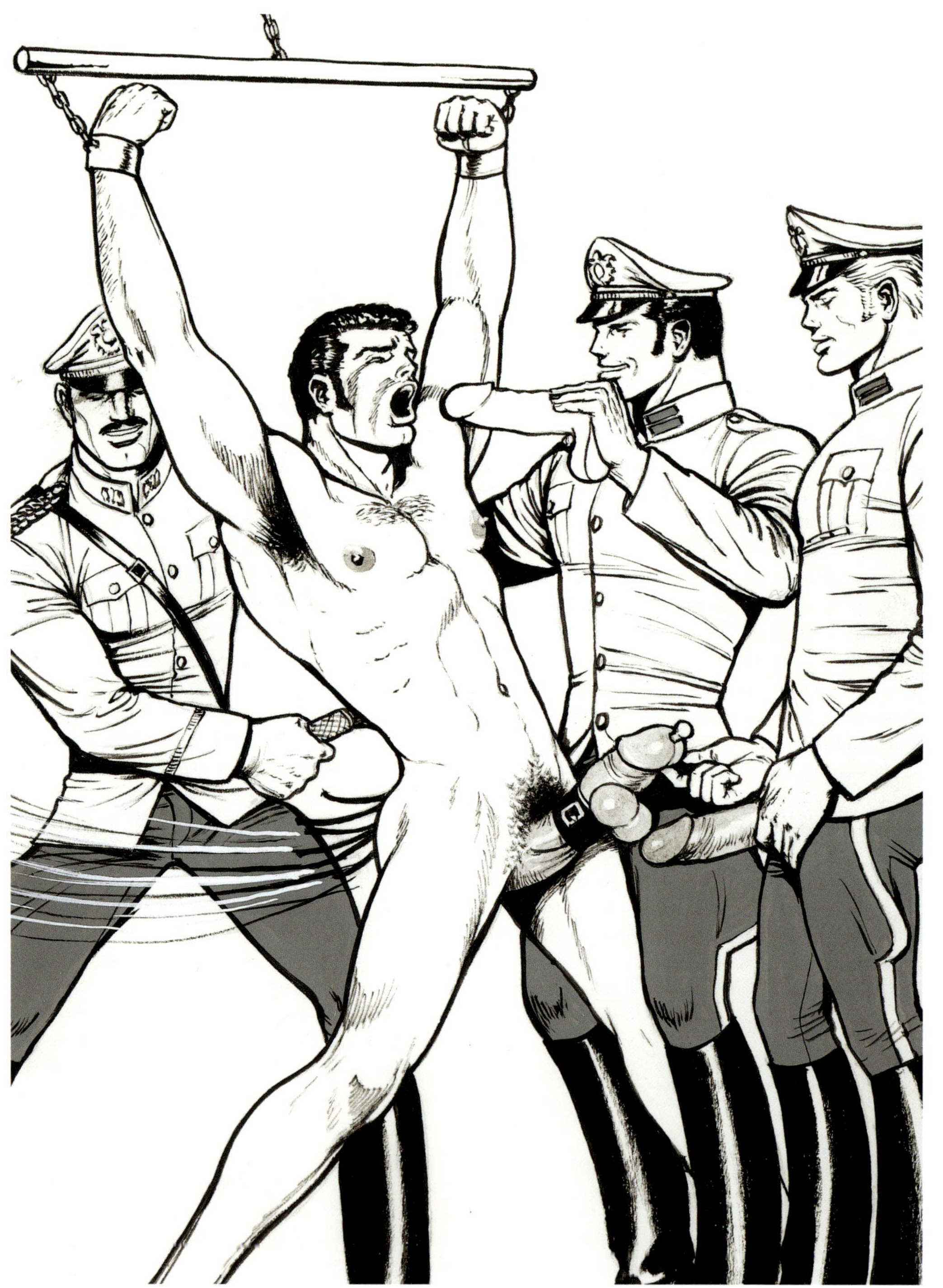

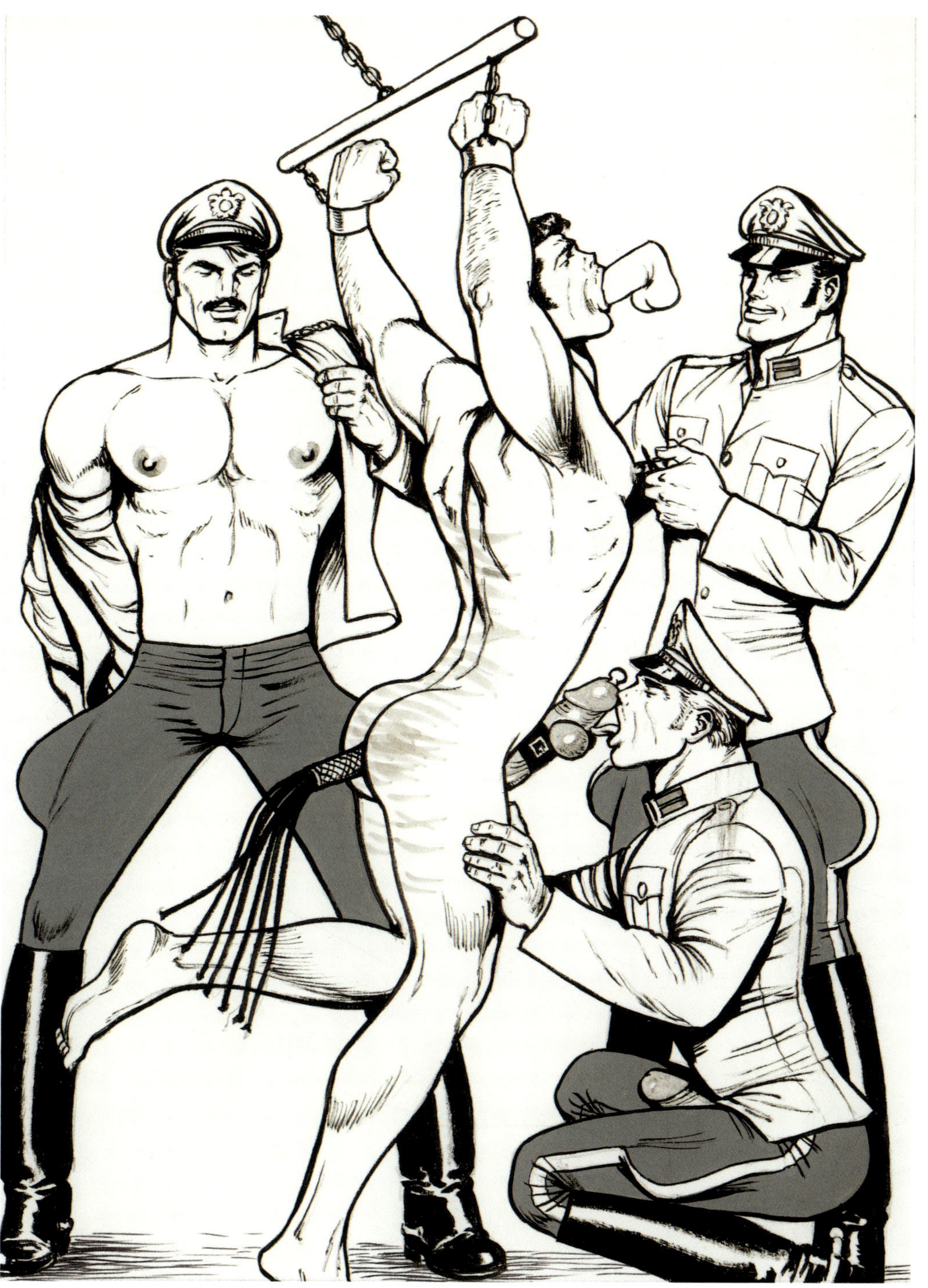

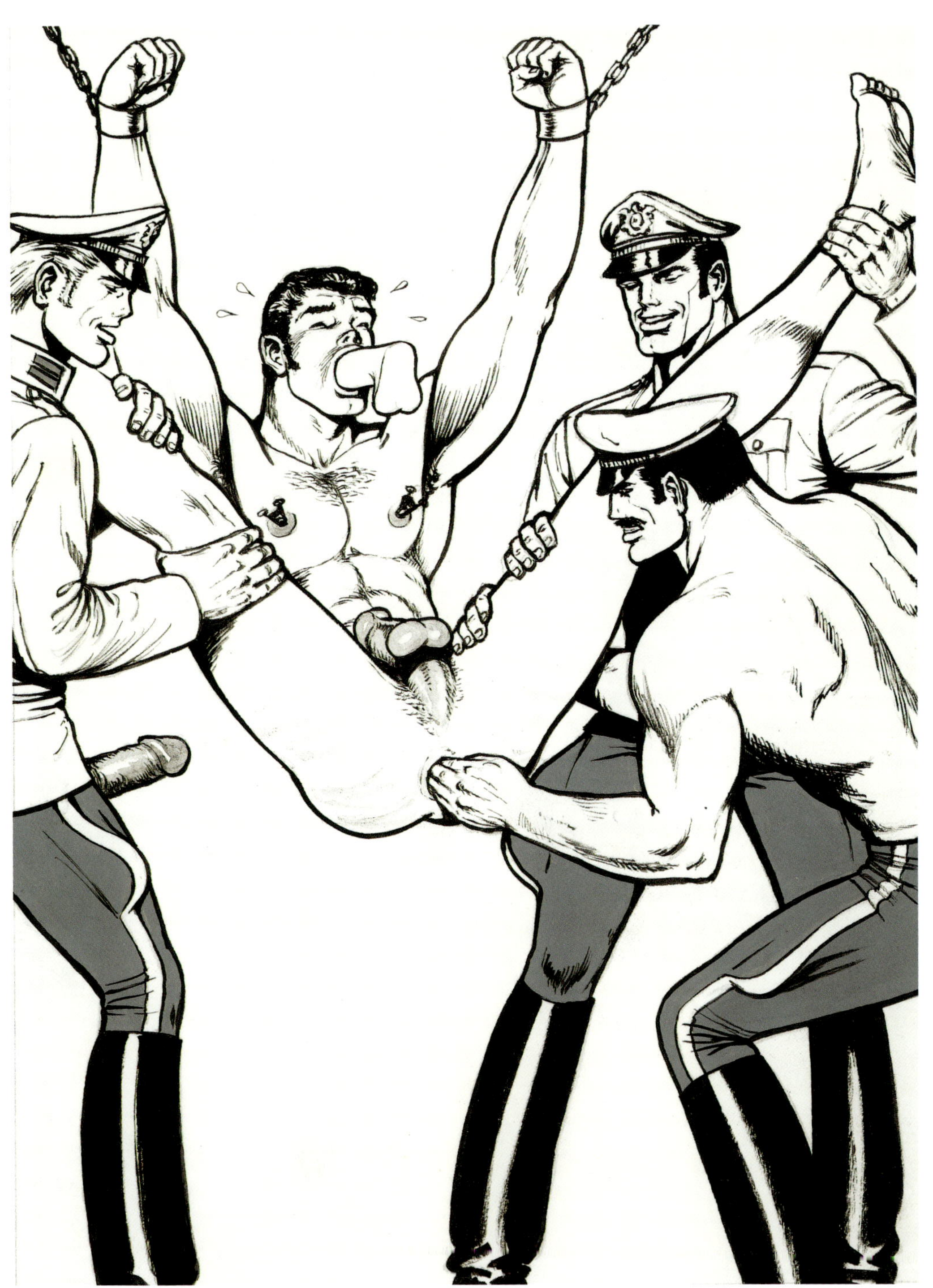

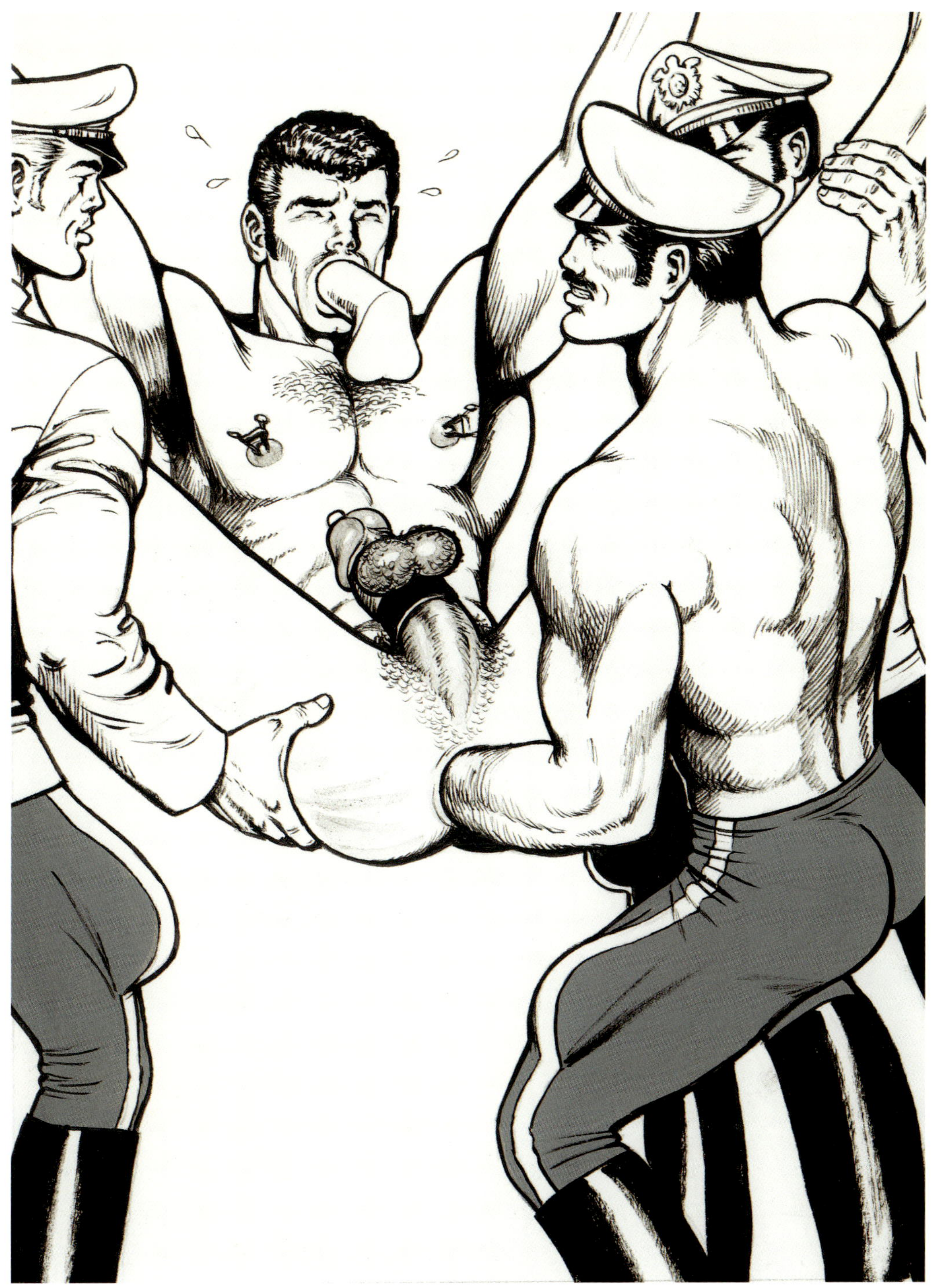

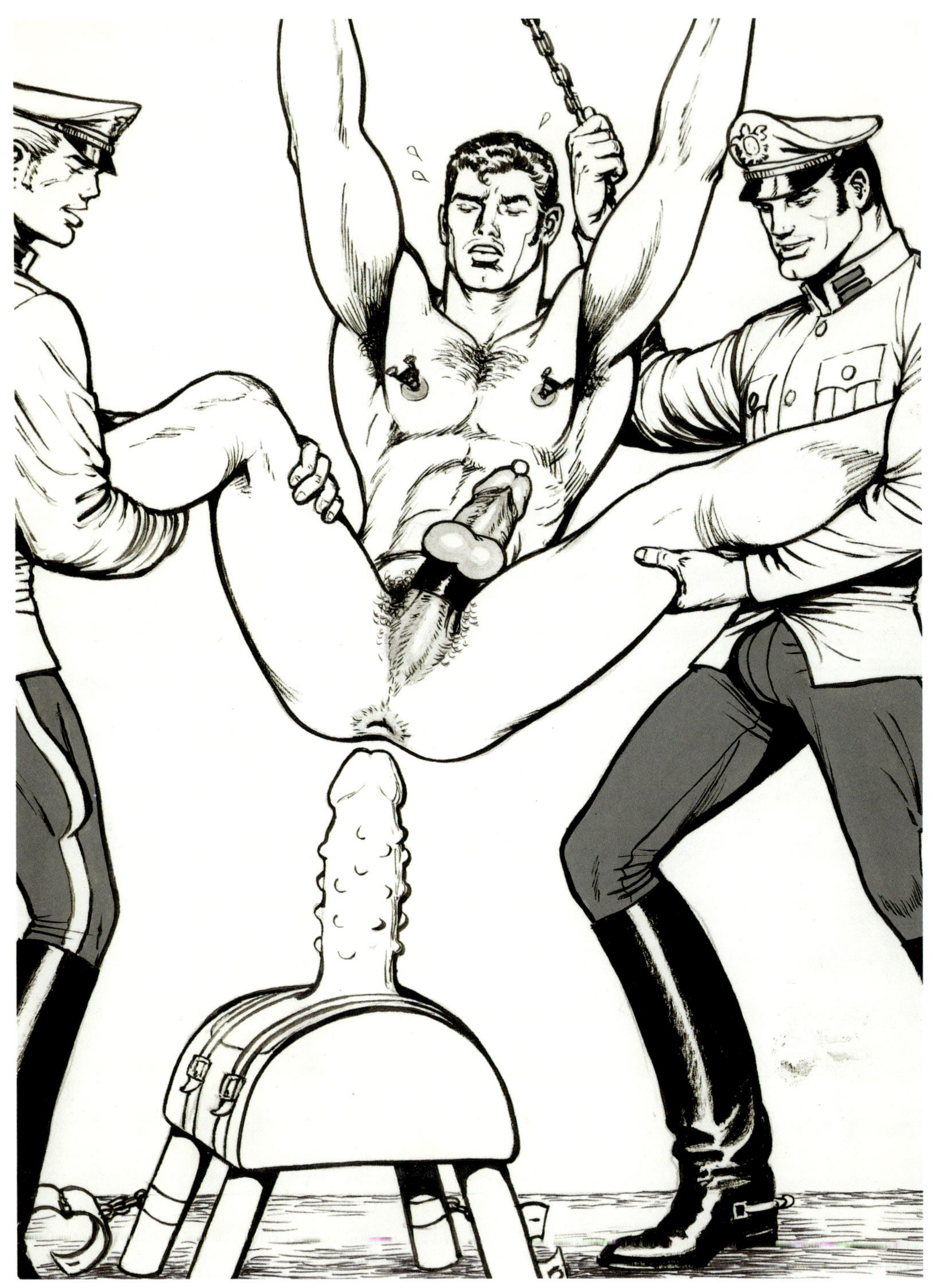

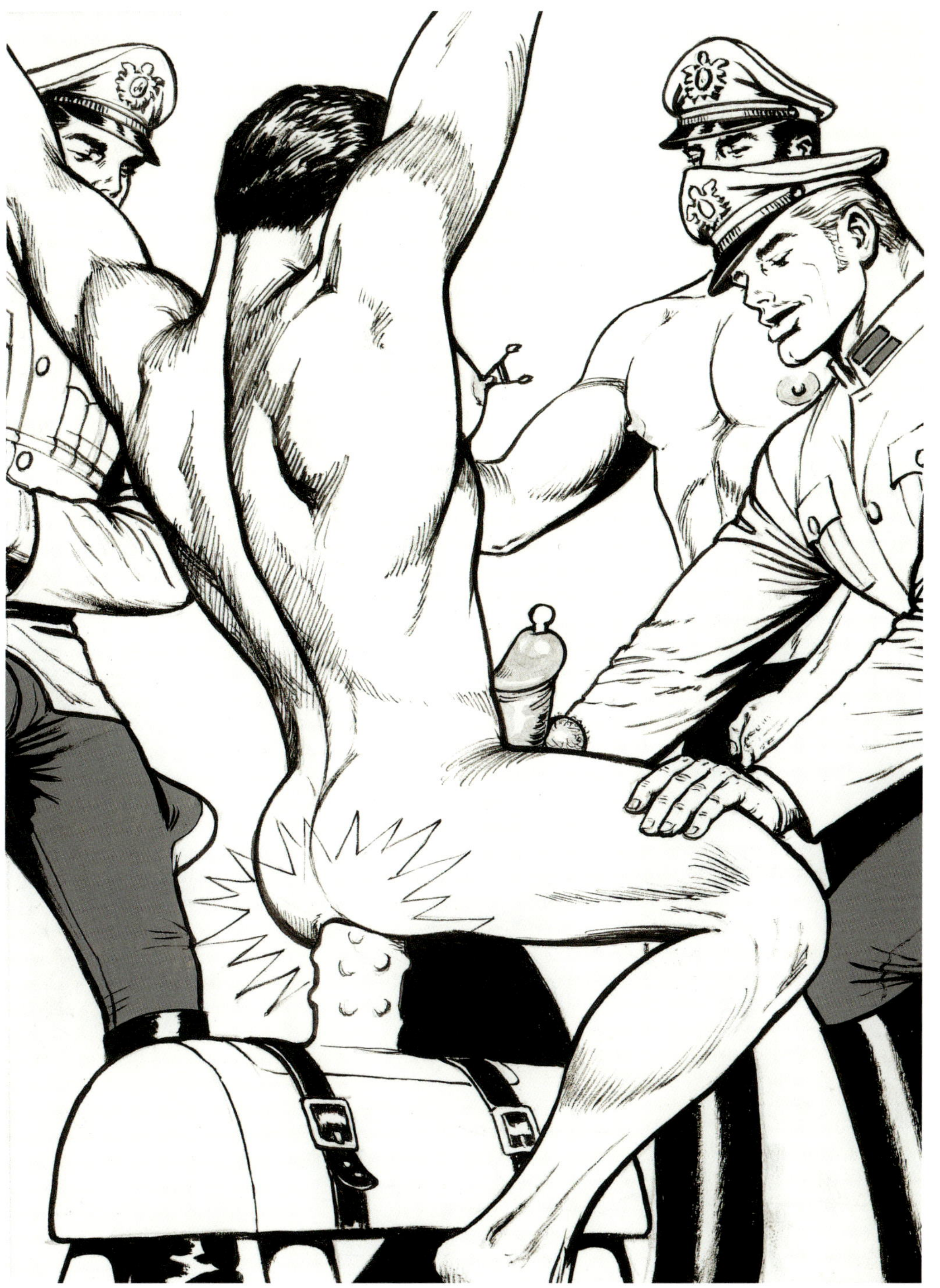

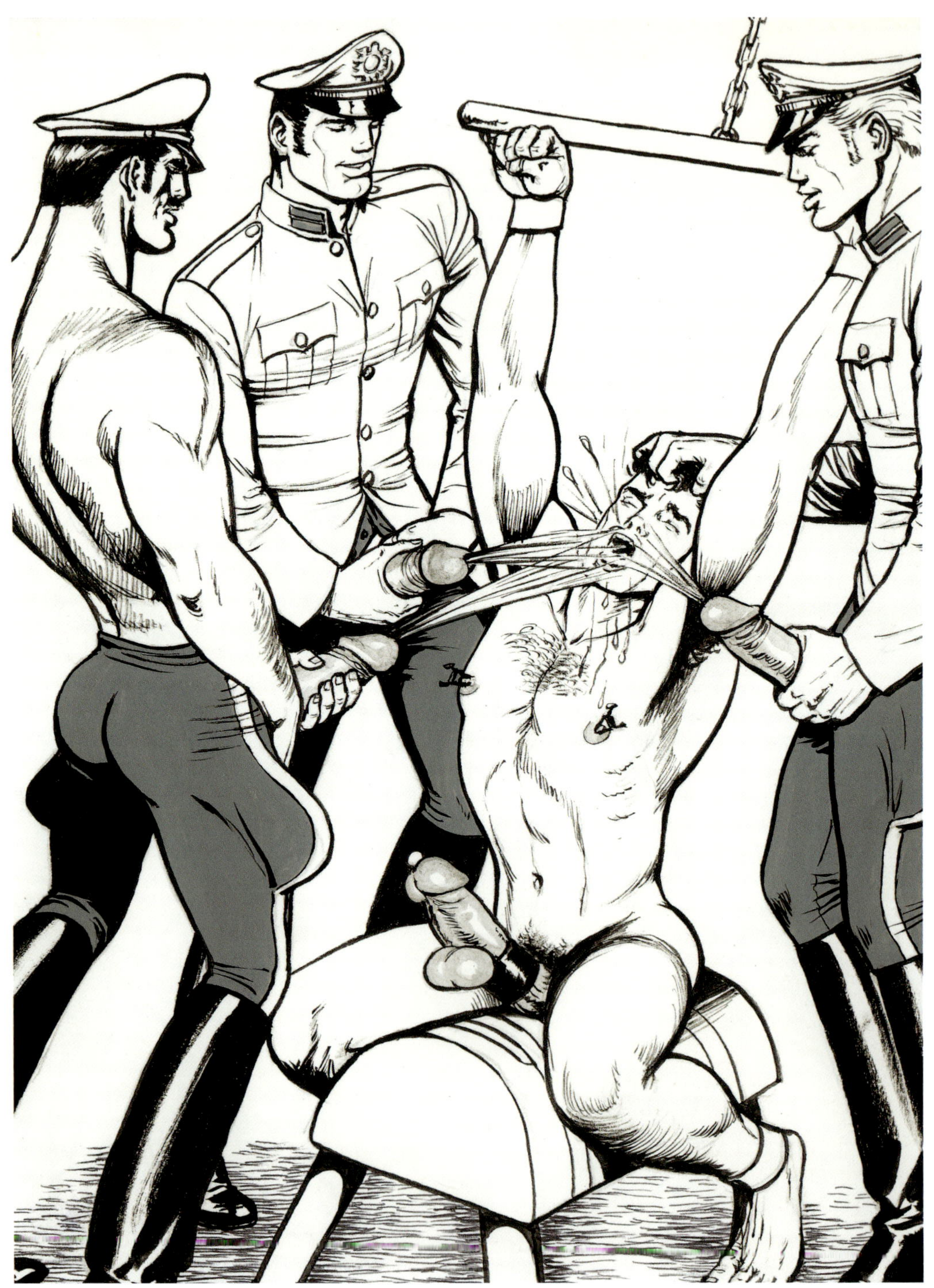

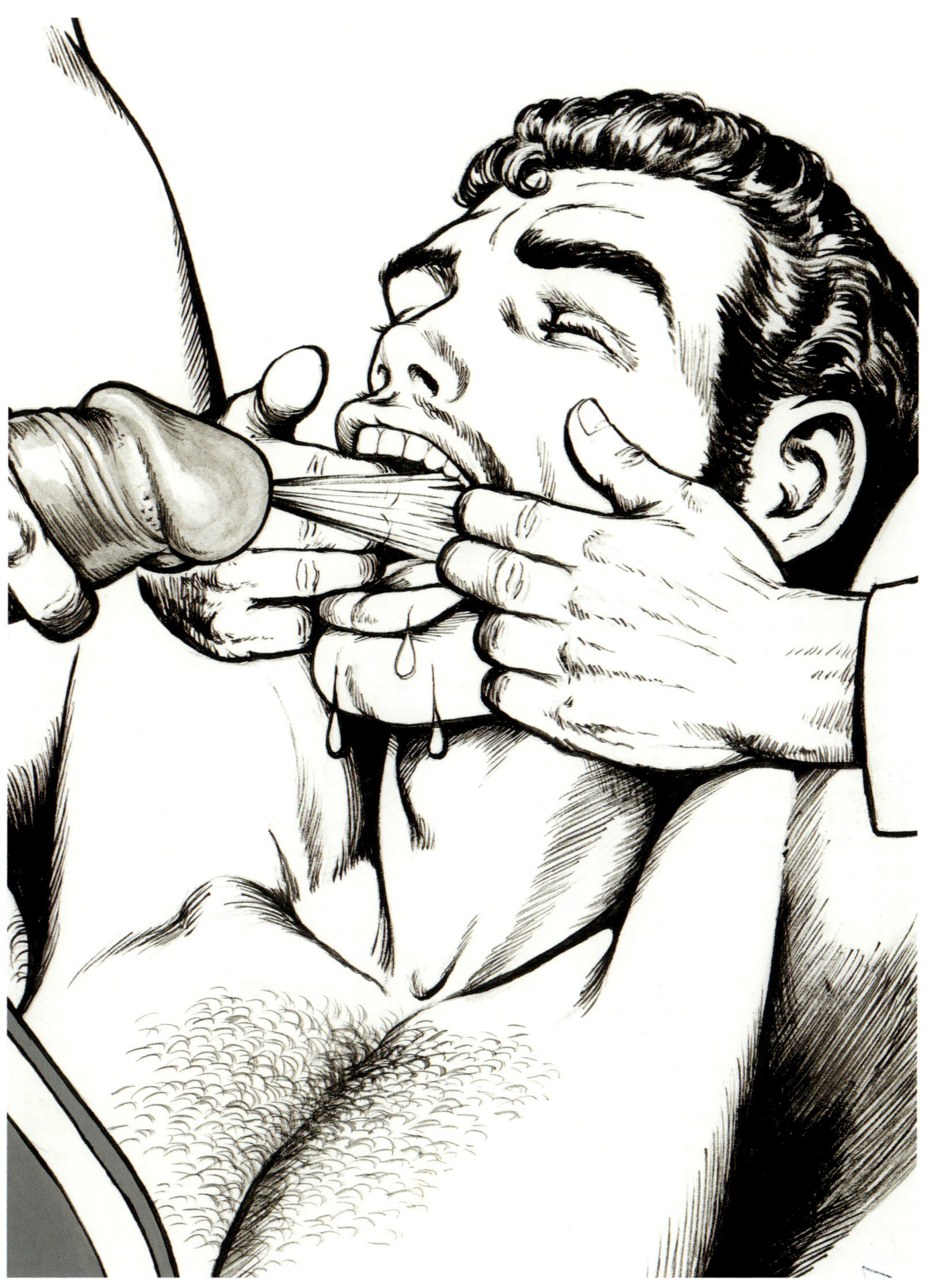

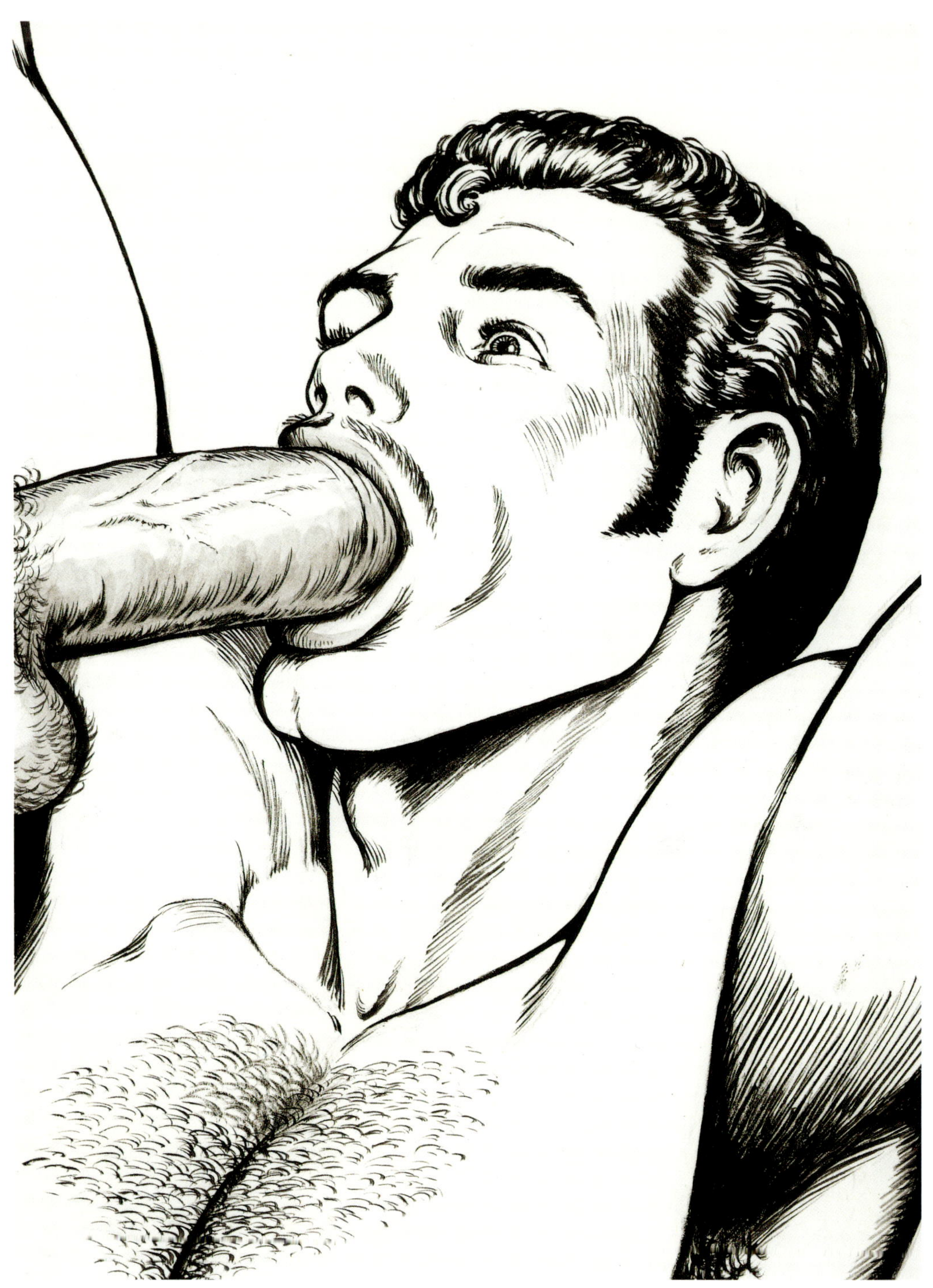

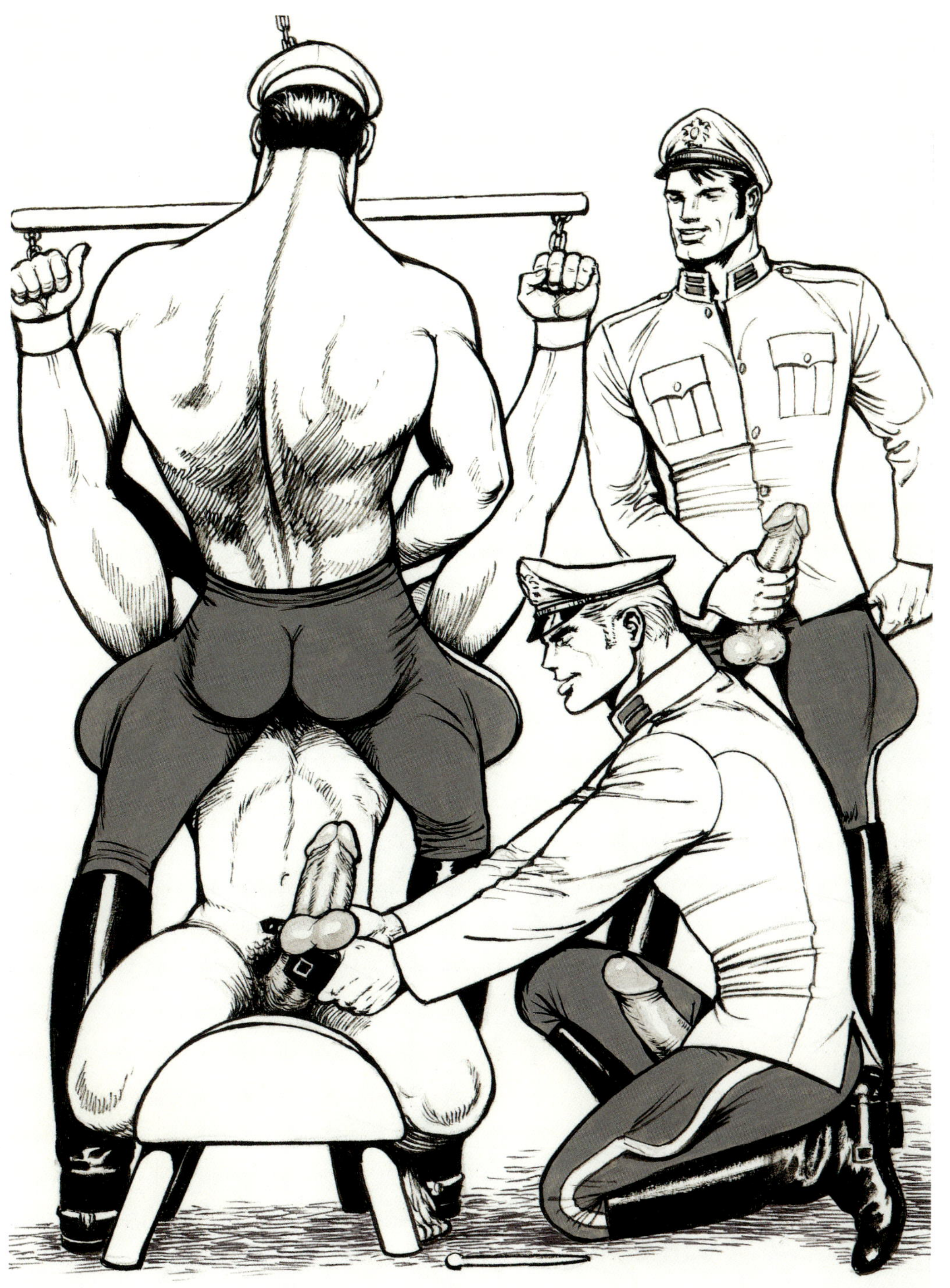

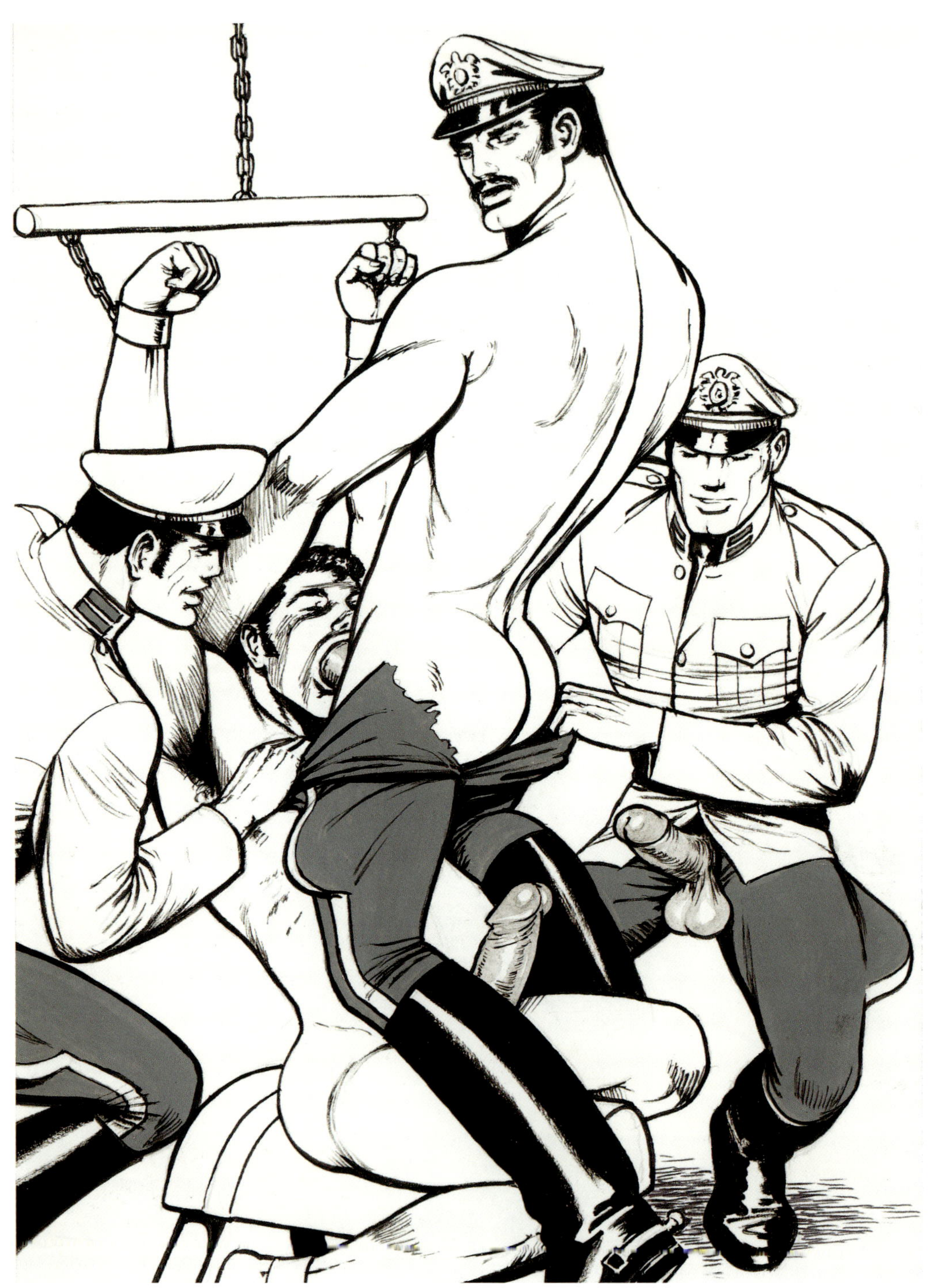

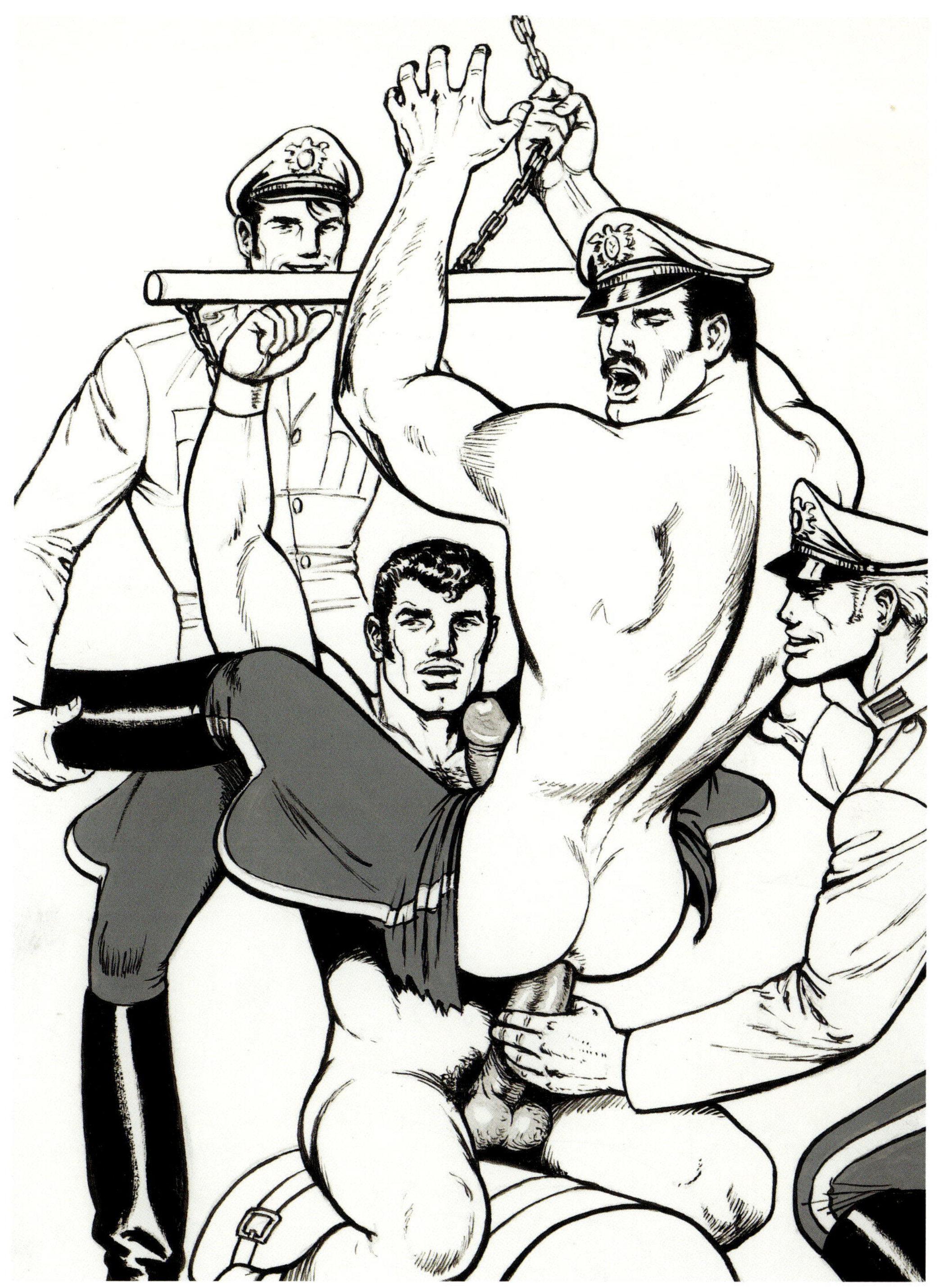

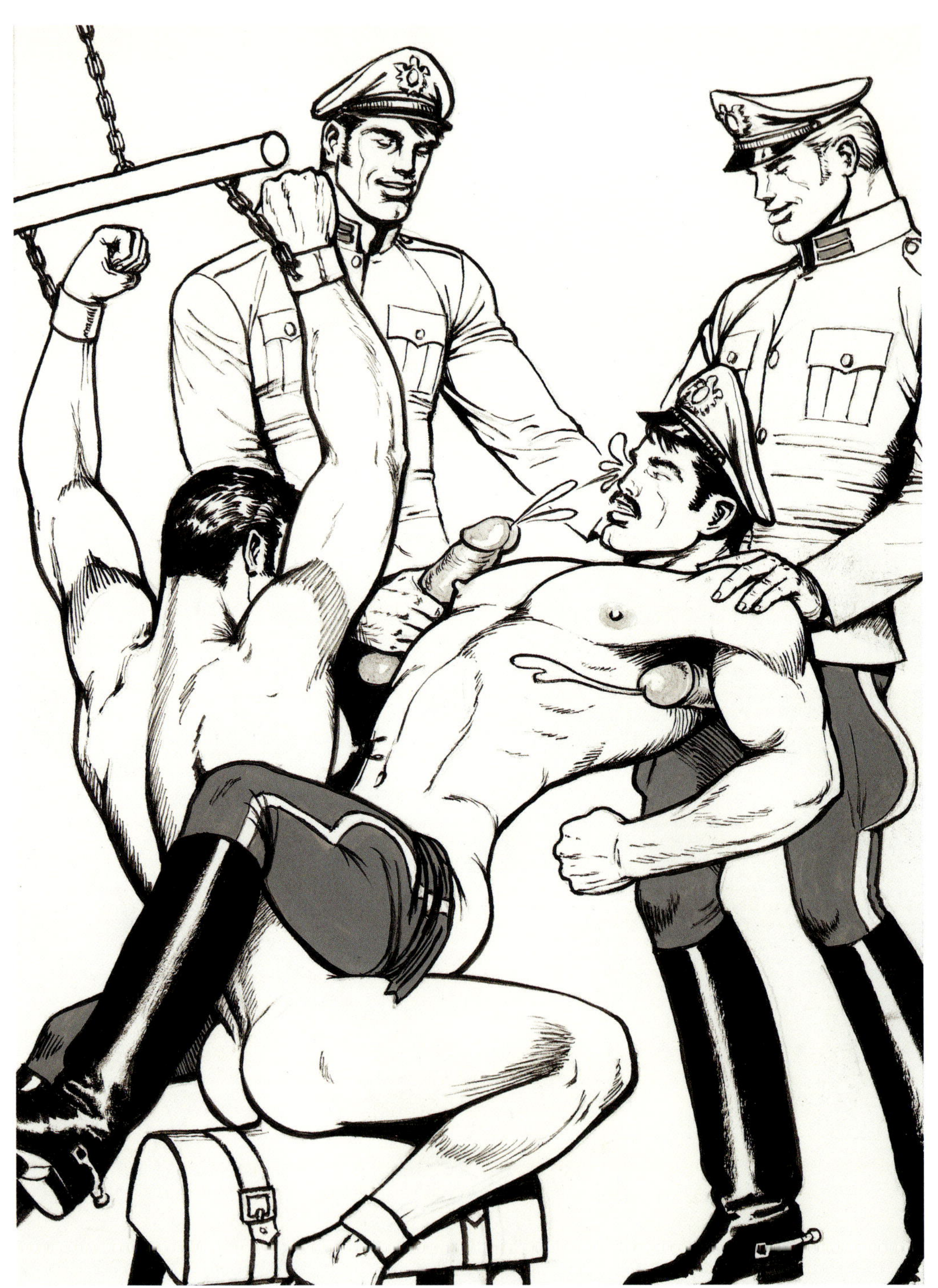

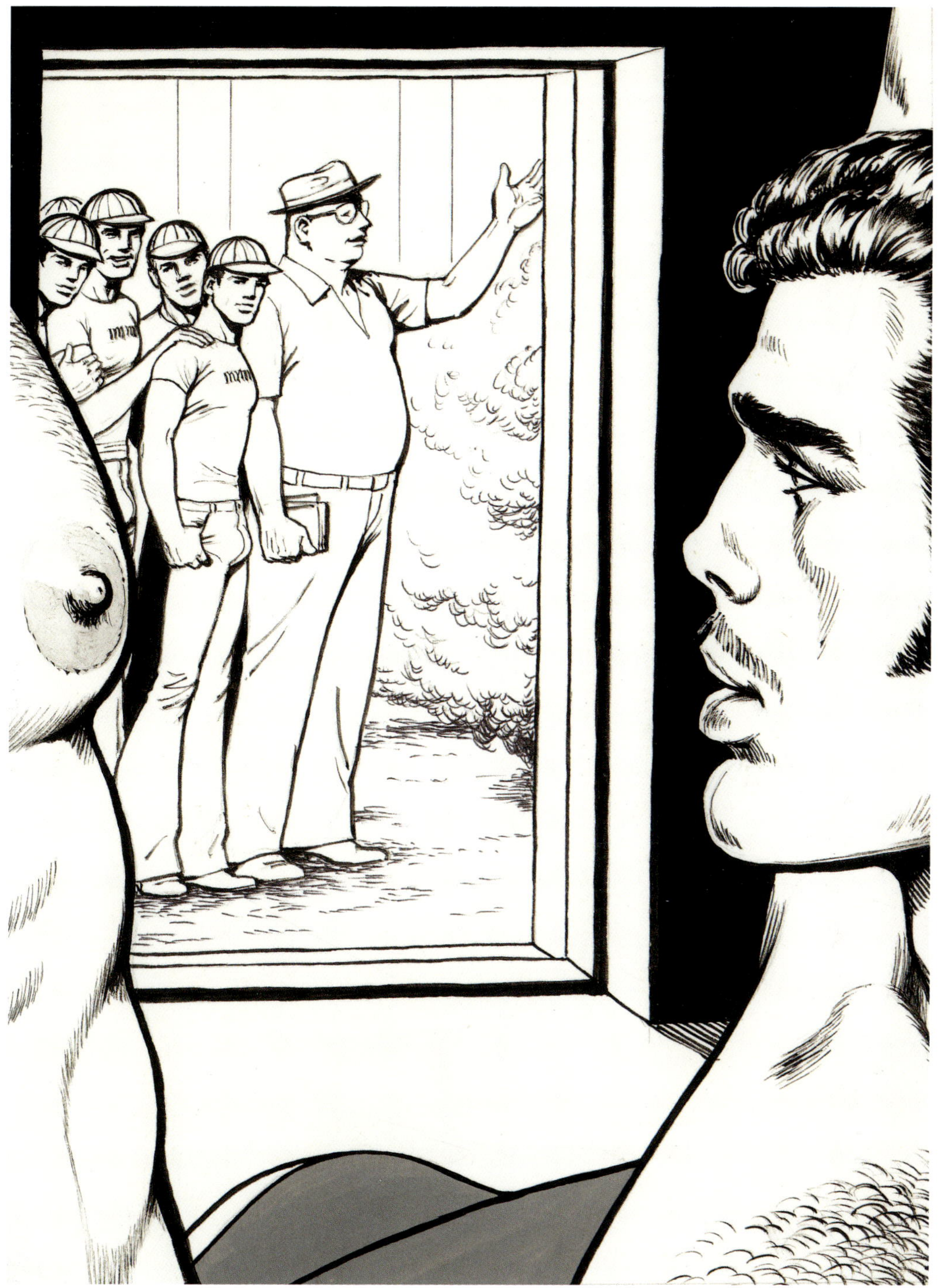

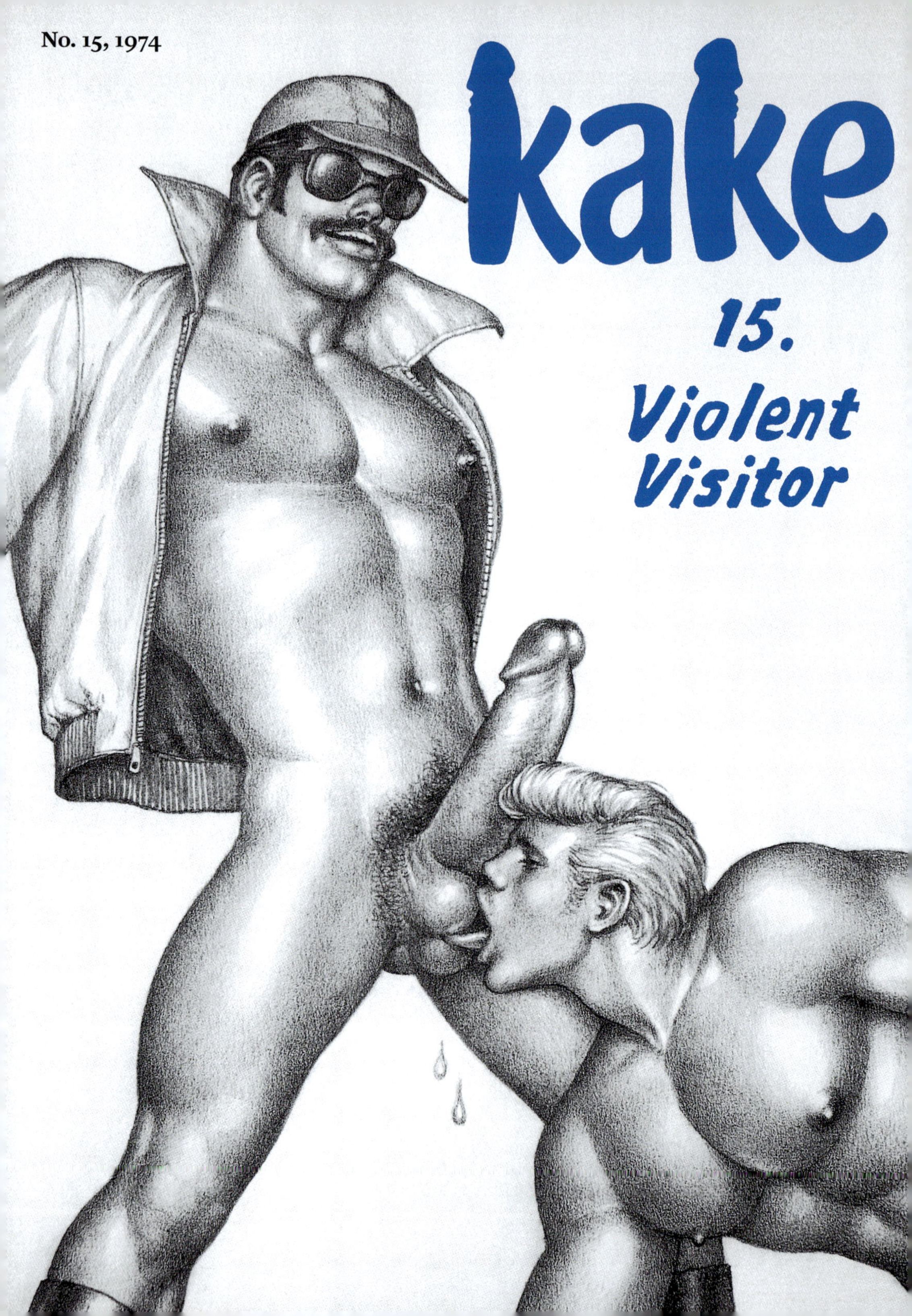
No. 15, 1974
kake
15.
Violent
Visitor

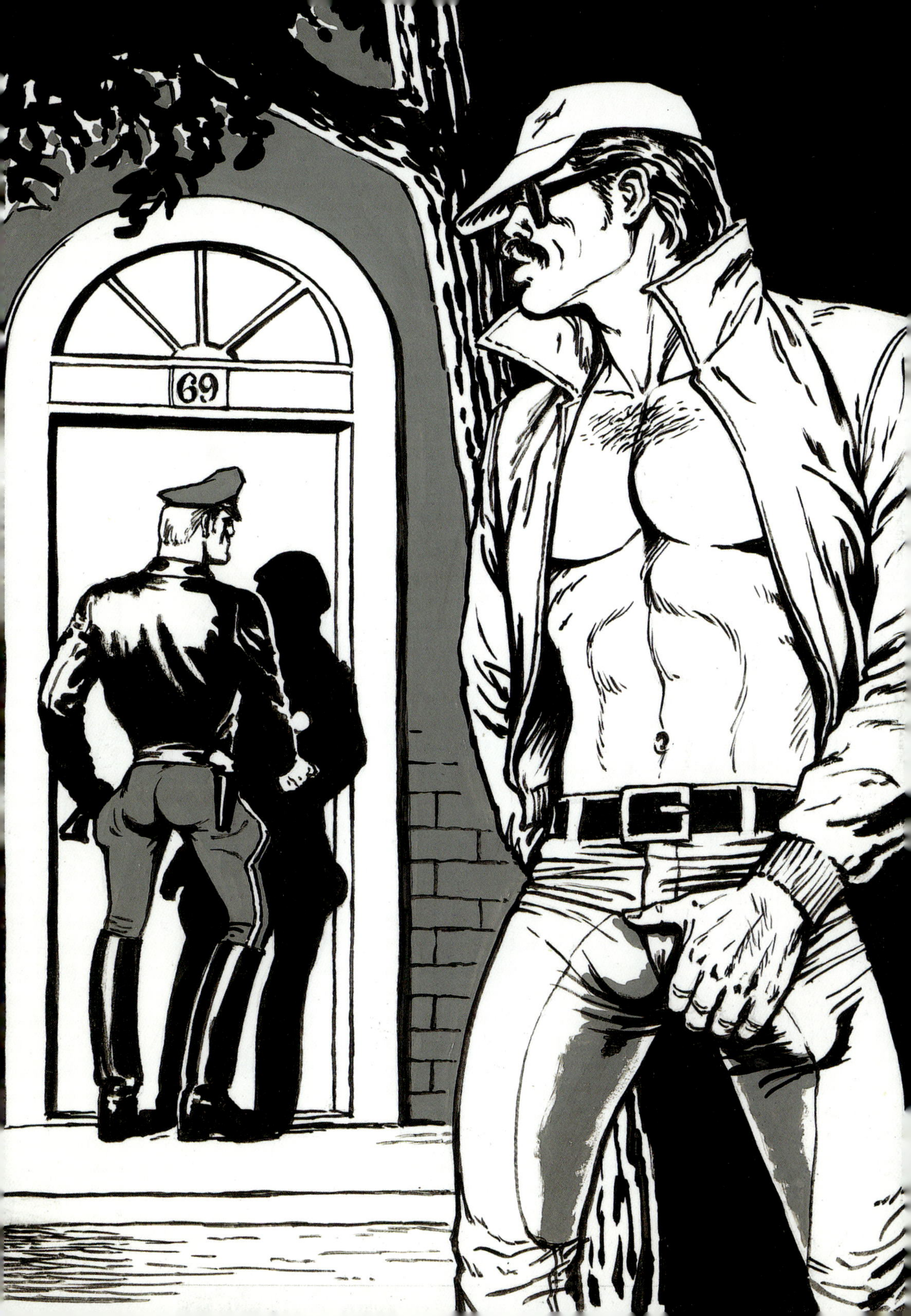
69

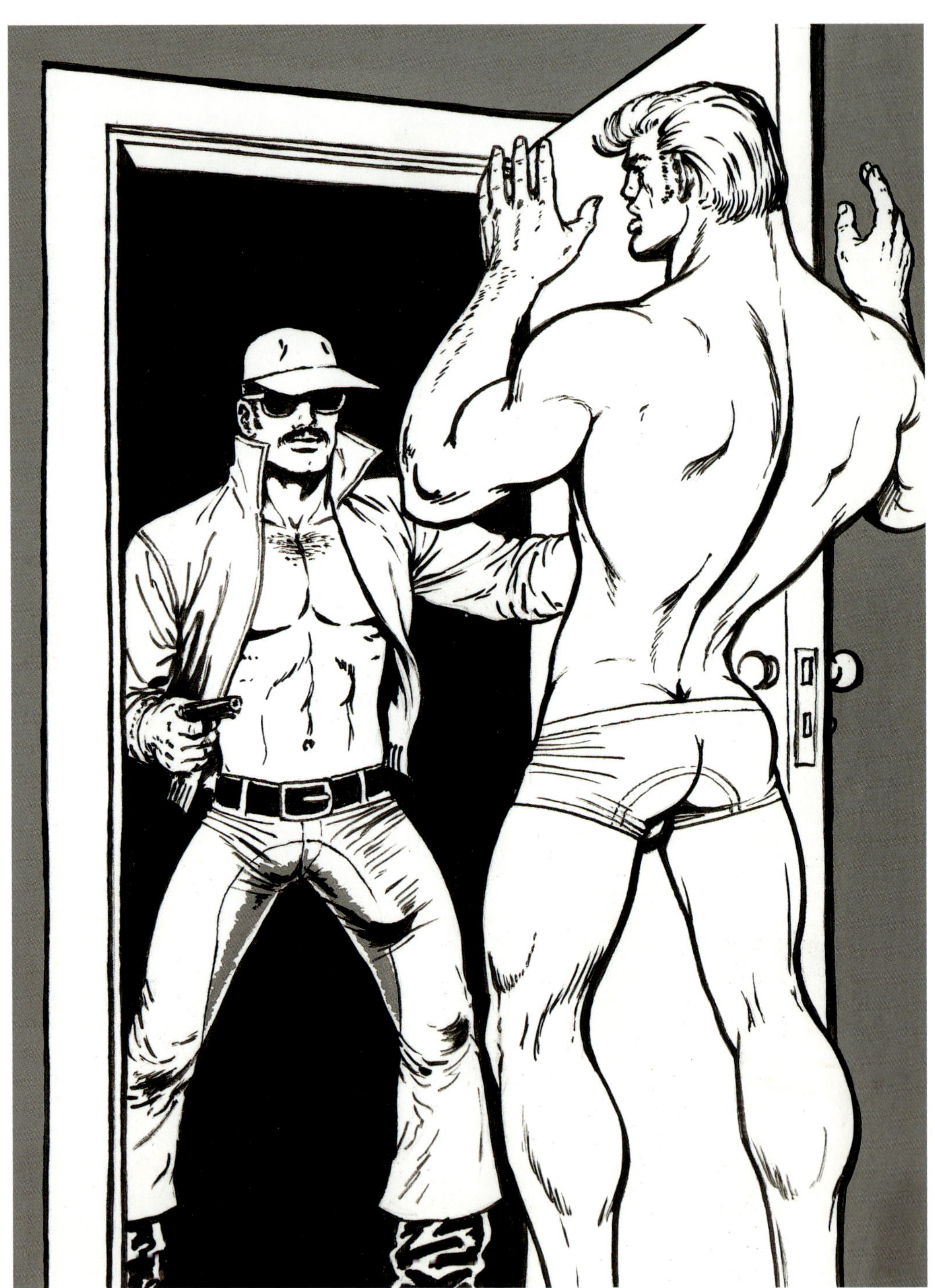

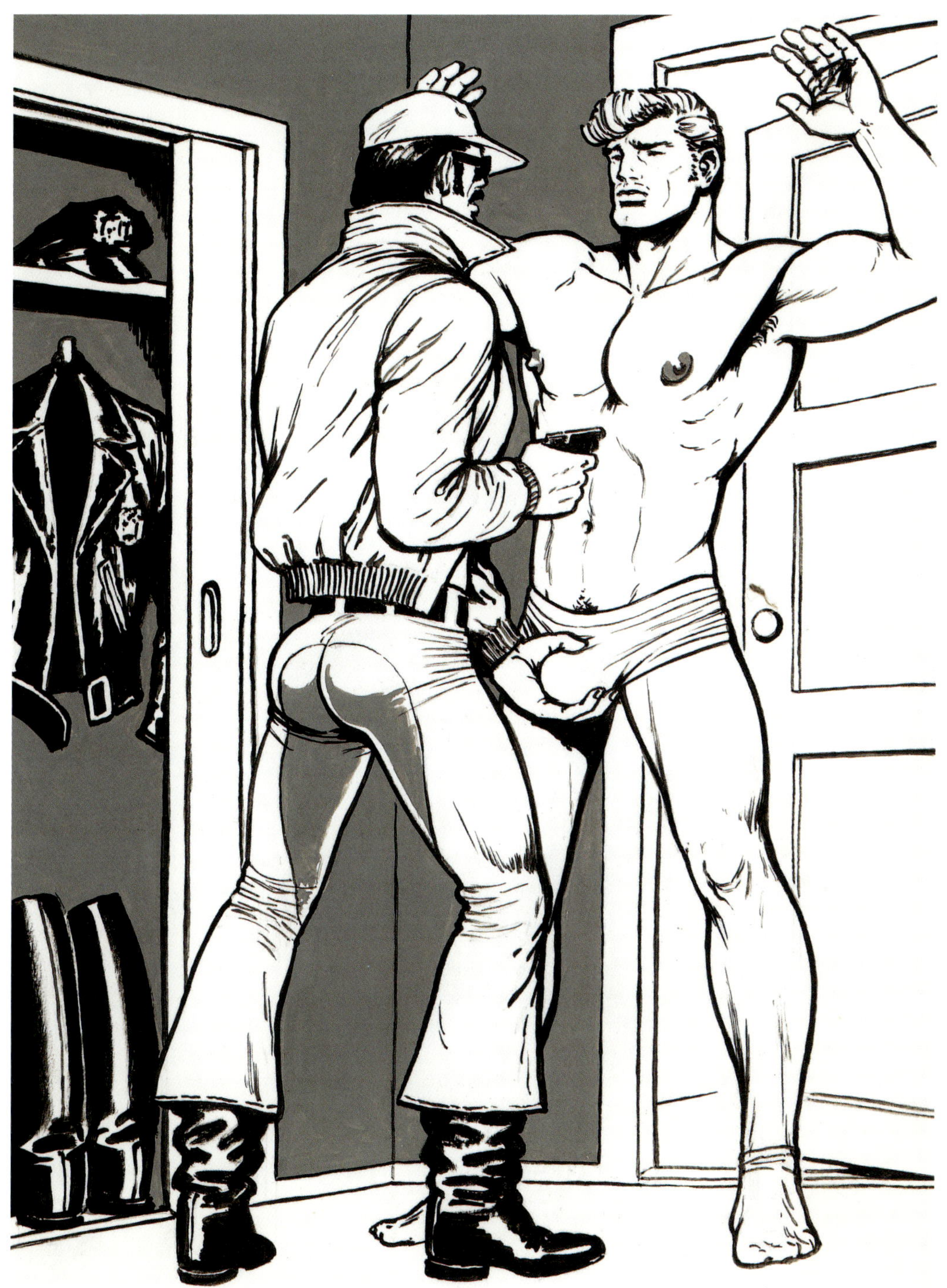

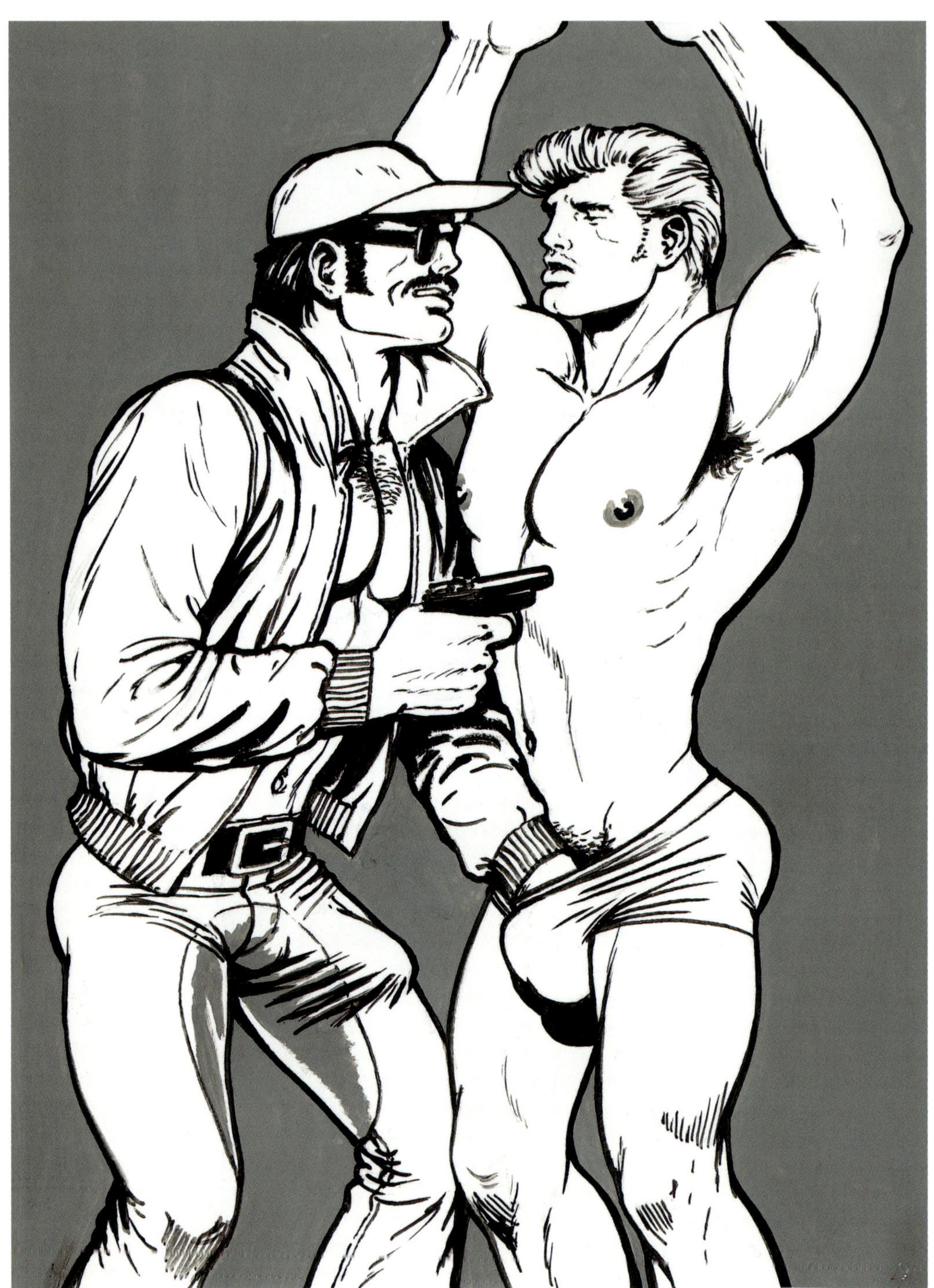

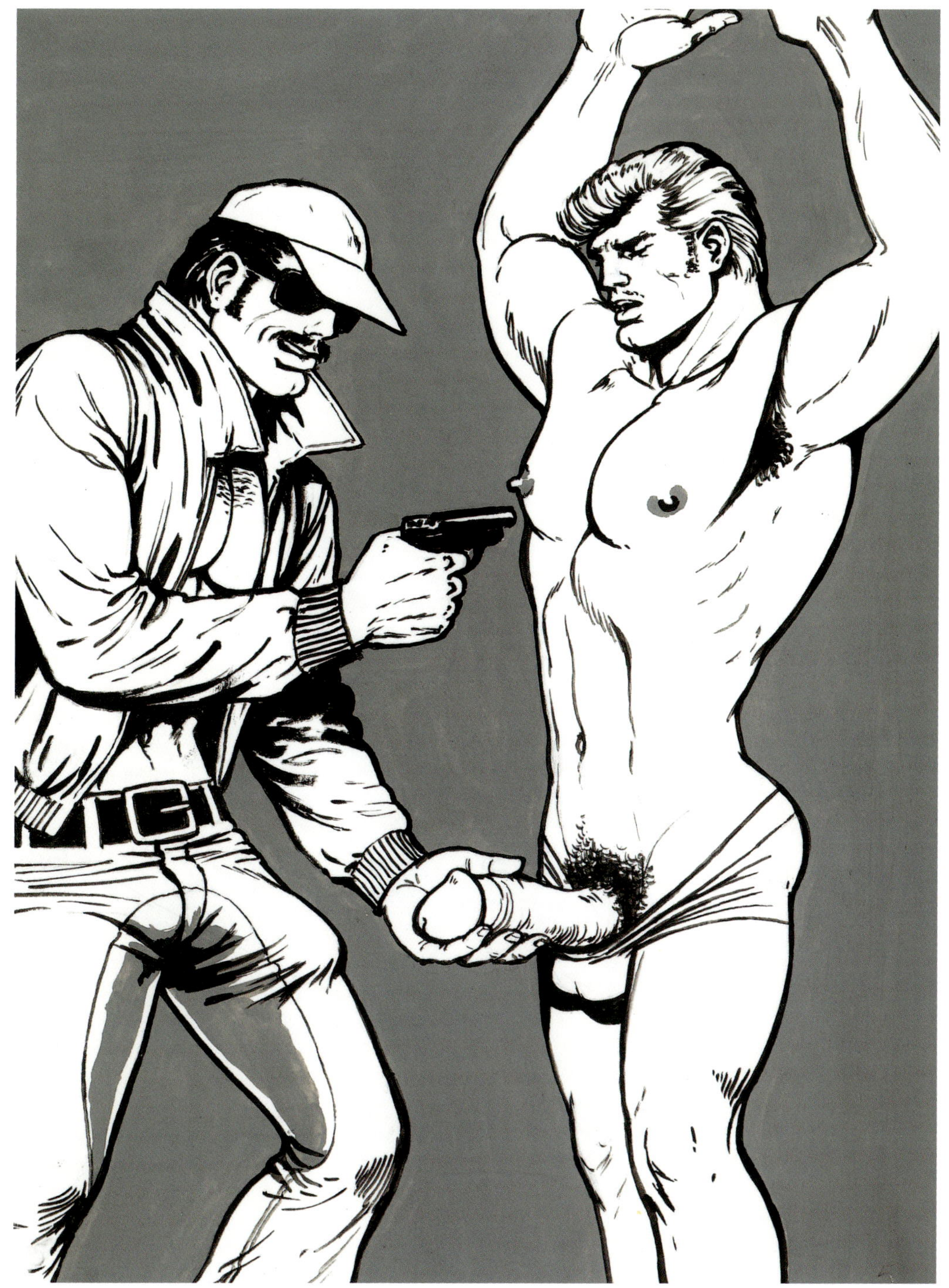

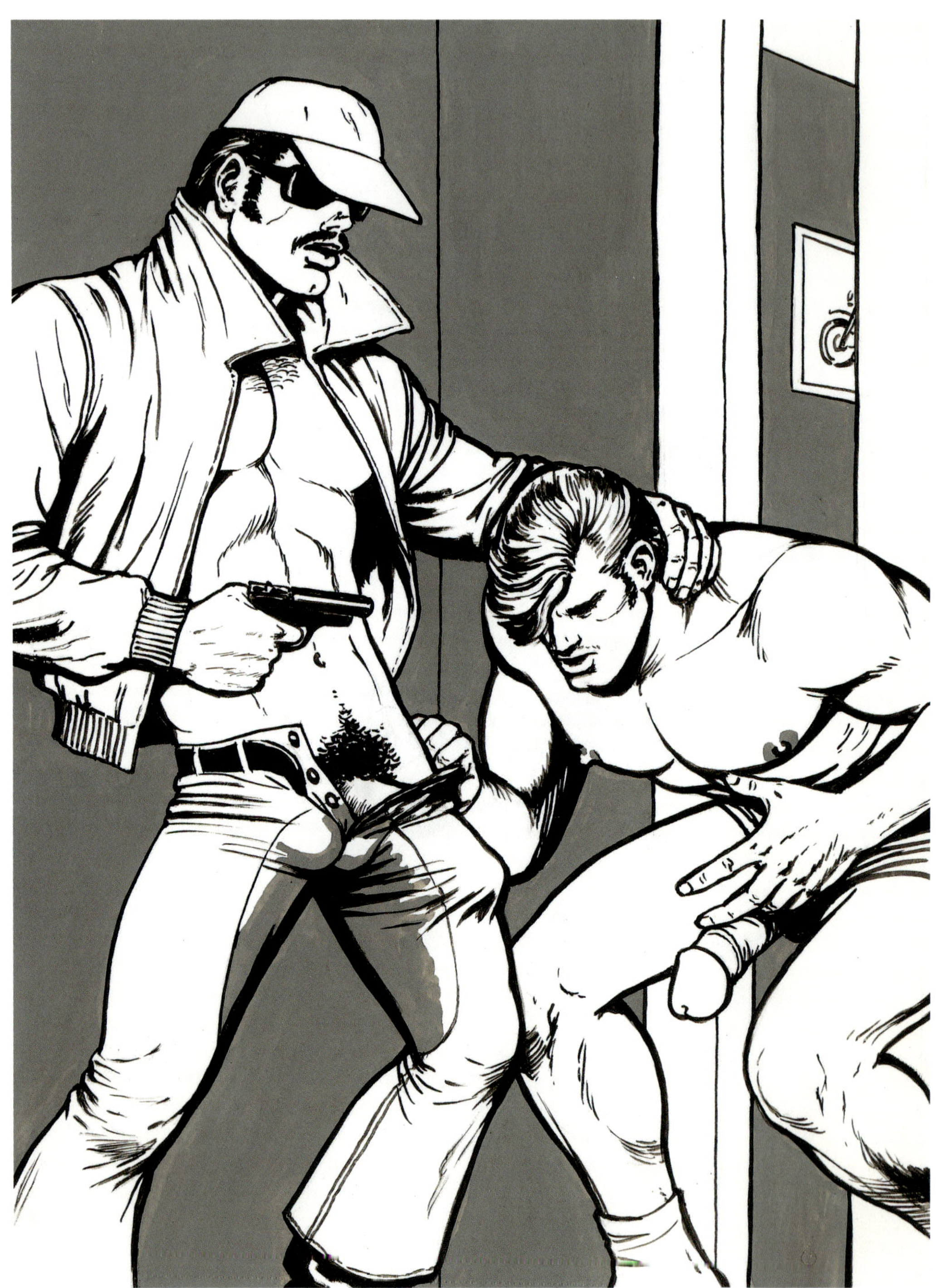

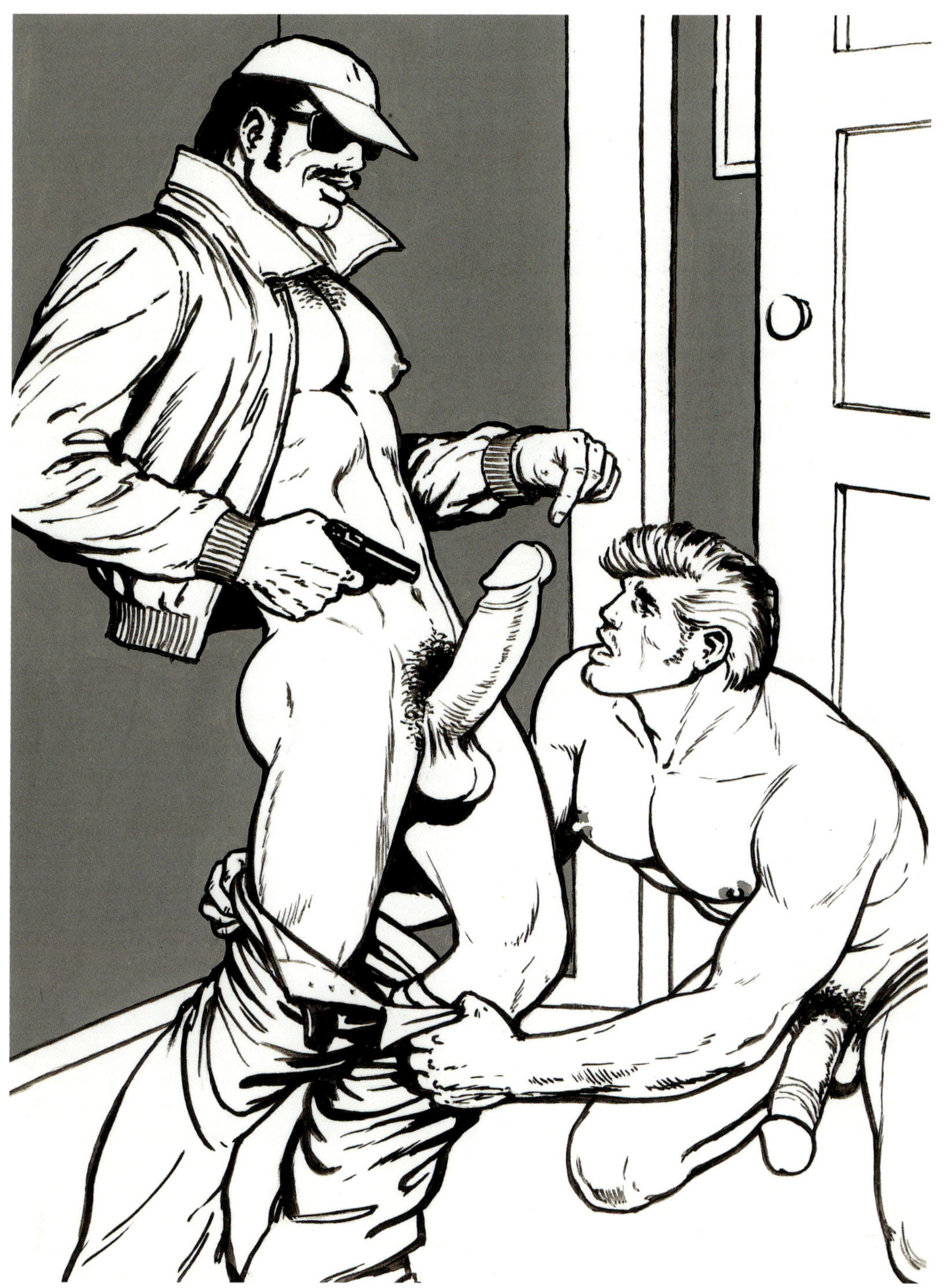

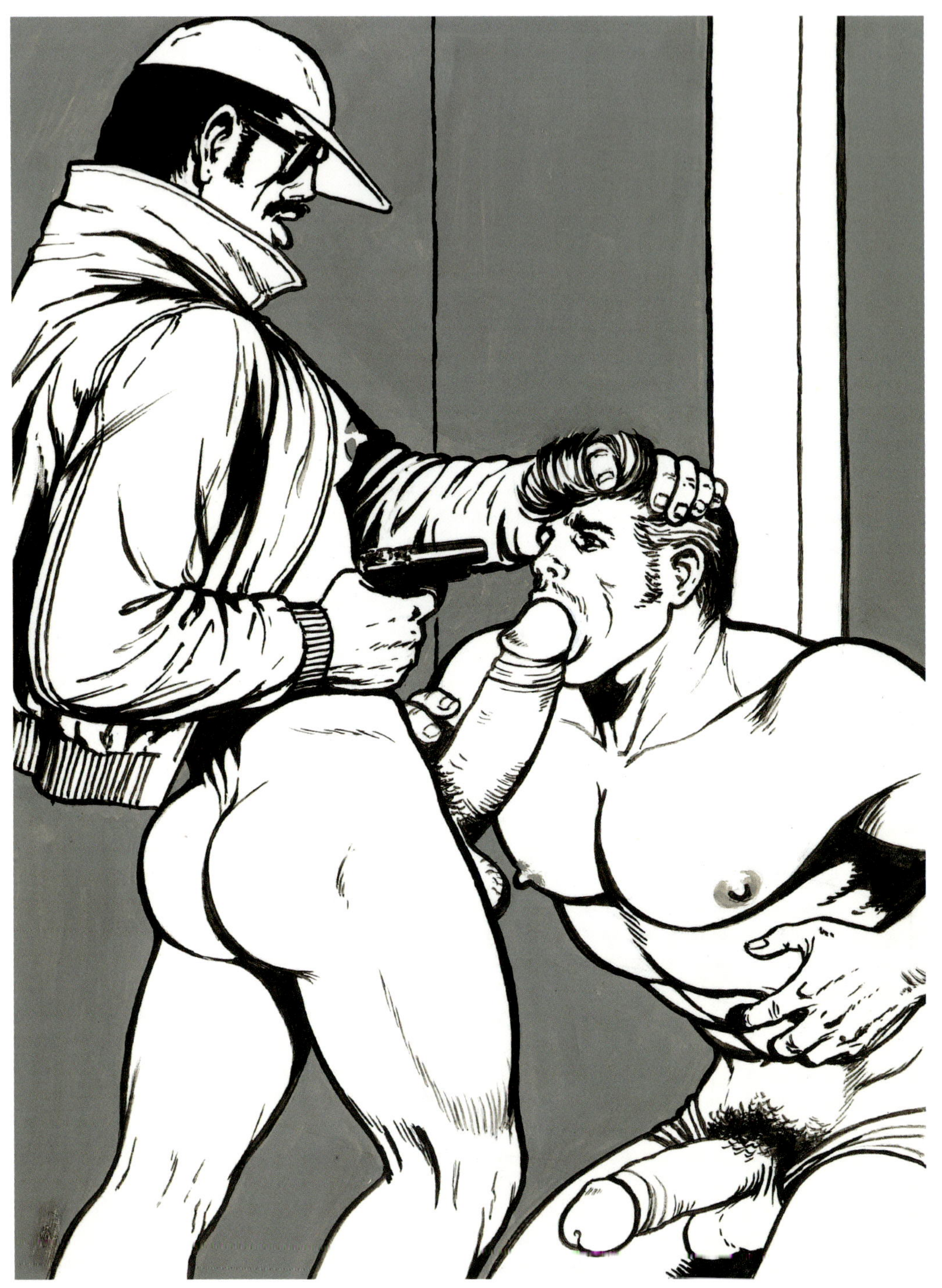

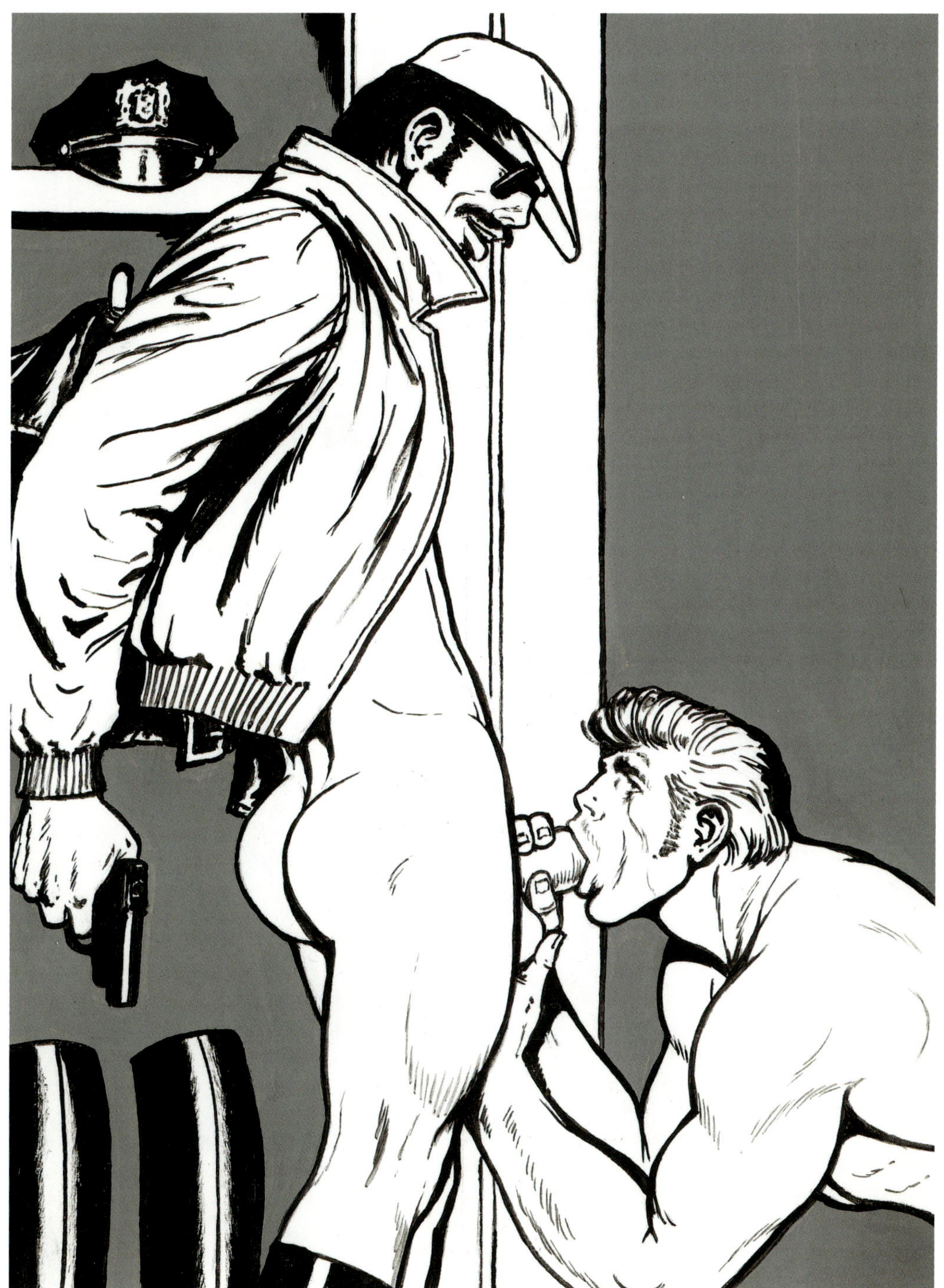

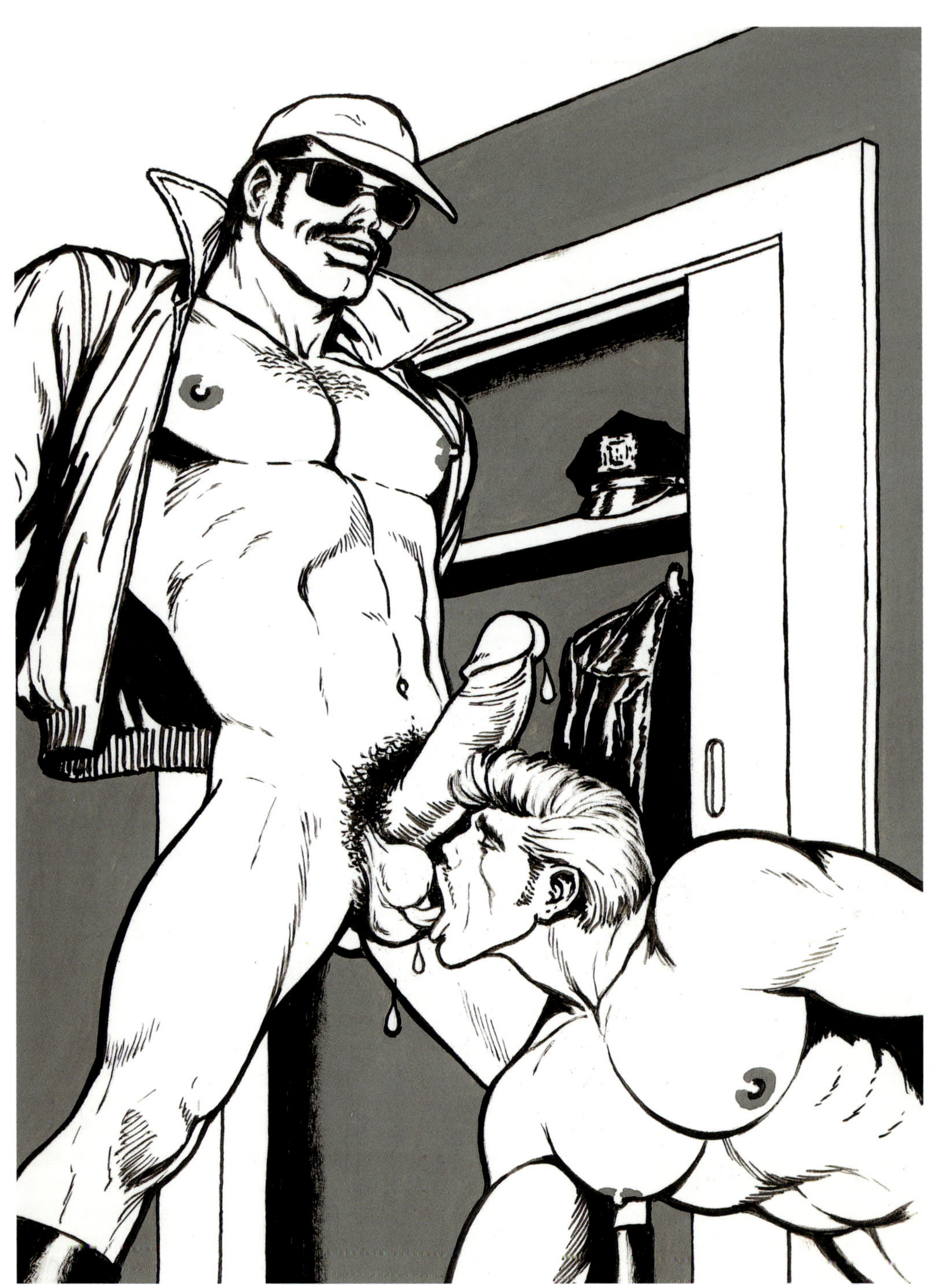

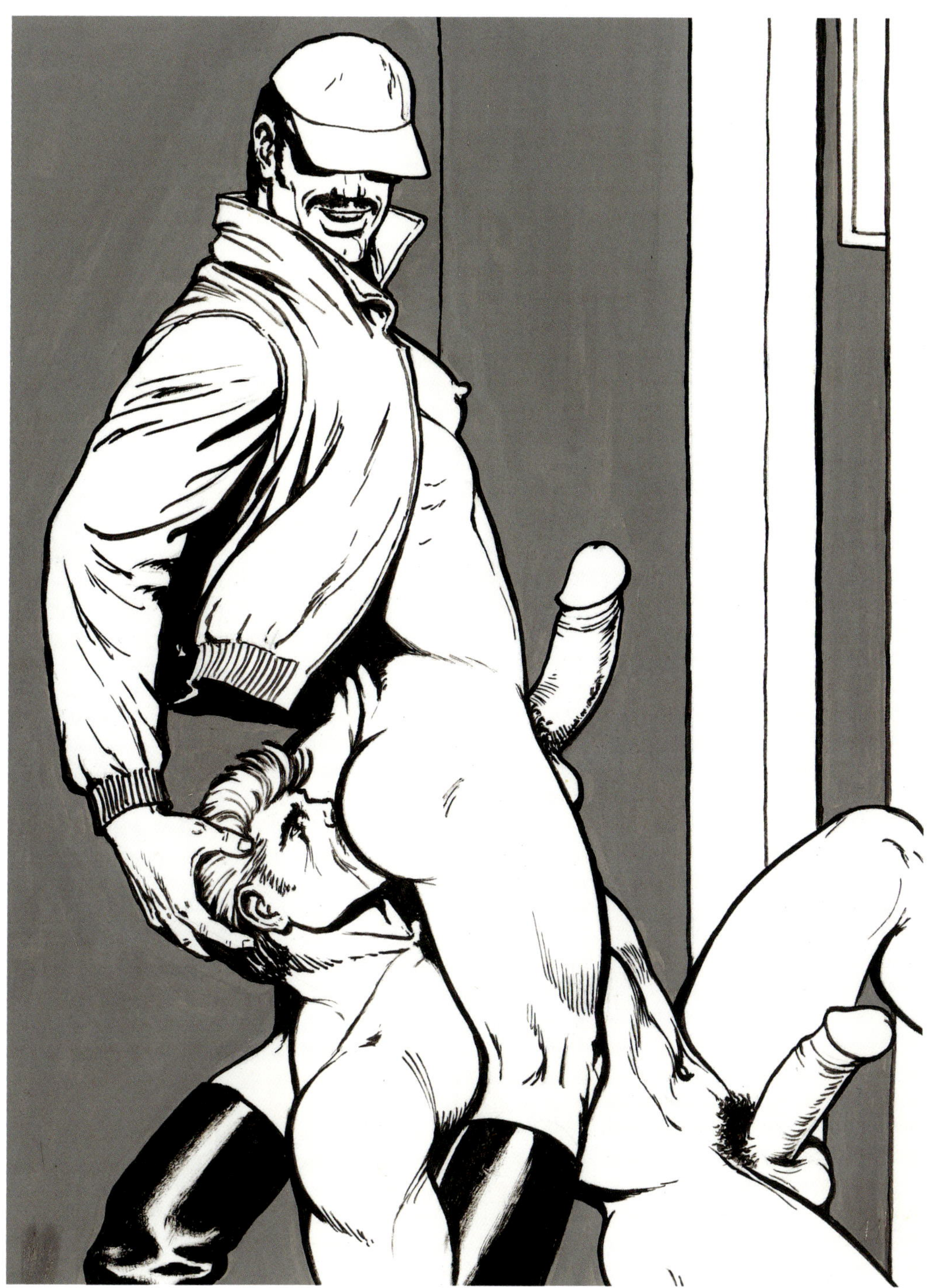

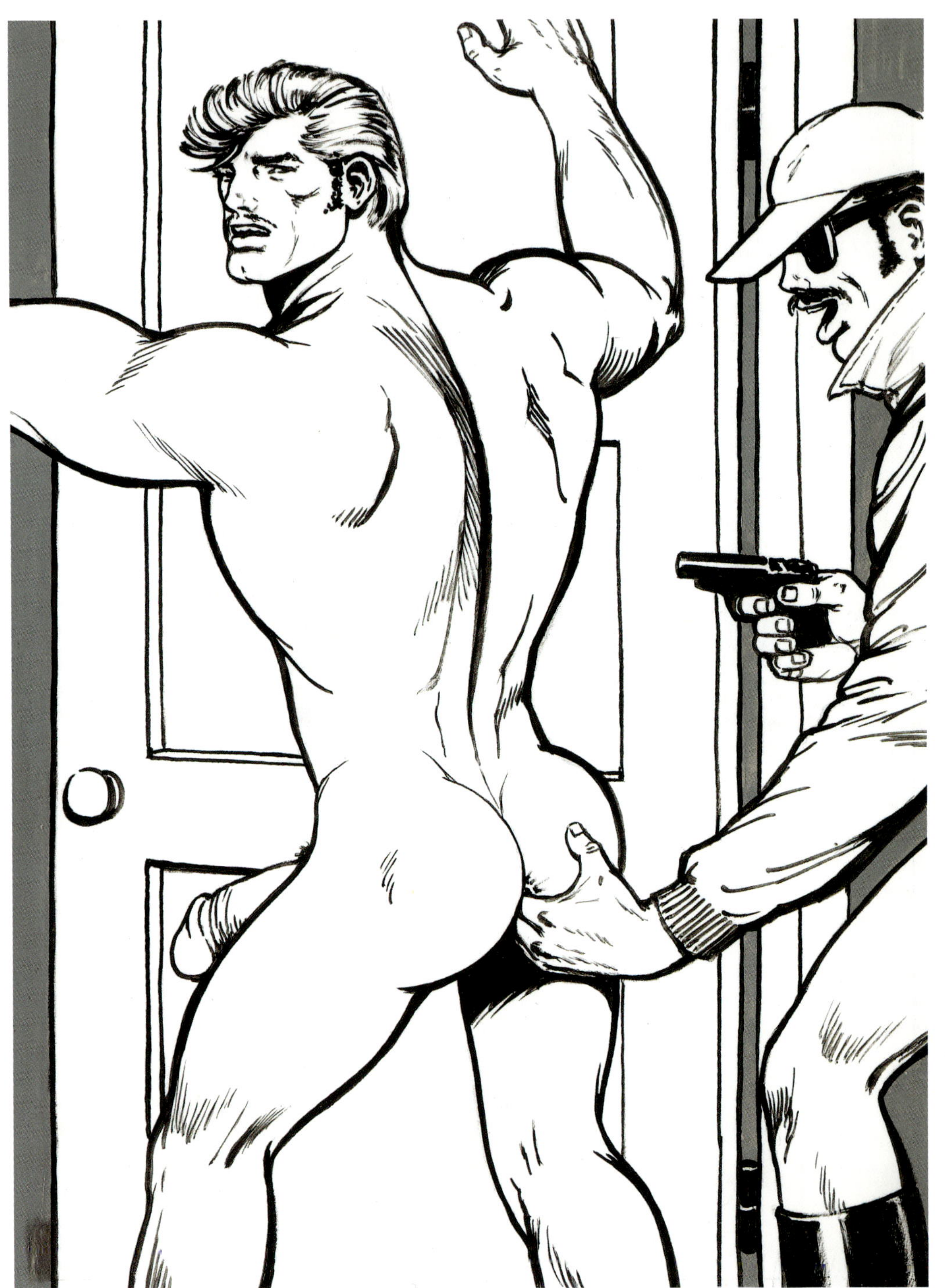

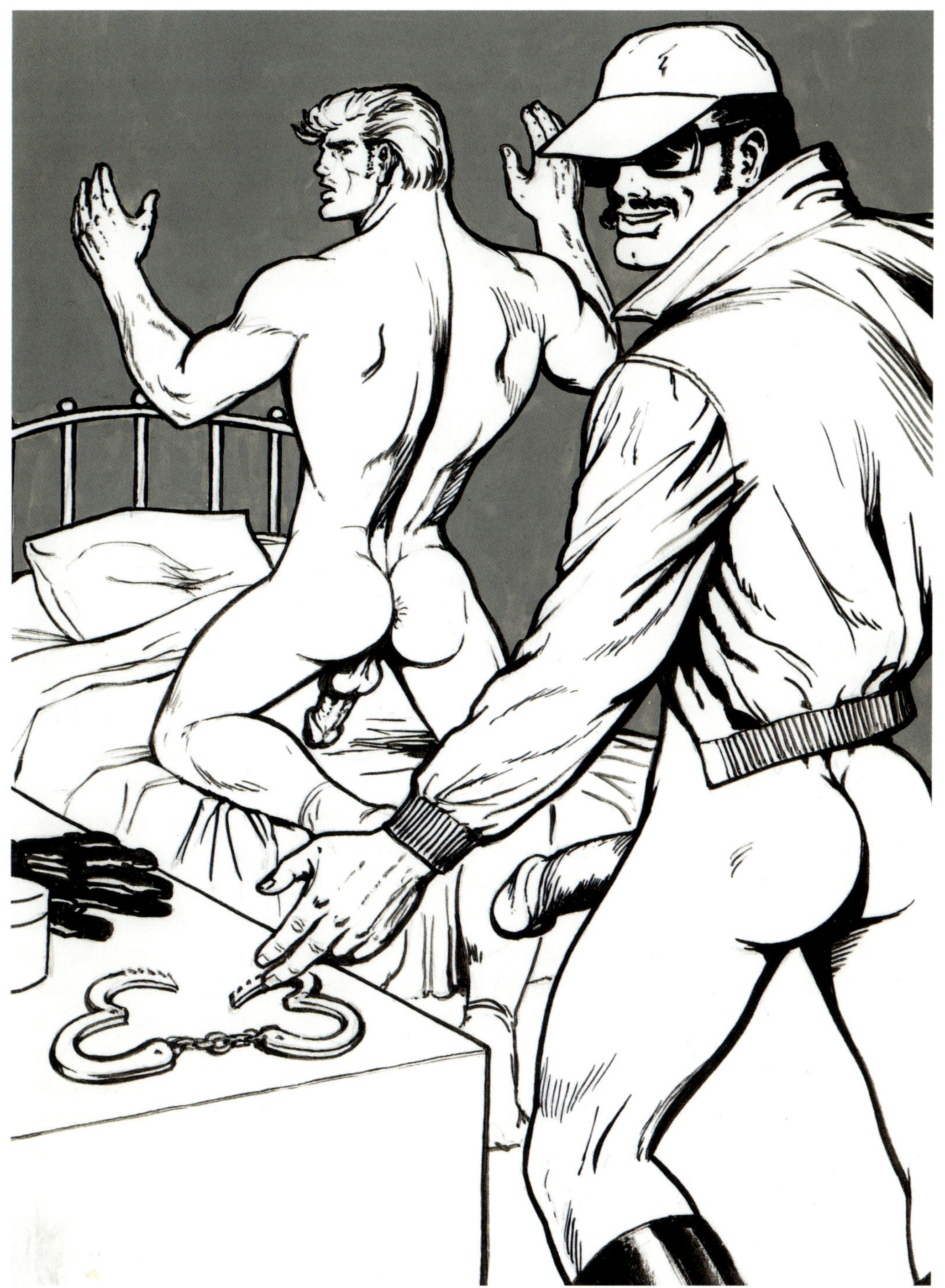

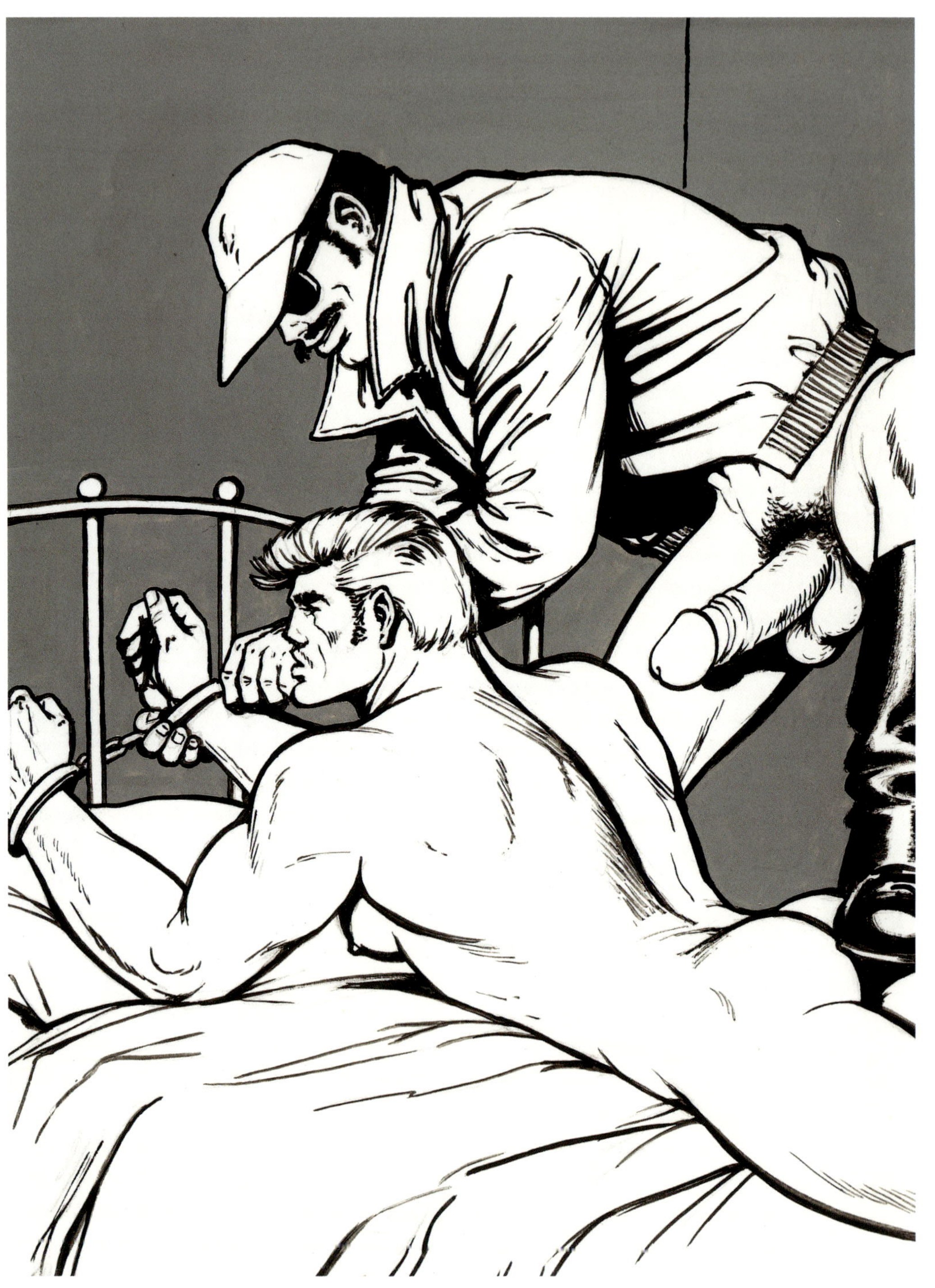

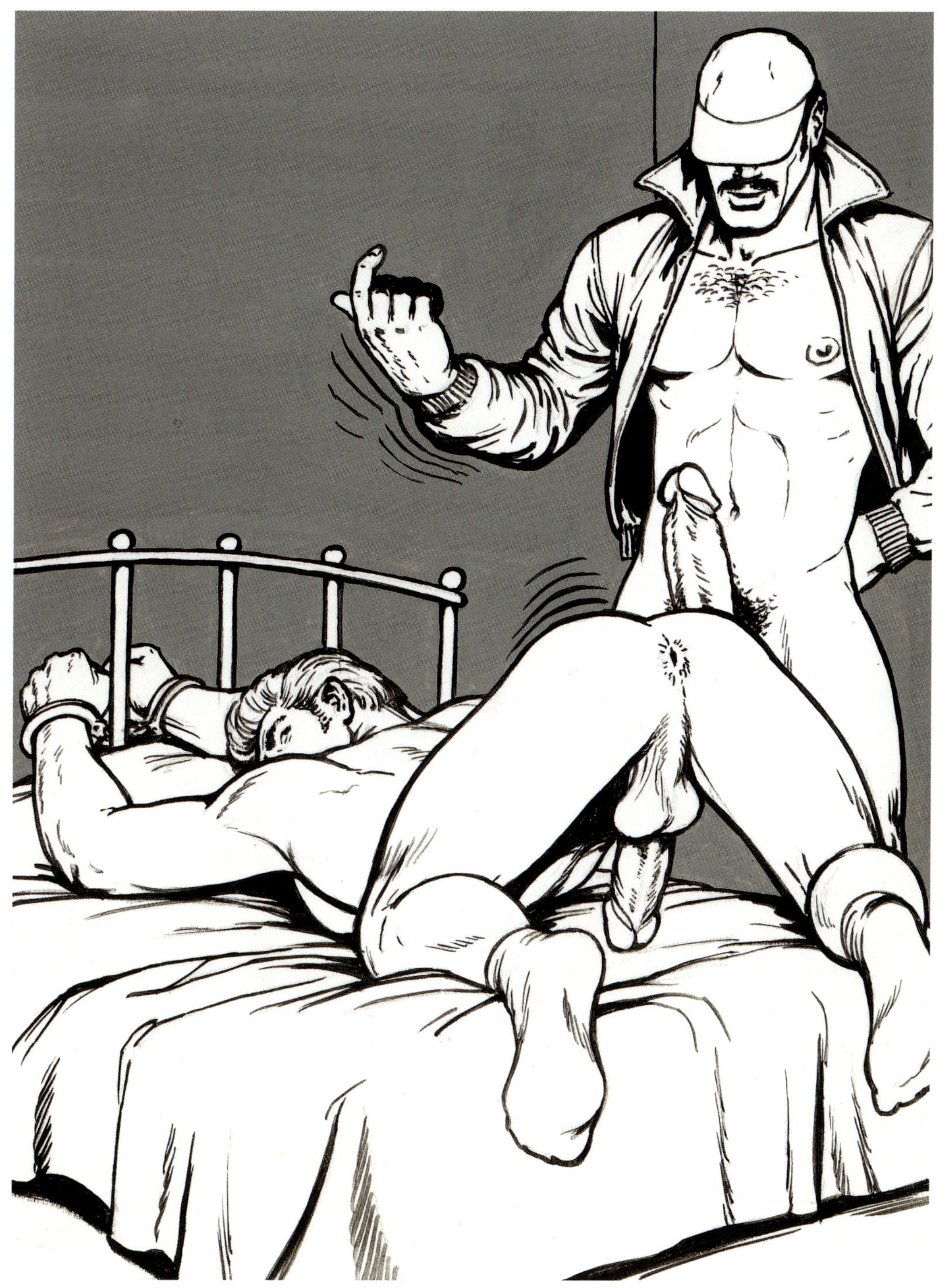

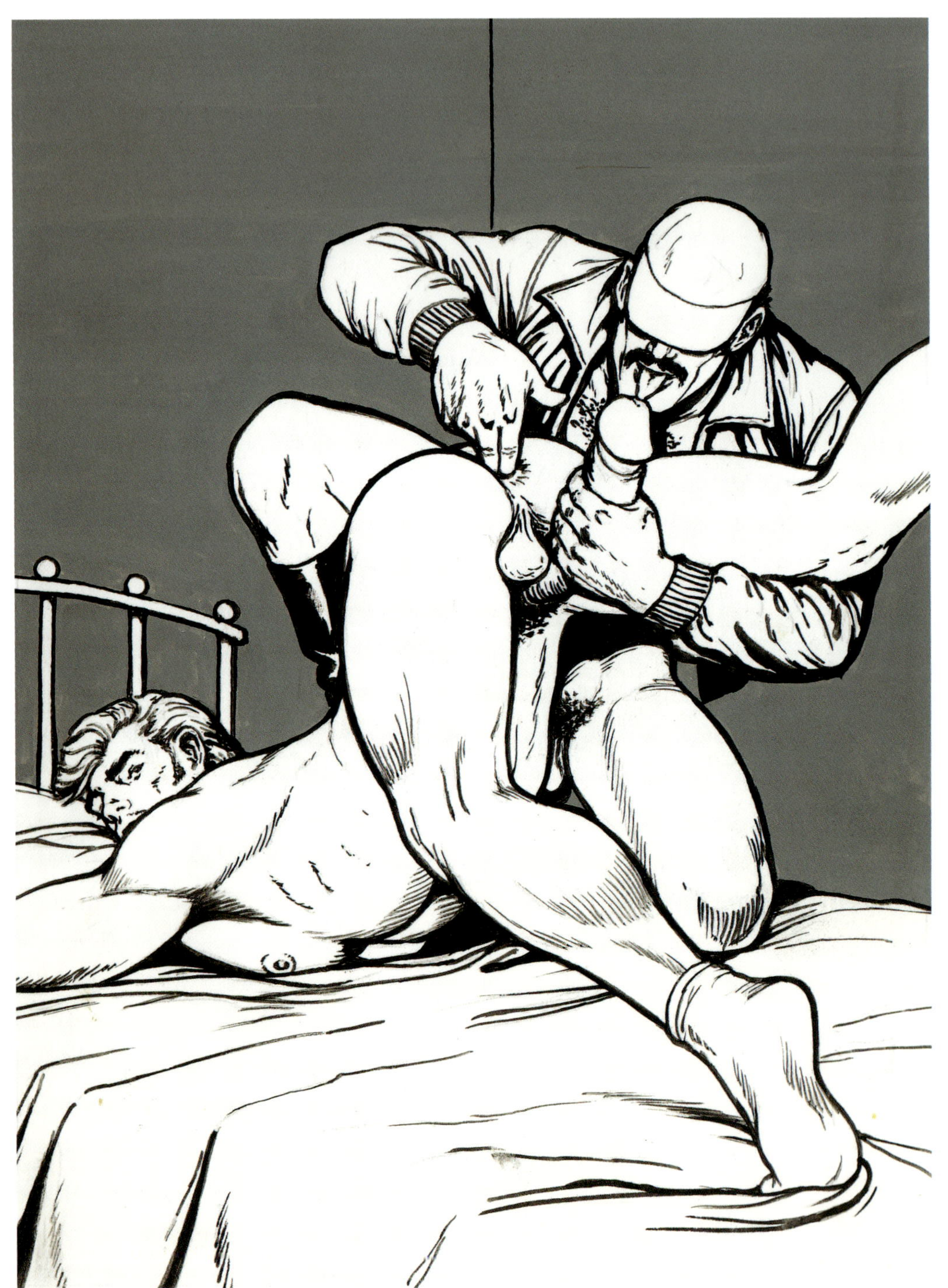

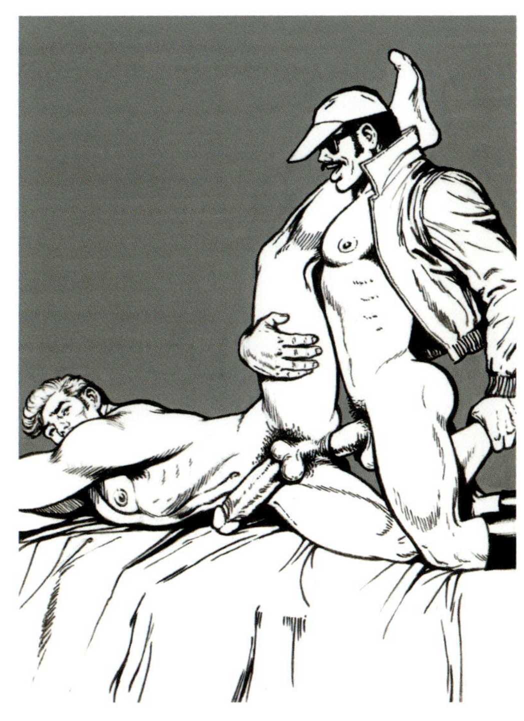
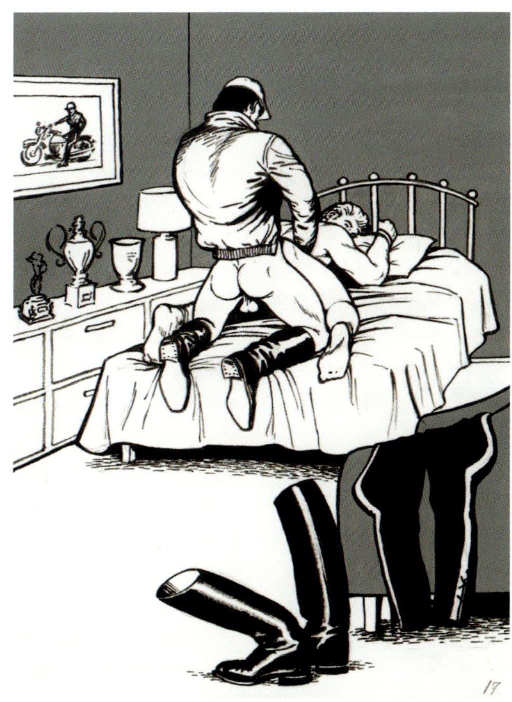
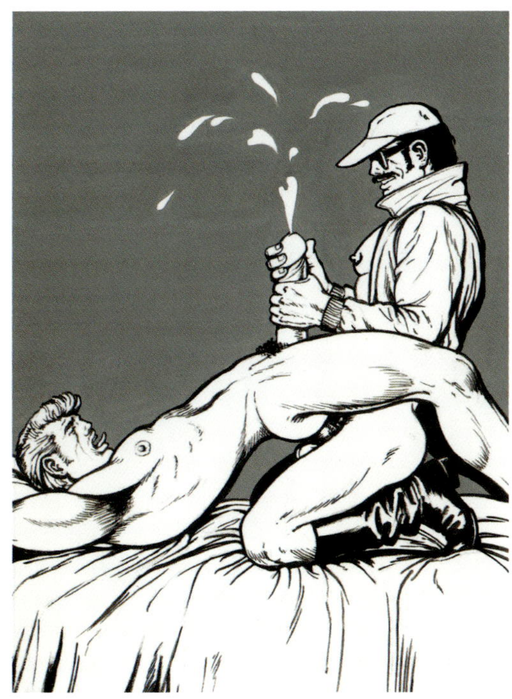
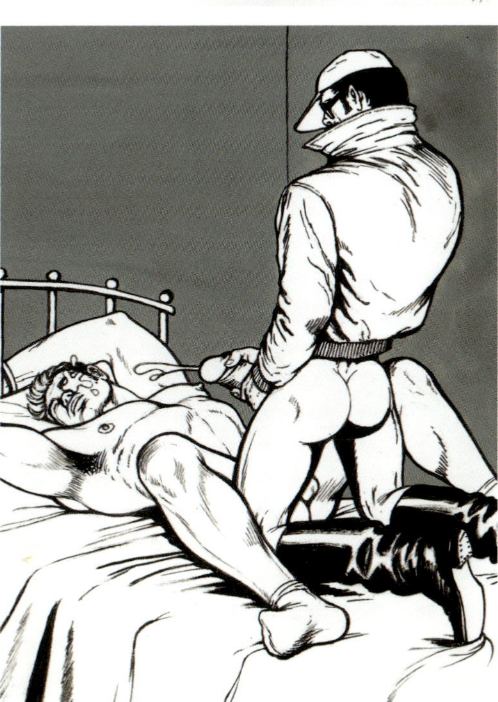

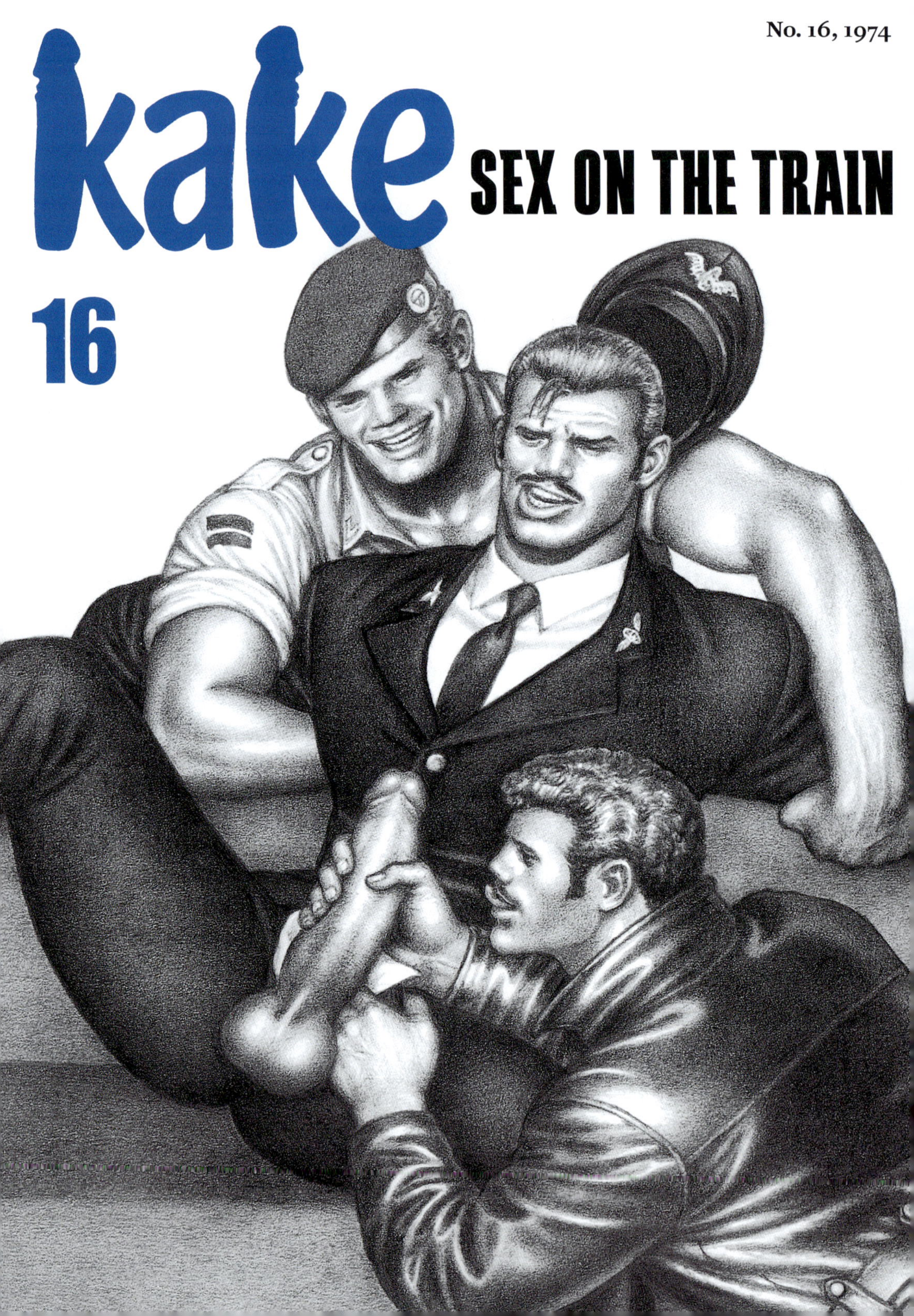
No. 16, 1974
kake
SEX ON THE TRAIN
16

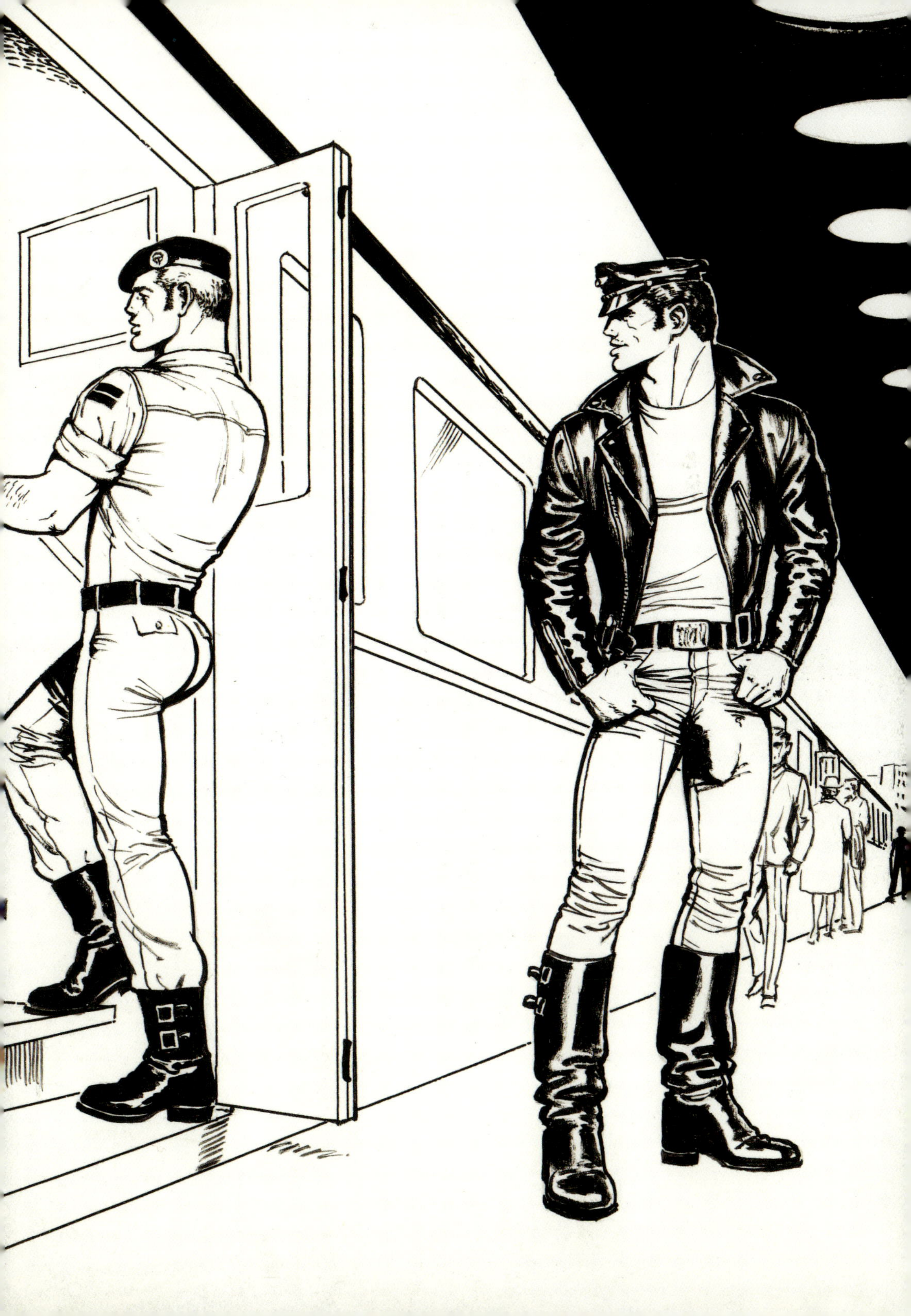

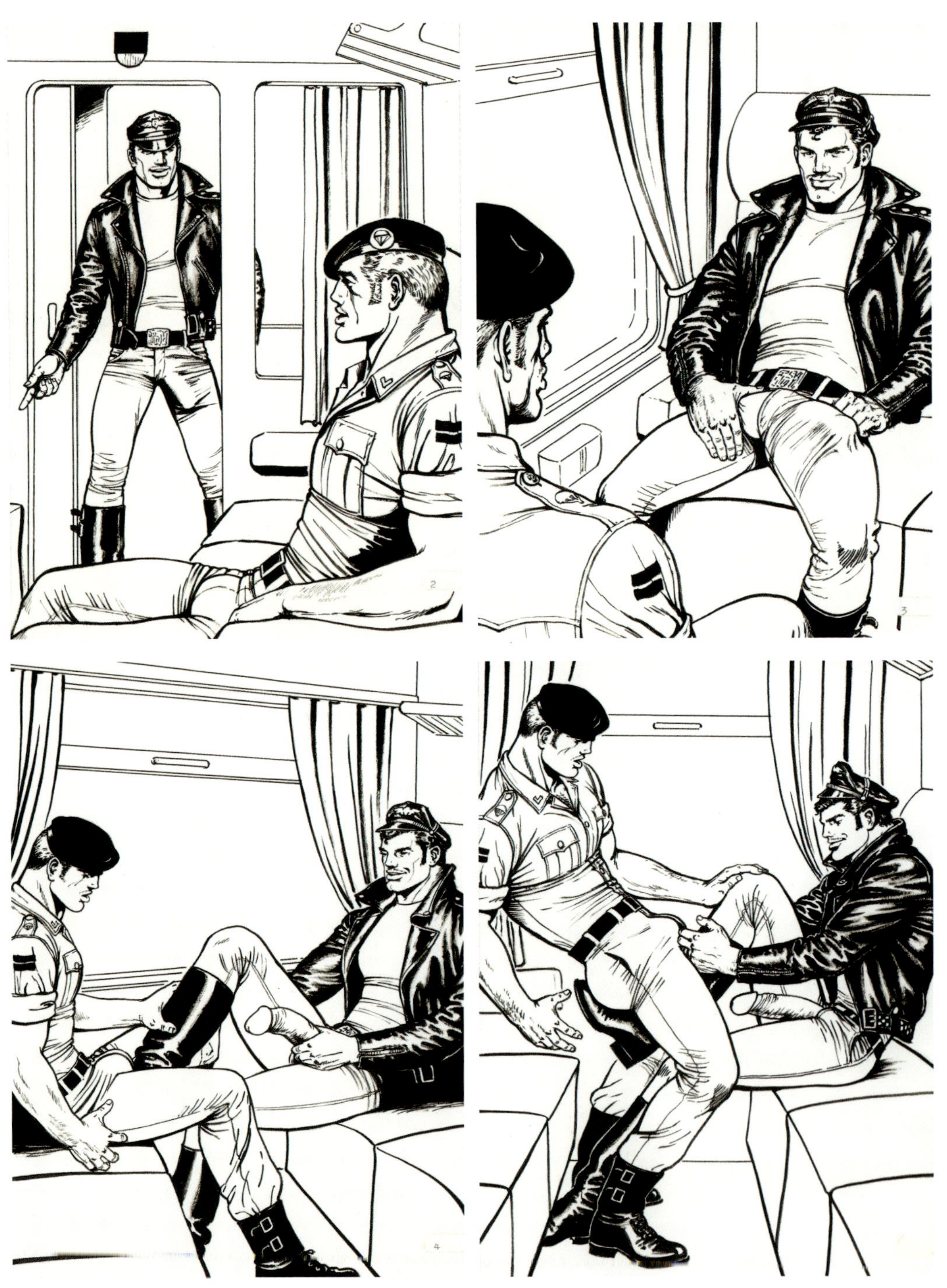

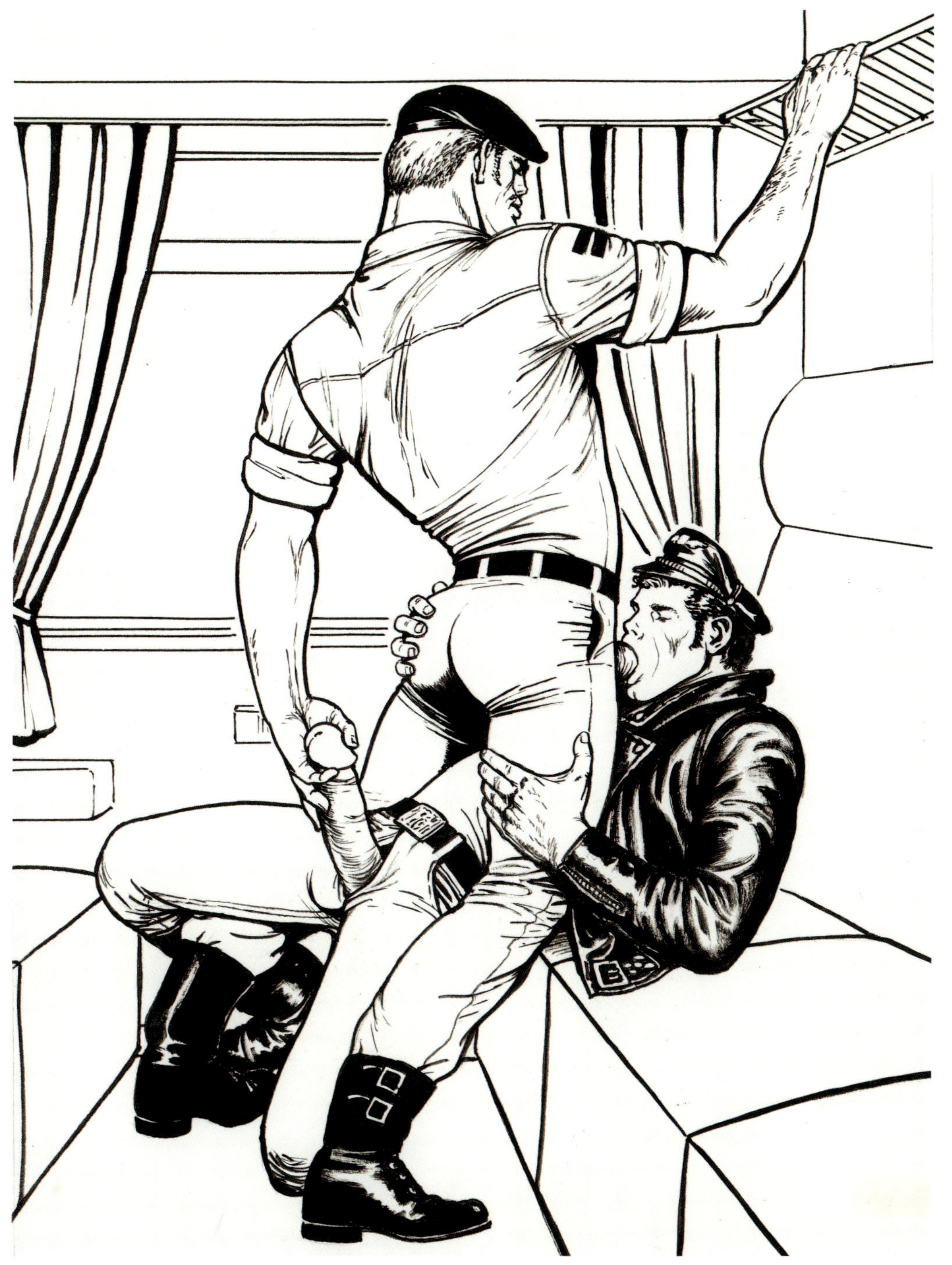

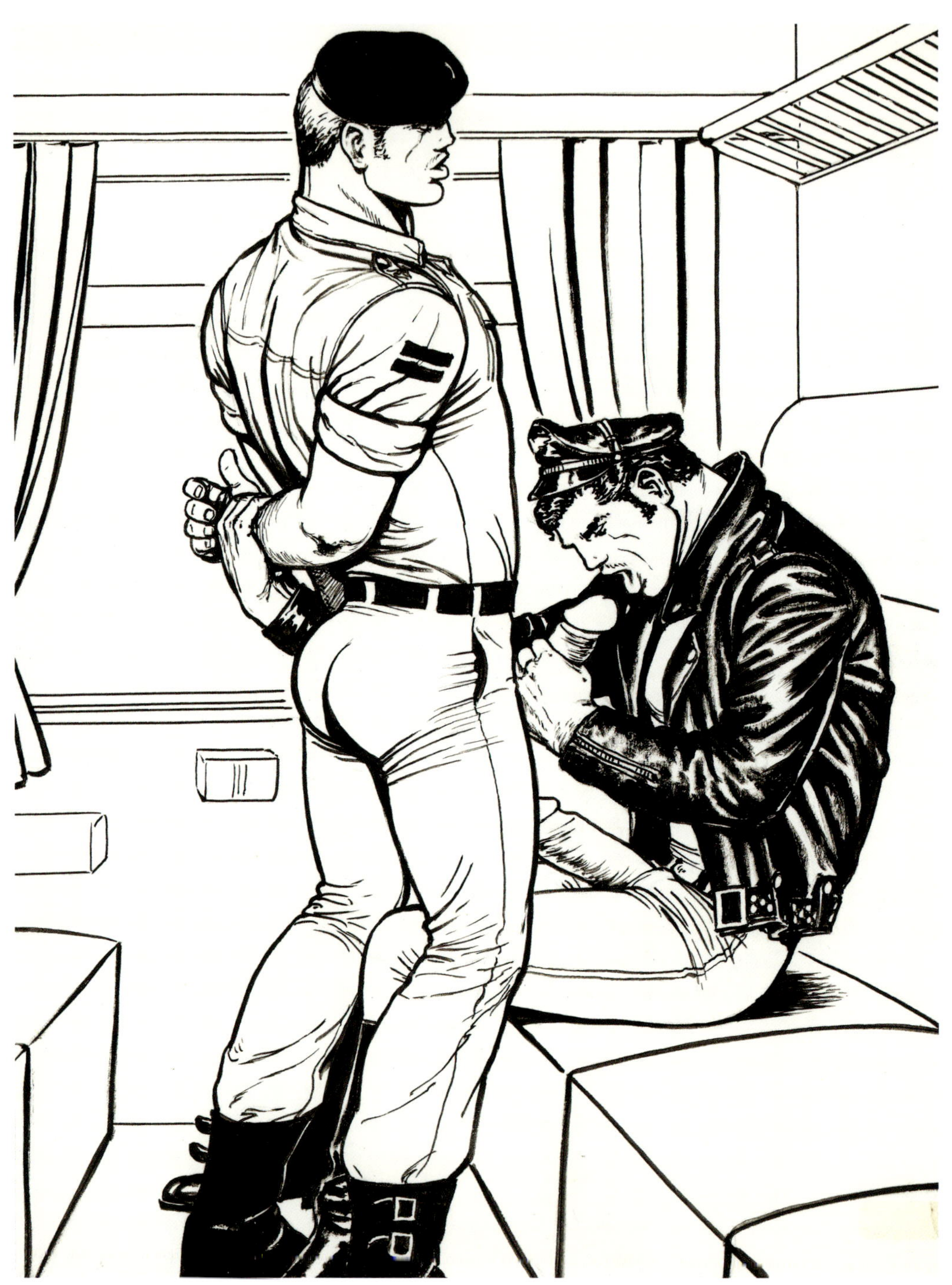

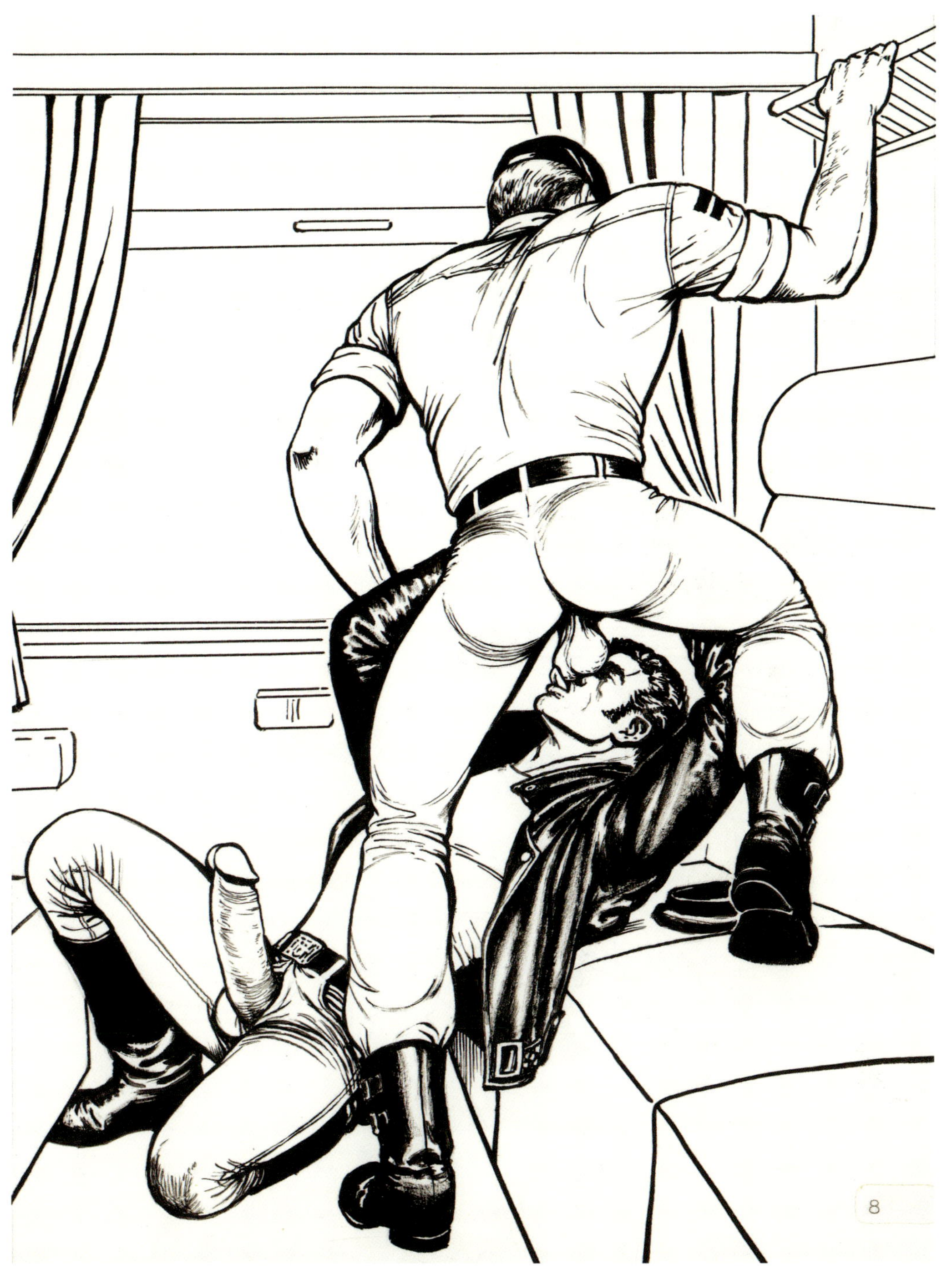

8

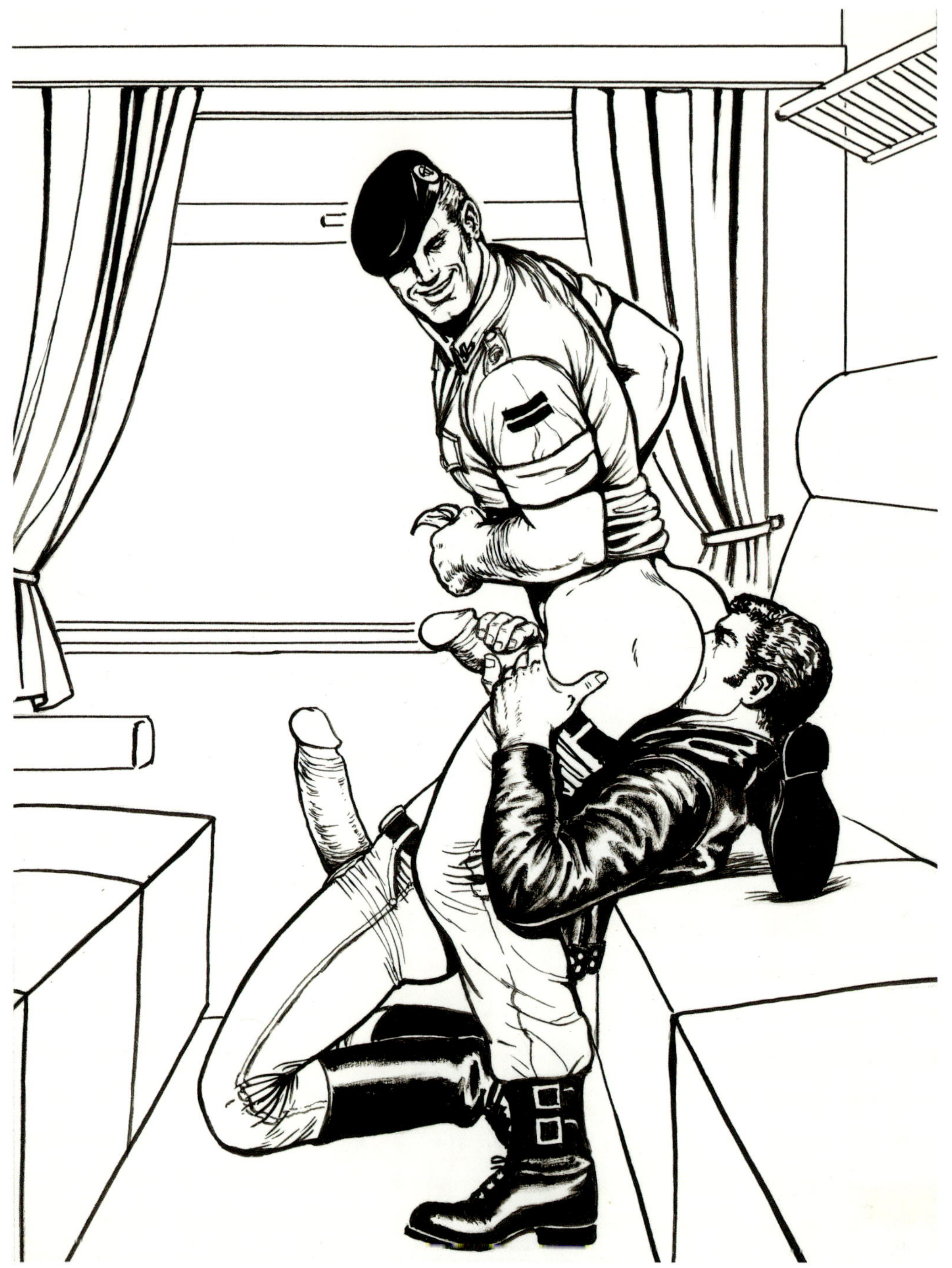

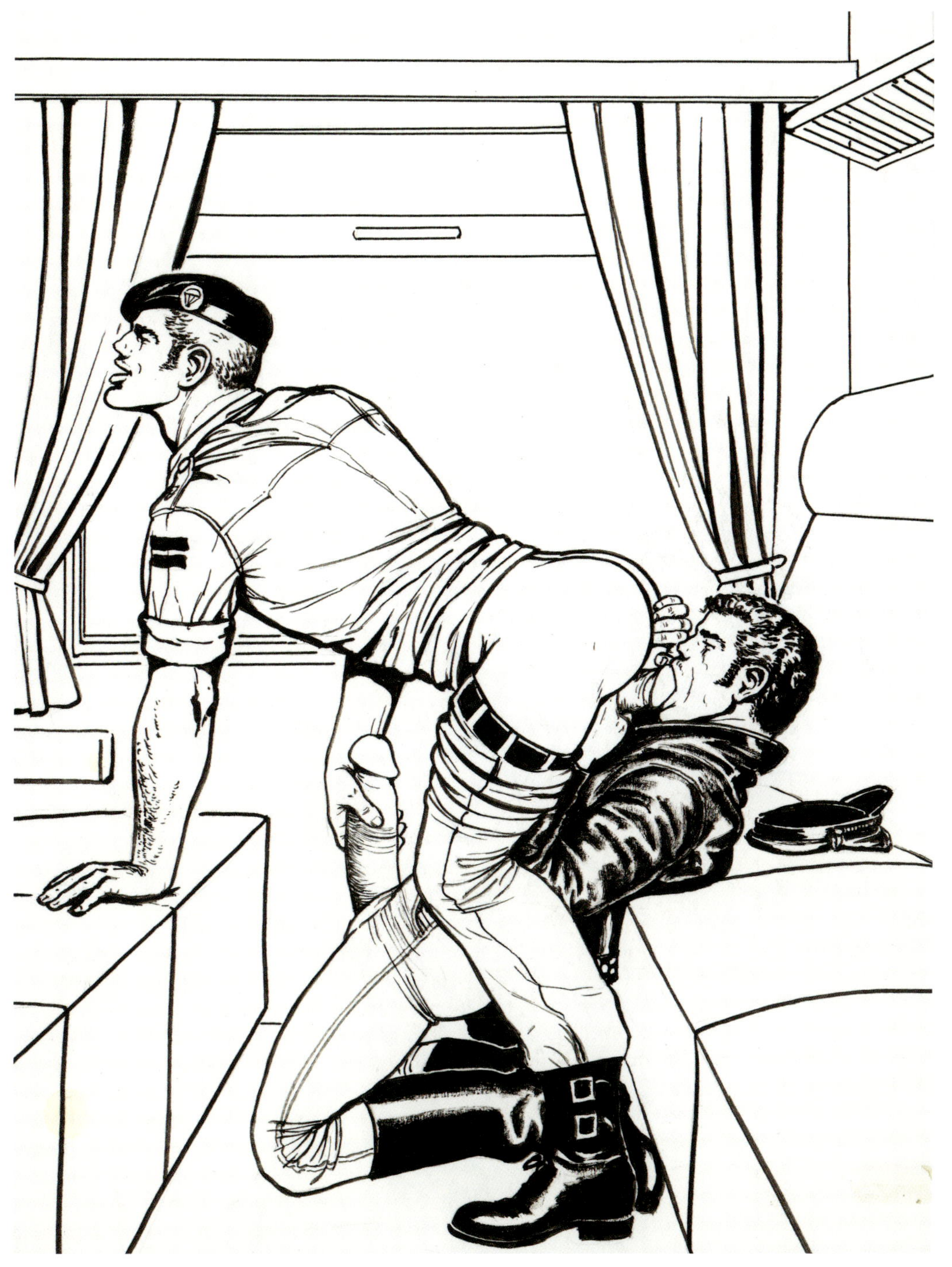

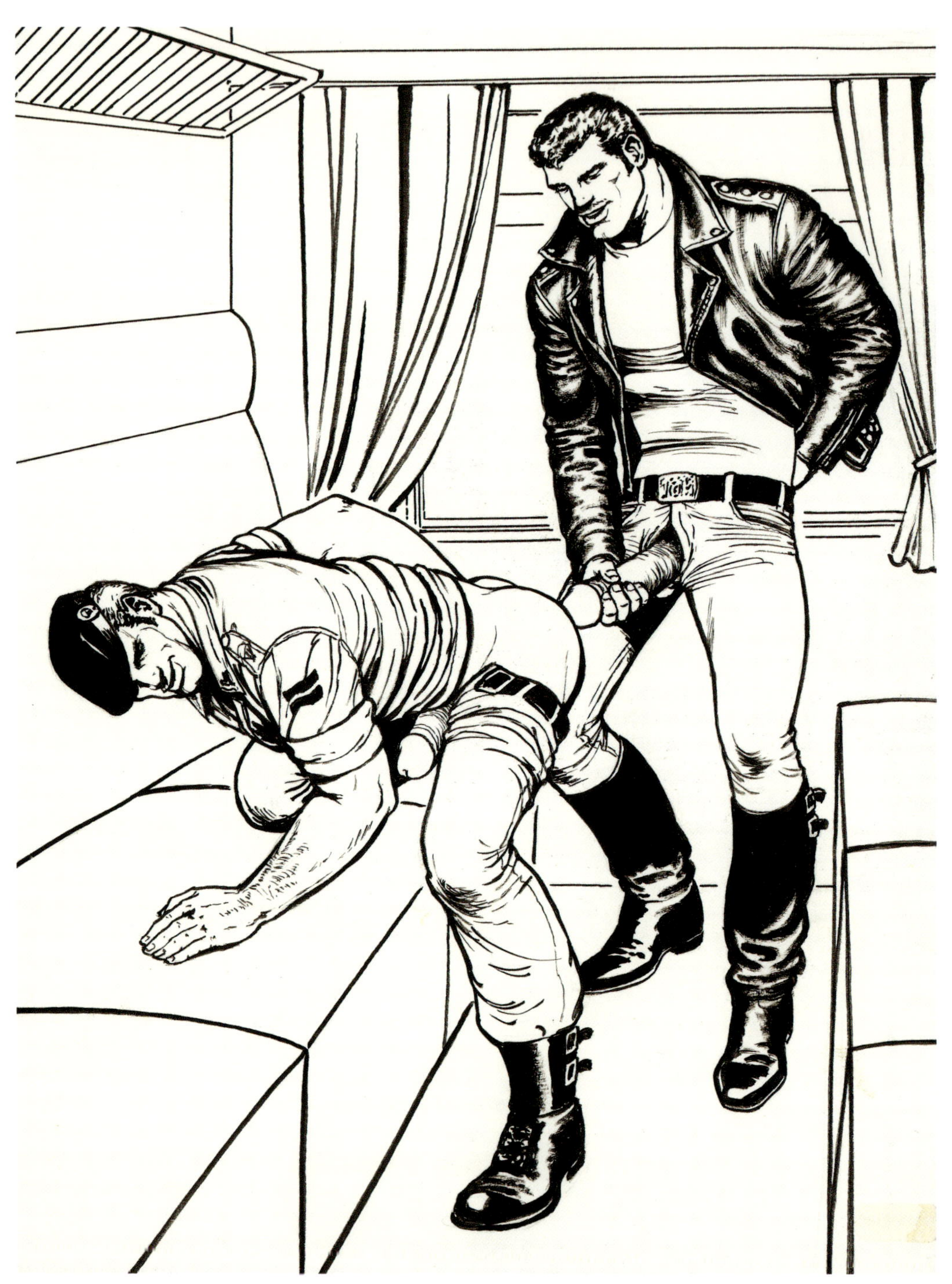

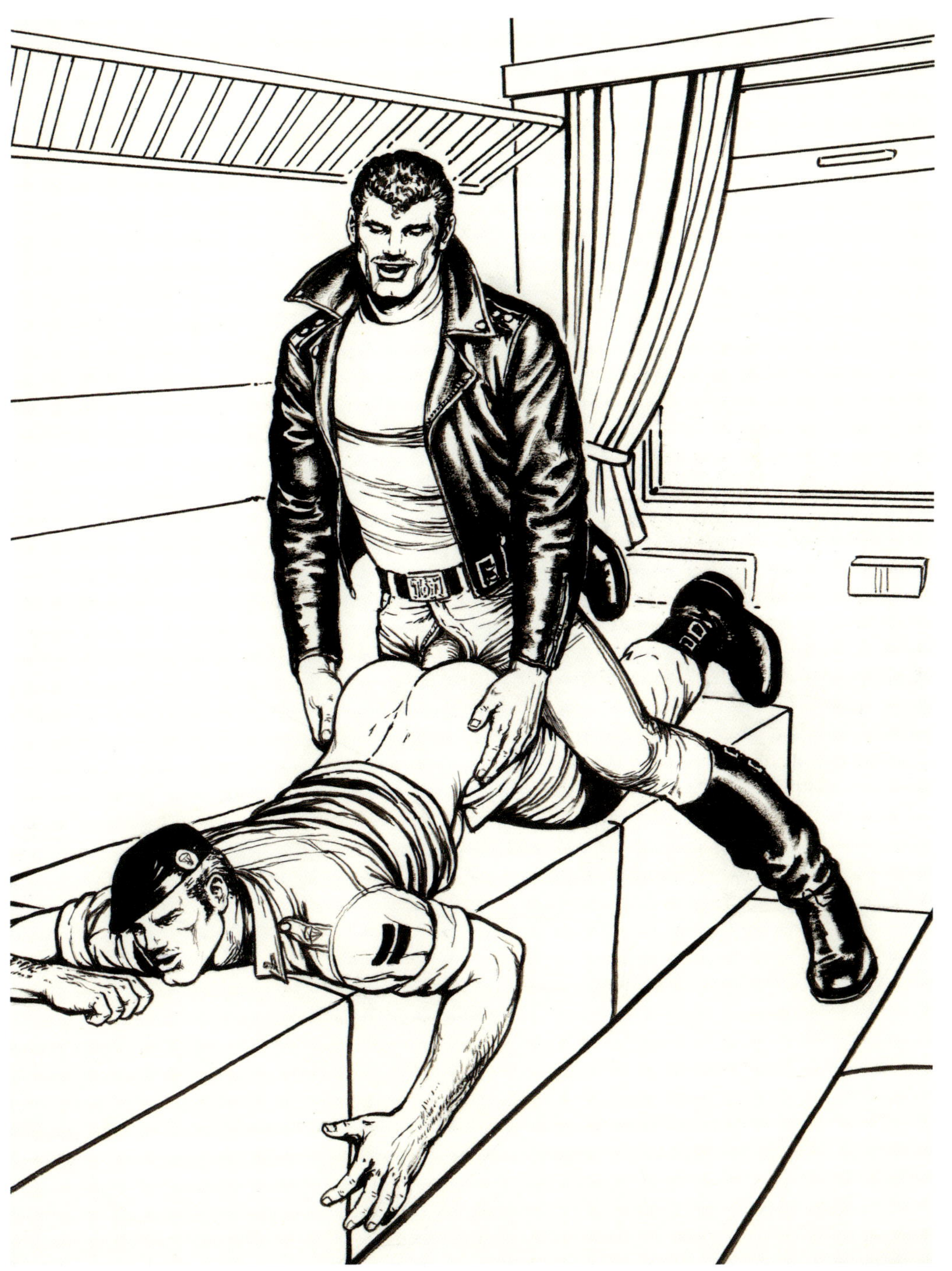

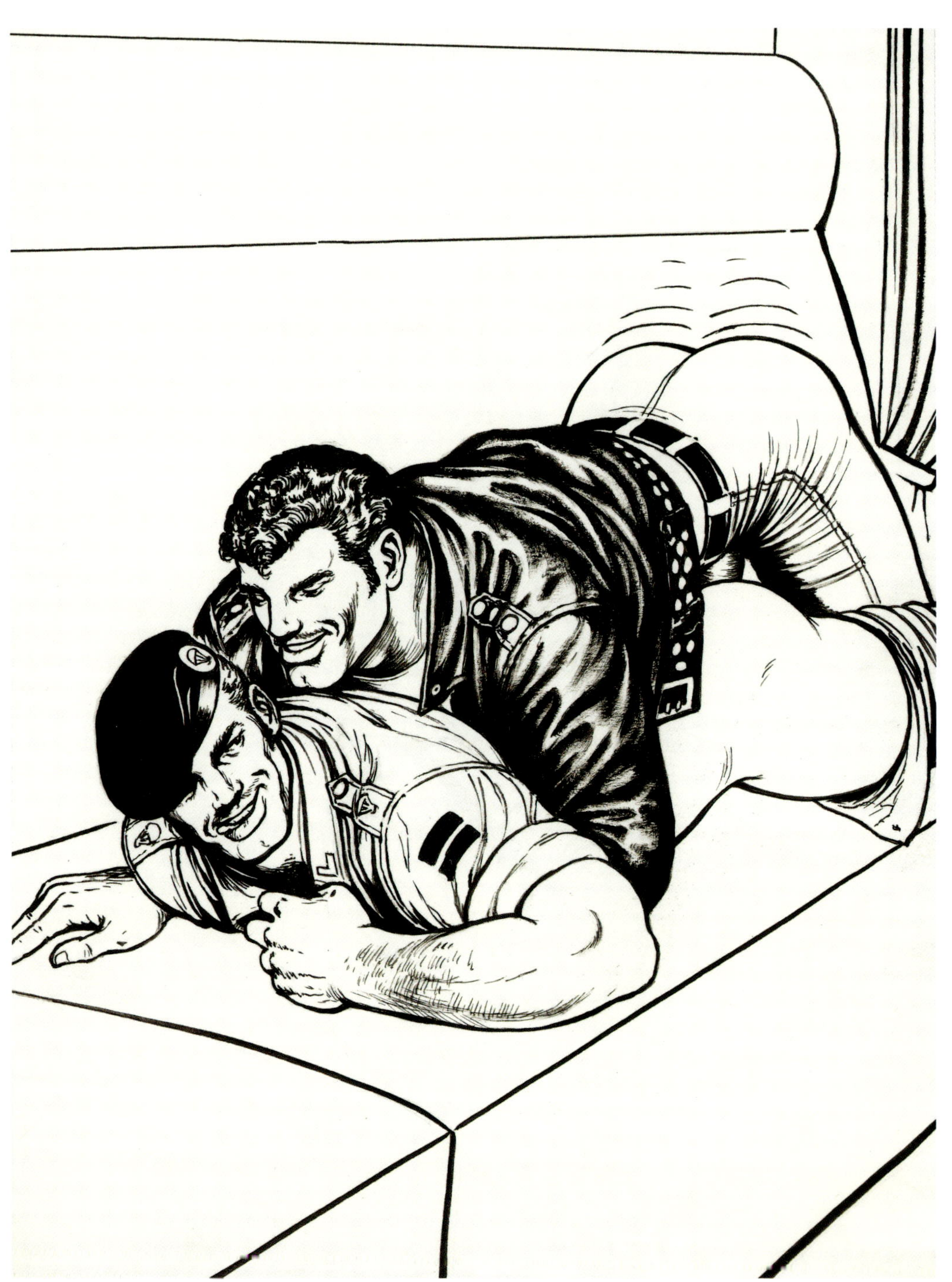

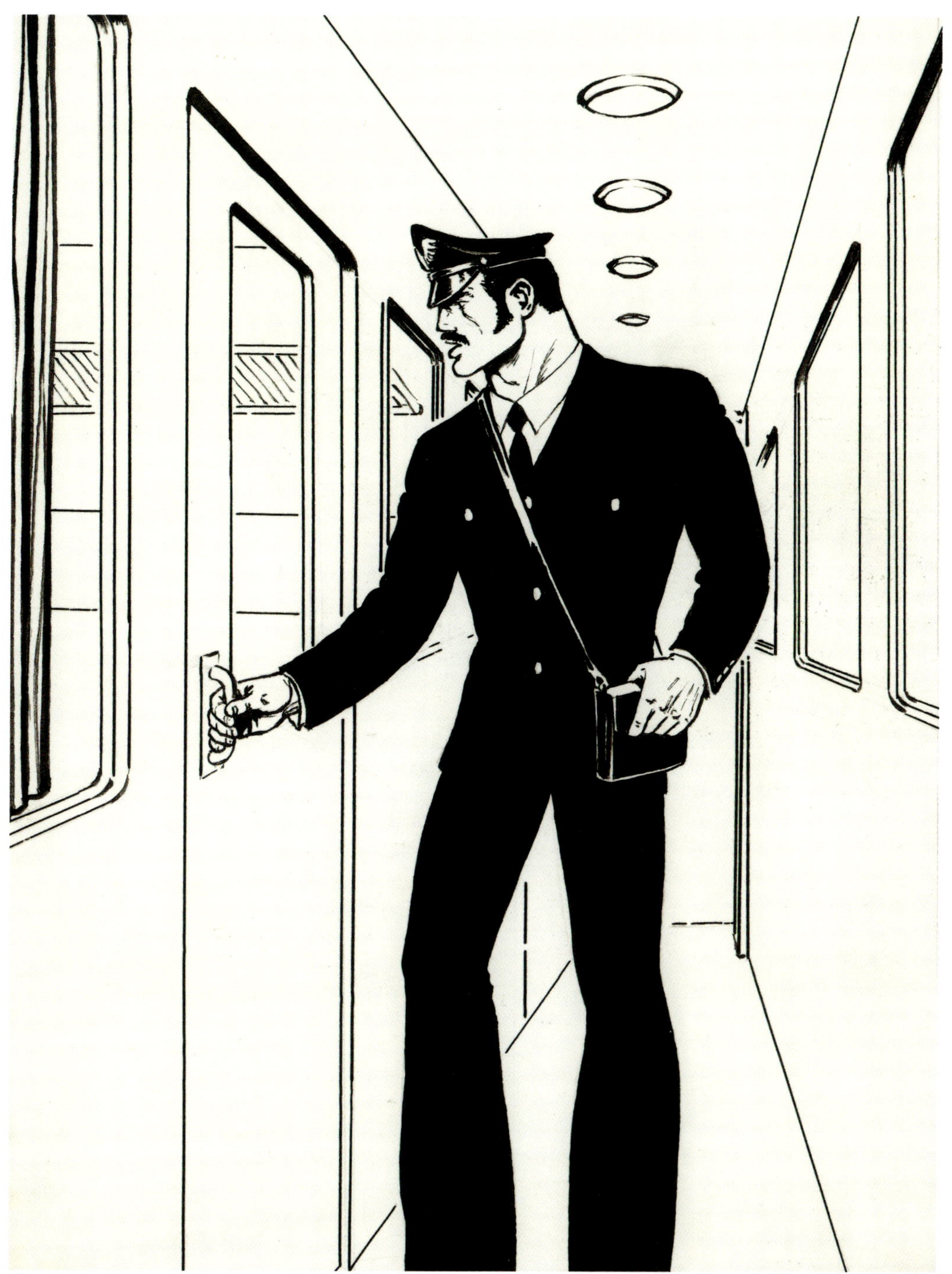

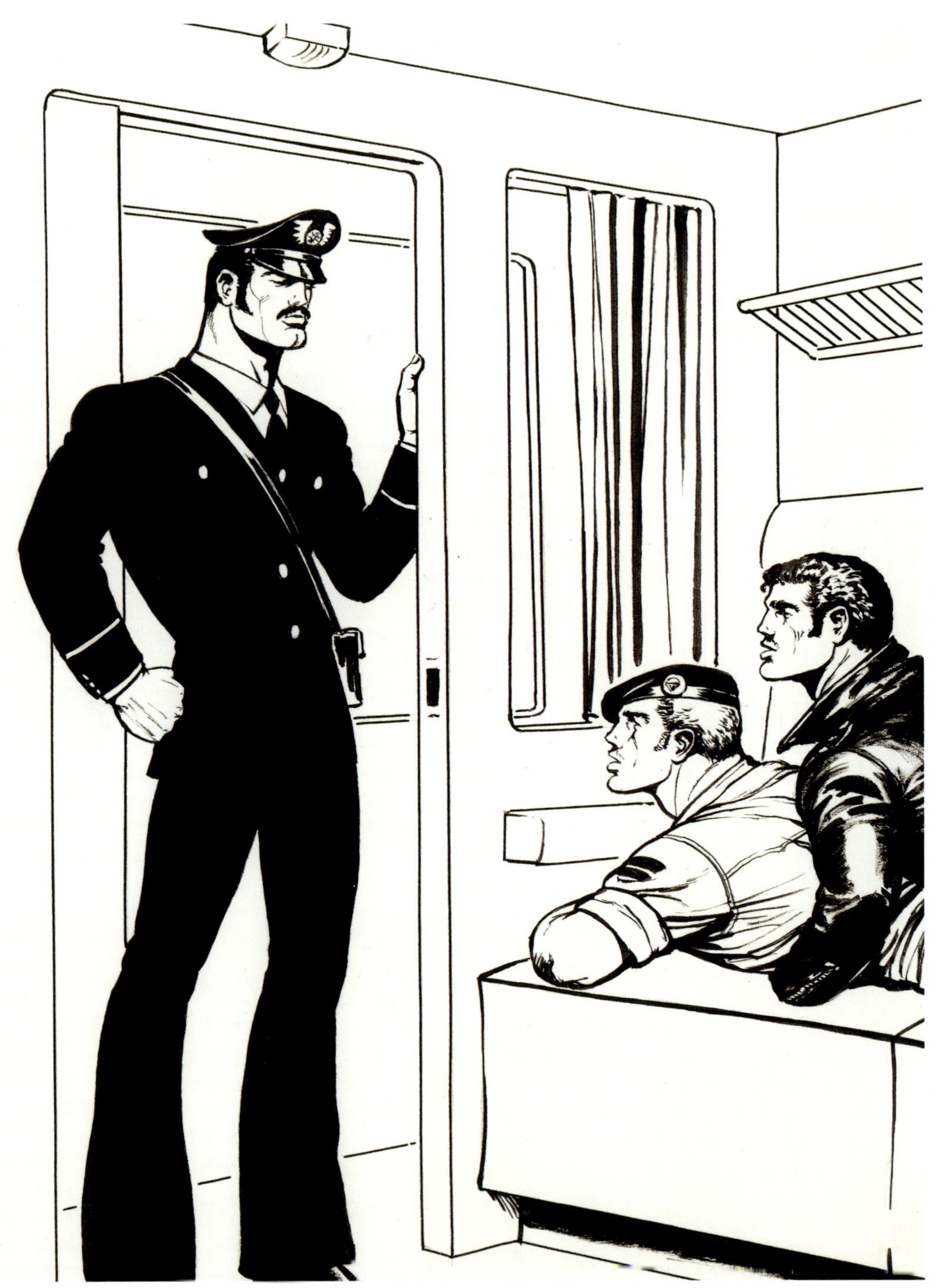

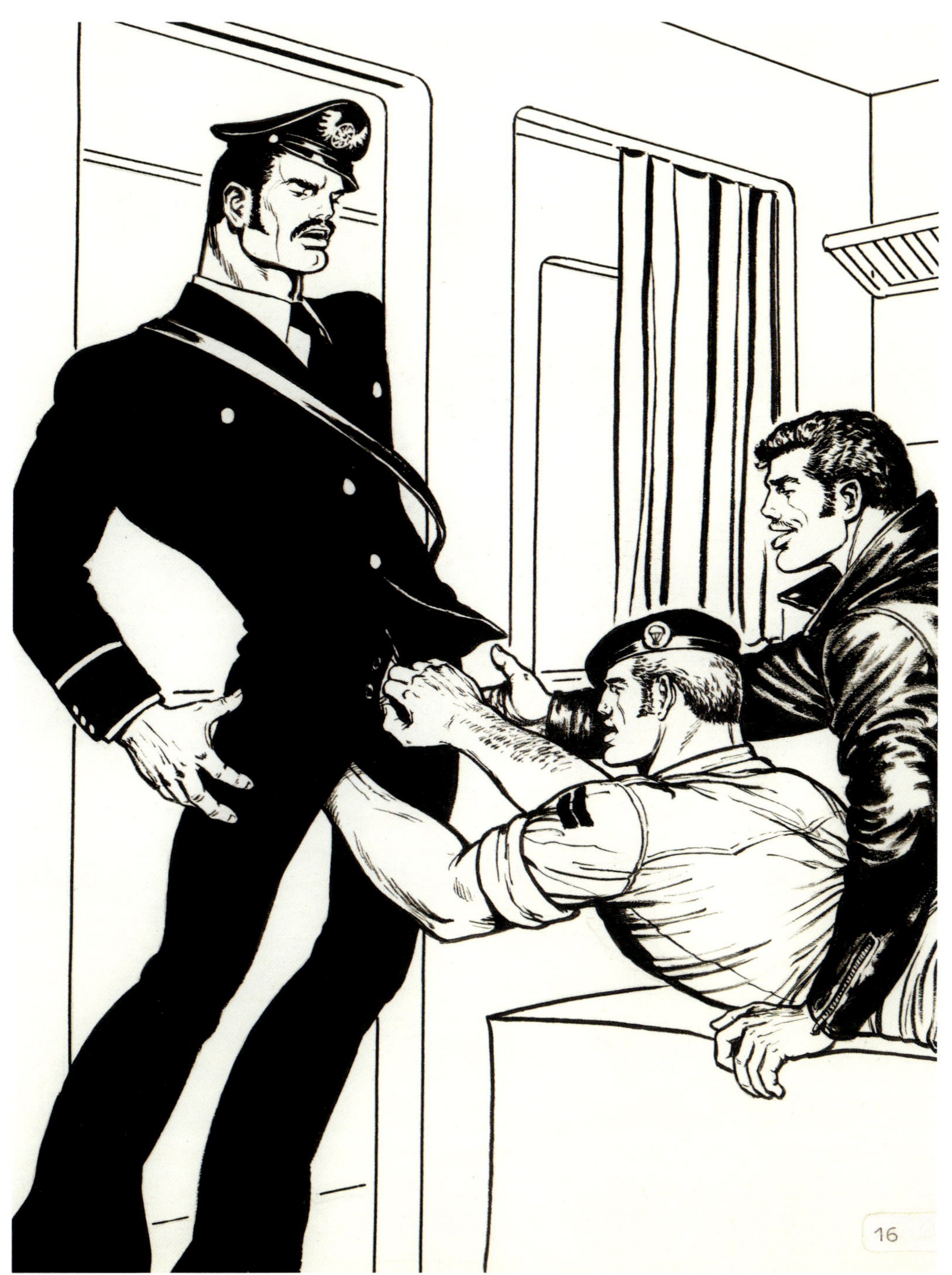

16

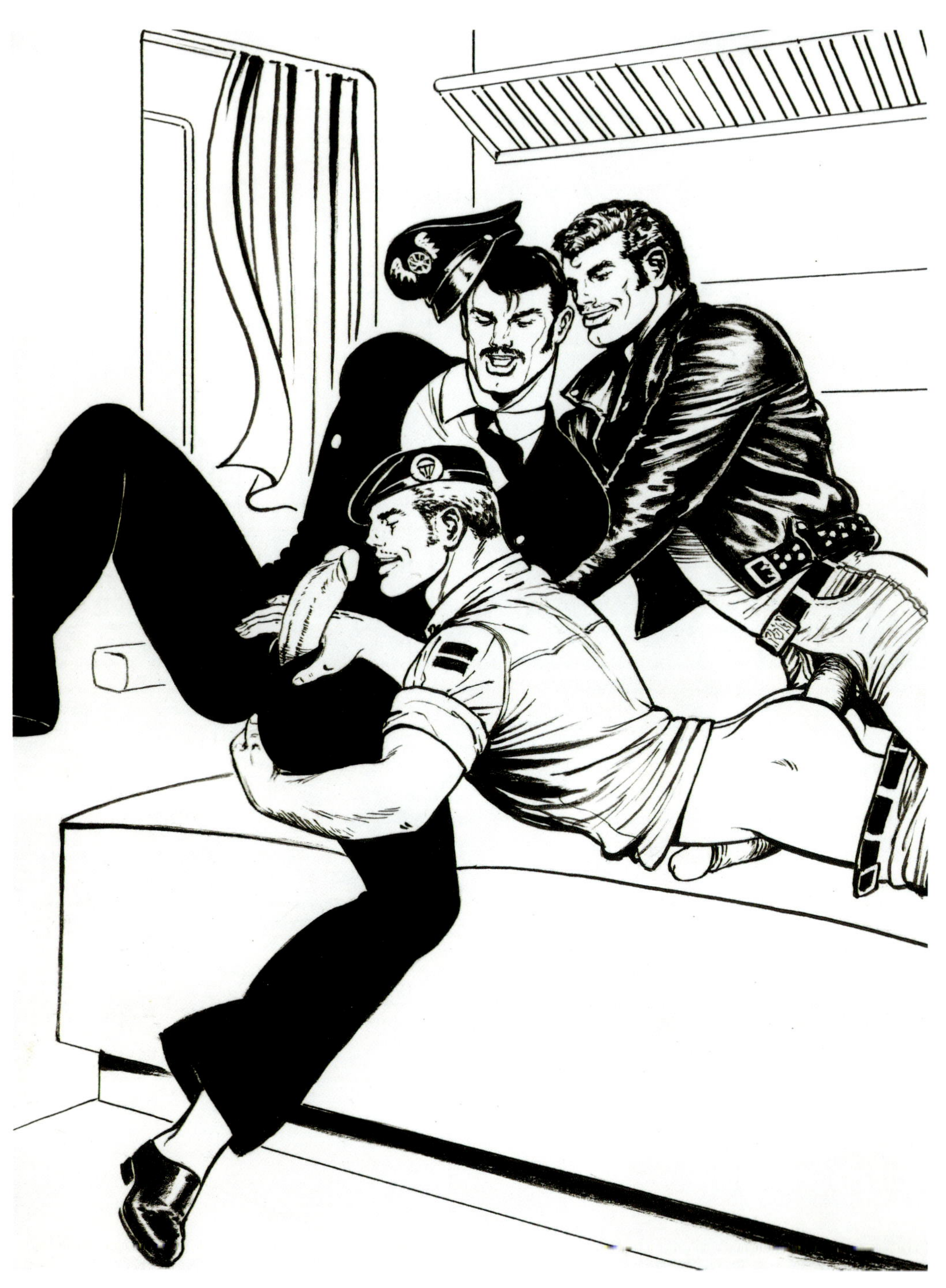

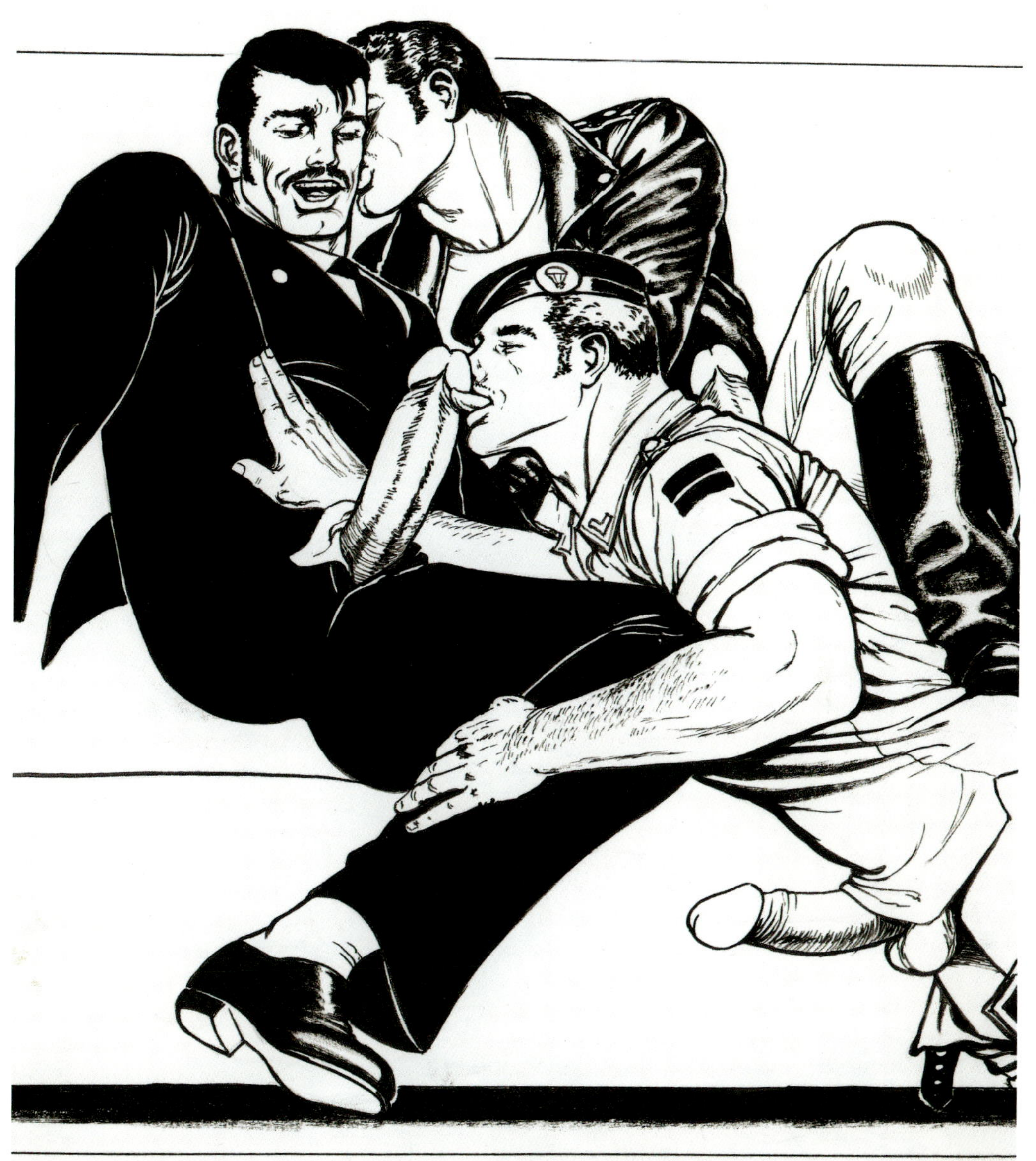

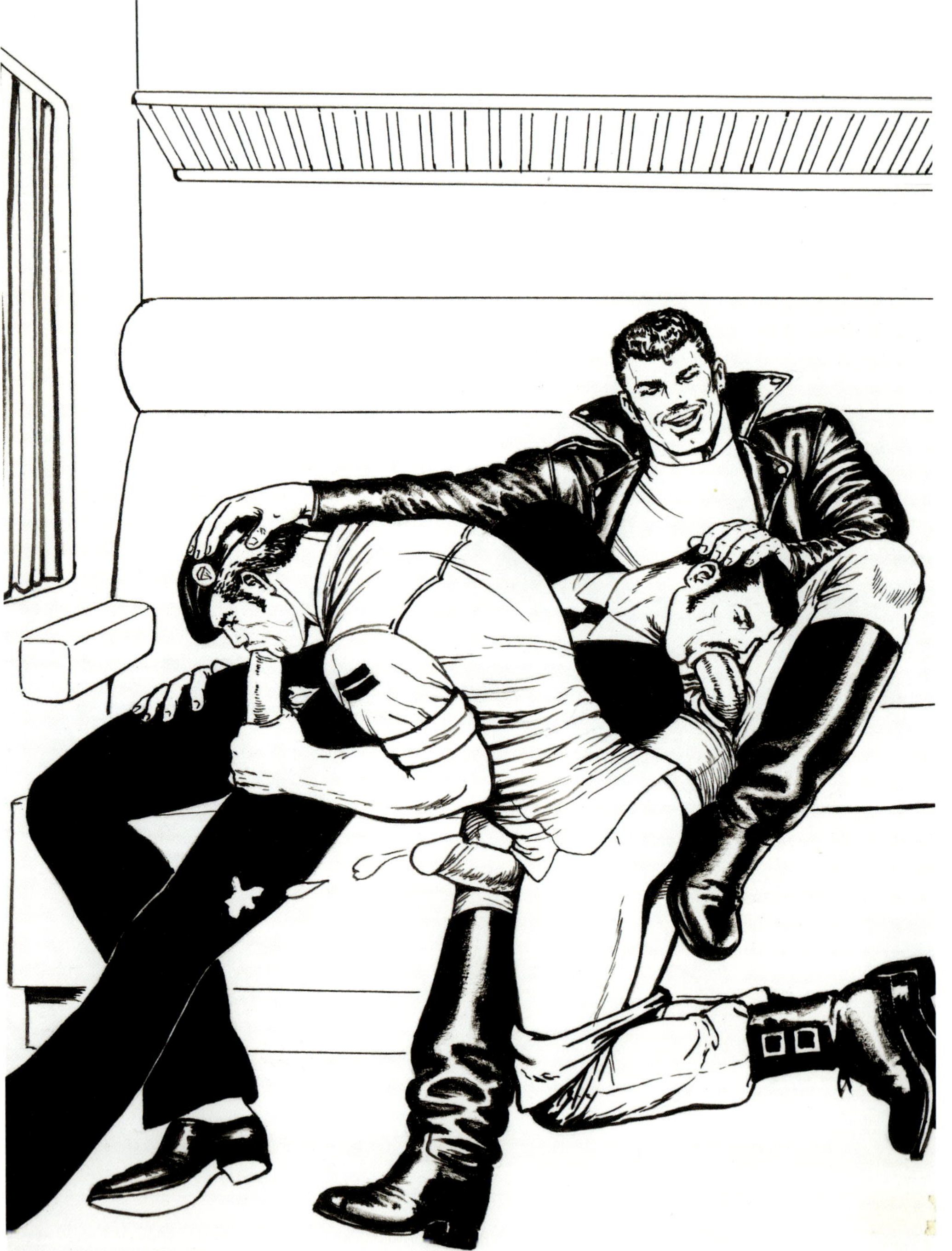

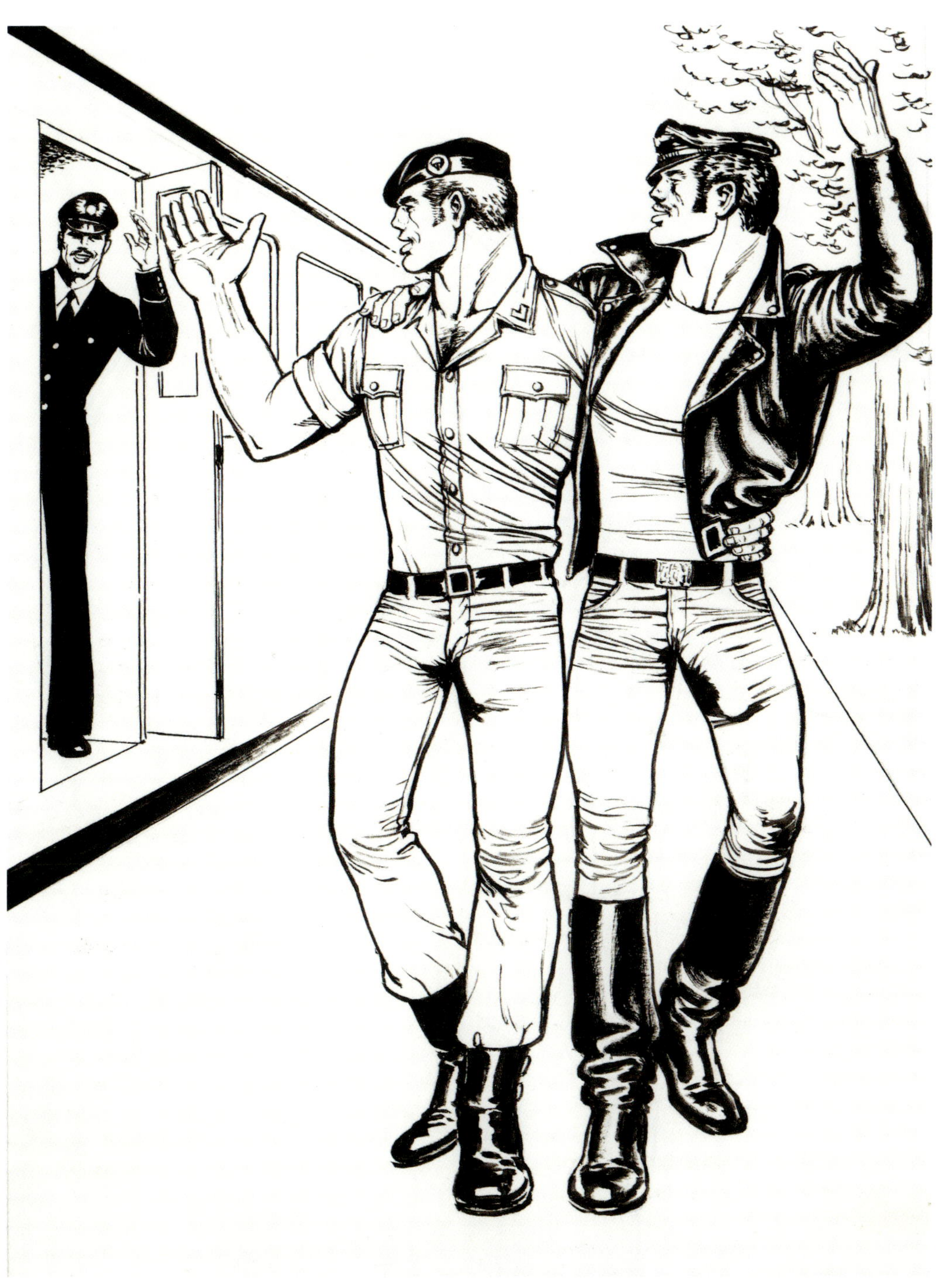

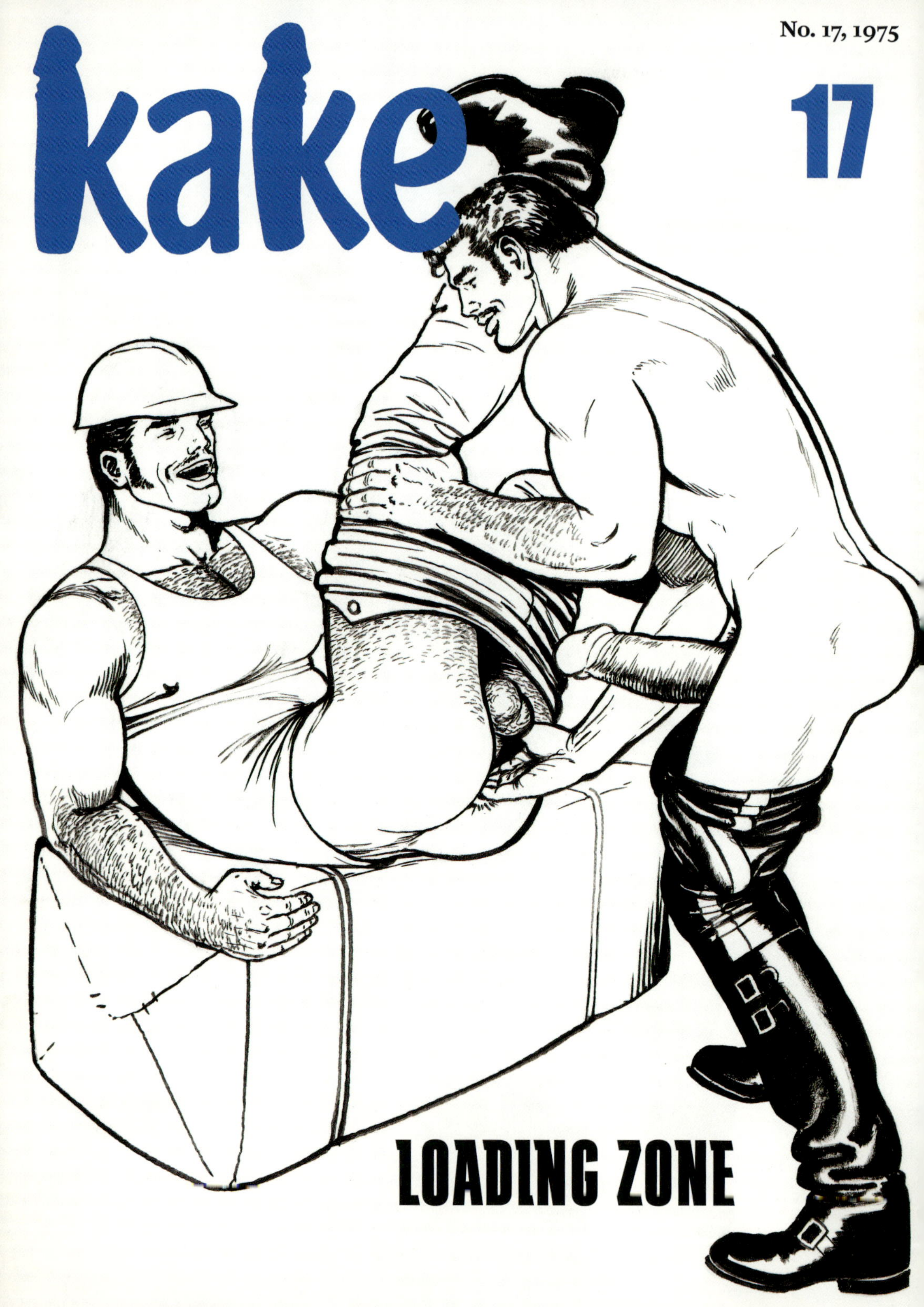

No. 17, 1975
17
kake
LOADING ZONE

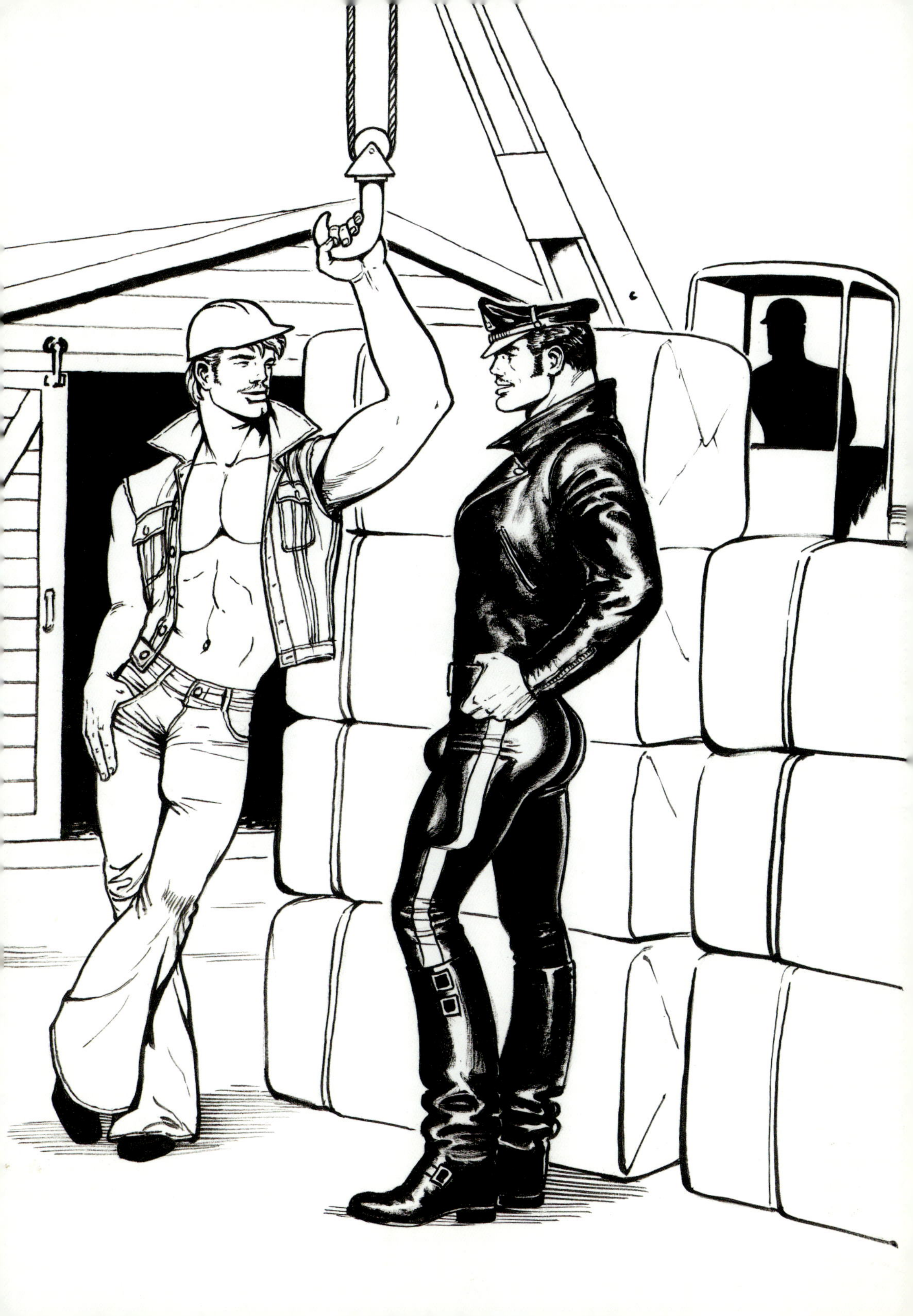

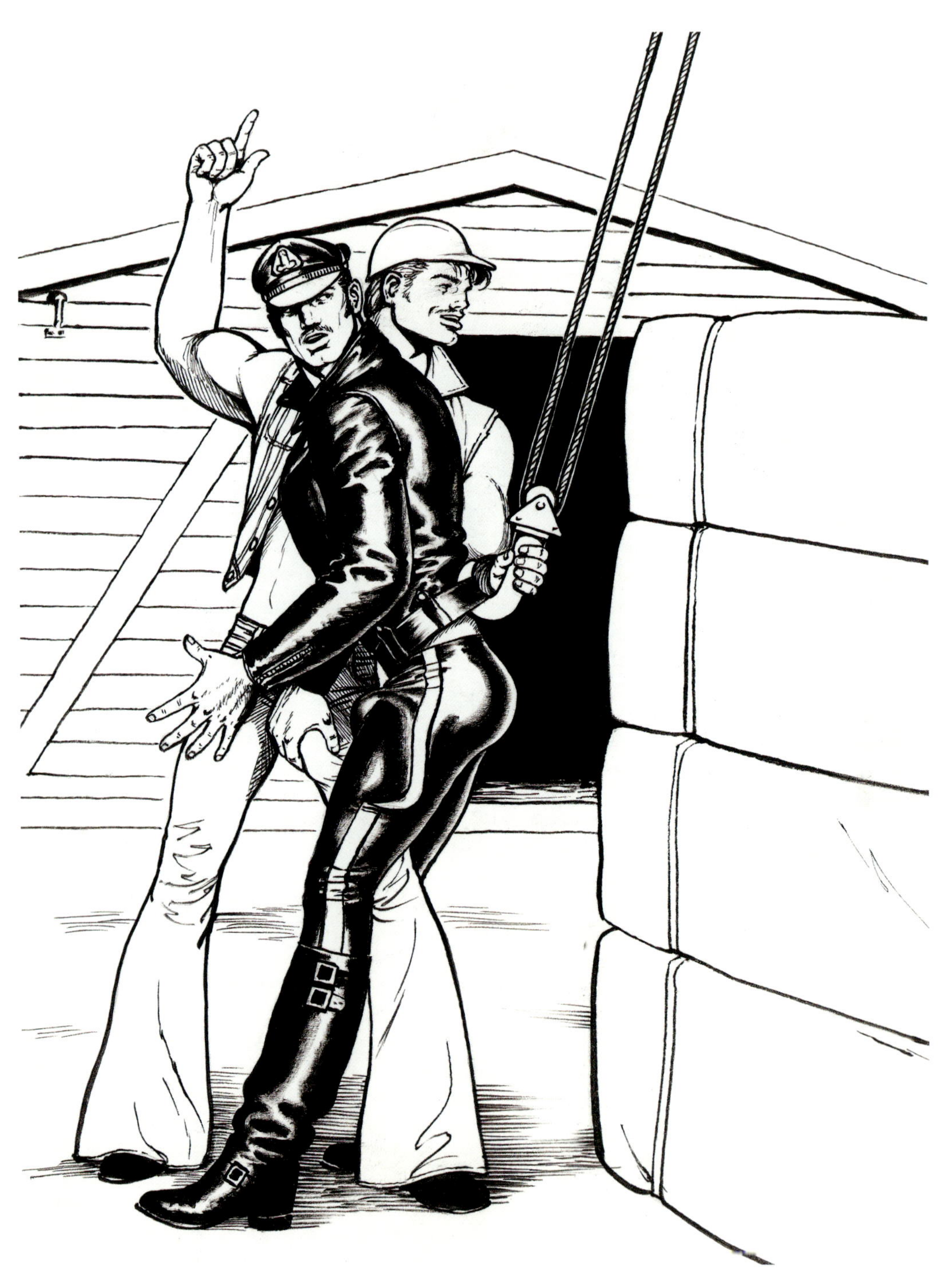

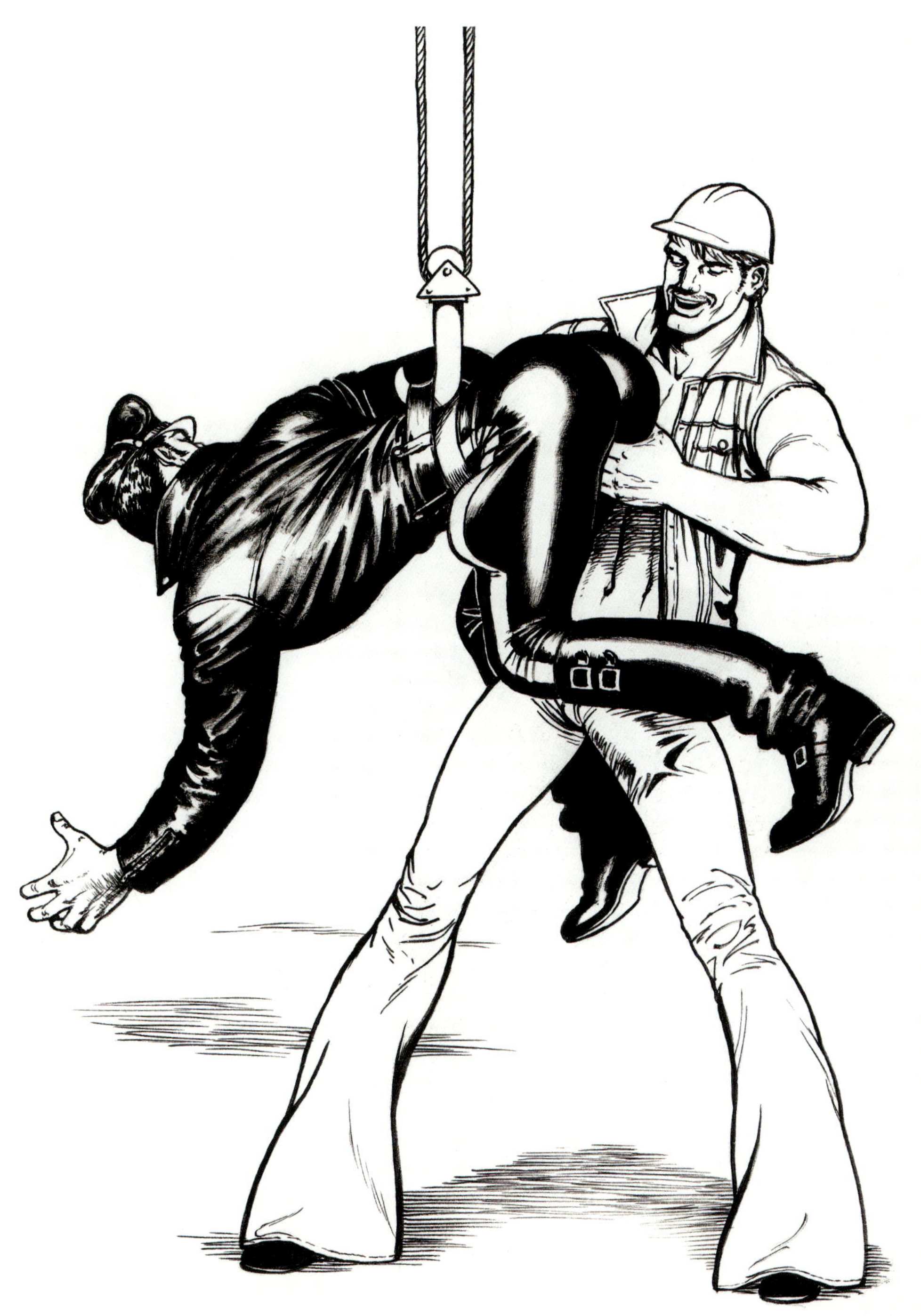

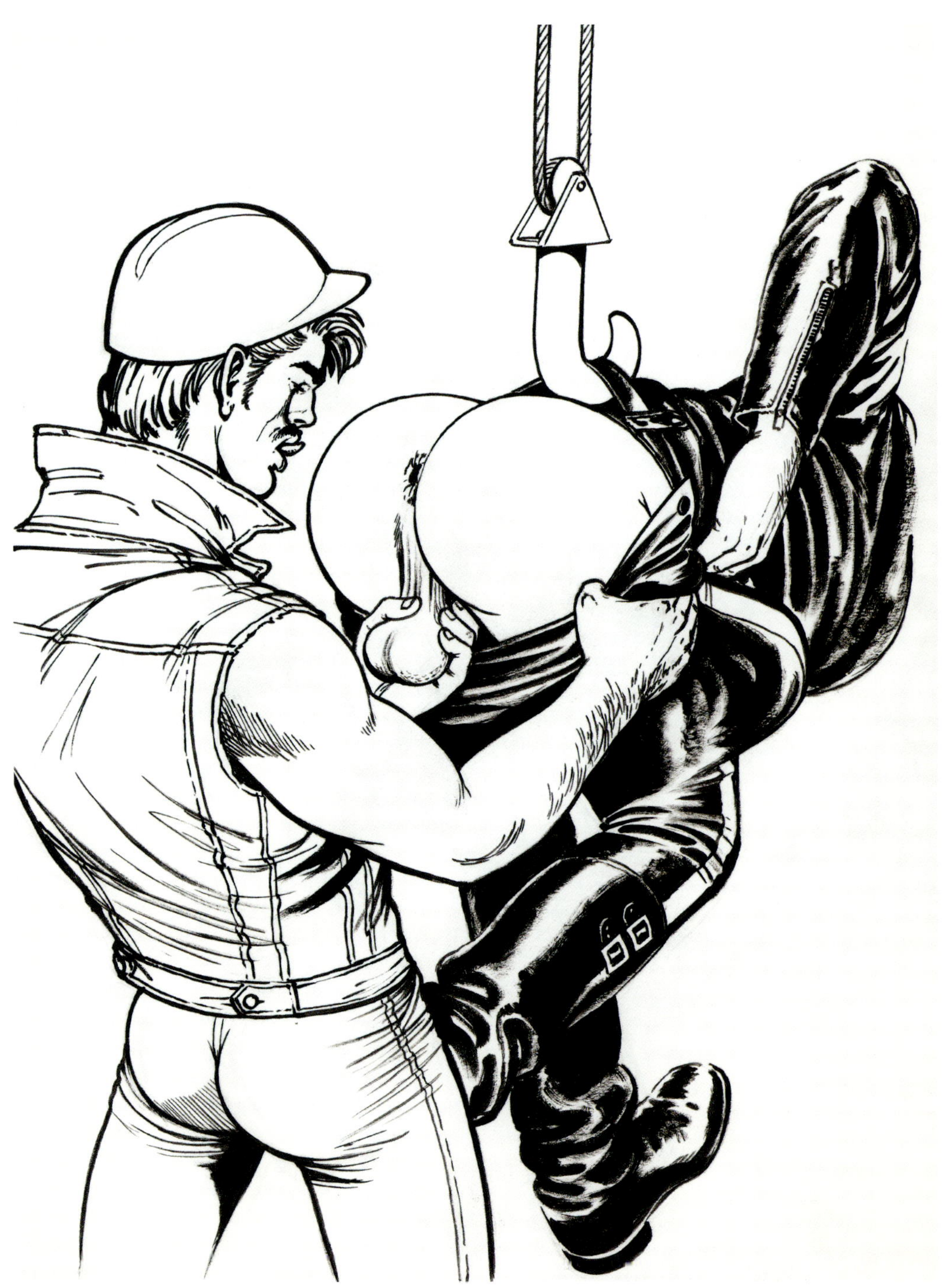

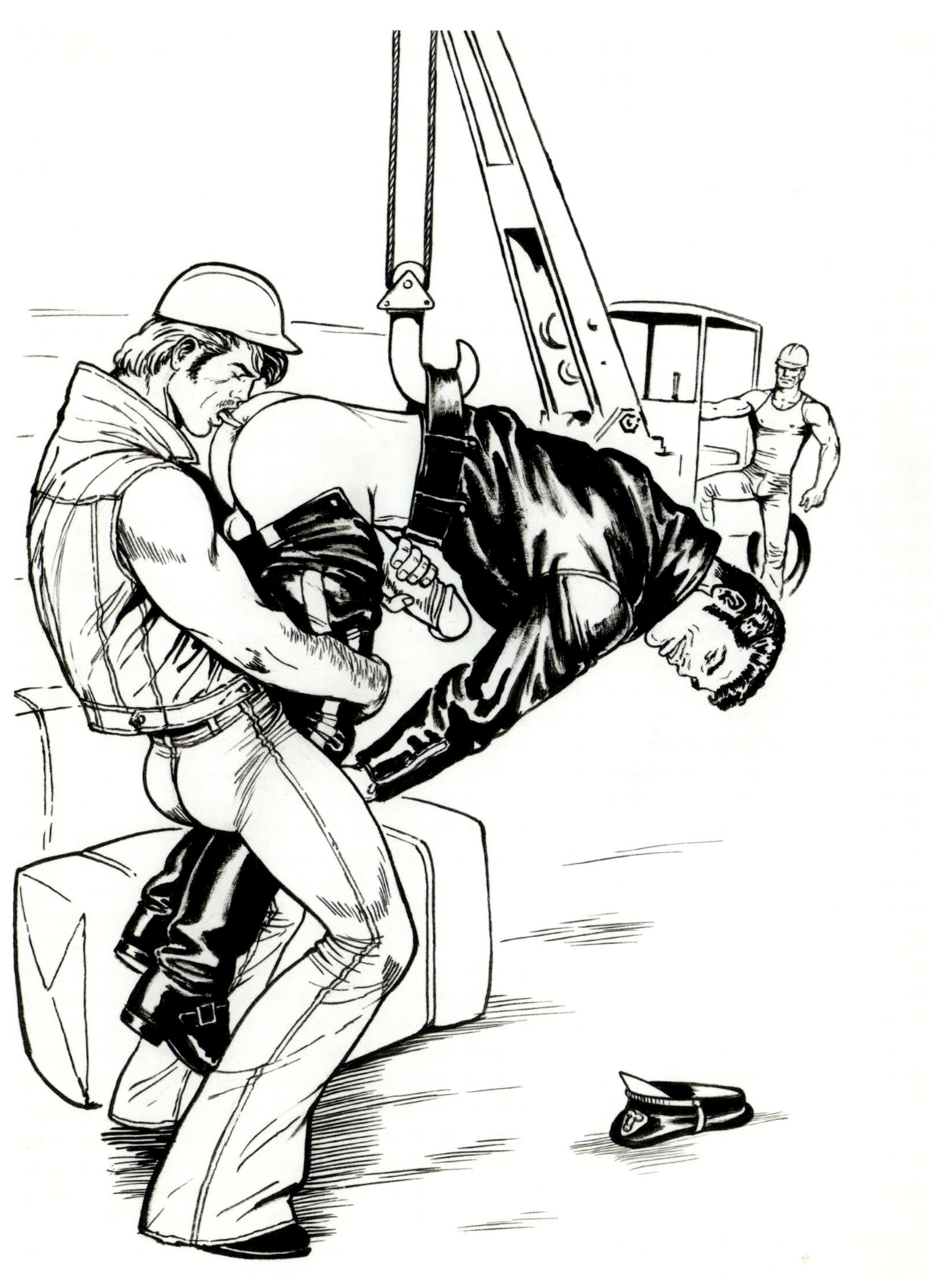

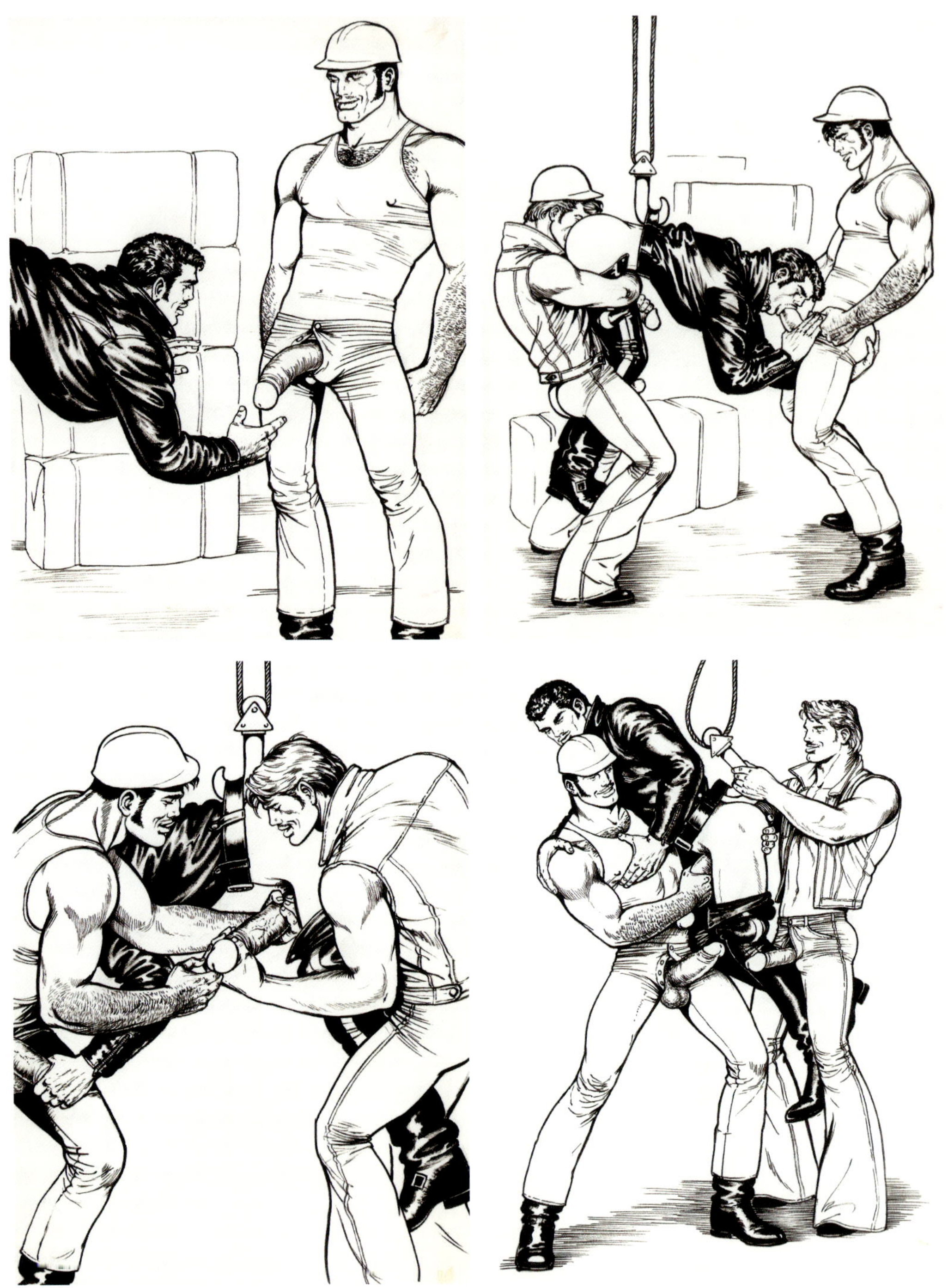

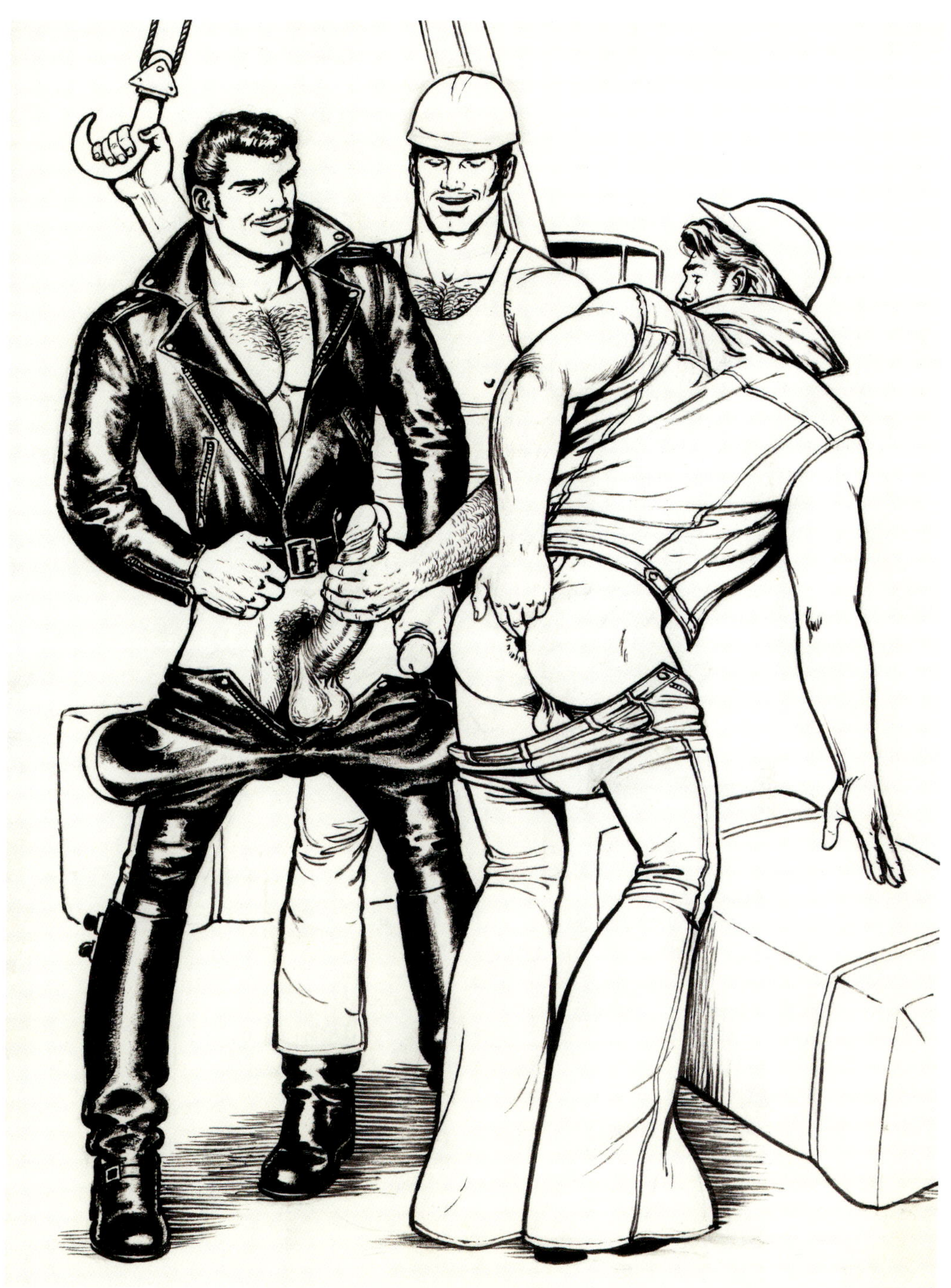

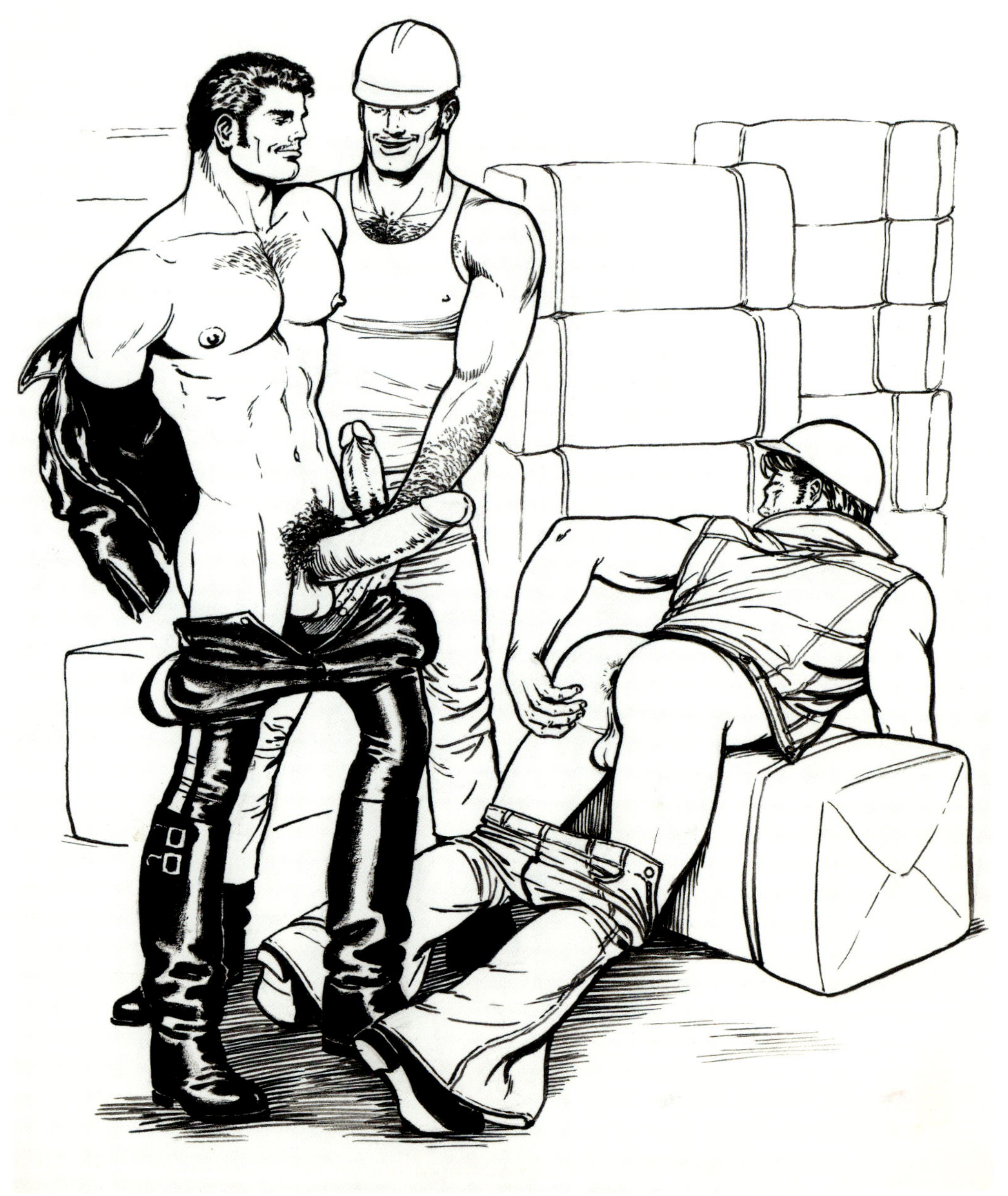

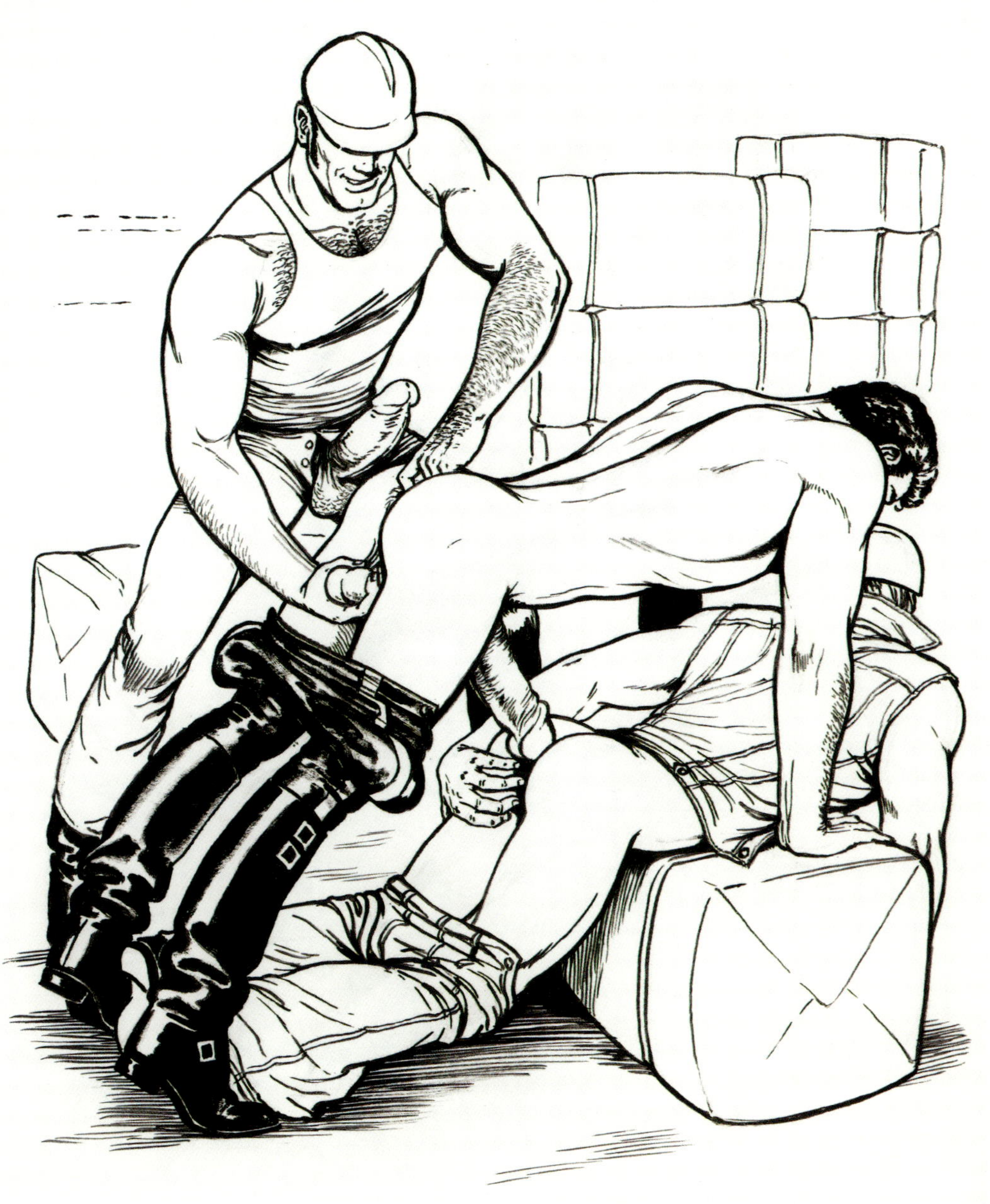

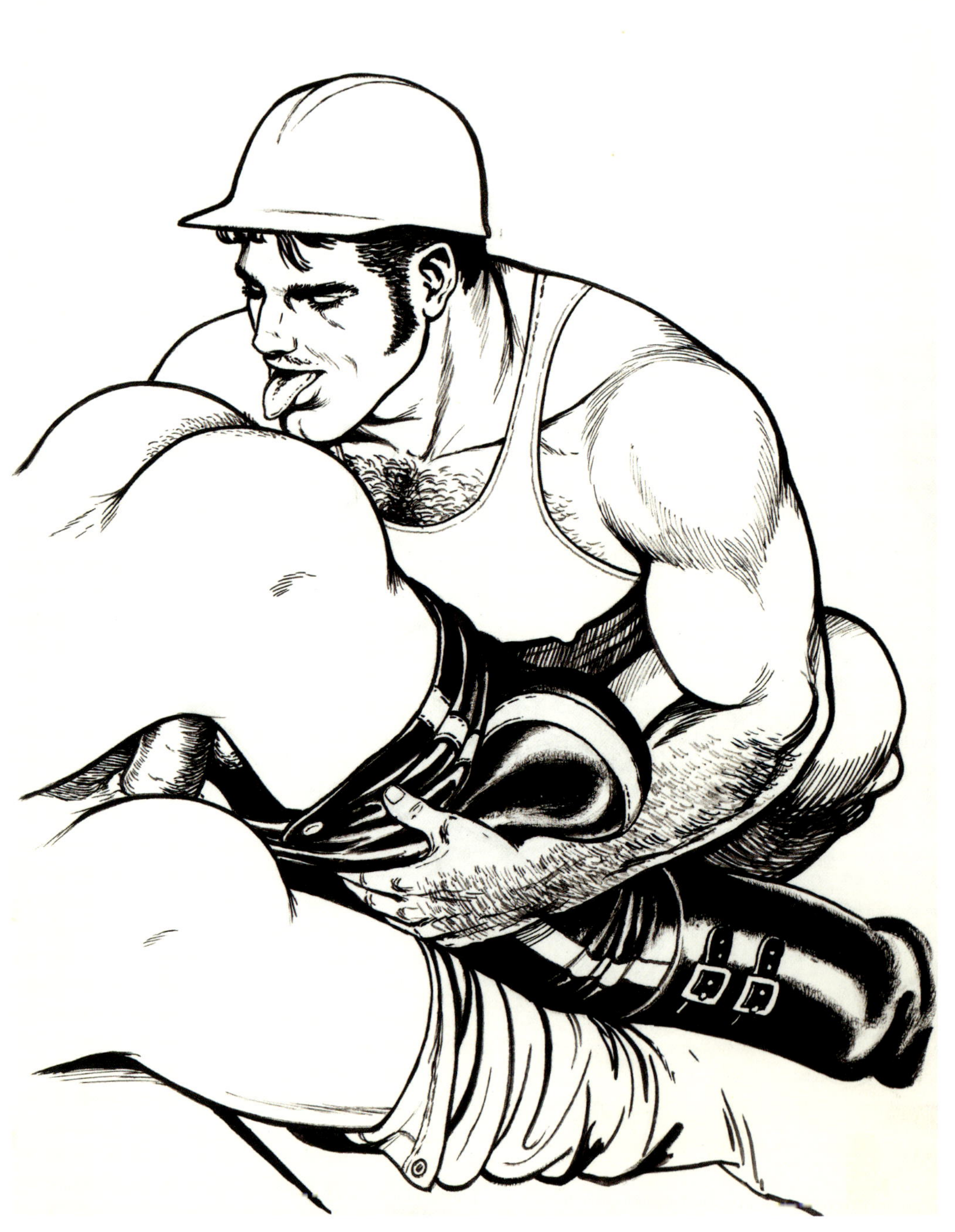

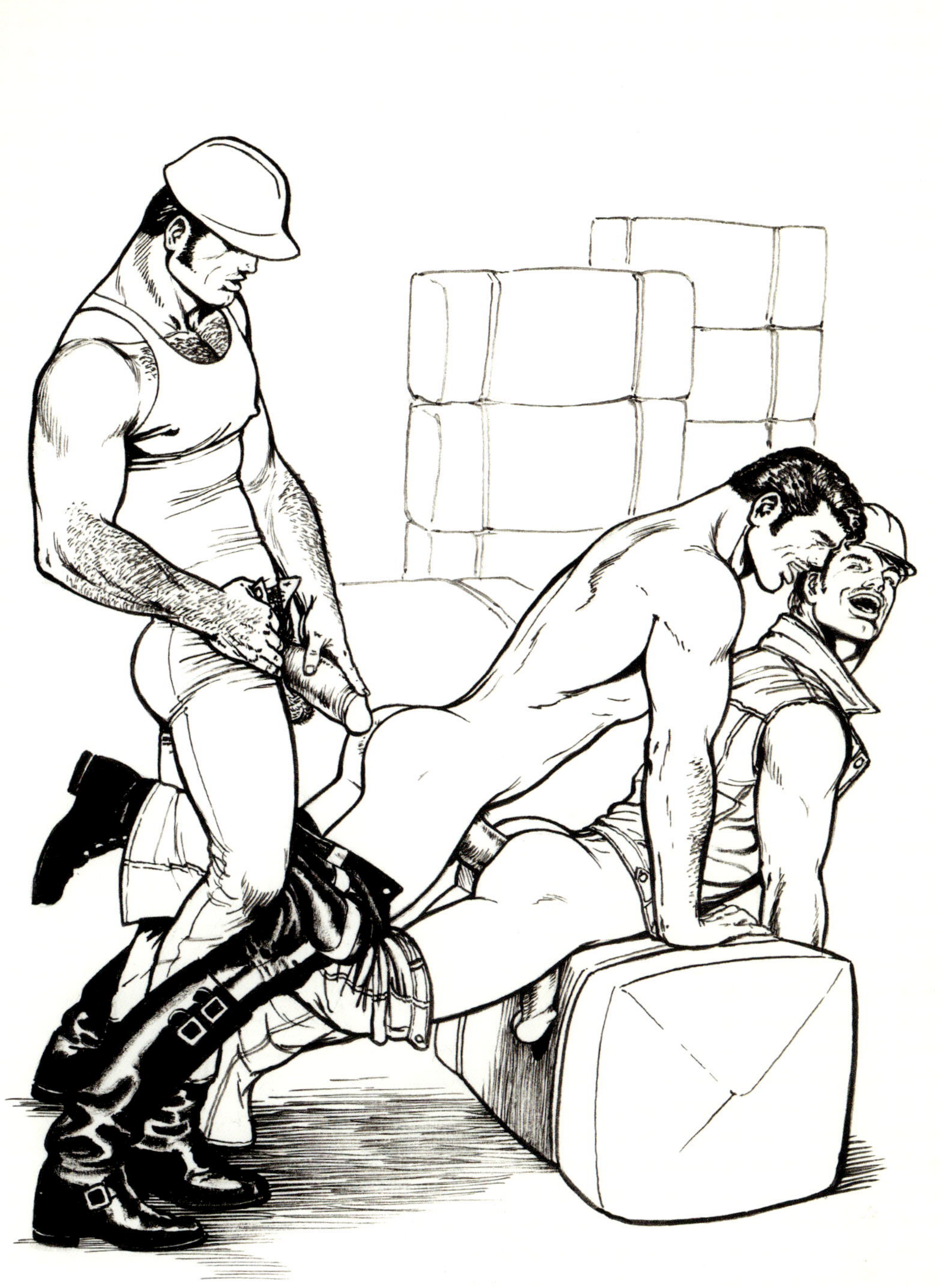

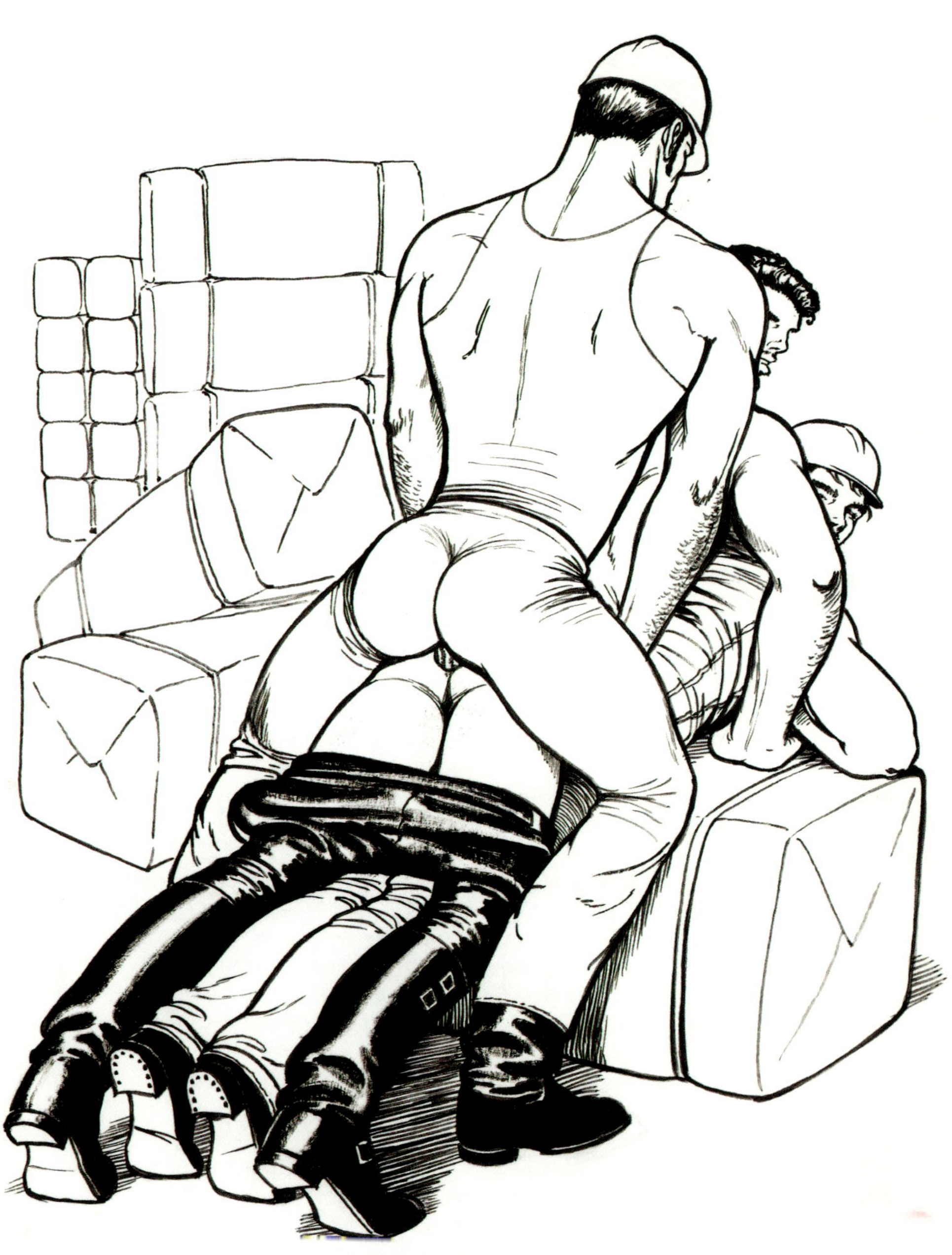

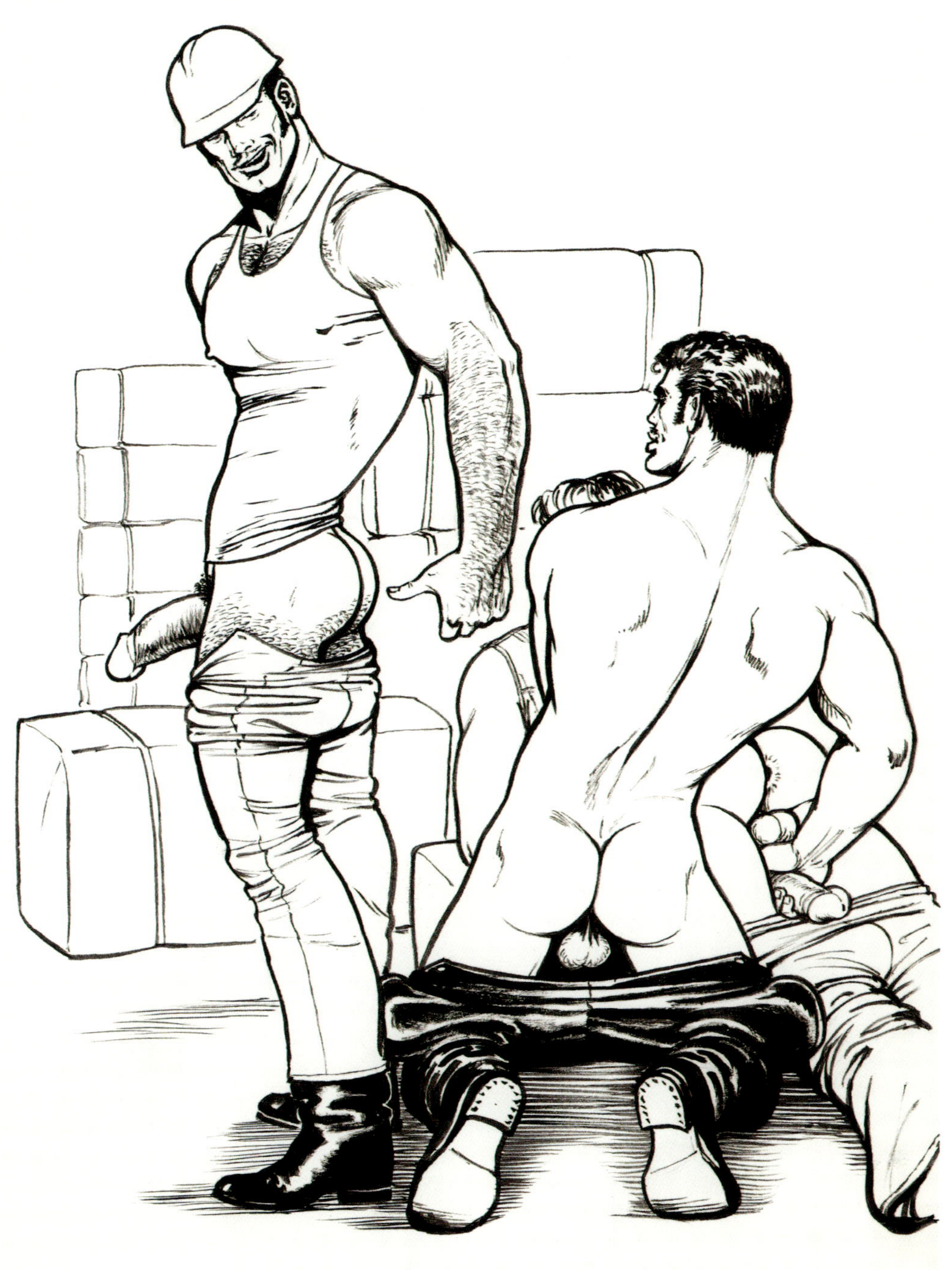

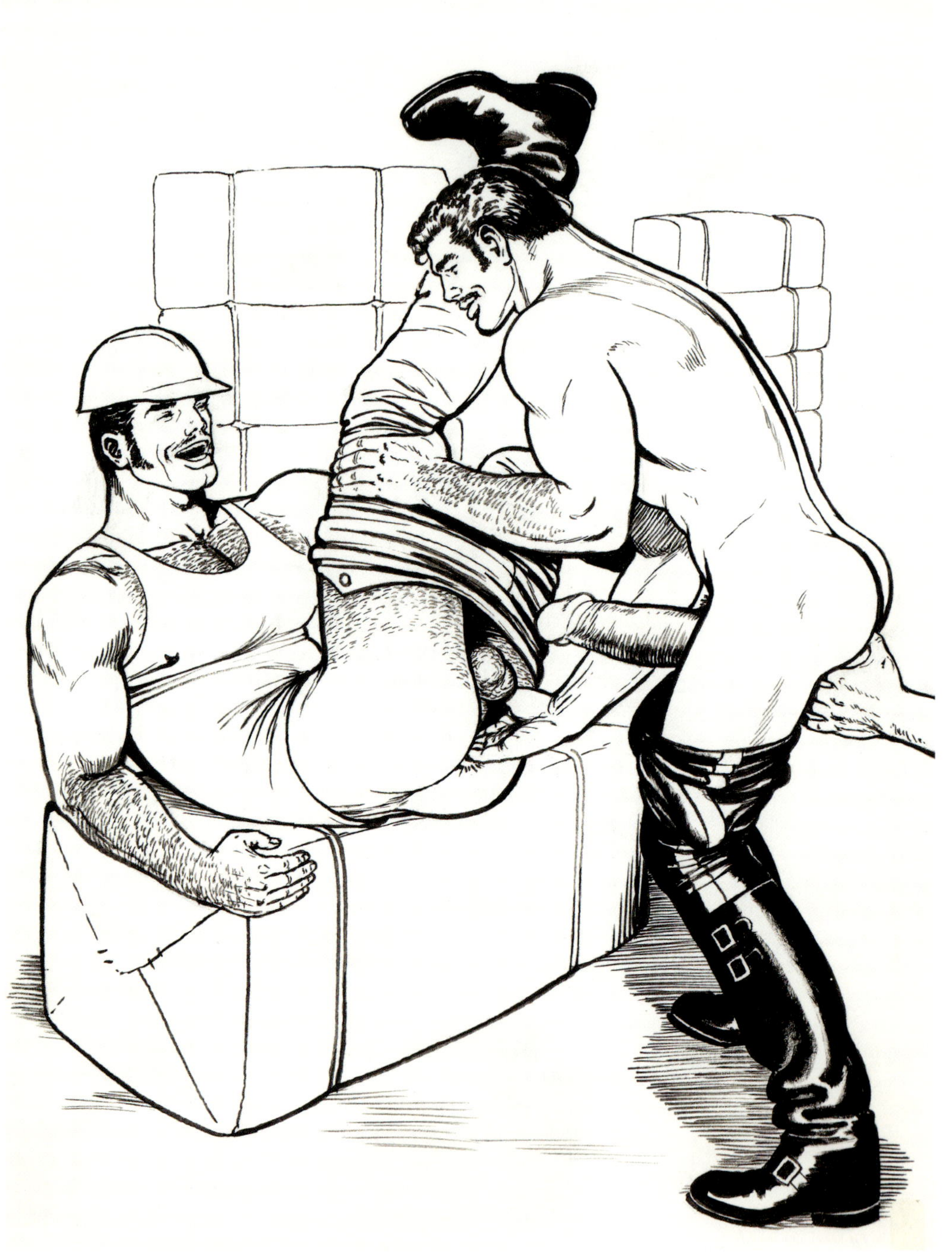

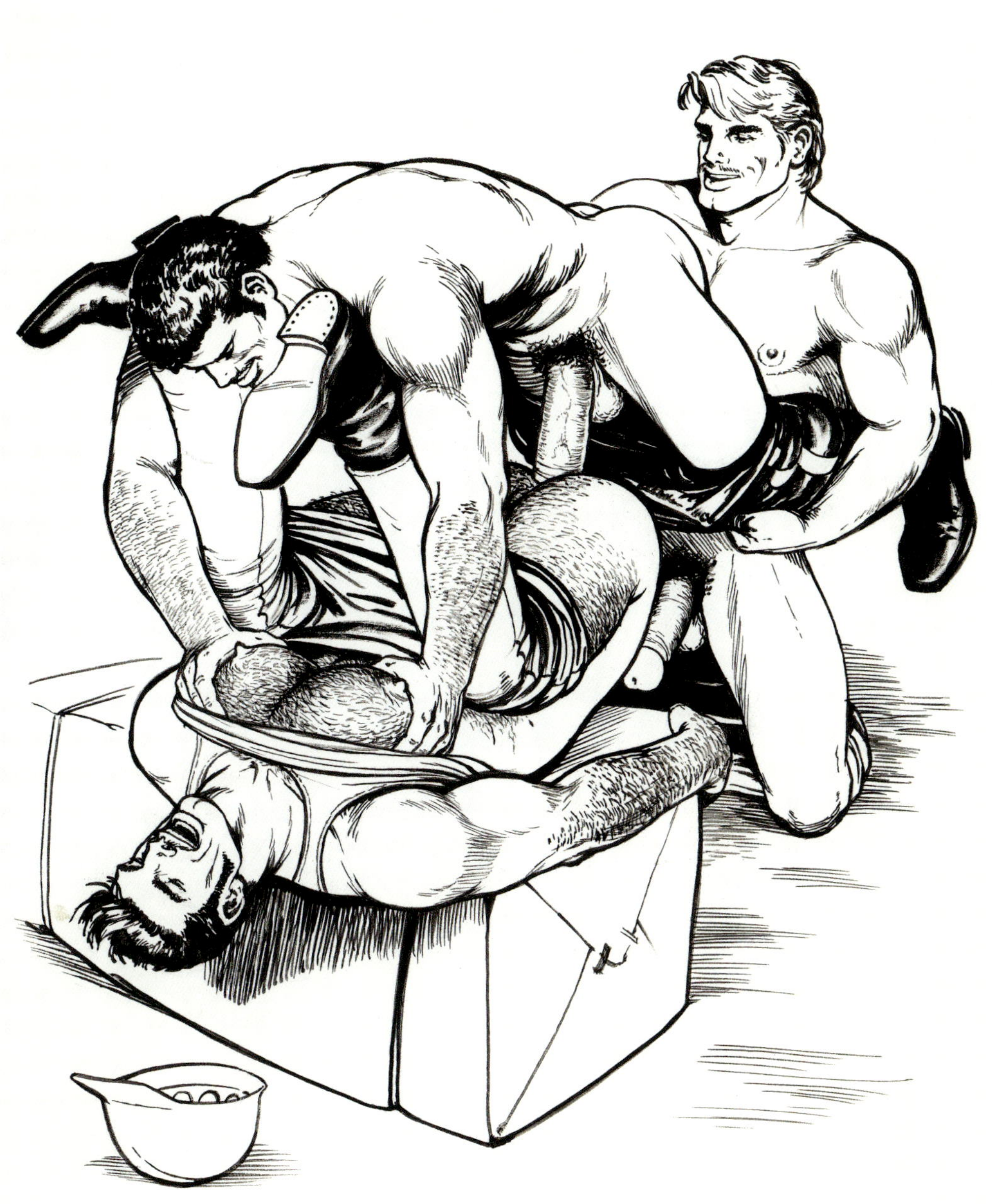

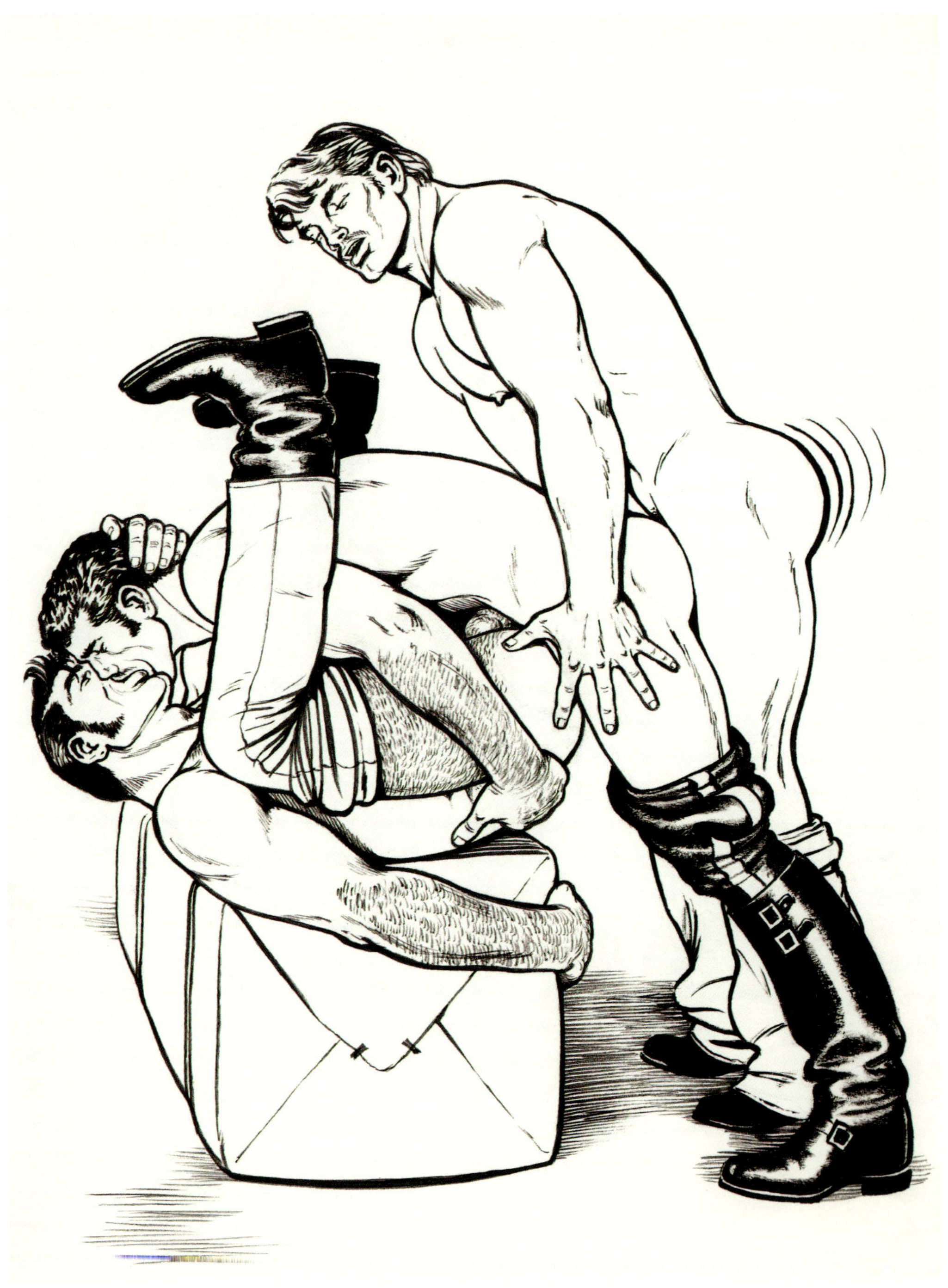

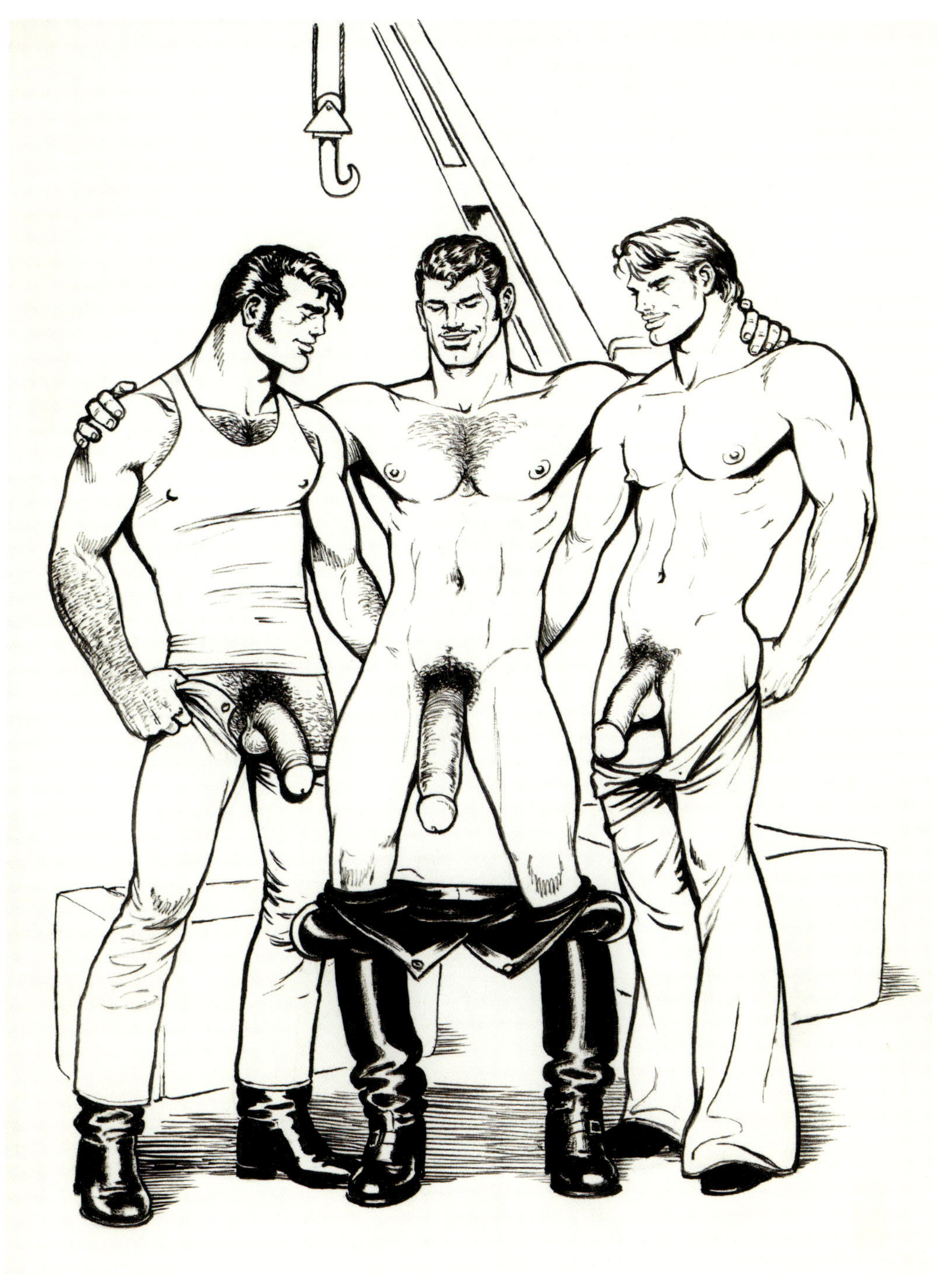

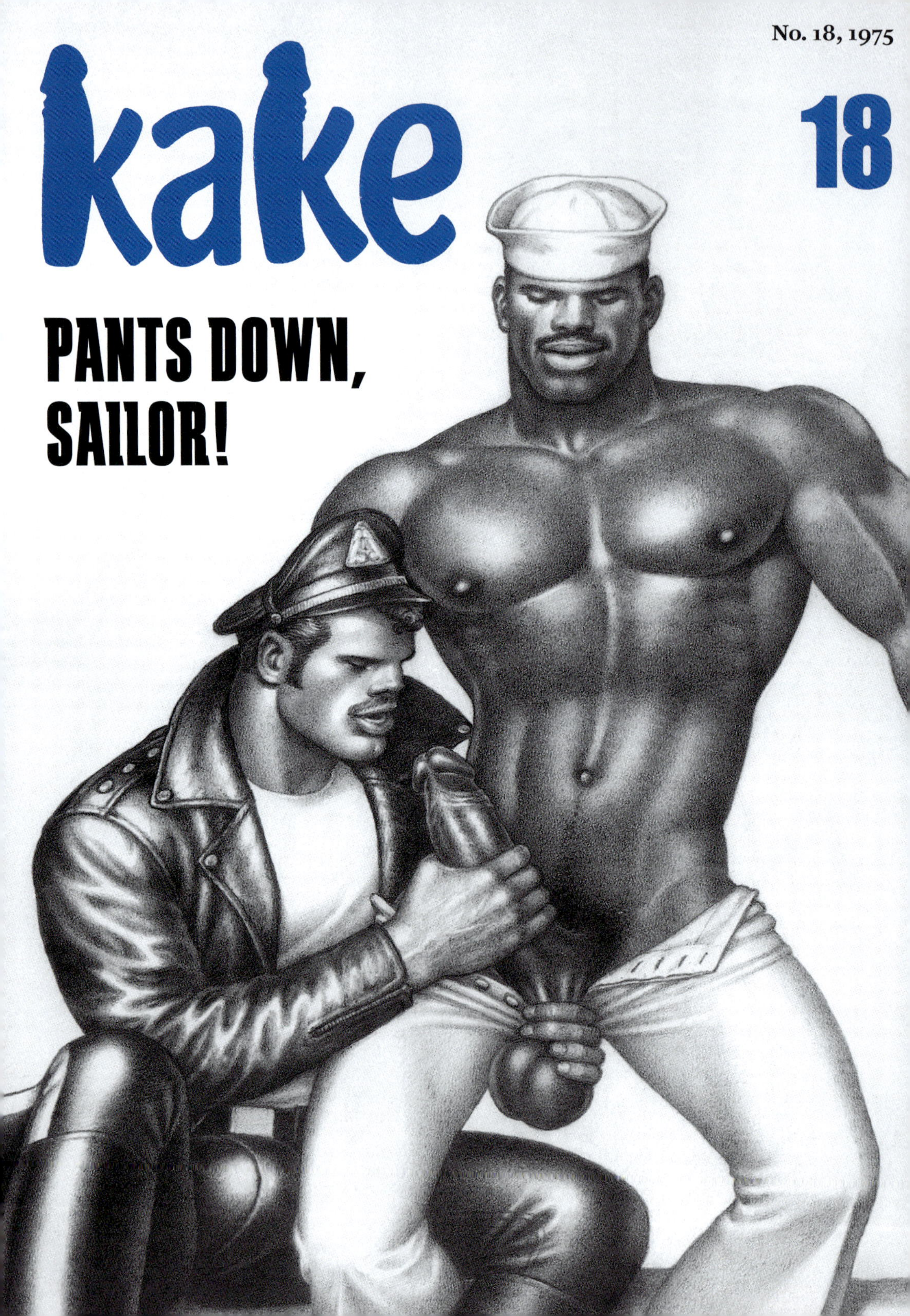

No. 18, 1975
kake
18
PANTS DOWN,
SAILOR!

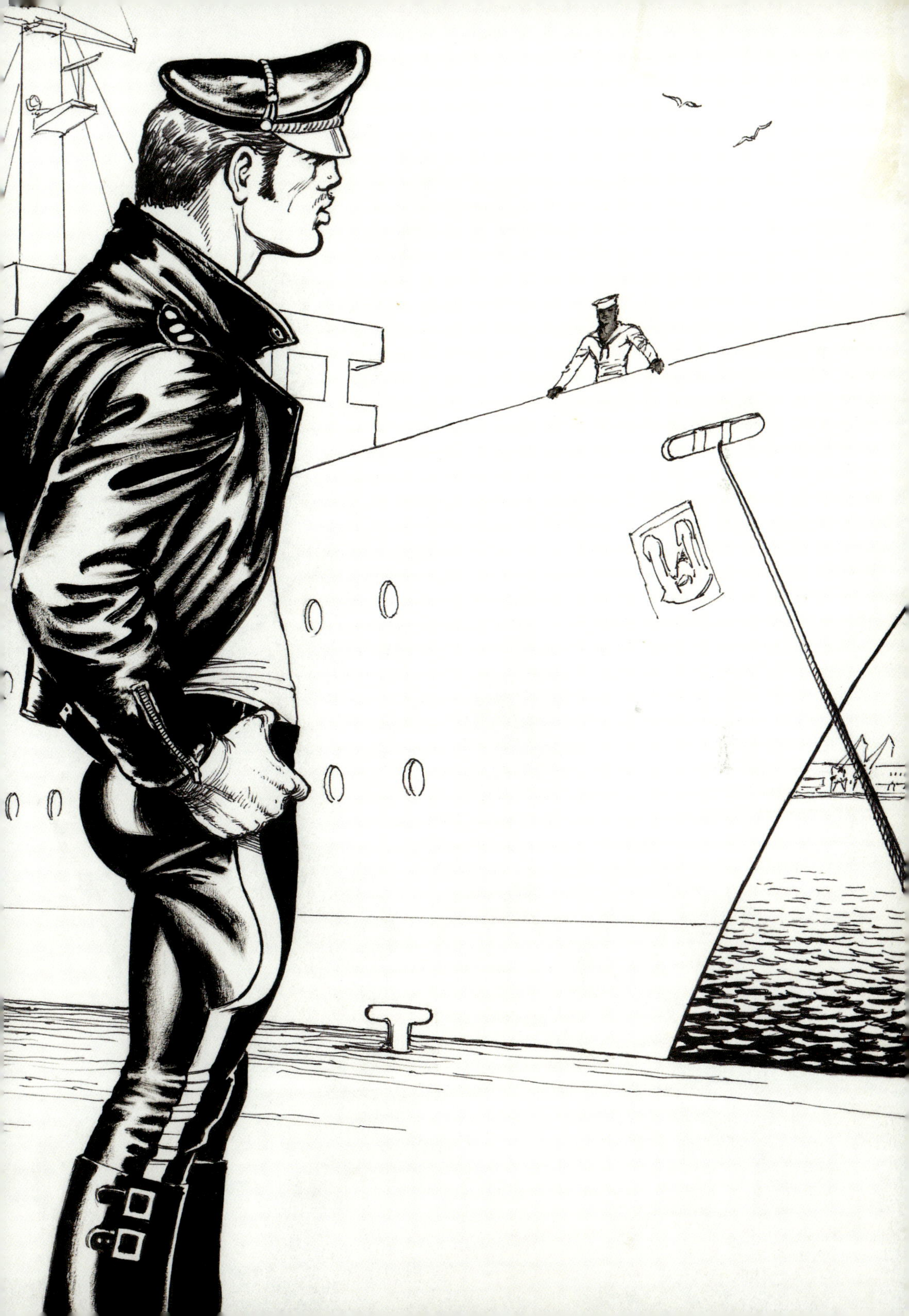

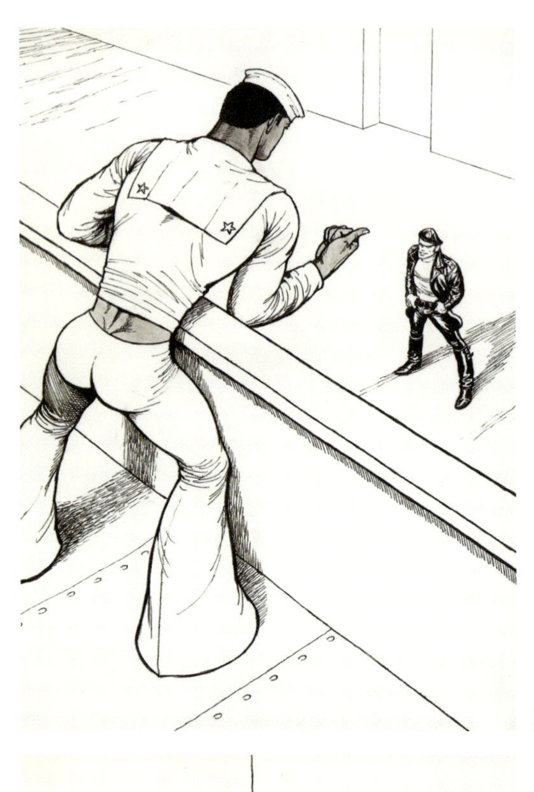
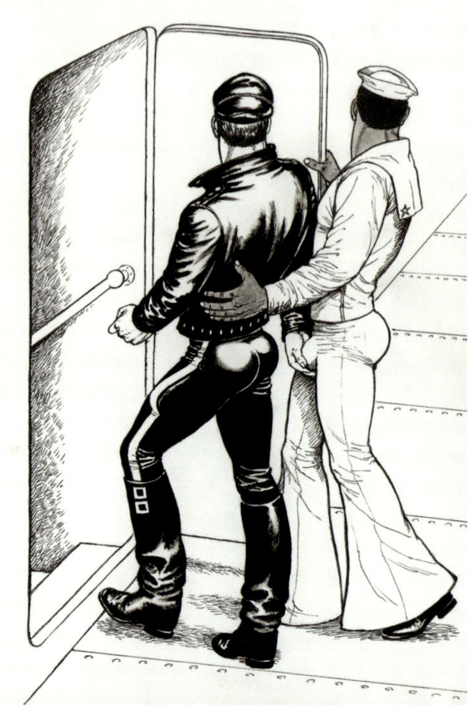
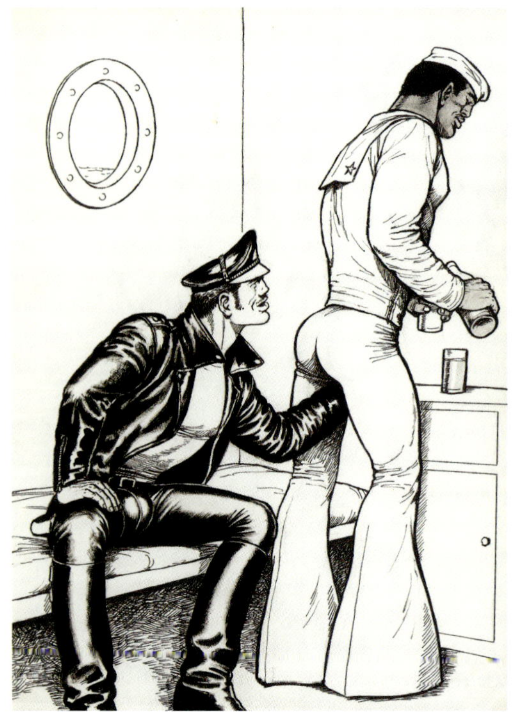
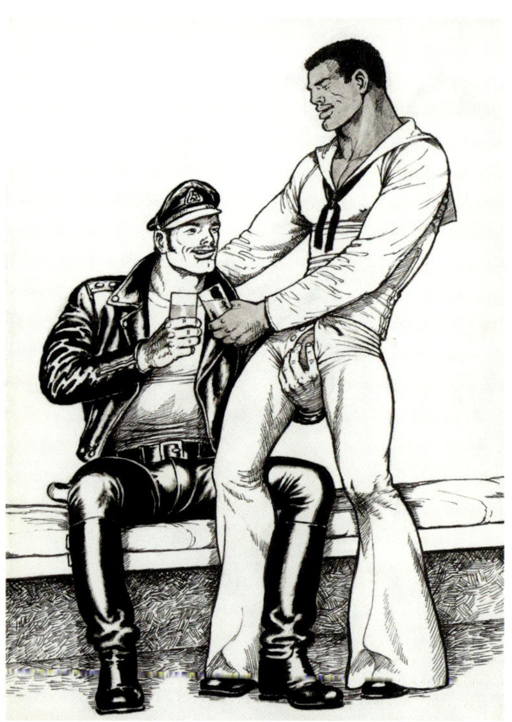

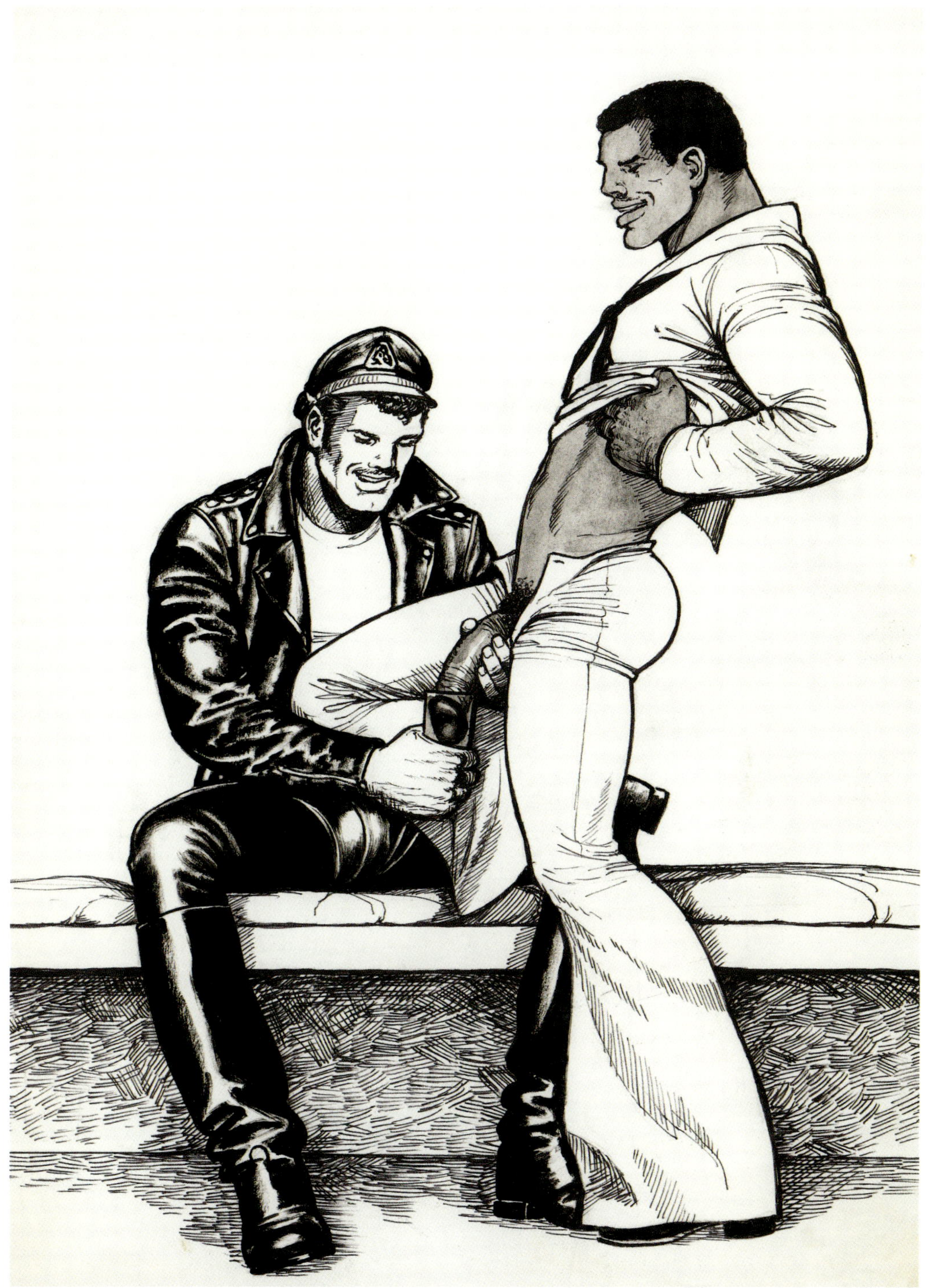

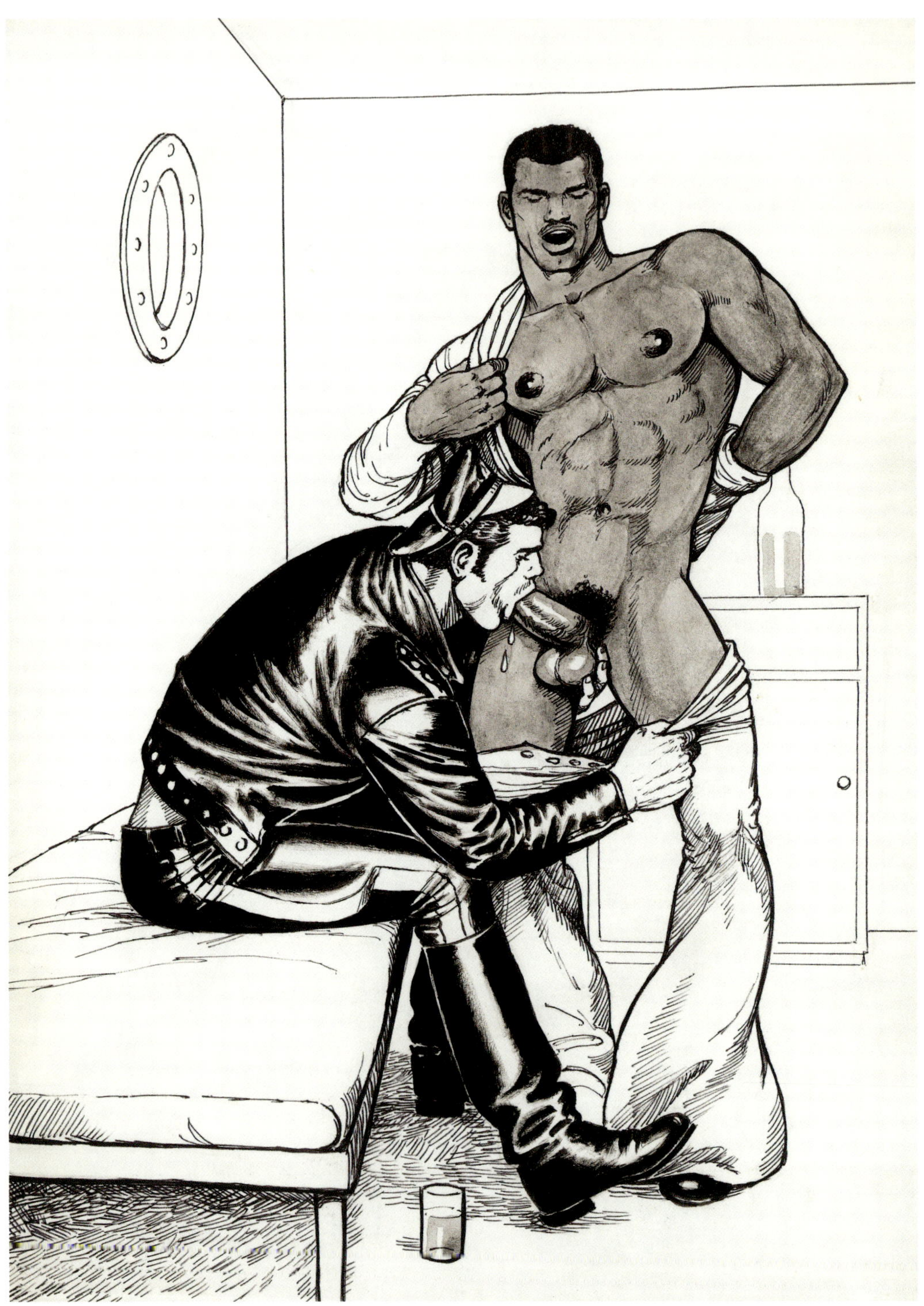

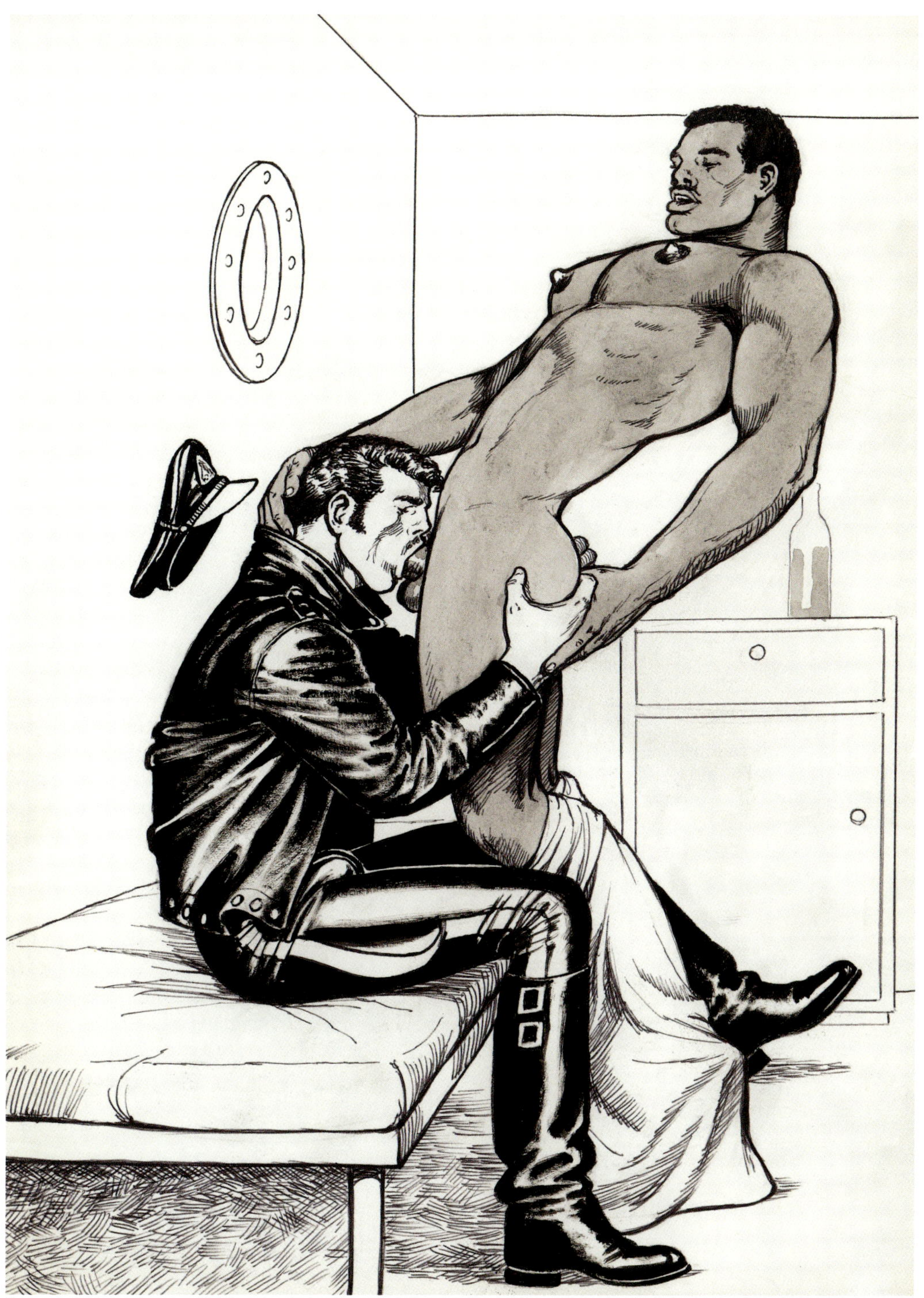

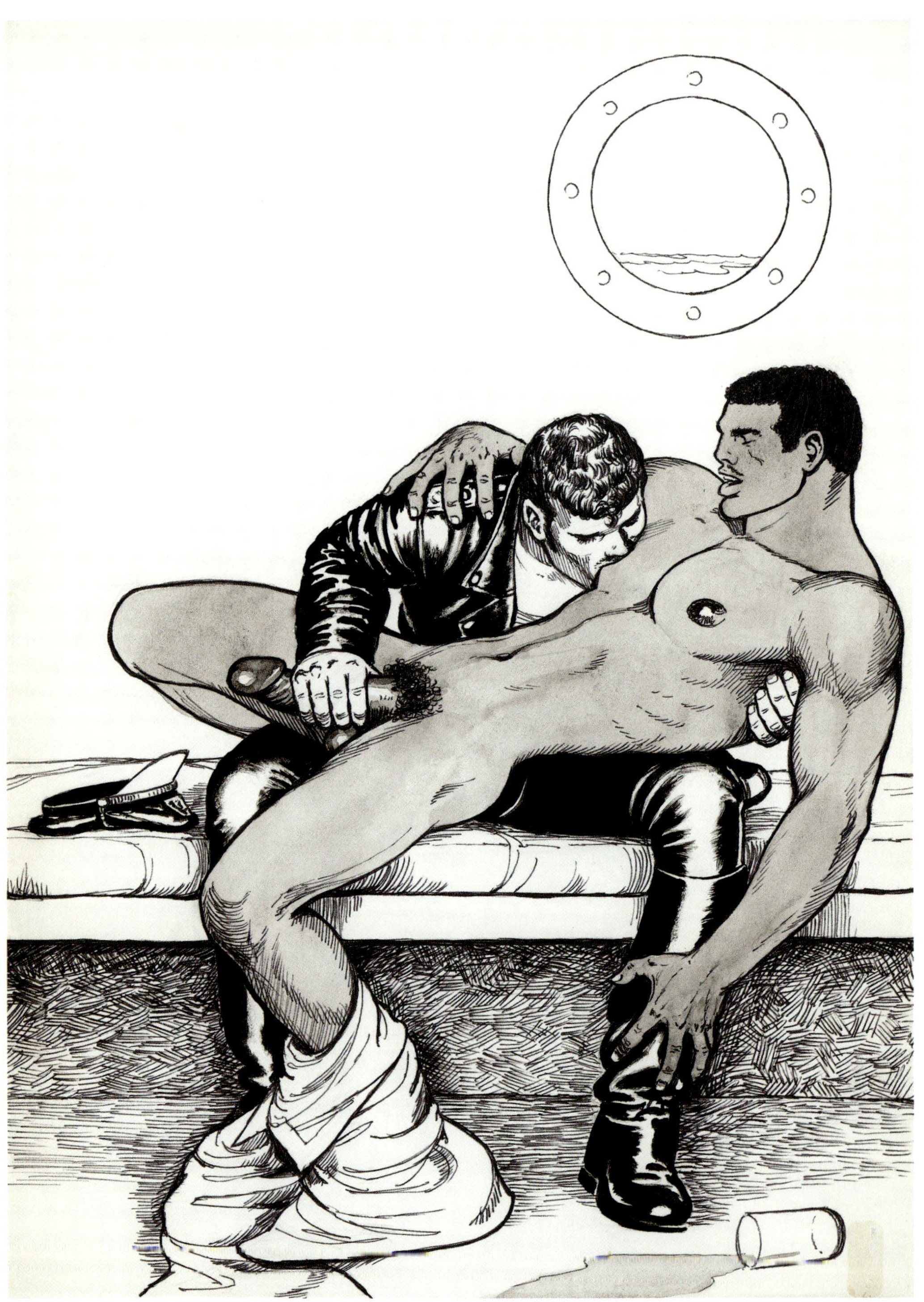

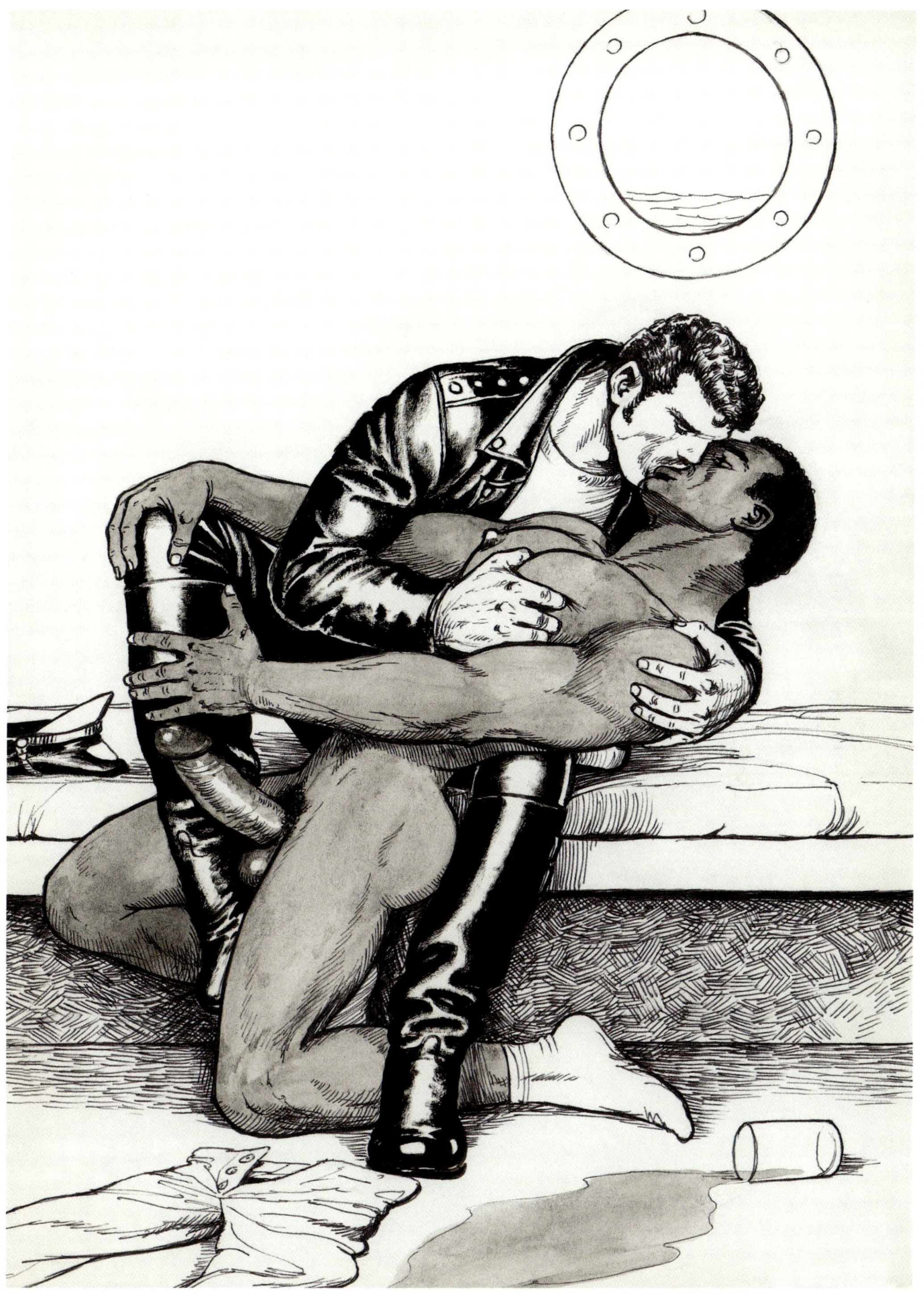

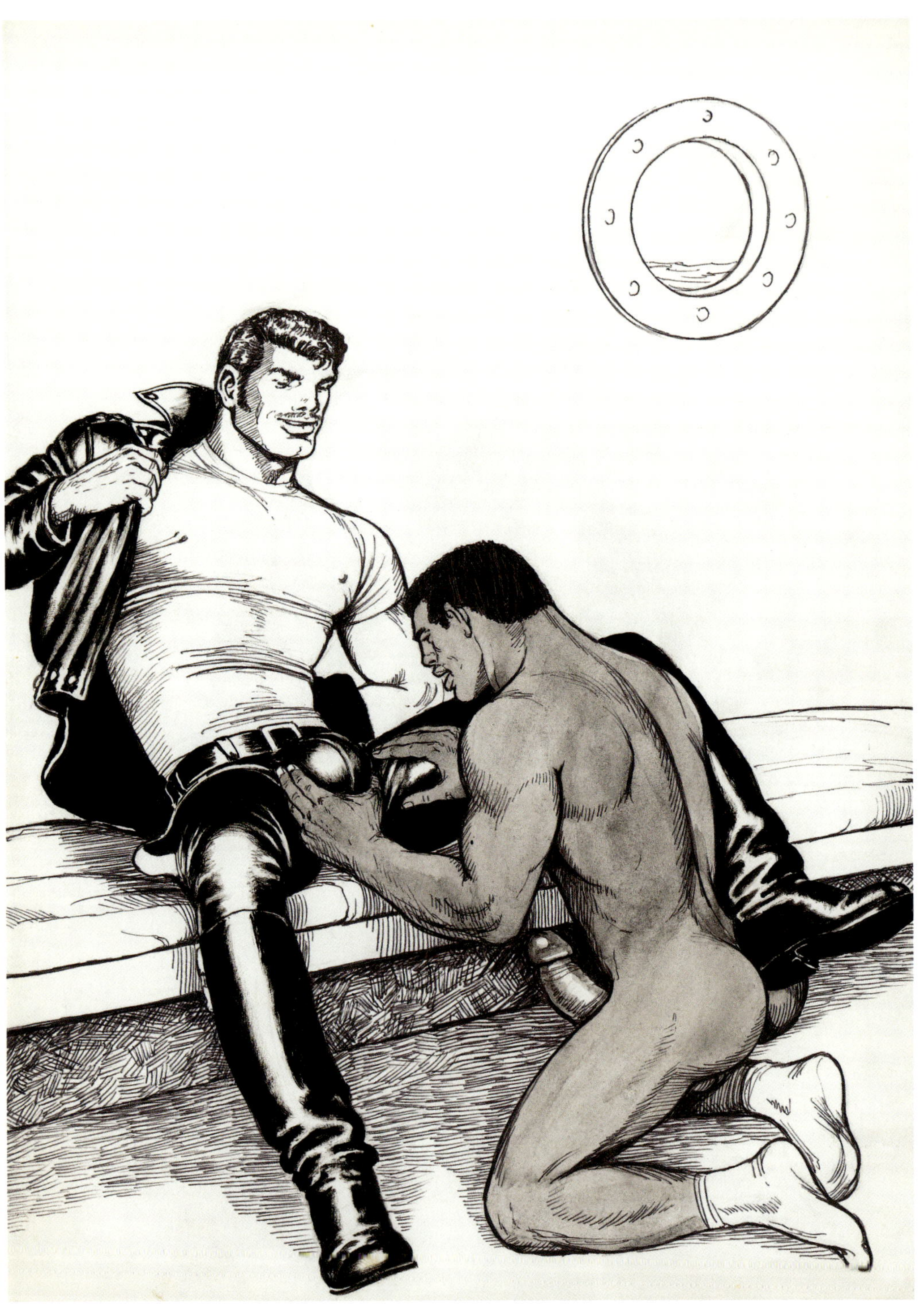

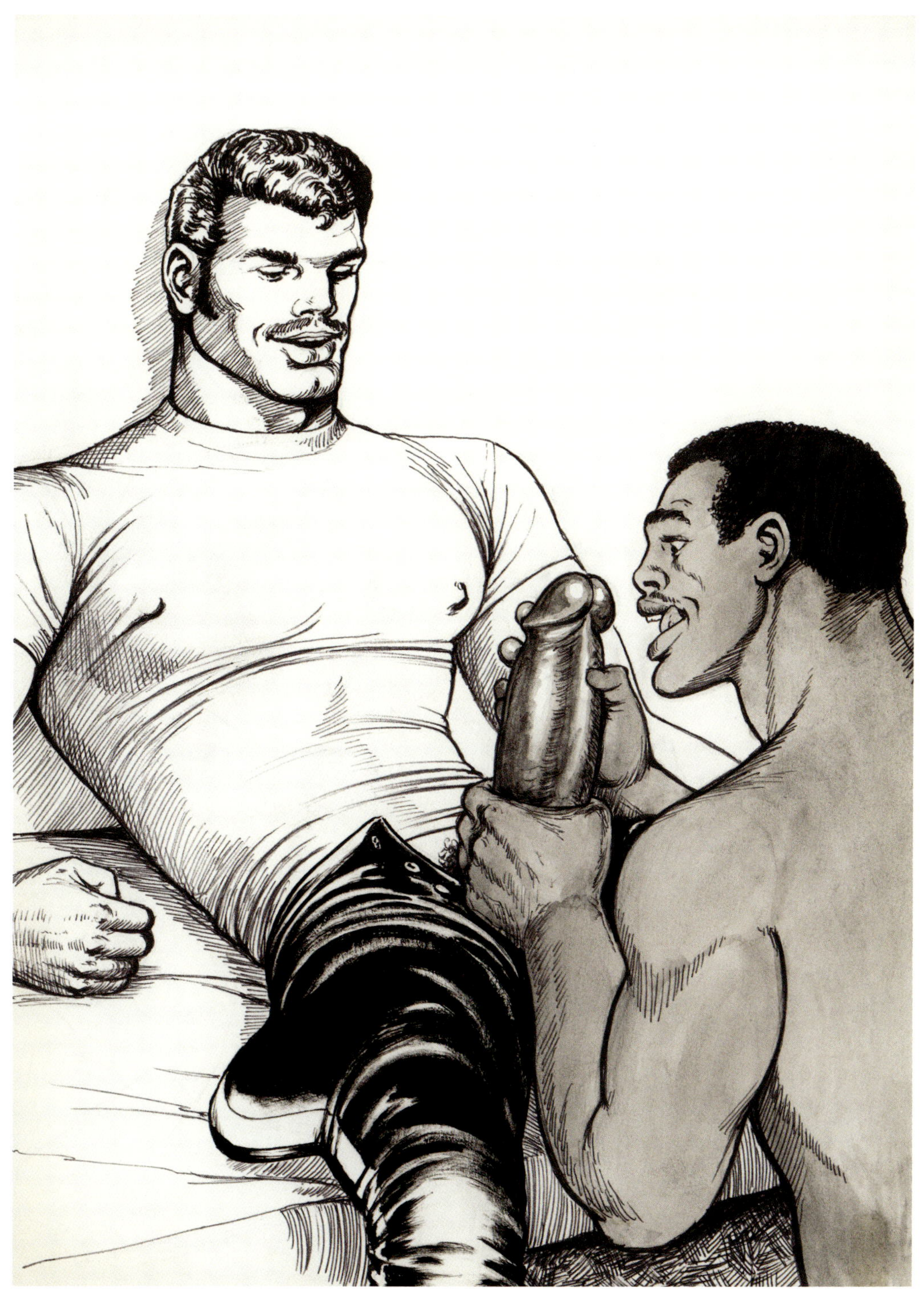

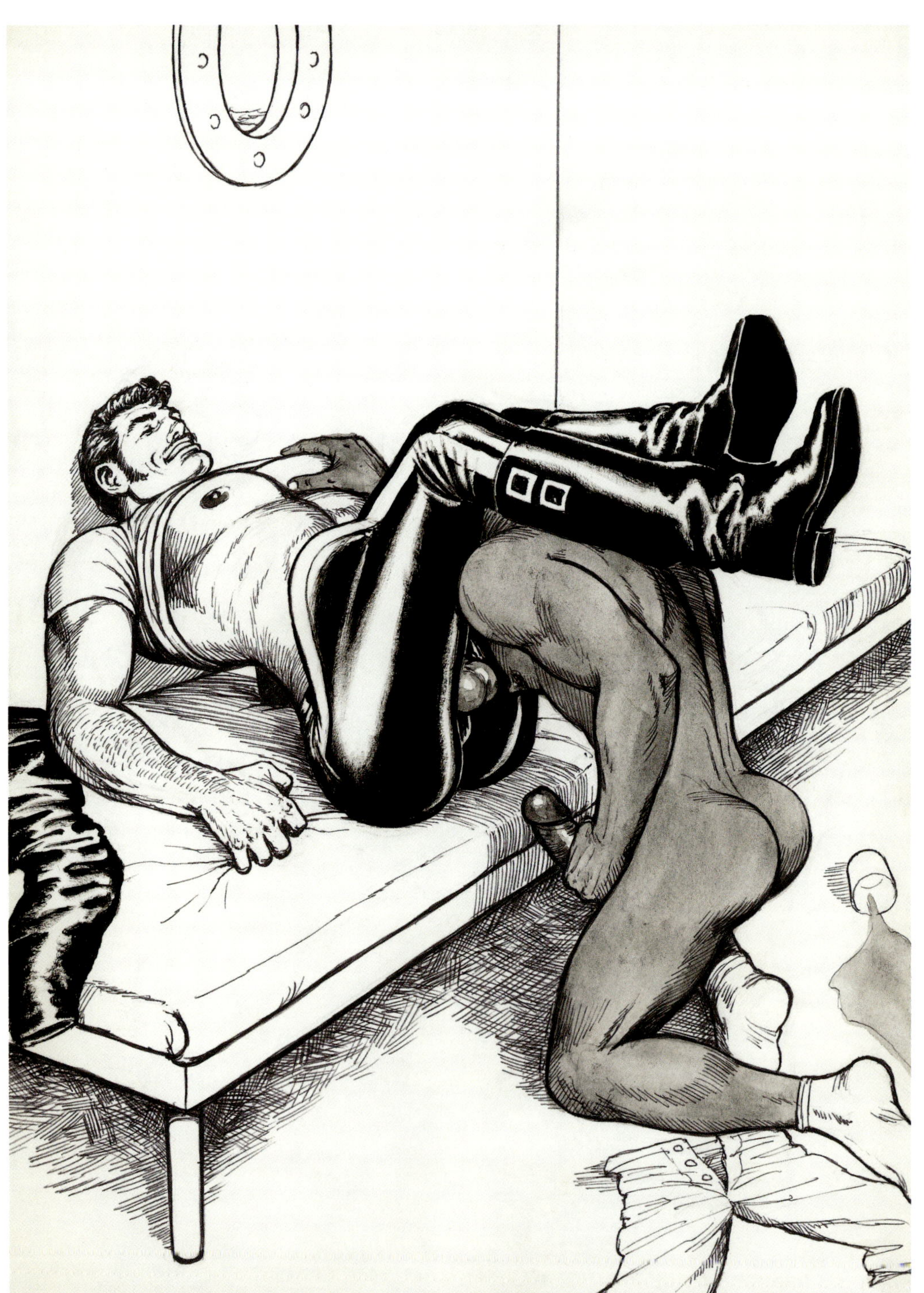

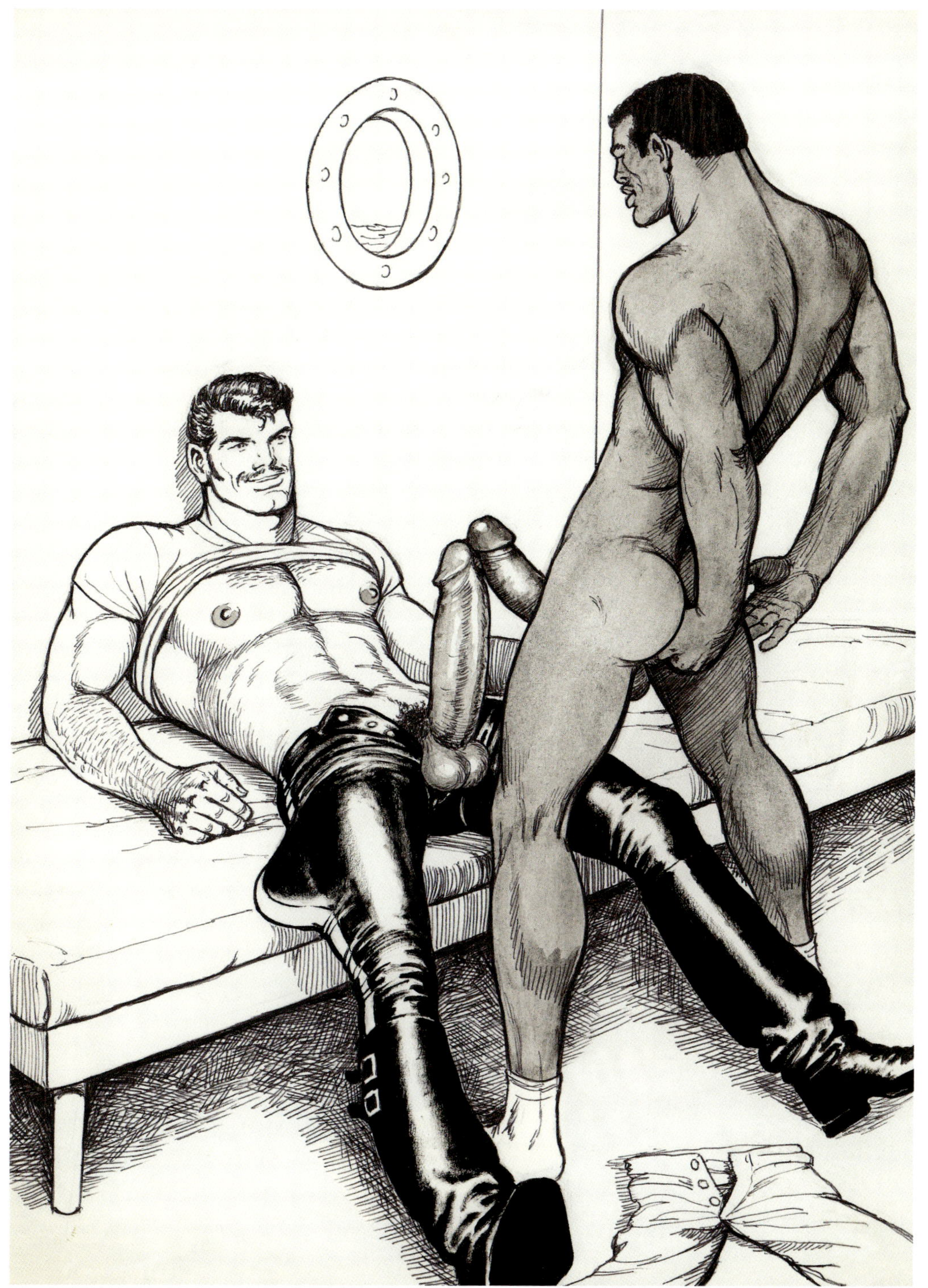

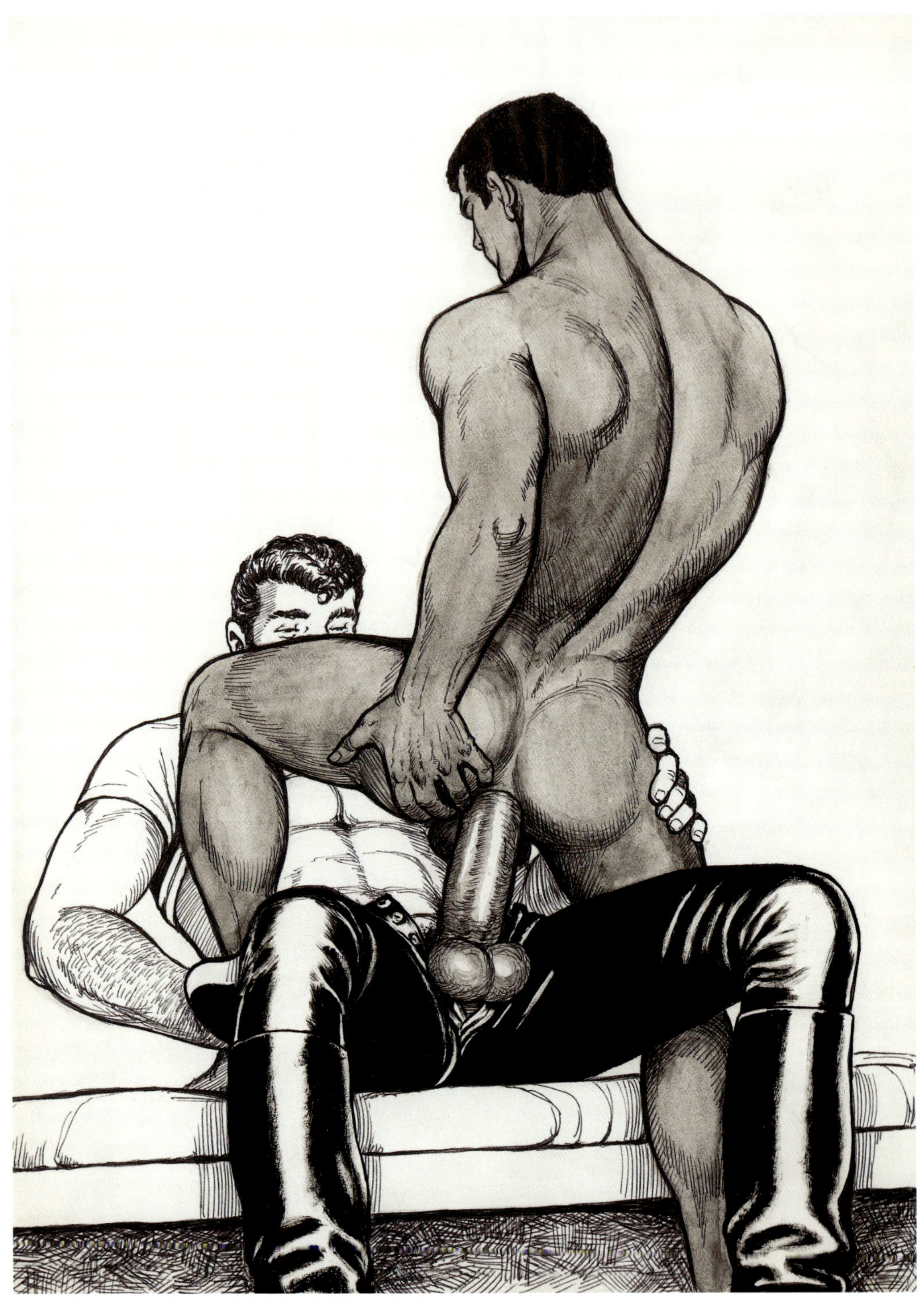

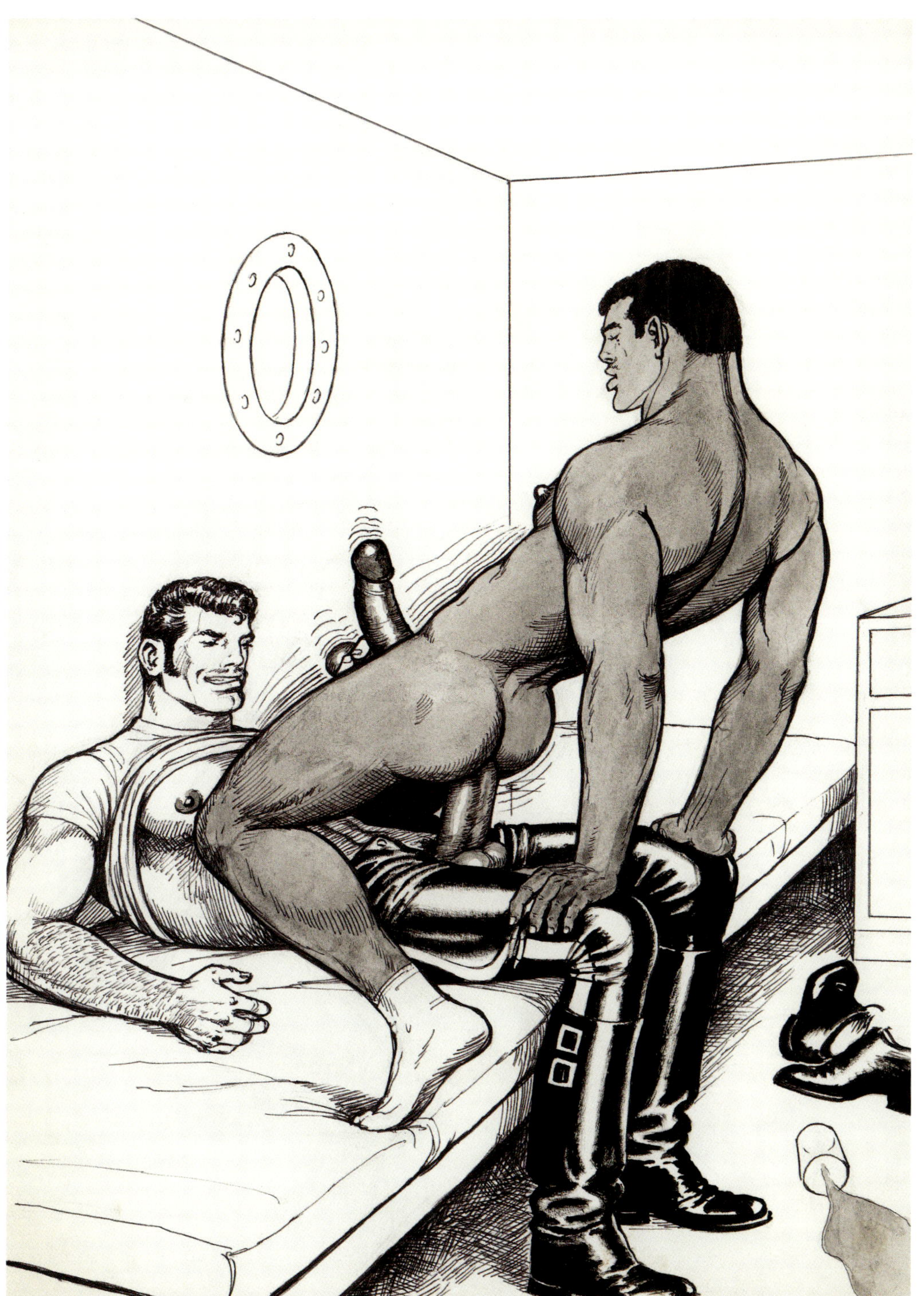

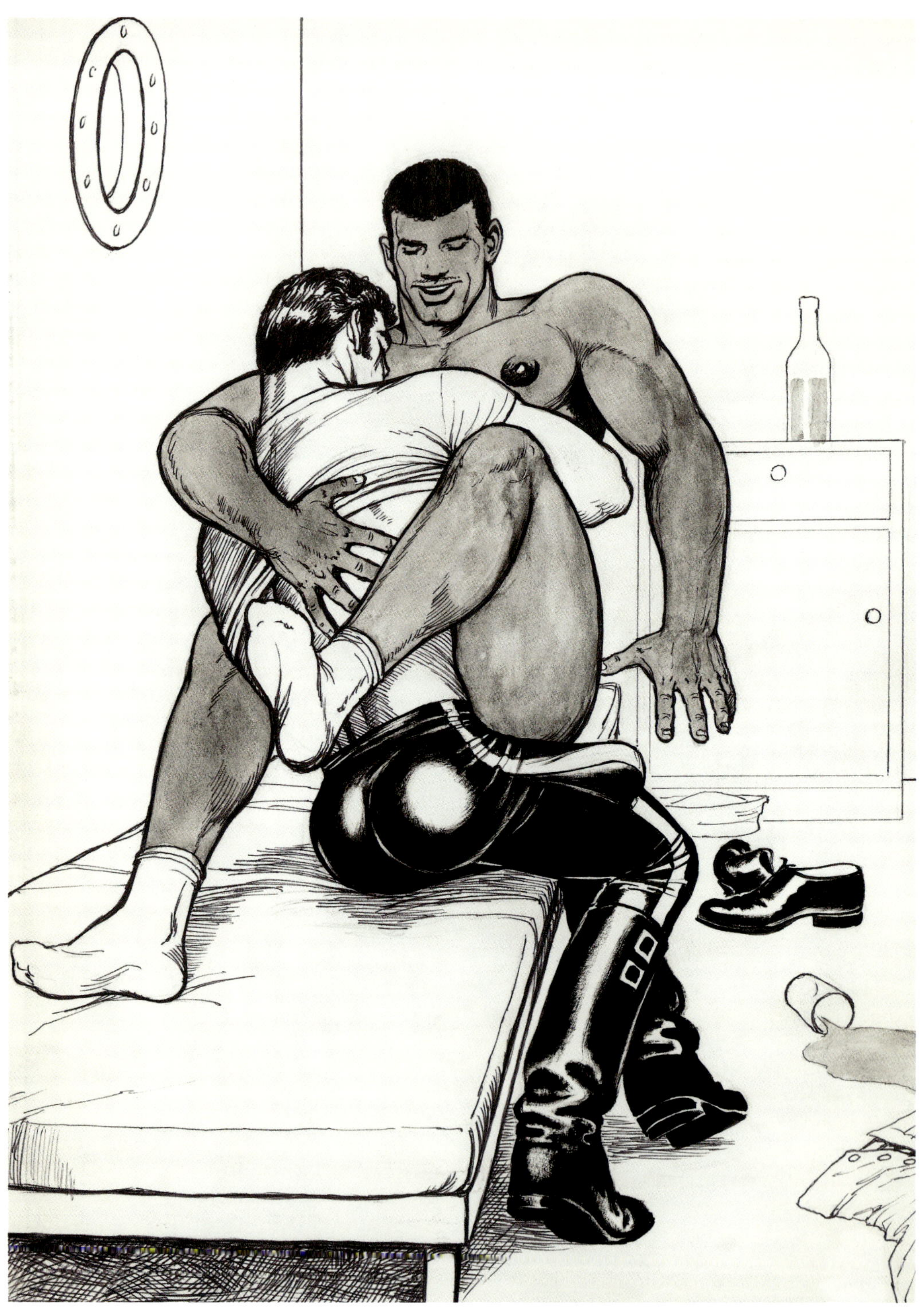

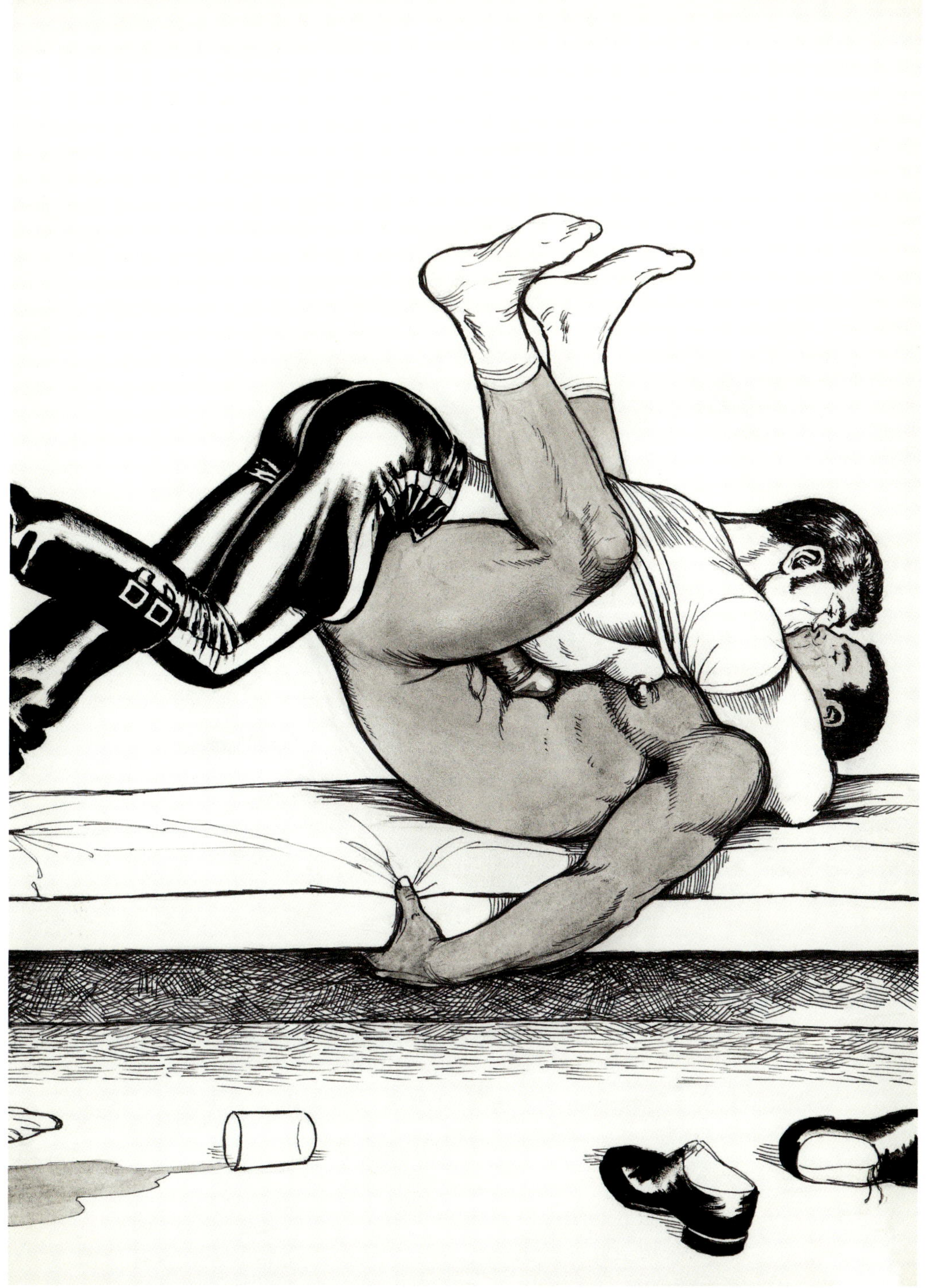

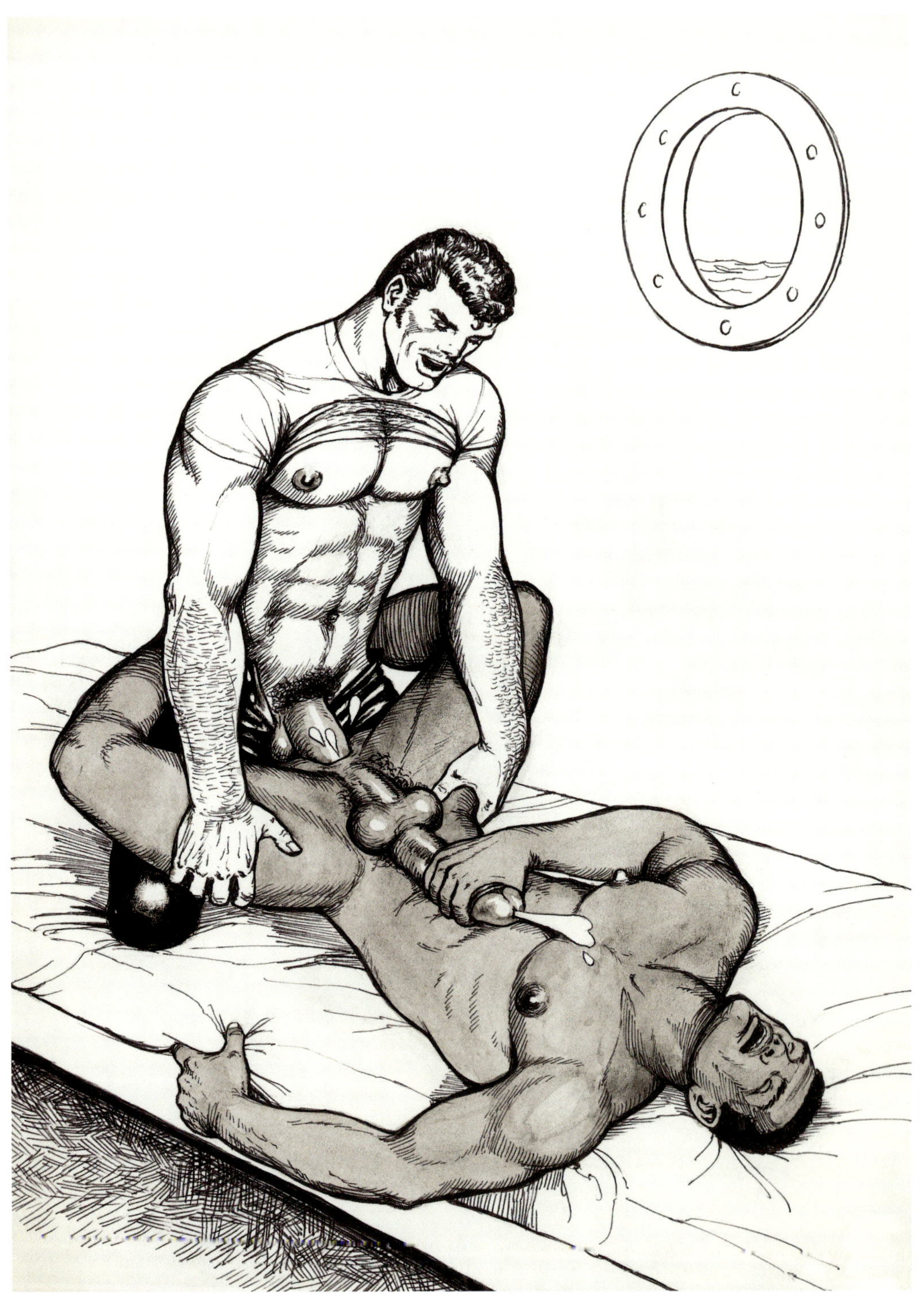

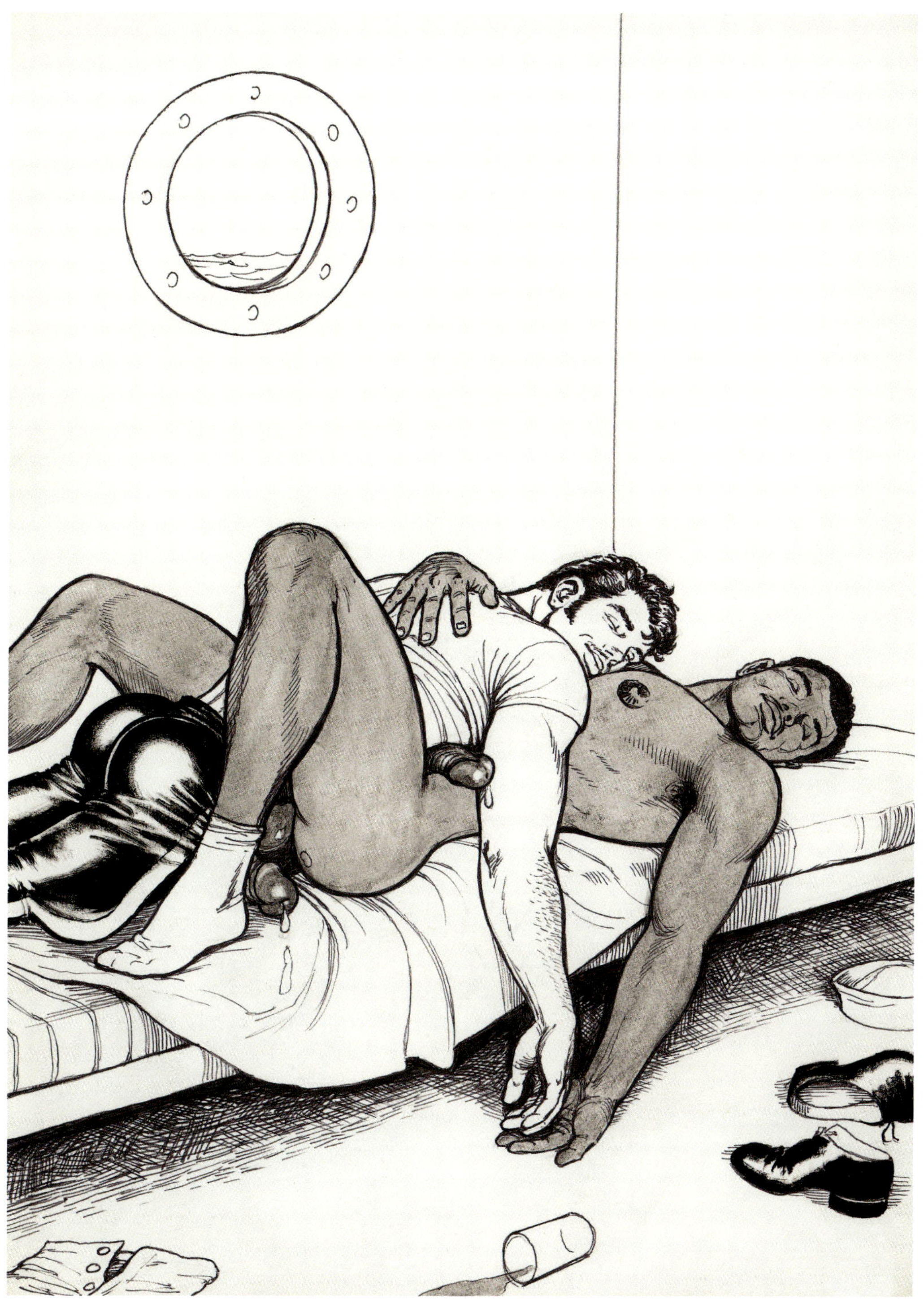

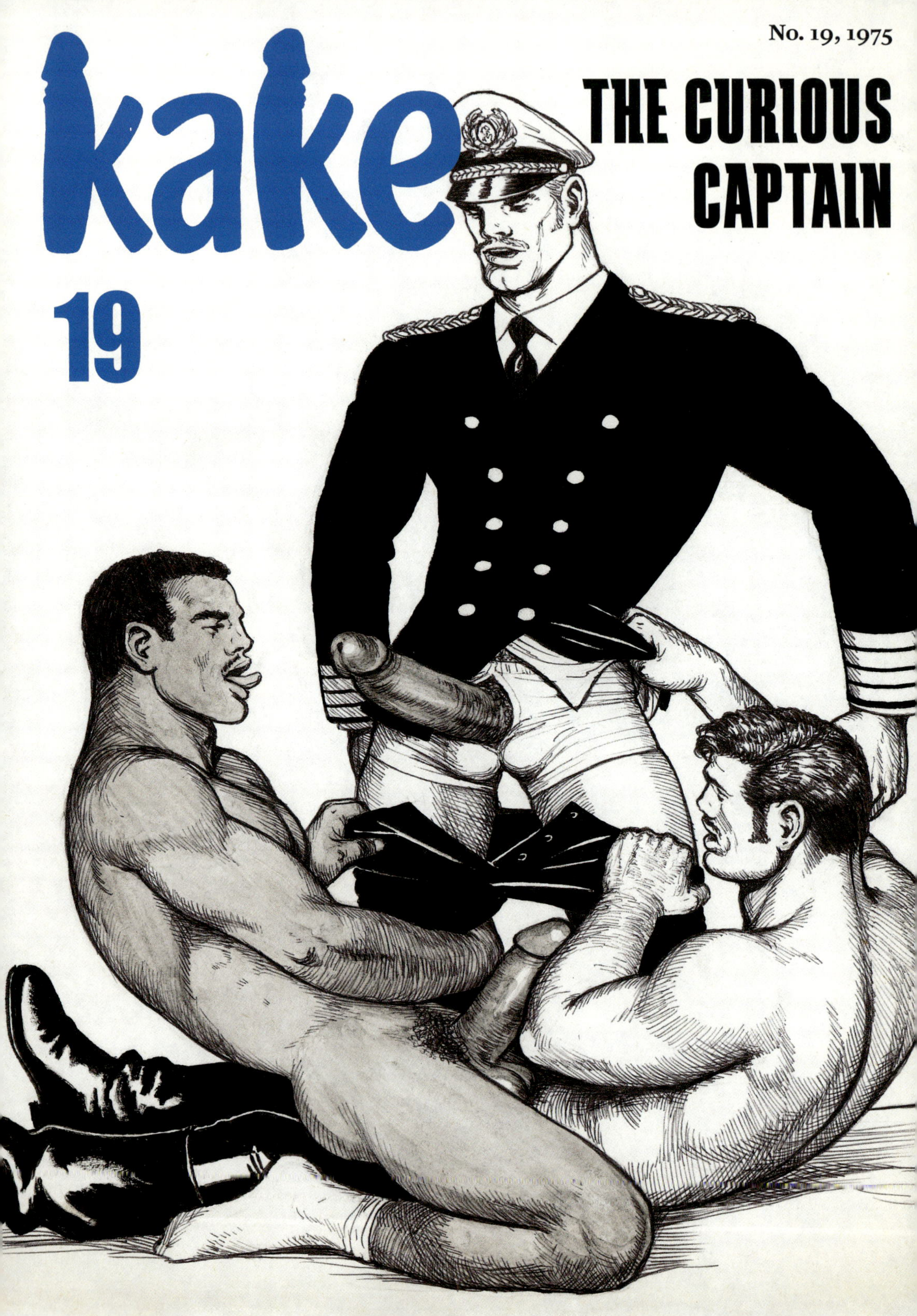
kake
19
No. 19, 1975
THE CURIOUS CAPTAIN

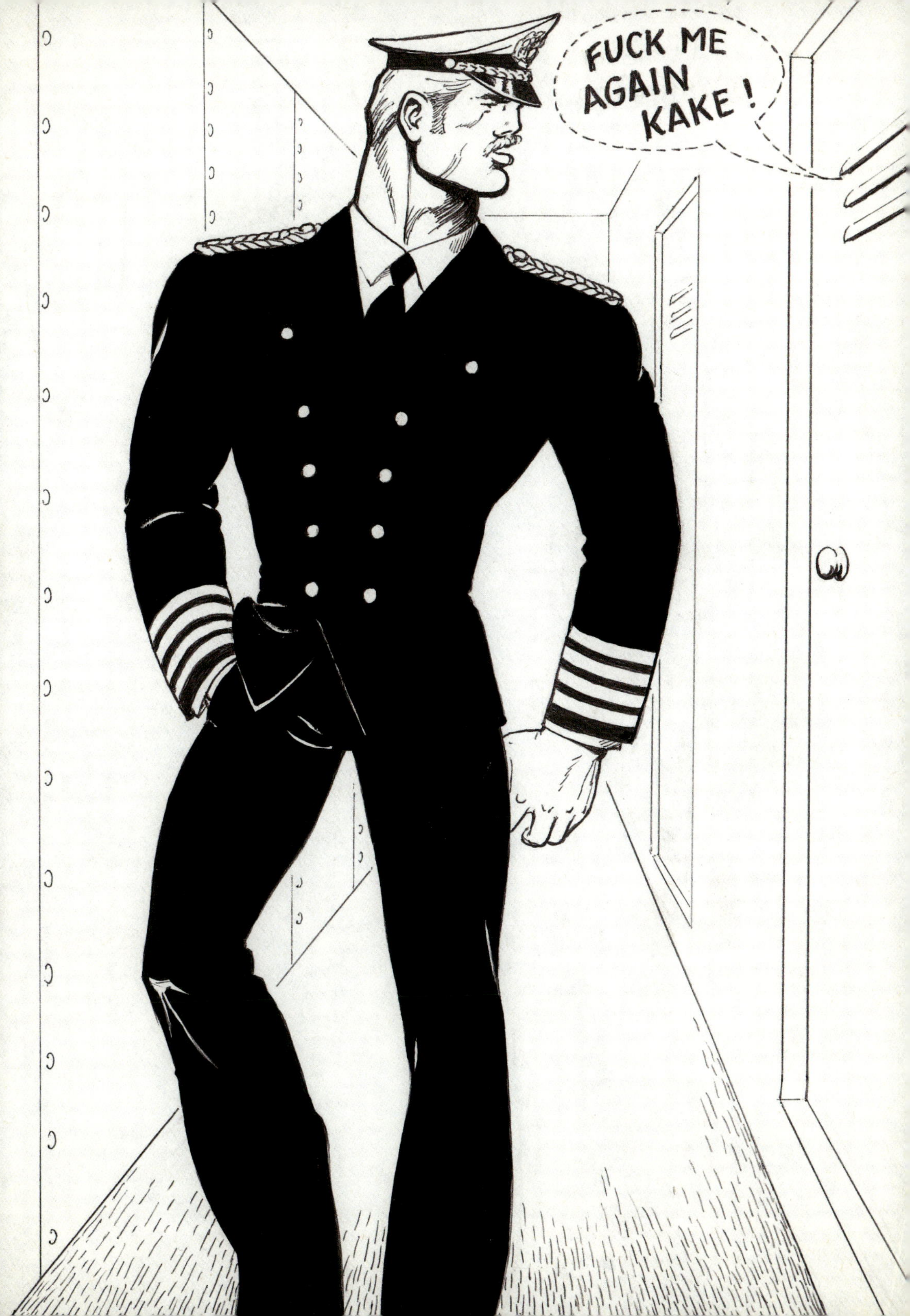

FUCK ME AGAIN KAKE !

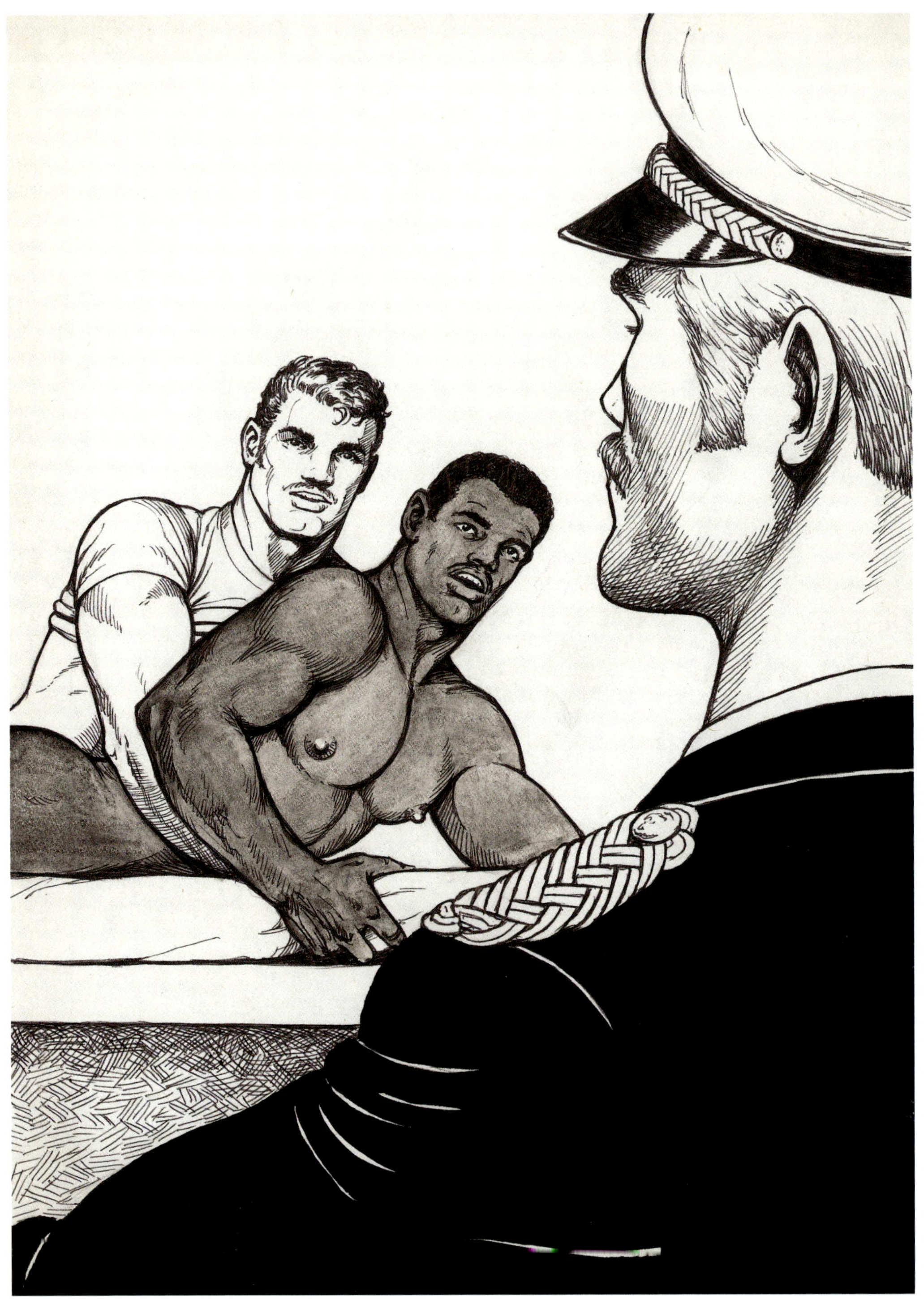

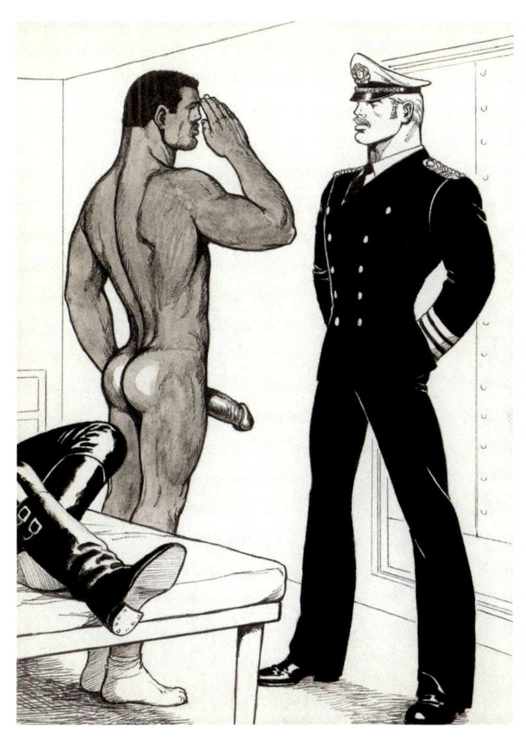

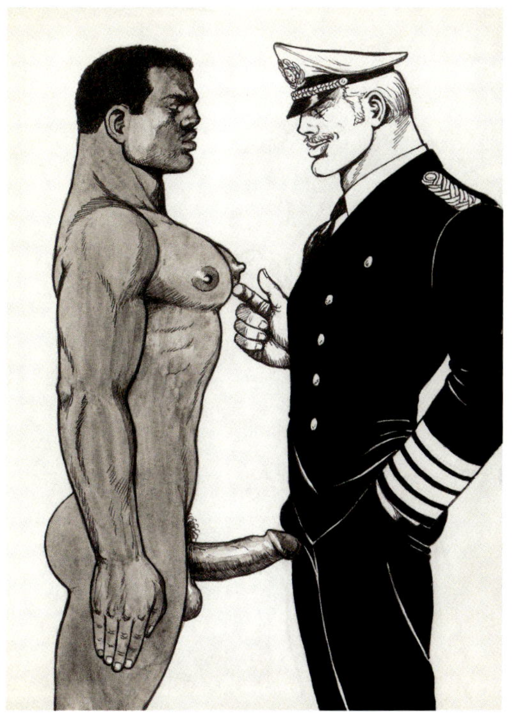

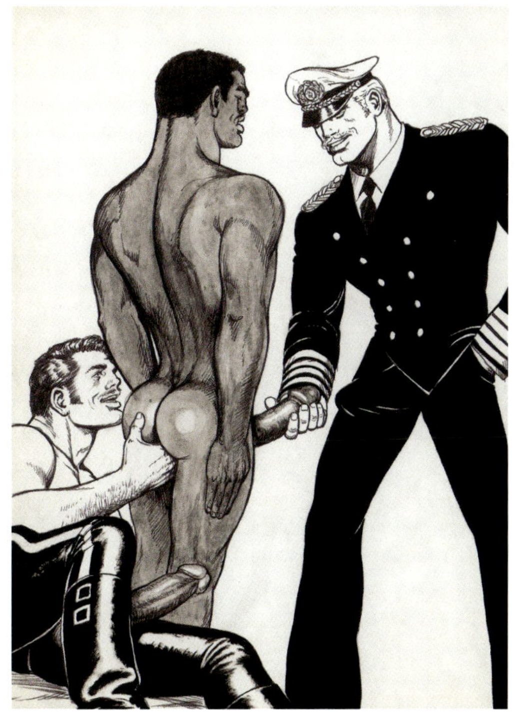

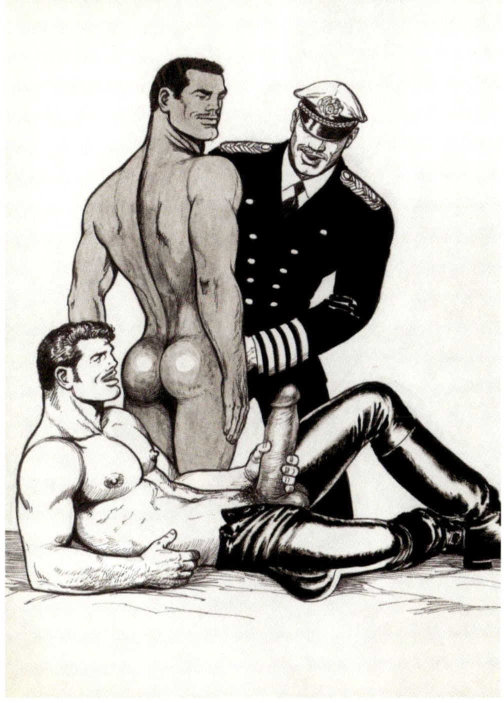

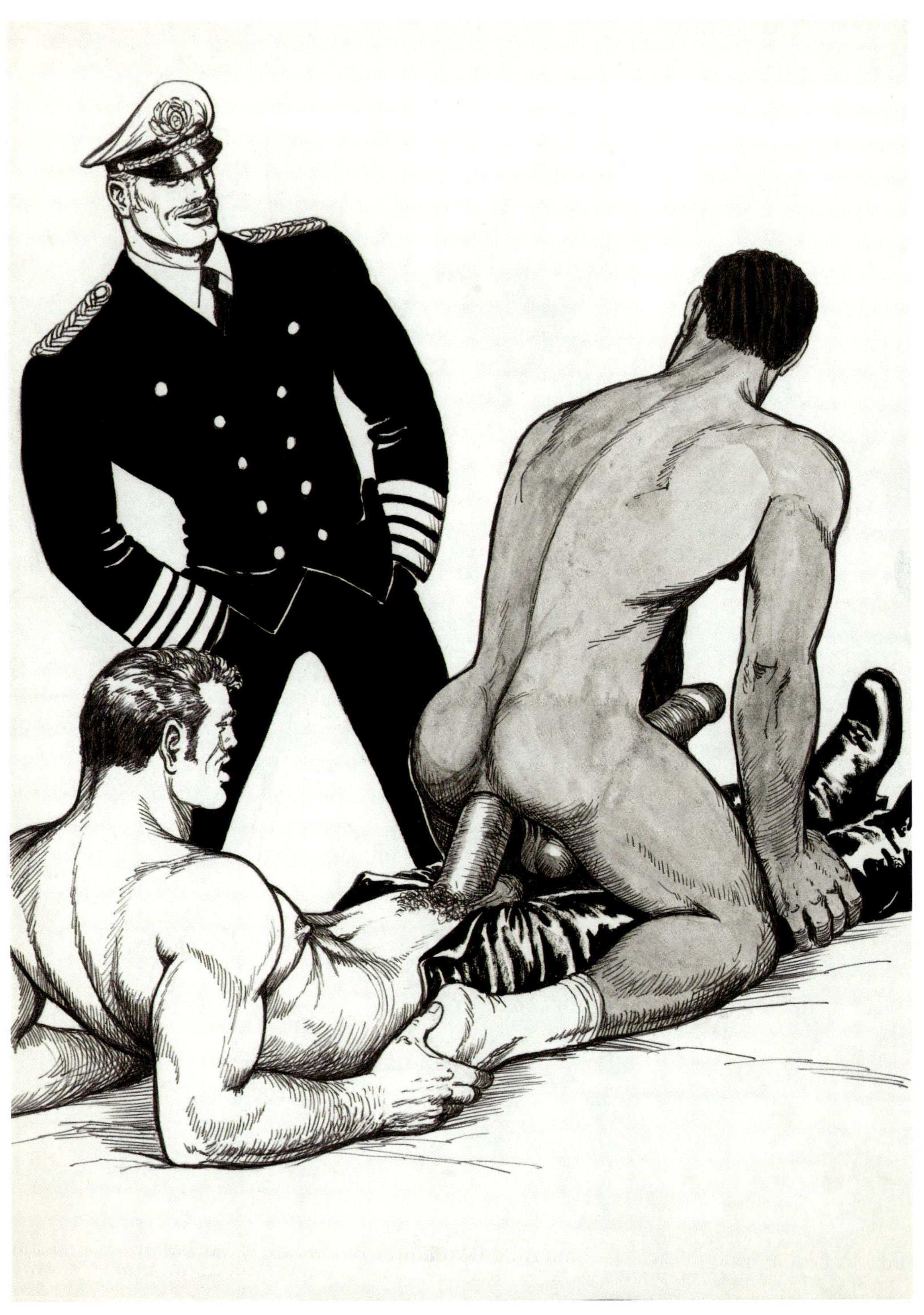

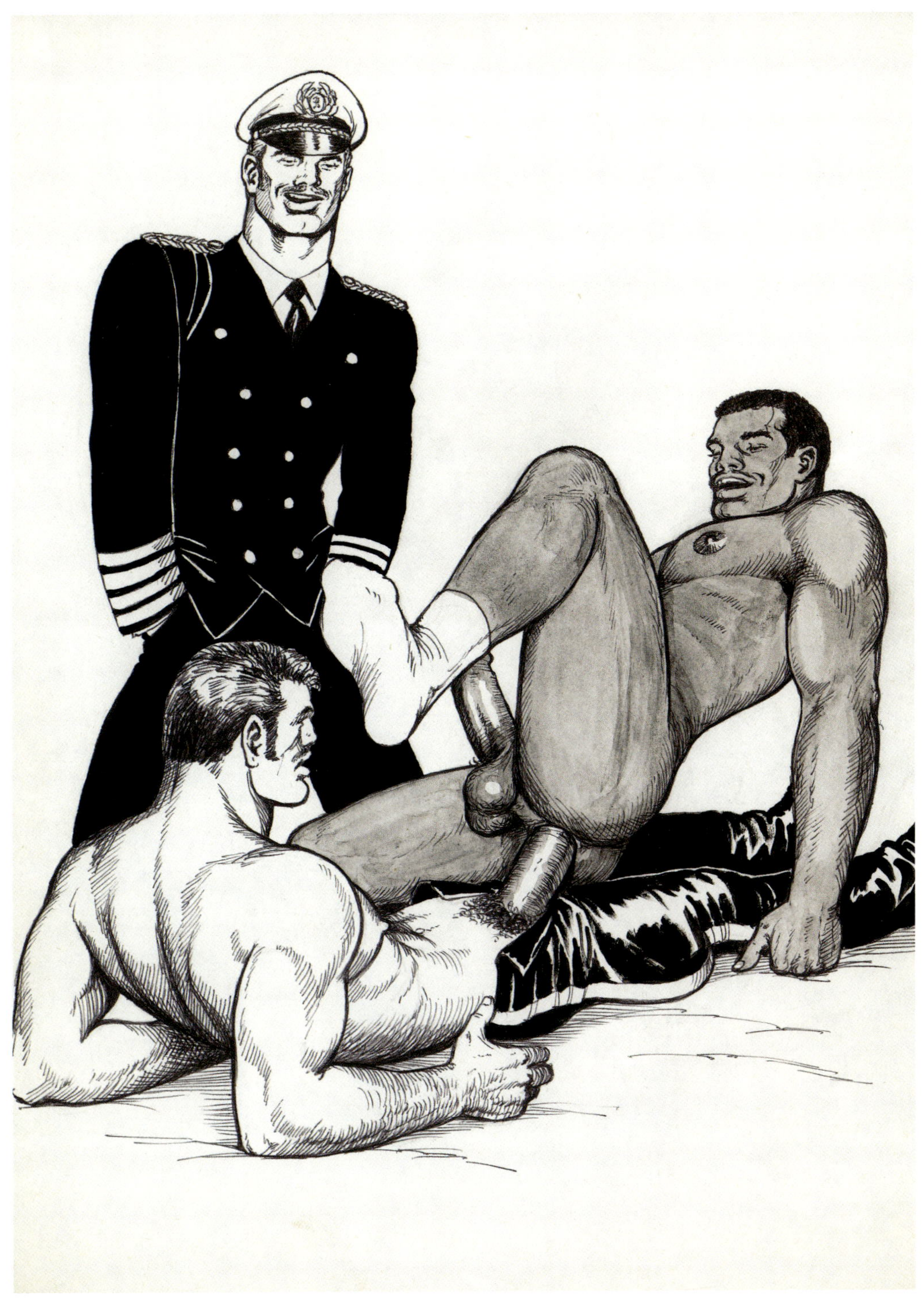

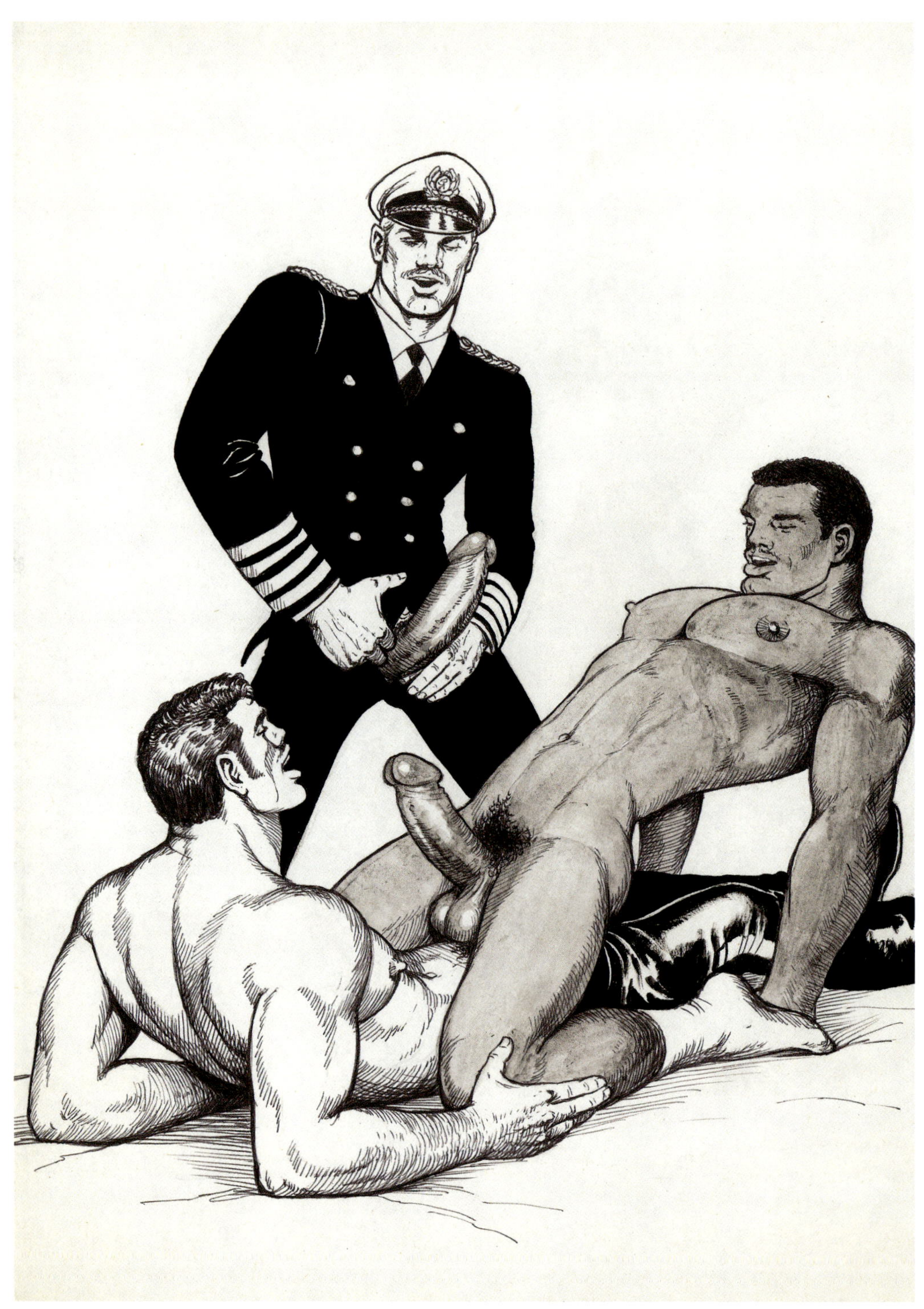

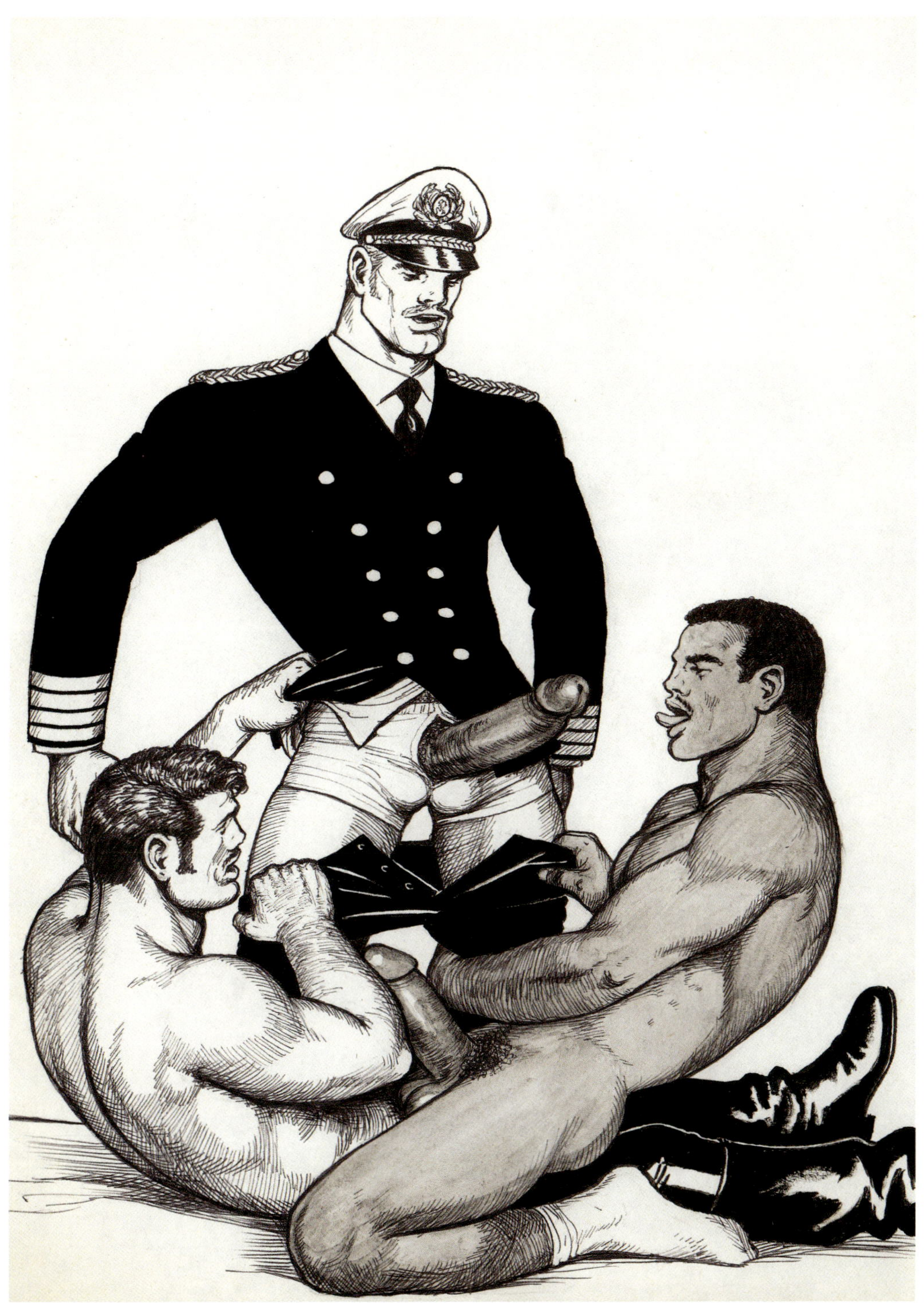

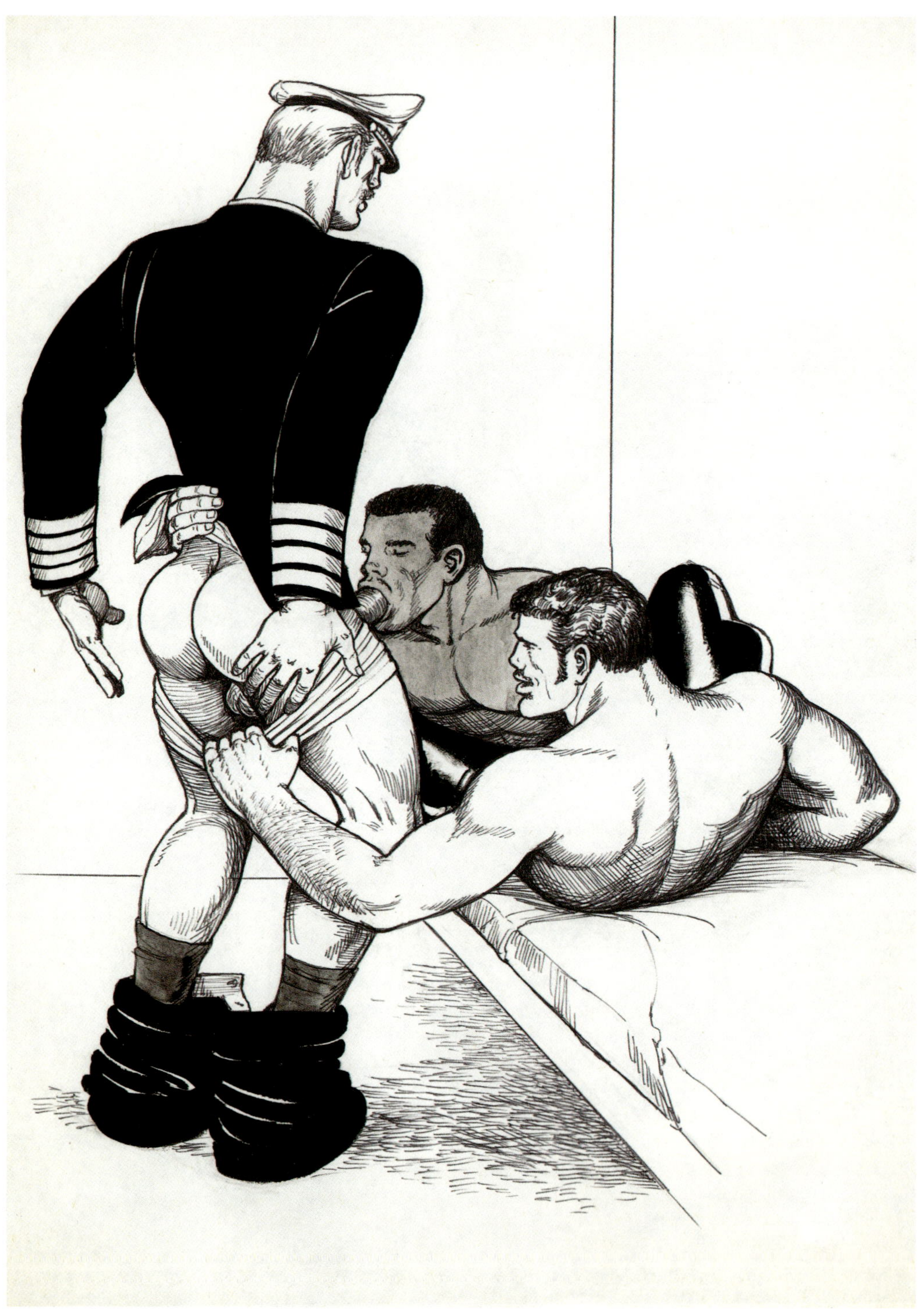

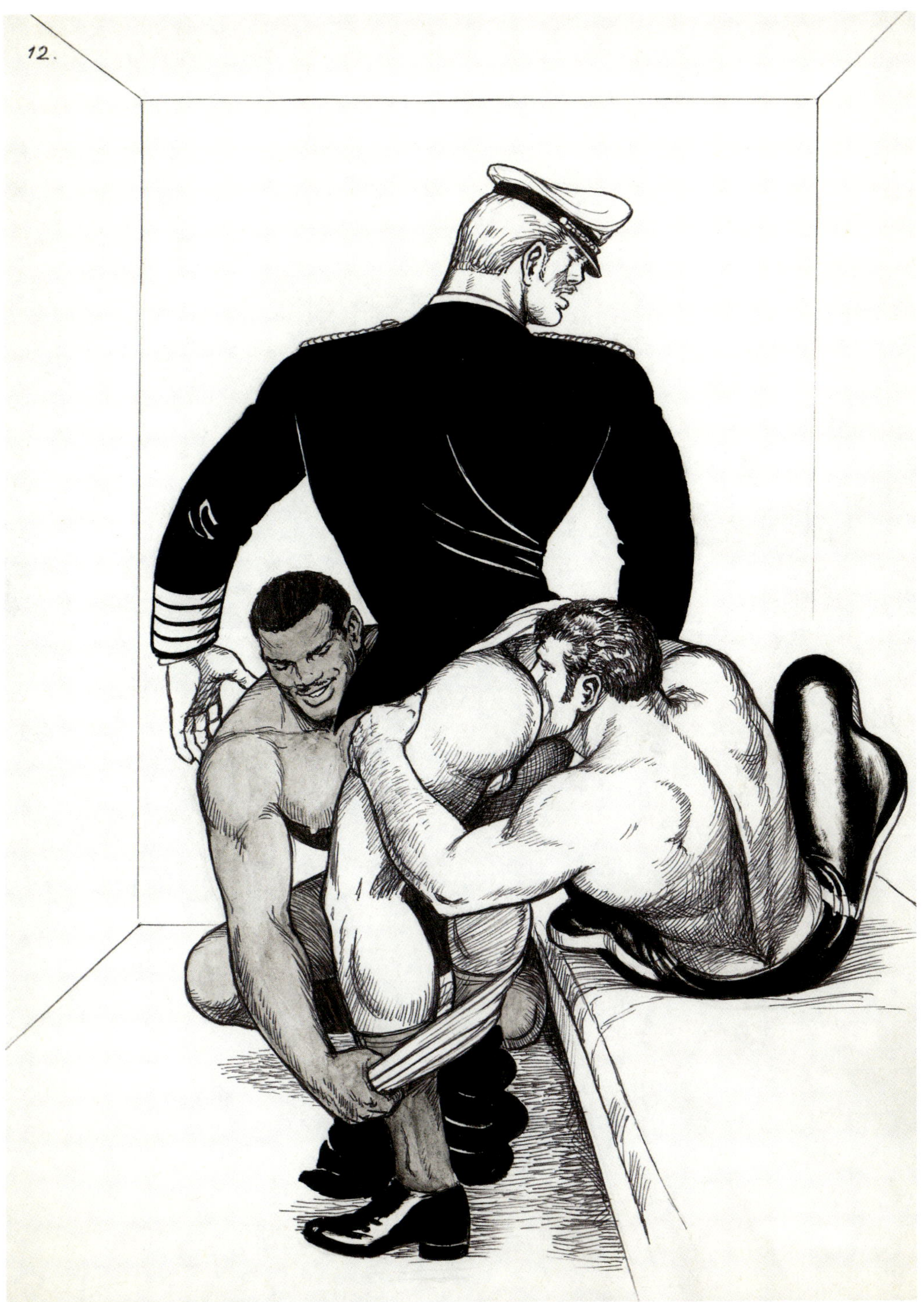

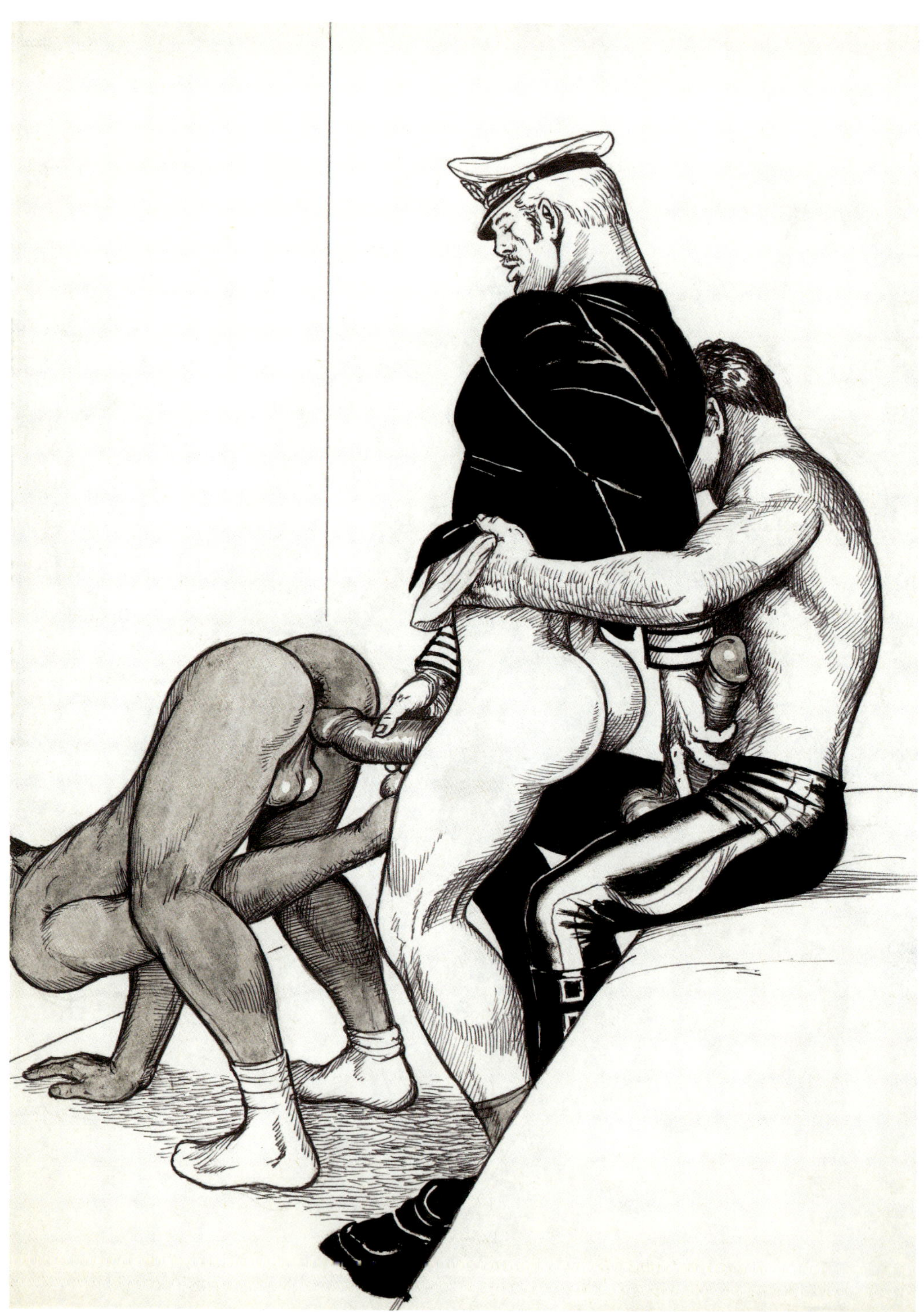

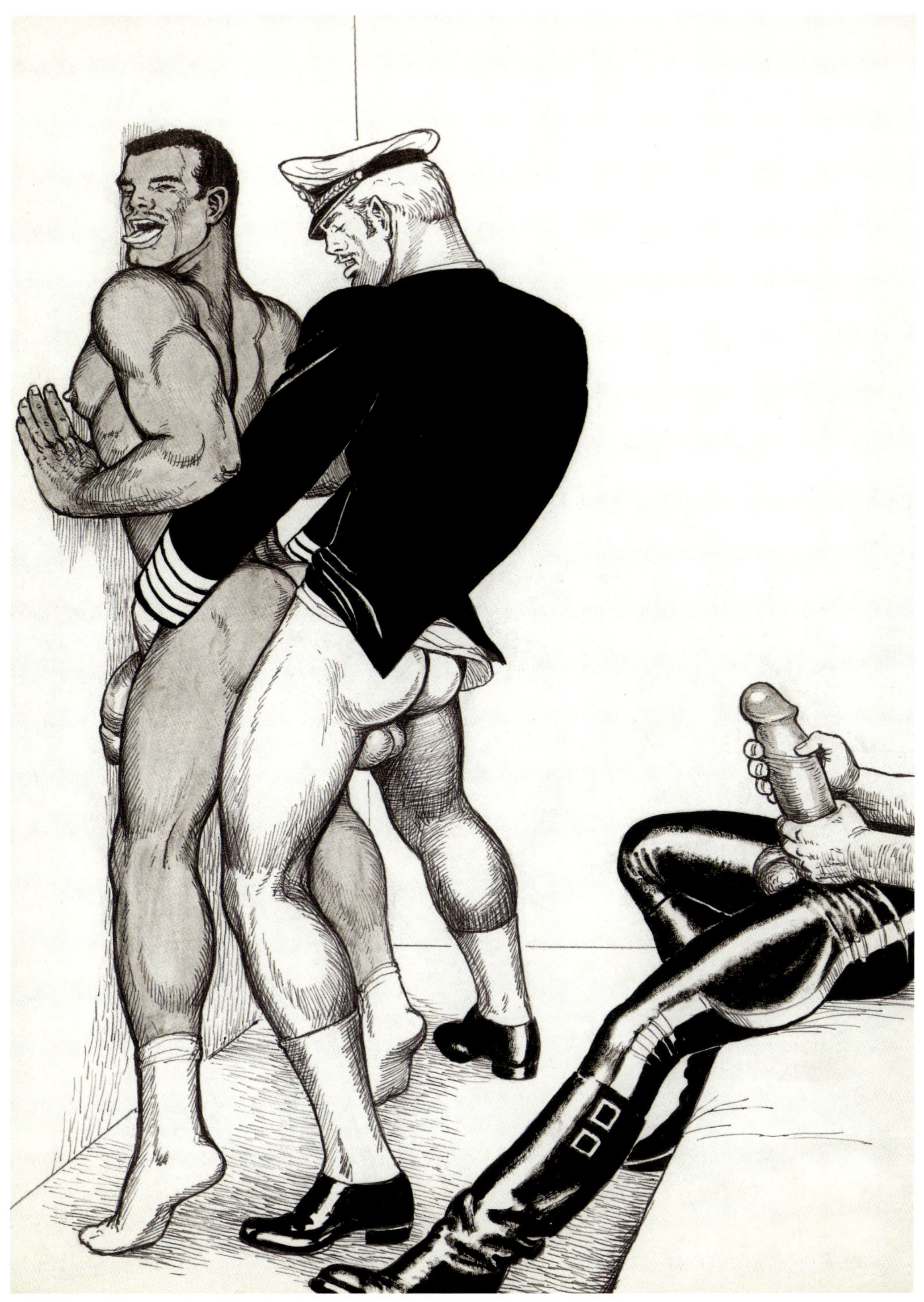

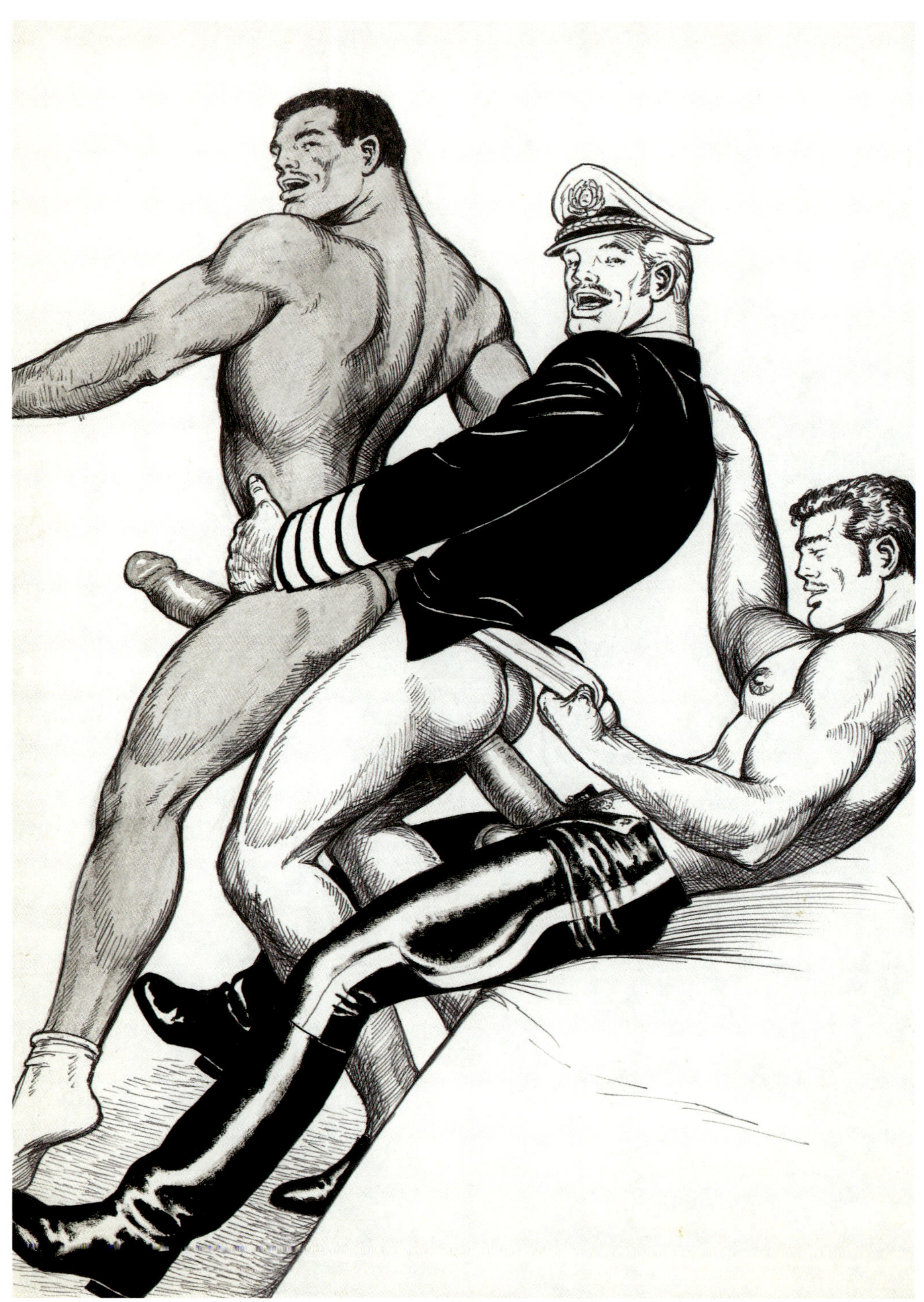

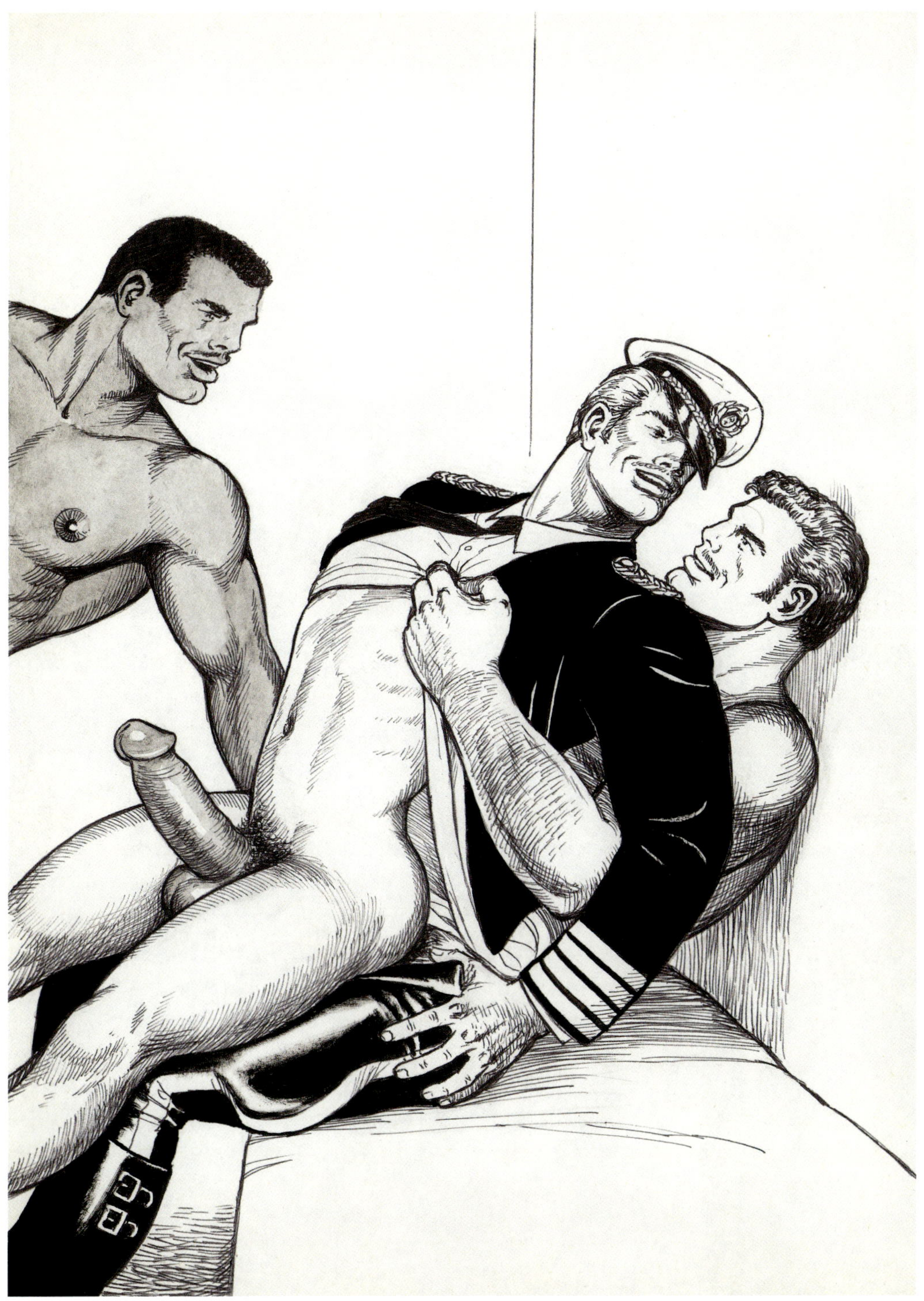

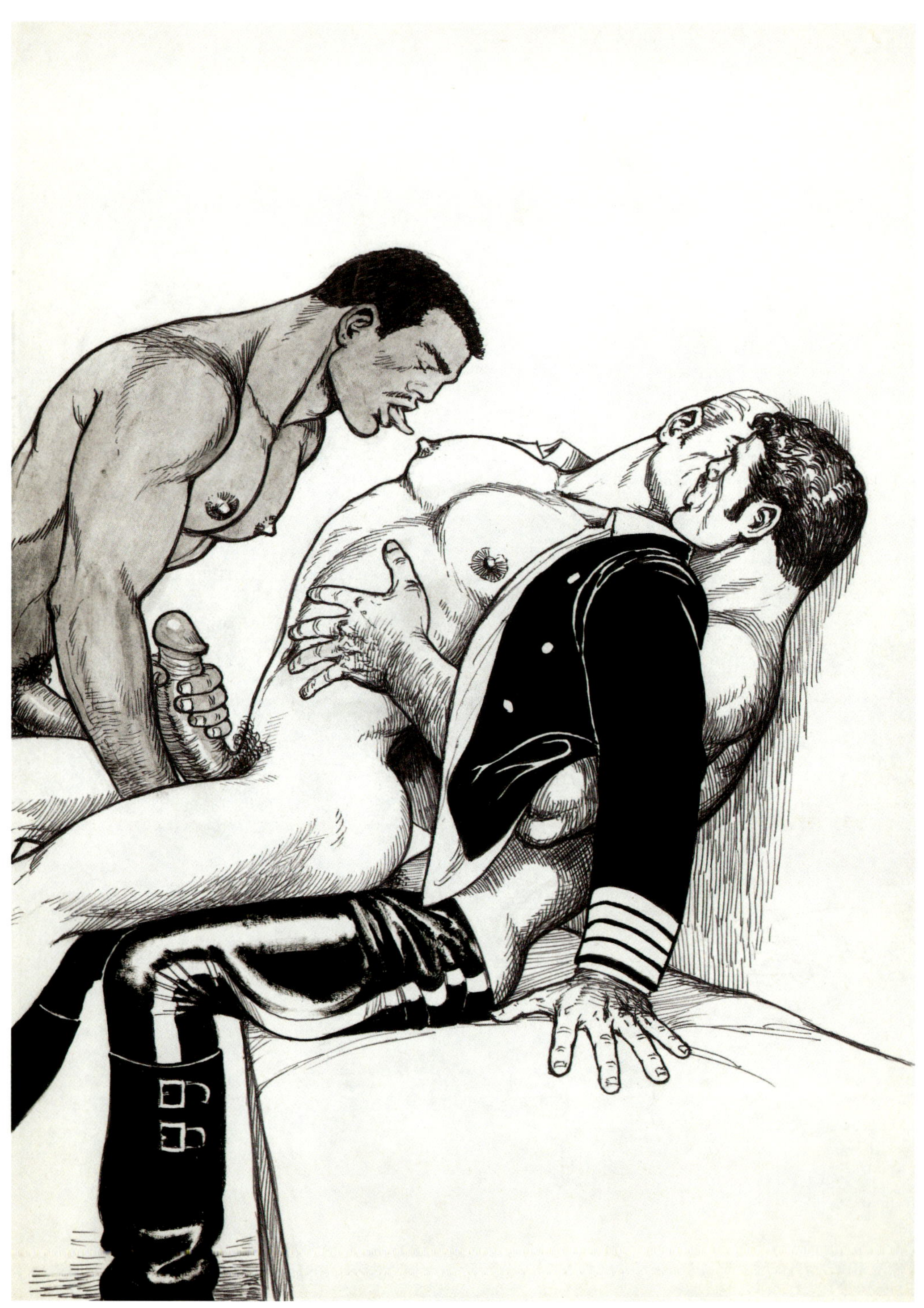

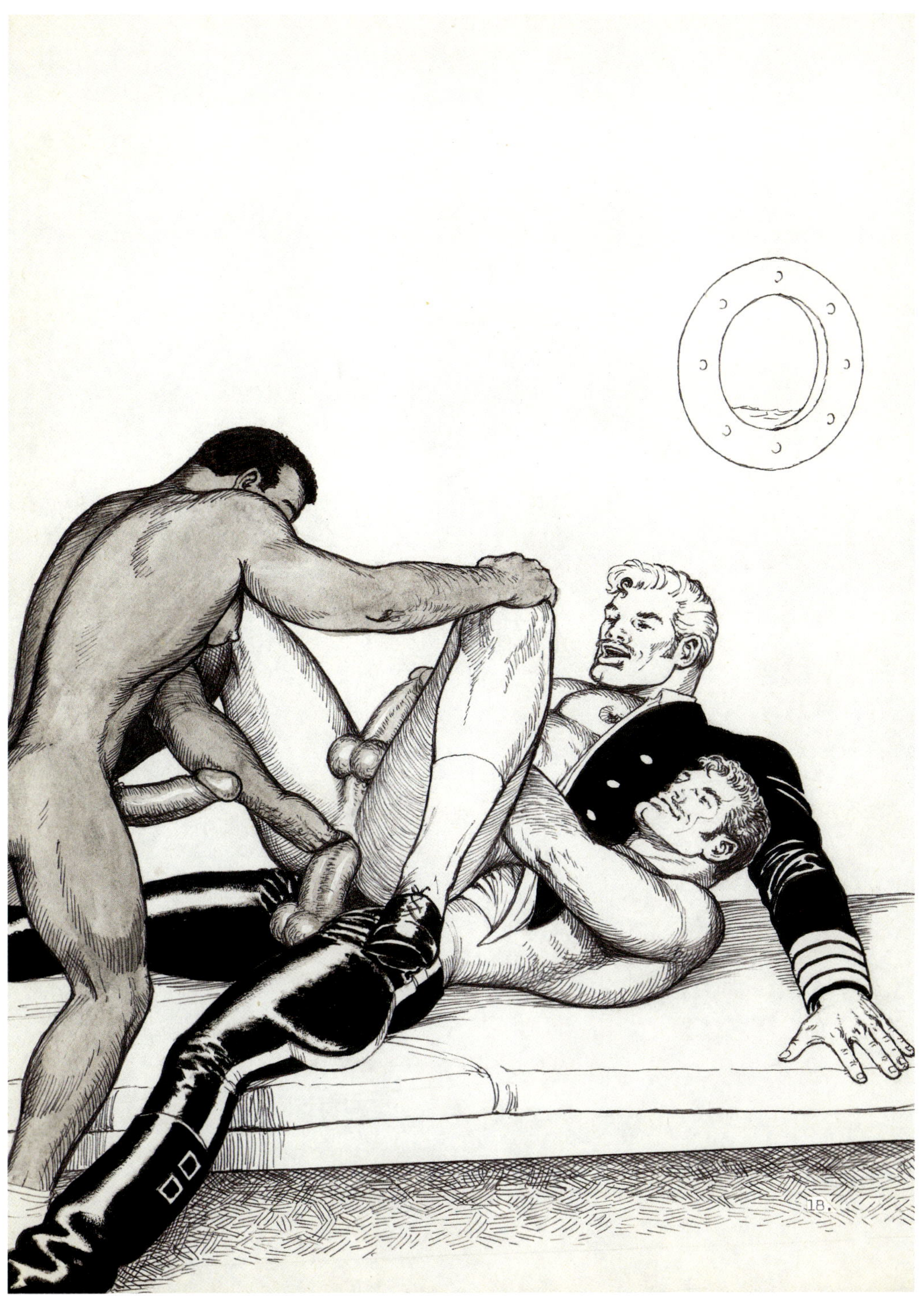

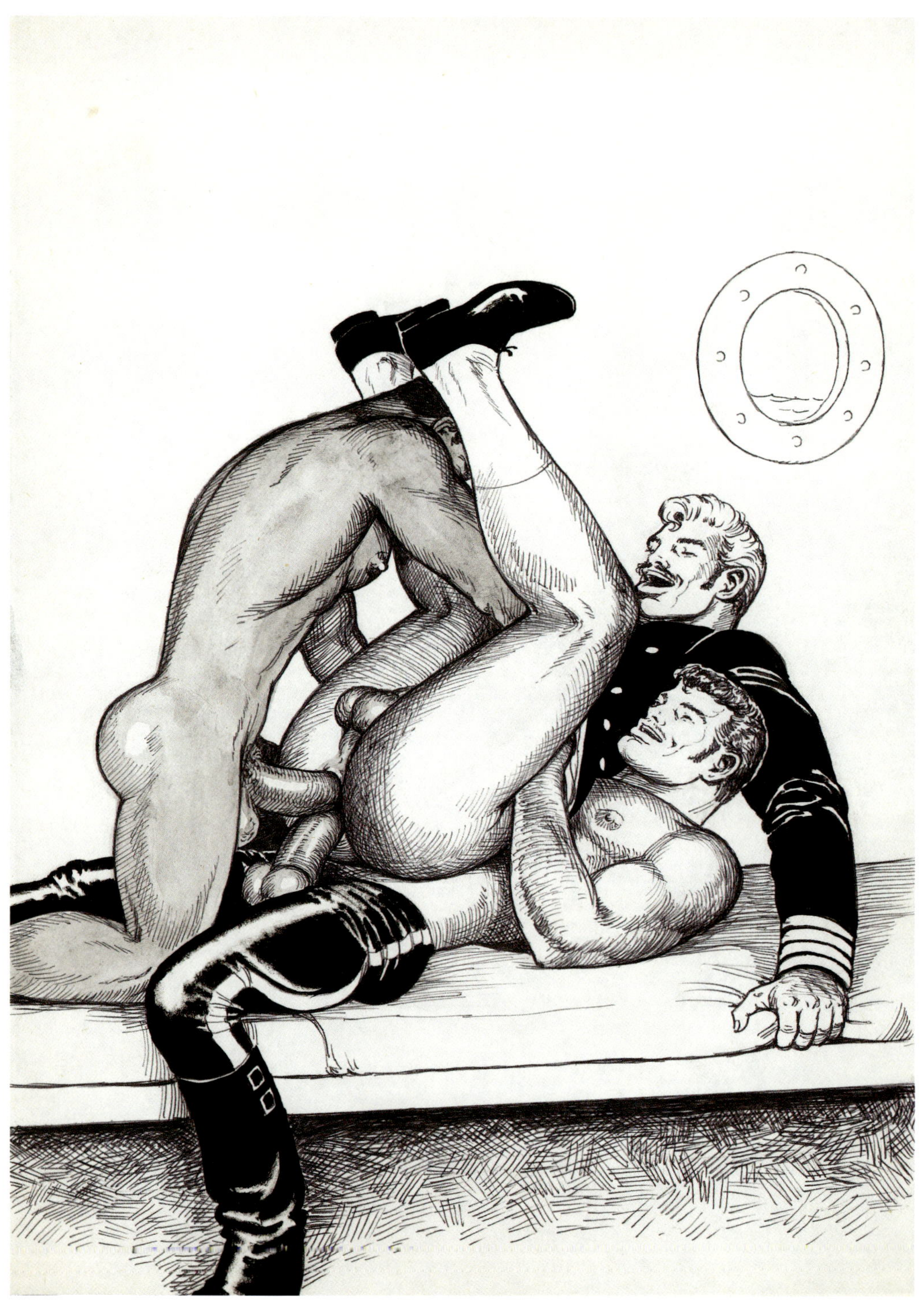

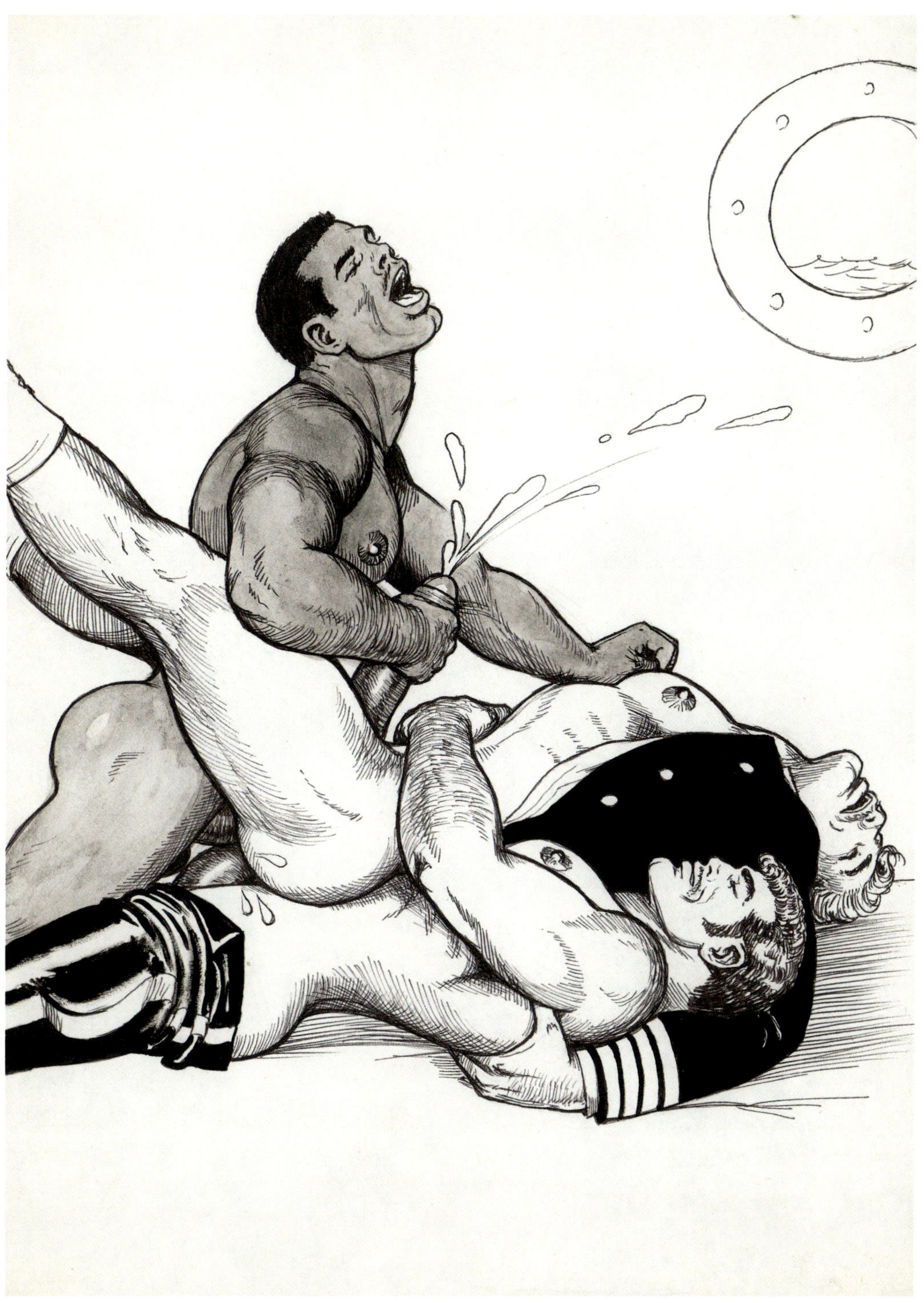

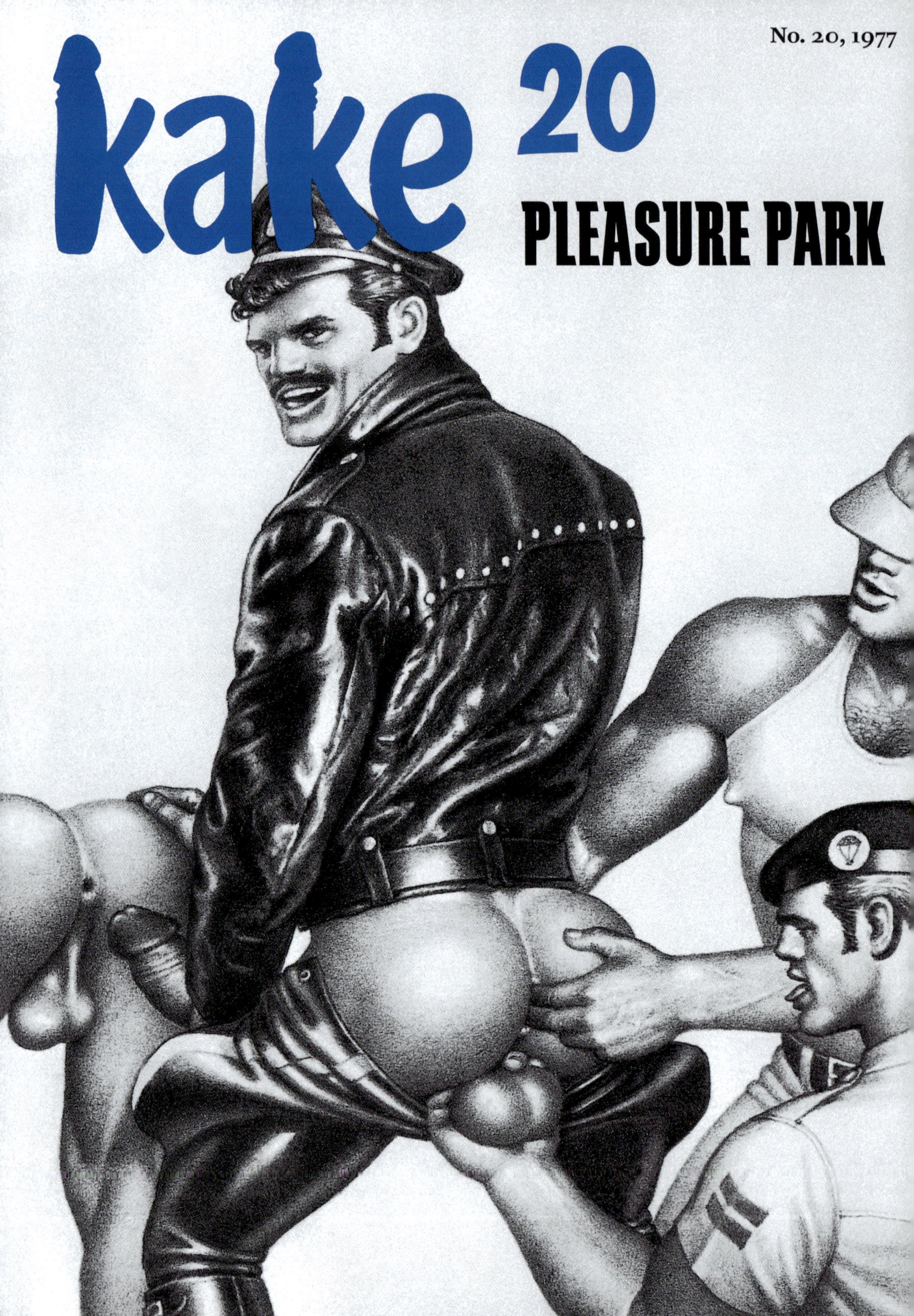

kake 20
No. 20, 1977
PLEASURE PARK

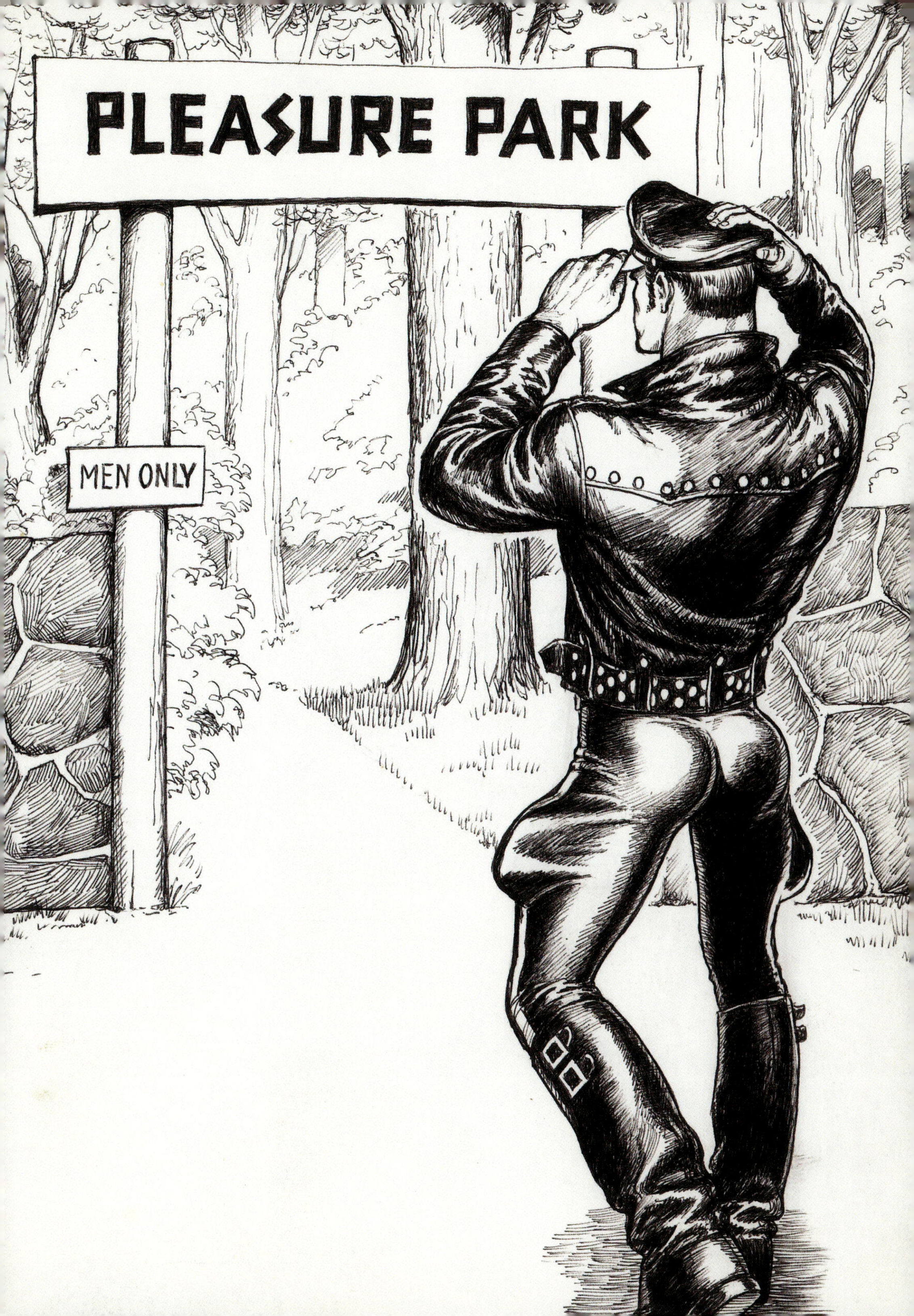
PLEASURE PARK
MEN ONLY

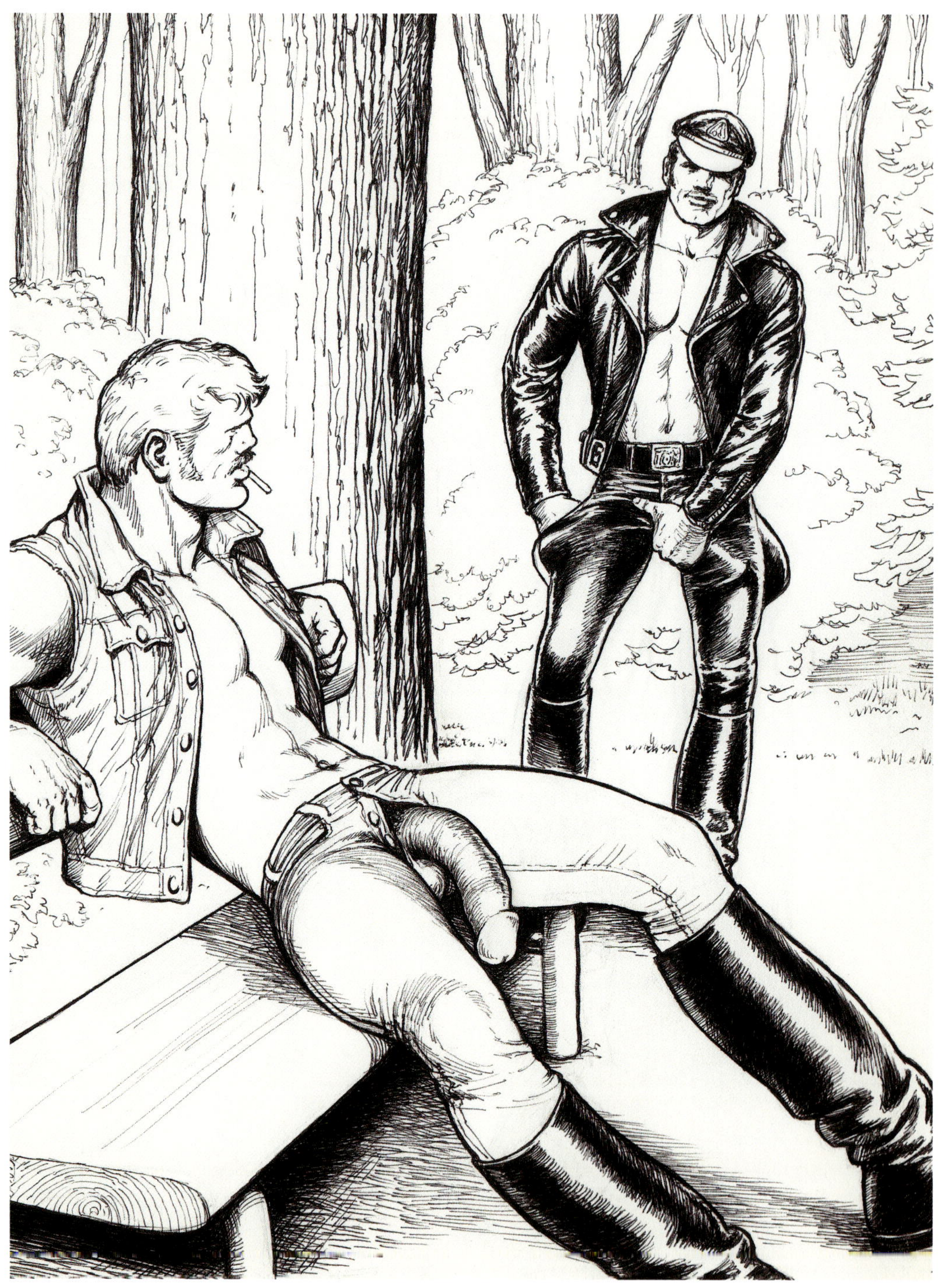

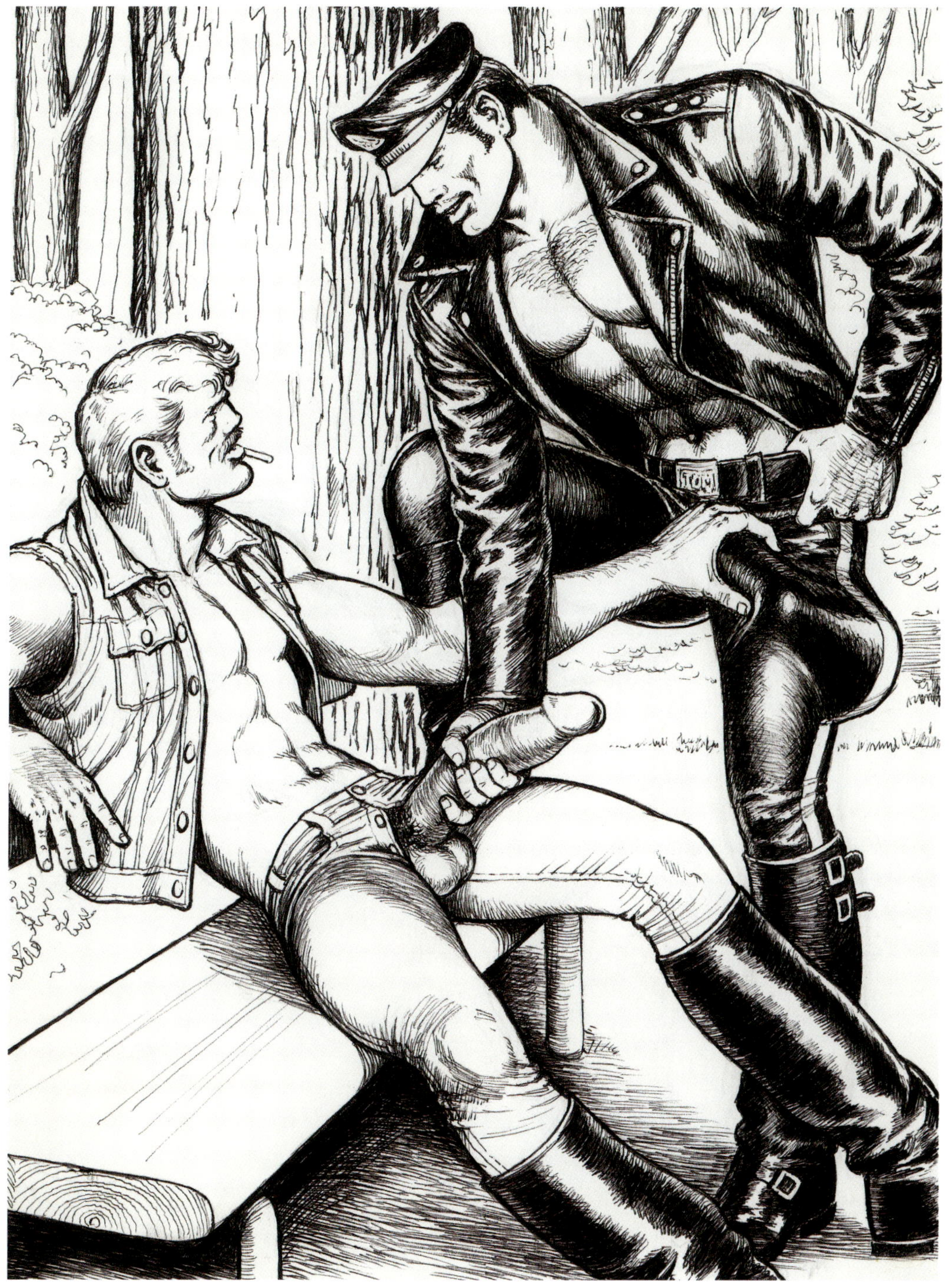

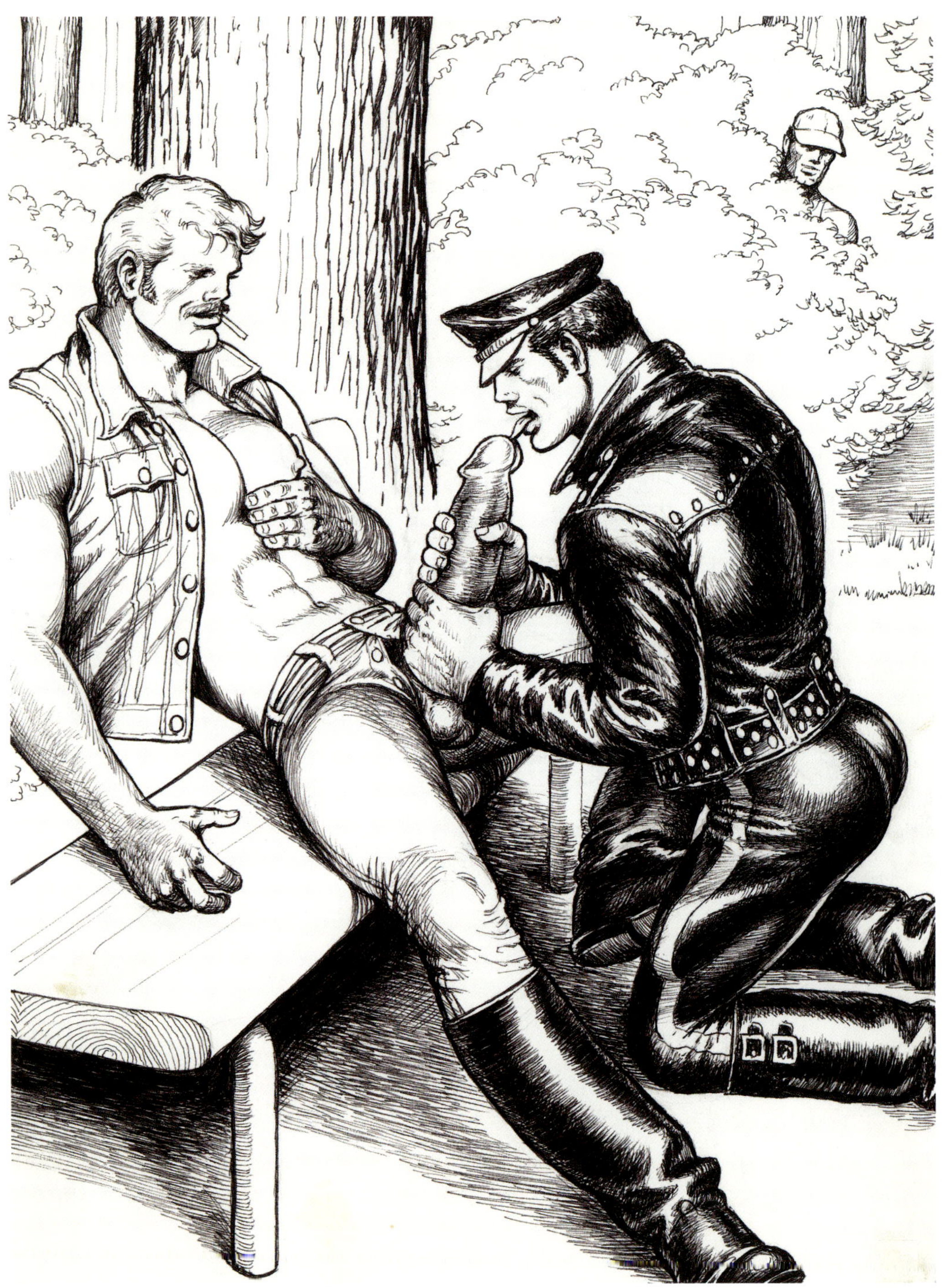

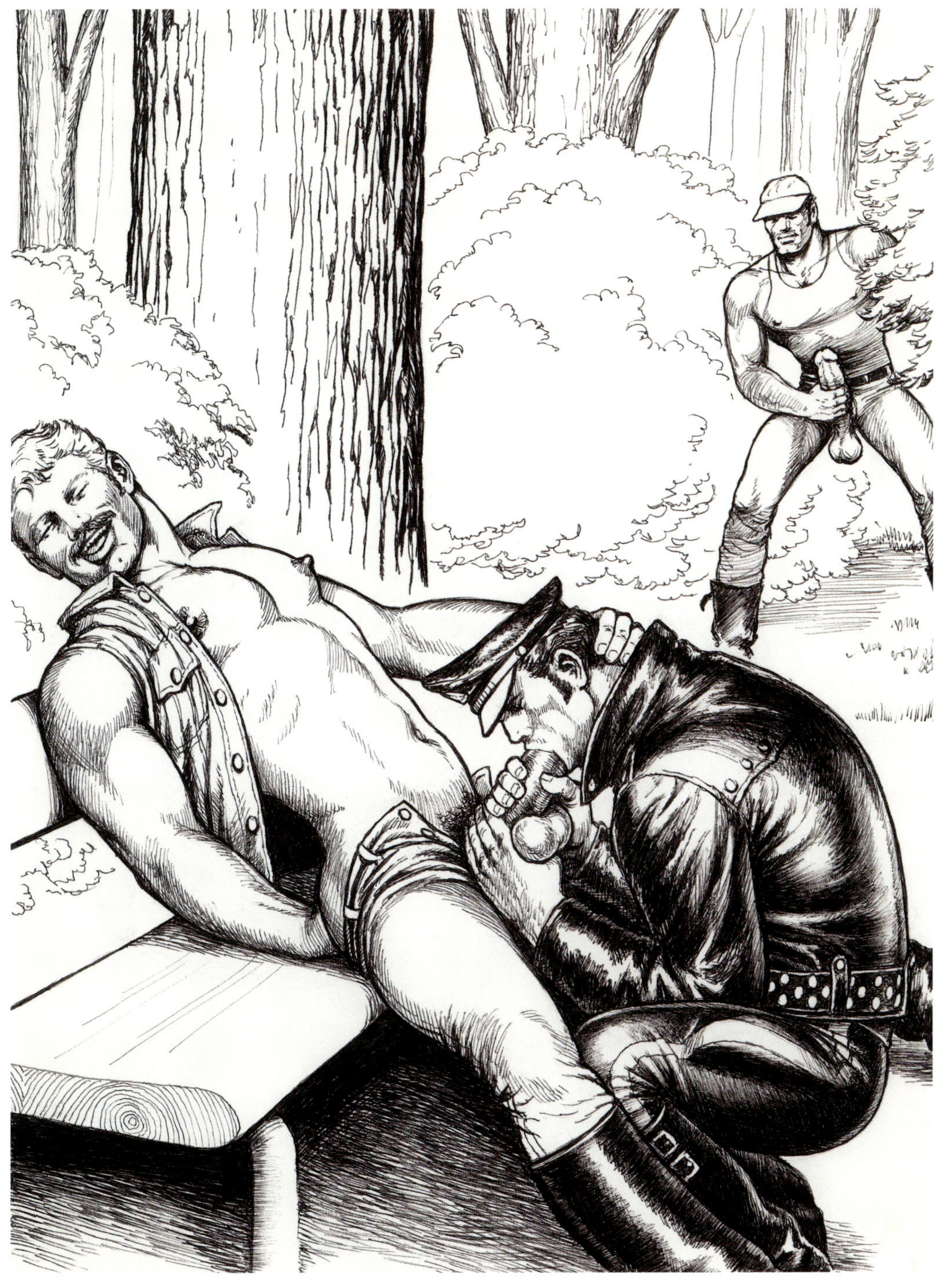

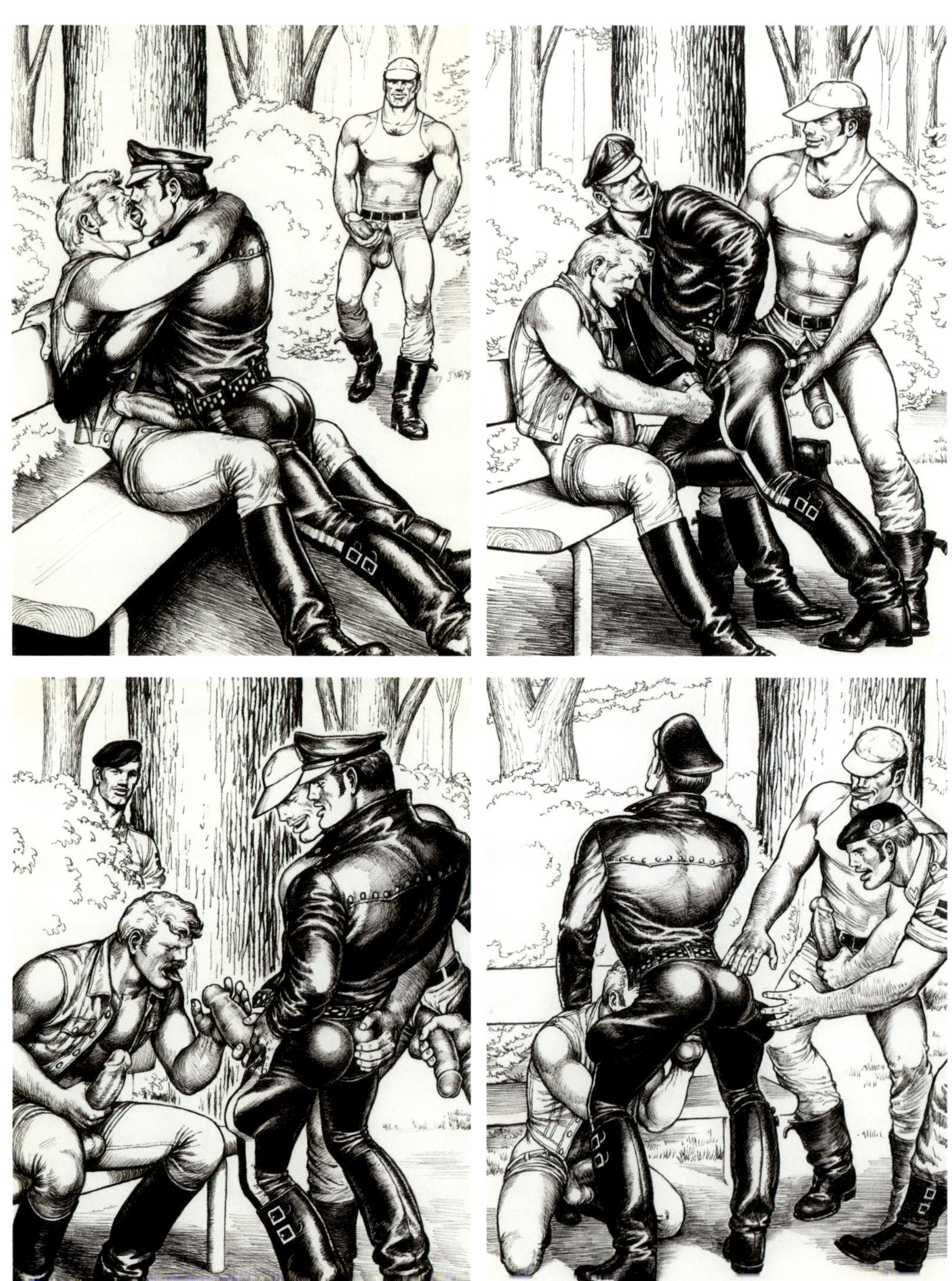

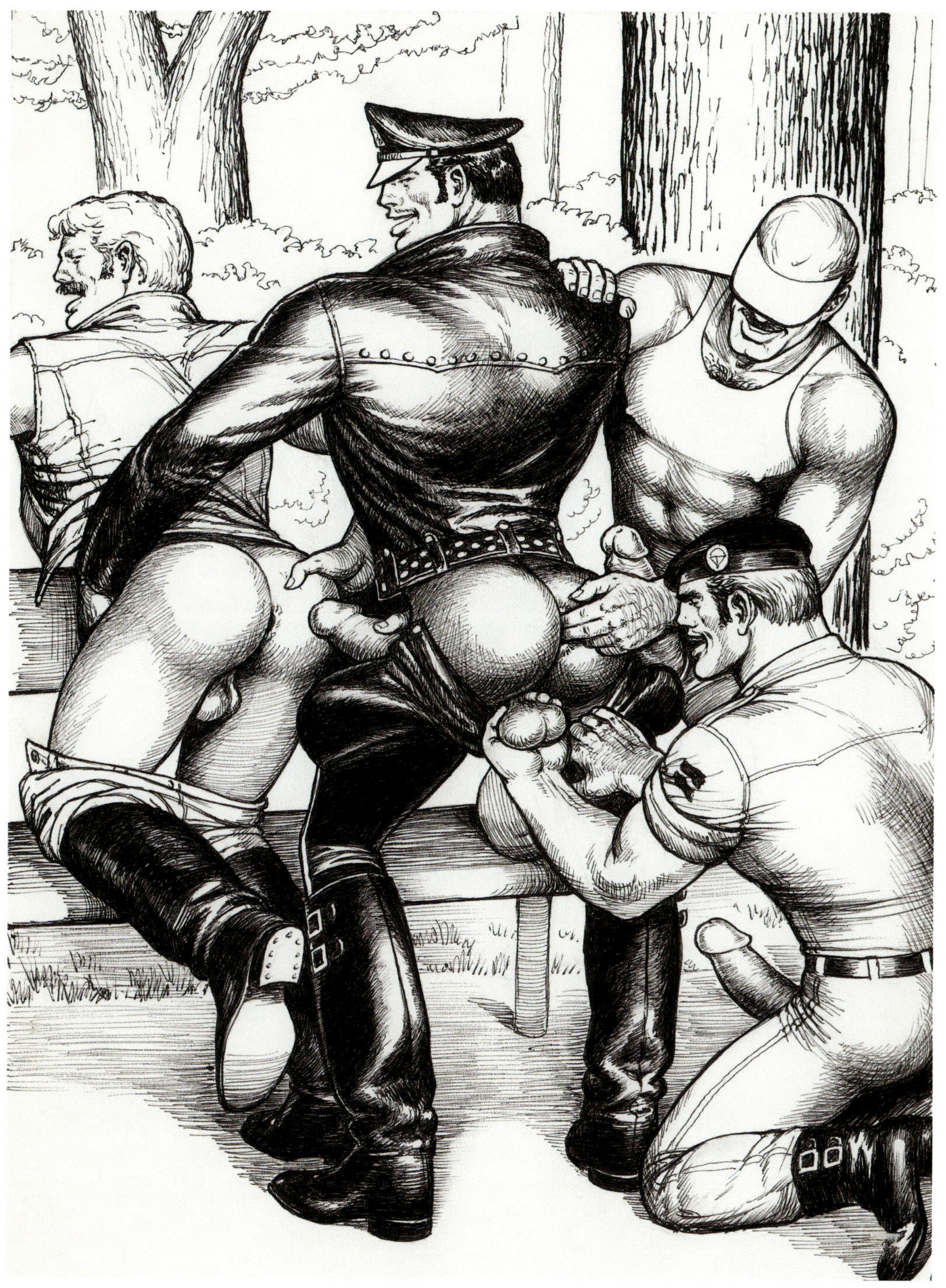

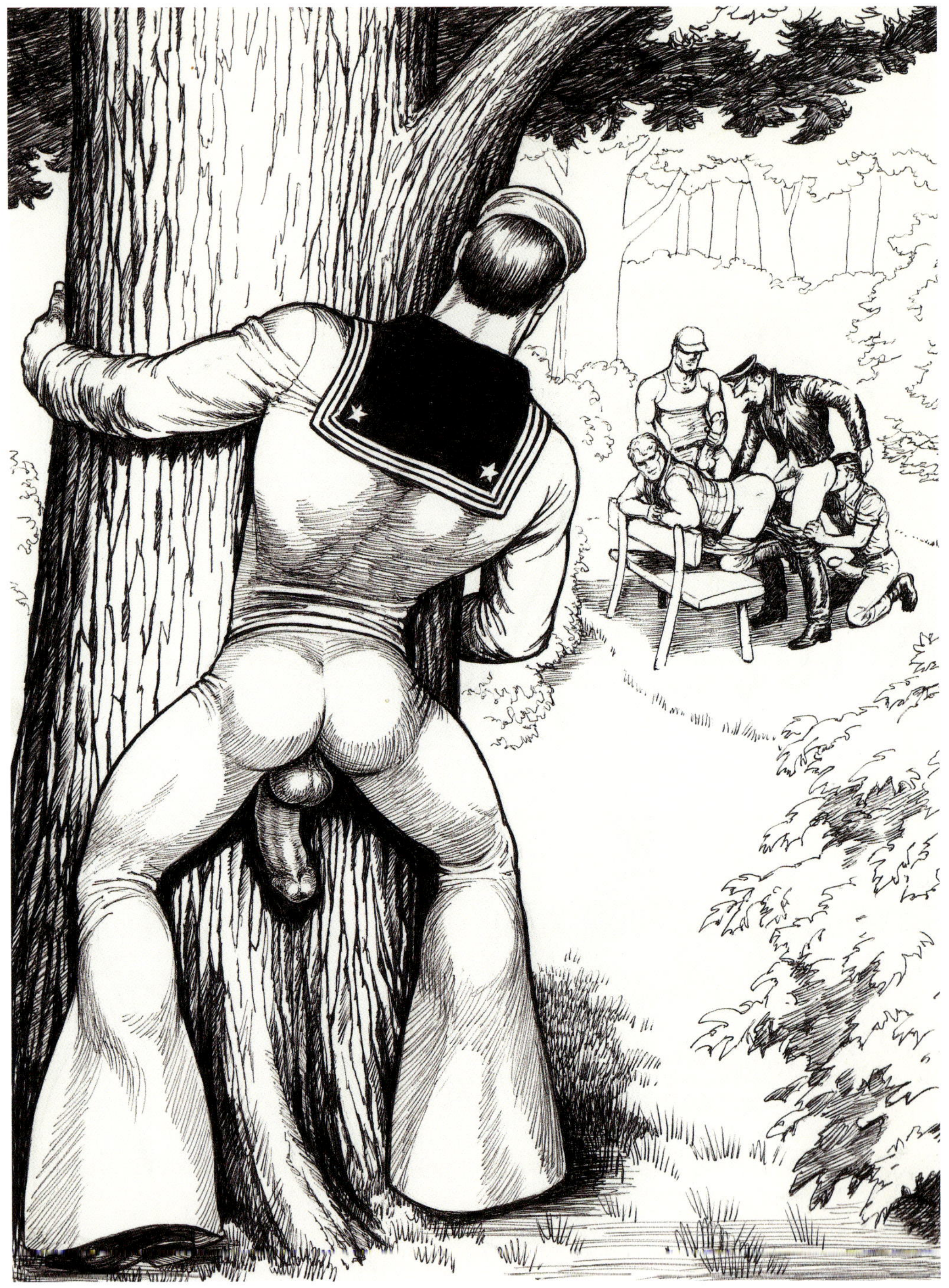

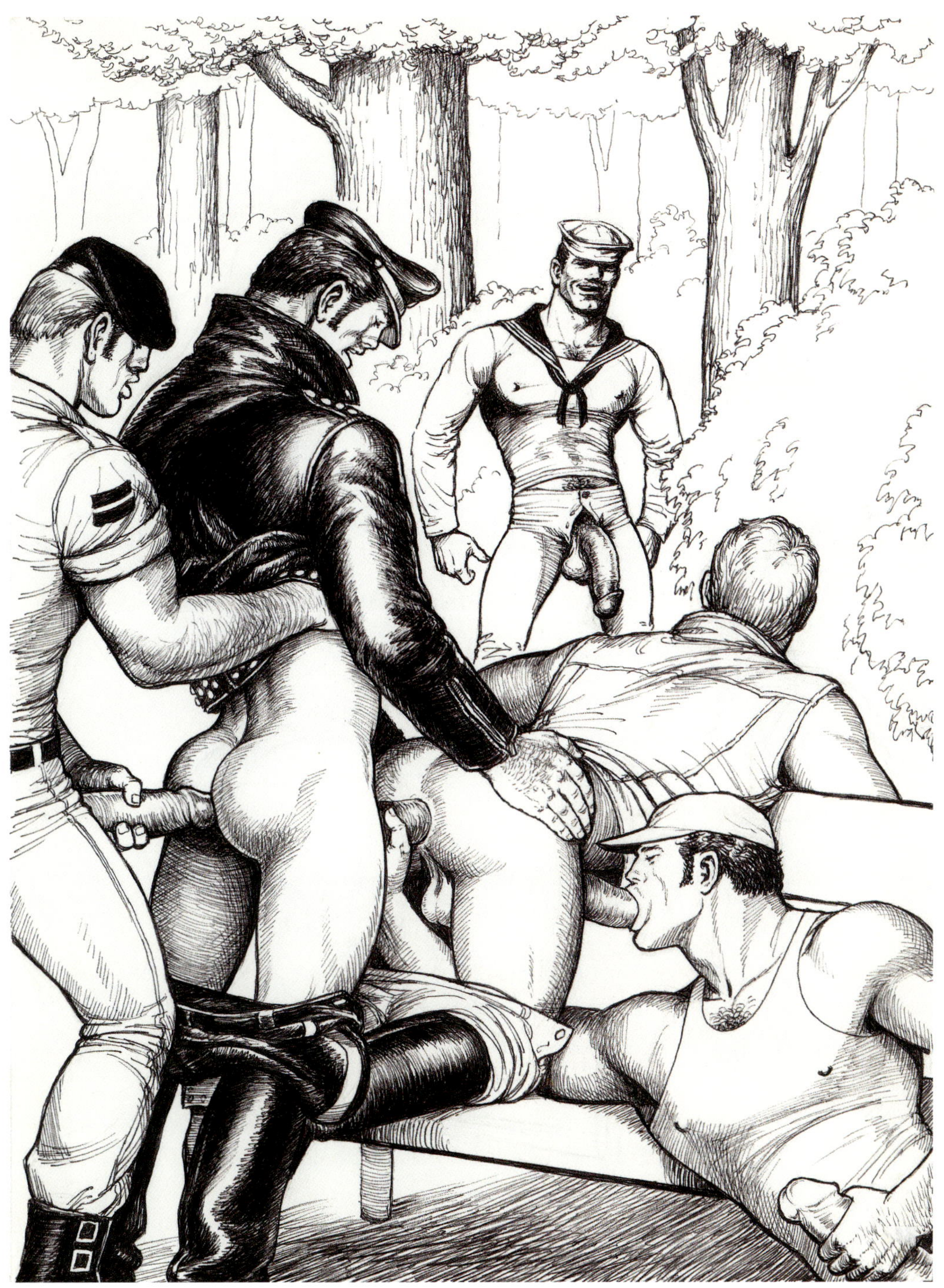

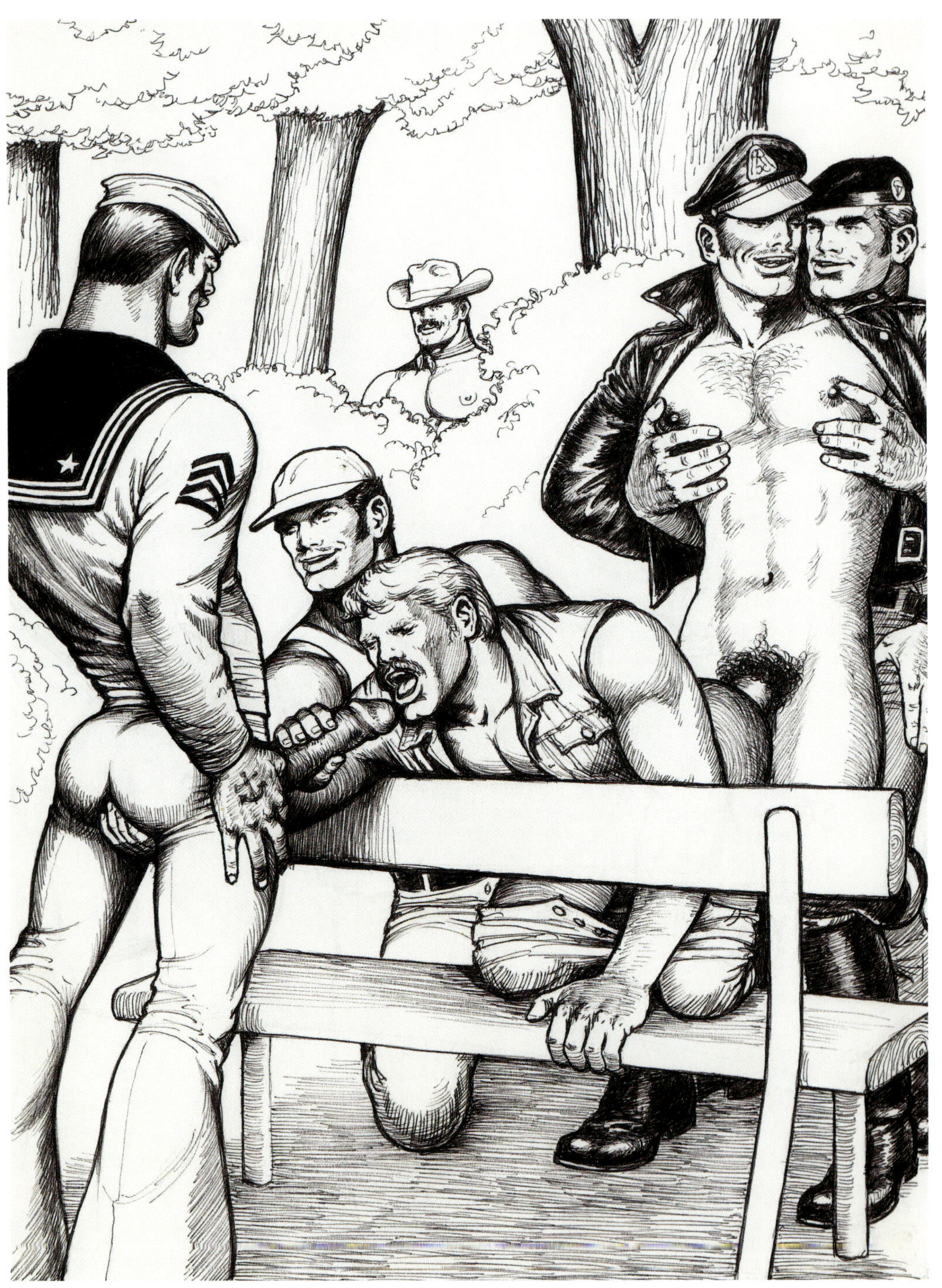

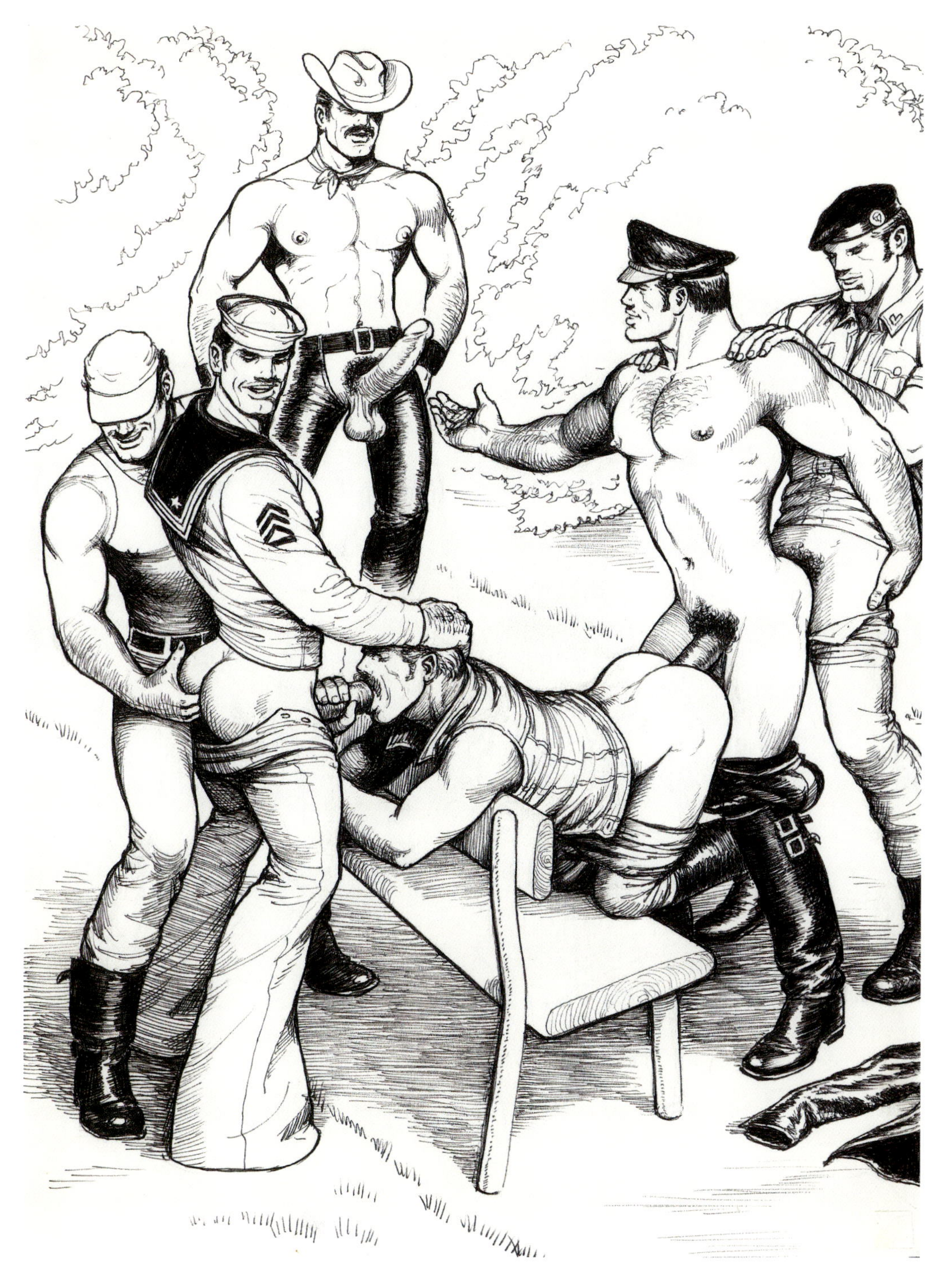

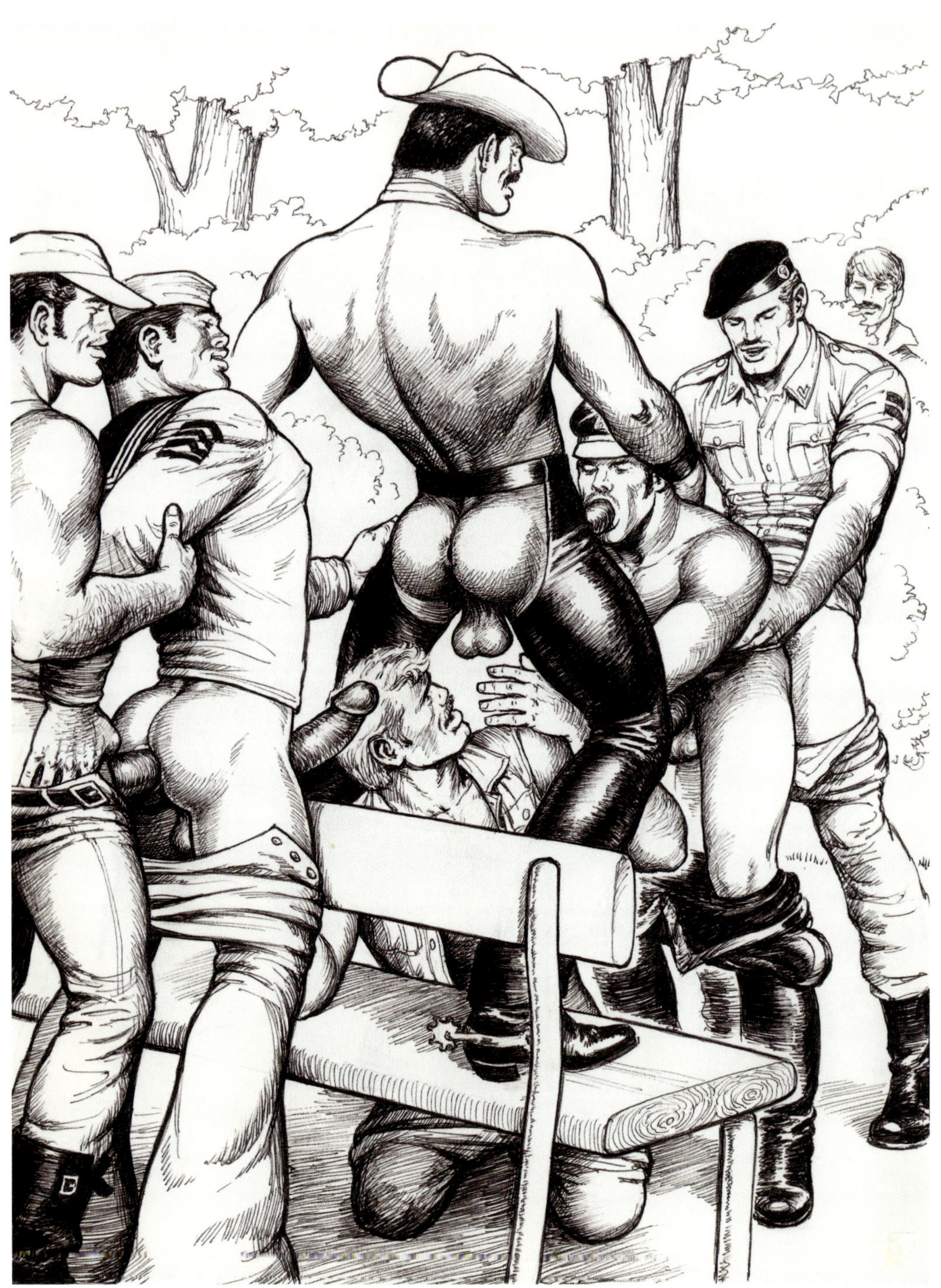

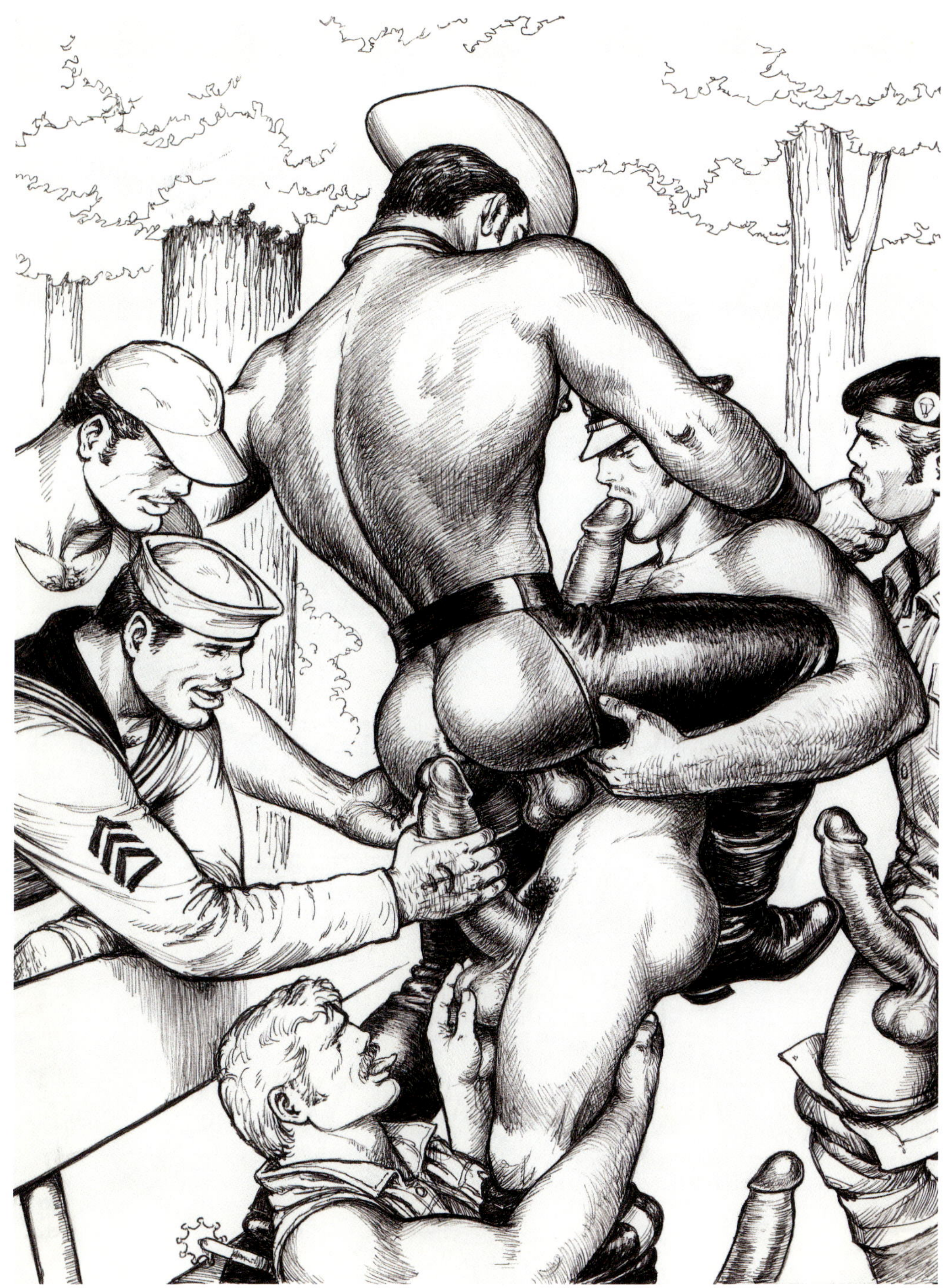

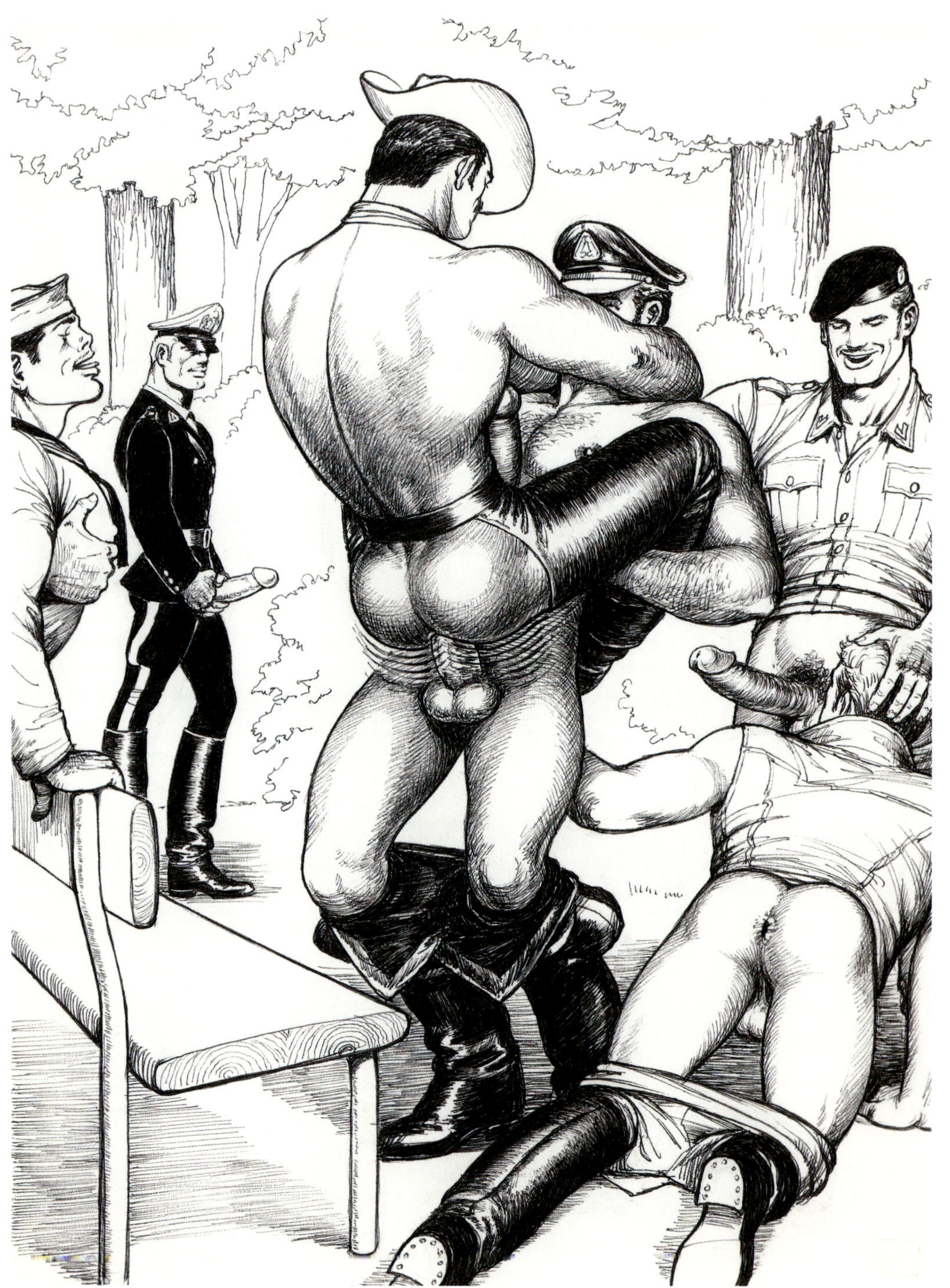

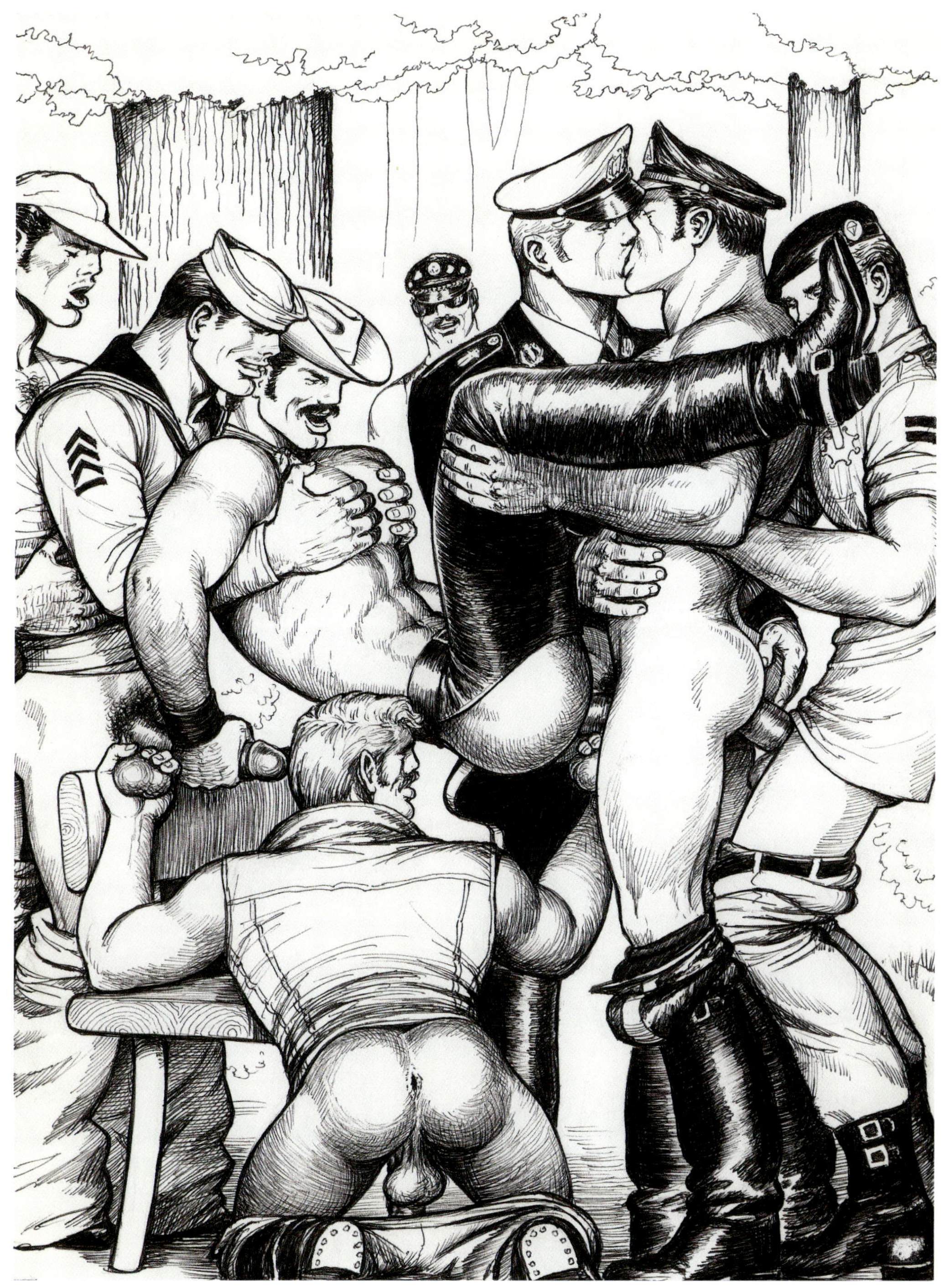

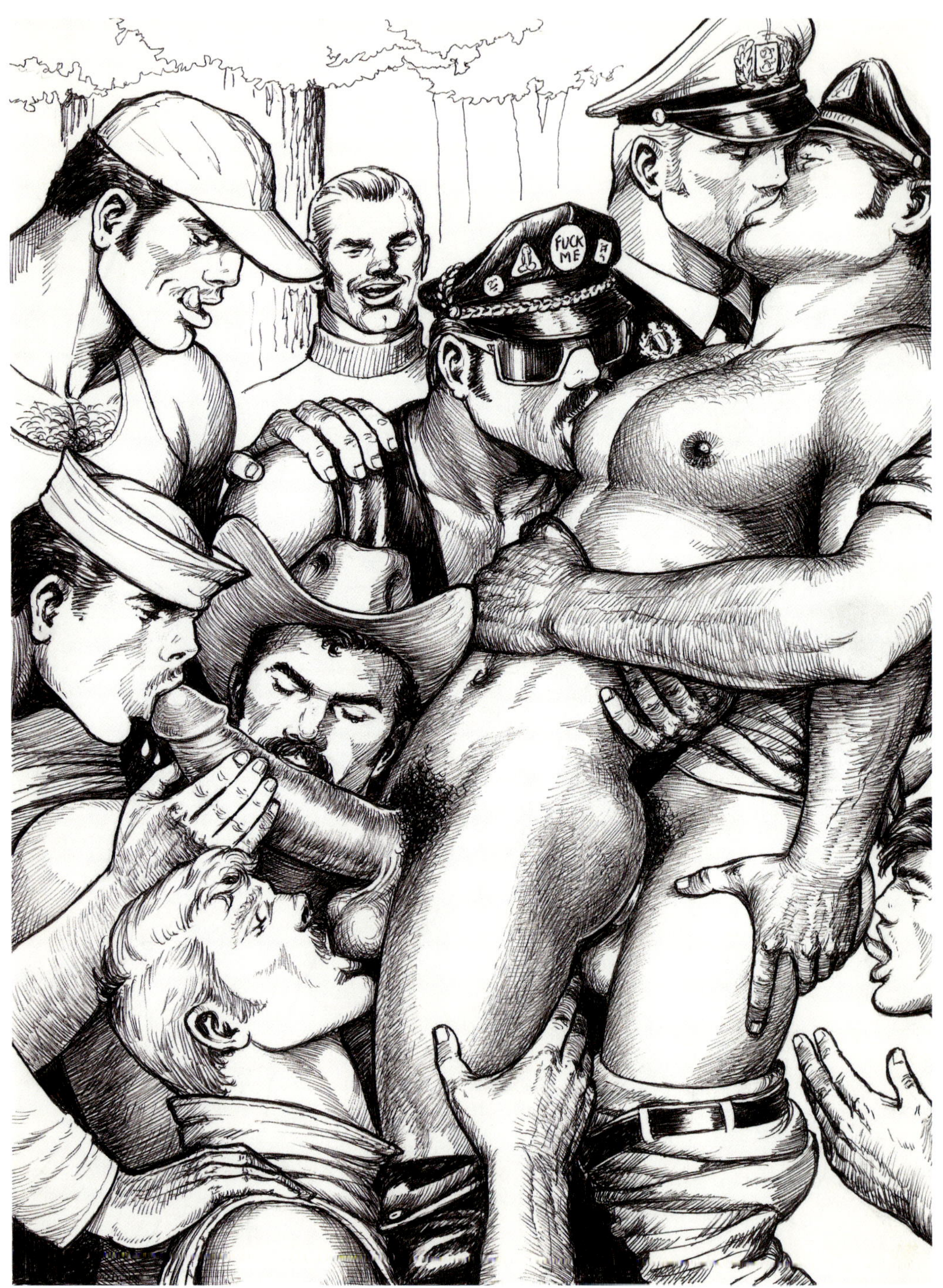
FUCK
ME

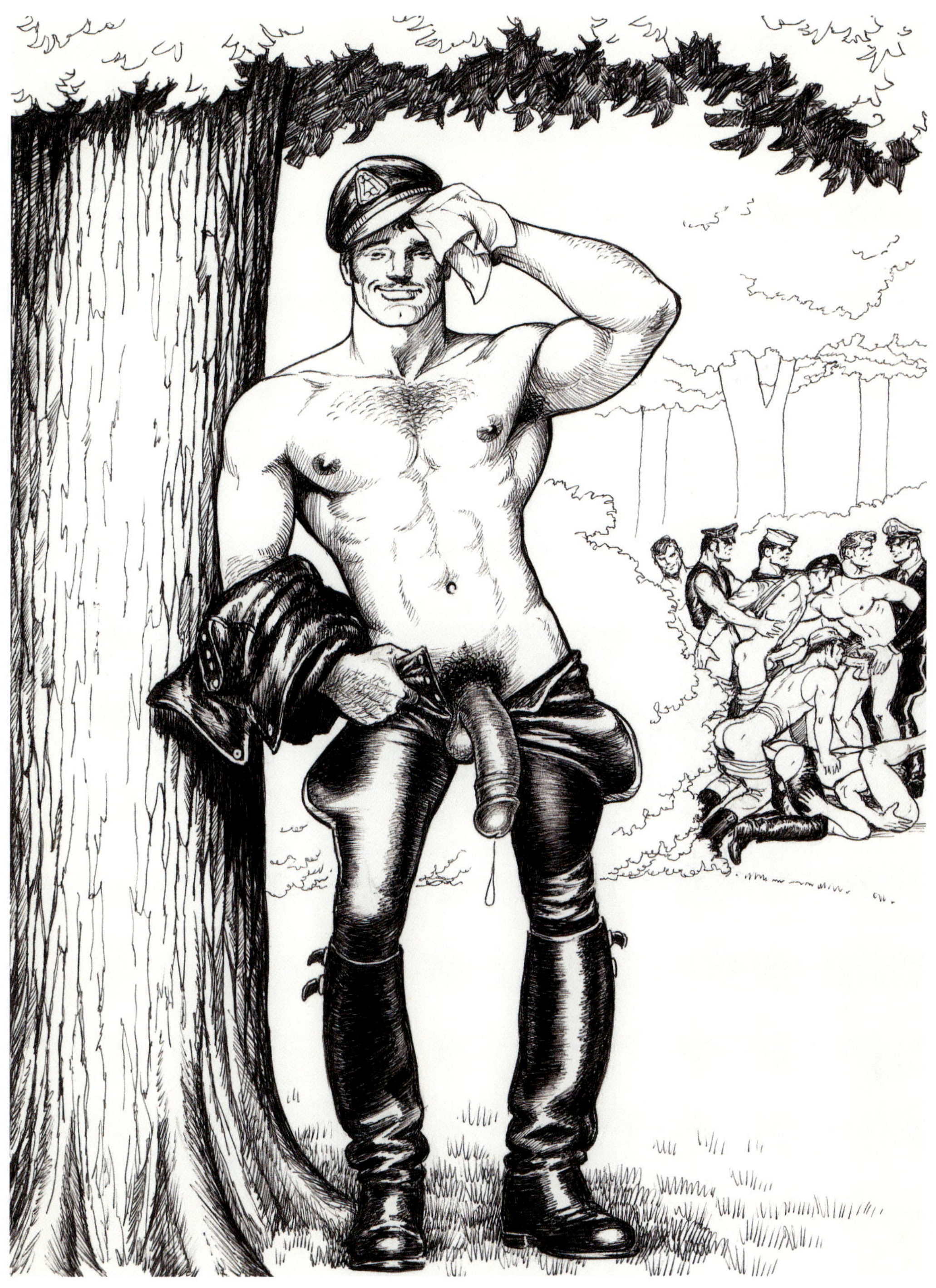

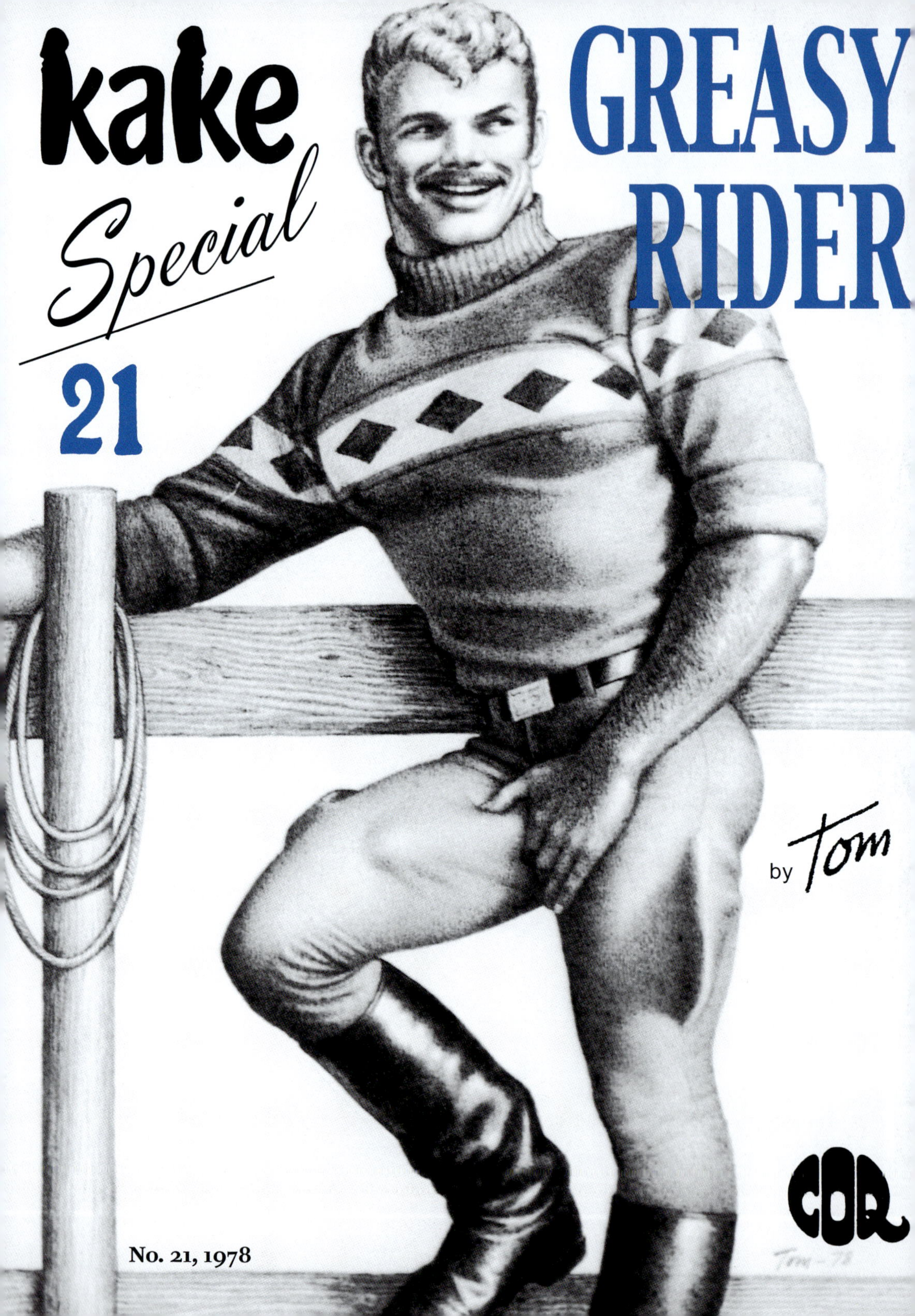

kake
Special
21
No. 21, 1978
GREASY RIDER
by Tom
CDR

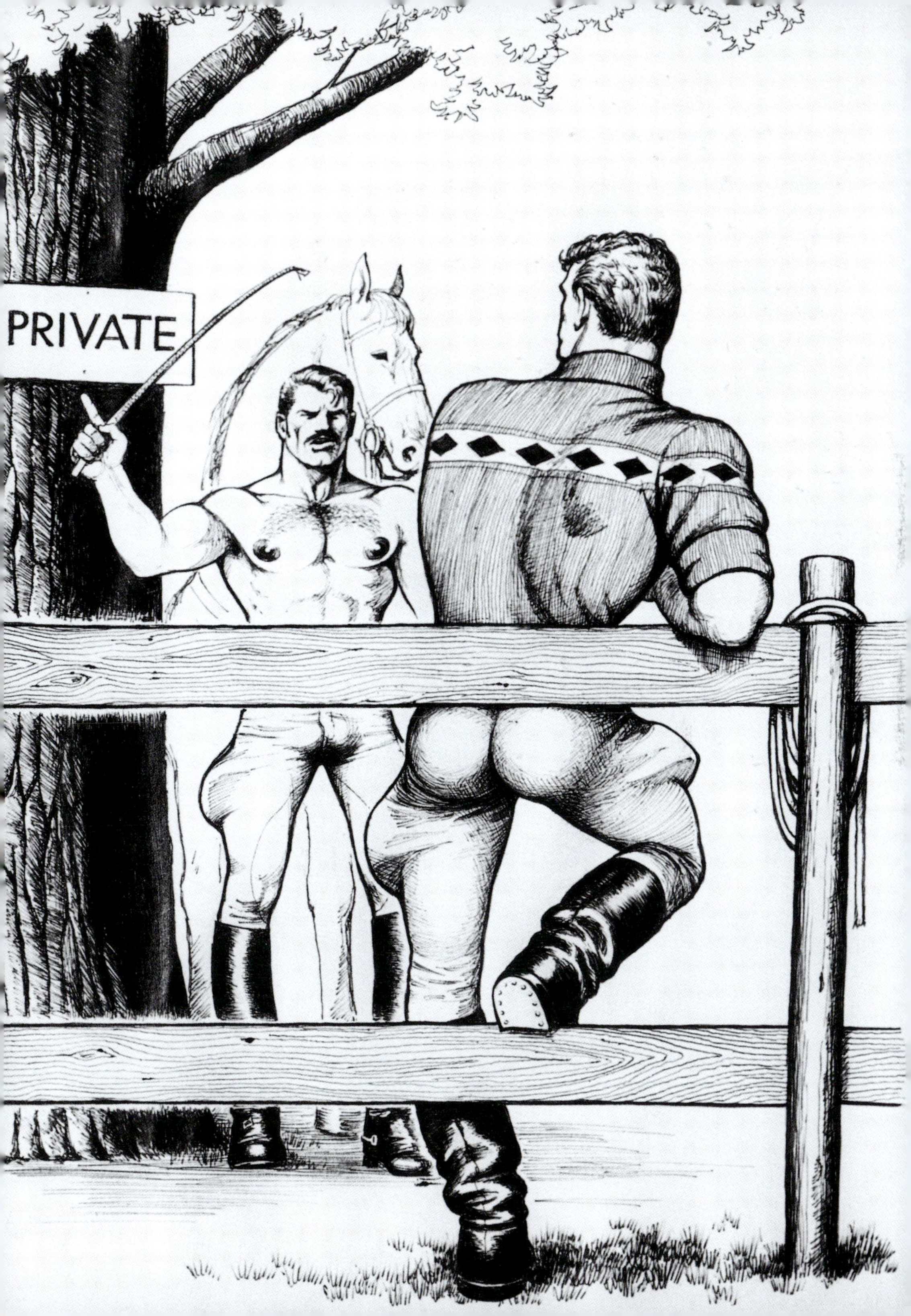
PRIVATE

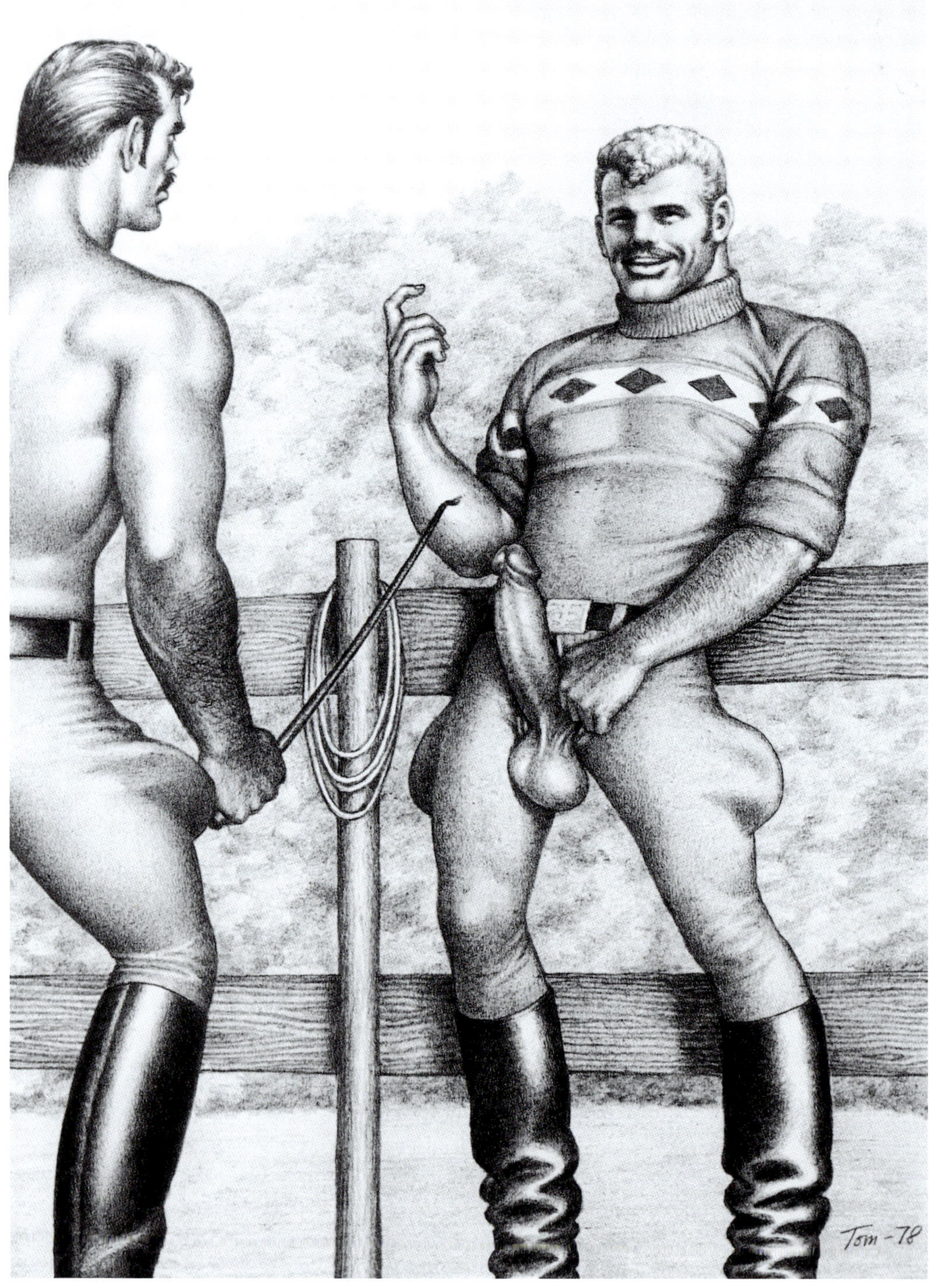

Tom -78

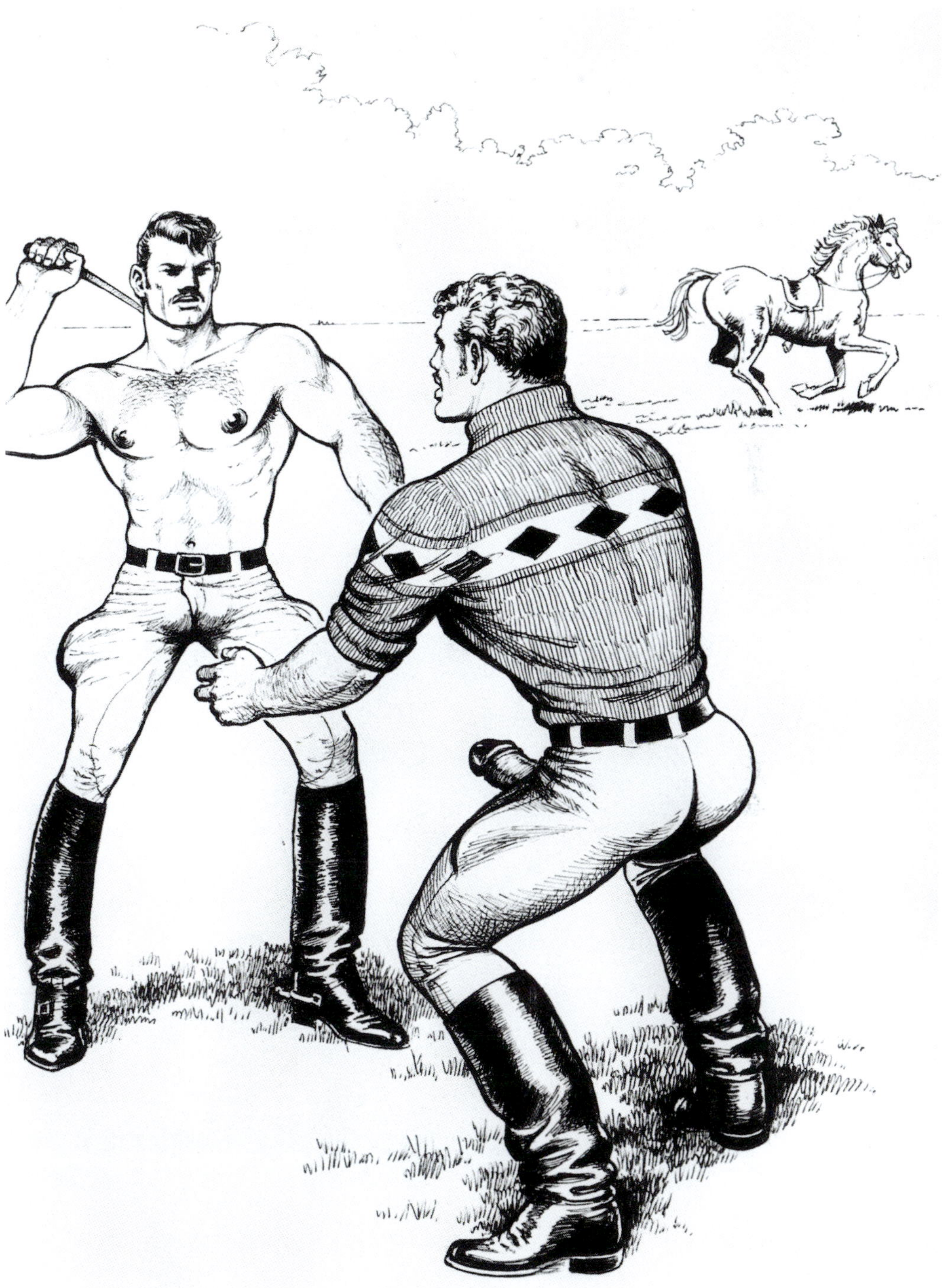

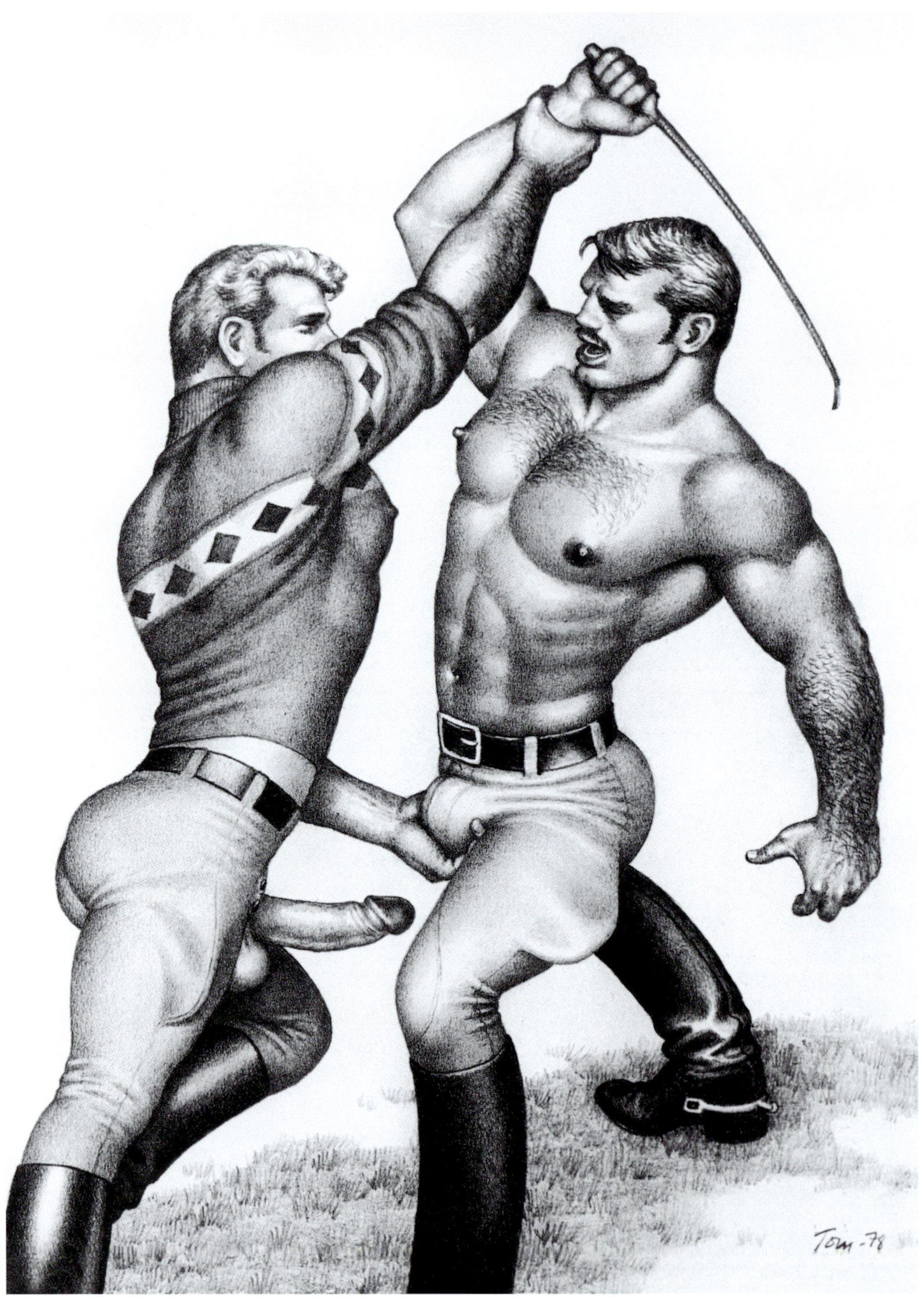

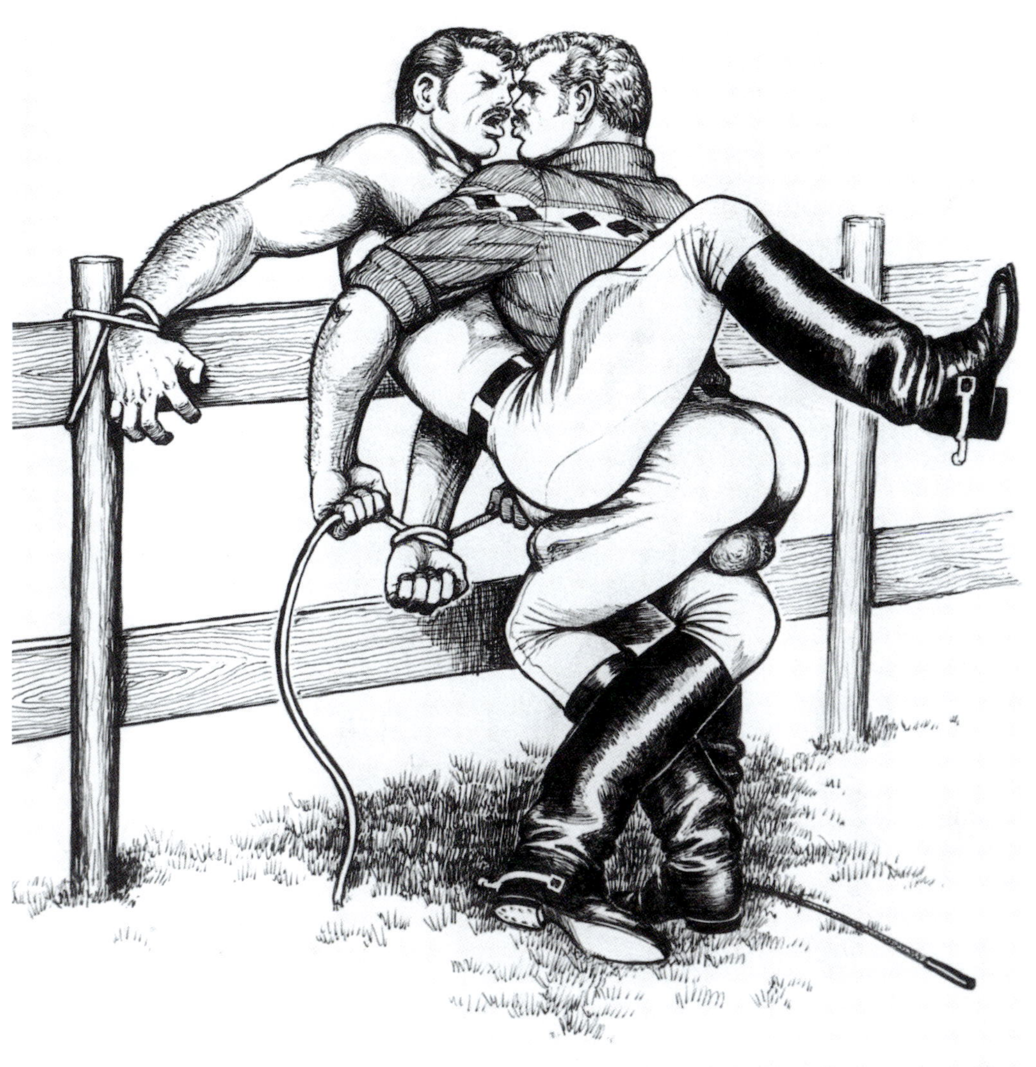

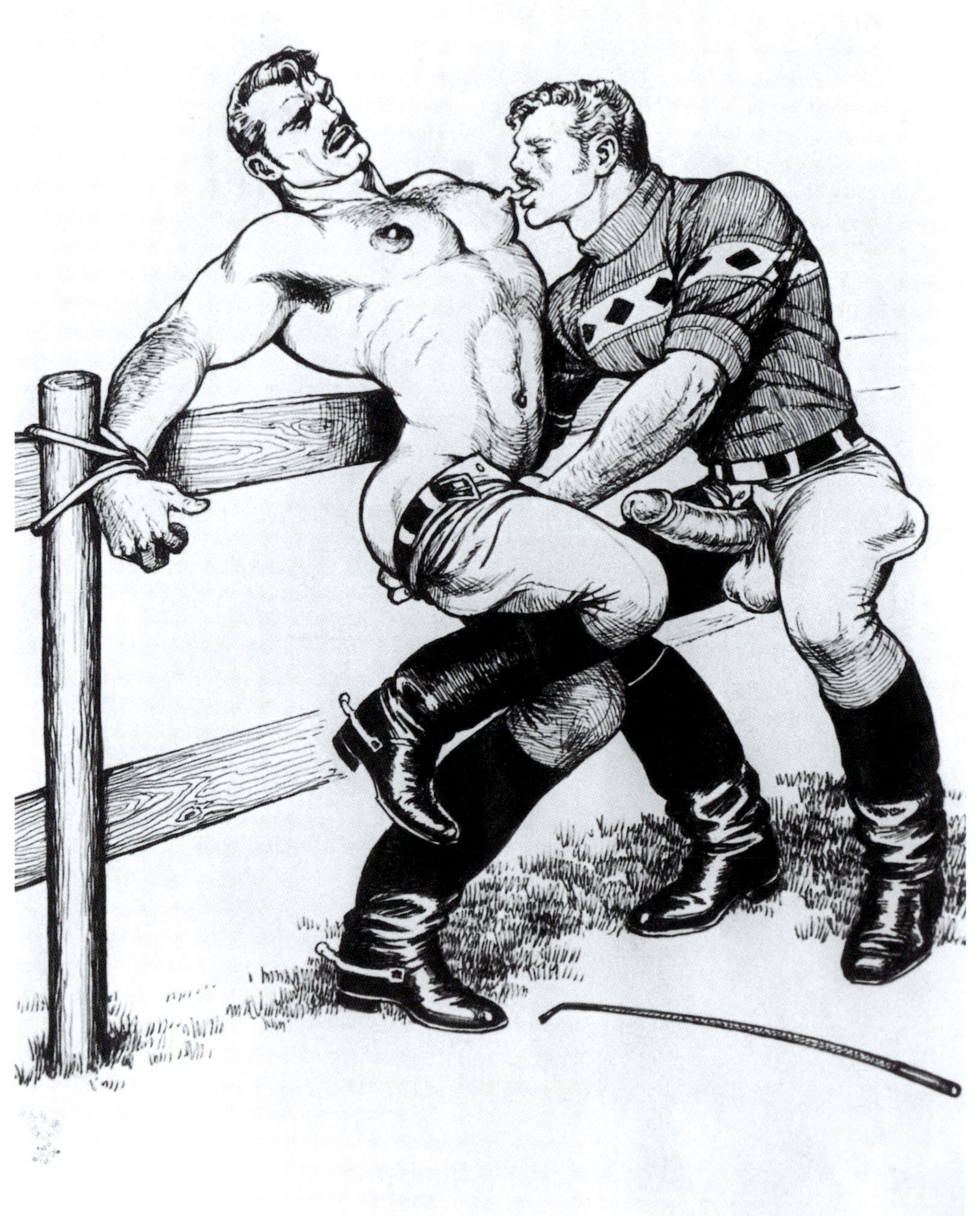

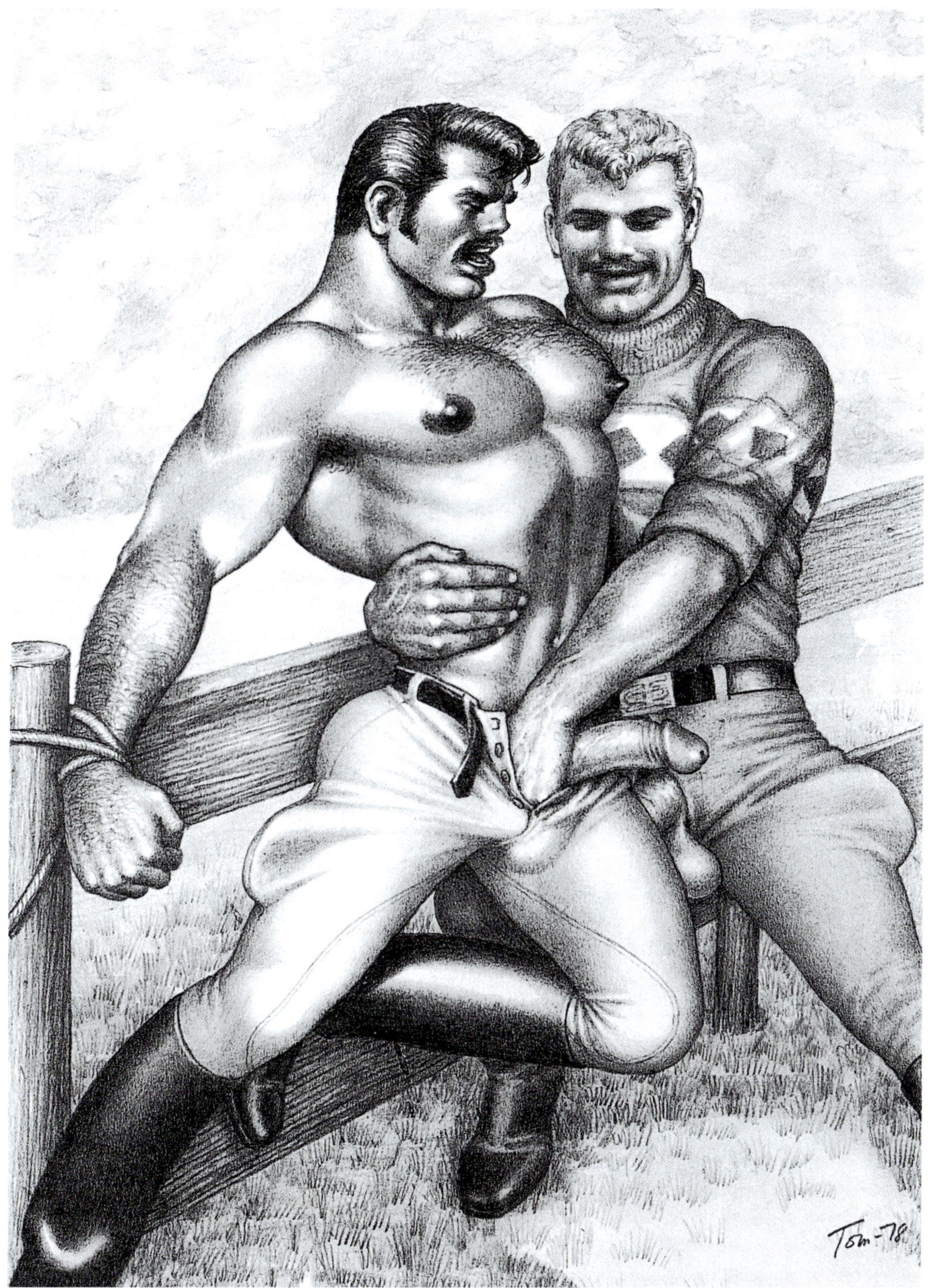

Tom-78

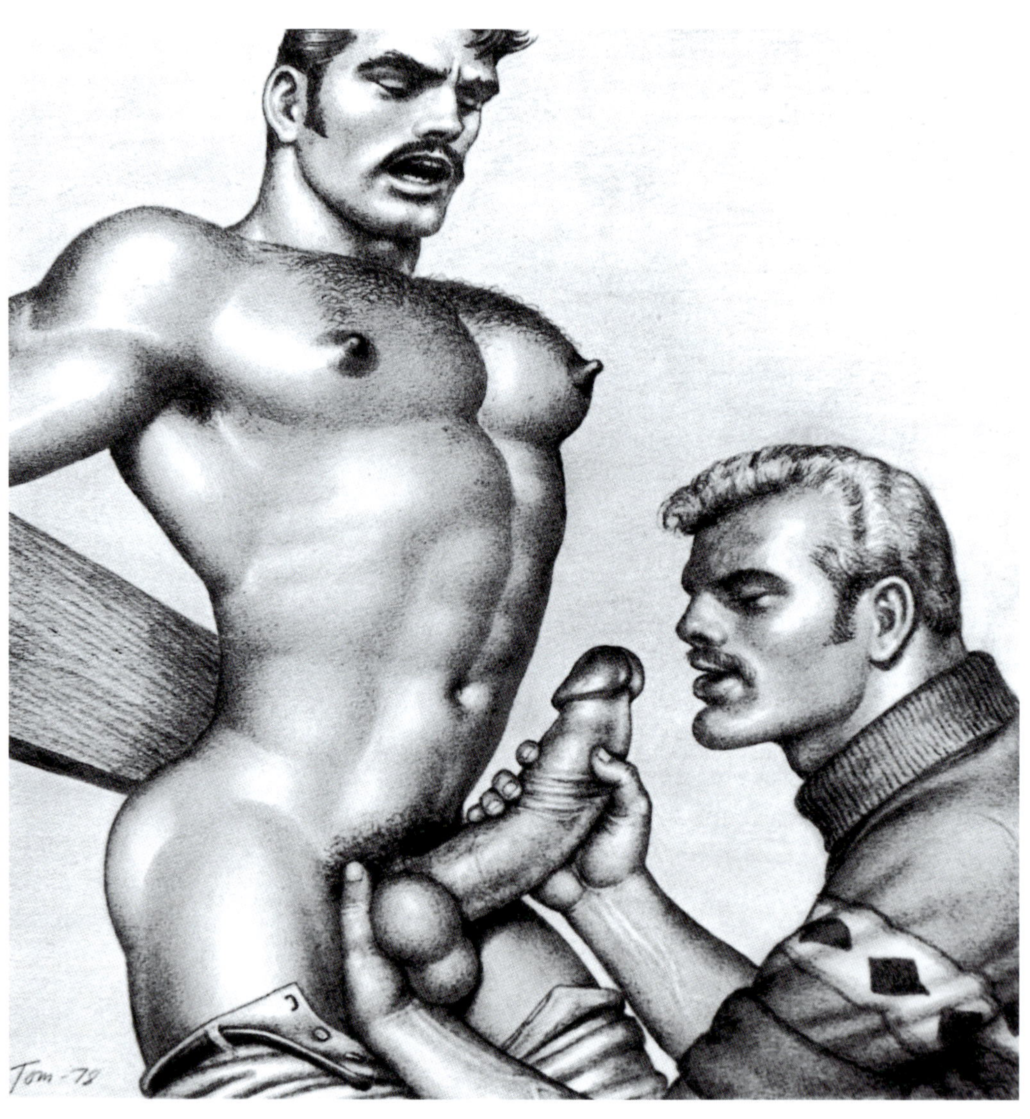

Tom -78

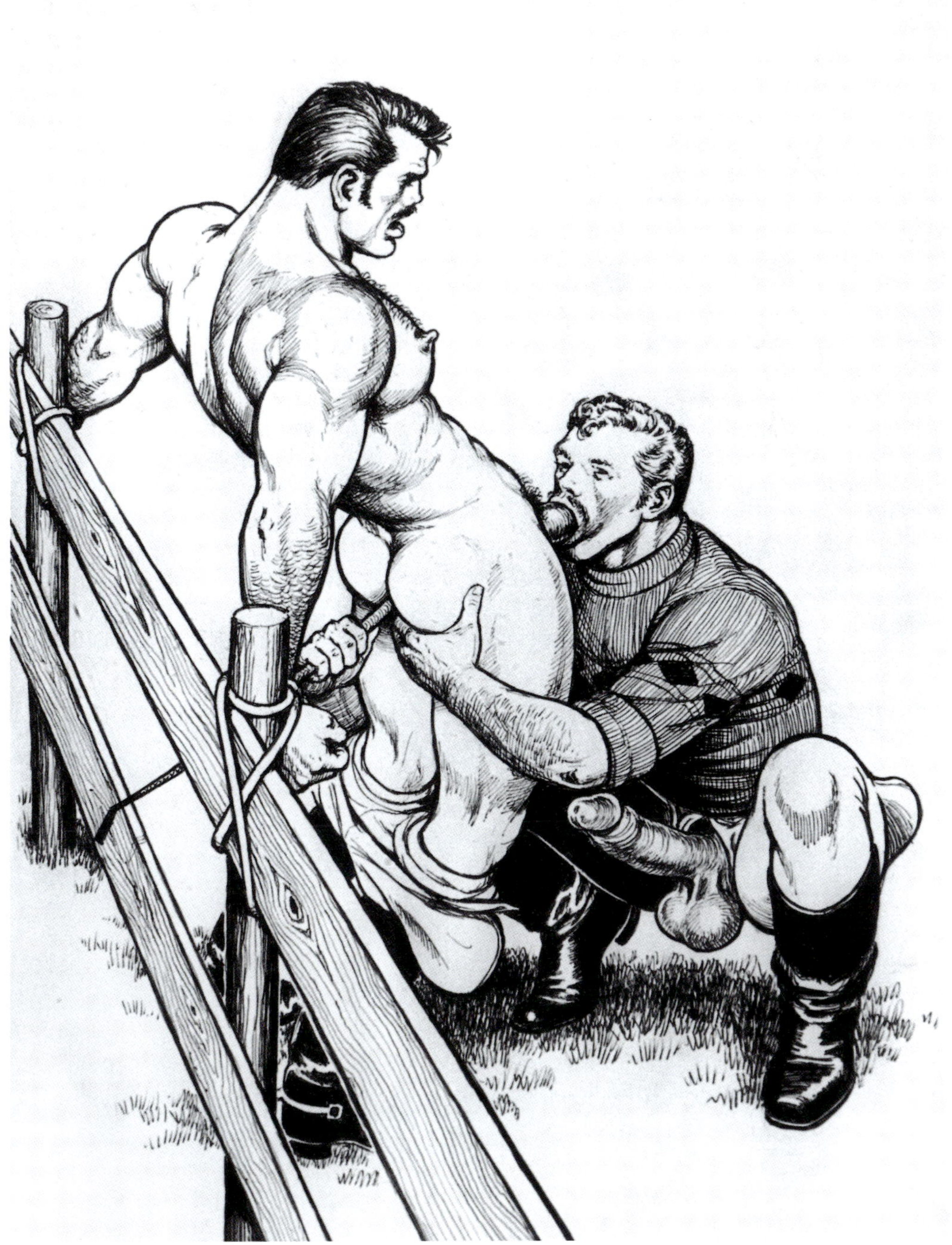

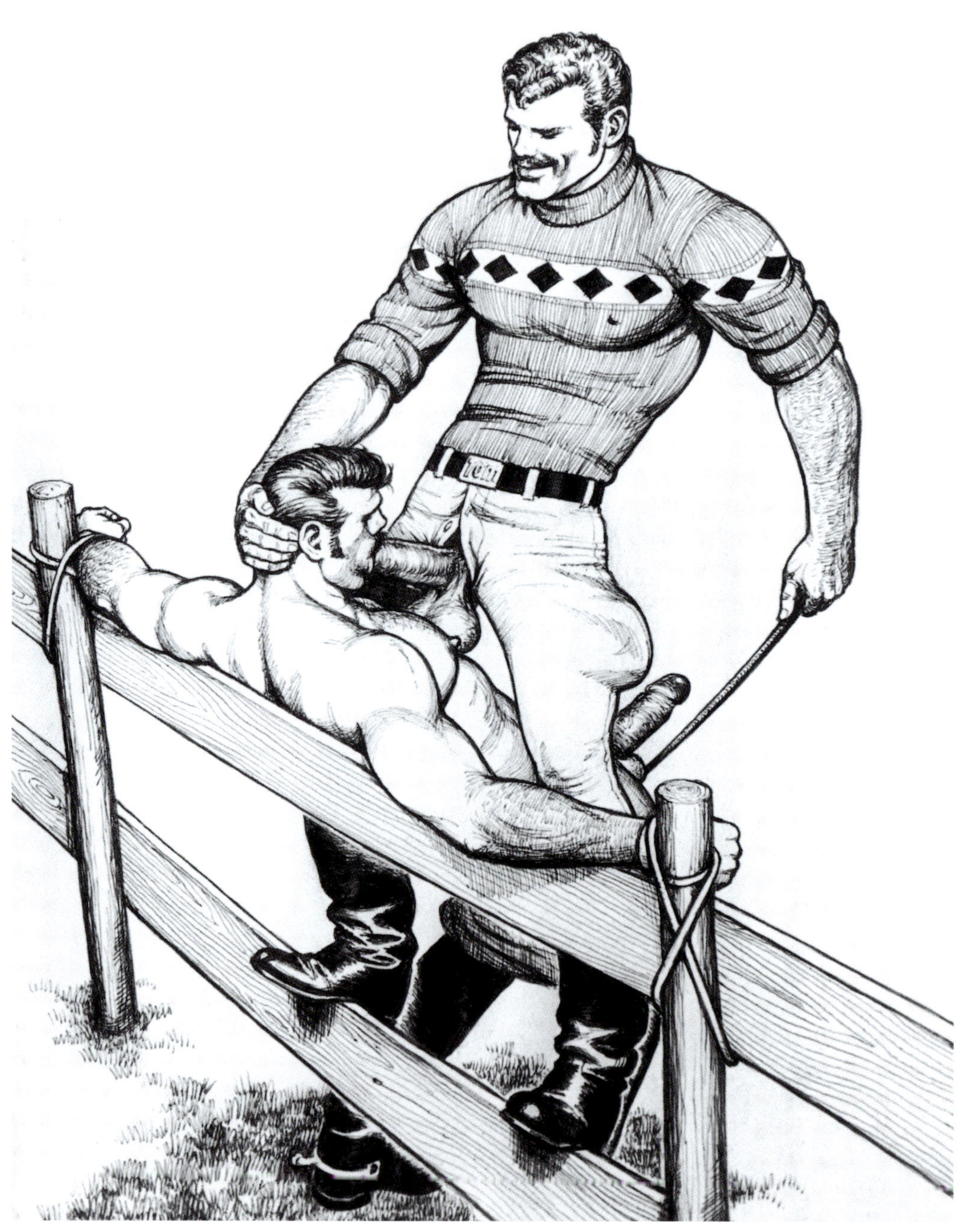

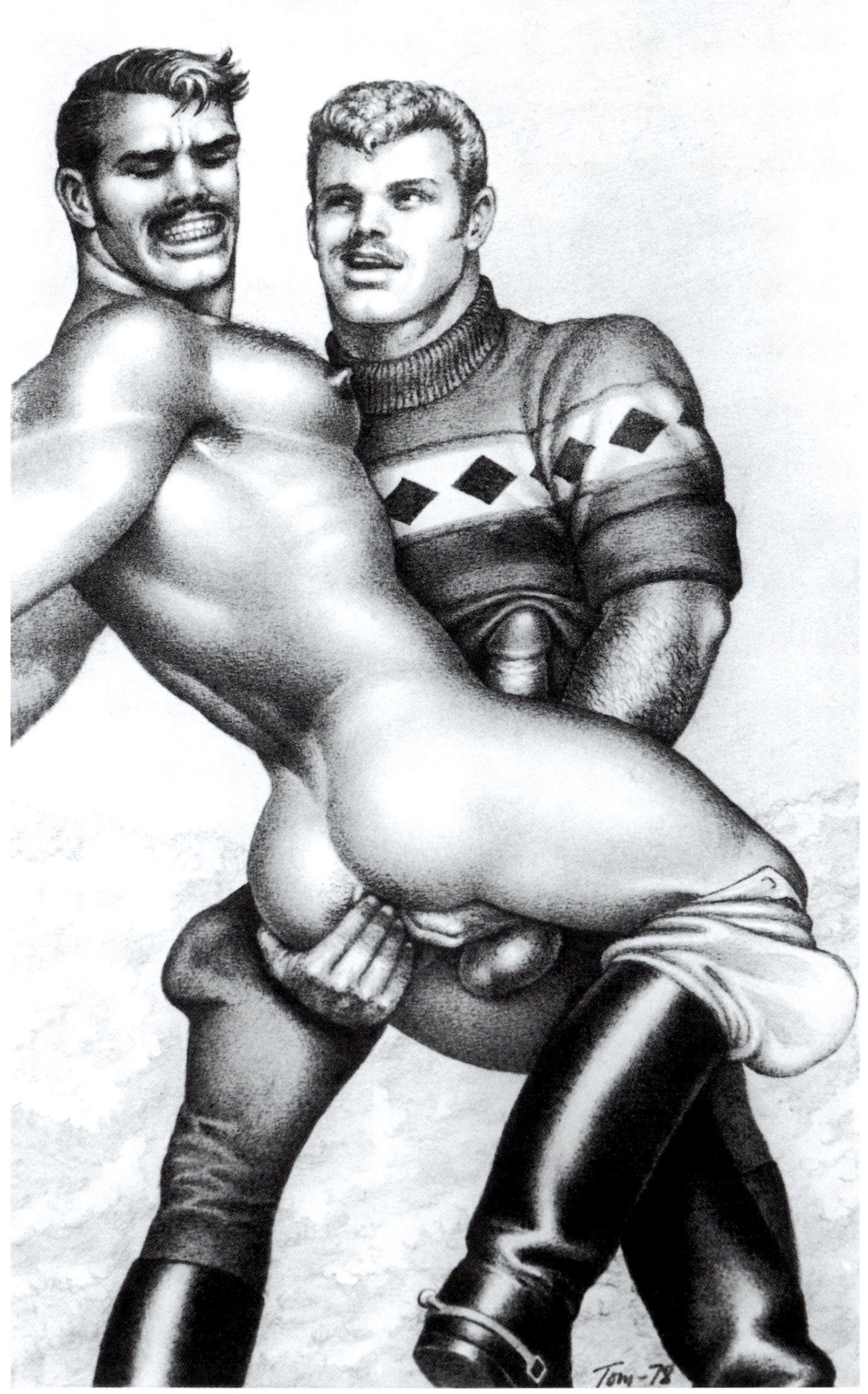

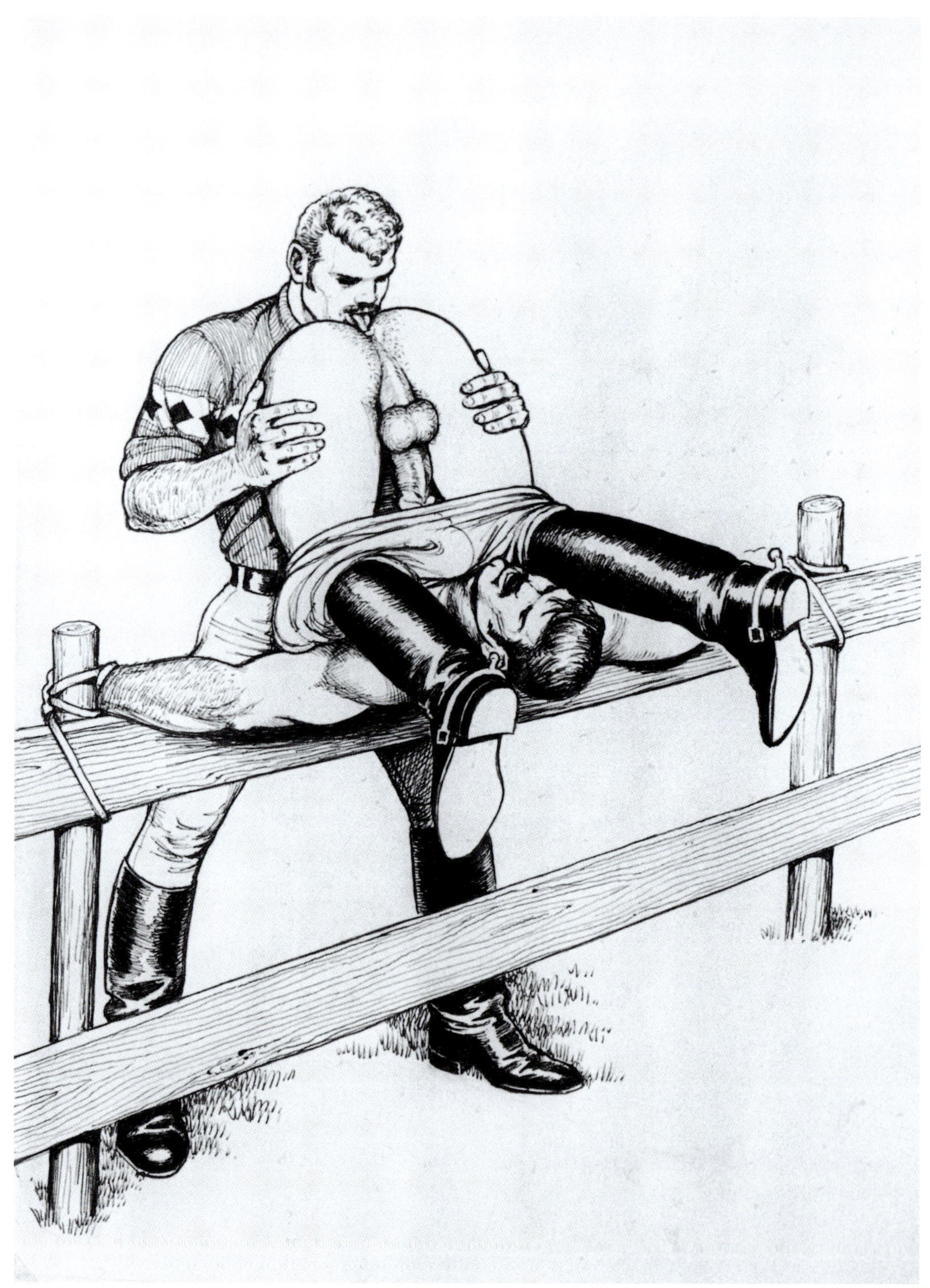

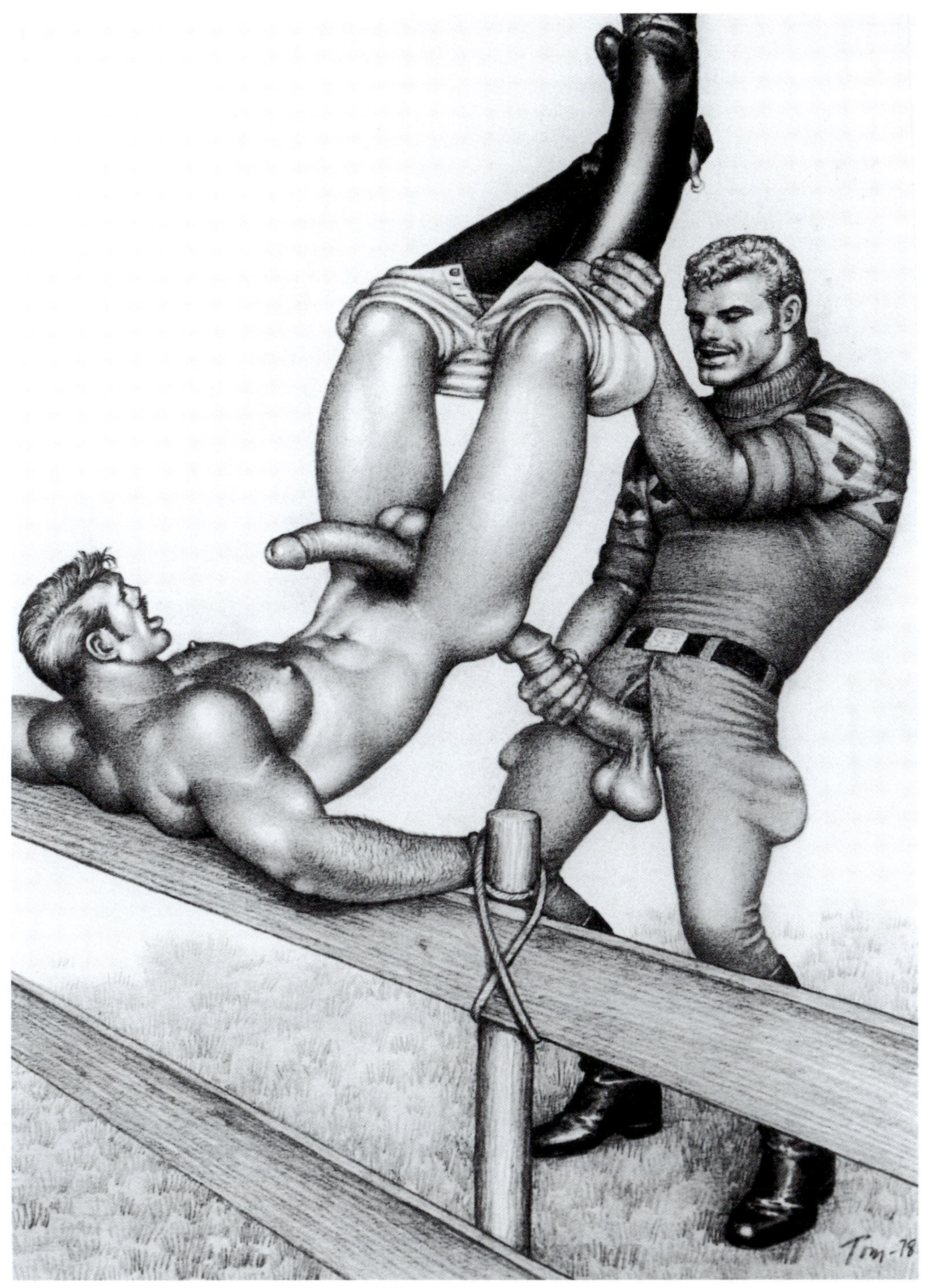

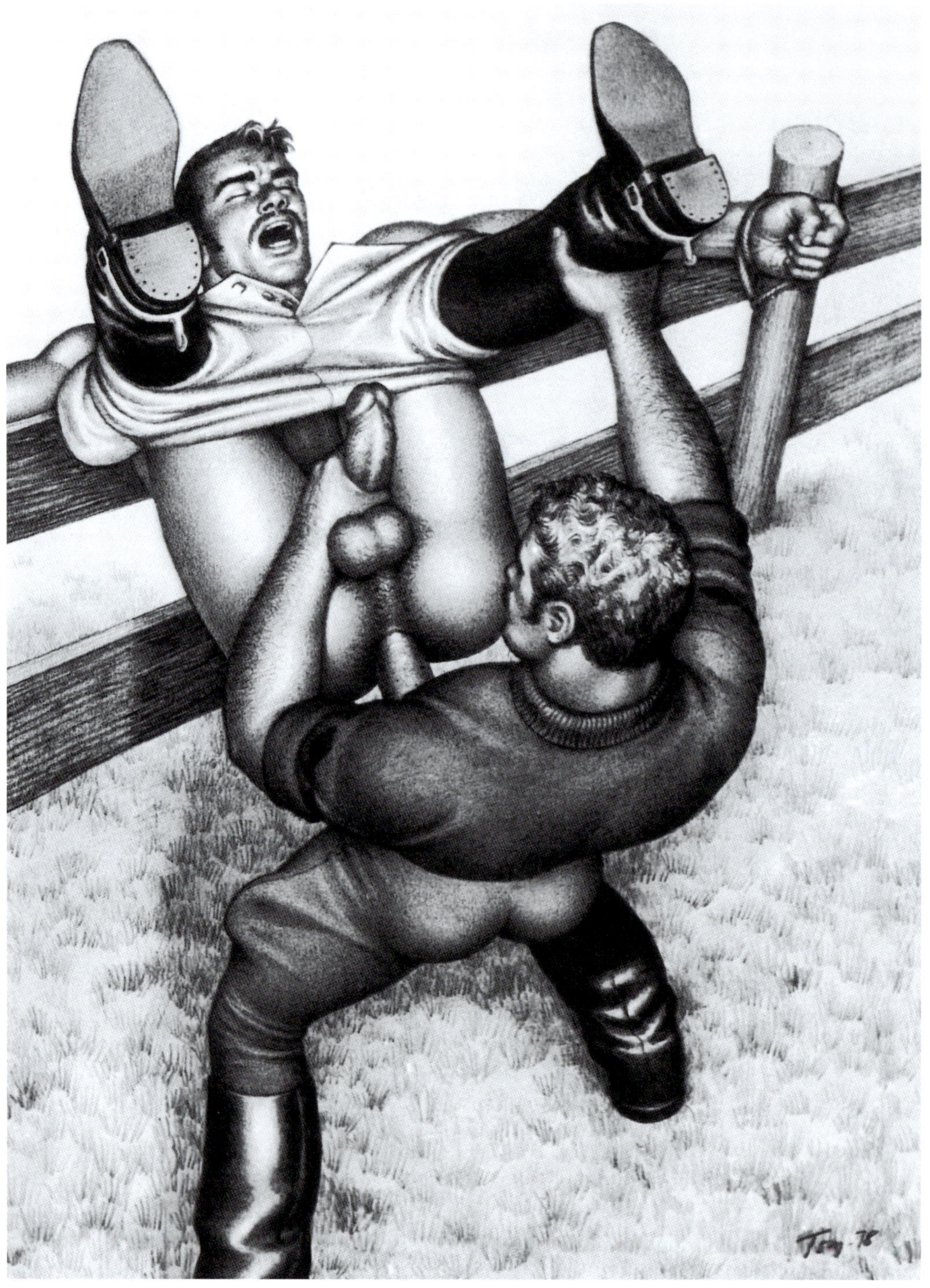

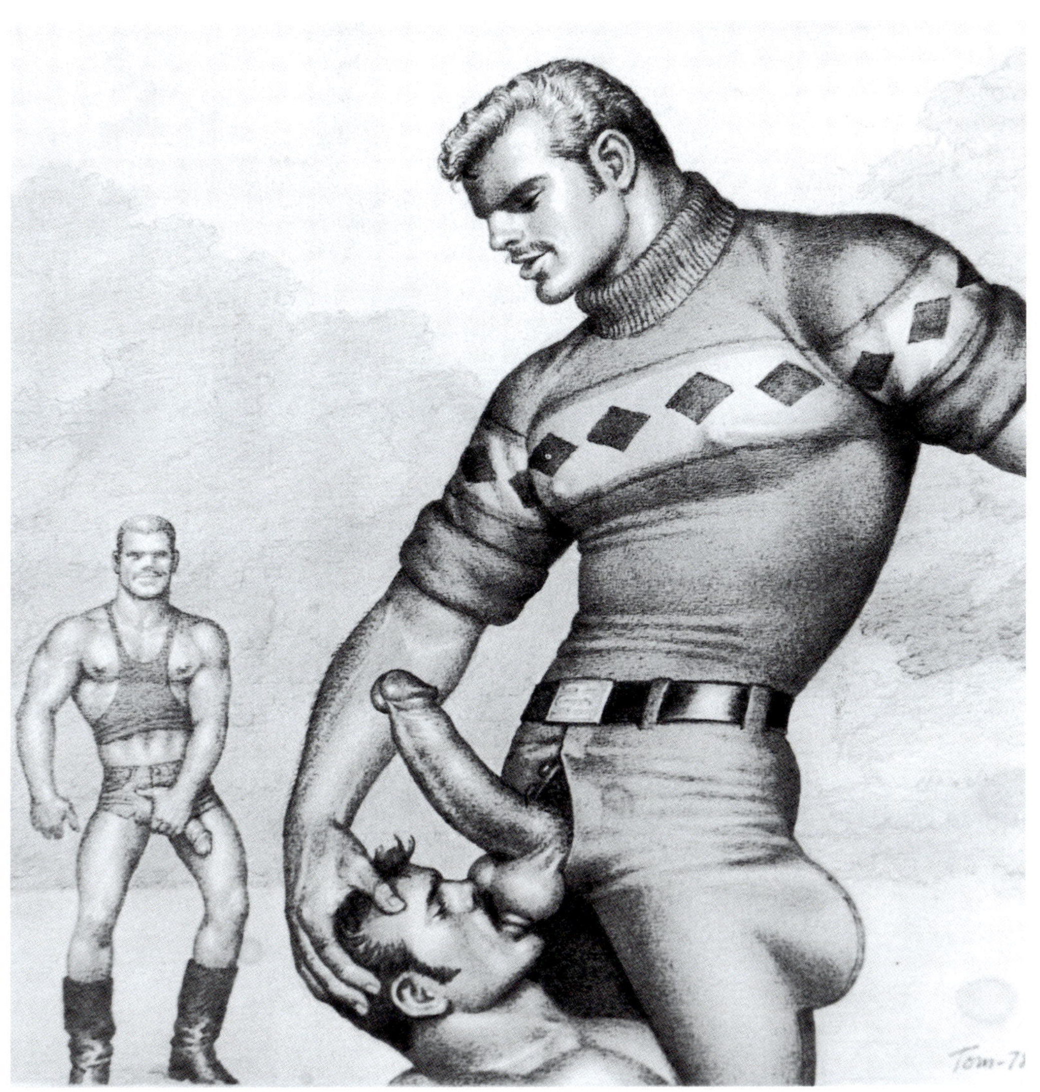

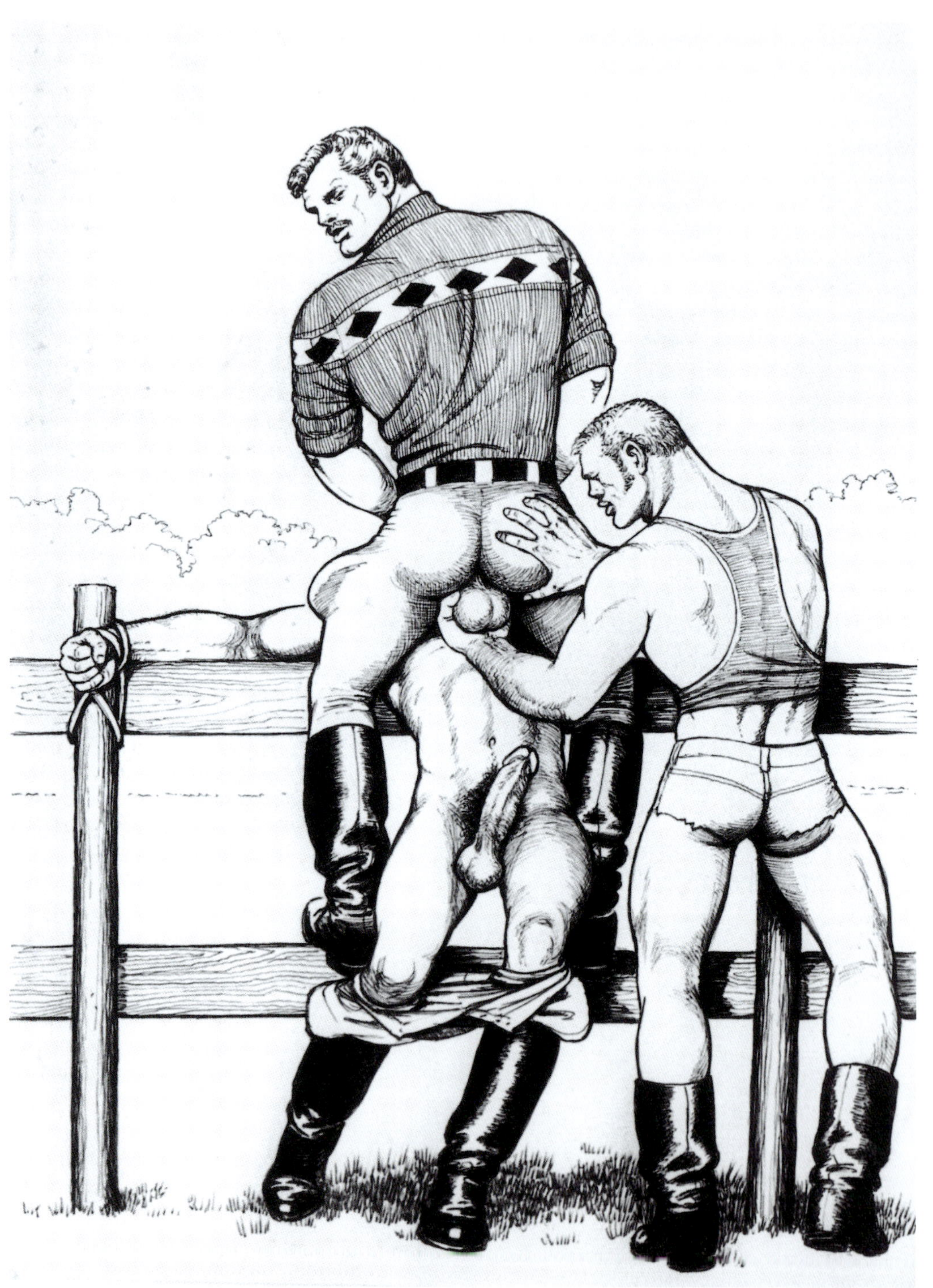

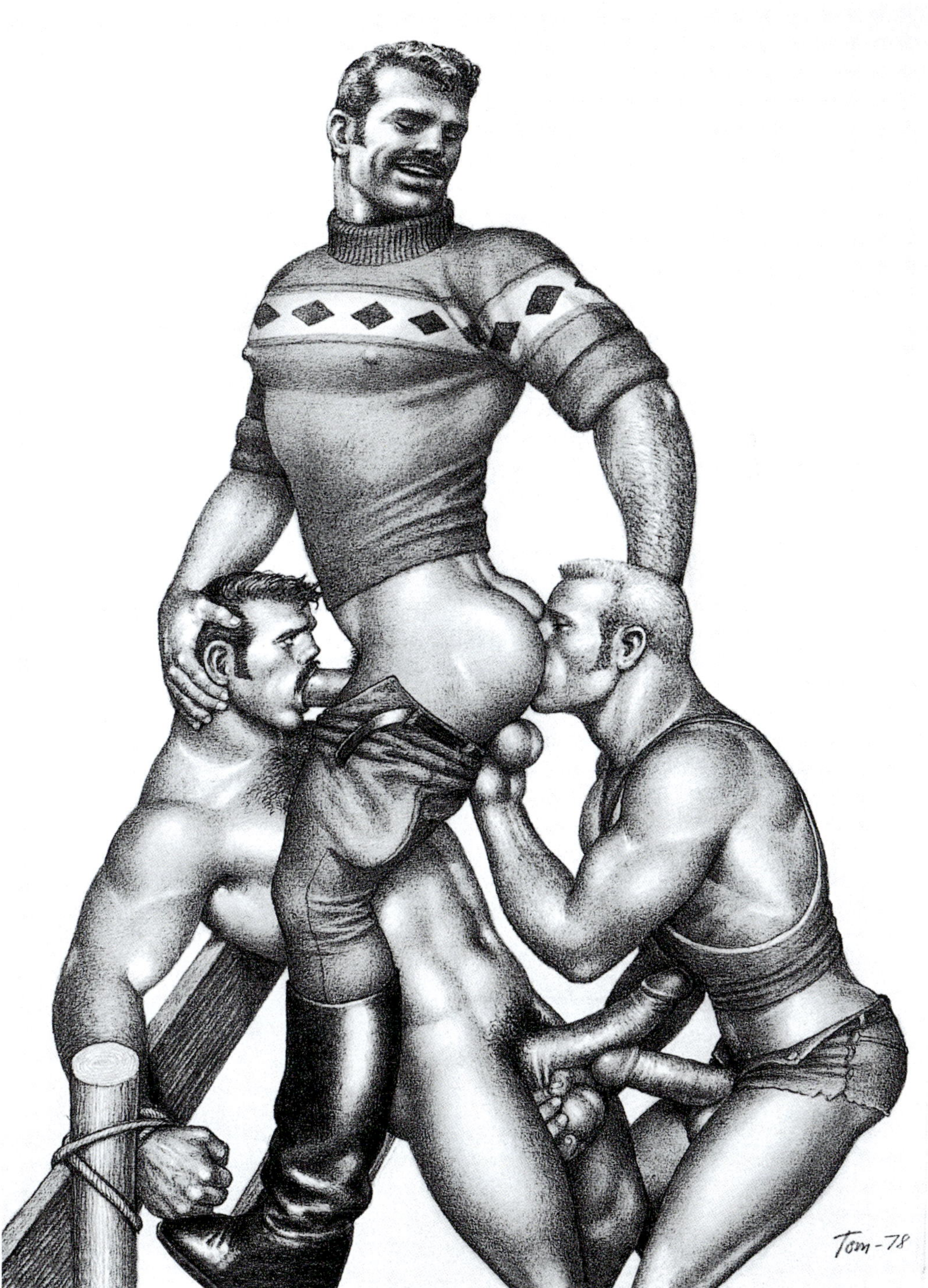

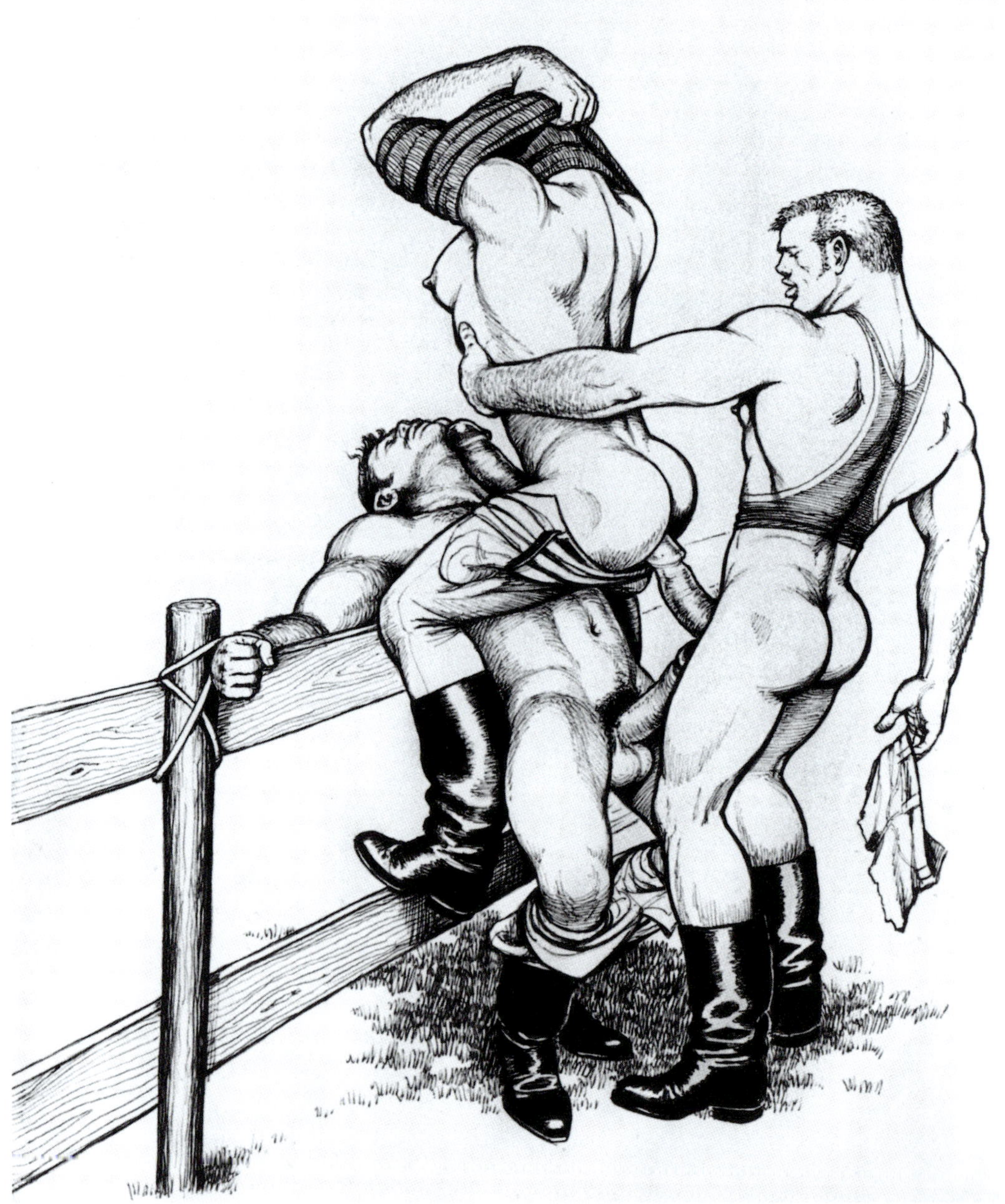

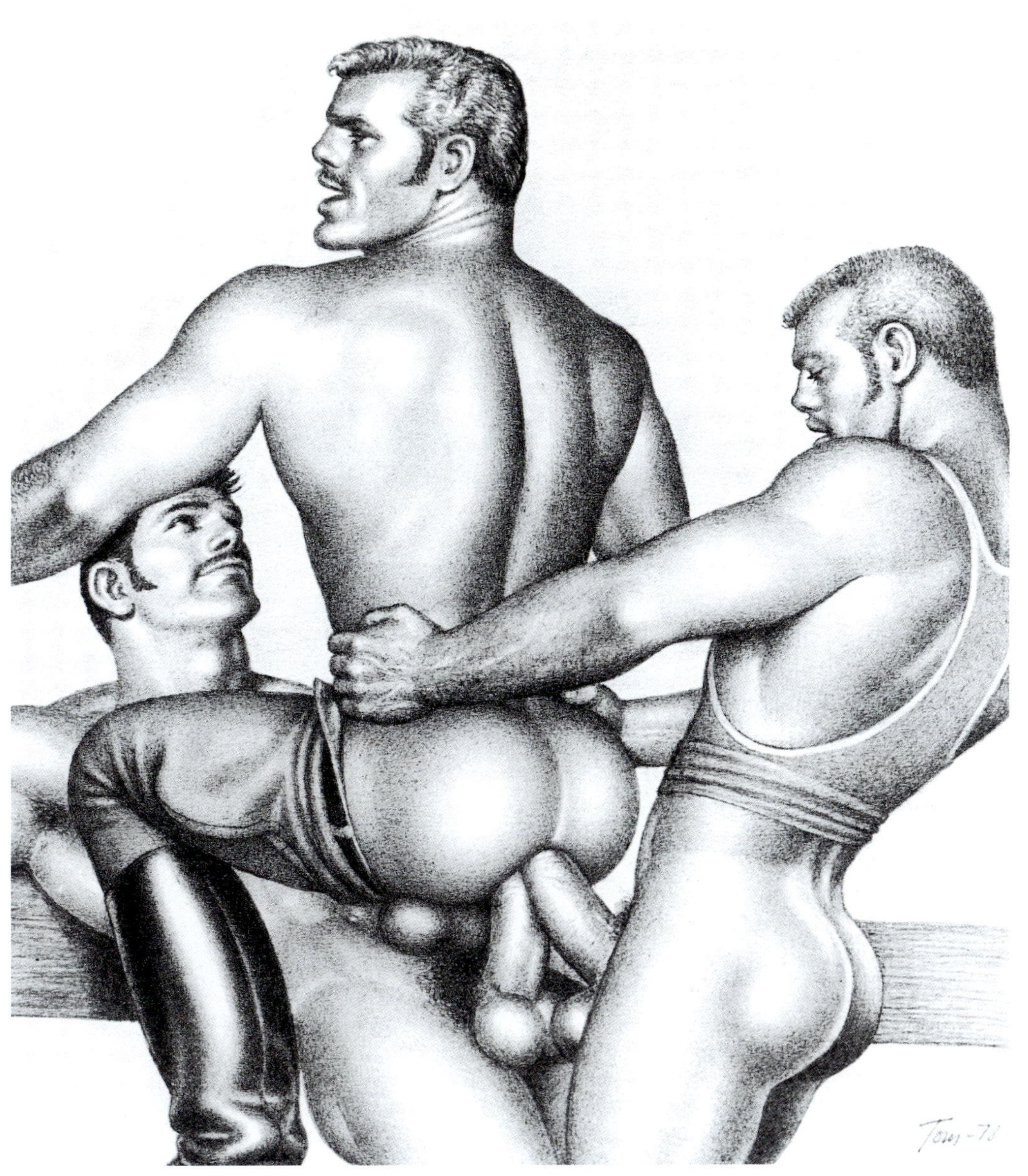

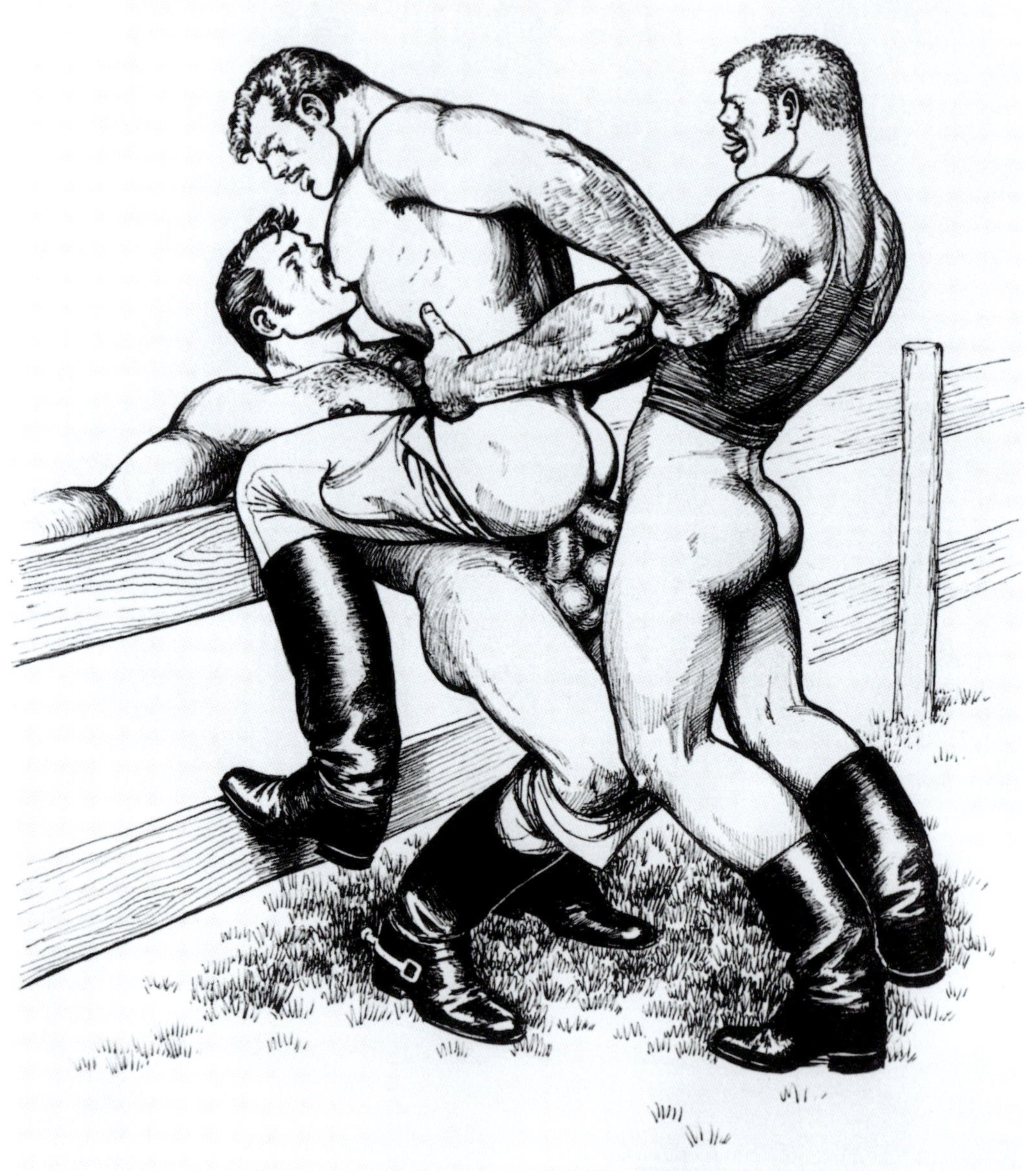

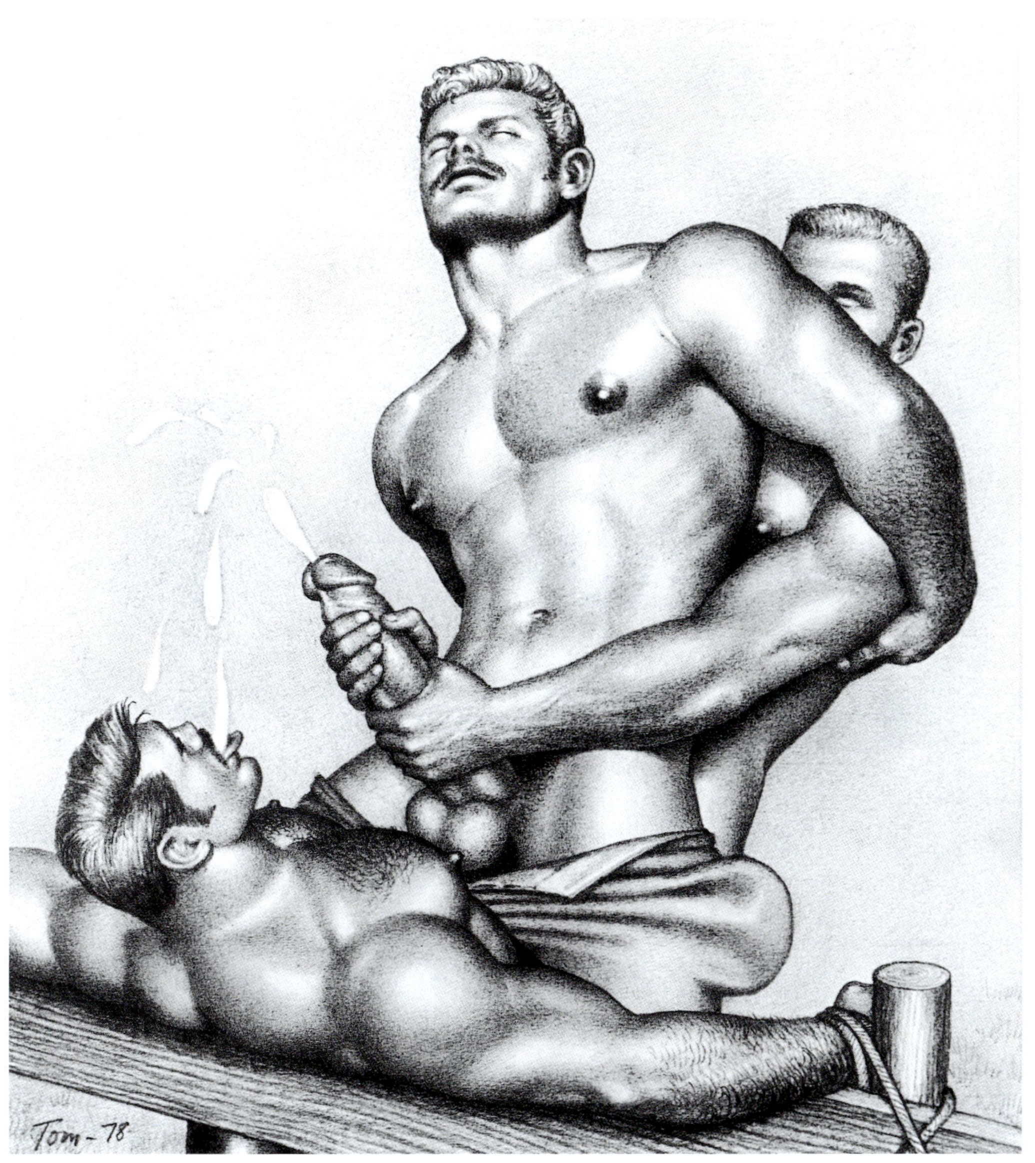

Tom-78

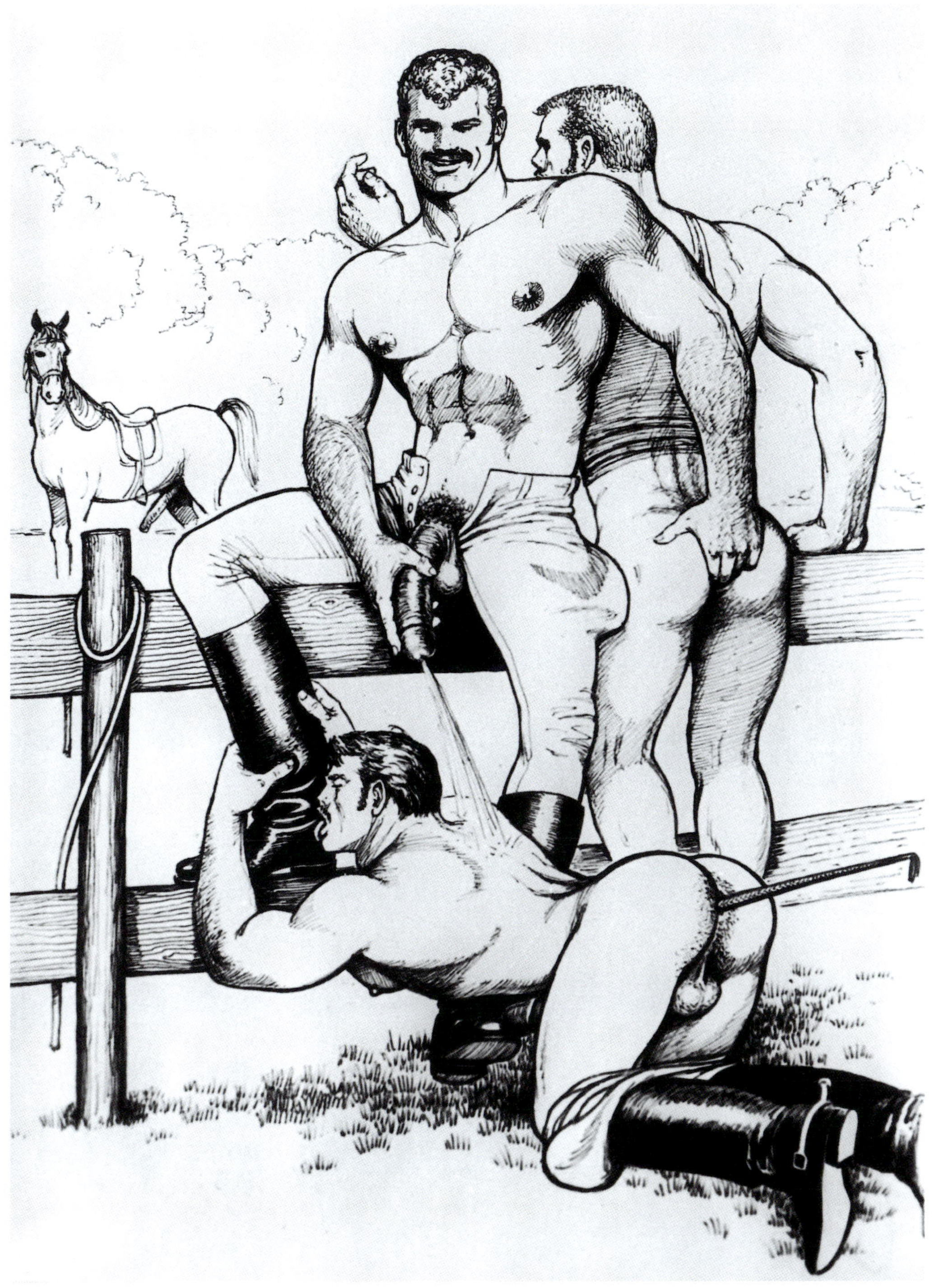

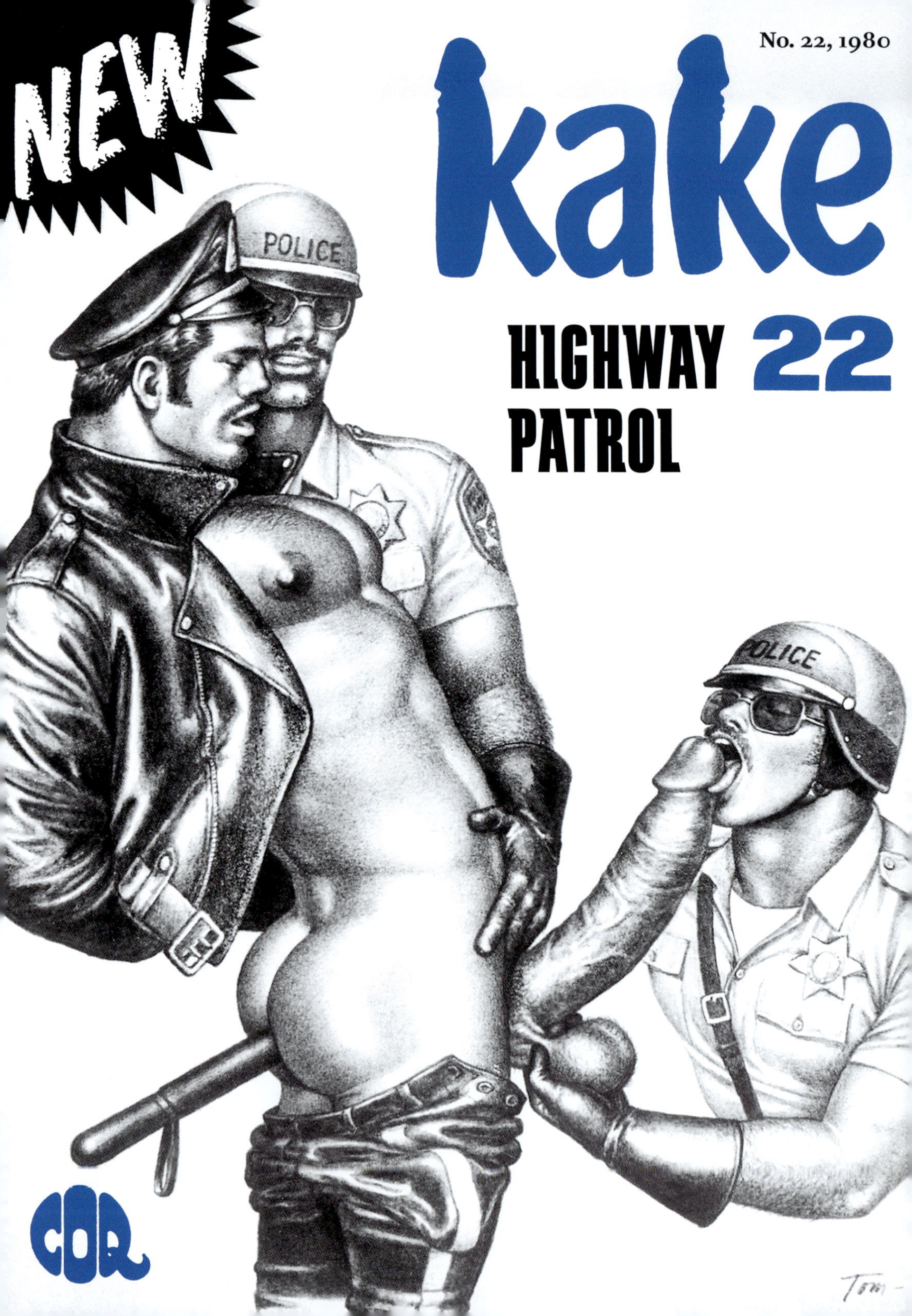
NEW
No. 22, 1980
kake
22
HIGHWAY PATROL
POLICE
POLICE
COQ
Tom

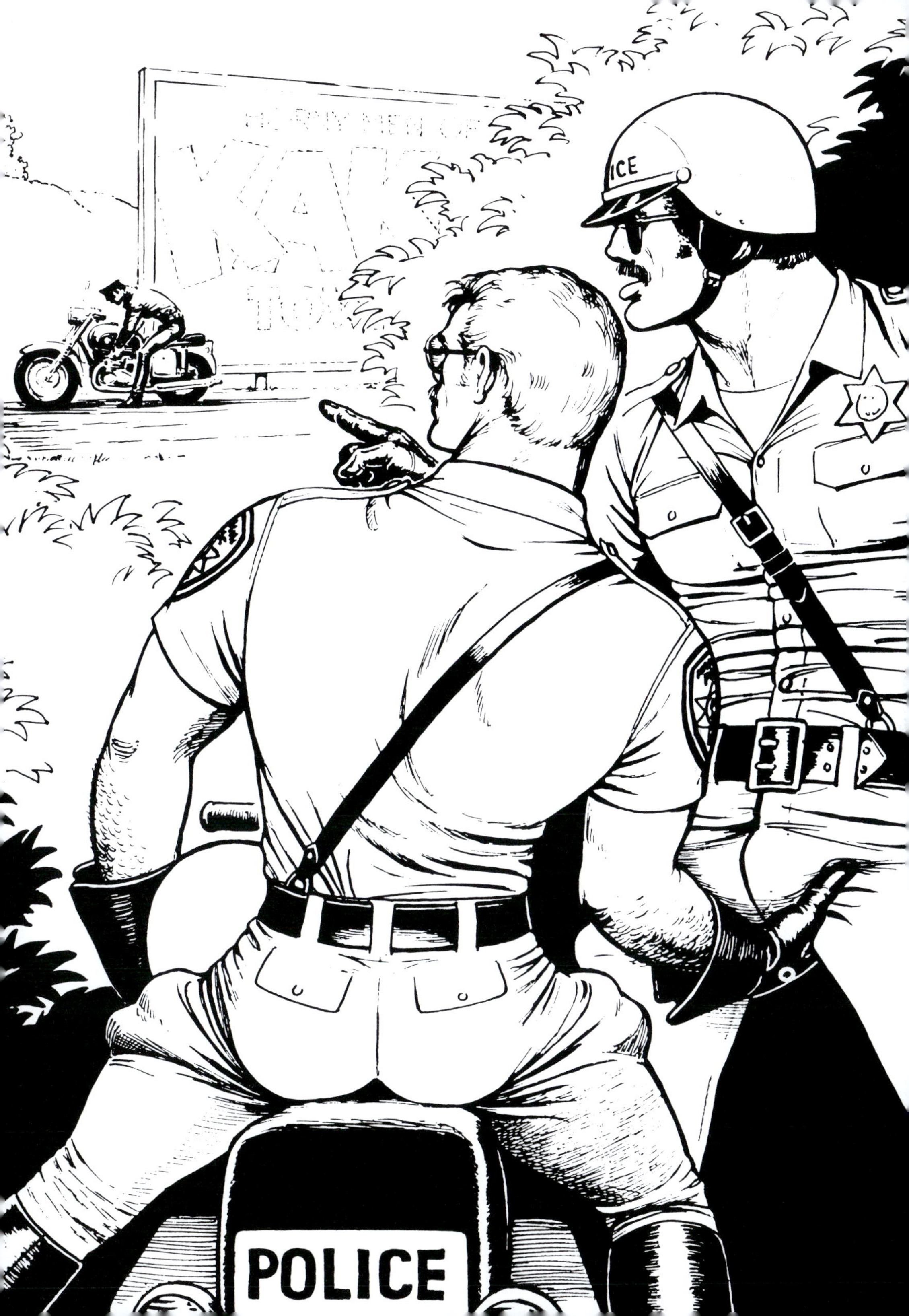
POLICE

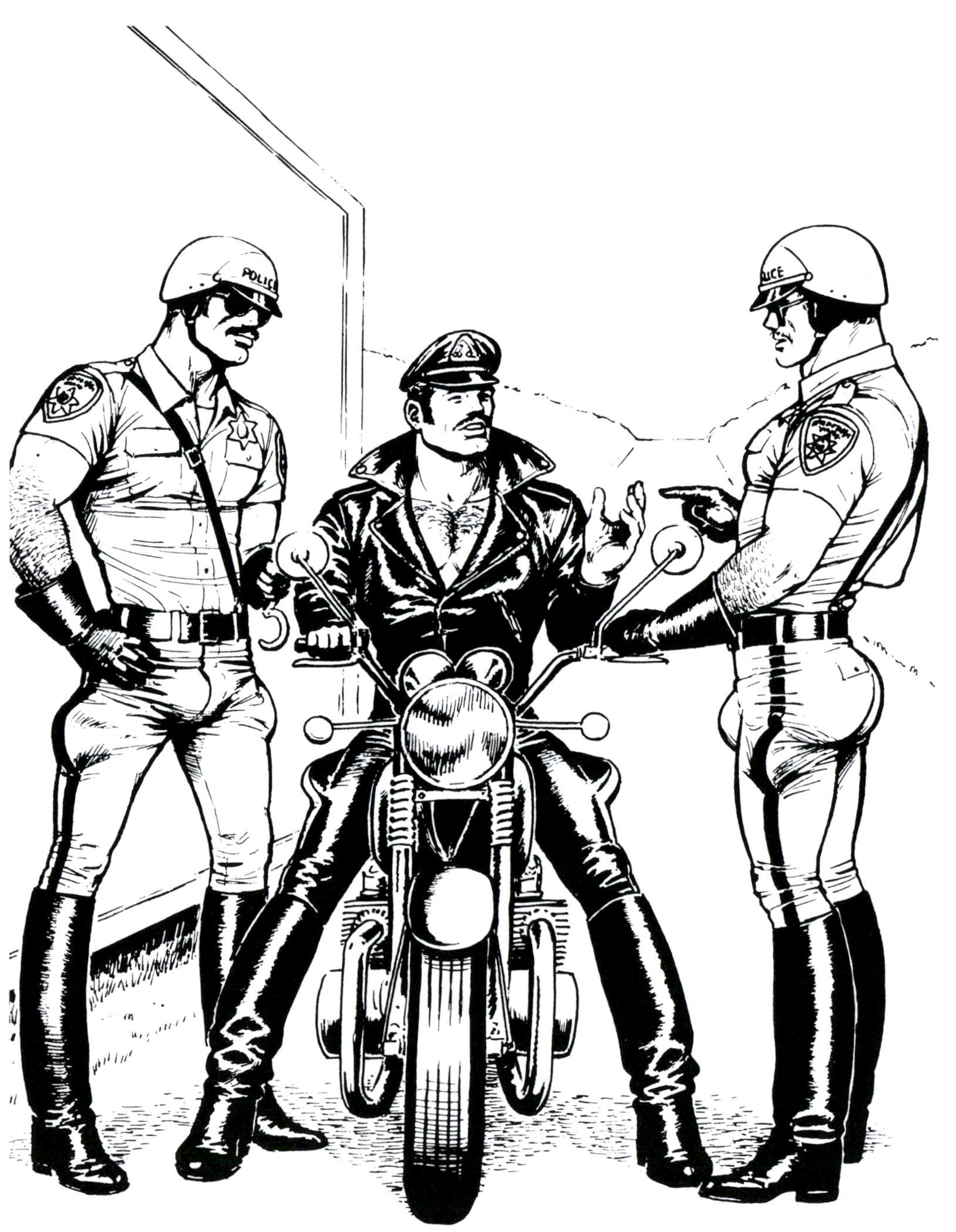

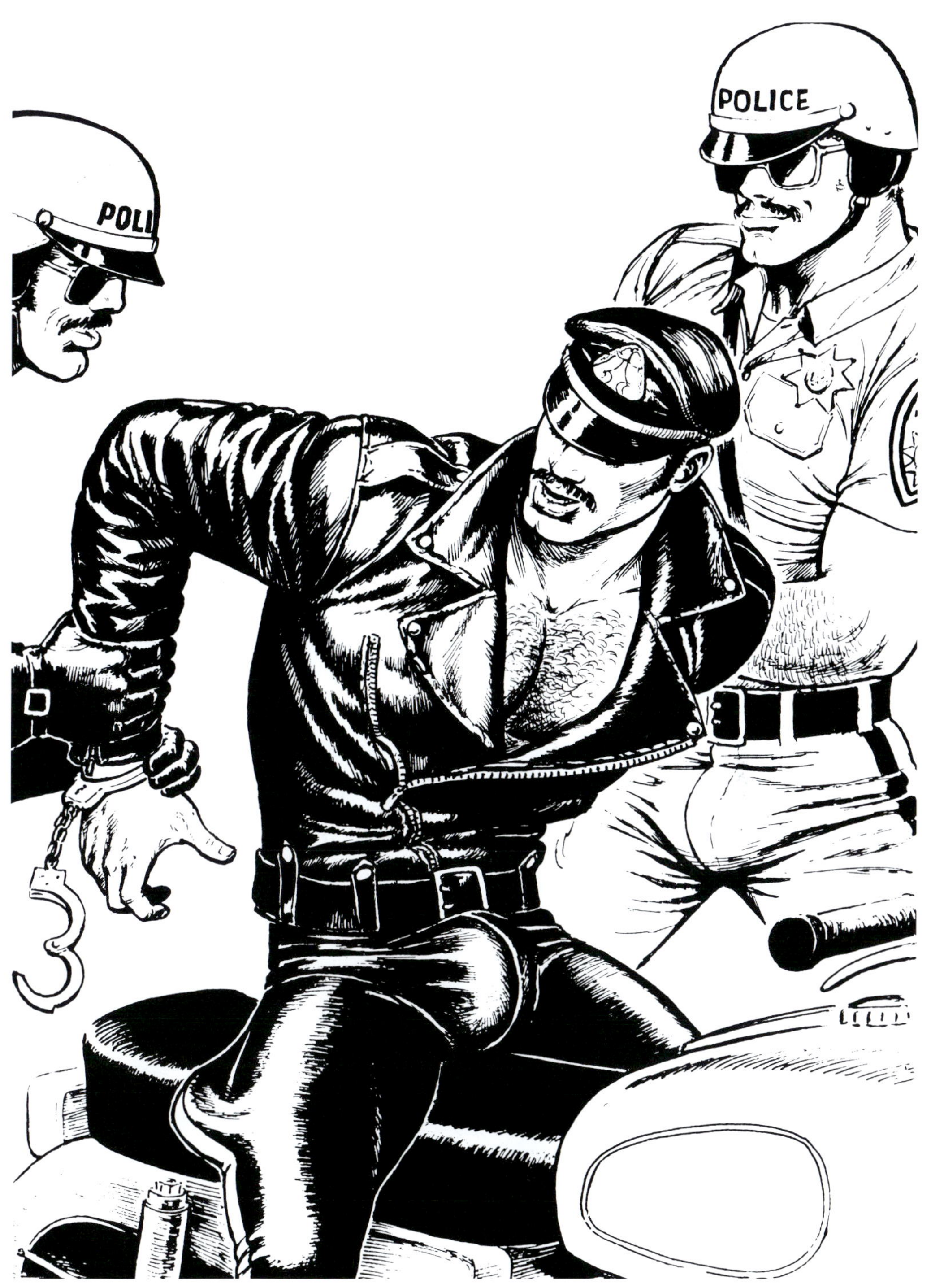
POLICE
POLI

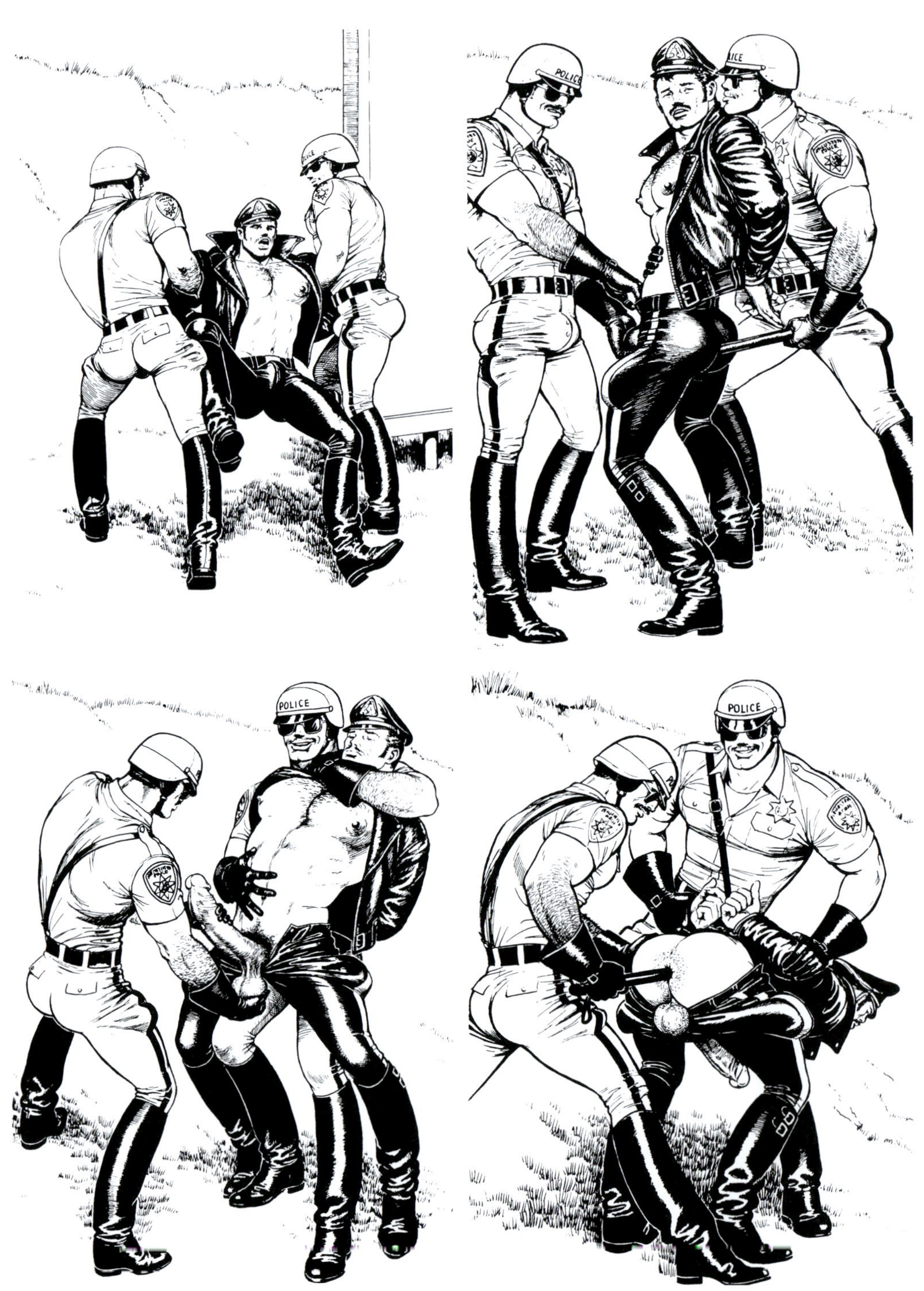

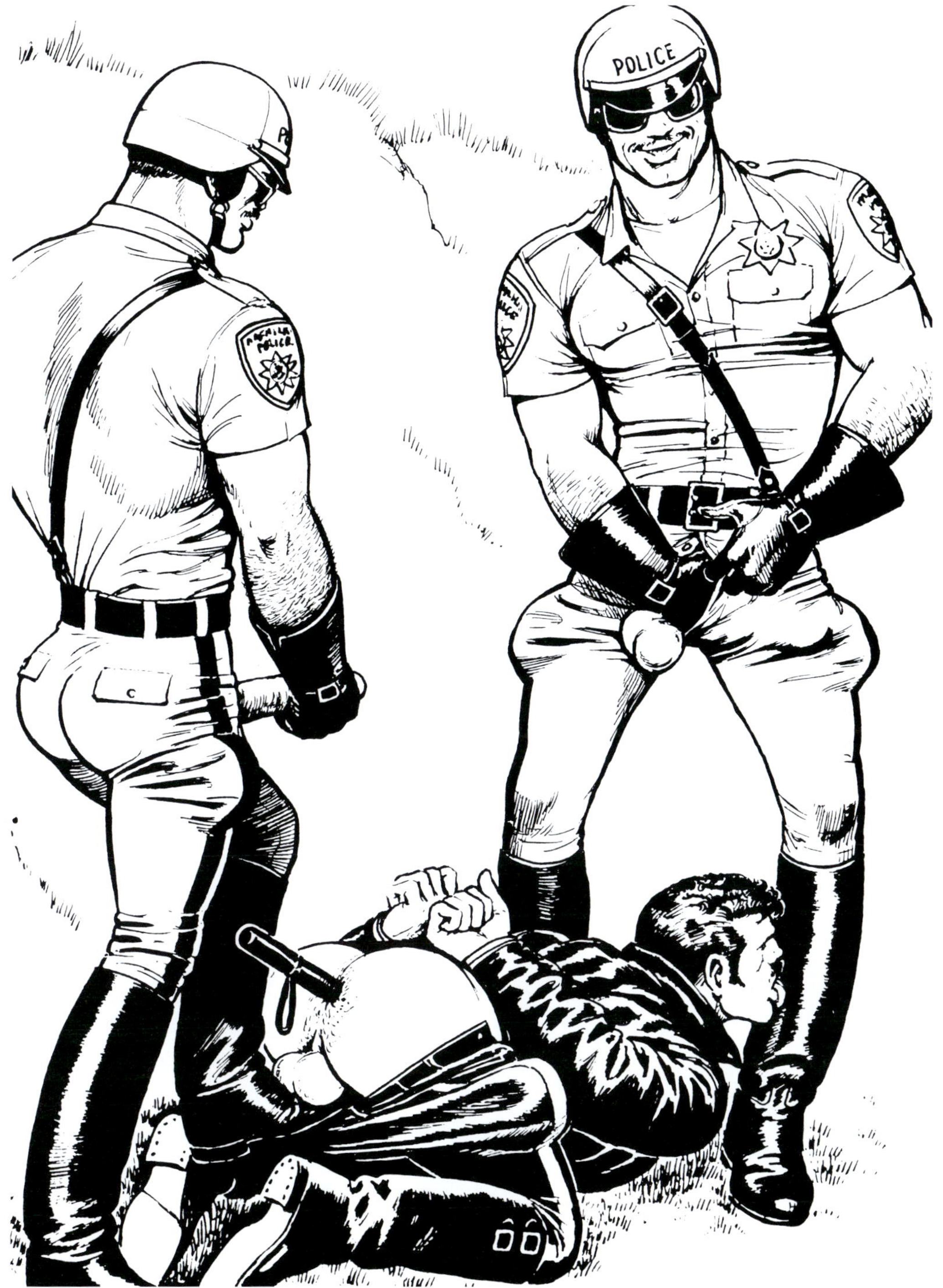

POLICE

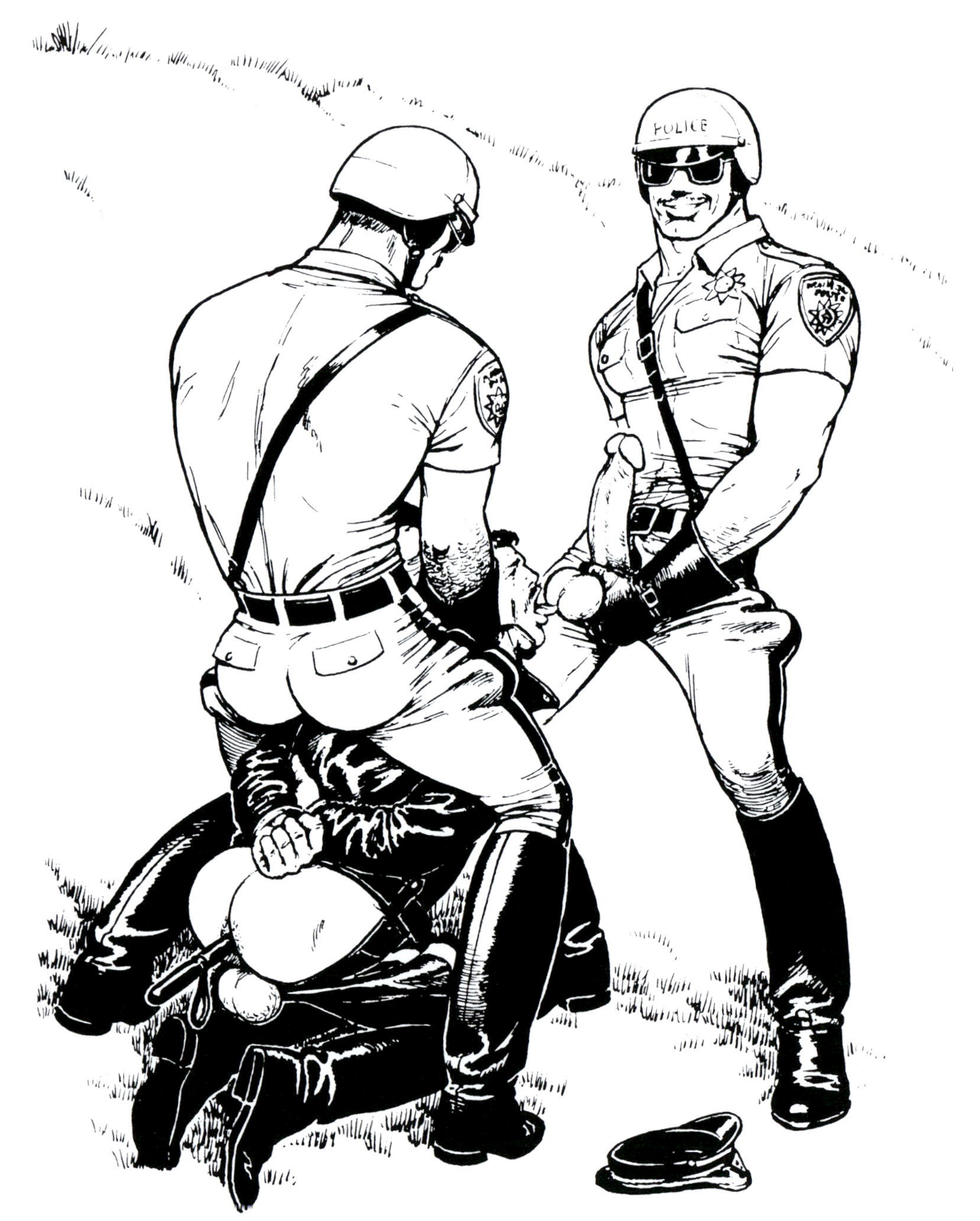

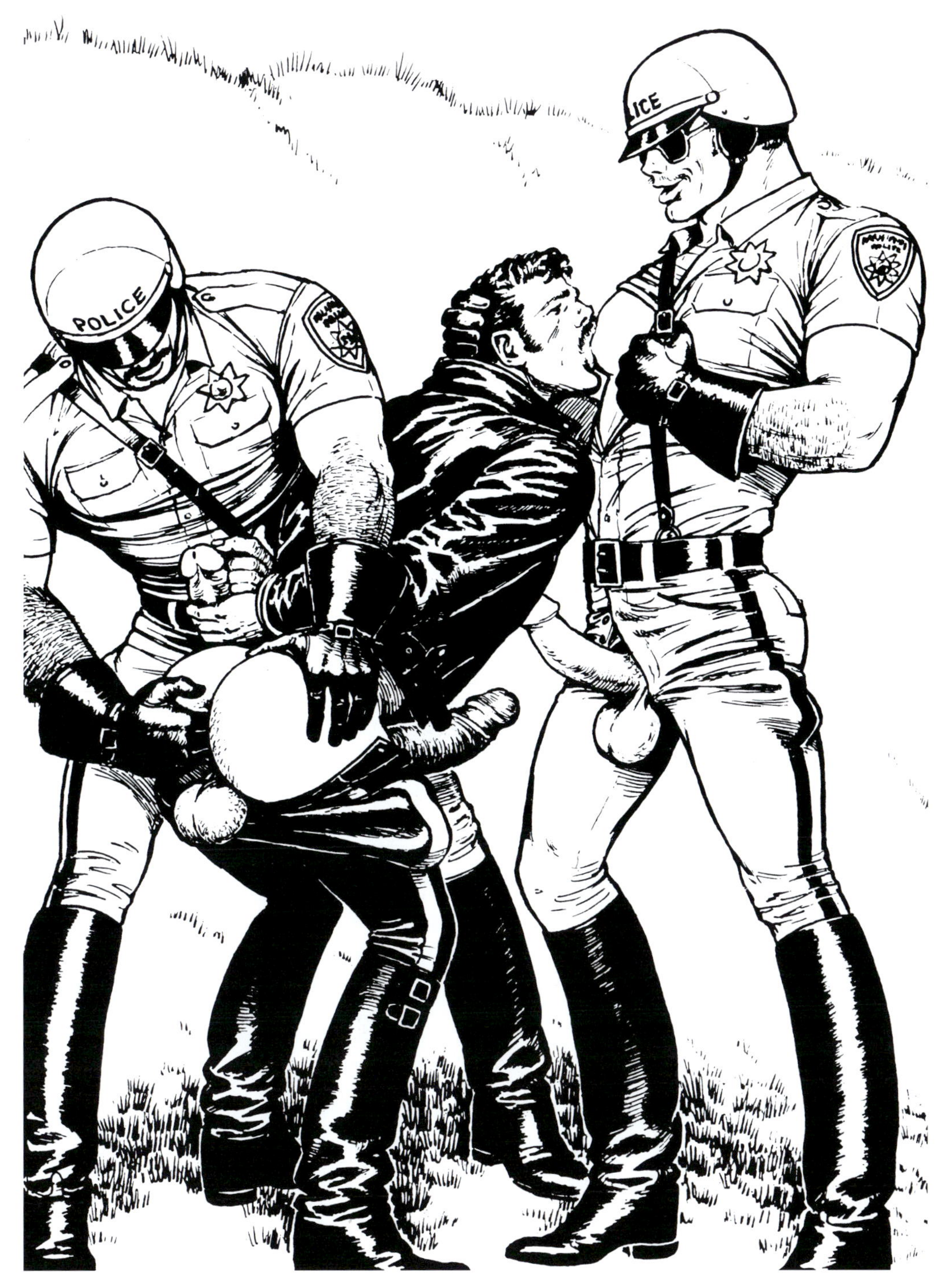

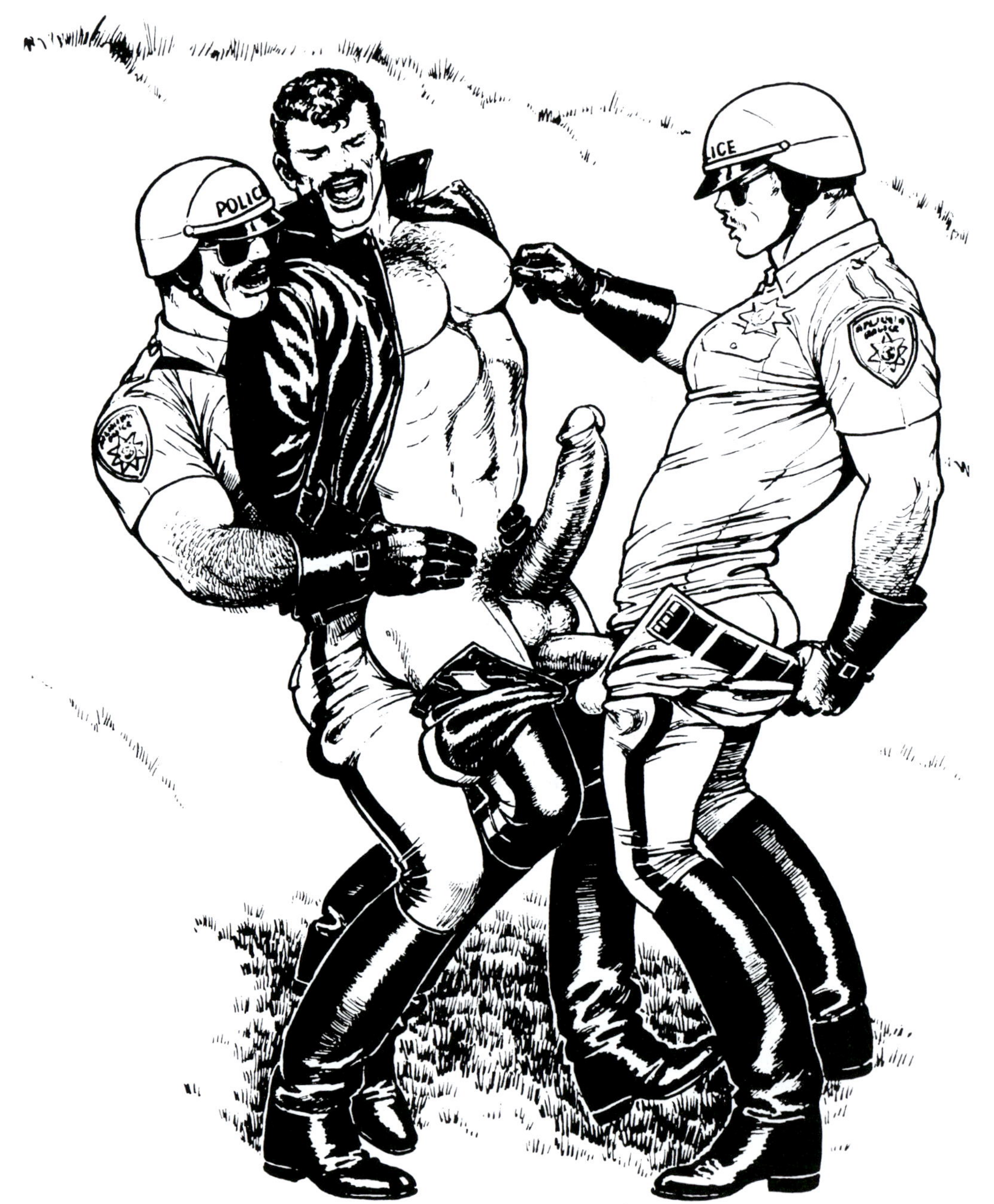

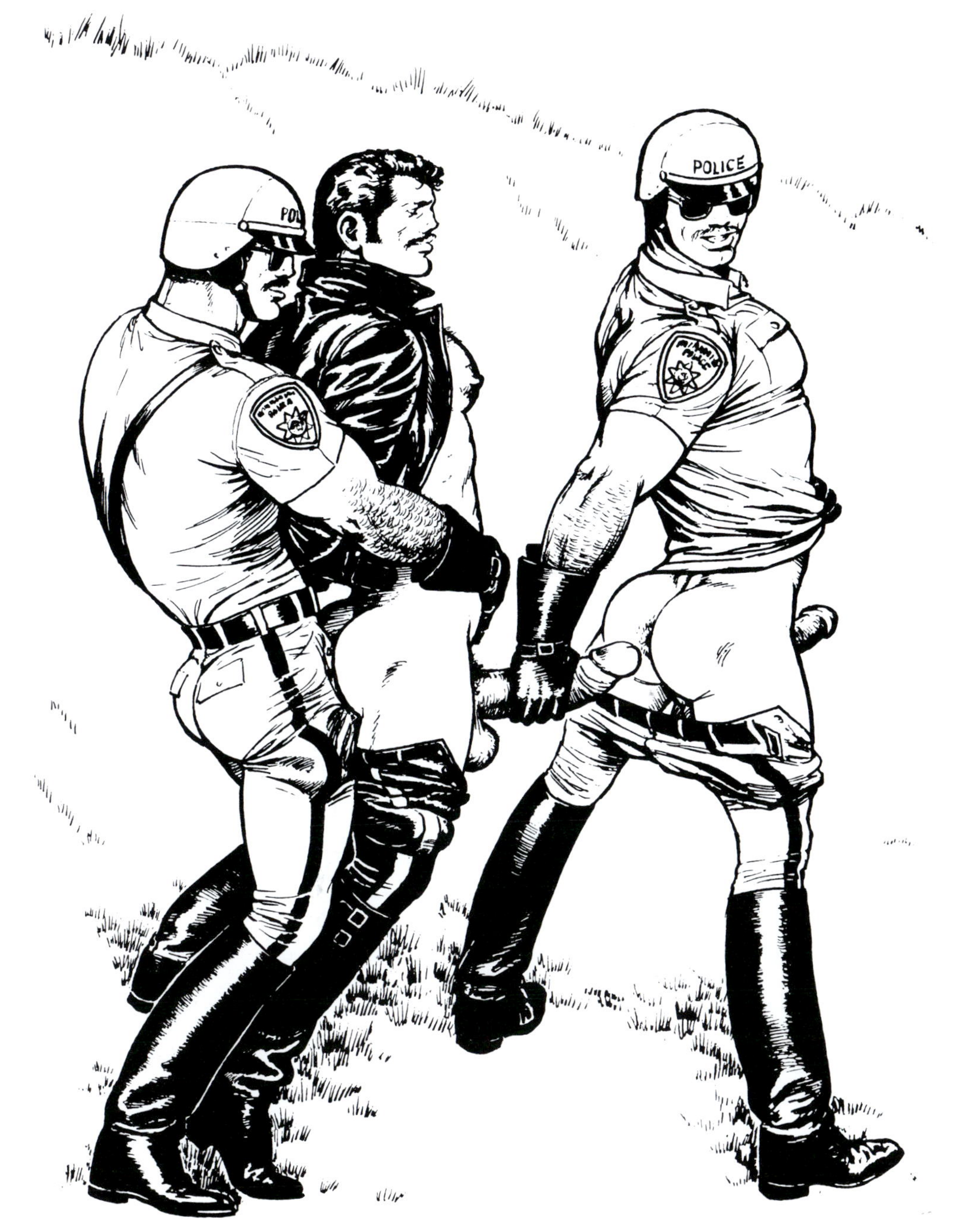

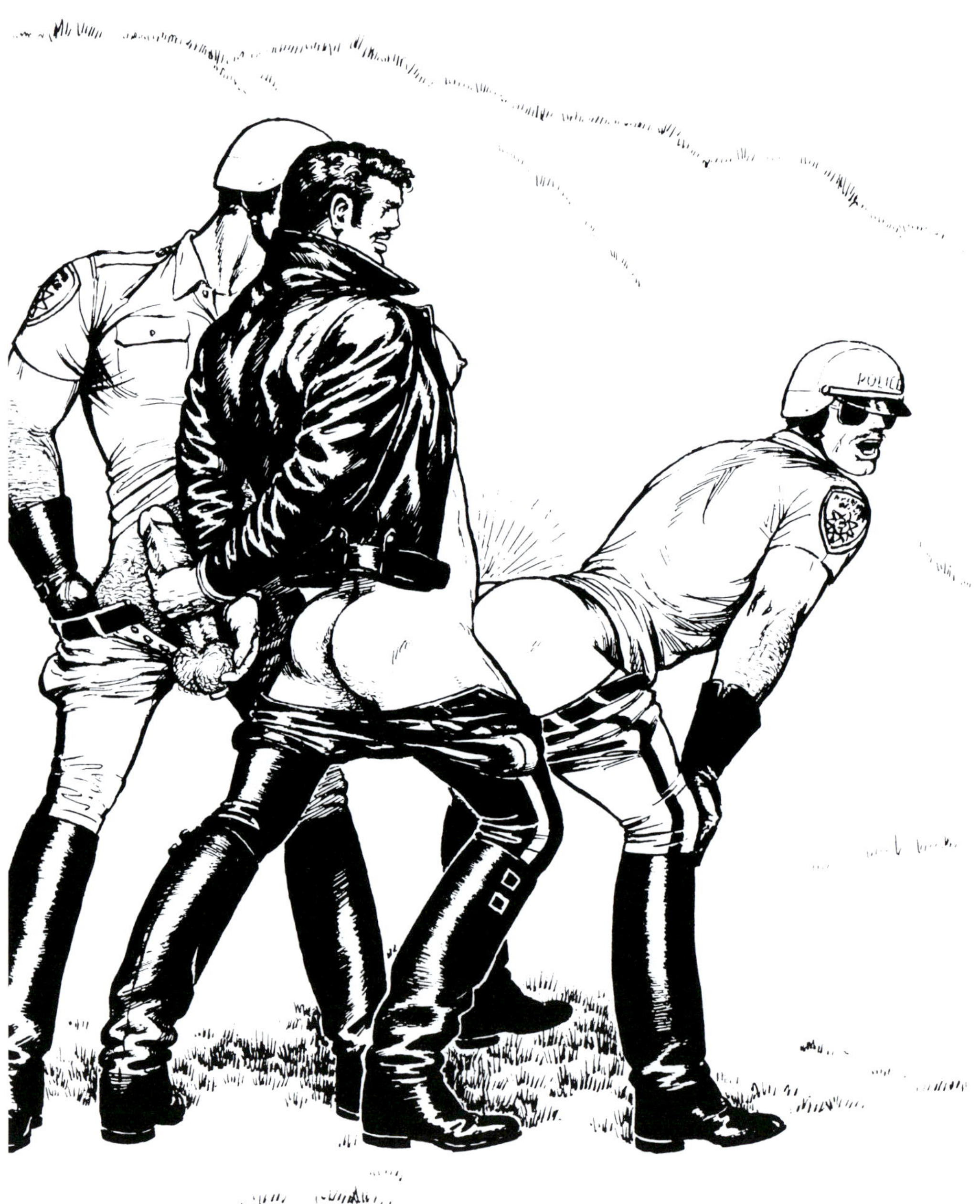

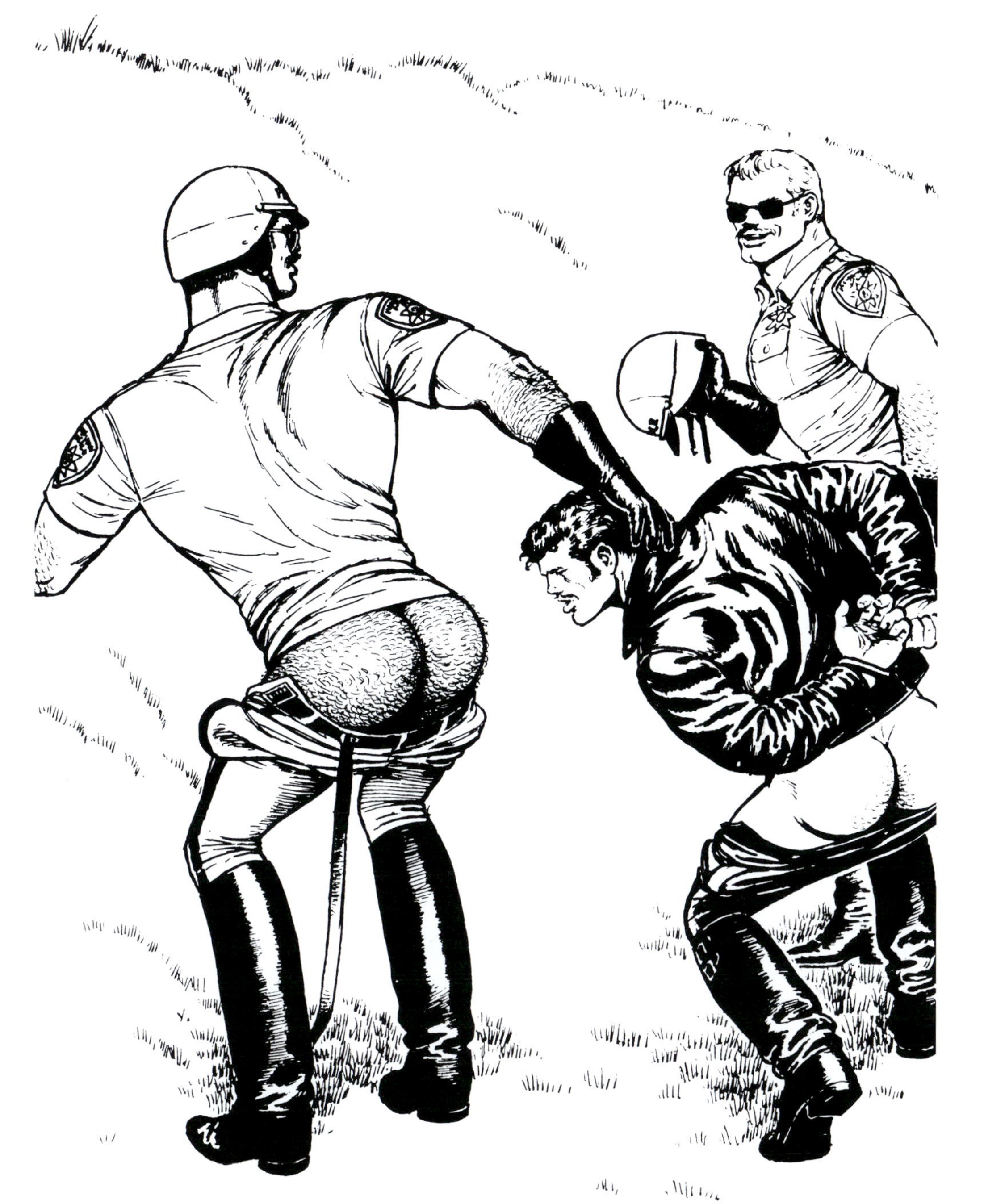

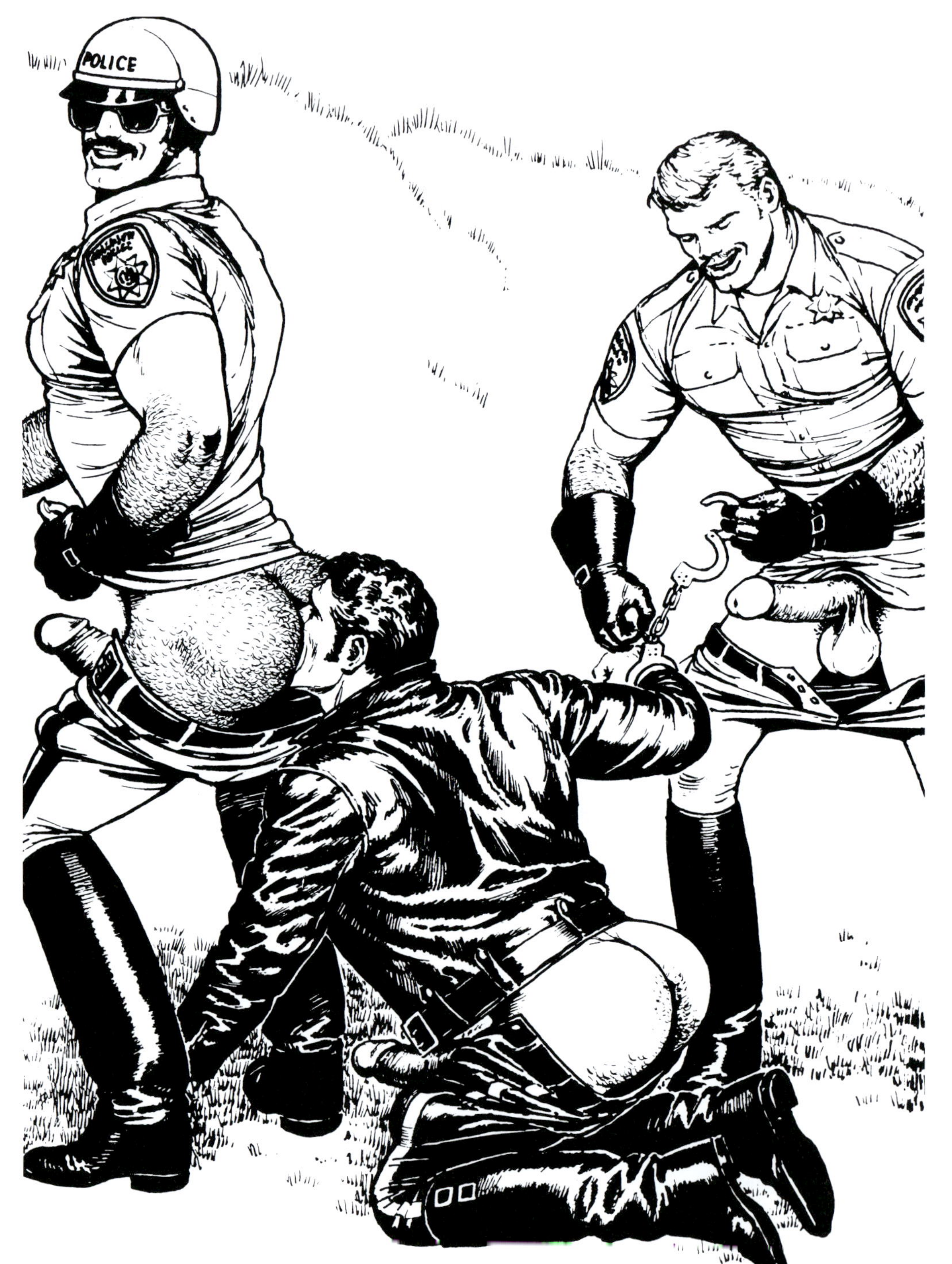
POLICE

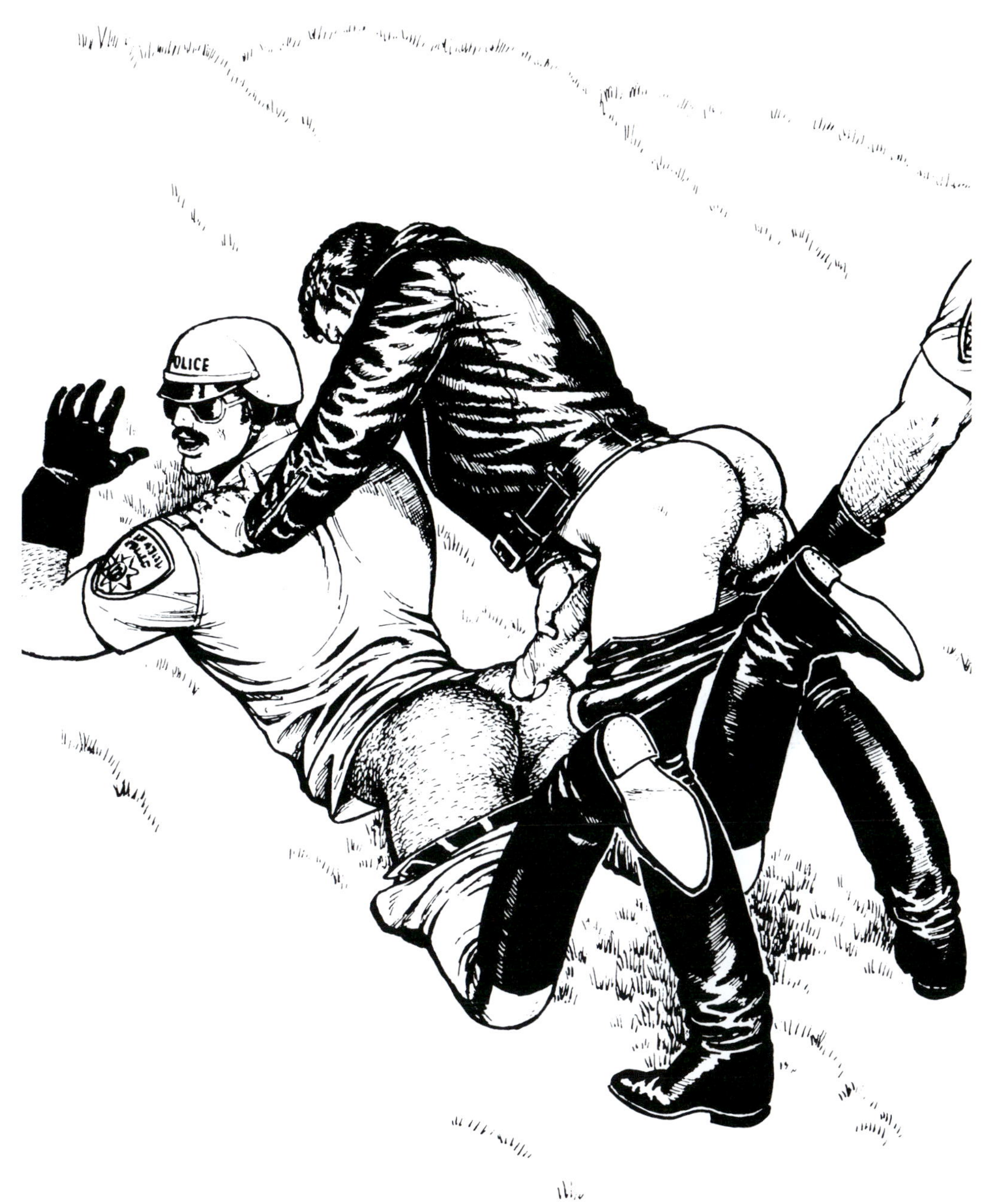

POLICE

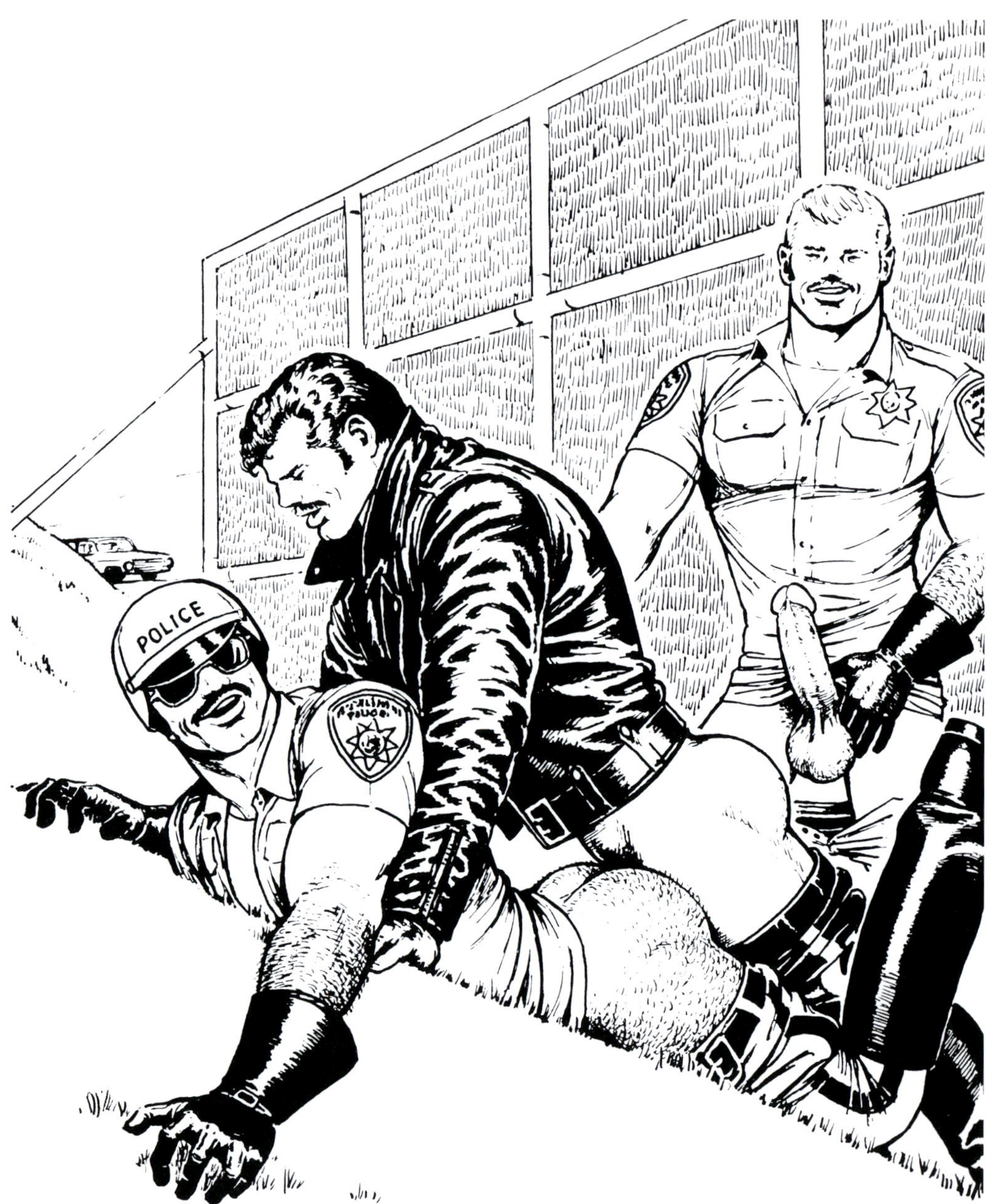

POLICE

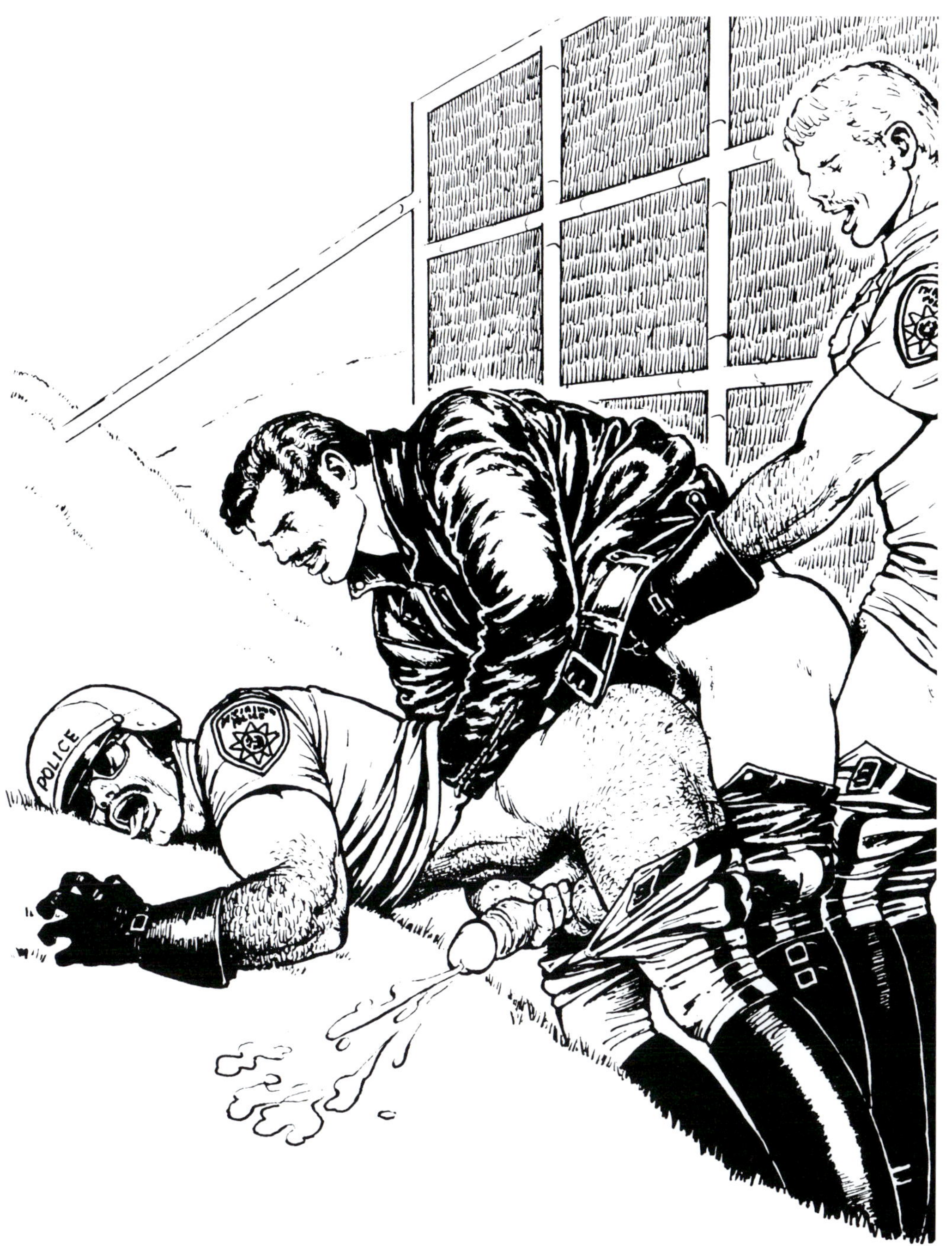

POLICE

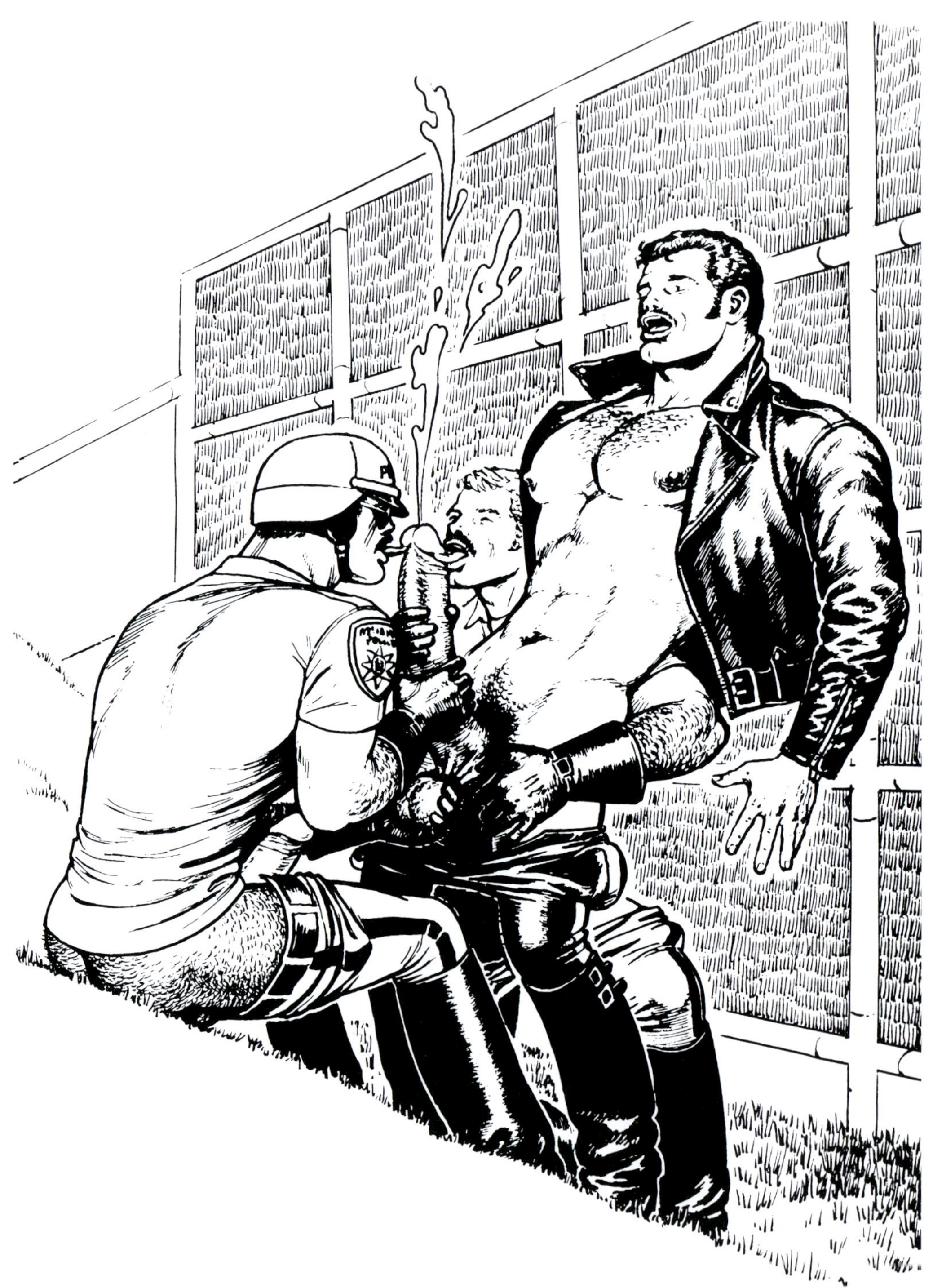

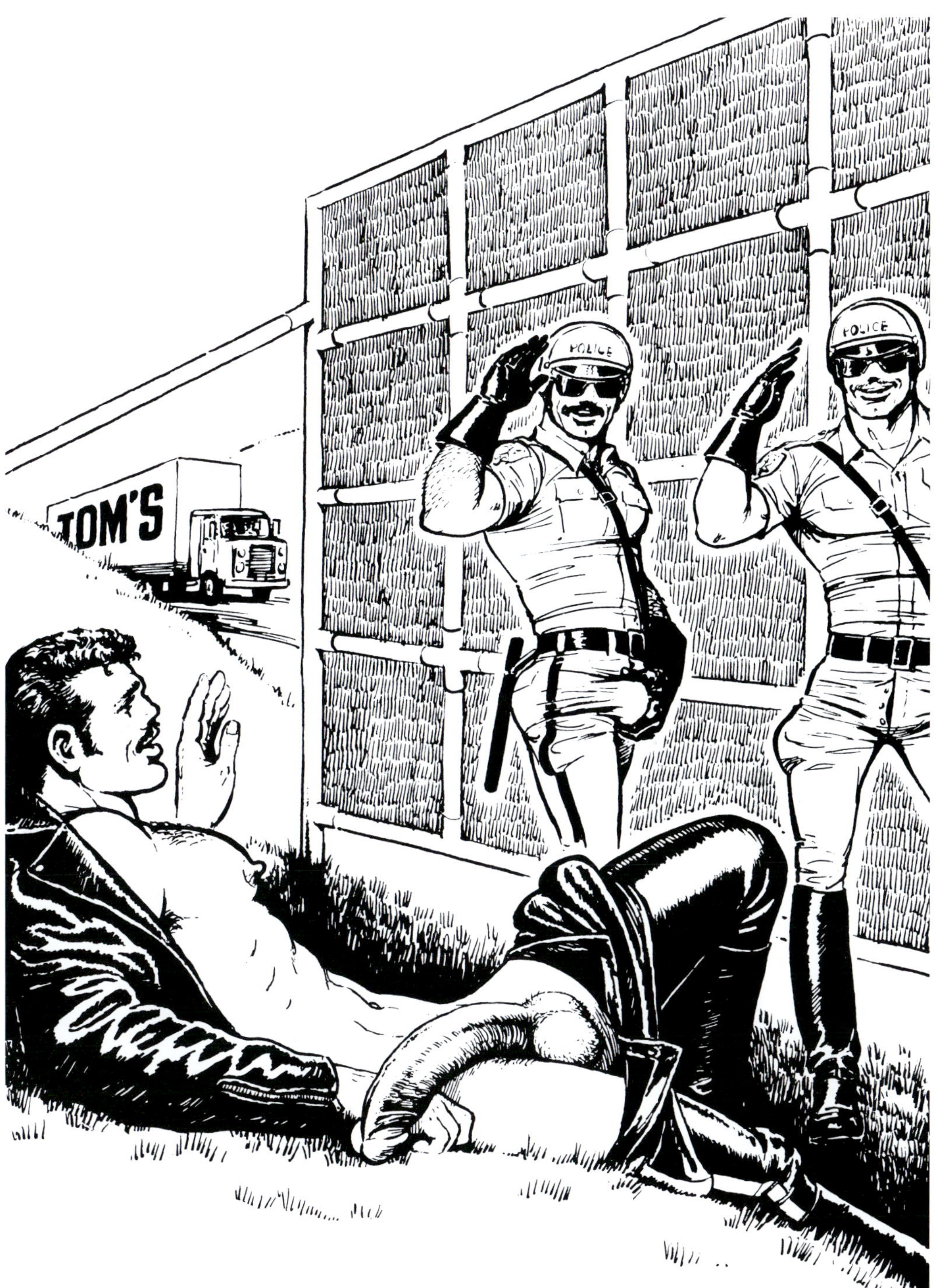

409

KAKE

IN THE WILD WEST

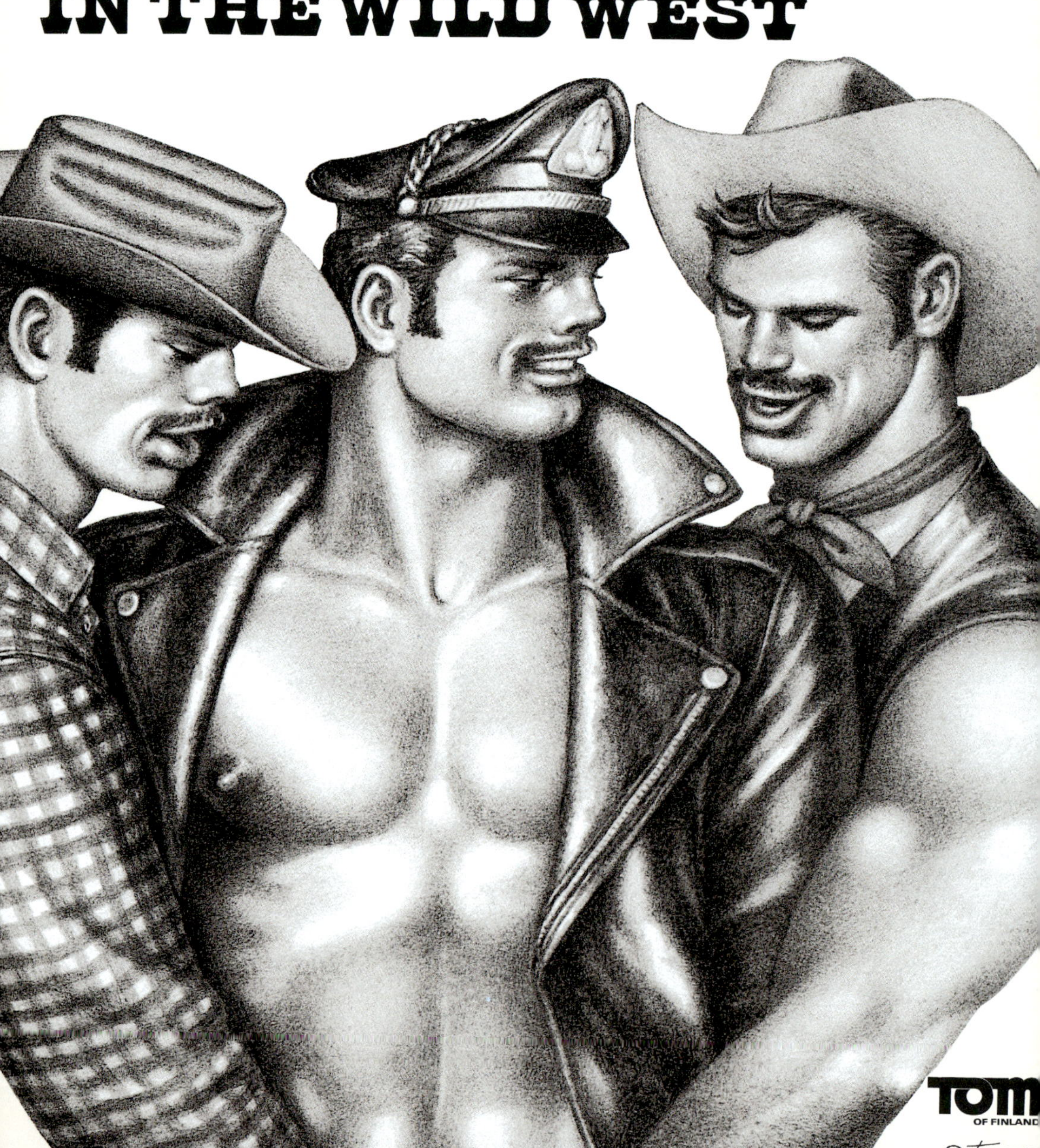

TOM
OF FINLAND

© Tom 1982

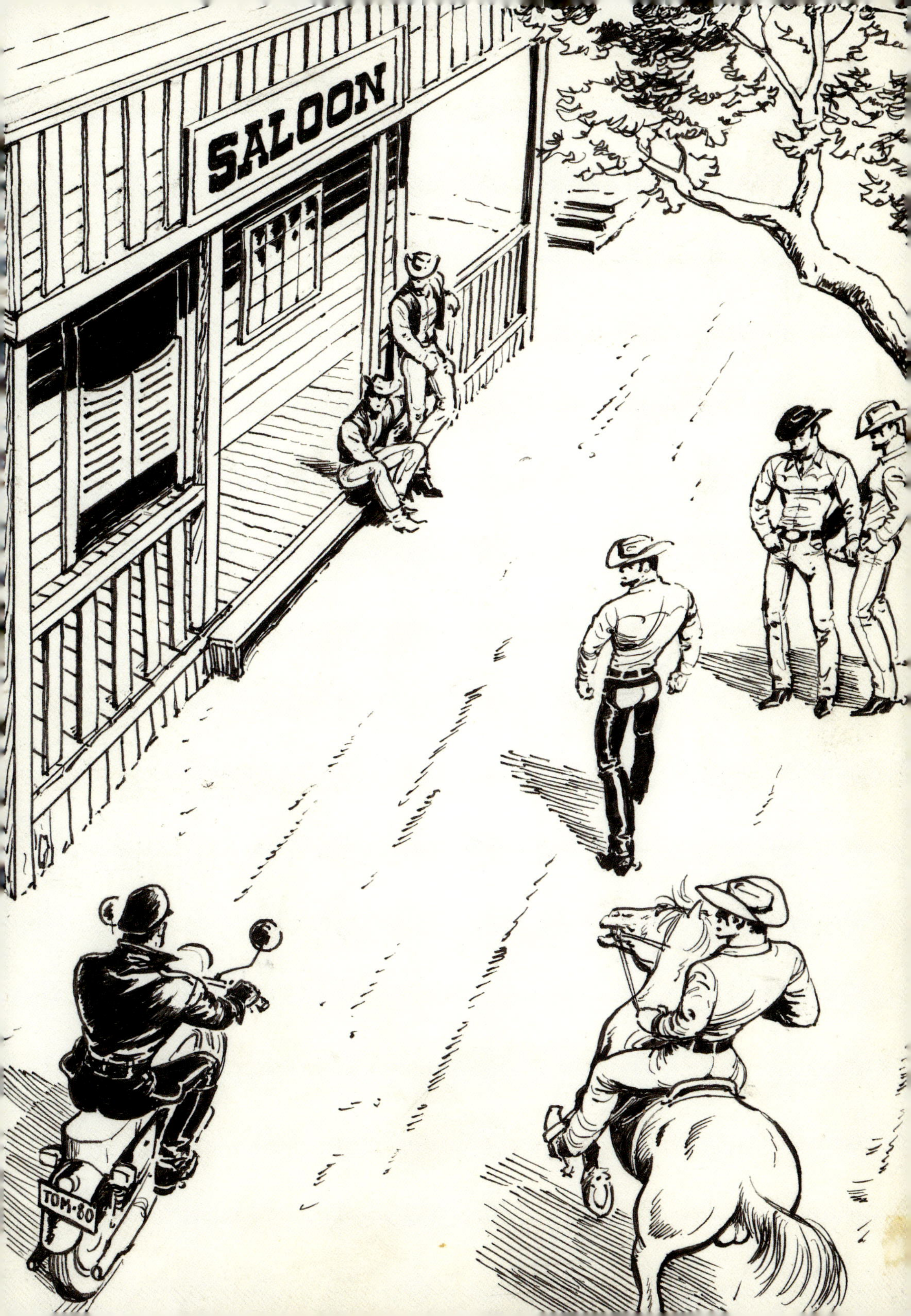
SALOON
TOM·80

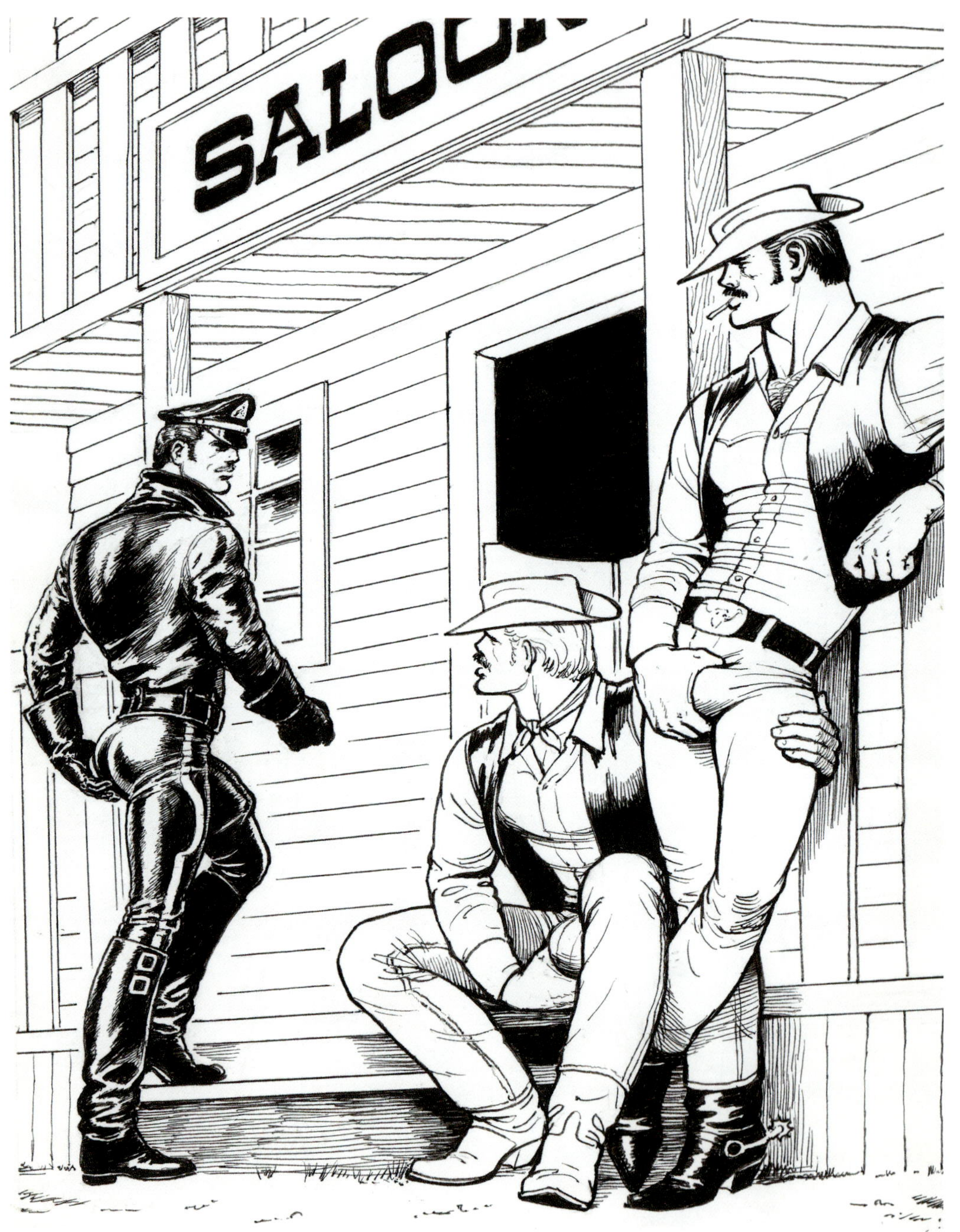

SALOON

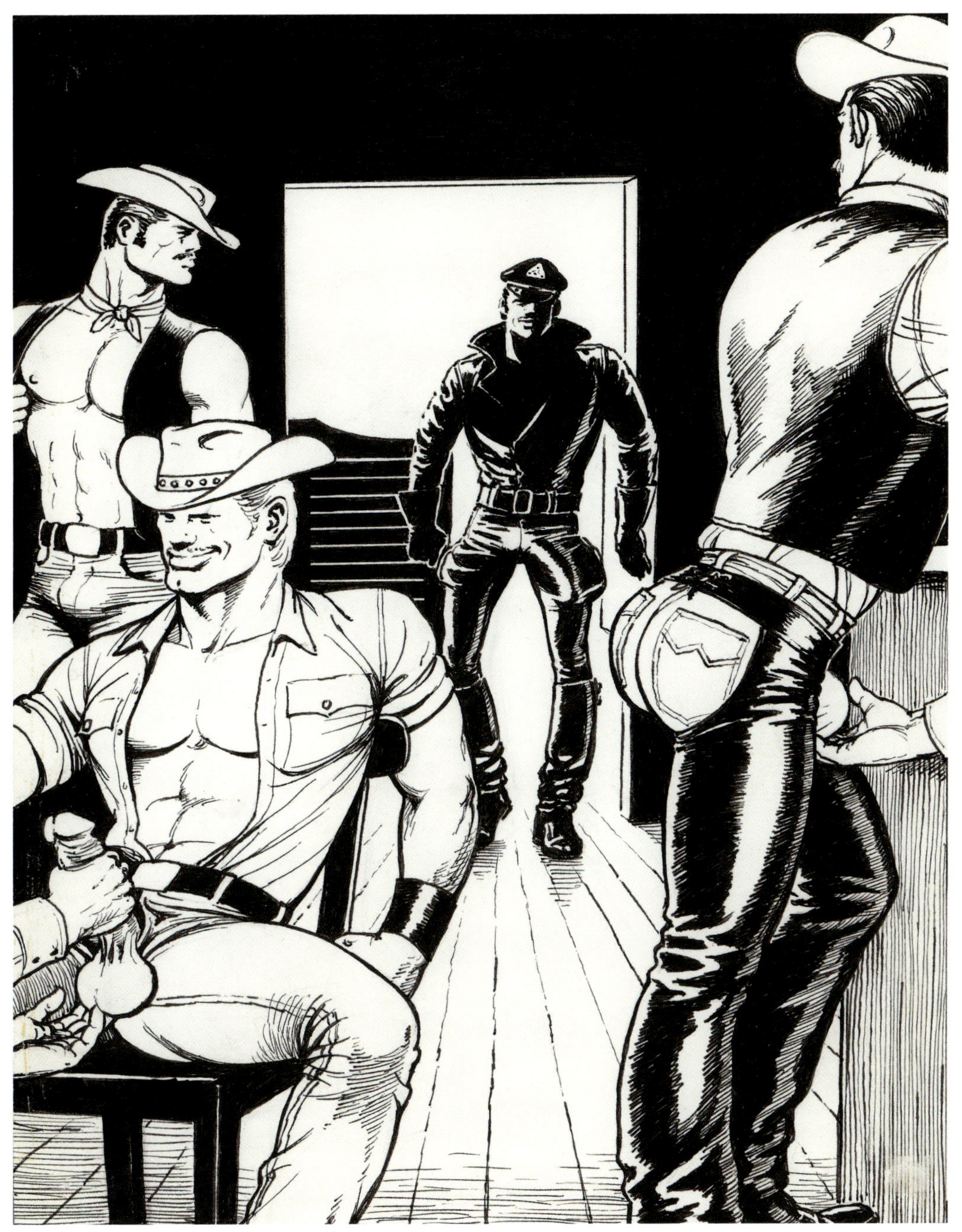

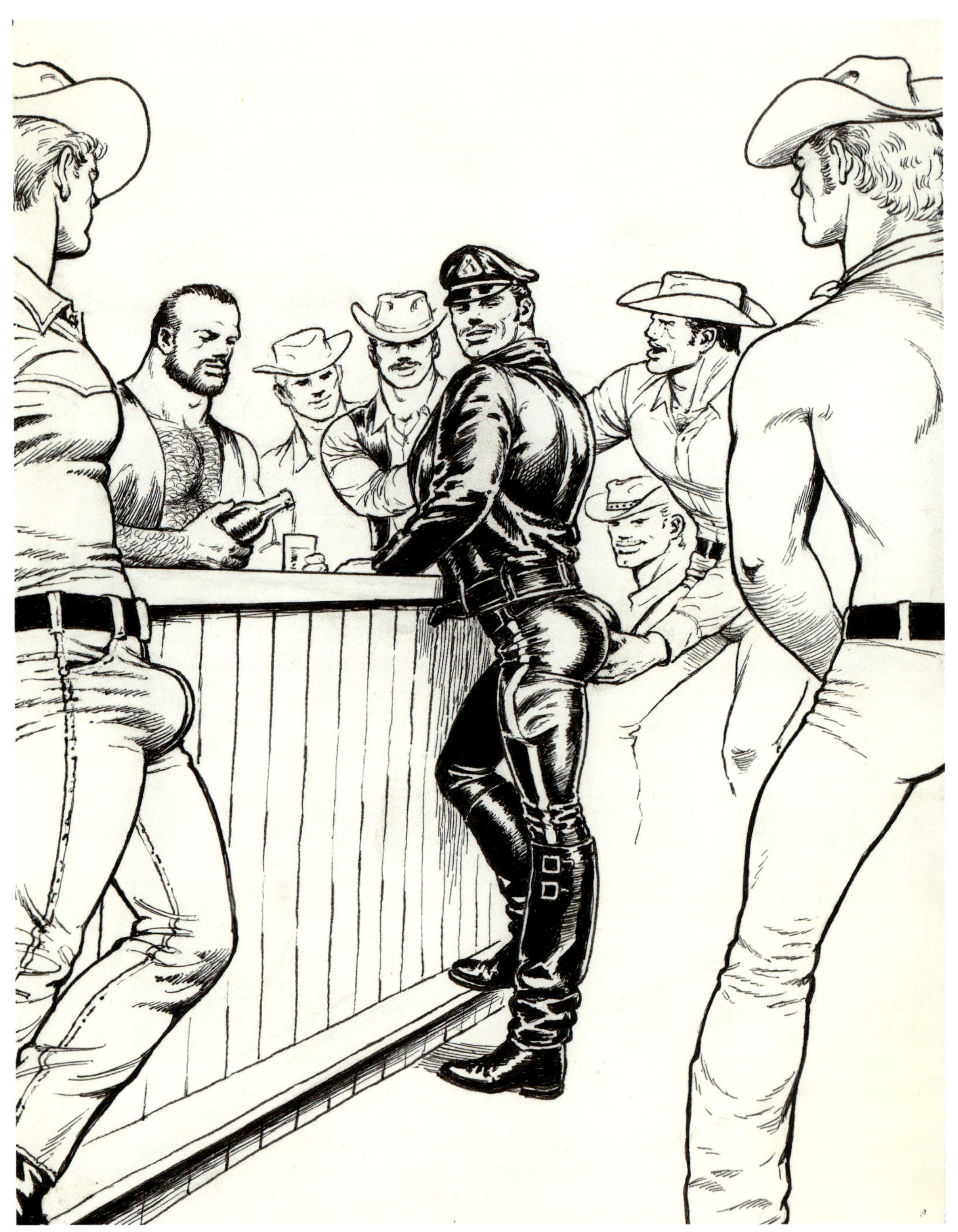

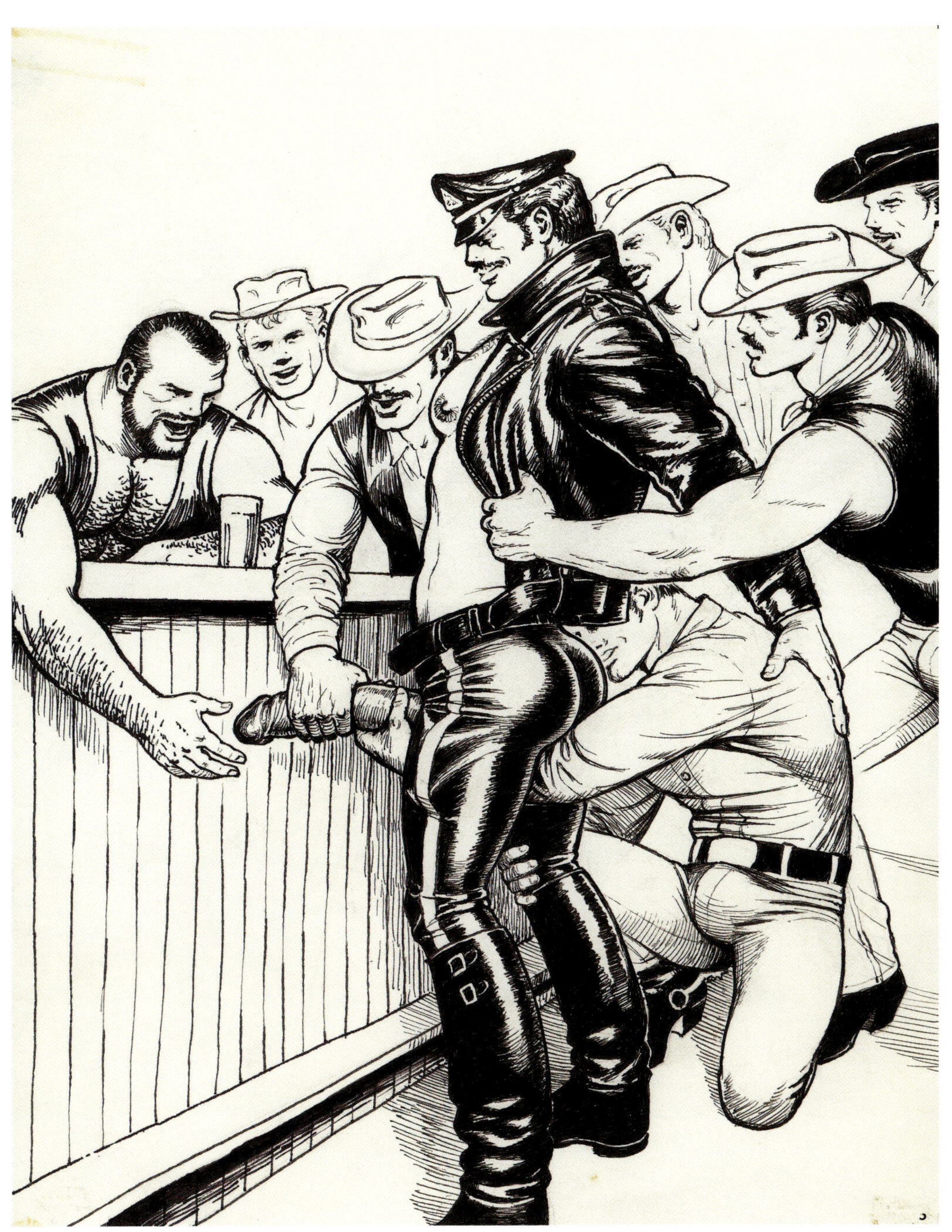

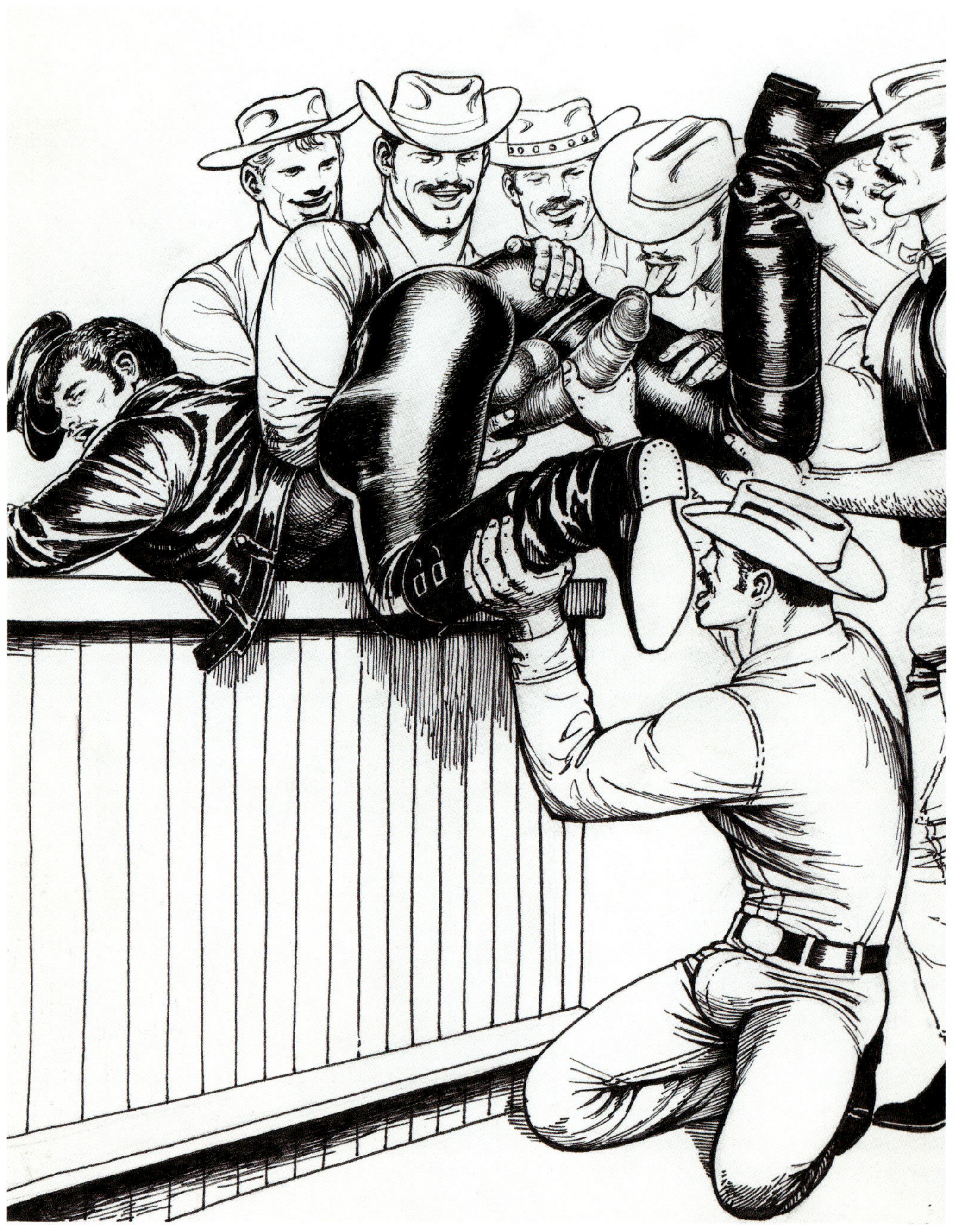

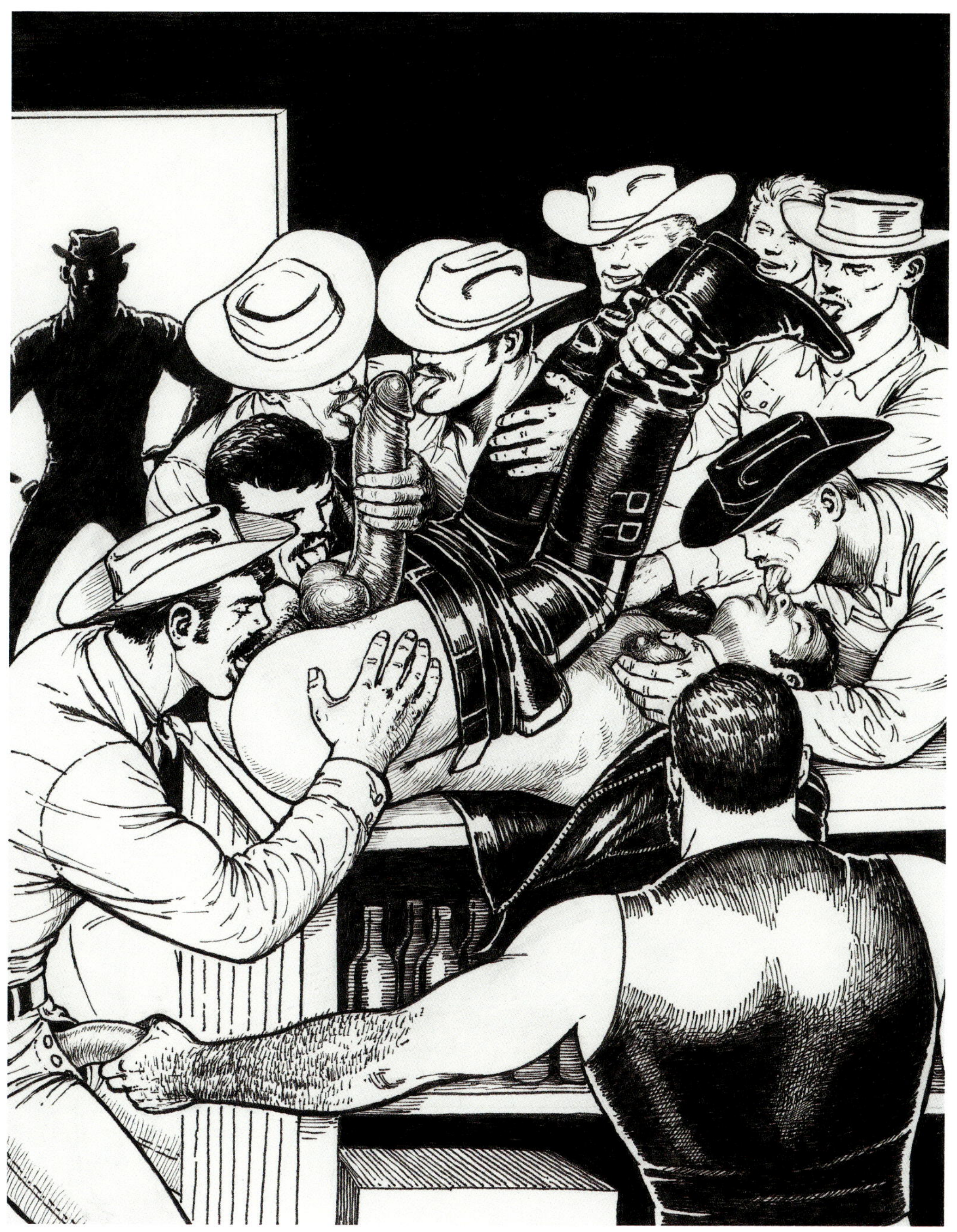

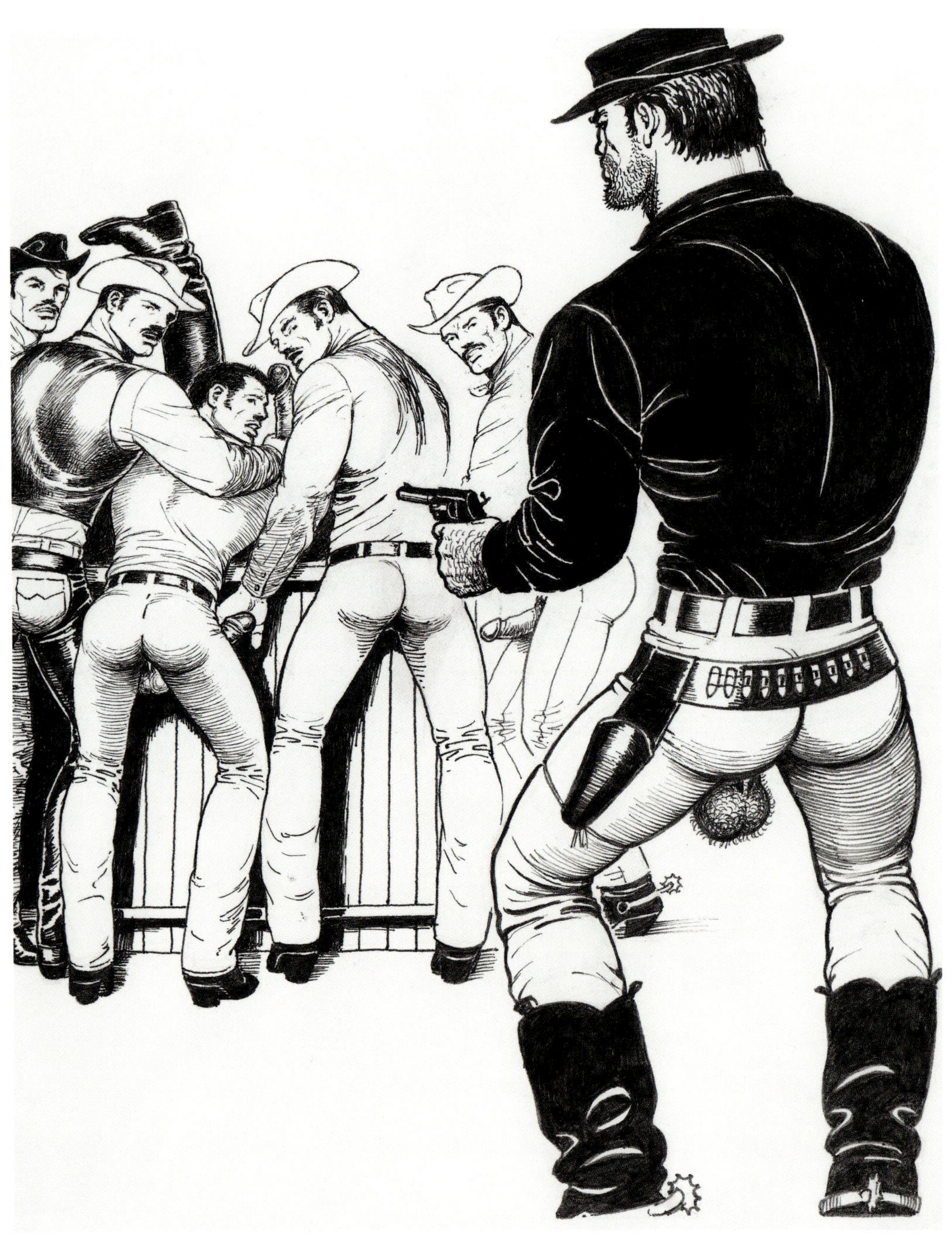

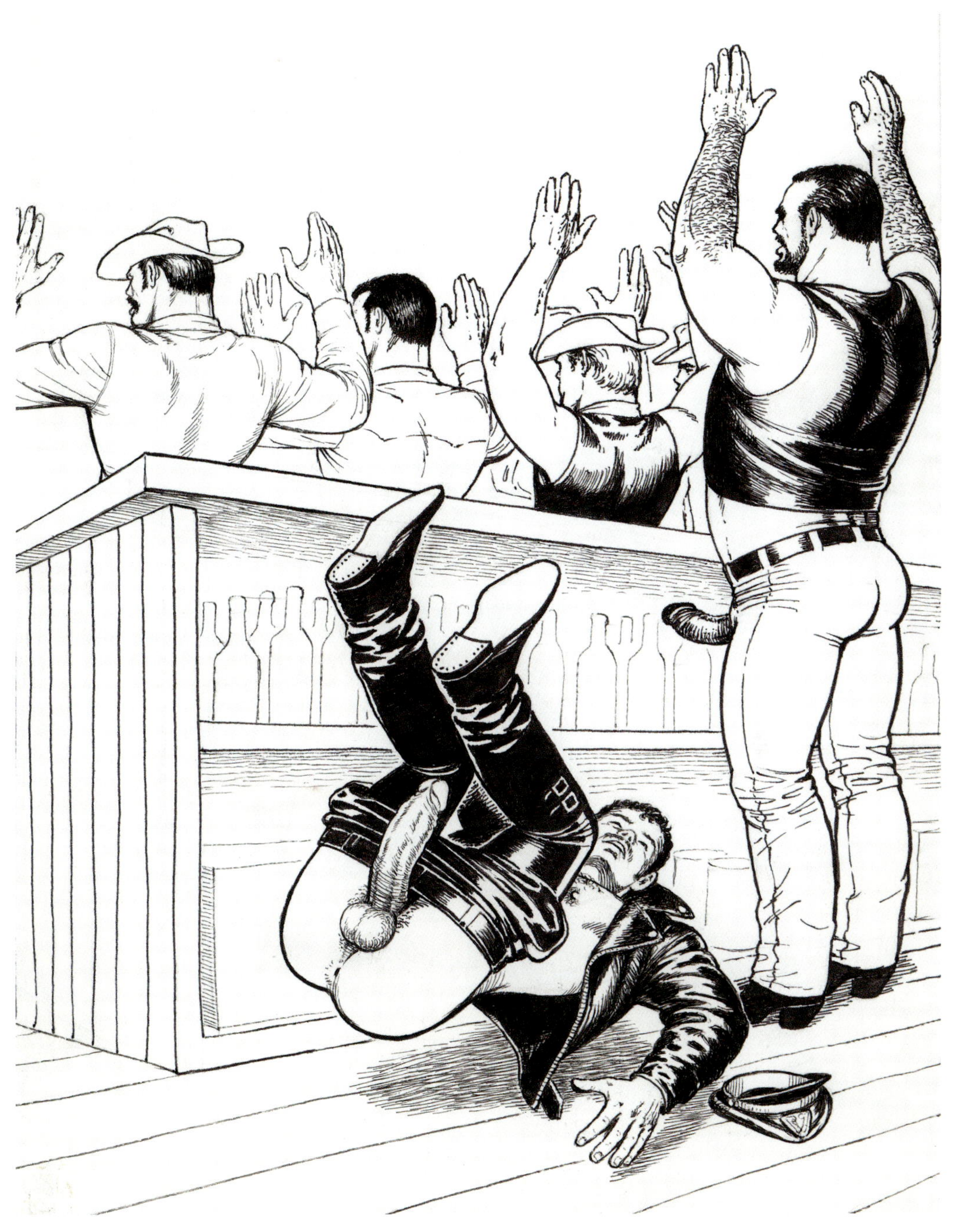

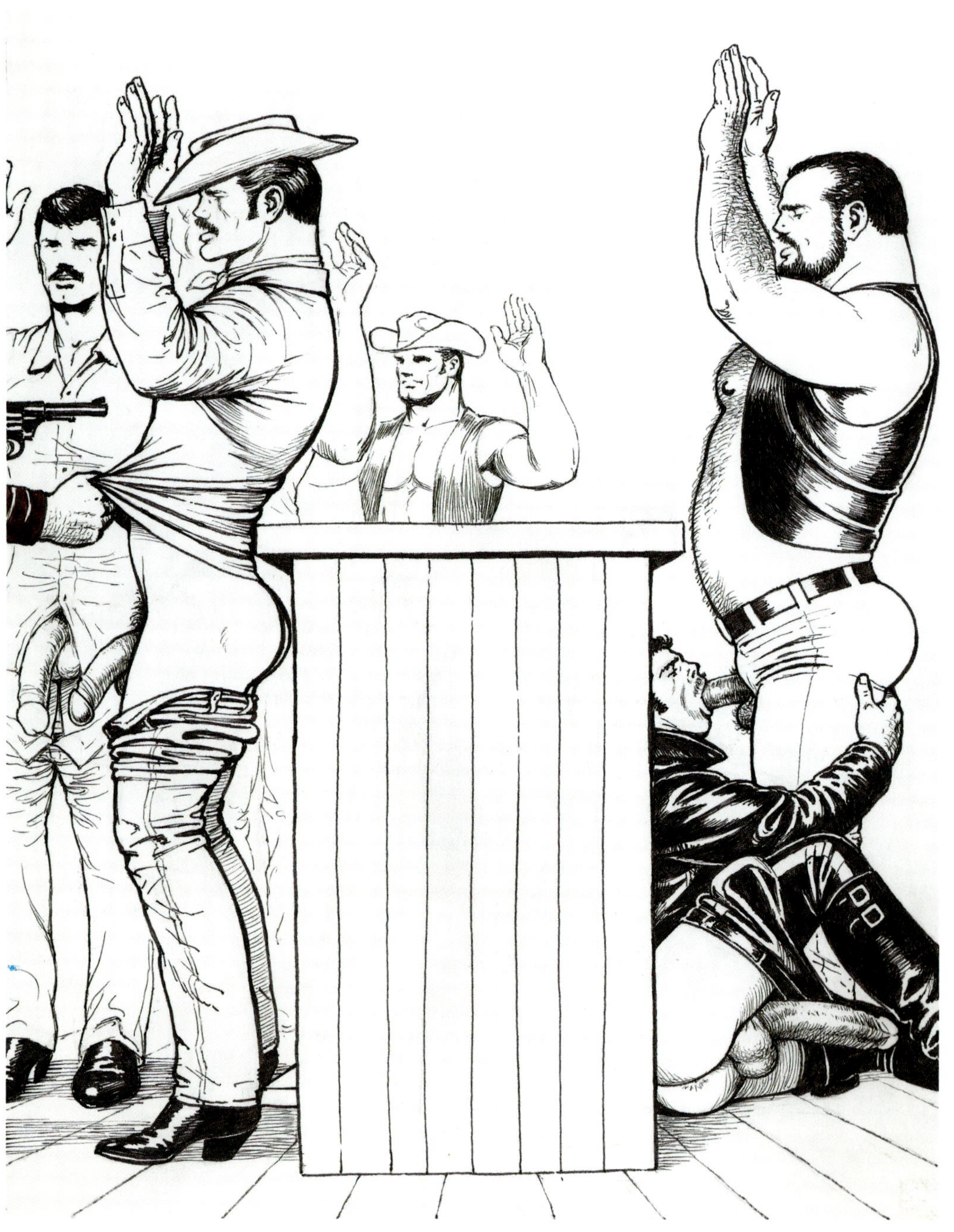

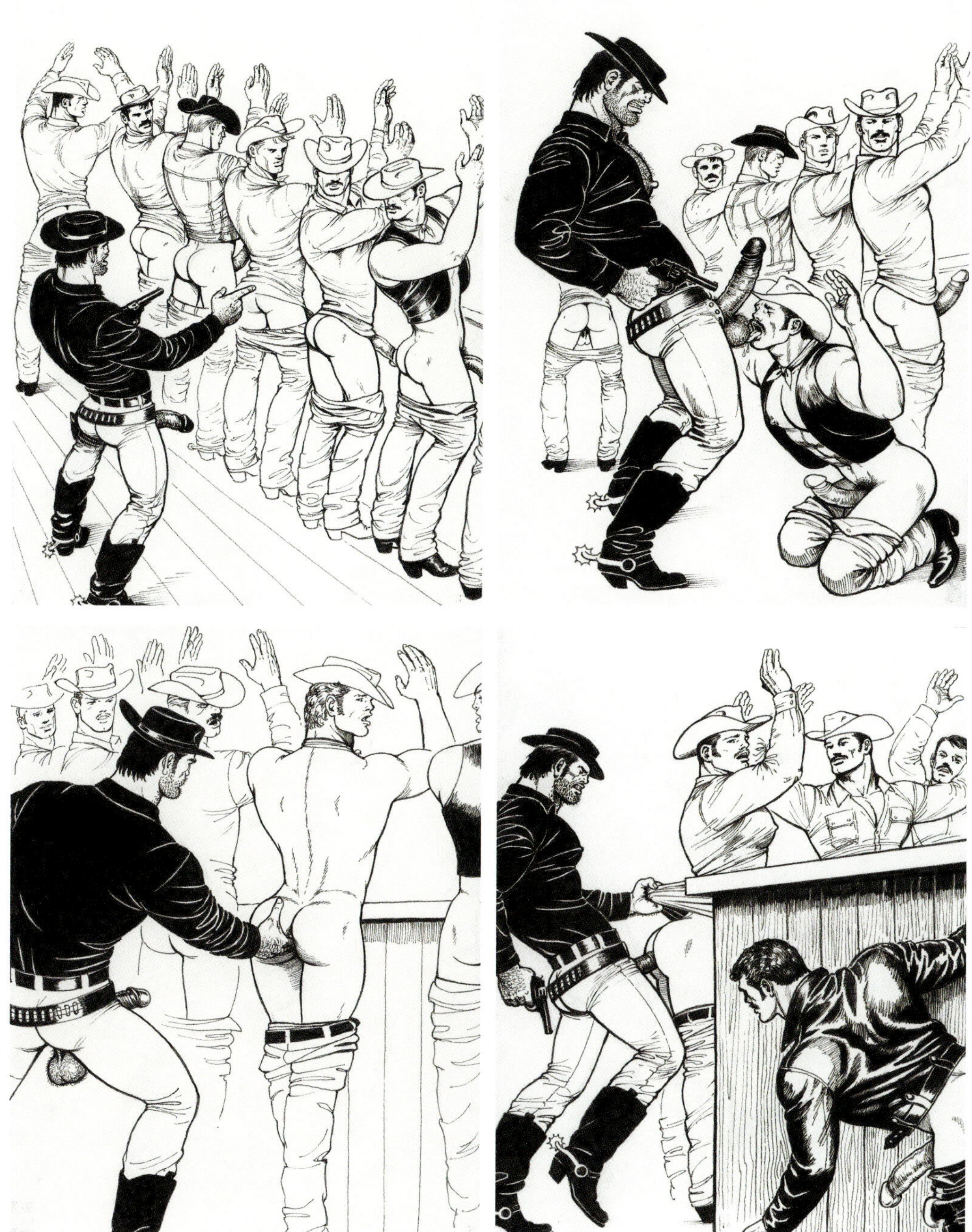

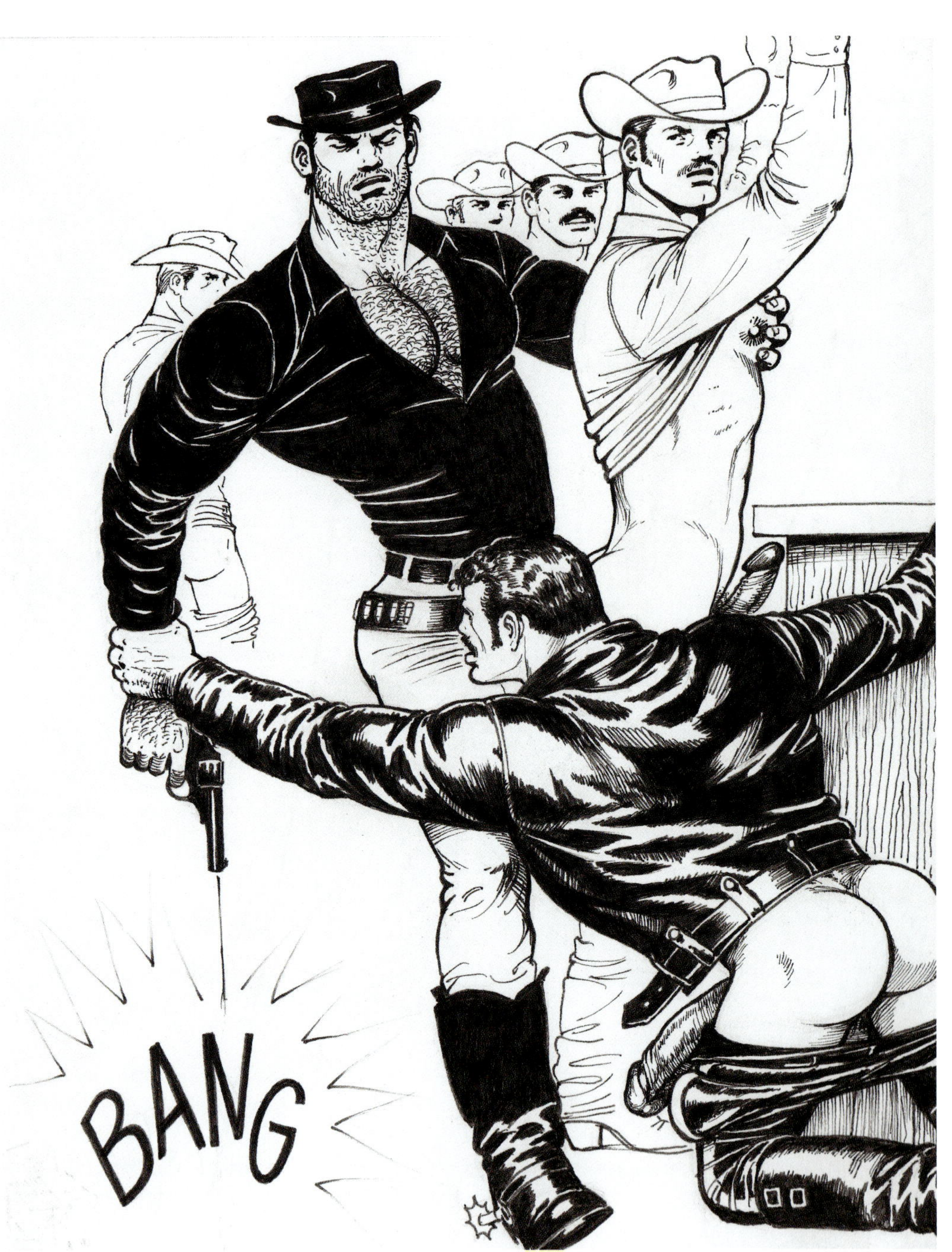
BANG

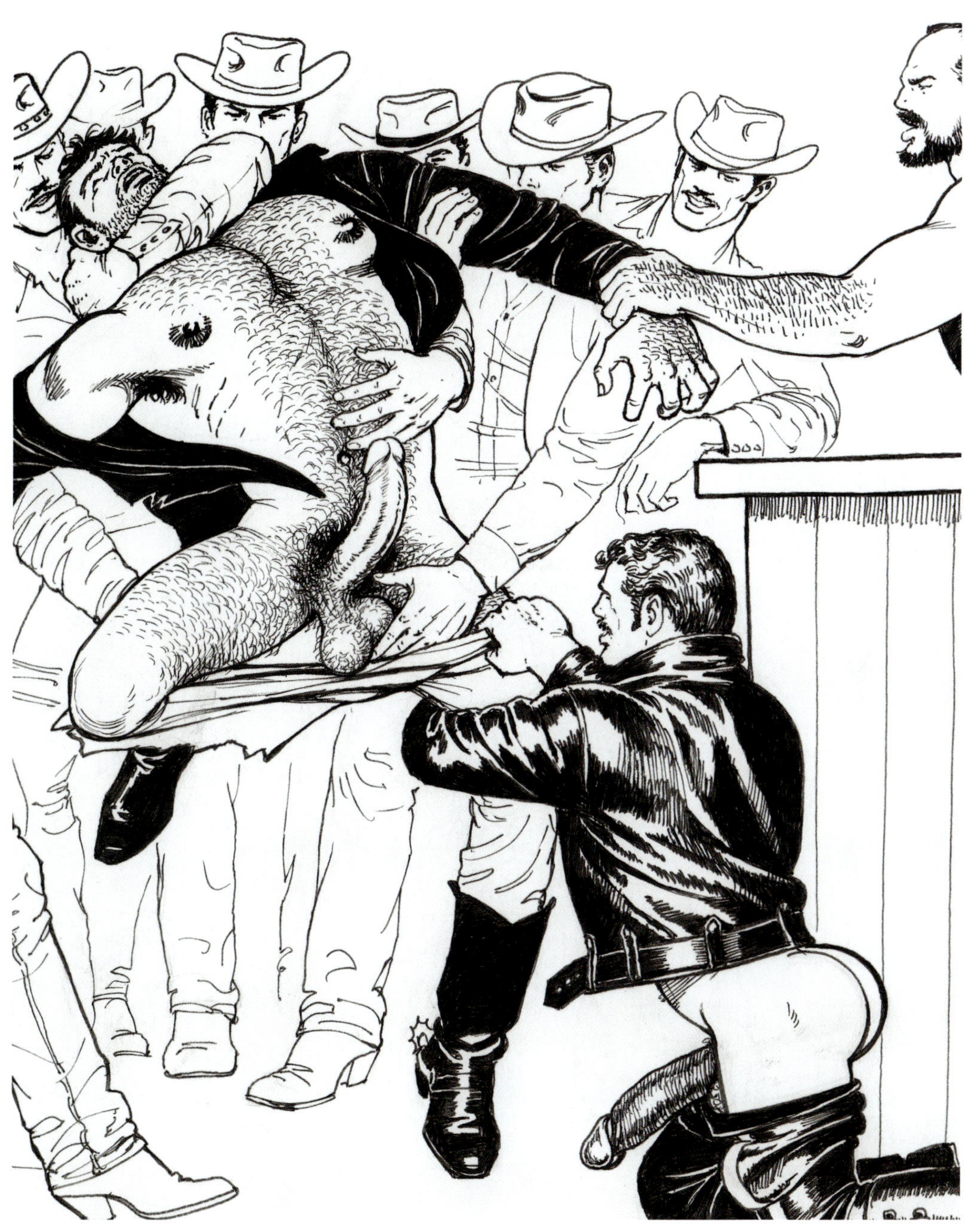

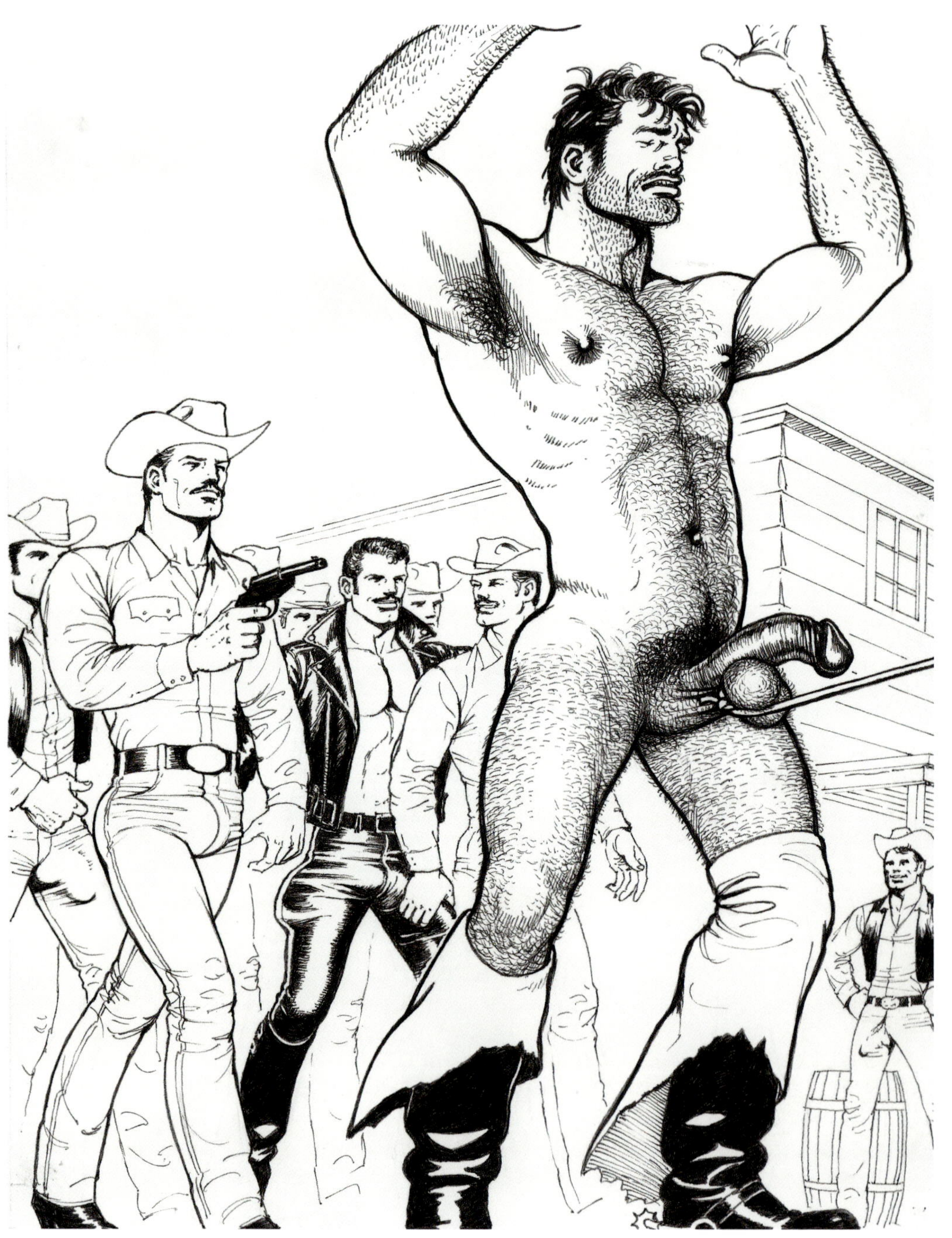

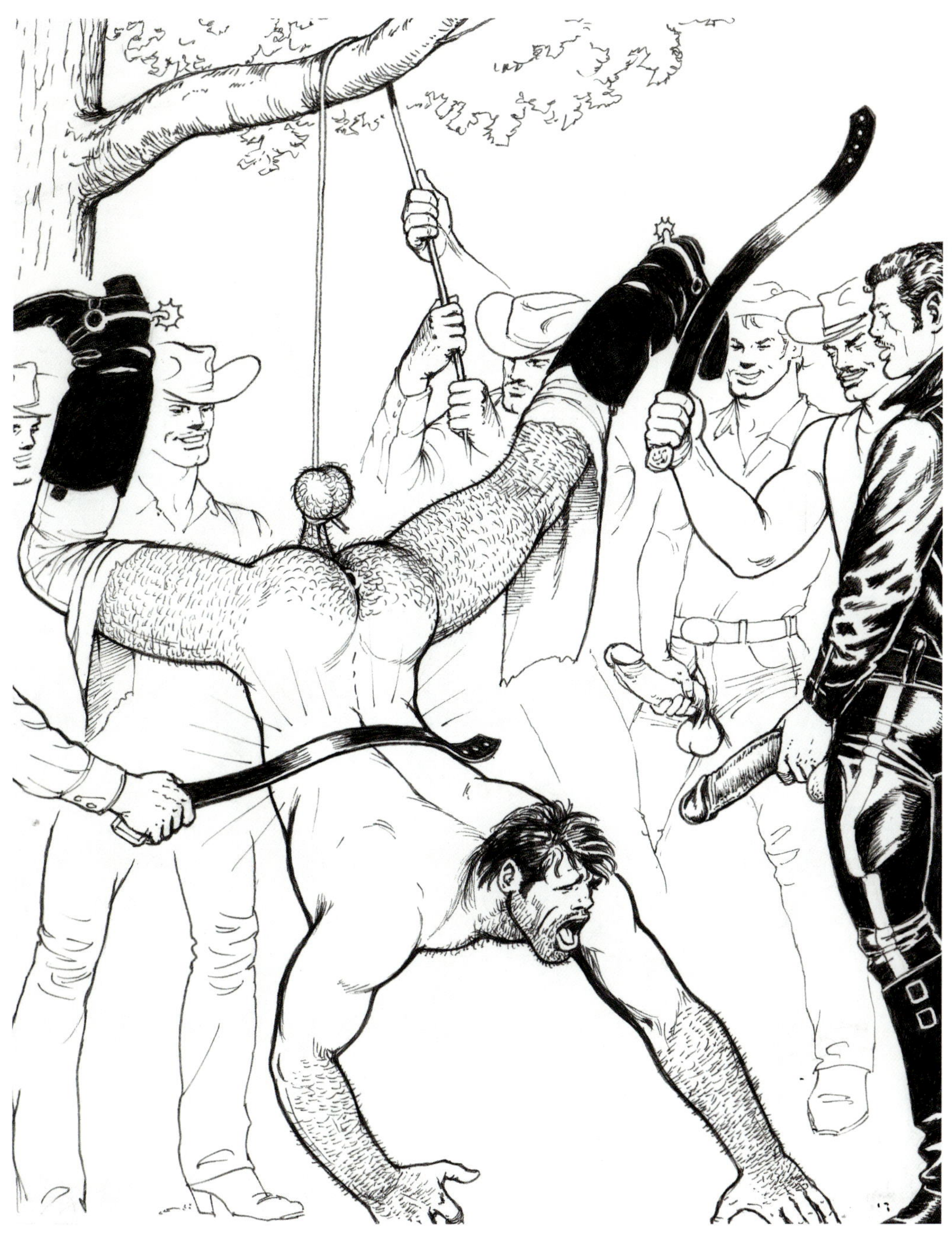

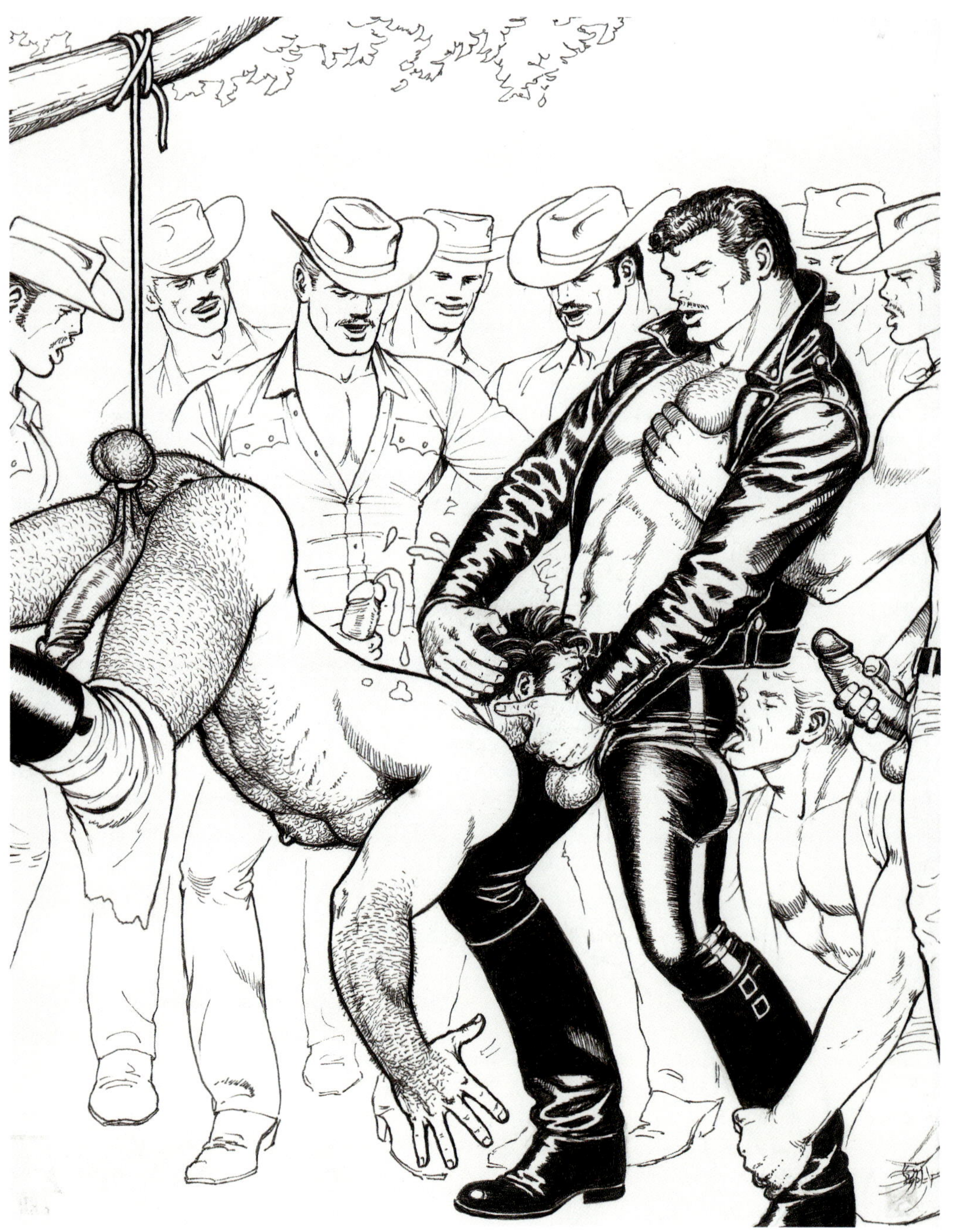

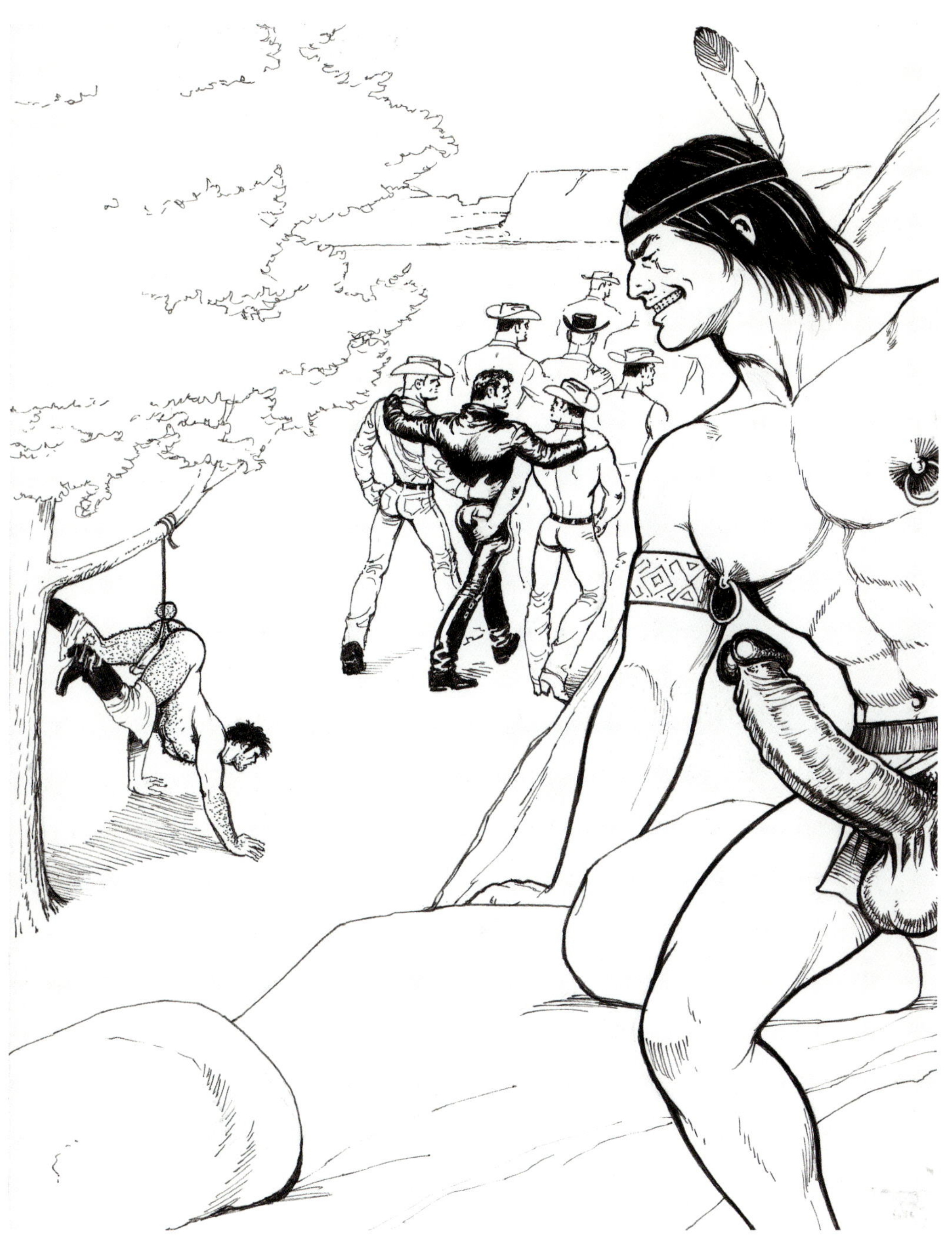

$10.

No. 24, 1984

KAKE

IN CANADA

24

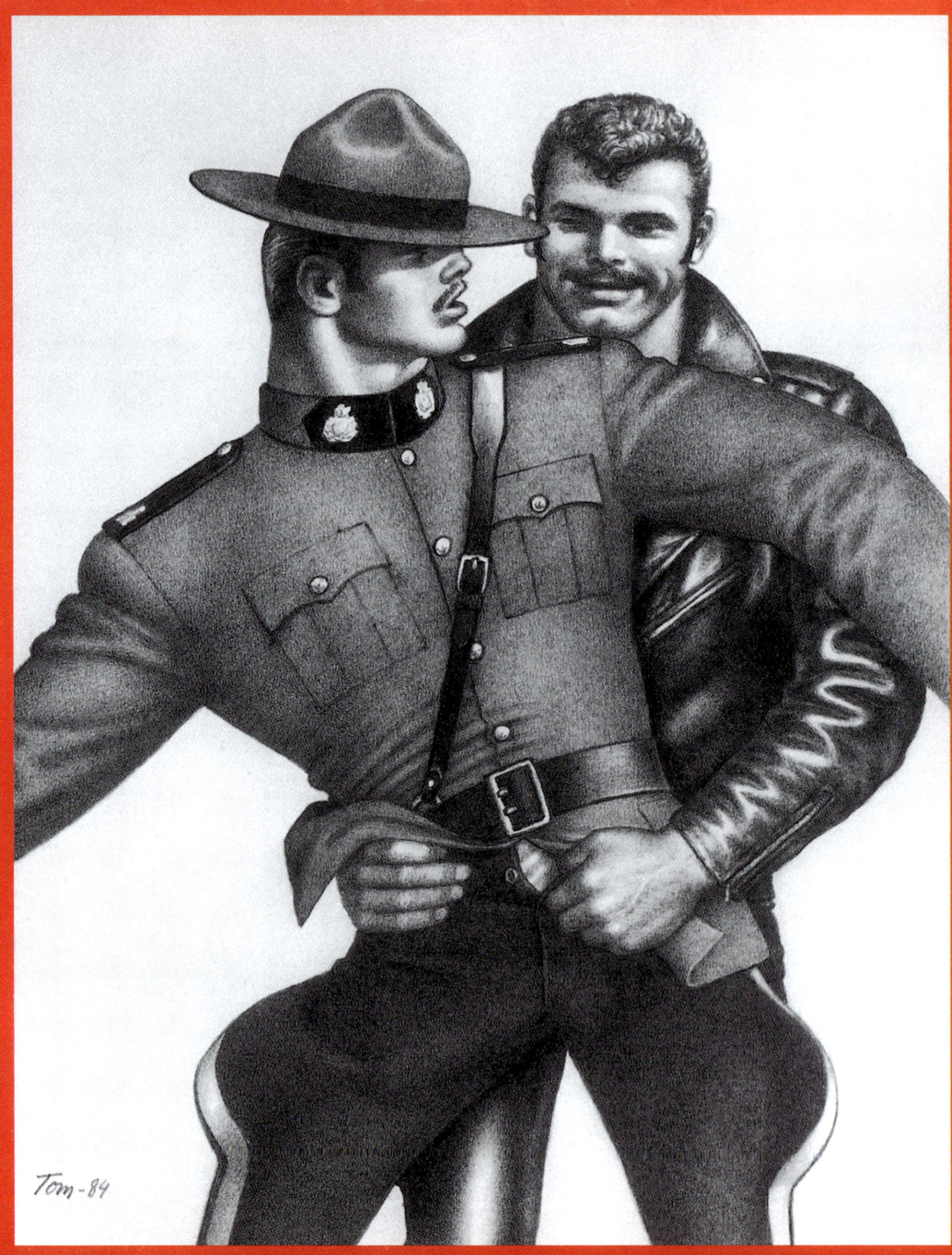

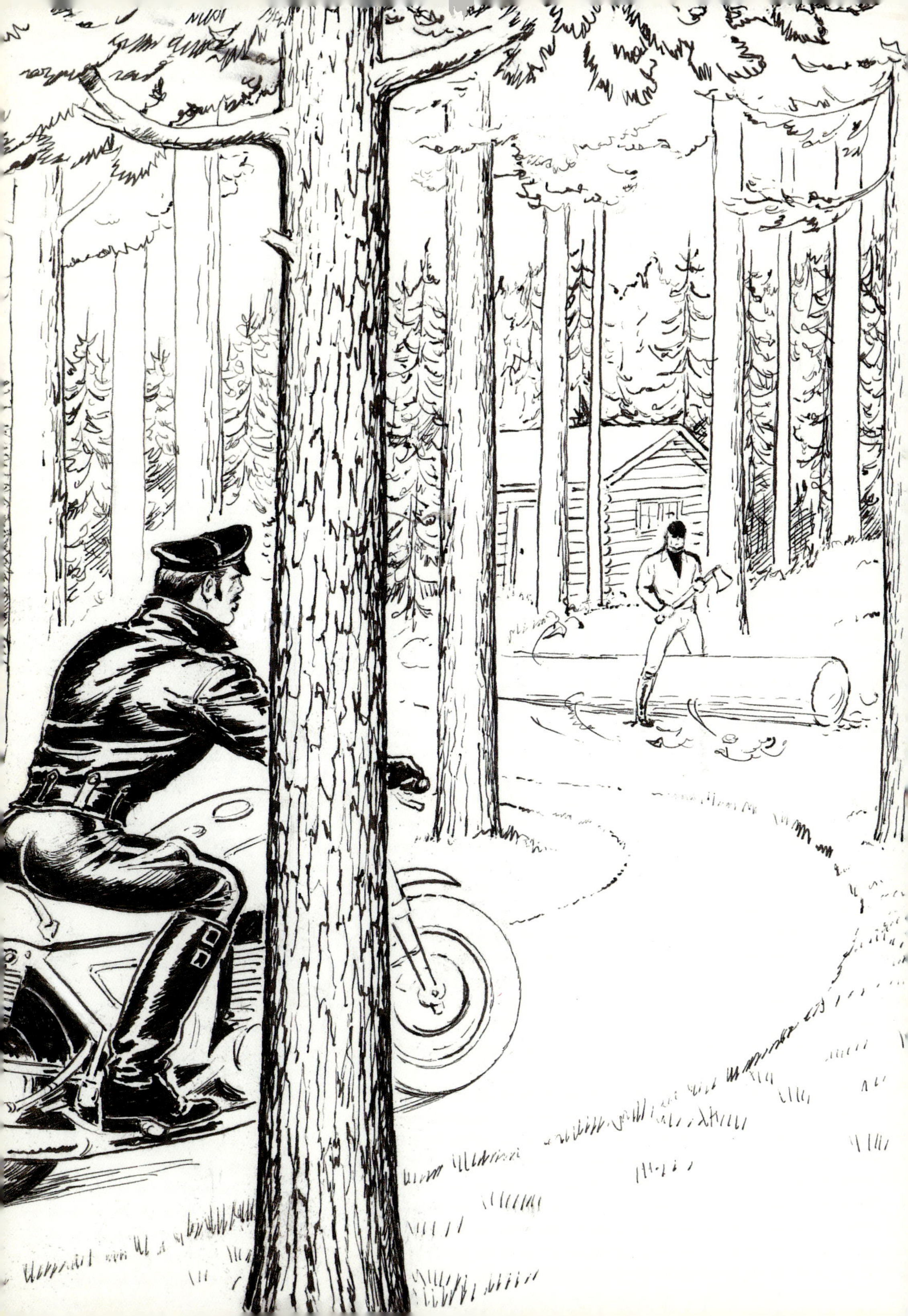

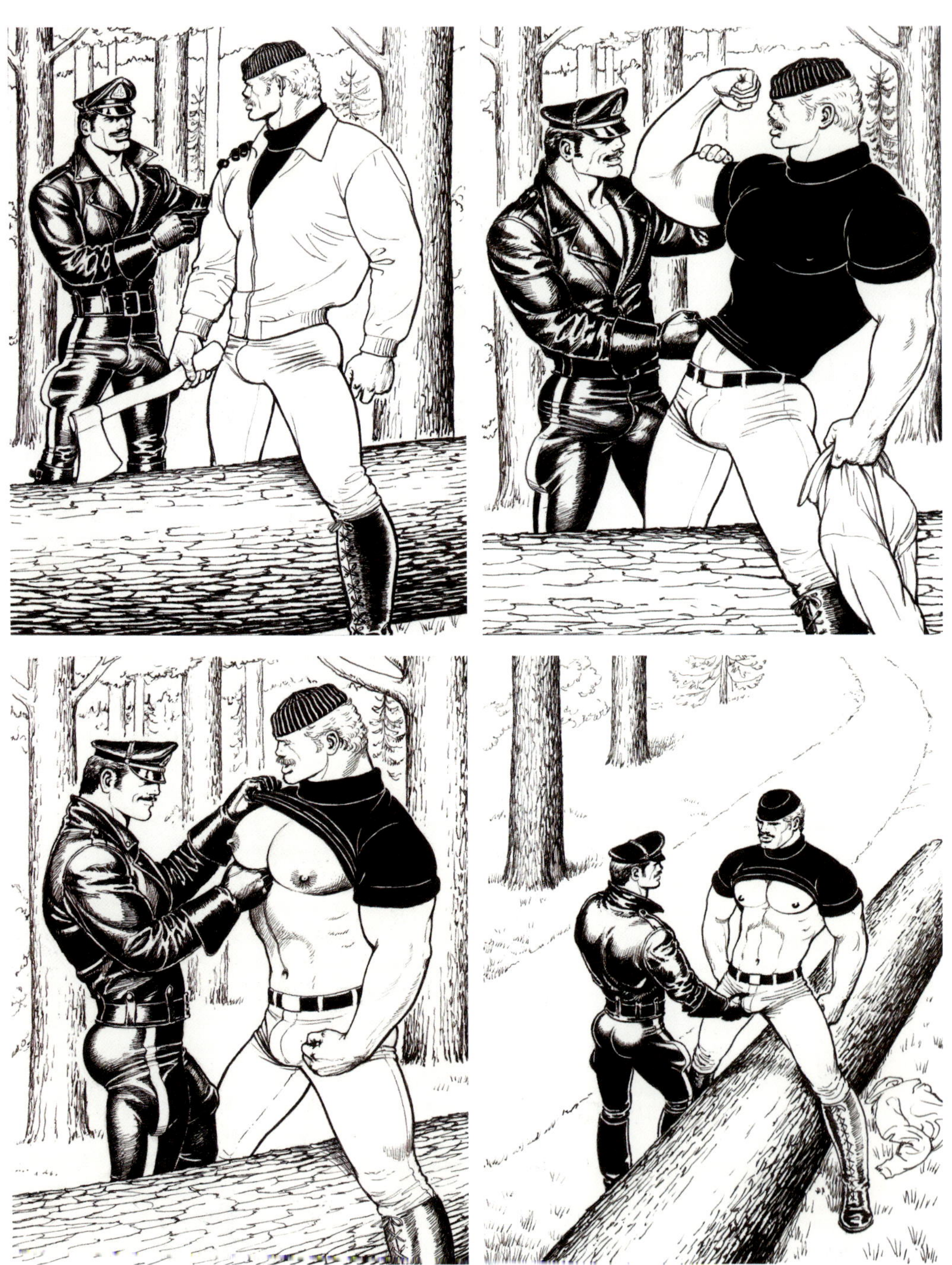

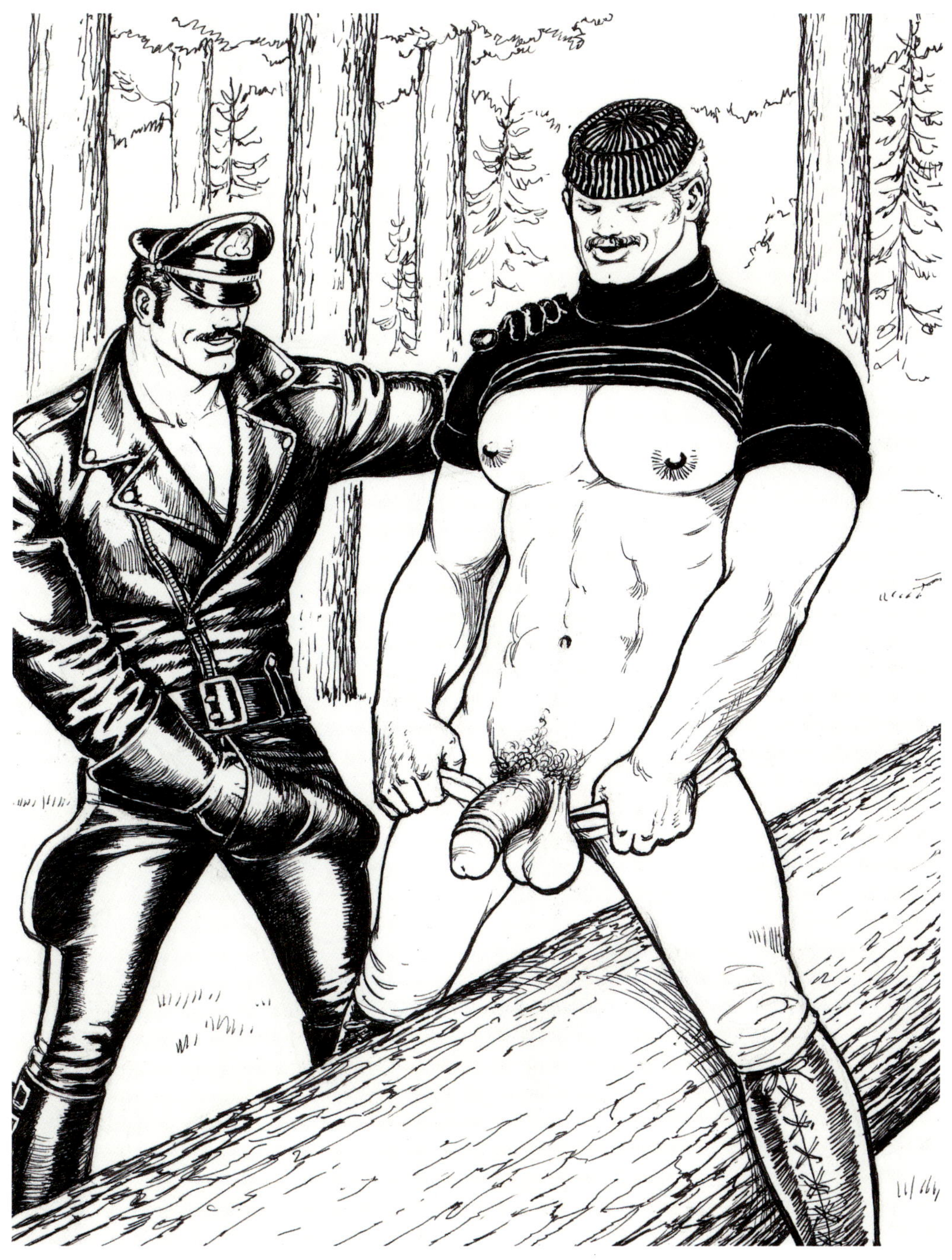

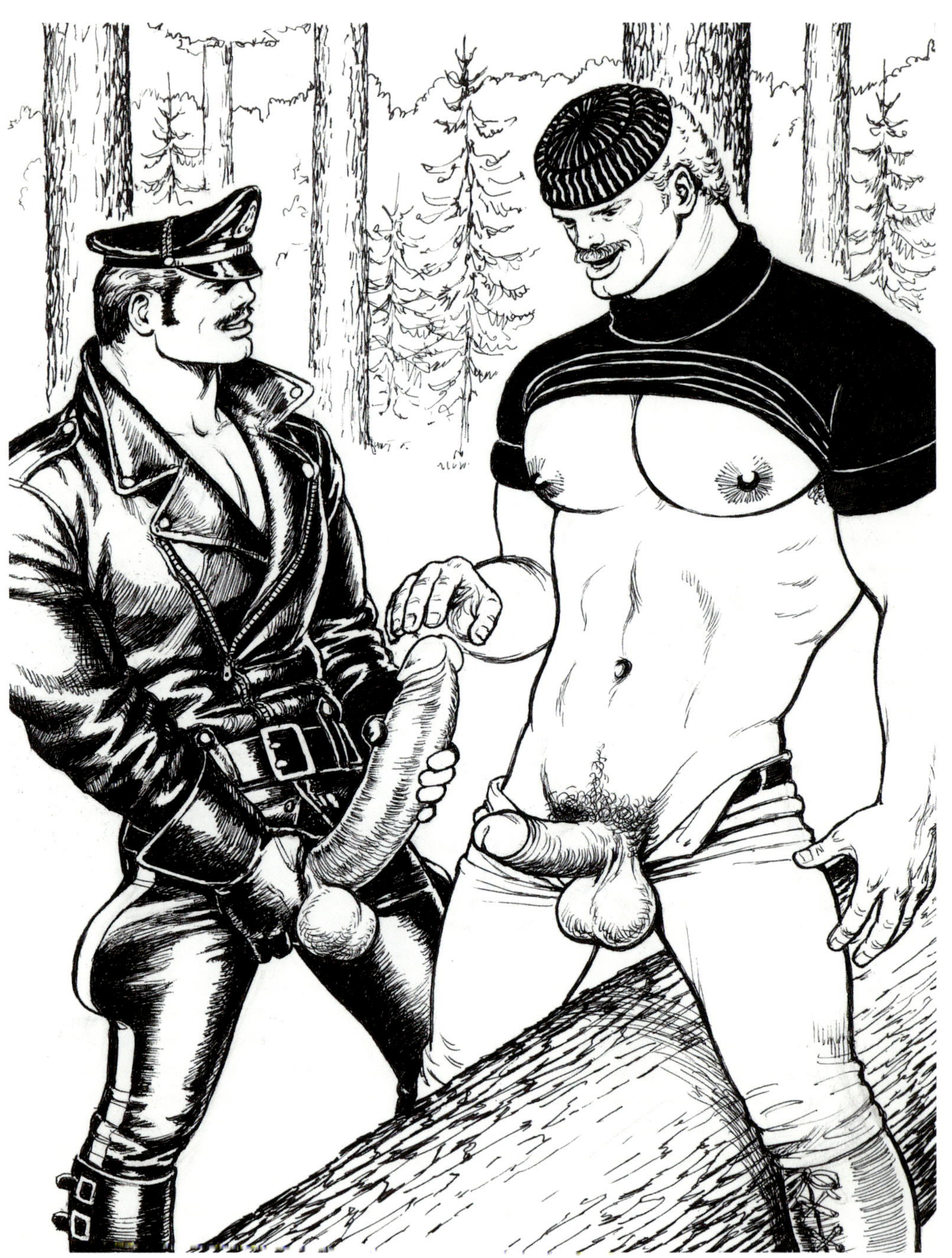

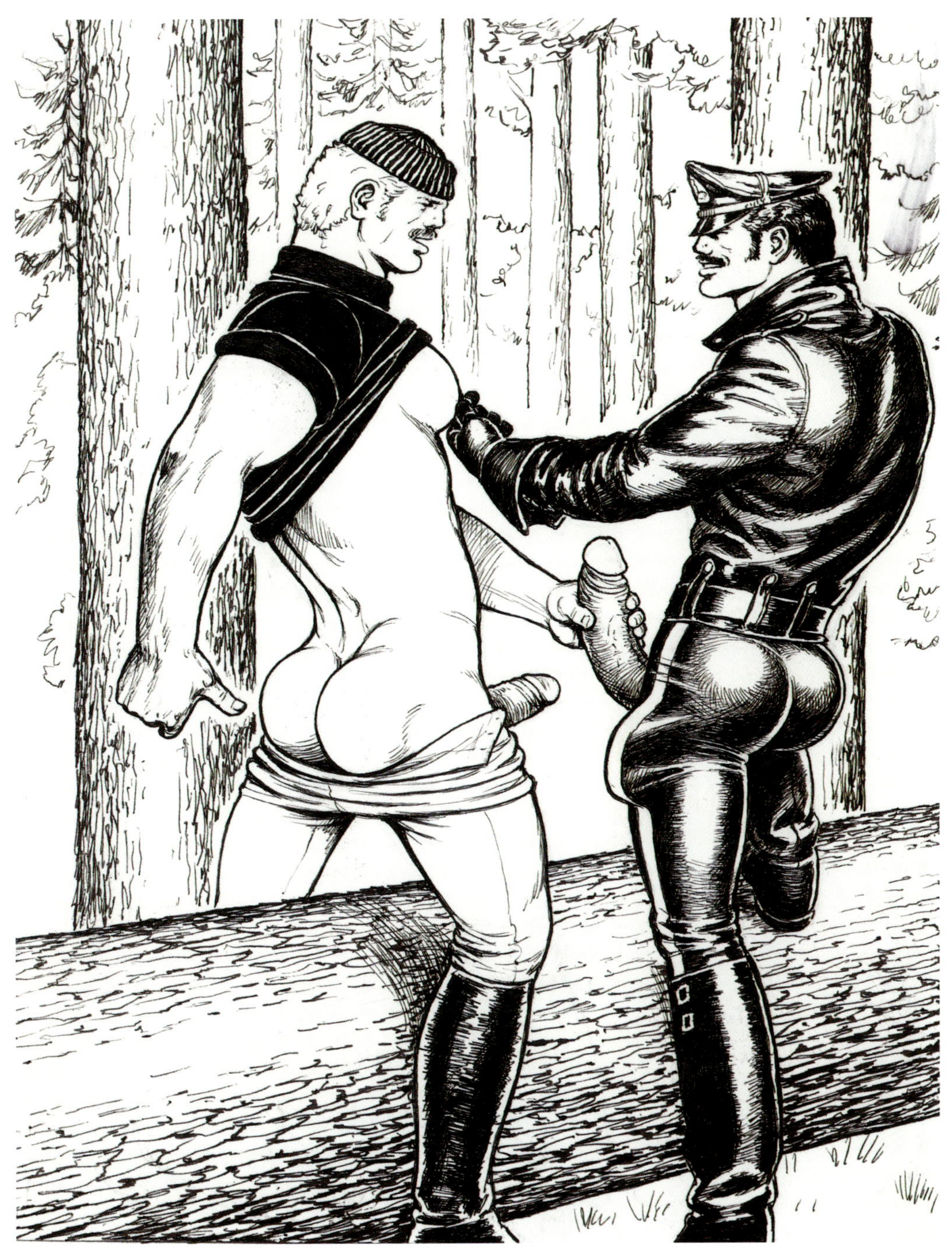

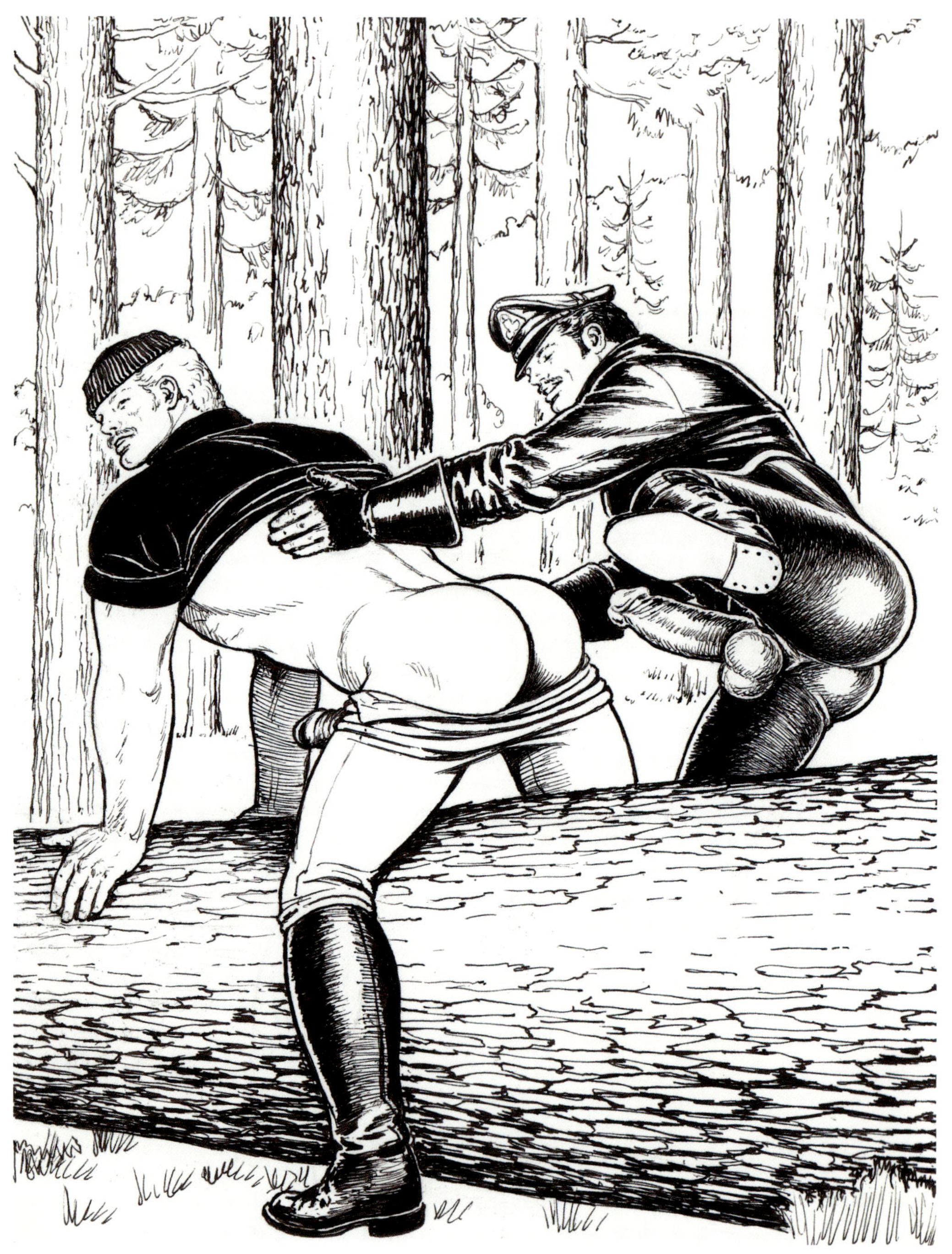

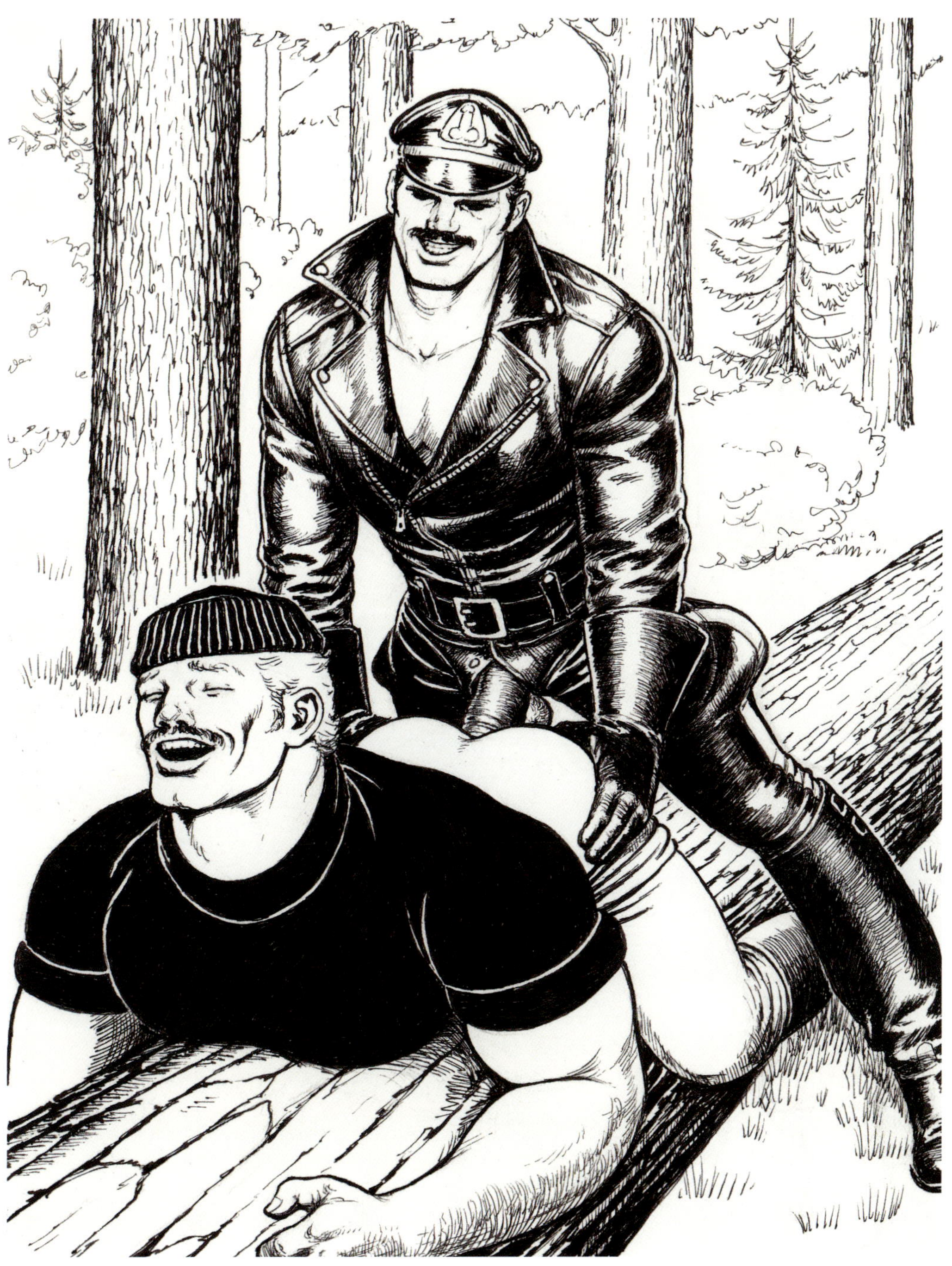

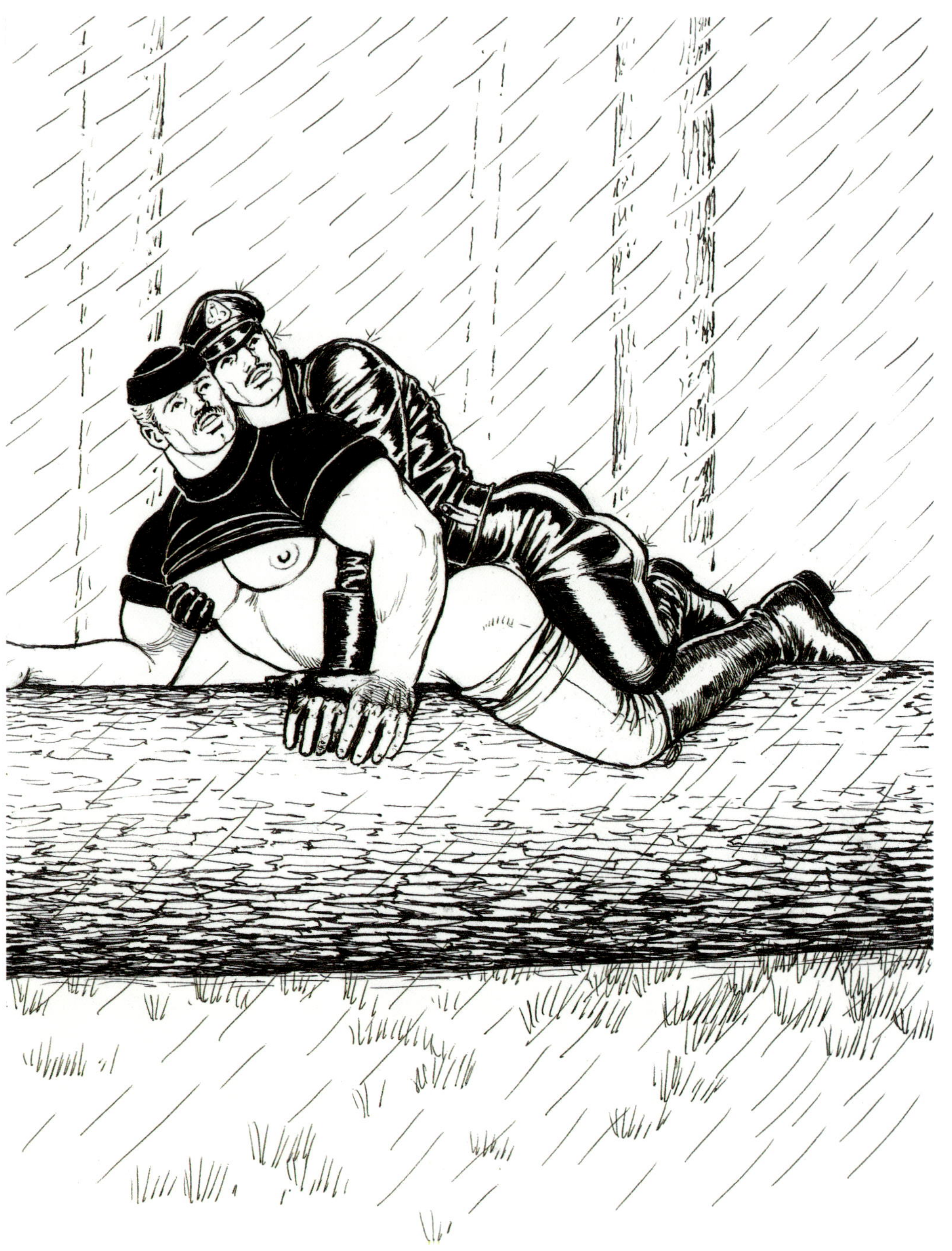

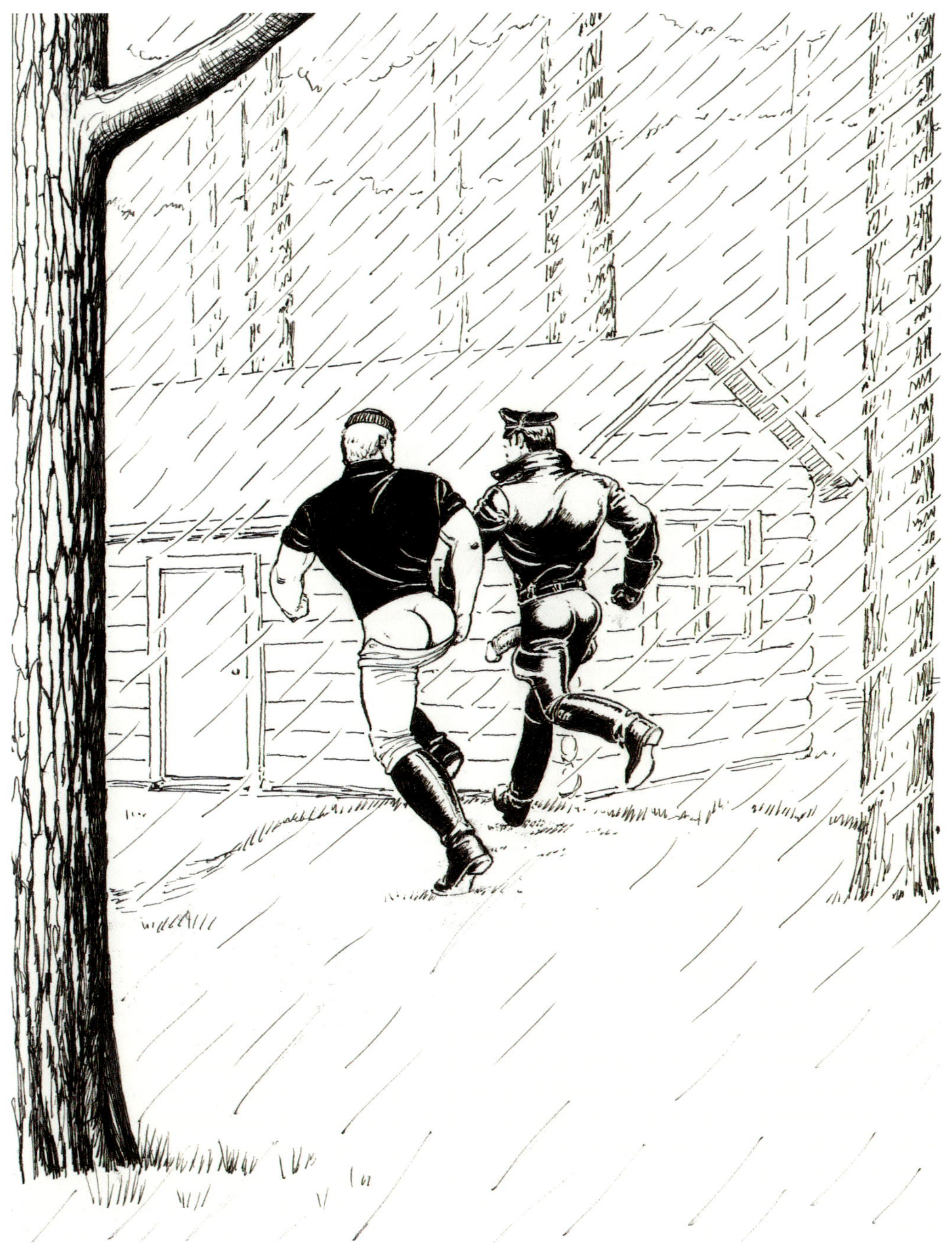

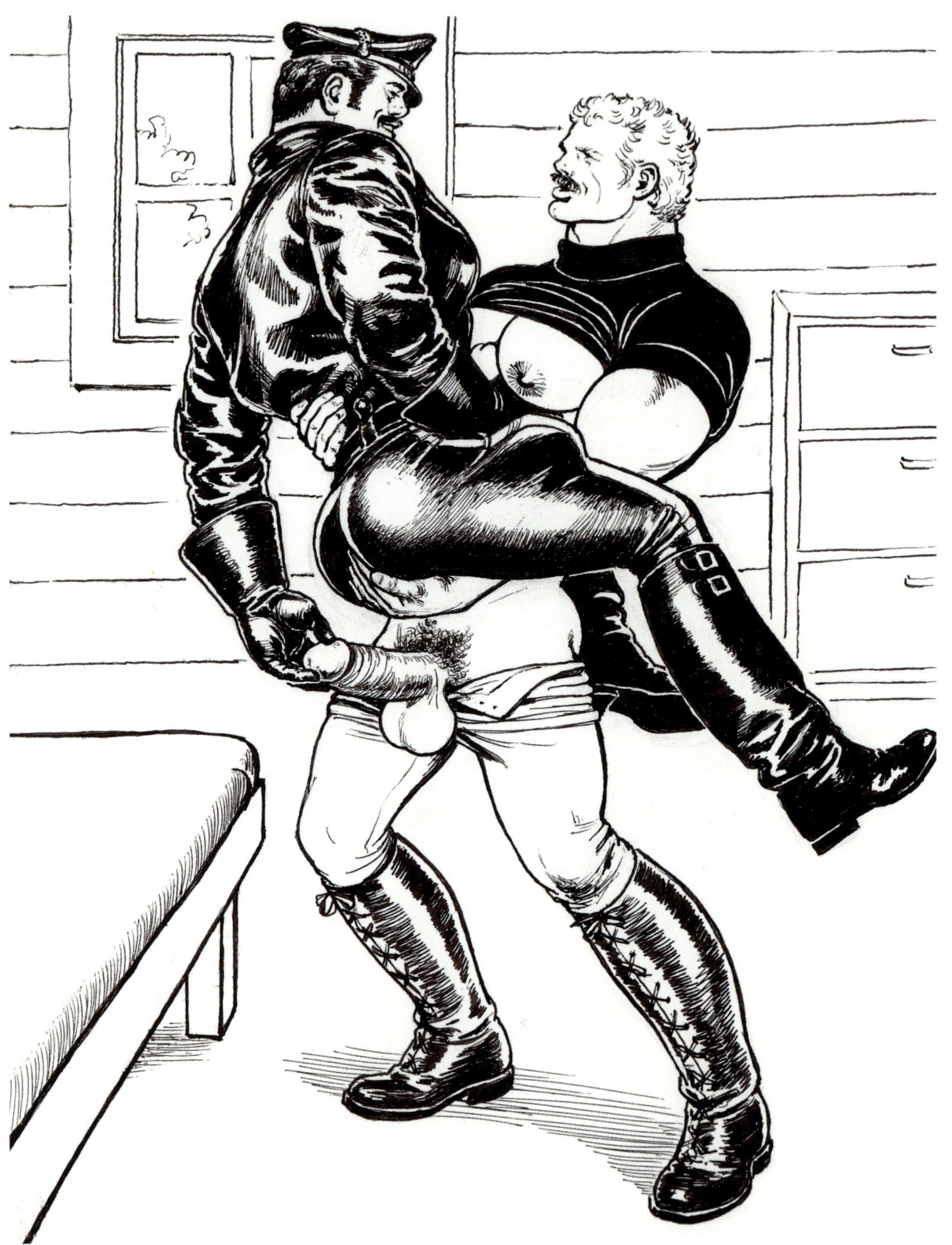

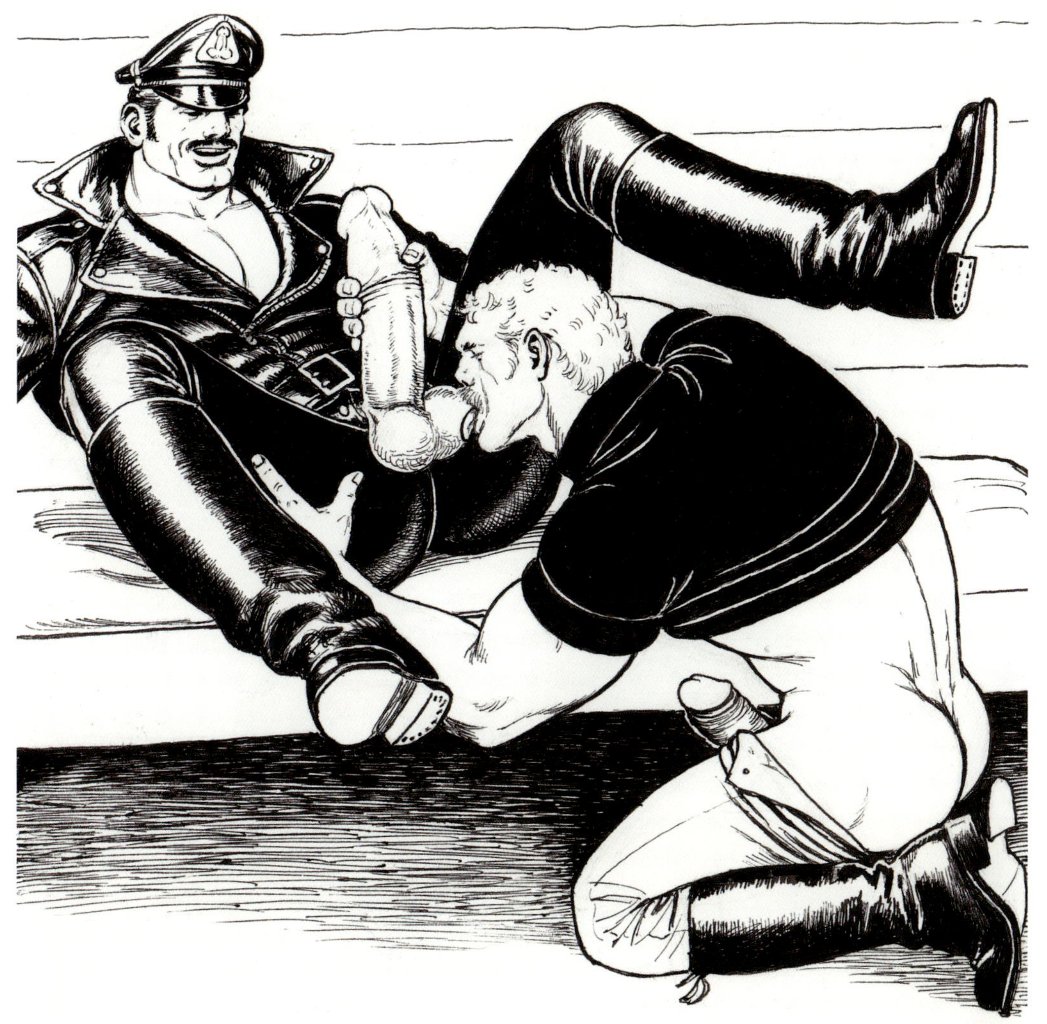

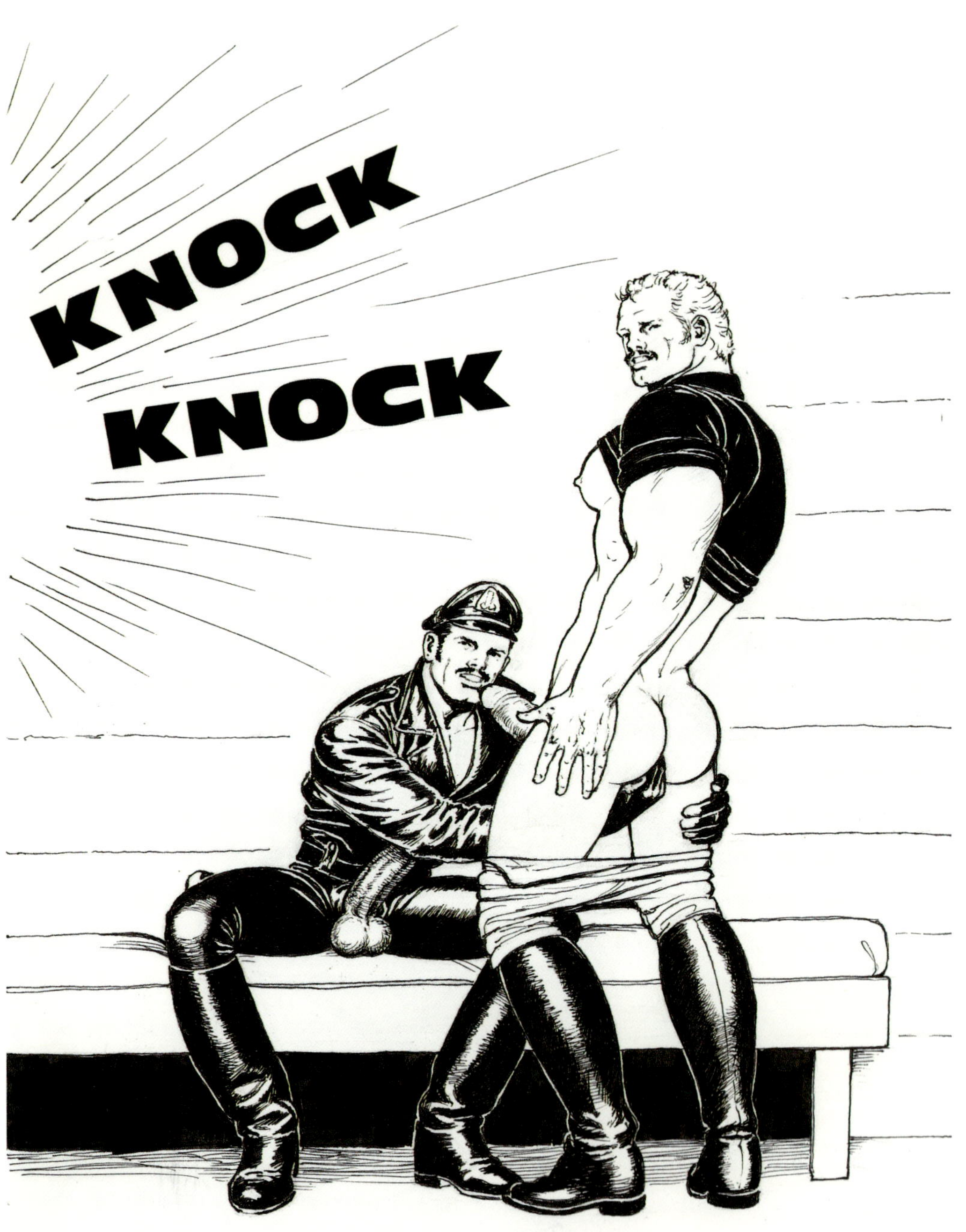

KNOCK
KNOCK

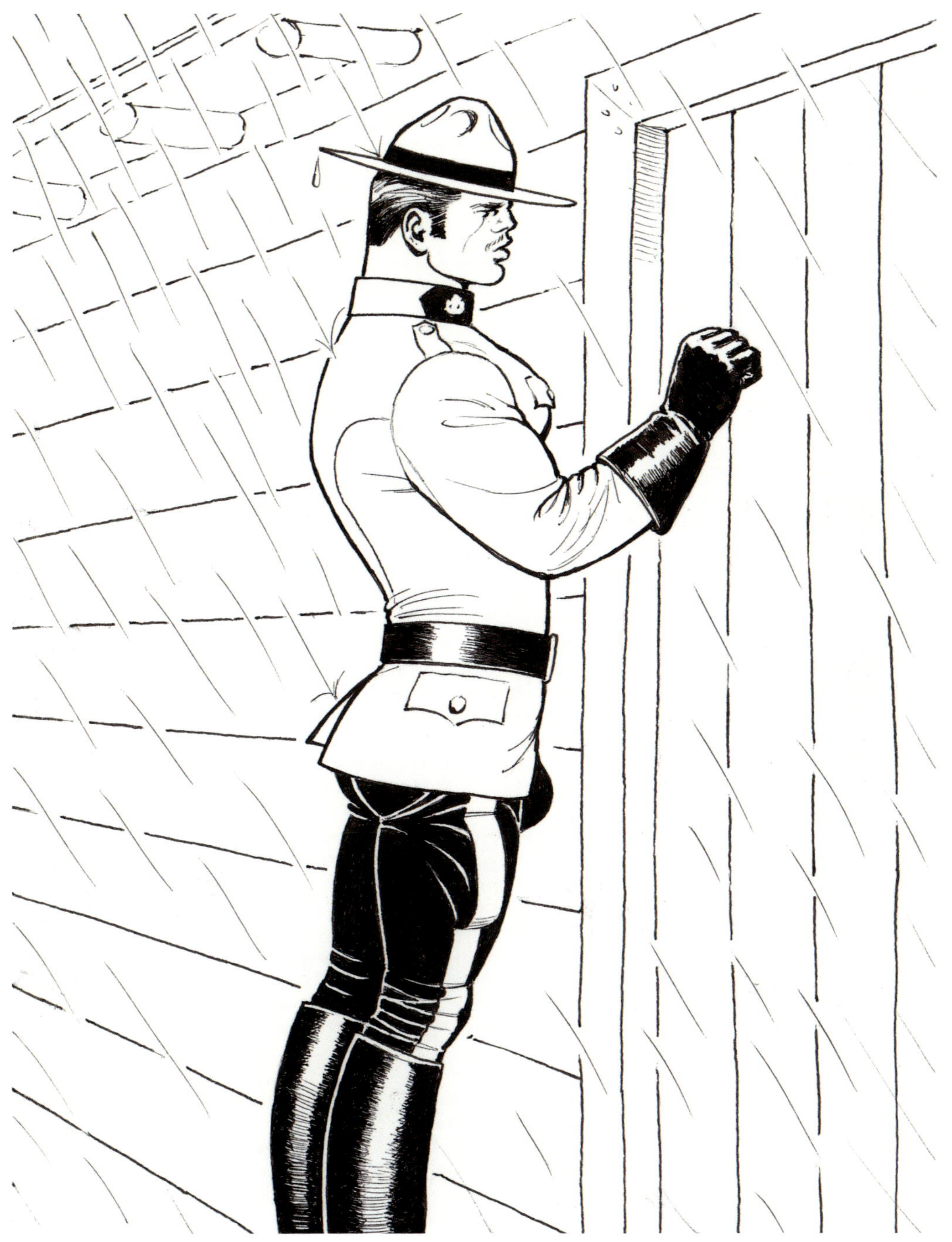

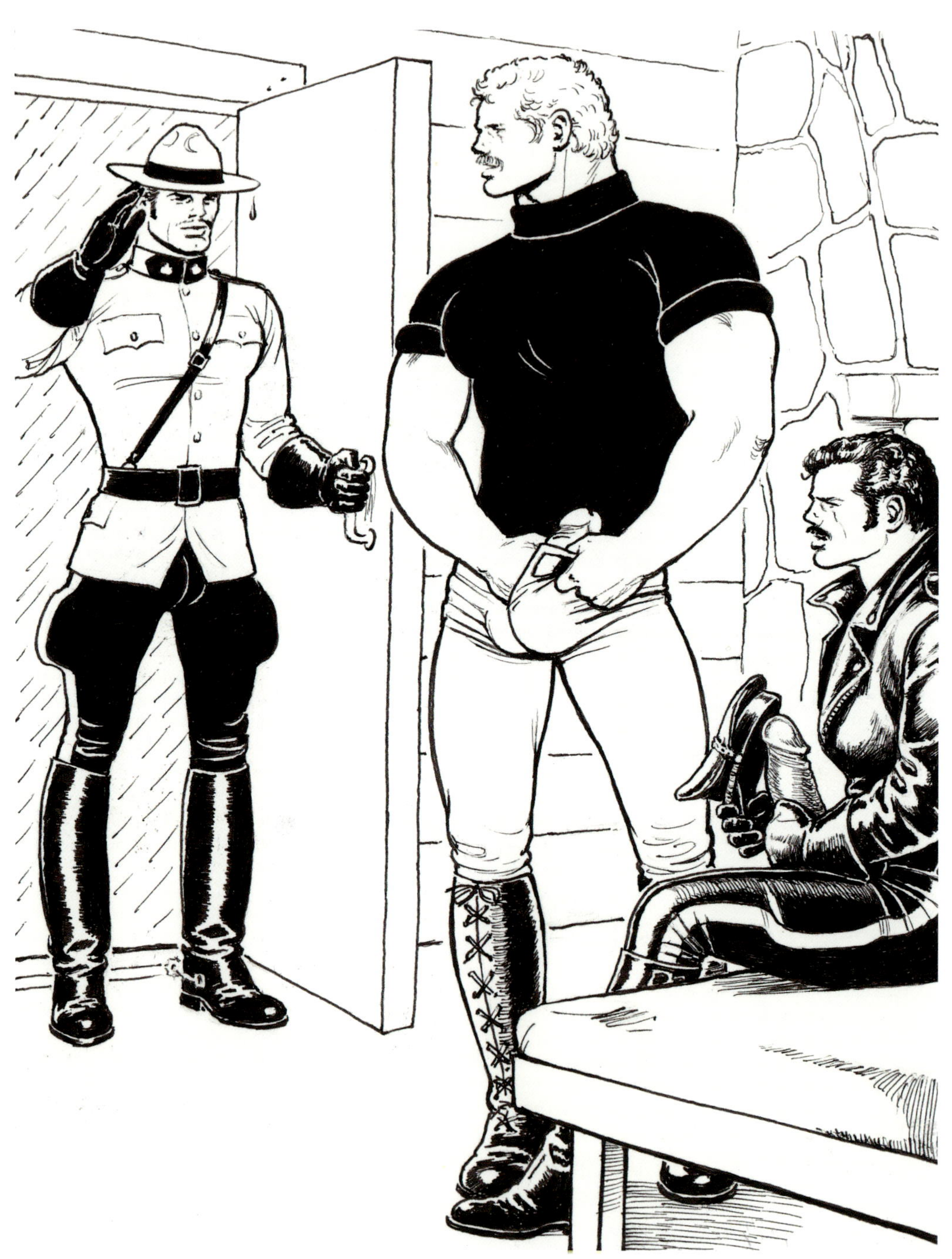

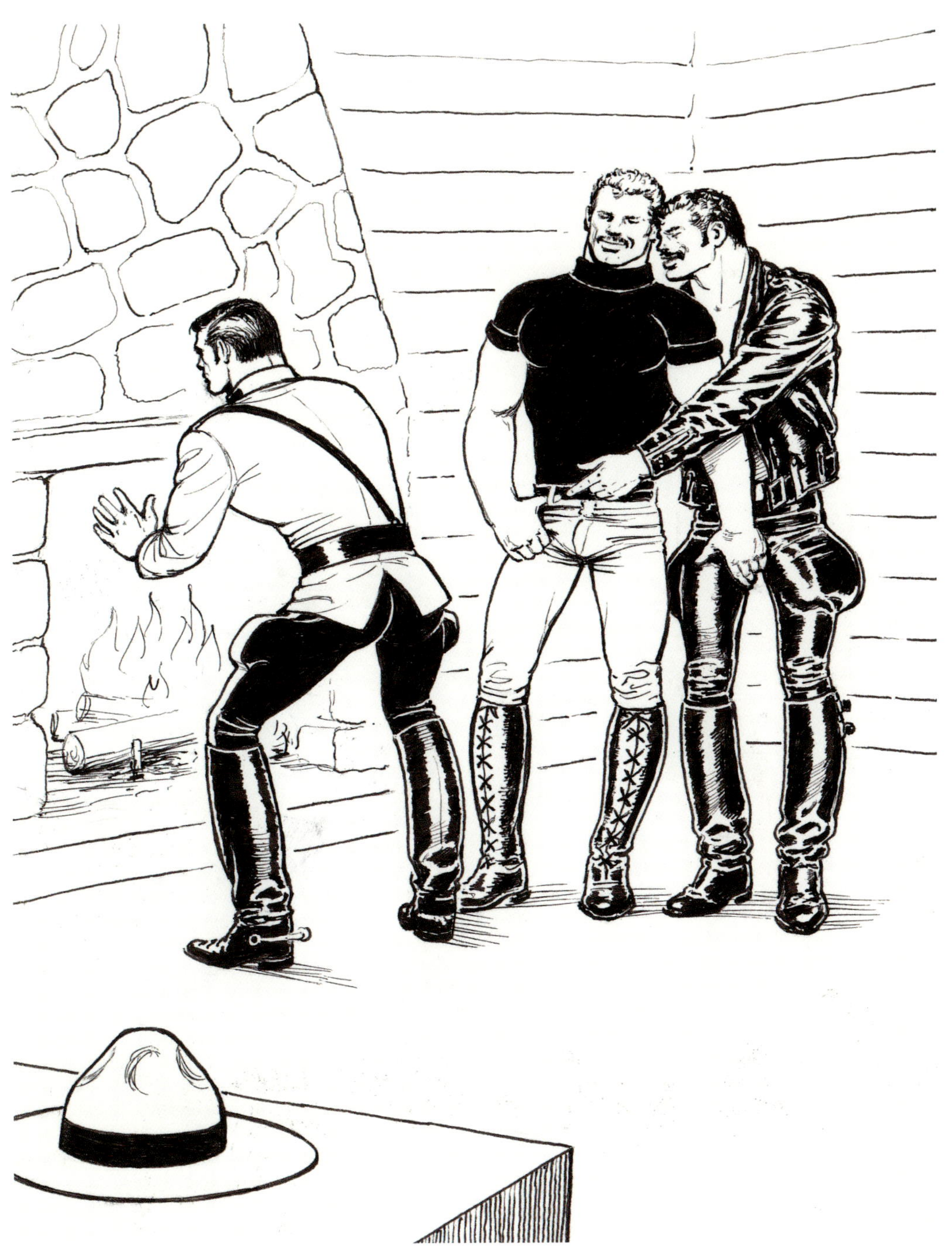

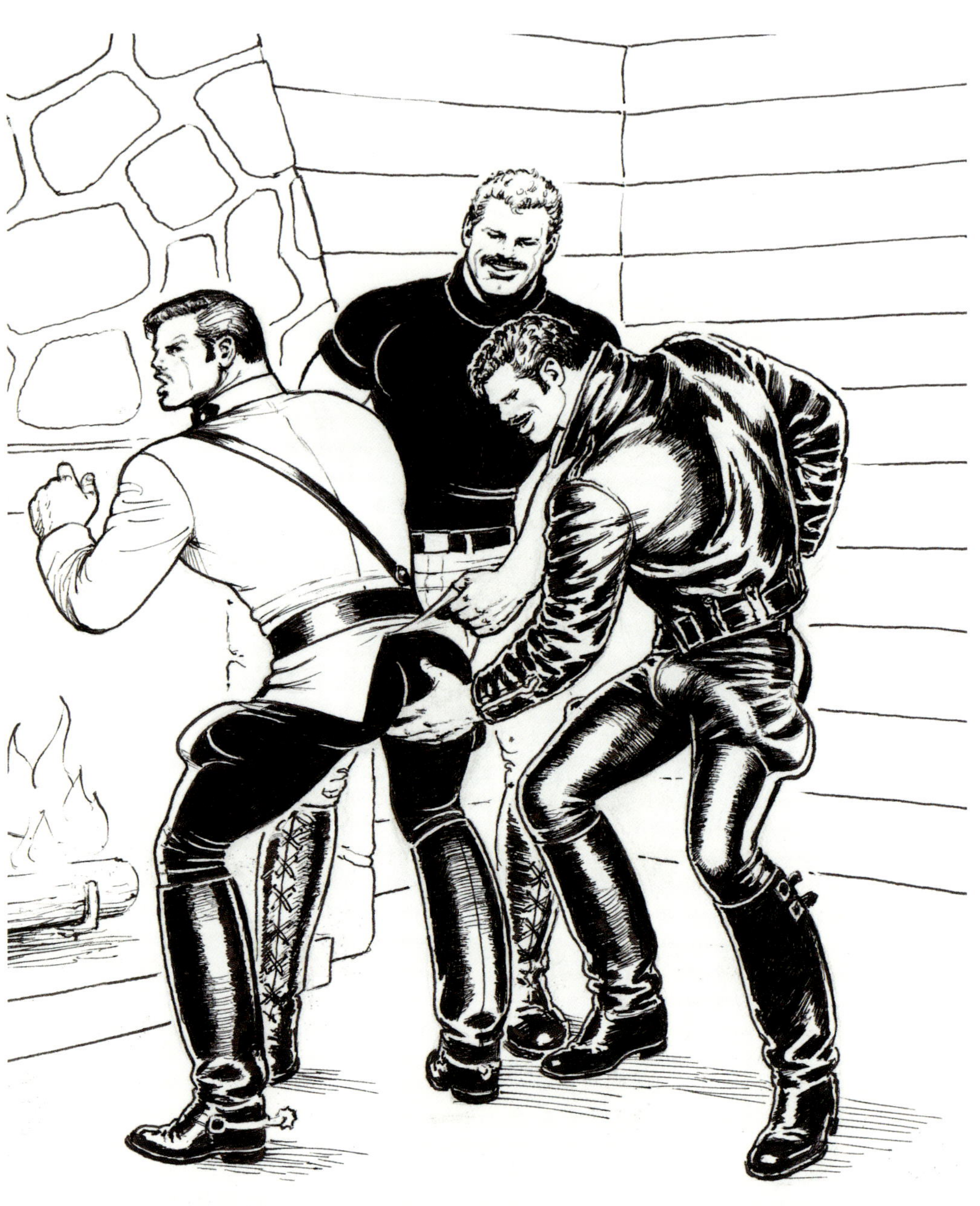

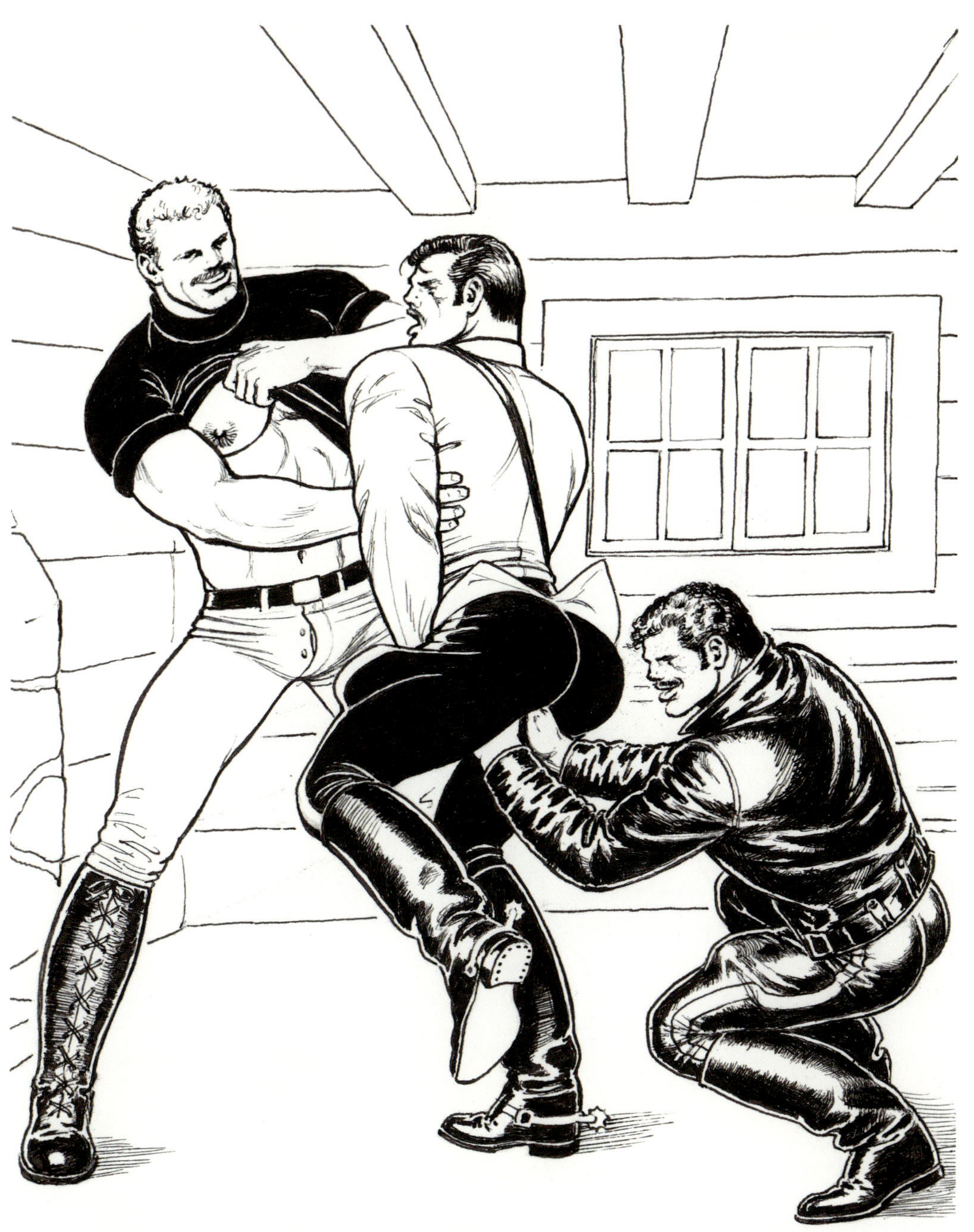

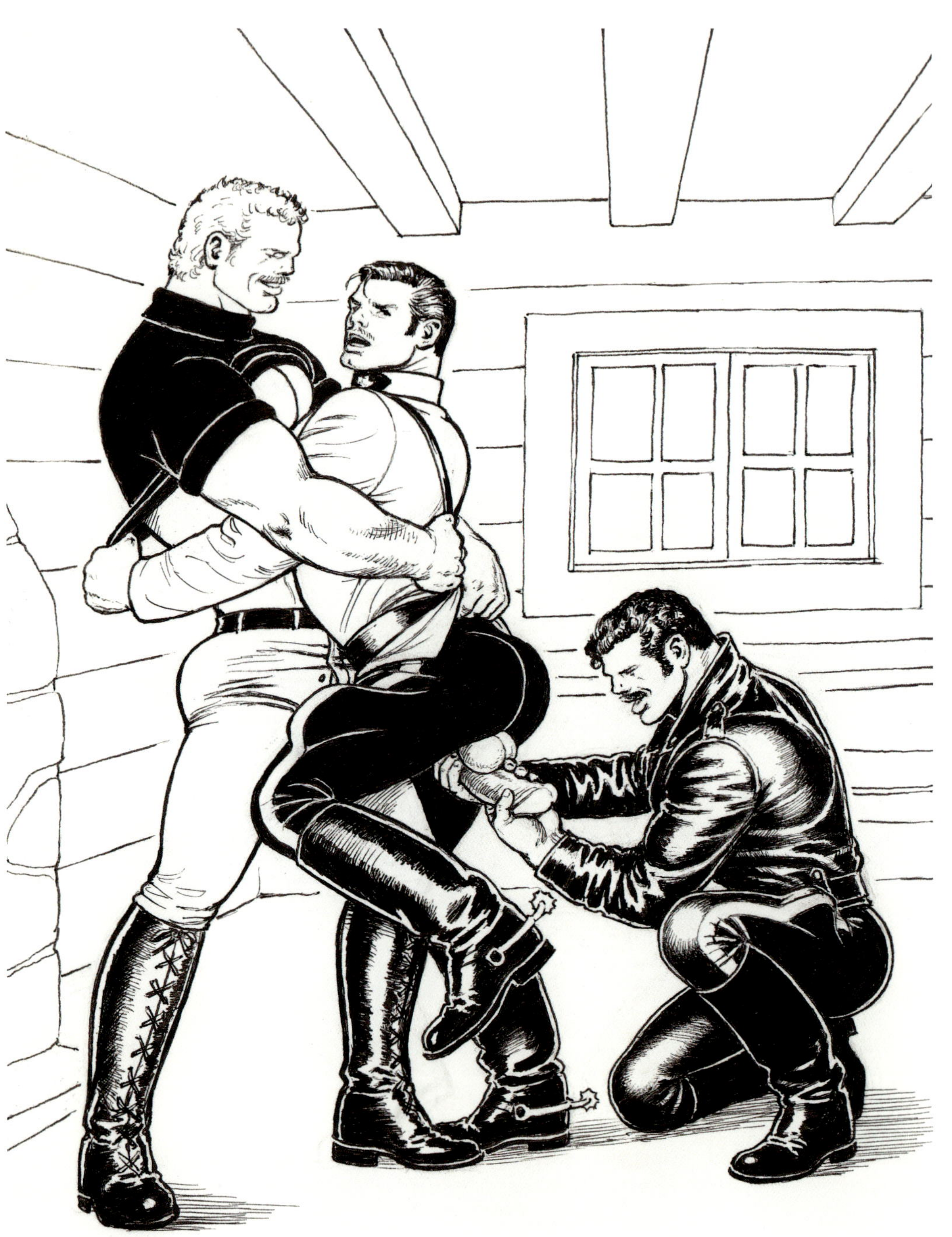

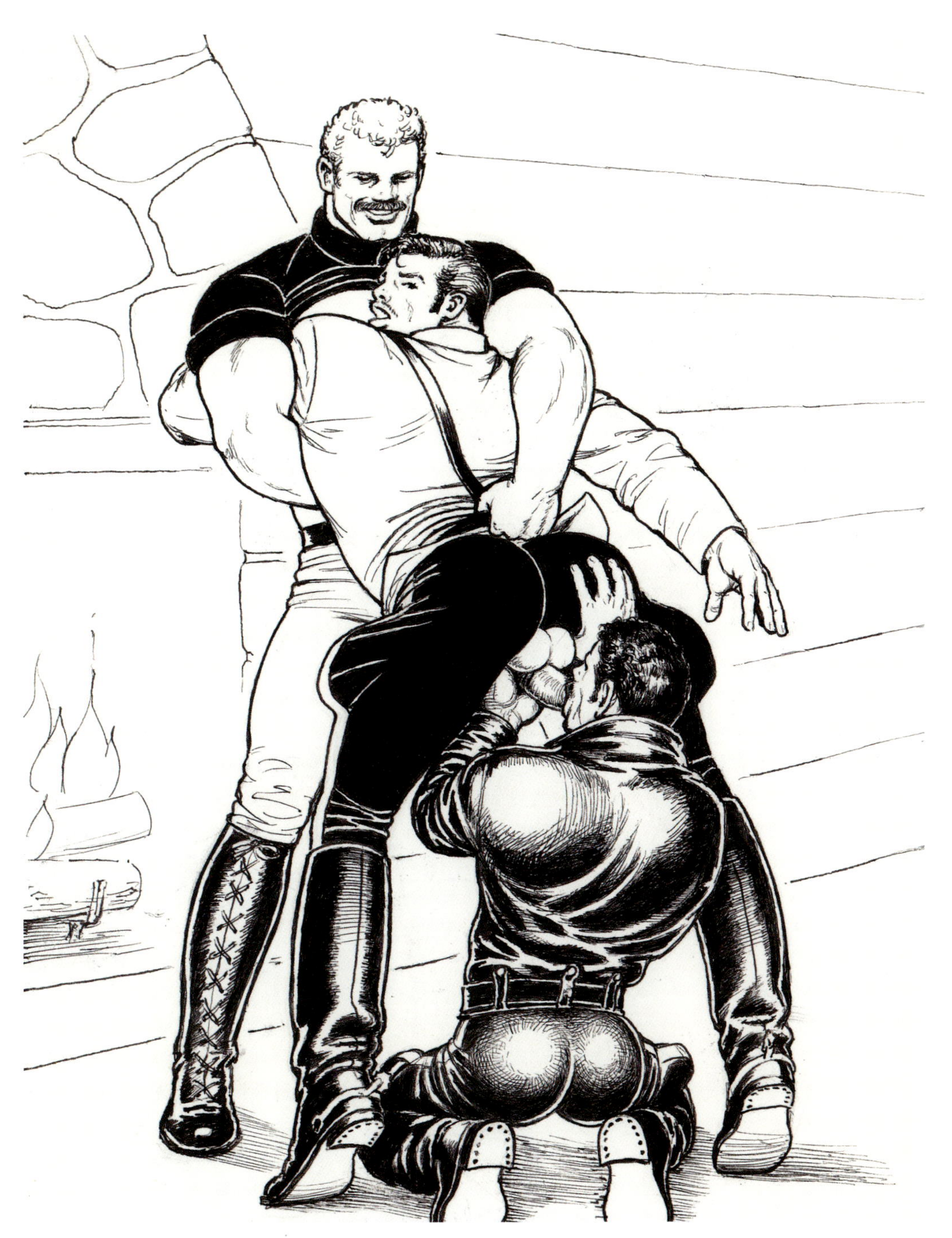

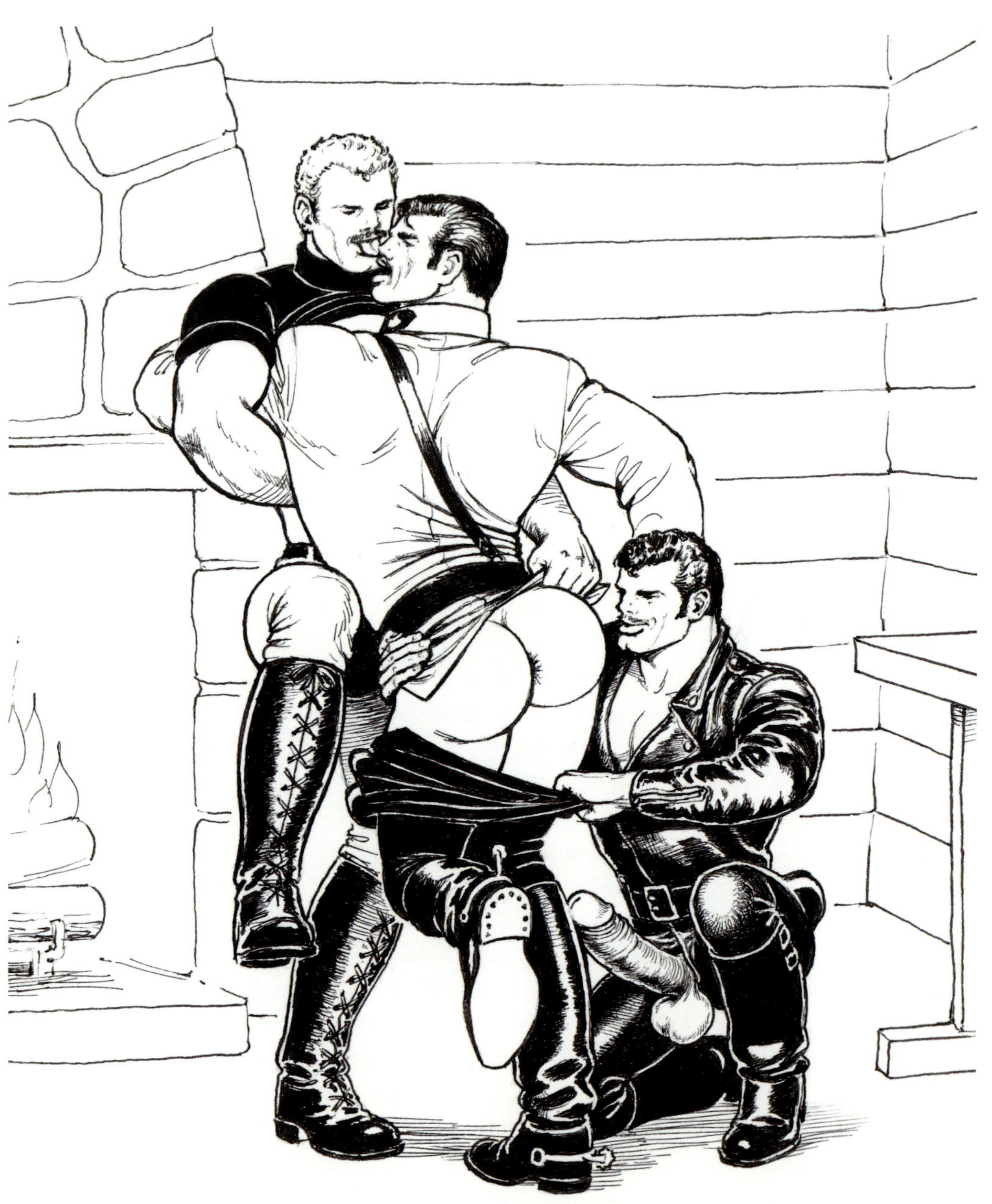

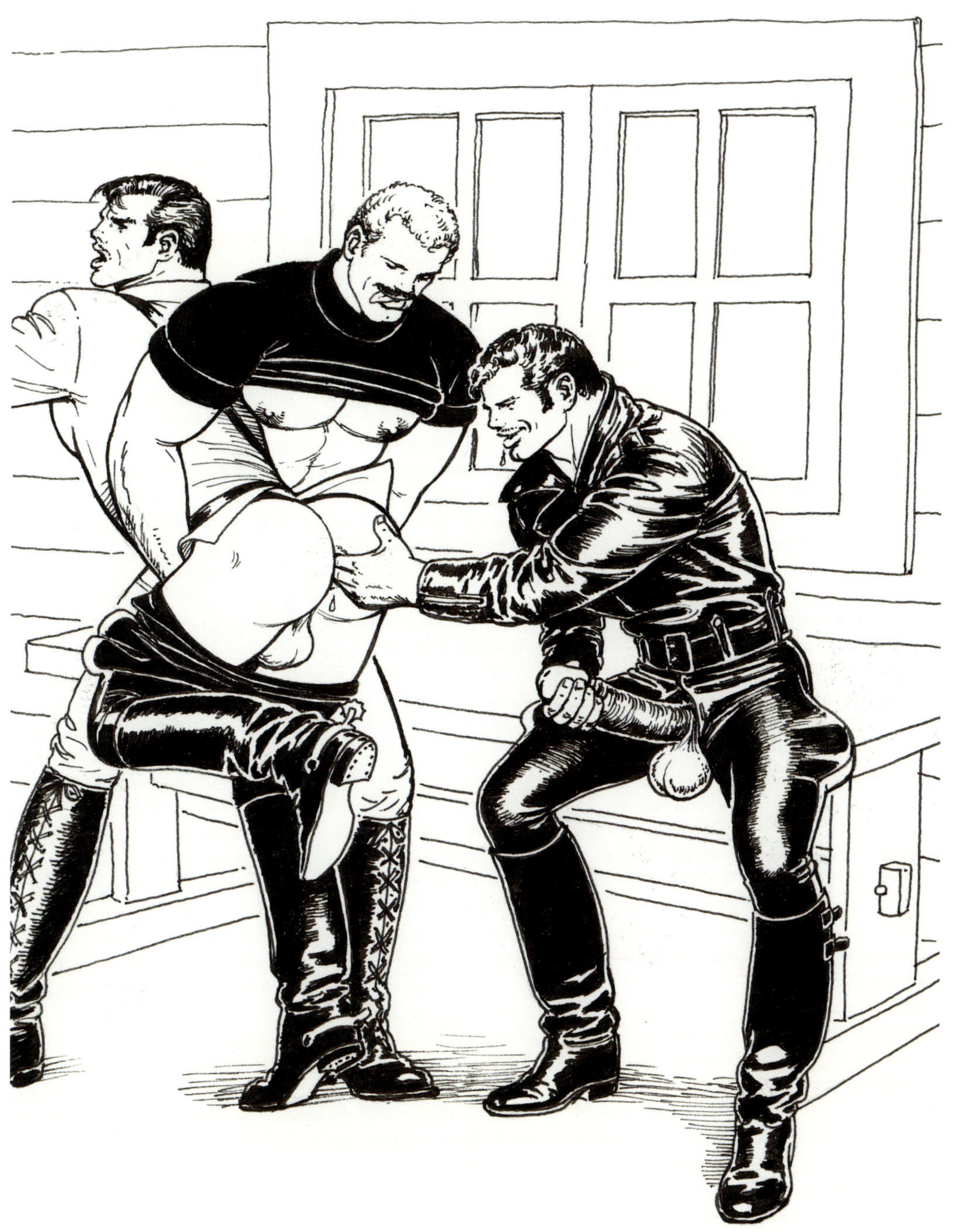

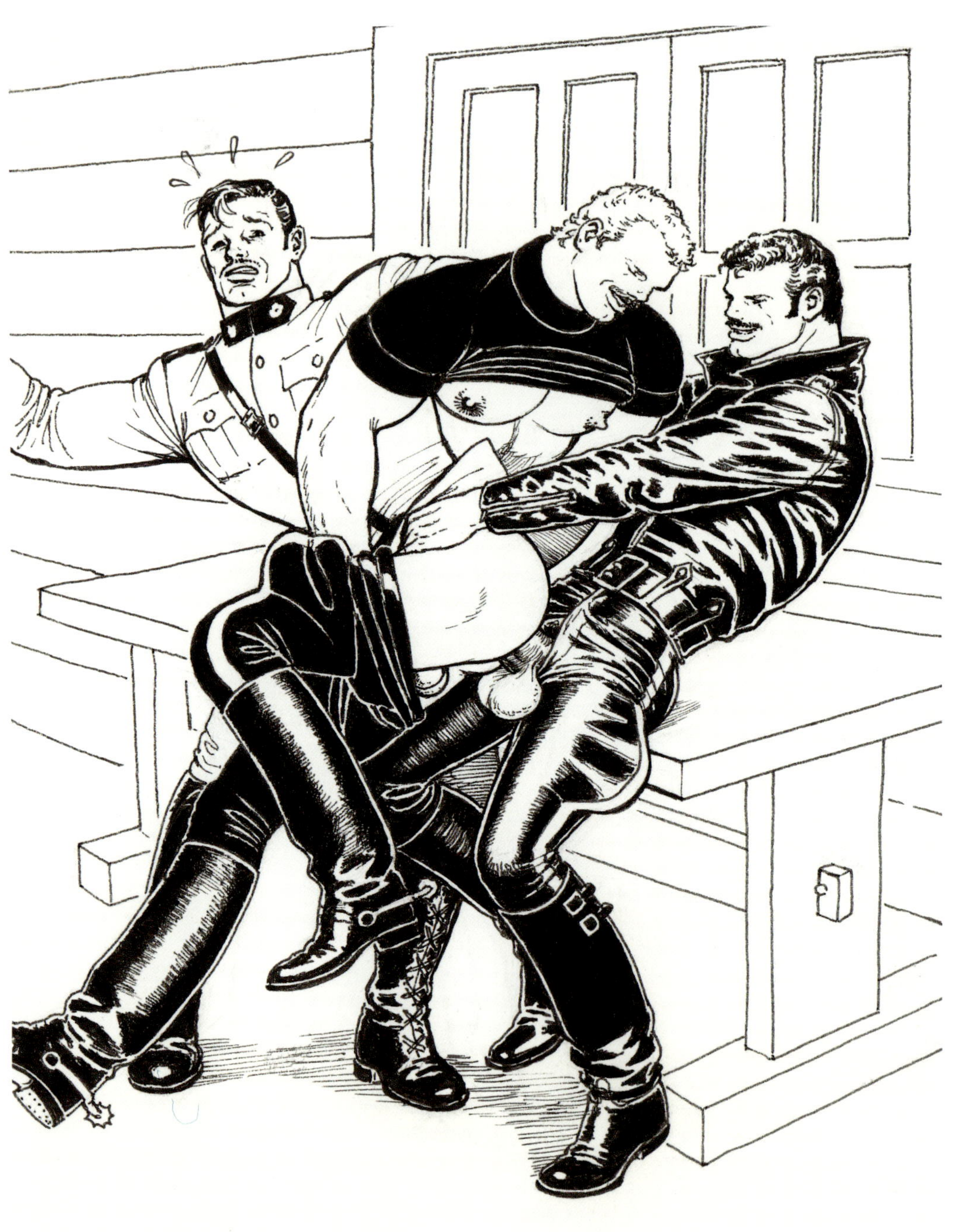

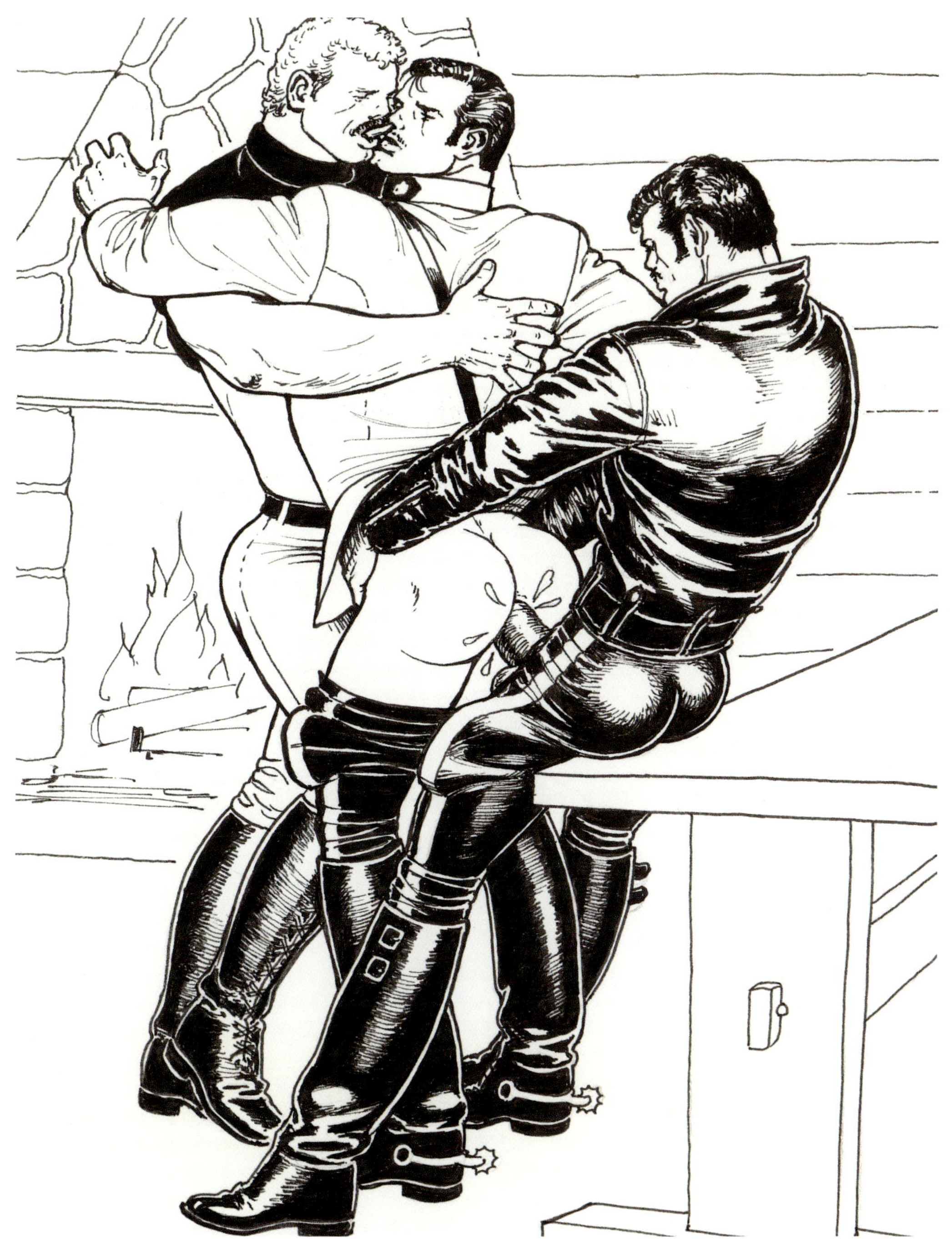

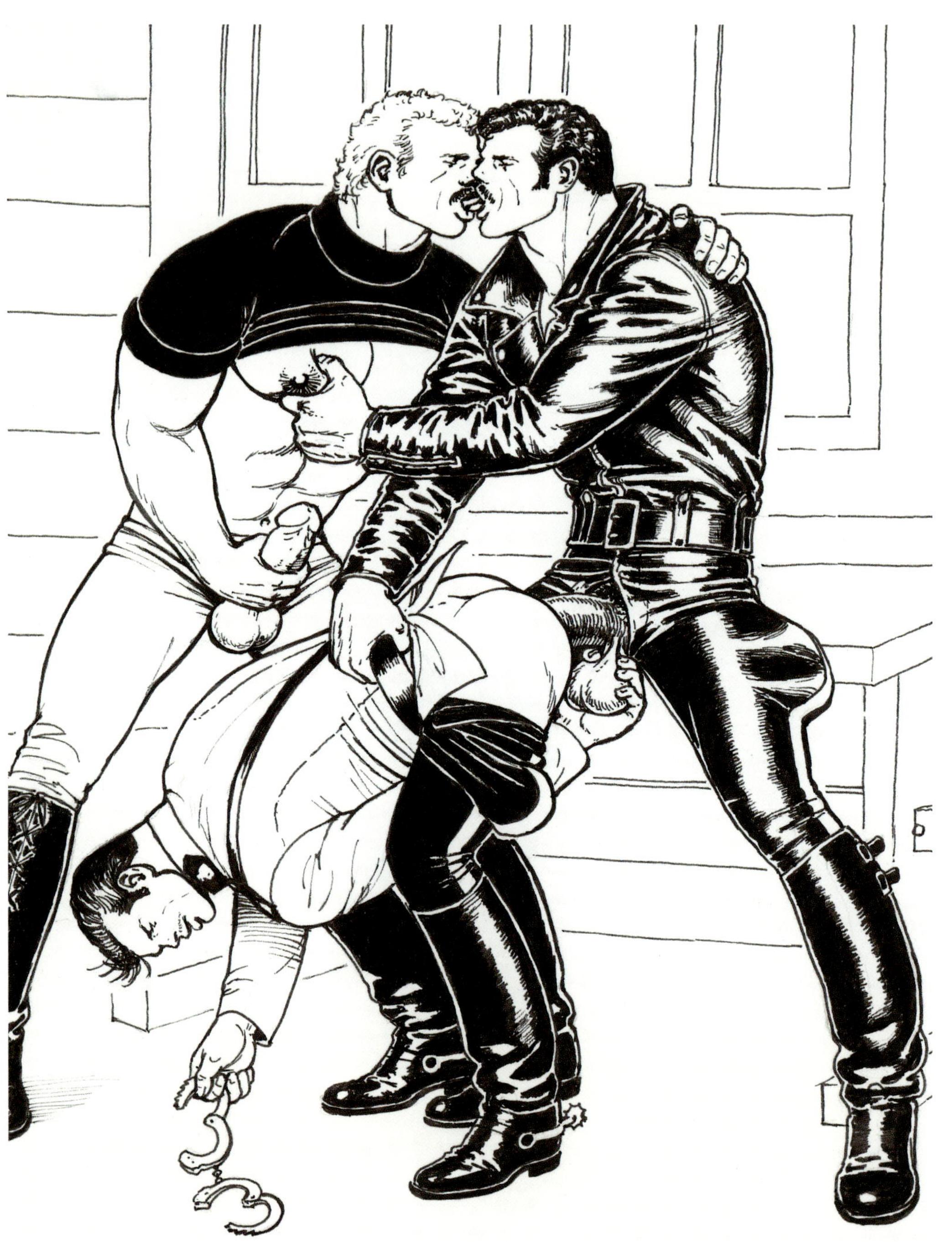

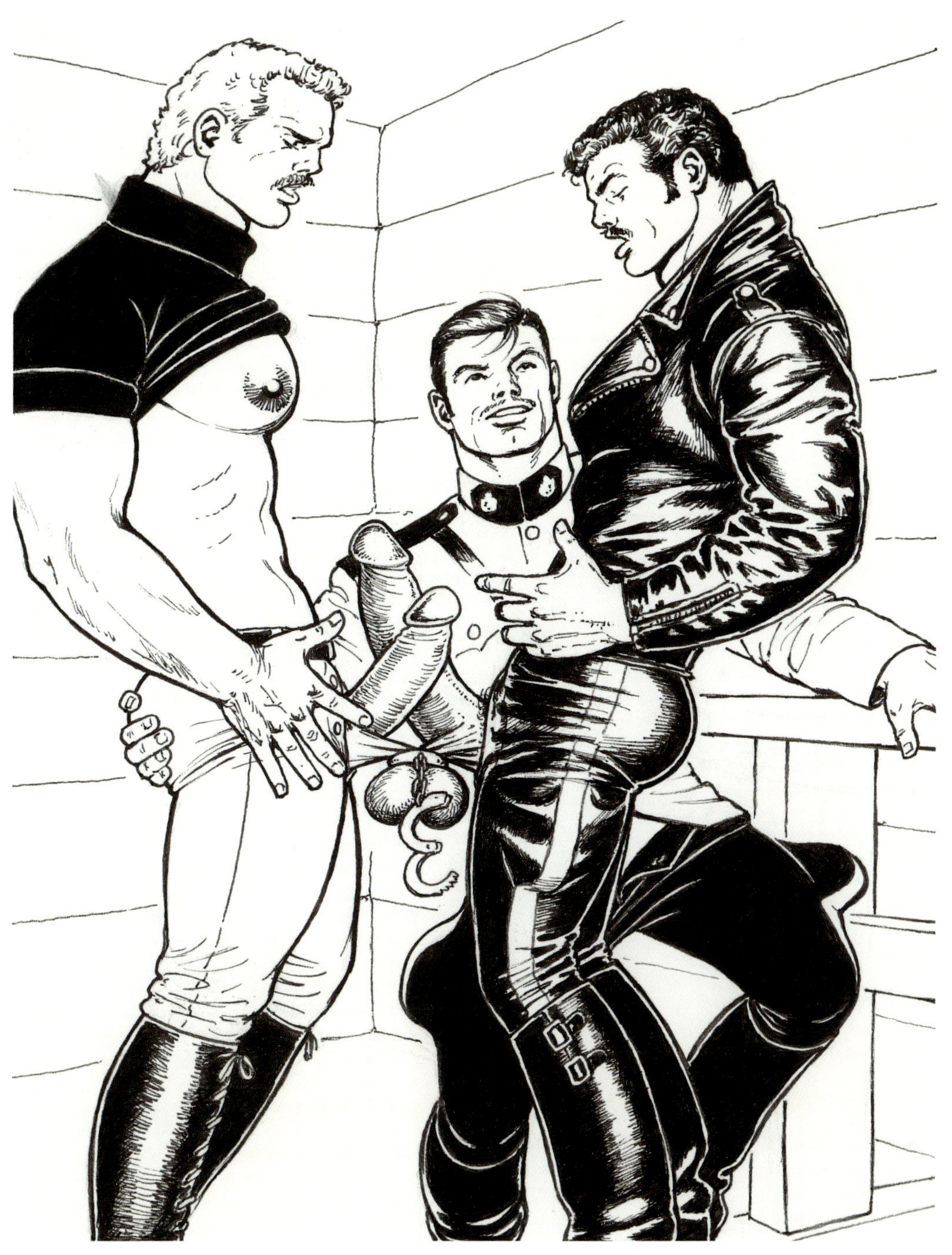

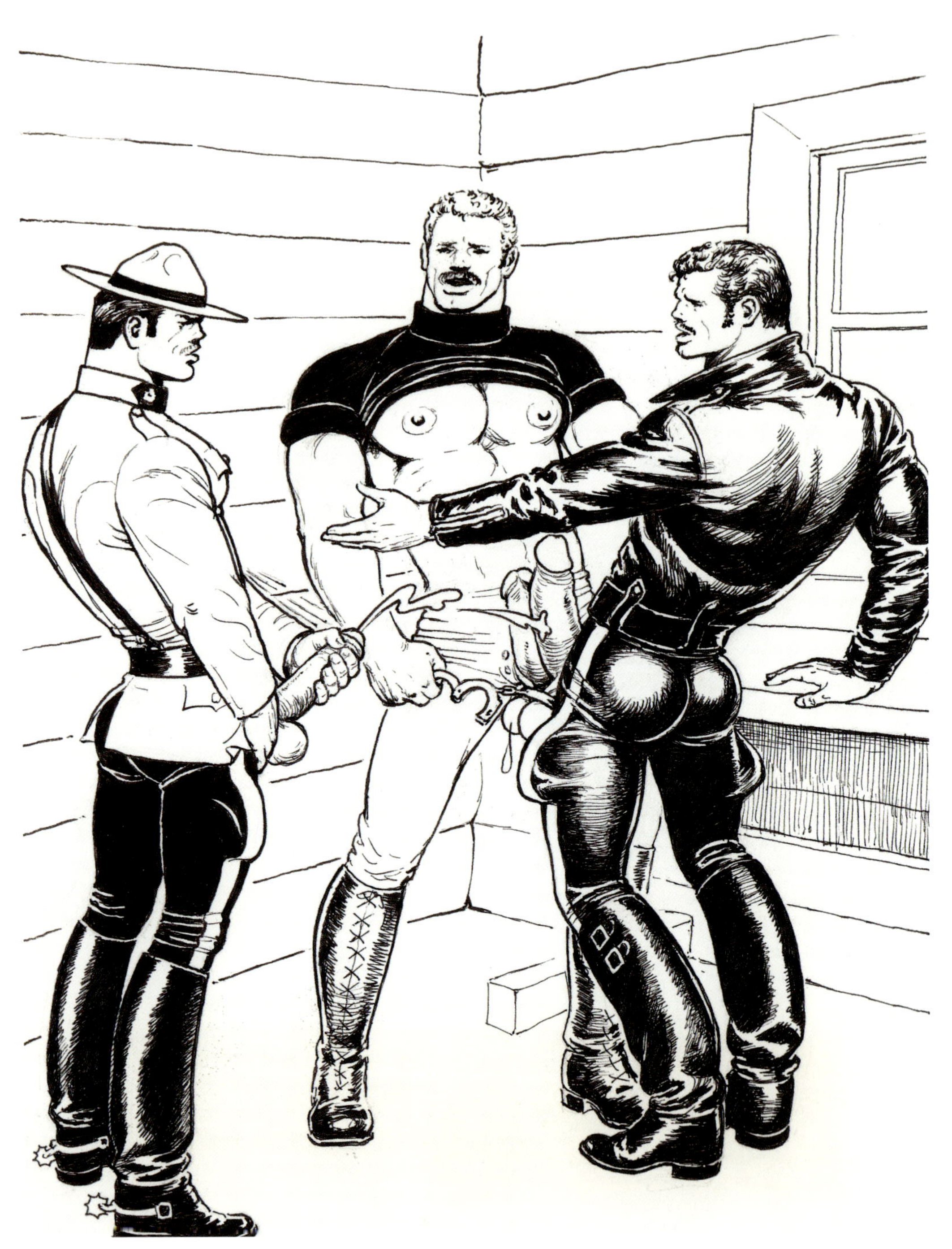

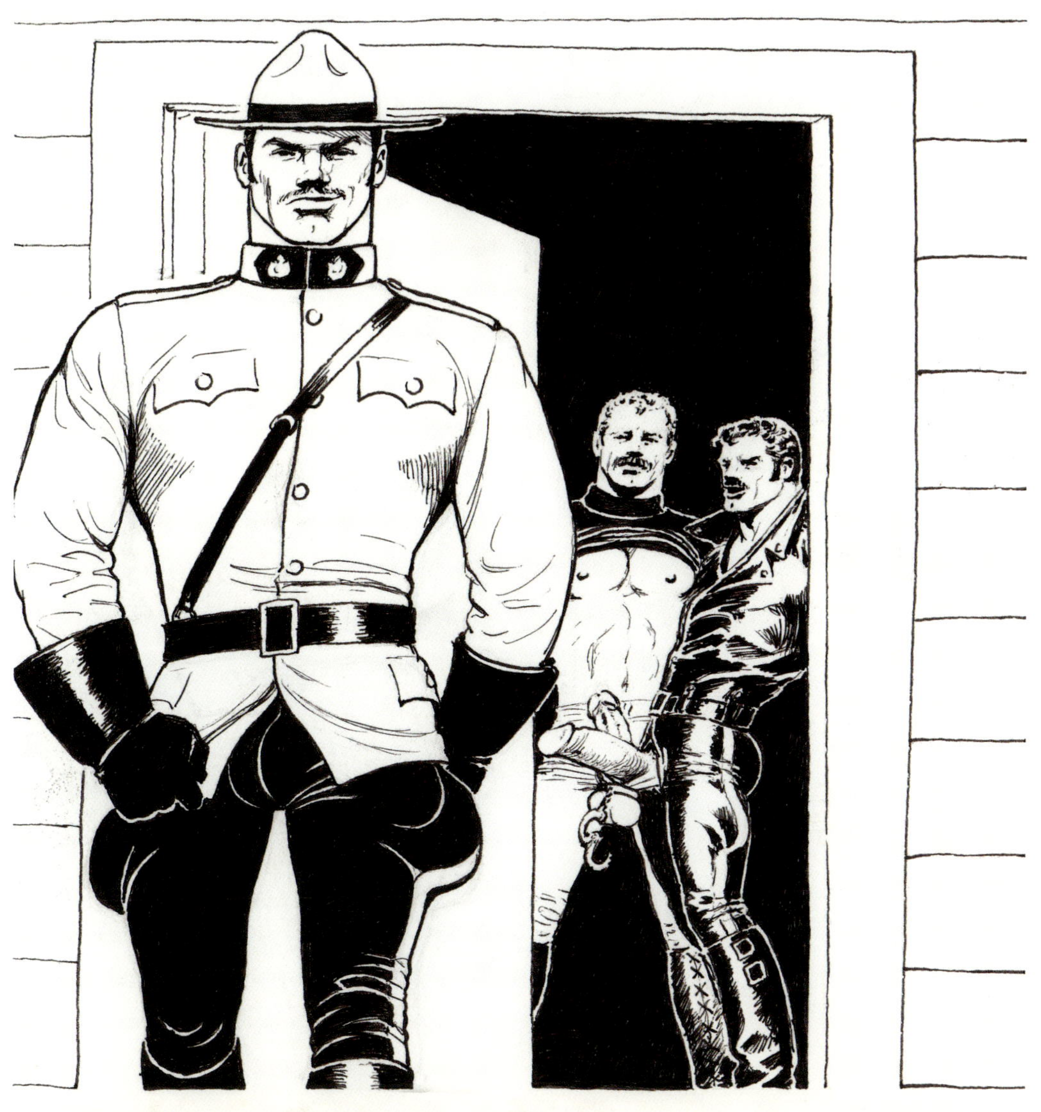

"The cop returned the next day to release them,
and begged Kake to push his monstrous cock into
his deep and waiting asshole again."

$11.0

No. 25, 1984

KAKE
POSTAL RAPE

25

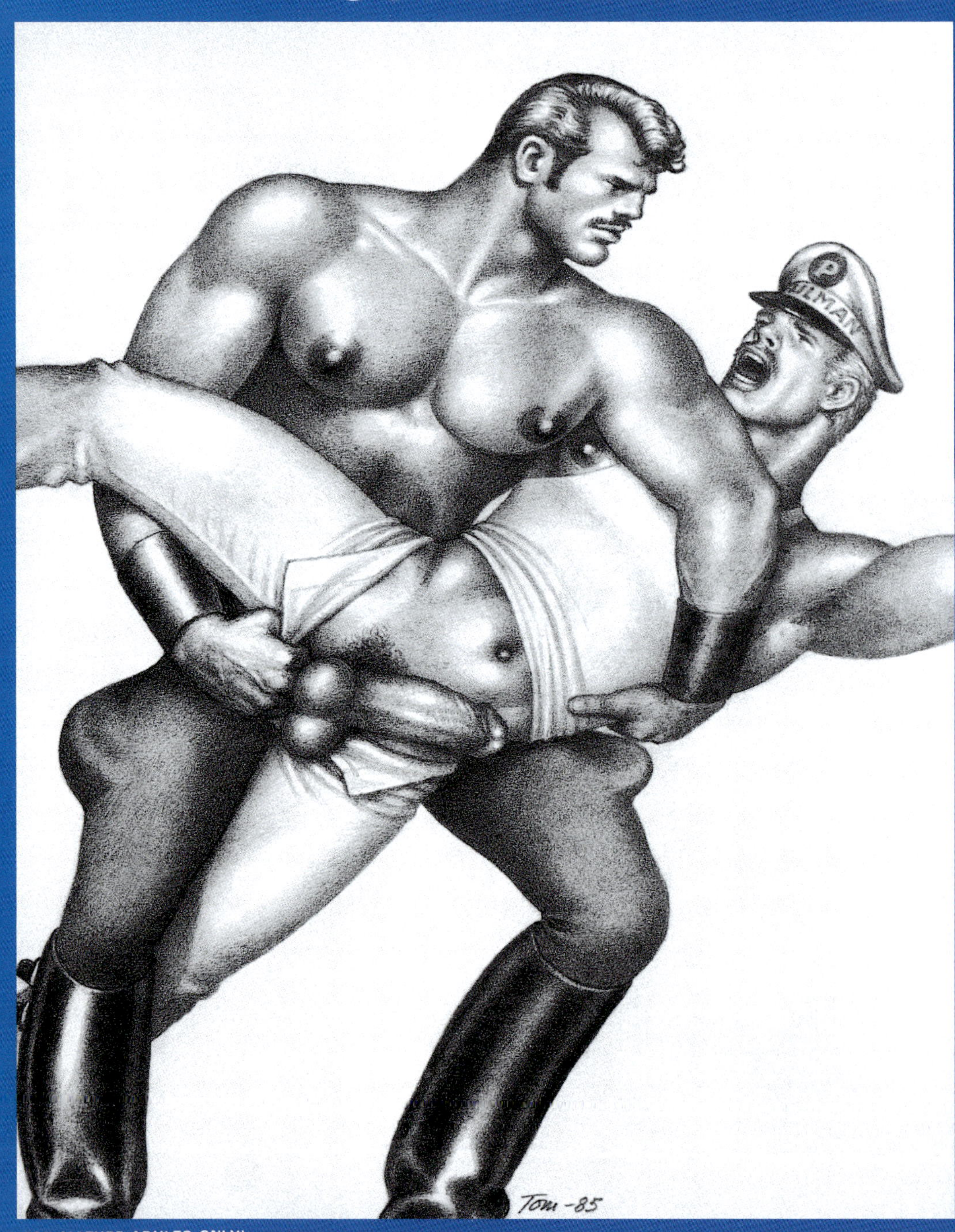

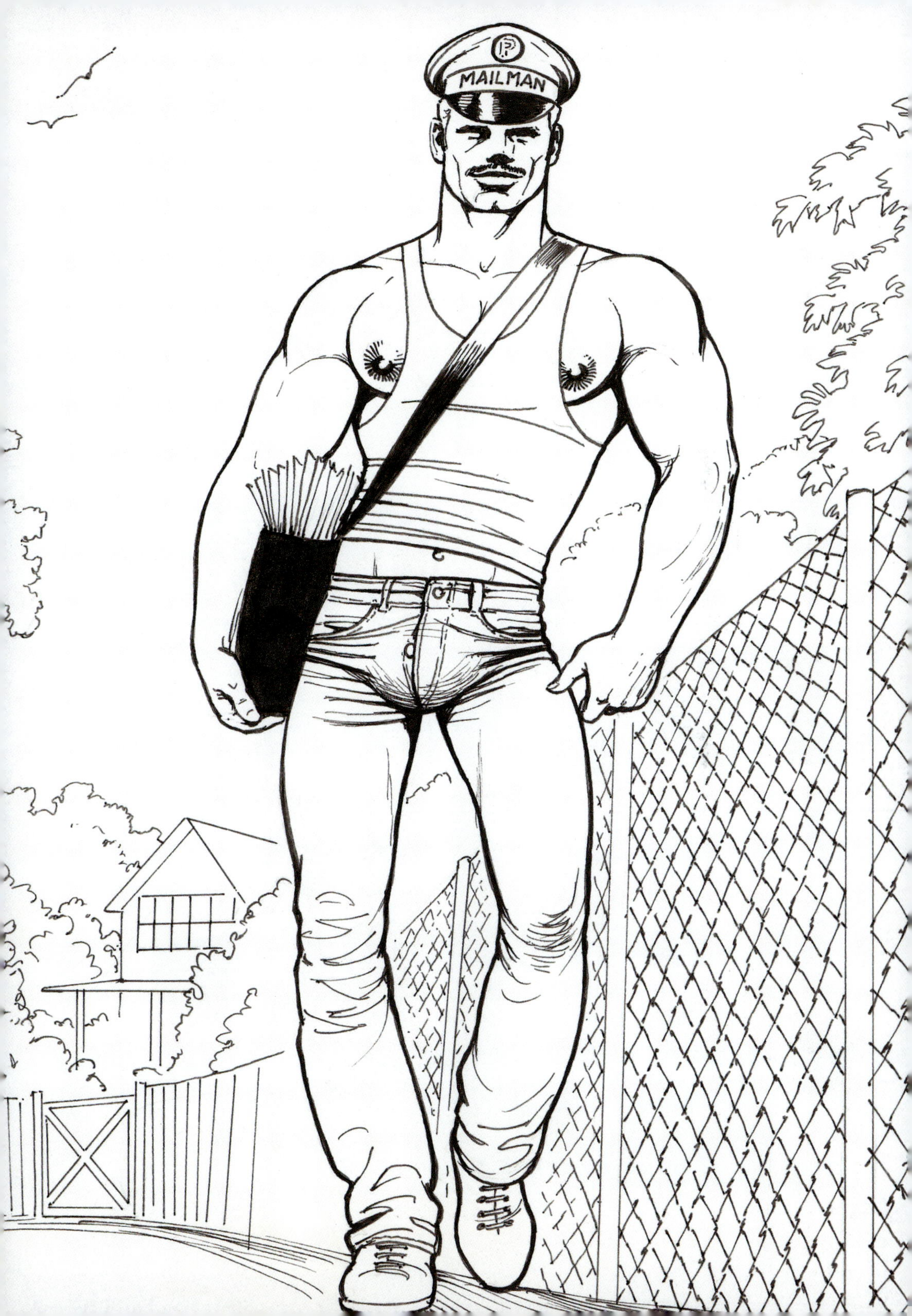
MAILMAN

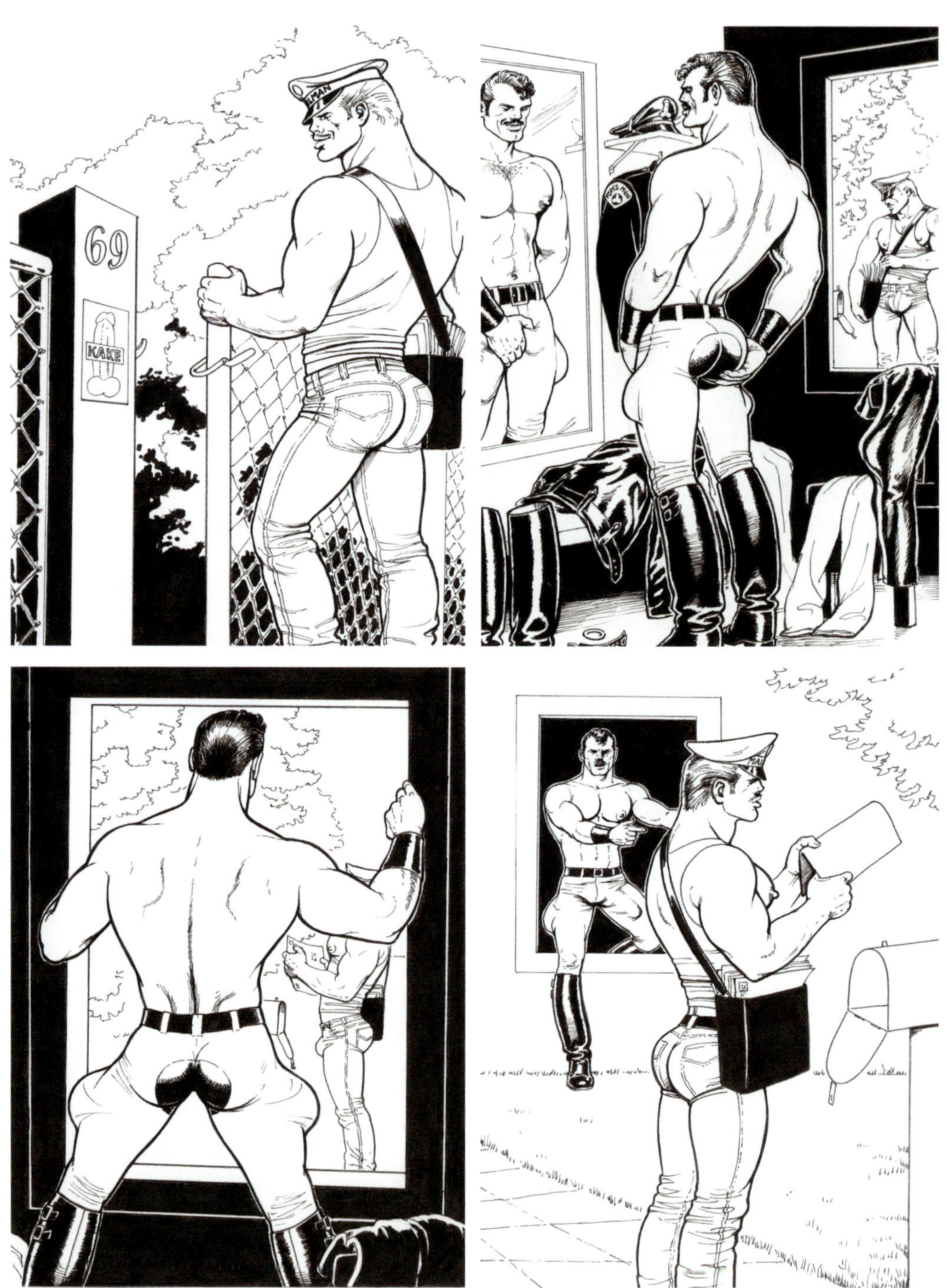
69
KAKE

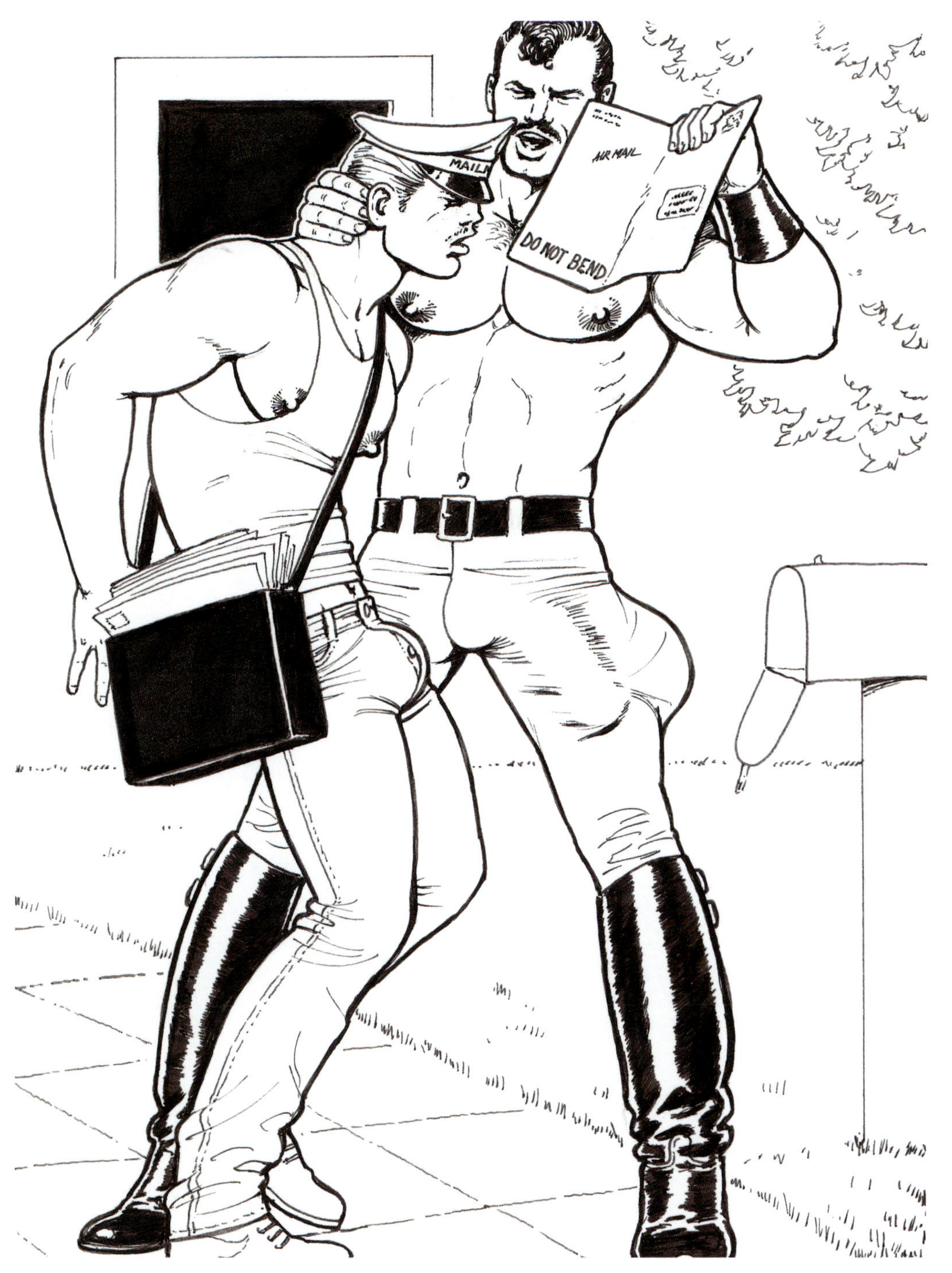
MAIL
AIR MAIL
DO NOT BEND

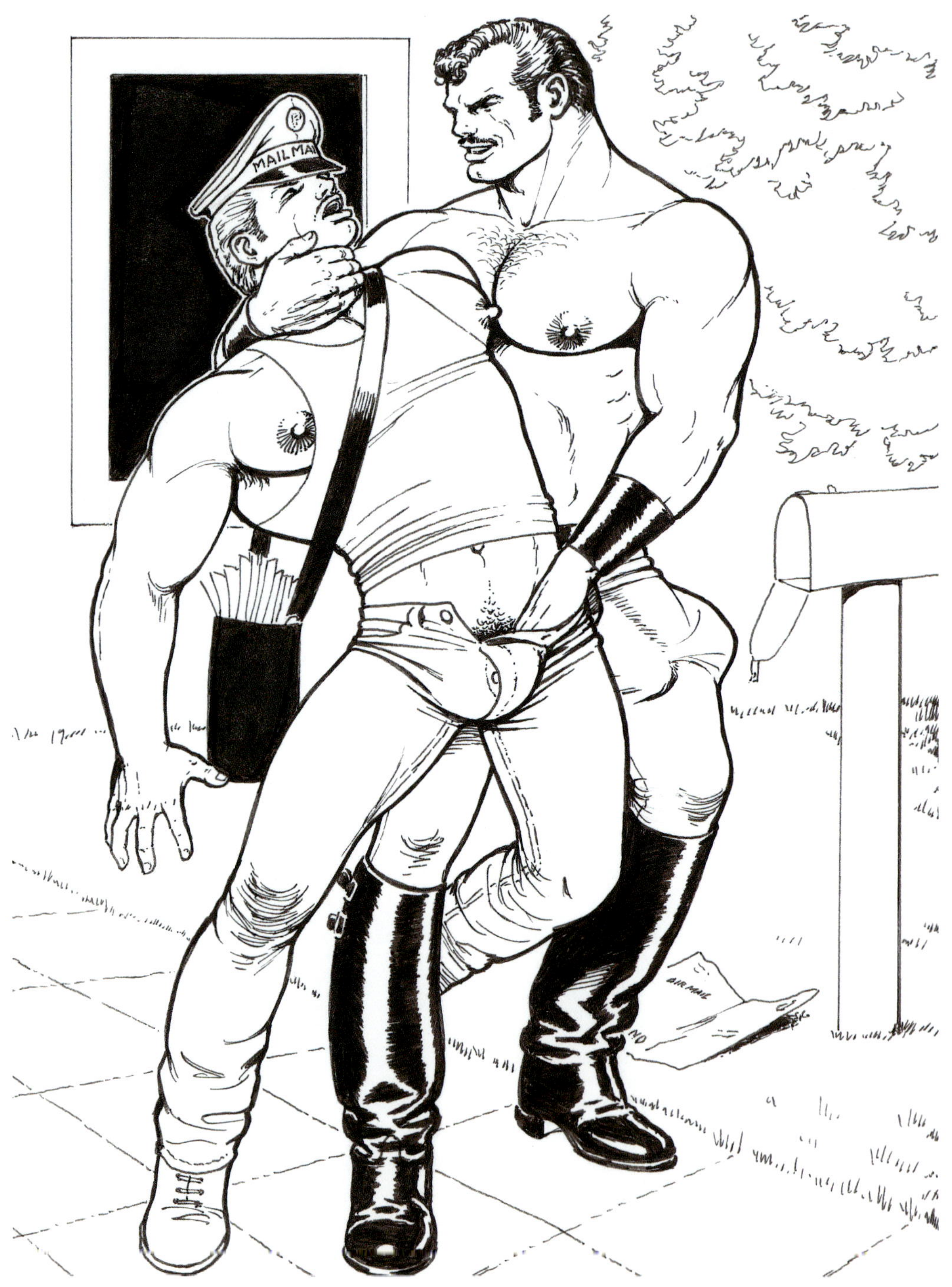

MAIL MAN
AIR MAIL

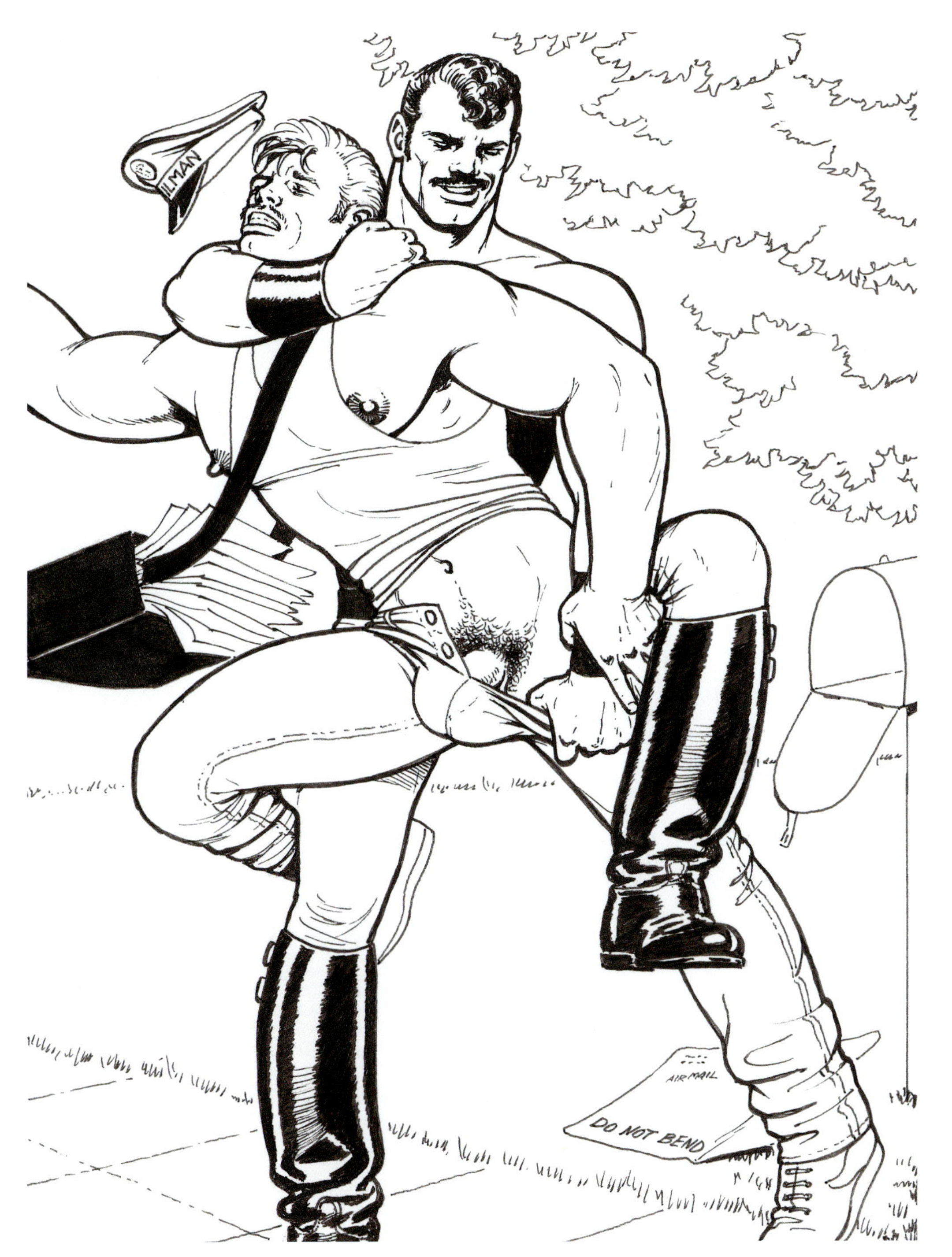

ILMAN
AIR MAIL
DO NOT BEND

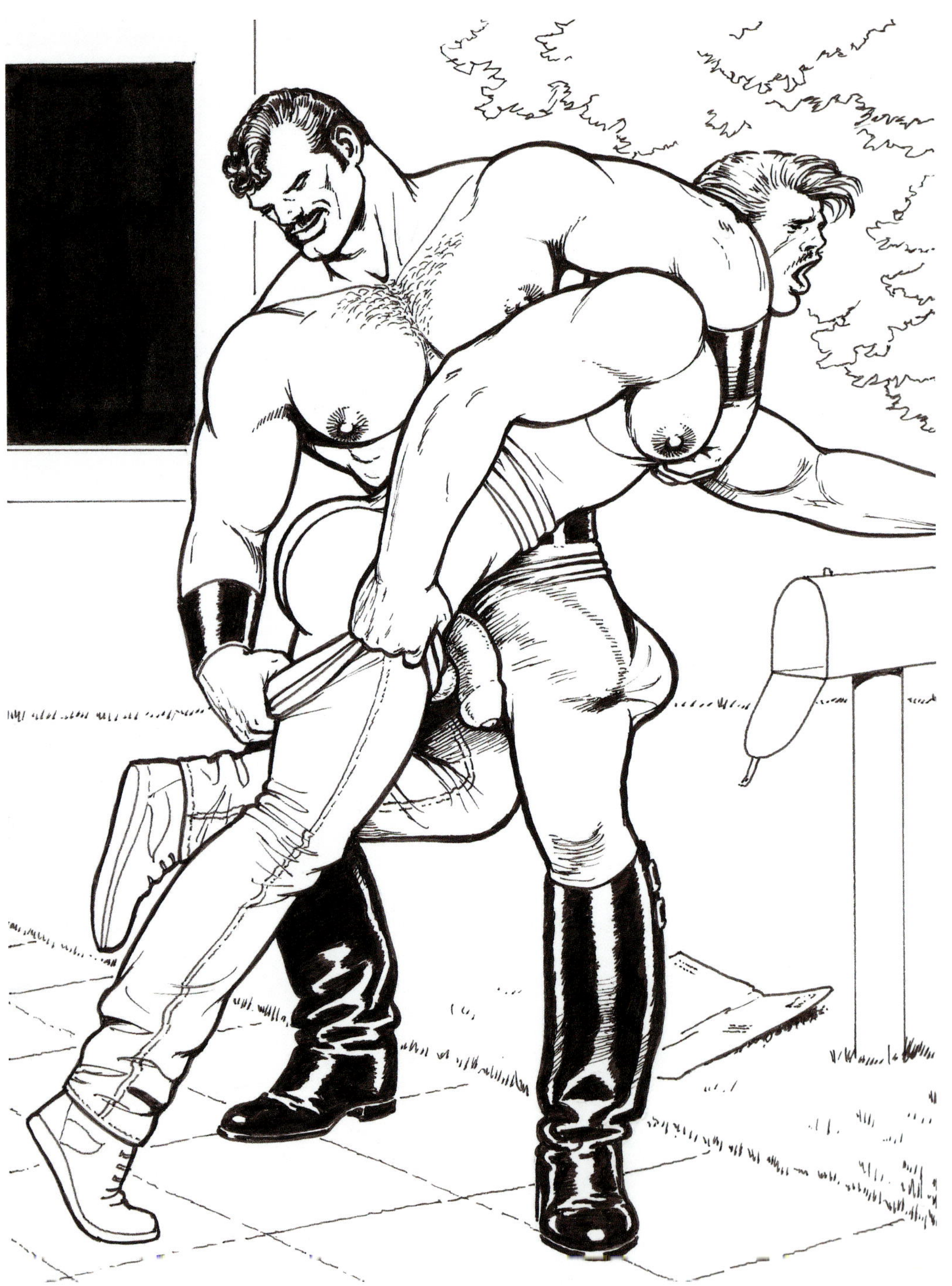

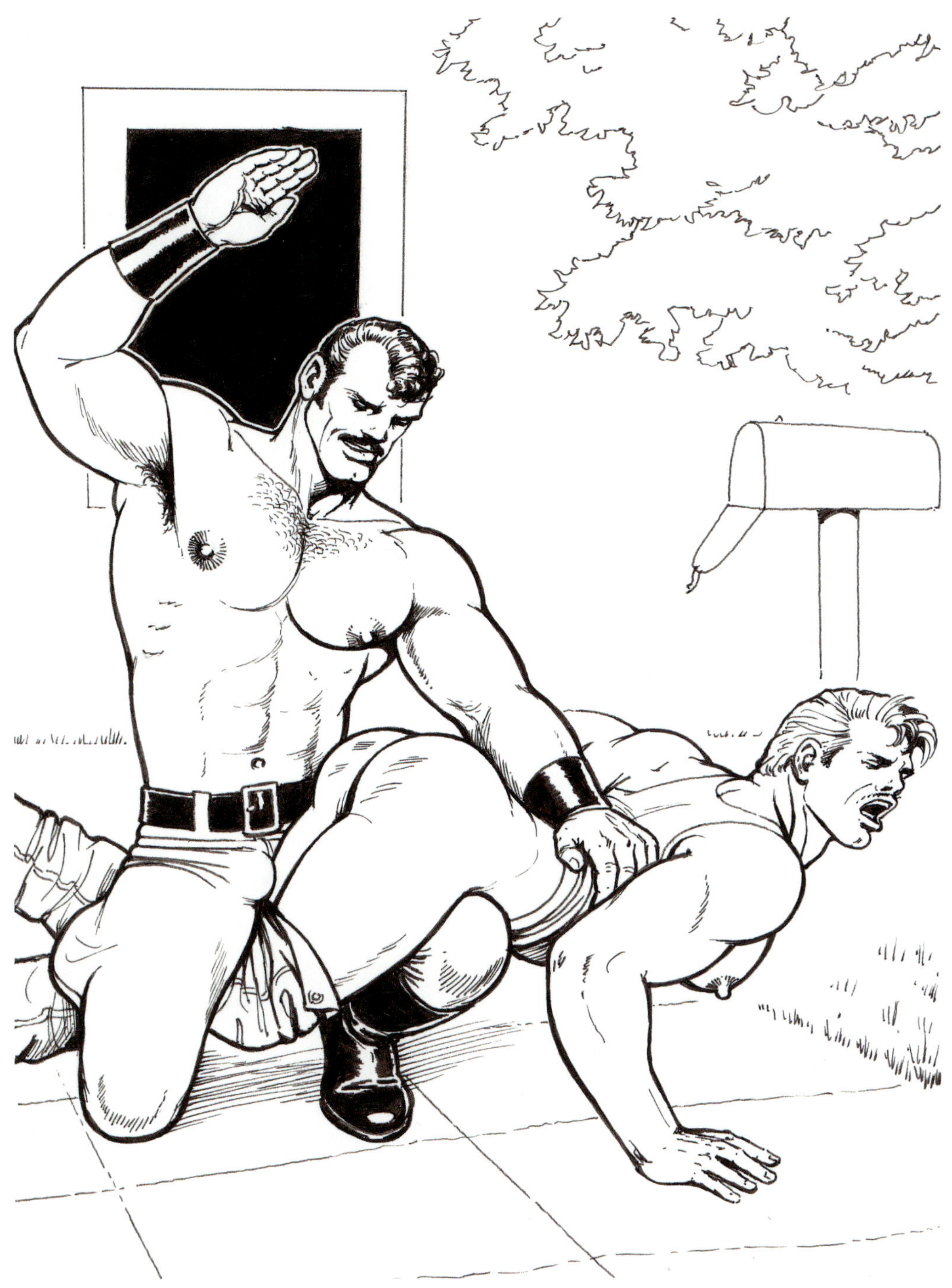

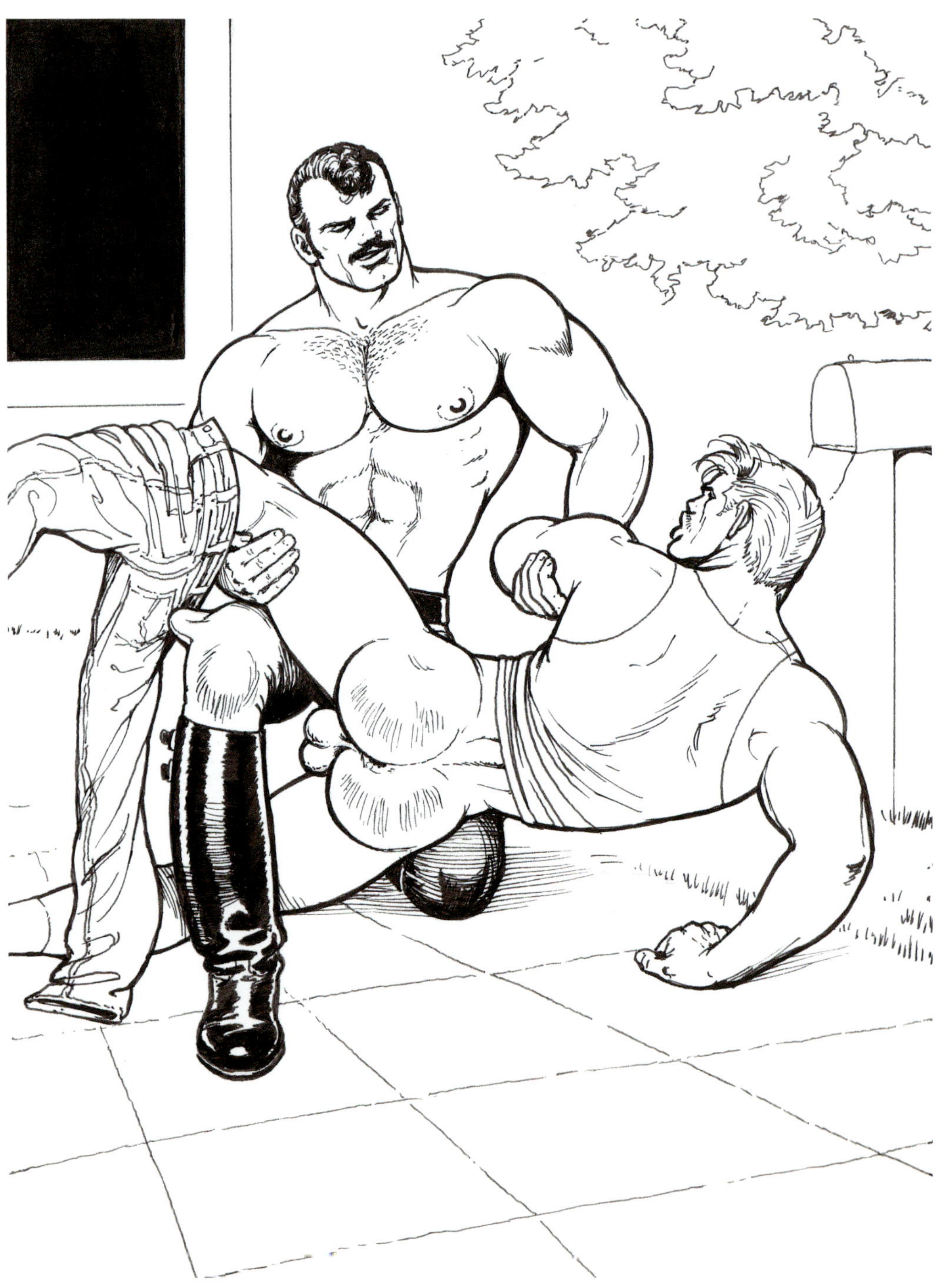

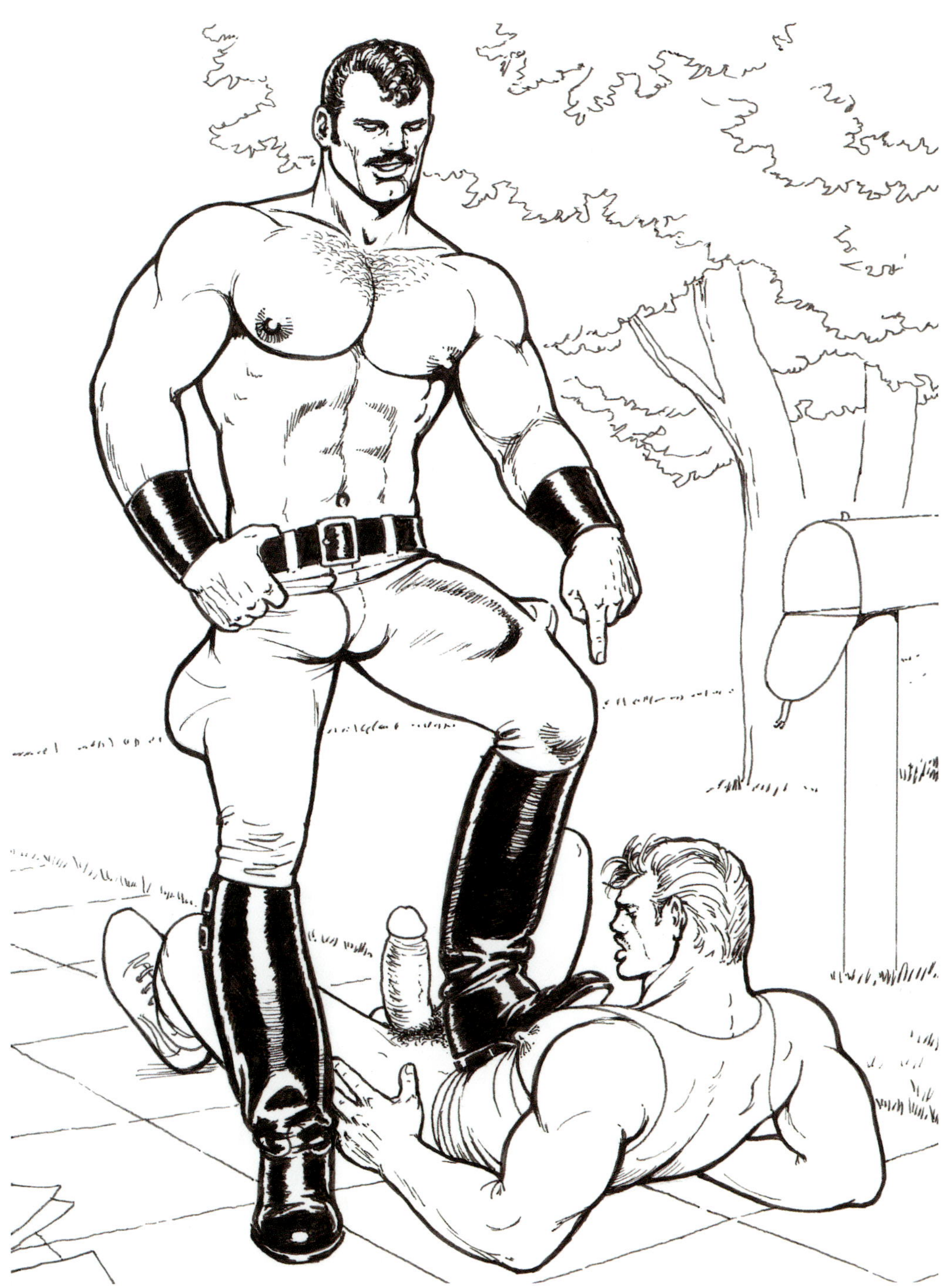

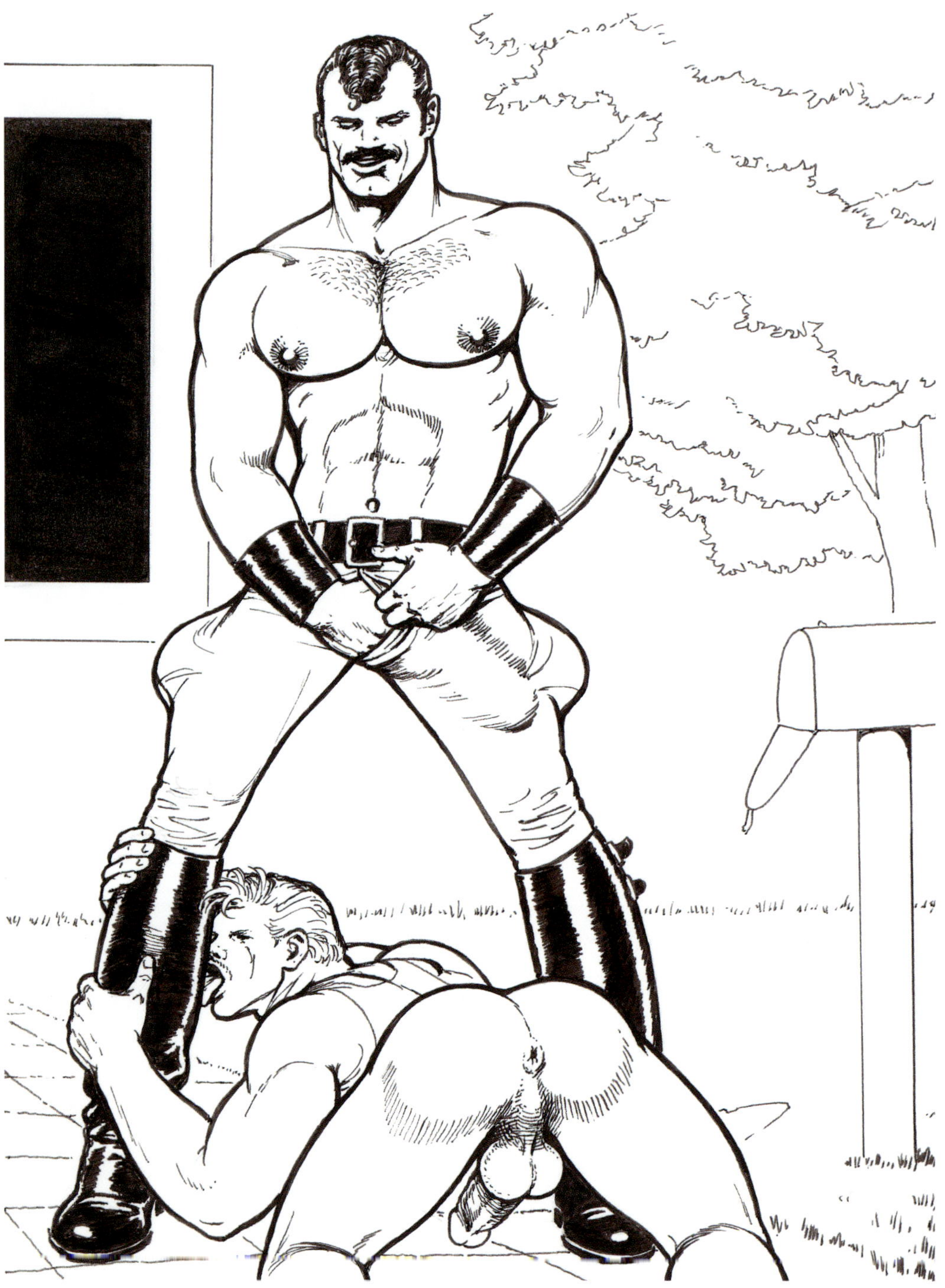

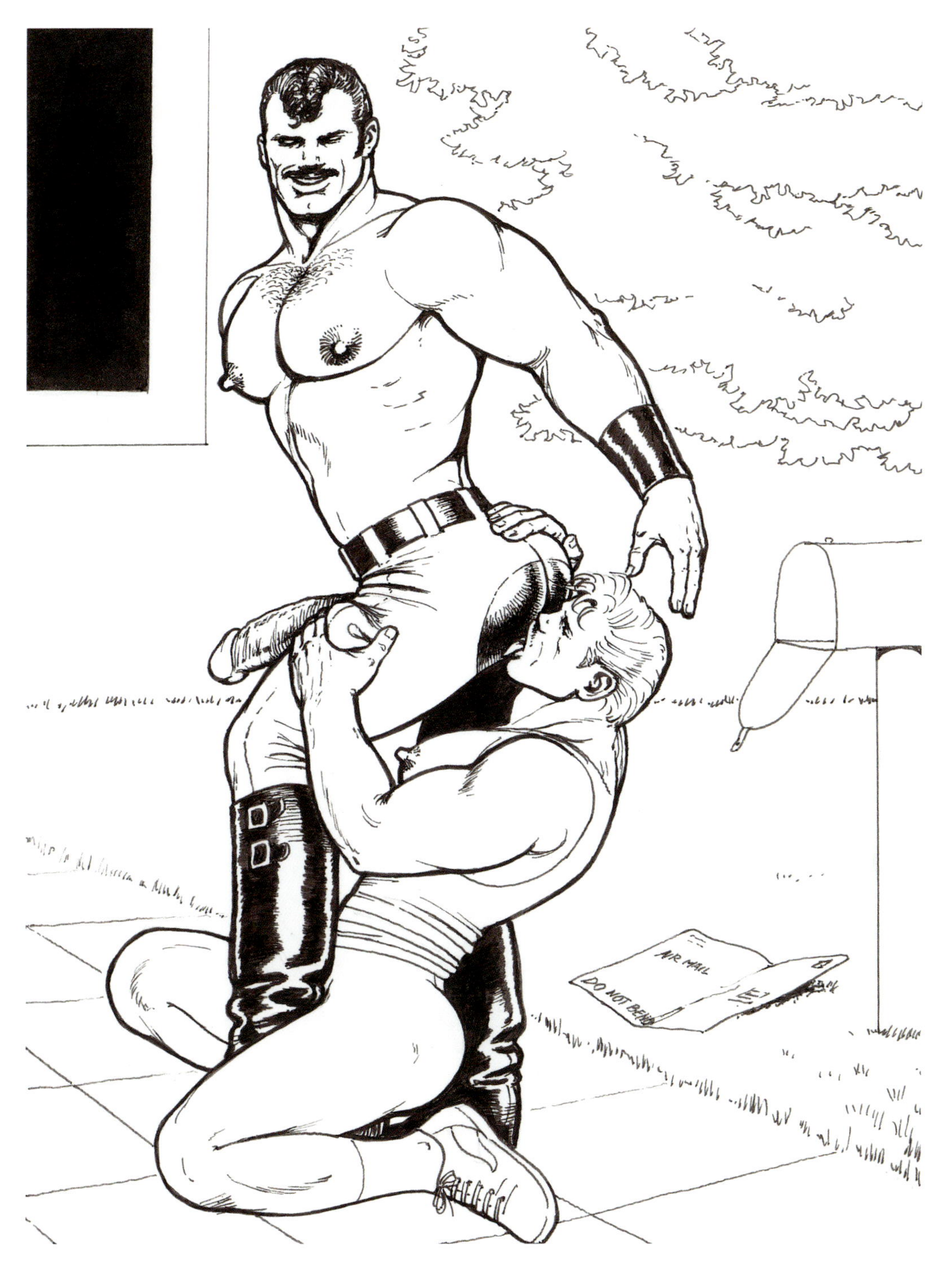

467

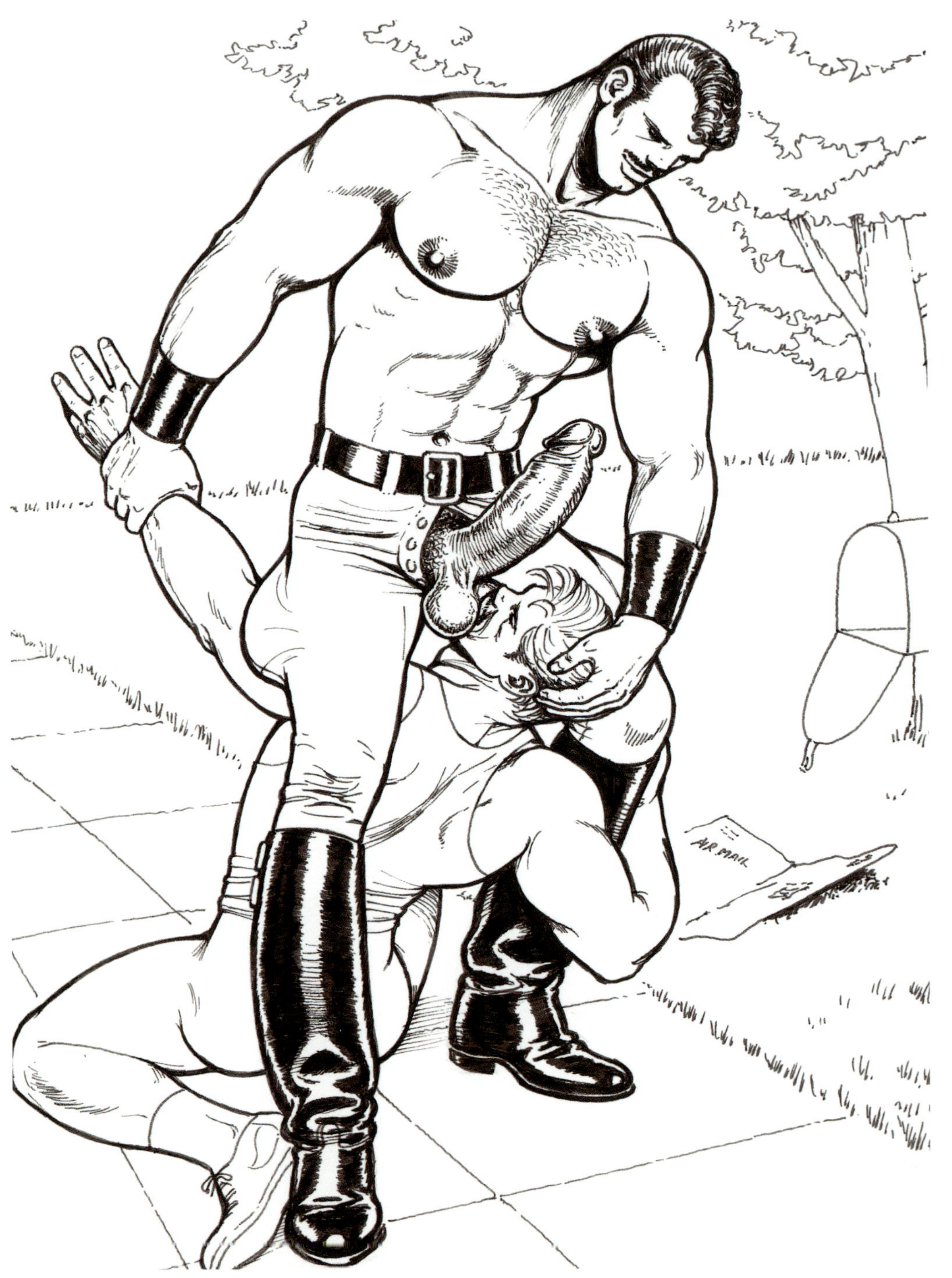
AIR MAIL

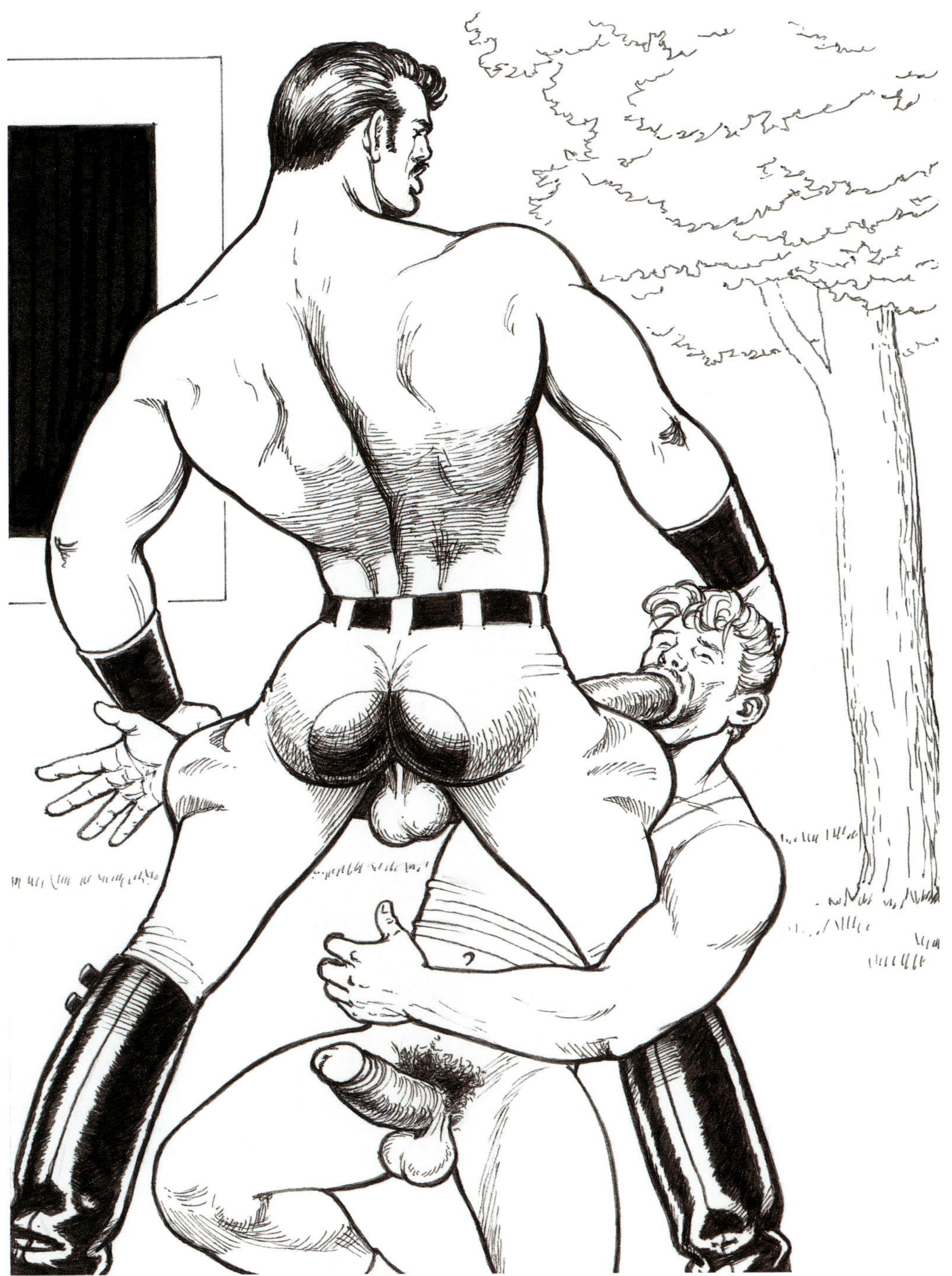

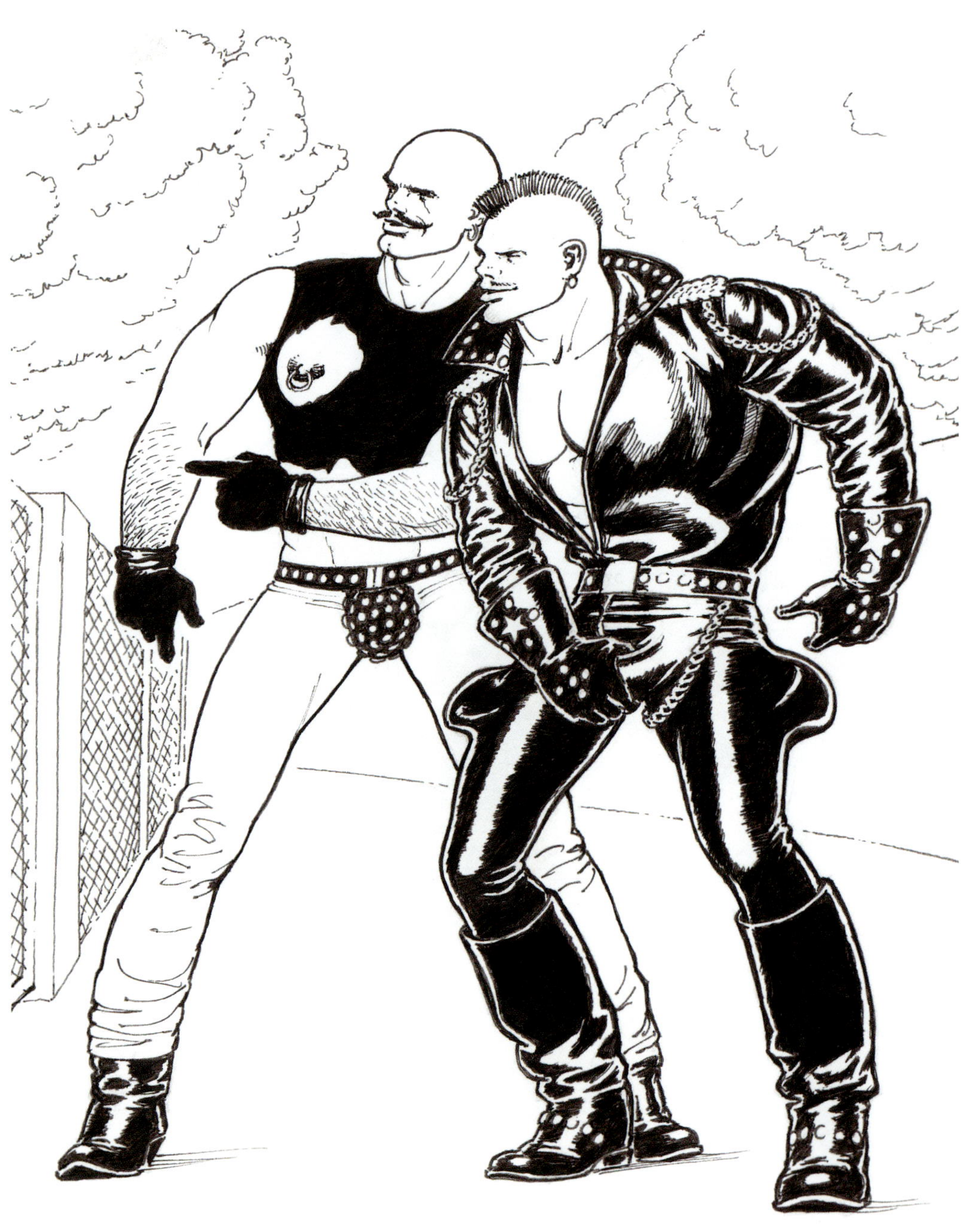

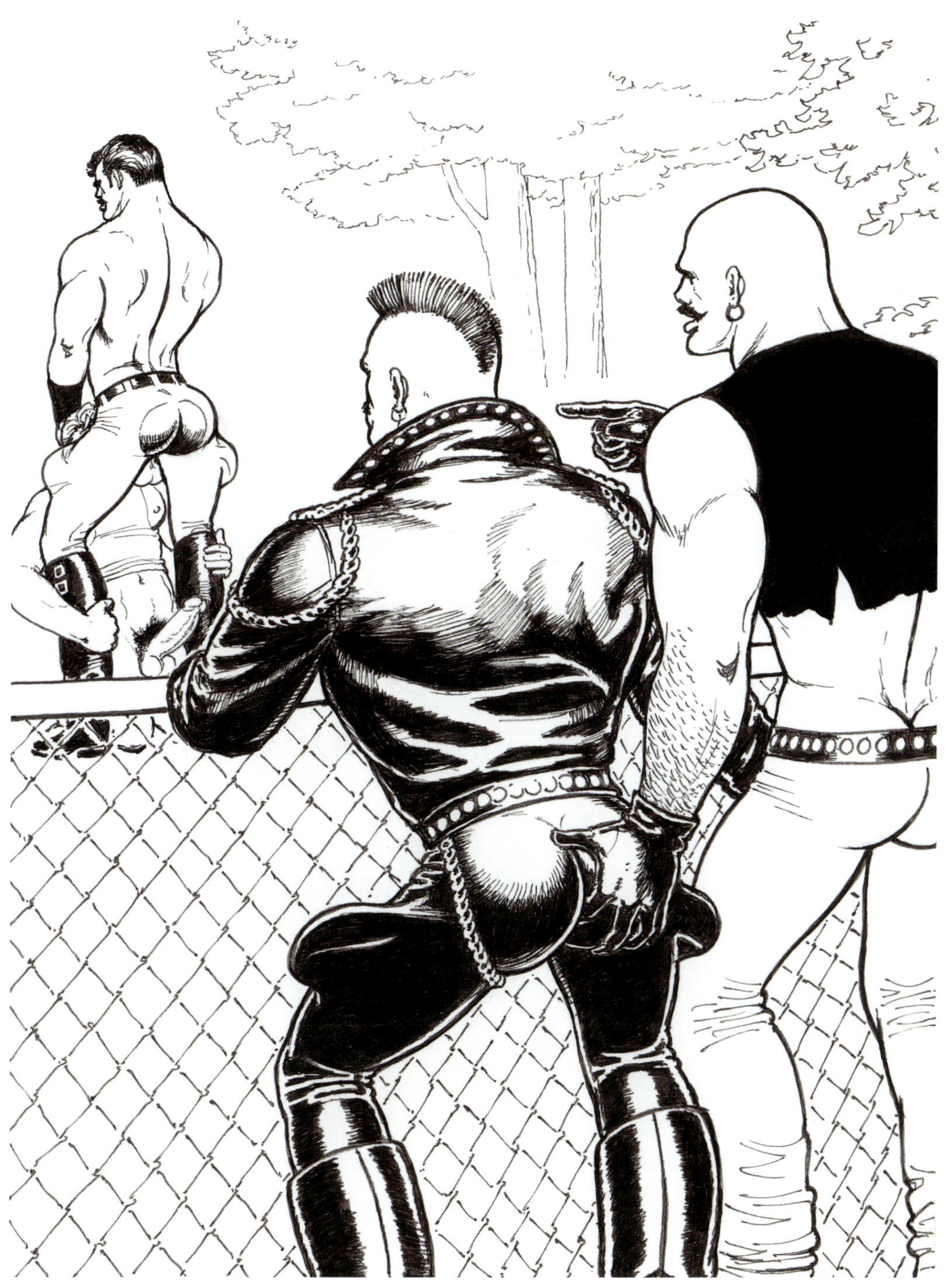

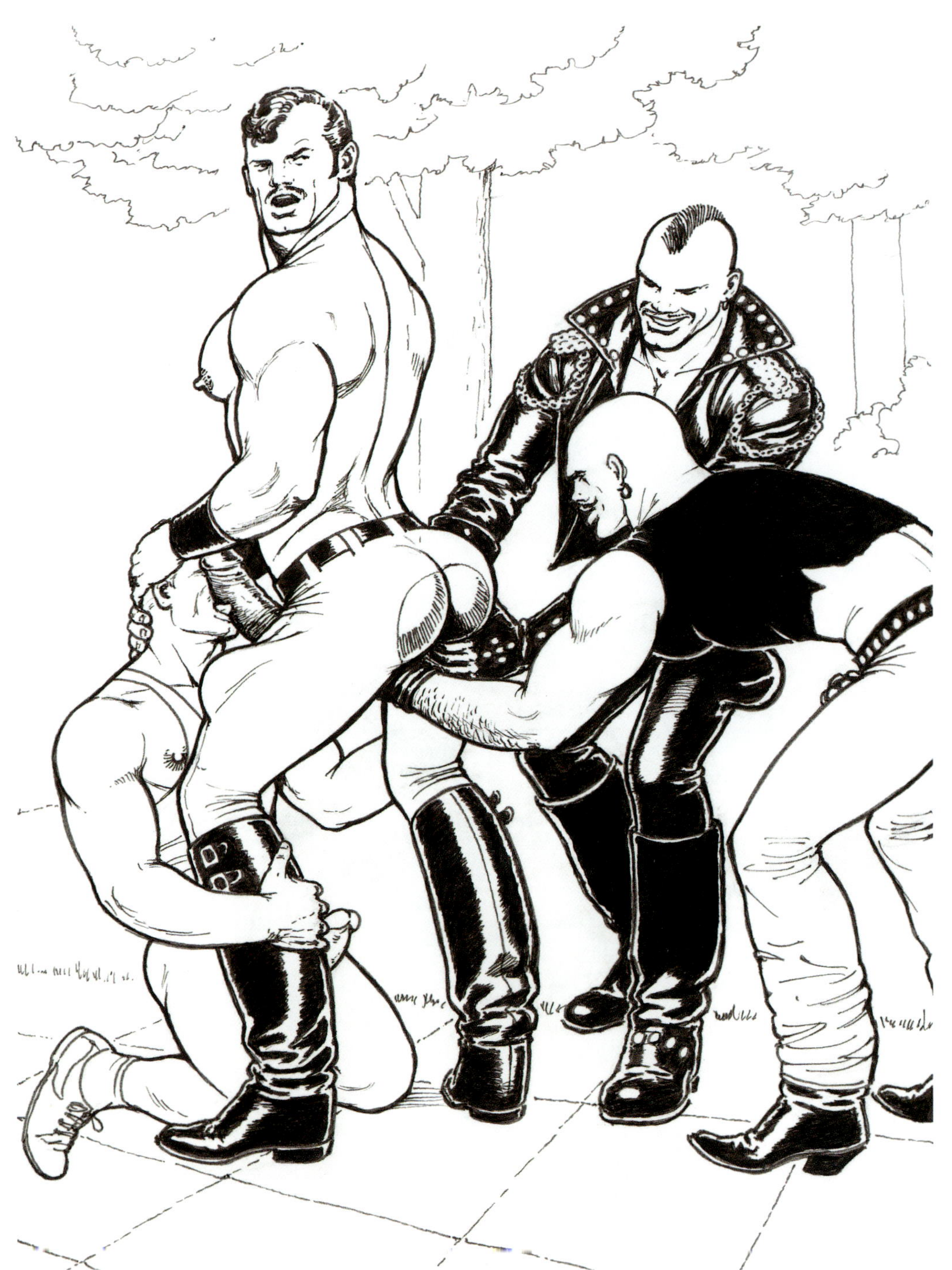

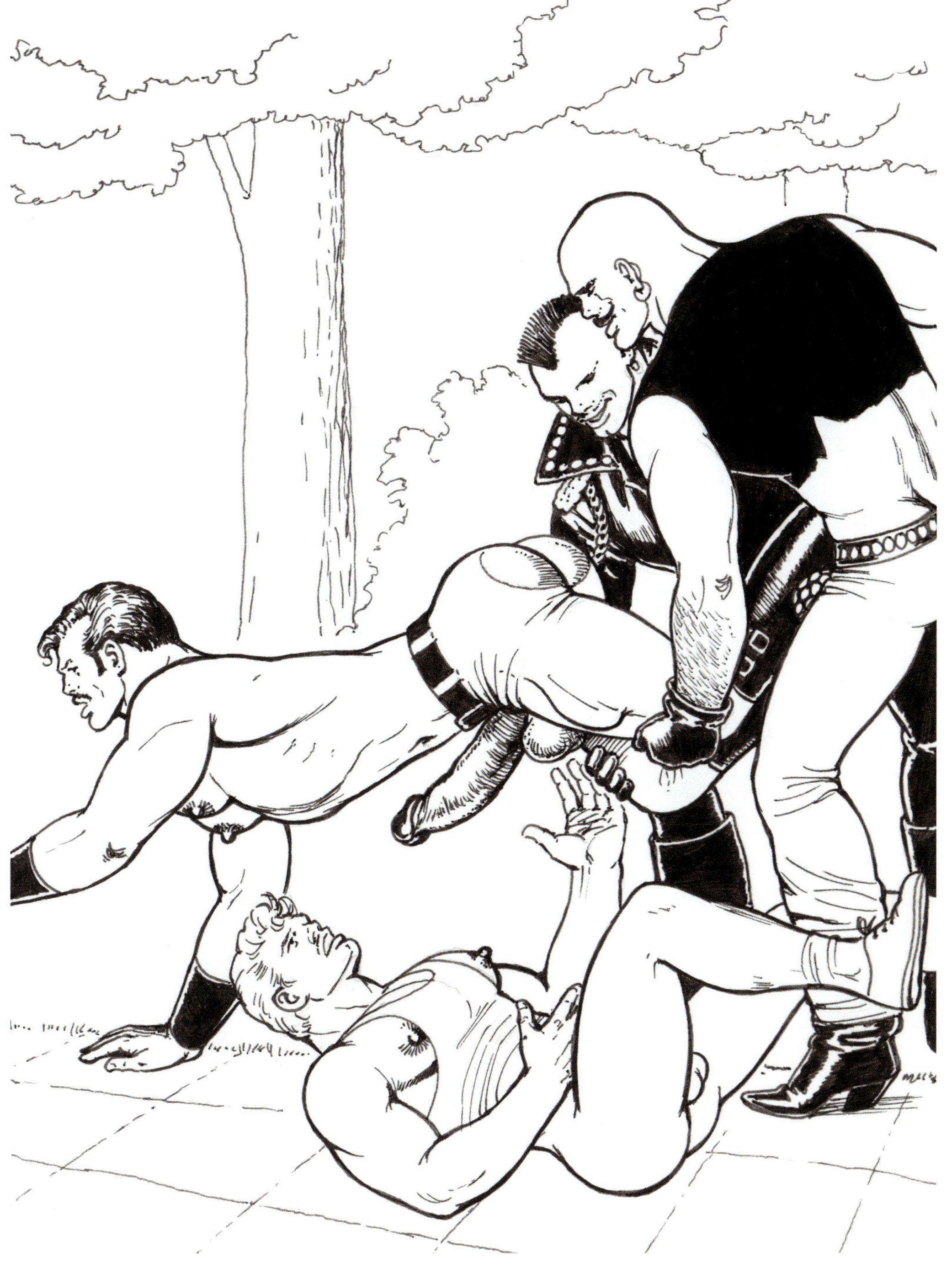

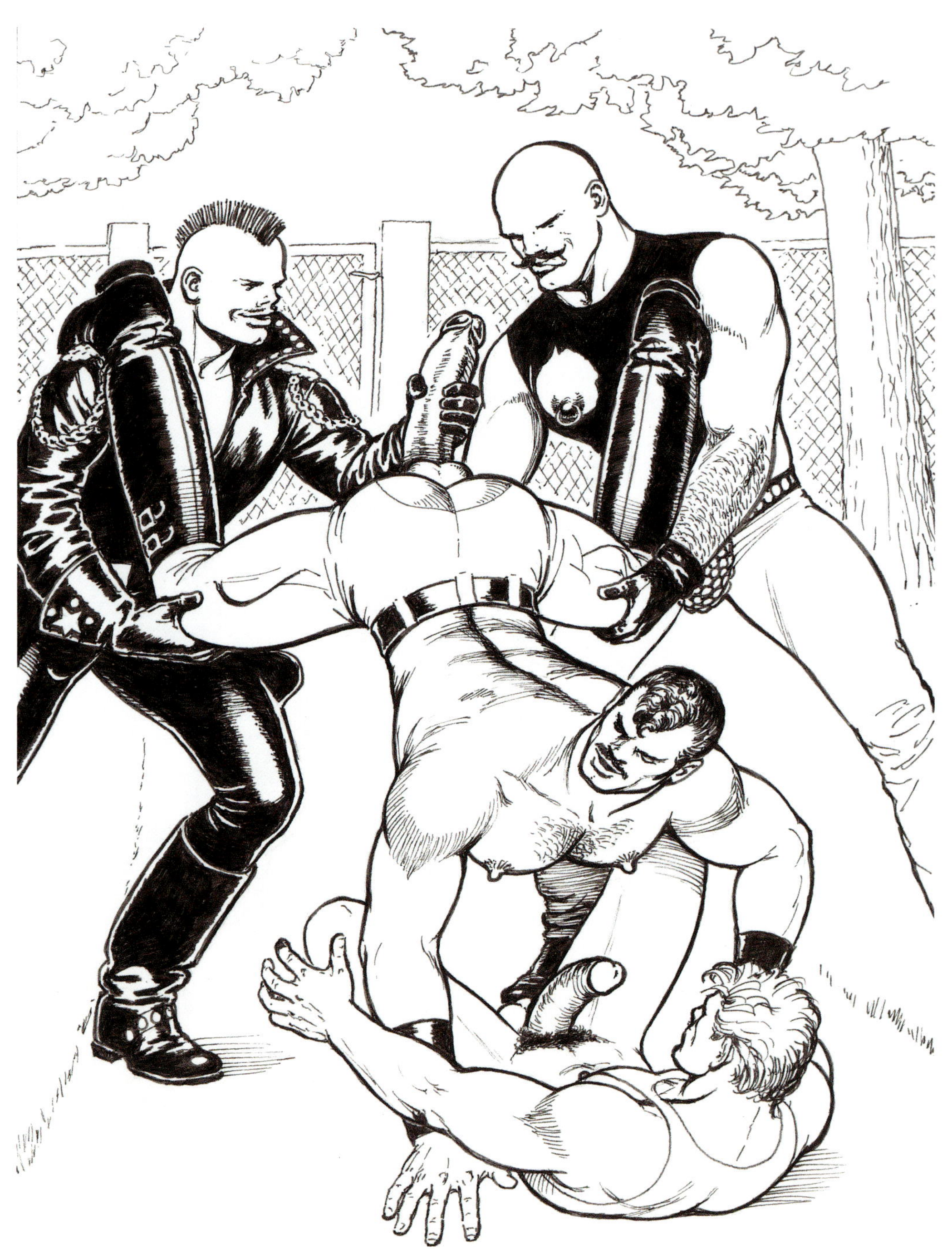

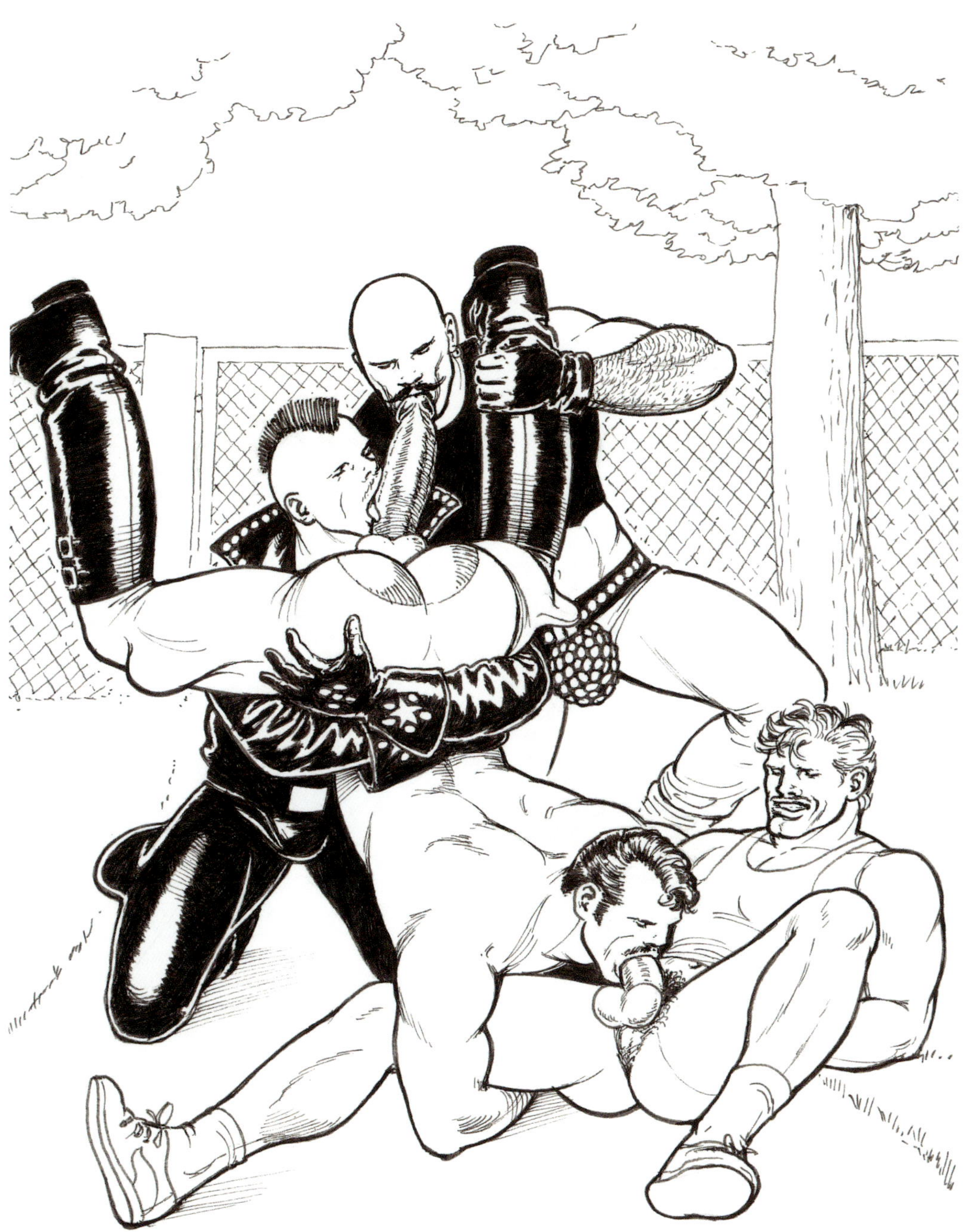

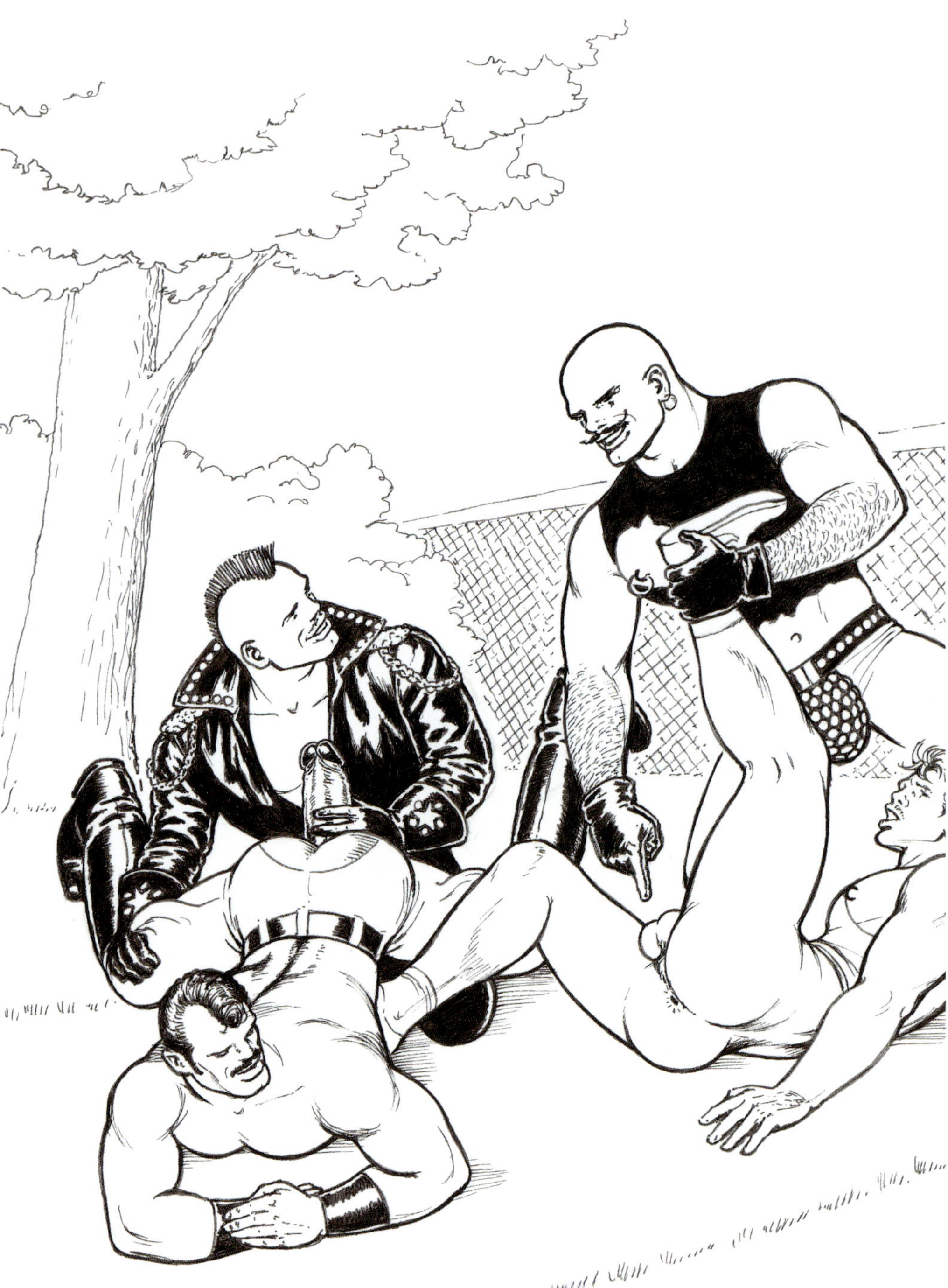

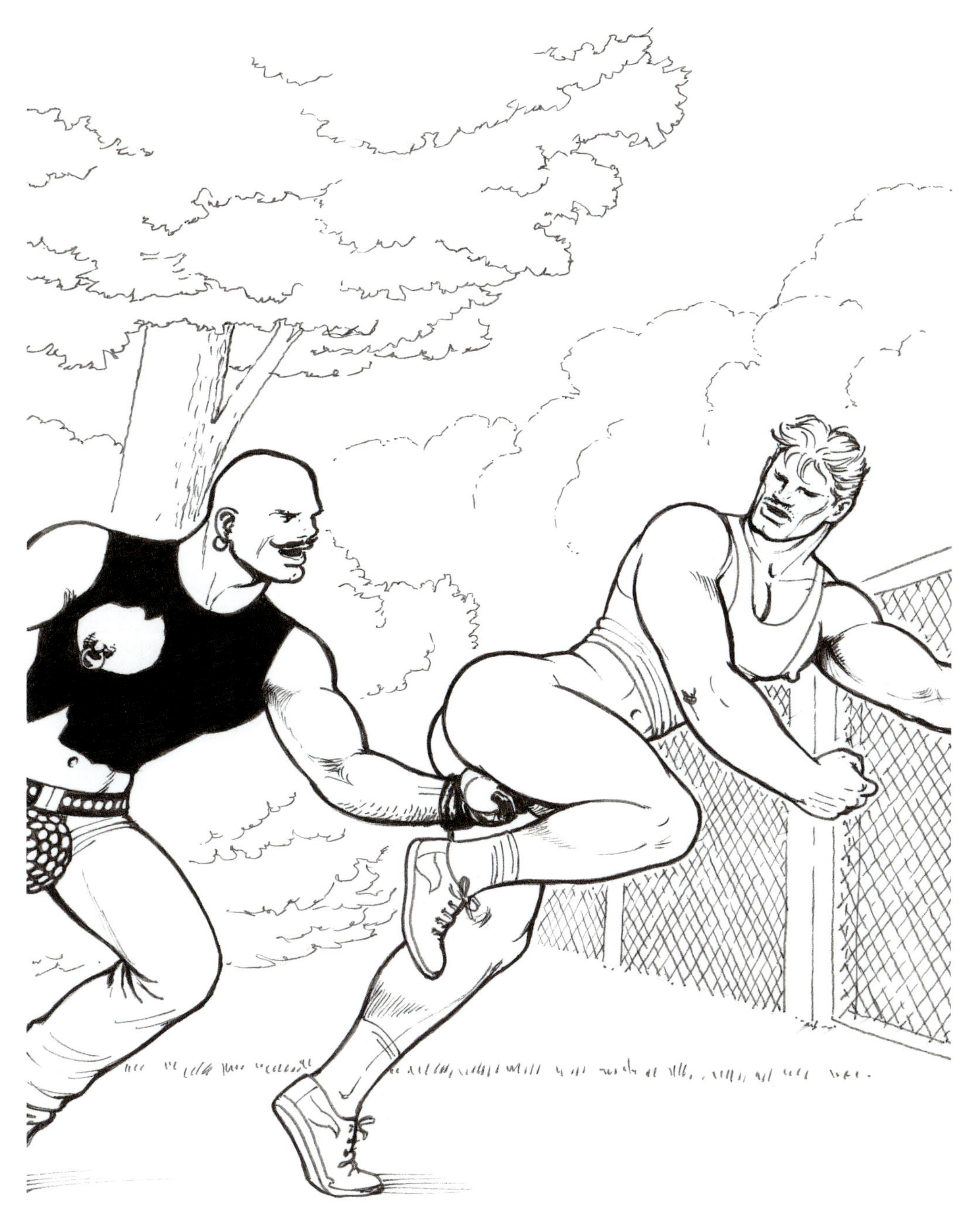

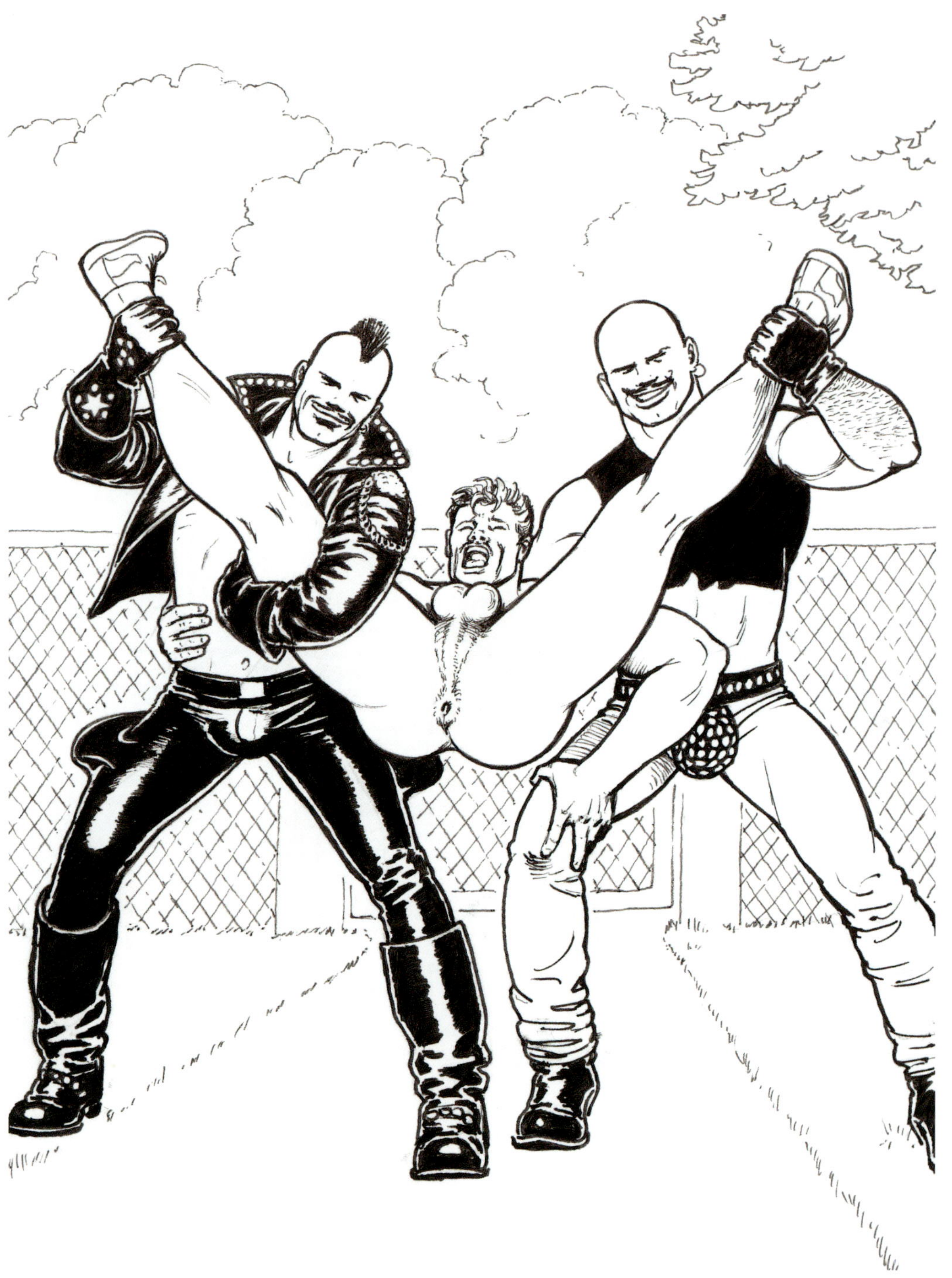

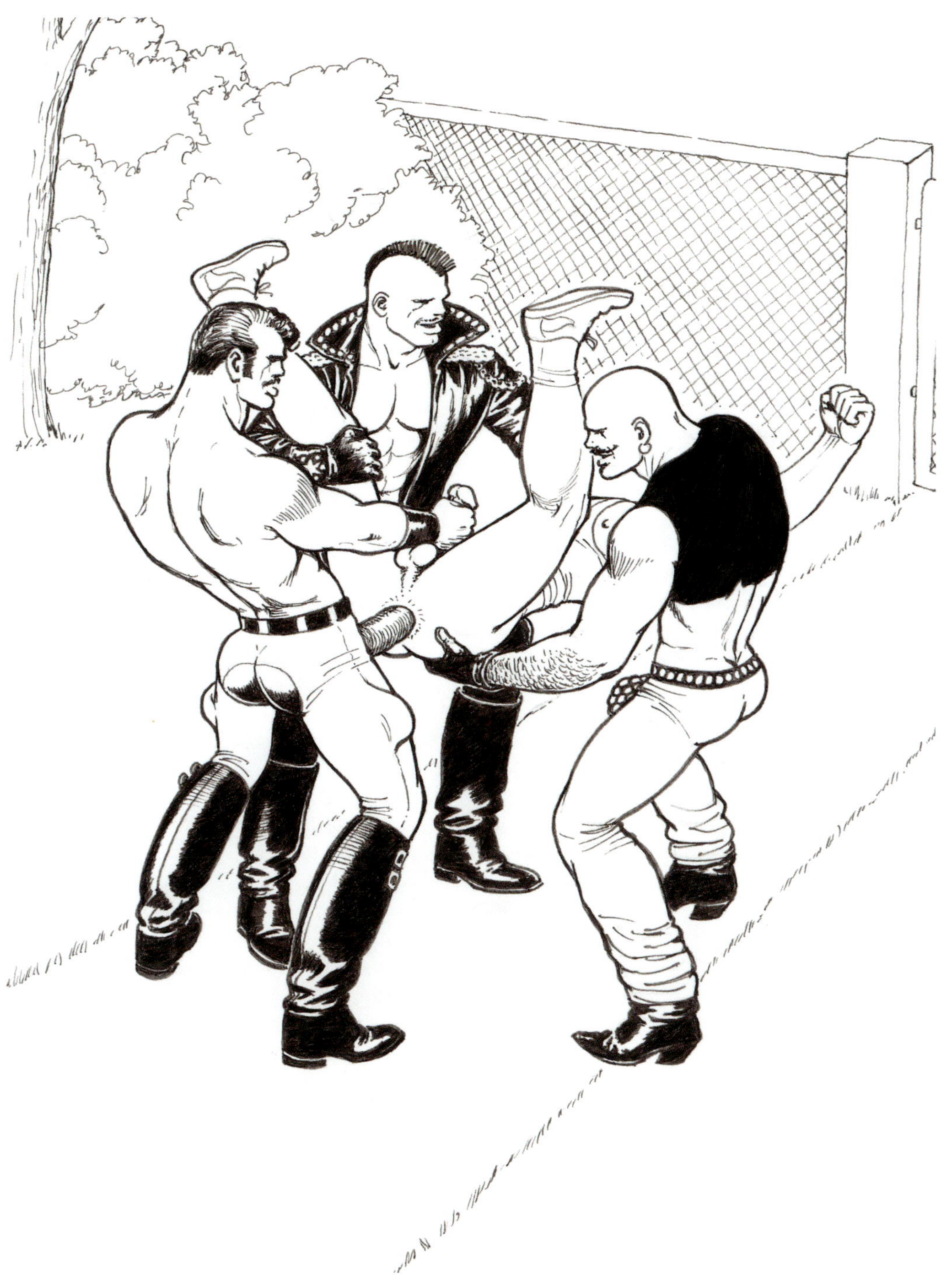

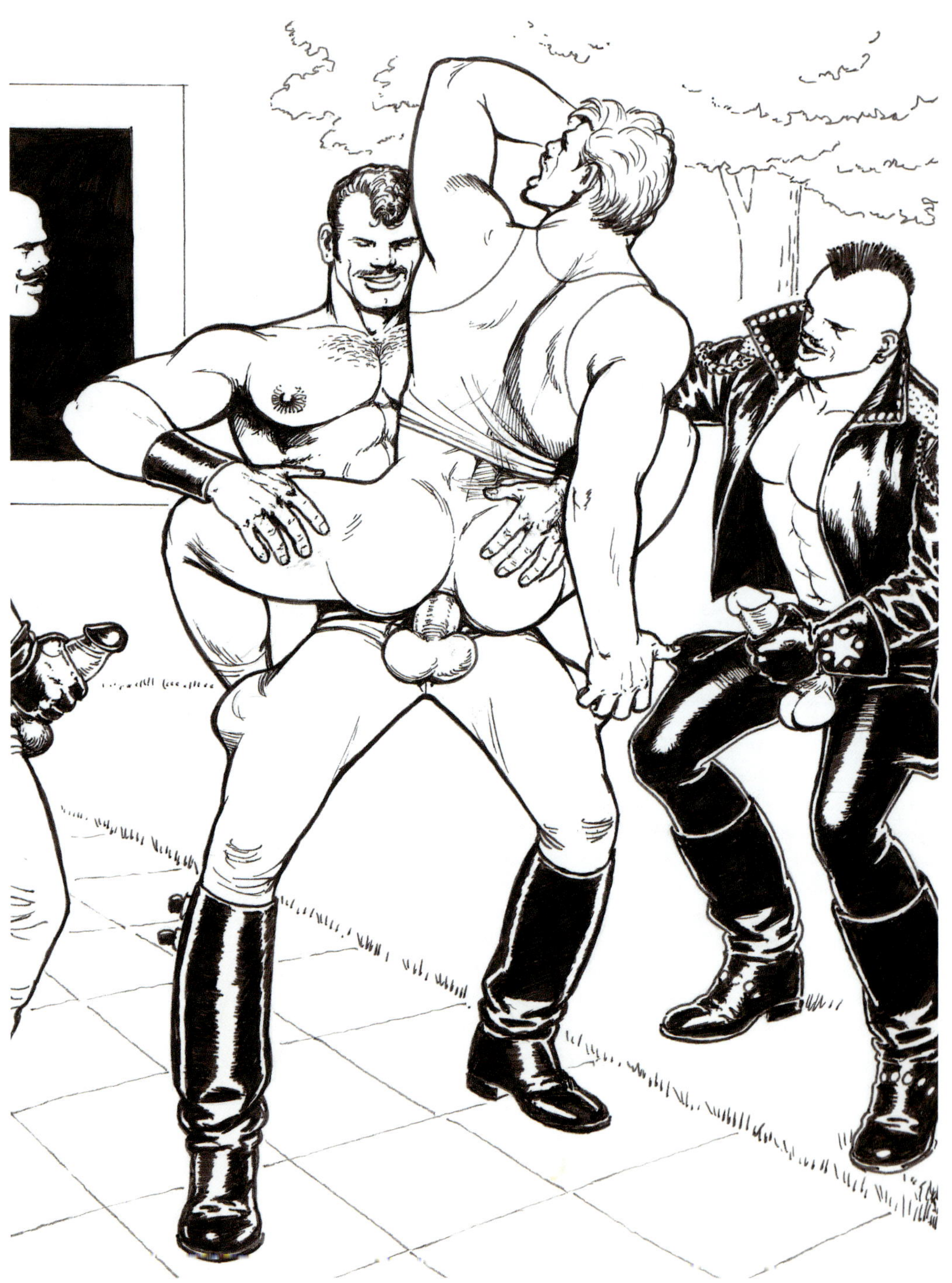

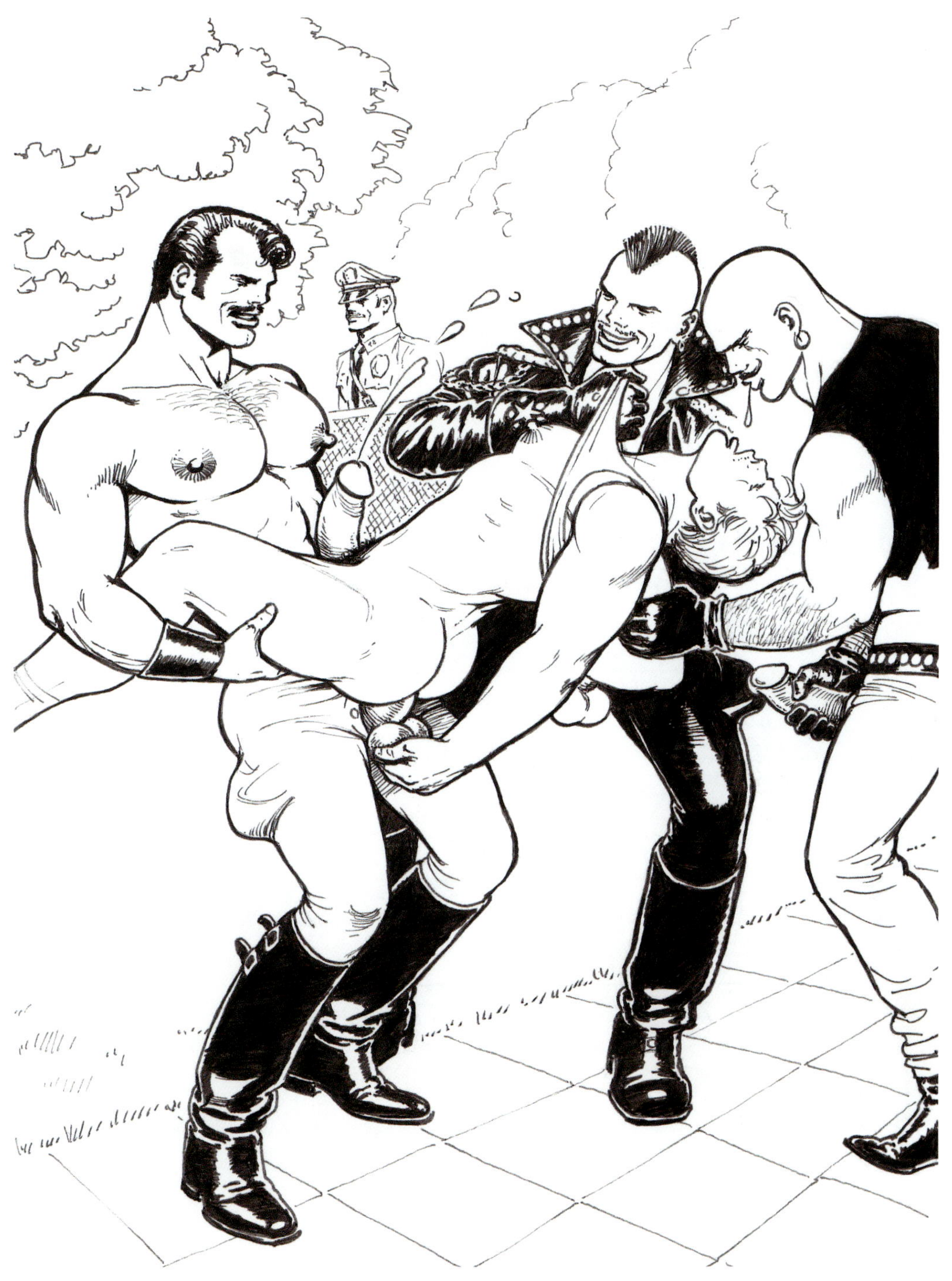

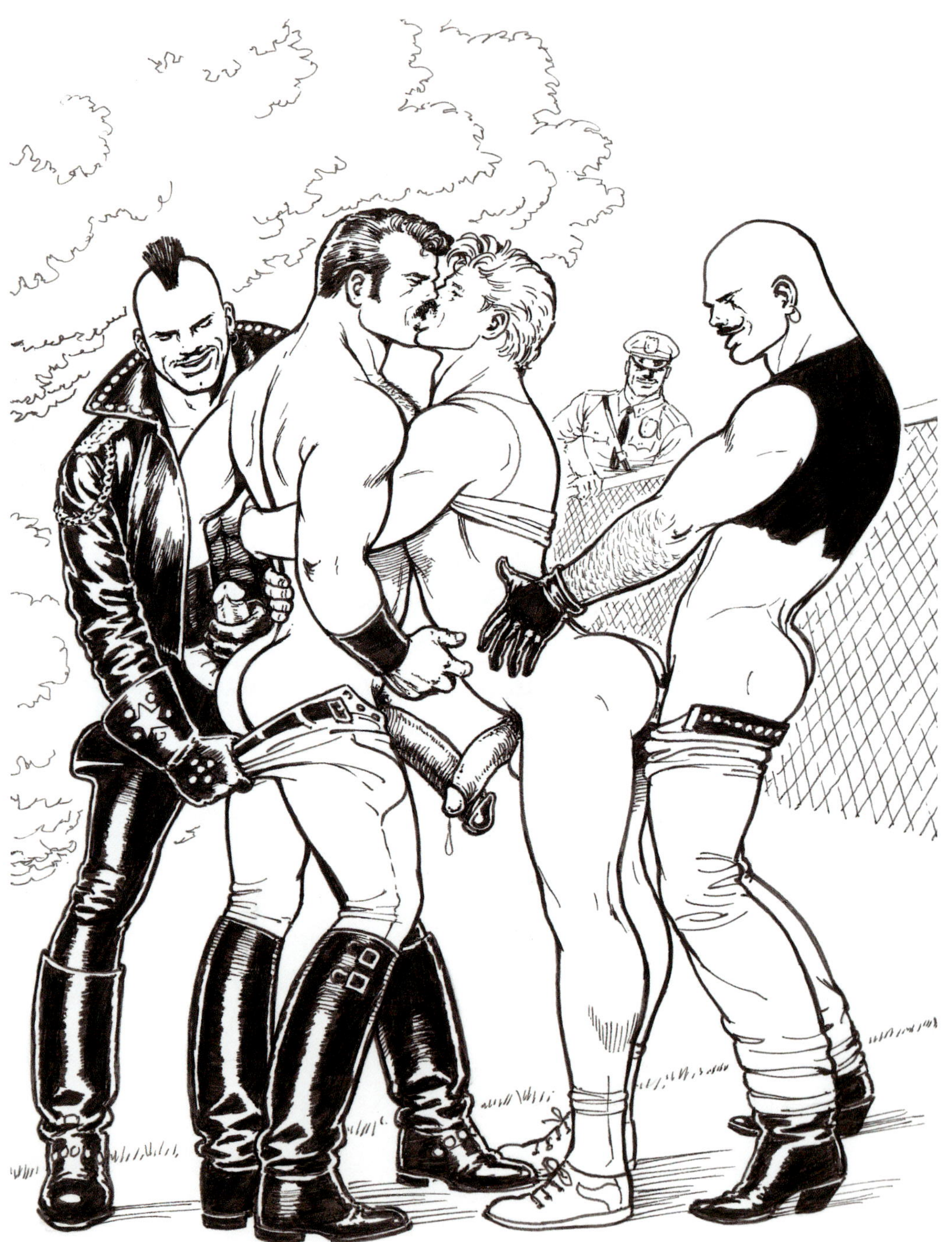

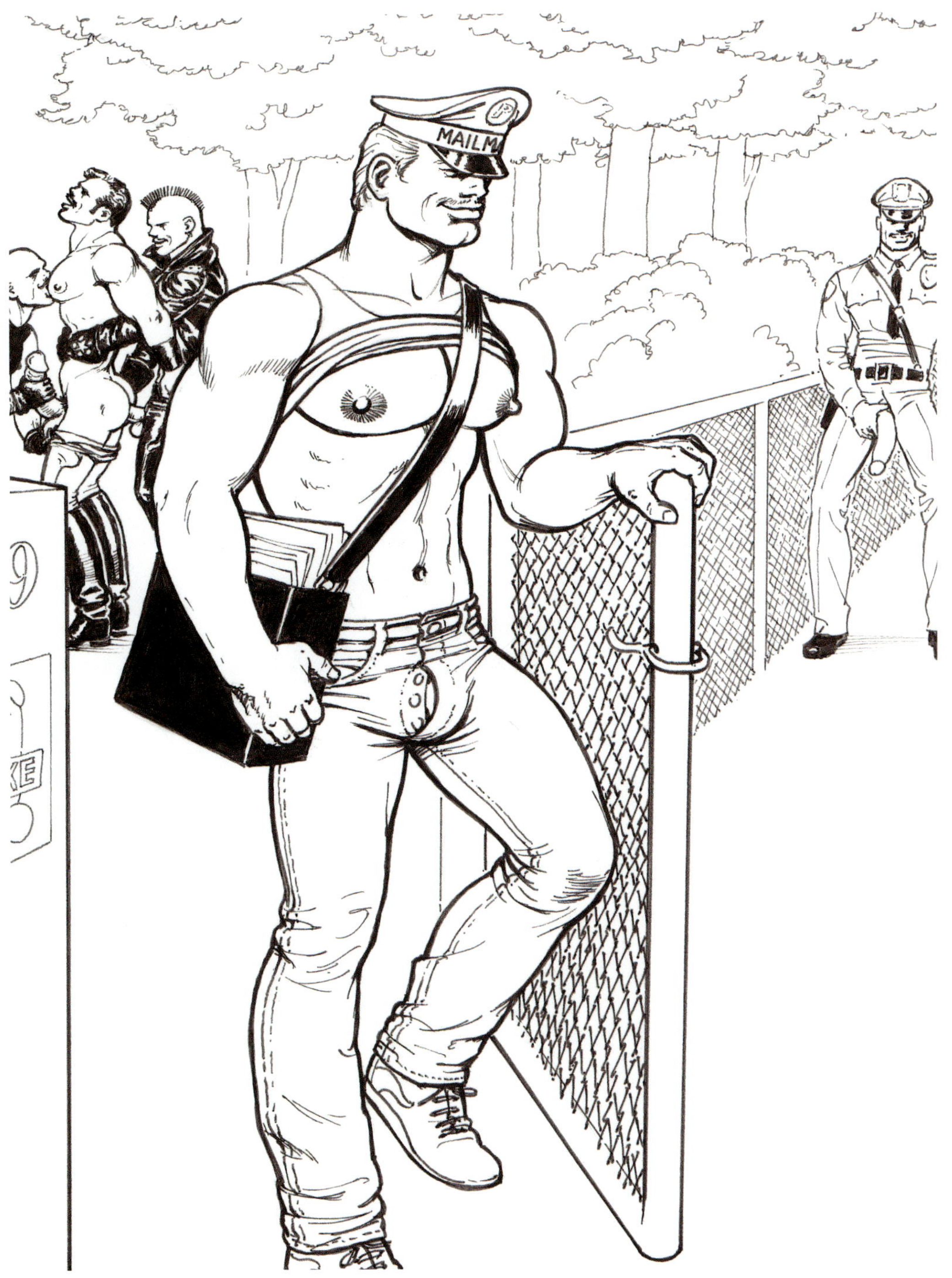
MAILM

$10.
No. 26, 1986
Tom
OF FINLAND
KAKE
OVERSEXED OFFICE   26

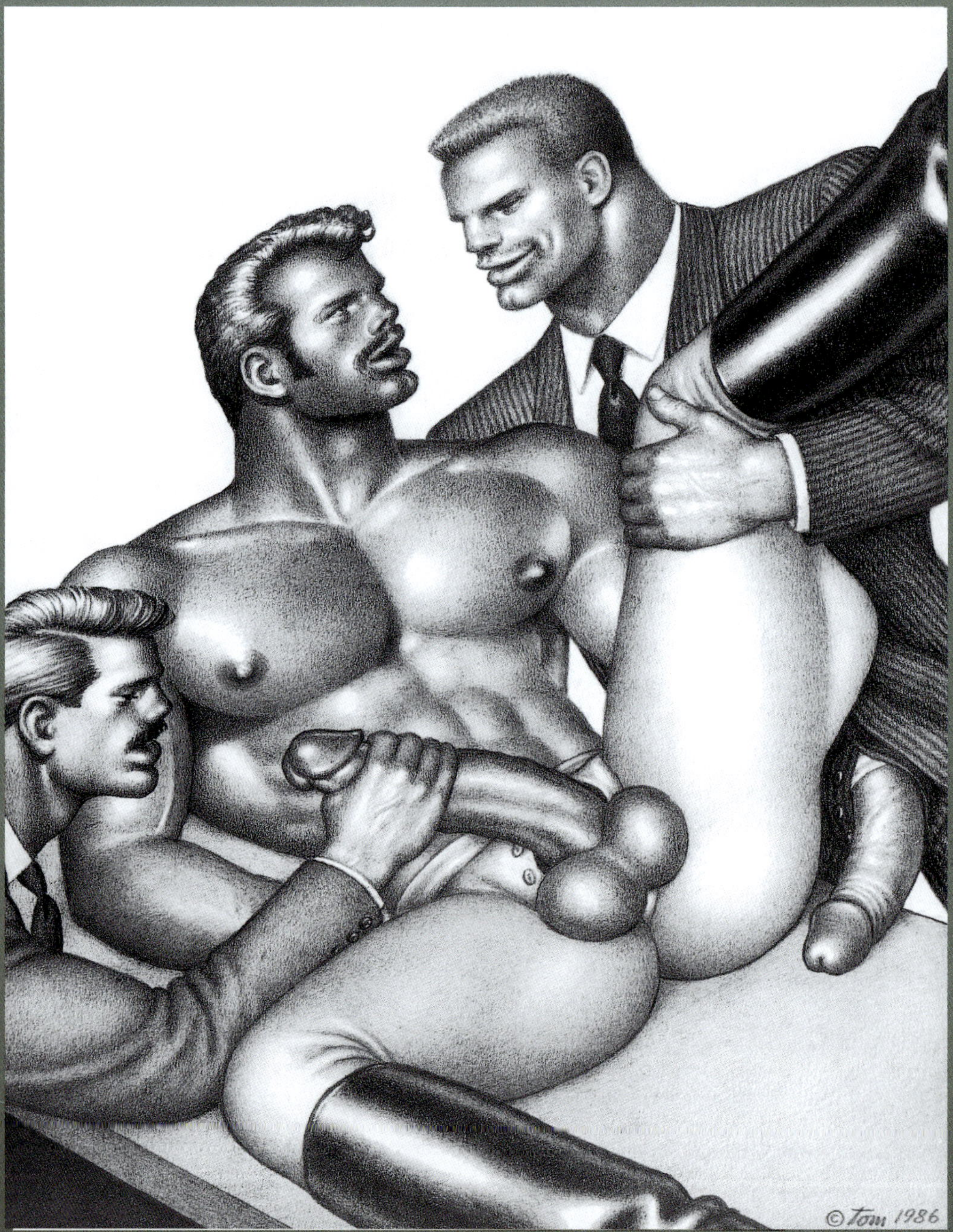
© Tom 1986

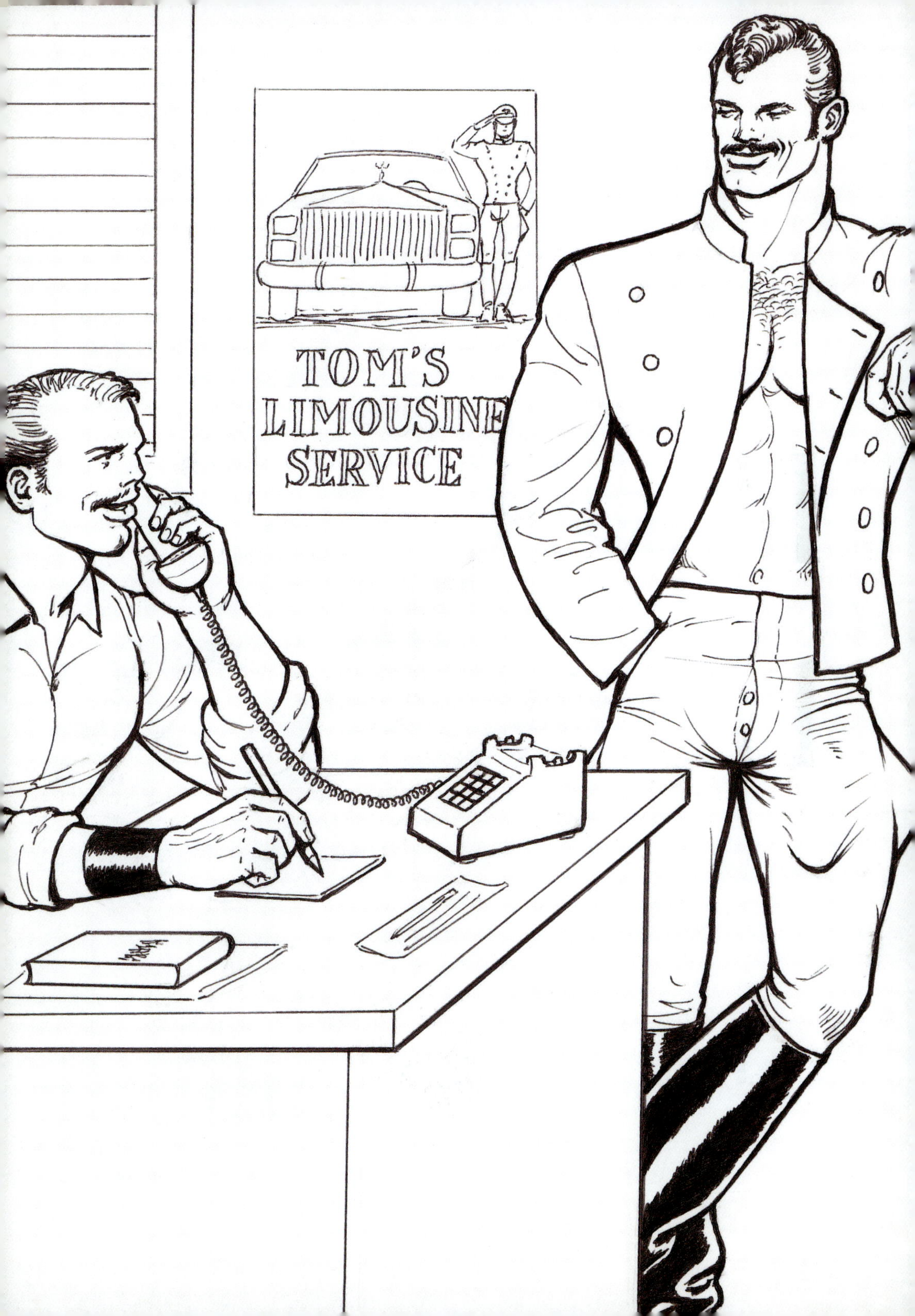

TOM'S
LIMOUSINE
SERVICE

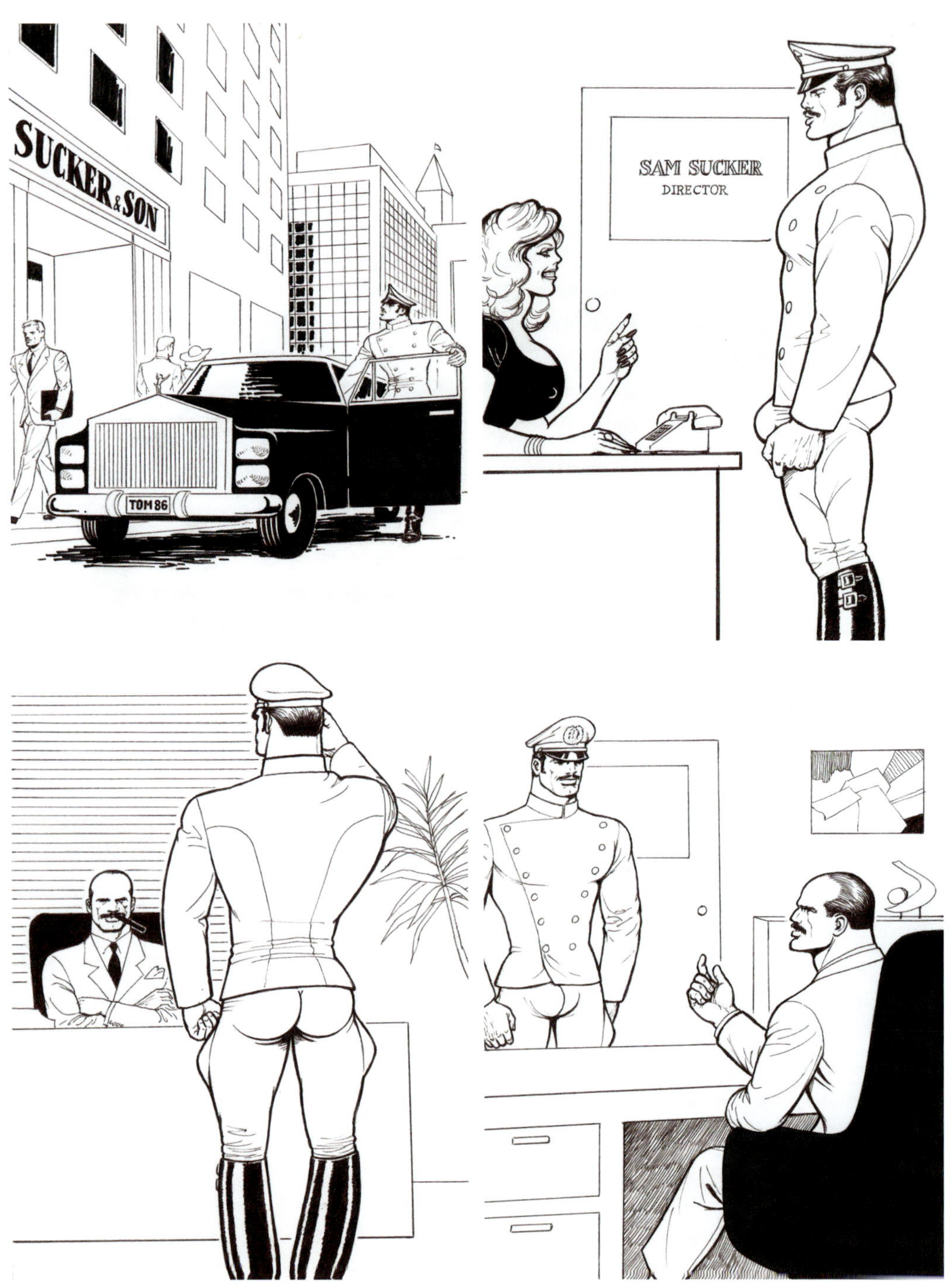

SUCKER & SON
TOM 86
SAM SUCKER
DIRECTOR

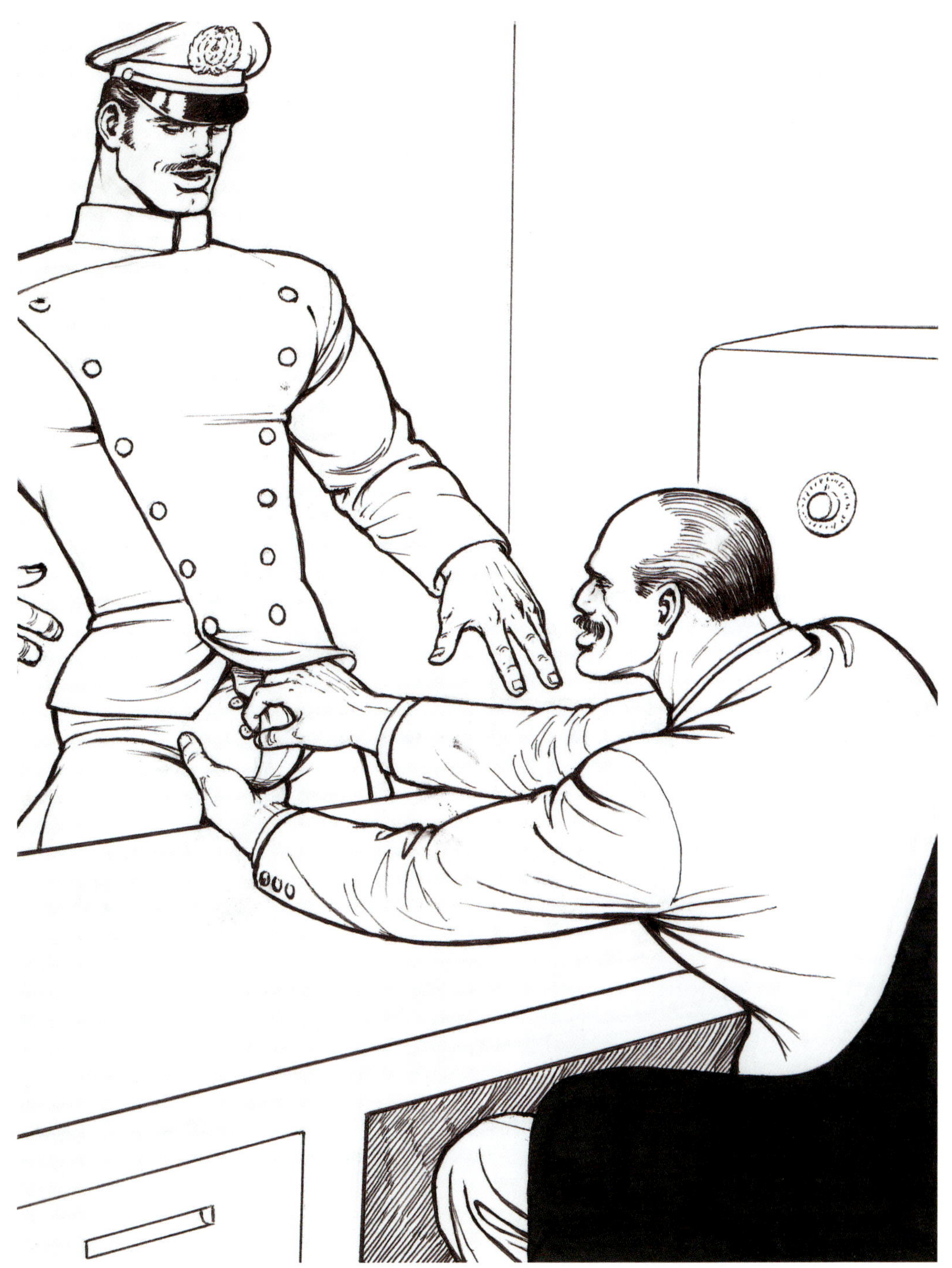

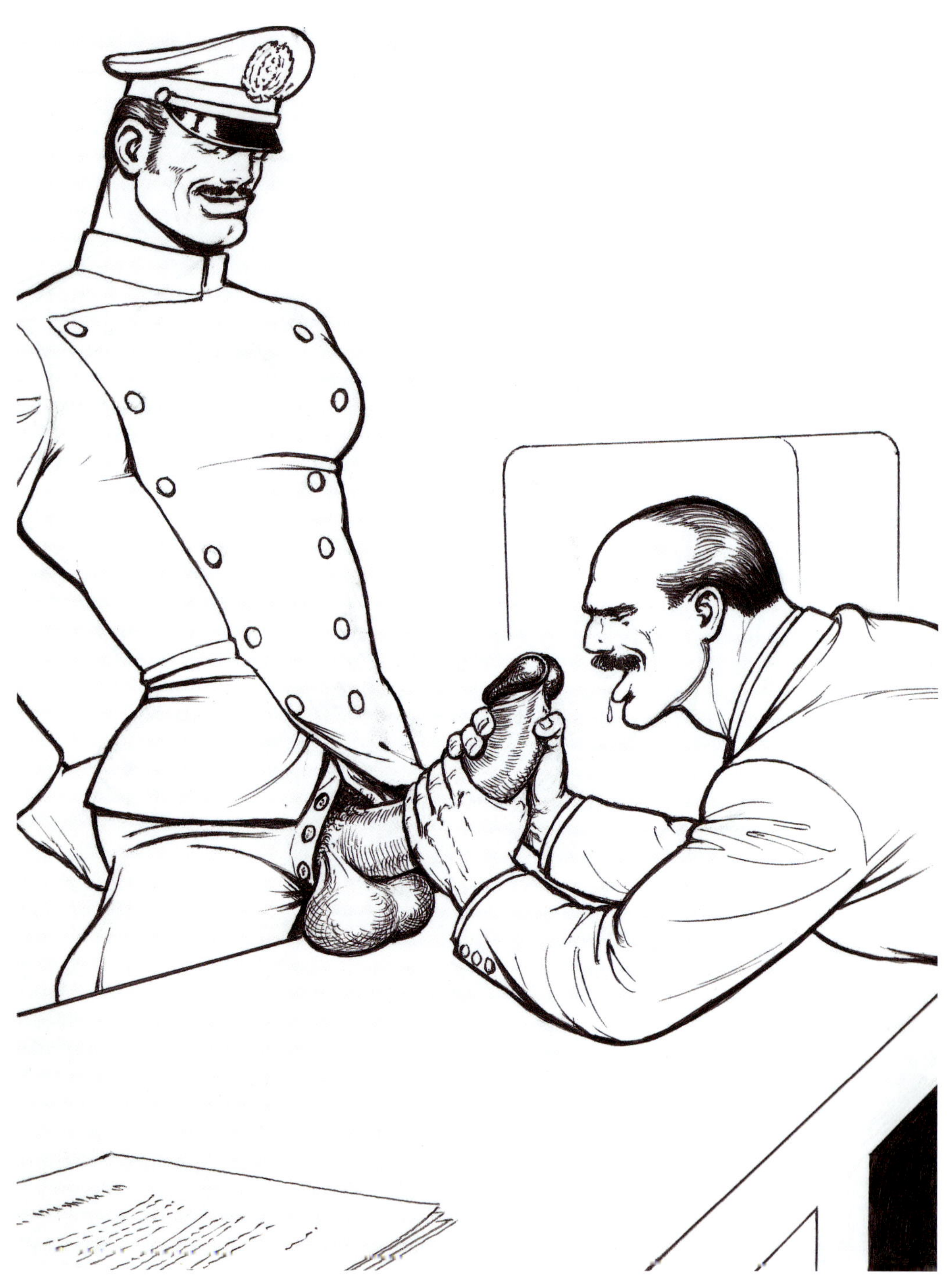

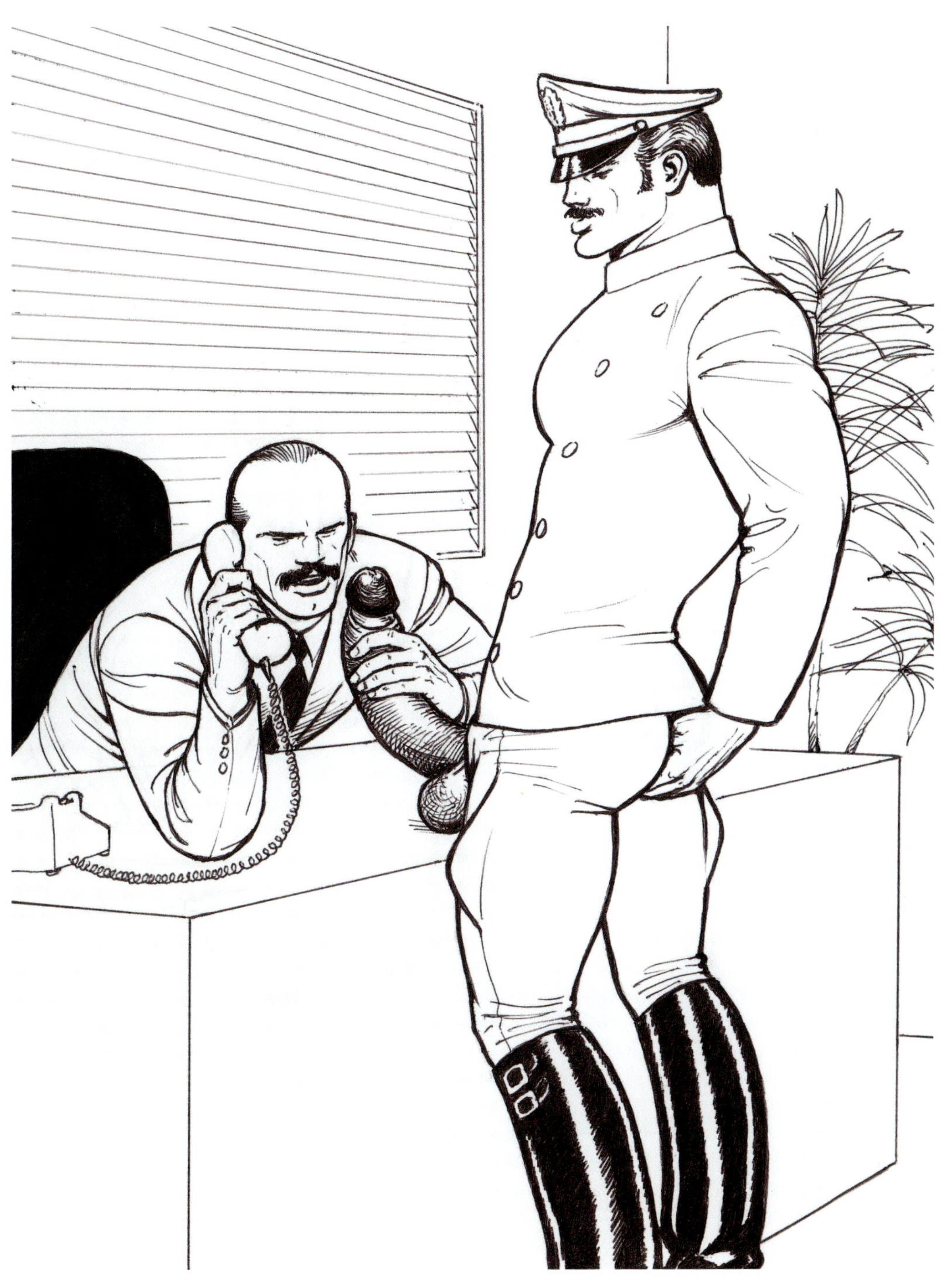

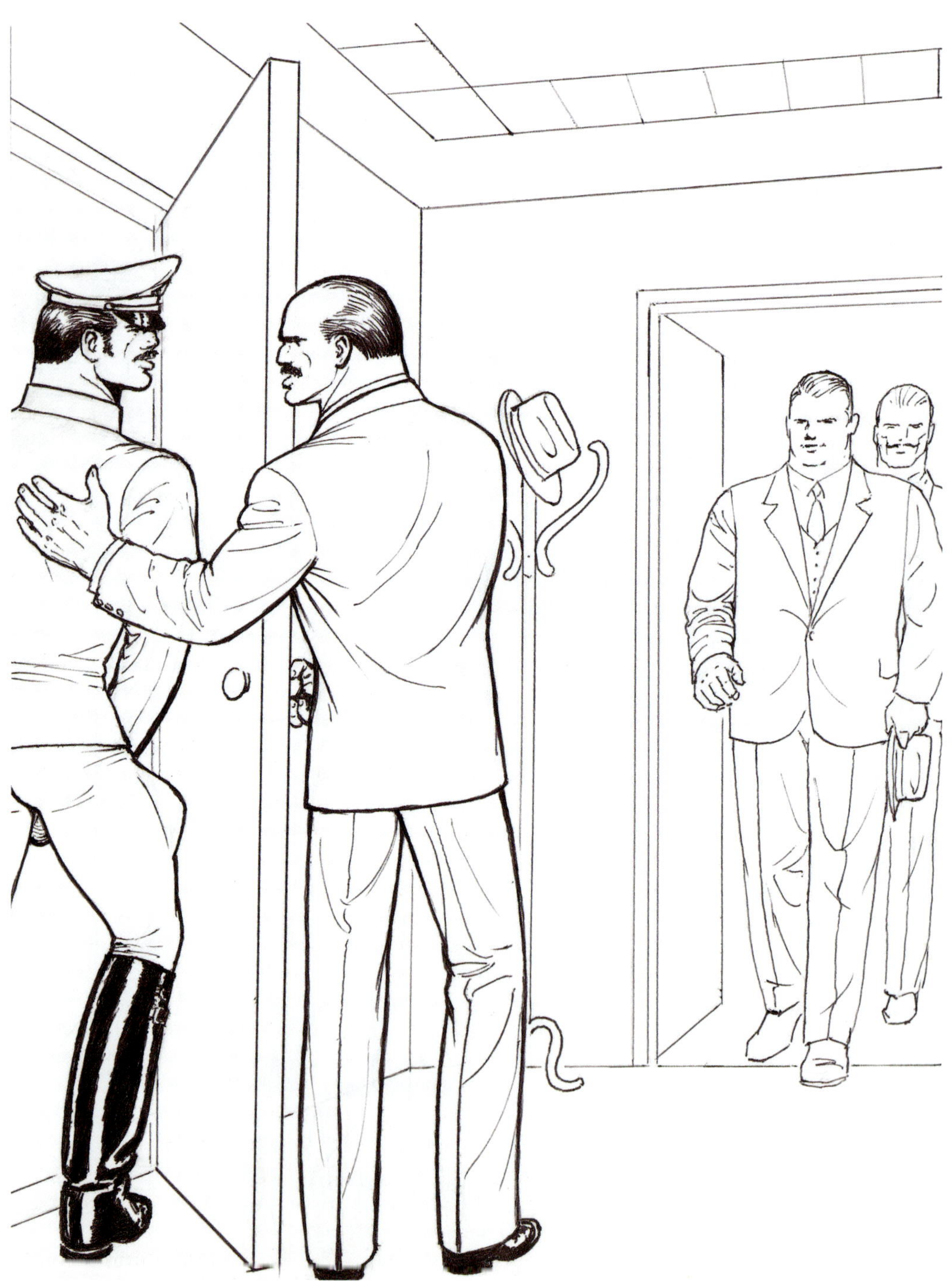

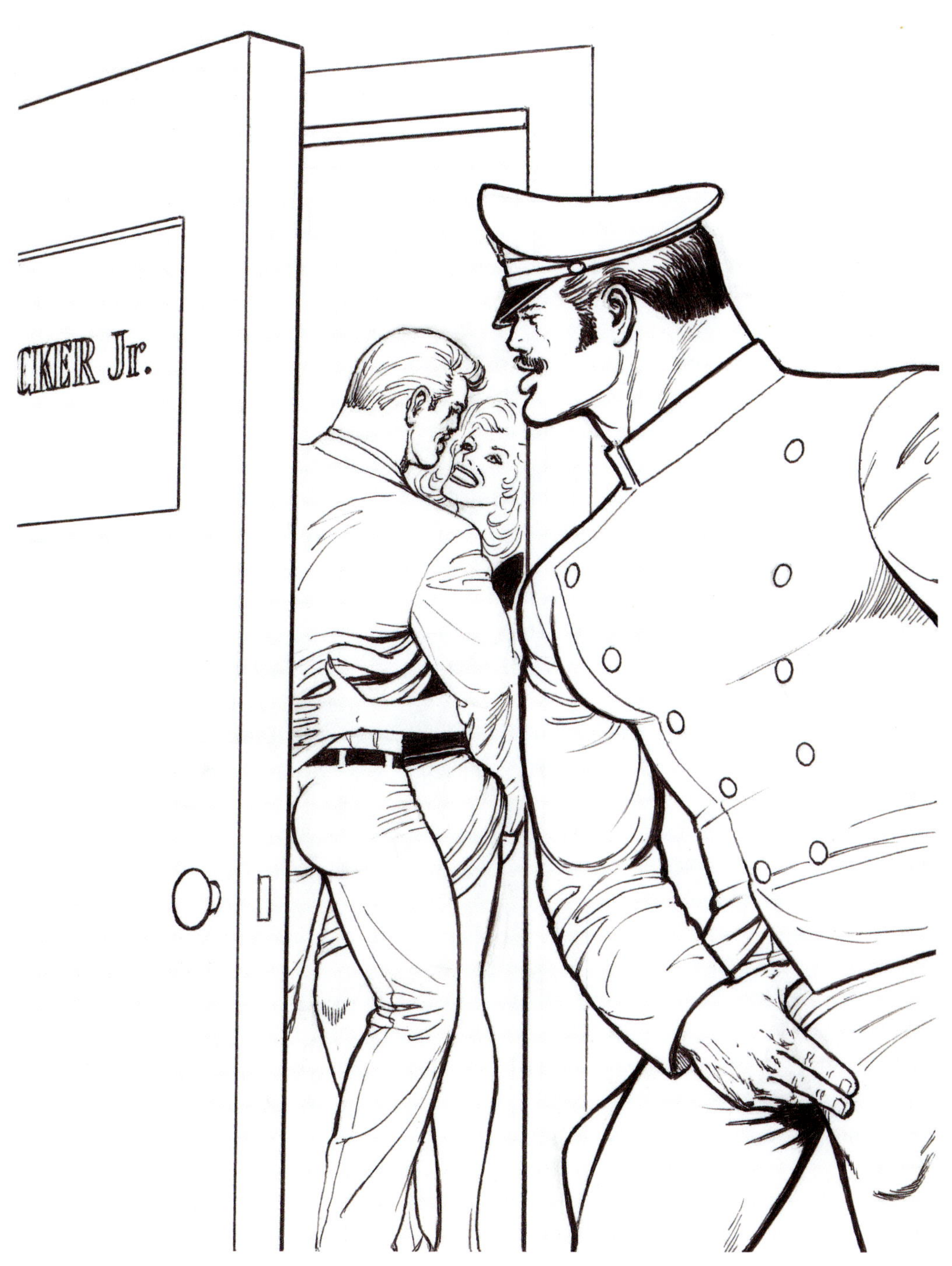
CKER Jr.

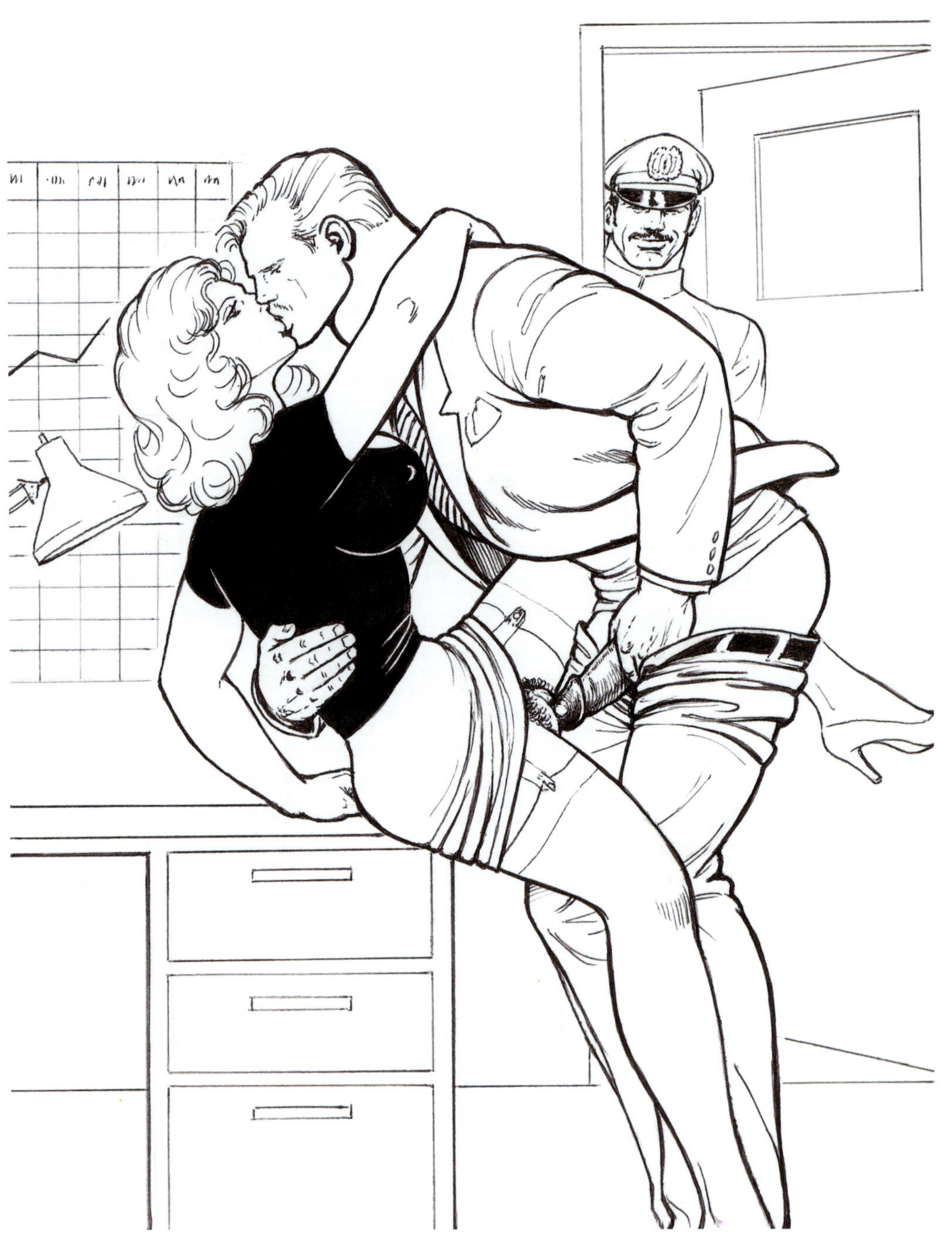

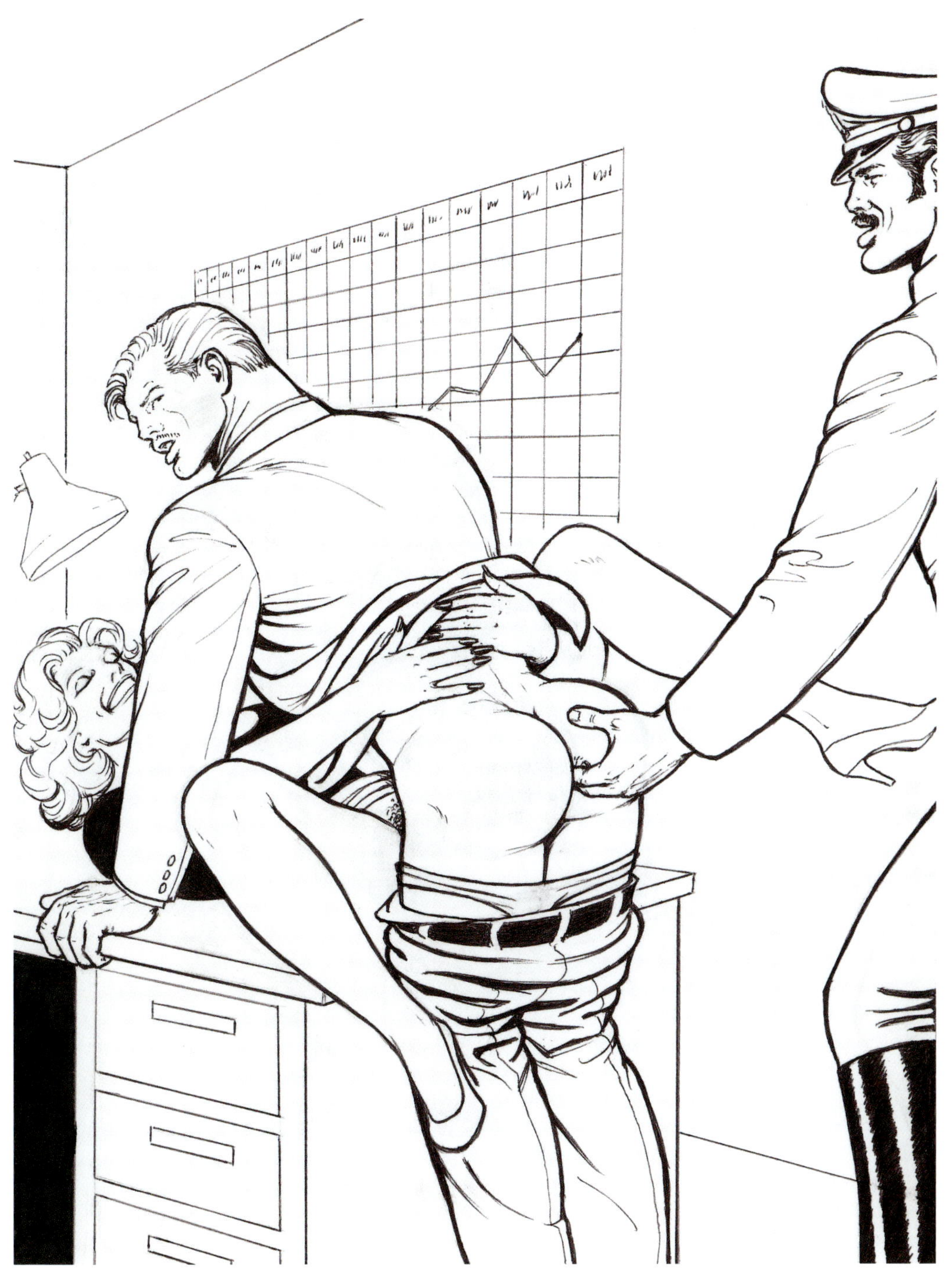

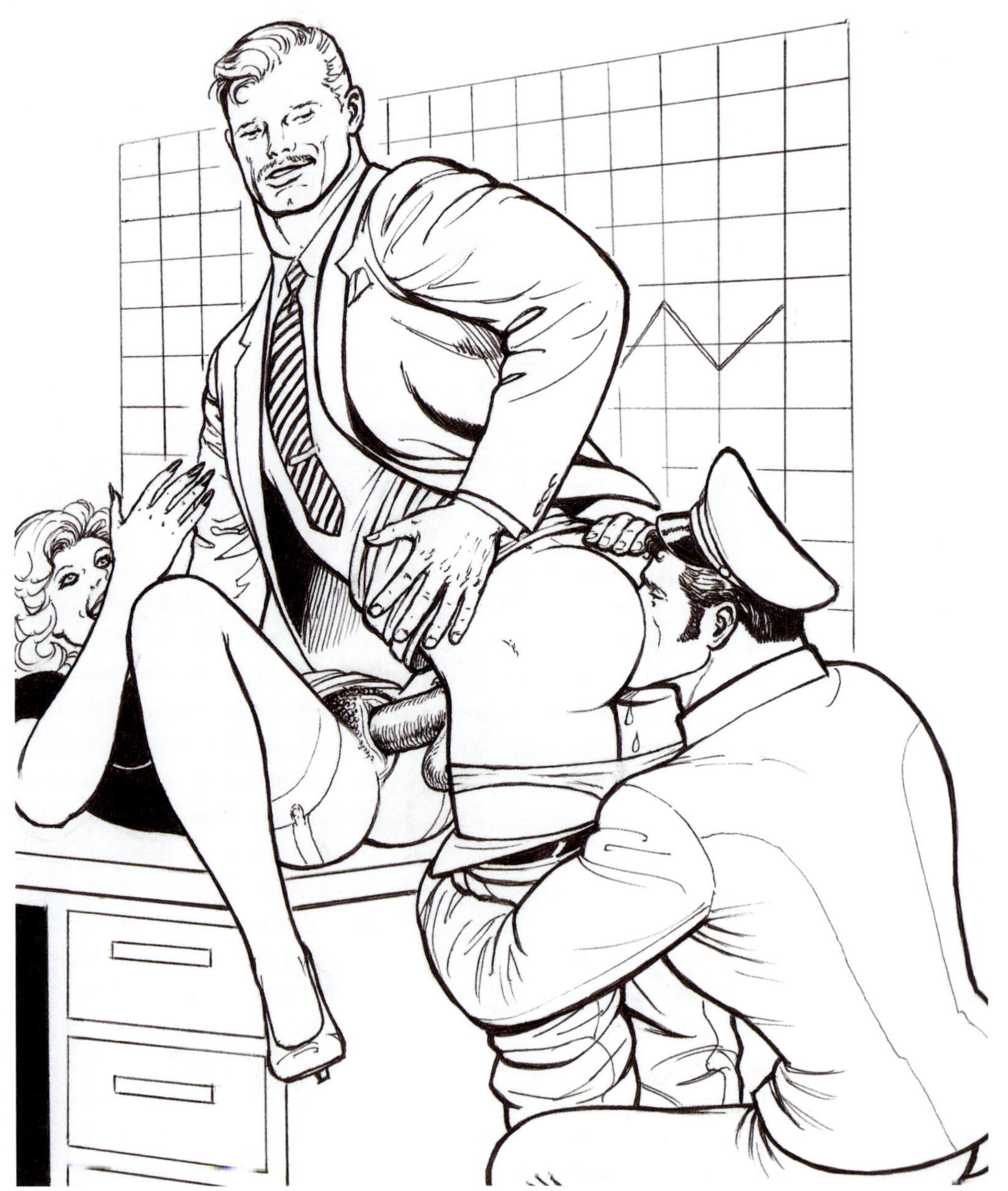

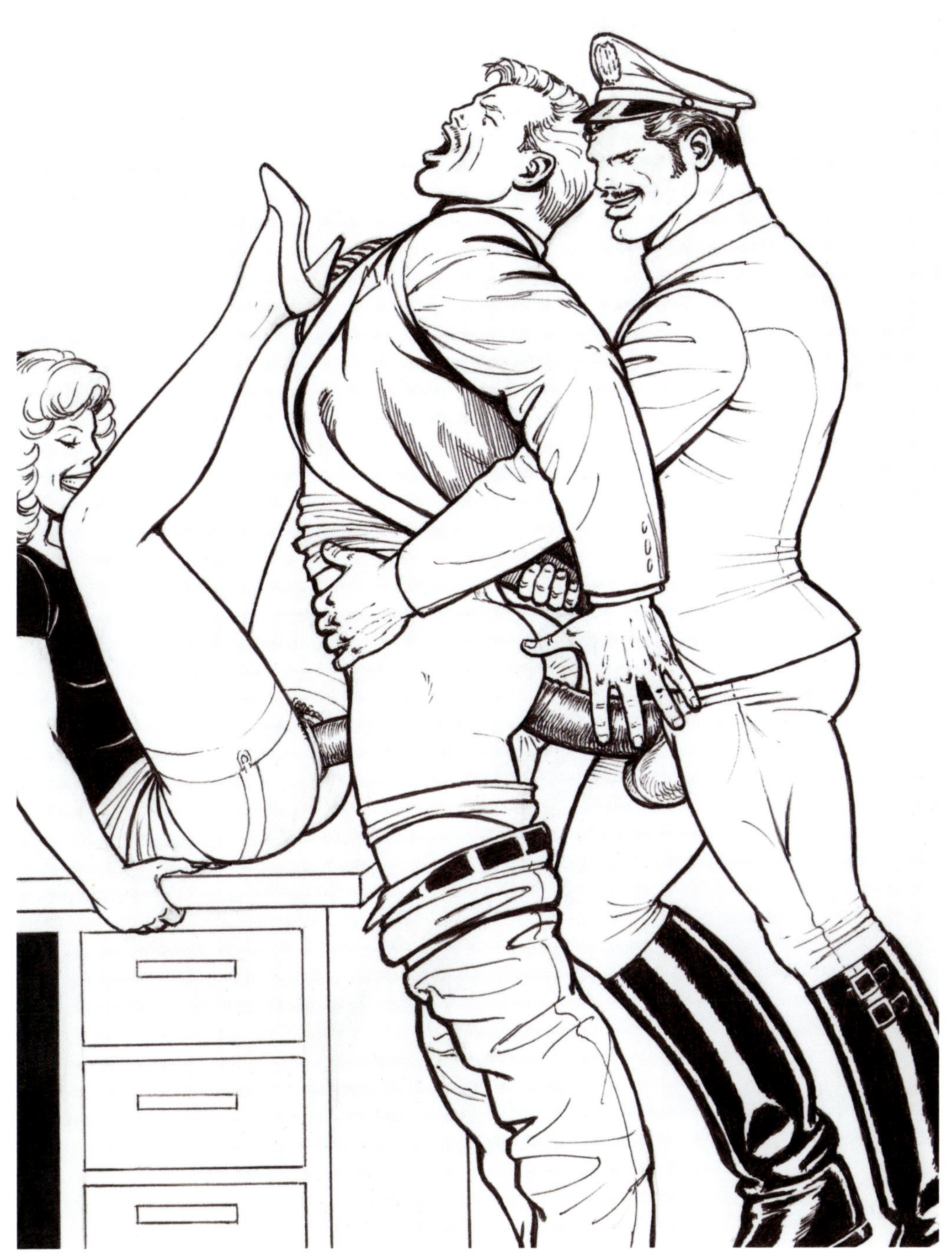

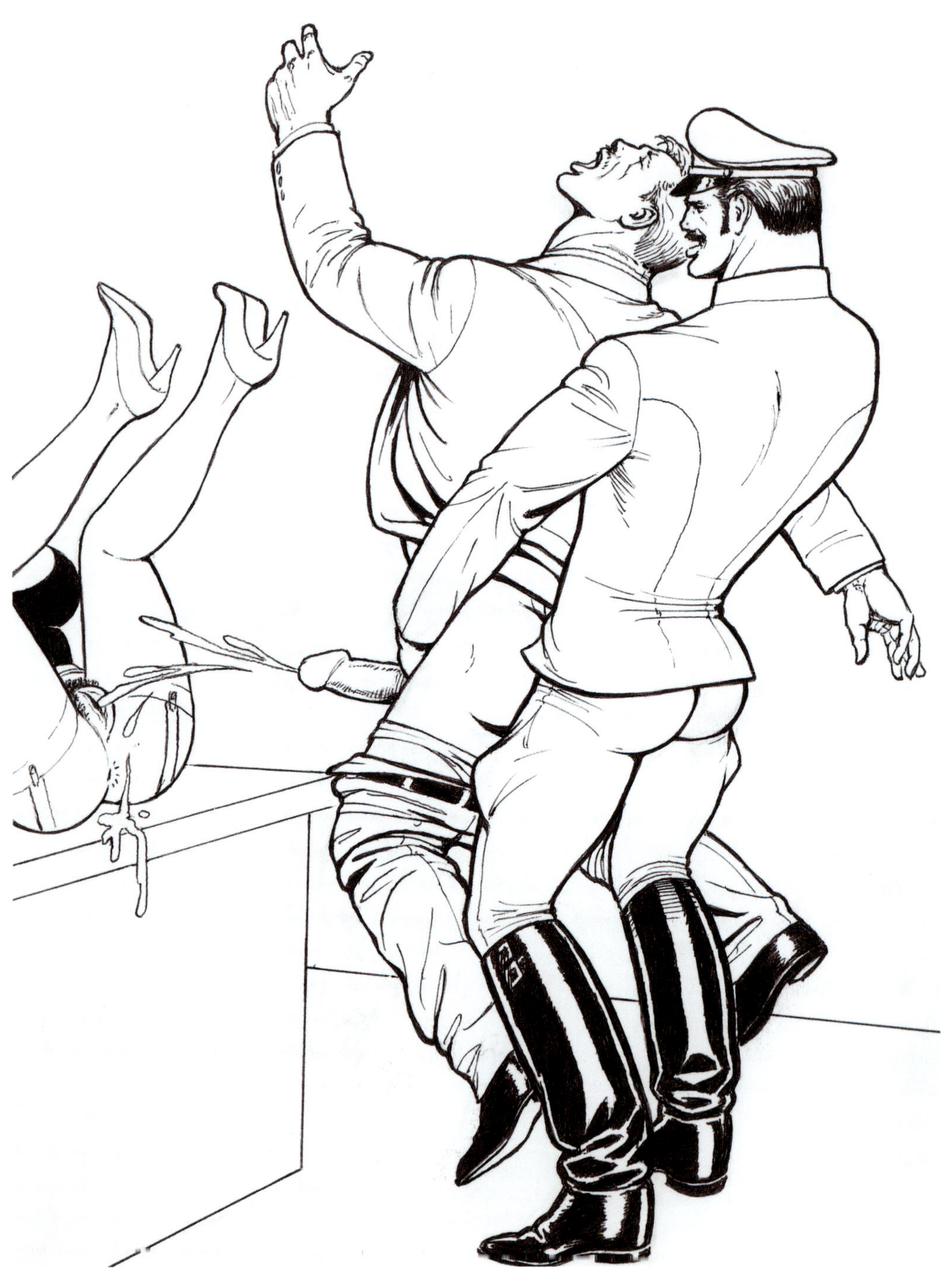

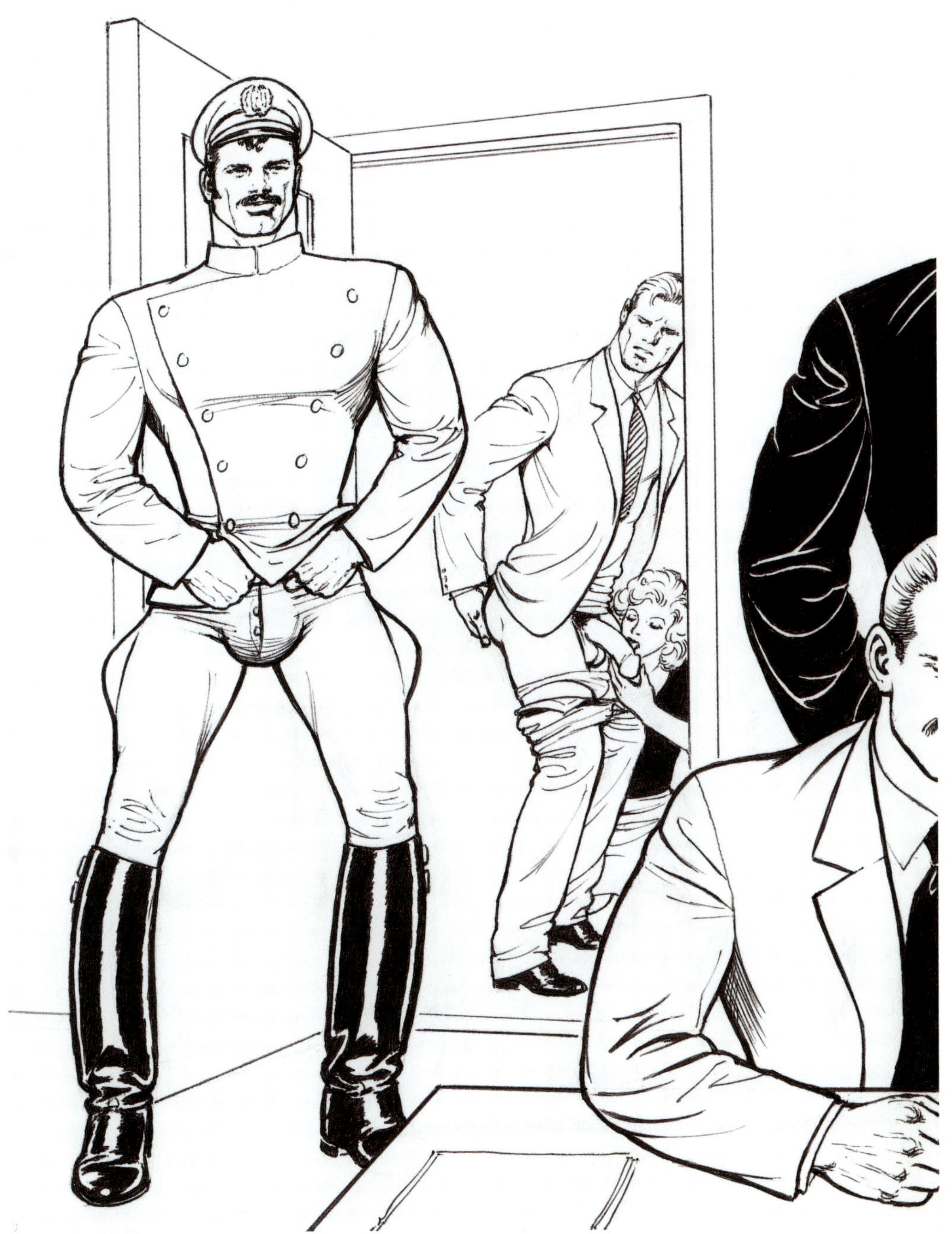

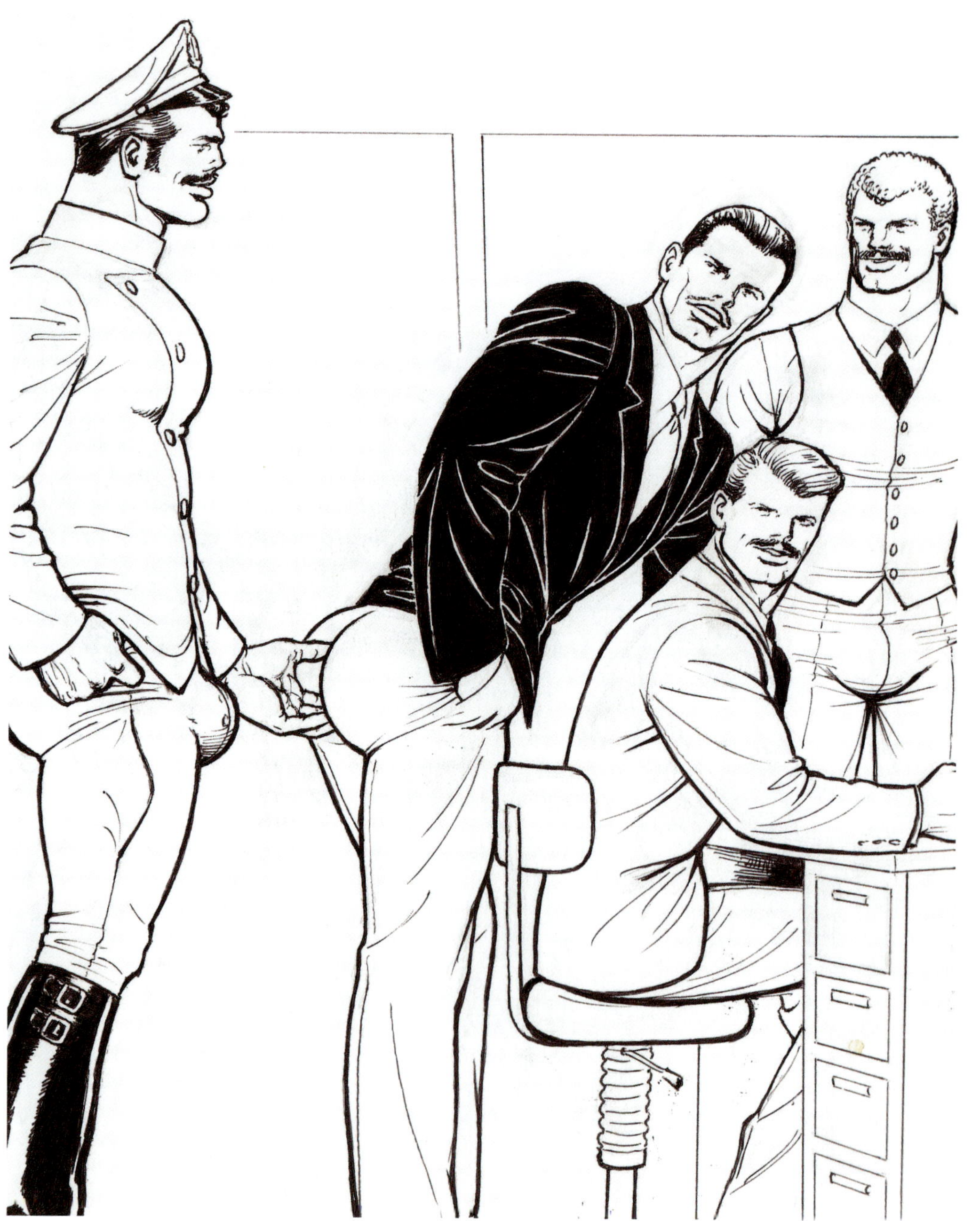

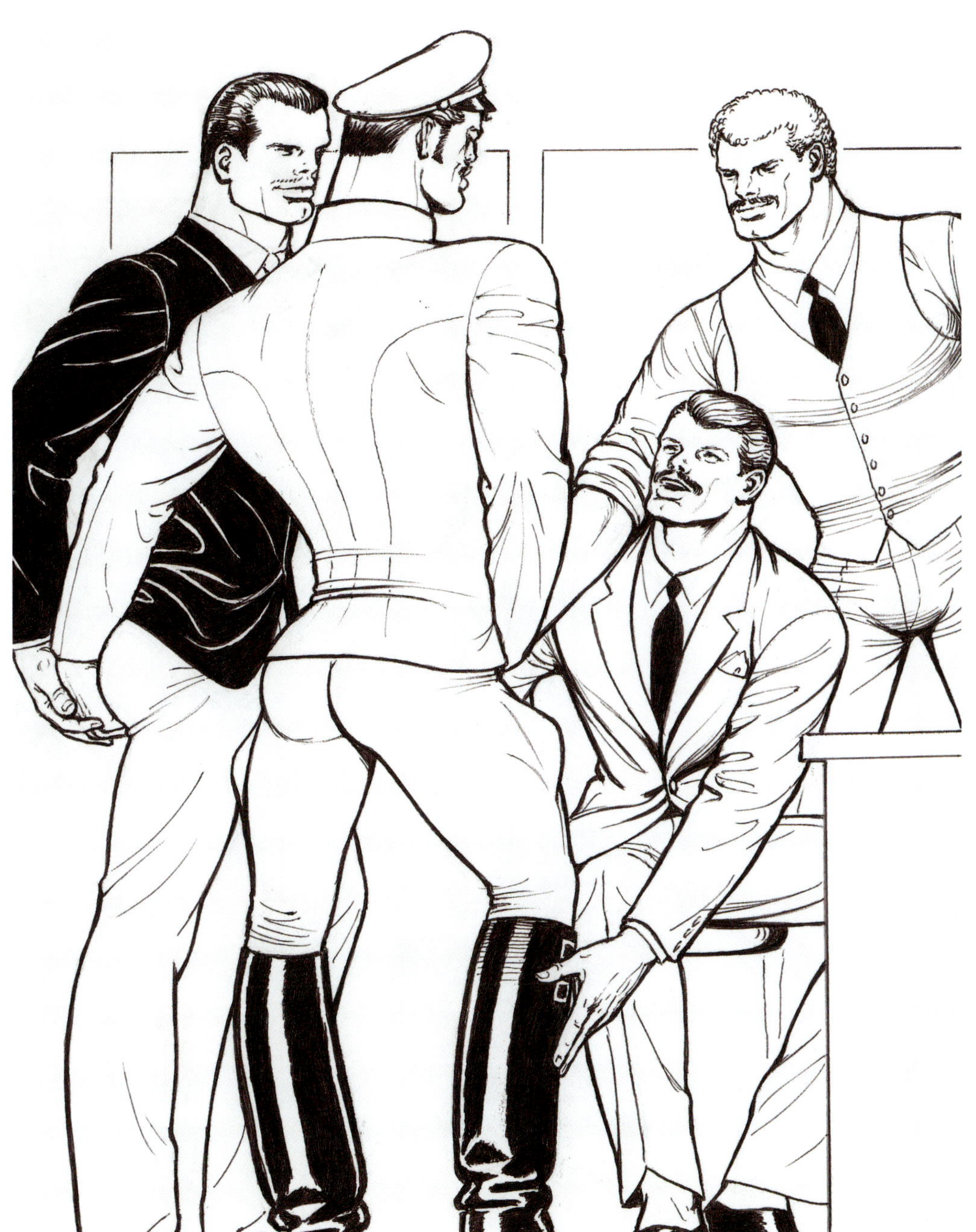

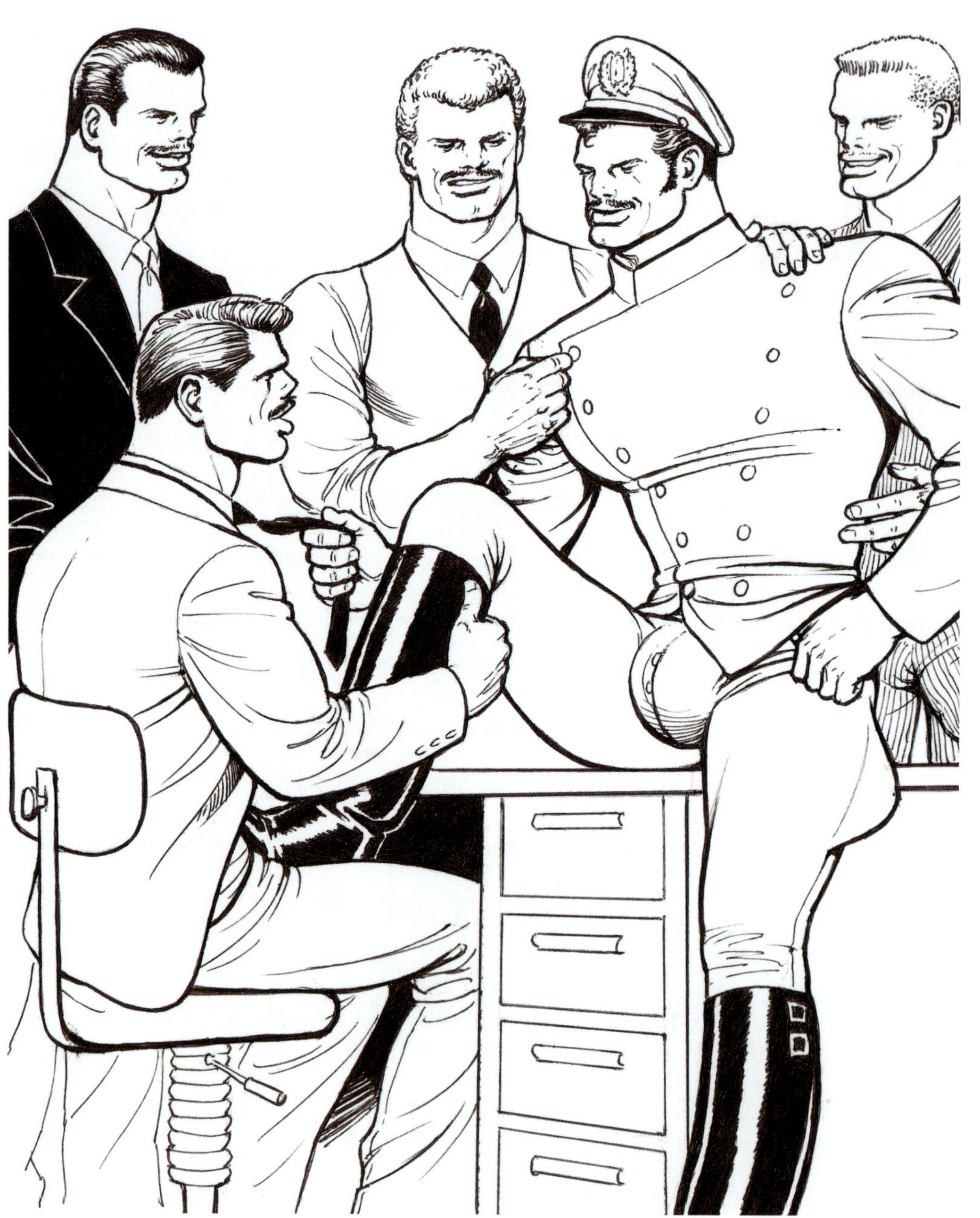

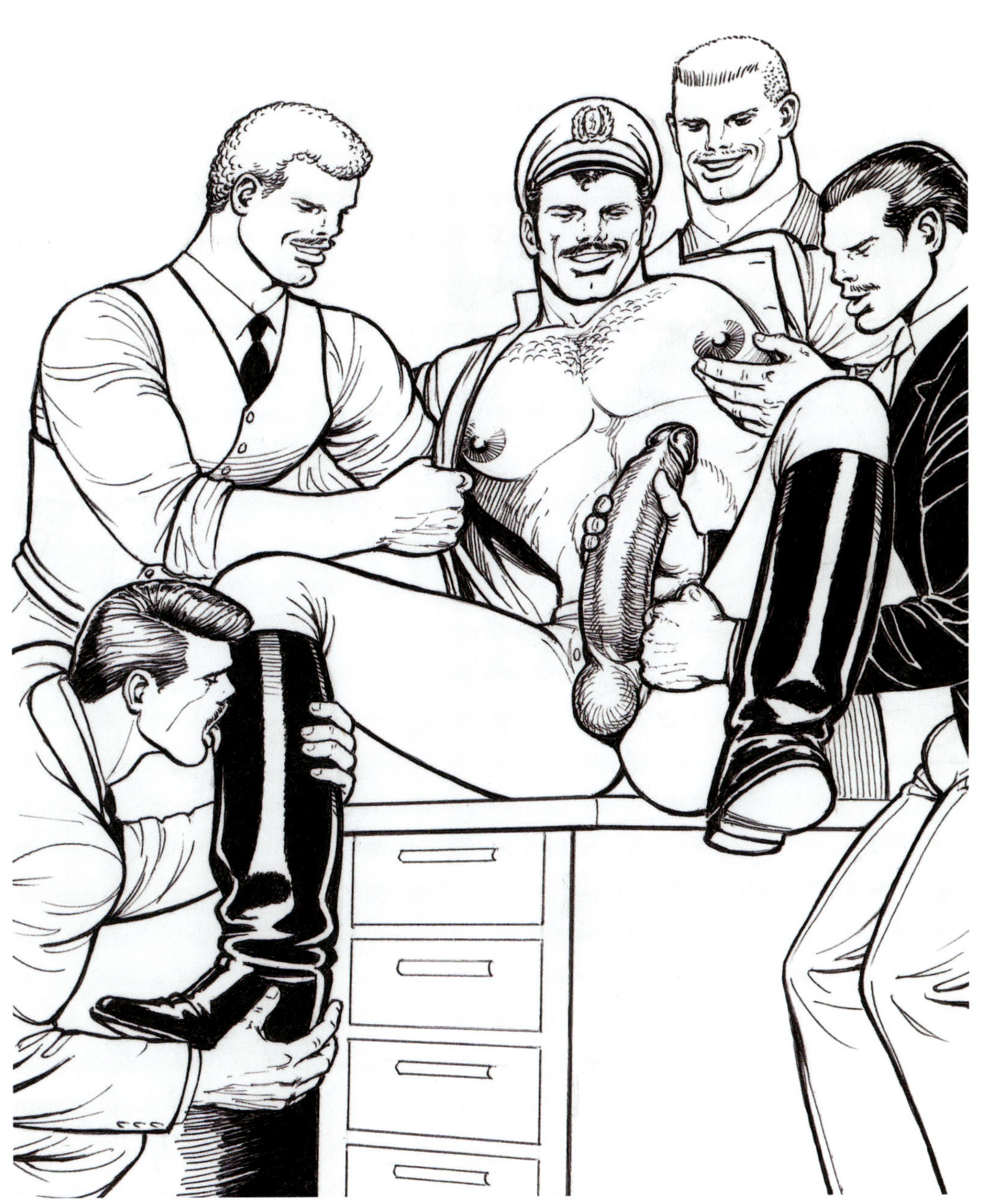

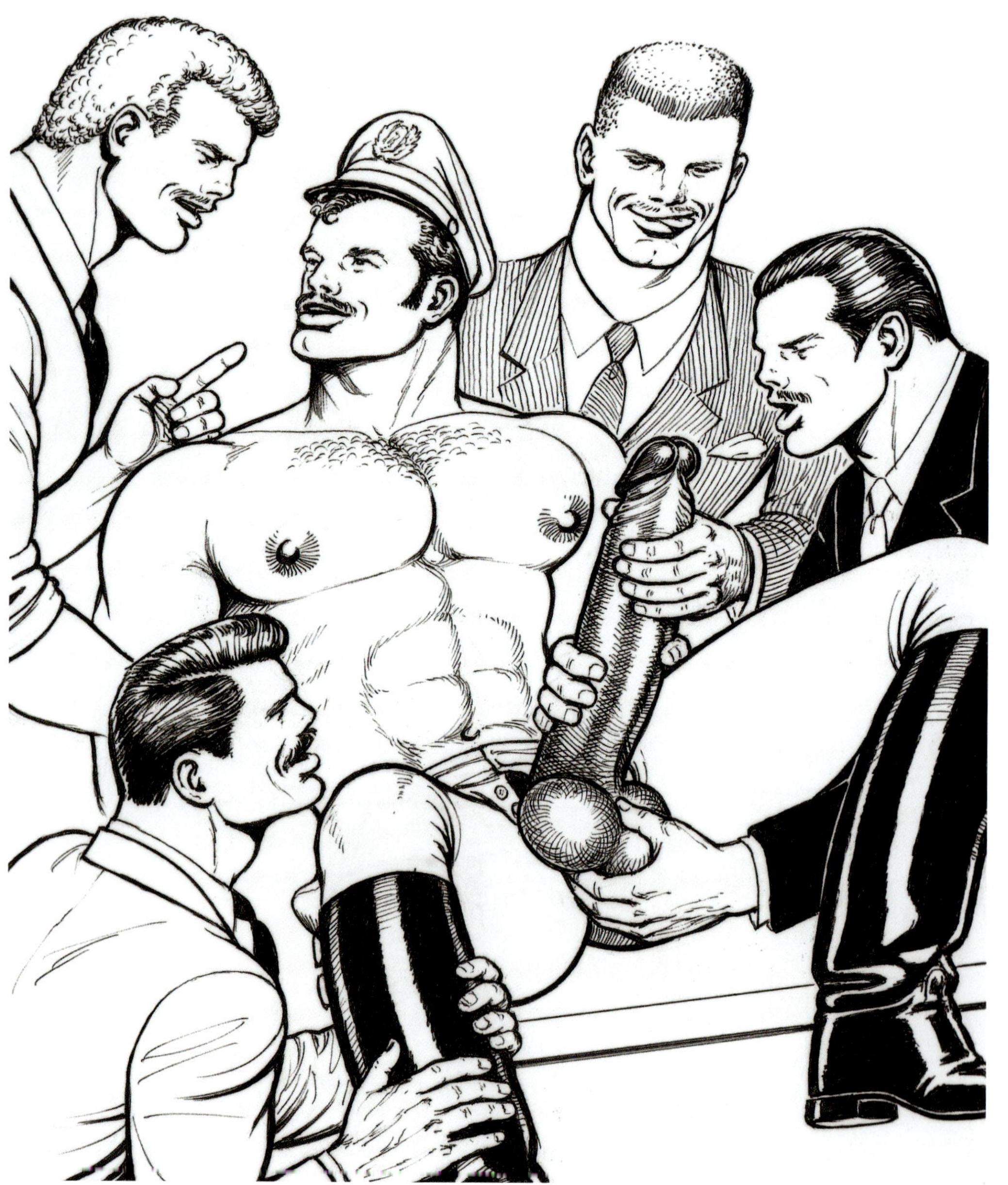

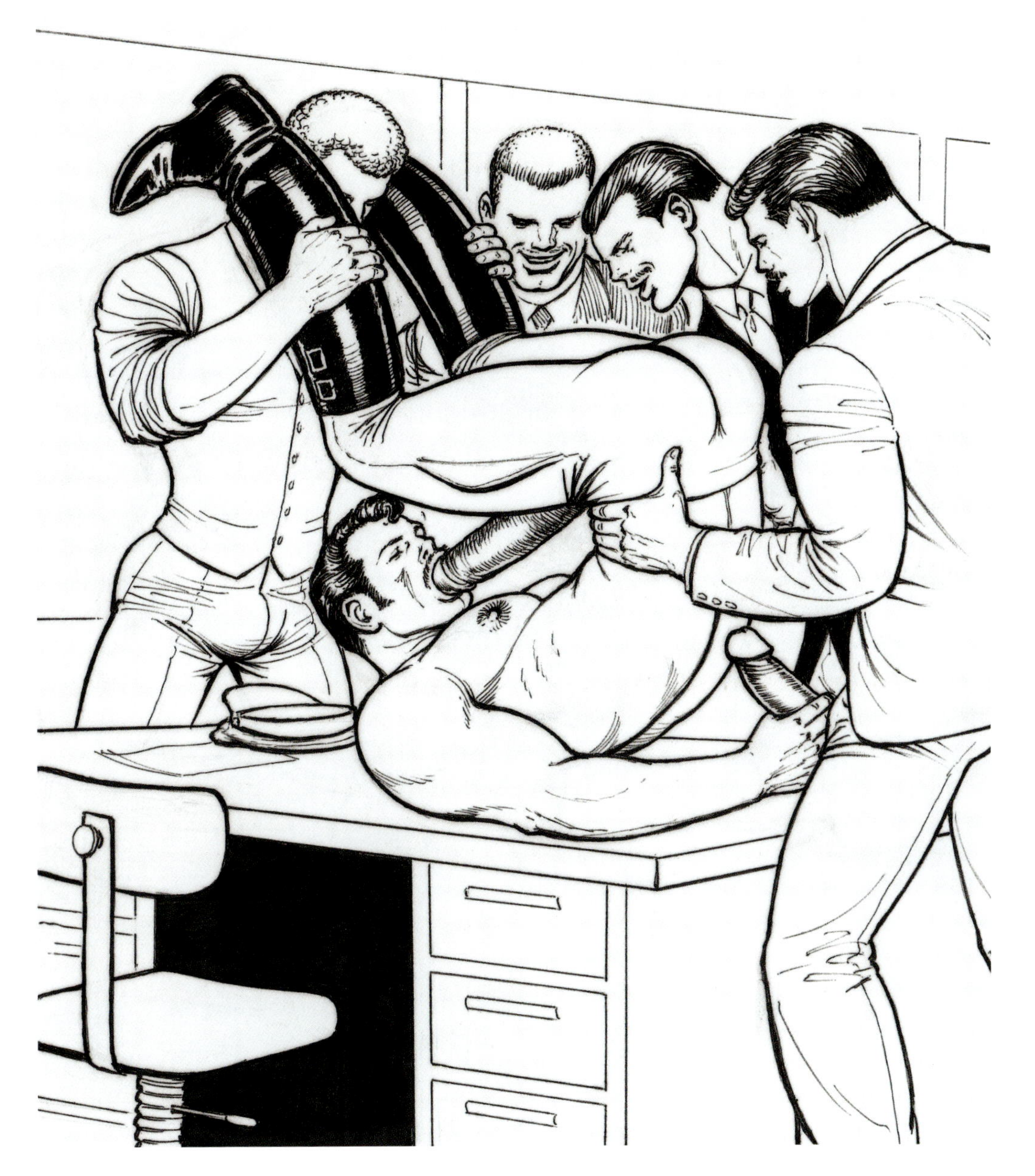

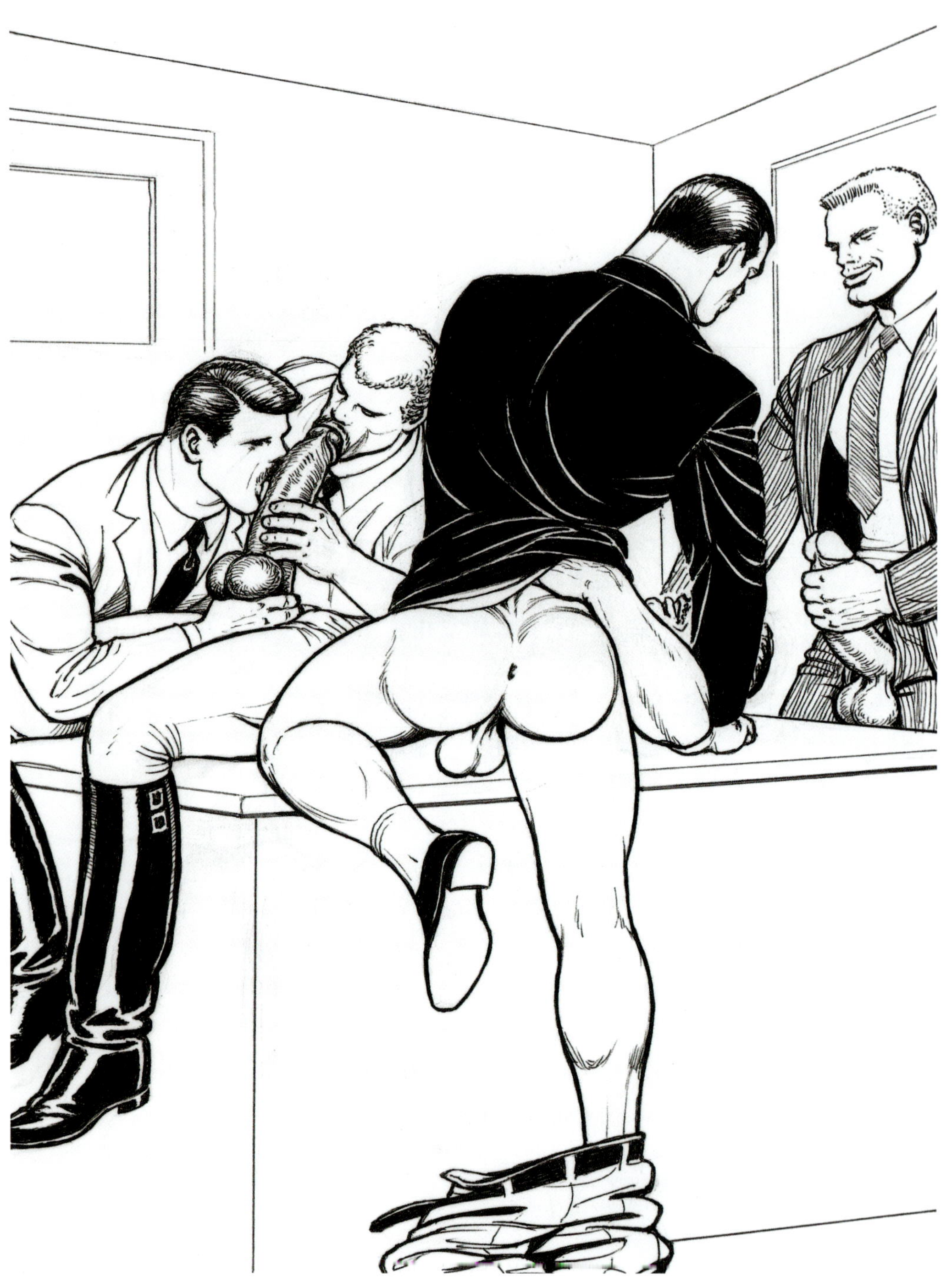

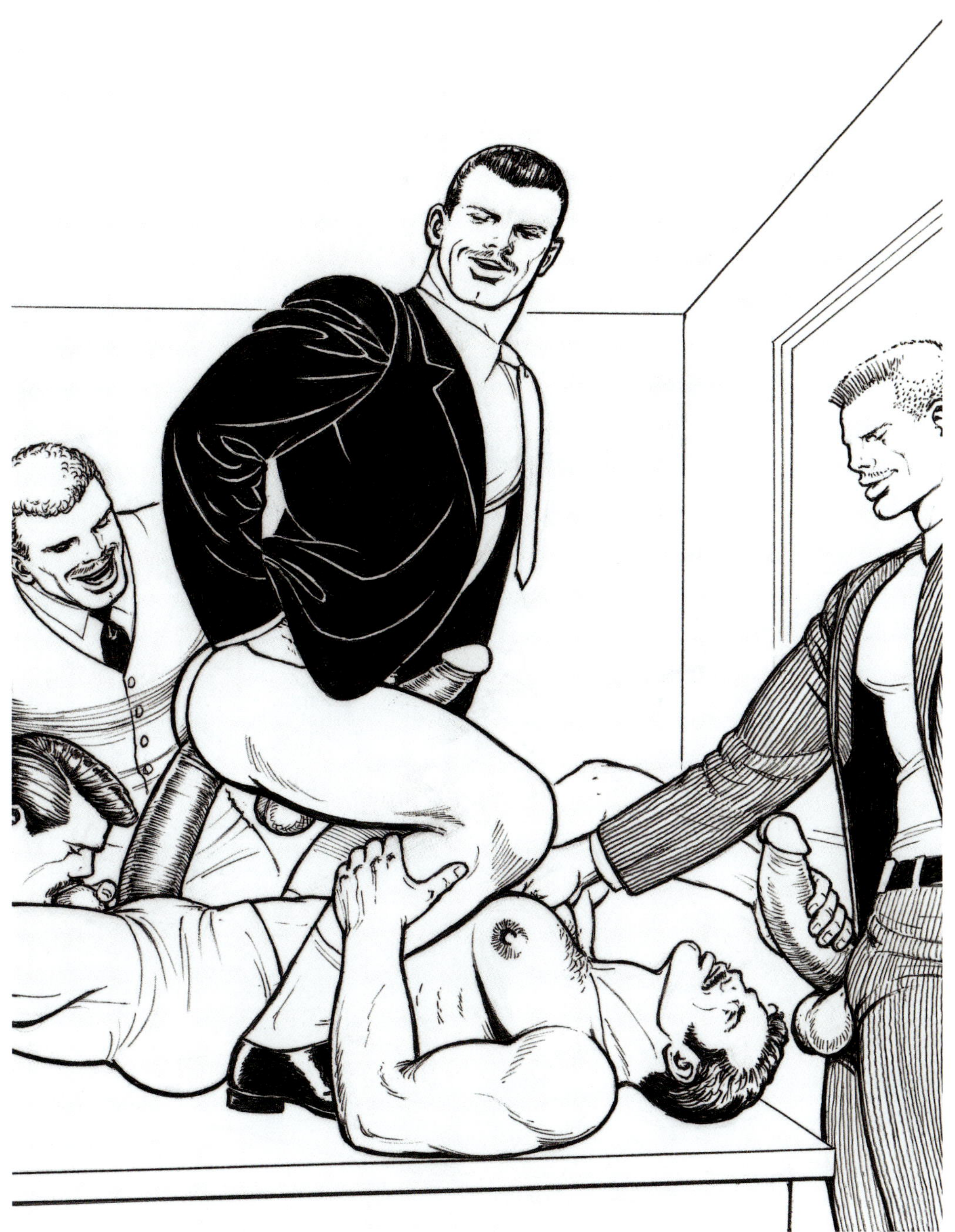

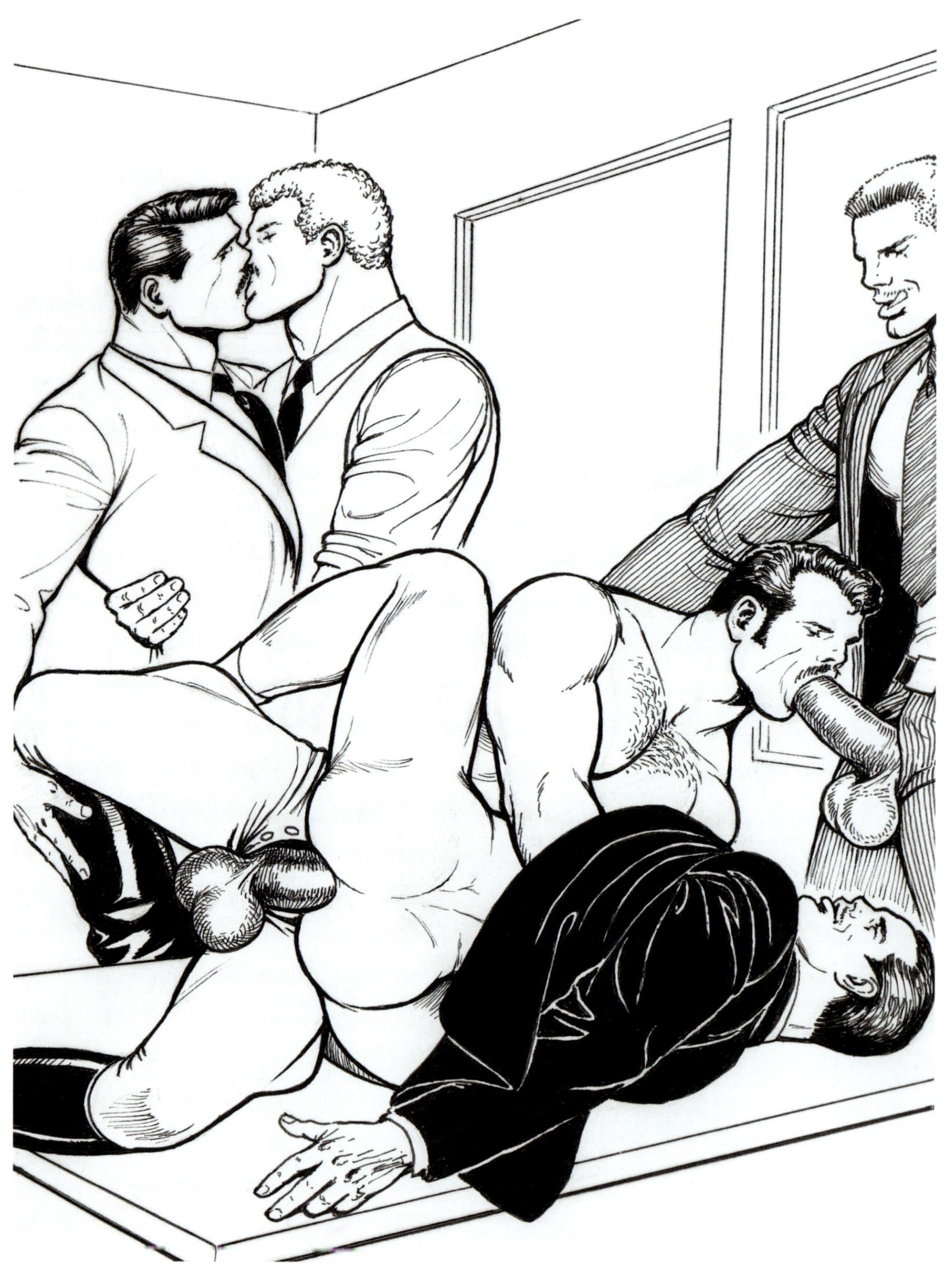

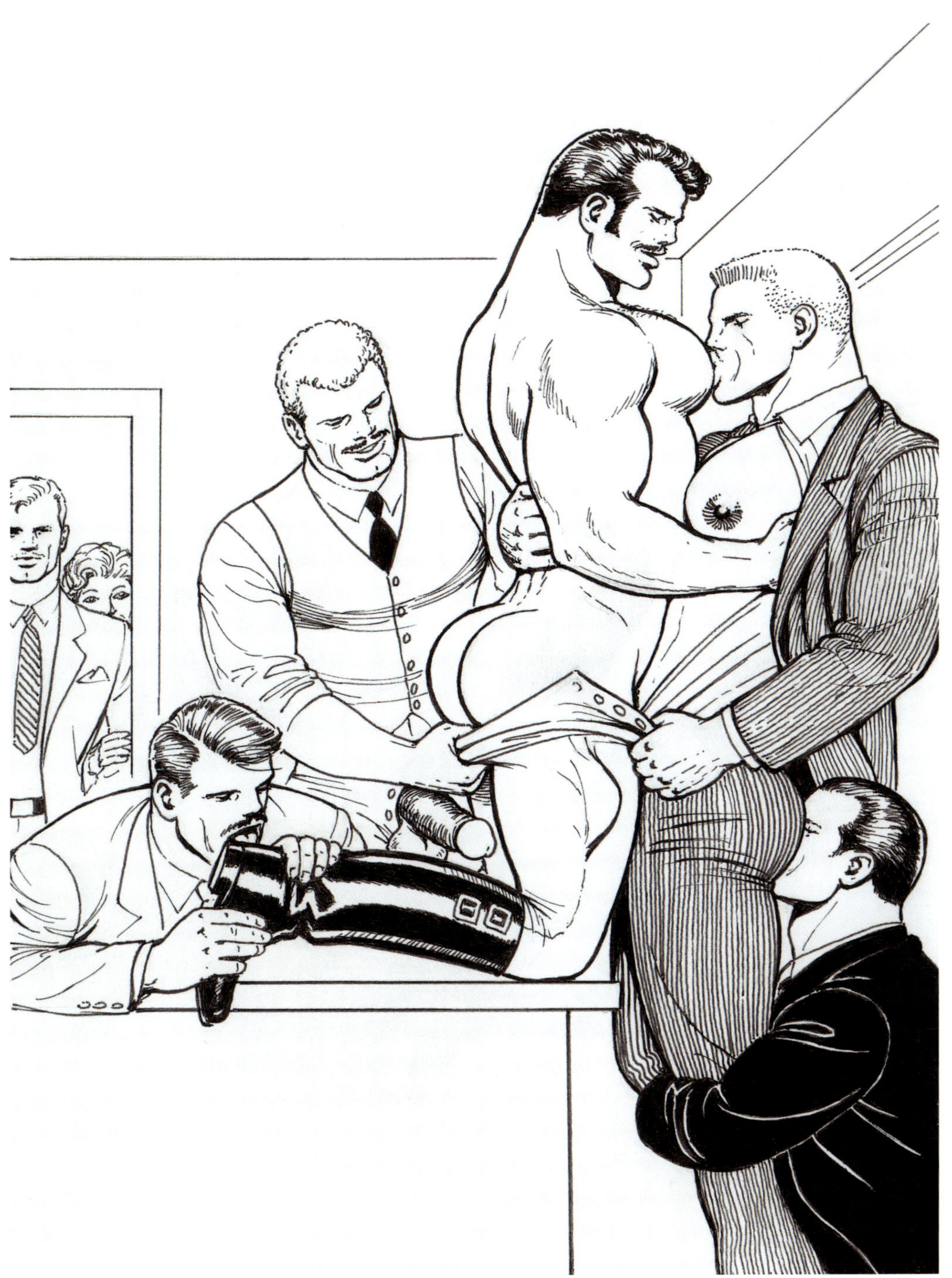

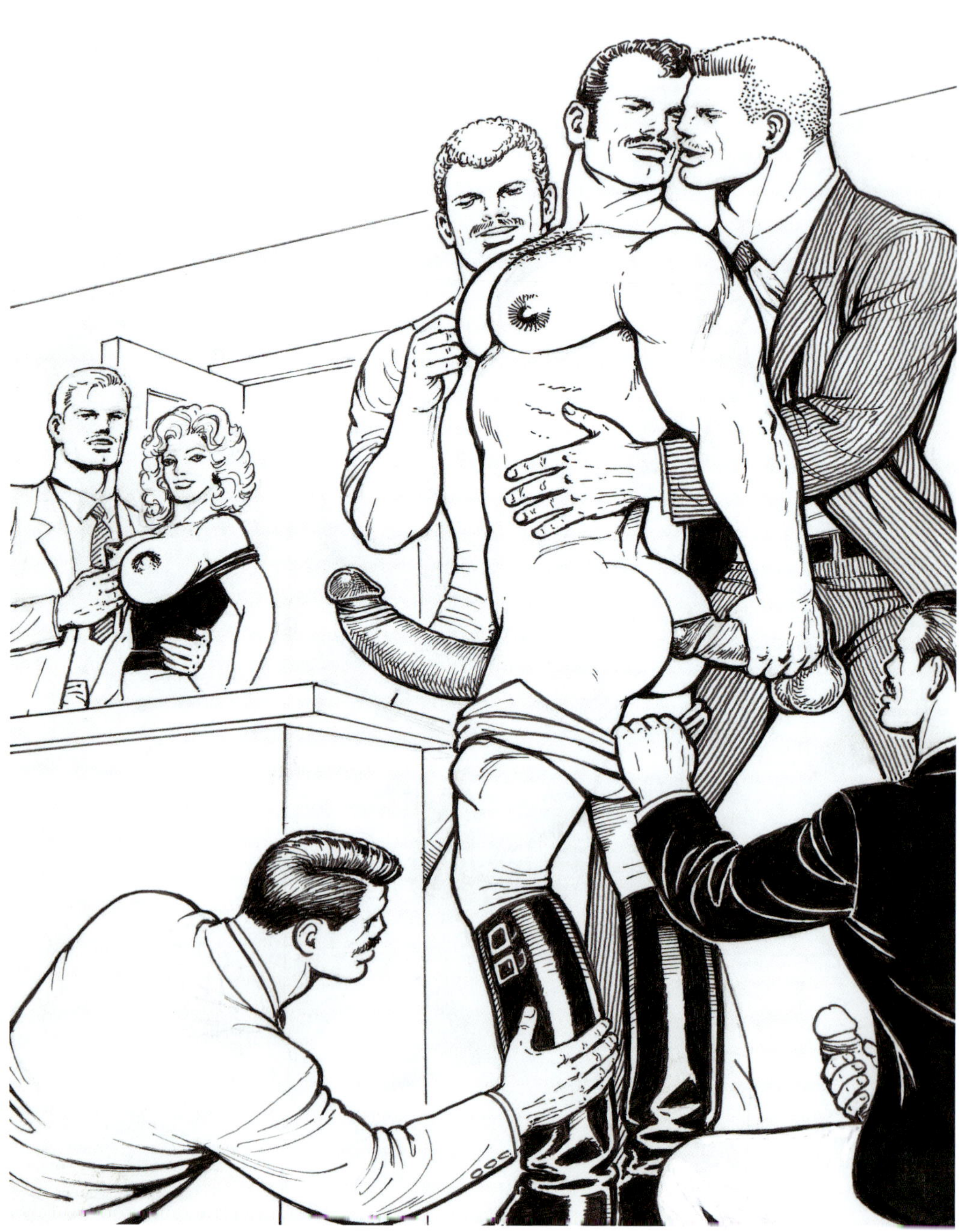

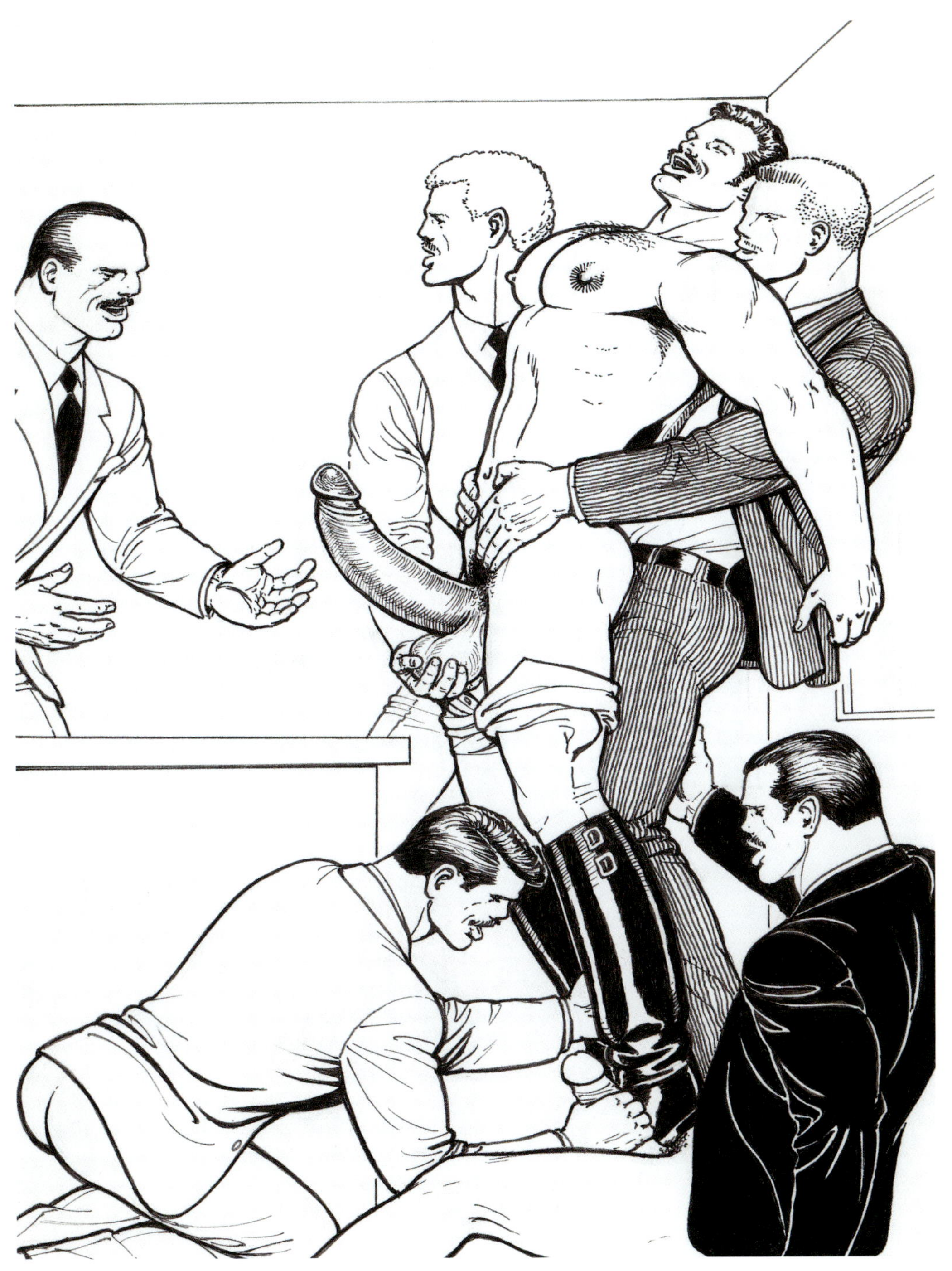

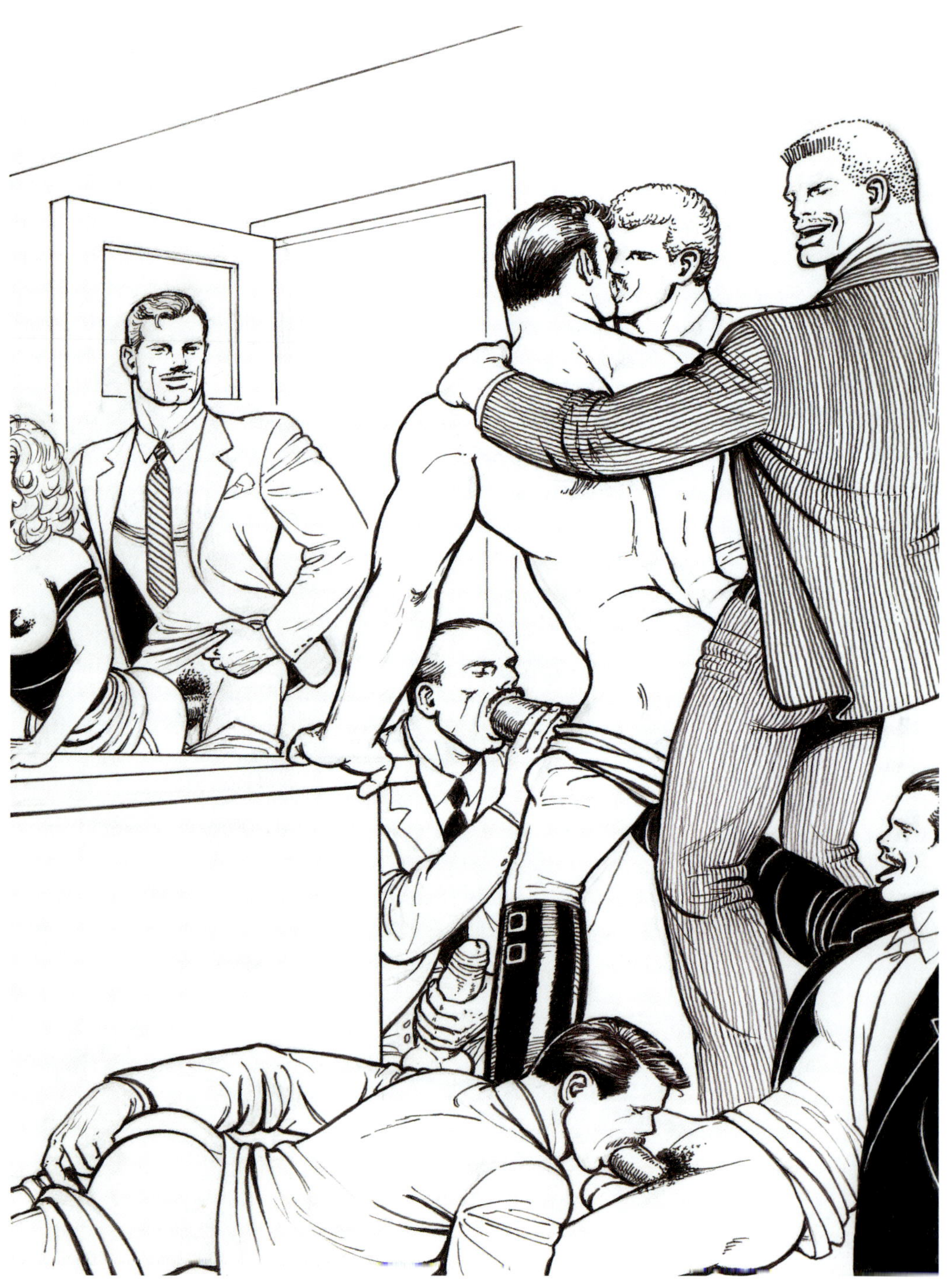

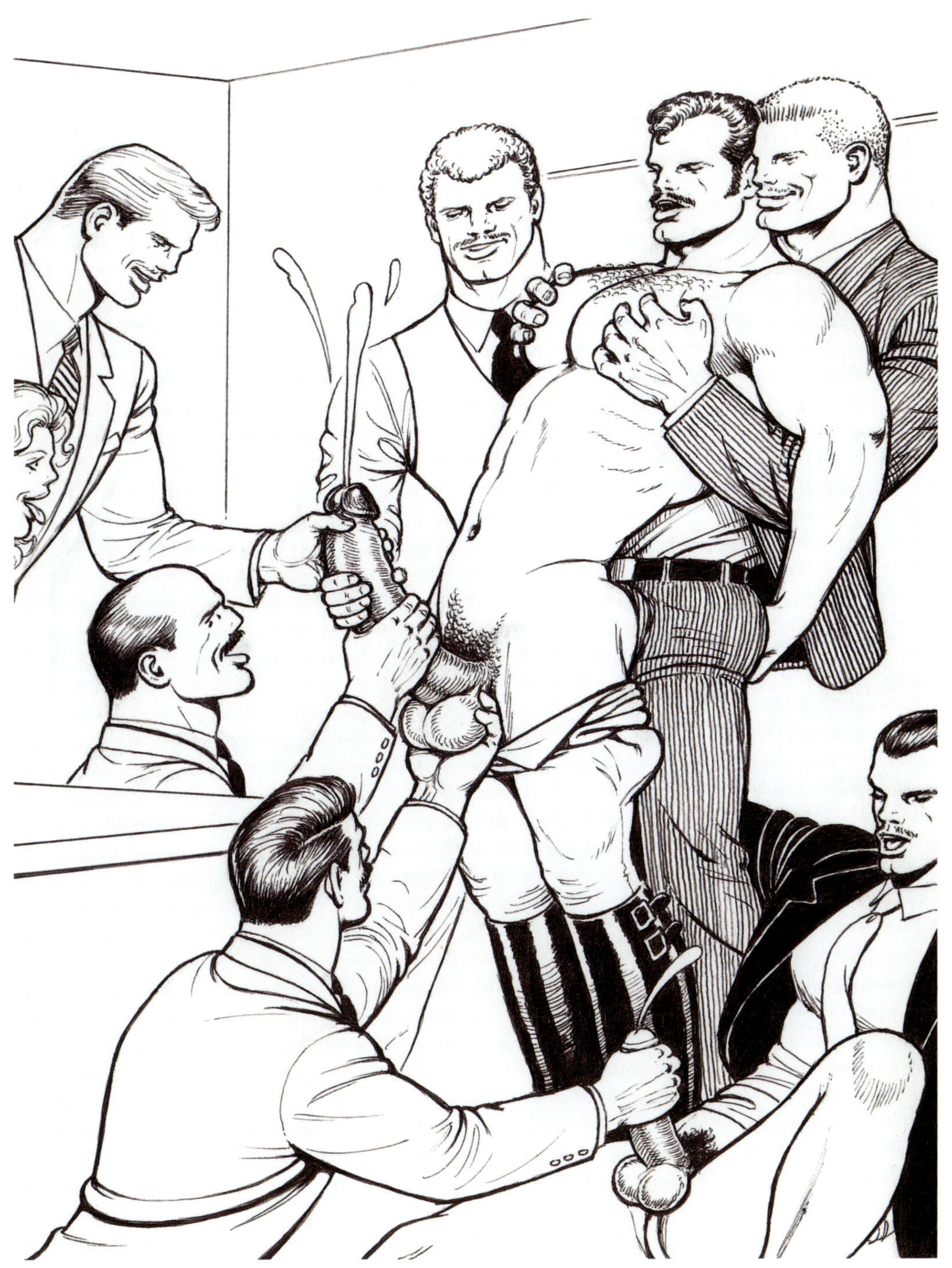

TOM OF FINLAND FOUNDATION

Protecting, Preserving, and Promoting Erotic Art

Tom of Finland Foundation (ToFF) was conceived by the artist Tom of Finland (born Touko Laaksonen) and his partner Durk Dehner in 1984 as a nonprofit visual arts organization to house and preserve the collective works of the artist. It has evolved into a support facility, archive and library serving all artists working in the field of human sexuality.

Today ToFF has over 500,000 visual records, documentation on nearly 4,000 works of art by Tom of Finland, and an art collection representing hundreds of other artists from around the world.

ToFF is only able to continue its work of protecting, preserving and promoting art and artists through the public's generous support including donations and participation in its membership and volunteer programs.

When in Los Angeles, you are invited to tour TOM House, ToFF's HQ and museum, where Tom spent much of the last decade of his life.

For more information:
www.tomoffinland.org
administration@tomoffinland.org
P.O. Box 26658, Los Angeles, CA 90026
+1 213 250 1685

Want to see more? Visit taschen.com to view our current publications, browse our latest magazine, and subscribe to our newsletter.

© 2026 TASCHEN GmbH
Hohenzollernring 53, D-50672 Köln
taschen.com

© Tom of Finland Foundation
All works by Tom of Finland are copyrights under international law.

Original edition: © 2008 TASCHEN GmbH
Edited by Dian Hanson, Los Angeles
German translation: Franca Fritz and
  Heinrich Koop
French translation: Frédéric Maurin

Printed in Bosnia-Herzegovina
ISBN 978-3-7544-0329-7